ROUTLEDGE ENCYCLOPEDIA OF TRANSLATION TECHNOLOGY

Routledge Encyclopedia of Translation Technology, second edition, provides a state-of-the-art survey of the field of computer-assisted translation. It is the first definitive reference to provide a comprehensive overview of the general, regional, and topical aspects of this increasingly significant area of study.

The *Encyclopedia* is divided into three parts:

- Part 1 presents general issues in translation technology, such as its history and development, translator training, and various aspects of machine translation, including a valuable case study of its teaching at a major university;
- Part 2 discusses national and regional developments in translation technology, offering contributions covering the crucial territories of China, Canada, France, Hong Kong, Japan, South Africa, Taiwan, the Netherlands and Belgium, the United Kingdom, and the United States;
- Part 3 evaluates specific matters in translation technology, with entries focused on subjects such as alignment, concordancing, localization, online translation, and translation memory.

The new edition has five additional chapters, with many chapters updated and revised, drawing on the expertise of over 50 contributors from around the world and an international panel of consultant editors to provide a selection of chapters on the most pertinent topics in the discipline. All the chapters are self-contained, extensively cross-referenced, and include useful and up-to-date references and information for further reading.

It will be an invaluable reference work for anyone with a professional or academic interest in the subject.

Chan Sin-wai is Professor-cum-Dean of the School of Humanities and Languages, Caritas Institute of Higher Education, Hong Kong. He was formerly Professor of the School of Humanities and Social Science, The Chinese University of Hong Kong, Shenzhen, and Professor at the Department of Translation, The Chinese University of Hong Kong.

ROUTLEDGE ENCYCLOPEDIA OF TRANSLATION TECHNOLOGY

Second Edition

Edited by Chan Sin-wai

LONDON AND NEW YORK

Designed cover image: Pobytov via Getty Images

Second edition published 2023
by Routledge
4 Park Square, Milton Park, Abingdon, Oxon, OX14 4RN

and by Routledge
605 Third Avenue, New York, NY 10158

Routledge is an imprint of the Taylor & Francis Group, an informa business

© 2023 selection and editorial matter, Chan Sin-wai; individual chapters, the contributors

First edition published by Routledge 2014

British Library Cataloguing-in-Publication Data
A catalogue record for this book is available from the British Library

Library of Congress Cataloging-in-Publication Data
Names: Chan, Sin-wai, editor.
Title: Routledge encyclopedia of translation technology/edited by Chan Sin-wai.
Other titles: Encyclopedia of translation technology
Description: Second edition. | Abingdon, Oxon; New York, NY:
Routledge, 2023. | Includes bibliographical references and index.
Identifiers: LCCN 2022046520 (print) | LCCN 2022046521 (ebook) |
ISBN 9780367767365 (hardback) | ISBN 9780367767372 (paperback) |
ISBN 9781003168348 (ebook)
Subjects: LCSH: Translating and interpreting–Technological Innovations–Encyclopedias. |
Translating and Interpreting–Encyclopedias. | LCGFT: Essays.
Classification: LCC P306.97.T73 R68 2023 (print) | LCC P306.97.T73 (ebook) |
DDC 418/.020285–dc23/eng/20220926
LC record available at https://lccn.loc.gov/2022046520
LC ebook record available at https://lccn.loc.gov/2022046521

ISBN: 978-0-367-76736-5 (hbk)
ISBN: 978-0-367-76737-2 (pbk)
ISBN: 978-1-003-16834-8 (ebk)

DOI: 10.4324/9781003168348

CONTENTS

Contents

FIGURES

TABLES

CONSULTANT EDITORS

Lynne Bowker
School of Translation and Interpreting
University of Ottawa, Canada

David Farwell
TALP, Research Centre, Universitat Politecnica de Catalunya
Barcelona, Spain

W. John Hutchins
University of East Anglia, the United Kingdom

Alan K. Melby
Department of Linguistics and English Language
Brigham Young University, the United States

William S-Y. Wang
Department of Electronic Engineering
Hong Kong Polytechnic University, Hong Kong

CONTRIBUTORS

Lars Ahrenberg is Emeritus Professor at the Department of Computer and Information Science, Linköping University, where he previously headed its NLP research. He received a BA in general linguistics and mathematics from Stockholm University and entered computational linguistics at Uppsala University at the beginning of the 1980s. Dr Ahrenberg's research spans several areas of NLP, including dialogue systems, grammar formalisms and syntactic analysis, corpus linguistics, terminology extraction, and translation technologies. He has published more than fifteen papers on methods and uses of word alignment. His current research interests include machine translation, translation evaluation, and the growing interface of translation technology and translation studies. Dr Ahrenberg was Editor-in-Chief of the *Northern-European Journal of Language Technology* for the period 2012–2017 and is a member of the Association for Computational Linguistics and the European Association for Machine Translation.

Bai Xiaojing is an associate professor at the Language Centre of Tsinghua University. She received her PhD in computer software and theory at the Institute of Computational Linguistics, Peking University, in 2004. Her main research interest is in computational linguistics, specifically corpus linguistics, computer-aided translation studies, and educational technology. She has published papers in *Chinese Translators Journal* and *Computer-Assisted Foreign Language Education* and was one of the contributors to *China Translation Yearbook*, *Routledge Handbook of Chinese Applied Linguistics*, and others. She is currently a member of the Professional Committee of Natural Language Generation under the Chinese Information Processing Society of China.

Lynne Bowker holds a BA and MA in translation (University of Ottawa, Canada), an MSc in computer applications for education (Dublin City University, Ireland) and a PhD in language engineering (University of Manchester Institute of Science and Technology, United Kingdom). She is currently a full professor at the School of Translation and Interpretation at the University of Ottawa, where her teaching and research focus on the use of computer tools in the disciplines of translation and terminology. Her publications include *Computer-Aided Translation Technology* (University of Ottawa Press, 2002) and *Working with Specialized Language: A Practical Guide to Using Corpora* (Routledge, 2002), as well as many articles and book chapters on various aspects of computer-aided translation. Additionally, she serves on the editorial board of the *International Journal of Corpus Linguistics* (John Benjamins Publishing Company) and the *International Journal* *of Lexicography* (Oxford University Press), as well as on the advisory board for *The Interpreter and Translator Trainer* (St. Jerome Publishing).

Sylviane Cardey, PhD and state thesis in linguistics, Member of the Institut universitaire de France, is Professor Emeritus (Classe exceptionelle) of Linguistics and Natural Language Processing at the University of Franche-Comté, Besançon, France. She was Director of the Centre de Recherche en Linguistique et Traitement Automatique des Langues Lucien Tesnière and created the natural language processing (NLP) programme at Besançon and the European Master Mundus Course in NLP and human language technology (HLT). Her research is fundamentally oriented and principally concerns the development of her systemic linguistics analysis model and its associated calculus. This work has led to applications in which quality is paramount. The principal applied research domains are in sense-mining, controlled languages, and machine translation (between languages of the same and different origins or families), where she has been lead partner in collaborative projects in France and internationally. She has several international collaborations, in particular in safety-critical environments, for example, with enterprises in the aircraft manufacturing and food-processing industries and for data protection. She has supervised forty-one PhDs; has written 145 international papers and a book, *Modelling Language* (2013); created the international conference series XTAL; and is a national and international expert. Sylviane Cardey is chevalier de la Légion d'honneur.

Chan Sin-wai is Professor-cum-Dean of the School of Humanities and Languages, Caritas Institute of Higher Education, Hong Kong. He was formerly Professor of the School of Humanities and Social Science, the Chinese University of Hong Kong, Shenzhen, and Professor at the Department of Translation, the Chinese University of Hong Kong. He was also Director of the Master of Arts in the Computer-Aided Translation Programme and Director of the Centre for Translation Technology. His teaching and research interests lie mainly in the areas of translation studies, translation technology, and bilingual lexicography. He is the Chief Editor of *Journal of Translation Technology*, published by the Chinese University of Hong Kong, and Editor of *International Journal of Techno-Humanities*. He has published more than sixty-six academic books in eighty-five volumes, mainly dictionaries and scholarly monographs, and translated works in different fields. He edited *An Encyclopaedia of Translation*, revised *Longman Dictionary of English Language and Culture* (bilingual edition), and authored *A Dictionary of Translation Technology* and *A Chinese-English Dictionary of the Human Body*. His book translations from Chinese into English include *An Exposition of Benevolence, Palaces of the Forbidden City, Letters of Prominent Figures in Modern China, Paintings and Calligraphy of Jao Tsung-I, Stories by Gao Yang, An Illustrated History of Printing in Ancient China, Famous Chinese Sayings Quoted by Wen Jiabao*, and *Selected Works of Cheng Siwei: Economic Reforms and Development in China*, Volume 2. He also translated *My Son Yo Yo* from English into Chinese. His most recent co-edited books include *Style, Wit and Word-Play* (2012) and *The Dancer and the Dance* (2013), both published by Cambridge Scholars Publishing. His most recent publications include *The Routledge Encyclopedia of the Chinese Language* (2016), *An Encyclopedia of Practical Translation* (2018), *The Human Factor in Machine* Translation (2018), *Routledge Encyclopedia of Traditional Chinese Culture* (2020), and *A Dictionary of Chinese Popular Sayings and Famous Quotes* (2021).

Venus Chan is an assistant professor at the Department of Humanities, Language and Translation of Hong Kong Metropolitan University, Hong Kong. She is the secretary of the Association of Translation Technology (ATT). Her main research interests are education technologies, applied linguistics, and interpreter and translator training. She is the Principal Investigator of some internal and external funded research projects, such as the Faculty Development Grant (University Grants Committee). In addition, she has served as a journal reviewer, academic advisor, and external examiner.

Freddy Y.Y. Choi created the C99 text segmentation algorithm during his PhD and has worked on a range of applied natural language processing projects with BBN Technologies, European Commission, BBC, Rolls-Royce, Finmeccanica, and the UK government over the last twenty years. He has a keen interest in making cutting-edge but imperfect artificial intelligence solution work in real-world applications.

Ian Castor Chow is currently a research fellow at the College of Design and Social Context of the RMIT University. He received his PhD in computational linguistics from City University of Hong Kong. His teaching and research areas include discourse analysis, corpus linguistics, computer-aided translation, localization, terminology management, and general education. Besides teaching and research, he also specialized in curriculum management and pedagogy in higher education. Before joining the RMIT University, he served as a general education manager of Chung Chi College and formerly a lecturer at the Department of Translation of the Chinese University of Hong Kong. He also taught computer-aided translation and localization courses at the Caritas Institute of Higher Education. His research interests include discourse analysis, corpus linguistics, language technology, ontology, and curriculum development.

Jennifer DeCamp is the Chief Scientist for Human Language Technology in MITRE Corporation's Department of Social, Behavioral, and Linguistic Sciences in their Center for Connected Government. Jennifer works with MITRE's five federally funded research and development centres (FFRDCs) to provide consulting to the US government on translation processes and technology. Jennifer has worked with translation for over thirty years, including as a translator, an editor, a professor of translation, an industry program manager, and a developer. She has worked extensively with the American Translators Association (ATA), the American Society for Testing and Materials (ASTM), the International Organization for Standardization (ISO), and other organizations to develop standards for improving translation and interpretation, particularly for advancing technology.

Christophe Declercq is a senior lecturer who graduated as a translator (Dutch/English/Russian) in 1998. After several years in the translation industry (including Yamagata Europe), he taught translation technology in the United Kingdom for twenty years, at Imperial College London first and University College London next. Christophe has been an evaluator for the European Commission on multilingual ICT projects (DG CONNECT, INEA) and was a member of the LIND board for its first ten years. In 2022 Christophe started at the University of Utrecht. He has been a visiting lecturer at universities in Belgium, France, the Netherlands, and the United Kingdom. Christophe has published several articles and chapters on translation and language technology.

Jorge Díaz Cintas is Professor of Translation and Founding Director (2013–2016) of the Centre for Translation Studies (CenTraS) at University College London. He is the author of numerous articles, special issues, and books on audiovisual translation, including *Subtitling: Concepts and Practices* (with Aline Remael, 2021). A pioneer in audiovisual translation, Jorge has trained translators-to-be across six continents; is a frequent speaker at international conferences and events; and has offered consultant services to the European Parliament, European Commission,

NATO, OOONA, and Netflix, among others. He is the Chief Editor of the Peter Lang series *New Trends in Translation Studies* and the recipient of the Jan Ivarsson Award (ESIST, 2014) and the Xènia Martínez Award (ATRAE, 2015) for invaluable services to the field of audiovisual translation.

Keiran J. Dunne is a professor of translation studies, Chair of the Department of Modern and Classical Language Studies, and a member of the faculty in the Institute for Applied Linguistics at Kent State University, where he teaches graduate courses on computer-assisted translation, localization, project management, and the language industry. Drawing upon more than fifteen years' experience as a French localization and technical translation subcontractor for Fortune 500 companies and other corporate clients, his research interests include localization, project management, quality management, terminology management, and the industrialization of translation. He is the editor of the collective volume *Perspectives on Localization* (2006) and the co-editor of the collective volume *Translation and Localization Project Management: The Art of the Possible* (2011). He is a member of the editorial advisory boards of the journal *Translation Spaces* and of the American Translators Association Scholarly Monograph Series.

David Farwell was a senior ICREA research scientist at the Catalonia Polytechnic University in Barcelona, Spain, from 2002 through 2011 and served as Director of the university's Centre for Language and Speech Applications and Technologies from 2009 through 2011. From 1985 through 2006, Dr Farwell was a research scientist at the Computing Research Laboratory, New Mexico State University, in Las Cruces, New Mexico. He received a PhD in linguistics in 1985 from the University of Illinois-Urbana. In 2012, he retired from active research. Dr Farwell was particularly active in the areas of machine translation, natural language processing, semantic representation and reasoning and computational pragmatics. During that time, he was Principal Investigator for three National Science Foundation projects, two US Defense Department projects, and two industry-funded projects. In addition, he participated in four European Commission Information and Communication Technologies projects, four Spanish Ministry of Science and Innovation projects, and an additional five US Defense Department projects. He has published well over 100 articles in conference proceedings, journals, and edited volumes, including some twenty-five on pragmatics-based machine translation. Additionally, he has given several invited talks, panel presentations, tutorials, and seminars, as well as chairing or participating in numerous conference organizing and programme committees.

Mikel L. Forcada was born in Caracas (Venezuela) in 1963 and is married with two children. He graduated in science in 1986 and got his PhD in chemistry in 1991. Since 2002 he has been Full Professor ('Catedràtic') of Computer Languages and Systems at the Universitat d'Alacant. Professor Forcada is also secretary of the European Association for Machine Translation, president of the Special Interest Group for Speech and Language Technologies for Minority Languages (SaLTMiL) of the International Speech Communication Association, and book review editor of the international journal *Machine Translation*. From the turn of the millennium on, Professor Forcada's interests have mainly focused on the field of translation technologies, but he has worked in fields as diverse as quantum chemistry, biotechnology, surface physics, machine learning (especially with neural networks), and automata theory. He is the author of seventeen articles in international journals (three in machine translation), forty-eight papers in international conferences (twenty-five in machine translation), and six book chapters (three on machine translation). Professor Forcada has headed several publicly and privately funded projects and has led the development of the machine translation systems interNOSTRUM (Spanish-Catalan) and Traductor Universia (Spanish-Portuguese). More recently (2004), he started the free/open-source machine translation platform Apertium (with more than twenty-six language pairs), where he is currently the President of the project management committee. He is also administrator of three more free software projects (Bitextor, Orthoepikon, Tagaligner) and co-founder of start-up company Prompsit Language Engineering (2006). Professor Forcada has participated in the scientific committees of more than twenty international conferences and workshops. Recently (2009–2010) he has been an ETS Walton Visiting Professor in the machine translation group at Dublin City University.

Ignacio Garcia is a senior lecturer at the School of Humanities and Communication Arts, University of Western Sydney, where he teaches in English–Spanish translation and translation technologies. He has published in academic and professional journals on translation memory, translation memory and machine translation integration, post-editing, and uses of machine translation for language learning. His current interest is in the deployment of digital technology to assist bilinguals to translate and everyone to interact in unfamiliar linguistic environments. He has also taught and published on Spanish and Latin American studies, having completed his PhD in this area.

Alejandro Bolaños García-Escribano, PhD, is Lecturer (Teaching) in Audiovisual Translation and Programme Director at University College London, UK, where he teaches translation and Spanish language and culture at both the Centre for Translation Studies and the Department of Spanish, Portuguese and Latin American Studies. He is also Senior Fellow of the Higher Education Academy and a member and chartered linguist of the Chartered Institute of Linguists. His research focuses on audiovisual translation in higher education and subtitling technologies. He also works as a freelance translator and subtitler.

Federico Gaspari is associate professor of English language and translation at the Department of Political Science of the University of Naples "Federico II" in Italy. He graduated in translation studies from the University of Bologna at Forlì (Italy), and then went on to earn a PhD in machine translation from the University of Manchester (UK). He has held lecturing and research positions at the Universities of Manchester, Salford, Bologna at Forlì, Macerata and Reggio Calabria "Dante Alighieri", and is affiliated to the ADAPT Centre of Dublin City University (Ireland), where he collaborates on European research projects focusing on language and translation technologies. His teaching and research interests include applied and descriptive English linguistics, translation technologies, specialised translation, translation theory, corpus linguistics and corpus-based translation studies. He has published widely on these topics and is a regular contributor to international conferences in these areas, as a programme committee member or speaker.

Marissa Griesel completed a bachelor's degree in computational linguistics as well as a master's degree in applied linguistic theory (cum laude) at North-West University (NWU), South Africa. The title of her thesis was "Syntactic Reordering as Pre-Processing in the Development of an English-Afrikaans Machine Translation System". As part of her MA, she spent three months as an exchange student at the University of Tilburg, the Netherlands. She worked as research assistant (2005–2007), project manager (2008), and later computational linguist (2009–2012) at the NWU's Centre for Text Technology (CTexT) and was involved in a wide range of projects, from compiling speech corpora to developing educational software. For example, she played an important role in the Autshumato project – the first machine translation system for various South African languages – and published numerous papers about the project. She also lectured in numerous HLT courses and led workshops for freelance translators in using computer-assisted translation (CAT) tools. She is currently enrolled as a PhD student at the NWU, investigating various ways of fast-tracking natural language processing for South African languages.

Stephen Helmreich worked as a computational linguist at the Computing Research Laboratory of New Mexico State University in Las Cruces, New Mexico, from 1988 through 2007, serving as Deputy Director from 2003–2007. He continued to work as a principal investigator in the Department of Information Sciences and Security Systems of the Physical Science Laboratory (also at New Mexico State University) until his retirement in 2009. He received a PhD in linguistics in 1996 from the University of Illinois-Urbana/Champaign. Dr Helmreich's areas of interest include machine translation, particularly interlingual approaches; computational morphology; and computational approaches to metaphor, metonymy, and other types of non-literal language. He was a principal investigator on seven projects and co-principal investigator on three more, including five NSF grants and five defence-related and funded projects. He also served as a board member of the Association of Machine Translation in the Americas and as treasurer from 2001–2006. He is the author or co-author of over forty papers. With Dr David Farwell, he has published a series of papers on pragmatics-based machine translation. They have also edited a series of workshop proceedings on interlingual machine translation.

W. John Hutchins is retired from the University of East Anglia (Norwich, United Kingdom), where he worked in the university library. He is the author of books and articles on linguistics, information retrieval, and in particular machine translation. Principal works include *Machine Translation: Past, Present, Future* (Chichester: Ellis Horwood, 1986); *An Introduction to Machine Translation* [with Harold Somers] (London: Academic Press, 1992); and *Early Years in Machine Translation: Memoirs and Biographies of Pioneers* (as editor; Amsterdam and Philadelphia: John Benjamins Publishing Company 2000). He was Editor of *MT News International* from 1991 until 1997 and the *Compendium of Translation Software* from 2000 until 2011. Since 2004 he has compiled the *Machine Translation Archive* (www.mt-archive.info), an electronic repository of publications on MT and related topics – now containing over 10,000 items. He has been a speaker at many machine translation conferences, the MT Summit conferences, the EAMT workshops and conferences, the Translating and Computer conferences and the AMTA conferences. He was President of the European Association for Machine Translation, 1995–2004, and President of the International Association for Machine Translation, 1999–2001. His website containing most of his publications is at www.hutchinsweb.me.uk.

Hitoshi Isahara is Professor of the Information and Media Center at Toyohashi University of Technology, Japan. He received his BE, ME, and PhD in electrical engineering from Kyoto University, Kyoto, Japan, in 1978, 1980, and 1995, respectively. His research interests include natural language processing and lexical semantics. Until December 2009, he was working at the National Institute of Information and Communications Technology (NICT), Japan, as a leader of the Computational Linguistics Group and a director of the Thai Computational Linguistics Laboratory (TCL). He was a guest professor at Kobe University Graduate School of Engineering, Japan, and part-time lecturer at Kyoto University Graduate School of Human and Environmental Studies and Doshisha University. He was a president of the International Association for Machine Translation (IAMT) and a president of the Asia-Pacific Association for Machine Translation (AAMT). He is working for ISO/TC37/SC4 and is a project co-leader of one of its working items. He is a board member of Gengo Shigen Kyokai (GSK, a linguistic resource association), Japan.

Kit Chunyu is a professor currently teaching and researching in computational linguistics and machine translation at the City University of Hong Kong. He obtained his BEng in computer science and technology from Tsinghua University (1985), MSc in computational linguistics from Carnegie Mellon University (1994), and PhD in computer science from the University of Sheffield (2001). He also holds an MA in applied linguistics from the Chinese Academy of Social Sciences (1988) and an MPhil in linguistics from the City University of Hong Kong (1993). His research interests include Chinese language processing, text mining, computational terminology, psycholinguistics, and poetry. He has published over 100 research papers in academic journals (including *Information Sciences, Journal of Artificial Intelligence Research, International Journal of Corpus Linguistics, Journal of Computer Science and Technology, Law Library Journal, Machine Translation,* and *Terminology*) and international conferences (including Association for Computational Linguistics (ACL), Conference on Computational Linguistics (COLING), Conference on Natural Language Processing (CoNLP), Empirical Methods in Natural Language Processing (EMNLP), and International Joint Conference on Artificial Intelligence (IJCAI)).

Olivia Kwong Oi Yee graduated from the University of Hong Kong with a first degree in psychology and obtained her PhD in computational linguistics from the University of Cambridge with a doctoral thesis on automatic word sense disambiguation. She is currently Assistant Professor in the Department of Chinese, Translation and Linguistics of the City University of Hong Kong. Her research interests cover natural language processing, corpus linguistics, and psycholinguistics, involving mainly English and Chinese. She has worked in many related areas, including lexical semantics, lexical resources, corpus development, bilingual corpus processing, translation lexicon extraction, name transliteration, mental lexicon and lexical access, and sentiment analysis, amongst others. Her work often focuses on multi-disciplinary and empirical approaches and has appeared in international journals and important international conferences. Recently she has published a monograph titled *New Perspectives on Computational and Cognitive Strategies for Word Sense Disambiguation*, which presents the topic from an integrated viewpoint. She has also been active in the research field, having been involved in the organization of many international conferences and having served on the editorial board of the journal *Computational Linguistics*.

Lee Tan is an associate professor at the Department of Electronic Engineering and the Director of the DSP and Speech Technology Laboratory, the Chinese University of Hong Kong. He was a visiting researcher at the Department of Speech, Music and Hearing, Royal Institute of Technology (KTH), Sweden, during 1997–1998. Lee Tan's research covers many different areas of speech processing and spoken language technologies, including automatic speech and speaker recognition, text-to-speech, spoken dialogue systems, prosody modelling, language identification, and music signal processing. He is a member of IEEE Signal Processing Society and a member of the International Speech Communication Association (ISCA). He was the Chairman of IEEE Hong Kong Chapter of Signal Processing during 2005–2006 and the General Chair of 2012 Oriental COCOSDA Conference. Currently he is an associate editor of the *EURASIP Journal on Advances in Signal Processing* and a workgroup chair of the ISCA Special Interest Group on Chinese Spoken Language Processing. Lee Tan received the Chinese University of Hong Kong Vice-Chancellor's Exemplary Teaching Award in 2005.

Li Chengze received his BEng from the University of Science and Technology of China in 2013 and PhD in computer science and engineering from the Chinese University of Hong Kong in 2020. Chengze is currently an assistant professor in the School of Computing and Information

Sciences, Caritas Institute of Higher Education, with research interests in 2D non-photorealistic media analysis and processing, computational photography, and computer graphics.

Lan Li works as an associate professor in the School of Humanities and Social Science, the Chinese University of Hong Kong, Shenzhen. She is a fellow of the Chartered Institute of Linguists, UK. She holds MPhil and PhD in applied linguistics from the University of Exeter, UK. She has been teaching English at the university level for over twenty years in the United Kingdom, Hong Kong, and Mainland China. Her research interests and publications cover lexicology, lexicography, corpus linguistics, professional communication, and sociolinguistics.

May Li is a professor and Director of MTI Center of Tongji University and Vice President of Shanghai Science & Technology Translation Society. She obtained her BA from Anhui University and MA and PhD from University of Manchester, UK. Her research interests cover translation technology, in particular machine translation post-editing (MTPE) and technical communication (TC). She has conducted research in MTPE and TC and translated and published books and papers, among which *Famous Chinese Gardens* won the National Publication Award in 2009. She was awarded the China Technical Communication Education Contribution Award in 2020 and obtained the copyright of two MTPE-related software programs in 2021.

Cindy McKellar completed a Bachelor Degree in Computational Linguistics followed by a Masters Degree in Applied Linguistic Theory (cum laude) at the North-West University (NWU), South Africa. The title of her M.A. thesis was 'Data selection and manipulation for statistical English-Afrikaans machine translation'. She is employed (2005-present) as a computational linguist at the NWU's Centre for Text Technology (CTexT). She has been and continues to be involved in a range of projects in the field of human language technology with special emphasis on the development of datasets for training machine translation as well as research and development in the field of machine translation for various South African language pairs.

Liu Qun is the Chief Scientist of Speech and Natural Language Processing of Huawei. He was a full professor at Dublin City University and the Theme Leader of the ADAPT Centre, Ireland, during July 2012 and June 2018. Before that, he was a professor in the Institute of Computing Technology (ICT), Chinese Academy of Sciences, for twenty years, where he founded and led the ICT NLP Research Group. He obtained his BSc, MSc, and PhD in computer science in the University of Science and Technology of China, Chinese Academy of Sciences, and Peking University, respectively. His research interests lie in the areas of natural language processing and machine translation. His main academic contributions are on Chinese language processing, syntax-based statistical machine translation, pre-trained language models (training, compression, applications), and so on. He has authored or co-authored more than 300 peer-reviewed research publications, which have been cited more than 12,000 times. He has supervised more than forty students to the completion of their MScs or PhDs. He has received the Google Research Award (2012), ACL Best Long Paper Award (2018), Qian Weichang First Prize for Chinese Information Processing Technologies, China National Second Prize for Progress in Science and Technology, and others. He was elected an ACL fellow in 2021.

Liu Xueting received her BEng in computer science and technology from Tsinghua University and her PhD in computer science and engineering from the Chinese University of Hong Kong in 2009 and 2014, respectively. She is currently an assistant professor in the School of Computing and Information Sciences, Caritas Institute of Higher Education. Her research interests include computational art, intelligent art, computer vision, and computer graphics.

Liu Yang is an associate professor in the Department of Computer Science and Technology at Tsinghua University, China. His research interests include natural language processing, Chinese information processing, and machine translation. He has published more than twenty papers in leading natural language processing journals and conferences, such as *Computational Linguistics*, conferences of the Association for Computational Linguistics (ACL), the Association for the Advancement of Artificial Intelligence (AAAI), Empirical Methods in Natural Language Processing (EMNLP), and Computational Linguistics (COLING). He won the COLING/ACL 2006 Meritorious Asian NLP Paper Award. He will serve as ACL 2014 Tutorial Co-Chair and ACL 2015 Local Arrangement Co-Chair.

Arle Lommel is a recognized expert in the fields of localization and translation. Widely published in the field, he focuses on both the technical and business aspects of the industry and how they relate to each other. As director of standards at LISA, he was responsible for submission of the TBX standard to ISO (now ISO 30042) and for driving standards development at LISA. In his other life, he holds a PhD in folkloristics and is trained as a linguist. He has worked extensively in the fields of ethnography, organology, and semiotics and has led the development of a visual identity and exhibit materials for Traditional Arts Indiana, a state-recognized folk arts agency in Indiana. His specialties include standards development, translation technology, translation and localization business, ethnographic research, and linguistics.

Elliott Macklovitch, a linguist by training, has been actively involved in machine and machine-aided translation since 1977, when he joined the TAUM group at the University of Montreal; this is the group that developed the MÉTÉO System, long considered one of the most successful applications in the history of machine translation. From 1986 to 1997, he worked at the Centre for Information Technology Innovation, an Industry Canada research lab, where he was responsible for the Translator's Workstation project. He returned to the University of Montreal in 1997 as Coordinator of the RALI Laboratory. The RALI has developed a number of innovative tools for translators, including the TransSearch system, which is now successfully marketed in Canada. Between 2000 and 2004, he served two terms as President of AMTA, the Association for Machine Translation in the Americas. Since leaving the RALI in 2009, he has worked as independent consultant in machine translation. His hobby is literary translation.

Alan K. Melby is professor emeritus of the Department of Linguistics and English Language at the Provo campus of Brigham Young University, United States. He received his BSc in mathematics, MA in linguistics, and PhD in computational linguistics from Brigham Young University. Professor Melby has been interested in terminology management and exchange since the mid-1980s. He has been involved in various efforts to develop terminology exchange formats. Professor Melby is an ATA-certified French-to-English translator. He worked on a machine translation project for a decade and does freelance translation and consulting in translation quality. He is a vice-president of the International Federation of Translators (FIT) and a member of the US delegation to the International Organization for Standardization, Technical Committee 37 for Terminology and Other Language Resources (ISO/TC37). In 2007, Professor Melby received the Eugen Wüster prize awarded by Infoterm for lifetime achievement in the area of terminology. In 2003, he received the Gode Medal, which is the most prestigious award of the American Translators Association presented to an individual or institution in recognition of outstanding service to the translation and interpreting professions. His book publications include and *The Possibility of Language: A Discussion of the Nature of Language, with Implications for Human and Machine Translation* (co-authored with Terry Warner) (Amsterdam 1995); *LACUS Forum XXVI – The Lexicon* (co-edited with Arle Lommel) (Lacus Fullerton 2000); *Multilingual Solutions* (SMP, Geneva 2000); *LACUS Forum XXVII – Speaking and Comprehending* (co-edited with Ruth Brend and Arle Lommel) (California 2001); and *Listening Comprehension, Laws, and Video: LACUS Forum XXIX – Linguistics and the Real World* (co-edited with Douglas Coleman, William Sullivan, and Arle Lommel) (Houston 2003).

Nie Jian-Yun is a professor at the Department of Computer Science and Operations Research, University of Montreal. His main research areas are information retrieval and natural language processing. He is a graduate from Southwest University in China, and he obtained a PhD from University Joseph Fourier of Grenoble, France. During his career of more than two decades, he has published widely in journals and conferences in these areas. In particular, he received the Best Paper award at SIGIR 1999 for his work on cross-language information retrieval using parallel web pages. Nie Jian-Yun has been invited to deliver keynote and invited speeches at a number of conferences. He is regularly invited to serve on programme committees and is a member of the editorial boards of several journals. More information about Professor Nie can be obtained from his website: www.iro.umontreal.ca/~nie.

Qian Duoxiu is an associate professor at Beihang University, Beijing, China. Her research interests include translation technology, corpus-based translation studies, and corpus rhetoric. Her publications have appeared in *Target: International Journal of Translation Studies, META: Journal of Translation Studies, Translation Review, Machine Translation, The ATA Chronicle, Terminology, Chinese Translators Association Journal, Perspectives: Studies in Translation Theory and Practice*, and other internationally refereed journals. Her *Computer-Aided Translation: A Coursebook* (in Chinese, Beijing: Foreign Language Teaching and Research Press, 2011) has been used by more than 200 universities in China. She can be reached at qianduoxiu@buaa.edu.cn.

Felipe Sánchez-Martínez, PhD, is a lecturer at the Departament de Lenguatges i Sistemes Informàtics (Universitat d'Alacant, Spain) and a member of the European Association for Machine Translation since 2009. He has published ten articles in international journals, five articles in Spanish journals, a book chapter, and more than thirty papers in international conferences. His main field of research is MT and the application of unsupervised corpus-based methods to build some of the modules and linguistic resources needed by rule-based MT systems; his doctoral dissertation focused on the unsupervised learning of part-of-speech taggers and structural transfer rules. He has also worked in the hybridization of MT systems and in the selection of the best MT system to use to translate a given sentence using only source-language information. He has participated in the design and development of the Apertium rule-based machine translation platform, where he is currently a member of the Project Management Committee, and in several projects funded by the Spanish government. Most of his undergraduate and graduate teaching involves translation and language technologies.

Martin Puttkammer completed his PhD in General Linguistics in 2014 at the North-West University (NWU) in South Africa and currently serves as the head of Centre for Text Technology at the NWU. He is a computational linguist specialising in natural language processing with more than 20 years of experience in research, development and university level teaching in the field of human language technologies. Puttkammer was directly involved in projects spanning 17 (resource-scarce) languages, including the release of more than 30 commercial software packages and more than 100 human language technology packages, ranging from machine translation systems and automatic morpho-syntactic analysis technologies, to spelling and grammar checkers.

Rolf Schwitter is a senior lecturer in the Centre for Language Technology at Macquarie University in Sydney, Australia. His main research interests are natural and formal language processing; in particular, controlled natural languages, knowledge representation, automated reasoning, and semantic technologies. Rolf received a PhD in computational linguistics from the University of Zurich. He designed and implemented controlled natural languages and tools for controlled natural language processing for a number of research projects and as a contractor for Data61 (formerly known as NICTA), for the DSTG, Australia's Defence Science and Technology Group, and for a company in the taxation domain.

Shih Chung-ling is Professor of English at National Kaohsiung First University of Science and Technology in Taiwan. Her research focuses and interests are broad, including machine translation (MT), computer-aided translation, corpus-based translation studies, translation studies, cultural studies, English teaching, and literature studies. Because of her MT and CAT research, she was invited to give a lecture at School of Foreign Languages of China University of Geosciences in China. She was also a keynote speaker at the International Conference organized by Guangdong University of Foreign Studies and hosted by Zhongnan University of Economics and Law in China. In addition to these, she has given lectures at some universities in Taiwan, transmitting the concept of controlled web cultural writing for effective multilingual MT application. She has completed a series of research with the grant of Taiwan's NSC, and part of the results is posted on her teaching website. Her research results can also be found in books such as *Helpful Assistance to Translators: MT and TM* (2006), *Real-Time Communication through Machine-Enabled Translation: Taiwan's Oracle Poetry* (2011), *Translation Research Models and Application* (2012), and others. Over thirty papers in her name have been published in various journals in Taiwan and abroad.

Mark Shuttleworth has been involved in translation studies research and teaching since 1993, first at the University of Leeds, Imperial College London, and University College London and now at Hong Kong Baptist University. His publications include the *Dictionary of Translation Studies*, as well as articles on translation technology, translator training, metaphor in translation, translation and the web, and Wikipedia translation. He also has an interest in the use of digital methodologies in translation studies research. His monograph, *Studying Scientific Metaphor in Translation*, was published in 2017, and he is currently working on a second edition of the *Dictionary*. Mark Shuttleworth has been invited as a keynote speaker to translation studies conferences in Poland, China, and Malaysia. He has also addressed industry conferences in the United Kingdom, Italy, and Brazil on the subject of translation technology and has provided training in the same area in Spain, Italy, Portugal, Finland, Tunisia, and Malaysia. He is a fluent speaker of Russian, German, Polish, and French and has some knowledge of a number of other languages. As and when time permits, he is active as a translator.

Siu Sai Cheong is Associate Professor in the School of Translation and Foreign Languages at the Hang Seng University of Hong Kong. He is Programme Director of the bachelor of translation with business and the master of arts in translation (computer-aided translation), and he was also Director of Deep Learning Research and Application Centre. His research focuses on translation technology and artificial intelligence for the creative industries. His publicly funded projects include "Machine Translation of IPO Documents" and "A Hybrid Approach to the

Translation of Government Press Releases", supported by the Innovation and Technology Fund and the Research Grants Council, respectively.

Antal van den Bosch held research positions at the experimental psychology labs of Tilburg University, the Netherlands, and the Université Libre de Bruxelles, Belgium (1993–1994); obtained his PhD in computer science at the Universiteit Maastricht, the Netherlands (1994–1997); and held several positions at Tilburg University (1997–2011), where he was appointed full professor in computational linguistics and AI in 2008. In 2011 he took on a full professorship in language and speech technology at Radboud University Nijmegen, the Netherlands. His research interests include memory-based natural language processing and modelling, machine translation, text analytics applied to historical texts and social media, and proofing tools. He is a member of the Netherlands Royal Academy of Arts and Sciences.

Leonoor van der Beek combines journalism with natural language processing. With an MA in the first and a PhD in the latter, she went to work in the search industry (Ask.com, Right-Now technologies) to improve the search experience by applying natural language processing techniques. In 2011, she published a book on the rise of natural language processing in the Netherlands and Flanders (*Van Rekenmachine tot Taalautomaat*). This book, commissioned by the University of Groningen, is based on interviews with pioneers in the field and gives insight on the early battles for automation of the translation process. van der Beek currently works on automated processing of structured and unstructured data for the Dutch e-commerce giant bol.com.

Gerhard B. van Huyssteen completed his PhD in linguistics in 2000 at the North-West University in South Africa. He is currently appointed as research professor at NWU and has published more than fifty local and international scholarly articles/papers/chapters in books. Although his core research focuses on Afrikaans morphology, most of his research was done on the development of numerous human language technology resources and applications for various South African languages. van Huyssteen is therefore best known for his contribution as a linguist in the development of real-world text-based computer applications and core computer technologies for Afrikaans and other South African languages. He serves on the expert panel of the South African National Centre for HLT and was (co-)guest editor of two special issues of journals focusing on HLT in South Africa. van Huyssteen is also actively involved in various initiatives to improve the spelling skills of language users.

Lucía Morado Vázquez is a senior research associate at the Department of Translation Technology of Faculty of Translation and Interpreting, University of Geneva, on the areas of localisation, computer-assisted translation tools, and information technology. Member of the Cod.eX Research Group, Lucía also collaborates with other universities and international institutions as course facilitator, research collaborator, and external examiner. She holds a PhD in localization from the Localisation Research Centre, University of Limerick, Ireland. In the last decade, Lucía has been an active member of the localisation standards ecosystem, and she is currently the co-chair of the XLIFF (XML Localisation Interchange File Format) Technical Committee.

Kara Warburton, with an MA and PhD in terminology (Université Laval, Canada, and City University of Hong Kong), is a classically educated terminologist, but she also has over twenty years of experience managing terminology in various production-oriented settings, including fifteen years at IBM and consulting engagements for a dozen or so enterprises, among them the World Bank and ISO. Also with a BA in translation (Université Laval) and a BA in education

(Dalhousie University, Canada), she has taught courses at universities in Canada and Hong Kong and provided training to language professionals in over fifty companies. Kara has been actively contributing to international standards and best practices in the field of terminology for over ten years and currently holds the position of International Chair of ISO Technical Committee 37, which sets standards for terminology and other types of language resources. She offers consultancy services in terminology management through Termologic (www.termologic.com).

Cecilia Wong Shuk Man is an assistant professor cum programme leader of the Bachelor of Arts (Hons.) in translation technology in the Caritas Institute of Higher Education in Hong Kong. She obtained her PhD in linguistics from the City University of Hong Kong. She taught at the City University of Hong Kong before joining the Hong Kong Polytechnic University in 2004. Since then, she has been the Course Lecturer for the Master of Arts in Computer Aided Translation Programme in the Chinese University of Hong Kong for eleven years. She has written several research articles on ontology processing, text analysis, and machine translation. Her research interests are machine translation, speech translation, and computer-aided translation.

Billy Wong Tak Ming is currently Deputy Director of the Institute for Research in Open and Innovative Education and Senior Research Coordinator of Hong Kong Metropolitan University. He received his PhD in computational linguistics from City University of Hong Kong. He has taught a range of courses on linguistics and computer-aided translation. His research interests include machine translation, corpus linguistics, and the impacts of technology on education. He has published more than 100 papers in academic journals, books, and international conferences, such as *Machine Translation, Babel, Intralinea*, and *Interactive Learning Environments*. He has also served as a guest editor of Springer's Education Innovation Series and journals including *International Journal of Mobile Learning and Organisation, Interactive Technology and Smart Education*, and *SN Computer Science*.

Sue Ellen Wright is a professor emerita of German and a former member of the Kent State University Institute for Applied Linguistics, where she taught computer applications for translators and German-to-English technical translation. She has served as chair of the American Translators Association Terminology Committee and is ATA certified for German-to-English translation. She is active as a terminology trainer and consultant for companies and institutions implementing terminology management in localization environments. She is engaged in the national and international standards community (ASTM International and the International Organization for Standardization) and chairs the US mirror committee (Technical Advisory Group) for ISO Technical Committee 37, Language and Terminology. Together with Professor Gerhard Budin of the University of Vienna, she compiled the *Handbook for Terminology Management* and is the author of many articles on applied terminology management in industry. She was the recipient of the Eugen Wüster Prize awarded by the International Information Centre for Terminology (Infoterm), the Center for Translation Studies (University of Vienna), and the Department of Planned Languages and Esperanto Museum (Austrian National Library) in 2010. She was the recipient of the ATA Alexander Gode medal in 2020.

Ye Meng is a teaching fellow in literature and applied linguistics, School of Education and English, at the University of Nottingham, Ningbo China. She holds a PhD in applied linguistics from Hong Kong Polytechnic University. Her research interests include corpus-assisted textual analysis, media discourse, and multimodal discourse analysis. To date, she has published in *Discourse & Communication, Language & Communication*, and so on.

Yu Shiwen was a professor of the Key Laboratory of Computational Linguistics (Peking University), Ministry of Education of PRC, and the Institute of Computational Linguistics at Peking University. He worked at Peking University after graduating from the Department of Mathematics of Peking University in 1964. His most representative academic achievement is the Comprehensive Language Knowledge Base (CLKB) based on the Grammatical Knowledge-Base of Contemporary Chinese. CLKB has made a great contribution to the development of Chinese information processing and won the second prize of the National Science and Technology Progress Award of PRC in 2011. Professor Yu also won the Lifetime Achievement Award of the Chinese Information Processing Society of China in 2011.

Federico Zanettin is Associate Professor of English Language and Translation at the University of Perugia, Italy. His research activity has focused mainly on two areas of translation studies, corpus-based studies and the translation of comic books, on which he has published and lectured widely. His publications include *Translation Driven Corpora: Corpus Resources for Descriptive and Applied Translation Studies* (2012), *Corpora in Translator Education* (co-editor, with Silvia Bernardini and Dominic Stewart, 2003), and *Comics in Translation* (editor, 2008).

Zhang Min, a distinguished professor and Director of the Research Institute of Intelligent Computing at Soochow University, received his BA and PhD in computer science from Harbin Institute of Technology in 1991 and 1997, respectively. From 1997 to 1999, he worked as a postdoctoral research fellow in Korean Advanced Institute of Science and Technology in South Korea. He began his academic and industrial career as a researcher at Lernout & Hauspie Asia Pacific (Singapore) in September 1999. He joined Infotalk Technology (Singapore) as a researcher in 2001 and became a senior research manager in 2002. He joined the Institute for Infocomm Research (Singapore) in 2003. He has co-authored more than 150 papers in leading journals and conferences. He was the recipient of several awards in China and oversea, including the 2013 Shuang Chuang Program (1000 Talent Program of Jiangsu Province), the second prize of the Ministry of Aerospace of China in 1995 and 1997, the 2008/2009 research achiever of the Institute for Infocomm Research, and the 2002 National Infocomm Award (group) at Singapore. He is the Vice President of COLIPS (2011–2013), a steering committee member of PACLIC (2011–present), an executive member of AFNLP (2013~2014), and a member of ACL (2006~).

Xiaojun Zhang 張霄軍 is an associate professor of Xi'an Jiaotong-Liverpool University and an honorary fellow of University of Liverpool. He was an academic staff and researcher at higher education institutes in China, Ireland, and the United Kingdom after he obtained his PhD in computational linguistics in 2008. He is a professional conduct committee member of the Association of Computational Linguistics and the deputy chair of the Translation Technology Education Society affiliated with the World Interpreting and Translation Teaching Association (WITTA). He is a scientific member for top conferences in natural language processing, such as EMNLP, Coling, LREC, CWMT, CCL, and AACL and a peer reviewer for international and national journals. His research interests cover translation technology, natural language processing, and practical translation.

Zhang Yihua is professor of linguistics and applied linguistics and the former director of the Center for Lexicographical Studies at Guangdong University of Foreign Studies and, concurrently, the Vice-President and Director of the Academic Committee of the China Association for Lexicography and Head of the Chinalex Bilingual Committee. Since 1998, he has authored numerous publications in lexicography, including 130 academic papers, ten academic works, three translation works, and eleven dictionaries. Among these, *English-Chinese Medical Dictionary* won the First Prize of the Fifth National Dictionary Award; *Illustrated English-Chinese Dictionary for Primary School Learners* won the Second Prize of the Fifth National Dictionary Award; and his monographs entitled *Semantics and Lexicographical Definition, Computational Lexicography, Contemporary Lexicography*, and *Meaning, Cognition and Definition,* as well as a number of published papers, have made a great impact on the teaching and research of lexicography in China. His books *Contemporary Lexicography* and *Study on Second Language Acquisition and Leaners' Dictionaries* won the Fourth and Eighth National Excellent Achievement Award of Humanities in Higher Institution, respectively.

PREFACE TO THE SECOND EDITION

Introduction

In recent decades, as a result of the rapid advances in computer science and other related disciplines, such as computational linguistics and terminology studies, translation technology has become a norm in translation practice, an important part of translation studies, a new paradigm of translation pedagogy, and a major trend in the industry. It is generally recognized that translation technology has become popular both in Asia and in the West. It is widely used by translation companies as an indispensable tool to conduct their business with high productivity and efficiency, by international corporations as a foundation for their global language solutions, by professional translators as a core component of their personal workstations, and by occasional users as an important means of multilingual information mining. The advent of translation technology has totally globalized and instantized translation and drastically changed the way we process, teach, and study translation. Translation technology has, in short, brought fundamental changes and additional dimensions to all aspects of the contemporary world of translation. The time has really come for us to sum up what has been done so far and what needs to be done in the future through the publication of the first encyclopedia on this important subject.

Definition of Translation Technology

The scope of this encyclopedia covers as far as possible all the concepts in the field and all the changes that translation technology has brought to it. This scope determines the way we define translation technology. According to Lynne Bowker, translation technology refers to different types of technology used in human translation, machine translation, and computer-aided translation, covering the general tools used in computing, such as word processors and electronic resources, and the specific tools used in translating, such as corpus-analysis tools and terminology management systems (Bowker 2002: 5–9). A broader definition is given in *A Dictionary of Translation Technology*, which describes translation technology as "a branch of translation studies that specializes in the issues and skills related to the computerization of translation" (Chan 2004: 258). This means that translation technology is inclusive of both computer-aided translation and machine translation. As machine translation serves basically as an aid to human translation without human intervention, it is considered a form of computer-aided translation. In this encyclopedia, translation technology covers computer-aided translation, machine translation, localization, and speech translation.

Aims of the Encyclopedia

The main purpose of preparing this *Routledge Encyclopedia of Translation Technology*, as mentioned, is to produce a comprehensive reference for scholars and specialists engaged in the study of translation technology and for general readers who are interested in knowing, learning, and using new concepts and skills of translation technology in translation practice. To meet the aspirations of these two groups of users, the contents of all the chapters in this encyclopedia are both academic and general and brief and self-contained, depending on the nature of the topic. Useful references and resources are given in chapters to show the scholarship that has been attained in relevant areas and what essential works are available for readers to delve deeper into the areas they are interested in.

To achieve these purposes, we have invited fifty-eight scholars and specialists working at academic institutions or private organizations in different parts of the world to contribute chapters to this encyclopedia. Their national or regional affiliations include, in alphabetical order, Australia, Belgium, Canada, China, France, Germany, Hong Kong, Ireland, Italy, Japan, the Netherlands, Singapore, South Africa, Spain, Sweden, Taiwan, the United Kingdom, and the United States. Contributions by scholars in these countries are in general comprehensive, informative, prospective, and well documented. As the first definitive encyclopedia of translation technology, this book aims to serve as an authoritative reference to scholars and students of both machine translation and computer-aided translation and lay a solid foundation for translation technology to undergo a rapid growth in the future.

Coverage of This Encyclopedia

This encyclopedia is structured in a way that facilitates the understanding of translation technology in all its aspects. It is divided into three parts: Part 1, "General Issues in Translation Technology", covers the general issues relating to both computer-aided translation and machine translation; Part 2, "The National/Regional Developments of Translation Technology", contains articles on the history and growth of translation technology in countries and regions where this technology is researched, developed, and widely used; and Part 3, "Specific Topics in Translation Technology", which has twenty-two chapters on the various aspects of machine translation and computer-aided translation, including topics such as alignment, concordancing, localization, online translation, and translation memory.

Part 1: General Issues in Translation Technology

Part 1 has four chapters on computer-aided translation and eleven chapters on machine translation. The first four chapters cover the general issues relating to the history, major concepts, major systems, and translator training of computer-aided translation. This part begins with a history of computer-aided translation in the last five decades by Chan Sin-wai of Caritas Institute of Higher Education, who divides the entire history of translation technology (1967–2013) into five periods: the period of germination (1967–1983), the period of steady growth (1984–1992), the period of rapid growth (1993–2003), the period of global development (2004–2013), and the period of new age (2013–2023).

The second chapter, also by the same author, is about the seven major concepts in computer-aided translation that shape the development of functions in translation technology. These concepts are: simulativity, emulativity, customizability, compatibility, controllability, productivity, and collaborativity.

The third chapter in this part is by Ignacio Garcia of Sydney University in Australia, who writes on computer-aided translation systems. He is of the view that computer-aided translation systems are software applications aimed at increasing translators' productivity while maintaining an acceptable level of quality. The use of these systems, restricted to technical translation in the nineties, has extended now to most types of translation, and most translators, including non-professionals, could benefit from using them.

The fourth chapter is by Lynne Bowker of the University of Ottawa, who discusses translator training in the context of translation technologies. She believes that just as translation has been affected by the use of computers, so too has the way in which translators are trained. Her chapter explores questions such as which types of tools are relevant for translators, what translators need to learn about technologies, who should be responsible for teaching translators about computer aids, and when technologies should be introduced into the curriculum. The answers are not always clear cut, but solutions and best practices are emerging.

The second half of Part 1 has chapters on various general aspects of machine translation, including its general aspects, history, systems, evaluation criteria, approaches, and teaching. It begins with a chapter by Liu Qun of Noah's Ark Lab of Huawei and Xiaojun Zhang of Xi'an Jiaotong-Liverpool University in China. Their chapter introduces the technology of machine translation (MT), also known as automatic translation. It defines machine translation; outlines its history; and describes its various approaches, evaluation methods, and applications. The second chapter is by W. John Hutchins, formerly of the University of East Anglia. He provides a history of machine translation from the "pioneering" research and the early operational systems (1950s and 1960s) to the dominance of rule-based systems (1967 to 1989) and finally to the emergence of corpus-based systems (in particular statistical approaches), translation memories, evaluation methods, and current applications.

The next five chapters cover five major approaches to machine translation: example-based machine translation, open-source machine translation, pragmatics-based machine translation, rule-based machine translation, and statistical machine translation. There is no chapter on neural machine translation, but this approach has been adequately covered in chapters on machine translation and deep learning and translation technology. Wong Tak-ming of Hong Kong Metropolitan University authored the chapter on example-based machine translation (EBMT), covering its history, the major issues related to translation examples, and the fundamental stages of translation for an EBMT system. The suitability issue is also discussed, showing the types of translation that are deemed suitable for EBMT and how it interoperates with other MT approaches. The second chapter on machine translation is by Mikel L. Forcada of the Universitat d'Alacant in Spain. It defines free/open-source (FOS) software and reviews its licensing and implications for machine translation as data-intensive software and the types of free/open-source MT systems and users and their use in business and research. It also surveys the existing free/open-source MT systems and looks into the challenges their systems face in the future. The third chapter in this part is on pragmatics-based machine translation by David Farwell, formerly of the Catalonia Polytechnic University in Barcelona, Spain, and Stephen Helmreich of the New Mexico State University in the United States. They hold the view that pragmatics-based machine translation relies on reasoning to determine speech act content and on belief ascription for modelling the participants in the translation process (source text author and audience, translator, intended audience of translation). The theoretical framework and computational platform are presented, along with an analysis of their benefits and shortcomings. Rule-based machine translation is the topic of the fourth chapter in this part, written by

Bai Xiaojing of Tsinghua University and Yu Shiwen of Peking University in China. According to the authors, the rule-based method had been dominant in machine translation research for several decades, and it is still functioning in present-day MT systems. Despite its difficulties and problems, this method is now gaining a new momentum, as the significance of linguistic research has been realized more than ever and the formalization of linguistic knowledge is growing and maturing. The fifth chapter in this part is on statistical machine translation. According to the authors of this chapter, Liu Yang of Tsinghua University and Zhang Min of Soochow University in China, statistical machine translation (SMT) is a machine translation paradigm that generates translations based on a probabilistic model of translation process, the parameters of which are estimated from parallel text. Modelling, training, and decoding are three fundamental issues in SMT, which has evolved from an early word-based approach to recent phrase-based and syntax-based approaches in the past decades. As a data-driven technology, it will continue to develop in the era of big data.

The last two chapters on machine translation are on its evaluation and teaching. Kit Chunyu of the City University of Hong Kong and Wong Tak-ming of Hong Kong Metropolitan University introduce the key issues and basic principles of computer(-aided) translation evaluation, covering its historical evolution, context-dependent multi-dimensional nature, and existing methodologies. The major evaluation approaches, including both manual and automatic, are presented with a full discussion of their strengths and weaknesses. Cecilia Wong Shuk Man, who has taught machine translation at the Chinese University of Hong Kong for a number of years and currently with Caritas Institute of Higher Education, recounts her experience in teaching machine translation at the MA in Computer-Aided Translation Programme of the Chinese University of Hong Kong.

Two new chapters have been added to this part. Venus Chan of Hong Kong Metropolitan University and Mark Shuttleworth of Hong Kong Baptist University authored the chapter on teaching translation technology. This chapter sets out to consider relevant theoretical contexts and pedagogical approaches and to provide a snapshot of current implementations of translation technology teaching. In the first part, rationale, course content, and approaches are all considered in some detail from a theoretical point of view. Following that, the second, more practical part offers an overview of different training types, enumerates the various types of technology that can most often be found in university-level curricula, and ends with a brief discussion of a selection of problems and challenges with which course designers and deliverers are currently faced. Throughout the chapter, the focus is mainly on university training, although other types are also briefly considered.

The last chapter in Part 1 is on artificial intelligence and translation. Liu Xueting and Li Chengze, both of Caritas Institute of Higher Education, hold the view that artificial intelligence (AI) is a large field of study that enables computers and machines to mimic the perception, learning, problem-solving, and decision-making capabilities of humans. The main challenge in AI-based translation comes from the difficulties in understanding the semantics of texts as well as understanding the syntactic structure of texts to translate them. This chapter starts from the rule-based machine translation approach to show how human-crafted rules can be used to translate texts and illustrate their limitations. It then moves on to statistical machine translation, which learns to translate automatically from a text corpus without too much human intervention. Recently, deep learning–based approaches in translation have emerged. The key component of deep learning is neural networks, which are used to extract text semantics and learn the translation patterns from the training data. The widely used attention mechanism in deep learning enables a very deep understanding of the word-level text and sentence relationships to enable precise translation.

Part 2: The National/Regional Developments of Translation Technology

The importance of studying translation technology from a global perspective cannot be over-emphasized. Part 2 of this encyclopedia contains chapters that describe the development of computer-aided translation and machine translation in some of the countries and regions where translation technology is studied, developed, and used. A number of countries in different regions have been selected to illustrate the development and application of translation technology in different social and cultural situations and at different levels of technological advancement. These countries and regions include Belgium, France, the Netherlands, and the United Kingdom in Europe; China, Hong Kong, Japan, and Taiwan in Asia; South Africa in Africa; and Canada and the United States in North America.

The first chapter, on China, is written by Qian Duoxiu of Beihang University in Beijing, China. Her chapter outlines the growth of translation technology in China from 1946 to the present, covering its major participants, achievements, applications, mainstream tools, and prospects.

The second chapter is by Elliott Macklovitch, former president of the Association for Machine Translation in the Americas. His chapter traces the evolution of translation technology in Canada, from the emergence of the first computerized aids (dedicated word processors), through the well-known success of the MÉTÉO system, to the development of innovative translator support tools like TransType. It also assesses the current use of cutting-edge technologies and automatic dictation for the production of high-quality translation.

Sylviane Cardey of the University of Franche-Comte in France writes on translation technology in France. According to the author, machine translation in France started at the time of the Cold War. She traces the development of machine translation in France from the 1950s to the present, focusing, in the latter part of her chapter, on six research centres and companies, the technologies they used, and the systems they produced. Two approaches to MT in France clearly stand out, one based on linguistic methods and the other on statistical methods.

Chan Sin-wai, Ian Castor Chow, and Wong Tak-ming jointly authored the chapter on translation technology in Hong Kong, focusing on the research projects, course offerings, research centres at local tertiary institutions, and the use of translation technology in Hong Kong's translation industry.

The situation of Japan is described by Hitoshi Isahara of Toyohashi University of Technology in Japan. He gives a historical overview of research and development of machine translation systems in Japan and then goes on to describe one of the latest government-funded MT projects, research activities related to pre- and post-editing, development of linguistic resource for MT systems, and research on evaluation of MT systems.

The only chapter on Africa is by Gerhard B. van Huyssteen, Marissa Griesel, and Martin Puttkammer, all of North-West University in South Africa. This chapter focuses on the history and state of the art of MT research and development in South Africa for South African languages. It first provides an overview of the lead-up to MT development in South Africa, highlighting some related research, as well as the development of tools and data that could support MT in South Africa indirectly. It then gives an overview of the first initiatives by the South African government to support the development of MT for South African languages. It also discusses individual research and development projects on MT for South African languages before describing in more detail the Autshumato project, South Africa's first consolidated national MT project for South African languages. It concludes with a look ahead to post-Autshumato initiatives and possibilities for MT in South Africa.

From Africa we turn back to Asia and introduce the situation of translation technology in Taiwan, written by Shih Chung-ling of the National Kaohsiung First University of Science and

Technology. This chapter describes the findings regarding translation technological (TT) development and the use of translation technology in Taiwan's translation industry, university education, and academic research. The author also makes some suggestions to address the inadequacy in the use of translation technology in the industry and academia through on-the-job training, joint lectures, and regular conferences and highlights the need to incorporate elements of translation technology in translation research in response to the changing situation of the field of translation.

Leonoor van der Beek of RightNow Technologies and Antal van den Bosch of Radboud University Nijmegen in the Netherlands write on translation technology in the Netherlands and Belgium. Their chapter highlights the development of the Eurotra, METAL, DLT, and Rosetta systems and examines the current state of translation in Dutch. According to the authors, researchers from Belgium and the Netherlands participated in large national and international projects in the 1980s. Disappointing results led to a decade of silence, but in the 2000s, new research projects embraced statistical and example-based machine translation. Dutch, with an estimated 25 million native speakers, is a source or target language in about 15% of current translation technology products.

The chapter on translation technology in the United Kingdom is by Christophe Declercq of University College London. He examines this topic under the headings of peculiar relations, education, devolution, and translation technology companies.

The last chapter of Part II is on translation technology in the United States, jointly written by Jennifer DeCamp, the chief scientist for human language technology at MITRE Corporation, and Jost Zetzsche, a German-American translator, Sinologist, and writer who lives in Oregon. To them, while the history of translation technology development in the United States has been highly international, there are certain unique features in the country that differentiate it from its development elsewhere. These include the extensive investment by the US military, the wide gulf between machine translation researchers and human translators, and the extensive involvement of religious groups in the development and use of translation technology. They provide a list of major events in the history of translation technology in the United States, highlighting the special features in each decade.

Part 3: Specific Topics in Translation Technology

Whereas topics in the first two parts, Part 1 and Part 2, are on the whole of a more general nature, the twenty-two topics in Part 3, written by twenty-eight scholars, are more specific to translation technology.

"Alignment", the first chapter of this part, is written by Lars Ahrenberg of Linköping University, Sweden. His chapter covers the main algorithms and systems for sentence and word alignment. The focus is on statistical properties of bi-texts and the way these properties are exploited for alignment in generative as well as discriminative and heuristic models. In addition, this chapter provides an overview of standard evaluation metrics for alignment performance, such as precision, recall, and alignment error rate.

Bi-text is the topic discussed by Alan K. Melby of Brigham Young University in the United States and Yves Savourel, a localization expert now residing in Colorado. Bitext is an idea from the 1980s that was originally intended to primarily assist human translators in retrieving instances of words and phrases as treated by other human translators, and it has also turned out to be the basis for many other aspects of translation technology, from translation memory to machine translation. In a sense, it has evolved from a purely descriptive mechanism to a framework for translation that makes it difficult to break out of a sentence-by-sentence correspondence between source and target languages.

Zhang Yihua of the Guangdong University of Foreign Studies, writes on computational lexicography, an area which is closely related to translation technology. Computational lexicography, according to the author, has gone through decades of development, and great achievements have been attained in building and using corpora, which contribute enormously to the development of lexicographical databases and computer-aided dictionary writing and publishing systems. Computer lexicography is also closely associated with machine translation, as all MT systems have electronic dictionaries.

The topic of concordancing is covered by Federico Zanettin of the University of Perugia, Italy. This chapter provides an historical overview of concordances and concordancers; describes how different types of corpus resources and tools can be integrated into a computer-assisted translation environment; and examines a set of parameters, including data search and display options, which may be used to evaluate concordancing applications.

Controlled languages, a topic of considerable interest to translation technologists, is covered by Rolf Schwitter of Macquaire University in Australia. Controlled languages are subsets of natural languages that use a restricted vocabulary and grammar in order to reduce or eliminate ambiguity and complexity. Some of these controlled languages are designed to improve communication between humans. Some of them make it easier for non-native speakers to read technical documentation. Some aim to improve the quality of machine translation, and another group of controlled languages serve as high-level interface languages to semantic systems where automated reasoning is important. It is generally recognized that corpus in important both in lexicography and translation technology.

The chapter on corpus is written by Lan Li of the Chinese University of Hong Kong, Shenzhen, and Mary Ye of the University of Nottingham, Ningbo, in China. Their chapter introduces the important advances in corpus-based translation studies; presents detailed information on standard monolingual and bilingual corpora; and argues that both can help translators to establish equivalence, terminology, and phraseology between languages. In addition, corpus-based quantitative and qualitative methods can help to verify, refine, or clarify translation theories.

The topic of editing has been dealt with from three perspectives – editing in translation technology, editing in audiovisual translation, and post-editing of machine translation. "Editing in Translation Technology" is authored by Christophe Declercq, of University College London, who also writes a chapter on translation technology in the United Kingdom in Part 2. He covers a number of areas in this topic, including language and translation technology, "traditional" translation technology and editing, cognitive processes and editing, forms of editing, revision and proof-reading, post-editing and machine translation, and post-editing guidelines.

"Editing in Audiovisual Translation" is authored by Alejandro Bolaños García-Escribano and Christophe Declercq, both of University College London. This chapter aims to provide an overarching description of concepts and issues involved with editing forms of audiovisual localization, particularly subtitling.

"Post-Editing of Machine Translation" is written by May Li of Jiaotong University in Shanghai, China. This chapter starts with a justification of why post-editing MT has become more prevalent in recent years. The common practice of post-editing is then introduced, with demonstrations of post-editing guidelines at different levels and with different organizations. The role of source text in post-editing is explored in relation to the increase of translation productivity. Data from a recent experiment of post-editing MT texts with and without source text between English and Chinese will be analysed in detail to show the impact of the source text on the time and quality of post-editing. Suggestions are provided to facilitate post-editing in a productive manner.

The topic of information retrieval and text mining is covered in the chapter co-authored by Kit Chunyu of the City University of Hong Kong and Nie Jian-Yun of the University of Montreal in Canada. This chapter divides information retrieval and text mining into three stages and describes the main operations of information retrieval and text mining.

Sue Ellen Wright, of Kent State University in the United States, explores the issues of language codes in this book. This chapter examines what a human language is, as well as other related concepts, such as language families and groups, language varieties, and dialects. The first part of the chapter provides an outline-like reference to the many stakeholders and standards used to encode or otherwise characterize languages and language varieties, while the second part of the chapter provides a more detailed review of the history and future directions affecting the creation, maintenance, and application of language identifiers, codes, and tags.

Keiran J. Dunne, also of Kent State University, authors the chapter on localization. This chapter examines localization and its evolution from the 1980s to the present, paying special attention to when, why, and how it arose; the ways it has changed over time; and its relationship to translation and internationalization.

Olivia Kwong Oi Yee, formerly of the Chinese University of Hong Kong, authors the chapter on natural language processing. According to her, the primary concern of natural language processing is the design and implementation of computational systems for analysing and understanding human languages to automate certain real-life tasks demanding human language abilities. It is typically a multidisciplinary endeavour, drawing on linguistics, computer science, mathematics, and psychology, amongst others, with particular focus on computational models and algorithms at its core.

The chapter on online translation is written by Federico Gaspari of the University of Bologna, Italy. The chapter concerns key aspects of online translation, focusing on the relationship between translators and the web, with a review of the latest trends in this area. A wide range of Internet-based resources, tools, and services for translators are presented, highlighting their key features and discussing their pros and cons.

Felipe Sanchez-Martinez of the Universitat d'Alacant in Spain writes on part-of-speech tagging. Part-of-speech tagging is a well-known problem and a common step in natural language processing applications; part-of-speech taggers try to assign the correct part of speech to all words of a given text. This chapter reviews the main approaches to part-of-speech tagging and its use in machine translation.

Segmentation is a topic covered by Freddy Y.Y. Choi. His chapter introduces text segmentation and covers all the elements that make up a working algorithm, key considerations in a practical implementation, and the impact of design decisions on the performance of a complete machine translation solution. The narrative offers a survey of existing design options and recommendations for advancing the state of the art and managing current limitations.

Lee Tan of the Chinese University of Hong Kong writes on speech translation. According to the author, speech translation is an advanced computer-based technology that enables speech communication between people who speak different languages. A speech translation system is an integration of speech recognition, machine translation, and speech synthesis. The latest systems are available as smartphone applications. They can perform translation of naturally spoken sentences and support multiple languages.

Jorge Díaz Cintas of University College London writes on subtitling and technology. His chapter highlights some of the most significant technological milestones that have taken place in the field of subtitling and considers more recent developments in this arena, such as machine translation and cloud subtitling.

Kara Warburton of the University of Illinois Urbana-Champaign writes on terminology management. Her chapter provides an introduction to terminology as a field of applied linguistics and a strategic pursuit in information technology. It covers relations to lexicology, basic concepts and principal theories, methods and workflows for managing terminologies, uses of terminology, connections with corpora, terminology databases, and standards and best practices.

Alan K. Melby and Sue Ellen Wright discuss translation memory and computer-aided translation in the contexts of translation environment tools; sub-segment identification; advantages of a translation memory; how to create, use, and maintain a translation memory; history of translation memory; and the future developments and industry impact of translation memory.

The chapter on translation management systems, written by Mark Shuttleworth of Hong Kong Baptist University, traces the history of translation management, studies its common features, and estimates the future of technology in the field of translation. Computerized translation management systems have been in existence since the late 1990s. They were introduced in order to enable translation companies and individual translators to remain in control of ever-increasing volumes of content and to facilitate the monitoring of business, process, and language aspects of translation and localization projects.

The last chapter, "Deep Learning and Translation Technology", is authored by Siu Sai Cheong of Hang Seng University of Hong Kong. This chapter discusses deep learning and its application to translation technology. It first explains what deep learning is and how it works, with an introduction to key concepts, such as artificial neural networks, activation functions, loss functions, forward propagation, backpropagation, and optimization. It then explores three approaches to machine translation with deep neural networks, which is followed by a discussion of the application of deep neural networks to speech translation, intersemiotic translation, and translation memory and a review of noteworthy trends.

Conclusion

With five leading scholars in the field serving as consultant editors and fifty-eight scholars and specialists contributing their chapters to this volume, this encyclopedia, the first of its kind, is a valuable and definitive reference in the field of translation technology. It is hoped that specialists and general readers will find this encyclopedia informative and useful, while professionals will find the knowledge they gain from this volume helpful in translation practice.

Bibliography

Bowker, Lynne (2002) *Computer-Aided Translation Technology: A Practical Introduction*, Ottawa: University of Ottawa Press.

Chan, Sin-wai (2004) *A Dictionary of Translation Technology*, Hong Kong: The Chinese University Press.

ON THE PUBLICATION OF THE SECOND EDITION

The publication of this second edition owes much to Andrea Hartill, senior publisher of Routledge, who suggested an enlarged and revised version of the first edition due to the rapid advances in the field of translation technology. This edition has five additional chapters, with many chapters updated and revised. It is hoped that it will better meet the needs of the increasing number of people who are interested in translation technology.

Chan Sin-wai

EDITOR'S ACKNOWLEDGEMENTS

First and foremost, I would like to thank Andrea Hartill, senior publisher of Routledge, for giving me an opportunity to fulfil my wish to edit the first encyclopaedia of translation technology. Without her support and encouragement, this volume would not have seen the light of day.

My most sincere gratitude goes to Professor David Pollard, former professor of translation and chairman of the Department of Translation of the Chinese University of Hong Kong. It was David's recommendation that resulted in the publication of this volume.

My thanks are due to all the five consultant editors of this encyclopaedia, Professor Lynne Bowker, Professor David Farwell, Dr W. John Hutchins, Professor Alan K. Melby, and Professor William S-Y, whose support for this volume is indispensable in its completion. Alan K. Melby, in particular, deserves a special note of thanks not only for his contribution of two articles but also for recommending prominent scholars in the field to contribute articles to this volume.

Last, I would like to thank Florence Li Wing Yee, my colleague at Caritas Institute of Higher Education, and Iola Ashby, editorial assistant at Routledge, for their efforts in the publication of this encyclopaedia.

PART 1

General

1

THE DEVELOPMENT OF TRANSLATION TECHNOLOGY

1967–2023

Chan Sin-wai

Introduction

The history of translation technology, or more specifically computer-aided translation, is short, but its development is fast. It is generally recognized that the failure of machine translation in the 1960s led to the emergence of computer-aided translation. The development of computer-aided translation from its beginning in 1967 as a result of the infamous ALPAC report (1966) to 2013, totalling 46 years, can be divided into four periods. The first period, which goes from 1967 to 1983, is a period of germination. The second period, covering the years between 1984 and 1993, is a period of steady growth. The third period, which is from 1993 to 2003, is a decade of rapid growth. The last period, which includes the years 2004 to 2013, is a period of global development.

1967–1983: A Period of Germination

Computer-aided translation, as mentioned, came from machine translation, while machine translation resulted from the invention of computers. Machine translation had made considerable progress in a number of countries from the time the first computer, ENIAC, was invented in 1946. Several events before the ALPAC report in 1966 are worth noting. In 1947, one year after the invention of the computer, Warren Weaver, president of the Rockefeller Foundation and Andrew D. Booth of Birkbeck College, London University, were the first two scholars who proposed to make use of the newly invented computer to translate natural languages (Chan 2004: 290–91). In 1949, Warren Weaver wrote a memorandum for peer review outlining the prospects of machine translation, known in history as "Weaver's Memorandum". In 1952, Yehoshua Bar-Hillel held the first conference on machine translation at the Massachusetts Institute of Technology, and some of the papers were compiled by William N. Locke and Andrew D. Booth into an anthology entitled *Machine Translation of Languages: Fourteen Essays*, the first book on machine translation (Locke and Booth 1955). In 1954, Leon Dostert of Georgetown University and Peter Sheridan of IBM used the IBM701 machine to make a public demonstration of the translation of Russian sentences into English, which marked a milestone in machine translation (Hutchins 1999: 1–16; Chan 2004: 125–26). In the same year, the inaugural issue of *Mechanical Translation*, the first journal in the field of machine translation, was published by the Massachusetts Institute

DOI: 10.4324/9781003168348-2

of Technology (Yngve 2000: 50–51). In 1962, the Association for Computational Linguistics was founded in the United States, and the journal of the association, *Computational Linguistics*, was also published. It was roughly estimated that by 1965, there were eighteen countries or research institutions engaged in studies on machine translation, including the United States, the former Soviet Union, the United Kingdom, Japan, France, West Germany, Italy, the former Czechoslovakia, the former Yugoslavia, East Germany, Mexico, Hungary, Canada, Holland, Romania, and Belgium (Zhang 2006: 30–34).

The development of machine translation in the United States since the late 1940s, however, fell short of expectations. In 1963, the Georgetown machine translation project was terminated, which signifies the end of the largest machine translation project in the United States (Chan 2004: 303). In 1964, the government of the United States set up the Automatic Language Processing Advisory Committee (ALPAC) of seven experts to enquire into the state of machine translation (ALPAC 1966; Warwick 1987: 22–37). In 1966, the report of the Committee, entitled *Languages and Machines: Computers in Translation and Linguistics*, pointed out that "there is no immediate or predictable prospect of useful machine translation" (ALPAC 1966: 32). As machine translation was twice as expensive as human translation, it was unable to meet people's expectations; the Committee recommended that resources to support machine translation be terminated. Its report also stated that "as it becomes increasingly evident that fully automatic high-quality machine translation was not going to be realized for a long time, interest began to be shown in machine-aided translation" (ALPAC 1966: 25). It added that machine translation should shift to machine-aided translation, which was "aimed at improved human translation, with an appropriate use of machine aids" (ALPAC 1966: iii), and that "machine-aided translation may be an important avenue toward better, quicker, and cheaper translation" (ALPAC 1966: 32). The ALPAC report dealt a serious blow to machine translation in the United States, which was to remain stagnant for more than a decade, and it also had a negative impact on research on machine translation in Europe and Russia. But this gave an opportunity for machine-aided translation to come into being. All these events show that the birth of machine-aided translation is closely related to the development of machine translation.

Computer-aided translation, nevertheless, would not be possible without the support of related concepts and software. It was no mere coincidence that translation memory, which is one of the major concepts and functions of computer-aided translation, came out during this period. According to W. John Hutchins, the concept of translation memory can be traced to the period from the 1960s to the 1980s (Hutchins 1998: 287–307). In 1978, when Alan K. Melby of the Translation Research Group of Brigham Young University conducted research on machine translation and developed an interactive translation system, Automated Language Processing Systems (ALPS), he incorporated the idea of translation memory into a tool called "Repetitions Processing", which aimed at finding matched strings (Melby 1978; Melby and Warner 1995: 187). In the following year, Peter Arthern, in his paper on the issue of whether machine translation should be used in a conference organized by the European Commission, proposed the method of "translation by text-retrieval" (Arthern 1979: 93). According to Arthern,

> This information would have to be stored in such a way that any given portion of text in any of the languages involved can be located immediately . . . together with its translation into any or all of the other languages which the organization employs.
>
> *(1979: 95)*

In October 1980, Martin Kay published an article entitled "The Proper Place of Men and Machines in Language Translation", at the Palo Alto Research Center of Xerox. He proposed to create a machine translation system in which the display on the screen is divided into two windows. The text to be translated appears in the upper window, and the translation will be composed in the bottom one to allow the translator to edit the translation with the help of simple facilities particular to translation, such as aids for word selection and dictionary consultation, which are labelled by Kay a *translator amanuensis* (1980: 9–18). In view of the level of word-processing capacities at that time, his proposal was inspiring to the development of computer-aided translation and exerted a huge impact on its research later on. Kay is generally considered a forerunner in proposing an interactive translation system.

It can be seen that the idea of translation memory was established in the late 1970s and 1980s. Hutchins believed that the first person to propose the concept of translation memory is Arthern. As Melby and Arthern proposed the idea almost at the same time, both could be considered forerunners. And it should be acknowledged that Arthern, Melby, and Kay made a great contribution to the growth of computer-aided translation in its early days.

The first attempt to deploy the idea of translation memory in a machine translation system was made by Alan K. Melby and his co-researchers at Brigham Young University, who jointly developed ALPS. This system provided access to previously translated segments which were identical (Hutchins 1998: 291). Some scholars classify this type of full match as a function of the first-generation translation memory systems (Gotti *et al.* 2005: 26–30; Kavak 2009; Elita and Gavrila 2006: 24–26). One of the major shortcomings of this generation of computer-aided translation systems is that sentences with full matching were very small in number, minimizing the reusability of translation memory and the role of the translation memory database (Wang 2011: 141).

Some researchers around 1980 began to collect and store translation samples with the intention of redeploying and sharing their translation resources. Constrained by the limitations of computer hardware (such as its limited storage space), the cost of building a bilingual database was high, and with the immaturity in the algorithms for bilingual data alignment, translation memory technology had been in a stage of exploration. As a result, a truly commercial computer-aided translation system did not emerge during the sixteen years of this period, and translation technology failed to make an impact on translation practice and the translation industry.

1984–1992: A Period of Steady Growth

The eight years between 1984 and 1992 were a period of steady growth for computer-aided translation and for some developments to take place. Corporate operation began in 1984, system commercialization in 1988, and regional expansion in 1992.

Company Operation

It was during this period that the first computer-aided translation companies, Trados in Germany and Star Group in Switzerland, were founded in 1984. These two companies later had a great impact on the development of computer-aided translation.

The German company was founded by Jochen Hummel and Iko Knyphausen in Stuttgart, Germany, in 1984. Trados GmbH came from TRAnslation and DOcumentation Software. This company was set up initially as a language service provider (LSP) to work on a translation project they received from IBM in the same year. As the company later developed computer-aided translation software to help complete the project, the establishment of Trados GmbH is regarded as the starting point of the period of steady growth in computer-aided translation (Garcia 2005: 18–31; www.lspzone.com).

Of equal significance was the founding of the Swiss company STAR AG in the same year. STAR, an acronym of software, translation, artwork, and recording, provided manual technical editing and translation with information technology and automation. Two years later, STAR opened its first foreign office in Germany in order to serve the increasingly important software localization market and later developed STAR software products, GRIPS, and Transit for information management and translation memory, respectively. At the same time, client demand and growing export markets led to the establishment of additional overseas locations in Japan and China. The STAR Group still plays an important role in the translation technology industry (www.star-group.net).

It can be observed that during this early period of computer-aided translation, all companies in the field were either established or operated in Europe. This Eurocentric phenomenon was going to change in the next period.

System Commercialization

The commercialization of computer-aided translation systems began in 1988, when Eiichiro Sumita and Yutaka Tsutsumi of the Japanese branch of IBM released the ETOC (Easy to Consult) tool, which was actually an upgraded electronic dictionary. Consultation of a traditional electronic dictionary was by individual words. It could not search phrases or sentences with more than two words. ETOC offered a flexible solution. When inputting a sentence to be searched into ETOC, the system would try to extract it from its dictionary. If no matches were found, the system would make a grammatical analysis of the sentence, taking away some substantive words but keeping the form words and adjectives which formed the sentence pattern. The sentence pattern would be compared with bilingual sentences in the dictionary database to find sentences with a similar pattern, which would be displayed for the translator to select. The translator could then copy and paste the sentence into the editor and revise the sentence to complete the translation. Though the system did not use the term translation memory and the translation database was still called a "dictionary", it nevertheless had essentially the basic features of translation memory of today. The main shortcoming of this system was that as it needed to do grammatical analyses, the programming of the system would be difficult and its scalability would be limited. If a new language were to be added, a grammatical analysis module would have to be programmed for the language. Furthermore, as the system could only work on perfect matching but not fuzzy matching, it drastically cut down on the reusability of translations (Sumita and Tsutsumi 1988: 2).

In 1988, Trados developed TED, a plug-in for text processor tool that was later to become, in expanded form, the first Translator's Workbench editor, developed by two people and their secretary (Brace 1992). It was around this time that Trados made the decision to split the company, passing the translation services part of the business to INK in the Netherlands, so that they could concentrate on developing translation software (www.translationzone.com).

Two years later, the company also released the first version of MultiTerm as a memory-resident multilingual terminology management tool for DOS, taking the innovative approach of storing all data in a single, freely structured database with entries classified by user-defined attributes (Eurolux Computers 1992: 8; www.translationzone.com; Wassmer 2011).

In 1991 STAR AG also released worldwide the Transit 1.0 ("Transit" was derived from the phrase "translate it") 32-bit DOS version, which had been under development since 1987 and used exclusively for in-house production. Transit featured the modules that are standard features of today's CAT systems, such as a proprietary translation editor with separate but synchronized windows for source and target language and tag protection, a translation memory engine, a terminology management component, and project management features. In the context of system development, the ideas of terminology management and project management began with Transit 1.0. Additional products were later developed for the implementation and automation of corporate product communications: TermStar, WebTerm, GRIPS, MindReader, SPIDER, and STAR James (www.star-group.net).

One of the most important events in this period is obviously the release of the first commercial system, Trados, in 1992, which marks the beginning of commercial computer-aided translation systems.

Regional Expansion

The year 1992 also marks the beginning of the regional expansion of computer-aided translation. This year witnessed some significant advances in translation software made in different countries. First, in Germany, Translator's Workbench I and Translator's Workbench II (the DOS version of Trados) were launched within the year, with Workbench II being a standalone package with an integrated editor. Translator's Workbench II comprises the TW II Editor (formally TED) and MultiTerm 2. Translator's Workbench II was the first system to incorporate a "translation memory" and alignment facilities into its workstation. Also of considerable significance was the creation by Matthias Heyn of Trados's T Align, later known as WinAlign, the first alignment tool on the market. In addition, Trados began to open a network of global offices, including in Brussels, Virginia in the United States, the United Kingdom, and Switzerland (Brace 1994; Eurolux Computers 1992; www.translationzone.com; Hutchins 1998: 287–307).

Second, in the United States, IBM launched its IBM Translation Manager/2 (TM/2), with an operating system/2 (OS/2) package that integrated a variety of translation aids within a Presentation Manager interface. TM/2 had its own editor and a translation memory feature which used fuzzy search algorithms to retrieve existing material from its translation database. TM/2 could analyse texts to extract terms. TM/2 came with lemmatizers, spelling lists, and other linguistic resources for nineteen languages, including Catalan, Flemish, Norwegian, Portuguese, Greek, and Icelandic. External dictionaries could also be integrated into TM/2, provided they were formatted in Standard Generalized Markup Language (SGML). TM/2 could be linked to logic-based machine translation (Brace 1992). This system is perhaps the first hybrid computer-aided translation system that was integrated with a machine translation system (Brace 1993; Wassmer 2011).

Third, in Russia, the PROMT Ltd was founded by two doctorates in computational linguistics, Svetlana Sokolova and Alexander Serebryakov, in St. Petersburg in 1991. At the beginning, the company mainly developed machine translation (MT) technology, which has been at the heart of the @promt products. Later, it began to provide a full range of translation solutions: machine translation systems and services, dictionaries, translation memory systems, and data mining systems (www.promt.com).

Fourth, in the United Kingdom, two companies specializing in translation software production were founded. First, Mark Lancaster established SDL International, which served as a service provider for the globalization of software (www.sdl.com). Second, ATA Software Technology Ltd, a London-based software house specializing in Arabic translation software, was established in 1992 by some programmers and Arabic software specialists. The company later developed a series of machine translation products (Arabic and English) and MT and TM hybrid systems, Xpro7, and an online translation engine (www.atasoft.com).

1993–2003: A Period of Rapid Growth

This period, covering the years from 1993 to 2003, is a period of rapid growth, due largely to (1) the emergence of more commercial systems, (2) the development of more built-in functions, (3) the dominance of Windows operating systems, (4) the support of more document formats, (5) the support of more languages for translation, and (6) the dominance of Trados as a market leader.

(1) The Emergence of More Commercial Systems

Before 1993, there were only three systems available on the market, Translator's Workbench II from Trados, IBM Translation Manager/2, and STAR Transit 1.0. During this ten-year period between 1993 and 2003, about twenty systems were developed for sale, including better-known systems such as Déjà Vu, Eurolang Optimizer (Brace 1994), WordFisher, SDLX, ForeignDesk, Trans Suite 2000, Yaxin CAT, Wordfast, Across, OmegaT, MultiTrans, Huajian, Heartsome, and Transwhiz. This means that there was a sixfold increase in commercial computer-aided translation systems during this period.

Déjà Vu is the name of a computer-aided translation system developed by Atril in Spain starting in 1993. A preliminary version of Déjà Vu, a customizable computer-aided translation system that combined translation memory technology with example-based machine translation techniques, was initially developed by ATRIL in June to fulfil its own need for a professional translation tool. At first, it worked with machine translation systems, but the experiments with machine translation were extremely disappointing, and subsequent experiences with translation memory tools exposed two main shortcomings: all systems ran under MS-DOS and were capable of processing only plain text files. Then ATRIL began considering the idea of writing its own translation memory software.

Déjà Vu 1.0 was released to the public in November 1993. It had an interface for Microsoft Word for Windows 2.0, which was defined as the first of its kind. Version 1.1 followed soon afterwards, incorporating several performance improvements and an integrated alignment tool (at a time when alignment tools were sold as expensive individual products), and setting a new standard for the translation tool market (www.atril.com).

Déjà Vu, designed to be a professional translation tool, produced acceptable results at an affordable price. Déjà Vu was a first in many areas: the first TM tool for Windows, the first TM tool to directly integrate into Microsoft Word, the first 32-bit TM tool (Déjà Vu version 2.0), and the first affordable professional translation tool.

In the following year, Eurolang Optimizer, a computer-aided translation system, was developed by Eurolang in France. Its components included the translator's workstation, pre-translation server with translation memory and terminology database, and project management tool for multiple languages and users (Brace 1994).

In Germany, Trados GmbH announced the release of the new Windows version of Translator's Workbench, which could be used with standard Windows word processing packages via the Windows DDE interface (Brace 1994). In June 1994, Trados released MultiTerm Professional 1.5, which was included in Translator's Workbench, which had fuzzy search to deliver successful searches even when words were incorrectly spelt, a dictionary-style interface, faster searches through use of new highly compressed data algorithms, drag-and-drop content into a word processor, and an integrated programming language to create powerful layouts (www.translationzone.com).

In Hungary, Tibor Környei developed the WordFisher for Microsoft Word macro set. The program was written in the WordBasic language. For translators, it resembled a translation memory program but provided a simpler interface in Word (Környei 2000).

In 1995, Nero AG was founded in Germany as a manufacturer of CD and DVD application software. Later, the company set up Across Systems GmbH as a division, which developed and marketed a tool of the same name for corporate translation management (CTM) that supported the project and workflow management of translations (Schmidt 2006; German 2009: 9–10).

During the first half of 1996, when Windows 95 was in its final stages of beta testing, Atril Development S.L. in Spain began writing a new version of Déjà Vu – not just porting the original code to 32 bits but adding a large number of important functionalities that had been suggested by users. In October, Atril released Déjà Vu beta v2.0. It consisted of the universal editor, Déjà Vu Interactive (DVI), the Database Maintenance module with an alignment tool, and a full-featured Terminology Maintenance module (Wassmer 2007: 37–38).

In the same year, Déjà Vu again was the first TM tool available for 32-bit Windows and shipped with a number of filters for DTP (desktop publishing) packages – including Frame-Maker, Interleaf, and QuarkXPress – and provided extensive project management facilities to enable project managers to handle large, multi-file, multilingual projects.

In 1997, developments in France and Germany deserve mentioning. In France, CIMOS released Arabic to English translation software An-Nakel El-Arabi, with features like machine translation, a customized dictionary, and translation memory. Because of its deep sentence analysis and semantic connections, An-Nakel El-Arabi could learn new rules and knowledge. CIMOS had previously released English to Arabic translation software (Multilingual 1997). In Germany, Trados GmbH released WinAlign as a visual text alignment tool as the first fully fledged 32-bit application in Trados. Microsoft decided to base its internal localization memory store on Trados and consequently acquired a share of 20% in Trados (www.translationzone.com).

The year 1998 marks a milestone in the development of translation technology in China and Taiwan. In Beijing, Beijing YaxinCheng Software Technology Co. Ltd. 北京雅信誠公司 was set up as a developer of translation software. It was the first computer-aided translation software company in China. In Taipei, the Inventec Corporation released Dr Eye 98 (譯典通) with instant machine translation, dictionaries, and termbases in Chinese and English (www.dreye.com.tw).

In the same year, the activities of SDL and International Communications deserve special mention. In the United Kingdom, SDL began to acquire and develop translation and localization software and hardware – both for its own use in client-specific solutions and to be sold as free-standing commercial products. At the end of the year, SDL also released SDLX, a suite of translation memory database tools. SDLX was developed and used in-house at SDL, and therefore was a mature product at its first offering (Hall 2000; Multilingual 1998). Another British company, International Communications, a provider of localization, translation, and multilingual communications services, released ForeignDesk v5.0 with the full support of Trados Translator's Workbench 2.0 and WinAlign, S-Tagger. Then, Lionbridge Technologies Inc. acquired it (known as Massachusetts-based INT'L.com at the transaction) and later in November 2001 decided to open-source the ForeignDesk suite free of charge under BSD licence. ForeignDesk was originally developed by International Communications around 1995 (Multilingual 2000).

In June 1999, Beijing YaxinCheng Software Technology Co. Ltd. established Shida CAT Research Centre (實達CAT研究中心), which later developed Yaxin CAT Bidirectional v2.5 (Chan 2004: 338). In June, SJTU Sunway Software Industry Ltd. acquired what was then one of the most famous CAT products in China, Yaxin CAT from Beijing YaxinCheng Software Technology Co. Ltd., and it released Yaxin CAT v1.0 in August. The release of this software signified, in a small way, that the development of computer-aided systems was no longer a European monopoly.

In France, the first version of the Wordfast PlusTools suite of CAT (computer-assisted translation) tools was developed. One of the developers was Yves A. Champollion, who incorporated Wordfast LLC later. There were only a few TM software packages available in the first version. It could be downloaded freely before 2002, although registration was required (www.wordfast.net/champollion.net).

In the United States, MultiCorpora R&D Inc. was incorporated, which was exclusively dedicated to providing language technology solutions to enterprises, governments, and language service providers (www.multicorpora.com).

In the United Kingdom, following the launch of SDL International's translation database tool, SDLX, SDL announced SDL Workbench. Packaged with SDLX, SDL Workbench memorized a user's translations and automatically offered other possible translations and terminology from a user's translation database within the Microsoft Word environment. In line with its "open" design, it was able to work with a variety of file formats, including Trados and pre-translated RTF files (Multilingual 1999).

The year 2000 was a year of activity in the industry. In China, Yaxin CAT v2.5 Bidirectional (English and Chinese) was released with new features like seventy-four topic-specific lexicons with six million terms free of charge, project analysis, project management, shared translation memory online, and simultaneous editing of machine output (Chen 2001).

In Germany, OmegaT, a free (General Public License, GPL) translation memory tool, was publicly released. The key features of OmegaT were basic (the functionality was very limited), free, open-source, and across operating systems, as it was programmed in Java (www.omegat.org; Prior 2003).

In Ireland, Alchemy Software Development Limited announced the acquisition of Corel CATALYST, which was designed to boost the efficiency and quality of globalizing software products and was used by over 200 software development and globalization companies worldwide (www.alchemysoftware.ie).

In the United Kingdom, SDL International announced in April the release of SDLX 2.0, which was a new and improved version of SDLX 1.03 (www.sdl.com). It also released SDL Webflow for managing multilingual website content (www.sdlintl.com).

In Germany, Trados relocated its headquarters to the United States in March and became a Delaware corporation.

In France, Wordfast v3.0 was released in September. The on-the-fly tagging and un-tagging of HTML (HyperText Markup Language) files was a major breakthrough in the industry. Freelance translators could translate HTML pages without worrying about the technical hurdles.

Not much happened in 2001. In Taiwan, Inventec Corporation released Dr Eye 2001, with new functions like online search engine, full-text machine translation from English to Chinese, machine translation from Japanese to Chinese, and a localization plug-in (Xu 2001). In the United Kingdom, SDL International released SDLX 4.0 with real-time translation, a flexible software licence, and enhanced capabilities. In the United States, Trados announced the launch of Trados 5 in two flavours, Freelance and Team (www.translationzone.com).

In contrast, the year 2002 was full of activity in the industry.

In North America, MultiCorpora R&D Inc. in Canada released MultiTrans 3, providing corpus-based translation support and language management solution. It also introduced a new translation technology called Advanced Leveraging Translation Memory (ALTM). This model provided past translations in their original context and required virtually no alignment maintenance to obtain superior alignment results. In the United States, Trados 5.5 (Trados Corporate Translation Solution) was released. MultiCorpora released MultiTrans 3.0, which introduced an optional client-server add-on, so it could be used in a web-based, multi-user environment or as a standalone workstation. Version 3 supported TMX and was also fully Unicode compliant (Locke and Giguère 2002: 51).

In Europe and the United Kingdom, SDL International released its new SDLX Translation Suite 4 and then later that year released the elite version of the suite. The SDLX Translation Suite features a modular architecture consisting of five to eight components: SDL Project Wizard, SDL Align, SDL Maintain, SDL Edit, and SDL TermBase in all versions, and SDL Analyse, SDL Apply, and SDLX AutoTrans in the Professional and Elite versions. (Wassmer 2003) In Germany, MetaTexis Software and Services released in April the first official version 1.00 of MetaTexis (www.metatexis.com).

In Asia, Huajian Corporation in China released Huajian IAT, a computer-aided translation system (www.hjtek.com). In Taiwan, Otek launched in July Transwhiz Power version (client/server structure), which aimed at enterprise customers (www.otek.com.tw). In Singapore, Heartsome Holdings Pte. Ltd. was founded to develop language translation technology (Garcia and Stevenson 2006: 77).

North America and Europe were active in translation technology in 2003.

In 2003, MultiCorpora R&D Inc. in Canada released MultiTrans 3.5, which had new and improved capabilities, including increased processing speed of automated searches, increased network communications speed, improved automatic text alignment for all languages, and optional corpus-based pre-translation. Version 3.5 also offered several new terminology management features, such as support for additional data types, additional filters, batch updates, and added import and export flexibility, as well as full Microsoft Office 2003 compatibility, enhanced Web security, and document analysis capabilities for a wider variety of document formats (Multilingual 2003). In the United States, Trados 6 was launched in April, and Trados 6.5 was launched in October with new features like auto concordance search, Word 2003 support, and access to an internet TM server (Wassmer 2004: 61).

In Germany, MetaTexis version 2.0 was released in October with a new database engine, and MetaTexis version Net/Office was released with new features that supported Microsoft PowerPoint and Excel files and Trados Workbench and could be connected with Logoport servers (www.metatexis.com).

In Russia, PROMT, a developer of machine translation products and services, released a new version, @promt XT, with new functions like processing PDF file formats, which made PROMT the first among translation software that supported PDF. Also, one of the editions, @promt Expert, integrated translation memory solutions (Trados) and a proprietary terminology extraction system (www.promt.com).

In France, Atril, which was originally founded in Spain but relocated its group business to France in the late 1990s, released Déjà Vu X (Standard, Professional, Workgroup, and Term Sever) (Harmsen 2008). Wordfast 4, which could import and translate PDF contents, was also released (www.wordfast.net).

Some developers of machine translation systems also launched new versions with a translation memory component, such as LogoVista, An-Nakel El-Arabi, and PROMT. Each of these systems was created with distinct philosophies in its design, offering its own solutions to problems and issues in the work of translation. This was aptly pointed out by Brace (1994):

> Eurolang Optimizer is based on an ambitious client/server architecture designed primarily for the management of large translation jobs. Trados Workbench, on the other hand, offers more refined linguistic analysis and has been carefully engineered to increase the productivity of single translators and small workgroups.

(2) The Development of More Built-in Functions

Computer-aided translation systems of the first and second periods were usually equipped with basic components, such as translation memory, terminology management, and translation editors. In this period, more functions were developed and more components were gradually integrated into computer-aided translation systems. Of all the new functions developed, tools for alignment, machine translation, and project management were most significant. Trados Translator's Workbench II, for example, incorporated T Align, later known as WinAlign, into its workstation (www.translationzone.com), followed by other systems such as Déjà Vu, SDLX, WordFisher, and MultiTrans. Machine translation was also integrated into computer-aided translation systems to handle segments not found in translation memories. IBM's Translation Manager, for example, introduced its Logic-Based Machine Translation (LMT) to run on IBM mainframes and RS/6000 Unix systems (Brace 1993). The function of project management was also introduced by Eurolang Optimizer in 1994 to better manage translation memory and terminology databases for multiple languages and users (Brace 1992).

(3) The Dominance of the Windows Operating System

Computer-aided translation systems created before 1993 were run either in the DOS or OS/2 system. In 1993, the Windows versions of these systems were first introduced, and they later became the dominant stream. For example, IBM and Trados GmbH released a Windows version of TM/2 and of Translator's Workbench, respectively, in mid-1993. More Windows versions came onto the market, such as the preliminary version of ATRIL's Déjà Vu 1.0 in June in Spain. Other newly released systems running on Windows included SDLX, ForeignDesk, Trans Suite 2000, Yaxin CAT, Across, MultiTrans, Huajian, and TransWhiz.

(4) The Support of More Document Formats

Computer-aided translation systems of this period could handle more document formats directly or with filters, including Adobe InDesign, FrameMaker, HTML, Microsoft PowerPoint, Excel, Word, QuarkXPress, and even PDF by 2003. Trados 6.5, for example, supported all the widely used file formats in the translation community, which allowed translators and translation companies to translate documents in Microsoft Office 2003 Word, Excel and PowerPoint, Adobe InDesign 2.0, FrameMaker 7.0, QuarkXPress 5, and PageMaker.

(5) The Support of Translation of More Languages

Translation memory is supposed to be language independent, but computer-aided translation systems developed in the early 1990s did not support all languages. In 1992, Translator Workbench Editor, for example, supported only five European languages, German, English, French, Italian, and Spanish, while IBM Translation Manager/2 supported 19 languages, including Chinese, Korean, and other OS/2-compatible character code sets. This was due largely to the contribution of Unicode, which provided the basis for the processing, storage, and interchange of text data in any language in all modern software, thereby allowing developers of computer-aided translation systems to gradually resolve obstacles in language processing, especially after the release of Microsoft Office 2000. Systems with Unicode support mushroomed, including Transit 3.0 in 1999, MultiTerm and WordFisher 4.2.0 in 2000, Wordfast Classic 3.34 in 2001, and Tr-AID 2.0 and MultiTrans 3 in 2002.

(6) *The Dominance of Trados as a Market Leader*

As a forerunner in the field, Trados became a market leader in this period. As observed by Colin Brace, "Trados has built up a solid technological base and a good market position" in its first decade. By 1994, the company had a range of translation software, including Trados Translator's Workbench (Windows and DOS versions), MultiTerm Pro, MultiTerm Lite, and MultiTerm Dictionary. Its technology in translation memory and file format was then widely used in other computer-aided translation systems, and its products were the most popular in the industry. From the late 1990s, a few systems began to integrate Trados's translation memory into their systems. In 1997, ProMemoria, for example, was launched with its translation memory component provided by Trados. In 1998, International Communications released ForeignDesk 5.0 with the full support of Trados Translator's Workbench 2.0, WinAlign, and S-Tagger. In 1999, SDLX supported import and export formats such as Trados and tab-delimited and CSV files. In 2000, Trans Suite 2000 was released with the capacity to process Trados RTF files. In 2001, Wordfast 3.22 could directly open Trados TMW translation memories (Translator's Workbench versions 2 and 3). In 2003, PROMT XT Export integrated Trados's translation memory. In October 2003, MetaTexis Net/Office 2.0 was released and was able to work with Trados Workbench.

2004–2013: A Period of Global Development

Advances in technology have given added capabilities to computer-aided translation systems. During the last nine years, while most old systems have been upgraded on a regular basis, close to thirty new systems have been released to the market. This situation has offered a wider range of choices for buyers to acquire systems with different packages, functions, operating systems, and prices.

One of the most significant changes in this period is the addition of new computer-aided translation companies in countries other than those mentioned previously. Hungary is a typical example. In 2004, Kilgray Translation Technologies was established by three Hungarian language technologists. The name of the company was made up of the founders' surnames: Kis Balázs (KI), Lengyel István (L), and Ugray Gábor (GRAY). Later, the company launched the first version of MemoQ, an integrated localization environment (ILE), in 2005. MemoQ's first version had a server component that enabled the creation of server projects. Products of Kilgray included MemoQ, MemoQ server, QTerm, and TM Repository (www.kilgray.com).

Another example is Japan. In Japan, Rozetta Corporation released TraTool, a computer-aided translation system with translation memory, an integrated alignment tool, an integrated terminology tool, and a user dictionary. The product is still commercially available, but no major improvement has been made since its first version (www.tratool.com).

Yet another example is Poland, where AidTrans Soft launched its AidTrans Studio 1.00, a translation memory tool. But the company was discontinued in 2010 (www.thelanguagedirectory.com/translation/translation_software).

New versions of computer-aided translation systems with new features are worth noting. In the United Kingdom, ATA launched a new Arabic memory translation system, Xpro7, which had the function of machine translation (www.atasoft.com). SDL Desktop Products, a division of SDL International, announced the launch of SDLX 2004. Its new features included TMX certification, seamless integration with enterprise systems such as online terminology and multilingual workflow management, adaptation of new file formats, synchronized web-enabled TM, and knowledge-based translation (www.sdl.com). In the United States, Systran released Systran Professional Premium 5.0, which contained integrated tools such as integrated translation memory with TMX support, a translator's workbench for post-editing, and ongoing quality analysis (www.systransoft.com). Multilizer Inc., a developer of globalization technologies in the United States, released a new version of Multilizer, which included multiuser translation memory with Translation Memory Manager (TMM), a standalone tool for maintaining Multilizer Translation Memory contents. TMM allowed editing, adding, and deleting translations, and also included a briefcase model for working with translations offline (www.multilizer.com).

In Ukraine, Advanced International Translations (AIT) started work on user-friendly translation memory software, later known as AnyMen, which was released in December 2008.

In 2005, translation technology moved further ahead with new versions and new functions.

In North America, MultiCorpora in Canada released MultiTrans 4, which built on the foundation of MultiTrans 3.7 and had a new alignment process that was completely automated (Multilingual 2005d). Trados, incorporated in the United States, produced Trados 7 Freelance, which supported twenty additional languages, including Hindi. At the operating-system level, Microsoft Windows 2000, Windows XP Home, Windows XP Professional, and Windows 2003 Server were supported. More file formats were now directly supported by TagEditor. MultiCorpora also introduced MultiTrans 4, which was designed to meet the needs of large organizations by providing the newest efficiencies for translators in the areas of text alignment quality, user friendliness, flexibility, and web access (www.multicorpora.com).

In Europe, Lingua et Machina, a memory translation tool developer, released SIMILIS v1.4, its second-generation translation tool. SIMILIS uses linguistic parsers in conjunction with the translation memory paradigm. This function allowed for the automatic extraction of bilingual terminology from translated documents. Version 1.4 brought compatibility with the Trados translation memory format (text and TMX) and a new language, German (Multilingual 2005b). In Switzerland, STAR Group released Transit XV Service Pack 14. This version extended its capabilities with a number of new features and support of 160 languages and language versions, including Urdu (India) and Urdu (Pakistan). It supported Microsoft Word 2003 files and had MySpell dictionaries. (Multilingual 2005a) PROMT released @promt 7.0 translation software, which supported the integrated translation memory, the first of its kind among PROMT's products (www.promt.com).

In the United Kingdom, SDL Desktop Products released the latest version of its translation memory tool SDLX 2005, which expanded the terminology QA check and automatically checked source and translations for inconsistent, incomplete, partial, or empty translations; corrupt characters; and consistent regular expressions, punctuation, and formatting. Language support had been added for Maltese, Armenian, and Georgian, and the system could handle more than 150 languages (Multilingual 2005c). In June, SDL International acquired Trados for £35 million. The acquisition provided extensive end-to-end technology and service solutions for global information assets (www.translationzone.com). In October, SDL Synergy was released as a new project management tool on the market.

In Asia, Huajian Corporation in China released Huajian Multilingual IAT network version (華建多語IAT網絡版) in June, and in October the Huajian IAT (Russian to Chinese) standalone version (www.hjtrans.com). In July, Beijing Orient Yaxin Software Technology Co. Ltd. released Yaxin CAT 2.0, which was a suite including Yaxin CAT 3.5, CAM 3.5, Server, Lexicons, Translation Memory Maintenance, and Example Base. In Singapore, Heartsome Holdings Pte. Ltd. released Heartsome Translation Suite, which was composed of three programs: an XLIFF editor in which source files were converted to XLIFF format and translated, a TMX editor that dealt with TMX files, and a dictionary editor that dealt with TBX files (Garcia and Stevenson 2006: 77). In Taiwan, Otek released Transwhiz 9.0 for English, Chinese, and Japanese languages (www.otek.com.tw).

Significant advances in translation technology were made in 2006, particularly in Europe, the United Kingdom, and the United States.

In Europe, Across Systems GmbH in Germany released its Corporate Translation Management 3.5 in September, which marked the start of the worldwide rollout of Across software (Multilingual 2006a). In the United Kingdom, SDL International released SDL Trados 2006 in February, which integrated with the Translators Workbench, TagEditor, and SDLX editing environments and SDL MultiTerm. It included new support for Quark, InDesign CS2, and Java (www.sdl.com). In the United States, MultiCorpora launched the TextBase TM concept. (www.multicorpora.com). Apple Inc. released AppleTrans in August, a text editor specially designed for translators, featuring online corpora which represented translation memory accessible through documents. AppleTrans helped users localize web pages (http://developer.apple.com). Lingotek, a language search engine developer in the United States, launched a beta version of a collaborative language translation service that enhanced a translator's efficiency by quickly finding meaning-based translated material for reuse. Lingotek's language search engine indexed linguistic knowledge from a growing repository of multilingual content and language translations instead of web pages. Users could then access its database of previously translated material to find more specific combinations of words for reuse. Such meaning-based searching maintained better style, tone, and terminology. Lingotek ran completely within most popular web browsers, including initial support for Internet Explorer and Firefox. Lingotek supported Word, Rich Text Format (RTF), Open Office, HTML, XHTML, and Excel formats, thereby allowing users to upload such documents directly into Lingotek. Lingotek also supported existing translation memory files that were TMX-compliant memories, thus allowing users to import TMX files into both private and public indices (Multilingual 2006b).

In 2007, Wordfast 5.5 was released in France. It was an upgrade from Wordfast 4, in which Mac support was completely overhauled. This version continued to offer translators collaboration community via a LAN. Each Wordfast license granted users the ability to search Wordfast's web-based TM and knowledge base, VLTM (www.wordfast.net). In Germany, in October, a group of independent translators and programmers under the GNU GPL license developed Anaphraseus, a computer-aided translation tool for creating, managing, and using bilingual translation memories. Originally, Anaphraseus was developed to work with the Wordfast TM format, but it could also export and import files in TMX format (http://anaphraseus.sourceforge.net). In Hungary, Kilgray Translation Technologies released MemoQ 2.0 in January. The main theme for the new version was networking, featuring a new resource server. This server not only stored translation memory and term bases but also offered the possibility of creating server projects that allowed for the easy distribution of work among several translators and ensured productivity at an early stage of the learning curve. Improvements on the client side included support for XML and Adobe FrameMaker MIF file formats, improvements to all other supported file formats, support for the Segmentation Rule eXchange standard, auto-propagation of translated segments, better navigation, and over a hundred more minor enhancements (Multilingual 2007a, 2007b). In Russia, MT2007, freeware, was developed by a professional programmer Andrew Manson. The main idea was to develop easy-to-use software with extensive features. This software lacked many features that leading systems had. In the United Kingdom, SDL International released SDL Trados 2007 in March, which had features such as a new concept of project delivery and supply chain; new one-central-view dashboard for the new project wizard, PerfectMatch; an automated quality assurance checker; and full support for Microsoft Office 2007 and Windows Vista.

In the United States, MultiCorpora's Advanced Leveraging launched WordAlign to boast the ability to align text at the individual term and expression level (www.multicorpora.com).

MadCap Software Inc., a multi-channel content authoring company, in May developed Mad-Cap Lingo, an XML-based, fully integrated help authoring tool and translation environment. MadCap Lingo offered an easy-to-use interface and complete Unicode support for all left-to-right languages for assisting localization tasks. Across Systems GmbH and MadCap Software announced a partnership to combine technical content creation with advanced translation and localization. In June, Alchemy Software Development Ltd. and MadCap Software, Inc., announced a joint technology partnership that combined technical content creation with visual TM technology.

In 2008, Europe again figured prominently in computer-aided translation software production. In Germany, in April, Across Systems GmbH released Across Language Server 4.0 Service Pack 1, which contained various extensions in addition to authoring, such as FrameMaker 8 and SGML support, context matching, and improvements for web-based translations via crossWeb (Multilingual 2008a). It also introduced in July its new language portal solution (later known as Across Language Portal) for large-scale organizations and multinational corporations, which allowed customers operating on an international scale to implement Web portals for all language-related issues and all staff levels that need to make use of language resources. At the same time Across released the latest update to the Across Language Server, offering many new functions for the localization of software user interfaces (www.across.net). In Luxembourg, Wordbee S.A. was founded as a translation software company focusing on web-based integrated CAT and management solutions (www.wordbee.com).

In Eastern Europe in September, Kilgray Translation Technologies in Hungary released MemoQ 3.0, which included a new termbase and provided new terminology features. It introduced full support for XLIFF as a bilingual format and offered the visual localization of RESX files. MemoQ 3.0 was available in English, German, Japanese, and Hungarian (http://kilgray. com). In Russia, in March, Promt released 8.0 version with major improvements in its translation engine; translation memory system with TMX file import support; and dialect support in English (UK and American), Spanish (Castilian and Latin American), Portuguese (Portuguese and Brazilian), German (German and Swiss), and French (French, Swiss, Belgian, Canadian) (www.promt.com). In Ukraine, Advanced International Translations (AIT) released AnyMen, a translation memory system compatible with Microsoft Word, in December. In Uruguay, Max-programs launched Swordfish version 1.0–0, a cross-platform computer-aided translation tool based on the XLIFF 1.2 open standard published by OASIS (www.maxprograms.com), in April. In November, this company released Stingray version 1.0–0, a cross-platform document aligner. The translation memories in TMX, CSV, or Trados TXT format generated by Stingray could be used in most modern computer-aided translation systems (www.maxprograms.com).

In Ireland, Alchemy Software Development, a company in visual localization solutions, released Alchemy PUBLISHER 2.0, which combined visual localization technology with translation memory for documentation, in July. It supported standard documentation formats, such as MS Word and XML; application platforms such as Windows 16/22/64x binaries; and web content formats such as HTML, ASP, and all derivative content formats (www.alchemysoftware.ie).

In North America, JiveFusion Technologies, Inc., in Canada officially launched Fusion One and Fusion Collaborate 3.0. The launches introduced a new method of managing translation memories. New features included complete contextual referencing. JiveFusion also integrated Fusion Collaborate 3.0 with TransFlow, a project and workflow management solution by Logo-soft (Multilingual 2008b). In the United States, in February, MadCap Software, Inc., released MadCap Lingo 2.0, which included the Darwin Information Typing Architecture standard, and support for Microsoft Word and a range of standard text and language formats. In September, it released MadCap Lingo 3.0, which included a new project packager function designed to bridge the gap between authors and translators who used other translation memory system software and a new TermBase Editor for creating databases of reusable translated terms.

In Asia, Yaxin CAT 4.0 was released in China in August with some new features, including a computer-aided project platform for project management and huge databases for handling large translation projects. In Taiwan, Otek released Transwhiz 10 for translating English, Chinese, and Japanese, with a fuzzy search engine and Microsoft Word workstation (www.otek.com.tw).

The year 2009 witnessed the development of Autshumato Integrated Translation Environment (ITE) version 1.0, a project funded by the Department of Arts and Culture of the Republic of South Africa. It was released by The Centre for Text Technology (CTexT) at the Potchefstroom Campus of the North-West University and University of Pretoria after two years of research and development. Although Autshumato ITE was specifically developed for the eleven official South African languages, it was in essence language independent and could be adapted for translating between any language pair.

In Europe, Wordfast released in January Wordfast Translation Studio, a bundled product with Wordfast Classic (for Microsoft Word) and Wordfast Pro (a standalone CAT platform). With over 15,000 licences in active use, Wordfast claimed it was the second most widely used translation memory tool (www.wordfast.net). In Germany, in May, Across Systems GmbH released Across Language Server 5.0, which offered several options for process automation as well as for workflow management and analysis. Approximately 50 connections were available for interacting with other systems (Multilingual 2009b). In September, STAR Group in Switzerland released Transit^NXT (Professional, Freelance Pro, Workstation, and Freelance). Service pack 1 for Transit NXT/TermStar NXT contained additional user interface languages for Chinese, Spanish, Japanese, and Khmer; enhanced alignment usability; support for QuarkXpress 7; and proofreading for internal repetitions.

In the United Kingdom, SDL announced in June the launch of SDL Trados Studio 2009 in the same month, which included the latest versions of SDL MultiTerm, SDL Passolo Essential, SDL Trados WinAlign, and SDL Trados 2007 Suite. New features included Context Match, AutoSuggest, and QuickPlace (www.sdl.com). In October, SDL released its enterprise platform SDL TM Server 2009, a new solution to centralize, share, and control translation memories (www.sdl.com).

In North America, JiveFusion Technologies Inc. in Canada released Fusion 3.1 in March to enhance current TMX compatibility and the capability to import and export to TMX while preserving the complete segment context (Multilingual 2009a). In the United States, Lingotek introduced software-as-a-service collaborative translation technology that combined the workflow and computer-aided translation capabilities of human and machine translation into one application. Organizations could upload new projects, assign translators (paid or unpaid), check the status of current projects in real time, and download completed documents from any computer with web access (Multilingual 2009c).

In Asia, in September, Beijing Zhongke LongRay Software and Technology Ltd. Co. in China released LongRay CAT 3.0 (standalone edition), a CAT system with translation memory, alignment, dictionary and terminology management, and other functions (www.zklr.com). In November, Foshan Snowman Computer Co. Ltd. released Snowman version 1.0 in China (www.gcys.cn). Snowman deserves mention because (1) Snowman was new; (2) the green trial version of Snowman could be downloaded free of charge; (3) Snowman was easy to use, as its interface was user friendly and the system was easy to operate; and (4) Snowman had the language pair of Chinese and English that caters to the huge domestic market as well as the market abroad.

Most of the activities relating to computer-aided translation in 2010 took place in Europe and North America.

In Germany, in August, Across Systems GmbH released Across Language Server v. 5 Service Pack 1, which introduced a series of new functionalities and modes of operation relating to the areas of project management, machine translation, crowdsourcing, and authoring assistance (http://new.multilingual.com). In October, MetaTexis version 3.0 was released, which imported filter for Wordfast Pro and Trados Studio translation memories and documents (www.metatexis.com). In France, in July, Wordfast LLC released Wordfast Pro 2.4 (WFP) with over sixty enhancements. This system was a standalone environment that featured a highly customizable interface, enhanced batch processing functionality, and increased file format support (www.wordfast.net). In October, Wordfast LLC created an application to support translation on the iPhone and iPad in the Wordfast Anywhere environment (www.wordfast.net). In Hungary, in February, Kilgray Translation Technologies released MemoQ 4.0, which was integrated with project management functions for project managers who wanted to have more control and enable translators to work in any translation tool. In October, the company released MemoQ 4.5, which had a rewritten translation memory engine and improvements to the alignment algorithm (www.kilgray.com). In France, in March, Atril released TeaM Server, which allowed translators with Déjà Vu Workgroup to work on multinational and multisite translation projects on a LAN or over the Internet, sharing their translations in real time, ensuring superior quality and consistency. TeaM Server also provided scalable centralized storage for translation memories and terminology databases. The size of translation repositories and the number of concurrent users were only limited by the server hardware and bandwidth (www.atril.com). In October, Atril released Déjà Vu X2 in four editions: Editor, Standard, Professional, and Workgroup. Its new features included DeepMiner data extraction engine, new StartView interface, and AutoWrite word prediction. In Switzerland, in October, STAR Group released Transit NXT Service Pack 3 and TermStar NXT. Transit NXT Service Pack 3 contained the following improvements: support of Microsoft Office 2007, InDesign CS5, QuarkXpress 8 and Quark Xpress 8.1 and PDF synchronization for MS Word files.

In the United Kingdom, in March, SDL released a new subscription level of its SDL Trados Studio, which included additional productivity tools for translators such as Service Pack 2, enabling translators to plug in to multiple automatic translation tools. The company also did a beta launch of SDL OpenExchange, inviting the developer community to make use of standard open application programming interfaces to increase the functionality of SDL Trados Studio (Multilingual 2010a). In September, XTM International released XTM Cloud, which was a totally online software-as-a-service (SaaS) computer-assisted translation tool set, combining translation workflow with translation memory, terminology management, and a fully featured translator workbench. The launch of XTM Cloud meant independent freelance translators had access to XTM for the first time (www.xtm-intl.com). In Ireland, in May, Alchemy Software Development Limited released Alchemy PUBLISHER 3.0, which supported all aspects of the localization workflow, including form translation, engineering, testing, and project management. It also provided a machine translation connector which was jointly developed by PROMT so that documentation formats could be machine translated (www.alchemysoftware.ie; www.promt.com).

In North America, in June, IBM in the United States released the open source version of OpenTM/2, which originated from the IBM Translation Manager. OpenTM/2 integrated with several aspects of the end-to-end translation workflow (www.opentm2.org). Partnering with the Localization Industry Standards Association (LISA), Welocalize, Cisco, and Linux Solution Group e.V. (LiSoG), IBM aimed to create an open source project that provided a full-featured, enterprise-level translation workbench environment for professional translators on the OpenTM/2 project. According to LISA, OpenTM/2 not only provided a public and open implementation of translation workbench environment that served as the reference implementation of existing localization industry standards, such as TMX, it also aimed to provide standardized access to globalization process management software (www.lisa.org; LISA 2010). In July, Lingotek upgraded its Collaborative Translation Platform (CTP) to a software-as-a-service product which combined machine translation, real-time community translation, and management tools (Multilingual 2010b). In September, MadCap Software, Inc., released Mad-Cap Lingo v4.0, which had a new utility for easier translation alignment and a redesigned translation editor. In December, Systran introduced Desktop 7 Product Suite, which included the Premium Translator, Business Translator, Office Translator, and Home Translator. Among them, Premium Translator and Business Translator were equipped with translation memory and project management features.

In South America, in April, Maxprograms in Uruguay released Swordfish II, which incorporated Anchovy version 1.0–0 as glossary manager and term extraction tool and added support for SLD XLIFF files from Trados Studio 2009 and Microsoft Visio XML Drawings, and so on (www.maxprograms.com).

In 2011, computer-aided translation was active in Europe and America.

In Europe, ATRIL/PowerLing in France released in May Déja Vu X2, a new version of its computer-assisted translation system, which had new features such as a DeepMiner data mining and translation engine, SmartView Interface, and a multi-file and multi-format alignment tool (Multilingual 2011). In June, Wordfast Classic v6.0 was released with features such as the ability to share TMs and glossaries with an unlimited number of users, improved quality assurance, AutoComplete, and improved support for Microsoft Word 2007/2010 and Mac Word 2011 (www.wordfast.net). In Luxembourg, in January, the Directorate-General for Translation of the European Commission released its one million segments of multilingual Translation Memory in TMX format in 231 language pairs. Translation units were extracted from one of its large shared translation memories in Euramis (European Advanced Multilingual Information System). This memory contained most, but not all, of the documents of the *Acquis Communautaire*, the entire body of European legislation, plus some other documents which were not part of the *Acquis*. In Switzerland, the STAR Group released in February Service Pack 4 for Transit NXT and TermStar NXT. Transit NXT Service Pack 4 contained the following improvements: support of MS Office 2010, support of Quicksilver 3.5l, and preview for MS Office formats. In Eastern Europe, in June, Kilgray Translation Technologies in Hungary released TM Repository, the world's first tool-independent Translation Memory management system (http://kilgray.com). Kilgray Translation Technologies later released MemoQ v 5.0 with the AuditTrail concept to the workflow, which added new improvements like versioning, tracking changes (to show the difference of two versions), X-translate (to show changes on source texts), and post-translation analysis on formatting tags (Kilgray Translation Technologies 2011).

In the United Kingdom, in March, XTM International released XTM 5.5, providing both Cloud and On-Premise versions, which contained customizable workflows, a new search and replace feature in Translation Memory Manager, and the redesign of XTM Workbench (www.xtm-intl.com).

In North America, in May, MultiCorpora R&D Inc. in Canada released MultiTrans Prism, a translation management system (TMS) for project management, translation memory, and terminology management (MultiCorpora 2011).

In 2012, the development of computer-aided translation in various places was considerable, and translation technology continued its march to globalization.

In North America, the development of computer-aided translation was fast. In Canada, Multi-Corpora, a provider of multilingual asset management solutions, released MultiTrans Prism version 5.5 in June. The new version featured a web editing server that extended control of the management of translation processes, and it could be fully integrated with content management systems. In September, Terminotix launched LogiTerm 5.2. Its upgrades and new features, including indexing TMX files directly in Bitext database, reinforced the fuzzy match window, and adjusted buttons (http://terminotix.com/news/newsletter). In December, MultiCorpora added new machine translation integrations to its MultiTrans Prism. The integration options include Systran, Google, and Microsoft (www.multicorpora.com). In Asia, there was considerable progress in computer-aided translation in China. Transn Information Technology Co., Ltd. released TCAT 2.0 as freeware early in the year. New features of this software include the Translation Assistant (翻譯助理) placed at the sidebar of Microsoft Office, pre-translation with TM and termbase, and source segment selection by highlighting (自動取句) (www.transn.com). In May, Foshan Snowman Computer Co. Ltd. released Snowman 1.27 and Snowman Collaborative Translation Platform (雪人CAT協同翻譯平臺) free version. The platform offers a server for a central translation memory and termbase so that all users can share their translations and terms, and reviewers can view the translations simultaneously with translators. It also supports online instant communication, document management, and an online forum (BBS) (www.gcys.cn). In July, Chengdu Urelite Tech Co. Ltd. (成都優譯信息技術有限公司), which was founded in 2009, released Transmate, including the standalone edition (beta), internet edition, and project management system. The standalone edition was freely available for download from the company's website. The standalone edition of Transmate was targeted at freelancers, and this beta release offered basic CAT functions, such as using TM and terminology during translation. It had features such as pre-translation, creating file-based translation memory, bilingual text export, and links to an online dictionary website and Google MT (www.urelitetech.com.cn).

Heartsome Translation Studio 8.0 was released by the Shenzhen Office of Heartsome in China. Its new features included pre-saving MT results and external proofreading file export in RTF format. The new and integrated interface also allowed the user to work in a single unified environment in the translation process (www.heartsome.net).

In Japan, Ryan Ginstrom developed and released Align Assist 1.5, which is freeware to align source and translation files to create translation memory. The main improvement of this version was the ability to set the format of a cell text (http://felix-cat.com). In October, LogoVista Corporation released LogoVista PRO 2013. It could support Microsoft Office 2010 64-bit and Windows 8. More Japanese and English words were included, and the total number of words in dictionaries was 6.47 million (www.logovista.co.jp).

In Europe, the developments of computer-aided translation systems are noteworthy.

In Czech Republic, in January, MemSource Technologies released MemSource Editor for translators as a free tool to work with MemSource Cloud and MemSource Server. The Editor was multiplatform and could be installed on Windows and Macintosh (www.memsource.com). In April, this company released MemSource Cloud 2.0. MemSource Plugin, the former CAT component for Microsoft Word, was replaced by the new MemSource Editor, a standalone translation editor. Other new features included adding comments to segments, version control, translation workflow (only in the Team edition), better quality assurance, and segmentation (http://blog.memsource.com). In December, MemSource Technologies released MemSource Cloud 2.8, which encrypted all communication by default. This release also included redesigned menu and tools. Based on the data about previous jobs, MemSource could suggest relevant linguistics for translation jobs (www.memsource.com).

In France, Wordfast LLC released Wordfast Pro 3.0 in April. Its new features included bilingual review, batch TransCheck, filter 100% matches, split and merge TXML files, reverse source/ target, and pseudo-translation (www.wordfast.com). In June, Atril and PowerLing updated Déjà

Vu X2. Its new features included an incorporated a PDF converter and a CodeZapper macro (www.atril.com).

In Germany, Across Language Server v 5.5 was released in November. New features such as linguistic supply chain management were designed to make project and resource planning more transparent. The new version also supported the translation of display texts in various formats and allowed the protection of the translation units to ensure uniform use (www. across.net).

In Hungary, in July, Kilgray Translation Technologies released MemoQ 6.0 with new features like predictive typing and several new online workflow concepts such as FirstAccept (assign job to the first translator who accepted it on the online workflow), GroupSourcing, Slicing, and Subvendor group (http://kilgray.com). In December, the company released MemoQ 6.2. Its new features included SDL package support, InDesign support with preview, new quality assurance checks, and the ability to work with multiple machine translation engines at the same time (http://kilgray.com).

In Luxembourg, in October, Wordbee designed a new business analysis module for its Wordbee translation management system, which provided a new dashboard where over a hundred real-time reports were generated for every aspect of the localization process (www.wordbee. com).

In Switzerland, STAR Group released Service Pack 6 for Transit^{NXT} and TermStar ^{NXT}. The improvements of Service Pack 6 of Transit^{NXT} contained support for Windows 8 and Windows Server 2012, QuarkXPress 9.0–9.2, InDesign CS6, integrated OpenOffice spell check dictionaries, and ten additional Indian languages (www.star-group.net).

In the United Kingdom, XTM International, a developer of XML authoring and translation tools, in April released XTM Suite 6.2. Its updates included a full integration with machine translation system, Asia Online Language Studio, and the content management system XTRF. In October, the company released XTM Suite 7.0 and a new XTM Xchange module in XTM Cloud intended to increase the supply chain. Version 7.0 included project management enhancements, allowing users to group files, assign translators to specific groups or languages, and create different workflows for different languages (www.xtm-intl.com).

During this period, the following trends are of note.

(1) Systematic Compatibility With Windows and Microsoft Office

Of the sixty-seven currently available systems on the market, only one does not run on the Windows operating system. Computer-aided translation systems have to keep up with the advances in Windows and Microsoft Office for the sake of compatibility. Wordfast 5.51j, for example, was released in April 2007, three months after the release of Windows Vista, and Wordfast 5.90v was released in July 2010 to support Microsoft Office Word 2007 and 2010.

(2) Integration of Workflow Control Into CAT Systems

Besides reusing or recycling translations of repetitive texts and text-based terminology, systems developed during this period added functions such as project management, spell check, quality assurance, and content control. Take SDL Trados Studio 2011 as an example. This version, which was released in September 2011, has a spell checking function for a larger number of languages and PerfectMatch 2.0 to track changes of the source documents. Most of the systems on the market can also perform "context match", which is an identical match with identical surrounding segments in the translation document and in the translation memory.

(3) Availability of Networked or Online Systems

Because of the fast development of new information technologies, most CAT systems during this period were sever-based, web-based, and even cloud-based CAT systems, which had huge storage of data. By the end of 2012, there were fifteen cloud-based CAT systems available on the market for individuals or enterprises, such as Lingotek Collaborative Translation Platform, SDL World Server, and XTM Cloud.

(4) Adoption of New Formats in the Industry

Data exchange between different CAT systems has always been a difficult issue to handle, as different systems have different formats, such as *dvmdb* for Déjà Vu X, and *tmw* for SDL Trados Translator's Workbench 8.0. These program-specific formats cannot be mutually recognizable, which makes it impossible to share data in the industry. In the past, LISA played a significant role in developing and promoting data exchange standards, such as Segmentation Rules eXchange (SRX), TMX, TBX (Term-Base eXchange) and XLIFF. It can be estimated that compliance with industry standards is also one of the future directions for better data exchange.

Translation Technology on the Fast Track: A Comparison of the Developments of Computer-Aided Translation With Human and Machine Translation

The speed of the development of translation technology in recent decades can be illustrated through a comparison of computer-aided translation with human translation and machine translation.

The Development of Human Translation

Human translation, in comparison with machine translation and computer-aided translation, has taken a considerably longer time and slower pace to develop. The history of human translation can be traced to 1122 BCE when, during the Zhou dynasty (1122–255 BCE), a foreign affairs bureau known as *Da xing ren* 大行人 was established to provide interpreting services for government officials to communicate with the twelve non-Han minorities along the borders of the Zhou empire (Chan 2009: 29–30). This is probably the first piece of documentary evidence of official interpreting in the world.

Since then a number of major events have taken place in the world of translation. In 285 BCE, there was the first partial translation of the Bible from Hebrew into Greek in the form of the Septuagint (Worth 1992: 5–19). In 250 BCE, the contribution of Andronicus Livius to translation made him the "father of translation" (Kelly 1998: 495–504). In 67, Zhu Falan made the first translation of a Buddhist sutra in China (Editorial Committee 1988: 103). In 1141, Robert de Retines produced the first translation of the Koran in Latin (Chan 2009: 47). In 1382, John Wycliffe made the first complete translation of the Bible in English (Worth 1992: 66–70). In 1494, William Tyndale was the first scholar to translate the Bible from the original Hebrew and Greek into English (Delisle and Woodsworth 1995: 33–35). In 1611, the King James Version of the Bible was published (Allen 1969). In 1814, Robert Morrison made the first translation of the Bible into Chinese (Chan 2009: 73). In 1945, simultaneous interpreting was invented at the Nuremberg Trials held in Germany (Gaiba 1998). In 1946, the United Bible Society was founded in New York (Chan 2009: 117). In 1952, the first conference on machine translation was held at the Massachusetts Institute of Technology (Hutchins 2000: 6, 34–35).

In 1953, the Federation Internationale des Traducteurs (FIT), or International Association of Translators, and the Association Internationale des Interpretes de Conference (AIIC), or the International Association of Conference Interpreters, were both founded in Paris (Haeseryn 1989: 379–84; Phelan 2001). In 1964, with the publication of *Toward a Science of Translating*, in which the concept of dynamic equivalent translation was proposed, Eugene A. Nida was referred to as the "father of translation theory" (Nida 1964). In 1972, James S. Holmes proposed the first framework for translation studies (1972/1987: 9–24, 1988: 93–98). In 1978, Even-Zohar proposed the polysystem theory (21–27).

A total of some seventeen major events took place during the history of human translation, which may be 3,135 years old. This shows that in terms of the mode of production, human translation has remained unchanged for a very long time.

The Development of Machine Translation

In comparison with human translation, machine translation has advanced enormously since its inception in the 1940s. This can be clearly seen from an analysis of the countries with research and development in machine translation during the last seventy years.

Available information shows that an increasing number of countries have been involved in the research and development of machine translation. This is very much in evidence since the beginning of machine translation in 1947. Actually, long before the Second World War was over and the computer was invented, Georges Artsrouni, a French-Armenian engineer, created a translation machine known as the Mechanical Brain. Later in the year, Petr Petrovič Smirnov-Troyanskij (1894–1950), a Russian scholar, was issued a patent in Moscow on 5 September for his construction of a machine which could select and print words while translating from one language into another or into several others at the same time (Chan 2004: 289).

But it was not until the years after the Second World War that the climate was ripe for the development of machine translation. The invention of computers, the rise of information theory, and the advances in cryptology all indicated that machine translation could be a reality. In 1947, the idea of using machines in translating was proposed in March by Warren Weaver (1894–1978), who was at that time the vice president of the Rockefeller Foundation, and Andrew D. Booth of Birkbeck College of the University of London. They wanted to make use of the newly invented computer to translate natural languages. Historically speaking, their idea was significant in several ways. It was the first application of the newly invented computers to non-numerical tasks, such as translation. It was the first application of the computer to natural languages, which was later to be known as computational linguistics. It was also one of the first areas of research in the field of artificial intelligence.

The following year witnessed the rise of information theory and its application to translation studies. The role of this theory has been to help translators recognize the function of concepts such as information load, implicit and explicit information, and redundancy (Shannon and Weaver 1949; Wiener 1954). On 15 July, Warren Weaver, director of the Rockefeller Foundation's natural sciences division, wrote a memorandum for peer review outlining the prospects of machine translation, known in history as "Weaver's Memorandum", in which he made four proposals to produce translations better than word-for-word translations (Hutchins 2000: 18–20).

The first machine translation system, the Georgetown-IBM system for Russian-English translation, was developed in the United States in June 1952. The system was developed by Leon Dostert and Paul Garvin of Georgetown University and Cuthbert Hurd and Peter Sheridan of IBM Corporation. This system could translate from Russian into English (Hutchins 1986: 70–78).

Russia was the second country to develop machine translation. At the end of 1954, the Steklov Mathematical Institute of the Academy of Sciences began work on machine translation under the directorship of Aleksej Andreevič Ljapunov (1911–1973), a mathematician and computer expert. The first system developed was known as FR-I, which was a direct translation system and was also considered one of the first generation of machine translation systems. The system ran on STRELA, one of the first generation of computers (Hutchins 2000: 197–204).

In the same year, the United Kingdom became the third country to engage in machine translation. A research group on machine translation, Cambridge Language Research Group, led by Margaret Masterman, was set up at Cambridge University, where an experimental system was tried on English-French translation (Wilks 2000: 279–98).

In 1955, Japan was the fourth country to develop machine translation. Kyushu University was the first university in Japan to begin research on machine translation (Nagao 1993: 203–08). This was followed by China, which began research on machine translation with a Russian-Chinese translation algorithm jointly developed by the Institute of Linguistics and the Institute of Computing Technology (Dong 1988: 85–91; Feng 1999: 335–40; Liu 1984: 1–14).

Two years later, Charles University in Czechoslovakia began to work on English-Czech machine translation (www.cuni.cz).

These six countries were the forerunners in machine translation. Other countries followed suit. In 1959, France set up the Centre d'Études de la Traduction Automatique (CETA) for machine translation (Chan 2009: 300). In 1960, East Germany had its Working Group for Mathematical and Applied Linguistics and Automatic Translation, while in Mexico, research on machine translation was conducted at the National Autonomous University of Mexico (Universidad Nacional Autonoma de Mexico) (www.unam.mx). In 1962, Hungary's Hungarian Academy of Sciences conducted research on machine translation. In 1964 in Bulgaria, the Mathematical Institute of the Bulgarian Academy of Sciences in Sofia set up the section of 'Automatic Translation and Mathematical Linguistics' to conduct work on machine translation (www.bas.bg; Hutchins 1986: 205–06). In 1965, the Canadian Research Council set up CETADOL (Centre de Traitement Automatique des Donnees Linguistiques) to work on an English-French translation system (Hutchins 1986: 224).

But with the publication of the ALPAC Report prepared by the Automatic Language Processing Advisory Committee of the National Academy of Sciences, which concluded with the comment that there was "no immediate or predictable prospect of useful machine translation", funding for machine translation in the United States was drastically cut, and interest in machine translation waned considerably (ALPAC 1966; Warwick 1987: 22–37). Still, sporadic efforts were made in machine translation. An important system was developed in the United States by Peter Toma, previously of Georgetown University, known as Systran, an acronym for System Translation. To this day, this system is still one of the most established and popular systems on the market. In Hong Kong, The Chinese University of Hong Kong set up the Hung On-To Research Laboratory for Machine Translation to conduct research into machine translation and developed a practical machine translation system known as the Chinese University Language Translator, abbreviated as CULT (Loh 1975: 143–55, 1976a: 46–50, 1976b: 104–05; Loh *et al.* 1978: 111–20; Loh and Kong 1979: 135–48). In Canada, the TAUM group at Montreal developed a system for translating public weather forecasts known as TAUM-METEO, which became operative in 1977.

In the 1980s, the most important translation system developed was the EUROTRA system, which could translate all the official languages of the European Economic Community (Arnold and Tombe 1987: 114–35; Johnson *et al.* 1985: 155–69; King 1982; King 1987: 373–91; Lau 1988: 186–91; Maegaard 1988: 61–65; Maegaard and Perschke 1991: 73–82; Somers

1986: 129–77; Way *et al.* 1997: 323–74). In 1983, Allen Tucker, Sergei Nirenburg, and others developed at Colgate University an AI-based multilingual machine translation system known as TRANSLATOR to translate four languages, English, Japanese, Russian, and Spanish. This was the beginning of knowledge-based machine translation in the United States (www.colgate.edu). The following year, Fujitsu produced ATLAS/I and ATLAS/II translation systems for translation between Japanese and English in Japan, while Hitachi and Market Intelligence Centre (QUICK) developed the ATHENE English–Japanese machine translation system (Chan 2009: 223). In 1985, the ArchTran machine translation system for translation between Chinese and English was launched in Taiwan and was one of the first commercialized English-Chinese machine translation systems in the world (Chen *et al.* 1993: 87–98). In the United States, the METAL (Mechanical Translation and Analysis of Languages) system for translation between English and German, supported by the Siemens Company in Munich since 1978 and developed at the University of Texas, Austin, became operative (Deprez *et al.* 1994: 206–12; Lehmann *et al.* 1981; Lehrberger 1981; Little 1990: 94–107; Liu and Liro 1987: 205–18; Schneider 1992: 583–94; Slocum *et al.* 1987: 319–50; White 1987: 225–40). In China, the TranStar English-Chinese Machine Translation System, the first machine-translation product in China, developed by China National Computer Software and Technology Service Corporation, was commercially available in 1988 (www.transtar.com.cn). In Taiwan, the BehaviorTran, an English-Chinese machine translation system, was also launched in the same year.

In the 1990s, Saarbrucken in Germany formed the largest and the most established machine translation group in 1996. The SUSY (Saarbrücker Ubersetzungssystem/Saarbrücken Machine Translation System) project for German to English and Russian to German machine translation was developed between 1972 and 1986 (rz.uni-sb.de). In 1997, *Dong Fang Kuai Che* 東方快車 (Orient Express), a machine translation system developed by the China Electronic Information Technology Ltd. in China, was commercially available (Chan 2004: 336), while in Taiwan, TransBridge was developed for internet translation from English into Chinese (www.transbridge.com.tw). The first year of the twenty-first century witnessed the development of BULTRA (BULgarian TRAnslator), the first English-Bulgarian machine translation tool, by Pro Langs in Bulgaria (Chan 2004: 339).

What has been presented shows very clearly that from the beginning of machine translation in 1947 until 1957, six countries were involved in the research and development of machine translation, which included the Massachusetts Institute of Technology and Georgetown University in the United States in 1952, the Academy of Sciences in Russia and Cambridge University in the United Kingdom in 1954, Kyushu University in Japan in 1955, the Institute of Linguistics in China in 1956, and Charles University in Czechoslovakia in 1957. By 2007, of the 193 countries in the world, 30 had conducted research on computer or computer-aided translation, 9 actively. This means that around 16% of all the countries in the world were engaged in machine translation, 30% of which are active in research and development. The 31 countries which have been engaged in the research and development of machine translation are: Belgium, Brazil, Bulgaria, Canada, China, Czechoslovakia, Denmark, Finland, France, Germany, Hungary, India, Italy, Japan, Korea, Macau, Malaysia, Mexico, the Netherlands, Luxemburg, Poland, Russia, Singapore, Slovenia, Spain, Sweden, Switzerland, Taiwan, Tunisia, the United Kingdom, and the United States. Of these, the most active countries are China and Japan in Asia; France, Germany, the Netherlands, the United Kingdom, and Russia in Europe; and Canada and the United States in North America. The huge increase in the number of countries engaged in machine translation and the fast development of systems for different languages and language pairs show that machine translation has advanced by leaps and bounds in the last sixty-five years.

Concluding Remarks on Translation Technology Before 2013

It should be noted that computer-aided translation has been growing rapidly in all parts of the world in the last forty-seven years since its inception in 1967. Drastic changes have taken place in the field of translation since the emergence of commercial computer-aided translation systems in the 1980s. In 1988, as mentioned, we only had the Trados system that was produced in Europe. Now we have more than 100 systems developed in different countries, including Asian countries such as China, Japan, and India and American countries, such as Canada and the United States. In the 1980s, very few people had any ideas about computer-aided translation, let alone translation technology. Now, it is estimated that there are around 200,000 computer-aided translators in Europe, and more than 6,000 large corporations in the world handle their language problems with the use of corporate or global management computer-aided translation systems. At the beginning, computer-aided translation systems only had standalone editions. Now, there are over 17 different types of systems on the market.

According to my research, the number of commercially available computer-aided translation systems from 1984 to 2012 is 86. Several observations on these systems can be made. First, about three computer-aided translation systems have been produced every year during the last twenty-eight years. Second, because of the rapid changes in the market, 19 computer-aided translation systems failed to survive in the keen competition, and the total number of current commercial systems stands at 67. Third, almost half of the computer-aided translation systems have been developed in Europe, accounting for 49.38%, while 27.16% of them have been produced in America.

All these figures show that translation technology has been on the fast track in the last five decades. It will certainly maintain its momentum for many years to come.

2013–2023: A New Scope and Definition of Translation Technology in a New Age

In the last ten years, considerable changes have taken place in the field of translation technology, which deserve our examination from the global as well as area-specific perspectives. A new scope and definition of translation technology have gradually emerged, giving a much clearer conception of the name and nature of translation technology.

After seven decades of development, translation technology is now generally accepted as an umbrella concept that covers the four areas of machine translation, computer-aided translation, localization, and speech translation, as shown in the following.

In the last ten years and in the years to come, with the rapid advances in technology and to meet the needs of society, there will be changes in the four areas of translation technology.

From a global perspective, four major changes are expected to take place.

(1) Multimedia Translation Will Be Emphasized

Attending to the needs of the less fortunate to create a fair world will be important to the world of translation in the years to come. That means other than text and speech translations, more attention will be given to, for example, sign language translation to meet the needs of the audially handicapped. Paralinguistic translation could be introduced, such as gestures, through computer graphics.

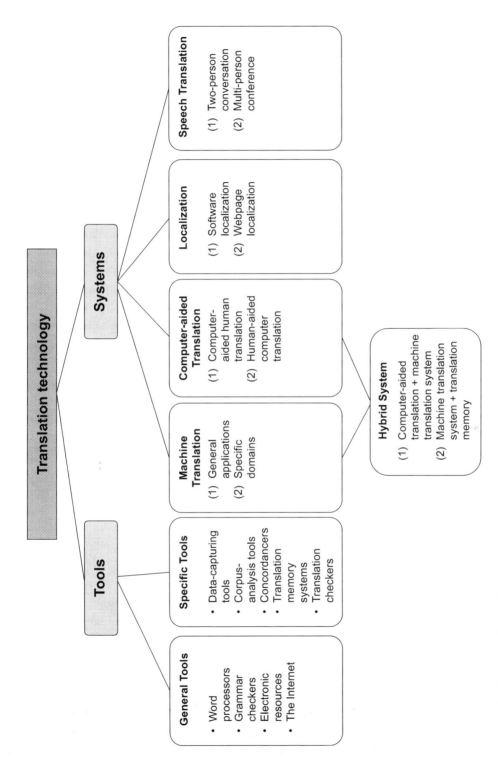

Figure 1.1 Typology of translation technology

(2) More Integrated Systems Will Be Introduced

Currently, hybrid forms of translation systems are popular. But the varied sources of data lower the quality of translation. In the future, it is hoped that integrated systems could be available. In other words, all the current forms of translation systems could be presented in an integrated system.

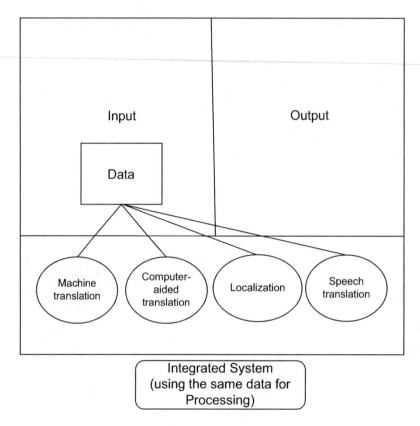

Figure 1.2   Integrated translation system

There are at least two major advantages in having such a system: first, more user-friendliness: users are free to use any form of translation system, and second, data consistency will be maintained. One of the major issues concerning the hybrid systems, such as CAT+MT and MT + TM (translation memory), is the inconsistency in data. MT systems linked to CAT systems have their own sources of data, whereas CAT data are prepared and given by the user. Then what is produced from a CAT system is different from what is produced from an MT system, which makes data editing very difficult. The proposed integrated system uses the same data for text generation, which is a huge advantage over a hybrid system.

(3) Reshuffling of Work Among Current Forms of Translation Technology

Currently there is a clear division of functions among the four types of translation technology. Machine translation is mainly information (textual) translation for all users, computer-aided translation is textual translation for professional translators, localization is software and webpage translation for product globalization, and speech translation is for dialogue interpretation for a specific pair of languages for tourists or daily conversations.

Table 1.1 Division of functions of translation technology

Type	Features	Target user
Machine translation	• Textual translation • Automatic • Fast • Bilingual/ multilingual • Information translation	• General users
Computer-aided translation	• Textual translation • Interactive • Bilingual/ multilingual	• Professional translators
Localization	• Software localization • Webpage localizations • Product globalization	• Localizers
Speech translation	• Conversational • Specific language pair	• Tourists • Business negotiation

(4) Shifting of Functions Could Take Place Soon

In the future, with the rapid advances of technology, there could be a shift of functions for different forms of translation. When machine translation, for example, is getting better and better, it could be an effective way of preparing draft translations for professional translators other than its function of information translation for people at large. When we have more useful data and automating functions, computer-aided (human) translation will soon move up to the stage of human-aided (machine) translation and eventually to automated computer-aided translation to replace machine translation. It is likely that speech translation will be the most popular tool for communication in the future, going beyond dialogue interpreting to more elaborate speech activities, such as business and political negotiations.

From an area-specific perspective, there will be major changes in machine translation, computer-aided translation, localization, and speech translation.

(5) Machine Translation

Machine translation is a useful means of speedy information translation. It has the advantages of

- fully automatic in text generation;
- high speed at 5,000 words/second;
- multilingual translation: can translate many languages; for example, Google Translate can translate 138 languages; and
- mainly interlingual translation.

But the disadvantages of machine translation are

- quality is in general unsatisfactory, with inaccuracies;
- it is time-consuming and labour intensive to post-edit the output; and
- it uses closed systems without human intervention.

(6) Partial Translation Systems Could Be Developed

Machine translation has been working mostly on full-text translation since its inception. Machine translation could make use of its computational capacities to work on partial translation, such as information translation in the forms of gist translation and abstracting. Gist translation is the production of the substance or general meaning of a speech or text or an outline translation of a text to provide an insight into the subject and overall content of the source text.

(7) Development of Intralingual Translation

It is noted that machine translation systems are dominantly interlingual systems. It is about time to consider developing intralingual translation systems, such as (a) Dialect-Putonghua system, such as Cantonese-Putonghua and Tibetan-Putonghua text translation systems and (b) interdialectal translation system, such as a Shanghainese–Cantonese text translation system.

(8) Development of Open Systems

All the current online systems are closed systems. They are not user friendly, as they do not allow users to make any changes to their databases to meet the needs of the user. In other words, what is wrongly translated will remain so, and users can only correct the same errors repeatedly. Things would improve enormously if machine translation systems could be open systems, allowing users to make lexical, syntactical, and textual changes without affecting the functionality of the system.

(9) Better Approach Needed for Better Output

In the last seven decades, experts in machine translation, in their effort to search for fully automatic high-quality translation (FAHQT), have tried more than twenty approaches in system design and construction. Despite their efforts, the output quality of machine translation is still unsatisfactory.

(10) Better Approach Needed for Better Output

This is because machine translation is imperfect in certain areas, including polysemy, parts of speech, syntactic ambiguity, context, proper noun translation, abbreviation translation, tense translation, long-sentence translation, source-equivalent translation, and language kinship. Obviously we need to have an approach that could deal with these issues adequately.

(11) More Domain-Specific Systems Are Needed

Poor translations will be generated when a domain-specific text is processed by a general application system. Likewise, a domain-specific system cannot translate a general text adequately. Due to market considerations, virtually all the systems available to us are general-application systems. It would be enormously helpful if translation systems for popular domains were developed, such as business, finance, sports, law, and entertainment.

(12) Use of MT by Professional Translators Will Be Popular

In the past, machine translation was despised by translators due to its poor output. Nowadays, 56% of professional translators in Europe use popular machine translation systems to prepare draft translations for them to work out acceptable and even publishable translations. The situation in other parts of the world will be similar in the future.

(13) Rapid Advances in MT Are Expected

Machine translation will continue to make rapid advances in the future, due to three factors: (1) rapid advances in artificial intelligence; (2) big data, including all the e-resources (e.g. e-books); and (3) new developments in neural science.

(14) Sentence-Breaking for Long Sentences

Machine translation is poor at translating long sentences. Shorter sentences are easier to process. Scholars have spent effort on the translation of long sentences in vain. Long sentences could be handled by pre-editing, by sentence-breaking functions in the system, or through human translation.

(15) Mobile Translation Will Be a Major Trend

Mobile translation will be a dominant trend in the future, for several reasons:

(1) the trend of machine translation is from desktop to mobile;
(2) with more inventions of digital devices, more mobile translation platforms will be available to us in the future;
(3) the large number of mobile phone users creates a huge demand for mobile translation; and
(4) the huge pool of bilingual/multilingual talents around the world will be able to use translation apps to make their contribution to mobile translation.

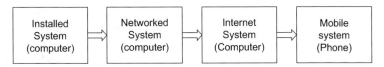

Figure 1.3 Mobile translation

(16) Crowdsourcing Will Be Popular

Crowdsourcing will become a major trend in translation. It has become increasingly popular, at least in China, to translate texts by crowdsourcing. Despite the lack of control over quality, this form of translating speeds up the translation of texts by many folds. If issues such as quality control and project management could be dealt with in a satisfactory manner, the future of crowdsourcing will be promising.

(17) Image Translation Will Gain Wider Acceptance

There has been a rapid rise of image translation. This is yet another emerging trend of great importance. It is most likely that people in the next generation will be interested more in images than in texts. Visual translation helps the visually handicapped people, as is the case with audio translation. Visual translation can be image-to-text or text-to-image.

Camera translation has been able to recognize and translate the text in a photo. It can also recognize the object in a photo, produce the name of the object, and translate the name into the target language. With the increase of visual data, great advances will be made in this area. Visual data has to be increased greatly to enable visual translation.

(18) Computer-Aided Translation

Computer-Aided Translation Has a Promising Future

Central to computer-aided translation is the concept of reusability, which is to use past bilingual documents to prepare data for the translation of current and new documents, as shown in Figure 1.4.

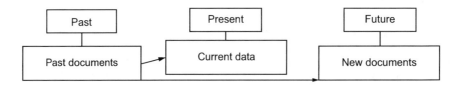

Figure 1.4 Process of computer-aided translation

In the span of fifty-two years, it has grown from obscurity to a global presence, being developed in a large number of countries in different continents, as shown in Figure 1.5.

(19) The Growth of Computer-Aided Translation Will Continue

Computer-aided translation will continue to be used by increasing numbers of translators. One major reason that accounts for its popularity is that with a very large translation memory database, translation generation can be done by selection, not by translation. This means translation can be done without translating. Terminological consistency in team translation can be maintained. This is not possible in the case of human translation. It has a lower cost, as material does not need to be translated. Higher volume is achieved for the same reason, and there is better management with the use of the project management platform.

At the same time, improvement should be made in a number of areas. (1) translation initialization is time consuming; (2) the creation and maintenance of terminology and translation memory databases is time consuming and labour intensive; (3) the reuse of stored data may be

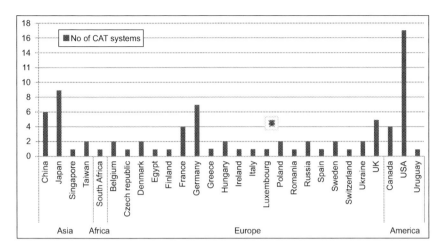

Figure 1.5 Global development of computer-aided translation

questionable, especially in the case of ad hoc translators; and (4) the speed of text generation is much slower than that of machine translation.

(20) Keen Challenges for Machine Translation

The role of computer-aided translation is decreasing when machine translation is getting better and better with the use of big data and artificial intelligence.

Big data is certainly good for both machine translation and computer-aided translation. We all know that data is king in computing. Without data, no machine can work. But the data we use have to be of high quality, relevant, and adequate.

(21) More User Friendly to Attract More Users

Computer-aided translation systems have to be more user friendly to attract more users. The development of computer-aided translation lags behind other three forms of translation technology, as it serves only a small number of target users, that is, professional translators, estimated to be around 600,000 in the world. How to enlarge the user population is another challenge we face if computer-aided translation is to survive in the competition or, in a more positive light, emulate machine translation. This has to do with the ease of operation of a computer-aided translation system and its accessibility to non-professionals.

(22) User Customization Should Be Introduced

Another challenge computer-aided translation faces is the role played by translators in system customization in the future. Should translators be always getting what they are given rather than playing a positive role to improve translation output for the system in use? A system that allows users to meet their own needs would be welcomed.

(23) Automating Computer-Aided Translation Is of Great Significance

Computer-aided translation has been with us for more than five decades. It is about time to elevate computer-aided translating to human-aided translation and eventually to automated computer-aided translation, which, hopefully, could serve as an alternative to or emulate machine translation by its human-quality translation output.

Several strategies will be used in automating computer-aided translation.

(1) the use of translator-manageable machine translation approaches to enable general syntactical transfer of data in textual translation;
(2) the use of readily available cleaned data to enable automatic translation;
(3) the automatic preparation of project-specific terminology and translation memory databases with the creation and use of two new tools: AutoTermSearch and AutoTMSearch; and
(4) the maintenance of quality through initially human editing, which eventually will be replaced by reference templates to close the gap of edit distance.

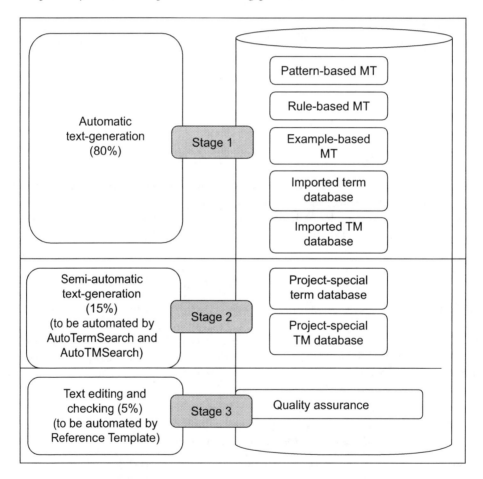

Figure 1.6   Automated computer-aided translation

(24)   Computer-Aided Interpreting Should Be Developed

Virtually all computer-aided systems are for translators, not interpreters. Computer-aided interpreting is a much-neglected area. Speech translation developers and interpreters should work together to come up with systems that could help interpreters in their work.

(25) **Localization**

Localization Is a Fast-Growing and Profitable Business

Localization is to customize software (software localization) or webpages (webpage localization) for a "local" audience. The main purpose of localization is to maximize the understandability and usability of a product so that it can be used in different parts of the world with optimal effectiveness.

The future of localization is promising, as the localization of software and webpages is a huge business for the translation industry. Localization of video games, in particular, has become increasingly important and profitable.

(26) **Simplifying the Task of Localization**

It is hoped that localization could be made simpler for translators or interpreters so that all that needs to be done can be done by them without relying on others. This means that the internationalization stage should be better prepared so that computer glitches would not occur, while the globalization of the product could be more culturally neutral.

(27) **Chinese Will Be the Number-One Localization Language in the World**

During its entire period of development, there have been changes in the languages for localization: from "dominant languages" (languages of the industrially more advanced countries, such as French and German), to "major languages" (such as English) and to "strategic languages" with new potential markets.

More recently, due to the size of its market, the Chinese language has become and will continue to be the number-one localization language in the world.

(28) **Partial Localization Will Be the Norm**

The degree of localization varies with the target users. Software and webpages can be "standardized", "semi-localized", "localized", "highly localized", and "culturally customized", depending on the necessity of translation.

In the future, when the world becomes increasingly globalized, partial localization rather than full localization will be the norm.

(29) **Localization as a Branch of Translation Studies**

At present, localization is generally regarded as an operational procedure in the translation industry, not an academic topic that deserves the attention of translation scholars.

Much effort is needed to examine the commercial, computational, linguistic, and theoretical aspects of localization from an academic perspective.

Speech Translation

Speech translation has been widely used as a means of communication for people from different language communities. It has a history of thirty-five years, which is relatively short when compared to machine translation or computer-aided translation. Speech translation systems are usually used in tourism and conversational discourse.

(30) Rapid Rise in the Number of Speech Translation Users

Speech translation will grow enormously in the future, as speech translation systems are convenient to use and have been widely used. The impact of speech translation is great, as the number of users has been on the increase and has outgrown other forms of translation technology. The e-speech of Google Translate, for example, has more than 500 million users. The number will continue to grow as tourism has prospered.

(31) Increase in the Number of Languages Needed

The number of languages currently available, which is estimated to be around 40, is relatively small when gauged against the total number of world languages (7,110) and languages for machine translation, which has around 150 languages. One major concern is the monopoly of some companies in the collection of voice data. Another concern is the infringement of privacy in data collection.

(32) Intralingual Systems Needed

Like machine translation systems, speech translation systems are interlingual to meet the need their target users, such as tourists. Intralingual systems should be developed to facilitate inter-dialectal communication, such as between Shanghainese and Cantonese.

(33) Open Speech Translation Systems Preferred

As in the case of machine translation, the speech signals in a speech translation system are not accessible to the user, and there is no way for a user to revise the speech corpus stored in the system. It is hoped that an open system will be designed to allow changes in data to be made to improve the quality of speech generation.

Conclusion

These thirty-three tendencies and suggestions have been explored with the intention of making translation technology more user friendly and matching users' expectations in the future. A remark to conclude the first chapter on translation technology is: The future of translation lies with technology, and translation technology is and will always be our future.

Additional Resources

http://anaphraseus.sourceforge.net.
http://blog.memsource.com.
http://developer.apple.com.
http://en.wikipedia.org/wiki/XLIFF.
http://felix-cat.com.
http://new.multilingual.com.
http://terminotix.com/news/newsletter.
http://wordfast.net/champollion.net.
www.across.net.
www.alchemysoftware.ie.

www.atasoft.com.
www.atril.com.
www.bas.bg.
www.colgate.edu.
www.cuni.cz.
www.dreye.com.tw.
www.gcys.cn.
www.heartsome.net.
www.hjtek.com.
www.hjtrans.com.
www.kilgray.com.
www.lisa.org.
www.logovista.co.jp.
www.lspzone.com.
www.maxprograms.com.
www.memsource.com.
www.metatexis.com.
www.multicorpora.com.
www.multilizer.com.
www.omegat.org.
www.opentm2.org.
www.otek.com.tw.
www.promt.com.
www.sdl.com.
www.sdlintl.com.
www.star-group.net.
www.systransoft.com.
www.thelanguagedirectory.com/translation/translation_software.
www.transbridge.com.tw.
www.translationzone.com.
www.transn.com.
www.transtar.com.cn.
www.tratool.com.
www.unam.mx.
www.urelitetech.com.cn.
www.wordbee.com.
www.wordfast.net.
www.xtm-intl.com.
www.zklr.com.

Bibliography

Allen, Ward (ed.) (1969) *Translating for King James*, Nashville: Vanderbilt University Press.

ALPAC (Automatic Language Processing Advisory Committee) (1966) 'Languages and Machines: Computers in Translation and Linguistics', *A Report by the Automatic Language Processing Advisory Committee, Division of Behavioral Sciences, National Academy of Sciences, National Research Council*, Washington, DC: National Academy of Sciences, National Research Council.

Arnold, Doug J. and Louis des Tombe (1987) 'Basic Theory and Methodology in EUROTRA', Sergei Nirenburg (ed.) *Machine Translation: Theoretical and Methodological Issues*, Cambridge: Cambridge University Press, 114–35.

Arthern, Peter J. (1979) 'Machine Translation and Computerized Terminology Systems: A Translator's Viewpoint', in Barbara M. Snell (ed.) *Translating and the Computer: Proceedings of a Seminar*, London: North-Holland Publishing Company, 77–108.

Brace, Colin (1992) 'Trados: Smarter Translation Software', *Language Industry Monitor*, Issue September–October. Available at: www.lim.nl/monitor/trados-1.html.

Brace, Colin (1993) 'TM/2: Tips of the Iceberg', *Language Industry Monitor*, Issue May–June. Available at: www.mt-archive.

Brace, Colin (1994) 'Bonjour, Eurolang Optimizer', *Language Industry Monitor*, Issue March–April. Available at: www.lim.nl/monitor/optimizer.html.

Chan, Sin-wai (2004) *A Dictionary of Translation Technology*, Hong Kong: The Chinese University Press.

Chan, Sin-wai (2009) *A Chronology of Translation in China and the West*, Hong Kong: The Chinese University Press.

Chen, Gang (2001) 'A Review on Yaxin CAT2.5', *Chinese Science and Technology Translators Journal* 14(2).

Chen, Shuchuan, Chang Jing-shin, Wang Jong-nae, and Su Keh-yih (1993) 'ArchTran: A Corpus-based Statistics-oriented English-Chinese Machine Translation System', in Sergei Nirenburg (ed.) *Progress in Machine Translation*, Amsterdam: IOP Press, 87–98.

Deprez, F., Greert Adriaens, Bart Depoortere, and Gert de Braekeleer (1994) 'Experiences with METAL at the Belgian Ministry of the Interior', *Meta* 39(1): 206–12.

Deslisle, Jean and Judith Woodsworth (eds.) (1995) *Translators Through History*, Amsterdam and Philadelphia: John Benjamins Publishing Company and UNESCO Publishing.

Dong, Zhendong (1988) 'MT Research in China', in Dan Maxwell, Klaus Schubert, and Toon Witkam (eds.) *New Directions in Machine Translation*, Dordrecht-Holland: Foris Publications, 85–91.

Editorial Committee 編寫組 (ed.) (1988) 《中國翻譯家詞典》(*A Dictionary of Translators in China*), Beijing: China Translation and Publishing Corporation 中國對外翻譯出版公司.

Elita, Natalia and Monica Gavrila (2006) 'Enhancing Translation Memories with Semantic Knowledge', in *Proceedings of the 1st Central European Student Conference in Linguistics*, 29–31 May 2006, Budapest, Hungary, 24–26.

Eurolux Computers (1992, September–October) 'Trados: Smarter Translation Software', *Language Industry Monitor* 11. Available at: www.lim.nl.

Even-Zohar, Itamar (1978) *Papers in Historical Poetics*, Tel Aviv: The Porter Institute for Poetics and Semiotics, Tel Aviv: Tel Aviv University.

Feng, Zhiwei 馮志偉 (1999) '〈中國的翻譯技術：過去、現在和將來〉(Translation Technology in China: Past, Present, and Future)', in Huang Changning 黃昌寧 and Dong Zhendong 董振東 (eds.) 《計算機語言學文集》(*Essays on Computational Linguistics*), Beijing: Tsinghua University Press, 335–440.

Gaiba, Francesca (1998) *The Origins of Simultaneous Interpretation: The Nuremberg Trial*, Ottawa: University of Ottawa Press.

Garcia, Ignacio and Vivian Stevenson (2005) 'Trados and the Evolution of Language Tools: The Rise of the De Facto TM Standard – and Its Future with SDL', *Multilingual Computing and Technology* 16(7).

Garcia, Ignacio and Vivian Stevenson (2006) 'Heartsome Translation Suite', *Multilingual* 17(1): 77. Available at: www.multilingual.com.

German, Kathryn (2009) 'Across: An Exciting New Computer Assisted Translation Tool', *The Northwest Linguist*: 9–10.

Gotti, Fabrizio, Philippe Langlais, Elliott Macklovitch, Didier Bourigault, Benoit Robichaud, and Claude Coulombe (2005) '3GTM: A Third-generation Translation Memory', in *Proceedings of the 3rd Computational Linguistics in the North-East (CLiNE) Workshop*, Gatineau, Québec, Canada, 26–30.

Haeseryn, Rene (1989) 'The International Federation of Translators (FIT) and Its Leading Role in the Translation Movement in the World', in Rene Haeseryn (ed.) *Roundtable Conference FIT-UNESCO: Problems of Translator in Africa*, Belgium: FIT, 379–84.

Hall, Amy (2000) 'SDL Announces Release of SDLX Version 2.0', *SDL International*. Available at: www.sdl.com/en/about-us/press/1999/SDL_Announces_Release_of_SDLX_Version_2_0.asp.

Harmsen, R. (2008) 'Evaluation of DVX'. Available at: http://rudhar.com.

Holmes, James S. (1972, 1987) 'The Name and Nature of Translation Studies', in Gideon Toury (ed.) *Translation Across Cultures*, New Delhi: Bahri Publications: Pvt. Ltd., 9–24.

Holmes, James S. (1988) 'The Name and Nature of Translation Studies', in James S. Holmes (ed.) *Translated! Papers on Literary Translation and Translation Studies*, Amsterdam: University of Amsterdam, 93–98.

Hutchins, W. John (1986) *Machine Translation: Past, Present and Future*, Chichester: Ellis Horwood.

Hutchins, W. John (1998) 'The Origins of the Translator's Workstation', *Machine Translation* 13(4): 287–307.

Hutchins, W. John (1999) 'The Development and Use of Machine Translation System and Computer-based Translation Tools', in Chen Zhaoxiong (ed.) *Proceedings of the International Conference on MT and Computer Language Information Processing*, Beijing: Research Center of Computer and Language Engineering, Chinese Academy of Sciences, 1–16.

Hutchins, W. John (2000) *Early Years in Machine Translation*, Amsterdam and Philadelphia: John Benjamins Publishing Company.

Johnson, R. I., Margaret King, and Louis des Tombe (1985) 'Eurotra: A Multilingual System under Development', *Computational Linguistics* 11(2–3): 155–69.

Kavak, Pinar (2009) 'Development of a Translation Memory System for Turkish to English', Unpublished MA dissertation, Boğaziçi University, Turkey.

Kay, Martin (1980) 'The Proper Place of Men and Machines in Language Translation', *Research Report CSL-80-11*, Xerox Palo Alto Research Center, Palo Alto, CA.

Kelly, Louis G. (1998) 'Latin Tradition', in Mona Baker (ed.) *Routledge Encyclopedia of Translation Studies*, London and New York: Routledge, 495–504.

Kilgray Translation Technologies (2011) 'What's New in MemoQ'. Available at: http://kilgray.com/products/memoq/whatsnew.

King, Margaret (1982) *EUROTRA: An Attempt to Achieve Multilingual MT*, Amsterdam: North-Holland Publishing Company.

King, Margaret (ed.) (1987) *Machine Translation Today: The State of the Art*, Edinburgh: Edinburgh University Press.

Környei, Tibor (2000) 'WordFisher for MS Word: An Alternative to Translation Memory Programs for Freelance Translators?', *Translation Journal* 4(1). Available at: http://accurapid.com/journal/11wf.htm.

Lau, Peter Behrendt (1988) 'Eurotra: Past, Present and Future', Catriona Picken (ed.) *Translating and the Computer 9: Potential and Practice*, London: The Association for Information Management, 186–91.

Lehmann, Winfred P., Winfield S. Bennett, Jonathan Slocum *et al.* (1981) *The METAL System*, New York: Griffiss Air Force Base.

Lehrberger, John (1981) *The Linguistic Model: General Aspects*, Montreal: TAUM Group, University of Montreal.

LISA (2010) 'IBM and the Localization Industry Standards Association Partner to Deliver Open-Source Enterprise-level Translation Tools'. Available at: www.lisa.org/OpenTM2.1557.0.html.

Little, Patrick (1990) 'METAL-Machine Translation in Practice', in Catriona Picken (ed.) *Translation and the Computer 11: Preparing for the Next Decade*, London: The Association for Information Management, 94–107.

Liu, Jocelyn and Joseph Liro (1987) 'The METAL English-to-German System: First Progress Report', *Computers and Translation* 2(4): 205–18.

Liu, Yongquan *et al.* 劉湧泉等 (1984) 《中國的機器翻譯》 (*Machine Translation in China*), Shanghai: Knowledge Press.

Locke, Nancy A. and Marc-Olivier Giguère (2002) 'Multitrans 3.0', *Multilingual Computing and Technology* 13(7): 51.

Locke, William Nash and Andrew Donald Booth (eds.) (1955) *Machine Translation of Languages: Fourteen Essays*, Cambridge, MA: MIT Press.

Loh, Shiu-chang (1975) 'Machine-aided Translation from Chinese to English', *United College Journal* 12(13): 143–55.

Loh, Shiu-chang (1976a) 'CULT: Chinese University Language Translator', *American Journal of Computational Linguistics Microfiche* 46: 46–50.

Loh, Shiu-chang (1976b) 'Translation of Three Chinese Scientific Texts into English by Computer', *ALLC Bulletin* 4(2): 104–05.

Loh, Shiu-chang and Kong Luan (1979) 'An Interactive On-line Machine Translation System (Chinese into English)', in Barbara M. Snell (ed.) *Translating and the Computer*, Amsterdam: North-Holland Publishing Company, 135–48.

Loh, Shiu-chang, Kong Luan, and Hung Hing-sum (1978) 'Machine Translation of Chinese Mathematical Articles', *ALLC Bulletin* 6(2): 111–20.

Maegaard, Bente (1988) 'EUROTRA: The Machine Translation Project of the European Communities', *Literary and Linguistic Computing* 3(2): 61–65.

Maegaard, Bente and Sergei Perschke (1991) 'Eurotra: General Systems Design', *Machine Translation* 6(2): 73–82.

Melby, Alan K. (1978) 'Design and Implementation of a Machine-assisted Translation System', in *Proceedings of the 7th International Conference on Computational Linguistics*, 14–18 August 1978, Bergen, Norway.

Melby, Alan K. and Terry C. Warner (1995) *The Possibility of Language: A Discussion of the Nature of Language, with Implications for Human and Machine Translation*, Amsterdam and Philadelphia: John Benjamins Publishing Company.

MultiCorpora Inc (2011) 'MultiCorpora Launches New Translation Management System'. Available at: www.multicorpora.com/news/multicorpora-launches-new-translation-management-system.

Multilingual (1997) 'CIMOS Releases Arabic to English Translation Software', *Multilingual*, 20 December 1997. Available at: http://multilingual.com/newsDetail.php?id=422.

Multilingual (1998) 'SDL Announces Translation Tools', *Multilingual*, 23 September 1998. Available at: http://multilingual.com/newsDetail.php?id=154.

Multilingual (1999) 'SDL Announces SDL Workbench and Product Marketing Executive', *Multilingual*, 22 February 1999. Available at: http://multilingual.com/newsDetail.php?id=12.

Multilingual (2000) 'Lionbridge to Acquire INT'L.com'. Available at: http://multilingual.com/newsDetail.php?id=1143.

Multilingual (2003) 'MultiCorpora R&D Releases MultiTrans 3.5', *Multilingual*, 17 October 2003. Available at: http://multilingual.com/newsDetail.php?id=3219.

Multilingual (2005a) 'STAR Releases Transit Service Pack 14', *Multilingual*, 15 April 2005. Available at: http://multilingual.com/newsDetail.php?id=4169.

Multilingual (2005b) 'SIMILIS Version 1.4 Released', *Multilingual*, 27 April 2005. Available at: http://multilingual.com/newsDetail.php?id=4187.

Multilingual (2005c) 'SDL Releases SDLX 2005', *Multilingual*, 5 May 2005. Available at: http://multilingual.com/newsDetail.php?id=4216.

Multilingual (2005d) 'MultiCorpora Announces the Release of MultiTrans 4', *Multilingual*, 31 August 2005. Available at: http://multilingual.com/newsDetail.php?id=4425.

Multilingual (2006a) 'Across Rolls out New Version 3.5', *Multilingual*, 20 November 2006. Available at: http://multilingual.com/newsDetail.php?id=5372.

Multilingual (2006b) 'Lingotek Announces Beta Launch of Language Search Engine', *Multilingual*, 15 August 2006. Available at: http://multilingual.com/newsDetail.php?id=5168.

Multilingual (2007a) 'Kilgray Releases Version 2.0 of MemoQ', *Multilingual*, 25 January 2007. Available at: http://multilingual.com/newsDetail.php?id=5467.

Multilingual (2007b) 'Quality Assurance Module Available for MemoQ', *Multilingual*, 4 April 2007.

Multilingual (2008a) 'Across Language Server 4.0 SP1', *Multilingual*, 21 April 2008. Available at: http://multilingual.com/newsDetail.php?id=6228.

Multilingual (2008b) 'Fusion One and Fusion Collaborate 3.0', *Multilingual*, 28 November 2008. Available at: http://multilingual.com/newsDetail.php?id=6568.

Multilingual (2009a) 'Fusion 3.1', *Multilingual*, 19 March 2009. Available at: http://multilingual.com/newsDetail.php?id=6734.

Multilingual (2009b) 'Across Language Server V.5', *Multilingual*, 13 May 2009. Available at: http://multilingual.com/newsDetail.php?id=6834.

Multilingual (2009c) 'Lingotek Launches Crowdsourcing Translation Platform', *Multilingual*, 22 October 2009. Available at: http://multilingual.com/newsDetail.php?id=7103.

Multilingual (2010a) 'SDL Trados Studio', *Multilingual*, 3 March 2010. Available at: http://multilingual.com/newsDetail.php?id=7298.

Multilingual (2010b) 'Collaborative Translation Platform 5.0', *Multilingual*, 27 July 2010. Available at: http://multilingual.com/newsDetail.php?id=7544.

Multilingual (2011) 'Déjà Vu X2', *Multilingual*, 24 May 2011. Available at: http://multilingual.com/newsDetail.php?id=933.

Nagao, Makoto (1993) 'Machine Translation: The Japanese Experience', in Sergei Nirenburg (ed.) *Progress in Machine Translation*, Amsterdam: IOS Press, 203–08.

Nida, Eugene A. (1964) *Toward a Science of Translating*, Leiden: E.J. Brill.

Phelan, Mary (2001) *The Interpreter's Resource*, Clevedon: Multilingual Matters Ltd.

Prior, Marc (2003) 'Close Windows, Open Doors', *Translation Journal* 7(1). Available at: http://accurapid.com/journal/23linux.htm.

rz.uni-sb.de.

Schmidt, Axel (2006, March) 'Integrating Localization into the Software Development Process', *TC World*.

Schneider, Thomas (1992) 'User Driven Development: METAL as an Integrated Multilingual System', *Meta* 37(4): 583–94.

Shannon, Claude L. and Warren Weaver (1949) *The Mathematical Theory of Communication*, Urbana: University of Illinois Press.

Slocum, Jonathan, Winfield S. Bennett, J. Bear, M. Morgan, and Rebecca Root (1987) 'METAL: The LRC Machine Translation System', in Margaret King (ed.) *Machine Translation Today: The State of the Art*, Edinburgh: Edinburgh University Press, 319–50.

Somers, Harold L. (1986) 'Eurotra Special Issue', *Multilingual* 5(3): 129–77.

Sumita, Eiichiro and Yutaka Tsutsumi (1988) 'A Translation Aid System Using Flexible Text Retrieval Based on Syntax-matching', in *Proceedings of the 2nd International Conference on Theoretical and Methodological*

Issues in Machine Translation of Natural Languages, Pittsburgh, PA: Carnegie Mellon University. Available at: www.mt-archive.info/TMI-1988-Sumita.pdf.

Wang, Zheng 王正 (2011) '〈翻譯記憶系統的發展歷程與未來趨勢〉 (Translation Memory Systems: A Historical Sketch and Future Trends)', 《編譯論叢》 (*Compilation and Translation Review*) 4(1): 133–60.

Warwick, Susan (1987) 'An Overview of Post-ALPAC Developments', in Margaret King (ed.) *Machine Translation Today: The State of the Art*, Edinburgh: Edinburgh University Press, 22–37.

Wassmer, Thomas (2003) 'SDLX TM Translation Suite 2003', *Translation Journal* 7(3).

Wassmer, Thomas (2004) 'Trados 6.5', *Multilingual Computing and Technology* 15(1): 61.

Wassmer, Thomas (2007) 'Comparative Review of Four Localization Tools: Déjà Vu, MULTILIZER, MultiTrans and TRANS Suite 2000, and Their Various Capabilities', *Multilingual Computing and Technology* 14(3): 37–42.

Wassmer, Thomas (2011) 'Dr Tom's Independent Software Reviews'. Available at: www.localizationworks.com/DRTOM/Trados/TRADOS.

Way, Andrew, Ian Crookston, and Jane Shelton (1997) 'A Typology of Translation Problems for Eurotra Translation Machines', *Machine Translation* 12(4): 323–74.

White, John S. (1987) 'The Research Environment in the METAL Project', in Sergei Nirenburg (ed.) *Machine Translation: Theoretical and Methodological Issues*, Cambridge: Cambridge University Press, 225–40.

Wiener, Norbert (1954) *The Human Use of Human Beings: Cybernetics and Society*, New York: Houghton Mifflin.

Wilks, Yorick (2000) 'Margaret Masterman', in W. John Hutchins (ed.) *Early Years in Machine Translation*, Amsterdam and Philadelphia: John Benjamins Publishing Company, 279–98.

Worth, Roland H. (1992) *Bible Translations: A History Through Source Documents*, Jefferson, NC and London: McFarland and Company, Inc., Publishers.

Xu, Jie (2001) 'Five Amazing Functions of Dr Eye 2001 (Dr Eye 2001 譯典通5大非凡功能)', 《廣東電腦與電訊》 (*Computer and Telecom*) 3.

Yngve, Victor H. (2000) 'Early Research at M.I.T. in Search of Adequate Theory', in W. John Hutchins (ed.) *Early Years in Machine Translation*, Amsterdam and Philadelphia: John Benjamins Publishing Company, 39–72.

Zhang, Zheng 張政 (2006) 《計算機翻譯研究》 (*Studies on Machine Translation*), Beijing: Tsinghua University Press清華大學出版社.

2

COMPUTER-AIDED TRANSLATION

Major Concepts

Chan Sin-wai

Introduction

When the term computer-aided translation is mentioned, we often associate it with the functions a computer-aided translation system offers, such as toolbars, icons, and hotkeys; the built-in tools we can use, such as online dictionaries and browsers; and the computational hitches we often encounter when working on a computer-aided translation project, such as chaotic code. What is more important is to see beyond the surface of computer-aided translation to the major concepts that shape the development of functions in translation technology.

Concepts, which are relatively stable, govern or affect the way functions are designed and developed, while functions, which are fast-changing, realize the concepts through the tasks they perform. As a major goal of machine translation is to help human translators, a number of functions in computer-aided translation systems have been created to enable machine processing of the source with minimal human intervention. Concepts, moreover, are related to what translators want to achieve in translating. Simply put, translators want to have a controllable (*controllability*) and customizable (*customizability*) system, which is compatible with file formats (*compatibility*) and language requirements and behaves as well as (*simulativity*) or even better than (*emulativity*) a human translator to allow them to work together (*collaborativity*) to produce quality translations (*productivity*). We have therefore identified seven major concepts which are important in computer-aided translation: simulativity, emulativity, productivity, compatibility, controllability, customizability, and collaborativity. These are arranged for better memorization by their acronym SEPCCCC.

Simulativity

The first concept of computer-aided translation is simulativity, which is about the method and ability of a computer-aided translation system to model the behaviour of a human translator by means of its functions, such as the use of concordancers in text analysis to model after comprehension on the part of the human translator and the creation of a number of quality assurance tools to follow the way checking is done by a human translator.

There are a number of ways to illustrate man–machine simulativity.

DOI: 10.4324/9781003168348-3

(1) Goal of Translation

The first is about the ultimate goal of translation technology. All forms of translation, machine translation, computer-aided translation, and human translation, aim at obtaining high-quality translations. In the case of machine translation, the goal of a fully automatic high-quality translation (FAHQT) is to be achieved with the use of a machine translation system without human intervention. In the case of computer-aided translation, the same goal is to be achieved with a computer-aided translation system that simulates the behaviour of a human translator through man–machine interaction.

(2) Translation Procedure

A comparison of the procedures of human translation with those of computer-aided translation shows that the latter simulates the former in a number of ways. In manual translation, various translation procedures have been proposed by translation scholars and practitioners, ranging from two-stage models to eight-stage ones, depending on the text type and purposes of translation. In machine translation and computer-aided translation, the process is known as technology-oriented translation procedure.

(a) Two-Stage Model

In human translation, the first type of translation procedure is a two-stage one, the stage of source text comprehension and the stage of target text formulation, as shown in Figure 2.1.

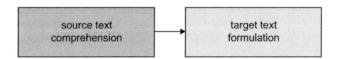

Figure 2.1 Two-stage model for human translation

This is a model for human translators with the ability of comprehension. As a computer-aided translation system does not have the ability of comprehension, it cannot model after human translation with this two-stage model. It can, however, work on a two-stage translation with the use of its system dictionary, particularly in the case of a language-pair–specific system.

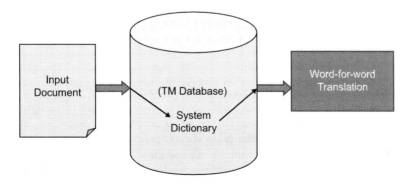

Figure 2.2 Two-stage dictionary-based language-pair–specific model

Another two-stage model of computer-aided translation is a terminology-based system, as shown in Figure 2.3.

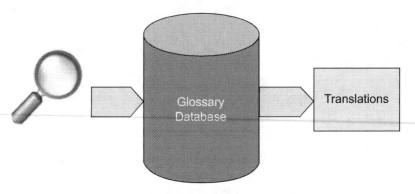

Figure 2.3 Two-stage terminology-based CAT system

(b) Three-Stage Models

The second type of translation procedure is a three-stage model. This section covers five variations of this model proposed by Eugene Nida and Charles Taber (1969), Wolfram Wilss (1982), Roger Bell (1991), Basil Hatim and Ian Mason, and Jean Delisle (1988) respectively. A three-stage example-based computer-aided translation system is shown to illustrate the simulation of human translation by computer-aided translation.

(I) MODEL BY EUGENE NIDA AND CHARLES TABER

The first model of a three-stage translation procedure involving the three phases of analysis, transfer, and restructuring was proposed by Eugene Nida and Charles Taber ([1969] 1982: 104). They intended to apply elements of Chomsky's transformational grammar to provide Bible translators with some guidelines when they translate ancient source texts into modern target texts, which are drastically different in languages and structures. Nida and Taber describe this three-stage model as a translation procedure in which

> the translator first analyses the message of the source language into its simplest and structurally clearest forms, transfers it at this level, and then restructures it to the level in the receptor language which is most appropriate for the audience which he intends to reach.
>
> *([1969] 1982: 484)*

Analysis is described by these two scholars as 'the set of procedures, including back transformation and componential analysis, which aim at discovering the kernels underlying the source text and the clearest understanding of the meaning, in preparation for the transfer' (Nida and Taber [1969] 1982: 197). Transfer, on the other hand, is described as the second stage 'in which the analysed material is transferred in the mind of the translator from language A to language B' ([1969] 1982: 104). Restructuring is the final stage in which the results of the transfer process are transformed into a 'stylistic form appropriate to the receptor language and to the intended receptors'.

In short, analysis, the first stage, is to analyse the source text; transfer, the second stage, is to transfer the meaning; and restructuring, the final stage, is to produce the target text. Their model is shown in Figure 2.4.

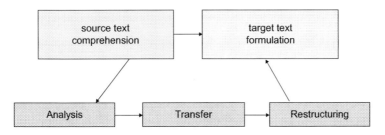

Figure 2.4   Three-stage model by Nida and Taber (1969)

(II) MODEL BY WOLFRAM WILSS

The second three-stage model was proposed by Wolfram Wilss (1982), who regards the translation procedure as a linguistic process of decoding, transfer, and encoding. His model is shown in Figure 2.5.

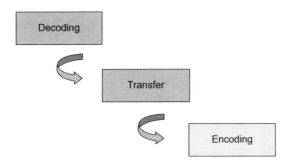

Figure 2.5   Three-stage model by Wolfram Wilss (1982)

(III) MODEL BY ROGER BELL

Another three-stage model of note is by Roger Bell, whose translation procedure framework is divided into three phases: the first phase is source text interpretation and analysis, the second translation process, and the third text reformulation. The last phase takes into consideration three factors: writer's intention, reader's expectation, and the target language norms (Bell 1991).

(IV) MODEL BY BASIL HATIM AND IAN MASON

This model, proposed by Basil Hatim and Ian Mason, is a more sophisticated three-stage model, which involves the three steps of source text comprehension, transfer of meaning, and target text assessment. At the source text comprehension level, text parsing, specialized knowledge, and intended meaning are examined. At the meaning transfer stage, consideration is given to

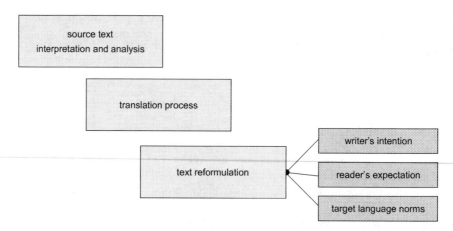

Figure 2.6 Model by Roger Bell

the lexical meaning, grammatical meaning, and rhetorical meaning. At the target text assessment level, attention is paid to text readability, target language conventions, and the adequacy of purpose.

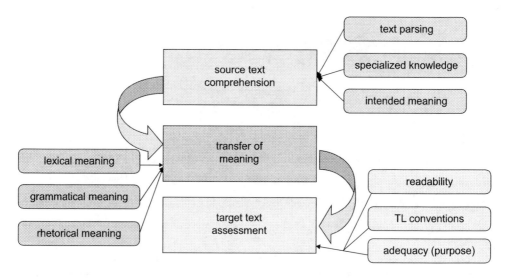

Figure 2.7 Three-stage model by Basil Hatim and Ian Mason

(V) MODEL BY JEAN DELISLE

The fourth model of a three-stage translation procedure was proposed by Jean Delisle (1988: 53–69). Deslisle believes that there are three stages in the development of a translation equivalence: comprehension, reformulation, and verification: 'comprehension is based on decoding linguistic signs and grasping meaning, reformulation is a matter of reasoning by analogy and re-wording concepts, and verification involves back-interpreting and choosing a solution' (1988: 53).

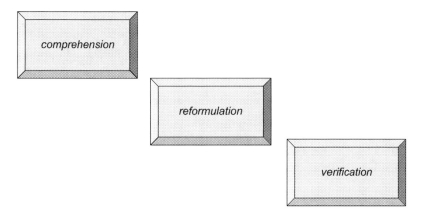

Figure 2.8　Three-stage model by Jean Delisle

Parallel to human translation, a three-stage model in computer-aided translation is the example-based system. The input text goes through the translation memory database and glossary database to generate fuzzy matches and translations of terms before getting the target text. The procedure of an example-based computer-aided translation system is shown in Figure 2.9.

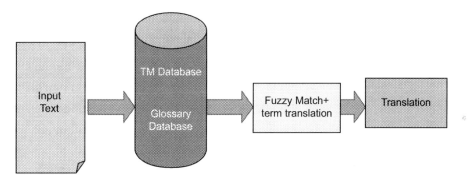

Figure 2.9　Three-stage example-based computer-aided translation model

(c)　Four-Stage Model

The third type of translation procedure is a four-stage one. A typical example is given by George Steiner ([1975] 1992), who believes that the four stages of translation procedure are knowledge of the author's time, familiarization with author's sphere of sensibility, original text decoding, and target text encoding.

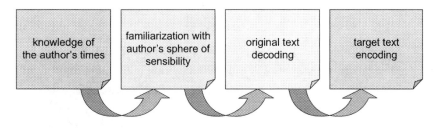

Figure 2.10　Model by George Steiner (1975)

For computer-aided translation, a four-stage model is exemplified by the webpage translation provided by Yaxin. The first stage is to input the Chinese webpage, the second stage is to process the webpage with the multilingual maintenance platform, the third stage is to process it with the terminology database, and the final stage is to generate a bilingual webpage. The Yaxin translation procedure is shown in Figure 2.11.

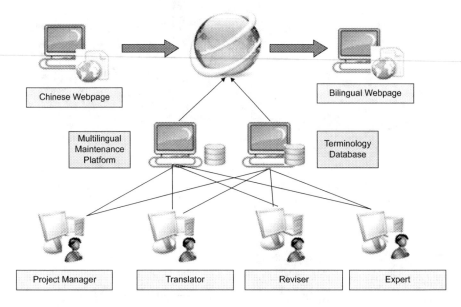

Figure 2.11   Yaxin's four-stage procedure

(d) Five-Stage Model

The fourth type of translation procedure is a five-stage one, as proposed by Omar Sheikh Al-Shabab (1996: 52). The first stage is to edit the source text, the second to interpret the source text, the third to interpret it in a new language, the fourth to formulate the translated text, and the fifth to edit the formulation.

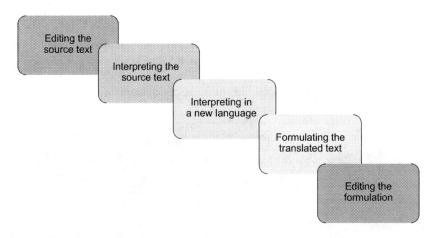

Figure 2.12   Model by Omar Sheikh Al-Shabab

In computer-aided translation, a five-stage model is normally practised. At the first stage, the initiating stage, tasks such as setting computer specifications, logging in to a system, creating a profile, and creating a project file are performed. At the second stage, the data preparation stage, the tasks involve data collection, data creation, and the creation of terminology and translation memory databases. At the third stage, the data processing stage, the tasks include data analysis, the use of system and non-system dictionaries, the use of concordancers, doing pre-translation, data processing by translation by computer-aided translation systems with human intervention or by machine translation systems without human intervention, or data processing by localization systems. At the fourth stage, the data editing stage, the work is divided into two types. One type is data editing for computer-aided translation systems, which is about interactive editing, the editing environments, matching, and methods used in computer-aided translation. Another type is data editing for computer translation systems, which is about post-editing and the methods used in human translation. At the last or fifth stage, the finalizing stage, the work is mainly updating databases.

The fives stages in computer-aided translation are illustrated in in Figure 2.13.

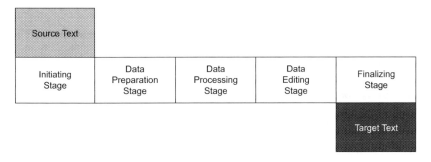

Figure 2.13   Five-stage technology-oriented translation procedure

It can be seen that though there are five-stage models in both human and computer-aided translation and the tasks involved are different, the concept of simulativity is at work at almost all stages.

(e) Eight-Stage Model

The fifth type of translation procedure is an eight-stage one, as proposed by Robert Bly (1983).

set down a literal version
find out the meaning of the poem
make it sound like English
make it sound like American
catch the mood of the poem
pay attention to sound
ask a native speaker to go over the version
make a final draft with some adjustments

Figure 2.14   Model by Robert Bly (1983)

Robert Bly, who is a poet, suggests an eight-stage procedure for the translation of poetry: (1) set down a literal version, (2) find the meaning of the poem, (3) make it sound like English, (4) make it sound like American, (5) catch the mood of the poem, (6) pay attention to sound, (7) ask a native speaker to go over the version, and (8) make a final draft with some adjustments.

In computer-aided translation, there is no eight-stage model. But other than the five-stage model, there is also a seven-stage model, which is shown in Figure 2.15.

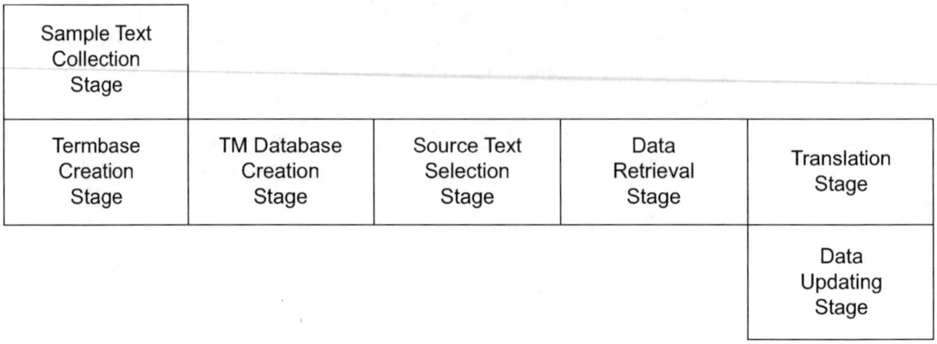

Sample Text Collection Stage				
Termbase Creation Stage	TM Database Creation Stage	Source Text Selection Stage	Data Retrieval Stage	Translation Stage
				Data Updating Stage

Figure 2.15   Seven-stage computer-aided translation procedure

The seven stages of computer-aided translation go from sample text collection to termbase creation, translation memory database creation, source text selection, data retrieval, source text translation, and finally data updating.

All in all, we can say that when compared to human translation, computer-aided translation is simulative, following some of the stages in human translation.

Emulativity

There are obviously some functions which are performable by a computer-aided translation system but not by a human translation. This is how technology can emulate human translation. Computer-aided translation, with the help of machine translation, simulates human translation, and it also emulates human translation in a number of areas, some of which are mentioned in the following.

Alt-Tag Translation

This function of machine translation allows the user to understand the meaning of text embedded within images (Joy 2002). The images on a web site are created by the IMG tag (inline image graphic tag), and the text that provides alternate message to viewers who cannot see the graphics is known as an ALT-tag, which stands for 'alternative text'. Adding an appropriate ALT tag to every image within one's web site will make a huge difference to its accessibility. As translators, our concern is the translation of the alternative text, as images are not to be translated anyway.

Chatroom Translation

Machine translation has the function to translate the contents of a chatroom, known as 'chat translation' or 'chatroom translation'. Chat translation systems are commercially available for the translation of the contents of a chatroom on a computer. As a chat is part of conversational discourse, all the theoretical and practical issues relating to conversational discourse can be applied to the study of chat translation. It should be noted that this kind of online jargon and addressivity are drastically different from what we have in other modes of communication.

The chatroom function is available in some systems, such as Fluency, as one of the resources. This function has to be purchased and enabled in the Fluency Chat Server to allow clients to be connected to this closed system for internal communications. For standalone version users, the function of chat will be provided by the Fluency Chat Server provided by its company, Western Standard (2011: 39).

Clipboard Translation

This is to copy a text to the clipboard from any Windows application for a machine translation system to translate the clipboard text, and the translated text can then be pasted into the original or any other location. One of the systems that translate clipboards is Atlas.

Conversion Between Metric and British Systems

A function that can be easily handled by machine translation but not so easily by human translation is the conversion of weight, volume, length, or temperature from metric to British or vice versa. Fluency, for example, can do metric/British conversion a target text box with the converted units.

Currency Conversion

Some computer-aided translation systems can do currency conversion. With the use of Currency Converter, a function in Fluency, and access to the Internet to get the currency conversion rates, systems can convert a currency in a country into the local country's currency. The number of currencies that can be handled by a system is relatively large. Fluency, for example, supports the conversion of currencies of around 220 countries. The conversion of multiple currencies is also supported.

Email Translation

This refers to the translation of emails by a machine translation system (Matsuda and Kumai 1999; Rooke 1985: 105–15). The first online and real-time email translation was done in 1994 by the CompuServe service, which provided translation service for emails from and to English and French, German, or Spanish. Email translation has since become a very important part of daily communication, and most web translation tools have email translators to translate emails. As emails are usually conversational and often written in an informal or even ungrammatical way, they are difficult for mechanical processing (Fais and Ogura 2001; Han *et al.* 2006). One of the systems that translates emails is Atlas.

Foreign Language Translation

One of the most important purposes of using translation software is to translate a source text, the language of which is unfamiliar to the user, so as to have its contents in a language familiar to the user. It is found that a majority of the commercial machine translation systems are for translation among Indo-European languages or major languages with a large number of speakers or users. Software programs for translation between major languages and minor languages are relatively small in number.

Gist Translation

Another area where machine translation differs fundamentally from human translation is gist translation, which refers to a translation output which expresses only a condensed version of the source text message. This type of rough translation is to get the essential information of what is in the text for a user to decide whether to translate it in full or not to serve a specific purpose.

Highlight and Translate

This function allows the user to highlight a part of the text and translate it into the designated language. The highlighted text is translated on its own without affecting the rest of the text.

Instant Transliteration

This refers to a function of machine translation which can transliterate the words of a text with a certain romanization system. In the case of Chinese, the Hanyu Pinyin Romanization system for simplified characters is used in mainland China, while the Wade-Giles Romanization system for traditional characters is used in Taiwan.

Mouse Translation

This is to translate sentences on a web page or in applications by simply clicking the mouse. Systems that provide mouse translation include Atlas.

Online Translation

This is the translation of a text by an online machine translation system which is available at all times on demand from users. With the use of an online translation service, the functions of information assimilation, message dissemination, language communication, translation entertainment, and language learning can be achieved.

Pre-Translation

Machine translation is taken to be pre-translation in two respects. The first is as a kind of preparatory work on the texts to be translated, including the checking of spelling, the compilation of dictionaries, and the adjustment of text format. The second is taken to be a draft translation of the source text which can be further revised by a human translator.

Sentence Translation

Unlike human translation, which works at the textual level, machine translation is sentential translation. In other words, machine translation is a sentence-by-sentence translation. This type of translation facilitates the work of post-editing, and methods which are frequently used in translating sentences in translation practice to produce effective translations can be used to produce good translations from machine translation systems.

Web Translation

This refers to the translation of information on a webpage from one language into another. Web translation tools are a type of translation tool that translate information on a webpage from one language into another. They serve three functions: (1) as an assimilation tool to transmit information to the user, (2) as a dissemination tool to make messages comprehensible, and (3) as a communication tool to enable communication between people with different language backgrounds.

Productivity

As translation technology is a field of entrepreneurial humanities, productivity is of great importance. Productivity in computer-aided translation is achieved through the use of technology, collective translation, recycling translations, reusing translations, professional competence, profit-seeking, labour-saving, and cost-saving.

Using Technology to Increase Productivity

The use of technology to increase productivity needs no explanation. As early as 1980, when Martin Kay discussed the proper place of humans and machines in language translation, he said:

> Translation is a fine and exacting art, but there is much about it that is mechanical and routine and, if this were given over to a machine, the productivity of the translator would not only be magnified but his work would become more rewarding, more exciting, more human.
>
> *(Kay 1980: 1)*

All computer-aided translation systems aim to increase translation productivity. In terms of the means of production, all translation nowadays is computer-aided translation, as virtually no one could translate without using a computer.

Collective Translation to Increase Productivity

Gone are the days when bilingual competence, pen and paper, and printed dictionaries made a translator. Gone are the days when a single translator did a long translation project all alone. It is true that in the past, translation was mainly done singly and individually. Translation was also done in a leisurely manner. At present, translation is done largely through team work linked by a server-based computer-aided translation system. In other words, translation is done in a collective manner.

Recycling Translations to Increase Productivity

To recycle a translation in computer-aided translation is to use exact matches automatically extracted from a translation memory database. To increase productivity, the practice of recycling translations is followed in computer-aided translation. Networked computer-aided translation systems are used to store centralized translation data, which are created by and distributed among translators. As this is the case, translators do not have to produce their own translations. They can simply draw from and make use of the translations stored in the bilingual database to form their translation of the source text. Translation is therefore produced by selection.

Reusing Translations to Increase Productivity

To reuse a translation in computer-aided translation is to appropriate terms and expressions stored in a term database and translation memory database. It should be noted that while in literary translation, translators produce translations in a creative manner, translators in practical translation reuse and recycle translations, as the original texts are often repetitive. In the present age, over 90% of translation work is in the area of practical translation. Computer-aided translation is ideal for the translation of repetitive practical writings. Translators do not have to translate the sentences they have translated before. The more they translate, the less they have to translate. Computer-aided translation therefore reduces the amount a translator needs to translate by eliminating duplicate work. Some systems, such as Across, allow the user to automatically reuse the existing translations from the translation memory. It can be seen that 'reduce, reuse, recycle' are three effective ways of increasing profitability (de Ilarraza *et al.* 2000).

Professional Competence to Increase Productivity

Translators have to work with the help of translation technology. The use of computer-aided translation tools has actually been extended to almost every type of translation work. Computer-aided translation tools are aiming at supporting translators and not at replacing them. They make sure that translation quality is maintained as 'all output is human input'. As far as the use of tools is concerned, professional translation is technological. In the past, translators used only printed dictionaries and references. Nowadays, translators use electronic concordancers, speech technology, online terminology systems, and automatic checkers. Translation is about the use of a workbench or workstation in translation work.

Translation competence or knowledge and skills in languages are not enough today. It is more realistic to talk about professional competence, which includes linguistic, cultural, translation, translator, and technological competence. Professional competence is important for translators, as it affects their career development. A remark made by Timothy Hunt is worth noting: 'Computers will never replace translators, but translators who use computers will replace translators who don't' (Sofer 2009: 88). What has happened in the field of translation technology shows that Hunt's remark may not be far off the mark. In the 1980s, very few people had any ideas about translation technology or computer-aided translation. Now, SDL alone has more than 180,000 computer-aided translators. The total number of computer-aided translators in the world is likely to be several times higher than that.

Profit-Seeking to Increase Productivity

Translation is in part vocational, in part academic. In the training of translators, there are courses on translation skills to foster their professionalism, and there are courses on translation theories to enhance their academic knowledge. But there are very few courses on translation as a business or as an industry. It should be noted that translation in recent decades has increasingly become a field of entrepreneurial humanities as a result of the creation of the project management function in computer-aided translation systems. This means translation is now a field of humanities which is entrepreneurial in nature. Translation as a commercial activity has to increase productivity to make more profits.

Labour-Saving to Increase Productivity

Computer-aided translation systems help to increase productivity and profits through labour-saving. Computer-aided translation is labour saving. It eliminates repetitive translation tasks.

Through reusing past translations, enormous labour is saved. Computer-aided translation tools support translators by freeing them from boring work and letting them concentrate on what they can do best over machines, that is, handling semantics and pragmatics. Generally, this leads to a broader acceptance by translators. The role of a translator, therefore, has changed drastically in the modern age of digital communication. Rather than simply translating the document, a computer-aided translator has to engage in other types of work, such as authoring, pre-editing, interactive editing, post-editing, term database management, translation memory database management, text alignment, and manual alignment verification. It is estimated that with the use of translation technology, the work that is originally done by six translators can be taken up by just one.

Cost-Saving to Increase Productivity

Computer-aided translation is also cost saving. It helps to keep the overhead cost down, as what has been translated needs not to be translated again. It helps to improve planning of budgets.

Other issues relating to cost should also be taken into account. First, the actual cost of the tool and its periodic upgrades. Second, the licensing policy of the system, which is about the ease of transferring licenses between computers or servers, the incurrence of extra charges for client licenses, the lending of licenses to one's vendors, freelancers, and the eligibility for free upgrades. Third, the cost that is required for support, maintenance, or training. Fourth, the affordability of the system to one's translators. Fifth, the user friendliness of the system to one's computer technicians and translators, which affects the cost of production.

Compatibility

The concept of compatibility in translation technology must be considered in terms of file formats, operating systems, intersystem formats, translation memory databases, terminology databases, and the languages supported by different systems.

Compatibility of File Formats

One of the most important concepts in translation technology is the type of data that needs to be processed, which is indicated by its format, being shown by one or several letters at the end of a filename. Filename extensions usually follow a period (dot) and indicate the type of information stored in the file. A look at some of the common file types and their file extensions shows that in translation technology, text translation is but one type of data processing, though it is the most popular one.

There are two major types of formats: general documentation types and software development types.

(I) General Documentation Types

(1) TEXT FILES

All computer-aided translation systems which use Microsoft Word as text editor can process all formats recognized by Microsoft Word. Throughout the development of translation technology, most computer-aided translation systems process text files (.txt). For Microsoft Word 2000–2003, text files were saved and stored as .doc (document text file/word processing file); for Microsoft Word 2007/2011, documents were saved and stored as .docx (document text file

[Microsoft Office 2007]) or .dotx (Microsoft Word 2007 Document Template). Other types of text files include .txt (text files), .txml (Wordfast files), and .rtf (Rich Text files).

All automatic and interactive translation systems can process text files, provided the text processing system has been installed on the computer before processing begins. Some of the computer-aided translation systems which can only translate text files include: Across, AidTrans-Studio, Anaphraseus (formerly known as OpenWordfast), AnyMen (.docx or higher), Araya, Autshumato Integrated Translation Environment (ITE), CafeTran, Déjà Vu, Esperantilo, Fluency, Fusion, OmegaT, Wordfast, and WordFisher. Computer-aided translation systems which can translate text files as well as other formats include CafeTran, Esperantilo, Felix, Fortis, GlobalSight, Google Translator Toolkit, Heartsome Translation Suite, Huajian IAT, Lingo, Lingotek, MadCap Lingo, MemoQ, MemOrg, MemSource, MetaTexis, MultiTrans, OmegaT+, Pootle, SDL-Trados, Similis, Snowman, Swordfish, TM-Database, Transit, Wordfast, XTM, and Yaxin.

(2) WEB-PAGE FILES

HyperText Markup Language (HTML) is a markup language that web browsers use to interpret and compose text, images, and other material into visual or audible web pages. HTML defines the structure and layout of a web page or document by using a variety of tags and attributes. HTML documents are stored as .asp (Active Server Pages), .aspx (Active Server Page Extended), .htm and .html (Hypertext Markup Language), .php (originally Personal Home Page, now Hypertext Preprocessor), .jsp (JavaServer Pages), .sgml (Standard Generalized Markup Language), .xml (Extensible Markup Language), and .xsl (Extensible Stylesheet Language) file formats, which have been available since late 1991. Due to the popularity of web pages, web translation has been an important part of automatic and interactive translation systems. Many systems provide comprehensive support for the localization of HTML-based document types. Web page localization is interchangeable with web translation or web localization.

Systems that handle HTML include Across, AidTransStudio, Alchemy Publisher, Araya, Atlas, CafeTran, CatsCradle, Déjà Vu, Felix, Fluency, Fortis, GlobalSight, Google Translator Toolkit, Heartsome Translation Suite, Huajian IAT, Lingo, Lingotek, LogiTerm, MemoQ, MemOrg, MetaTexis, MultiTrans, Okapi Framework, OmegaT, OmegaT+, Open Language Tools, Pootle, SDL-Trados, Similis, Snowman, Swordfish, TM-Database, TransSearch, Transit, Transolution, and XTM.

(3) PDF FILES

Portable Document Format (PDF) (.pdf) is a universally accepted file interchange format developed by Adobe in the 1990s. The software that allows document files to be transferred between different types of computers is Adobe Acrobat. A PDF file can be opened by the document format, which might require editing to make the file look more like the original or can be converted to an .rtf file for data processing by a computer-aided translation system.

Systems that can translate Adobe PDF files and save them as Microsoft Word documents include Alchemy Publisher, CafeTran, Lingo, Similis, and Snowman.

(4) MICROSOFT OFFICE POWERPOINT FILES

Microsoft PowerPoint is a presentation program developed to enable users to create anything from basic slide shows to complex presentations, which are composed of slides that may contain text, images, and other media. Types of Microsoft Office PowerPoint files include .ppt (general file extension), .pps (PowerPoint slideshow), .pot (PowerPoint template), and Microsoft PowerPoint 2007/2011, which are saved as .pptx (Microsoft PowerPoint Open XML document), .ppsx (PowerPoint Open XML slideshow), .potx (PowerPoint Open XML Presentation Template), and .ppsm (PowerPoint 2007 macro-enabled slideshow).

Systems that can handle PowerPoint files include Across, AidTransStudio, Alchemy Publisher, CafeTran, Déjà Vu, Felix, Fluency, Fusion, GlobalSight, Lingotek, LogiTerm, MadCap Lingo, MemoQ, MemSource, MetaTexis, SDL-Trados, Swordfish, TM-Database, Transit, Wordfast, XTM, and Yaxin.

(5) MICROSOFT EXCEL FILES

Different types of Microsoft Excel files include .xls (spreadsheet), .xlt (template), Microsoft Excel 2007 .xlsx (Microsoft Excel Open XML document), .xltx (Excel 2007 spreadsheet template), and .xlsm (Excel 2007 macro-enabled spreadsheet).

The computer-aided translation systems that can translate Excel files include Across, AidTransStudio, Déjà Vu, Felix, GlobalSight, Lingotek, LogiTerm, and MemoQ, MemOrg, MetaTexis, MultiTrans, Snowman, Wordfast, and Yaxin.

(6) MICROSOFT ACCESS FILES

This is one of the computer-aided translation systems which can handle Access with .accdb (Access 2007–2010) file extension is Déjà Vu.

(7) IMAGE FILES

The processing of image data, mainly graphics and pictures, is important in computer-aided translation. The data are stored as .bmp (bitmap image file), .jpg (Joint Photographic Experts Group), and .gif (Graphics Interchange Format). One of the computer-aided translation systems that is capable of handling images is CafeTran.

(8) SUBTITLE FILES

One of the most popular subtitle file types on the market is .srt (SubRip Text). OmegaT is one of the computer-aided systems that support subtitle files.

(9) ADOBE INDESIGN FILES

Adobe InDesign is desktop publishing software. It can be translated without the need of any third-party software by Alchemy Publisher and AnyMem. For Alchemy Publisher, .indd files must be exported to an .inx format before they can be processed. Other computer-aided translation systems that support Adobe InDesign files include Across, Déjà Vu, Fortis, GlobalSight, Heartsome Translation Suite, Okapi Framework, MemoQ, MultiTrans, SDL-Trados, Swordfish, Transit, and XTM.

(10) ADOBE FRAMEMAKER FILES

Adobe FrameMaker is an authoring and publishing solution for XML. FrameMaker files, .fm, .mif, and .book, can be opened directly by a system if it has Adobe FrameMaker installed.

Computer-aided translation systems that can translate Adobe FrameMaker files include Across and Alchemy Publisher (which requires a PPF created by Adobe FrameMaker before translating it; Alchemy Publisher supports FrameMaker 5.0, 6.0, 7.0, 8.0, 9.0, FrameBuilder 4.0, and FrameMaker + SGML), CafeTran, Déjà Vu, Fortis, GlobalSight, Heartsome Translation Suite, Lingo, Lingotek, MadCap Lingo, MemoQ, MetaTexis, MultiTrans, SDL-Trados, Swordfish, Transit, Wordfast, and XTM.

(11) ADOBE PAGEMAKER FILES

Systems that support Adobe PageMaker 6.5 and 7 files include Déjà Vu, GlobalSight, MetaTexis, and Transit.

(12) AUTOCAD FILES

AutoCAD, developed and first released by Autodesk, Inc., in December 1982, is a software application for computer-aided design (CAD) and drafting which supports both 2D and 3D formats. This software is now used internationally as the most popular drafting tool for a range of industries, most commonly in architecture and engineering.

Computer-aided translation systems that support AutoCad include CafeTran, Transit, and TranslateCAD.

(13) DTP TAGGED TEXT FILES

DTP stands for desktop publishing. A popular desktop publishing system is QuarkXPress.

Systems that support desktop publishing include Across, CafeTran, Déjà Vu, Fortis, GlobalSight, MetaTexis, MultiTrans, SDL-Trados, and Transit.

(14) LOCALIZATION FILES

Localization files include files with the standardized format for localization .xliff (XML Localization Interchange File Format) files, .ttx (XML font file format) files, and .po (portable object) files.

Computer-aided translation systems which process XLIFF files include Across Language Server, Araya, CafeTran, Esperantilo, Fluency, Fortis, GTranslator, Heartsome translation Suite, MadCap Lingo, Lingotek, MemoQ, Okapi Framework, Open Language Tools, Poedit, Pootle, Swordfish, Transolution, Virtaal, and XTM.

(II) *Software Development Types*

(1) JAVA PROPERTIES FILES

Java Properties files are simple text files that are used in Java applications. The file extension of a Java Properties file is *.properties* (Java Properties File).

Computer-aided translation systems that support Java Properties files include Déjà Vu, Fortis, Heartsome Translation Suite, Lingotek, Okapi Framework, OmegaT+, Open Language Tools, Pootle, Swordfish, and XTM.

(2) OPENOFFICE.ORG/STAROFFICE

StarOffice of the Star Division was a German company that ran from 1984 to 1999. It was succeeded by OpenOffice.org, an open-source version of StarOffice owned by Sun Microsystems

(1999–2009) and Oracle Corporation (2010–2011), which ran from 1999–2011. Currently it is Apache OpenOffice. The format of OpenOffice is .odf (OpenDocument Format).

Computer-aided translation systems which process this type of file include AidTransStudio, Anaphraseus, CafeTran, Déjà Vu, Heartsome Translation Suite, Lingotek, OmegaT, OmegaT+, Open Language Tools, Pootle, Similis, Swordfish, Transolution, and XTM.

(3) WINDOWS RESOURCE FILES

These are simple script files containing startup instructions for an application program, usually a text file containing commands that are compiled into binary files such as .exe and .dll. File extensions include .rc (record columnar file) and .resx (NET XML Resource Template). Computer-aided translation systems that process this type of file include Across, Déjà Vu, Fortis, Lingotek, MetaTexis, and Okapi Framework.

Compatibility of Operating Systems

One of the most important factors which determined the course of development of computer-aided translation systems is their compatibility with the current operating systems on the market. It is therefore essential to examine the major operating systems running from the beginning of computer-aided translation in 1988 to the present, which include, among others, Microsoft Windows and Mac OS.

Microsoft Operating Systems

In the world of computing, Microsoft Windows has been the dominant operating system. From 1981 to 1995, the x86-based MS-DOS (Microsoft Disk Operating System) was the most commonly used system, especially for IBM compatible personal computers. Trados's Translator's Workbench II, developed in 1992, is a typical example of a computer-aided translation system working on DOS.

DOS was supplemented by Microsoft Windows 1.0, a 16-bit graphical operating environment, released on 20 November 1985 (Windows 2012). In November 1987, Windows 1.0 was succeeded by Windows 2.0, which existed to 2001. Déjà vu 1.0, released in 1993, was one of the systems compatible with Windows 2.0. Windows 2.0 was supplemented by Windows 286 and Windows 386.

Then came Windows 3.0, succeeding Windows 2.1x. Windows 3.0, with a graphical environment, is the third major release of Microsoft Windows and was released on 22 May 1990. With a significantly revamped user interface and technical improvements, Windows 3 became the first widely successful version of Windows and a rival to Apple Macintosh and the Commodore Amiga on the GUI front. It was followed by Windows 3.1x. During its lifespan from 1992–2001, Windows 3.1x introduced various enhancements to the still MS-DOS–based platform, including improved system stability, expanded support for multimedia, TrueType fonts, and workgroup networking. Trados's Translator's Workbench, released in 1994, was a system that was adaptable to Windows 3.1x.

Except for Windows and DOS, OS/2 was also one of the operating systems that supported computer-aided translation systems, especially in the late 1980s and early 1990s.

Apple Operating Systems

Mac OS (1984–2000) and OS X (2001–) are two in a series of graphical user interface–based operating systems developed by Apple Inc. for their Macintosh line of computer systems. Mac

OS was first introduced in 1984 with the original Macintosh, and this series was ended in 2000. OS X, first released in March 2001, is a series of Unix-based graphical interface operating systems. Both series share a general interface design but have very different internal architectures.

Only one computer-aided translation system, AppleTrans, is designed for OS X. Its initial released was announced in February 2004, and the latest updated version was version 1.2(v38) released in September 2006, which runs on Mac OS X 10.3 or later.

Another computer-aided translation system, Wordfast Classic, was released to upgrade its support of the latest text processor running on Mac OS X, such as Wordfast Classic 6.0, which is compatible with MS Word 2011 for Mac.

Other computer-aided translation systems that can run on Mac OS or OS X are cross-platform software, rather than software developed particularly for Mac. Examples are Java-based applications, such as Autshumato, Heartsome, OmegaT, Open Language Tools, and Swordfish. Besides, all cloud-based systems can support Mac OS and OS X, including Wordbee, XTM Cloud, Google Translator's Toolkit, Lingotek Collaborative Translation Platform, MemSource Cloud, and WebWordSystem.

OS/2 is a series of computer operating systems, initially created by Microsoft and IBM, then later developed by IBM exclusively. The name stands for Operating System/2.

Up to 1992, the early computer-aided translation systems ran either on MS-DOS or OS/2. For example, IBM Translation Manager/2 (TM/2) was released in 1992 and ran on OS/2. ALPS's translation tool also ran on OS/2. But OS/2 had a much smaller market share compared with Windows in the early 1990s. Computer-aided translation system developers therefore gradually shifted from OS/2 and MS-DOS to Windows or discontinued the development of OS/2- and MS-DOS–compatible computer-aided translation systems. By the end of the 1990s, most computer-aided translation systems mainly ran on Windows, although some developers offered operating-system customization services upon request. OS/2 4.52 was released in December 2001. IBM ended its support of OS/2 on 31 December 2006.

Compatibility of Databases

Compatibility of Translation Memory Databases

Translation Memory eXchange (TMX), created in 1998, is widely used as an interchange format between different translation memory formats. TMX files are XML files whose format was originally developed and maintained by Open Standards for Container/Content Allowing Reuse (OSCAR) of the Localization Industry Standards Association. The latest official version of the TMX specification, version 1.4b, was released in 2005. In March 2011, Localization Industry Standards Association (LISA) was declared insolvent; as a result, its standards were moved under the Creative Commons license and the standards specification relocated. The technical specification and a sample document of TMX can be found on the website of the Globalization and Localization Association.

TMX has been widely adopted and is supported by more than half of the current computer-aided translation systems on the market. The total number of computer-aided translation systems that can import and export translation memories in TMX format is 54: Across, Alchemy Publisher, Anaphraseus, AnyMem, Araya, ATLAS, Autshumato, CafeTran, Crowdin, Déjà Vu, EsperantiloTM, Felix, Fluency, Fortis, Fusion, GE-CCT, GlobalSight, Google Translator Toolkit, Heartsome, Huajian IAT, Lingotek, LogiTerm, LongRay CAT, MadCap Lingo, MemoQ, MemSource, MetaTexis, MT2007, MultiTrans, OmegaT, OmegaT+, Open Language Tools, OpenTM2, OpenTMS, PROMT, SDL Trados, Snowball, Snowman, Swordfish, Systran, Text

United, The Hongyahu, TM Database, Transit, Translation Workspace, Transwhiz, TraTool, WebWordSystem, Wordbee Translator, Wordfast Classic and Wordfast Pro, XTM, Yaxin CAT, and 翻訳ブレイン (Translation Brain).

Compatibility of Terminology Databases

Compatibility of terminology databases is best illustrated by TermBase eXchange (TBX), which covers a family of formats for representing the information in a high-end termbase in a neutral intermediate format in a manner compliant with the Terminological Markup Framework (TMF) (Melby 2012: 19–21).

Termbase Exchange is an international standard as well as an industry standard. The industry standard version differs from the ISO standard only by having different title pages. LISA, the host organization for OSCAR that developed Termbase Exchange, was dissolved in February 2011. In September 2011, the European Telecommunications Standards Institute (ETSI) took over maintenance of the OSCAR standards. ETSI has established an interest group for translation/localization standards and a liaison relationship with the International Organization for Standardization (ISO) so that TBX can continue to be published as both an ISO and industry standard.

There are many types of termbases in use, ranging from huge termbases operated by governments, to medium-size termbases maintained by corporations and non-governmental organizations, to smaller termbases maintained by translation service providers and individual translators. The problem addressed by the designers of term exchange was that existing termbases are generally not interoperable. They are based on different data models that use a variety of data categories. And even if the same data category is used for a particular piece of information, the name of the data category and the values allowed for the data category may be different.

Compatibility of Rules

Segmentation Rules Exchange

Segmentation Rules eXchange (SRX) is an XML-based standard that was maintained by Localization Industry Standards Association, until it became insolvent in 2011, and this standard is now maintained by the Globalization and Localization Association (GALA).

Segmentation Rules eXchange provides a common way to describe how to segment text for translation and other language-related processes. It was created when it was realized that translation memory exchange leverage was lower than expected in certain instances due to differences in how tools segment text. Segmentation Rules eXchange is intended to enhance the translation memory exchange so that translation memory data that are exchanged between applications can be used more effectively. Having the segmentation rules that were used when a translation memory was created will increase the leverage that can be achieved when deploying the translation memory data.

Compatibility With the Languages Supported

As computer-aided translation systems cannot identify languages, language compatibility is an important concept in translation technology. There are a large number of languages and sublanguages in the world, totalling 6,912. But the number of major languages that computers can process is relatively small. It is therefore important to know whether the languages that require machine processing are supported by a system.

With the aid of Unicode, most of the languages in the world are supported in popular computer-aided translation systems. Unicode is a computing industry standard for the consistent encoding, representation, and handling of text expressed in most of the world's writing systems.

There are basically two major types of language and sublanguage codes. Some systems, such as OmegaT and XTM, use letters for language codes (two or three letters) and language-and-region codes (two + two letters), which can be selected from a drop-down list. OmegaT follows the ISO 639 Code Tables in preparing its code list. French for example, is coded *fr*, with the language and region code for French (Canada) as *fr-CA*.

The following is a list of languages supported by Wordfast Classic and XTM, two of the nine computer-aided translation systems chosen for analysis in this chapter.

Wordfast Classic

Wordfast can be used to translate any of the languages supported by Microsoft Word. The number of languages supported by Microsoft is ninety-one, with a number of sub-languages for some major languages.

[*Afro-Asiatic*] Arabic (Algeria), Arabic (Bahrain), Arabic (Egypt), Arabic (Iraq), Arabic (Jordan), Arabic (Kuwait), Arabic (Lebanon), Arabic (Libya), Arabic (Morocco), Arabic (Oman), Arabic (Qatar), Arabic (Saudi Arabia), Arabic (Syria), Arabic (Tunisia), Arabic (U.A.E.), Arabic (Yemen), Hebrew, Maltese

[*Altaic*] Azeri (Cyrillic), Azeri (Latin), Japanese, Korean, Turkish

[*Austro-Asiatic*] Vietnamese

[*Austronesian*] Indonesian, Malay (Brunei Darussalam), Malaysian

[*Basque*] Basque

[*Dravidian*] Kannada, Malayalam, Tamil, Telugu

[*Indo-European*] Afrikaans, Albanian, Armenian, Assamese, Belarusian, Bengali, Bulgarian, Byelorussian, Catalan, Croatian, Czech, Danish, Dutch, Dutch (Belgian), English (Australia), English (Belize), English (Canadian), English (Caribbean), English (Ireland), English (Jamaica), English (New Zealand), English (Philippines), English (South Africa), English (Trinidad), English (U.K.), English (US), English (Zimbabwe), Faroese, Farsi, French (Belgian), French (Cameroon), French (Canadian), French (Congo), French (Cote d'Ivoire), French (Luxembourg), French (Mali), French (Monaco), French (Reunion), French (Senegal), French (West Indies), Frisian (Netherlands), Gaelic (Ireland), Gaelic (Scotland), Galician, German, German (Austria), German (Liechtenstein), German (Luxembourg), Greek, Gujarati, Hindi, Icelandic, Italian, Kashmiri, Konkani, Latvian, Lithuanian, Macedonian (FYRO), Marathi, Nepali, Norwegian (Bokmol), Norwegian (Nynorsk), Oriya, Polish, Portuguese, Portuguese (Brazil), Punjabi, Rhaeto-Romance, Romanian, Romanian (Moldova), Russian, Russian (Moldova), Sanskrit, Serbian (Cyrillic), Serbian (Latin), Sindhi, Slovak, Slovenian, Sorbian, Spanish (Argentina), Spanish (Bolivia), Spanish (Chile), Spanish (Colombia), Spanish (Costa Rica), Spanish (Dominican Republic), Spanish (Ecuador), Spanish (El Salvador), Spanish (Guatemala), Spanish (Honduras), Spanish (Nicaragua), Spanish (Panama), Spanish (Paraguay), Spanish (Peru), Spanish (Puerto Rico), Spanish (Spain),

Spanish (Traditional), Spanish (Uruguay), Spanish (Venezuela), Swedish, Swedish (Finland), Swiss (French), Swiss (German), Swiss (Italian), Tajik, Ukrainian, Urdu, Welsh

[*Kartvelian*] Georgian

[*Niger-Congo*] Sesotho, Swahili, Tsonga, Tswana, Venda, Xhosa, Zulu

[*Sino-Tibetan*] Burmese; Chinese, Chinese (Hong Kong SAR), Chinese (Macau SAR), Chinese (Simplified), Chinese (Singapore), Chinese (Traditional), Manipuri, Tibetan

[*Tai-Kadai*] Laotian, Thai

[*Turkic*] Tatar, Turkmen, Uzbek (Cyrillic), Uzbek (Latin)

[*Uralic*] Estonian, Finnish, Hungarian, Sami Lappish

XTM

There are 157 languages available in XTM, not including varieties within a single language. These languages are as follows:

[*Afro-Asiatic*] Afar, Amharic, Arabic, Hausa, Hebrew, Maltese, Oromo, Somali, Sudanese Arabic, Syriac, Tigrinya,

[*Altaic*] Azeri, Japanese, Kazakh, Korean, Mongolian, Turkish,

[*Austro-Asiatic*] Khmer, Vietnamese

[*Austronesian*] Fijian, Indonesian, Javanese, Malagasy, Malay, Māori, Nauru, Samoan, Tagalog, Tetum, Tonga

[*Aymaran*] Aymara,

[*Bantu*] Kikongo

[*Basque*] Basque

[*Constructed Language*] Esperanto, Interlingua, Volapuk

[*Dravidian*] Kannada, Malayalam, Tamil, Telugu

[*English Creole*] Bislama,

[*Eskimo-Aleut*] Greenlandic, Inuktitut, Inupiaq

[*French Creole*] Haitian Creole

[*Hmong-Mien*] Hmong

[*Indo-European*] Afrikaans, Armenian, Assamese, Asturian, Bengali, Bihari, Bosnian, Breton, Bulgarian, Byelorussian, Catalan, Corsican, Croatian, Czech, Danish, Dari, Dhivehi, Dutch, English, Faroese, Flemish, French, Frisian, Galician, German, Greek, Gujarati, Hindi, Icelandic, Irish, Italian, Kashmiri, Konkani, Kurdish, Latin, Latvian, Lithuanian, Macedonian, Marathi, Montenegrin, Nepali, Norwegian, Occitan, Oriya, Pashto, Persian, Polish, Portuguese, Punjabi, Rhaeto-Romance, Romanian, Russian, Sanskrit, Sardinian, Scottish Gaelic, Serbian, Sindhi, Singhalese, Slovak, Slovenian, Sorbian, Spanish, Swedish, Tajik, Ukrainian, Urdu, Welsh, Yiddish,

[*Kartvelian*] Georgian

[*Ngbandi-based Creole*] Sango

[*Niger-Congo*] Chichewa, Fula, Igbo, Kinyarwanda, Kirundi, Kiswahili, Lingala, Ndebele, Northern Sotho, Sesotho, Setswana, Shona, Siswati, Tsonga, Tswana, Twi, Wolof, Xhosa, Yoruba, Zulu

[*Northwest Caucasian*] Abkhazian

[*Quechuan*] Quechua

[*Romanian*] Moldavian

[*Sino-Tibetan*] Bhutani, Burmese, Chinese, Tibetan

[*Tai-Kadai*] Laotian, Thai

[*Tupí*] Guarani

[*Turkic*] Bashkir, Kirghiz, Tarar, Turkmen, Uyghur, Uzbek

[*Uralic*] Estonian, Finnish, Hungarian

Several observations can be made from the languages supported by the current eleven systems.

(1) The number of languages supported by language-specific systems is small, as they need to be supplied with language-specific dictionaries to function well. Yaxin is best for English–Chinese translation, covering two languages, while most non-language-specific systems support around or above 100 languages.
(2) For the seven systems developed in Europe, the United Kingdom, and the United States, Across, Deja Vu, MemoQ, OmegaT, SDL Trados, Wordfast, and XTM, the Indo-European languages take up around 51.89%, while the non-Indo-European languages are 48.11%. Table 2.1 shows the details.

Controllability

One of the main differences between human translation and computer-aided translation lies in the degree of control over the source text. In human translation, there is no need, or rather it is

Table 2.1 Statistics of languages supported by seven CAT systems

Name of the System	Number of Languages Supported	Number of Language Families Supported	Number and Percentage of Indo-European Languages	Number and Percentage of Non-Indo-European Languages
Across	121	18	61 (50.41%)	60 (49.59%)
Deja Vu	132	21	66 (50%)	66 (50%)
MemoQ	102	16	54 (52.94%)	48 (47.06%)
OmegaT	90	14	48 (53.33%)	42 (46.67%)
SDL Trados	115	18	62 (53.91%)	53 (46.09%)
Wordfast	91	13	54 (59.34%)	37 (40.66%)
XTM	157	26	68 (43.31%)	89 (56.69%)

not the common practice, to control how and what the author should write. But in computer-aided translation, control over the input text may not be inappropriate, as the output of an unedited or uncontrolled source language text is far from satisfactory (Adriaens and Macken 1995: 123–41; Allen and Hogan 2000: 62–71; Arnold *et al.* 1994; Hurst 1997: 59–70; Lehtola and Bounsaythip 1998: 16–29; Mitamura 1999: 46–52; Murphy *et al.* 1998; Nyberg *et al.* 2003: 245–81; Ruffino 1985: 157–62).

The concept of controllability is realized in computer-aided translation by the use of controlled language and the method of pre-editing.

Controllability by the Use of Controlled Language

An effective means of achieving controllability in translation technology is controlled language. The idea of controlled language was created, partly at least, as a result of the problems with natural languages which are full of complexities, ambiguities, and robustness (Nyberg *et al.* 2003: 245–81). A strong rationale for controlled language is that a varied source text generates a poor target text, while a controlled source text produces a quality target text. (Bernth 1999) Controlled language is therefore considered necessary (Caeyers 1997: 91–103; Hu 2005: 364–72).

Controlled language, in brief, refers to a type of natural language developed for specific domains with a clearly defined restriction on controlled lexicons, simplified grammars, and style rules to reduce the ambiguity and complexity of a text so as to make it easier to be understood by users and non-native speakers and processed by machine translation systems (Chan 2004: 44; Lux and Dauphin 1996: 193–204).

Control over the three stages of a translation procedure, which are the stage of inputting a source text, the stage of transfer, and the stage of text generation, is generally regarded as a safe guarantee of quality translation. Control of the source text is in the form of controlled authoring, which makes the source text better for computer processing (Allen 1999; Chan 2004: 44; van der Eijk and van Wees 1998: 65–70; Zydron 2003). The text produced is a 'controlled language text' (Melby 1995: 1). There is also control over the transfer stage. The output of a machine translation system is known as 'controlled translation' (Carl 2003: 16–24; Gough and Way 2004: 73–81; Rico and Torrejon 2004; Roturier 2004; Torrejon 2002: 107–16) or a 'controlled target language text' (Chan 2004: 44). In short, a controlled text is easier to process by machine translation systems to produce quality output.

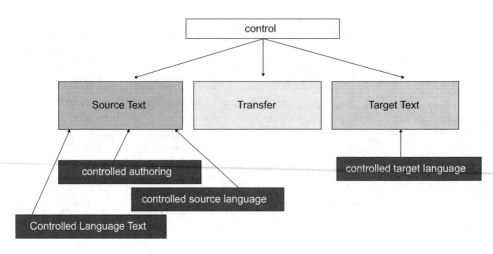

Figure 2.16 Controlled language

Goals and Means of Controlled Language

Controlled language is used by both humans and computers. The goals of controlled language are to make the source text easier to read and understand. These goals are to be achieved at the lexical and sentential levels.

At the lexical level, controlled language is about the removal of lexical ambiguity and the reduction in homonymy, synonymy, and complexity. This is achieved by one-to-one correspondence in the use and translation of words, known as one-word one-meaning. An example is to use only the word 'start' but not similar words such as 'begin', 'commence', 'initiate', and 'originate'. The second method is to use the preferred language, such as the use of American English but not British English. The third method is to have a limited basic vocabulary (Bjarnestam 2003; Chen and Wu 1999; Probst and Levin 2002: 157–67; Wasson 2000: 276–81), which can be illustrated by the use of a controlled vocabulary of 3,100 words in aircraft-maintenance documentation at the European Association of Aerospace Industries (AECMA) in 1980 (AECMA 1995).

At the sentential level, controlled language is about the removal of syntactical ambiguity; the simplification of sentence structures; limitations on sentence length; and constraints on voice, tense, and other grammatical units. To do all these, there are a limited number of strictly stipulated writing rules to follow. The European Association of Aerospace Industries had fifty-seven writing rules. Short sentences are preferred over long and complex sentences. There is also a limit on the number of words in a sentence. For procedural text, there should be no more than twenty words. For descriptive texts, the number is twenty-five. There are also rules governing grammatical well-formedness (Loong 1989: 281–97), restricted syntax, the use of passive construction in procedural texts, and structural clarity by the use of parallel structures. At the suprasentential level, there is a limit of six sentences in a paragraph, the maximum number of clauses in a sentence, and the use of separate sentences for sequential steps in procedural texts.

This means setting limits on the length of a sentence, such as setting the number of words at twenty, using only the active voice, and expressing one instruction or idea by one sentence.

Controlled Language Checkers

Controlled language cannot be maintained manually; it relies on the use of different kinds of checkers, which are systems to ensure that a text conforms to the rules of a particular controlled language (Fouvry and Balkan 1996: 179–92). There is the automatic rewriting system, which is specially developed for controlled language, rewriting texts automatically into controlled language without changing the meaning of the sentences in the original in order to produce a high-quality machine translation. There is the controlled language checker, which is software that helps an author to determine whether a text conforms to the approved words and writing rules of a particular controlled language.

Checkers can also be divided into two types: in-house controlled language checker and commercial controlled language checker. In-house controlled language checkers include the Perkins Approved Clear English (PACE) of Perkins Engines Ltd., the Controlled English of Alcatel Telecom, and the Boeing Simplified English Checker of the Boeing Company (Wojcik and Holmback 1996: 22–31). For commercial controlled language checkers, there are a number of popular systems. The LANTmaster Controlled Checker, for example, is a controlled language checker developed by LANT in Belgium. It is based on work done for the Mechanical Translation and Analysis of Languages (METAL) machine translation project. It is also based on the experience of the Simplified English Grammar and Style Checker (SECC) project (Adriaens 1994: 78–88; Adriaens and Macken 1995: 123–41). The MAXit Checker is another controlled language software developed by Smart Communications Incorporation to analyse technical texts written in controlled or simplified English with the use of more than 8,500 grammar rules and artificial intelligence to check the clarity, consistency, simplicity, and global acceptance of the texts. The Carnegie Group also produced ClearCheck, which performs syntactic parsing to detect such grammatical problems as ambiguity (Andersen 1994: 227).

Advantages and Disadvantages of Controlled Language

The advantages of controlled language translation are numerous, including high readability, better comprehensibility, greater standardization, easier computer processing, greater reusability, increased translatability, improved consistency, improved customer satisfaction, improved competitiveness, greater cost reduction in global product support, and enhanced communication in global management.

There are a number of disadvantages in using controlled language, such as expensive system construction, high maintenance cost, time-consuming authoring, and a restrictive checking process.

Controlled Language in Use

As the advantages of using controlled language outweigh its disadvantages, companies started to use controlled language as early as the 1970s. Examples of business corporations which used controlled languages include Caterpillar Fundamental English (CFE) of the Caterpillar Incorporation in 1975 (Kamprath *et al.* 1998: 51–61; Lockwood 2000: 187–202); Smart Controlled English of Smart Communications Ltd. in 1975; Douglas Aircraft Company in 1979; the European Association of Aerospace Industries (AECMA) in 1980; the KANT Project at the Center for Machine Translation, Carnegie Mellon University, in 1989 (Allen 1995; Carbonell *et al.* 1992: 225–35; Mitamura *et al.* 1994: 232–33; Mitamura and Nyberg 1995: 158–72; Mitamura *et al.* 2002: 244–47; Nyberg and Mitamura 1992: 1069–73; Nyberg *et al.* 1997; Nyberg 1998: 1–7; Nyberg and Mitamura 2000: 192–95); the PACE of Perkins Engines Ltd. in 1989;

ScaniaSwedish in Sweden in 1995 (Almqvist and Hein 1996: 159–64; Hein 1997); General Motors in 1996; Ericsson English in Sweden in 2000; Nortel Standard English in the United Kingdom in 2002; and Oce Technologies English in Holland in 2002.

Controlled Language in Computer-Aided Translation Systems

The concept of controlled language is realized in controlled authoring in computer-aided translation systems. Authoring checking tools are used to check and improve the quality of the source text. There is an automatic rewriting system which is usually used as a tool to realize controlled authoring. One of the computer-aided translation systems that perform controlled authoring is Star Transit. This system provides automatic translation suggestions from the translation memory database from a speedy search engine, and it is an open system that can integrate with many authoring systems.

Customizability

Customizability, etymologically speaking, is the ability to be customized. More specifically, it refers to the ability of a computer or computer-aided translation system to adapt itself to the needs of the user. Customizing a general-purpose machine translation system is an effective way to improve MT quality.

Editorial Customization

Pre-editing is in essence a process of customization. The customization of machine translation systems, which is a much-neglected area, is necessary and essential, as most software on the market is for general use and not for specific domains. Practically, system customization can be taken as part of the work of pre-editing as we pre-edit words and expressions to facilitate the production of quality translation.

The degree of customization depends on the goals of translation and the circumstances and type of text to be translated.

Language Customization

It is true that there are many language combinations in computer-aided translation systems to allow the user to choose any pair of source and target languages when creating a project, yet many users only work with a limited set of source and target languages. XTM, a cloud-based system, allows the user to set language combinations through the Data section. In the language combinations section, the project administrator or user can reduce and customize the available languages to be used, set the language combinations for the entire system, and set specific language combinations for individual customers (XTM International 2012: 15).

Language customization in XTM, for example, can be conducted on the Customize tab, where there are three options for the user to modify and use language combinations. The first option is 'system default language combinations', which is the full set of unmodified language combinations. The second option is 'system defaults with customized language combinations', which is the full set of language combinations in which the user may have customized some parameters. The third option is 'customized language combinations only', which includes only the language combinations that the user has customized. It is possible to add or delete the source and target languages in the selected customized option.

Lexigraphical Customization

Lexicographical customization is best shown in the creation of custom dictionaries for each customer, other than the dictionaries for spell checking. This means that multiple translators working on projects for the same customer will use the same custom dictionary.

Linguistic Customization

As far as linguistic customization is concerned, there are basically two levels of customization: lexical customization and syntactical customization.

Lexical Customization

Lexical customization is to customize a machine translation system by preparing a customized dictionary, in addition to the system dictionary, before translating. This removes the uncertainties in translating ambiguous words or word combinations. It must be pointed out, however, that the preparation of a customized dictionary is an enormous task, involving a lot of work in database creation, maintenance, and management.

Syntactical Customization

Syntactical customization, on the other hand, is to add sentences or phrases to the database to translate texts with many repetitions. Syntactical customization is particularly important when there is a change of location for translation consumption. The translation memory databases built up in Hong Kong for the translation of local materials, for example, may not be suitable for the production of translations targeted at non–Hong Kong readers, such as those in mainland China.

Resource Customization

Website Customization

Some computer-aided translation systems allow the user to create resource profile settings. Each profile in Fluency, for example, has four customized uniform resource locators (URLs) associated with it. URLs are the Internet addresses of information. Each document or file on the Internet has a unique address for its location. Fluency allows the user to have four URLs of one's preference, two perhaps for specialized sites and two general sites.

Machine Translation System Customization

Some systems are connected to installed machine translation systems the terminology databases of which can be customized for the generation of output, thus achieving terminological consistency in the target text.

Collaborativity

Collaborativity is about continuously working and communicating with all parties relating to a translation project, from the client to the reviewer, in a shared work environment to generate the best benefits of team work. Computer-aided translation is a modern mode of translation production that works best in team translation. In the past and decreasingly at present, individual translation has been the norm of practice. At present and increasingly in the future, team translation is the standard practice.

A number of systems, such as Across and Wordfast, can allow users to interact with each other through the translation memory server and share translation memory assets in real time.

Translation is about management. The translation business operates on projects. Translation technology is about project management, about how work is to be completed by translation teams. With the use of translation technology, the progress of translation work is under control and completed with higher efficiency. The best way to illustrate this point is project collaboration, which allows translators and project managers to easily access and distribute projects and easily monitor their progress.

The work of translation in the present digital era is done almost entirely online with the help of a machine translation or computer-aided translation system. This can be illustrated with SDL-Trados 2007 Synergy, which is a computer-aided translation system developed by SDL International and generally considered the most popular translation memory system on the market at that time.

Workflow of a Translation Project

To start a project, the first stage of the workflow is the creation of a termbase and a translation memory database, as shown in Figure 2.17.

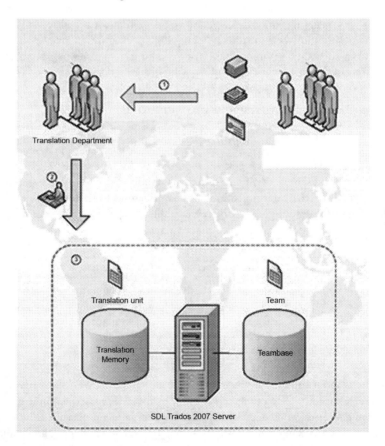

Figure 2.17 Workflow of a translation project: the first stage

In other words, when the project manager has any publications, files, or web pages to translate, they will send them to the translators of a department or unit or freelancers for processing. They will create translation units and term databases from these pre-translated documents and save these databases in the SDL-Trados 2007 Server. This is the first stage of the workflow.

After the creation of translation memory and term databases, as shown in Figure 2.18, the project manager can then initiate a translation project and monitor its progress with the use of SDL-Trados 2007 Synergy (as indicated by 1). They can assign and distribute source files to in-house and/or freelance translators by emails (as indicated by 2). Translators can then do the translation by (1) reusing the translation memory and terms stored in the databases and (2) adding new words or expressions to the translation memory and term databases (as indicated by 3). When translation is done, translators send their translated files back to the project manager on or before the due date (as indicated by 4). When the project manager receives the translated files, they update the project status, finalize the project, and mark it as 'complete' (as indicated by 5).

To make sure that SDL-Trados 2007 Synergy has a smooth run, a technical support unit to maintain the SDL-Trados server may be necessary (as indicated by 6).

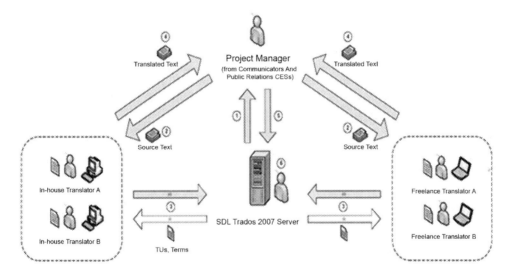

Figure 2.18 Workflow of a translation project: the second stage

A translation team usually consists of the following members.

Project Manager

A project manager is a professional in the field of project management. The responsibilities of a project manager include the following:

(1) Plan, execute, and close projects;

When planning a project, the project manager works on the overall resources and budget of the project. When executing a project, the project manager can add or import customers and subcontract projects.

(2) create clear and attainable project objectives;

(3)   build the project requirements; and
(4)   manage cost, time, and scope of projects.

Terminologist

A terminologist is one who manages terms in the terminology database. There are two types of terminologists: (1) customer-specific terminologists who can only access the terminology of one customer and (2) global experts who can access all the terms in the systems for all customers.

Conclusion

This chapter is possibly the first attempt to analyse the concepts that have governed the growth of functionalities in computer-aided translation systems. As computing science and related disciplines advance, more concepts will be introduced and more functions will be developed accordingly. However, it is believed that most of the concepts discussed in this chapter will last for a long time.

Additional Resources

www.alchemysoftware.ie/index.html.
www.helicon.co.at/aboutus.html.
www.internetworldstats.com/stats.htm.
www.lisa.org/Glossary.
www.passolo.com.
www.schaudin.com.
www2.multilizer.com/company.

Bibliography

Adriaens, Geert (1994) 'Simplified English Grammar and Style Correction in an MT Framework: The LRE SECC Project', in *Translating and the Computer 16*, London: The Association for Information Management, 78–88.

Adriaens, Geert and Lieve Macken (1995) 'Technological Evaluation of a Controlled Language Application: Precision, Recall and Convergence Tests for SECC', in *Proceedings of the 6th International Conference on Theoretical and Methodological Issues in Machine Translation* (*TMI-95*), 5–7 July 1995, University of Leuven, Leuven, Belgium, 123–41.

AECMA (1995) *A Guide for the Preparation of Aircraft Maintenance Documentation in the International Aerospace Maintenance Language-Issue 1*, Brussels, Belgium.

Allen, Jeffrey (1995) 'Review of the Caterpillar KANT English-French MT System', *Internal Technical Report*, Peoria, IL: Technical Information Department, Caterpillar Inc.

Allen, Jeffrey (1999) 'Adapting the Concept of "Translation Memory" to "Authoring Memory" for a Controlled Language Writing Environment', in *Translating and the Computer 20*, London: The Association for Information Management.

Allen, Jeffrey and Christopher Hogan (2000) 'Toward the Development of a Post-editing Module for Raw Machine Translation Output: A Controlled Language Perspective', in *Proceedings of the 3rd International Workshop on Controlled Language Applications (CLAW 2000)*, 29–30 April 2000, Seattle, WA, 62–71.

Almqvist, Ingrid and Anna Sågvall Hein (1996) 'Defining ScaniaSwedish-Controlled Language for Truck Maintenance', in *Proceedings of the 1st International Workshop on Controlled Language Applications* (*CLAW-96*), Leuven, Belgium, 159–64.

Al-Shabab, Omar Sheikh (1996) *Interpretation and the Language of Translation: Creativity and Convention in Translation*, London: Janus Publishing Company.

Andersen, Peggy (1994) 'ClearCheck Demonstration', in *Proceedings of the 1st Conference of the Association for Machine Translation in the Americas: Technology Partnerships for Crossing the Language Barrier (AMTA-1)*, 5–8 October 1994, Columbia, MD, 227.

Arnold, Doug J., Lorna Balkan, R. Lee Humphreys, Seity Meijer, and Louisa Sadler (1994) *Machine Translation: An Introductory Guide*, Manchester and Oxford: NCC Blackwell.

Bell, Roger T. (1991) *Translation and Translating: Theory and Practice*, London and New York: Longman.

Bernth, Arendse (1999) *Tools for Improving E-G MT Quality*, Yorktown Heights: IBM T.J. Watson Research Center.

Bjarnestam, Anna (2003) 'Internationalizing a Controlled Vocabulary Based Search Engine for Japanese', in *Proceedings of the Localization World Conference 2003*, 14–16 October 2003, Seattle, WA.

Bly, Robert (1983) *The Eight Stages of Translation*, Boston: Rowan Tree Press.

Caeyers, Herman (1997) 'Machine Translation and Controlled English', in *Proceedings of the 2nd Workshop of the European Association for Machine Translation: Language Technology in Your Organization?*, 21–22 May 1997, University of Copenhagen, Copenhagen, Denmark, 91–103.

Carbonell, Jaime G., Teruko Mitamura, and Eric H. Nyberg (1992) 'The KANT Perspective: A Critique of Pure Transfer (and Pure Interlingua, Pure Statistics, . . .)', in *Proceedings of the 4th International Conference on Theoretical and Methodological Issues in Machine Translation of Natural Languages: Empiricist vs Rationalist Methods in MT (TMI-92)*, Montreal, Quebec, Canada, 225–35.

Carl, Michael (2003) 'Data-assisted Controlled Translation', in *Proceedings of the Joint Conference Combining the 8th International Workshop of the European Association for Machine Translation and the 4th Controlled Language Applications Workshop: Controlled Language Translation (EAMT-CLAW-2003)*, Dublin City University, Ireland, The United Kingdom, 16–24.

Chan, Sin-wai (2004) *A Dictionary of Translation Technology*, Hong Kong: The Chinese University Press.

Chen, Kuang-Hua and Chien-Tin Wu (1999) 'Automatically Controlled-vocabulary Indexing for Text Retrieval', in *Proceedings of the International Conference on Research in Computational Linguistics (ROCLING-XII)*, Taipei, Taiwan.

de Ilarraza, Arantxa Diaz, Aingeru Mayor, and Kepa Sarasola (2000) 'Reusability of Wide-coverage Linguistic Resources in the Construction of Multilingual Technical Documentation', in *Proceedings of the International Conference on Machine Translation and Multilingual Applications in the New Millennium (MT-2000)*, University of Exeter, England, The United Kingdom.

Delisle, Jean (1988) *Translation: An Interpretive Approach*, Patricia Logan and Monica Creery (trans.), Ottawa and London: University of Ottawa Press.

Fais, Laurel and Kentaro Ogura (2001) 'Discourse Issues in the Translation of Japanese Email', in *Proceedings of the 5th Pacific Association for Computational Linguistics Conference (PACLING-2001)*, Fukuoka, Japan.

Fouvry, Frederik and Lorna Balkan (1996) 'Test Suites for Controlled Language Checkers', in *Proceedings of the 1st International Workshop on Controlled Language Applications*, Katholieke Universiteit, Leuven, Belgium, 179–92.

Gough, Nano and Andy Way (2004) 'Example-based Controlled Translation', in *Proceedings of the 9th Workshop of the European Association for Machine Translation: Broadening Horizons of Machine Translation and Its Applications*, Foundation for International Studies, Malta, 73–81.

Han, Benjamin, Donna Gates, and Lori S. Levin (2006) 'Understanding Temporal Expressions in Emails', in *Proceedings of the Human Language Technology Conference-Annual Meeting of the North American Chapter of the Association for Computational Linguistics (HLT-NAACL-2006)*, New York.

Hein, Anna Sagvall (1997) 'Scania Swedish – A Basis for Multilingual Translation', in *Translating and the Computer 19*, London: The Association for Information Management.

Hu, Qingping 胡清平 (2005) '〈受控語言及其在漢英機器翻譯裏的應用前景〉(Controlled Language and Its Prospective Application in Chinese-English Machine Translation)', in Luo Xuanmin 羅選民 (ed.) 《語言認識與翻譯研究》(*Language, Cognition and Translation Studies*), Beijing: Foreign Language Press 外文出版社, 364–72.

Hurst, Matthew F. (1997) 'Parsing for Targeted Errors in Controlled Languages', in Ruslan Mitkov and Nicolas Nicolov (eds.) *Recent Advances in Natural Language Processing*, Amsterdam and Philadelphia: John Benjamins Publishing Company, 59–70.

Joy, Lorna (2002) 'Translating Tagged Text-Imperfect Matches and a Good Finished Job', in *Translating and the Computer 24*, London: The Association for Information Management.

Kamprath, Christine, Eric Adolphson, Teruko Mitamura, and Eric H. Nyberg (1998) 'Controlled Language Multilingual Document Production: Experience with Caterpillar Technical English', in *Proceedings of the 2nd International Workshop on Controlled Language Applications (CLAW-98)*, Language Technologies Institute, Carnegie Mellon University, Pittsburgh, PA, 51–61.

Kay, Martin (1980) 'The Proper Place of Men and Machines in Language Translation', *Research Report CSL-80-11*, Xerox Palo Alto Research Center, Palo Alto, CA.

Lehtola, Aarno, Jarno Tenni, and Catherine Bounsaythip (1998) 'Controlled Language – An Introduction', in *Proceedings of the 2nd International Workshop on Controlled Language Applications*, Carnegie Mellon University, Pittsburgh, PA, 16–29.

Lockwood, Rose (2000) 'Machine Translation and Controlled Authoring at Caterpillar', in Robert C. Sprung (ed.) *Translating into Success: Cutting-edge Strategies for Going Multilingual in a Global Age*, Amsterdam and Philadelphia: John Benjamins Publishing Company, 187–202.

Loong, Cheong Tong (1989) 'A Data-driven Control Strategy for Grammar Writing Systems', *Machine Translation* 4(4): 281–97.

Lux, Veronika and Eva Dauphin (1996) 'Corpus Studies: A Contribution to the Definition of a Controlled Language', in *Proceedings of the 1st International Workshop on Controlled Language Applications (CLAW-96)*, Leuven, Belgium, 193–204.

Matsuda, Junichi and Hiroyuki Kumai (1999) 'Transfer-based Japanese–Chinese Translation Implemented on an E-mail System', in *Proceedings of MT Summit VII: MT in the Great Translation Era*, 13–17 September 1999, Kent Ridge Digital Labs, Singapore.

Melby, Alan K. (1995) *The Possibility of Language: A Discussion of the Nature of Language, with Implications for Human and Machine Translation*, Amsterdam and Philadelphia: John Benjamins Publishing Company.

Melby, Alan K. (2012) 'Terminology in the Age of Multilingual Corpora', *The Journal of Specialized Translation* 18: 7–29.

Mitamura, Teruko (1999) 'Controlled Language for Multilingual Machine Translation', in *Proceedings of MT Summit VII: MT in the Great Translation Era*, Singapore, 46–52.

Mitamura, Teruko and Eric H. Nyberg (1995) 'Controlled English for Knowledge Based MT: Experience with the KANT System', in *Proceedings of the 6th International Conference on Theoretical and Methodological Issues in Machine Translation (TMI-95)*, Leuven, Belgium, 158–72.

Mitamura, Teruko, Eric H. Nyberg, Kathy Baker, Peter Cramer, Jeongwoo Ko, David Svoboda, and Michael Duggan (2002) 'The KANTOO MT System: Controlled Language Checker and Lexical Maintenance Tool', in Stephen D. Richardson (ed.) *AMTA-02: Proceedings of the 5th Conference of the Association for Machine Translation in the Americas, Machine Translation: From Research to Real Users*, 6–12 October 2002, Tiburon, CA, 244–47.

Mitamura, Teruko, Eric H. Nyberg, and Jaime G. Carbonell (1994) 'KANT: Knowledge-based, Accurate Natural Language Translation', in *Proceedings of the 1st Conference of the Association for Machine Translation in the Americas: Technology Partnerships for Crossing the Language Barrier (AMTA-1)*, 5–8 October 1994, Columbia, MD, 232–33.

Murphy, Dawn, Jane Mason, and Stuart Sklair (1998) 'Improving Translation at the Source', in *Translating and the Computer 20*, London: The Association for Information Management.

Nida, Eugene A. and Charles A. Taber (1969) *The Theory and Practice of Translation*, Leiden: Brill.

Nyberg, Eric H., Christine Kamprath, and Teruko Mitamura (1998) 'The KANT Translation System: From R&D to Large-Scale Deployment', *LISA Newsletter* 2(1): 1–7.

Nyberg, Eric H. and Teruko Mitamura (1992) 'The KANT System: Fast, Accurate, High-quality Translation in Practical Domains', in *Proceedings of the 14th International Conference of Computational Linguistics (COLING-92)*, 23–28 August 1992, Nantes, France, 1069–73.

Nyberg, Eric H. and Teruko Mitamura (2000) 'The KANTOO Machine Translation Environment', in John S. White (ed.) *Envisioning Machine Translation in the Information Future*, Berlin: Springer Verlag, 192–95.

Nyberg, Eric H., Teruko Mitamura, and Jaime G. Carbonell (1997) 'The KANT Machine System: From R&D to Initial Deployment', in *LISA Workshop on Integrating Advanced Translation Technology*, Seattle and Washington, DC.

Nyberg, Eric H., Teruko Mitamura, and Willem-Olaf Huijsen (2003) 'Controlled Language for Authoring and Translation', in Harold L. Somers (ed.) *Computers and Translation: A Translator's Guide*, Amsterdam and Philadelphia: John Benjamins Publishing Company, 245–81.

Probst, Katharina and Lori S. Levin (2002) 'Challenges in Automated Elicitation of a Controlled Bilingual Corpus', in *Proceedings of the 9th International Conference on Theoretical and Methodological Issues in Machine Translation (TMI-2002)*, Keihanna, Japan, 157–67.

Rico, Celia and Enrique Torrejon (2004) 'Controlled Translation as a New Translation Scenario – Training the Future User', in *Translating and the Computer 26*, London: The Association for Information Management.

Rooke, Robert (1985) 'Electronic Mail', in Catriona Picken (ed.) *Translation and Communication: Translating and the Computer 6*, London: The Association for Information Management, 105–15.

Roturier, Johann (2004) 'Assessing Controlled Language Rules: Can They Improve Performance of Commercial Machine Translation Systems?', *Translating and the Computer 26*, London: The Association for Information Management.

Ruffino, J. Richard (1985) 'The Impact of Controlled English on Machine Translation', in Patricia E. Newman (ed.) *American Translators Association Conference-1985*, Medford, NJ: Learned Information, Inc., 157–62.

Sofer, Morry (2009) *The Translator's Handbook*, Rockville: Schreiber Publishing.

Steiner, George ([1975] 1992) *After Babel: Aspect of Language and Translation*, 2nd edition, Oxford: Oxford University Press.

Torrejón, Enrique (2002) 'Controlled Translation: A New Teaching Scenario Tailor-made for the Translation Industry', in *Proceedings of the 6th Workshop of the European Association for Machine Translation: Teaching Machine Translation*, Manchester, UK, 107–16.

van der Eijk, Pim and Jacqueline van Wees (1998) 'Supporting Controlled Language Authoring', in *Proceedings of the 3rd Workshop of the European Association for Machine Translation: Translation Technology: Integration in the Workflow Environment*, Geneva, Switzerland, 65–70.

Wasson, Mark (2000) 'Large-scale Controlled Vocabulary Indexing for Named Entities', in *Proceedings of the 6th Applied Natural Language Processing Conference*, Seattle, WA, 276–81.

Western Standard (2011) 'Fluency Translation Suite 2011Fluency User Manual V2.5.04', Utah: © 2009–2011 Western Standard Translation. Available at: www.westernstandard.com/FluencyInstalls/Fluency-Documentation.pdf.

Wilss, Wolfram (1982) *The Science of Translation: Problems and Methods*, Tubingen: Gunter Narr Verlag.

Wojcik, Richard H. and Heather Holmback (1996) 'Getting a Controlled Language off the Ground at Boeing', in *Proceedings of the 1st International Workshop on Controlled Language Applications (CLAW-96)*, Belgium: Katholieke Universiteit Leuven, 22–31.

XTM International Ltd. (2012) *XTM for CMS Explained*, Bucks: XTM International Ltd. Available at: www.xtm-intl.com/files/content/xtm/resources/XTM%20for%20CMS%20Explained%202012-01.pdf.

Zydron, Andrzeg (2003) 'xml:tm – Using XML Technology to Reduce the Cost of Authoring and Translation', in *Translating and the Computer 25*, London: The Association for Information Management.

3

COMPUTER-AIDED TRANSLATION SYSTEMS

Ignacio Garcia

Introduction

Computer-aided translation (CAT) systems are software applications created with the specific purpose of facilitating the speed and consistency of human translators, thus reducing the overall costs of translation projects while maintaining the earnings of contracted translators and an acceptable level of quality. At its core, every CAT system divides a text into 'segments' (normally sentences, as defined by punctuation marks) and searches a bilingual memory for identical (*exact match*) or similar (*fuzzy match*) source and translation segments. Search and recognition of terminology in analogous bilingual glossaries is also standard. The corresponding search results are then offered to the human translator as prompts for adaptation and reuse.

CAT systems were developed from the early nineties to respond to the increasing need of corporations and institutions to target products and services toward other languages and markets (localization). Sheer volume and tight deadlines (simultaneous shipment) required teams of translators to work concurrently on the same source material. In this context, the ability to reuse vetted translations and to consistently apply the same terminology became vital. Once restricted to technical translation and large localization projects in the nineties, CAT systems have since expanded to cater to most types of translation, and most translators, including non-professionals, can benefit now from them.

This overview of CAT systems includes only those computer applications specifically designed with translation in mind. It does not discuss word processors, spelling and grammar checkers, and other electronic resources which, while certainly of great help to translators, have been developed for a broader user base. Nor does it include applications such as concordancers which, although potentially incorporating features similar to those in a typical CAT system, have been developed for computational linguists.

Amongst the general class of translation-focused computer systems, this will centre only on applications that assist human translators by retrieving human–mediated solutions, not those that can fully provide a machine-generated version in another language. Such machine translation (MT) aids will be addressed only in the context of their growing presence as optional adjuncts in modern-day CAT systems.

CAT systems fundamentally enable the reuse of past (human) translation held in so-called translation memory (TM) databases and the automated application of terminology held in

DOI: 10.4324/9781003168348-4

terminology databases. These core functionalities may be supplemented by others such as alignment tools to create TM databases from previously translated documents and term extraction tools to compile searchable term bases from TMs, bilingual glossaries, and other documents. CAT systems may also assist in extracting the translatable text out of heavily tagged files and in managing complex translation projects with large numbers and types of files, translators, and language pairs while ensuring basic linguistic and engineering quality assurance.

CAT systems have variously been known in both the industry and literature as CAT tools, TM, TM tools (or systems or suites), translator workbenches or workstations, translation support tools, or latterly translation environment tools (TEnTs). Despite describing only one core component, the vernacular term TM has been widely employed: as a label for a human-mediated process, it certainly stands in attractive and symmetrical opposition to MT. Meanwhile, the CAT acronym has been considered rather too catholic in some quarters for encompassing strict translation-oriented functionality plus other more generic features (word processing, spell checking, etc.).

While there is presently no consensus on an 'official' label, CAT will be used here to designate the suites of tools that translators will commonly encounter in modern work flows. Included within this label will be the so-called localization tools – a specific sub-type which focuses on the translation of software user interfaces (UIs) rather than the 'traditional' user help and technical text. Translation memory or TM will be used in its actual and literal sense as the database of stored translations.

Historically, CAT system development was somewhat *ad hoc*, with most concerted effort and research going into MT instead. CAT grew organically, in response to the democratization of processing power (personal computers opposed to mainframes) and perceived need, with the pioneer developers being translation agencies, corporate localization departments, and individual translators. Some systems were built for in-house use only, others to be sold.

Hutchins' *Compendium of Translation Software: Directory of Commercial Machine Translation Systems and Computer-Aided Translation Support Tools* lists (from 1999 onwards) 'all known systems of machine translation and computer-based translation support tools that are currently available for purchase on the market' (Hutchins 1999–2010: 3). In this *Compendium*, CAT systems are included under the headings of 'Terminology management systems', 'Translation memory systems/components', and 'Translator workstations'. As of January 2005, said categories boasted 23, 31, and 9 products respectively (with several overlaps), and although a number have been discontinued and new ones created, the overall figures have not changed much during the past decade. Some *Compendium* entries have left a big footprint in the industry, while others do not seem used outside the inner circle of the developer.

The essential technology, revolving around sentence-level segmentation, was fully developed by the mid-nineties. The offerings of leading brands would later increase in sophistication, but for over a decade the gains centred more on stability and processing power than any appreciably new ways of extracting extra language-data leverage. We refer to this as the classic period, discussed in the next section. From 2005 onwards, a more granular approach towards text reuse has emerged; the amount of addressable data expanded, and the potential scenarios for CAT usage have widened. These new trends are explored in the 'Current CAT Systems' section.

Classic CAT Systems (1995–2005)

The idea of computers assisting the translation process is directly linked to the development of MT, which began circa 1949. Documentary references to CAT, as we understand it today, are already found in the Automatic Language Processing Advisory Committee (ALPAC) report of

1966, which halted the first big wave of MT funding in the United States. In that era of vacuum tube mainframes and punch-cards, the report understandably found that MT (*mechanical transla-tion*, as it was mostly known then) was a more time-consuming and expensive process than the traditional method, then frequently facilitated by dictation to a typist. However, the report did support funding for computational linguistics, and in particular for what it called the 'machine-aided human translation' then being implemented by the Federal Armed Forces Translation Agency in Mannheim. A study included in the report (Appendix 12) showed that translators using electronic glossaries could reduce errors by 50% and increase productivity by over 50% (ALPAC 1966: 26, 79–86).

CAT systems grew out of MT developers' frustration at being unable to design a product which could truly assist in producing faster, cheaper, and yet still useable translation. While terminology management systems can be traced back to Mannheim, the idea of data-basing translations per se did not surface until the eighties. During the typewriter era, translators presumably kept paper copies of their work and simply consulted them when the need arose. The advent of the personal computer allowed document storage as softcopy, which could be queried in a more convenient fashion. Clearly, computers might somehow be used to automate those queries, and that is pre-cisely what Kay ([1980] 1997: 3–23) and Melby (1983: 174–77) proposed in the early eighties.

The Translation Support System (TSS) developed by Automated Language Processing Sys-tems (ALPS) in Salt Lake City, Utah, in the mid-eighties is considered the first prototype of a CAT system. It was later re-engineered by INK Netherlands as INK TextTools (Kingscott 1999: 7). Nevertheless, while the required programming was not overly complicated, the conditions were still not ripe for the technology's commercialization.

By the early nineties this had changed: micro-computers with word processors displaced the typewriter from the translators' desks. Certain business-minded and technologically proficient translators saw a window of opportunity. In 1990, Hummel and Knyphausen (two German entrepreneurs who had founded Trados in 1984 and had already been using TextTools) launched their MultiTerm terminology database, with the first edition of the Translator's Workbench TM tool following in 1992. Also in 1992, IBM Deustchland commercialized its in-house devel-oped Translation Manager 2, while large language service provider STAR AG (also German) launched its own in-house system, Transit, onto the market (Hutchins 1998: 418–19).

Similar products soon entered the arena. Some, such as Déjà Vu, first released in 1993, still retain a profile today; others, such as the Eurolang Optimiser, well-funded and marketed at its launch (Brace 1992), were shortly discontinued. Of them all, it was Trados – thanks to successful European Commission tender bids in 1996 and 1997 – that found itself the tool of choice of the main players and, thus, the default industry standard.

By the mid-nineties, translation memory, terminology management, alignment tools, file conversion filters and other features were all present in the more advanced systems. The main components of that technology, which would not change much for over a decade, are described in the following.

The Editor

A CAT system allows human translators to reuse translations from translation memory databases and apply terminology from terminology databases. The editor is the system front-end that translators use to open a source file for translation and query the memory and terminology data-bases for relevant data. It is also the workspace in which they can write their own translations if no matches are found and the interface for sending finished sentence pairs to the translation memory and terminology pairs to the term base.

Some classic CAT systems piggy-backed their editor onto third-party word processing software, typically Microsoft Word. Trados and Wordfast were the best-known examples during this classic period. Most, however, decided on a proprietary editor. The obvious advantage of using a word-processing package such as Word is that users would already be familiar with its environment. The obvious disadvantage, however, is that if a file could not open normally in Word, then it could not be translated without prior processing in some intermediary application capable of extracting its translatable content. A proprietary editor already embodies such an intermediate step, without relying on Word to display the results.

Whether bolt-on or stand alone, a CAT system editor first segments the source file into translation units, enabling the translator to work on them separately and the program to search for matches in the memory. Inside the editor window, the translator sees the active source segment displayed together with a workspace into which the system will import any hits from the memory and/or allow a translation to be written from scratch. The workspace can appear below (vertical presentation) or beside (horizontal or tabular presentation) the currently active segment.

The workflow for classic Trados in both its configurations, as Word macro, and the later proprietary Tag Editor is the model for vertical presentation. The translator opens a segment, translates with assistance from matches if available, then closes this segment and opens the next. Any TM and glossary information relevant to the open segment appear in a separate window, called Translator's Workbench. The inactive segments visible above and below the open segment provide the translator with co-text. Once the translation is completed and edited, the result is a bilingual ('uncleaned') file requiring 'clean up' into a monolingual target-language file. This model was followed by other systems, most notably Wordfast.

When the source is presented in side-by-side, tabular form, Déjà Vu being the classic example, the translator activates a particular segment by placing the cursor in the corresponding cell; depending on the (user adjustable) search settings, the most relevant database information is imported into the target cell on the right, with additional memory and glossary data presented either in a sidebar or at bottom of screen.

Independently of how the editor presents the translatable text, translators work either in interactive mode or in pre-translation mode. When using their own memories and glossaries, they most likely work in interactive mode, with the program sending the relevant information from the databases as each segment is made 'live'. When memories and glossaries are provided by an agency or the end client, the source is first analysed against them and then any relevant entries either sorted and sent to the translators or directly inserted into the source file in a process known as *pre-translation*. Translators apparently prefer the interactive mode, but, during this period, most big projects involved pre-translation (Wallis 2006).

The Translation Memory

A translation memory, or TM, the original coinage attributed to Trados founders Knyphausen and Hummel, is a database that contains past translations, aligned and ready for reuse in matching pairs of source and target units. As we have seen, the basic database unit is called a segment and is normally demarcated by explicit punctuation – it is therefore commonly a sentence, but can also be a title, caption, or the content of a table cell.

A typical TM entry, sometimes called a translation unit, or TU, consists of a source segment linked to its translation, plus relevant metadata (e.g. time/date and author stamp, client name, subject matter, etc.). The TM application also contains the algorithm for retrieving a matching translation if the same or a similar segment arises in a new text.

When the translator opens a segment in the editor window, the program compares it to existing entries in the database:

> If it finds a source segment in the database that precisely coincides with the segment the translator is working on, it retrieves the corresponding target as an *exact match* (or a *100% match*); all the translator need do is check whether it can be reused as-is, or whether some minor adjustments are required for potential differences in context.

> If it finds a databased source segment that is similar to the active one in the editor, it offers the target as a *fuzzy match* together with its degree of similarity, indicated as a percentage and calculated on the Levenshtein distance, i.e. the minimum number of insertions, deletions or substitutions required to make it equal; the translator then assesses whether it can be usefully adapted, or if less effort is required to translate from scratch; usually, only segments above a 70% threshold are offered, since anything less is deemed more distracting than helpful.

> If it fails to find any stored source segment exceeding the pre-set match threshold, no suggestion is offered; this is called a *no match*, and the translator will need to translate that particular segment in the conventional way.

How useful a memory is for a particular project will not only depend on the number of segments in the database (simplistically, the more the better) but also on how related they are to the source material (the closer, the better). Clearly, size and specificity do not always go hand-in-hand.

Accordingly, most CAT tools allow users to create as many translation memories as they wish – thereby allowing individual TMs to be kept segregated for use in specific circumstances (a particular topic, a certain client, etc.) and ensuring internal consistency. It has also been common practice among freelancers to periodically dump the contents of multiple memories into one catch-all TM, known in playful jargon as a 'big mama'.

Clearly, any active TM is progressively enhanced because its number of segments grows as the translator works through a text, with each translated segment sent by default to the database. The more internal repetition, the better, since as the catchphrase says, 'with TM one need never translate the same sentence twice'. Most reuse is achieved when a product or a service is continually updated with just a few features added or altered – the ideal environment being technical translation (Help files, manuals and documentation), where consistency is crucial and repetition may be regarded stylistically as virtue rather than vice.

There have been some technical variations of strict sentence-based organization for memories. Star-Transit uses file pairs as reference materials indexed to locate matches. Canadian developers came up with the concept of *bi-texts*, linking the match not to an isolated sentence but to the complete document, thus providing context. LogiTerm (Terminotix) and MultiTrans (Multi-Corpora) are the best current examples, with the latter referring to this as TextBased (rather than sentence-based) TM. In current systems, however, the lines of differentiation between stress on text or on sentence are blurred, with conventional TM indicating also when an exact match comes from the same context by naming it, depending on the brand, *context, 101%, guaranteed* or *perfect* match, and text-based able to import and work with sentence-based memories. All current systems can import and export memories in Translation Memory eXchange (TMX) format, an open XML standard created by Open Standards for Container/Content Allowing Re-use (OSCAR), a special interest group of the Localization Industry Standards Association (LISA).

The Terminology Feature

To fully exploit its data-basing potential, every CAT system requires a terminology feature. This can be likened conceptually to the translation memory of reusable segments but instead functions at term level by managing searchable/retrievable glossaries containing specific pairings of source and target terms plus associated metadata.

Just as the translation memory engine does, the terminology feature monitors the currently active translation segment in the editor against a data base – in this case, a bilingual glossary. When it detects a source term match, it prompts with the corresponding target rendering. Most systems also implement some fuzzy terminology recognition to cater for morphological inflections.

As with TMs, bigger is not always better: specificity being equally desirable, a glossary should also relate as much as possible to a given domain, client, and project. It is therefore usual practice to compile multiple term bases which can be kept segregated for designated uses (and, of course, periodically dumped into a 'big mama' term bank too).

Term bases come in different guises, depending upon their creators and purposes. The functionalities offered in the freelance and enterprise versions of some CAT systems tend to reflect these needs.

Freelance translators are likely to prefer unadorned bilingual glossaries which they build up manually – typically over many years – by entering source and target term pairings as they go. Entries are normally kept in local computer memory and can remain somewhat *ad hoc* affairs unless subjected to time-consuming maintenance. A minimal approach offers ease and flexibility for different contexts, with limited (or absent) metadata supplemented by the translator's own knowledge and experience.

By contrast, big corporations can afford dedicated bureaus staffed with trained terminologists to both create and maintain industry-wide multilingual term bases. These will be enriched with synonyms, definitions, examples of usage, and links to pictures and external information to assist any potential users, present or future. For large corporate projects it is also usual practice to construct product-specific glossaries that impose uniform usages for designated key terms, with contracting translators or agencies being obliged to abide by them.

Glossaries are valuable resources, but compiling them more rapidly via database exchanges can be complicated due to the variation in storage formats. It is therefore common to allow export/import to/from intermediate formats such as spreadsheets, simple text files, or even TMX. This invariably entails the loss or corruption of some or even all of the metadata. In the interests of enhanced exchange capability, a Terminology Base eXchange (TBX) open standard was eventually created by OSCAR/LISA. Nowadays most sophisticated systems are TBX compliant.

Despite the emphasis traditionally placed on TMs, experienced users will often contend that it is the terminology feature which affords the greatest assistance. This is understandable if we consider that translation memories work best in cases of incremental changes to repetitive texts, a clearly limited scenario. By contrast, recurrent terminology can appear in any number of situations where consistency is paramount.

Interestingly, terminology features – while demonstrably core components – are not always 'hard-wired' into a given CAT system. Trados is one example, with its MultiTerm tool presented as a stand-alone application beside the company's translation memory application (historically the Translator's Workbench). Déjà Vu on the other hand, with its proprietary interface, has bundled everything together since inception.

Regardless, with corporations needing to maintain lexical consistency across user interfaces, Help files, documentation, packaging and marketing material, translating without a terminology feature has become inconceivable. Indeed, the imposition of specific vocabulary can be so strict that many CAT systems have incorporated quality assurance (QA) features which raise error flags if translators fail to observe authorized usage from designated term bases.

Translation Management

Technical translation and localization invariably involve translating great numbers (perhaps thousands) of files in different formats into many target languages using teams of translators. Modest first generation systems, such as the original Wordfast, handled files one at a time and catered to freelance translators in client-direct relationships. As globalization pushed volumes and complexities beyond the capacities of individuals and into the sphere of translation bureaus or language service providers (LSPs), CAT systems began to acquire a management dimension.

Instead of the front end being the translation editor, it became a 'project window' for handling multiple files related to a specific undertaking – specifying global parameters (source and target languages, specific translation memories and term bases, segmentation rules) and then importing a number of source files into that project. Each file could then be opened in the editor and translated in the usual way.

These changes also signalled a new era of remuneration. Eventually all commercial systems were able to batch-process incoming files against the available memories, and pre-translate them by populating the target side of the relevant segments with any matches. Effectively, that same analysis process meant quantifying the number and type of matches as well as any internal repetition, and the resulting figures could be used by project managers to calculate translation costs and time. Individual translators working with discrete clients could clearly project-manage and translate alone and reap any rewards in efficiency themselves. However, for large agencies with demanding clients, the potential savings pointed elsewhere.

Thus, by the mid-nineties, it was common agency practice for matches to be paid at a fraction of the standard cost per word. Translators were not enthused about these so-called 'Trados discounts' and complained bitterly on the Lantra-L and Yahoo Groups CAT systems user's lists.

As for the files themselves, they could be of varied types. CAT systems would use the relevant filters to extract from those files the translatable text to present to the translator's editor. Translators could then work on text that kept the same appearance, regardless of its native format. Inline formatting (bold, italics, font, colour, etc.) would be displayed as read-only tags (typically numbers displayed in colours or curly brackets), while structural formatting (paragraphs, justification, indenting, pagination) would be preserved in a template to be reapplied upon export of the finished translation. The proper filters made it possible to work on numerous file types (desktop publishers, HTML encoders, etc.) without purchasing the respective licence or even knowing how to use the creator software.

Keeping abreast of file formats was clearly a challenge for CAT system developers, since fresh converter utilities were needed for each new release or upgrade of supported types. As the information revolution gathered momentum and file types multiplied, macros that sat on third-party software were clearly unwieldy, so proprietary interfaces became standard (witness Trados shift from Word to Tag Editor).

There were initiatives to normalize the industry so that different CAT systems could talk effectively to each other. The XML Localisation Interchange File Format (XLIFF) was created by the Organization for the Advancement of Structured Information Standards (OASIS) in 2002 to simplify the processes of dealing with formatting within the localization industry. However, individual CAT designers did not embrace XLIFF until the second half of the decade.

By incorporating project management features, CAT systems had facilitated project sharing amongst teams of translators using the same memories and glossaries. Nevertheless, their role was limited to assembling a translation 'kit' with source and database matches. Other in-house or third party systems (such as LTC Organiser, Project-Open, Projetex, and Beetext Flow) were used to exchange files and financial information between clients, agencies, and translators. Workspace by Trados, launched in 2002 as a first attempt at whole-of-project management within a single CAT system, proved too complex and was discontinued in 2006. Web based systems capable of dealing with these matters in a much simpler and more effective fashion started appearing immediately afterwards.

Alignment and Term Extraction Tools

Hitherto the existence of translation memories and term bases has been treated as a given, without much thought as to their creation. Certainly, building them barehanded is easy enough, by sending source and target pairings to the respective database during actual translation. But this is slow and ignores large amounts of existing matter that has already been translated known variously as parallel corpora, bi-texts, or legacy material.

Consider for example the Canadian Parliament's Hansard record, kept bilingually in English and French. If such legacy sources and their translations could be somehow lined up side by side (as if already in a translation editor), then they would yield a resource that could be easily exploited by sending them directly into a translation memory. Alignment tools quickly emerged at the beginnings of the classic era precisely to facilitate this task. The first commercial alignment tool was T Align, later renamed Trados WinAlign, launched in 1992.

In the alignment process parallel documents are paired, segmented, and coded appropriately for import into the designated memory database. Segmentation would follow the same rules used in the translation editor, theoretically maximizing reuse by treating translation and alignment in the same way within a given CAT system. The LISA/OSCAR Segmentation Rules eXchange (SRX) open standard was subsequently created to optimize performance across systems.

Performing an alignment is not always straightforward. Punctuation conventions differ between languages, so the segmentation process can frequently chunk a source and its translation differently. An operator must therefore work manually through the alignment file, segment by segment, to ensure exact correspondence. Alignment tools implement some editing and monitoring functions as well so that segments can be split or merged as required and extra or incomplete segments detected, to ensure a perfect 1:1 mapping between the two legacy documents. When determining whether to align apparently attractive bi-texts, one must assess whether the gains achieved through future reuse from the memories will offset the attendant cost in time and effort.

Terminology extraction posed more difficulties. After all, alignments could simply follow punctuation rules; consistently demarcating terms (with their grammatical and morphological inflections and noun and adjectival phrases) was another matter. The corresponding tools thus began appearing towards the end of the classic period and likewise followed the same well-worn path from standalones (Xerox Terminology Suite being the best known) to full CAT system integration.

Extraction could be performed on monolingual (usually the source) or bilingual text (usually translation memories) and was only semi-automated. That is, the tool would offer up terminology candidates from the source text, with selection based on frequency of appearance. Since an unfiltered list could be huge, users set limiting parameters such as the maximum number of words a candidate could contain, with a stopword list applied to skip the function words. When term-mining from translation memories, some programs were also capable of proposing translation candidates from the target text. Whatever their respective virtues, term extractors could only propose: everything had to be vetted by a human operator.

Beyond purely statistical methods, some terminology extraction tools eventually implemented specific parsing for a few major European languages. After its acquisition of Trados in 2006, SDL offered users both its SDLX PhraseFinder and Trados MultiTerm Extract. PhraseFinder was reported to work better with those European languages that already had specific algorithms, while MultiTerm Extract seemed superior in other cases (Zetzsche 2010: 34).

Quality Assurance

CAT systems are intended to help translators and translation buyers by increasing productivity and maintaining consistency even when teams of translators are involved in the same project. They also contribute significantly to averting errors through automated quality assurance features that now come standard in all commercial systems.

CAT QA modules perform linguistic controls by checking terminology usage, spelling, and grammar, and confirming that any non-translatable items (e.g. certain proper nouns) are left unaltered. They can also detect if numbers, measurements, and currency are correctly rendered according to target language conventions. At the engineering level, they ensure that no target segment is left untranslated and that the target format tags match the source tags in both type and quantity. With QA checklist conditions met, the document can be confidently exported back to its native format for final proofing and distribution.

The first QA tools (such as QA Distiller, Quintillian, or Error Spy) were developed as third-party standalones. CAT systems engineers soon saw that building in QA made technical and business sense, with Wordfast leading the way.

What is also notable here is the general trend of consolidation, with QA tools following the same evolutionary path as file converters, word count and file analysis applications, alignment tools, and terminology extraction software. CAT systems were progressively incorporating additional features, leaving fewer niches where third-party developers could remain commercially viable by designing plug-ins.

Localization Tools: A Special CAT System Sub-Type

The classic-era CAT systems described previously worked well enough with Help files, manuals and web content in general; they fell notably short when it came to software user interfaces (UIs) with their drop-down menus, dialogue boxes, pop-up help, and error messages. The older class of texts retained a familiar aspect, analogous to a traditional, albeit electronically enhanced, 'book' presentation of sequential paragraphs and pages. The new texts of the global information age operated in a far more piecemeal, visually oriented and random-access fashion, with much of the context coming from their on-screen display. The contrast was simple yet profound: the printable versus the viewable.

Moreover, with heavy computational software (for example, 3D graphics) coded in programming languages, it could be problematic just identifying and extracting the translatable (i.e. displayable) text from actual instructions. Under the circumstances, normal punctuation rules were of no use in chunking, so localizers engineered a new approach centred on 'text strings' rather than segments. They also added a visual dimension – hardly a forte of conventional CAT – to ensure the translated text fitted spatially without encroaching on other allocated display areas.

These distinctions were significant enough to make localization tools notably different from the CAT systems described previously. However, to maintain consistency within the UI and between the UI *per se* and its accompanying Help and documentation, the linguistic resources (glossaries, and later memories too) were shared by both technologies.

The best known localization tools are Passolo (now housed in the SDL stable) and Catalyst (acquired by major US agency TransPerfect). There are also many others, both commercial (Multilizer, Sisulizer, RCWinTrans) and open source (KBabel, PO-Edit). Source material aside, they all operated in much the same way as their conventional CAT brethren, with translation memories, term bases, alignment and term extraction tools, project management, and QA.

Eventually, as industry efforts at creating internationalization standards bore fruit, software designers ceased hard-coding translatable text and began placing it in XML-based formats instead. Typical EXE and DLL files give way to Java and .NET, and more and more software (as opposed to text) files could be processed within conventional CAT systems.

Nowadays, the distinctions which engendered localization tools are blurring, and they no longer occupy the field exclusively. There are unlikely to disappear altogether, however, since new software formats will always arise and specialized tools will always address them faster.

CAT Systems Uptake

The uptake of CAT systems by independent translators was initially slow. Until the late nineties, the greatest beneficiaries of the leveraging and savings were those with computer power – corporate buyers and language service providers. But CAT ownership conferred an aura of professionalism, and proficient freelancers could access the localization industry (which, as already remarked, could likewise access *them*). In this context, from 2000, most professional associations and training institutions became keen allies in CAT system promotion. The question of adoption became not if but which one – with the dilemma largely hinging on who did the translating and who commissioned it and epitomized by the legendary Déjà Vu versus Trados rivalry.

Trados had positioned itself well with the corporate sector, and for this reason alone was a pre-requisite for certain jobs. Yet by and large freelancers preferred Déjà Vu, and while today the brand may not be so recognizable, it still boasts a loyal user base.

There were several reasons Déjà Vu garnered such a loyal following. Freelancers considered it a more user-friendly and generally superior product. All features came bundled together at an accessible and stable price, and the developer (Atril) offered comprehensive – and free – after sales support. Its influence was such that its basic template can be discerned in other CAT systems today. Trados meanwhile remained a rather unwieldy collection of separate applications that required constant and expensive upgrades. For example, freelancers purchasing Trados 5.5 Freelance got rarefied engineering or management tools such as WorkSpace, T-Windows, and XML Validator but had to buy the fundamental terminology application MultiTerm separately (Trados 2002). User help within this quite complex scenario also came at a price.

The pros and cons of the two main competing packages, and a degree of ideology, saw passions run high. The Lantra-L translators' discussion list (founded in 1987, the oldest and one of the most active at the time) would frequently reflect this, especially in the famed Trados vs. Déjà Vu *holy wars*, the last being waged in August 2002.

Wordfast, which first appeared in 1999 in its 'classic' guise, proved an agile competitor in this environment. It began as simple Word macro akin to the early Trados, with which it maintained compatibility. It also came free at a time when alternatives were costly and began to overtake even Déjà Vu in freelancers' affections. Users readily accepted the small purchase price the developer eventually set in October 2002.

LogiTerm and especially MultiTrans also gained a significant user base during the first years of the century. MetaTexis, WordFisher, and TransSuite 2000 had also a small but dedicated base that shows in their users' Yahoo Groups. Completing the panorama were a number of in-house only systems, such Logos' Mneme and Lionbridge's ForeignDesk. However, the tendency amongst most large translation agencies was to either stop developing and buy off the shelf (most likely Trados) or launch their own offerings (as SDL did with its SDLX).

There are useful records for assembling a snapshot of relative CAT system acceptance in the classic era. From 1998 onwards, CAT system users began creating discussion lists on Yahoo Groups, and member numbers and traffic on these lists give an idea of respective importance. By June 2003, the most popular CAT products, ranked by their list members, were Wordfast (2205) and Trados (2138), then Déjà Vu (1233) and SDLX (537). Monthly message activity statistics were topped by Déjà Vu (1169), followed by Wordfast (1003), Trados (438), Transit (66), and SDLX (30).

All commercial products were Trados compatible, able to import and export the RTF and TTX files generated by Trados. Windows was the default platform in all cases, with only Word-fast natively supporting Mac.

Not all activity occurred in a commercial context. The free and open source software (FOSS) community also needed to localize software and translate documentation. That task fell less to conventional professional translators and more to computer-savvy and multilingual collectives who could design perfectly adequate systems without the burden of commercial imperatives. OmegaT, written in Java and thus platform independent, was and remains the most developed open software system.

Various surveys on freelancer CAT system adoption have been published, amongst them LISA 2002, eColore 2003, and LISA 2004, with the most detailed so far by London's Imperial College in 2006. Its most intriguing finding was perhaps not the degree of adoption (with 82.5% claiming ownership) or satisfaction (a seeming preference for Déjà Vu) but the 16% of recipients who reported buying a system without ever managing to use it (Lagoudaki 2006: 17).

Current CAT Systems

Trados was acquired by SDL in 2005, to be ultimately bundled with SDLX and marketed as SDL Trados 2006 and 2007. The release of SDL Trados Studio 2009 saw a shift that finally integrated all functions into a proprietary interface; MultiTerm was now included in the licence but still installed separately. Curiously, there has been no new alignment tool while SDL has been at the Trados helm: it remains WinAlign, still part of the 2007 package which preserves the old Trans-lator's Workbench and Tag Editor. Holders of current Trados licences (Studio 2011 at time of writing) have access to all prior versions through downloads from SDL's website.

Other significant moves were occurring: Lingotek, launched in 2006, was the first fully web-based system and pioneered the integration of TM with MT. Google released its own web-based Translator Toolkit in 2009, a CAT system pitched for the first time at non-professionals. Déjà Vu along with X2, Transit with NXT, and MultiTrans with Prism (latest versions at writing) have all kept a profile. Wordfast moved beyond its original macro (now Wordfast Classic) to Java-coded Wordfast Professional and web-based Wordfast Anywhere.

Translation presupposes a source text, and texts have to be written by someone. Other soft-ware developers had looked at this supply side of the content equation and begun creating authoring tools for precisely the same gains of consistency and reuse. Continuing the consolida-tion pattern we have seen, CAT systems began incorporating them. Across was the first, linking to crossAuthor. The flow is not just one way: Madcap, the developer of technical writing aid Flare, has moved into the translation sphere with Lingo.

Many other CAT systems saw the light in the last years of the decade and will also gain a mention later when illustrating new features now supplementing the ones carried out from the classic era. Of them, MemoQ (Kilgray), launched in 2009, seems to have gained considerable freelance following.

The status of CAT systems – their market share, and how they are valued by users – is less clear cut than it was ten years ago when Yahoo Groups user lists at least afforded some comparative basis. Now developers seek tighter control over how they receive and address feedback. SDL Trados led with its Ideas, where users could propose and vote on features to extend functionality, then with SDL OpenExchange, allowing the more ambitious to develop their own applications. Organizing conferences, as memoQfest does, is another way of both showing and garnering support.

The greatest determining factors throughout the evolution of CAT have been available computer processing power and connectivity. The difference in scope between current CAT systems and those in the 1990s can be better understood within the framework of two trends: cloud computing, where remote (internet) displaced local (hard drive) storage and processing, and Web 2.0, with users playing a more active role in web exchanges.

Cloud computing in particular has made it possible to meld TM with MT, access external databases, and implement more agile translation management systems capable of dealing with a myriad of small changes with little manual supervision. The wiki concept and crowd sourcing (including crowd-based QA) have made it possible to harness armies of translation aficionados to achieve outbound-quality results. Advances in computational linguistics are supplying grammatical knowledge to complement the purely statistical algorithms of the past. Sub-segmental matching is also being attempted. On-screen environments are less cluttered and more visual, with translation editors capable of displaying in-line formatting (fonts, bolding, etc.) instead of coded tags. Whereas many editing tasks were ideally left until after re-export to native format, CAT systems now offer advanced aids – including Track Changes – for revisers too. All these emerging enhanced capabilities, which are covered in the following, appropriately demarcate the close of the classic CAT systems era.

From the Hard Drive to the Web Browser

Conventional CAT systems of the 1990s installed locally on a hard drive; some, such as Wordfast, simply ran as macros within Word. As the technology expanded with computer power, certain functionalities would be accessed over a LAN and eventually on a server. By the middle 2000s, some CAT systems were already making the connectivity leap to software as a service (SaaS).

The move had commenced at the turn of this century with translation memories and term bases. These were valuable resources, and clients wanted to safeguard them on servers. This forced translators to work in 'web-interactive' mode – running their CAT systems locally but accessing client-designated databases remotely via a login. It did not make all translators happy: it gave them less control over their own memories and glossaries and made work progress partially dependent on internet connection speed. Language service providers and translation buyers, however, rejoiced. The extended use of Trados-compatible tools instead of Trados had often created engineering hitches through corrupted file exports. Web access to databases gave more control and uniformity.

The next jump came with Logoport. The original version installed locally as a small add-in for Microsoft Word, with the majority of computational tasks (databasing and processing) now performed on the server. Purchased by Lionbridge for in-house use, it has since been developed into the agency's current GeoWorkz Translation Workspace.

The first fully online system arrived in the form of Lingotek, launched in 2006. Other web-based systems soon followed: first Google Translator Toolkit and Wordfast Anywhere, then

Crowd.in, Text United, Wordbee, and XTM Cloud, plus open source GlobalSight (Welocalize) and Boltran. Traditional hard drive-based products also boast web-based alternatives, including SDL Trados (WorldServer) and Across.

The advantages of web-based systems are obvious. Where teams of translators are involved, a segment just entered by one can be almost instantly reused by all. Database maintenance becomes centralized and straightforward. Management tasks can also be simplified and automated – most convenient in an era with short content lifecycles, where periodic updates have given way to streaming changes.

Translators themselves have been less enthused, even though browser-based systems neatly circumvent tool obsolescence and upgrade dilemmas (Muegge 2012: 17–21). Among Wordfast adherents, for example, the paid Classic version is still preferred over its online counterpart, the free Wordfast Anywhere. Internet connectivity requirements alone do not seem to adequately explain this, since most professional translators already rely on continuous broadband for consulting glossaries, dictionaries and corpora. As countries and companies invest in broadband infrastructure, response lag times seem less problematic too. Freelancer resistance thus presumably centres on the very raison d'être of web-based systems: remote administration and resource control.

Moving to the browser has not favoured standardization and interoperability ideals either. With TMX having already been universally adopted and most systems being XLIFF compliant to some extent, retreating to isolated log-in access has hobbled further advances in cross-system communicability. A new open standard, the Language Interoperability Portfolio (Linport), is being developed to address this. Yet as Translation Automation User Society (TAUS) has noted, the translation industry still is a long way behind the interoperability achieved in other industries such as banking or travel (Van der Meer 2011).

Integrating Machine Translation

Research into machine translation began in the mid-twentieth century. Terminology management and translation memory happened to be just as an offshoot of research into full automation. The lack of computational firepower stalled MT progress for a time, but it was renewed as processing capabilities expanded. Sophisticated and continually evolving MT can be accessed now on demand through a web browser.

Although conventional rule-based machine translation (RBMT) is still holding its ground, there is a growing emphasis on statistical machine translation (SMT), for which, with appropriate bilingual and monolingual data, it is easier to create new language-pair engines and customize existing ones for specific domains. What is more, if source texts are written consistently with MT in mind output can be significantly improved again. Under these conditions, even free online MT engines such as Google Translate and Microsoft Bing Translator, with *light* (or even no) postediting may suffice, especially when *gisting* is more important than stylistic correctness.

Postediting, the manual 'cleaning up' of raw MT output, once as marginal as MT itself, has gradually developed its own principles, procedures, training, and practitioners. For some modern localization projects, enterprises may even prefer customized MT engines and trained professional posteditors. As an Autodesk experiment conducted in 2010 showed, under appropriate conditions, MT postediting also 'allows translators to substantially increase their productivity' (Plitt and Masselott 2010: 15).

Attempts at augmenting CAT with automation began in the nineties, but the available desktop MT was not really powerful or agile enough, trickling out as discrete builds on CD-ROM. As remarked, Lingotek in 2006 was the first to launch a web-based CAT integrated with a mainframe powered MT; SDL Trados soon followed suit, and then all others. With machines now producing useable first drafts, there are potential gains in pipelining MT-generated output to translators via their CAT editor. The payoff is twofold: enterprises can do so in a familiar environment (their chosen CAT system), whilst leveraging from legacy data (their translation memories and terminology databases).

The integration of TM with MT gives CAT users the choice of continuing working the traditional way (accepting or repairing *exact* matches, repairing or rejecting the *fuzzy* ones and translating from the source the *no matches*) or to populate those *no matches* with – MT solutions for treatment akin to conventional fuzzy matches: modify if deemed helpful enough, or discard and translate from scratch.

While the process may seem straightforward, the desired gains in time and quality are not. As noted before, fixing fuzzy matches below a certain threshold (usually 70%) is not viable; similarly, MT solutions should at least be of gisting quality to be anything other than a hindrance. This places translation managers at a decisional crossroad: trial and error is wasteful, so how does one *predict* the suitability of a text before MT processing?

Unfortunately, while the utility of MT and postediting for a given task clearly depends on the engine's raw output quality, as yet there is no clear way of quantifying it. Standard methods such as the bilingual evaluation understudy (BLEU) score (Papineni 2002: 311–18) measure MT match quality against a reference translation and thus cannot help to exactly predict performance on a previously untranslated sentence. Non-referenced methods, such as those based on confidence estimations (Specia 2011: 73–80), still require fine-tuning.

The next generation of CAT systems will foreseeably ascribe segments another layer of metadata to indicate whether the translation derives from MT (and if so which) and the steps and time employed achieving it. With the powerful analytic tools currently emerging, we might shortly anticipate evidence-based decisions regarding the language pairs, domains, engines, post editors, and specific jobs for which MT integration into CAT localization workflow makes true business sense.

Massive External Databases

Traditionally, when users first bought a CAT system, it came with empty databases. Unless purchasers were somehow granted external memories and glossaries (from clients, say) everything had to built up from zero. Nowadays that is not the only option, and from day one it is possible to access data in quantities that dwarf any translator's – or, for that matter, entire company's – lifetime output.

Interestingly, this situation has come about partly through SMT, which began its development using published bilingual corpora – the translation memories (minus the metadata) of the European Union. The highly usable translations achieved with SMT were a spur to further improvement, not just in the algorithms but in data quality and quantity as well. Since optimal results for any given task depend on feeding the SMT engine domain-specific information, the greater the volume one has, the better, and the translation memories created since the nineties using CAT systems were obvious and attractive candidates.

Accordingly, corporations and major language service providers began compiling their entire TM stock too. But ambitions did not cease there, and initiatives have emerged to pool *all* available data in such a way that it can be sorted by language, client and subject matter. The most notable include the TAUS Data Association (TDA, promoted by the Translation Automation User Society TAUS), MyMemory (Translated.com), and Linguee.com.

Now, these same massive translation memories that have been assembled to empower SMT can also significantly assist human translation. Free online access allows translators to tackle problematic sentences and phrases by querying the database, just as they would with the concordance feature in their own CAT systems and memories. The only hitch is working within a separate application and transferring results across: what would be truly useful is the ability to access such data without ever needing to leave the CAT editor window. It would enable translators to query worldwide repositories of translation solutions and import any *exact* and *fuzzy* matches directly.

Wordfast was the first to provide a practical implementation with its Very Large Translation Memory (VLTM); it was closely followed by the Global, shared TM of the Google Translator Toolkit. Other CAT systems have already begun incorporating links to online public translation memories: MultiTrans has enabled access to TDA and MyMemory since 2010, and SDL Trados Studio and memoQ had MyMemory functionality soon afterwards.

Now that memories and glossaries are increasingly accessed online, it is conceivable that even the most highly resourced corporate players might also see a benefit to increasing their reach through open participation, albeit quarantining sensitive areas from public use. Commercial secrecy, ownership, prior invested value, and copyright are clearly counterbalancing issues, and the trade-off between going public and staying private is exercising the industry's best minds. Yet recent initiatives (e.g. TAUS) would indicate that the strain of coping with sheer translation volume and demand is pushing irrevocably toward a world of open and massive database access.

Sub-Segmental Reuse

Translation memory helps particularly with internal repetition and updates and also when applied to a source created for the same client and within the same industry. Other than that, a match for the average-size sentence is a coincidence. Most repetition happens below the sentence level, with the stock expressions and conventional phraseology that make up a significant part of writing. This posed a niggling problem, since it was entirely possible for sentences which did not return fuzzy matches to contain shorter *perfect* matches that were going begging.

Research and experience showed that low-value matches (usually under 70%) overburdened translators, so most tools were set to ignore anything under a certain threshold. True, the concordancing tool can be used to conduct a search, but this is inefficient (and random), since it relies on the translator's first identifying the need to do so, and it takes additional time. It would be much better if the computer could find and offer these phrase-level (or 'sub-segmental') matches all by itself – automated concordancing, so to speak.

Potential methods have been explored for years (Simard and Langlais 2001: 335–39) but have proven elusive to achieve. The early leader in this field was Déjà Vu, with its Assemble feature, which offered portions that had been entered into the term base, lexicon, or memory when no matches were available. Some translators loved it; others found it distracting (Garcia 2003).

It is only recently that all major developers have engaged with the task, usually combining indexing with predictive typing, suggestions popping up as the translator types the first letters. Each developer has its own implementation and jargon for sub-segmental matching: MultiTrans and Lingotek, following TAUS, call it Advanced Leveraging; memoQ refers to Longest Substring Concordance; Star-Transit has Dual Fuzzy, and Déjà Vu X2 has DeepMiner. Predictive typing is variously described as AutoSuggest, AutoComplete, AutoWrite, and so on.

A study sponsored by TAUS in 2007 reported that sub-segmental matching (or advanced leveraging in TAUS-speak), increased reuse by an average of 30% over conventional reuse at sentence level only.

As discovered with the original Déjà Vu Assemble, what is a help to some is a distraction to others, so the right balance is needed between what (and how many) suggestions to offer. Once that is attained, one can only speculate on the potential and gains of elevating sub-segmental match queries from internal databases to massive external ones.

CAT Systems Acquire Linguistic Knowledge

In the classic era, it was MT applications that were language specific, with each pair having its own special algorithms; CAT systems were the opposite, coming as empty vessels that could apply the same databasing principles to whatever language combination the user chose. First-generation CAT systems worked by seeking purely statistical match-ups between new segments and stored ones; as translation aids they could be powerful but not 'smart'.

The term extraction tool Xerox Terminology Suite was a pioneer in introducing language-specific knowledge within a CAT environment. Now discontinued, its technology resurfaced in the second half of the decade in the Similis system (Lingua et Machina). Advertised as a 'second-generation translation memory', Similis boasts enhanced alignment, term extraction, and sub-segmental matching for the seven European Union languages supported by its linguistic analysis function.

Canada-based Terminotix has also stood out for its ability to mix linguistics with statistics, to the extent that its alignments yield output which for some purposes is deemed useful enough without manual verification. Here an interesting business reversal has occurred. As already noted, CAT system designers have progressively integrated third-party standalones (file converters, QA, alignment, term extraction), ultimately displacing their pioneers. But now that there is so much demand for SMT bi-texts, quick and accurate alignments have become more relevant than ever. In this climate, Terminotix has bucked the established trend by unbundling the alignment tool from its LogiTerm system and marketing it separately as Align Factory.

Apart from alignment, term extraction is another area where tracking advances in computational linguistics can pay dividends. Following the Xerox Terminology Suite model, SDL, Terminotix and MultiCorpora have also created systems with strong language specific term extraction components. Early in the past decade term extraction was considered a luxury, marketed by only the leading brands at a premium price. By decade's end, all newcomers (Fluency, Fortis, Snowball, Wordbee, XTM) were including it within their standard offerings.

Now at least where the major European languages are concerned, the classic 'tabula rasa' CAT paradigm no longer stands, and although building algorithms for specific language pairs remains demanding and expensive, more CAT language specialization will assuredly follow.

Upgrades to the Translator's Editor

Microsoft Word-based TM editors (such as Trados Workbench and Wordfast) had one great blessing: translators could operate within a familiar environment (Word) whilst remaining oblivious to the underlying coding that made the file display. Early proprietary interfaces could handle other file types but could become uselessly cluttered with inline formatting tags (displayed as icons in Tag Editor, paint-brushed sections in SDLX, or a numeric code in curly brackets).

If for some reason the file had been not properly optimized at the source (e.g. text pasted in from a PDF, OCR output with uneven fonts, etc.), the number of tags could explode and negate any productivity benefits entirely. If a tag were missing, an otherwise completed translation could not be exported to native format – a harrowing experience in a deadline-driven industry. Tags were seemingly the bane of a translator's existence. The visual presentation was a major point of differentiation between conventional CAT systems and localization tools. That situation has changed somewhat, with many proprietary editors edging closer to a seamless 'what-you-see-is-what-you-get' view.

Conventional CAT has not particularly facilitated the post-draft editing stage either. A decade ago, the best available option was probably in Déjà Vu, which could export source and target (plus metadata) to a table in Word for editing, then import it back for finalization (TM update, export to native format).

In word processing, Track Changes has been one effective way to present alterations in a document for another to approve. It is only at the time of writing that this feature is being developed for CAT systems, having emerged almost simultaneously in SDL Trados and MemoQ.

Where to From Here?

A decade ago, CAT systems were aimed at the professional translator working on technical text and tended to be expensive and cumbersome. The potential user base is now much broader, and costs are falling. Several suites are even free, such as OmegaT, Virtaal, GlobalSight, and other open source tools, but also the Google Translation Toolkit and Wordfast Anywhere. Many at least have a free satellite version, so that while the project creator needs a licence, the person performing the translation does not: Across, Lingotek memoQ, MemSource, Similis, Snowball, Text United, Wordbee, and others.

One sticking point for potential purchasers was the often hefty up-front licence fee and then feeling 'locked in' by one's investment. Web based applications (Madcap Lingo, Snowball, Text United, Wordbee) have skirted this obstacle by adopting a subscription approach, charged monthly or on the volume of words translated. This allows users to both shop and move around.

Modern CAT systems now assist with most types of translation and suit even the casual translator engaged in sporadic work. Some translation buyers might prefer to have projects done by bilingual users or employees in the belief that subject matter expertise will offset a possible lack of linguistic training. Another compensating factor is sheer numbers: if there are enough people engaged in a task, results can be constantly monitored and if necessary corrected or repaired. This is often referred to as crowdsourcing. For example, Facebook had its user base translate its site into various languages voluntarily. All CAT systems allow for translators to work in teams, but some – like Crowd.in, Lingotek, or Translation WorkSpace – have been developed specifically with mass collaboration in mind.

A decade ago, CAT systems came with empty memory and terminology databases. Now, MultiTrans, SDL Trados Studio, and memoQ can directly access massive databases for matches and concordancing; Logiterm can access Termium and other major term banks. In the past, CAT systems aimed at boosting productivity by reusing *exact* and *fuzzy* matches and applying terminology. Nowadays, they can also assist with non-match segments by populating with MT and postediting or, if preferred, enhancing manual translation with predictive typing and sub-segmental matching from existing databases.

As for typing per se, history is being revisited with a modern twist. In the typewriter era, speed could be increased by having expert translators dictate to expert typists. With the help of speech recognition software, dictation has returned for major supported languages at least.

Translators have been using stand-alone speech recognition applications in translation editor environments over the last few years. However, running heavy programs concurrently (say Trados and Dragon NaturallySpeaking) can strain computer resources. Aliado.SAT (speech-aided translation) is the first system that is purpose-built to package TM (and MT) with speech recognition.

Translators who are also skilled interpreters might perhaps achieve more from 'sight translating' than from MT postediting or assembling sub-segmental strings or predictive typing. The possibilities seem suggestive and attractive. Unfortunately, there are still no empirical studies to describe how basic variables (text type, translator skill profile) can be matched against different approaches (MT plus post editing, sub-segmental matching, speech recognition, or combinations thereof) to achieve optimal results.

Given all this technological ferment, one might wonder how professional translation software will appear by the end of the present decade. Technology optimists seem to think that MT postediting will be the answer in most situations, making the translator-focused systems of today redundant. Pessimists worry even now that continuous reuse of matches from internal memory to editor window, from memory to massive databases and STM engines, and then back to the editor, will make language itself fuzzier; they advocate avoidance of the technology altogether except for very narrow domains.

Considering recent advances, and how computing in general and CAT systems in particular have evolved, any prediction is risky. Change is hardly expected to slacken, so attempting to envision state-of-the-art in 2020 would be guesswork at best. What is virtually certain is that by then, the systems of today will look as outdated as DOS-based software looks now.

While it is tempting to peer into possible futures, it is also important not to lose track of the past. That is not easy when change is propelling us dizzyingly and distractingly forward. But if we wish to fully understand what CAT systems have achieved in their first twenty years, we need to comprehensively document their evolution before it recedes too far from view.

Further Reading and Relevant Resources

With the Hutchings *Compendium* now discontinued, the TAUS Tracker web page may soon become the best information repository for products under active development. Just released, it contained only 27 entries at the time of writing (even major names such as Déjà Vu or Lingotek have not made its list yet). ProZ's CAT Tool comparison – successor to its popular 'CAT Fight' feature that was shelved some years ago – also proposes to help freelance translators make informed decisions by compiling all relevant information con CAT systems in one place.

ProZ, the major professional networking site for translators, includes also 'CAT Tools Support' technical forums and Group buy schemes. There are also user bases on Yahoo Groups, some of which (Déjà Vu, Wordfast, the old Trados) are still quite active; these CAT Tool Support forums allow for a good appraisal of how translators engage with these products.

The first initiative to use the web to systematically compare features of CAT systems was Jost Zetzsche's TranslatorsTraining.com. Zetzsche is also the author of *The Tool Kit* newsletter, now rebranded *The Tool Box*, which has been an important source of information and education on CAT systems (which he calls TEnTs, or 'translation environment tools'). Zetzsche has also authored and regularly updated the electronic book *A Translator's Tool Box for the 21st Century: A Computer Primer for Translators*, now in its tenth edition.

Of the several hard copy industry journals available in the nineties (*Language Industry Monitor*, *Language International*, *Multilingual Computing and Technology*, and others), only *Multilingual* remains and continues offering reviews of new products (and new versions of established ones) as well as general comments on the state of the technology. Reviews and comments can also be found in digital periodicals such as *Translation Journal*, *ClientSide News*, or *TCWorld*; they can be found also in newsletters published by translators' professional organizations (*The ATA Chronicle*, *ITI Bulletin*), and academic journals such as *Machine Translation* and *Journal of Specialised Translation*.

Articles taken from these and other sources may be searched from within the Machine Translation Archives, a repository of articles also compiled by Hutchings. Most items related to CAT systems will be found in the 'Methodologies, techniques, applications, uses' section under 'Aids and tools for translators' and also on 'Systems and project names'.

Bibliography

ALPAC (Automatic Language Processing Advisory Committee) (1966) *Language and Machines: Computers in Translation and Linguistics, A Report by the Automatic Language Processing Advisory Committee*, Division of Behavioral Sciences, National Academy of Sciences, National Research Council, Washington, DC.

Brace, Colin (1992, March–April) 'Bonjour, Eurolang Optimiser', *Language Industry Monitor*. Available at: www.lim.nl/monitor/optimizer.html.

Garcia, Ignacio (2003) 'Standard Bearers: TM Brand Profiles at Lantra-L', *Translation Journal* 7(4).

Hutchins, W. John (1998) 'Twenty Years of Translating and the Computer', in *Translating and the Computer 20*, London: The Association for Information Management.

Hutchins, W. John (1999–2010) 'Compendium of Translation Software: Directory of Commercial Machine Translation Systems and Computer-aided Translation Support Tools'. Available at: www.hutchinsweb.me.uk/Compendium.htm.

Kay, Martin (1980/1997) 'The Proper Place of Men and Machines in Language Translation', *Machine Translation* 12(1–2): 3–23.

Kingscott, Geoffrey (1999, November) 'New Strategic Direction for Trados International', *Journal for Language and Documentation* 6(11). Available at: www.crux.be/English/IJLD/trados.pdf.

Lagoudaki, Elina (2006) 'Translation Memories Survey', Imperial College London. Available at: www3.imperial.ac.uk/portal/pls/portallive/docs/1/7294521.PDF.

Melby, Alan K. (1983) 'Computer Assisted Translation Systems: The Standard Design and a Multi-level Design', in *Proceedings of the ACL-NRL Conference on Applied Natural Language Processing*, Santa Monica, CA, 174–77.

Muegge, Uwe (2012) 'The Silent Revolution: Cloud-based Translation Management Systems', *TC World* 7(7): 17–21.

Papineni, Kishore A., Salim Roukos, Todd Ward, and Zhu Wei-Jing (2002) 'BLEU: A Method for Automatic Evaluation of Machine Translation', in *Proceedings of the 40th Annual Meeting of the Association for Computational Linguistics, ACL-2002*, 7–12 July 2002, University of Pennsylvania, Philadelphia, PA, 311–18.

Plitt, Mirko and François Masselot (2010) 'A Productivity Test of Statistical Machine Translation: Post-editing in a Typical Localisation Context', *The Prague Bulletin of Mathematical Linguistics* 93: 7–16.

Simard, Michel and Philippe Langlais (2001) 'Sub-sentential Exploitation of Translation Memories', in *Proceedings of the MT Summit VIII: Machine Translation in the Information Age*, Santiago de Compostela, Spain, 335–39.

Specia, Lucia (2011) 'Exploiting Objective Annotations for Measuring Translation Post-editing Effort', in *Proceedings of the 15th Conference of the European Association for Machine Translation (EAMT 2011)*, Leuven, Belgium, 73–80.

TAUS (Translation Automation User Society) (2007) 'Advanced Leveraging: A TAUS Report'. Available at: www.translationautomation.com/technology-reviews/advanced-leveraging.html.

Trados (2002) *Trados 5.5 Getting Started Guide*, Dublin: Trados.

van der Meer, Jaap (2011) 'Lack of Interoperability Costs the Translation Industry a Fortune: A TAUS Report'. Available at: www.translationautomation.com/reports/lack-of-interoperability-costs-the-translation-industry-a-fortune.

Wallis, Julian (2006) 'Interactive Translation vs. Pre-translation in the Context of Translation Memory Systems: Investigating the Effects of Translation Method on Productivity, Quality and Translator Satisfaction', Unpublished MA Thesis in Translation Studies, University of Ottawa, Ottawa.

Zetzsche, Jost (2004) *The Tool Box Newsletter*, Winchester Bay: International Writers' Group.

Zetzsche, Jost (2010, March) 'Get Those Things Out of There!', *The ATA Chronicle*: 34–35.

Zetzsche, Jost (2012) *A Translator's Tool Box for the 21st Century: A Computer Primer for Translators* (version 10), Winchester Bay: International Writers' Group.

4

TRANSLATION TECHNOLOGIES

Translator Training

Lynne Bowker

Over the past seventy-five years, computer technology has evolved considerably and has become increasingly prevalent in most areas of society. The translation profession is no exception, and this field has witnessed changes in the way that translation work is approached and carried out as a result of the increasing availability and integration of computer-based tools and resources. Indeed, translation technologies have become so firmly embedded in the translation profession that it now seems unthinkable for a translator to approach the task of translating without the use of some kind of computer tool.

If the task of translation itself has been affected by the use of computers, so too has the way in which translators are educated, which now necessarily includes training in the use of technologies. The need to integrate training in the use of computer-aided translation (CAT) and machine translation (MT) tools into translator education programs has introduced a host of challenges, raising questions such as the following, among others: Which types of tools are relevant for translators? What do translators need to learn about technologies? Who should be responsible for teaching translators about computer aids? When should technologies be introduced into the curriculum? The answers to such questions are not always clear cut, and they may be influenced by practical considerations that differ from one educational institution to the next. Nevertheless, over the past few decades, translation technologies have staked claim to a place in the translation curriculum. Kenny (2020) provides a thorough overview of the history of translation technology education, so the focus here will look more toward the current and future situation and to some of the possible solutions and best practices that are emerging as translator educators continue to grapple with the challenges associated with translation technologies.

Why Do Translators Need to Learn About Translation Technologies?

There is a longstanding debate about whether translation constitutes an art, a craft, or a science. Indeed some purists take the attitude that true translation is something best learned in the absence of technology. However, the reality of the twenty-first century is such that the vast majority of practising translators need to be able to leverage the possibilities offered by computer tools in order to remain competitive and to meet the evolving demands of the marketplace. In 2016, the translation technology company SDL conducted a survey of close to 3,000 professionals around the world who were involved in some way with translation technology (e.g. freelance

DOI: 10.4324/9781003168348-5

translators, translation agency employees, translators in private- and public-sector organizations) (SDL 2016). Key findings include that 90 percent of respondents agree that translation technology helps them to work more quickly, and 72 percent believe that they would lose competitive advantage if they stopped using translation productivity tools such as translation memories or MT. At the time of the survey, which was conducted just as neural machine translation (NMT) was being introduced, 40 percent of those who answered were already using MT tools, and nearly two-thirds of these MT users felt that it made them more efficient. Based on the overall survey results, SDL (2016) determined that embracing translation technology, particularly MT, constitutes an obvious way of boosting translation productivity moving forward.

Fuelled by a host of societal, political, economic, and technological trends, the demand for translation as a means of cutting through language barriers has grown exponentially in recent decades. Among these trends, we have witnessed:

- the shift to an information society with a knowledge-based economy;
- the creation and expansion of political and economic unions and agreements (e.g. the European Union, the North American Free Trade Agreement);
- the development of new and increasingly sophisticated products (e.g. digital cameras, smart phones, medical equipment), which often require extensive accompanying documentation;
- the globalization of commerce and the rise of e-commerce;
- the popularity of international entertainment (e.g. videogames and streaming services for films and series); and
- the growth of the World Wide Web coupled with the desire for localized content.

In the face of such trends, the volume of text to be translated worldwide has increased significantly, and the demand for translation far outstrips the supply of qualified translators. What is more, on top of the increased volume of text to be translated and the relative shortage of qualified workers, deadlines for producing translations are getting ever shorter as organizations strive to provide multiple language versions of the same document or product at the same time. Taken in combination, these trends are putting translators around the world under enormous pressure.

In addition to all these pragmatic and market-oriented reasons for integrating technology into the translation profession more fully, Kenny (2020: 499) argues convincingly that

> a well-informed understanding of how translation and technology go hand in hand should form a part not just of any sharply focused, professionally oriented translator training programme, but also of any more broadly defined education in translation studies.

In this vein, Kenny (2020) emphasizes that a solid technological education can make an important contribution to the development of critical citizenship more broadly (e.g. some of the more influential technologies currently in use in the translation industry, such as NMT, incorporate the same machine learning methods as those used in other areas of our economy and society). Indeed, Bowker (2019) has suggested that translation educators even have a social responsibility to educate those outside the profession in the critical use of tools that are now widely available to the general public, such as free online MT tools.

For both the present and future translators who are faced with the prospect of processing higher volumes of text in seemingly ever shorter turnaround times, translation technologies present an attractive option for helping them to increase productivity and throughput. However, translation tools cannot merely be assimilated into the translator's workflow without any effort.

To this end, institutes of higher education, as well as professional translators' associations, are offering different types of education aimed at helping language professionals to make the most of various translation technologies.

For example, the European Master's in Translation (EMT) is a quality designation that has been developed for MA university programs in translation (EC-DGT 2021). This designation is awarded to higher education translation programs in Europe that meet agreed-upon professional standards and market demands. At its heart is the EMT competence framework, which was first introduced in 2009 and then revised in 2017 and again in 2022 (EC-DGT 2022). The framework considers that translator education teaches a combination of knowledge and skills, and that it should equip students not only with a deep understanding of the processes involved but also with the ability to perform and provide a translation service to high professional and ethical standards. The EMT competence framework defines five main areas of competence: technology, along with language and culture, translation, personal and interpersonal, and service provision. According to the EMT framework, the technology competence includes all the knowledge and skills used to implement present and future translation technologies within the translation process, as well as basic knowledge of machine translation technologies and the ability to implement machine translation according to potential needs (EC-DGT 2022).

Meanwhile, associations for language professionals, such as the American Translators Association (ATA 2022) and the Institute of Translation and Interpreting (ITI 2022) in the United Kingdom, to name just a couple, regularly address technology-related issues as part of their conferences, workshops, seminars and professional publications.

Which Types of Tools Are Relevant for Translators?

Before considering some possible approaches to technology-related education, and the accompanying challenges that they present, let us begin with a brief survey of some of the different types of technologies that may appear in a translation education context. Note that the goal here is not to describe specific features of these tools nor to explain how they work – such descriptions can be found elsewhere in this volume – but rather to provide a general idea of different categories of tools to show the variety of technologies available to translators and to provide a very general indication of how these might fit into the translation curriculum.

The range of general office software, in particular word processors or text editors, but also spreadsheets and desktop publishing programs, are among those tools used most regularly by translators in their daily work. In addition, translators regularly find themselves needing to use general tools such as applications for converting, compressing, or transferring files, as well as cloud-based storage (EC-DGT 2022). In the past, when the presence of computers in our everyday lives was far less ubiquitous, and before the plethora of specialized and sophisticated translation technologies had arrived on the market, training in the use of these more basic tools was sometimes integrated into the translator training curriculum. Nowadays, as computers have become increasingly prevalent, translation students arriving in the translation classrooms in the twenty-first century are undoubtedly more computer savvy than were their counterparts in preceding decades. Nevertheless, while these students might be comfortable with the basic functions of such programs, there may still be considerable room for them to develop into "power users" who can optimize the functionality of a word processor or other type of office software. However, since the translation curriculum must make room for intensive learning with regard to the more specialized technologies now in existence, the training provided for the more basic tools must come in other forms. For example, translator education institutes may keep on hand a series of tutorials and exercises covering the more advanced features of office tools and encourage students to do these independently so that they might be better prepared for the program. Similarly, students may organize or participate in peer-to-peer training sessions, where they share tips and tricks that they have acquired for making better use of general software. Some educational institutions may offer computer training workshops or seminars organized through a central student services or computer services unit. Finally, many professional associations, such as the previously mentioned ATA or ITI, offer workshops or training sessions on a range of tools – from the general to the more specialized – and students may be directed towards these offerings. This will not only provide an opportunity to learn about a tool, but it also helps students to develop a professional network and instils the important notion that lifelong learning – particularly in relation to technology – is essential for continued success in the translation profession.

Electronic resources, such as term banks, glossaries or dictionaries, as well as resources such as pre-constructed online corpora and associated processing tools such as concordancers (e.g. Linguee, Glosbe, TradooIT), will likely find a place in a translator education program (EC-DGT 2022). Again, while the use of pre-existing resources might seem relatively intuitive, an early and gradual introduction to technologies allows students to build a solid foundation. In addition to giving students a chance to learn how to search pre-constructed corpora, documentation courses may also provide translator trainees with an opportunity to learn how to design and compile their own "do-it-yourself" corpora, as recommended by Bowker and Pearson (2002), among others. This requires learning how to critically evaluate texts to decide whether they can usefully be included in a corpus. It also entails learning how to interpret the output of a concordancer, taking into account the limitations of the corpus.

The use of terminology management systems, which allow students to build and query their own termbases, will undoubtedly be incorporated into a terminology course or specialized translation course on a translator education program. These tools can be used in standalone mode, and students learn how to design term record templates, record terminological information, and search for solutions within the termbase. Monolingual and multilingual term extractors, which seek to automatically identify potential terms in an electronic corpus, may also be introduced in a terminology or specialized translation course.

Translation memory (TM) systems, which are used to interrogate associated databases of previously translated texts along with their corresponding source texts, are typically introduced in a course dedicated to translation technologies. These tools are normally at the heart of a larger tool suite, sometimes referred to as a Translation Environment Tool (TEnT) or translator's workstation. As part of this larger suite, they may interact with other tools, such as word processors, terminology management systems, concordancers, and machine translation systems; however, in many cases, students learn about these different modules independently. From a didactic viewpoint, this makes sense as students can more manageably digest information about the underlying concepts and the operation of the individual components. However, as we will see in an upcoming section, this approach does not facilitate an understanding of the way the different tools interact, nor of the ways in which users must interact with the tools in order to optimize their performance.

Once considered a tool for replacing translators, machine translation systems are now more widely accepted as a technology that requires some interaction with a professional translator, such as in the form of pre- or post-editing. In the past, MT systems were frequently left out of the curriculum of translator training programs altogether, or given only cursory attention, on the grounds that such tools were not used by practising professionals. This was certainly true in the past, when the output of the older rule-based MT systems was often so poor that post-editing was more labour intensive and time consuming than was translating from scratch. However, with the introduction of first statistical and then neural approaches to MT, the quality of MT output has improved such that, while not perfect, it may nonetheless represent a viable starting point (e.g. Castilho *et al.* 2017). Therefore, professional translators are increasingly working with MT systems in some form. For example, an MT system may be integrated with a translation memory system in order to generate possible solutions when none is found in the translation memory database. Alternatively, an MT system may be used to produce a complete initial draft to be post-edited by a translator. It is therefore becoming necessary to include at least an introduction to MT as part of the regular translation curriculum (EC-DGT 2022). Bowker and Buitrago Ciro (2019) refer to this notion as machine translation literacy instruction. Additional specialized training may be added to provide guidance in pre-editing or writing for translation (e.g. Bowker and Buitrago Ciro 2019), as well as in post-editing, where translators learn techniques for revising the output of an MT system (e.g. Guerberof Arenas and Moorkens 2019). Indeed, recent studies emphasize the need to train students specifically in post-editing of NMT output not only because employers increasingly desire those skills but also because the task of post-editing NMT appears to require competences that resemble those needed for conventional translation or revision. Finally, Massey and Ehrensberger-Dow (2017) point to another valid reason as to why students need to learn about MT when they observe that it is by understanding the tool's functioning, along with its strengths and weaknesses, that students can appreciate the added value of human translation and be able to deliver this when needed.

Several other types of tools address more targeted or specialized types of translation, and even interpreting. For instance, localization tools, such as those used in the translation and adaptation of software, websites, videogames, and other digital products, include functions that allow translators to extract text strings from the software code and to reinsert them back into the code once they have been translated (Jiménez-Crespo 2013; O'Hagan and Mangiron 2013). In addition, localization tools make it possible to adapt other elements of software or websites, such as shortcut keys, colours, or currency or date formats, so that they are more appropriate to users from another culture. Localization tools may be introduced as part of a core course in translation technologies, but they are more likely to be examined in detail as part of a specialized elective course dedicated to localization, if such a specialization is offered as part of a given translator training program. A similarly specialized set of tools are those used for dubbing, subtitling or audiovisual translation (e.g. Díaz-Cintas 2008). These tools may not be introduced as part of the regular curriculum but may be included in a course on audiovisual translation if such a course is part of the program. The same goes for computer-aided interpreting (CAI) tools. These were somewhat slower to evolve than CAT tools, but they are growing in importance as part of interpreter training programs. Fantinouli and Prandi (2018), for example, present a training proposal for teaching tools for remote interpreting, as well as teaching tools that can be used in preparation for interpreting assignments and even in a simultaneous interpreting booth. Finally, Desjardins (2017) addresses the question of translation in the context of online social media (OSM) and argues that translation students need to also acquire OSM competencies to be competitive in the workplace.

Translation workflow tools are another type of tool that are making their way into the translation curriculum as part of project management training or a practicum, for example (EC-DGT 2022). These tools are designed to help manage translation projects where there are multiple team members who must share resources and work with the same texts. They also have features that facilitate interactions between clients and translators, such as a means of placing an order or sending an estimate or an invoice. While these tools do not typically get addressed in core translation technology courses, they may be introduced in courses that deal with professional issues or courses that focus on project management (Mitchell-Schuitevoerder 2020), if such electives are part of the translation program in question. Another place where such tools might come into play is in the context of a work placement, whether this takes place externally in the field or as part of a model such as a "simulated translation bureau", which aims to familiarize students with new ways of working and with new technologies (Buysschaert *et al.* 2018). In a similar vein, a practicum or a project management course might be a venue for introducing new tools and technologies such as wiki-based collaborative authoring or collaborative terminology management platforms, which are designed with a view to facilitating work by translators who collaborate online.

Finally, voice recognition tools, which allow users to dictate a text directly into a word processor or text editor, have not yet become commonplace on the translator training curriculum, but this is beginning to change (Zapata and Quirion 2016). This is in part because, until recently, the technology did not produce accurate enough results to make it worthwhile for translators to adopt a dictation approach to working. However, it is likely that voice recognition tools will feature more prominently in the translation curriculum in coming years since these tools offer yet another potential means of boosting productivity.

While this list is not exhaustive, it has nonetheless provided a general idea of the broad range of technologies that might be introduced in a translator training program. It has also suggested, in a general way, where these tools might currently be found in the curriculum of many programs.

Which Specific Tools Should Be Included in the Curriculum?

The previous section introduced an extensive range of types of tools that trainee translators are likely to encounter as part of their studies. As the number of tools available in each category continues to rise, translator trainers are faced with the dilemma of having to select specific products to represent these different categories of tools in order to give students an opportunity to get some practical hands-on experience. A host of factors may influence the decision about which tools to select, and as part of that decision process, translation technology trainers have long been aware that one of the main challenges is the so-called "skills versus knowledge" debate. In other words, should a university course attempt to train translators how to use the leading TM tools on the market (e.g. to increase their chances of employment)? Or should it aim to impart knowledge of the technology in a more generic way in order to equip students with the ability to evaluate and to learn to use such tools themselves? Most trainers try to attempt a tricky balancing act between these two positions. As noted previously, the EMT competence framework assumes that translator education programs will teach a combination of knowledge and skills; in other words, they will strive to impart knowledge, and this will necessarily involve facilitating the development of some specific skills as students learn to apply the general principles through working with particular tools (EC-DGT 2022).

The good news in this scenario is that, if one goal is to teach students the underlying principles that are common across a particular category of tool, then the decision about which particular tool is chosen becomes less important. However, in order to allow trainees to develop critical evaluation skills, an educational institution should not focus on a single tool for training purposes. Moreover, there is a good argument to be made that having a minimum of two to three tools available for observation makes it much easier to distinguish the basic features of the tool type in general from the specificities or options of an individual product.

Undoubtedly, a fundamental understanding of the underlying concepts and principles, as can be obtained from studying a small number of tools, is essential. However, ideally, any training program should be flexible enough to adapt to evolving commercial needs. In the case of translation technology, there would seem to be at least two further arguments to be made in favour of exposing the students to an even wider selection of tools during the course of their training. First, as noted, there is a plethora of tools available on the market today, and even if a translator is in a position where they are able to work with only a single tool, it will first be necessary to select this tool. Deciding which tool can best meet the needs at hand is a task that can be facilitated through a comparative evaluation. Therefore, if translators are going to find themselves needing to conduct such comparative evaluations, they will be better equipped to do so if they have previously been given the opportunity to gain such experience by evaluating and comparing a selection of tools as part of their training. In addition, the reality of today's market is that translators are much more likely to need to be able to use multiple tools. That being the case, students will surely benefit from having the chance to learn and experiment with several tools as part of their studies. In addition, the more exposure they have to a variety of tools, the less likely they are to be naïve users once they enter the workforce.

Another consideration is the complexity of the tools selected. Kappus and Ehrensberger-Dow (2020) emphasize that the increasing reliance on technology has serious ergonomic implications for translators since poor ergonomic design can result in cognitive overload. If more than one tool of a certain type is to be learned, it may make sense to begin with one that integrates fewer "extra" features. As numerous trainers logically point out, translators with strong basic computer skills can more easily graduate to using complex software. Kappus and Ehrensberger-Dow (2020) suggest that when students are first learning to use translation technology, they could begin with tools that have lean interfaces in order to be able to concentrate more on the decision-making process without having to shift their attention between different areas of the screen. Indeed, newer users may be less intimidated by a "core" tool package containing only the main functions that they are likely to use than by a product that includes numerous additional programs whose uses may be less clear or less commonly required (e.g. functions intended to assist in managing complex workflow, dealing with heavily coded documents, and other similar tasks). Moreover, the volume of accompanying documentation for these programs is also likely to be more manageable for a new user, such as a student, when the product itself is more targeted to specific, translation-centred functions. Additional features and tools can be introduced to students once they have mastered the basics. The general consensus seems to be that every tool has its strengths and weaknesses, and the choice of which one to use depends on the job at hand. Still, the fact remains that if multiple tools must be learned, there is a certain logic to learning the most straightforward tool first and working up to a more complex system.

If the cost of purchasing multiple tools in a single category is prohibitive for a translator training institute, one option may be to try to incorporate the use of demo versions of some tools. Most commercial products do create and distribute demo versions with a view to allowing potential clients to have an opportunity to test and evaluate the tool before committing to it. However, these demo versions are often restricted in some way (e.g. time-limited versions, limited functionality), which may hinder their usefulness as a teaching tool. Depending on the way in which the functionality is limited, it may be more or less feasible for a demo version to be usefully incorporated into a training program.

It may be more attractive for an educational institution to turn instead to freely available open source products and to incorporate these into training programs. In this way, students can be introduced to a wider range of products and can have the opportunity to learn multiple tools and to comparatively evaluate them. Open source tools have the added advantage that they can be installed by students on their own computers and used outside the requirements of specific courses. This may encourage students to begin using tools more extensively and to allow them to start building up resources – such as translation memory and terminology databases – early on, before they even get started on their career. Moreover, even if translators end up switching from using a free TM system during their student days to using a commercial product after graduation or later in their career, or if they end up using multiple tools, it is becoming increasingly easy to transfer TM databases and termbases between different systems – including between free systems and commercial products – without a great loss of time or investment of effort.

What Do Translators Need to Learn About Translation Technologies?

Once translator trainers have acquired a selection of tools for translation students to work with, an important question becomes *what* students need to learn about these tools. Some tools can be extremely sophisticated, each incorporating a variety of features and functions that work in a slightly different manner, are referred to by a different proprietary term, or are accessed through a different style of interface. It is clear, therefore, that any training must involve learning the particular steps required to operate a given tool. In other words, trainers certainly need to provide students with step-by-step instructions for using this tool. As part of this, Kappus and Ehrensberger-Dow (2020) emphasize the need to take ergonomics into account when teaching students about translation technologies, which includes teaching students how to individualize their tool settings to optimize the ergonomics in order to reduce effort and otherwise suit their own needs.

However, as noted, while it is clearly important for translator training institutes to turn out graduates whose overall skill set is in line with the needs of the market, this market is somewhat volatile. Therefore, technology training cannot be set up solely to address the latest trends but must take a more balanced approach that includes providing students with transferable skills, such as the ability to engage in critical analysis and problem solving. Therefore, in addition to providing a "how to" manual, instructors must also seek to provide a framework that goes beyond merely describing a tool's features or explaining *how* it functions. In other words, to prepare translators to become effective users of translation technologies, trainers need to provide opportunities for students to learn not only *how* but also *whether*, *when*, and *why* to use a given tool. Speaking specifically about MT, Bowker and Buitrago Ciro (2019) use the term "MT literacy" to emphasize that students need to develop not only techno-procedural skills but also cognitive skills that will allow them to become critical users of tools. Although Bowker and Buitrago Ciro (2019: 33) are referring to MT in particular, this general idea can be applied to translation technologies more broadly. For instance, for each category of tool that is being learned, students should be given a series of tasks and questions for reflection that will encourage them, as tool users, to reflect on *why* it might be helpful to adopt a given tool as well as to consider what a tool can and cannot do, and the positive and negative effects that tool use may have on the translator, the translation process and product, or even more broadly on society.

As noted previously, Kenny (2020) stresses that part of technology training in translator education is to ensure that translators are able to function as good digital citizens, which includes being able to evaluate the implications of tool use, such as from an ethical perspective. Until relatively recently, there had been less emphasis on the deeper implications of these technologies, including how they fit within the wider spectrum of cultural, social, political, professional, and ethical concerns, and this in spite of the fact that

> Many of these questions about ethical aspects of new [translation] technologies are difficult to separate from broader sociocultural issues. Technological developments have occurred alongside, and played a part in, major ongoing shifts in social structures, migration patterns, trade, information and employment.
>
> *(Drugan 2019: 250)*

It is therefore becoming increasingly common for translator education to make a greater effort to consider ethical issues, and this applies to the teaching of translation technologies also. Bowker (2021) outlines a complex web of technology-related ethical issues that might rightfully find a place in a translation curriculum, such as ownership of translation resources, privacy and confidentiality of translation data, professional identity of translators, productivity and payment, translators' codes of ethics, machine bias, and the potential contribution of tools to linguistic hegemony or linguistic diversity.

It is clear that translation technology cannot be taught or understood in a vacuum, so translator training programs must provide opportunities for practical hands-on experience with tools in order to support theoretical understanding. This practical experience may in turn stand students in good stead as they reach the job market. This is one argument for integrating technology use more widely across a program rather than limiting its use to a core course specifically on technologies.

Where in the Curriculum Should Translators Learn About Translation Technologies?

Teaching and learning translation technologies are not straightforward tasks. As alluded to previously, one factor that may hinder students from developing a well-rounded understanding of technologies may be the fact that, in many cases, the opportunity to learn about translation technologies may be restricted to a "core" course dedicated solely to this subject. Such core courses are certainly valuable, and in fact are essential to understanding the underlying principles of how tools work and how they may be useful. Moreover, core courses provide opportunities for comparative evaluation of different tools as well as in-depth exploration of a fuller range of the features offered by the tools. In short, these courses provide an occasion for students to think about technology. However, in these courses, tools are often examined in isolation rather than as part of an integrated translation environment or interactive tool suite. For example, the features of a terminology management system may be explored in some depth by working with this tool in stand-alone mode; however, the practices needed to optimize the tool for use in conjunction with a translation memory system might not be adequately addressed. Because these "core" courses do not always provide students with sufficient opportunity to use the tools in the context of an actual translation project, it means they may not be thinking specifically about how tool performance is affected by – or can affect – the translation process and product, and how they themselves can best interact with tools to achieve optimal results.

In some contemporary translator training programs, a main drawback to the way that translation technologies are taught can thus be summarized as a lack of integration on two levels. First, as noted, tools are primarily viewed in isolation rather than as part of an integrated translation environment. This approach, which introduces students to the basic functions of the tools, is necessary as a first stage of teaching and learning where knowledge and instructional content are broken down for easy digestion. However, it does not allow students to appreciate fully how the performance and use of these tools fits into the bigger picture of translation practice. Therefore, the next stage of learning requires evaluating the task in its natural wider context, which many include as part of a larger interactive tool suite.

Second, in some translator training programs, the tools are only seen and used in "core" courses – that is, courses with a specific focus on technology – rather than being integrated across a range of applied courses in the translator training program. The resulting gap between theory and practice does not provide students with an accurate picture of how they, as future translators, are likely to work – and in fact may be expected or required to work – in many professional contexts. To truly learn how tools fit into the translation process, technology-related tasks must be contextualized rather than severed from realistic experience.

Another challenge that may arise in "core" courses is that students work with various language pairs and directions. Whereas practical translation classes tend to focus on a specific language pair, core technology courses often bring together a mixed language group, which often requires technology trainers to provide source texts or research questions in a lingua franca, and some students must work in the "wrong" direction or with their less dominant language, which may not be an authentic experience for them. Moreover, in such contexts, trainers may not be able to provide in-depth assessments or feedback since they may not be experts in all the languages or language directions used by the students.

This lack of integration is not usually a result of trainers' unwillingness or failure to recognize the importance of technologies. Indeed, many educators recognize that integrating technologies more fully across the translator training curriculum could benefit students (and their eventual employers). However, many challenges are involved in achieving this goal. The question then remains: how can translator trainees' needs be met effectively in a university context?

Situated learning promotes the use of tools as aids in practical translation courses as well as in core technology courses and offers a chance for reflection on the role and impact of translation technologies in the bigger picture. Active and situated learning strategies are increasingly being adopted in numerous facets of translator education. Using this approach, learning takes place in an environment that simulates as much as possible an authentic workplace setting. In the case of translation technology education, this means embedding tool use in practical translation courses, or adopting a project-based approach to translation technology as recommended by Mitchell-Schuitevoerder (2020), rather than contributing to the siloization of tools by restricting their use to the "core" technology courses.

Under such realistic conditions, students work and build knowledge and skills in a collaborative fashion, thus taking on the role of active learners rather than passive receivers of potentially abstract and decontextualized knowledge, which may appear divorced from real-world requirements or practices. The challenge for translator educators is to establish a framework that will support the embedding of technologies into – and especially across – translator education programs. For some programs, an effective way to introduce situated learning is through internships, co-operative education options, or work placements. While many such opportunities involve students working in the field, there are also approaches, such as the simulated translation bureau (STB) solution proposed by Buysschaert *et al.* (2018), who describe this as follows:

> In STBs, teams of students set themselves up as a (fictitious) translation agency as part of their course and run their agency under mock-realistic circumstances, which vary from one course to another. They work on authentic tasks, though not necessarily "live". The bureaus typically run alongside other courses students take as part of their studies.

As Buysschaert *et al.* (2018) emphasize, the STB model offers practice in providing translation services in a professional context, practice in applying suitable translation technologies in a realistic context, and practice in training competences related to team work, planning, and time management. As a result, it addresses many of the requirements identified in the EMT competence framework (EC-DGT 2022), including those focusing on technology.

When Should Translators Learn About Translation Technologies?

As discussed by Kelly (2005: 113), decisions about sequencing the different elements of a translator training program (e.g. theory, practice, language skills) have long been debated. Moreover, the simple time pressures of trying to prepare students to translate professionally with a limited number of course hours mean that choices of content at each stage must be carefully weighed to maximize results. With regard to technology, there is no consensus on when tools should be introduced. On the one hand, students will benefit from the opportunity to practice realistic work habits by using such tools early and often, but on the other hand, they need a certain amount of translation experience to avoid becoming naive users of technology.

Dillon and Fraser (2006: 69), for example, suggest that inexperienced translators do not have the breadth or depth of knowledge needed to allow them to properly evaluate the advantages or disadvantages of using a given tool. Meanwhile, Bowker (2005: 19) observes that novice translators sometimes exhibit "blind faith" in technologies because they lack the confidence or experience required to critically evaluate the tools' output.

Of course, it is worth noting that translators use many different kinds of tools, ranging from the relatively straightforward word processors and term banks to the more sophisticated corpus processing tools, translation memories and beyond. Common sense suggests that it should be possible to introduce more general tools earlier in the translator training process, while reserving some of the more complex tools for later integration. With an early and gradual introduction to technologies, students will build a solid foundation, and with these strong basic computer skills in place, they will be better positioned to graduate to using more specialized tools.

Although there may be no straightforward answer to *when* tools should be introduced, simply not introducing them is not a reasonable solution. Rather, observations such as those made previously seem to reinforce the notion that more and better training in technology use for translation is needed. The translation classroom offers an unparalleled venue for students to observe when using technology has helped them to find good solutions, when it has not, and why. Such discussions can help to develop students' judgment not only about technologies, but also about translation strategies in general.

The previously mentioned work placement options – whether in the field or in a simulated form (e.g. Buysschaert *et al.* 2018) – often come towards the end of a program, and they are specifically designed to allow students to knit together the various types of skills and knowledge that they have acquired in individual courses.

It is also worth noting that as the role of technology continues to take on greater importance in the language professions as a whole, a number of institutions have introduced graduate programs where translation technologies are the focus of the program, rather than being just one part of a more general translation program. For instance, Dublin City University (Ireland) has offered an MSc in translation technology for a number of years, while 2019 saw the launch of a new European master's in technology for translation and interpreting delivered by a consortium of the University of Wolverhampton (UK), the University of Malaga (Spain), the New Bulgarian University (Bulgaria), and Ghent University (Belgium). In these more technology-focused programs, students may learn additional technical skills such as programming or artificial intelligence and machine learning (e.g. how to train a translation engine). Indeed, some translator trainers, such as Mellinger (2017), envision that the technical skill of learning how to tune an MT engine in the context of post-editing may provide an advantage to a translator who is able to articulate specific suggestions for improvement to MT system designers.

Finally, as already mentioned, translators will need to be prepared to keep learning about new technologies or better ways to optimize existing technologies throughout the course of their career. In this regard, the continuing education or professional development opportunities offered by higher education institutes or professional associations (e.g. ATA, ITI) will be invaluable.

Additional Challenges to Integrating Technologies Into Translator Training

In addition to the challenges discussed previously, numerous other obstacles can hinder the successful integration of technologies into a translation program. Some are practical in nature, such as lack of access to appropriate hardware and software. Hopefully, such issues will become increasingly less problematic as prices for computer-related products continue to drop and partnership agreements between universities and tools vendors become more commonplace, and as open source tools become fully developed. However, a number of thorny issues remain, and are less straightforward to address, though some tentative solutions are proposed below.

Managing Expectations by Encouraging Critical Reflection

One significant challenge presented by translation technologies is the management of expectations with regard to what these tools can and cannot do. In their enthusiasm to reap the aggressively marketed potential benefits associated with translation technology use, some less experienced translators and technology users may have expectations of tools that go far beyond the capacities of today's technologies, and certainly beyond their intended uses. As observed by Dillon and Fraser (2006: 75), inexperienced translators seem to have "an uncharacteristically positive view of TM [translation memory]", coupled with "a higher level of ignorance of the limitations of TM". This type of attitude may result either in disillusionment with tools when these expectations are not met or – even more seriously – in uncritical reliance on the output of these tools. While gains in income, productivity, and quality are often reported, problems can arise from uncritical use of tools, such as inappropriately recycling the contents of a translation memory or applying one tool in a context that more properly calls for the use of another. In the context of translation technologies, those translators who have developed keen critical reflection skills will be the ones best placed to determine where the benefits and pitfalls lie in relation to tool use.

Experienced translator educators, who have witnessed some unfortunate results arising from uncritical attitudes, may be understandably reluctant to use technologies in class or to introduce them into translator education before students have acquired enough experience to be critical of tools' output. Without a coherent structure to guide the implementation of technologies in a translator education program, and in the absence of reflection by both educators and students about the contexts and ways in which tools may (and, equally importantly, should not) be used, it is difficult to bring these two extremes together in a way that allows tools to be implemented to their – and more importantly their users' – best advantage.

To mitigate this situation, translator trainers might consider presenting the practical instructions for the use of tools in a framework that accents both background knowledge and critical thinking. For example, rather than simply adopting the tutorials provided by the tool developers, it could be useful for translator trainers to augment these by including as an introduction to each tutorial or exercise the essential information for understanding what the tool is designed to do, how it can be useful to a translator, and how it compares to some other tools or approaches. This type of information aims to help users determine whether a tool is of particular interest and to lead them to consider whether it may meet their personal needs. The tutorials and exercises could be accompanied by a series of questions for reflection on key points about the tools (e.g. user reactions to a tool and its use, comparisons to other similar tools they may have used, advantages and disadvantages compared to a manual approach and/or to using other tools, situations in which the tool might be useful). This encourages users to consider the tool at a relatively high level based on both background knowledge and practical experience rather than simply on the basis of whether they were able to accomplish a specific required task with it. This goes beyond the approach used by many others in the field, as few of the tutorials and resources that are provided by developers encourage evaluation and comparison of tools according to users' specific needs. However, these are among the most important aspects of instruction in translation technologies, and they will go a long way toward helping educators and users to manage expectations surrounding technology use in the field of translation.

Expanding and Centralizing Resources for Increased Accessibility

Another problem facing trainers is the lack of easy access to authentic complementary resources (e.g. relevant exercises, sample termbases, corpora, bitexts, sample source texts suitable for technological processing) required to introduce these tools to students and to work with them in a realistic way. Tools such as terminology management systems and translation memory systems are "empty" when first installed, and users must create relevant term records and corpora to build up the termbases and TM databases. In a similar vein, term extractors are designed to operate on corpora, but to get realistic and usable results, these corpora must be well designed and reasonably large. Designing and compiling these resources and accompanying exercises can be time consuming and labour intensive. For educators who already have a very full schedule, this additional workload can act as a deterrent, preventing them from effectively introducing computerized translation tools to students and working with them in the non-core courses.

A related challenge that may hinder the successful integration of tools into a wider range of translation courses is a lack of centralization and management of technology-related resources. All too often, tutorials, exercises, and resources developed for use with particular tools are dispersed among the various educators who create and use them and thus are not known to or available for use by others. Storing and organizing various types and versions of documents relating to different tools, as well as coordinating their use in different courses, also pose challenges for instructors. Moreover, when educators leave an institution, the resources and expertise they have developed are not always passed on to others and may be lost. As a result of these obstacles, work may be duplicated unnecessarily and overall coverage of tools and their functions may be uneven, with the risk that some elements may be covered repeatedly in different courses while others are neglected altogether, leaving students both frustrated and ill prepared with regard to tool use.

By pooling resources such as corpora, termbases, or translation memory databases and storing them in a central and easily accessible location (e.g. using a course management system or shared directory), trainers could have access to a wider range of materials to provide a more authentic and situated learning experience for their students.

Training the Trainers

It is widely recognized that a key question when contemplating a more integrated approach to technology training is whether the trainers who teach other subjects (e.g. terminology, specialized translation) are comfortable using the relevant tools. As it has been barely a quarter century since technology has really begun to permeate a wide range of translation activities, some instructors likely received their own training before technologies were incorporated into the translation curriculum in any significant way. While they are almost inevitably aware of the increasingly important role of technology in the field, they will not necessarily be familiar with the finer details of the tools and/or may not have considered how such tools could be used in teaching. It is tempting to dismiss this as a generational issue that will be resolved as senior trainers retire and are replaced by colleagues who are familiar with technologies. However, because tools are evolving rapidly and because instructors who specialize in other areas of translation may not have the time or inclination to keep up with the latest technologies, it is actually an ongoing challenge.

Nevertheless, in spite of the fact that they may not currently integrate translation tools into their teaching, many trainers are acutely aware of the benefits that such integration could bring. Many feel that they themselves would need further training to become highly proficient users (particularly of specialized software) and especially to be able to teach others. However, encouragingly, among those trainers who are not yet familiar with relevant tools, there is an obvious interest in learning. It would therefore seem that a resource for helping such educators to learn more about translation technologies would be welcome and useful. One such effort is the Collection of Electronic Resources in Translation Technologies (CERTT) project, based at the University of Ottawa in Canada. The general idea is to provide a point for "one-stop shopping" – a single centralized and relatively comprehensive resource that both instructors and students can access to find everything they need to begin using, or to facilitate or increase their use of, translation technologies as part of their academic experience (Bowker and Marshman 2010; Marshman and Bowker 2012).

In addition to the previously mentioned continuing education opportunities offered by professional associations, there has also been a noticeable trend in setting up summer schools that focus on technology training. Several institutions in both Europe and North America regularly offer specialized technology training (e.g. through summer schools) aimed more precisely at addressing this specific need for "training the trainers". Moreover, following the global COVID-19 pandemic, as more attention is being paid to offering training in an online format, there will undoubtedly be an increase in online technology training opportunities in the coming years.

The literature has also underlined a growing recognition of the benefits to be gained by universities and industry working more closely (e.g. Angelone *et al.* 2020), which could certainly include having some aspects of technology training delivered by part-time professors who also work in industry. Doherty and Kenny (2014) offer one example of an industry-academia partnership for translation technology training.

Addressing the Needs of a Wide Range of Student Learners

Once translator trainers have developed necessary resources and knowledge and feel ready to integrate these more fully into their teaching, they then face another challenge. One of the most constant and greatest challenges in teaching technologies is that students arrive in translation classes with varying degrees of technological competence. Course groups may include students with an advanced grasp of and significant experience with tools alongside those who have little experience and who may even be intimidated by information technology. Thus trainers must walk a metaphorical tightrope trying to ensure that the more technologically savvy students are not bored, while the more technologically challenged ones are not frustrated or overwhelmed. Moreover, the latter may experience considerable difficulties in courses that involve technologies, perhaps particularly when these are not the main focus of a course but rather tools intended to facilitate learning, discussion, and practice. Clearly, when students find using tools the greatest challenge in these courses, the effect is quite the opposite. In such a case, it is important for the trainer to ensure that tools-related difficulties do not become the focus of the learning situation, overshadowing the larger objective of learning to translate.

On a related note, it is clear that individuals learn differently and thus have different training preferences (Kelly 2005: 47). When learning about translation technologies, some prefer a classroom setting, others want to do exercises independently, and still others favour using documentation or videos that explain tools and their uses. Initial comfort and confidence levels may also influence the effectiveness of different learning strategies. For instance, users who initially have better general computer skills may be better able to learn to use new tools independently. Accommodating these varied learning styles and needs requires a flexible approach.

While this chapter has focused heavily on the needs of students who are preparing for a career in the language industries, it is worth taking a moment to consider that other groups are emerging who may benefit from some type of training in translation technologies. For instance, now that many machine translation systems are freely available online, a large number of people are using these tools for a wide range of purposes, for everything from researching their family history to publishing academic research in another language. Bowker (2019) has argued that translation educators have a social responsibility to help people outside the language professions to learn to use these tools critically, and Bowker (2020) reports on an experience of offering a workshop to international students through a university library in order to help these non-translation students to develop their machine translation literacy skills.

Concluding Remarks

Early users of translation technologies primarily had to come to grips with understanding and applying them as quickly as possible, often without any formal instruction. Meanwhile, translator trainers had to contend with developing expertise, designing methodologies, and preparing curricula and resources required to teach these tools. Even today, there are numerous challenges to be faced by educators as they seek to comprehensively organize, categorize, and contextualize the bewildering and evolving array of tools and technologies available to translation professionals. The diverse approaches to overcoming these challenges reflect the diverse backgrounds and circumstances of the trainers, as well as shifting societal norms and the state of flux that characterizes technology development in general.

The integration of new tools into courses will always require preparation and effort on the part of trainers. In addition, technical difficulties cannot be avoided completely. However, it is much better for students to begin to come to grips with new technologies and their associated challenges during their studies rather than waiting until they enter the high-volume, high-stress environment of today's professional workplace. Students who begin their careers with established and tested translation practices that work for them are better prepared to continue these good practices in their professional life. Moreover, the literature highlights the fact that students who have already developed basic skills are more likely to be able to adapt easily to new tools and situations (e.g. to a new tool used by an employer or client). By allowing students to become more familiar and more comfortable with CAT and MT tools gradually and by giving them access to a range of tools throughout their program of studies, students should be able to significantly improve comfort levels with technologies and knowledge of the field and also develop better and more realistic translation practices throughout their training.

Finally, by encouraging a fuller integration of technologies in the academic life of students and trainers, we hope the a translator training program will better reflect current practice in the translation field today, including the necessary integration of effective CAT and MT tool use into the translator's day-to-day work. As pointed out by Kiraly (2000: 13), there is a difference between helping students to develop "translation competence", which gives them the skills to produce an acceptable target text in one language on the basis of a text written in another, and aiding them in the acquisition of "translator competence", which also involves assisting them with the development of a host of other skills, including proficiency in new technologies. In the words of Kiraly (2000: 13–14):

> Translator competence does not primarily refer to knowing *the* correct translation for words, sentences or even texts. It does entail being able to use tools and information to create communicatively successful texts that are accepted as good translations within the community concerned. . . . With the changes in the translation profession in mind, it is time to reconsider the viability of conventional approaches for educating translators, which date back almost half a century, when the translation profession was something altogether different from what it is today.

Bibliography

American Translators Association (ATA) (2022). Available at: www.atanet.org/.

Angelone, Erik, Maureen Ehrensberger-Dow, and Gary Massey (eds.) (2020) *The Bloomsbury Companion to the Language Industry Studies*, London: Bloomsbury.

Bowker, Lynne (2005) 'Productivity vs Quality? A Pilot Study on the Impact of Translation Memory Systems', *Localisation Focus* 4(1): 13–20.

Bowker, Lynne (2019) 'Machine Translation Literacy as a Social Responsibility', in Gilles Adda, Khalid Choukri, Irmgada Kasinskaite-Buddeberg, Joseph Mariani, Hélène Mazo, and Sakti Sakriani (eds.) *Proceedings of the First International Conference on Language Technology for All (LT4All)*, Paris: UNESCO/ELDA, 104–07.

Bowker, Lynne (2020) 'Machine Translation Literacy Instruction for International Business Students and Business English Instructors', *Journal of Business and Finance Librarianship* 25(1): 25–43.

Bowker, Lynne (2021) 'Translation Technology and Ethics', in Kaisa Koskinen and Nike K. Pokorn (eds.) *The Routledge Handbook of Translation and Ethics*, London: Routledge, 263–78.

Bowker, Lynne and Jairo Buitrago Ciro (2019) *Machine Translation and Global Research: Towards Improved Machine Translation Literacy in the Scholarly Community*, Bingley: Emerald.

Bowker, Lynne and Elizabeth Marshman (2010) 'Toward a Model of Active and Situated Learning in the Teaching of Computer-aided Translation: Introducing the CERTT Project', *Journal of Translation Studies* 13(1–2): 199–226.

Bowker, Lynne and Jennifer Pearson (2002) *Working with Specialized Language: A Practical Guide to Using Corpora*, London: Routledge.

Buysschaert, Joost, María Fernández-Parra, Koen Kerremans, Maarit Koponen and Gys-Walt van Egdom (2018) 'Embracing Digital Disruption in Translator Training: Technology Immersion in Simulated Translation Bureaus', *Revista Tradumàtica* 16: 125–33.

Castilho, Sheila, Joss Moorkens, Federico Gaspari, Iacer Calixto, John Tinsley and Andy Way (2017) 'Is Neural Machine Translation the New State of the Art?', *Prague Bulletin of Mathematical Linguistics* 108: 109–20.

Desjardins, Renée (2017) *Translation and Social Media*, Basingstoke: Palgrave Macmillan.

Díaz-Cintas, Jorge (2008) *The Didactics of Audiovisual Translation*, Amsterdam: John Benjamins.

Dillon, Sarah and Janet Fraser (2006) 'Translators and TM: An Investigation of Translators' Perceptions of Translation Memory Adoption', *Machine Translation* 20(2): 67–79.

Doherty, Stephen and Dorothy Kenny (2014) 'The Design and Evaluation of a Statistical Machine Translation Syllabus for Translation Students', *The Interpreter and Translator Trainer* 8(2): 295–315.

Drugan, Joanna (2019) 'Ethics', in Piers Rawling and Philip Wilson (eds.) *The Routledge Handbook of Translation and Philosophy*, London: Routledge, 243–55.

European Commission Directorate-General for Translation (EC-DGT) (2022) 'European Master's in Translation Competence Framework 2022'. Available at: https://ec.europa.eu/info/sites/default/files/about_the_european_commission/service_standards_and_principles/documents/emt_competence_fwk_2022_en.pdf.

European Commission Directorate-General for Translation (EC-DGT) (2021) 'European Master's in Translation (EMT) Explained'. Available at: https://ec.europa.eu/info/resources-partners/european-masters-translation-emt/european-masters-translation-emt-explained_en.

Fantinuoli, Claudio and Bianca Prandi (2018) 'Teaching Information and Communication Technologies: A Proposal for the Interpreting Classroom', *Trans-kom* 11(2): 162–82.

Guerberof Arenas, Ana and Joss Moorkens (2019) 'Machine Translation and Post-Editing Training as Part of a Master's Programme', *JoSTrans: Journal of Specialised Translation* 31: 217–38.

Institute of Translation and Interpreting (ITI) (2022) Available at: www.iti.org.uk/.

Jiménez-Crespo, Miguel A. (2013) *Translation and Web Localization*, London: Routledge.

Kappus, Martin and Maureen Ehrensberger-Dow (2020) 'The Ergonomics of Translation Tools: Understanding When Less is More', *The Interpreter and Translator Trainer* 14(4): 386–404.

Kelly, Dorothy (2005) *A Handbook for Translator Trainers*, Manchester: St. Jerome Publishing.

Kenny, Dorothy (2020) 'Technology and Translator Training', in Minako O'Hagan (ed.) *The Routledge Handbook of Translation and Technology*, London: Routledge, 498–515.

Kiraly, Don (2000) *A Social Constructivist Approach to Translator Education*, Manchester: St. Jerome Publishing.

Marshman, Elizabeth and Lynne Bowker (2012) 'Translation Technologies as Seen Through the Eyes of Educators and Students: Harmonizing Views with the Help of a Centralized Teaching and Learning Resource', in Séverine Hubscher-Davidson and Michal Borodo (eds.) *Global Trends in Translator and Interpreter Training: Mediation and Culture*, London and New York: Continuum, 69–95.

Massey, Gary and Maureen Ehrensberger-Dow (2017) 'Machine Learning: Implications for Translator Education', *Lebende Sprachen* 62(2): 300–12.

Mellinger, Christopher (2017) 'Translators and Machine Translation: Knowledge and Skills Gaps in Translator Pedagogy', *The Interpreter and Translator Trainer* 11(4): 280–93.

Mitchell-Schuitevoerder, Rosemary (2020) *A Project-based Approach to Translation Technology*, London: Routledge.

O'Hagan, Minako and Carmen Mangiron (2013) *Game Localization*, Amsterdam: John Benjamins.

SDL (2016) 'SDL Translation Technology Insights'. Available at: www.sdltrados.com/landing/lsp/Translation-Technology-Insight.html.

Zapata, Julián and Jean Quirion (2016) 'La traduction dictée interactive et sa nécessaire intégration à la formation des traducteurs', *Babel* 62(4): 531–51.

5

MACHINE TRANSLATION

General

Liu Qun and Zhang Xiaojun

Definition: Machine Translation

Machine translation (MT) is a sub-field of computational linguistics (CL) or natural language processing (NLP) that investigates the use of software to translate text or speech from one natural language to another. The central core of MT itself is the automation of the full translation process, which is different from related terms such as machine-aided human translation (MAHT), human-aided machine translation (HAMT) and computer-aided translation (CAT).

History

1950s and 1960s: Pioneers

The idea of MT may be traced back to the 17th century (Hutchins and Somers 1992: 5). In 1629, René Descartes proposed an idea of universal language to share one symbol in different tongues. The possibilities of using computers to translate natural languages were proposed as early as 1947 by Warren Weaver of the Rockefeller Foundation and Andrew D. Booth, a British scientist. In the next two years, Weaver was urged by his colleagues to elaborate on his ideas. In 1949, he wrote a memorandum entitled "Translation" which concludes his four proposals and assumptions on mechanical translation: (1) the problem of multiple meaning might be tackled by examinations of immediate contexts, (2) there may be logical features common in all languages, (3) the cryptographic methods concerned with the basic statistical properties of communication can be applied in mechanical translation and (4) there may be linguistic universals. These proposals were practiced and realized by successors completely or partially, and each proposal was regarded as an important approach in later MT studies.

Yehoshua Bar-Hillel was one of the successors and practitioners. He was appointed as the first full-time researcher in MT by Massachusetts Institute of Technology (MIT) in 1951. One year later, he convened the first MT conference at MIT to outline the future research on MT clearly. The MIT conference in 1952 brought together those who had contact with MT and who might have a future interest. Two years later, on 8 January 1954, the first public demonstration of an MT system was reported by US newspapers. In the report, the demonstration system used only 250 words and six grammar rules to translate 49 Russian sentences into English, and it achieved success. It was the result of a joint project by IBM staff and members of the Institute

DOI: 10.4324/9781003168348-6

of Linguistics at Georgetown University. The IBM-Georgetown demonstration had attracted a great deal of attention, which was impressive to stimulate the large-scale funding of MT research in the United States and the world. It marked the beginning of MT as a reality from the idea of the use of computer to translate proposed by Weaver seven years earlier.

After the 1954 demonstration, MT study became a 'multimillion dollar affair' in the United States. The decade from 1956 to 1966 filled with high expectations to MT. The emergence of electronic brains created all kinds of expectations in people and institutions, and some researchers hoped to solve the problem of MT early on. More and more major funding went into the field. Under sufficient funding, various methods were tried in MT research. By the mid-1960s, MT research groups had been established in many countries throughout the world, including most European countries (Germany, France, Hungary, Czechoslovakia, Bulgaria and Belgium), China, Mexico and Japan, as well as the United States. Unfortunately, most of them set on a misguided and unattainable goal of MT research, fully automatic high-quality (FAHQ) translation.

Mid-1960s: The ALPAC Report

Optimism dominated MT research in the 1950s because of rising expectations. Developments in formal linguistics such as syntax seemed to ensure great improvement in translation quality. However, disillusion caused by 'semantic barriers' grew as the complexity of the linguistic problems became more and more apparent and researchers saw no straightforward solutions.

In 1959, Bar-Hillel proposed his second survey report on MT research, questioning the goals and expectations of the whole field of MT research. In 1960, he revised the report and published it in the journal *Advances in Computers*, where he was highly critical of any MT group that declared FAHQ translation its long-term aim. He suggested that MT should adopt less ambitious goals but more cost-effective use of man–machine interaction. But the report was read only within MT, circles and it was relatively unnoticed. The validity of Bar-Hillel's argument was not seen until the release of the Automatic Language Processing Advisory Committee (ALPAC) report six years later.

In 1964, the National Academy of Sciences of the United States formed ALPAC to examine the prospects of MT research. The famous report released two years later showed, among other things, that MT output was not cheaper or faster than full human translation, with the conclusion that "there is no immediate or predicable prospect of useful machine translation". The committee suggested that funding should rather go into basic linguistic research and the development of methods to improve human translation, for there was no advantage in using MT systems. Funding for MT in the United States stopped almost entirely as a consequence. While the ALPAC report may have unfairly considered only the goal of high-quality translation, it shows the dangers of over-promising the abilities of MT systems. The ALPAC report was widely regarded as narrow, biased and short-sighted. It also misjudged the economics of the computer-based translation industry.

Fortunately, the negative impact of the ALPAC report did not stop research in other countries. MT research stepped into a quiet decade after the release of the ALPAC report in 1966.

1970s: Revival

One of the reasons for the strong negative attitude of the ALPAC report to MT was translation needs. In the United States, the main activity had concentrated on English translation of Russian scientific and technical materials. With the worsening of relationship between the United States and Soviet Union in the Cold War, the requirement of translation between English and Russian was changed. However, in Canada and Europe, the translation needs were quite different. To the Canadian government, English–French translation was required to meet the demand of its bicultural policy. For the European countries, there were growing demands for translation from and into all European Community languages. Therefore, the focus of MT activity switched from the United States to Canada and Europe in the 1970s.

In Montreal in Canada, a project named Traduction Automatique à l'Université de Montréal (TAUM) generated two MT systems: Q-system and Météo system. Q-system formalized a computational metalanguage for manipulating linguistic strings and trees in natural language processing. Météo system translated weather forecasts at close to 80,000 words per day or 30 million words per year. Météo has been successfully doing this job since 1976, and it was designed for the restricted vocabulary and limited syntax of meteorological reports.

Between 1960 and 1971, the group at Grenoble University in France established by Bernard Vauquois developed an interlingua system CETA for translating Russian into French. An interlingua, namely "pivot language", was used at the grammatical level (Slocum 1985: 1–17).

Russian MT research was greatly affected by Igor Mel'čuk's meaning-text model (Kahane 2003: 546–69), which was an ambitious interlingua system that combined a stratificational dependency approach with a strong emphasis on lexicographic aspects of an interlingua.

The United States MT research was also revived from the mid-1970s. The Linguistics Research Center (LRC) at Texas adopted a similar model of "pivot language" in its METAL system. Another famous system, Systran, was founded in 1968. The Russian–English system has been used by the US Air Force since 1970. A French–English version was bought by the European Commission in 1976, and thereafter systems for more European language pairs were developed. The Xerox Corporation used Systran to translate technical manuals starting in 1978. There is another long-established system named Logos, which was an English–Vietnamese system for translating aircraft manuals during the 1970s. The Logos system was based on a direct translation approach. The Pan American Health Organization in Washington has successfully developed and widely used two systems for translating Spanish to English and back since the 1970s.

1980s and 1990s: Diversity

Research from the 1980s had three main strands: (1) transfer systems, (2) new kinds of interlingua systems and (3) corpus-based MT research.

The Grenoble group began development of the second-generation linguistic-based transfer system Ariane in the 1980s. Different from the previous pivot language tree, the Ariane system could incorporate different levels and types of representation on single labelled tree structures. Ariane did not become an operational system and ceased in the late 1980s but became part of the Eurolang project in the 1990s, and the Grenoble team has continued MT research in this project.

The Mu system was developed at the University of Kyoto under Makoto Nagao in the 1980s. The features of the Mu system were case grammar analysis; dependency tree presentation; and GRADE, a programming environment for grammar writing (Nagao and Tsujii 1986: 97–103). Since 1986, the Mu system has been converted into an operational system in practice.

From the mid-1970s to the late 1980s, the group at Saarbrücken (Germany) developed SUSY. It was a highly modular multilingual transfer system focusing on the in-depth treatment of inflected languages such as Russian and German (Maas 1977: 582–92). The Eurotra project of European Community in the 1980s aimed to construct an advanced multilingual transfer system for translation among all the European Community languages. It was designed to combine lexical, logical syntactic information and semantic information in different level interfaces. In that period, Eurotra was regarded as the best linguistics-based design (de Roeck 1981: 298–303).

There was a general revival of interest in interlingua systems during the latter half of the 1980s. Some groups used knowledge-based methods from research on artificial intelligence

(AI). The DLT system was a leader of development in this field in the 1990s (Witkam 1988: 756–59). It was a multilingual interactive system operating over computer networks with each terminal as a translating machine from and into one language only. Its interlingua was a modified form of Esperanto. Another interlingua project was Rosetta (Landsbergn 1982: 175–81), which explored the use of Montague grammar in interlingual representations. After the Mu system, MT research in Japan showed a wide variety of approaches. The PIVOT system from NEC was a typical interlingua system which was available commercially (Muraki 1987: 113–15). The LUTE project of NTT was a knowledge-based experiment (Nomura *et al.* 1985: 621–26). Investigations of AI methods in MT research began in the mid-1970s focusing on preference semantics and semantic templates. Roger Schank at Yale University later developed an expert system for text "understanding" (Schank and Abelson 1977). The KANT prototype system of the Carnegie-Mellon team was designed as "meaning-oriented MT in an interlingua paradigm" to translate computer manuals for English and Japanese in both directions (Nyberg III and Mitamura 1992: 1069–73). The core of the system was the interlingual representation form of networks of propositions.

Rule-based machine translation (RBMT) research has continued in both transfer and interlingua systems since 1990. The CAT2 system at Saarbrücken (Sharp 1988) and PaTrans transfer system in Denmark (Orsnes *et al.* 1996: 1115–18) were two fruits of the Eurotra project. The Eurolang project developed ten language pairs between English, French, German, Italian and Spanish and produced a translator's workstation, Optimizer (Seite *et al.* 1992: 1289–93). Another remarkable European MT project, LMT stood for 'logic programming MT' and implemented translation in Prolog in combination with a lexical approach. In 1994, LMT was sold to IBM to be modules of TranslationManager/2. CATALYST at Carnegie-Mellon University, ULTRA at New Mexico State University and UNITRAN at the University of California were all rule-based domain-adopted interlingual systems in the 1990s.

Since the end of the 1980s, the dominance of linguistic rules-based approaches was broken by the appearance of new corpus-based methods and strategies. First, an IBM research group purely based on statistical methods developed an MT system, which paved the way to statistical machine translation (SMT). Second, a Japanese group sought methods on translation examples, namely example-based machine translation (EBMT).

In 1988, with the development of speech recognition, the IBM group with the Candide project began to look for the application of statistics in MT. Their research was based on the vast French and English texts of Canadian parliamentary debate reports to align phrases, word groups and individual words and calculate the probabilities that any segment in the source language corresponded to the segment in the aligned target language. The results were acceptable. To improve the results, the IBM group proposed introducing more sophisticated statistical methods in the 1990s (Vogel *et al.* 1996: 836–41; Och and Ney 2003: 19–51).

Example-based experiments were begun at the end of the 1980s. Makoto Nagao had first proposed this idea in 1984. An underlying assumption was that translation often involves the finding or recalling of analogous examples. The example-based approach extracted and selected the equivalent aligned translation segments from a parallel corpus as examples in the translation process (Nagao 1984: 173–80).

2000s and Early 2010s: Dominance of Statistical Machine Translation

SMT systems were being developed in a large number of academic and commercial systems. IBM Research pioneered the research on SMT, in particular word-based SMT methods based on the IBM Model 1–5 (Brown *et al.* 1993: 263–313), which also provide the theoretical basis for word alignment, which is fundamental to all other SMT methods. The modern statistical phrase-based models are rooted in works by Franz Och and his colleagues (Och and Weber 1998: 985–89; Och *et al.* 1999: 20–28; Och 2002; Och and Ney 2004: 417–47) and based on later works by Philipp Koehn and his colleagues (Koehn *et al.* 2003: 48–54). Various syntax-based models were proposed and researched to utilize syntax information in translation. Typical syntax-based models include inverse transduction grammar (Wu 1995: 1328–35), hierarchical phrase-based models (Chiang 2005: 265–70, 2007: 201–28), string-to-tree models (Galley *et al.* 2004: 273–80; Galley *et al.* 2006: 961–68) and tree-to-string models (Liu *et al.* 2006: 609–16; Huang *et al.* 2006: 66–73).

Open source tools are broadly used in the SMT research community. GIZA++ is an implementation of the IBM word-based models and hidden Markov model (HMM), and it is commonly used for word alignment. The code was developed at a Johns Hopkins University summer workshop and later refined by Och and Ney (Al-Onaizan *et al.* 1999; Och and Ney 2000: 440–47). Moses is an implementation of a phrase-based decoder, including training. It was developed at the University of Edinburgh and also enhanced during a Johns Hopkins University summer workshop (Koehn *et al.* 2007: 177–80).

MT evaluation is another highlight of MT research in the new century. Many automatic MT metrics have been proposed and broadly used in MT research. The National Institute of Standards and Technology (NIST) evaluation is the oldest and most prestigious open evaluation campaign. The International Workshop on Spoken Language Translation (IWSLT) evaluation campaign has a stronger focus on speech translation. The Workshop on Machine Translation (WMT) evaluation campaign targets translation between European languages. These campaigns also generate standard test sets, manual evaluation data and reference performance numbers (Koehn 2010).

Mid-2010s Onwards: Paradigm Shift to Neural Machine Translation

Along with the great success deep learning (DL) obtained in image and speech processing, researchers had increasing interest in applying DL technologies in NLP tasks, typically MT.

There was a short period in which researchers endeavoured to leverage DL to improve the capacity of the main components of SMT such as translation models, reordering models and language models (Devlin *et al.* 2014: 1370–80). Shortly after that period, end-to-end (E2E) neural machine translation (NMT) (Sutskever *et al.* 2014; Bahdanau *et al.* 2015), which uses neural networks to directly map between source and target languages based on an encoder–decoder or transformer framework, quickly become the mainstream MT technology both in the research community and on the market. Unlike in SMT, where multiple components are trained separately in a pipeline manner, all the components are trained together with a single loss function in E2E NMT.

NMT is a totally new paradigm compared with SMT, although it still follows the data-driven approach. In NMT, words are first converted to numerical vectors and fed to a neural network. Then all the computing happens in a continuous numerical space rather than the symbolic space represented by linguistic units of words, phrases, sentences and so on. Only in the final decoding step are target words are generated from the hidden states, as well as continuous vectors of neural networks. Due to the massive use of vector or tensor operations in neural network training and inference, the most popular hardware to run NMT systems are devices with chips like graphics processing units (GPUs) rather than traditional CPUs.

Although still suffering from problems like low-resource training data in specific language pairs and domains, hallucination and so on, NMT outperforms previous MT methods significantly. It even achieves "human parity" (Hassan *et al.* 2018) in certain scenarios.

Approaches

Vauquois's Triangle

MT approaches can be categorized by the depth of intermediary representations used in translation process: direct, transfer and interlingua, which are often depicted by Vauquois's Triangle (1968: 254–60).

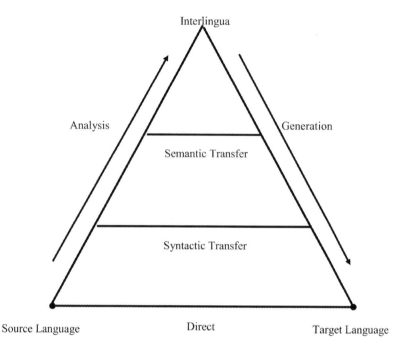

Figure 5.1 Vauquois's Triangle

In this triangle, the transfer approach is subcategorized to a syntactic transfer approach and semantic transfer approach.

Direct

In the direct approach, the target language sentence is translated directly from the source word sequence, possibly with analysis in certain individual linguistic phenomena. No general syntactic or semantic analysis is conducted, and the most (even only) important resource for this approach is a dictionary. That is the reason it is also called a dictionary-based approach.

Transfer

In the transfer approach, intermediary structures are defined for both source and target languages. The translation process is divided into three phases: analysis from the source language sentence to the source intermediary structure, transfer from the source intermediary structure to the target intermediary structure and generation from the target intermediary structure to the target sentence.

Independent analysis means the characteristics of the target language are not considered in the analysis phrase, which will lead to a source intermediary structure which can be used for MT into various target languages. Independent generation means the characteristics of the source language are not considered in the generation phrase, that is to say, the target intermediary structure can be used for MT from various source languages.

In the syntactic transfer approach, the transfer process mainly occurs at the syntactic level. Thus the system may have components of morphological analysis, syntactic analysis, syntactic transfer, syntactic generation and morphological generation.

In the semantic transfer approach, the transfer process mainly occurs at the semantic level. Accordingly, the system may have components of morphological analysis, syntactic analysis, semantic analysis, semantic transfer, semantic generation, syntactic generation and morphological generation.

Interlingua

In the interlingua approach, a universal representation is defined for all the source and target languages. The translation process only contains two phrases: analysis and generation. The interlingual approach is regarded as an appropriate method for multilingual MT because it dramatically reduces the number of components compared with those needed in the direct or transfer approach. An interlingua can be a structured representation such as a logic expression, a semantic network, a knowledge representation and so on, or an artificial or natural language representation. It is also called a knowledge-based approach (Nirenburg 1989: 5–24; Carbonell *et al.* 1978) when a knowledge representation is used as an interlingua. An interlingua is also called a pivot language, a meta-language or a bridge language. Practices in some large-scale projects showed that an interlingua approach using a human-defined presentation may encounter uncontrollable complexity when many languages are involved (Nagao 1989; Patel-Schneider 1989: 319–51). Web-based translation services such as Google Translate, Bing Translator and so on usually adopt English as a pivot language to support MT between tens of other languages.

Other terms used for categorizing MT approaches include rule-based, example-based, statistical and hybrid MT.

Rule-Based

A RBMT system uses rules to direct the process of MT. In a RBMT system, rules are encoded by experts with their linguistic insights. Although the automatically extracted rules are also used in some EBMT or SMT approaches, they are not RBMT approach because they do not use human-encoded rules. In a RBMT system, rules may be used in all the components. Table 5.1

Table 5.1 Rules used in a RBMT system adopting a semantic transfer approach

Analysis	Morphological Analysis	Source Morphological Rules
	Syntactic Analysis (Parsing)	Source Grammar
	Semantic Analysis	Source Semantic Rules
Transfer	Lexical Transfer	Bilingual Lexicon
	Syntactic Transfer	Syntactic Mapping Rules
	Semantic Transfer	Semantic Mapping Rules
Generation	Semantic Generation	Target Semantic Rules
	Syntactic Generation	Target Grammar
	Morphological Generation	Target Morphological Rules

lists the components and corresponding rules used in a typical RBMT system adopting a semantic transfer approach:

Not all these components and rules are necessary for a practical RBMT system. Some of them may be omitted or merged, depending on the specific language pairs or the algorithms used. Also, it is possible to have additional components or rule bases for a specific purpose.

The rule-based paradigm provides a mechanism for linguists and computer scientists working together to develop a MT system: computer scientists can focus on algorithm design and implementation, while linguistic experts on construction of rule bases and lexicons. The development of a RBMT system is time consuming and labour intensive, and that of a commercial RBMT system may take several years. Human-encoded rules suffer from the low coverage of linguistic phenomena and conflicts between rules, which leads to unsatisfied translation quality when handling large-scale real-life texts.

Example-Based

In an EBMT system, a sentence is translated by analogy (Nagao 1984: 173–80). A number of existing translation pairs of source and target sentences are used as examples, which is also called a parallel corpus. When a new source sentence is to be translated, examples are retrieved to find similar ones on the source side to match. Then the target sentence is generated by imitating the translation of the matched examples. Because the hit rate for long sentences is very low, usually the examples and the source sentence are broken down into small fragments. Word alignment is necessary between the source and target examples so that the correspondent target part can be located when only a part of the source example is matched. The typical process of EBMT includes the following phases: (1) Example retrieval: Indexing on examples should be built for fast retrieval on large number of examples against the input source sentence. Fuzzy match or partial match should be supported in example retrieval. (2) Source sentence decomposing: The input source sentence is decomposed into fragments to match example fragments or lexicon entries. (3) Fragment translation: Each matched source fragment is translated according the word alignment between source and target examples. (4) Target sentence recombination: The translation of the source fragments are assembled into the target sentence. It is very common to introduce a syntactic parser in the EBMT approach (Sato and Nagao 1990: 247–52). In such a case, an example fragment may be a sub-tree of a syntactic structure instead of a word sequence.

EBMT provides a technique to improve translation quality by increasing the size of the corpus only and to obtain natural output sentences without deep analysis on the source side. EBMT may result in a high-quality translation when high-similarity examples are found. On the contrary, when there is no example found with high similarity, the translation quality may be very low.

Memory-based MT is also called the translation memory (TM) approach, which is broadly used in CAT. TM is a sentence-aligned parallel corpus which is usually accumulated by the user him/herself. When a new source sentence is to be translated, the TM is searched, and if there are one or more sentences matched with higher similarity than a certain threshold, the aligned target sentence of the most similar source sentence in the translation memory will be output without any modification. The memory-based approach provides a reference translation for every source sentence, and the output must be post-edited if the source sentence is not matched with 100% similarity or the post-editor does not satisfy the output translation at all. The TM approach is regarded as a special case of EBMT.

Statistical

The basic idea of SMT (Brown *et al.* 1990: 79–85; Brown *et al.* 1993: 263–313; Koehn and Knight 2009) is to mathematically model the probability of a target sentence being the translation of a given source sentence $P(T|S)$, which is called a translation model. Once the translation model is defined and implemented, the problem of translating a source sentence into a target sentence is converted to searching a target sentence with the highest translation probability $\hat{T} = \mathrm{argmax}\ P(T\ |\ S)$. Such a searching process is decoding. For a given translation model, its parameters can be obtained from a given parallel in a training process.

A translation model is usually decomposed to several specific models under a certain framework to model the translation probability in different aspects.

An early framework is the source channel model (Brown *et al.* 1990: 79–85). In this model, first a target sentence is generated by an information source described by a language model $P(T)$; then the target sentence is transmitted through an information channel described by a reverse translation model $P(S|T)$, and finally the source sentence is output. With the source sentence observed, decoding can be viewed as a search process of finding the optimal target sentence $\hat{T} = \mathrm{argmax}_S\ P(T)P(S\ |\ T)$. The main contribution of the source channel model is introducing the language model to SMT. While the translation model ensures source and target sentences with the same meaning, the language model guarantees the target sentence is fluent.

A more general framework is the log-linear model (Och and Ney 2002: 295–302). In this model, the translation probability is defined as a log-linear combination based on a set of feature functions:

$$P(T\ |\ S) = \frac{\exp\left(\sum_i \lambda_i h_i(S,T)\right)}{\sum_{T'} \exp\left(\sum_i \lambda_i h_i(S,T')\right)}$$

where $h_i(S,T)$ is an arbitrary real function defined on source sentence S and target sentence T, and the denominator is a constant for normalization. Thus the decoding can be viewed as a search process to find a target sentence with the highest translation probability $\hat{T} = \mathrm{argmax}_T \sum_i \lambda_i h_i(S,T)$.

The log-linear framework takes the source channel framework as a special case, where there are only two features, log $P(T)$ and log $P(S\ |\ T)$, and the parameters are both equal to 1. In a log-linear model, the parameter i can be obtained in the process of tuning against a specific target function on the provided development data without overlapping with the training data. Features usually include one or more language models, translation models, reordering models, the length of the output sentence, lexicon features and so on. The log-linear model provides the possibility to incorporate any useful features in MT and to balance the effectiveness of all the features by tuning the parameters discriminatively.

Language models and translation models are the most important models in SMT. The most commonly used language model is the n-gram model. Translation models can be classified into several different formalisms depending on the language units used: word-based models, phrase-based models and syntax-based models.

Word-based models calculate sentence translation probability based on word-to-word translation tables. IBM Models 1–5 (Brown *et al.* 1993: 263–313) are typical word-based translation models with increasing complexity. IBM Model 1 only considers word-to-word translation probabilities, while the later models introduce more sophisticated factors, such as distortion probability, which characterizes word reordering, and fertilization probability, which depicts one-to-many mappings between words. IBM models can be trained on a sentence-aligned corpus using an expectation-maximization (EM) algorithm which results in the model parameters as well as the word alignment on the training corpus. HMM is an improved version of IBM Model 2 which models the distortion probability as a hidden Markov chain (Vogel *et al.* 1996: 836–41).

Phrase-based models (Och 2002; Koehn *et al.* 2003: 48–54) are built based on phrase tables which record phrase-to-phrase translation probabilities. Phrase-based models can capture the local context while translating a word and thus outperform word-based models significantly. However, phrase-based models fail to capture long-distance dependency.

Syntax-based models are built based on synchronized grammars. Rule tables are used to record the probabilities of synchronized syntax rules. A translation rule consists of a source rule, a target rule, and a correspondence between variables in source and target rules. There are many formalisms for syntax-based models depending on the characters of syntax information utilized: some of them, such as stochastic bracketing inverse transduction grammar (Wu 1995: 1328–35) and the hierarchical phrase-based model (Chiang 2005: 263–70), do not use linguistic syntax labels; others use linguistic syntax labels in source side (e.g. tree-to-string model) (Liu *et al.* 2006: 609–16; Huang *et al.* 2006: 66–73), target side (e.g. string-to-tree model) (Galley *et al.* 2004: 273–80; Galley *et al.* 2006: 961–68) or both sides (e.g. tree-to-tree model). Syntax-based models can capture long-distance dependencies between words and perform better than phrase-based models on language pairs with very different syntax structures.

Training of language models is on a monolingual corpus while that of translation models is on a parallel corpus. Word-based models (IBM Models 1–5 and HMM) can be trained directly from a sentence-aligned corpus using EM algorithms, and the model parameters and the word alignments will be generated in the same time (Brown *et al.* 1993: 263–313). The training processes of phrase-based models and syntax-based models are based on the word alignments generated by word-based models, which are also called phrase extraction (Koehn *et al.* 2003: 48–54) and rule extraction (Galley *et al.* 2006: 941–68), respectively.

Decoding is searching an optimal target sentence from the space of all possible target sentences for a given sentence. The stack search algorithm is the most commonly used algorithm for decoding in SMT, where partial translation candidates are grouped in different stacks and a threshold is used for each stack to prune low-possibility candidates. The decoding algorithm is closely related to the utilized translation model. For word-based and phrase-based models, the decoding usually runs in a left-to-right style, which means the words in the target sentence are generated from left to right, while for syntax-based models, it goes in a bottom–up style, which means the small pieces of target sentences are generated first and large pieces are merged from these small pieces.

Tuning is training the parameters for the log-linear model in a development data set, which is usually in the same domain as the test data. The parameters are tuned to obtain the best score with regard to certain automatic evaluation metrics in the development data. The minimal error rate training (MERT) (Och 2003: 160–67) algorithm is the most commonly used tuning algorithm. Other tuning algorithms are also proposed to improve the performance when a large number of features are used.

Neural

NMT aims to directly map natural languages using neural networks. Compared with SMT, NMT is capable of learning representations from data without the need to design features to capture translation regularities manually. To address the problem of long sentence sparsity, Sutskever *et al.* (2014) propose using a Recurrent Neural Network (RNN) to encode the source context into a vector representation. However, this may make it difficult for neural networks to deal with long-distance dependencies, and the translation quality of the original encoder-decoder framework decreases significantly with the increase of sentence length. To address this problem, Bahdanau *et al.* (2015) introduce an attention mechanism to dynamically select relevant source context for generating a target word. The basic idea of attention is to find relevant source context for target word generation. The major difference of attention-based NMT from the original encoder-decoder framework is the way to calculate source context. The latter only uses the last source hidden state to initialize the first target hidden state. It is unclear how the source context controls the generation of target words, especially for words near the end of long sentences. In contrast, the attention mechanism enables each source word to contribute to the generation of a target word according to attention weight regardless of the position of the target word. This strategy proves very effective in improving translation quality, especially for long sentences. Therefore, the attention-based approach has become the *de facto* approach in NMT.

The introduction of Transformers (Vaswani *et al.* 2017: 5998–6008) brought NTM to an ever higher level compared with the RNN-based method. First, in a Transformer, all the words are connected with each other directly, which further alleviates the problems brought by long-distance dependencies. Second, a Transformer can better leverage the power of GPUs by updating the hidden states for all the words in parallel rather than sequentially. The key idea of a Transformer is self-attention, where the strength of the connection between two words is calculated dynamically based on the representation of the two words. Due to these advantages, Transformers gradually became a standard neural structure for NMT.

The success of NMT greatly expanded the research community as well as the scope of MT research. Topics like multilingual translation, low-resource translation, unsupervised translation, document-level translation, non-autoregressive translation, speech translation, simultaneous translation, multimodal translation and so on have attracted much more attention than in the SMT era and achieved significant progress.

Quality Evaluation and Estimation

MT evaluation refers to assessing a MT system from various aspects, where translation quality is its main concern.

Human Evaluation

Human evaluation is the most reliable method for MT quality evaluation. It can be divided into: (1) scoring-based human evaluation: Human evaluators are asked to score each system's outputs sentence by sentence, and the average score on all the sentences and evaluators is the final score of a system. The most common metrics for human scoring are adequacy and fluency. Adequacy reflects how much meaning of the source sentence is conveyed in the target sentence, while fluency measures to what degree the target sentence is smooth idiomatically and grammatically. (2) Rank-based human evaluation: Human evaluators are asked to rank the results of the same sentence given by part or all of the system. An overall ranking of all systems is finally generated by synthesizing all the human assessments. (3) Post–edit-based human evaluation: Human post-editors are asked to post-edit all the results given by every sentence. Finally a human translation edit rate (HTER) (Snover *et al.* 2006: 223–31) is calculated for each system based on the system results and post-edited correspondences. (4) Direct assessment (DA): DA assesses the quality of MT by crowd-sourcing segment-level evaluations (Graham *et al.* 2015: 1183–91; Graham *et al.* 2016: 3124–34). It achieves a better inter-annotator agreement, reproducibility and consistency compared to the previous methods. (5) Multidimensional quality metrics (MQM)

(Lommel *et al.* 2015; Freitag *et al.* 2021: 1460–74): MQM provides a hierarchical framework with various types of translation errors which can be tailored to different application scenarios.

Automatic Evaluation

Human evaluation is expensive and time consuming and is not suitable for frequent use during research and development. Various automatic evaluation methods are proposed. Word error rate (WER) is defined based on the Levenshtein distance between the system output and the reference translation. Position-independent error rate (PER) calculates the word error rate by treating the sentence as a bag of words and ignoring the word order. TER (translation error rate) (Snover *et al.* 2006: 223–31) considers the shift operation in addition to the insertion, deletion and substitution operations used in WER. BLEU (Papineni *et al.* 2002: 311–18) computes the n-gram precision rather than word error rate against multiple references and has become the most commonly used metric to evaluate machine translation. METEOR (metric for evaluation of translation with explicit ordering) (Banerjee and Lavie 2005: 65–72; Lavie and Agarwal 2007: 228–31) takes further consideration of stemming and synonyms for evaluation. Diagnostic metrics (Yu 1993: 117–26; Zhou *et al.* 2008: 1121–28) calculate correctness on a number of linguistic check-points that are pre-defined and distributed in the test sentences rather than the score of each sentence, which provide a better understanding of the system from a linguistic point of view.

ML-based MT metrics, like Better Evaluation as Ranking (BEER) (Stanojević and Sima'an 2014: 414–19), chrF (Popović 2015: 392–95), CharacTER (Wang *et al.* 2016: 505–10) and Blend (Ma *et al.* 2017: 598–603) can achieve better correlation with human evaluation, but their usage is rather limited because they need human-annotated data to train and are much more complex and language dependent compared with lightweight metrics like BLEU, TER and METEOR.

With the prevalent use of pre-trained language models (PLMs) in NLP, PLM-based MT metrics such as BERTScore (Zhang *et al.* 2020) and BLEURT (Sellam *et al.* 2020: 7881–92) have been proposed and reach an higher level with regard to the correlation with human evaluation.

Automatic Quality Estimation

Because the current MT quality is not stable, many users hope to know the translation quality before they use it. Automatic quality estimation technologies are developed for this purpose (Specia *et al.* 2009: 28–35). Quality estimation can be done on the sentence level or word level. Usually a statistical classifier is trained to predict the translation quality for each sentence or word.

Application

Although MT does not reach the so-called ideal FAHQ, it can be applied in many cases with acceptable quality.

The most popular MT application may be the online translation services provided by search engines such as Google Translate, Bing Translator and Baidu Translation. Such products support translation between tens of languages and provide application programming interfaces (APIs) for other applications.

Another type of application for MT is integration with CAT tools. MT is used for post-editing by professional translators and brings significant improvement to their work efficiency.

MT is also used in online or offline human interaction situations through integration with tools such as instant messenger and email.

The combination of MT with other technologies also produces a diversity of applications, for example, speech translations, snapshot translations and cross-lingual information retrieval.

The improvement of translation quality brought by NMT has been extending application scenarios broadly. Personal translation devices or mobile phone apps which support speech translation and photo translation in addition to text translation are commonly used by international tourists all over the world.

Bibliography

Al-Onaizan, Y., J. Curin, M. Jahr, *et al.* (1999) *Statistical Machine Translation. Technical Report*, John Hopkins University Summer Workshop.

Bahdanau, D., K. Cho, and Y. Bengio (2015) 'Neural Machine Translation by Jointly Learning to Align and Translate', in *Proceedings of 3rd International Conference on Learning Representations*, 7–9 May, San Diego.

Banerjee, S. and A. Lavie (2005) 'METEOR: An Automatic Metric for MT Evaluation with Improved Correlation with Human Judgement', in *Proceedings of the ACL Workshop on Intrinsic and Extrinsic Evaluation Measures for Machine Translation and/or Summarization*, Ann Arbor, MI, 65–72.

Brown, P. F., J. Cocke, S. A. D. Pietra, *et al.* (1990) 'A Statistical Approach to Machine Translation', *Computational Linguistics* 16(2): 79–85.

Brown, P. F., S. A. Della-Pietra, V. J. Della-Pietra, *et al.* (1993) 'The Mathematics of Statistical Machine Translation', *Computational Linguistics* 19(2): 263–313.

Carbonell, J. G., R. E. Cullinford, and A. V. Gershman (1978) 'Knowledge-based Machine Translation', *Technical Report*, New Haven, CT: Yale Univ Dept of Computer Science.

Chiang, D. (2005) 'A Hierarchical Phrase-Based Model for Statistical Machine Translation', in *Proceedings of the 43rd Annual Meeting of the Association of Computational Linguistics (ACL)*, Ann Arbor, MI, 263–70.

Chiang, D. (2007) 'Hierarchical Phrase Based Translation', *Computational Linguistics* 33(2): 201–28.

Devlin, J., R. Zbib, Z. Huang, T. Lamar, R. M. Schwartz, and J. Makhoul (2014) 'Fast and Robust Neural Network Joint Models for Statistical Machine Translation', in *Proceedings of the 52nd Annual Meeting of the Association for Computational Linguistics*, 23–25 June, Baltimore, MD, 1370–80.

Dugast, L., J. Senellart, and P. Koehn (2007) 'Statistical Post-Editing on SYSTRAN's Rule-Based Translation System', in *Proceedings of the Second Workshop on Statistical Machine Translation*. Stroudsburg, PA, 220–23.

Freitag, M., G. Foster, D. Grangier, V. Ratnakar, Q. Tan, and W. Macherey (2021) 'Experts, Errors, and Context: A Large-Scale Study of Human Evaluation for Machine Translation', *Transactions of the Association for Computational Linguistics* 9: 1460–74.

Galley, M., J. Graehl, K. Knight, *et al.* (2006) 'Scalable Inference and Training of Context-Rich Syntactic Translation Models', in *Proceedings of the 21st International Conference on Computational Linguistics and 44th Annual Meeting of the Association for Computational Linguistics*, Sydney, Australia, 961–68.

Galley, M., M. Hopkins, K. Knight, *et al.* (2004) 'What's in a Translation Rule?', in *HLT-NAACL 2004: Main Proceedings*, Boston, MA, 273–80.

Graham, Y., T. Baldwin, M. Dowling, M. Eskevich, T. Lynn, and L. Tounsi (2016) 'Is All That Glitters in Machine Translation Quality Estimation Really Gold?', in *Proceedings of the 26th International Conference on Computational Linguistics (COLING 2016): Technical Papers*, 3124–34.

Graham, Y., T. Baldwin, and N. Mathur (2015) 'Accurate Evaluation of Segment-Level Machine Translation Metrics', in *Proceedings of the 2015 Conference of the North American Chapter of the Association for Computational Linguistics: Human Language Technologies*, 1183–91.

Hassan, H., A. Aue, C. Chen, V. Chowdhary, J. Clark, C. Federmann, X. Huang, M. Junczys-Dowmunt, W. Lewis, M. Li, S. Liu, T. Liu, R. Luo, A. Menezes, T. Qin, F. Seide, X. Tan, F. Tian, L. Wu, S. Wu, Y. Xia, D. Zhang, Z. Zhang, and M. Zhou (2018) 'Achieving Human Parity on Automatic Chinese to English News Translation', *arXiv preprint arXiv:1803.05567*.

Huang, L., K. Knight, and A. Joshi (2006) 'Statistical Syntax-Directed Translation with Extended Domain of Locality', in *Proceedings of AMTA*, Boston, MA, 66–73.

Hutchins, W. J. and H. L. Somers (1992) *An Introduction to Machine Translation*, London: Academic Press.

Kahane, S. (2003) 'The Meaning-Text Theory', in *Dependency and Valency: An International Handbook of Contemporary Research*, Berlin and New York: Walter de Gruyter, 546–69.

Koehn, P. (2010) *Statistical Machine Translation*, Cambridge: Cambridge University Press.

Koehn, P., H. Hoang, A. Birch, *et al.* (2007) 'Moses: Open Source Toolkit for Statistical Machine Translation', in *Proceedings of the 45th Annual Meeting of the Association of Computational Linguistics (ACL)*, Prague, Czech Public, 177–80.

Koehn, P. and K. Knight (2009) 'U.S. Patent No. 7,624,005', Washington, DC: U.S. Patent and Trademark Office.

Koehn, P., F. J. Och, and D. Marcu (2003) 'Statistical Phrase-Based Translation', in *Proceedings of Proceedings of the 2003 Conference of the North American Chapter of the Association for Computational Linguistics on Human Language*, Stroudsburg, PA, 48–54.

Landsbergn, J. (1982) 'Machine Translation Based on Logically Isomorphic Montague Grammars', in *Proceedings of the Ninth International Conference on Computational Linguistics*, Prague, 175–81.

Lavie, A. and A. Agarwal (2007) 'METEOR: An Automatic Metric for MT Evaluation with High Levels of Correlation with Human Judgments', in *Proceedings of the Second Workshop on Statistical Machine Translation*, Prague, Czech Republic, 228–31.

Liu, Y., Q. Liu, and S. Lin (2006) 'Tree-to-String Alignment Template for Statistical Machine Translation', in *Proceedings of COLING-ACL*, Sydney, Australia, 609–16.

Lommel, A., A. Burchardt, and H. Uszkoreit (eds.) (2015) 'Multidimensional Quality Metrics (MQM) Definition'. www.qt21.eu/mqm-definition/definition-2015-12-30.html.

Ma, Q., Y. Graham, S. Wang, and Q. Liu (2017) 'Blend: A Novel Combined MT Metric Based on Direct Assessment – CASICT-DCU Submission to WMT17 Metrics Task', in *Proceedings of the Second Conference on Machine Translation*, 598–603.

Mass, H. D. (1977) 'The Saarbrücken Automatic Translation System (SUSY)', in *Overcoming the Language Barrier*, München: Verlag Dokumentation, 585–92.

Muraki, K. (1987) 'PIVOT: Two-Phase Machine Translation System', in *Machine Translation Summit*, Tokyo: Ohmsha Ltd., 113–15.

Nagao, M. (1984) 'A Framework of a Mechanical Translation Between Japanese and English by Analogy Principle', in *Artificial and Human Intelligence*, New York: Elsevier North-Holland Inc., 173–80.

Nagao, M. (1989) *Machine Translation: How Far Can It Go?* Oxford: Oxford University Press.

Nagao, M. and J. Tsujii (1986) 'The Transfer Phase of the Mu Machine Translation System', in *COLING '86 Proceedings of the 11th Conference on Computational Linguistics*, Bonn, Germany, 97–103.

Nirenburg, S. (1989) 'Knowledge-Based Machine Translation', *Machine Translation* 4(1): 5–24.

Nomura, H., S. Naito, Y. Katagiri, *et al.* (1985) 'Experimental Machine Translation Systems: LUTE', in *Proceedings of Second European-Japanese Workshop on Machine Translation*, 621–26.

Nyberg III, E. H. and T. Mitamura (1992) 'The KANT System: Fast, Accurate, High-Quality Translation in Practical Domains', in *Proceedings of the 14th Conference on Computational Linguistics*, Nates, France, 1069–73.

Och, F. J. (2002) 'Statistical Machine Translation: From Single-word Models to Alignment Templates', PhD thesis, RWTH Aachen, Germany.

Och, F. J. (2003) 'Minimum Error Rate Training in Statistical Machine Translation', in *Proceedings of the 41st Annual Meeting on Association for Computational Linguistics*, Stroudsburg, PA, 160–67.

Och, F. J. and H. Ney (2000) 'Improved Statistical Alignment Models', in *Proceedings of the 38th Annual Meeting of the Association of Computational Linguistics*, Stroudsburg, PA, 440–47.

Och, F. J. and H. Ney (2002) 'Discriminative Training and Maximum Entropy Models for Statistical Machine Translation', in *Proceedings of the 40th Annual Meeting on Association for Computational Linguistics*, Stroudsburg, PA, 295–302.

Och, F. J. and H. Ney (2003) 'A Systematic Comparison of Various Statistical Alignment Models', *Computational Linguistics* 29(1): 19–51.

Och, F. J. and H. Ney (2004) 'The Alignment Template Approach to Statistical Machine Translation', *Computational Linguistics* 30(4): 417–49.

Och, F. J., C. Tillman, and H. Ney (1999) 'Improved Aligned Models for Statistical Machine Translation', in *Proceedings of the Joint Conference of Empirical Methods in Natural Language Processing and Very Large Corpora*. Maryland, 20–28.

Och, F. J. and H. Weber (1998) 'Improving Statistical Natural Language Translation with Categories and Rules', in *Proceedings of the 36th Annual Meeting of the Association of Computational Linguistics*, Montreal, Canada, 985–89.

Orsnes, B., B. Music, and B. Maegaard (1996) 'PaTrans – A Patent Translation System', in *Proceedings of the 16th Conference on Computational Linguistics*, Copenhagen, Denmark, 1115–18.

Papineni, K., K. Roukos, T. Ward, *et al.* (2002) 'Bleu: A Method for Automatic Evaluation of Machine Translation', in *Proceedings of ACL*, Philadelphia, PA, 311–18.

Patel-Schneider, P. F. (1989) 'A Four-Valued Semantics for Terminological Logics', *Artificial Intelligence* 38(3): 319–51.

Popović, M. (2015) 'chrF: Character N-Gram F-Score for Automatic MT Evaluation', in *Proceedings of the Tenth Workshop on Statistical Machine Translation*, 392–95.

Roeck, A. D. (1981) 'Anatomy of Eurotra: A Multilingual Machine Translation System', in *Actes du Congrès international informatique et sciences humaines*, Liège: Université de Liège, 298–303.

Rosti, A. V. I., N. F. Ayan, B. Xiang, *et al.* (2007) 'Combining Outputs from Multiple Machine Translation Systems', in *Proceedings of the North American Chapter of the Association for Computational Linguistics Human Language Technologies*, Rochester, NY, 228–35.

Sato, S. and M. Nagao (1990) 'Toward Memory-Based Translation', in *Proceedings of the 13th Conference on Computational Linguistics*, Stroudsburg, PA, 247–52.

Schank, R. C. and R. P. Abelson (1977) *Scripts, Plans, Goals, and Understanding: An Inquiry Into Human Knowledge Structures*, Hillsdale, NJ: Lawrence Erlbaum.

Seite, B., D. Bachut, D. Maret, *et al.* (1992) 'Presentation of Eurolang Project', in *Proceedings of the 14th Conference on Computational Linguistics*, Nates, France, 1289–93.

Sellam, T., D. Das, and A. Parikh (2020) 'BLEURT: Learning Robust Metrics for Text Generation', in *Proceedings of the 58th Annual Meeting of the Association for Computational Linguistics*, 7881–92.

Sharp, R. (1988) 'CAT2 – Implementing a Formalism for Multi-Lingual MT', *Paper Presented at 2nd International Conference on Theoretical and Methodological Issues in Machine Translation of Natural Language*, 3–6 June 1988, Pittsburgh, PA.

Slocum, J. (1985) 'A Survey of Machine Translation: Its History, Current Status, and Future Prospects', *Computational Linguistics* 11(1): 1–17.

Snover, M., B. Dorr, R. Schwartz, *et al.* (2006) 'A Study of Translation Edit Rate with Targeted Human Annotation', in *Proceedings of Association for Machine Translation in the Americas*, Cambridge, MA, 223–31.

Specia, L., M. Turchi, N. Cancedda, *et al.* (2009) 'Estimating the Sentence-Level Quality of Machine Translation Systems', in *Proceedings of 13th Conference of the European Association for Machine Translation*, Barcelona, Spain, 28–37.

Stanojević, M. and K. Sima'an (2014) 'Beer: Better Evaluation as Ranking', in *Proceedings of the Ninth Workshop on Statistical Machine Translation*, 414–19.

Sutskever, I., O. Vinyals, and Q. V. Le (2014) 'Sequence to Sequence Learning with Neural Networks', in *Advances in Neural Information Processing Systems 27 (Proceedings of NIPS 2014)*.

Vaswani, A., N. Shazeer, N. Parmar, J. Uszkoreit, L. Jones, A. Gomez, L. Kaiser, and I. Polosukhin (2017) 'Attention Is All You Need', in *Proceedings of 31st Conference on Neural Information Processing Systems (NIPS 2017)*, Long Beach, CA, 5998–6008.

Vauquois, B. (1968) 'A Survey of Formal Grammars and Algorithms for Recognition and Transformation in Machine Translation', in *Proceedings of the IFIP Congress-6*, 1114–22.

Vogel, S., H. Ney, and C. Tillmann (1996) 'HMM-based Word Alignment in Statistical Translation', in *Proceedings of the 16th Conference on Computational Linguistics*, Copenhagen, Denmark, 836–41.

Wang, W., J. T. Peter, H. Rosendahl, and H. Ney (2016) 'CharacTER: Translation Edit Rate on Character Level', in *Proceedings of the First Conference on Machine Translation: Volume 2, Shared Task Papers*, 505–10.

Witkam, T. (1988) 'DLT: An Industrial R and D Project for Multilingual MT', in *Proceedings of the 12th Conference on Computational Linguistics*, Budapest, Hungary, 756–59.

Wu, D. (1995) 'Stochastic Inversion Transduction, Grammars, with Application to Segmentation, Bracketing, and Alignment of Parallel Corpora', in *Proceedings of the 14th International Joint Conference on Artificial Intelligence*, San Francisco, CA, 1328–35.

Xia, F. and M. McCord (2004) 'Improving a Statistical MT System with Automatically Learned Rewrite Patterns', in *Proceedings of the 20th International Conference on Computational Linguistics*, Stroudsburg, PA, 508–14.

Yu, Shiwen (1993) 'Automatic Evaluation of Output Quality for Machine Translation Systems', *Machine Translation* 8(1–2): 117–26.

Zhang, T., V. Kishore, F. Wu, K. Q. Weinberger, and Y. Artzi (2020) 'BERTScore: Evaluating Text Generation with BERT', in *Proceedings of ICLR 2020*.

Zhou, Ming, Bo Wang, Shujie Liu, Mu Li, Dongdong Zhang, and Tiejun Zhao (2008) 'Diagnostic Evaluation of Machine Translation Systems Using Automatically Constructed Linguistic Check-Points', in *Proceedings of the 22nd International Conference on Computational Linguistics (Coling 2008)*, August 2008, Manchester, the United Kingdom, 1121–28.

6

MACHINE TRANSLATION
History of Research and Applications

W. John Hutchins

From 1949 to 1970

Within a few years of the first appearance of the 'electronic calculators', research had begun on using computers as aids for translating natural languages. The major stimulus was a memorandum in July 1949 by Warren Weaver, who put forward possible lines of research. One was a statistical approach expressed as a dictum that 'When I look at an article in Russian, I say: "This is really written in English, but it has been coded in some strange symbols. I will now proceed to decode"'. Weaver referred also to war-time success in code-breaking, from developments by Shannon in information theory and speculations about universal principles underlying natural languages (Weaver 1949: 15–33). Within a few years research had begun at many US universities, and in 1954 the first public demonstration of the feasibility of translation by computer was given, in a collaboration of IBM and Georgetown University (Hutchins 2004: 102–14). Although using a very restricted vocabulary and grammar, it was sufficiently impressive to stimulate massive funding of what became known from that date as 'machine translation' (MT).

This first decade saw the beginnings of the three basic approaches to MT. The first was the 'direct translation' model, where programming rules were developed for translation specifically from one source language (SL) into one particular target language (TL) with a minimal amount of analysis and syntactic reorganization. The second approach was the 'interlingua' model, based on abstract language-neutral representations (codes or symbols independent of both SL and TL), where translation would then be in two stages, from SL to the interlingua and from interlingua to TL. The third approach was less ambitious: the 'transfer approach', where conversion was through a transfer stage from abstract (i.e. disambiguated) representations of SL texts to equivalent TL representations; in this case, translation comprised three stages: analysis, transfer, and generation (or synthesis). (For a general historical survey of MT, see Hutchins 1986.)

At the University of Washington, Erwin Reifler led a team on German–English and Russian–English translation, which later led to the IBM system developed by Gilbert King on a special memory device (the 'photoscopic disk') developed for the US Air Force and in operation from 1958. The largest MT group in the United States was at Georgetown University, which did not continue with the method used in the 1954 experiment but based its system on rules derived from traditional grammars. There were three levels of analysis: morphological (including identification of idioms), syntagmatic (agreement of nouns and adjectives, government of verbs,

DOI: 10.4324/9781003168348-7

modification of adjectives, etc.), and syntactic (subjects and predicates, clause relationships, etc.) Much of the linguistic research for the Russian-English system was undertaken by Michael Zarechnak; the program was based on work by Petr Toma (later designer of Systran) and by Antony Brown (his SLC program for French–English). In this form it was successfully demonstrated in 1961 and 1962, and as a result, Russian–English systems were installed at Euratom in Ispra (Italy) in 1963 and at the Oak Ridge National Laboratory of the US Atomic Energy Commission in 1964.

Anthony Oettinger at Harvard University adopted in a gradualist approach. From 1954 to 1960 his group concentrated on the compilation of a massive Russian–English dictionary to serve as an aid for translators (a forerunner of the now common computer-based dictionary aids), to produce crude word-for-word translations for scientists familiar with the subject and as the basis for more advanced experimental work. From 1959 research turned to a method of syntactic analysis originally developed at the National Bureau of Standards under Ida Rhodes. This 'predictive syntactic analyser' sought to identify permissible sequences of grammatical categories (nouns, verbs, adjectives, etc.) and to predict the probabilities of the following categories. Multiple parsings were generated to examine all possible predictions, but the results were often unsatisfactory, and by 1965 the Harvard group had effectively ceased MT research.

Research at the Massachusetts Institute of Technology, started by Bar-Hillel in 1951, was directed by Victor Yngve from 1953 until its end in 1965. Whereas other groups saw syntax as an adjunct to lexicographic transfer, as a means of resolving ambiguities and rearranging TL output, Yngve placed syntax at the centre: translation was a three-stage process, a SL grammar analysed input sentences as phrase structure representations, a 'structure transfer routine' converted them into equivalent TL phrase structures, and the TL grammar rules produced output text. An important contribution of MIT was the development of the first string-handling programming language (COMIT). Eventually the limitations of the 'syntactic transfer' approach became obvious, and in 1964 Yngve acknowledged that MT research had come up against 'the semantic barrier . . . and that we will only have adequate mechanical translations when the machine can "understand" what it is translating' (279).

There were other US groups at the University of Texas led by Winfried Lehmann and at the University of California led by Sydney Lamb (who developed his 'stratificational' model of language), both linguistics-based models. There were, however, no American groups taking the interlingua approach. This was the focus of projects elsewhere. At the Cambridge Language Research Unit, Margaret Masterman and her colleagues adopted two basic lines of research: the development of a prototype interlingua producing crude 'pidgin' (essentially word-for-word) translations and the development of tools for improving and refining MT output, primarily by means of the rich semantic networks of a thesaurus (conceived as lattices of interlocking meanings.) At Milan, Silvio Ceccato concentrated on the development of an interlingua based on conceptual analysis of words (species, genus, activity type, physical properties, etc.) and their possible correlations with other words in texts.

In the Soviet Union research was as vigorous as in the United States and showed a similar mix of empirical and basic theoretical approaches. At the Institute of Precision Mechanics, the research under D.Y. Panov on English-Russian translation was on lines similar to that at Georgetown, but with less practical success – primarily from lack of adequate computer facilities. More basic research was undertaken at the Steklov Mathematical Institute by Aleksej A. Ljapunov, Olga S. Kulagina, and Igor A. Mel'čuk (of the Institute of Linguistics) – the latter working on an interlingua approach that led eventually to his 'meaning-text' model. This combined a stratificational dependency approach (six strata: phonetic, phonemic, morphemic, surface syntactic, deep syntactic, semantic) with a strong emphasis on lexicographic aspects of an interlingua. Fifty universal 'lexical functions' were identified at the deep syntactic stratum covering paradigmatic relations (e.g. synonyms, antonyms, verbs and their corresponding agentive nouns, etc.) and a great variety of syntagmatic relations (e.g. inceptive verbs associated with given nouns, *conference: open, war: break out*; idiomatic causatives, *compile: dictionary, lay: foundations*, etc.) Interlingua investigations were consonant with the multilingual needs of the Soviet Union and undertaken at a number of other centres. The principal one was at Leningrad State University, where a team under Nikolaj Andreev conceived an interlingua not as an abstract intermediary representation but as an artificial language complete in itself with its own morphology and syntax and having only those features statistically most common to a large number of languages.

By the mid-1960s MT research groups had been established in many countries throughout the world, including most European countries (Hungary, Czechoslovakia, Bulgaria, Belgium, Germany, France, etc.), China, Mexico, and Japan. Many of these were short lived; an exception was the project which began in 1960 at Grenoble University (see next section).

In the 1950s optimism had been high; developments in computing and in formal linguistics, particularly in the area of syntax, seemed to promise great improvement in quality. There were many predictions of imminent breakthroughs and of fully automatic systems operating within a few years. However, disillusion grew as the complexity of the linguistic problems became more and more apparent. In a review of MT progress, Bar-Hillel (1960: 91–163) criticized the prevailing assumption that the goal of MT research should be the creation of fully automatic high-quality translation (FAHQT) systems producing results indistinguishable from those of human translators. He argued that it was not merely unrealistic, given the current state of linguistic knowledge and computer systems, but impossible in principle. He demonstrated his argument with the word *pen*. It can have at least two meanings (a container for animals or children and a writing implement). In the sentence *The box was in the pen*, we know that only the first meaning is plausible; the second meaning is excluded by our knowledge of the normal sizes of (writing) pens and boxes. Bar-Hillel contended that no computer program could conceivably deal with such 'real world' knowledge without recourse to a vast encyclopaedic store.

By 1964, the US government sponsors had become increasingly concerned at the lack of progress; they set up the Automatic Language Processing Advisory Committee (ALPAC), which concluded in its report (ALPAC 1966) that MT was slower, less accurate, and twice as expensive as human translation and that 'there is no immediate or predictable prospect of useful machine translation'. It saw no need in the United States for further investment in MT research; instead it recommended the development of machine aids for translators, such as automatic dictionaries, and continued support in basic research in computational linguistics.

The ALPAC report brought a virtual end to MT research in the United States for over a decade, and it had great impact elsewhere in the Soviet Union and in Europe. However, MT research did continue in Canada, France, and Germany. Within a few years, Peter Toma, one of the members of the Georgetown University project, had developed Systran for operational use by the USAF (1970) and NASA (in 1974/5), and shortly afterwards Systran was installed by the Commission of the European Communities for translating from English into French (1976) and later between other Community languages.

Throughout this period, research on MT became an 'umbrella' for much contemporary work in structural and formal linguistics (particularly in the Soviet Union), semiotics, logical semantics, mathematical linguistics, quantitative linguistics, and nearly all of what would now be called computational linguistics and language engineering (terms already in use since early 1960s). Initially, there were also close ties with cybernetics and information theory. In general, throughout the early period, work on MT (both theoretical and practical) was seen to be of wide relevance in many fields concerned with the application of computers to 'intellectual' tasks;

this was true in particular for the research on 'interlingua' aspects of MT, regarded as significant for the development of 'information languages' to be used in document retrieval systems.

From 1970 to 1989

Research did not stop completely, however, after ALPAC. Even in the United States, groups continued for a few more years at the University of Texas and at Wayne State University. But there was a change of direction. Where 'first-generation' research of the pre-ALPAC period (1956–1966) had been dominated by mainly 'direct translation' approaches, the 'second generation' post-ALPAC was to be dominated by 'indirect' models, both interlingua and transfer based.

In the 1960s in the United States and the Soviet Union, MT activity had concentrated on Russian-English and English-Russian translation of scientific and technical documents for a relatively small number of potential users, most of whom were prepared to overlook mistakes of terminology, grammar, and style in order to be able to read something which they would have otherwise not known about. Since the mid-1970s the demand for MT has come from quite different sources with different needs and different languages. The administrative and commercial demands of multilingual communities and multinational trade have stimulated the demand for translation in Europe, Canada, and Japan beyond the capacity of the traditional translation services. The demand is now for cost-effective machine-aided translation systems which can deal with commercial and technical documentation in the principal languages of international commerce.

At Montreal, research began in 1970 on a syntactic transfer system for English-French translation. The Traduction Automatique de l'Université de Montréal (TAUM) project had two major achievements: first the Q-system formalism for manipulating linguistic strings and trees (later developed as the Prolog programming language) and second the Météo system for translating weather forecasts. Designed specifically for the restricted vocabulary and limited syntax of meteorological reports, Météo has been successfully operating since 1976 (since 1984 in a new version). The TAUM group attempted to repeat this success in another field, that of aviation manuals, but failed to overcome the problems of complex noun compounds and phrases, and the project ended in 1981.

A similar fate met the ITS system at Brigham Young University. This was a transfer-based interactive multilingual system based on Eldon G. Lytle's junction grammar. The aim was a commercial system, but an internal evaluation in 1979 – a decade after the project had begun – concluded that the system had become too complex and recommended the development of practical computer aids for translators (cf. ALPS, subsequently).

Throughout the 1980s research on more advanced methods and techniques continued. For most of the decade, the dominant strategy was that of 'indirect' translation via intermediary representations, sometimes interlingual in nature, involving semantic as well as morphological and syntactic analysis and sometimes non-linguistic 'knowledge bases'. There was an increasing emphasis on devising systems for particular subject domains and for particular specific purposes, for monolingual users as well as bilingual users (translators), and for interactive operation rather than batch processing.

The most notable research projects were the GETA-Ariane system at Grenoble; SUSY and ASCOF at Saarbrücken; Mu at Kyoto; DLT at Utrecht; Rosetta at Eindhoven; the knowledge-based MT project at Carnegie-Mellon University (Pittsburgh); and two ambitious international multilingual projects: Eurotra, supported by the European Communities, involving teams in each member country, and the Japanese CICC project with participants in China, Indonesia, and Thailand.

Between 1960 and 1971 the group established by Bernard Vauquois at Grenoble University developed an interlingua system for translating Russian mathematics and physics texts into French. The 'pivot language' of Centre d'Etudes pour la Traduction Automatique (CETA) was a formalism for representing the logical properties of syntactic relationships. It was not a pure interlingua, as it did not provide interlingual expressions for lexical items; these were translated by a bilingual transfer mechanism. Syntactic analysis produced first a phrase-structure (context-free) representation, then added dependency relations, and finally a 'pivot language' representation in terms of predicates and arguments. After substitution of TL lexemes (French), the 'pivot language' tree was converted first into a dependency representation and then into a phrase structure for generating French sentences. A similar model was adopted by the group at Texas during the 1970s in its METAL system: sentences were analysed into 'normal forms', semantic propositional dependency structures with no interlingual lexical elements.

By the mid-1970s, the future of the interlingua approach was in doubt. The main problems identified were attributed to the rigidity of the levels of analysis (failure at any one stage meant failure to produce any output at all), the inefficiency of parsers (too many partial analyses which had to be 'filtered' out), and in particular loss of information about surface forms of the SL input which might have been used to guide the selection of TL forms and the construction of acceptable TL sentence structures.

After the disappointing results of its interlingua system, the Grenoble group (Groupe d'Etudes pour la Traduction Automatique, GETA) began development of its influential Ariane system. Regarded as the paradigm of the 'second-generation' linguistics-based transfer systems, Ariane influenced projects throughout the world in the 1980s. Of particular note were its flexibility and modularity, its algorithms for manipulating tree representations, and its conception of static and dynamic grammars. However, like many experimental MT systems, Ariane did not become an operational system, and active research on the system ceased in the late 1980s.

Similar in conception to the GETA-Ariane design was the Mu system developed at the University of Kyoto under Makoto Nagao. Prominent features of Mu were the use of case grammar analysis and dependency tree representations and the development of a programming environment for grammar writing (GRADE). Another experimental system was developed at Saarbrücken (Germany), a multilingual transfer system, SUSY (Saarbrücker Übersetzungssystem), displaying a heterogeneity of techniques: phrase structure rules, transformational rules, case grammar and valency frames, dependency grammar, the use of statistical data, and so on.

The best-known project of the 1980s was the Eurotra project of the European Communities. Its aim was the construction of an advanced multilingual transfer system for translation among all the Community languages – on the assumption that the 'direct translation' approach of the Communities' Systran system was inherently limited. Like GETA-Ariane and SUSY, the design combined lexical, logico-syntactic, and semantic information in multilevel interfaces at a high degree of abstractness. No direct use of extralinguistic knowledge bases or of inference mechanisms was made, and no facilities for human assistance or intervention during translation processes were to be incorporated. A major defect was the failure to tackle problems of the lexicon, both theoretically and practically; by the end of the 1980s, no operational system was in prospect, and the project ended.

During the latter half of the 1980s, there was a general revival of interest in interlingua systems, motivated in part by contemporary research in artificial intelligence and cognitive linguistics. The Distributed Language Translation (DLT) system at the BSO software company in Utrecht (The Netherlands), under the direction of Toon Witkam, was intended as a multilingual interactive system operating over computer networks, where each terminal was to be a translating machine from and into one language only. Texts were to be transmitted between terminals in an intermediary language, a modified form of Esperanto. A second interlingua project in the Netherlands was the Rosetta project at Philips (Eindhoven) directed by Jan Landsbergen. The aim was to explore the use of Montague grammar in interlingual representations and, as a secondary goal, the exploration of the reversibility of grammars, that is, grammatical rules and transformations that could work in both directions between languages.

In the latter half of the 1980s Japan witnessed a substantial increase in MT research activity. Most of the computer companies (Fujitsu, Toshiba, Hitachi, etc.) began to invest large sums into an area which government and industry saw as fundamental to the coming 'fifth generation' of the information society. The research, initially greatly influenced by the Mu project at Kyoto University, showed a wide variety of approaches. While transfer systems predominated, there were also interlingua systems, such as the PIVOT system at NEC, and the Japanese-funded multilingual multinational project from the mid 1980s to the mid 1990s, already mentioned.

As in the previous decade, many research projects were established in the 1980s outside North America, Western Europe, and Japan – in Korea (sometimes in collaborative projects with Japanese and American groups); in Taiwan (e.g. the ArchTran system); in mainland China at a number of institutions; and in Southeast Asia, particularly in Malaysia.

There was also an increase in activity in the Soviet Union. From 1976 most research was concentrated at the All-Union Centre for Translation in Moscow. Systems for English-Russian (AMPAR) and German-Russian translation (NERPA) were developed based on the direct approach, but there was also work under the direction of Yurij Apres'jan based on Mel'čuk's 'meaning-text' model – Mel'čuk himself had been obliged to leave the Soviet Union in 1977. This led to the advanced transfer systems FRAP (for French-Russian) and ETAP (for English-Russian). Apart from this group, however, most activity in the Soviet Union focused on the production of relatively low-level operational systems, often involving the use of statistical analyses – where the influence of the 'Speech Statistics' group under Raimund Piotrowski (Leningrad State University) has been particularly significant for the development of many later commercial MT systems in Russia.

During the 1980s, many researchers believed that the most likely means for improving MT quality would come from natural language processing research within the context of artificial intelligence (AI). Investigations of AI methods in MT began in the mid-1970s with Yorick Wilks's work on 'preference semantics' and 'semantic templates'. A number of projects applied knowledge-based approaches – some in Japan (e.g. the LUTE project at NTT and the ETL research for the Japanese multilingual project), others in Europe (e.g. at Saarbrücken and Stuttgart), and many in North America. The most important group was at Carnegie-Mellon University in Pittsburgh under Jaime Carbonell and Sergei Nirenburg, which experimented with a number of knowledge-based MT systems (Goodman and Nirenburg 1991).

The 1980s witnessed the emergence of a variety of operational MT systems. First there were a number of mainframe systems. Best known is Systran, operating in many pairs of languages; others were Logos for German-English translation and for English-French in Canada, the internally developed systems for Spanish-English and English-Spanish translation at the Pan American Health Organization, systems developed by the Smart Corporation for large organizations in North America, and the Metal system from Siemens for German-English translation, and major systems for English–Japanese and Japanese–English translation came from Japanese computer companies Fujitsu, Hitachi, and Toshiba.

The wide availability of microcomputers and text-processing software led to a commercial market for cheaper MT systems, exploited in North America and Europe by companies such as ALPS, Weidner, Linguistic Products, Tovna, and Globalink and by many Japanese companies, such as Sharp, NEC, Oki, Mitsubishi, and Sanyo. Other microcomputer-based systems came from China, Taiwan, Korea, Bolivia, and Eastern and Central Europe, like PROMT from Russia.

Finally, not least, there was the beginning of systems offering some kind of translation for spoken language. These were the phrase-book and PC-based systems which included the option of voice output from written text – it seems that Globalink in 1995 was the earliest. But automatic speech synthesis of text-to-text translation is not at all the same as genuine 'speech-to-speech translation'. Research on speech translation did not start until the late 1980s (see subsequently).

Applications of MT up to 2000: Translation Tools

Until the middle of the 1990s, there were just two basic ways in which machine translation systems were used. The first was the traditional large-scale system mounted on mainframe computers in large companies. The purpose was to use MT in order to produce publishable translations. The output of MT systems were thus revised (post-edited) by human translators or editors familiar with both source and target languages. Revision for MT differs from the revision of traditionally produced translations; the computer program is regular and consistent with terminology, unlike the human translator, but typically it contains grammatical and stylistic errors which no human translator would commit. Hence, there was opposition from translators (particularly those with the task of post-editing), but the advantages of fast and consistent output have made large-scale MT cost effective. In order to improve the quality of the raw MT output, many large companies included methods of 'controlling' the input language (by restricting vocabulary and syntactic structures) in order to minimize problems of disambiguation and alternative interpretations of structure and thus improve the quality. Companies such as the Xerox Corporation used Systran systems with a 'controlled language' from the late 1970s (Elliston 1978: 149–58) for the translation of English language documents into Scandinavian languages. Many companies followed their example, and the Smart Corporation specializes to this day in setting up 'controlled language' MT systems for large companies in North America. In a few cases, it was possible to develop systems specifically for the particular 'sublanguage' of the texts to be translated, as in the Météo system mentioned previously. Indeed, nearly all systems operating in large organizations are in some way 'adapted' to the subject areas they operate in: earth moving machines, job applications, health reports, patents, police data, and many more.

Personal computers became widely marketed in the early 1980s, and software for translation became available soon afterwards: ALPS (later Alpnet) in 1983, Weidner in 1984 (later acquired by the Japanese company Bravis). They were followed from the mid-1980s onwards by many companies marketing PCs – including most of the Japanese manufacturers of PCs – and covering an increasingly wide range of language pairs and on an increasingly wide range of operating systems. Since the mid-1990s, a huge range of translation software has been available (Hutchins 2003: 161–74).

What has always been uncertain is how purchasers have been using these PC systems. In the case of large-scale (mainframe) 'enterprise' systems, it is clear that MT is used to produce drafts which are then edited by bilingual personnel. This may also be the case for PC systems: it may be that they have been and are used to create 'drafts' which are edited to a higher quality. On the other hand, it seems more likely that users want just to get some idea of the contents (the basic 'message') of foreign texts and are not concerned about the quality of translations. This usage is generally referred to as 'assimilation' (in contrast to the use for publishable translations: 'dissemination'). We know (anecdotally) that some users of PC systems have trusted them too much and have sent 'raw' (unedited) MT translations as if they were as good as human translations.

The same comments apply to the marketing since the early 1990s of hand-held translation devices or 'pocket translators'. Many, such as the Ectaco range of special devices, are in effect computerized versions of the familiar phrase-book or pocket dictionary and are clearly marketed primarily to the tourist and business traveller. The small dictionary sizes are obviously limited. Although sold in large numbers, there is no indication of how successful in actual use they may be. Recently, since the end of the 1990s, they have been largely replaced by online MT services (see subsequently).

Mainframe, client–server, and PC systems are overwhelmingly 'general purpose' systems; that is, they are built to deal with texts in any subject domain. Of course, 'enterprise' systems (particularly controlled language systems) are over time focused on particular subject areas, and adaptation to new areas is offered by most large MT systems (such as Systran). A few PC-based systems are available for texts in specific subject areas such as medical texts and patents (the English/Japanese Transer systems). On the whole, however, PC systems deal with specific subjects by the provision of subject glossaries. For some systems the range of dictionaries is very wide, embracing most engineering topics, computer science, business and marketing, law, sports, cookery, music, and so on.

Few translators have been happy with fully automatic translation. In particular they do not want to be post-editors of poor-quality output. They prefer dedicated computer-based aids, in particular since the early 1990s the availability of 'translation memories'. An early advocate of translation aids was Martin Kay (1980), who criticized the current approaches to MT as technology driven rather than user driven. He argued that the real need was assistance in translation tasks. These aids include facilities for multilingual word processing, creating in-house glossaries and termbanks, receiving and sending texts over telecommunication networks, accessing remote sources of information, publishing quality documents, and using interactive or batch MT systems when appropriate. Above all, translators need access to previous translations in 'translation memories', that is, bilingual corpora of aligned sentences and text segments. Translators can find examples of existing translations of text which match or are similar to those in hand. Not only is consistency improved and quality maintained, but sections of repetitive texts are not translated again unnecessarily. Ideas for translation memories date back to proposals by Arthern (1979) and Kay (1980), but it was not until the early 1990s that they came onto the market with systems from Trados, SDL, Atril, Champollion, and so on. Systems which integrate a variety of aids are known as translator's workstations or workbenches and have been commercially available from a number of vendors (Trados, STAR, IBM). (For a historical survey see Hutchins 1998: 287–307.)

A special application of MT since the early 1990s has been the localization of software products. (For a survey, see Esselink 2003: 67–86.) Software producers seek to market versions of their systems in other languages, simultaneously or very closely following the launch of the version in the original language (usually English), and so localization has become a necessity in the global markets of today. The repetitive nature of the documentation (e.g. software manuals), changing little from one product to another and from one edition to the next, made the use translation memories and the development of 'controlled' terminologies for MT systems particularly attractive. But localization involves more than just translation of texts. It means the adaptation of products (and their documentation) to particular cultural conditions, ranging from correct expression of dates (day-month-year vs. month-day-year), and times (12-hour vs. 24-hour), address conventions and abbreviations to the reformatting (re-paragraphing) and re-arranging of complete texts to suit expectations of recipients.

Corpus-Based MT Research – 1989 to the Present

The dominant framework of MT research until the end of the 1980s was based on essentially linguistic rules of various kinds: rules for syntactic analysis, lexical rules, rules for lexical transfer, rules for syntactic generation, rules for morphology, and so on. The rule-based approach was most obvious in the dominant transfer systems of the 1980s (Ariane, Metal, SUSY, Mu, and Eurotra), but it was also the basis of all the various interlingua systems – both those which were essentially linguistics oriented (DLT and Rosetta) and those which were knowledge based (KANT). Rule-based methods continued into the 1990s: the CAT2 system (a by-product of Eurotra) at Saarbrücken; the Catalyst project at Carnegie-Mellon University (a domain-specific knowledge-based system) for the Caterpillar company; a project at the University of Maryland based on the linguistic theory of 'principles and parameters'; and Pangloss, ARPA-funded research at Carnegie-Mellon, Southern California, and New Mexico State University.

Since 1989, however, the dominance of the rule-based approach has been broken by the emergence of new methods and strategies which are now loosely called 'corpus-based' methods. The most dramatic development was the revival of a purely statistics-based approach to MT in the Candide project at IBM, first reported in 1988 (Brown *et al.* 1988, 1990: 79–85) and developed to its definitive form in 1993 (Brown *et al.* 1993: 263–311). Statistical methods were common in the earliest period of MT research (such as the distributional analysis of texts at the RAND Corporation), but the results had been generally disappointing. With the success of newer stochastic techniques in speech recognition, the IBM team at Yorktown Heights began to look again at their application to MT. The distinctive feature of Candide was that statistical methods were used as the sole means of analysis and generation; no linguistic rules were applied. The researchers at IBM acknowledged that their approach was in effect a return to the statistical approach suggested by Warren Weaver (1949). The system was tested on the large corpus of French and English texts contained in the reports of Canadian parliamentary debates (the Canadian Hansard). What surprised most researchers (particularly those involved in rule-based approaches) was that the results were so acceptable: almost half the phrases translated either matched exactly the translations in the corpus, expressed the same sense in slightly different words, or offered other equally legitimate translations.

Stages of translation in statistical machine translation (SMT) systems are: first alignment of bilingual corpora (i.e. texts in original language and texts in target language or texts in comparable corpora which are not directly alignable), either by word or phrase; then frequency matching of input words against words in the corpus and extraction of most probable equivalents in the target language ('decoding'); reordering of the output according to most common word sequences using a 'language model', a monolingual corpus providing word frequencies of the TL; and finally production of the output in the target language. In broad terms, the process was in effect a revival of the 'direct translation' approach of some MT pioneers (see the quote from Weaver previously) but refined, of course, by sophisticated statistical techniques.

Since this time, statistical machine translation has become the major focus of most MT research groups, based primarily on the IBM model, but with many subsequent refinements (Ney 2005). The original emphasis on word correlations between source and target languages has been replaced by correlations between 'phrases' (i.e. sequences of words, not necessarily 'traditional' noun phrases, verb phrases, or prepositional phrases), the inclusion of morphological and syntactic information, and the use of dictionary and thesaurus resources. Subsequent refinements have been the inclusion of structural information (usually dependency relations) in hierarchical trees similar to some earlier rule-based systems. For transfer from source to target, SMT systems incorporate string-to-string (or phrase-to-string) transfer relations based on the bilingual corpora, and the output is revised (corrected) via frequency information from monolingual corpora ('language models'). The SMT approach has been applied to an ever-widening range of language pairs. The main centres for SMT research are the universities of Aachen, Edinburgh, and Southern California, and they have been recently joined by the Google Corporation. There are a number of ambitious SMT projects. Within Europe and funded by the European Union is the Euromatrix project involving many European researchers in an 'open' network under the general leadership of the Edinburgh centre. The project began in 2006 (Koehn 2007) with the aim of developing SMT systems between all the languages of the European Union. Some language pairs already exist, many in different versions, particularly between languages such as English, French, German, and Spanish. A major effort of the project has been the development of SMT for 'minor' languages not previously found in MT systems, such as Estonian, Latvian, Slovenian, Macedonian, and so on. The project does not exclude rule-based methods when appropriate (i.e. as hybrid systems – see subsequently), and given the complexity of translation and the range of types of languages, is it presumed that multiple approaches will be essential. (An insightful summary of achievements in SMT systems for translation of European languages is found in Koehn *et al.* [2009: 65–72].) Apart from the Euromatrix project, groups active in Europe include researchers at many German and Spanish universities; researchers at the Charles University Prague, who have made fundamental contributions to the SMT of morphologically rich languages (Czech and others); and researchers in the Baltic countries.

The second major 'corpus-based' approach – benefiting likewise from improved rapid access to large databanks of text corpora – was what is known as the 'example-based' (or 'memory-based') approach (Carl and Way 2003). Although first proposed in 1981 by Makoto Nagao (1984: 173–80), it was only towards the end of the 1980s that experiments began, initially in some Japanese groups and during the DLT project mentioned previously. The underlying hypothesis of example-based machine translation (EBMT) is that translation by humans often involves the finding or recalling of analogous examples, that is, how a particular expression or some similar phrase has been translated before. The EBMT approach is founded on processes of extracting and selecting equivalent phrases or word groups from a databank of parallel bilingual texts, which have been aligned either by statistical methods (similar perhaps to those used in SMT) or by more traditional rule-based methods. For calculating matches, some research groups use semantic methods, for example, a semantic network or a hierarchy (thesaurus) of domain terms; other groups use statistical information about lexical frequencies in the target language. A major problem is the re-combination of selected target language examples (generally short phrases) in order to produce fluent and grammatical output. Nevertheless, the main advantage of the approach (in comparison with rule-based approaches) is that since the texts have been extracted from databanks of actual translations produced by professional translators, there is an assurance that the results should be idiomatic. Unlike SMT, there is little agreement on what might be a 'typical' EBMT model (cf. Turcato and Popowich 2003: 59–81), and most research is devoted to example-based methods which might be applicable to any MT system (rule-based or statistical).

Although SMT is now the dominant framework for MT research, it is recognized that the two corpus-based approaches are converging in many respects: SMT systems are making more use of phrase-based alignments and of linguistic data, and EBMT systems are making wider use of statistical analysis techniques.

Increasingly, resources for MT (components, algorithms, corpora, etc.) are widely available as 'open source' materials. For SMT, well-known examples are: GIZA++ for alignment and the Moses basic translation engine. For rule-based MT, there is the Apertium system from Spain, which has been the basis of MT systems for Spanish, Portuguese, Galician, Catalan, Welsh, Swedish, Danish, Slovenian, and so on.

Many researchers believe that the future of MT lies in the development of hybrid systems combining the best of the statistical and rule-based approaches. In the meantime, however, until a viable framework for hybrid MT appears, experiments are being done with multi-engine systems and with adopting statistical techniques with rule-based (and example-based) systems. The multi-engine approach involves the translation of a given text by two or more different MT architectures (SMT and RBMT, for example) and the integration or combination of outputs for the selection of the 'best' output – for which statistical techniques can be used (in what are called 'combination systems'). An example of appending statistical techniques to rule-based MT is 'statistical post-editing', the submission of the output of an RBMT system to a 'language model' of the kind found in SMT systems.

Evaluation

Evaluations of MT systems date back to the earliest years of research: Miller and Beebe-Center (1956: 73–80) were the first; Henisz-Dostert evaluated the Georgetown Russian–English system (Henisz-Dostert 1967: 57–91), and John Carroll (1966: 55–66) did a study that influenced the negative conclusions of ALPAC – all were based on human judgments of comprehensibility, fluency, fidelity, and so on, and all were evaluations of Russian–English systems. In the years from 1970 to 1990, the European Commission undertook in-depth evaluations of the Systran English–French and English–Italian systems before they were adopted (Van Slype 1979: 59–81). In the 1990s there were numerous workshops dedicated specifically to the problems of evaluating MT, such as Falkedal (1991), Vasconcellos (1992), and the workshops attached to many MT conferences. The methodologies developed by the Japan Electronic Industry Development Association (Nomura and Isahara 1992: 11–12) and those designed for the evaluation of ARPA (later DARPA)-supported projects were particularly influential (ARPA 1994), and MT evaluation proved to have significant implications for evaluation in other areas of computational linguistics and other applications of natural language processing. Initially, most measures of MT quality were performed by human assessments of such factors as comprehensibility, intelligibility, fluency, accuracy, and appropriateness – for such evaluation methods, the research group at ISSCO has been particularly important – such as King *et al.* (2003: 224–31). However, human evaluation is expensive in time and effort, and so efforts have been made, particularly since 2000, to develop automatic (or semi-automatic) methods.

One important consequence of the development of the statistics-based MT models has in fact been the application of statistical analysis to the automatic evaluation of MT systems. The first metric was BLEU from the IBM group, followed later by the National Institute for Standards and Techniques (NIST); for BLEU, see Papineni *et al.* (2002: 311–18); for NIST, see Doddington (2002: 138–45). Both have been applied by (D)ARPA in its evaluations of MT projects supported by US research funds.

BLEU and NIST (and other subsequently developed metrics such as METEOR) are based on the availability of human produced translations (called 'reference texts'). The output from an MT system is compared with one of more 'reference texts'; MT texts which are identical or very close to the 'reference' in terms of word sequences score highly, and MT texts which differ greatly either in individual word occurrences or in word sequences score poorly. The metrics tend to rank rule-based systems lower than SMT systems even though the former are often more acceptable to human readers. Nevertheless, current automatic evaluation is undeniably valuable for monitoring whether a particular system (SMT or EBMT) has improved over time. Many researchers are currently seeking metrics which produce results more closely matching human judgments or, indeed, metrics based directly on collaborative human evaluations from 'crowd sourcing' (e.g. using Mechanical Turk, as in Callison-Burch 2009: 286–95).

A consequence of the change from rule-based approaches to statistics-based methods has been that MT researchers no longer need to have considerable knowledge of the source and target languages of their systems; they can rely upon metrics based on human-produced 'reference texts' to suggest improvements; furthermore, the use of statistics-based methods means that researchers can produce systems much more quickly than with the previous laborious rule-based methods.

Speech Translation Since 1990

Reports of the speech translation research in Japan appeared from 1988 onwards (e.g. the research at ATR, by Tomita *et al.* 1988: 57–77). Reports of the JANUS system at Carnegie-Mellon came in 1993 (Woszczyna *et al.* 1993: 195–200), and in the same year, there was news of the Verbmobil project based in Germany (Wahlster 1993: 127–35) and of the SLT project in the SRI group in Cambridge (Rayner *et al.* 1993: 217–22). The NESPOLE research project came in 2001 (Lavie *et al.* 2001)

The research in speech translation is faced with numerous problems, not just variability of voice input but also the nature of spoken language. By contrast with written language, spoken language is colloquial, elliptical, context dependent, interpersonal, and frequently in the form of dialogues. MT has focused primarily on well-formed, technical, and scientific language and has tended to neglect informal modes of communication. Speech translation therefore represents a radical departure from traditional MT. Some of the problems of spoken language translation may be reduced by restricting communication to relatively narrow domains. Business communication was the focus of the government-funded research at a number of German universities (the Verbmobil project), where the aim was the development of a system for three-way negotiation between English, German, and Japanese (Wahlster 2000). The focus of the ATR research in Japan has been telephone communication between English and Japanese, primarily in the area of booking hotel accommodation and registration for conferences. The potentialities of speech translation in the area of health communication are obvious. Communication may be from doctor to patient or interactive or may be via a screen displaying possible 'health' conditions. Examples are the MedSLT project from SRI where voice input locates potential phrases, and the translation is output by speech synthesis (Rayner and Bouillon 2002: 69–76) and the interactive multimodal assistance provided by the Converser system (Seligman and Dillinger 2006). A somewhat similar 'phrasebook' approach is found in the DIPLOMAT system from Carnegie-Mellon (Frederking *et al.* 1997: 261–62). The system was developed for the US Army for communication from English to Serbo-Croat, Haitian Creole, and Korean: spoken input is matched against fixed phrases in the database, and translations of the phrases are output by a speech synthesizer. Nearly all the systems were somewhat inflexible and limited in range – the weakest point continues to be speech recognition.

One of the most obvious applications of speech translation is the assistance of tourists in foreign countries. In most cases, translation is restricted to 'standard' phrases extracted from corpora of dialogues and interactions in tourist situations, although, in recent years, researchers have turned to systems capable of dealing with 'spontaneous speech'. Despite the amount of research in an apparently highly restricted domain, it is clear that commercially viable products are still some way in the future.

Usage and Applications Since 1990

Since the early 1990s, the use of unrevised MT output has grown greatly, such that now it may well be true that 'raw' unedited MT is the principal form in which people encounter translation from any source.

For the general public, the main source of translation since the mid-1990s has been the availability of free MT services on the Internet (Gaspari and Hutchins 2007: 199–206). Initially, online MT services in the early 1990s were not free. In 1988 Systran in France offered a subscription to its translation software using the French postal service's Minitel network. At about the same time, Fujitsu made its Atlas English–Japanese and Japanese–English systems available through the online service Niftyserve. Then in 1992 CompuServe launched its MT service (based on the Intergraph DP/Translator), initially restricted to selected forums, but which proved highly popular, and in 1994 Globalink offered an online subscription service – texts were submitted online and translations returned by email. A similar service was provided by Systran Express. However, it was the launch of AltaVista's Babelfish free MT service in 1997 (based on the various Systran MT systems) that attracted the greatest publicity. Not only was it free, but results were (virtually) immediate. Within the next few years, the Babelfish service was joined by FreeTranslation (using the Intergraph system), Gist-in-Time, ProMT, PARS, and many others; in most cases, these were online versions of already existing PC-based (or mainframe) systems. The great attraction of these services was (and is) that they are free to users – it is evidently the expectation of the developers that free online use will lead either to sales of PC translation software, although the evidence for this has not been shown, or to the use of fee-based 'valued-added' post-editing services offered by providers such as FreeTranslation. While online MT has undoubtedly raised the profile of MT for the general public, there have, of course, been drawbacks.

To most users the idea of automatic translation was something completely new – many users 'tested' the services by inputting sentences containing idiomatic phrases, ambiguous words and complex structures, and even proverbs and deliberately opaque sayings, and not surprisingly, the results were unsatisfactory. A favourite method of 'evaluation' was back translation: translation into another language and then back into the original language (Somers 2007: 209–33). Not surprisingly, users discovered that MT suffered from many limitations – all well known to company users and to purchasers of PC software. Numerous commentators have enjoyed finding fault with online MT and by implication with MT itself. On the other hand, there is no doubt that the less knowledge users have of the language of the original texts, the more value they attach to the MT output, and some users must have found that online MT enabled them to read texts which they would have previously had to pass over.

Largely unknown by the general public is the use of MT systems by the intelligence services. The languages of most interest are, for obvious reasons, Arabic, Chinese, and Persian (Farsi). The older demand for translation from Russian (see previously) has almost disappeared. The need is for the translation of huge volumes of text. The coming of statistical machine translation has answered this need to a great extent: SMT systems are based on large corpora, often concentrating on specific topics (politics, economics, etc.), and the systems can be delivered quickly. As a sideline, we may mention one intriguing application of SMT methods to the decipherment of ancient languages (Ravi and Knight 2011: 12–21) – reviving the cryptographic speculations of Weaver in 1949 (see the previous section).

Collaboration in the acquisition of lexical resources dates from the beginning of MT research (e.g. the Harvard Russian–English dictionary was used by the MT project at the National Physical Laboratory). A notable effort in the late 1980s was the Electronic Dictionary Research project in the late 1980s, supported by several Japanese computer manufacturing companies. The need grew with the coming of corpus-based systems (see previously). Since the latter part of the 1990s, large lexical resources have been collected and made available in the United States through the Linguistic Data Consortium and in Europe through the European Language Resources Association (ELRA), which in 1998 inaugurated its major biennial series of conferences devoted to the topic – the Language Resources and Evaluation Conferences (LREC). The

Internet itself is now a source for lexical data, such as Wikipedia. One of the earliest examples of 'mining' bilingual texts from the World Wide Web was described by Resnick (1999: 527–34).

The languages most often in demand and available commercially are those from and to English. The most frequently used pairs (for online MT services and apparently for PC systems) are English/Spanish and English/Japanese. These are followed by (in no particular order) English/French, English/German, English/Italian, English/Chinese, English/Korean, and French/German. Other European languages such as Catalan, Czech, Polish, Bulgarian, Romanian, Latvian, Lithuanian, Estonian, and Finnish were more rarely found in the commercial PC market or online until the last decade. Until the middle of the 1990s, Arabic/English, Arabic/French, and Chinese/English were also rare, but this situation has now changed for obvious political reasons. Other Asian languages have been relatively neglected: Malay, Indonesian, Thai, Vietnamese, and even major languages of India: Hindu, Urdu, Bengali, Punjabi, Tamil, and so on. And African languages (except Arabic dialects) are virtually invisible. In terms of population these are not 'minor' languages – many are among the world's most spoken languages. The reason for neglect is a combination of low commercial viability and lack of language resources (whether for rule-based lexicons and grammars or for statistical MT corpora). There is often no word-processing software (indeed, some languages lack scripts), no spellcheckers (sometime languages lack standard spelling conventions), no dictionaries (monolingual or bilingual) and indeed a general lack of language resources (e.g. corpora of translations) and of qualified and experienced researchers (for an overview, see Somers 2003: 87–103).

Summary

Machine translation has come a long way from its tentative and speculative beginnings in the 1950s. We can see three stages of development, each spanning two decades. The first twenty years include the pioneering period (1949–1966) when numerous different approaches were investigated: dictionary-based word-for-word systems, experiments with interlinguas, syntax-based systems with multiple levels of analysis, and the first operational systems (IBM and Georgetown). The period ended with the influential ALPAC report of 1966. The next two decades (1967–1989) saw the development of linguistic rule-based systems, mainly in the framework of transfer grammars and experiments with sophisticated interlingua and artificial intelligence systems; in the same decade there was increased application of MT for commercial users, including the use of controlled languages and sublanguages and applications such as localization, and there were also the first computer-based translation aids. The third period, since the early 1990s, has seen the domination of corpus-based approaches, translation memories, example-based MT, and in particular statistical MT, but there has also been much greater attention to evaluation methods; lastly, applications and usages of MT have widened markedly, most significantly by the access to and use of MT and resources over the Internet.

Bibliography

ALPAC (1966) *Languages and Machines: Computers in Translation and Linguistics*. A Report by the Automatic Language Processing Advisory Committee, Division of Behavioral Sciences, National Academy of Sciences, National Research Council, Washington, DC: National Academy of Sciences, National Research Council.

ARPA (1994) *ARPA Workshop on Machine Translation*, 17–18 March 1994, Sheraton Premier Hotel at Tyson's Corner, Vienna, Austria.

Arthern, Peter J. (1979) 'Machine Translation and Computerized Terminology Systems: A Translator's Viewpoint', in Barbara M. Snell (ed.) *Translating and the Computer: Proceedings of a Seminar*, London, 14 November 1978, Amsterdam: North-Holland Publishing Company, 77–108.

Bar-Hillel, Yehoshua (1960) 'The Present Status of Automatic Translation of Languages', *Advances in Computers* 1: 91–163.

Brown, Peter F., John Cocke, Stephen A. Della Pietra, Vincent J. Della Pietra, Fredrik Jelinek, John D. Lafferty, Robert L. Mercer, and Paul S. Roossin (1990) 'A Statistical Approach to Machine Translation', *Computational Linguistics* 16(2): 79–85.

Brown, Peter F., John Cocke, Stephen A. Della Pietra, Vincent J. Della Pietra, Fredrik Jelinek, Robert L. Mercer, and Paul S. Roossin (1988) 'A Statistical Approach to French/English Translation', in *Proceedings of the 2nd International Conference on Theoretical and Methodological Issues in Machine Translation of Natural Languages*, 12–14 June 1988, Center for Machine Translation, Carnegie Mellon University, Pittsburgh, PA.

Brown, Peter F., Stephen A. Della Pietra, Vincent J. Della Pietra, and Robert L. Mercer (1993) 'The Mathematics of Statistical Machine Translation: Parameter Estimation', *Computational Linguistics* 19(2): 263–311.

Callison-Burch, Chris (2009) 'Fast, Cheap, and Creative: Evaluating Translation Quality Using Amazon's Mechanical Turk', in *EMNLP-2009: Proceedings of the 2009 Conference on Empirical Methods in Natural Language Processing*, 6–7 August 2009, Singapore, 286–95.

Carl, Michael and Andy Way (eds.) (2003) *Recent Advances in Example-based Machine Translation*, Dordrecht: Kluwer Academic Publishers.

Carroll, John B. (1966) 'An Experiment in Evaluating the Quality of Translations', *Mechanical Translation and Computational Linguistics* 9(3–4): 55–66.

Doddington, George (2002) 'Automatic Evaluation of Machine Translation Quality Using N-gram Co-occurrence Statistics', in *HLT 2002: Human Language Technology Conference: Proceedings of the 2nd International Conference on Human Language Technology Research*, 24–27 March 2002, San Diego, CA, 138–45.

Elliston, John S. G. (1978) 'Computer-aided Translation: A Business Viewpoint', in Barbara M. Snell (ed.) *Translating and the Computer: Proceedings of a Seminar*, 14 November 1978, London and Amsterdam: North-Holland Publishing Company, 149–58.

Esselink, Bert (2003) 'Localisation and Translation', in Harold L. Somers (ed.) *Computers and Translation: A Translator's Guide*, Amsterdam and Philadelphia: John Benjamins Publishing Company, 67–86.

Falkedal, Kirsten (ed.) (1991) *Proceedings of the Evaluators' Forum*, 21–24 April 1991, Les Rasses, Vaud, Switzerland.

Frederking, Robert E., Ralf D. Brown, and Christopher Hogan (1997) 'The DIPLOMAT Rapid-deployment Speech MT System', in Virginia Teller and Beth Sundeim (eds.) *Proceedings of the MT Summit VI: Machine Translation: Past, Present, Future*, 29 October–1 November 1997, San Diego, CA, 261–62.

Gaspari, Federico and W. John Hutchins (2007) 'Online and Free! Ten Years of Online Machine Translation: Origins, Developments, Current Use and Future Prospects', in *Proceeding of the MT Summit XI*, 10–14 September 2007, Copenhagen, Denmark, 199–206.

Goodman, Kenneth and Sergei Nirenburg (eds.) (1991) *The KBMT Project: A Case Study in Knowledge-based Machine Translation*, San Mateo, CA: Morgan Kaufmann Publishers.

Henisz-Dostert, Bozena (1967) 'Experimental Machine Translation', in William M. Austin (ed.) *Papers in Linguistics in Honor of Léon Dostert*, The Hague: Mouton, 57–91.

Hutchins, W. John (1986) *Machine Translation: Past, Present, Future*, Chichester: Ellis Horwood and New York: Halsted Press.

Hutchins, W. John (1998) 'The Origins of the Translator's Workstation', *Machine Translation* 13(4): 287–307.

Hutchins, W. John (2003) 'Commercial Systems: The State of the Art', in Harold L. Somers (ed.) *Computers and Translation: A Translator's Guide*, Amsterdam and Philadelphia: John Benjamins Publishing Company, 161–74.

Hutchins, W. John (2004) 'The Georgetown-IBM Experiment Demonstrated in January 1954', in Robert E. Frederking and Kathryn B. Taylor (eds.) *Proceedings of Machine Translation: From Real Users to Research: Proceedings of the 6th Conference of the Association for Machine Translation in the Americas, AMTA 2004*, 28 September–2 October 2004, Washington, DC and Berlin: Springer Verlag, 102–14.

Kay, Martin (1980) 'The Proper Place of Men and Machines in Language Translation', *Research Report CSL-80-11, Xerox Palo Alto Research Center*, Palo Alto, CA.

King, Margaret, Andrei Popescu-Belis, and Eduard Hovy (2003) 'FEMTI: Creating and Using a Framework for MT Evaluation', in *Proceedings of Machine Translation Summit IX: Machine Translation for Semitic Languages: Issues and Approaches*, 23–27 September 2003, New Orleans, Louisiana, 224–31.

Koehn, Philipp (2007) 'EuroMatrix – Machine Translation for All European Languages', *Invited Talk at MT Summit XI*, 10–14 September 2007, Copenhagen, Denmark.

Koehn, Philipp (2009) *Statistical Machine Translation*, Cambridge: Cambridge University Press.

Koehn, Philipp, Alexandra Birch, and Ralf Steinberger (2009) '462 Machine Translation Systems for Europe', in *MT Summit XII: Proceedings of the 12th Machine Translation Summit*, 26–30 August 2009, Ottawa, Ontario, Canada, 65–72.

Lavie, Alon, Chad Langley, Alex Waibel, Fabio Pianesi, Gianni Lazzari, Paolo Coletti, Loredana Taddei, and Franco Balducci (2001) 'Architecture and Design Considerations in NESPOLE!: A Speech Translation System for E-commerce Applications', in *HLT-2001: Proceedings of the 1st International Conference on Human Language Technology Research*, 18–21 March 2001, San Diego, CA.

Miller, George A. and J. G. Beebe-Center (1956) 'Some Psychological Methods for Evaluating the Quality of Translations', *Mechanical Translation* 3(3): 73–80.

Nagao, Makoto (1984) 'A Framework of a Mechanical Translation between Japanese and English by Analogy Principle', in Alick Elithorn and Ranan Banerji (eds.) *Artificial and Human Intelligence*, Amsterdam: North-Holland Publishing Company, 173–80.

Ney, Hermann (2005) 'One Decade of Statistical Machine Translation', in *Proceedings of the MT Summit X: The 10th Machine Translation Summit*, 12–16 September 2005, Phuket, Thailand, i-12–i-17.

Nomura, Hirosato and Hitoshi Isahara (1992) 'The JEIDA Methodology and Survey', in Muriel Vasconcellos (ed.) *MT Evaluation: Basis for Future Directions: Proceedings of a Workshop Sponsored by the National Science Foundation*, 2–3 November 1992, San Diego, CA, 11–12.

Papineni, Kishore, Salim Roukos, Todd Ward, and Zhu Wei-Jing (2002) 'BLEU: A Method for Automatic Evaluation of Machine Translation', in *Proceedings of the 40th Annual Meeting of the Association for Computational Linguistics, ACL-2002*, 7–12 July 2002, University of Pennsylvania, Philadelphia, PA, 311–18.

Ravi, Sujith and Kevin Knight (2011) 'Deciphering Foreign Language', in *Proceedings of the 49th Annual Meeting of the Association for Computational Linguistics*, 19–24 June 2011, Portland, OR, 12–21.

Rayner, Manny, Hiyan Alshawi, Ivan Bretan, David Carter, Vassilios Digalakis, Björn Gambäck, Jaan Kaja, Jussi Karlgren, Bertil Lyberg, Steve Pulman, Patti Price, and Christer Samuelsson (1993) 'A Speech to Speech Translation System Built from Standard Components', in *HLT '93: Proceedings of the Workshop on Human Language Technology*, 21–24 March 1993, Plainsboro, NJ, 217–22.

Rayner, Manny and Pierrette Bouillon (2002) 'Flexible Speech to Speech Phrasebook Translator', in *Proceedings of the ACL-2002 Workshop on Speech-to-speech Translation*, 11 July 2002, Philadelphia, PA, 69–76.

Resnick, Philip (1999) 'Mining the Web for Bilingual Text', in *ACL-1999: Proceedings of the 37th Annual Meeting of the Association for Computational Linguistics*, 20–26 June 1999, University of Maryland, College Park, MD, 527–34.

Seligman, Mark and Mike Dillinger (2006) 'Usability Issues in an Interactive Speech-to-speech Translation System for Healthcare', in *HLT-NAACL 2006: Proceedings of the Workshop on Medical Speech Translation*, 9 June 2006, New York, NY, 1–8.

Somers, Harold L. (2003) 'Translation Technologies and Minority Languages', in Harold L. Somers (ed.) *Computers and Translation: A Translator's Guide*, Amsterdam and Philadelphia: John Benjamins Publishing Company, 87–103.

Somers, Harold L. (2007) 'Machine Translation and the World Wide Web', in Ahmad Kurshid, Christopher Brewster, and Mark Stevenson (eds.) *Words and Intelligence II: Essays in Honor of Yorick Wilks*, Dordrecht: Springer Verlag, 209–33.

Tomita, Masaru, Marion Kee, Hiroaki Saito, Teruko Mitamura, and Hideto Tomabechi (1988) 'Towards a Speech-to-speech Translation System', *Interface: Journal of Applied Linguistics* 3(1): 57–77.

Turcato, Davide and Fred Popowich (2003) 'What Is Example-based Machine Translation?', in Michael Carl and Andy Way (eds.) *Recent Advances in Example-based Machine Translation*, Dordrecht: Kluwer Academic Publishers, 59–81.

van Slype, Georges (1979) 'Critical Study of Methods for Evaluating the Quality of Machine Translation', *Final Report BR19142*, Brussels: Bureau Marcel van Dijk [for] European Commission.

Vasconcellos, Muriel (ed.) (1992) 'MT Evaluation: Basis for Future Directions: Proceedings of a Workshop Sponsored by the National Science Foundation', 2–3 November 1992, San Diego, CA.

Wahlster, Wolfgang (1993) 'Verbmobil: Translation of Face-to-face Dialogs', in *Proceedings of the MT Summit IV: International Cooperation for Global Communication*, 20–22 July 1993, Kobe, Japan, 127–35.

Wahlster, Wolfgang (ed.) (2000) *Verbmobil: Foundations of Speech-to-speech Translation*, Berlin: Springer Verlag.

Weaver, Warren (1949) 'Translation'. Reprinted in William N. Locke and Andrew D. Booth (eds.) *Machine Translation of Languages: Fourteen Essays*, Cambridge, MA: Technology Press of the Massachusetts Institute of Technology, 15–33.

Woszczyna, Monika, Noah Coccaro, Andreas Eisele, Alon Lavie, Arthur E. McNair, Thomas Polzin, Ivica Rogina, Carolyn P. Rose, Tilo Sloboda, Masaru Tomita, Junya Tsutsumi, Naomi Aoki-Waibel, Alex H. Waibel, and Wayne Ward (1993) 'Recent Advances in JANUS: A Speech Translation System', in *Proceedings of the 5th International Conference on Theoretical and Methodological Issues in Machine Translation of Natural Languages: MT in the Next Generation (TMI-93)*, 14–16 July 1993, Kyoto, Japan, 195–200.

Yngve, Victor H. (1964) 'Implications of Mechanical Translation Research', *Proceedings of the American Philosophical Society* 108(4): 275–81.

7

EXAMPLE-BASED MACHINE TRANSLATION

Billy Wong Tak Ming

Introduction

Machine translation (MT) is the mechanization and automation of the process of translating from one natural language into another. Translation is a task which needs to tackle the 'semantic barriers' between languages using real-world encyclopaedic knowledge and requires a full understanding of natural language. Accordingly different approaches have been proposed for addressing the challenges involved in automating this task. At present the major approaches include rule-based machine translation (RBMT), which heavily relies on linguistic analysis and representation at various linguistic levels, as well as example-based machine translation (EBMT), statistical machine translation (SMT), and neural machine translation (NMT), which follow a more general corpus-based methodology to make use of parallel corpora as primary resource.

This chapter presents an overview of the EBMT technology. In brief, EBMT involves extracting knowledge from existing translations (examples) in order to facilitate translation of new utterances. A comprehensive review of EBMT can be found in Somers (2003: 3–57) and Way (2010: 177–208).

After reviewing the history of EBMT and the controversies it has generated over the past decades, we will examine the major issues related to examples, including example acquisition, granularity, size, representation, and management. The fundamental stages of translation for an EBMT system will be discussed with attention to the various methodologies and techniques belonging to each stage. Finally the suitability of EBMT will be discussed, showing the types of translation that are deemed suitable for EBMT and how EBMT interoperates with other MT approaches.

Origin

The idea of using existing translation data as the main resource for MT is most notably attributed to Nagao (1984: 173–80). Around the same time, there were other attempts at similarly exploiting parallel data as an aid of human translation. Kay (1980, 1997: 3–23), for example, introduced the concept of translation memory (TM), which has become an important feature in many computer-aid translation (CAT) systems. TM can be understood as a 'restricted form of EBMT' (Kit *et al.* 2002: 57–78) in the sense that both involve storing and retrieving previous

DOI: 10.4324/9781003168348-8

translation examples; nevertheless in EBMT, the translation output is produced by the system, while in TM, this is left to human effort. Arthen (1978: 77–108) on the other hand proposes 'a programme which would enable the word processor to "remember" whether any part of a new text typed into it had already been translated, and to fetch this part together with the translation'. Similarly, Melby's (1995) ALPS system, one of the earliest commercial MT systems, which dates back to the 1970s, incorporated what they called a 'repetition processing' tool.

Conceptually, Nagao's EBMT attempts to mimic human cognitive behaviour in translating as well as language learning:

> Man does not translate a simple sentence by doing deep linguistic analysis, rather, man does the translation, first, by properly decomposing an input sentence into certain fragmental phrases, . . . then by translating these phrases into other language phrases, and finally by properly composing these fragmental translations into one long sentence. The translation of each fragmental phrase will be done by the analogy translation principle with proper example as its reference.
>
> *(Nagao 1984: 175)*

Nagao (1992) further notes:

> Language learners do not learn much about a grammar of a language. . . . They just learn what is given, that is, a lot of example sentences, and use them in their own sentence compositions.
>
> *(ibid.: 82)*

Accordingly, there are three main components of EBMT: (1) matching source fragments against the examples, (2) identifying the corresponding translation fragments, and then (3) recombining them to give the target output.

A major advantage of EBMT over RBMT is its ability to handle extra-grammatical sentences, which, though linguistically correct, cannot be accounted for in the grammar of the system. EBMT also avoids the intractable complexity of rule management, which can make it difficult to trace the cause for failure or to predict the domino effect of the addition or deletion of a rule. EBMT addresses such inadequacies by incorporating the 'learning' concept for handling the translation of expressions without structural correspondence in another language (Nagao 2007: 153–58) and also by extending the example base simply by adding examples to cover various kinds of language use.

Definition

EBMT offers high flexibility in the use of examples and implementation of each of the three components (matching, alignment, and recombination), leading to systems with, for instance, rule-based matching or statistical example recombination. The underlying principle for EBMT, according to Kit *et al.* (2002: 57–78), is to 'remember everything translated in the past and use everything available to facilitate the translation of the next utterance' where 'the knowledge seems to have no overt formal representation or any encoding scheme. Instead . . . in a way as straightforwardly as text couplings: a piece of text in one language matches a piece of text in another language'.

EBMT implies the application of examples – as the main source of system knowledge – at run-time, as opposed to a pre-trained model where bilingual data are only used for training in advance but not consulted during translation. Examples can be pre-processed and represented in the form of a string (sentence or phrase), template, tree structure, and/or other annotated representations appropriate for the matching and alignment processes.

Examples

Acquisition

As it relates to the source of system knowledge, example acquisition is critical to the success of EBMT. Examples are typically acquired from translation documents, including parallel corpora and multilingual webpages, as well as from TM databases. Multilingual texts from sources such as the European and Hong Kong parliaments constitute high-quality data. The Europarl corpus (Koehn 2005: 79–86), for example, covers twenty language pairings. The Bilingual Laws Information System (BLIS) of Hong Kong corpus (Kit *et al.* 2003: 286–92, 2004: 29–51, 2005: 71–78) provides comprehensive documentation of the laws of Hong Kong in Chinese–English bilingual versions aligned at the clause level, with 10 million English words and 18 million Chinese characters. Legal texts like this are known to be more precise and less ambiguous than most other types of text. In the past decades, the growing number of web-based documents represents another major source of parallel texts (Resnik 1998: 72–82; Ma and Liberman 1999: 13–17; Kit and Ng 2007: 526–29; Tiedemann 2016: 384).

Possible sources of examples include such highly parallel bitexts, which, though increasingly available, still remain limited in volume, language, and register coverage, especially for certain language pairs. Efforts have also been made to collect comparable non-parallel texts such as multilingual news feeds from news agencies. They are not exactly parallel but convey overlapping information in different languages; hence some sentences/paragraphs/texts can be regarded as meaning equivalent. Shimohata *et al.* (2003: 73–80) describe such as 'shar[ing] the main meaning with the input sentence despite lacking some unimportant information. It does not contain information additional to that in the input sentence'. In order to facilitate the development of an 'example-based rough translation' system, a method is proposed to retrieve such meaning equivalent sentences from non-parallel corpora using lexical and grammatical features such as content words, modality, and tense. Munteanu and Marcu (2005: 477–504), on the other hand, propose to accomplish the same purpose by means of machine learning strategy.

Apart from gathering available resources, new bitexts can also be 'created' by using an MT system to translate monolingual texts into target languages. Gough *et al.* (2002: 74–83) report on experiments in which they first decomposed sentences into phrases and then translated them with MT systems. The resulting parallel phrases could then be used as examples for an EBMT system. The output quality proved better than that from translating the whole input sentence via online MT systems.

Granularity and Size

In principle, an example can be as simple as a pair of translated texts in two languages of any size at any linguistic level: word, phrase, clause, sentence, and even paragraph. Thus, a bilingual dictionary can be viewed as a 'restricted example base', that is, translation aligned at the word level. There were also attempts to build bilingual lexicons of multiword expressions as examples from parallel corpora (Semmar and Laib 2017). More flexibly, an example can simply be a pair of text chunks of an arbitrary length, not necessarily matching a linguistically meaningful structure or constituent.

In practice, because sentence boundaries are relatively easier to identify than those of finer linguistic constituents, the most common 'grain-size' for examples is the sentence. Example sentences, however, have to be decomposed into smaller chunks in the process of matching and recombination. There is usually a trade-off between granularity and recall of examples: the larger the example, the lower the probability to reuse. On the other hand, the smaller the example, the greater the probability of ambiguity. For examples at the word level, it is not surprising to find many source words with multiple possible target counterparts. An optimal balance may be better achieved at the sub-sentential level. Cranias *et al.* (1994: 100–04) state that 'the potential of EBMT lies in the exploitation of fragments of text smaller than sentences'.

Another important consideration is the size of the example base. In general, the translation quality of an EBMT system improves as the example base is enlarged. However, there may be a ceiling on the number of examples after which further addition of examples will not further improve the quality and may even degrade the system performance. The speed of computation also depends on the number of examples: the more examples, the longer the processing time required at run time.

Representation and Management

There are a number of representation schemas proposed for storing examples. The simplest representation is in the form of text string pairs aligned at various granularity levels without additional information. Giza++ (Och and Ney 2003: 19–51) is one of the most popular choices for implementing word-level alignment. On the other hand, Way and Gough (2003: 421–57) and Gough and Way (2004b: 95–104) discuss an approach based on bilingual phrasal pairs, that is, 'marker lexicon'. Their approach follows the marker hypothesis (Green 1979: 481–96), which assumes that every natural language has its own closed set of lexemes and morphemes for marking the boundary of syntactic structure. Alternatively, Kit *et al.*'s (2003: 286–92, 2004: 29–51) lexical-based clause alignment approach achieves a high alignment accuracy via reliance on basic lexical resources.

Examples may be annotated with various kinds of information. Similar to conventional RBMT systems, many attempts at EBMT stored examples as syntactic tree structures following constituency grammar (Kotzé *et al.* 2017: 249–82). This offers the advantage of clear boundary definition, ensuring that example fragments are well-formed constituents. Later works such as Al-Adhaileh and Kong (1999: 244–49) and Aramaki *et al.* (2001: 27–32, 2005: 219–26) employed dependency structures linking lexical heads and their dependents in a linguistic expression. Planas and Furuse (1999: 331–39) presents a multi-level lattice representation combining typographic, orthographic, lexical, syntactic, and other information. Forcada (2002) represents sub-sentential bitexts as a finite-state transducer. In their data-oriented translation model, Way (2001: 66–80, 2003: 443–72) and Hearne and Way (2003: 165–72) use linked phrase-structure trees augmented with semantic information. In Microsoft's MT system reported in Richardson *et al.* (2001: 293–98) and Brockett *et al.* (2002: 1–7), a graph structure 'logical form' is used for describing labelled dependencies among content words, with information about word order and local morphosyntactic variation neutralized. Liu *et al.*'s (2005: 25–32) 'tree string correspondence' structure has only a parse tree in the source language, together with the target string and the correspondences between the leaf nodes of the source tree and the target substrings. Chua *et al.* (2017: 242–58) introduce a semantic compositional structure to represent the semantic information of examples and maintain the semantic structure of an input sentence throughout the recombination of examples.

A unique approach to EBMT which does without a parallel corpus is reported in Markantonatou *et al.* (2005: 91–98) and Vandeghinste *et al.* (2005: 135–42). Their example base consists only of a bilingual dictionary and monolingual corpora in the target language. In the translation process, a source text is first translated word for word into the target language using the dictionary. The monolingual corpora are then used to help determine a suitable translation in case of multiple possibilities, and to guide a correctly ordered recombination of target words. This approach is claimed to be suitable for language pairs without a sufficiently large parallel corpus available.

Webster *et al.* (2002: 79–91) links EBMT with semantic web technology and demonstrates how a flat example base can be developed into a machine-understandable knowledge base. Examples of statutory laws of Hong Kong in Chinese–English parallel versions are enriched with metadata describing their hierarchical structures and inter-relationships in Resource Description Framework (RDF) format, thus significantly improving example management and sub-sentential alignment.

In some systems, similar examples are combined and generalized as templates in order to reduce the size of the example base and improve example retrieval performance. Equivalence classes such as 'person's name', 'date', 'city's name', and linguistic information like gender and number that appear in examples with the same structure are replaced with variables. For example, the expression '*John Miller flew to Frankfurt on December 3rd*' can be represented as '<PER-SON-M> *flew to* <CITY> *on* <DATE>', which can easily be matched with another sentence '*Dr Howard Johnson flew to Ithaca on 7 April 1997*' (Somers 2003: 3–57). To a certain extent such example templates can be viewed as 'a special case of translation rules' (Maruyama and Watanabe 1992: 173–84) in RBMT. In general the recall rate of example retrieval can be improved by this approach but possibly with precision trade-off. Instances of studies of example templates include Malavazos *et al.* (2000), Brown (2000: 125–31), McTait (2001: 22–34), and Salam *et al.* (2018).

Examples need to be pre-processed before being put to use and be properly managed. For instance, Zhang *et al.* (2001: 247–52) discuss the pre-processing tasks of English–Chinese bilingual corpora for EBMT, including Chinese word segmentation, English phrase bracketing, and term tokenization. They show that a pre-processed corpus improves the quality of language resources acquired from the corpus: the average length of Chinese and English terms was increased by around 60 percent and 10 percent, respectively, and the coverage of bilingual dictionary by 30 percent.

When the size of the example base is scaled up, there is the issue of example redundancy. Explained in Somers (2003: 3–57), overlapping examples (source side) may mutually reinforce each other or be in conflict, depending on the consistency of translations (target side). Whether such redundancy needs to be constrained depends on the application of examples: a prerequisite for systems relying on frequency for tasks such as similarity measurement in example matching or a problem to be solved where this is not the case.

Stages

Matching

The first task of EBMT is to retrieve examples which closely match the source sentence. This process relies on a measure of text similarity and is one of the most studied areas in EBMT. Text similarity measurement is a task common in various applications of natural language processing, with many measures available. It is also closely related to how examples are represented and stored and accordingly can be performed on string pairs or annotated structures. In order to better utilize available syntactic and semantic information, it may be further facilitated by language resources like thesauri and a part-of-speech tagger.

When examples are stored as string pairs at the sentence level, they may first need to be decomposed into fragments to improve example retrieval. In Gough *et al.* (2002: 74–83) and Gough and Way (2004b: 95–104), example sentences are split into phrasal lexicons with the aid of a closed set of specific words and morphemes to 'mark' the boundary of phrases. Kit *et al.* (2002: 57–78) uses a multi-gram model to select the best sentence decomposition with the highest occurring frequencies in an example base. Roh *et al.* (2003: 323–29) discusses two types of segmentation for sentences: 'chunks' that include proper nouns, time adverbs, and lexically fixed expressions and 'partitions' that are selected by syntactic clues such as punctuation, conjunctions, relatives, and main verbs.

The similarity measure for example matching can be as simple as a character-based one. Two string segments are compared for the number of characters required for modification, whether in terms of addition, deletion, or substitution, until the two are identical. This is known as edit-distance, which has been widely applied in other applications like spell-checking, translation memory, and speech processing. It offers the advantages of simplicity and language independence and avoids the need to pre-process the input sentence and examples. Nirenburg *et al.* (1993: 47–57) extends the basic character-based edit-distance measure to account for necessary keystrokes in editing operations (e.g. deletion = 3 strokes, substitution = 3 strokes). Somers (2003: 3–57) notes that in languages like Japanese, certain characters are more discriminatory than others; thus the matching process may only focus on these key characters.

Nagao (1984: 173–80) employs word-based matching as the similarity measure. A thesaurus is used for identifying word similarity on the basis of meaning or usage. Matches are then permitted for synonyms and near-synonyms in the example sentences. An early method of this kind was reported on Sumita and Iida (1991: 185–92), where similarity between two words is measured by their distance in a hierarchically structured thesaurus. In Doi *et al.* (2005: 51–58), this method is integrated with an edit-distance measure. Highlighting an efficiency problem in example retrieval, they note that real-time processing for translation is hard to achieve, especially if an input sentence has to be matched against all examples individually using a large example base. Accordingly, they propose the adoption of multiple strategies, including search space division, word graphs, and the A⋆ search algorithm (Nilsson 1971), to improve retrieval efficiency. In Aramaki *et al.* (2003: 57–64), example similarity is measured based on different weights assigned to content and function words in an input string that are matched with an example, together with their shared meaning as defined in a dictionary. Liu and Yves (2021: 513–22) present a hybrid method to retrieve similar example sentences by combining n-gram matching, fuzzy matching based on edit distance, and contextual similarity search based on sentence embeddings.

The availability of annotated examples with linguistic information allows the implementation of similarity measures with multiple features. In the multi-engine Pangloss system (Nirenburg *et al.* 1994: 78–87), the matching process combines several variously weighted requirements including exact matches, number of word insertions or deletions, word-order differences, morphological variants, and parts of speech. Chatterjee (2001) discusses the evaluation of sentence similarity at various linguistic levels, that is, syntactic, semantic, and pragmatic, all of which need to be considered in the case of dissimilar language pairs where source and target sentences with the same meaning may vary in their surface structures. A linear similarity evaluation model is then proposed which supports a combination of multiple individually weighted linguistic features.

For certain languages, the word-based matching process requires pre-processing of both the input sentences and examples in advance. This may include tokenization and word segmentation for languages without clear word boundaries like Chinese and Japanese and lemmatization for morphologically rich languages such as Arabic.

When examples are stored as structured objects, the process of example retrieval entails more complex tree-matching. Typically it may involve parsing an input sentence into the same representation schema as examples, searching the annotated example base for best matched examples, and measuring similarity of structured representations. Liu *et al.* (2005: 25–32) presents a measure of syntactic tree similarity accounting for all the nodes and meaning of headwords in the trees. Aramaki *et al.* (2005: 219–26) proposes a tree matching model, whose parameters include the size of tree fragments; their translation probability; and context similarity of examples, which is defined as the similarity of the surrounding phrases of a translation example and an input phrase.

Recombination

After a set of translation examples are matched against an input sentence, the most difficult step in the EBMT process is to retrieve their counterpart fragments from the example base and then combine them into a proper target sentence. The problem is twofold, as described by Somers (2003: 3–57): (1) identifying which portion of an associated translation example corresponds to which portion of the source text and (2) recombining these portions in an appropriate manner. The first is partially solved when the retrieved examples are already decomposed from sentences into finer fragments, either at the beginning when they are stored or at the matching stage. However, in case more than one example is retrieved, or multiple translations are available for a source fragment, there arises the question of how to decide which alternative is better.

Furthermore, the recombination of translation fragments is not an independent process but closely related to the representation of examples. How examples are stored determines what information will be available for performing recombination. In addition, as the final stage of EBMT, the performance of recombination is to a large extent affected by the output quality from the previous stages. Errors occurring at the matching stage or earlier are a kind of noise which interferes with recombination. McTait (2001: 22–34) shows how tagging errors resulting from applying part-of-speech analysis to the matching of examples unexpectedly lowers both the recall of example retrieval and accuracy of translation output. Further complications occur when examples retrieved do not fully cover the input sentence in question.

The most critical point in recombination is to adjust the fragment order to form a readable, at best grammatical, sentence in the target language. Since each language has its own syntax to govern how sentential structures are formed, it will not work if the translation fragments are simply sequenced in the same order as in the source sentence. However, this is the approach of some EBMT systems, such as that reported in Way and Gough (2003: 421–57). In Doi and Sumita (2003: 104–10), it is claimed that such a simple approach is suitable for speech translation, since sentences in a dialog usually do not have complicated structures, and many long sentences can be split into mutually independent portions.

With reference to a text-structured example base, Kit *et al.* (2002: 57–78) suggest that it is preferable to use the probabilistic approach for recombination. Taking an empirical case-based knowledge engineering approach to MT, they give an example of a tri-gram language model and point out some other considerations such as insertion of function words for better readability. Techniques in SMT have also been used in the hybrid EBMT-SMT models of Groves and Way (2005a: 301–23, 2005b: 183–90), which uses Pharoah (Koehn 2004: 115–24), a decoder for selecting a translation fragment order in the highest probability, and the MaTrEx system (Du *et al.* 2009: 95–99), which uses another decoder called Moses (Koehn *et al.* 2007: 177–80).

For EBMT systems using examples in syntactic tree structures, where the correspondence between source and target fragments are labelled explicitly, recombination is then a task of tree unification. For instance, in Sato (1995: 31–49), possible word-dependency structures of translation are first generated based on the retrieved examples, and the best translation candidate is then selected by a number of criteria such as the size and source-target context of examples. In Wantanabe (1995: 269–91), where examples are represented as graphs, the recombination involves a kind of graph unification, which they refer to as a 'gluing process'. In Aramaki *et al.* (2005: 219–26), the translation examples stored in a dependency structure are first combined, with the source dependency relation preserved in the target structure, and then output with the aid of a probabilistic language model to determine the word order.

Other systems without annotated example bases may be equipped with information about probable word alignment from dictionaries or other resources that can facilitate the recombination process (e.g. Kaji *et al.* 1992: 672–78; Matsumoto *et al.* 1993: 23–30). Some systems, like Franz *et al.* (2000: 1031–35), Richardson *et al.* (2001: 293–98), and Brockett *et al.* (2002: 1–7), rely on rule-based generation engines supplied with linguistic knowledge of target languages. Alternatively, in Nederhof (2001: 25–32) and Forcada (2002), recombination is carried out via a finite state transition network (FSTN), according to which translation generation becomes akin to giving a 'guided tour' from the source node to the target node in the FSTN.

A well-known problem in recombination, namely 'boundary friction' (Nirenburg *et al.* 1993: 47–57; Collins 1998), occurs when translation fragments from various examples need to be combined into a target sentence. Grammatical problems often occur because words with different syntactic functions cannot appear next to each other. This is especially true for certain highly inflected languages like German. One solution is to smooth the recombined translation by adjusting the morphological features of certain words in the translation or inserting some additional function words based on a grammar or probabilistic model of the target language. Another proposal from Somers *et al.* (1994) is to attach each fragment with 'hooks' indicating the possible contexts of the fragment in a corpus, that is, the words and parts-of-speech which can occur before and after. Fragments which can be connected together are shown in this way. Brown *et al.* (2003: 24–31) put1 forth the idea of translation-fragment overlap. They find that examples with overlapping fragments are more likely to be combined into valid translations if there are sentences in an example base that also share these overlapping fragments. Based on their study of the occurrence frequencies of combined fragments from the Internet, Gough *et al.* (2002: 74–83) find that valid word combinations usually have much higher occurrence frequencies than invalid ones.

Suitability

Sublanguage Translation

EBMT is usually deemed suitable for sublanguage translation, largely due to its reliance on text corpora, most of which belong to specific domains. In other words, EBMT systems are optimized to texts in the same domain as their examples. The contribution of an example domain to improving EBMT translation quality is illustrated in Doi *et al.* (2003: 16–18). A system with more 'in-domain examples' (domain of input sentences matches with that of examples) performs better than those with either only out-of-domain examples or fewer in-domain examples. One negative finding in Denoual (2005: 35–42), however, shows that given the same number of examples, homogeneous data (in-domain) yield neither better nor worse EBMT quality than heterogeneous data (mixed domain). Even though the usefulness of in-domain examples is not yet completely clear, EBMT has been widely adopted in different specific areas, including translation of sign language (Morrissey *et al.* 2007: 329–36), DVD subtitles (Flanagan 2009: 85–92), idioms (Anastasiou 2010), and medicine publications (Ehab *et al.* 2018: 131–135).

A series of works in Gough and Way (2003: 133–40, 2004a: 73–81) and Way and Gough (2005: 1–36) further substantiates the suitability of EBMT for domain-specific translation. Their system is based on examples written in controlled language (CL), a subset of natural language whose grammar and lexicon are restricted in order to minimize ambiguity and complexity. In return, their system outperforms both RBMT and SMT systems in evaluation, largely due to the fact that RBMT suffers from greater complexity in fine-tuning its system to support CL, while SMT requires extremely large volumes of training text, which is hard to come by for CL. An EBMT system, on the other hand, can be developed with smaller amounts of training examples.

Interoperation With Other MT Paradigms

While there may be few 'pure' EBMT systems (Lepage and Denoual 2005: 81–90; Somers *et al.* 2009: 53–60), example-based method has been widely integrated with other MT approaches to provide complementary advantages. Mention of interoperability of EBMT occurs as early as in Furuse and Iida (1992: 139–50), which notes that 'an example-based framework never contradicts other frameworks such as a rule-based and a statistically based framework, nor is it difficult to integrate it with them'.

The following discussion reviews how EBMT was combined with rule-based and statistical systems.

With RBMT

Since its initial proposal, EBMT has long been applied as a solution for what is too difficult to resolve in RBMT. This includes notably special linguistic expressions such as Japanese adnominal particle constructions (Sumita *et al.* 1990: 203–11; Sumita and Iida 1991: 185–92), 'parameterizable fixed phrases' in economics news stories (Katoh and Aizawa 1994: 28–33), compound nouns, and noun phrases which are syntactically and semantically idiosyncratic (Yamabana *et al.* 1997: 977–82), all of which can be handled by simply collecting translation examples to cover them.

The strengths and weaknesses of the two approaches are more thoroughly analysed in Carl *et al.* (2000: 223–57). In general, applying EBMT to longer translation units (phrasal) ensures better translation quality but lower coverage of the types of source texts that can be reliably translated. In contrast, applying RBMT to shorter translation units (lexical) enables a higher coverage but inferior output quality to EBMT. An MT system architecture is accordingly proposed to integrate the two approaches. Source chunks in an input sentence are first matched by an example-based module against an example base. The unmatched parts and the reordering of translated chunks are then handled by a rule-based module.

With SMT

Statistical methods have been widely used in EBMT, including example retrieval (Doi *et al.* 2005: 51–58), as well as matching and recombination (Liu *et al.* 2005: 25–32). Example-based methods can also be utilized to assist SMT. Marcu (2001: 386–93) built a translation memory from a bilingual corpus with statistical methods to train SMT models. Langlais and Simard (2002: 104–13) integrated bilingual terminologies into an SMT system, leading to improved translation performance. Watanabe and Sumita (2003: 410–17) designed an example-based SMT decoder that can retrieve translation examples from a parallel corpus whose source part is similar to the input sentence and modify the target part of the example to produce translation output. Based on a series of experiments carried out by Groves and Way (2005a: 301–23, 2005b: 183–90, 2006: 115–24) involving the addition of example chunks to an SMT system, they note that, 'while there is an obvious convergence between both paradigmatic variants, more gains are to be had from combining their relative strengths in novel hybrid systems'. There has been also a number of attempts to integrate example-based methods with phrase-based SMT, such as Mrinalini *et al.* (2018), who adopted this approach to handle the out-of-vocabulary problem, and Kozerenko *et al.* (2019: 445–50), who dealt with the construction of syntax structure of texts based on representations of phrase structures.

Summary

In general, the main idea of EBMT is simple: from all that was translated in the past, use whatever is available to facilitate the translation of the next utterance. How translation data (examples) are stored and applied (in matching and recombination) can vary, as long as the examples are used in run-time. Being empirical in nature, the example base represents real language use, covers the constructions which really occur, and is relatively easy to extend – simply adding more examples. This is particularly true for examples stored as bilingual string pairs, which have benefited and will continue to benefit from the massively growing number of documents on the web. The problem of developing MT systems for language pairs suffering from a scarcity of resources has been to some extent resolved.

The current status of EBMT also reveals, however, the possible constraints of this approach. So far there is no publicly available MT system purely based on the example-based approach, except a few on a limited scale for research purposes. Most systems exhibit a certain degree of hybridity with other MT approaches (on the other hand, the example-based method has also been widely applied in other MT paradigms). From a practical perspective, it is perhaps more pragmatic to focus on how the strength of example-based methods can be adequately utilized, together with other available methods, to tackle various kinds of translation problems.

Bibliography

Al-Adhaileh, Mosleh Hmoud, and Enya Kong Tang (1999) 'Example-based Machine Translation Based on the Synchronous SSTC Annotation Schema', in *Proceedings of the Machine Translation Summit VII: MT in the Great Translation Era*, Singapore, 244–49.

Anastasiou, Dimitra (2010) *Idiom Treatment Experiments in Machine Translation*, Newcastle upon Tyne: Cambridge Scholars Publishing.

Aramaki, Eiji, Sadao Kurohashi, Hideki Kashioka, and Naoto Kato (2005) 'Probabilistic Model for Example-based Machine Translation', in *Proceedings of the Machine Translation Summit X: 2nd Workshop on Example-based Machine Translation*, Phuket, Thailand, 219–26.

Aramaki, Eiji, Sadao Kurohashi, Hideki Kashioka, and Hideki Tanaka (2003) 'Word Selection for EBMT Based on Monolingual Similarity and Translation Confidence', in *Proceedings of the HLT-NAACL 2003 Workshop on Building and Using Parallel Texts: Data Driven Machine Translation and Beyond*, Edmonton, Canada, 57–64.

Aramaki, Eiji, Sadao Kurohashi, Satoshi Sato, and Hideo Watanabe (2001) 'Finding Translation Correspondences from Parallel Parsed Corpus for Example-based Translation', in *Proceedings of the Machine Translation Summit VIII: Machine Translation in the Information Age*, Santiago de Compostela, Spain, 27–32.

Arthern, Peter J. (1978) 'Machine Translation and Computerized Terminology Systems: A Translator's Viewpoint', in *Proceedings of Translating and the Computer*, London: ASLIB, 77–108.

Brockett, Chris, Takako Aikawa, Anthony Aue, Arul Menezes, Chris Quirk, and Hisami Suzuki (2002) 'English–Japanese Example-based Machine Translation Using Abstract Linguistic Representations', in *Proceedings of the COLING-02 Workshop: Machine Translation in Asia*, Taipei, Taiwan, 1–7.

Brown, Ralf D. (2000) 'Automated Generalization of Translation Examples', in *Proceedings of the 18th International Conference on Computational Linguistics (COLING-00)*, Saarbrücken, Germany, 125–31.

Brown, Ralf D., Rebecca Hutchinson, Paul N. Bennett, Jaime G. Carbonell, and Peter Jansen (2003) 'Reducing Boundary Friction Using Translation-fragment Overlap', in *Proceedings of the Machine Translation Summit IX*, New Orleans, LA, 24–31.

Carl, Michael, Catherine Pease, Lonid L. Iomdin, and Oliver Streiter (2000) 'Towards a Dynamic Linkage of Example-based and Rule-based Machine Translation', *Machine Translation* 15(3): 223–57.

Chatterjee, Niladri (2001) 'A Statistical Approach for Similarity Measurement between Sentences for EBMT', in *Proceedings of the Symposium on Translation Support Systems (STRANS)*, Kanpur, India.

Chua, Chong Chai, Tek Yong Lim, Lay-Ki Soon, Enya Kong Tang, and Bali Ranaivo-Malançon (2017) 'Meaning Preservation in Example-based Machine Translation with Structural Semantics', *Expert Systems with Applications* 78: 242–58.

Collins, Brona (1998) 'Example-based Machine Translation: An Adaptation Guided Retrieval Approach', PhD thesis, Trinity College, Dublin.

Cranias, Lambros, Harris Papageorgiou, and Stelios Piperidis (1994) 'A Matching Technique in Example-based Machine Translation', in *Proceedings of the 15th International Conference on Computational Linguistics (COLING-94)*, Kyoto, Japan, 100–04.

Denoual, Etienne (2005) 'The Influence of Example-data Homogeneity on EBMT Quality', in *Proceedings of the Machine Translation Summit X: 2nd Workshop on Example-based Machine Translation*, Phuket, Thailand, 35–42.

Doi, Takao and Eiichiro Sumita (2003) 'Input Sentence Splitting and Translating', in *Proceedings of the HLT-NAACL Workshop on Building and Using Parallel Texts: Data Driven Machine Translation and Beyond*, Edmonton, Canada, 104–10.

Doi, Takao, Eiichiro Sumita, and Hirofumi Yamamoto (2003) 'Adaptation Using Out-of-Domain Corpus within EBMT', in *Proceedings of the HLT-NAACL: Conference Combining Human Language Technology Conference and the North American Chapter of the Association for Computational Linguistics*, Edmonton, Canada, 16–18.

Doi, Takao, Hirofumi Yamamoto, and Eiichiro Sumita (2005) 'Graph-based Retrieval for Example-based Machine Translation Using Edit Distance', in *Proceedings of the Machine Translation Summit X: 2nd Workshop on Example-based Machine Translation*, Phuket, Thailand, 51–58.

Du, Jinhua, He Yifan, Sergio Penkale, and Andy Way (2009) 'MaTrEx: The DCU MT System for WMT 2009', in *Proceedings of the EACL: The 4th Workshop on Statistical Machine Translation*, Athens, Greece, 95–99.

Ehab, Rana, Eslam Amer, and Mahmoud Gadallah (2018) 'Example-Based English to Arabic Machine Translation: Matching Stage Using Internal Medicine Publications', in *Proceedings of the 7th International Conference on Software and Information Engineering*, Cairo, Egypt, 131–35.

Flanagan, Marian (2009) 'Using Example-based Machine Translation to Translate DVD Subtitles', in *Proceedings of the 3rd International Workshop on Example-based Machine Translation*, Dublin, Ireland, 85–92.

Forcada, Mikel L. (2002) 'Using Multilingual Content on the Web to Build Fast Finite-state Direct Translation Systems', in *The 2nd ELSNET TMI Workshop on MT Roadmap*, Keihanna, Japan.

Franz, Alexander, Keiko Horiguchi, Duan Lei, Doris Ecker, Eugene Koontz, and Kazami Uchida (2000) 'An Integrated Architecture for Example-based Machine Translation', in *Proceedings of the 18th International Conference on Computational Linguistics (COLING-00)*, Saarbrücken, Germany, 1031–35.

Furuse, Osamu and Hitoshi Iida (1992) 'An Example-based Method for Transfer-driven Machine Translation', in *Proceedings of the 4th International Conference on Theoretical and Methodological Issues in Machine Translation: Empiricist vs. Rationalist Methods in MT (TMI-92)*, Montréal, Canada, 139–50.

Gough, Nano and Andy Way (2003) 'Controlled Generation in Example-based Machine Translation', in *Proceedings of the Machine Translation Summit IX*, New Orleans, LA, 133–40.

Gough, Nano and Andy Way (2004a) 'Example-based Controlled Translation', in *Proceedings of the 9th Conference of the European Association for Machine Translation (EAMT-04)*, Valetta, Malta, 73–81.

Gough, Nano and Andy Way (2004b) 'Robust Large-scale EBMT with Marker-based Segmentation', in *Proceedings of the 10th Conference on Theoretical and Methodological Issues in Machine Translation (TMI-04)*, Baltimore, LA, 95–104.

Gough, Nano, Andy Way, and Mary Hearne (2002) 'Example-based Machine Translation via the Web', in *Proceedings of the 5th Conference of the Association for Machine Translation in the Americas, Machine Translation: From Research to Real Users (AMTA-02)*, California, 74–83.

Green, T. R. G. (1979) 'The Necessity of Syntax Markers: Two Experiments with Artificial Languages', *Journal of Verbal Learning and Behavior* 18(4): 481–96.

Groves, Declan and Andy Way (2005a) 'Hybrid Data-driven Models of Machine Translation', *Machine Translation* 19(3–4): 301–23.

Groves, Declan and Andy Way (2005b) 'Hybrid Example-based SMT: The Best of Both Worlds?', in *Proceedings of the ACL Workshop on Building and Using Parallel Texts: Data-driven Machine Translation and Beyond*, Ann Arbor, MI, 183–90.

Groves, Declan and Andy Way (2006) 'Hybridity in MT: Experiments on the Europarl Corpus', in *Proceedings of the 11th Conference of the European Association for Machine Translation (EAMT-06)*, Oslo, Norway, 115–24.

Hearne, Mary and Andy Way (2003) 'Seeing the Wood for the Trees: Data-oriented Translation', in *Proceedings of the Machine Translation Summit IX*, New Orleans, LA, 165–72.

Kaji, Hiroyuki, Yuuko Kida, and Yasutsugu Morimoto (1992) 'Learning Translation Templates from Bilingual Text', in *Proceedings of the 14th International Conference on Computational Linguistics (COLING-92)*, Nantes, France, 672–78.

Katoh, Naoto and Teruaki Aizawa (1994) 'Machine Translation of Sentences with Fixed Expressions', in *Proceedings of the 4th Conference on Applied Natural Language Processing*, Stuttgart, Germany, 28–33.

Kay, Martin (1980) *The Proper Place of Men and Machines in Translation*, Palo Alto, CA: Xerox Palo Alto Research Center (Reprinted in Machine Translation (1997) 12(1–2): 3–23).

Kit, Chunyu, Pan Haihua, and Jonathan J. Webster (2002) 'Example-based Machine Translation: A New Paradigm', in Chan Sin-wai (ed.) *Translation and Information Technology*, Hong Kong: The Chinese University Press, 57–78.

Kit, Chunyu and Jessica Y. H. Ng (2007) 'An Intelligent Web Agent to Mine Bilingual Parallel Pages via Automatic Discovery of URL Pairing Patterns', in *Proceedings of the 2007 IEEE/WIC/ACM International Conferences on Web Intelligence and Intelligent Agent Technology – Workshops: Workshop on Agents and Data Mining Interaction (ADMI-07)*, California, 526–29.

Kit, Chunyu, Jonathan J. Webster, Sin King Kui, Pan Haihua, and Li Heng (2003) 'Clause Alignment for Bilingual HK Legal Texts with Available Lexical Resources', in *Proceedings of the 20th International Conference on the Computer Processing of Oriental Languages (ICCPOL-03)*, Shenyang, China, 286–92.

Kit, Chunyu, Jonathan J. Webster, Sin King Kui, Pan Haihua, and Li Heng (2004) 'Clause Alignment for Bilingual HK Legal Texts: A Lexical-based Approach', *International Journal of Corpus Linguistics* 9(1): 29–51.

Kit, Chungyu, Liu Xiaoyue, Sin King Kui, and Jonathan J. Webster (2005) 'Harvesting the Bitexts of the Laws of Hong Kong from the Web', in *Proceedings of the 5th Workshop on Asian Language Resources (ALR-05)*, Jeju Island, Korea, 71–78.

Koehn, Philipp (2004) 'Pharaoh: A Beam Search Decoder for Phrase-based Statistical Machine Translation Models', in *Proceedings of the 6th Conference of the Association for Machine Translation in the Americas (AMTA-04)*, Springer, Berlin, 115–24.

Koehn, Philipp (2005) 'Europarl: A Parallel Corpus for Statistical Machine Translation', in *Proceedings of the Machine Translation Summit X: 2nd Workshop on Example-based Machine Translation*, Phuket, Thailand, 79–86.

Koehn, Philipp, Hiu Hoang, Alexandra Birch, Chris Callison-Burch, Marcello Federico, Nicola Bertoldi, Brooke Cowen, Shen Wade, Christine Moran, Richard Zens, Chris Dyer, Ondrej Bojar, Alexandra Constantin, and Evan Herbst (2007) 'Moses: Open Source Toolkit for Statistical Machine Translation', in *ACL Proceedings of the Interactive Poster and Demonstration Sessions*, Prague, Czech Republic, 177–80.

Kotzé, Gideon, Vincent Vandeghinste, Scott Martens, and Jörg Tiedemann (2017) 'Large Aligned Treebanks for Syntax-based Machine Translation', *Language Resources and Evaluation* 51(2): 249–82.

Kozerenko, Elena, Alexander Khoroshilov, Alexei Khoroshilov, Yuri Nikitin, and Yuri Kalinin (2019) 'Introduction of Phrase Structures into the Example-Based Machine Translation System', in *Proceedings of the 6th International Conference on Computational Science and Computational Intelligence*, Las Vegas, USA, 445–50.

Langlais, Philippe and Michel Simard (2002) 'Merging Example-based and Statistical Machine Translation: An Experiment', in *Proceedings of the 5th Conference of the Association for Machine Translation in the Americas on Machine Translation (AMTA-02)*, Tiburon, CA, 104–13.

Lepage, Yves and Etienne Denoual (2005) 'The "Purest" EBMT System Ever Built: No Variables, No Templates, No Training, Examples, Just Examples, Only Examples', in *Proceedings of the Machine Translation Summit X: 2nd Workshop on Example-based Machine Translation*, Phuket, Thailand, 81–90.

Liu, Yuan and Yves Lepage (2021) 'Covering a Sentence in Form and Meaning with Fewer Retrieved Sentences', in *Proceedings of the 35th Pacific Asia Conference on Language, Information and Computation*, Shanghai, China, 513–22.

Liu, Zhanzi, Wang Haifeng, and Wu Hua (2005) 'Example-based Machine Translation Based on TSC and Statistical Generation', in *Proceedings of the Machine Translation Summit X: 2nd Workshop on Example-based Machine Translation*, Phuket, Thailand, 25–32.

Ma, Xiaoyi and Mark Y. Liberman (1999) 'Bits: A Method for Bilingual Text Search over the Web', in *Proceedings of the Machine Translation Summit VII*, Singapore, 13–17.

Malavazos, Christos, Stelios Piperidis, and George Carayannis (2000) 'Towards Memory and Template-based Translation Synthesis', in *Proceedings of MT2000: Machine Translation and Multilingual Applications in the New Millennium*, 1–8 January 2000, Exeter, the United Kingdom.

Marcu, Daniel (2001) 'Towards a Unified Approach to Memory- and Statistical-based Machine Translation', in *Proceedings of the 39th Annual Meeting of the Association for Computational Linguistics (ACL-01)*, Toulouse, France, 386–93.

Markantonatou, Stella, Sokratis Sofianopoulos, Vassiliki Spilioti, Yiorgos Tambouratzis, Marina Vassiliou, Olga Yannoutsou, and Nikos Ioannou (2005) 'Monolingual Corpus-based MT Using Chunks', in *Proceedings of the Machine Translation Summit X: 2nd Workshop on Example-based Machine Translation*, Phuket, Thailand, 91–98.

Maruyama, Hiroshi and Hideo Watanabe (1992) 'Tree Cover Search Algorithm for Example-based Translation', in *Proceedings of the 4th International Conference on Theoretical and Methodological Issues in Machine Translation: Empiricist vs. Rationalist Methods in MT (TMI-92)*, Montréal, Canada, 173–84.

Matsumoto, Yuji, Hiroyuki Ishimoto, and Takehito Utsuro (1993) 'Structural Matching of Parallel Texts', in *Proceedings of the 31st Annual Meeting of the Association for Computational Linguistics (ACL-93)*, Columbus, OH, 23–30.

McTait, Kevin (2001) 'Linguistic Knowledge and Complexity in an EBMT System Based on Translation Patterns', in *Proceedings of the Machine Translation Summit VIII: Workshop on Example-based Machine Translation*, Santiago de Compostela, Spain, 22–34.

Melby, Alan K. and Terry Warner (1995) *The Possibility of Language: A Discussion of the Nature of Language*, Amsterdam and Philadelphia: John Benjamins Publishing Company.

Morrissey, Sara, Andy Way, Daniel Stein, Jan Bungeroth, and Hermann Ney (2007) 'Combining Data-driven MT Systems for Improved Sign Language Translation', in *Proceedings of the Machine Translation Summit XI*, Copenhagen, Denmark, 329–36.

Mrinalini, K., T. Nagarajan, and P. Vijayalakshmi (2018) 'Pause-Based Phrase Extraction and Effective OOV Handling for Low-Resource Machine Translation Systems', *ACM Transactions on Asian and Low-Resource Language Information Processing* 18(2): Article no 12.

Munteanu, Dragos and Daniel Marcu (2005) 'Improving Machine Translation Performance by Exploiting Comparable Corpora', *Computational Linguistics* 31(4): 477–504.

Nagao, Makoto (1984) 'A Framework of a Mechanical Translation between Japanese and English by Analogy Principle', in Alick Elithorn and Ranan Banerji (eds.) *Artificial and Human Intelligence*, Amsterdam: North Holland, 173–80.

Nagao, Makoto (1992) 'Some Rationales and Methodologies for Example-based Approach', in *Proceedings of the International Workshop on Fundamental Research for the Future Generation of Natural Language Processing (FGNLP)*, Manchester, England, 82–94.

Nagao, Makoto (2007) 'An Amorphous Object Must Be Cut by a Blunt Tool', in Khurshid Ahmad, Christopher Brewster, and Mark Stevenson (eds.) *Words and Intelligence II: Essays in Honor of Yorick Wilks*, Dordrecht: Springer, 153–58.

Nederhof, Mark-Jan (2001) 'Approximating Context-free by Rational Transduction for Example-based MT', in *Proceedings of the ACL-EACL Workshop: Data-driven Machine Translation*, Toulouse, France, 25–32.

Nilsson, Nils J. (1971) *Problem-solving Methods in Artificial Intelligence*, New York: McGraw-Hill.

Nirenburg, Sergei, Stephen Beale, and Constantine Domashnev (1994) 'A Full-text Experiment in Example-based Machine Translation', in *Proceedings of the International Conference on New Methods in Language Processing (NeMLaP)*, Manchester, the United Kingdom, 78–87.

Nirenburg, Sergei, Constantine Domashnev, and Dean J. Grannes (1993) 'Two Approaches to Matching in Example-based Translation', in *Proceedings of the 5th International Conference on Theoretical and Methodological Issues in Machine Translation: MT in the Next Generation (TMI-93)*, Kyoto, Japan, 47–57.

Och, Franz and Hermann Ney (2003) 'A Systematic Comparison of Various Statistical Alignment Models', *Computational Linguistics* 29(1): 19–51.

Planas, Emmanuel and Osamu Furuse (1999) 'Formalizing Translation Memories', in *Proceedings of the Machine Translation Summit VII*, Singapore, 331–39.

Resnik, Philip (1998) 'Parallel Strands: A Preliminary Investigation into Mining the Web for Bilingual Text', in *Proceedings of the 3rd Conference of the Association for Machine Translation in the Americas (AMTA-98)*, Langhorne, PA, 72–82.

Richardson, Stephen D., William B. Dolan, Arul Menezes, and Jessie Pinkham (2001) 'Achieving Commercial-quality Translation with Example-based Methods', in *Proceedings of the Machine Translation Summit VIII*, Santiago de Compostela, Spain, 293–98.

Roh, Yoon-Hyung, Munpyo Hong, Choi Sung-Kwon, Lee Ki-Young, and Park Sang-Kyu (2003) 'For the Proper Treatment of Long Sentences in a Sentence Pattern-based English-Korean MT System', in *Proceedings of the Machine Translation Summit IX*, New Orleans, 323–29.

Salam, Khan Md Anwarus, Setsuo Yamada, and Nishino Tetsuro (2018) 'Improve Example-Based Machine Translation Quality for Low-Resource Language Using Ontology', *International Journal of Networked and Distributed Computing* 5(3): 176–91.

Sato, Satoshi (1995) 'MBT2: A Method for Combining Fragments of Examples in Example-based Machine Translation', *Artificial Intelligence* 75(1): 31–49.

Semmar, Nasredine and Meriama Laib (2017) 'Building Multiword Expressions Bilingual Lexicons for Domain Adaptation of an Example-Based Machine Translation System', in *Proceedings of the International Conference Recent Advances in Natural Language Processing*, Varna, Bulgaria, 661–70.

Shimohata, Mitsuo, Eiichiro Sumita, and Yuji Matsumoto (2003) 'Retrieving Meaning-equivalent Sentences for Example-based Rough Translation', in *Proceedings of the HLT-NAACL 2003 Workshop on Building and Using Parallel Texts: Data Driven Machine Translation and Beyond*, Edmonton, Canada, 73–80.

Somers, Harold L. (2003) 'An Overview of EBMT', in Michael Carl and Andy Way (eds.) *Recent Advances in Example-based Machine Translation*, Dordrecht: Kluwer Academic Publishers, 3–57.

Somers, Harold L., Sandipan Dandapat, and Sudip Kumar Naskar (2009) 'A Review of EBMT Using Proportional Analogies', in *Proceedings of the 3rd International Workshop on Example-based Machine Translation*, Dublin, Ireland, 53–60.

Somers, Harold L., Ian McLean, and Danny Jones (1994) 'Experiments in Multilingual Example-based Generation', in *Proceedings of the 3rd Conference on the Cognitive Science of Natural Language Processing (CSNLP-94)*, Dublin, Ireland.

Sumita, Eiichiro and Hitoshi Iida (1991) 'Experiments and Prospects of Example-based Machine Translation', in *Proceedings of the 29th Annual Meeting of the Association for Computational Linguistics (ACL-91)*, Berkeley, CA, 185–92.

Sumita, Eiichiro, Hitoshi Iida, and Hideo Kohyama (1990) 'Translating with Examples: A New Approach to Machine Translation', in *Proceedings of the 3rd International Conference on Theoretical and Methodological Issues in Machine Translation (TMI-90)*, Texas, 203–11.

Tiedemann, Jörg (2016) 'OPUS – Parallel Corpora for Everyone', *Baltic Journal of Modern Computing* 4(2): 384.

Vandeghinste, Vincent, Peter Dirix, and Ineke Schuurman (2005) 'Example-based Translation without Parallel Corpora: First Experiments on a Prototype', in *Proceedings of the Machine Translation Summit X: The 2nd Workshop on Example-based Machine Translation*, Phuket, Thailand, 135–42.

Watanabe, Hideo (1995) 'A Model of a Bi-directional Transfer Mechanism Using Rule Combinations', *Machine Translation* 10(4): 269–91.

Watanabe, Taro and Eiichiro Sumita (2003) 'Example-based Decoding for Statistical Machine Translation', in *Proceedings of the Machine Translation Summit IX*, New Orleans, LO, Los Angeles, CA, 410–17.

Way, Andy (2001) 'Translating with Examples', in *Proceedings of the Machine Translation Summit VIII: Workshop on Example-Based Machine Translation*, Santiago de Compostela, Spain, 66–80.

Way, Andy (2003) 'Translating with Examples: The LFG-DOT Models of Translation', in Michael Carl and Andy Way (eds.) *Recent Advances in Example-based Machine Translation*, Dordrecht: Kluwer Academic Publishers, 443–72.

Way, Andy (2010) 'Panning for EBMT Gold, or "Remembering Not to Forget"', *Machine Translation* 24(3–4): 177–208.

Way, Andy and Nano Gough (2003) 'wEBMT: Developing and Validating an Example-based Machine Translation System Using the World Wide Web', *Computational Linguistics* 29(3): 421–57.

Way, Andy and Nano Gough (2005) 'Controlled Translation in an Example-based Environment', *Machine Translation* 19(1): 1–36.

Webster, Jonathan J., Sin King Kui, and Hu Qinan (2002) 'The Application of Semantic Web Technology for Example-based Machine Translation (EBMT)', in Chan Sin-wai (ed.) *Translation and Information Technology*, Hong Kong: The Chinese University Press, 79–91.

Yamabana, Kiyoshi, Shin-ichiro Kamei, Kazunori Muraki, Shinichi Doi, Shinko Tamura, and Kenji Satoh (1997) 'A Hybrid Approach to Interactive Machine Translation – Integrating Rule-based, Corpus-based, and Example-based Method', in *Proceedings of the 15th International Joint Conference on Artificial Intelligence (IJCAI-97)*, Nagoya, Japan, 977–82.

Zhang, Ying, Ralf Brown, Robert Frederking, and Alon Lavie (2001) 'Pre-processing of Bilingual Corpora for Mandarin-English EBMT', in *Proceedings of the Machine Translation Summit VIII*, Santiago de Compostela, Spain, 247–52.

8

OPEN-SOURCE MACHINE TRANSLATION TECHNOLOGY

Mikel L. Forcada

Free/Open-Source Software

Free software,[1] as defined by the Free Software Foundation, is software that (a) may be freely executed for any purpose, (b) may be freely examined to see how it works and may be freely modified to adapt it to a new need or application (for that, source code, that is, the text of the program as the programmer sees and edits it,[2] must be available, hence the alternative name *open-source*, see subsequently), (c) may be freely redistributed to anyone, and (d) may be freely improved and released to the public so that the whole community of users benefits (source code must be available for this too). These freedoms are regulated by a license, which is packaged with each piece of free software. The Open Source Initiative establishes an alternative definition[3] of *open-source software* which is roughly equivalent, as the most important free licenses are also open source. The joint term free/open-source will be used in this chapter. Free/open-source licenses are legally based on copyright law; therefore, the freedoms they grant are protected by law in almost every country in the world.

Note that in English, the word *free* is ambiguous: free software advocates explain that it means 'free as in *freedom*, not as in *free beer*'; some use the word *libre* as an alternative to avoid the second sense.[4] Examples of free/open-source software include the LibreOffice and OpenOffice.org word-processing alternatives to Microsoft Word, the Firefox web browser, or the GNU/Linux family of operating systems.

Note also that, in contrast, the term *freeware* is the usual name for software that is distributed free of charge (free as in 'free beer') but does not necessarily grant the four freedoms explained previously (for instance, there may be no way to access the source code).

For most users ('end users' in the jargon of the software industry), the difference between freeware and free/open-source software may not be directly relevant, unless they are particularly conscious about knowing what the software is actually doing in their computer (if the source is available, a programmer can determine, for instance, if the program is respecting the user's private information stored in the computer). If the user is happy about the program as is, freeware is probably fine (two typical examples of freeware would be Acrobat Reader, used to read PDF files; the Opera web browser; or Adobe Flash Player, used to view multimedia content). However, if the user wants to get involved in efforts to improve the program, having access to the source in free/open-source software makes it possible to recruit people with the necessary

DOI: 10.4324/9781003168348-9

programming skills to do it. Free/open-source software is frequently developed collaboratively by communities of experts that share their improvements (in free/open-source projects), constantly improve the code, and periodically release new versions of the software.

An optional property that some free/open-source software licenses may have is called *copyleft*, which is obviously a pun on the word *copyright*. When the free/open-source license for a piece of software has copyleft, it means that derivatives (modifications) of this software can only be distributed using exactly the same free/open-source license and therefore may not be distributed as non-free/closed-source software. *Copylefted* licenses provide a way to encourage modifications to be contributed back to the community so that a shared pool of software, a *commons*,[5] is created. The most popular free/open-source license for software, the GNU General Public License, or GPL for short,[6] is a typical *copylefted* license. There are also some popular non-copylefted licenses such as the Apache License,[7] the MIT License,[8] or the three-clause BSD license.[9]

Machine Translation Software: Licensing

Machine translation (MT) software is special in the way it strongly depends on data.

One can distinguish two main kinds of MT: *rule-based* (or *knowledge-based*) *machine translation* (RBMT) [→?], which uses linguistic and translation knowledge, created and conveniently encoded by experts, to perform the translations, and *corpus-based* (or *data-driven*) *machine translation* (CBMT) [→?] which automatically *learns* information learned from (usually very large) corpora of *parallel text*, where all sentences come with their translations. Of course, there is a wide range of hybrid approaches between these two extremes.

On the one hand, rule-based machine translation depends on *linguistic data* such as morphological dictionaries (which specify, for instance, that *went* is the past tense of *go*); bilingual dictionaries (specifying, for instance, that a French translation of *go* is *aller*); grammars that describe, for instance, the use of the verb *do* in English interrogative and negative clauses; and *structural transfer* rule files describing how structures are transformed from one language to another, for instance, to turn English genitive constructions such as *the teacher's library* into the Spanish construction *la biblioteca del profesor*.

On the other hand, corpus-based machine translation (such as *statistical machine translation* [→?], for example, Koehn 2010) depends, as noted, on the availability of data, in most cases, of sentence-aligned parallel text, where, for instance, *Machine translation software is special* comes with its French translation *Les logiciels de traduction automatique sont spéciaux*.

The choice of rule-based versus corpus-based MT depends on the actual language setting and the actual translation tasks that will be tackled. For some language pairs, it may be quite hard to obtain and prepare the amounts of sentence-aligned parallel text (on the order of millions of words) required to get reasonable results in 'pure' corpus-based machine translation such as statistical machine translation (SMT), so hard that it might be much easier to encode the available expertise into the language data files (dictionaries, grammar rule files, etc.) needed to build a rule-based machine translation system. For other language pairs, translated texts may be readily available in sufficient amounts, and it may be much easier to filter and sentence-align those texts and then train a statistical machine translation system.

In either case, one may clearly distinguish three components: first, an *engine*, the program that performs the translation (also called *decoder* in statistical machine translation); second, the *data* (either linguistic data or parallel corpora) needed for that particular language pair; and, third, optionally, *tools* to maintain these data and turn them into a format which is suitable for the engine to use (for instance, in statistical machine translation, parallel text is used to *learn* a statistical translation table containing sub-sentential translation units – *phrase pairs* in statistical

MT parlance – such as '*machine translation* = *traduction automatique*' and probability information associated to each such pair).

Commercial Machine Translation

Most commercial machine translation systems are rule-based (although machine translation systems with a strong corpus-based component have started to appear).[10] Most RBMT systems have engines with proprietary technologies which are not completely disclosed (indeed, most companies view their proprietary technologies as their main competitive advantage). Linguistic data are not easily modifiable by end users either; in most cases, one can only add new words or user glossaries to the system's dictionaries, and perhaps some simple rules, but it is not possible to build complete data for a new language pair and use it with the engine.

Free/Open-Source Machine Translation

On the one hand, for a rule-based machine translation system to be free/open-source, source code for the engine and tools should be distributed as well as the 'source code' (expert-editable form) of linguistic data (dictionaries, translation rules, etc.) for the intended pairs. It is more likely for users of the free/open-source machine translation to change the linguistic data than to modify the machine translation engine; for the improved linguistic data to be used with the engine, tools to maintain them should also be distributed under free/open-source licenses. On the other hand, for a corpus-based machine translation system such as a statistical machine translation system, source code both for the programs that learn the statistical translation models from parallel text as well as for the engines (decoders) that use these translation models to generate the most likely translations of new sentences should be distributed along with data such as the necessary sentence-aligned parallel texts.[11]

Machine Translation That Is Neither Commercial nor Free/Open-Source

The previous sections have dealt with commercial machine translation and free/open-source machine translation. However, the correct dichotomy would be between free/open-source MT versus 'non-free/closed-source' MT; indeed, there are a number of systems that do not clearly fit in the categories considered in the last two sections.

For example, there are MT systems on the web that may be freely used (with a varying range of restrictions); some are demonstration or reduced versions of commercial systems, whereas some other freely available systems are not even commercial.[12] The best examples of web-based MT systems which are not free/open-source but may be freely used for short texts and web pages are Google Translate[13] and Microsoft's Bing Translator:[14] both are basically corpus-based systems. Finally, another possibility would be for the MT engine and tools not to be free/open-source (even using proprietary technologies) but just to be simply freely or commercially available and fully documented, with linguistic data being distributed openly (open-source linguistic data), but there is no such system available.

Types of Free/Open-Source Machine Translation Systems and Users

Distributing machine translation systems under free/open-source licenses gives their target users full access to machine-translation technologies. As the target users of free/open-source machine translation systems are very varied, one may find many different types of systems. Note that we are referring here to systems that may be downloaded and installed, either to be used offline or to set up a web service.

There are systems which may easily be installed in a few clicks and directly used (some call these 'zero-install' systems): For instance, Apertium-Caffeine,[15] part of the Apertium platform (see subsequently) is a small package that runs immediately after download in any computer where a Java run-time environment has been installed and prompts the user for the language pairs they would like to have available. It translates plain text as soon as it is typed or pasted in the input window, and it is aimed at casual users needing a quick translation for short texts when an Internet connection is not available. A related program, Apertium-Android,[16] offers similar 'offline' translation functionalities for devices running the Android operating system.

There are also free/open-source machine translation systems aimed at professional translators using computer-aided translation [→?] environments. For instance, for those using the (also free/open-source) OmegaT CAT system,[17] [→?] Apertium-OmegaT,[18] also part of the Apertium project, is available for easy installation as an extension (or *plug-in*). It allows translators to get a quick offline translation for segments in their job for which the system cannot find a match in their translation memories.

There are complete fully fledged free/open-source machine translation systems whose installation and usage requires a certain degree of technical expertise. Among the rule-based machine translation systems, OpenLogos, Apertium, and Matxin are designed to be installed on computers running the GNU/Linux operating system (although they may also be installed on other operating systems). They offer support for different kinds of text formats and are aimed at heavy usage by more than one user, possibly remotely through a web interface; they are also intended to serve as platforms for research and development. Among corpus-based machine translation systems, with similar target users and expected usages, the prime example would be the statistical machine translation system Moses; installation (and training on suitable corpora) is a bit more challenging,[19] even if efforts have been made to simplify the process.

Free/Open-Source Machine Translation in Business

Free/open-source machine translation may be used to engage in basically the same kinds of business as non-free/closed-source machine translation, with differences that will be described immediately.

(1) The business of companies who would otherwise sell machine translation software licenses is probably the one that changes most with free/open-source machine translation. On the one hand, if the company has developed the system and therefore owns the right to distribute it, it may want to release a reduced-functionality or 'basic' version under a free/open-source license while marketing end-user licenses for a fully functional or 'premium' system for a fee, as it is done with some non-free/closed-source software. On the other hand, if the company has not developed the system but the license is not a 'copylefted' license requiring the distribution of source when distributing a modified system (see section 1 previously), it may produce a non-free/closed-source derivative of an existing free/open-source system and sell licenses to use them.

(2) Other companies sell services around a particular machine translation system, such as installing, configuring, or customizing the system for a particular user (for instance, to deal with their particular terminology, document formats, document style, etc.); their business in the free/open-source setting changes significantly. Companies marketing such services for a non-free/closed-source system may do so by means of a specific (often exclusive) agreement

with the company producing the system, which provides them with tools that other companies would not have access to; this reduces competition. In the case of free/open-source software, the same kinds of services could be offered by any company, as the software is usually available to them as third parties under a general free/open-source license (and that software includes usually the necessary tools to customize or adapt the system). Access to the source code of the system adds flexibility to the kind of services they can market. But using free/open-source may expose service companies to strong competition by other companies having exactly the same access rights to the software: therefore, the deeper the knowledge of the system, the sharper the competitive edge of the company (with machine translation developers having the sharpest edge of all if they decide to market these services). Note that the usage of free/open-source licenses shifts a good part of the business from a license-centred model to a service-centred model, which happens to be less vulnerable, for instance, to loss of revenue due to unlicensed distribution of copies.

(3) A third group of companies offer value-added web-based machine translation (translation of documents in specific formats, translated chat rooms, online computer-aided translation systems, etc.). They are currently under strong competition by the main web-based machine translation companies, namely Google and Microsoft; therefore, they have to add value to web-based machine translation. In the non-free/closed-source setting, web-based translation companies have to buy a special license, different from end-user licenses, from machine translation manufacturers or their resellers; in the free/open-source setting, no fees are involved, and, as in the second group, the additional flexibility provided by full access to the source allows these companies to offer innovative services that would be more difficult to develop with non-free/closed-source software; they could develop and deploy these services themselves or hire one of the companies in the third group, who are competing to offer services based on the same free/open-source machine translation system.

(4) The fourth group comprises professional translators and translation agencies. Instead of investing in licenses for non-free/closed-source systems, they could either instal and use the free/open-source system 'as is' and save in license fees; they could additionally hire one of the service companies in the second group previously to customize it for their needs. In the case of a free/open-source system, more than one company could actually offer the service: better prices could arise from the competition; in turn, professional translators and translation agencies could offer more competitive translation prices to their customers.

Note that free/open-source machine translation systems often have active (and enthusiastic) user and developer communities that may make technical support available to any of these businesses. Businesses themselves may choose to engage in the activity of these communities to ensure a better technical support in the future. These interactions may result in improved services or products.

Free/Open-Source Machine Translation in Research

Machine translation research is undoubtedly very active in view of its relevance in an increasingly globalized world. Many researchers and developers have adopted free/open-source licensing models to carry out and disseminate their research. A clear indicator of this is the fact that over the last decade, many free/open-source MT systems and resources have been released.[20] Series of specialized conferences and workshops such as Machine Translation Marathons[21] or International Workshops on Free Rule Based Machine Translation (FreeRBMT)[22] have been devoted to free/open-source machine translation.

The benefits of using free/open-source MT systems for research are varied. On the one hand, free/open-source development radically guarantees the reproducibility of any experiments, a key point in the advance of any scientific field, and lowers the bar for other researchers to engage in research in that field (Pedersen 2008: 465–70). On the other hand, it makes it easier for end users to benefit earlier from the latest advances in the field; in particular, as the systems may be freely used, businesses and industries become direct and early beneficiaries of the research that has gone into building them, and the technology advances reach its end users much faster. Finally, as Pedersen (ibid.) also notes, the fact that the software is distributed and probably pooled makes it possible for the software to survive changes in the staff of research groups or the mere passage of time.

In fact, the existence of actively developed free/open-source machine translation platforms has contributed to the consolidation of what are now considered standard or state-of-the-art approaches to machine translation: consider, for instance, statistical machine translation, where the combination of the free/open-source packages GIZA++ (Och and Ney 2003: 19–51) and Moses (Koehn *et al.* 2007: 177–80) has become the de facto 'baseline' system, both in research and in industry. Some of the free-open/source MT systems featured in section 6 are also designed to be platforms on their own; as a result, there has never been a wider option for researchers starting to do research in this field.

These benefits may be used as arguments to encourage public administrations to preferentially fund machine translation research projects whose developments are to be released under free/open-source licences, as they encourage fast transfer of technology to all interested parties in society; this is for instance, the point of Streiter *et al.* (2006: 267–89). It certainly makes complete sense for publicly funded machine translation technologies to be freely and openly available to the society that directly or indirectly supports those public institutions with their taxes. Indeed, there is a tendency for research projects that explicitly commit to the free/open-source development to receive more public funding: for instance, the European Union's seventh Framework Programme explicitly lists as a sought outcome of the research that it will fund in the field of Information and Communication Technologies in 2013 (European Commission 2012: 50, 54) that 'a European open-source MT system becomes the most widely adopted worldwide'.

A Survey of Free/Open-Source Machine Translation Technologies

Knowledge- or Rule-Based Free/Open-Source Machine Translation Systems

Among the existing knowledge- or rule-based free/open-source machine translation systems, Apertium will be described in detail and Matxin and OpenLogos in less detail; other systems will also be mentioned at the end of this section.

Apertium

Apertium[23] (Forcada *et al.* 2011: 124–44) is a platform for rule-based MT – with an active community of hundreds of developers around it – which can be used to build machine translation systems for many language pairs, initiated in 2004 as part of a project funded by the Spanish Ministry of Industry, Tourism and Commerce. The design of Apertium is simple, as it was initially aimed at translating between closely related languages such as Spanish and Portuguese to produce draft translations to be post-edited [→?]. The core idea is that of building on top of the intuitive notion of word-for-word translation by tackling, using the minimum amount of linguistic analysis possible, the main problems encountered by such a crude approximation: solving the ambiguity of certain lexical items (such as *books*, which can be a noun in *the books* or a verb in *He books*), identifying multi-word lexical items that need to be translated as a whole (such as *machine translation → traduction automatique* and not *→ traduction de machine*), ensuring locally the right word order (*the blue lamp → la lampe bleue*, *Peter's telephone → le téléphone de Peter*), agreement (*the blue lamps → les lampes bleues*), and so on. Such a simple formulation of the translation strategy makes it easy for people to help in the development of linguistic data for Apertium language pairs or even to start new language pairs.

Even if this design was not initially aimed at less related language pairs, there also exist Apertium translators for these pairs, not with the objective of producing a draft needing a reasonable amount of post-editing (which would be impossible with such a simple design) but rather to provide readers with the gist or general idea of a text written in a language that would otherwise be impenetrable to them. For instance, someone who does not know any Basque will not be able to make any sense of the sentence *Nire amaren adiskideak loreak erosi ditu*. However, the Apertium Basque–English translator (currently under development) produces the approximate translation *My mother's friend the flowers he has bought*, which is quite intelligible for an English speaker even if rather hard to post-edit into *My mother's friend has bought the flowers*.

Apertium as a platform provides a language-independent engine; a well-defined, XML-based format to encode linguistic data; and the tools needed to manage these data and to turn them into the format used by the engine. The Apertium engine is a modular pipeline that processes the text by incrementally transforming it as follows:

(1) Any formatting information (fonts, font weights, etc.) is detected and hidden so that work concentrates on the actual text.

(2) All words are morphologically analysed. For instance, the word *books* previously could be analysed as *book*, noun, plural, or *book*, verb, present tense, third person singular. Multi-word lexical units such as *machine translation* are also detected and marked in this step.

(3) For words such as *books*, one of the morphological analyses is chosen according to context (this is commonly called *part-of-speech tagging* [→?]). This may be done in one or two steps. The first step is optional and uses *constraints* or rules such as 'the word *the* cannot be followed by a personal form of a verb'. The second step uses statistical information obtained from texts about the distribution of word classes of neighbouring words to decide, for instance, that *like* is more likely to be a preposition than a verb in *run like the wind*.

(4) Morphologically analysed words are looked up in a bilingual dictionary and translations are attached to them: *book*, noun, plural *→livre*, noun, masculine, plural (default translation); *cahier*, noun, masculine, plural (alternative translation). Multi-word lexical units are translated as a whole: *machine translation*, noun, singular *→ traduction automatique*, noun, feminine, singular.

(5) In recent Apertium versions, one of these translations is chosen using lexical selection rules which may be hand-written or learned from a bilingual corpus of sentences and their translations. If this module is not available, the default translation is chosen.

(6) One or more modules apply (in cascade) the *structural transfer rules* for the language pair to ensure the correct word order, agreement, and so on and produce an adequate translation. For instance, a rule detects the English sequence article–adjective–noun and translates it into French as article–noun–adjective while making sure that the adjective received the gender of the noun in French, to ensure, for instance, that *the blue lamp* is translated into *la lampe bleue*. Another rule may be used to decide that the translation of the English preposition *in* should be *à* before a place name, so that *in the house → dans la maison* but *in Paris → à Paris*.

(7) Structural transfer rules do not deliver target-language words in their final form but rather in their 'morphologically analysed' form. A module is needed to turn, for example, *bleu*, adjective, feminine, singular into *bleue*.

(8) The last linguistic processor takes care of some inter-word phenomena such as *la + élection* → *l'élection, de + égalité* → *d'égalité, viendra + il ?* → *viendra-t-il?* and so on.

(9) Formatting information hidden in the first step is placed back into the appropriate positions of the text.

This particular design may be classified as a transfer architecture [→?] (Hutchins and Somers 1992: 75), in particular, a shallow-transfer architecture; it may also be seen as what Arnold *et al.* (1994: sec. 4.2) call a *transformer* architecture (Arnold *et al.* 1994).

To perform some of these operations, Apertium uses source- and target-language dictionaries describing their morphology, bilingual dictionaries, disambiguation rules, structural transfer (structure transformation) rules, and so on. All this information is encoded in clearly specified formats based on XML [→?] and grouped in language-pair packages that can be installed on demand. The modularity of the engine reflects on the internal modularity of language-pair packages: for instance, the Spanish–Portuguese and the Spanish–French language pair use essentially the same Spanish morphological dictionary.

At the time of writing this chapter, thirty-three stable[24] language pairs are available from Apertium. Many of them include small languages which are not supported by any other machine translation systems such as Breton, Asturian, and Occitan or Nynorsk (one of the two Norwegian languages). The free/open-source setting in Apertium, which uses the GNU General Public License for all its packages, makes it particularly attractive for minor-language experts to contribute their expertise in the creation of resources, as it is guaranteed that these will be available to the whole language community.

Apertium is one of the most-installed rule-based free/open-source machine translation systems. On the one hand, it has been included in some major GNU/Linux operating system distributions such as Debian and Ubuntu. On the other hand, it is so fast[25] and frugal that it may be installed in devices running the Android operating system; used as a plug-in in the most popular free/open-source computer-aided translation toolkit, OmegaT; or installed in a single click on any Java-enabled computer, regardless of the operating system.

Matxin

Matxin[26] (Mayor *et al.* 2011: 53–82) was born in the same project as Apertium as the first publicly available machine translation system for Basque, a less-resourced language, and shares some components with it (for instance, monolingual and bilingual dictionaries and the code processing them). Matxin translates from Spanish to Basque (and from English to Basque). The authors (ibid.) declare that they designed this system for assimilation purposes (to be useful for Basque readers to understand Spanish text), although it has also been used by volunteers in marathon-like events to populate the Basque Wikipedia.[27] Unlike Apertium, Matxin works by performing a deep morphological and syntactical analysis of the source sentence, which delivers a parse tree (a mixed dependency/constituency tree).[28] This is needed because of the stark morpho-syntactic divergence between English or Spanish on the one hand and Basque on the other hand. The source parse tree, encoded as an XML [→?] structure, is transformed into a target-language parse tree which is then used to generate the Basque sentence. Transformations use rich linguistic knowledge: for instance, verb sub-categorization frames – describing the arguments taken by each verb together with their case – are used to inform the choice of the correct translation of prepositions and verb chunks, and the order of words in the target language is determined independently of that of words in the source language. Matxin has also been used as a platform to perform machine translation research, for instance, on hybrid rule-based/statistical machine translation (España-Bonet *et al.* 2011: 554–61), and its extension to language pairs not involving Basque has also been explored (Mayor and Tyers 2009: 11–17). The free/open-source version of Matxin (which has a more reduced vocabulary than the one that may be used on the web) is distributed under the GNU General Public License and may be installed by moderately expert users on computers running the GNU/Linux operating system.

OpenLogos

OpenLogos[29] is the free/open-source version (released by the German Research Center for Artificial Intelligence; DFKI)[30] of a historical commercial machine translation system, Logos, which was developed by the Logos Corporation from 1970 to 2000. OpenLogos translates from German and English into French, Italian, Spanish, and Portuguese. It uses an incremental or cascaded pipeline structure, and a particular internal symbolic representation called SAL ('semantico-syntactic abstract representation'). The designers of OpenLogos (Barreiro *et al.* 2011: 107–26) claim that this endows the system with the ability to deal with ambiguity and other particularly hard related cognitive problems in ways which differ from those of other rule-based systems and which, according to the authors, are inspired in neural computation. The authors argue that OpenLogos is unique in the way it applies rules to the input stream and that this makes its customization to application-specific needs very easy with the tools provided with the system. OpenLogos is also distributed under the GNU General Public License and may only be installed by expert users on the GNU/Linux operating system. Public development in the project site[31] appears to have ceased around 2011.

Research Systems

There are a few other free/open-source rule-based systems, but they are experimental and are not widely distributed or packaged to be easily installed. An example of these research systems has been recently described by Bond *et al.* (2011: 87–105). Their system tackles the problem of translation as one of meaning preservation, by using precise grammars for both the analysis of the source language and the generation of the target language, an explicit semantic representation of language meaning and statistical methods to select the best translation among those possible. Using only free/open-source components, they describe the building of a Japanese–English system with slightly better human evaluation results than a Moses statistical machine translation system trained on a suitable corpus.

Data-Driven or Corpus-Based Free/Open-Source Machine Translation Systems

Due to their nature, data-driven or corpus-based free/open-source machine translation systems usually require the existence of sentence-aligned parallel corpora containing translations of good quality, related to the texts one aims to translate, and usually in very large amounts, substantially larger than the usual translation memories [→?] used in computer-aided translation [→?]. This means that *training* is a necessary step before one starts to translate.

The following paragraphs describe the most famous free/open-source corpus-based system, the statistical machine translation system Moses, in detail, and then go on to briefly describe other systems.

Moses

Moses (Haddow 2012) is a statistical machine translation [→?] system; it is probably the most widely used and installed free/open-source machine translation system. Hieu Hoang, a PhD student in the University of Edinburgh, started it as a successor to a freely available but not free/open-source research system called Pharaoh[32] (Koehn 2004: 115–24). The first version of Moses was made available in 2005, and one can say it became an instant success, partly because the license used (the GNU Lesser General Public License),[33] a partially copylefted license (unlike the GPL which is *fully copylefted*), was perceived as being more adequate for commercial usage. Moses development has successfully attracted funding from the European Commission.[34]

As Pharaoh, Moses provides a *decoder*, that is, a program that performs the translation, but also a series of training tools to process the sentence-aligned parallel texts (parallel corpus) and extract the necessary information (the translation table) for the decoder.[35] Moses is what in statistical machine translation jargon is called a *phrase*-based system [→?]: new translations are performed by breaking down the source sentences into smaller units called *phrases* (sequences of words, not necessarily *phrases* in the linguistic sense) and assembling the available translations of these smaller units, stored as *phrase* pairs in the translation table, into the *most likely* translation, according to the probabilistic information stored with the *phrase* pairs as well as a probabilistic model of the target language. Recent versions of Moses can also learn advanced ('hierarchical') models of translation equivalence, in which phrase pairs are embedded. Examples of phrase pairs would be (*basically depends on, depend fondamentalement de*) or (*statistical machine translation, traduction automatique statistique*).

Moses is not a monolithic system and integrates external components:

- Training relies on existing tools such as *word aligners* [→?], which are trained on the parallel corpus to establish translation links between the words in the source sentence and those in the target sentence, and then used to extract the *phrase* pairs. The preferred word aligner in Moses is GIZA++ (Och and Ney 2003: 19–51), which is also free/open-source (under the GNU General Public License). Moses used to rely also on external software to train and use probabilistic models of the target language, but now it has one of them fully integrated as part of the main *decoder*.
- Models trained with Moses depend on a few parameters. One can run a Moses-trained system with preset values of these parameters, but one usually sets a small part of the training corpus apart (a *development* corpus) and uses it to automatically *tune* it so that translation performance on that corpus is maximized. This means that Moses has to rely on software that computes *automatic evaluation measures* that compare the output of the system with the *reference* translation given in the reference corpus. Some of this software (for example, the one that computes BLEU [→?], one of the most widely used such measures) comes bundled with Moses, but one can easily integrate other evaluation measures perceived as giving a better indication of translation quality.
- Training can make use of the linguistic information provided by morphological analysers or part-of-speech taggers (such as the ones available from the Apertium system previously). By using 'factored models' that *factor* in that linguistic information to help in the probabilistic estimation. Moses can also use source-language and target-language parsers to help train *hierarchical phrase*-based models in which *phrase* pairs may contain *variables* that represent a set of smaller *phrase* pairs. For instance, the phrase (X *depends on, depend* X *de*) has a variable X that could be instantiated by the phrase pairs (*basically, fondamentalement*) or (*radically, radicalement*) to obtain translations such as (*basically depends on, depend fondamentalement de*) or (*radically depends on, depend radicalement de*).

Moses has become the *de facto* baseline system in machine translation research: performance of new systems is always compared with that of a Moses-trained statistical machine translation system. This may be due to the free/open-source nature of Moses, which allowed unrestricted usages and therefore could be seen not only as a readily available research platform but also as a path towards industrial or commercial applications.

Moses may be installed in GNU/Linux-based and in Windows-based systems, and recently successful use of the *decoder* in Android-based devices has been reported. The standard distribution of Moses requires certain expertise to install; however, there are initiatives like *Moses for Mere Mortals*[36] or even commercial installers[37] to make installation easier. Web services such as LetsMT!,[38] KantanMT,[39] or SmartMATE[40] offer Moses training and translation online. Many companies offer translation services powered by Moses-trained systems.

Other Systems

JOSHUA

Joshua[41] (Li *et al*. 2009: 135–39) is a free/open-source statistical machine translation *decoder* that implements *hierarchical* machine translation models (also implemented in Moses). One important feature of Joshua is that it is written in Java, which makes it possible to install in most operating systems through the available Java support. Installing Joshua requires a certain level of expertise, and one has to install other packages in advance, as it only provides a decoder. Like Moses, Joshua is distributed under the GNU Lesser General Public License.

CUNEI

Cunei[42] (Phillips 2011: 161–77) is a free/open-source corpus-based machine translation platform that combines the traditional example-based MT [→?] and statistical MT paradigms, which allows to integrate additional contextual information in the translation process. Like Moses, Cunei translates by segmenting the new source sentence in all possible contiguous subsegments ('phrases') and looking for examples where they appear; in contrast to Moses, it then takes advantage of the context (document type, genre, alignment probability, etc.) in which the examples were found by using the distance between the new sentence and each of the actual matching examples in the example base; in this way Cunei builds features that model the relevance of the 'phrase' and that are tuned on a development set as usual in statistical MT. Cunei can be considered a research system requiring a certain level of expertise to install it and train it; unfortunately, its designer, Aaron Phillips, has given up maintaining it as of July 2012. Cunei is distributed using the MIT License, a non-copylefted free/open-source license.

CMU-EBMT

CMU-EBM[43] (Carnegie-Mellon University Example-Based Machine Translation; Brown 2011: 179–95) may be called a classical example-based MT system, capable of learning a lexicon, performing word and *phrase* alignment, and indexing and looking up a corpus, but it also brings in some also uses typical statistical MT techniques: target-language modelling, decoding, and parameter tuning. Like Cunei, installation and usage require a certain level of expertise. CMU-EBMT is distributed under the GNU General Public License and has not released any new version since May 2011.

MARIE

Marie[44] provides a statistical machine translation decoder, which is an alternative to the phrase-based decoder used in Moses: it uses *bilingual language modelling*, that is, it models translation as the search for the best sequence or chain of sub-sentential translation units using an explicit statistical model to model sub-chains of length N called N-grams. Marie is distributed under the GNU General Public License but has not released any versions since 2005.

GREAT

Great (Gonzalez and Casacuberta 2011: 145–60) also resorts to *bilingual language modelling* like Marie, but it uses general probabilistic finite-state models instead of N-grams. The authors reports competitive results with standard *phrase*-based models like Moses (see previously) obtained faster and using a smaller amount of memory for the statistical translation model. A recent version, iGreat,[45] enhanced to be used in interactive machine translation environments, is distributed under the GNU General Public License.

PBMBMT

The Tilburg University phrase-based memory-based machine translation system[46] (PBMBMT) implements a kind of example-based machine translation in which the translation of new words and *phrases* in the sentence is modelled as the search for the k best equivalents in the given context using a classifier based on the 'nearest neighbour' strategy, using a suitable distance or dissimilarity measure. The system is available under the GNU General Public License and is suited primarily for research purposes.

OPENMATREX

OpenMaTrEx[47] (Dandapat *et al.* 2010: 121–26) is a basically a wrapper around Moses that uses alternative example-based methods (based on the idea of *marker words*) to extract linguistically motivated *phrase* pairs, which can be added to the Moses phrase tables. OpenMaTrEx is licensed under the GNU General Public License. The last release was in May 2011.

Challenges for Free/Open-Source MT Technology

There are two main challenges faced by free/open-source MT technology:

User-friendliness: The free/open-source machine translation technologies available are diverse and cover the two main paradigms: rule-based and corpus-based. However, most of the systems require a fair level of expertise, on the one hand, to install and set up (which involves training in the case of corpus-based machine translation) and, on the other hand, to execute (for instance, most of them assume a command-line interface, i.e., offer no graphical interface). Their integration in the usual professional environment (e.g. to be used from computer-aided translation software in conjunction with translation memories) has barely started. This lack of end-user friendliness is surely delaying the adoption of systems that have obtained substantial public and private funding and is one of the main challenges faced.

Unification: The multiplicity of systems, each one having different requirements, installation procedures, and user interfaces, is another major hindrance to users who would like to switch technologies when choosing tasks to obtain the best possible results. Integrating all the free/open-source systems in a single platform with unified installation procedures, standardized application-oriented interfaces, and user-friendly interfaces is another main challenge, which should in principle be easier to tackle when free/open-source software is involved but remains basically open.

Notes

1 The reader will find a definition at www.gnu.org/philosophy/free-sw.html.
2 Access to the source is not necessary for users to run the program.
3 See www.opensource.org/docs/definition.php. The concept of 'open-source' is more of an operational, business-friendly concept that avoids the political overtones usually associated with the position of the Free Software Foundation.
4 Which gives rise to a common acronym: FLOSS, free/libre/open-source software.
5 The notion of software commons draws from the existing meaning of *commons* as 'a piece of land subject to common use'; its current usage refers to a body of related free/open-source software which is shared and developed by an online community and also to systems that host that commons to allow this sharing and development, such as SourceForge (www.sourceforge.net) or GitHub (www.github.com).
6 www.gnu.org/licenses/gpl.html.
7 www.apache.org/licenses/LICENSE-2.0.
8 http://opensource.org/licenses/MIT.
9 http://opensource.org/licenses/BSD-3-Clause.
10 AutomaticTrans (www.eng.automatictrans.es), SDL Language Weaver (www.sdl.com/products/sdl-enterprise-language-server/).
11 This last requirement may sound strange to some but is actually the SMT analog of distributing linguistic data for a RBMT system.
12 This is the case, for example, of three non-commercial but freely available machine translation systems between Spanish and Catalan: interNOSTRUM (www.internostrum.com), which has thousands of daily users, and two less-known but powerful systems called SisHiTra (http://sishitra.iti.upv.es. González *et al.* 2006) and N-II (www.n-ii.org).
13 http://translate.google.com.
14 www.bing.com/translator.
15 http://wiki.apertium.org/wiki/Apertium-Caffeine.
16 http://wiki.apertium.org/wiki/Apertium_On_Mobile.
17 www.omegat.org.
18 http://wiki.apertium.org/wiki/Apertium-OmegaT.
19 www.statmt.org/moses/?n=Development.GetStarted.
20 For a list of free/open-source machine translation software, see www.fosmt.org.
21 The last Machine Translation Marathon, the seventh one, was held in September 2012: www.statmt.org/mtm12.
22 The last FreeRBMT was held in Sweden in 2012: www.chalmers.se/hosted/freerbmt12-en.
23 www.apertium.org.
24 'Stable' does not imply any claim about the quality of the translations; it is rather a development concept referring to the fact that those language-pair packages do not contain any internal errors or inconsistencies and do not produce any problems when used with the Apertium engine. Forcada *et al.* (2011) report evaluation results for selected language pairs.
25 With speeds in the range of tens of thousands of words a second in regular desktop computers.
26 http://matxin.sourceforge.net.
27 http://eu.wikipedia.org/wiki/Wikiproiektu:OpenMT2_eta_Euskal_Wikipedia.
28 The source-language syntactical parser in Matxin was written specifically for this system and is currently part of the (also free/open-source) Freeling language analysis toolbox (http://nlp.lsi.upc.edu/freeling; Padró and Stanilovsky 2012).
29 There is another free/open-source project called OpenLogos which has no relation to this machine translation system.
30 http://sourceforge.net/apps/mediawiki/openlogos-mt.
31 www.sourceforge.net/projects/openlogos-mt.
32 www.isi.edu/licensed-sw/pharaoh.

33 www.gnu.org/copyleft/lesser.html.
34 Projects EuroMatrix, EuroMatrix+ and MosesCore.
35 As well as many other tools, for instance, to tune the statistical models for maximum performance in a held-out portion of the training.
36 http://code.google.com/p/moses-for-mere-mortals.
37 www.precisiontranslationtools.com. It also provides a free/open-source 'community edition' called DOMY (do Moses yourself): www.precisiontranslationtools.com/products/software-requirements-domt-desktop.
38 www.letsmt.eu.
39 www.kantanmt.com.
40 www.smartmate.co.
41 http://joshua-decoder.org.
42 www.cunei.org.
43 http://sourceforge.net/projects/cmu-ebmt.
44 www.talp.upc.edu/index.php/technology/tools/machine-translation-tools/75-marie.
45 http://sourceforge.net/projects/igreat.
46 http://ilk.uvt.nl/mbmt/pbmbmt.
47 www.openmatrex.org.

Bibliography

Arnold, Doug J., Lorna Balkan, R. Lee Humphreys, Seity Meijer, and Louisa Sadler (1994) *Machine Translation: An Introductory Guide*, Manchester and Oxford: NCC Blackwell. Available at: www.essex.ac.uk/linguistics/external/clmt/MTbook.

Barreiro, Anabela, Bernard Scott, Walter Kasper, and Bernd Kiefer (2011) 'OpenLogos Machine Translation: Philosophy, Model, Resources and Customization', *Machine Translation* 25(2): 107–16.

Bond, Francis, Stephen Oepen, Eric Nichols, Dan Flickinger, Erik Velldal, and Petter Haugereid (2011) 'Deep Open-source Machine Translation', *Machine Translation* 25(2): 87–105.

Brown, Ralf D. (2011) 'The CMU-EBMT Machine Translation System', *Machine Translation* 25(2): 179–95.

Dandapat, Sandipan, Mikel L. Forcada, Declan Groves, Sergio Penkale, John Tinsley, and Andy Way (2010) 'OpenMaTrEx: A Free/Open-Source Marker-Driven Example-based Machine Translation System', in Hrafn Loftsson, Eiríkur Rögnvaldsson, and Sigrún Helgadóttir (eds.) *Advances in Natural Language Processing: 7th International Conference on NLP, IceTAL 2010*, 16–18 August 2010, Reykjavík, Iceland, 121–26.

España-Bonet, Cristina, Gorka Labaka, Arantza Diaz de Ilarraza, Lluis Màrquez, and Kepa Sarasola (2011) 'Hybrid Machine Translation Guided by a Rule-based System', in *Proceedings of the 13th Machine Translation Summit*, 19–23 September 2011, Xiamen, China, 554–61.

European Commission (2012) *ICT – Information and Communication Technologies: Work Programme 2013*, Luxembourg: EU Publications Office.

Forcada, Mikel L., Mireia Ginestí-Rosell, Jacob Nordfalk, Jim O'Regan, Sergio Ortiz-Rojas, Juan Antonio Pérez-Ortiz, Felipe Sánchez-Martínez, Gema Ramírez-Sánchez, and Francis M. Tyers (2011) 'Apertium: A Free/Open-source Platform for Rule-based Machine Translation', *Machine Translation* 25(2): 127–44.

González, Jorge and Francisco Casacuberta (2011) 'GREAT: Open Source Software for Statistical Machine Translation', *Machine Translation* 25(2): 145–60.

Haddow, B. (coord. 2012) 'Moses Core Deliverable D.1.1: Moses Specification'. Available at: www.statmt.org/moses/manual/Moses-Specification.pdf.

Hutchins, W. John and Harold L. Somers (1992) *An Introduction to Machine Translation*, London: Academic Press. Available at: www.hutchinsweb.me.uk/IntroMT-TOC.htm.

Koehn, Philipp (2004) 'Pharaoh: A Beam Search Decoder for Phrase-based Statistical Machine Translation', in Robert E. Frederking and Kathryn B. Taylor (eds.) *Proceedings of Machine Translation: From Real Users to Research: Proceedings of the 6th Conference of the Association for Machine Translation in the Americas, AMTA 2004*, 28 September–2 October 2004, Washington, DC, and Berlin: Springer Verlag, 115–24.

Koehn, Philipp (2010) *Statistical Machine Translation*, Cambridge: Cambridge University Press.

Koehn, Philipp, Hieu Hoang, Alexandra Birch, Chris Callison-Burch, Marcello Federico, Nicola Bertoldi, Brooke Cowan, Wade Shen, Cristine Moran, Richard Zens, Chris Dyer, Ondřej Bojar, Alexandra Constantin, and Evan Herbst (2007) 'Moses: Open Source Toolkit for Statistical Machine Translation', in *Proceedings of the 45th Annual Meeting of the Association for Computational Linguistics*, 25–27 June 2007, Prague, Czech Republic, 177–80.

Li, Zhifei, Chris Callison-Burch, Chris Dyer, Juri Ganitkevitch, Sanjeev Khudanpur, Lane Schwartz, Wren N. G. Thornton, Jonathan Weese, and Omar F. Zaidan (2009) 'Joshua: An Open Source Toolkit for Parsing-based Machine Translation', in *Proceedings of 4th Workshop on Statistical Machine Translation (StatMT '09)*, 30–31 March 2009, Athens, Greece, 135–39.

Lluis Padro and Evgeny Stanilovsky (2012) "FreeLing 3.0: Towards Wider Multilinguality": in Nicoletta Calzolari, Khalid Choukri, Thierry Declerck, Mehmet Ugur Dogan, Bente Maegaard, Joseph NMariani,m Asuncion Moreno, Jan Odijk, and Stelios Piperidis (eds) *Proceedings of the Eighth International Conference on Language Resources and Evaluation*, European Language Resources Association.

Mayor, Aingeru, Iñaki Alegria, Arantza Díaz de Ilarraza, Gorka Labaka, Mikel Lersundi, and Kepa Sarasola (2011) 'Matxin: An Open-source Rule-based Machine Translation System for Basque', *Machine Translation* 25(1): 53–82.

Mayor, Aingeru and Francis M. Tyers (2009) 'Matxin: Moving Towards Language Independence', in Juan Antonio Pérez-Ortiz, Felipe Sánchez-Martínez, and Francis M. Tyers (eds.) *Proceedings of the 1st International Workshop on Free/Open-Source Rule-based Machine Translation*, 2–3 November 2009, Alacant, Spain, 11–17.

Och, Franz Josef and Hermann Ney (2003) 'A Systematic Comparison of Various Statistical Alignment Models', *Computational Linguistics* 29(1): 19–51.

Pedersen, Ted (2008) 'Empiricism Is Not a Matter of Faith', *Computational Linguistics* 34(3): 465–70.

Phillips, Aaron B. (2011) 'Cunei: Open-Source Machine Translation with Relevance-based Models of Each Translation Instance', *Machine Translation* 25(2): 161–77.

Streiter, Oliver, Kevin P. Scannell, and Mathias Stuflesser (2006) 'Implementing NLP Projects for Non-central Languages: Instructions for Funding Bodies, Strategies for Developers', *Machine Translation* 20(4): 267–89.

9

PRAGMATICS-BASED MACHINE TRANSLATION

David Farwell and Stephen Helmreich

Introduction

There are three basic computational strategies for fully automatic machine translation (MT). (1) The algorithm, using a stochastic model induced from large amounts of extant data, substitutes source language surface forms (strings) for target language surface forms. (2) Alternatively, using linguistic rule bases, it converts source language surface forms into some sort of abstract representation (possibly syntactic, ideally semantic), which it then manipulates in such a way as to make it suitable for generating a target language equivalent. (3) Or, using a knowledge base, context modeling and inferencing engine, it converts the text into a representation of what the author intended to communicate and then uses that representation as the target interpretation for the translation generated. The first of these strategies is referred to as the *direct method* (and its current instantiations as *statistical* or *example-based* MT), while the second is referred to as the *transfer method* (or, in some cases, where the representation is in fact semantic, the *interlingual method*). The third strategy alone may be referred to as pragmatics-based MT (PBMT) since it is in fact attempting to model the communicative intent associated with a text as opposed to its linguistic form or content *per se*.

Pragmatics-based MT, then, relies on:

- the use of context to interpret source language utterances and to produce target language equivalents,
- a context of the utterance which crucially includes nested belief environments which are constructed and modified through ascription during processing,
- a discourse context consisting of a knowledge base which is accessed for constructing or modifying the utterance context,
- context-sensitive (non-monotonic) inferencing within the context to resolve ambiguities during interpretation or to select expressions during production.

Within pragmatics-based approaches to machine translation, it is important to note that there are three distinct levels of analysis: that of identifying the intended information content of an utterance (the locutionary level), that of identifying the underlying communicative intent

DOI: 10.4324/9781003168348-10

of an utterance (the illocutionary level) and that of identifying the intended effect of the utterance (the perlocutionary level) (Austin 1975; Searle 1969). In particular, the illocutionary level includes more than simply the type of speech act. It also includes the intended implications of the information content.

These levels may be illustrated in the following exchange between the characters Coulomb and Constance in a scene from the film *Jesus of Montreal* (1989). Coulomb, an actor and playwright, has been living in the apartment of his good friend and collaborator Constance while revising the script of a Passion play. He normally is out all day researching the life of Christ at a local library or organizing the staging of the play itself. But on this day he returns early to the apartment. After entering, he takes off his coat and tries unsuccessfully to hang it up as he proceeds to the back of the apartment where there is a bookshelf with various books of interest. The coat, falling from the hook, knocks something over, making a bit of noise. Shortly thereafter Constance emerges from her bedroom in a robe. Coulomb, thinking he may have found her in a compromising situation asks, whispering, if she would like him to leave. She shakes her head while and then turns, cracks open the bedroom door and says in a calm voice, *Ben, écoutes, sors* (Ok. Listen. Come on out), *On va pas jouer une scène de Feydeau* (We are not acting out a scene from Feydeau).

This last line in particular is relevant to the discussion because its English subtitle is 'This isn't a bedroom farce', which is not only a possible translation but a very good one. This is because, while at the locutionary level, 'We are not acting out a scene from Feydeau' is perfectly appropriate, at the illocutionary level and therefore at the perlocutionary level, it is quite likely to fail. The reasoning is as follows. Constance wishes to let the person in the bedroom (who is a priest, as it turns out, and thus might well fear being caught in a compromising situation) know that there will be no negative consequences in his being discovered. So, since Constance knows that Feydeau was a turn of the (20th) century playwright who was famous for writing bedroom farces and Constance also believes that the person in the bedroom knows who Feydeau was, in saying 'We are not acting out a scene from Feydeau', she is in fact telling the priest that the situation in which they find themselves is not one in which he needs to conceal his identity, that is, a scene in a bedroom farce, a scene typical of a play by Feydeau. In telling this to the priest, Constance is trying to allay his fears of coming out.

What is interesting here in regard to the subtitling is that the translator feels that the English-speaking audience of the film will likely not know who Feydeau is or that he was famous for writing bedroom farces. Therefore, they will not understand the illocutionary intent or intended perlocutionary effect of what Constance said. So instead of translating on the basis of the locutionary level, the subtitle is based on the illocutionary level, which presumably the English-speaking audience would understand. Were it the case that the meaning at the illocutionary level were equally opaque, that is, that the audience is unlikely to know what a bedroom farce is, the translator might have chosen to base the subtitle directly on the intended perlocutionary effect, perhaps something like 'Do not worry about being discovered, it is safe to come out'.

In the remainder of this chapter, (1) a pragmatics-based approach to machine translation is motivated, (2) the theoretical framework for developing such an approach is presented, (3) the requirements for a computational platform on which to implement such a system are outlined, (4) various advantages to the approach are discussed and (5) some serious difficulties with the approach are addressed. The objective is, on the one hand, to provide an introduction to pragmatics-based machine translation and, on the other, to demonstrate the importance of pragmatics for high-quality MT.

Motivation

Theoretical Motivation

The theoretical motivation for pursuing pragmatics-based approaches to machine translation derives from linguistic phenomena which can only be accounted for by positing an extra-linguistic context. These include such processes as resolving references; recovering ellipted information; interpreting metonymy and metaphor; and resolving lexical, semantic and syntactic ambiguity. These are, of course, mainly problematic as source language phenomena and therefore prerequisite for arriving at an accurate interpretation, but they also may come into play as target language phenomena and relevant for formulating a fluent translation.

Resolving references, for instance, is especially relevant when translating into a language whose pronominal anaphors reflect gender from a language whose anaphors are gender neutral. For example, the Spanish translation of:

> The gardeners used dull chain saws to prune the trees and so several of them were damaged.

might be:

> Los jardineros utilizaron motosierras desafiladas para podar los arboles así que **varios de ellos** fueron dañad**os**.

or it might be:

> Los jardineros utilizaron motosierras desafiladas para podar los arboles así que **varias de ellas** fueron dañad**as**.

The choice depends on whether it was the saws or the trees that were damaged, that is to say, depending on the referent for 'several of them'. What is crucial, however, is that the decision (saws or trees) is based on one's knowledge of typical scenarios related to pruning trees. It is likely, for instance, that it was the trees rather than the saws that were damaged since dull chainsaws tend to rip and burn limbs rather than cut them. But such reasoning can easily be overridden should later (or previous) context happen to shed additional light on the situation (see Farwell and Helmreich 2000: 1–11 for further discussion).

As for recovering ellipted information, it is often necessary when translating from a language that favors nominalization and/or noun compounding into a language that tends to favor oblique or sentential complements. For example, the translation into Spanish of:

> . . . *the expansion of US small business investment* . . .

is either:

> . . . *la expansión de las inversiones **de las pequeñas** empresas en los EEUU* . . .

or

> . . . *la expansión de las inversiones **en las pequeñas** empresas en los EEUU* . . .

Here, the choice depends on whether *small business investment* is understood as 'investment on the part of small business' or 'investment in small business'. That interpretation, in turn, will depend on what the translator understands to be the state of the world at the time that the description was intended to apply.

Pragmatics is equally crucial for interpreting metonymy and metaphor. For instance, in order to translate *is rippling across* in the following text, it is prerequisite that the translator understand that the expression is being used metaphorically to express the notion that a particular practice (not a phenomena that is literally given to wavelike behavior) is spreading from school to school just as small waves spread out from some initial epicenter. It would not be good practice to translate:

> . . . *the story of how it [incorporating leadership skills into core curricula] all started and why* ***it is rippling across*** *the globe,. . . .*

as:

> . . . *la historia de cómo empezó todo y por qué* ***se está ondulando por*** *todo el mundo, . . .*

since the reader might well become confused about the meaning. Rather, the translator would better serve the audience of the translation by unpacking the metaphor along the lines of:

> . . . *la historia de cómo empezó todo y por qué* ***se está extendiendo por*** *todo el mundo, . . .*

This is perhaps more prosaic but certainly communicates more clearly the original intent of the source text.

The need for pragmatics can similarly be motivated in situations involving the interpretation of metonymy or lexical, syntactic or semantic disambiguation. In fact, there is ample theoretical motivation for developing pragmatics-based approaches to MT.

Empirical Motivation

Still, some would argue that the sorts of phenomena discussed here are not all that common in the mundane world of newspaper articles, parliamentary proceedings, business communication and so on and that the know-how and labor required for implementing such a system far exceed the benefits that would be derived. Nonetheless, there is important empirical motivation for pragmatics-based approaches to MT as well.

Such motivation can be found in the comparative analysis of multiple translations of a given text by different translators. Placing such translations side by side, it is possible to identify equivalent translation units, observe the addition or omission of information and variations in the translators' perspectives on what the author of the original text intended to communicate and which aspects of that information are viewed as more or less important. It is possible to identify as well any outright errors on the part of the translators.

For a limited range of texts, such an analysis has been carried out (see Helmreich and Farwell 1998: 17–39, for a more detailed account). From a corpus of 125 Spanish language newswire articles and their translation into English by two independent professional translators, three sets of articles and translations were aligned on the basis of translation units, and the translations were compared in terms of literal graphological equivalence.[1] If comparable translation units were graphologically the same, these units were set aside. If the units were graphologically different, the difference was attributed to one of three categories: error on the part of one of the translators, alternative paraphrastic choices or variation in the underlying beliefs of the translators about the author and audience of the source language text, the audience of the translation or the world in general.

By way of example, the following is a headline from one of the articles in the data set: Source language text:

Acumulación de víveres por anuncios sísmicos en Chile

Translation 1:

Hoarding Caused by Earthquake Predictions in Chile

Translation 2:

STOCKPILING OF PROVISIONS BECAUSE OF PREDICTED EARTHQUAKES IN CHILE

First the data is segmented into translation units and equivalents: (1) *Acumulación de víveres/ Hoarding/STOCKPILING OF PROVISIONS*; (2) *por/Caused by/BECAUSE OF*; (3) *anuncios sísmicos/Earthquake Predictions/PREDICTED EARTHQUAKES*; (4) *en Chile/in Chile/IN CHILE*. Next the translation equivalents are compared at the graphological level. Here, the first three pairs differ but the fourth pair, aside from capitalization, is the same. As a result, the fourth pair is set aside.

With regard to each of the remaining pairs, the next step is to categorize them as either due to translator error (here there are no examples), due to alternative choices of paraphrase (here, on the face of it, exemplified by the second pair) or due to differing beliefs about the source text author's intent or the target audience's background knowledge (here exemplified by the first and third pairs).

Finally, differing chains of reasoning leading to the differing translations must be inferred. For instance, the choice of 'hoarding' indicates that the first translator believes the agents of the action are behaving selfishly and irrationally, whereas the choice of 'stockpiling' indicates that the second translator believes that the agents of the action are behaving calmly and rationally. The choice of 'earthquake predictions' indicates that the first translator believes that it is the predictions that are the reason for the action, whereas the choice of 'predicted earthquakes' indicates that the second translator believes that it is possible earthquakes that are the cause of the action. Together, the differing translations set the reader up with rather different expectations of what the article is about.

The result of the analysis of a small data set consisting of roughly 352 phrasal translation units was that 142 units, or roughly 40%, differed with respect to at least one internal element. All together, there were a total of 184 differences of which 160 were lexical and 24 were syntactic. Of the 184 differences, the source of 27, or 15%, could be attributed to translator errors (9 to carelessness – roughly divided equally between the translators, 13 to source language interference – again roughly divided equally between the translators and 5 to mistranslations). The source of 70 differences, or 38%, could be attributed to paraphrastic variation (including 60 lexical and 10 syntactic). Finally, the source of 75 differences, or 41%, could be attributed to differing assumptions on the part of the translators (67 being related to the interpretation of the source language text and 8 being related to assumptions about the target audience's background knowledge).[2]

179

Thus, far from being uncommon, translation variations derived from differing beliefs on the parts of the translators account for 41% of all variations and 16% of all units translated. This is a significant portion of the translator's output and should be recognized as such.[3] The fact is that pragmatics is every bit as crucial in processing language and in translating from one language to another as lexis, morpho-syntax and semantics.

Theoretical Framework

PBMT aims, at some level of abstraction, to model the human translation process. A human translator implicitly ascribes knowledge and beliefs to the author of the source language text or utterance, to the addressees of that text and to the intended audience of the translation. The translator then uses these models as a basis for reasoning about the original intent of the source text and about the appropriateness of any translation. Therefore, a pragmatics-based approach needs to model the translator's ascription of relevant beliefs about the world (both shared and unshared) to:

(1) the author of the source text, including the author's beliefs about the beliefs of the addressees of that text,
(2) the audience of the translation.

Needless to say, this model is dynamic, changing with each new text segment processed, since the translator assumes that the author assumes that the addresses of the text have all updated their views of the author's view of the world (if not their own view of the world) in accordance with the author's intended interpretation of that text segment. In addition, the updated view will include any potential inferences that may be expected to follow from the locutionary content. The translator also assumes that the intended audience of the translation will have updated its view of the author's view of the world (if not their own view of the world) in accordance with the intended interpretation of the translation as well as any potential inferences that may be expected to follow from it.

Thus the goal is to model the translator's knowledge of the world (including the translator's knowledge of the two linguistic systems and associated sets of cultural conventions relevant to the translation at hand), the translator's view of the author's knowledge of the world and of the intended audience of the source text (including knowledge of the source language and associated cultural conventions) and the translator's view of the world knowledge of target audience of the translation (including knowledge of the target language and associated cultural conventions).

These knowledge models are then used as background knowledge to support the two component tasks of the translation process, interpreting what the author intended to express by way of the source language text and then formulating an expression in the target language in such a way as to communicate that intended content to the degree possible to the audience of the translation in as a similar a manner as possible.

Discourse and Utterance Contexts

This background knowledge (or *discourse context*) is the source of all the beliefs that enter into play during interpretation and restatement. It may include beliefs about specific people, places and past events, types of people, objects and events, the source language and communicative strategies, the social and cultural conventions of the setting of the communication and so on.

By way of concrete illustration, consider the following text and translations from the data set described previously that was used for empirically motivating PBMT. It comes from an article about the booming real estate market in Moscow in the early 1990s, and here the author quotes a Moscow real estate agent who is talking to a perspective buyer. The agent says:

> . . . *los 300 metros cuadrados **del tercer piso** estaban disponibles pero fueron aquilados . . . , sólo queda **el segundo piso** . . . .*

While one translator rendered this excerpt as:

> . . . *the 300 square meters of **the third floor** were available . . ., but they were rented. . . . All that is left is **the second floor** . . . .*

the second translated it as:

> . . . *the 300 square meters on **the fourth floor** were available, but they were rented . . . ; only **the third floor** remains. . . .*

It is important to note that, despite appearances, both translations are appropriate and both are potentially accurate. They may even be expressing the same information. The reason for the apparent contradiction is that the two translators have differing beliefs about the story naming conventions that enter into play either during interpretation or during restatement or both. The specific conventions in question are:

Convention 1: In Europe and elsewhere, people refer to the story that is at ground level as the ground floor, to the next level up as the first floor, to the level after that as the second floor and so on.

Convention 2: In the United States and elsewhere, people refer to the story that is at ground level as the first floor, the next level up as the second floor, the level after that as the third floor and so on.

Very briefly, while the first translator (*tercer piso | third floor, segundo piso | second floor*) assumes that the floor naming convention is the same for both the source language participants and the audience of the translation, the second translator (*tercer piso | fourth floor, segundo piso | third floor*) assumes that Convention 1 applies during interpretation (possibly because the building is in Moscow) and that Convention 2 applies during restatement (possibly because the intended audience of the translation is American).

The knowledge that has been introduced during the actual discourse is the *utterance context*. It also is a source for the beliefs that enter into play during interpretation and restatement. It constitutes the foreground knowledge as well as serving as the interpretation of the discourse thus far. It is the knowledge with which new information must be made consistent and coherent. It includes beliefs about the objects and events mentioned or implied during prior discourse and about the current state of the discourse, especially any unresolved issues (those objects, situations and events whose connection to the interpretation have yet to be established).

With respect to our example, the utterance context includes information that the author had mentioned in the article prior to the current text fragment such as:

- the commercial real estate market in Moscow is rapidly expanding,
- there is a great demand for commercial properties,
- properties are renting at $700 to $800 per square meter per year,

- properties are renting at the highest prices in the world apart from Tokyo and Hong Kong,
- the market is dominated by legal uncertainty and the usual result that the rich get richer.

While it is not entirely clear how this knowledge affects the interpretation or restatement of the text fragment in question, it may be that the second translator decided to apply Convention 1 during interpretation because he or she assumed that it is the convention that Muscovites follow.

Interpretation

The process of interpretation may be described in a semi-formal manner as follows.

To begin, a source language expression, E_i (e.g. *el tercer piso*), is provided with a semantic representation, p (i.e. third floor), which needs to be interpreted, that is, added to the current source-language utterance context (call it $SLUC_h$) in a coherent fashion.[4]

Next, any beliefs that provide information relevant to the interpretation are inferred on the basis of beliefs drawn from the utterance and discourse contexts. For instance, it may be that b_4 (that the author is referring to the fourth story of the building) follows from p (third floor) and b_1 (Convention 1), resulting in one particular updated source language interpretation, $SLUC_{i1}$, or that b_5 (that the author is referring to the third story) follows from p (third floor) and b_2 (Convention 2), resulting in a second updated source language interpretation, $SLUC_{i2}$. Or it may be that b_6 (that the author is referring to some other story) follows from p (third floor) and b_3 (some other convention), resulting in yet a third updated source language interpretation, $SLUC_{i3}$. Finally, from these possible interpretations, that which is most compatible with the prior utterance context is selected as the intended updated interpretation ($SLUC_i$), for example, $SLUC_{i1}$, by the second translator and either $SLUC_{i1}$ or $SLUC_{i2}$ (or neither) by the first translator.

Restatement

The process of restatement is more complex. First, the beliefs used to support the interpretation of the source text segment need to be identified. Next these beliefs must be integrated into the target language utterance context in order to produce the intended interpretation of the translation. Then, a translation is formulated which expresses that intended interpretation.

Somewhat more formally, the source language utterance context as it stood prior to interpreting E_i is first subtracted from the utterance context resulting from the interpretation of E_i, i.e., $SLUC_{i1}$ or $SLUC_{i2}$, thus isolating only those beliefs that were used to arrive at $SLUC_{i1}$, or $SLUC_{i2}$, (e.g. b_4 – that the author is referring to the fourth story – and b_1 – Convention 1, or b_5 – that the author is referring to the third story – and b_2 – Convention 2, respectively). That is to say, what are left are only those beliefs and inferences that were necessary in order to establish $SLUC_{i1}$ or $SLUC_{i2}$ given p.

Next, in order to formulate the translation, the intended interpretation of the yet-to-be-formulated translation is partially created by updating the target language utterance context using the set of new beliefs (i.e. b_4 and b_1, or b_5 and b_2) so long as these are compatible with the target language discourse and utterance contexts. Note that, in the case of the second translation, b_1 may not be compatible with the discourse context of the audience of the translation.

At this point a target language expression, $E_i{}^*$, having the semantic representation p^*, is formulated such that its interpretation in the context of the target language interaction is equivalent to that derived in the source language interaction, i.e., b_4 – that the author is referring to the fourth story or, alternatively, b_5 – that the author is referring to the third story. This then results in the updated utterance context for the translation, $TLUC_i$, as well as the expression used for the translation, $E_i^\star$, along with its semantic interpretation, $p^\star$.

Equivalence

Within a pragmatics-based approach, there are two basic notions of equivalence. First, there is *core equivalence*. This is measured in terms of the similarity of authors' intentions as represented by the source language interpretation that was used as a basis for the translation, for example, $SLUC_i$, and the translator's intentions as represented by the preferred interpretation of the translation, for example, $TLUC_i$ (for example, the levels above ground level and the beliefs and inferences required to identify it). The greater the overlap and consistency of the beliefs making up these two interpretations, the greater the core equivalence between the source language text and translation.

In addition to core equivalence, there is a broader notion of *extended equivalence*, which is measured in terms of the pair wise similarity (and difference) between the other possible interpretations of the source language text and translation (e.g. $SLUC_{i1}$, $SLUC_{i2}$, . . . vs TLI_1, TLI_2, . . .). Here, equivalence would be based not simply on the primary interpretations of the source language text and translation but on all the other possible interpretations of the source language text and of their translations as well.

Computational Platform

The computational platform needed for a PBMT system is necessarily complex. Since the novel part of the system involves inferencing to and from intended perlocutionary effect using contextual information, the source text input will be represented as a set of logical propositions. This, in turn, suggests an interlingual approach to MT as a substrate for any pragmatic reasoning, since such approaches provide a source text with a meaning representation. Thus, the basic requirements include:

- a knowledge base,
- a belief ascription component,
- a default reasoning component,
- an analysis component,
- a generation component.

The Knowledge Base

There are a number of interlingual MT systems that could serve as a substrate (Nyberg and Mitamura 1992: 1069–73; Dorr *et al.* 1995: 221–50; Levin *et al.* 2000: 3–25; Mitamura and Nyberg 2000: 192–95, etc.), which differ somewhat in the nature of the interlingual representation but more so in the semantic depth of that representation. The deeper the representation, the more useful it is for pragmatic reasoning. One of the deeper systems is that of Mahesh and Nirenberg (1995) and Nirenburg and Raskin (2004). It includes the following modules, which are assumed as an appropriate basis for a PBMT system:

- Ontology – a conceptual knowledge base of objects, properties, relations and activities;
- Onomasticon – a database of proper names of people, places and other objects;
- Fact Database – episodic knowledge of people, places and events.

Together, these modules determine the discourse context. Linguistic knowledge bases for each of the relevant languages that are used for providing meaning representations for expressions and generating expressions given meaning representations include the lexicons and lexical, syntactic and semantic rules.

Pragmatic Reasoning Components

Logical Inferencing for Speech Act Analysis

Given a semantic interpretation of an input (or set of such interpretations), the pragmatic reasoning components aim to identify the illocutionary and the perlocutionary intents, that is, what the author was *doing* in producing the input expression and how the author intended the audience to react.

To reach these interpretive levels requires a default reasoning mechanism. For example, the application of a floor-naming convention must be the result of default reasoning, since there is neither concrete factual information about the particular convention used by the author or audience of the translation, nor is there some absolute generalization that can allow certainty in this specific case. However, there are default generalizations ('Europeans generally use Convention 2') as well as other default inferences ('The article was written in Castilian, so the author is likely to be European') that would allow a default conclusion to be reached about what convention to adopt in interpreting the source text. Similar reasoning would exist for choosing the convention to apply for the target audience. One such default inferencing system is Att-Meta (Barnden *et al.* 1994a: 27–38, 1994b), which also deals with metaphorical input. Other possibilities might include Nottelmann and Fuhr (2006: 17–42), Motik (2006) and Hustadt *et al.* (2007: 351, 384), to name a few more recent systems.

A speech act identifier such as Levin *et al.* (2003) is used as a first step in identifying a plausible speech act. However, a PBMT system must be able to identify indirect speech acts and be alert to unusual sequences of overt speech acts, such as, two successive questions by two different interlocutors. If a question such as 'Do you know where Bin Laden is?' is answered with another question, it might be a request for clarification of the question (e.g. 'Do you mean Osama Bin Laden or Mohammed bin Laden?'), it might be a request for clarification of the questioner's perlocutionary intent ('Why do you want to know?' or 'What makes you think I know the answer?') or it might even be a refusal to answer ('What do you take me for, a GPS system?').

In addition, it should be clear that the 'speech act' level of representation of a source language expression might be several degrees removed from that of its semantic content. For example, in interpreting a yard sign that says, 'Only an ass would walk on the grass' not only must the speech act be recognized as a command rather than an informative statement but the content of the command must be clear as well: *Please do not walk on the grass.*

Belief Ascription for Participant Modeling

Finally, PBMT requires that the translator's view of the differing beliefs of the source language author and addressees as well as those of the target language audience guide translation choices.

Therefore, a simple, univocal reasoning system is insufficient. The system must have the capacity to attribute different beliefs to at least these three participants in the translation process: the source language author and addressees and the target language audience. In some translation scenarios, it may even be necessary to attribute differing beliefs to the people described in the source language text. Otherwise, if all the beliefs of all the participants are merged into a single model, it would undoubtedly be inconsistent, disallowing anything to be deduced.

One possible belief ascription system that could be used for participant modeling is the View-Gen system (Ballim and Wilks 1991). This system creates complex embedded belief contexts, or viewpoints, that allow each participant to reason independently. Within the viewpoint of each participant, a different set of assumptions can be held about each topic of conversation, allowing for conflicting beliefs. In addition, participants may have their own views of other participants' viewpoints (which may or may not correspond to that participant's viewpoint). Such embedded viewpoints allow, for instance, for a translator to reason about a source text author's reference to a story in a building and then later reason about whether the audience of the translation should work out the same referent. Other approaches have been described by Maida (1991: 331–83); Alechina and Logan (2002: 881–88); and more recently Alechina *et al.* (2009: 1–15), Alechina and Logan (2010: 179–97), Wilks (2011: 337–44) and Wilks *et al.* (2011: 140–57).

Generator

Once the system has identified the meaning of an input text, the likely speech act and illocutionary intent and the perlocutionary intent of the author, this information is then used to generate a translation.

Given the lack of information about how to incorporate pragmatic information in the production of an output sentence (Goodman and Nirenberg 1991; Hovy 1993: 341–86), the PBMT system falls back on a generate-and-test paradigm.

The system first attempts a translation of the semantic content of the utterance using the IL substrate. The semantic representation of this target text is then placed in the target audience's belief space and the attempt is made to deduce an illocutionary and perlocutionary intent. If the results are the same as those of the original text, the translation may stand.

However, if unsuccessful, a translation is produced on the basis of the illocutionary level interpretation and the test is repeated. If the representation of the perlocutionary intent for the translation is equivalent to that of the source language document, it is assumed to be an acceptable translation.

If not, as a last resort, a translation based on the representation of the perlocutionary intent would be sent to the generator.

Benefits of Pragmatics-Based Machine Translation

Evidence provided thus far indicates that human translators translate on the basis of the communicative intent behind the source language text, as opposed to solely on the basis of its meaning. Section 4 discusses how a computational platform could be constructed that would emulate this translation process. However, the question remains whether this system could solve some of the difficult problems that arise from pragmatic phenomena such as reference resolution, the interpretation of metaphor and metonymy, the recovery of ellipted information and morphosyntactic and lexical disambiguation. For each of these problem areas a PBMT system could be expected to perform more adequately than other types of MT.

In addition, quantitative analysis of multiple translations of the same texts indicates that approximately 16% (1/6) of all translation units in a text differ because of differing beliefs. This holds true whether the study is of entire texts (Farwell and Helmreich 1997a: 125–31, 1997b) or of selected aspects of multiple texts (Helmreich and Farwell 2004: 86–93). In such situations, neither translation is wrong, but each variant is based on differing analyses of the intent of the author or of the common knowledge of the audience of the translation. The remainder of this section focuses on such situations, showing how a PBMT system would deal with them.

User-Friendly Translation

In some cases, the analysis of the source document may provide reasonable illocutionary and perlocutionary intents, but the reasoning that led to that analysis cannot be reconstructed in the target language due to the lack of a crucial belief on the part of the audience of the translation. Compensating for that missing information in the formulation of the translation is what has been referred to as *user-friendly translation* (Farwell and Helmreich 1997a: 125–31).

An example of this is the translation of *On va pas jouer un scène de Feydeau*. As indicated in Section 1, reaching the appropriate level of interpretation requires inferencing from the playwright Feydeau to the kinds of plays he wrote, namely bedroom farces. Such information is likely to be lacking on the part of the English-speaking audience. Therefore, following the generation plan outlined in Section 4, the PBMT system would replace the text based on the locutionary content with a text based on the representation of the illocutionary intent, i.e., 'this is not a bedroom farce'.

A similar situation arises when the illocutionary and perlocutionary intents depend on an inference from the form of the utterance, rather than the content. Examples would include poetry (alliteration, rhyme, assonance) and, frequently, jokes such as puns.

In both these cases, the intent of the source language author is twofold. In poetry, the author, on the one hand, intends that the content be understood and yet, on the other, the author intends to create an emotional (perhaps subliminal) effect through the poetic devices used. If the corresponding content of the target language text does not employ words with a similar effect, then that intended poetic effect fails to be captured. A PBMT system that could translate poetry would be able to identify such devices and select words and phrases in the target language that produce the same effect to the degree possible, perhaps even sacrificing aspects of the locutionary content.

In the case of puns and other jokes, the humor may depend on reference to two different scenarios at the same time (Rankin 1984), often through the use of ambiguous words or phonetically similar patterns. For example, the joke:

- *Why do sharks swim in salt water?*
- *Because pepper water makes them sneeze.*

depends on the dual language-specific oppositions between salt water/fresh water and salt/pepper. In French, the expression for 'salt water' is *eau to mer* (sea water) and its opposite is *eau douce* (sweet water), so a literal translation of 'pepper water' would fail to be humorous. A PBMT system should be capable of recognizing this dual intent, and providing an alternative translation of 'pepper water' as, perhaps, 'eau de cologne' while at the same time substituting *stink* for *sneeze* (see Farwell and Helmreich 2006 for further discussion).

Alternatively, inferencing in the target language belief space might not fail and yet produce a different communicative intent from that originally intended by the author of the original text. In such cases, a PBMT system needs to adjust the translation in such a way as to insure that the desired inferences are made, blocking any unwanted inference while accommodating an alternative but appropriate default belief.

An example this phenomenon is the switching of story-naming conventions during target language generation as described earlier in Section 3. The differing default beliefs in the source and target cultures (not necessarily languages) result in differing illocutionary intents in regard to which story is actually being referred to, given the same semantic content. In such cases, the PBMT system would be capable of replacing the translation based on the locutionary content with one that would have the same illocutionary intent, given the different default conventions.

A generalization of this case involves any system of measurement or counting which differs across languages or cultures: metric versus English measures, various temperature scales (Fahrenheit, Centigrade, Kelvin), shoe sizes, dress sizes, numbering of Biblical psalms and the 10 commandments, musical keys and so on.

A measuring system includes a number of conceptual items: the content (what is to be measured, e.g. temperature), a starting point (e.g. the freezing point of water), a scale itself (for continuous measures, e.g., the temperature shift measured by one unit), a name for the system (e.g. Fahrenheit, Centigrade, etc.) and names for the scales themselves (e.g. for musical scales, the letters A, B, C, . . . G). Most frequently these conceptual items are not named explicitly in the text. Temperature system, for instance, is usually not mentioned, so it must be inferred from the discourse and utterance contexts.

If a reference is made to a temperature of 32 degrees, the PBMT system could, for example, determine by default reasoning that the source language audience would interpret the temperature as degrees Fahrenheit, while the target language audience prefers to use Centigrade measurements. Then two translation options are available: (1) clarify the source language usage by inserting 'Fahrenheit' into the translation or (2) translate the reference to '32 degrees' to '0 degrees' (Centigrade).

Translation Based on High-Level Beliefs

The situations described in the previous section required adjustments of the translation in order to accommodate differing beliefs on the part of the audience of the translation and to support the inferencing needed for arriving at the desired interpretation. However, some of the more interesting variation between human translations may be due to the translators' attempt to maintain cohesion at the level of the text as a whole. Because of this, differences in the translators' assessments of what the over-arching perlocutionary intent of the author of the source text is result in different patterns of lexical choice, each of which tends to cohere on the basis of connotation.

For instance, one article from the corpus described in Section 2 concerned the murder trial in Brazil of a person who was alleged to have killed a union leader (see Farwell and Helmreich 1997b for details). In this case, the two translations differed according to whether the translator believed the trial involved a straightforward murder or a political assassination. Thus, the words derived from the Spanish *asesinar* (i.e. *asesinado*, *asesino*, etc.) were consistently translated by words derived from 'murder' or 'kill' by one translator and by words derived from 'assassinate' by the other, depending on their global viewpoint. Similarly, the victim was described as a 'union member' by the first translator or as a 'labor leader' by the second. The surrounding conflict was described as between 'landholders' and 'small farmers' by the first translator or as between 'landowners' and 'peasants' by the second. In each case the connotations of the words selected for the first translation imply a simple criminal trial, whereas the connotations of the words selected for the second translation imply a trial due to and influenced by politics. Overall, these two patterns of lexical selection account for some 60% of the beliefs-based differences in the translations.

Another article from the same corpus described people buying up supplies in response to press stories about a possible future earthquake (see Farwell and Helmreich 1997a: 125–31 for details). In this case, the translators seemed to differ as to whether the article was about a government lapse in which an overly precise statement about an impending earthquake led to a rational response by people to stockpile supplies or about a reasonable government statement that was overblown by the local media, resulting in irrational hoarding. These two views are epitomized by the translations of the article's headline *Acumulación de víveres por anuncios sísmicos* as either *Hoarding Due to Earthquake Prediction*, on the one hand, or as *Stockpiling because of Predicted Earthquakes*, on the other. As mentioned before, the choice of 'hoarding' indicates that the first translator believes the agents of the action are behaving selfishly and irrationally, while the choice of 'earthquake predictions' indicates it is a prediction that is the reason for their action. On the other hand, the choice of 'stockpiling' indicates that the second translator believes that the agents of the action are behaving calmly and rationally, while the choice of 'predicted earthquakes' implies that it is a possible earthquake that is the cause of the action. These general tendencies to select expressions that, on the one hand, exaggerate the panic of the people, minimize the likelihood of an earthquake and place the role of the press in a negative light by the first translator or that, on the other, convey the measured reaction of the people, maximize the likelihood of an earthquake and place the role of government in a negative light by the second translator are prevalent throughout the translations. In fact, the two differing assumptions about the source text author's general perlocutionary intent accounts for roughly half the belief-based differences in the translations.

In both these texts, the translators reached different conclusions about the over-arching perlocutionary intent of the author of the source text. These conclusions were arrived at through inferencing largely on the basis of implicit (not explicit) propositions or beliefs. In fact, there are several reasonable chains of reasoning that might link semantic content to illocutionary intent to perlocutionary intent. Because of this, PBMT systems must be capable of finding several differing inference chains, since any one of them might potentially guide the generation of an alternative coherent translation.

Finally, the translator reaches conclusions not only about the beliefs of the source language author and addressees and target language audience but also about the purpose of the translation itself. The translator will take into account whether the translation is for assimilation or dissemination, whether a particular detail is vital to an argument, whether the target audience will be scrutinizing the translation for each detail (as in the case of a piece of evidence or a legal document) or whether some details are irrelevant in the end. In this latter case, it is likely that some inferencing would be avoided altogether (such as, for instance, exactly which story of the Moscow building was being rented in the example in Section 3).

Evaluation

In regard to the evaluation of MT quality, ideally it should be based on the notion of equivalence discussed in Section 3. As noted, this is defined by the similarity and difference between the interpretations of the source language text and the translation in terms of their component beliefs and inferences. But if the goal is to measure pragmatic equivalence, objective evaluation is complicated, to say the least. Automatic evaluation at this point is completely implausible. Subjective evaluation might appear to be more plausible, but, even so, it will be exceedingly problematical given the open-endedness of the inferencing process and would clearly be very human intensive. Nevertheless, to broach the subject, it is first important to understand what constitutes pragmatic equivalence and then attempt to develop evaluation methodologies that are sensitive to that specific notion.

The actual comparison of interpretations, whether for core equivalence or extended equivalence, may be quantitative, based simply on the number of beliefs and inferences used to arrive at the interpretations of the source text or its translation. Or the comparison may be qualitative, based on the prepositional content of those beliefs and inferences used, their 'currency', the 'transparency' of their connection to or their consistency with the source language and target language utterance and discourse contexts.

In a perfect world, evaluation would consist of automatically or manually inspecting the number and similarity of content of the beliefs and the inferences used. To do this requires that those beliefs and inferences be explicitly represented. Yet, to date, no pragmatics-based MT system exists and, even if there were one, no reference translations exist whose underlying beliefs and inferences have been made explicit.

Currently, automated evaluation methodologies are entirely inappropriate for capturing any notion of equivalence based on the similarity of interpretations of the source language text and translation. These techniques are based on comparing MT output with human-produced reference translations in terms of overlapping character sequences. This tells us nothing at all about beliefs and inferences that make up the compared interpretations. Still, were there a PBMT system that produced translations, no doubt its output could be compared alongside any other MT output. The problem would merely be that there would be no way of knowing whether a given translation having a relatively low rank was in fact inferior to a translation with a higher rank. For instance, clearly 'We are not acting out a scene from Feydeau' will not score as well against 'This is not a scene from a bedroom farce' as a reference translation, or vice versa, and yet neither is obviously an inferior translation.

As for manual evaluation, there is the very time-consuming and human-intensive sort of analysis that was carried out during the comparative analysis of multiple translations described in Section 2.2. This process could in theory be made more objective by increasing the number of evaluators, although even this may not entirely feasible – there are simply too many possible alternative interpretations and inferred connections to expect the analysts to always agree on a particular set. Still, traditional human evaluation methodologies such as those developed by such organizations as the American Translation Association (www.atanet.org/certification/aboutexams_overview.php), though human intensive, should at least be amenable to tolerating differing translations arising from differing interpretations on the part of the translators or translation systems. Perhaps not altogether practical and probably not so objective, they are nonetheless more reliable and flexible (for further discussion, see Farwell and Helmreich 2003: 21–28).

Critical Analysis

In addition to the problems concerning evaluation described in the previous section, pragmatics-based MT systems face a number of other serious challenges that must be met before they will have sufficient coverage to be deployed. These challenges are found both in the representation of linguistic phenomena and knowledge of the world as well as in the modeling of the translation process and the implementation of various crucial components.

To begin, the representation of many linguistic phenomena, particularly semantic and pragmatic, is often weakly motivated and incomplete. For example, one important area of overlap between semantics and pragmatics is reference resolution. In part the task of resolving reference requires deciding whether a given reference is to specific entity (real or imaginary) in the context of a description of a particular event as opposed to some generic entity in the context of a generalization. To wit, in:

The elephant (that we keep in our back yard) *is eating the grass.*

the elephant is being used to refer to some particular individual. By contrast, in:

Elephants eat grass.

189

elephants is being used to refer to some indefinitely large set of arbitrary individuals. Where the former sentence is being used to describe a particular event, the latter is being used to make a generalization, to describe a situation that, in the abstract, could happen.

The problem for representation systems is how to capture the semantics and pragmatics of reference. There are many possible taxonomies that might be offered but none that is generally accepted. One system, motivated by referring to expressions in English (Farwell and Wilks 1991: 19–24), entails a fourfold classification that includes: (1) the pragmatic distinction between referring to a specific entity or entities, as in the first example previously, or referring generically, as in the second example; (2) the semantic distinction between referring to a particular individual (*the elephant, the elephants*) or to an arbitrary individual (*an elephant, elephants*); and (3) the pragmatic distinction between whether a reference is to individuals that the speaker presumes the addressee can identify (*the elephant, that elephant*) or to individuals that the speaker presumes the addressee cannot identify (*an elephant, some elephants*). Finally, a fourth deictic distinction is made in the case of references to specific, particular, identifiable individuals, which is whether that individual is nearby (*this elephant*), remote (*that elephant*) or neutral (*the elephant*).

Although this system is motivated by English referring expressions, the intent is to provide a general framework for classifying any reference made in any language and deciding whether corresponding references in a text and its translation are equivalent. Unfortunately, the extent to which the framework is successful is unclear since it can be difficult to identify where it is correct and where it fails or whether its distinctions are too fine-grained or not fine-grained enough. Thus, while perhaps useful for comparing references in languages which generally mark types of reference explicitly, such as English or Spanish, it is difficult to apply and leads to a good deal of ambiguity in languages in which most types of reference are implicit, such as Chinese. It simply is not well enough defined or well enough evaluated for deciding such issues. What is more troubling, as with reference, so too with the descriptive taxonomies for time/tense, aspect, modality, voice, case, grammatical relations, functional relations, rhetorical relations, speech acts and so on that are generally but vaguely understood.

In addition to being weakly motivated and incomplete, representations of linguistic phenomena and knowledge of the world are essentially arbitrary and often vague. As a result, they are not very amenable to annotation or evaluation. It can be rather difficult to confidently categorize concrete instances, with the result that training annotators and preparing training materials, as well as the task of annotation itself, are at best an art. For instance, suppose you are attempting to categorize the meaning of *proposed* in:

> The Czech Minister of Transportation, Jan Strasky, proposed on Saturday that the State buy back the shares held by Air France.

given DECLARE_A_PLAN, PRESENT_FOR_CONSIDERATION, INTEND or ASK_TO_MARRY as possible choices. While ASK_TO_MARRY is relatively easy to rule out, a case might be made for any of the other three choices with the result that different annotators might well make different choices. This results in lower inter-annotator agreement, which, in turn, reduces our confidence in the quality of the annotated corpus. For an extensive discussion of text annotation for interlingual content and the evaluation of inter-annotator agreement, see Dorr *et al.* 2008: 197–243.

In addition to the challenges of adequate representation, PBMT faces a number of serious deficiencies in terms of the computational infrastructure[5] available today. Among the more important are the size and granularity of the ontology, the ability to reason with uncertainty within an open-world context and the open-endedness of beliefs ascription. While progress has clearly been made in the last decade in all these areas, there remains much yet to be done.

Notes

1 The translations were done as part of the evaluation corpus for a US government–run machine translation evaluation and so were carefully supervised and done professionally, and the translators were given identical instructions about the translation – they were neither to add nor delete any information in the translation.

2 In addition there were twelve differences that were a consequence of translator choices about other elements within the same translation unit.

3 This is especially interesting since the translators were instructed to keep the translations as 'close' as possible, maintaining lexical and structural equivalence to the degree possible.

4 Actually it may have various semantic representations that will be filtered down to one in part on the basis of establishing a coherent connection to prior text.

5 It should be pointed out that no PBMT systems exist today. A small prototype system, ULTRA (Farwell and Wilks 1991), was abandoned prior to implementation of the required context modeling and inferencing mechanisms. The Mikrokosmos KBMT system (Mahesh and Nirenberg 1995) was certainly an important step in the direction of PBMT but has never been fully developed nor thoroughly tested.

Additional Resources

www.atanet.org/certification/aboutexams_overview.php.

Bibliography

Alechina, Natasha and Brian Logan (2002) 'Ascribing Beliefs to Resource Bounded Agents', in *Proceedings of the 1st International Joint Conference on Autonomous Agents and Multi-Agent Systems (AAMAS '02)*, 15–19 July 2002, Bologna, Italy, 2: 881–88.

Alechina, Natasha and Brian Logan (2010) 'Belief Ascription under Bounded Resources', *Synthese* 173(2): 179–97.

Alechina, Natasha, Brian Logan, Hoang Nga Nguyen, and Abdur Rakib (2009) 'Reasoning about Other Agents' Beliefs under Bounded Resources', in John-Jules Ch. Meyer and Jan Broersen (eds.) *Knowledge Representation for Agents and Multi-Agent Systems: First International Workshop, KRAMAS 2008, Sydney, Australia, September 17, 2008, Revised Selected Papers*, Berlin: Springer Verlag, 1–15.

Austin, J. L. (1975) *How to Do Things with Words*, Cambridge, MA: Harvard University Press.

Ballim, Afzal and Yorick Wilks (1991) *Artificial Believers: The Ascription of Belief*, Hillsdale, NJ: Lawrence Erlbaum.

Barnden, John A., Stephen Helmreich, Eric Iverson, and Gees C. Stein (1994a) 'An Integrated Implementation of Simulative, Uncertain and Metaphorical Reasoning about Mental States', in Jon Doyle, Erik Sandewall, and Pietro Torasso (eds.) *Principles of Knowledge Representation and Reasoning: Proceedings of the 4th International Conference*, 24–27 May 1994, San Mateo, CA: Morgan Kaufmann Publishers, 27–38.

Barnden, John A., Stephen Helmreich, Eric Iverson, and Gees C. Stein (1994b) 'Combining Simulative and Metaphor-based Reasoning about Beliefs', in *Proceedings of the 16th Annual Conference of the Cognitive Science Society*, Hillsdale, NJ: Lawrence Erlbaum, 21–26.

Dorr, Bonnie J., Joseph Garman, and Amy Weinberg (1995) 'From Syntactic Encodings to Thematic Roles: Building Lexical Entries for Interlingual MT', *Machine Translation* 9(3–4): 221–50.

Dorr, Bonnie J., Rebecca J. Passonneau, David Farwell, Rebecca Green, Nizar Habash, Stephen Helmreich, Eduard Hovy, Lori Levin, Keith J. Miller, Teruko Mitamura, Owen Rambow, and Advaith Siddharthan (2008) 'Interlingual Annotation of Parallel Text Corpora: A New Framework for Annotation and Evaluation', *Natural Language Engineering* 16(3): 197–243.

Farwell, David and Stephen Helmreich (1997a) 'User-friendly Machine Translation: Alternate Translations Based on Differing Beliefs', in Virginia Teller and Beth Sundeim (eds.) *Proceedings of the MT Summit VI: Machine Translation: Past, Present, Future*, 29 October–1 November 1997, San Diego, CA, 125–31.

Farwell, David and Stephen Helmreich (1997b) 'Assassins or Murders: Translation of Politically Sensitive Material', in *Proceedings of the 26th Annual Meeting of Linguistics Association of the Southwest*, October 1997, University of California at Los Angeles, CA.

Farwell, David and Stephen Helmreich (2000) 'An Interlingual-based Approach to Reference Resolution', in *Proceedings of ANLP/NAACL 2000 Workshop on Applied Interlinguas: Practical Applications of Interlingual Approaches to NLP*, 30 April 2000, Seattle, WA, 1–11.

Farwell, David and Stephen Helmreich (2003) 'Pragmatics-based Translation and MT Evaluation', in *Proceedings of Workshop on Machine Translation Evaluation: Towards Systematizing MT Evaluation and the 9th Machine Translation Summit (MT Summit IX)*, 23–27 September 2003, New Orleans, LA, 21–28.

Farwell, David and Stephen Helmreich (2006) 'Pragmatics-based MT and the Translation of Puns', in Jan Tore Lønning and Stephen Oepen (eds.) *Proceedings of the 11th Annual Conference of the European Association for Machine Translation (EAMT)*, 19–20 June 2006, Department of Computer Science, Oslo University, Oslo, Norway.

Farwell, David and Yorick Wilks (1991) 'ULTRA: A Multilingual Machine Translator', in *Proceedings of the Machine Translation Summit III*, 1–4 July 1991, Seattle, WA, 19–24.

Goodman, Kenneth and Sergei Nirenberg (1991) *The KBMT Project: A Case Study in Knowledge-based Machine Translation*, San Mateo, CA: Morgan Kaufmann Publishers.

Helmreich, Stephen and David Farwell (1998) 'Translation Differences and Pragmatics-based MT', *Machine Translation* 13(1): 17–39.

Helmreich, Stephen and David Farwell (2004) 'Counting, Measuring, Ordering: Translation Problems and Solutions', in Robert E. Frederking and Kathryn B. Taylor (eds.) *Proceedings of Machine Translation: From Real Users to Research: Proceedings of the 6th Conference of the Association for Machine Translation in the Americas, AMTA 2004*, 28 September–2 October 2004, Washington, DC, Berlin: Springer Verlag, 86–93.

Hovy, Eduard (1993) 'Automated Discourse Generation Using Discourse Structure Relations', *Artificial Intelligence: Special Issue on Natural Language Processing* 63(1–2): 341–86.

Hustadt, Ullrich, Boris Motik, and Ulrike Sattler (2007) 'Reasoning in Description Logics by a Reduction to Disjunctive Datalog', *Journal of Automated Reasoning* 39(3): 351–84.

Jésus de Montréal (1989) Dir. Denys Arcand, Orion Classics, Film.

Levin, Lori, Chad Langley, Alon Lavie, Donna Gates, Dorcas Wallace, and Kay Peterson (2003) 'Domain Specific Speech Acts for Spoken Language Translation', in *Proceedings of the 4th SIGdial Workshop of Discourse and Dialogue*, 5–6 July 2003, Sapporo, Japan.

Levin, Lori, Alon Lavie, Monika Woszczyna, Donna Gates, Marsal Galvadà, Detlef Koll, and Alex Waibel (2000) 'The Janus-III Translation System: Speech-to-speech Translation in Multiple Domains', *Machine Translation* 15(1–2): 3–25.

Mahesh, Kavi and Sergei Nirenberg (1995) 'A Situated Ontology for Practical NLP', in *Proceedings on the Workshop on Basic Ontological Issues in Knowledge Sharing, International Joint Conference on Artificial Intelligence-95*, 19–21 August 1995, Montreal, Canada.

Maida, Anthony S. (1991) 'Maintaining Mental Models of Agents Who Have Existential Misconceptions', *Artificial Intelligence* 50: 331–83.

Mitamura, Teruko and Eric Nyberg (2000) 'The KANTOO Machine Translation Environment', in John S. White (ed.) *Envisioning Machine Translation in the Information Future: Proceedings of 4th Conference of the Association for Machine Translation in the Americas*, 10–14 October 2000, Cuernavaca, Mexico, 192–95.

Motik, Boris (2006) 'Reasoning in Description Logics Using Resolution and Deductive Databases', Unpublished doctoral thesis, Univesität Karlsruhe (TH), Karlsruhe, Germany.

Nirenberg, Sergei and Victor Raskin (2004) *Ontological Semantics*, Cambridge, MA: MIT Press.

Nottelmann, Henrik and Norbert Fuhr (2006) 'Adding Probabilities and Rules to Owl Lite Subsets Based on Probabilistic Datalog', *International Journal of Uncertainty, Fuzziness and Knowledge-Based Systems* 14(1): 17–42.

Nyberg, Eric H. and Teruko Mitamura (1992) 'The Kant System: Fast, Accurate, High-quality Translation in Practical Domains', in *Proceedings of the 14th International Conference on Computational Linguistics (COLING-92)*, 23–28 August 1992, Nantes, France, 1069–73.

Rankin, Victor (1984) *Semantic Mechanisms of Humor*, Dordrecht: D. Reidel Publishing Company.

Searle, John R. (1969) *Speech Acts: An Essay in the Philosophy of Language*, Cambridge: Cambridge University Press.

Wilks, Yorick (2011) 'Protocols for Reference Sharing in a Belief Ascription Model of Communication', in *Advances in Cognitive Systems: Papers from the 2011 AAAI Fall Symposium (FS-11-01)*, 4–6 November 2011, Arlington, VA, 337–44.

Wilks, Yorick, Simon Worgan, Alexiei Dingli, Roberta Catizone, Roger Moore, Debora Field, and Weiwei Cheng (2011) 'A Prototype for a Conversational Companion for Reminiscing about Images', *Computer Speech and Language* 25(2): 140–57.

10

RULE-BASED MACHINE TRANSLATION

Bai Xiaojing and Yu Shiwen

Introduction

In the field of computational linguistics, rationalism and empiricism prevailed alternately as the dominant method of research in the past few decades (Church 2011). The early development of machine translation (MT) systems, accordingly, featured the shift between these two methods. The past decade has witnessed a remarkable upsurge of neural machine translation (NMT) (Tan *et al.* 2020). Being a radically different paradigm for the task of automatic translation, NMT is in a more dominant position of MT research now. Recent efforts also focus on introducing pre-trained models to NMT to improve the quality of translation (Wang and Li 2021).

Having been replaced by NMT as the mainstream method, the MT paradigm introduced in this chapter nevertheless played a typical and strategic role in the history of MT development. More importantly, when data, algorithm, and computing power are jointly contributing to the great success of NMT, human knowledge of language, which features in rule-based machine translation, may have new roles to play. (Zhou 2019; Tan *et al.* 2020) For these purposes, among others, the rule-based approach to MT is reviewed here.

Rule-based machine translation, abbreviated as RBMT and also known as knowledge-based machine translation, relies on morphological, syntactic, semantic, and contextual knowledge about both the source and the target languages, respectively, and the connections between them to perform the translation task. The linguistic knowledge assists MT systems through computer-accessible dictionaries and grammar rules based on theoretical linguistic research. This rationalist approach contrasts with the empiricist approach, which views the translation process as a proba-bilistic event and therefore features statistical translation models derived from language corpora.

MT systems were generally rule-based before the late 1980s. Shortly after Warren Weaver issued a memorandum in 1949, which practically stimulated the MT research, Georgetown University and IBM collaborated to demonstrate a Russian–English machine translation system in 1954. The system was reported to work with six rules instructing operations such as selection, substitution, and movement, which applied to words and sentences in the sample. Despite being merely a showcase designed specifically for a small sample of sentences, this demonstration is still the first actual implementation of RBMT. In the years that followed, the rule-based approach dominated the field of MT research and was further explored, leading to a deeper division among the direct model, the transfer model, and the interlingua model. There was a change

DOI: 10.4324/9781003168348-11

of direction from the direct model to the other two 'indirect' models as a result of the ALPAC report in 1966. Particularly in the latter half of the 1970s and the early 1980s, MT research revived from the aftermath of ALPAC and featured the predominance of the syntax-based transfer model (Hutchins 1994, 2004, 2010).

Whereas statistical analysis was found in the background, assisting rationalists when they took center stage, corpus-based statistical methods emerged with considerable effectiveness at the end of the 1980s (Hutchins 1994). The rule-based approach, though retreating to the background, developed its new framework using unification and constraint-based grammars (Hutchins 2010). The new millennium saw more efforts on the development of hybrid MT, leveraging and combining the strengths of statistical models and linguistic rules. There were reflections on the rationalist positions being overshadowed and expectations for richer linguistic representations to be made better use of in machine translation (Church 2011).

The Three Models

The three basic models of RBMT start from different linguistic premises. All of them require source language (SL) analysis and target (TL) synthesis, but with varying types, amounts, and depths of analysis and accordingly different bases for synthesis. Figures 10.1, 10.2, and 10.3 depict the general design of the three models, in which dictionaries may include more than just lexical equivalents, and grammars refer broadly to all the necessary morphologic, syntactic, semantic, and contextual rules.

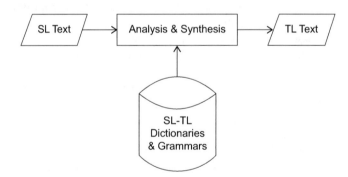

Figure 10.1 The direct model

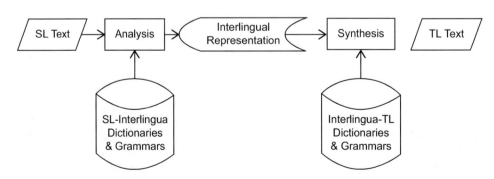

Figure 10.2 The interlingual model

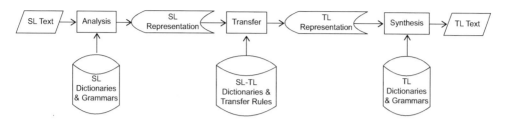

Figure 10.3   The transfer model

The Direct Model

The direct model is based on the assumption that translation tasks mainly require the lexical transfer between the languages involved. It takes an SL sentence as a string of words, retrieves their lexical equivalents in TL from accessible bilingual dictionaries, and reorganizes these equivalents into the corresponding TL sentence. A minimal amount of morphological (and occasionally syntactic) analysis and word reordering are included, with relevant linguistic knowledge stored in the dictionaries or simply described by algorithms and then expressed by program codes. The direct translation model can be employed to handle a finite number of sentence patterns for language pairs with similar syntactic features.

Early designs of MT systems generally adopted this model, a typical example of which is the system developed at the University of Washington mainly during the 1950s. Sponsored by the US Air Force, the Washington MT system produced word-for-word translation from Russian to English, with inadequate results. Bilingual dictionaries were so constructed that they assisted not only the selection of lexical equivalents but also the solution of other problems related to SL analysis and TL synthesis. For example, by searching the dictionary, the system was able to resolve the ambiguity arising from homographs. The Russian verb *dokhodyat*, which could correspond to *reach*, *ripen*, or *are done*, was only translated as *ripen* if followed by a noun labeled in the dictionary as fruit or vegetable. There were also entries in the dictionaries that gave rules for reordering the English output (Hutchins 1986).

Nevertheless, the translation process is still simplified in the direct model. When the complexity of language became more recognized, and particularly after the ALPAC report was issued, more attention was diverted to the other two models that promised a closer look at the linguistic problems in translation.

The Interlingual Model

The interlingual model starts from the premise that semantico-syntactic intermediary representations can be found to link different languages, which take the form of interlingual symbols independent of both SL and TL. The translation process consists of two language-specific steps: SL analysis that leads to the conversion from SL texts to their interlingual representations and TL synthesis that produces TL texts based on the interlingual representations. The representations are expected to be unambiguous and express the full content of SL texts, which include their morphological, syntactic, semantic, and even contextual information. Real projects and systems vary in their focus on the semantic or syntactic aspects of the texts.

A typical example of the interlingua-based MT is the Machine Translation System for Japan and its Neighboring Countries, the research and development of which started in 1987. Five languages were involved, Chinese, Indonesian, Malaysian, Thai, and Japanese. The interlingua in this system was used to represent four kinds of information: events and facts, speaker view, intension, and sentence structure (Tanaka *et al.* 1989). In most cases, interlinguas are designed for specific systems, but the DLT translation system developed in the Netherlands during the 1980s also adopted a modified form of Esperanto as the interlingua (Hutchins 1994).

The interlingual model offers an economical way to develop multilingual translation systems. It allows SL analysis and TL synthesis to work separately. Therefore, for a translation task among *N* languages, an interlingua-based MT system handles *2 × N* language pairs between the interlingua and the *N* languages, while the same translation task requires a direct translation system or a transfer-based system to handle *N × (N − 1)* language pairs. The advantage of the interlingua-based system increases when *N* is larger than 3. However, the difficulty in designing an adequate interlingua is also evident, as the language-independent representations are supposed to cover various language-specific phenomena and categories.

The Transfer Model

The transfer model takes a sentence as a structure other than a linear string of words as it is taken in the direct model, and the syntactic view of the structure is commonly adopted. A sentence *Time flies like an arrow* (S1) in English, for instance, may be treated as a combination of a noun phrase and a verb phrase shown in Figure 10.4, where the noun phrase may in turn consist of a noun, and the verb phrase may consist of a verb and a prepositional phrase.

It is not possible to enumerate all the sentences in a natural language, which are actually infinite in number, but it is possible to find a finite number of structures that represent the vast majority of the sentences. Accordingly, it is not feasible to build an MT system that stores the TL translation for all possible SL sentences, but it is feasible to find for a finite number of structures in one language their equivalent structures in another language. Figure 10.5 presents

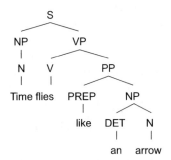

Figure 10.4   The syntactic tree for S1: *Time flies like an arrow*

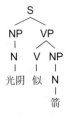

Figure 10.5   The syntactic tree for S2: 时光飞驰如一支箭

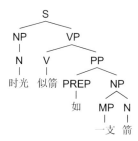

Figure 10.6   The syntactic tree for S3: 光阴似箭

the syntactic structure of the sentence时光飞驰如一支箭 (S2) in Chinese, which corresponds to the syntactic structure of S1. An important basis for the transfer model is the structural correspondence between the languages involved. It is not necessary, however, for the equivalent structures of two languages to be exactly the same. For example, in光阴似箭 (S3), which is a more appropriate Chinese translation of S1, the Chinese VP (似箭) corresponds to the English VP (*flies like an arrow*) in S1, but its syntactic structure (V+N) is obviously different from that of the English VP (V+PREP+DET+N). Figure 10.6 displays the syntactic structure of S3.

The non-linear structural view leaves more room for the transfer model, which operates in three main steps: analysis, transfer, and synthesis. An SL sentence is first analyzed to yield an abstract representation of its internal structure, which is then converted to the equivalent TL representation through the transfer stage. The last step is to generate a surface structure for the TL representation, which is the TL translation for the SL input sentence. Representations in this model are specific to either SL or TL and are thus different from those language-independent ones in the interlingual model. SL analysis carries much weight in the transfer model, which can be done on different levels – morphological, syntactic, semantic, and contextual.

Morphological analysis helps identify SL words, which is the first step toward any deeper analysis. In English and most European languages, words are generally separated by spaces. In English, tokenization is performed for contracted forms like *don't* and *we're*, for words followed by punctuation marks like commas and periods, for abbreviations like *U.S.A.*, and so on. Lemmatization is performed to find the lemma for a given word in its inflected forms, which, for example, determines that *flies* is the third-person singular form in the simple present tense of the lemma *fly*. Ambiguity arises, however, as *flies* is also the plural form of the noun lemma *fly*, which can either be resolved by the dictionary information on collocation or left for syntactic rules to handle. In Chinese, word boundaries have to be detected in the first place, as there are no spaces between words. Thus, S2 is segmented as 时光/飞驰/如/箭. Ambiguity arises again, for example, when the Chinese string 一个人 is analyzed, which can be either 一/个/人 or 一/个人, since 个人 is a justified word entry in the dictionary. To segment it properly, the occurrence of the numeral 一 before the classifier 个 has to be described either in a dictionary entry or by a rule. The grammatical categories of particular words are determined in syntactic analysis, but some morphological clues are also collected for that use. For example, the endings –*ing* and –*ed* in English generally signal verbs, and the endings –*ness* and –*ation* signal nouns.

Syntactic analysis helps identify the syntactic structure of an SL sentence: the grammatical categories of words, the grouping of them, and the relation between them. For S1, the MT system consults the dictionary to determine the grammatical category of each word: *time* being a noun, *flies* being an inflected verb, *like* being a preposition, *an* being a determiner, and *arrow* being a noun. Syntactic rules are then applied to build a syntactic tree for the sentence. Context-free grammar (CFG) is a formal grammar commonly used to describe the syntactic structure of sentences, which can be coded into computer program languages. The following are two sets of CFG rewrite rules describing the structures of S1 and S3, respectively.

Rule Set 1:

S → NP+VP
NP→N
VP→V+PP
PP→PREP+NP
NP→DET+N

Rule Set 2:

S → NP+VP
NP→N
VP→V+NP

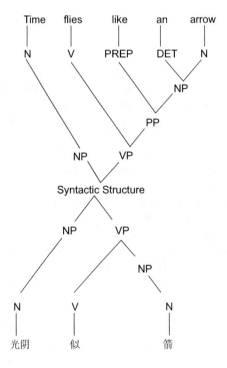

Figure 10.7   Syntactic transfer

If SL analysis stops at the syntactic level, the SL syntactic tree will then be transferred to the corresponding TL syntactic tree. Figure 10.7 offers a better view of the structural correspondence between the two syntactic trees in Figures 10.4 and 10.6. Based on the TL syntactic structure, equivalent TL words are finally retrieved from the dictionary to form the TL translation. In most cases, appropriate morphological forms of TL words are to be derived.

There are, however, ambiguities left unresolved on the syntactic level, for which semantic analysis of SL sentences is needed. In S3 and S4, the prepositional phrases headed by *with* can modify either the verb phrase *bought a table* or the noun phrase *a table*.

S3: *I bought a table with three dollars.*
S4: *I bought a table with three legs.*
S5: *She found a young girl with a telescope.*

To resolve such an ambiguity, dictionaries and rules are supposed to describe the semantic connection between *dollar* and *buy* (with *dollar* playing the role of an instrument in relation to the verb *buy*) and the semantic connection between *leg* and *table* (with *leg* being a part of *table*). The same analysis does not work for S5, however, as it is possible for the prepositional phrase *with a telescope* to modify the verb phrase *found a young girl* or to modify the noun phrase *a young girl*. In the former case, *telescope* plays the role of an instrument and, in the latter case, the role of an accompaniment. The ambiguity is left to contextual analysis, which entails the formalization of a more sophisticated mechanism of reasoning.

Difficulties and Problems

Several decades of MT research and development have unarguably demonstrated the complexity of human natural languages and the complexity of the translation tasks between them. Difficulties and problems in RBMT also arose from these complexities. As the first substantial attempt at the non-numerical use of computers, MT received great attention and was given high expectation. It is the ALPAC report that gave this attempt the first official evaluation and serious reflection, and as a consequence, disillusion with RBMT research came. Though the report was later viewed as biased (Hutchins 2010), it promoted more investigations on the structure and meaning of language and more research on the indirect rule-based models that involve closer syntactic and semantic considerations.

Frequently mentioned shortcomings of RBMT were mainly concerned with the sufficiency of rules and dictionaries, the method and cost of building them, the handling of ambiguities and idiomatic expressions in language, the system adaptability in new domains, and so on. These concerns attracted great attention and gave rise to new MT paradigms when large-scale parallel corpora became available and new translation models emerged.

Formalized Linguistic Knowledge: Great Demand, High Cost, and Appropriate Description

Linguistic knowledge is accessible to computers only when it is formalized. In RBMT, this is achieved through dictionaries and grammar rules.

With dictionaries, the initial concern was about the limited storage capacity and the slow accessing speed of computers, which turned out to be much easier to settle. The persisting concern, by contrast, is the huge and varying demand for linguistic knowledge to be formalized in dictionaries.

Take inflection as an example. There are different types of inflection for different grammatical categories, which complicates the task of morphological analysis. In Russian and German, nouns, pronouns, and numerals are inflected for gender, number, and case (six cases in Russian and four in German); adjectives, when modifying a noun, have to be inflected depending on the gender, number, and case of the noun and additionally inflected to indicate comparative and superlative meanings. English, though an inflected language, presents a lower degree of inflection on nouns: there are singular and plural forms for nouns; the case of nouns only has a remnant marker – the possessive indicator *'s*; few nouns are inflected for gender. The word *actor* usually refers to a man in plays or films whose job is acting, while the word *actress* refers to a woman for the same job. These, however, do not denote the grammatical gender. Pronouns are inflected for case (e.g. *I* as the nominative, *me* as the accusative, *my* as the possessive), number (e.g. *he/him* as the singular forms, *they/them* as the plural forms), and gender (e.g. *he/him* as the masculine forms, *she/her* as the feminine forms). The inflection of adjectives in English is not dependent on nouns. Instead, they have comparative and superlative forms of their own. The inflection of verbs is also complicated. When used as predicates, English verbs have finite forms that agree with the subjects in person and number. Inflection makes morphological analysis easier and more reliable, but it requires well-designed frameworks, development guidelines, knowledge representation schemes, and a huge amount of manual work to formalize all this inflectional information and thereby to make use of it in morphological and syntactic analyses. For less inflected languages such as Chinese, other types of linguistic knowledge are formalized to assist morphological and syntactic analyses, with comparable demand and cost.

With grammar rules, there are further concerns. The balance between the number and the coverage of rules has to be considered in the first place. While a small number of rules usually fail to cover diversifying linguistic phenomena, a large number of them may give rise to conflict among themselves. In addition, the generalization of rules has to be appropriate in order to maximize their coverage of linguistic phenomena but minimize errors. The inappropriate description of linguistic knowledge in this sense works negatively on the effectiveness of RBMT.

Semantic and Contextual Ambiguities: The High-Hanging Fruit

In regular communication, people rely on strings of words to exchange information. To translate the information from one language to another, an RBMT system has to recognize the underlying structure of the strings theoretically through morphological, syntactic, semantic, and contextual analysis. While there is more physical evidence for morphological and syntactic relations in some languages, semantic and contextual relations are harder to identify and define in all languages. In addition to the English examples in Section 2.3 (sentences S3, S4, and S5), here are examples in Chinese.

> S6: 猴子[Monkeys] 吃[eat] 香蕉[bananas]。Monkeys eat bananas.
> S7: 学生[Students] 吃[eat] 食堂[dining hall]。Students have their meals in the dining hall.
> S8: 老乡[The folks] 吃[eat] 大碗[big bowls]。The folks eat with big bowls.

Syntactically, 吃 *chi [to eat]* is a verb, taking nouns like 香蕉, 食堂, and 大碗 to form predicate-object constructions. But to translate these sentences into English, semantic information is needed to specify that the verb 吃 indicates an action by the animal, and therefore it requires an agent and a patient in the sentence, and that the agent is usually an animal specified by a noun and the patient a kind of food specified by another noun. Further, semantic markers are needed to distinguish 猴子 (animal), 学生 (animal, human), 老乡 (animal, human) and 苹果 (food), 食堂 (location), 大碗 (instrument), respectively. In the examples, therefore, the semantic roles of 食堂 and 大碗 as the objects of the verb 吃 are not patients but the location and the instrument, respectively.

Similarly, to understand a sentence correctly, the context beyond sentence boundaries is also essential. For instance, whether the sentence 小张打针去 is translated into *Xiao Zhang has gone to take an injection* or *Xiao Zhang has gone to give an injection* is decided by the contextual fact that Xiao Zhang is a patient or a nurse. Contextual information is more dynamic than semantic information, the formalization of which, accordingly, is more complex in design and implementation.

Research on MT, particularly studies on RBMT, makes greater use of the morphological and syntactic evidence. A moderate amount of semantic and contextual analysis has been explored, which helps to resolve some ambiguities left behind by morphological and syntactic analyses. An important reason behind these is the assumption that semantic and contextual information of language is in general less detectable and more difficult to formalize. However, after the low-hanging fruit has been picked up during the past decades of MT research (Church 2011), it is strategically important and practically necessary to have more focused and collaborated efforts on semantic and contextual analysis.

Domain Adaptability

One of the judgments on the 1954 Georgetown-IBM demonstration involves the domain restriction of the system, which was designed specifically to handle a particular sample of a small number of sentences mainly from organic chemistry based on a limited vocabulary of 250 words. The six rules worked well on the sentence patterns in the sample (Hutchins 2010). It is possible for the system to work on sentences outside the sample, but it requires an expansion of the embedded dictionary in the first place. Further, either these new sentences have to conform to the patterns of those in the sample, or new rules have to be added to cover the new input sentences.

Although organic chemistry is a subfield with a considerably small number of lexical items and typical sentence patterns, the Georgetown-IBM demonstration did not cover all of them (Hutchins 2004). It is now well understood that MT systems are developed to meet widely differing translation needs. This is particularly true with RBMT systems, which rely heavily on dictionaries and grammar rules. The adaptation of RBMT systems, therefore, is more concerned with the adaption of the corresponding dictionaries and grammar rules covering the domain-specific morphological, syntactic, semantic, and contextual information.

Failure to adapt to new domains has been listed as one of the weaknesses of RBMT systems, but the other side of the coin is the acknowledgement that the performance of RBMT systems can be greatly improved through domain-specific adaptation – the adaptation of domain-specific dictionaries and grammar rules. An example of domain-specific RBMT can be found in the well-known Météo system, which was developed at Montreal to translate weather forecasts (Hutchins 2010).

Formalized Description of Linguistic Knowledge

The significance of linguistic knowledge in MT has been repeatedly reflected upon, which leads to an ever-growing understanding of the role that linguistic knowledge plays in MT. In the case of RBMT particularly, difficulties and setbacks help to reveal, one after another, the necessity of morphological, syntactic, semantic, and contextual information. A more fundamental issue, however, is how to represent linguistic knowledge so that it can be processed and utilized by MT systems. Basically, there are two types of formalized knowledge representations: dictionaries and grammar rules on the one hand and corpora on the other. As explicit representations, the former adopt formal structures, such as relational databases and rewrite rules; as implicit representations, the latter use linear strings of words.

RBMT is in principle working with the explicit type. To handle an infinite number of sentences, RBMT systems rely on dictionaries that store the information about the finite number of words (in SL and TL, respectively) and on grammar rules that describe the relationship between words.

Dictionaries

Being an indispensable component in almost all RBMT systems, dictionaries may store morphological, syntactic, semantic, and contextual information about the languages involved. There are several important considerations when a dictionary is designed and constructed for RBMT.

(1) *Purpose*

To design a language knowledge base, it is necessary, above all, to decide whether it is to serve the special purpose of a specific system, as the adaptation of the knowledge base for new tasks requires significant investment of resources. A general-purpose dictionary is independent of any particular processing system and irrelevant even to any computational theory or algorithm. It is supposed to record the basic linguistic facts. Adaptation is needed if such a dictionary is to work in a RBMT system designed for another specific domain.

(2) *Structure*

The structure of a dictionary determines its way of storing and managing linguistic information. A suitable structure ensures the efficient use of a dictionary. The earliest dictionaries in RBMT systems were only consulted to find the TL equivalents of SL words, and the dictionary structure was therefore quite simple. As the understanding grows concerning the complex mechanism of natural languages and the complicated process of translation, the structure of dictionaries evolves accordingly. Relational databases, for example, provide a means to manage large amounts of morphological, syntactic, semantic, and lexical equivalence information efficiently. A database can be a collection of tables designed for particular grammatical categories. The attribute–value system makes it easy to describe a range of attributes for each linguistic entry. This can also be achieved by complex feature structures, but relational databases, by contrast, are more convenient for manual input and more efficient for computer access. In Table 10.1, the classifiers that collocate with the nouns in the four entries are clearly specified.

Table 10.1 A sample table for nouns

Word	POS	Individual Classifier	Container Classifier	Measure Classifier
人	n	个		
书	n	本，册	箱	
锁	n	把		
糖	n	块	袋，罐	克，斤

Relational databases can be converted to other forms of knowledge representation conveniently to suit the specific purpose of application systems.

(3) *Word Classification vs. Feature Description*

To build a dictionary, it is necessary to integrate word classification with feature description. Theoretically, describing the features of words is another way of classifying and distinguishing them. But due to the complexity of language, words of the same grammatical category, with many shared features, may still have distinctive ones. Similarly, words from different grammatical categories may also have shared features. Such being the case, word classification and feature description complement each other to achieve better coverage of the facts of real language use.

Relational databases provide an efficient solution to the combination of the two processes – defining the grammatical category of each word, on the one hand, and, more importantly, adding elaborate description of various linguistic features for each word, on the other.

(4) Expert Knowledge vs. Computer-Aided Corpus Study

The development of a dictionary requires enormous resources. Developed countries or regions enjoy financial advantages but find it unrealistic to engage high-level linguists in the tedious and tiresome work because of the high costs of manpower. Therefore, the development of dictionaries in those countries relies mainly on technology to automate the acquisition of knowledge. With the advance of computer science and the Internet, there are more machine-readable dictionaries and texts available, which benefits the development of new dictionaries. Obviously, the development also relies heavily on the engagement of linguists, the progress of theoretical linguistic research, and collaboration between computer science and linguistics.

In addition to expert knowledge, computer-aided corpus study is also necessary. Different from the linguistic evidence based on linguists' reflections upon language use, corpus data come from communication in real contexts, which may add greatly to the existing understanding of language. Annotated corpora, with the imposed explicit linguistic annotations, can also assist the learning of linguistic features. There are computer tools that help analyze corpus data and thereby retrieve linguistic knowledge efficiently and accurately. Further, corpus data can also be used to verify the content of dictionaries, thus increasing their credibility.

(5) Selection of Entries and Their Attributes

The selection of entries and their attributes to be included in a dictionary is based on a clear understanding of the goal that the dictionary is to achieve. In RBMT, it is to assist SL analysis and TL synthesis, so syntactic and semantic considerations are usually valued. For example, a Chinese dictionary shall have an entry for the verb 花 as in 花钱 *[to spend (money)]* and another entry for the noun 花 as in 鲜花 *[(fresh) flower]*. For the verb entry, the dictionary may describe its transitivity, the feature of its collocating nouns, adverbs, auxiliaries, and so on, and for the noun entry, the dictionary may describe its collocating classifiers, its function as subjects and objects, and so on.

Beside those previously mentioned, there are other considerations when dictionaries are constructed for RBMT, which include, for example, the standardization of language, the change of language, word formation, and so on.

Grammar Rules

Another important component in RBMT systems is the set of grammar rules that account for the main procedures of analysis and synthesis. There are also transfer rules, particularly in the transfer model, which link the representations of two languages together.

Research on RBMT has greatly encouraged the development of formal linguistics. An important focus of theoretical linguistic research in RBMT is placed on formal grammars, examples of which are phrase structure grammar (PSG), generalized phrase structure grammar

(GPSG), head-driven phrase structure grammar (HPSG), lexical functional grammar (LFG), and so on. Rules of these formal grammars have been used to describe the structure of natural language sentences precisely.

In PSG, a classic formal grammar first proposed by Noam Chomsky in 1957, a grammar consists of: i) a finite set of nonterminal symbols, none of which appear in sentences formed from the grammar; ii) a finite set of terminal symbols, which appear in strings formed from the grammar; iii) a start symbol, which is a distinguished nonterminal; and iv) a finite set of rewrite rules (also called production rules), each in the form of $a \rightarrow b$ (a being a string of an arbitrary number of symbols with at least one nonterminal and b being a string of an arbitrary number of symbols, including an empty string). Constraints on rewrite rules lead to different varieties of PSG. In the other grammars mentioned previously, feature structures and unification are introduced, adding more precision to the procedures of analysis and synthesis. For example, rules in LFG present simultaneously two distinct but interrelated levels of structures: constituent structure and functional structure, the former being a conventional phrase structure tree and the latter involving syntactic functions or features like subject, object, complement, adjunct, and so on. The following is an example of the functional structure for the sentence *A girl handed the baby a toy* (Kaplan and Bresnan 1982).

$$
\begin{bmatrix}
\text{SUBJ} & \begin{bmatrix} \text{SPEC} & \text{A} \\ \text{NUM} & \text{SG} \\ \text{PRED} & \text{"girl"} \end{bmatrix} \\
\text{TENSE} & \text{PAST} \\
\text{PRED} & \text{"hand ((}\uparrow\text{ SUBJ), (}\uparrow\text{ OBJ), (}\uparrow\text{ OBJ2))"} \\
\text{OBJ} & \begin{bmatrix} \text{SPEC} & \text{THE} \\ \text{NUM} & \text{SG} \\ \text{PRED} & \text{"baby"} \end{bmatrix} \\
\text{OBJ2} & \begin{bmatrix} \text{SPEC} & \text{A} \\ \text{NUM} & \text{SG} \\ \text{PRED} & \text{"boy"} \end{bmatrix}
\end{bmatrix}
$$

Figure 10.8   The functional structure in LFG

A pair of an attribute and its value may represent either a syntactic feature such as past tense (TENSE PAST) or a semantic feature such as the predicate-argument specification (PRED 'hand<($\uparrow$SUBJ), ($\uparrow$OBJ), ($\uparrow$OBJ2)'), which defines the mapping between, for instance, the argument SUBJ and the function SUBJ in this functional structure.

The complexity of language in general makes it difficult for grammar rules to capture the nuances of genuine word usages. The new and promising corpus-based statistic approach emerged, making it possible to cover detailed language use, particularly collocation between words. While bringing vigorous development to MT research, the new method requires the support of powerful computers and the time-consuming construction and processing of large-scale corpora. A balance can be achieved between formal grammars and corpora by adopting a new form for the traditional dictionaries – using relational databases to record more specific linguistic information.

Language Knowledge Base

The term *language knowledge base* offers a more inclusive and consistent way to refer to a machine-readable repository of linguistic knowledge collected, represented, organized, and thereafter utilized. It is usually more sophisticated in design, development, and integration compared with the traditional dictionaries and rule sets in RBMT. The Comprehensive Language Knowledge Base (CLKB) developed at Peking University in China, for instance, is a collection of a grammatical knowledge base of word entries, a phrase structure knowledge base, an annotated monolingual corpus, a bilingual parallel corpus, a multilingual concept dictionary, and a term bank, which embodies the knowledge expansion from words to sentences and texts, from syntactical level to semantic level, from monolingual to multilingual, and from general domain to specific domain (Yu *et al.* 2011).

(1) Rule-Based Automatic MT Evaluation

The evaluation of MT output quality supports the advance of MT research, and the automation of this task ensures a higher level of efficiency, objectiveness, and consistency. There has been MT evaluation ever since the start of MT research, but for quite a long time, evaluations were done manually, the most famous example of which delivered the ALPAC report. The report compared the translations of MT systems with human translation to evaluate their intelligibility and fidelity.

Methods for the automatic evaluation of MT output quality are also split between rule-based and statistical ones. MTE, the first automatic evaluation system for MT, was developed at Peking University, China, during the 1980s and 1990s to evaluate the output quality of English–Chinese translation systems. Six classes of test points (Yu 1993) were defined: words, idioms, morphology, elementary grammar, moderate grammar, and advanced grammar. The following are some examples:

> *Spring* is the first season in a year.
> It is a *spring* bed.
> Test point: word sense ambiguity

> Are the students playing football?
> Are the students playing football *your classmates*?
> Test point: garden path sentence

A context-free formal language, TDL, was designed to describe the specific test pointes and their corresponding marking criterion. For example:

> SL sentence: They got up *at six this morning*.
> R→(492:1)★$A[的]$B$C★
> R→(492:0)★
> $A→早晨/上午
> $B→六/6
> $C→点钟/点/时
> ##

where 492 is the code for the test point, 1 and 0 are the scores, and / separates alternatives. If an MT system produces 早晨六点 instead of 六点早晨 as a translation for the SL sentence, it scores 1; otherwise, it scores 0.

This rule-based method using test points can clearly locate the strengths and flaws of a system, but the definition of test points requires huge amount of manual work, for which corpus-based automatic extraction has been implemented (Zhou *et al.* 2008).

In contrast, the commonly used statistical method for MT evaluation is based on n-grams, with which all grams of a sentence are treated equally. The evaluation does not help distinguish the strengths and flaws of an MT system. In this respect, the rule-based approach can be more effective, focusing on particular test points – linguistic problems or difficulties – in SL analysis and TL synthesis.

Conclusion

Research on RBMT has played an important role in promoting the overall progress of MT. Despite the dominating influence of the statistical approach since the end of 1980s and the breakthrough made by NMT in the last ten years, the linguistic premises and assumptions of RBMT are still valued. While the insufficiency of linguistic knowledge is bypassed in NMT, particularly with a pre-trained model, we still expect that an increasing understanding of human languages could help solve the challenging problems, such as the interpretation of NMT, the design of better translation models, and so on (Tan *et al.* 2020), which leads to a more promising future of MT research.

Bibliography

Chomsky, Noam (1957) *Syntactic Structure*, The Hague: Mouton.

Church, Kenneth (2011) 'A Pendulum Swung Too Far', in *Linguistic Issues in Language Technology – LiLT*, CSLI Publications, 6. https://doi.org/10.33011/lilt.v6i.1245

Dong, Zhendong 董振東, Dong Qiang 董強, and He Changling 郝長伶 (2011) 〈下一站在哪裡?〉 (Where Is the Next Stop?),《中文信息學報》(*Journal of Chinese Information Processing*) 25(6): 3–11.

Hutchins, John (1986) *Machine Translation: Past, Present, Future*, New York: Halsted.

Hutchins, John W. (1994) 'Research Methods and System Designs in Machine Translation: A Ten-Year Review, 1984–1994', in *Proceedings of the International Conference 'Machine Translation: Ten Years on'*, 12–14 November 1994, Cranfield University, England.

Hutchins, John W. (2004) 'The Georgetown-IBM Experiment Demonstrated in January 1954', *Machine Translation: From Real Users to Research: The 6th Conference of the Association for Machine Translation in the Americas (AMTA 2004)*, September 28–October 2, 2004, Washington, DC.

Hutchins, John W. (2010) "Machine Translation: A Concise History', *Journal of Translation Studies: Special issue: The Teaching of Computer-aided Translation* 13(1–2): 29–70, ed. Chan Sin-wai.

Kaplan, Ronald and Joan Bresnan (1982) 'Lexical-functional Grammar: A Formal System for Grammatical Representation', in J. Bresnan (ed.). *The Mental Representation of Grammatical Relations*, Cambridge, MA: MIT Press, 173–281.

Tan, Zhixing, Shuo Wang, Zonghan Yang, Gang Chen, Xuancheng Huang, Maosong Sun, and Liu Yang (2020) 'Neural Machine Translation: A Review of Methods, Resources, and Tools', *AI Open* 1: 5–21.

Tanaka, Hozumi, Shun Ishizaki, Akira Uehara, and Hiroshi Uchid (1989) 'A Research and Development of Cooperation Project on a Machine Translation System for Japan and Its Neighboring Countries', in *Proceedings of the MT Summit II*, 16–18 August 1989, Munich, Germany, 146–51.

Wang, Mingxuan and Lei Li (2021) 'Pre-training Methods for Neural Machine Translation', in *Proceedings of the 59th Annual Meeting of the Association for Computational Linguistics and the 11th International Joint Conference on Natural Language Processing: Tutorial Abstracts*, Online. Association for Computational Linguistics, 21–25.

Yu, Shiwen (1993) 'Automatic Evaluation of Output Quality for Machine Translation Systems', *Machine Translation* 8: 117–26.

Yu, Shiwen 俞士汶 (ed.) (2003) 《計算語言學概論》 (*Introduction to Computational Linguistics*). Beijing: The Commercial Press 商務印書館.

Yu, Shiwen 俞士汶, Sui Zhifang 穗志方, and Zhu Xuefeng 朱學鋒 (2011) 〈綜合型語言知識庫及其前景〉 (A Comprehensive Language Knowledge Base and Its Prospect)《中文信息學報》(*Journal of Chinese Information Processing*) 25(6): 12–20.

Zhou, Ming, Bo Wang, Shujie Liu, Mu Li, Dongdong Zhang, and Tiejun Zhao (2008) 'Diagnostic Evaluation of Machine Translation Systems Using Automatically Constructed Linguistic Check-Points', in

Proceedings of the 22nd International Conference on Computational Linguistics (Coling 2008), Manchester, August 2008.

Zhou, Zhihua (2019) 'Abductive Learning: Towards Bridging Machine Learning and Logical Reasoning', *Science China Information Science* 62(7): 076101. https://doi.org/10.1007/s11432-018-9801-4.

冯志伟. 自然语言机器翻译新论[M]. 北京:语文出版社, 1995.

董振东,董强,郝长伶. 下一站在哪里?. 中文信息学报[J], 2011, 25(06): 3–11.

俞士汶,穗志方,朱学锋. 综合型语言知识库及其前景[J], 2011, 25(06): 12–20.

俞士汶主编. 计算语言学概论[M]. 北京：商务印书馆，2003.

11

STATISTICAL MACHINE TRANSLATION

Liu Yang and Zhang Min

Overview

Statistical machine translation (SMT) is a machine translation paradigm that generates translations based on a probabilistic model of translation process, the parameters of which are estimated from parallel text.

SMT was firstly introduced by Warren Weaver in 1949. He suggested that statistical techniques from Claude Shannon's information theory might make it possible to use computers to translate between natural languages automatically. However, this idea could hardly become reality at the time due to limited computer resources. Thanks to the improvement in computer power and the increasing availability of machine-readable text, a group of researchers at IBM TJ Watson Research Center launched the 'Candide' project to re-introduce statistical techniques to machine translation in 1991. Since then, SMT has seen a resurgence in popularity and become one of the most widely studied machine translation methods.

The major difference between SMT and conventional rule-based MT lies in the acquisition of translation knowledge. Rule-based translation systems often require the manual development of linguistic rules, which can be costly, time consuming, and hardly generalizable to other languages. Alternatively, SMT pursues a data-driven approach to acquiring translation knowledge. SMT systems are usually based on statistical models whose parameters, namely translation knowledge in SMT systems, can be derived from the analysis of machine-readable parallel text automatically. Therefore, SMT systems are language independent because they are not tailored to any specific pair of languages.

Generally, there are three fundamental problems in statistical machine translation:

(1) *Modeling*. The heart of statistical machine translation is the probabilistic modeling of the translation process. Early statistical machine translation systems are based on *generative* translation models where a generative story is designed to describe how a computer translates natural languages step by step. Significant advances have been made by the introduction of *discriminative* models in 2002. As discriminative models are capable of incorporating a great deal of diverse and overlapping knowledge sources as features, it has become the mainstream in modern SMT systems. From the perspective of basic translation unit, statistical machine translation has evolved from modeling flat structures (i.e. word, phrase) to hierarchical structures (i.e. syntactic trees) in the past two decades.

DOI: 10.4324/9781003168348-12

(2) *Training*. As a data-driven approach, SMT estimates the parameters of translation models from parallel corpus automatically. This is called training or parameter estimation. The parameters of generative models are usually probability distributions on unobserved latent variables such as word-to-word translation sub-models, distortion models, and so on. While the expectation maximization (EM) algorithm is widely used for word-based models, phrase-based and syntax-based models usually resort to simple and efficient heuristic methods for parameter estimation. To estimate the parameters of discriminative models, which are usually real-valued feature weights of log-linear models, the most widely used algorithm is minimum error rate training that can directly optimize feature weights with respect to the final evaluation metric.

(3) *Decoding*. Given estimated translation model parameters and an unseen source language text, the goal of decoding is to find a target language text that maximizes translation probability. Due to the diversity of natural languages, the search space of SMT is often prohibitively large. Therefore, SMT systems have to use approximate search algorithms instead of exhaustive search in practice. The decoding algorithms in SMT can be roughly divided into two broad categories with respect to the order of generating target language words: left-to-right and bottom-up. Left-to-right decoding algorithms, which run in quadratic time, are mainly used in phrase-based systems where stacks are maintained to store promising partial translations. Bottom-up decoding algorithms (e.g. the CYK algorithm) are mainly used in syntax-based systems and generally run in cubic time.

Word-based SMT

The initial statistical machine translation system was based on word-based models, in which the basic unit of translation is word (Brown *et al.* 1993: 233–312).

Given a source language sentence $f_1^J = f_1 \cdots f_J$, how likely a target language sentence $e_1^I = e_1 \cdots e_I$ is a translation of the source language sentence can be denoted by a probability distribution $P\left(e_1^I \mid f_1^J\right)$. Therefore, the goal of statistical machine translation is to build a translation model, train the model parameters, and search for the optimal translation with highest translation probability.

Originating from Shannon's information theory, word-based translation models apply the Bayes theorem to make the search of optimal translations dependent on two models: an inverse translation model $P\left(f_1^J \mid e_1^I\right)$ that assigns a probability that the source language sentence f_1^J is a translation of the target language sentence e_1^I and a language model $P(e_1^I)$ that assigns a probability of the target sentence e_1^I:

$$P\left(e_1^I \mid f_1^J\right) = \frac{P\left(f_1^J \mid e_1^I\right) \times P\left(e_1^I\right)}{P\left(f_1^J\right)}$$

Intuitively, the inverse translation model $P\left(f_1^J \mid e_1^I\right)$ evaluates the fidelity of a translation while the language model $P(e_1^I)$ evaluates the fluency.

Brown *et al.* (1993) propose five translation models with increasing expressive power, namely IBM models 1–5. All IBM models are based on an important notion in statistical machine translation: word alignment. Word alignment indicates the correspondence between the words of source and target language sentences. Figure 11.1 shows a word alignment for a Chinese-English sentence pair. The dashed lines denote alignment links. It is introduced into translation models as a latent variable.

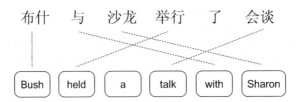

Figure 11.1 Word alignment

Therefore, the translation probability that a target language sentence is translated into a source language sentence is equal to the sum of alignment models over all possible word alignments between the two sentences:

$$P\left(f_1^J \mid e_1^I\right) = \sum_{a_1^J} P\left(f_1^J, a_1^J \mid e_1^I\right)$$

As the IBM models are generative models, each of them is based on a generative story that describes how to transform a target language sentence to a source language sentence step by step. The generative story for IBM models 1 and 2 is as follows:

(1) Given a target language sentence e_1^I, decide the length J of the corresponding source language sentence f_1^J;
(2) For each source language position j ranging from 1 to J:

    (a) Decide which target language word e_{a_j} is aligned to the current source language position j;
    (b) Decide what the source language word f_j is given the aligned target language word e_{a_j}.

This generative story can be exactly described by a probabilistic model in a mathematical way. The three types of decisions in the generative story correspond to three sub-models in the translation model: length sub-model, alignment sub-model, and translation sub-model. While IBM models 1 and 2 share with the same length and translation sub-models, they differ in the choice of alignment sub-models. IBM model 1 assumes the alignment distribution is uniform. In contrast, IBM model 2 uses an alignment sub-model that depends on positions of words.

IBM models 3–5 are based on more sophisticated generative stories. They are different from simpler IBM models 1–2 because of the introduction of fertility, which explicitly describes the fact that a target language word can be aligned to multiple source language words. The generative story for IBM model 3 is as follows (Knight 1999: 607–15):

(1) For each target language word e_i, choose a fertility ϕ_i, which is the number of source language words that will be generated from the target language word and depends only on the target word.
(2) Generate source language words from the NULL target language word.
(3) Generate source language words from the non-NULL target language words according the corresponding fertilities.
(4) Move all the non-spurious words in the source language sentence.
(5) Insert spurious words in the remaining open positions.

IBM models 3–5 are usually called fertility-based models. They have more parameters than IBM models 1–2. The most important parameters are the fertility, distortion, and translation sub-models.

The parameters of IBM models can be estimated from a given parallel training corpus consisting of a set of sentence pairs. Often, the unknown parameters are determined by maximizing the likelihood of the parallel training corpus using the expectation maximization algorithm. Note that the parameters of the statistical translation models are optimized using maximum likelihood estimation (MLE), which is not related to alignment and translation evaluation metrics used in practice.

Training IBM models often involves the computation of the alignment with highest probability, namely Viterbi alignment. While there exist simple polynomial algorithms for IBM models 1 and 2, computing Viterbi alignments for the fertility-based models is non-trivial. As suggested by Brown *et al.* (1993: 233–312), an efficient hill-climbing algorithm is widely used in finding Viterbi alignments for fertility-based models. The basic idea is to first compute the Viterbi alignment of a simple model. Then this alignment is iteratively improved with respect to the alignment probability of fertility models by modifying the current alignment.

As the decoding problem for word-based models is NP-complete (Knight 1999: 607–15), a sensible strategy is to examine a large subset of promising translations and choose just one from that. The stack-based decoding algorithm, which was first introduced in the domain of speech recognition, has been widely used in word-based SMT decoders. By building translations incrementally and storing partial translations in a stack (i.e. a priority queue), the decoder conducts an ordered best-first search in the search space. Other decoding algorithms include greedy and integer programming algorithms (Germann *et al.* 2001: 228–35).

Manning and Schutze (1999) point out a number of drawbacks of word-based models:

(1) No notion of phrases. The models relate only to individual words and do not model relationships between phrases.
(2) Non-local dependencies. The models fail to capture non-local dependencies that are important in translation.
(3) Morphology. Morphologically related words (e.g. *like, likes, liked*) are treated as separate symbols.
(4) Sparse data problems. Estimates for rare words are unreliable.

Although word-based models are not widely used today, word alignments generated by word-based models still play an important role in training more advanced phrase-based and syntax-based translation models.

Phrase-Based SMT

While word-based models only consider how each individual word is translated, phrase-based models are based on the intuition that a better way is to translate and move phrases as a unit in machine translation. A phrase in phrase-based models is usually a sequence of consecutive words. It is not necessarily a phrase in any syntactic theory.

The generative story of phrase-based models is as follows:

(1) Given a target language sentence, segment it into a sequence of phrases. Suppose that the number of source language phrases is identical to that of target language phrases.
(2) Permutate the target language phrases
(3) Translate each target language phrase into a source language phrase one by one and form the source language sentence.

Figure 11.2 shows an example of phrase-based translation. Each block represents a phrase. The dashed lines denote the correspondence between Chinese and English phrases.

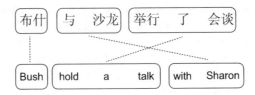

Figure 11.2   Phrase-based SMT

Therefore, there are three sub-models in phrase-based models: phrase segmentation, phrase reordering, and phrase translation. For simplicity, most phrase-based models typically assume a uniform distribution over segmentations.

Unlike word-based models that use an EM algorithm for parameter estimation, phrase-based models often resort to an efficient heuristic way to learn model parameters. Typically, training phrase-based models begins by training word-based models to generate word alignments for the parallel corpus. Then the word-aligned parallel corpus is used to extract aligned phrase pairs. As IBM models assume that each source language word is aligned to at most one target language word, they cannot align a multiword phrase in the source language with a multiword in the target language. Therefore, a method call symmetrization is proposed to produce many-to-many word alignments (Och and Ney 2004: 417–49). First, two separate word-based aligners are trained to produce a source-to-target alignment and a target-to-source alignment, respectively. Then the two alignments are combined in a heuristic way to get an alignment that maps phrases to phrases. After getting symmetrized word alignments, all phrase pairs that are consistent with word alignments are extracted. A consistent phase pair is one in which all words are aligned only to each other and not to any external words in the training instance. Once all the aligned phrase pairs are collected from the entire training corpus, the maximum likelihood estimates for the phrase translation probability of a particular pair can be computed as relative frequencies in two translation directions, respectively.

The distortion sub-model is an important component in phrase-based statistical machine translation. It models the distortion between source and target language phrases resulted from the divergence of word orders in natural languages. For example, while subject-verb-object (SVO) languages such as English often put the object after the verb (e.g. *I like you*), subject-object-verb (SOV) languages such as Japanese place object before the verb. A simple distortion sub-model widely used in phrase-based SMT is distance-based model (Koehn *et al.* 2003: 49–54). It measures the distance between positions of a phrase in two languages. The distortion probability thus means the probability of two consecutive target language phrases being separated in source language by a span of a particular length. Often this simple distortion model penalizes large distortions by giving lower probability. A problem with the distance-based model is that it is only conditioned on movement distance while some phrases are reordered more frequently than others. Therefore, lexicalized distortion models conditioned on actual phrases are proposed to alleviate the problem. Lexicalized distortion models consider three types of orientation of a phrase: monotone, swapping, and discontinuous. The probability distribution can be estimated from the word-aligned parallel corpus. When extracting each phrase pair, the orientation type of a phrase pair is also extracted in that specific occurrence. A variation to the way phrase orientation statistics are collected is that phrase-based orientation models use phrases both at training and decoding time. A further improvement is hierarchical orientation model that is able to detect swaps or monotone arrangements between very large blocks. Although lexicalized distortion models are powerful than the distance-based model, they face the problem of sparse data, as a particular phrase pair may occur only a few times in the training data. Therefore, it is hard to obtain reliable estimates from training data.

Phrase-based SMT uses a stack decoding algorithm to search for optimal translations. The basic intuition is to maintain a sequence of priority queues with all partial translation hypotheses together with their scores. The decoding algorithm begins by searching for a phrase-translation table to collect possible translation options. Each of these translation options consists of a source language phrase, the target language phrase, and phrase translation probabilities. The decoder needs to search through combinations of these options to find the best translation. The target language sentence is generated from left to right in the form of partial translation hypothesis (hypothesis for short). Each hypothesis is associated with a cost to guide the search. The cost combines the current cost of the phrase with an estimate of the future cost. The current cost is the product of translation, distortion, and language model probabilities. The future cost is an estimate of the cost of translating the uncovered words in the source language sentence. As it is too expensive to estimate the future cost of distortion models, phrase-based SMT typically uses a Viterbi algorithm to compute the product of translation and language model probabilities. As the search space is exponential, most phrase-based decoders use pruning techniques to constrain the search space. For every stack, only the most promising hypotheses are kept, and unlikely hypotheses are pruned. An important risk-free pruning technique is hypothesis recombination. It can safely discard degenerate hypotheses that cannot be part of the best translation.

While SMT originated from the noisy channel model, discriminative models have become the mainstream nowadays. In a discriminative model such as a log-linear model (Och and Ney 2004: 417–49), the language model and the translation model can be treated as features:

$$P\left(e_1^I \mid f_1^J\right) = \frac{exp\left(\sum_{m=1}^M \lambda_m h_m\left(e_1^I, f_1^J\right)\right)}{Z}$$

where $h(\cdot)$ are feature functions, λs are feature weights, and Z is a partition function.

In practice, sub-models of generative translation models are still the most important feature functions in the log-linear model. The flexible architecture of discriminative framework has the advantage of allowing for arbitrary overlapping features to include useful knowledge sources in the translation process. In modern SMT systems, log-linear models are trained to directly optimize evaluation metrics using a method called minimum error rate training.

Quirk and Corston-Oliver (2006: 62–69) summarize advantages and disadvantages of phrase-based SMT as follows:

- Advantages

  - Non-compositionality. Phrases capture the translations of non-compositional phrases as a unit instead of reconstructing them word by word awkwardly.
  - Local reordering. Local reordering decisions are memorized in phrases.
  - Contextual information. Local context is incorporated in phrases.

- Disadvantages

  - Exact substring match; no discontiguity. Discontinuous translation pairs are not allowed in most phrase-based SMT systems.
  - Global reordering. Phrases provide no effective global re-ordering strategy.

- Probability estimation. Long phrases are most likely to contribute important translational and ordering information and but are most subject to sparse data issues.
- Partition limitation. Uniform distribution of phrase segmentation is problematic.

Despite these drawbacks, phrase-based models are still a simple and powerful mechanism for machine translation and have been widely used in commercial MT systems.

Syntax-Based SMT

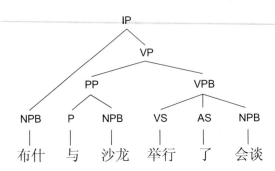

Figure 11.3 Phrase-structure parse tree

While both word-based and phrase-based models cast translation as a problem of permutating and concatenating flat structures, recent work in SMT has focused on modeling hierarchical syntactic structures. These syntax-based models attempt to assign a parallel syntactic tree structure to a pair of sentences in different languages, with the goal of translating the sentences by applying reordering operations on the trees. The mathematical model for these parallel structures is known as a *synchronous grammar* (also called a transduction grammar).

A synchronous grammar describes a structurally correlated pair of languages. From a generative perspective, a synchronous grammar is capable of generating pairs of related strings in two languages. A number of synchronous grammars and formalisms have been used since the late 1990s, most of which are generalizations of context-free grammars to the bilingual scenario:

- Synchronous context-free grammar (SCFG)
- Inversion transduction grammar (ITG)
- Synchronous tree substitution grammar (STSG)

A *synchronous context-free grammar* is like a CFG, but its productions have two related right-hand sides, namely the source language side and the target language side. The most well-known SCFG-based model is the hierarchical phrase-based translation model proposed by Chiang (2007: 201–28). As a hierarchical phrase can contain other phrases, it is capable of capturing reordering of phrases. For example, the SCFG rule

$$X \rightarrow (与\ X_1\ 举行\ 了\ X_2, \text{held a } X_2 \text{ with } X_1)$$

captures the different ordering of words in two languages, where X denotes a non-terminal and the subscripts denote the correspondence between non-terminals.

Formally, a hierarchical phrase pair corresponds to an SCFG production rule. Each right-hand side is a string of terminals and non-terminals. The model assumes that there is a one-to-one correspondence between non-terminal occurrences in the two right-hand sides. An SCFG derivation begins with a pair of linked start symbols. At each step, two linked non-terminals are rewritten by applying a production rule. Recursively applying SCFG rules generates a pair of sentences in two languages. As a data-driven approach, the bulk of SCFG consists of automatically extracted rules. The training corpus of the SCFG-based model is the same with phrase-based models: word-aligned parallel corpus. SCFG rules that are consistent with word alignment can be extracted from the training data in two steps. First, the extraction algorithm identifies initial phrase pairs in the same way as phrase-based SMT does. Second, the algorithm looks for phrases that contain other phrases and replaces sub-phrases with non-terminal symbols. As this scheme can generate a very large number of rules, a number of constraints are used to filter the grammar to achieve a reasonable grammar size. Besides SCFG rules learned from real-world data, Chiang (2007: 201–28) also introduce glue rules to concatenate partial translations in a monotonic way. Unlike phrase-based decoders that use a stack algorithm, the decoder for SCFG is a CYK parser. Given a source language sentence, the decoder finds the yield on the target language side of the single best derivation that has the source yield of the input sentence. It organizes the hypotheses in a chart whose cells are sets of hypotheses. A problem faced by an SCFG-based decoder is that language model integration becomes more expensive because the decoder needs to maintain target language words at both ends of a partial translation, whereas a phrase-based decoder only needs to do this at one end because the translation is always growing from left to right. Therefore, the integration of language model increases the decoding complexity of SCFG-based decoders. To alleviate this problem, Chiang (ibid.) proposes a method called *cube pruning* to discard most of less promising hypotheses. Cube pruning has been widely used in modern phrase-based and syntax-based SMT systems. In summary, as a logical outgrowth of phrase-based model, the hierarchical phrase-based model is the first syntax-based model that empirically shows that moving from flat structures to hierarchical structures significantly improves translation quality.

Inversion translation grammar (Wu 1997: 337–403) is a synchronous grammar for synchronous parsing of source and target language sentences. It builds a synchronous parse tree to indicate the correspondence as well as permutation of blocks (i.e. consecutive word sequences). There are three types of production rules. A lexical rule $X \rightarrow f / e$ generates two words or phrases in two languages simultaneously. A non-terminal rule in square brackets $X \rightarrow [X X]$ generates two blocks in a monotone order. A non-terminal rule in angle brackets $X \rightarrow \langle X X \rangle$ generates two blocks in an inverted order. Generally, ITG can be seen as a special case of SCFG. Any ITG can be converted into an SCFG of rank two. Therefore, the decoder of an ITG-based SMT system is also a CYK parser. Xiong *et al.* (2006: 521–28) introduce a maximum entropy-based reordering model for ITG. Instead of assigning a uniform distribution to non-terminal rules, they propose to make the decision on merging order dependent on the specific blocks.

Syntax-based models using SCFG and ITG only take the fundamental idea from syntax, as they do not exploit any linguistically syntactic structures. By contrast, syntax-based models that use *synchronous tree substitution grammars* usually leverage real linguistic parse trees. In an STSG, the productions are pairs of elementary trees, and the leaf non-terminals are linked just as in synchronous CFG. Depending on whether linguistic parse trees are used, syntax-based models can be roughly divided into four categories:

- String-to-String. No linguistic syntax is used. SCFG-based and ITG-based models are typically string-to-string.
- String-to-Tree. Linguistic syntax is used only on the target side.
- Tree-to-String. Linguistic syntax is used only on the source side.
- Tree-to-Tree. Linguistic syntax is used on both sides.

The string-to-tree models (Yamada and Knight 2001: 523–30; Galley *et al.* 2004: 273–80; Galley *et al.* 2006: 961–68) exploit linguistic syntax only on the target side. Galley *et al.* (2004) propose an algorithm called GHKM to learn string-to-tree rules from word-aligned, target side parsed parallel corpus. Like phrases and hierarchical phrases, these syntactically motivated trans-formation rules must be consistent with word alignment. The GHKM algorithm distinguishes between two types of STSG rules: minimal and composed. While minimal rules are atomic and cannot be decomposed, composed rules can be formed out of smaller rules. String-to-tree mod-els cast translation as a parsing problem: the decoder parses a source language sentence using the source projection of a synchronous grammar while building the target sub-translations in paral-lel. As string-to-tree rules usually have multiple non-terminals that make decoding complexity generally exponential, synchronous binarization (Zhang *et al.* 2006: 256–63) is a key technique for applying the CYK algorithm to parsing with string-to-tree rules. This can be done by fac-toring each STSG rules into two SCFG rules. While phrase structure trees are successfully used in string-to-tree models, recent work on dependency trees further proves the benefit of exploit-ing linguistic syntax (Shen *et al.* 2010: 649–71).

Tree-to-string models (Liu *et al.* 2006: 609–16; Huang *et al.* 2006; Mi *et al.* 2008: 206–14) explicitly use source parse trees and divide decoding into two separate steps: parsing and transla-tion. A parser first parses a source language sentence into a parse tree, and then a decoder converts the tree to a translation on the target side. The decoding algorithm visits each node in the input source tree in a top-down order and tries to match each translation rules against the local sub-tree rooted at the node. Compared with the CKY algorithm used in string-to-string and string-to-tree decoders, tree-to-string decoding is much simpler and faster: there is no need for synchronous binarization, and tree parsing generally runs in linear time. However, despite these advantages, tree-to-string systems suffer from a major drawback: they only use 1-best parse trees to guide trans-lation, which potentially introduces translation mistakes due to the propagation of parsing errors. This problem can be elegantly alleviated by using packed forests, which encodes exponentially many parse trees in a polynomial space (Mi and Huang 2008: 206–14). Taking a packed forest as input can be regarded as a compromise between taking a string and a single tree: decoding is still fast yet does not commit to a single parse. In addition, packed forests can also be used for translation rule extraction, which helps alleviate the propagation of parsing errors into rule sets.

Tree-to-tree models (Eisner 2003: 205–08; Quirk *et al.* 2005: 271–79; Zhang *et al.* 2008: 559–67; Liu *et al.* 2009: 558–66; Chiang 2010: 1443–52) explicitly use parse trees on both sides. The decoding algorithm for tree-to-tree translation can be either parsing or tree parsing. The tree parsing algorithm takes a source tree as input and produces a target tree (Eisner 2003: 205–08; Quirk *et al.* 2005: 271–79; Zhang *et al.* 2008: 559–67; Liu et al. 2009: 558–66). By contrast, the parsing algorithm takes a source sentence as input and generates source and target trees simultaneously (Chiang 2010: 1443–52).

The choice of syntax-based models depends on the availability of parsers. For example, string-to-tree models might be suitable for translating a resource-scarce language into a resource-rich language such as English. Similarly, tree-to-string models might work better for translating English into a resource-scarce language that has no high accuracy parsers.

The most frequently cited disadvantages of syntax-based SMT are

- Availability and accuracy of parsers. For most natural languages, there are no high-accuracy parsers. Even for resource-rich languages such as English, parsers usually only work well for limited domains. Therefore, the applicability of syntax-based SMT is severely limited.
- Huge grammar size. Syntax-based models usually learn a very large number of rules as compared with phrase-based models, which leads to high memory requirement.

- Decoding complexity. Syntax-based decoders are significantly slower than phrase-based decoders.

Despite these disadvantages, syntax-based models have undergone rapid development and started to be used in commercial MT systems.

To conclude, the past two decades have witnessed the rapid development of statistical machine translation, moving from modeling flat structures (e.g. word, phrase) to hierarchical structures (e.g. tree). As the central goal of machine translation is to ensure meaning equivalence between the input and output, semantics-based SMT is clearly an important future direction awaiting exploration. In addition, although SMT is claimed to be language independent, most systems are designed and tested for resource-rich languages such as English, Chinese, Arabic, and French. How to use SMT techniques to deal with other natural languages in the world, most of which are resource scarce and significantly different from English, remains a big challenge.

Bibliography

Brown, Peter F., Stephen A. Della Pietra, Vincent J. Della Pietra, and Robert L. Mercer (1993) 'The Mathematics of Statistical Machine Translation: Parameter Estimation', *Computational Linguistics* 1(2): 233–312.

Chiang, David (2007) 'Hierarchical Phrase-based Translation', *Computational Linguistics* 33(2): 201–28.

Chiang, David (2010) 'Learning to Translate with Source and Target Syntax', in *Proceedings of the 48th Annual Meeting of the Association for Computational Linguistics*, 11–16 July 2010, Uppsala, Sweden, 1443–52.

Eisner, Jason (2003) 'Learning Non-isomorphic Tree Mappings for Machine Translation', in *ACL '03 Proceedings of the 41st Annual Meeting on Association for Computational Linguistics*, 7–12 July 2003, Sapporo, Japan, 2: 205–08.

Galley, Michel, Jonathan Graehl, Kevin Knight, Daniel Marcu, Steve DeNeefe, Wei Wang, and Ignacio Thayer (2006) 'Scalable Inference and Training of Context-rich Syntactic Translation Models', in *Proceedings of ACL 2006*, 17–21 July 2006, Sydney, Australia, 961–68.

Galley, Michel, Mark Hopkins, Kevin Knight, and Daniel Marcu (2004) 'What's in a Translation Rule?', in *Proceedings of HLT-NAACL 2004*, 2–7 May 2004, Boston, MA, 273–80.

Germann, Ulrich, Michael Jahr, Kevin Knight, Daniel Marcu, and Kenji Yamada (2001) 'Fast Decoding and Optimal Decoding for Machine Translation', in *Association for Computational Linguistics: 39th Annual Meeting and 10th Conference of the European Chapter: Workshop Proceedings: Data-driven Machine Translation*, 6–11 July 2001, Toulouse, France, 228–35.

Huang, Liang, Kevin Knight, and Aravind Joshi (2006) 'Statistical Syntax-directed Translation with Extended Domain of Locality', in *Proceedings of the 7th Conference of the Association for Machine Translation in the Americas (AMTA 2006)*, 8–12 August 2006, Boston, MA.

Knight, Kevin (1999) 'Decoding Complexity in Word-replacement Translation Models', *Computational Linguistics* 25(4): 607–15.

Koehn, Philipp, Franz J. Och, and Daniel Marcu (2003) 'Statistical Phrase-based Translation', in *NAACL '03 Proceedings of 2003 Conference of the North American Chapter of the Association for Computational Linguistics on Human Language Technology*, 27 May–1 June 2003, Edmonton, Canada, 1: 49–54.

Liu, Yang, Liu Qun, and Shouxun Lin (2006) 'Tree-to-string Alignment Template for Statistical Machine Translation', in *ACL-44 Proceedings of the 21st International Conference on Computational Linguistics and the 44th Annual Meeting of the Association for Computational Linguistics*, 20 July 2006, Sydney, Australia, 609–16.

Liu, Yang, Yajuan Lü, and Liu Qun (2009) 'Improving Tree-to-tree Translation with Packed Forests', in *ACL '09 Proceedings of the Joint Conference of the 47th Annual Meeting of the ACL and the 4th International Joint Conference on Natural Language Processing of the AFNLP*, 2–7 August 2009, Singapore, 2: 558–66.

Manning, Chris and Hinrich Schutze (1999) *Foundations of Statistical Natural Language Processing*, Cambridge, MA: MIT Press.

Mi, Haitao and Liang Huang (2008) 'Forest-based Translation Rule Extraction', in *EMNLP '08 Proceedings of the Conference on Empirical Methods in Natural Language Processing*, 25–27 October 2008, Honolulu, HI, 206–14.

Mi, Haitao, Liang Huang, and Liu Qun (2008) 'Forest-based Translation', in *Proceedings of 46th Annual Meeting of the Association for Computational Linguistics: Human Language Technologies (ACL-08: HLT)*, 15–20 June 2008, the Ohio State University, Columbus, OH, 192–99.

Och, Franz and Hermann Ney (2004) 'The Alignment Template Approach to Statistical Machine Translation', *Computational Linguistics* 30(4): 417–49.

Quirk, Chris and Simon Corston-Oliver (2006) 'The Impact of Parse Quality on Syntactically-informed Statistical Machine Translation', in *Proceedings of EMNLP 2006*, 22–23 July 2006, Sydney, Australia, 62–69.

Quirk, Chris, Arul Menezes, and Colin Cherry (2005) 'Dependency Treelet Translation: Syntactically Informed Phrasal SMT', in *ACL '05 Proceedings of the 43rd Annual Meeting on Association for Computational Linguistics*, 25–30 June 2005, University of Michigan, MI, 271–79.

Shen, Libin, Jinxi Xu, and Ralph Weischedel (2010) 'String-to-dependency Statistical Machine Translation', *Computational Linguistics* 36(4): 649–71.

Wu, Dekai (1997) 'Stochastic Inversion Transduction Grammars and Bilingual Parsing of Parallel Corpora', *Computational Linguistics* 23(3): 377–403.

Xiong, Deyi, Liu Qun, and Shouxun Lin (2006) 'Maximum Entropy Based Phrase Reordering Model for Statistical Machine Translation', in *ACL-44 Proceedings of the 21st International Conference on Computational Linguistics and the 44th Annual Meeting of the Association for Computational Linguistics*, 20 July 2006, Sydney, Australia, 521–28.

Yamada, Kenji and Kevin Knight (2001) 'A Syntax-based Statistical Translation Model', in *Association for Computational Linguistics: 39th Annual Meeting and 10th Conference of the European Chapter: Workshop Proceedings: Data-driven Machine Translation*, 6–11 July 2001, Toulouse, France, 523–30.

Zhang, Hao, Liang Huang, Daniel Gildea, and Kevin Knight (2006) 'Synchronous Binarization for Machine Translation', in *HLT-NAACL '06 Proceedings of the Main Conference on Human Language Technology Conference of the North American Chapter of the Association of Computational Linguistics*, 4–9 June 2006, New York, NY, 256–63.

Zhang, Min, Hongfei Jiang, Aiti Aw, Haizhou Li, Chew Lim Tan, and Sheng Li (2008) 'A Tree Sequence Alignment-based Tree-to-tree Translation Model', in *ACL 2008, Proceedings of the 46th Annual Meeting of the Association for Computational Linguistics*, 15–20 June 2008, Columbus, OH, 559–67.

12

EVALUATION IN MACHINE TRANSLATION AND COMPUTER-AIDED TRANSLATION

Kit Chunyu and Billy Wong Tak Ming

Introduction

Machine translation (MT) and *computer-aided translation* (CAT) both serve the same purpose of enhancing translation efficiency via the utilization of a computer. MT refers specifically to the automation of translation by means of available computer technology. It has pursuing fully automatic high-quality translation (FAHQT) as its ultimate goal, which was criticized by some MT pioneers (e.g. Bar Hillel and Martin Kay) a few decades ago as an unrealistic objective to strive for but has been pursued since the very beginning of MT by many other MTers through several generations of methodology and technology with notable but still limited successes. CAT is intended to provide suitable utilities with necessary language resources to assist human translation, aiming at maximizing the productivity of translation by means of combining the strengths of both sides.

Translation has become an industry that needs MT/CAT systems as 'machines' to facilitate translation production at various levels of automation. Typical utilities they provide to support human translation include monolingual/bilingual dictionaries and term banks (with terminology management tools), translation examples as in the form (and name) of translation memory, and so on. Besides, it is even more fundamental that CAT incorporates MT as one of its facilities to provide an initial version of a translation of a certain quality, as high as possible, for human translators to post-edit into a final version up to their quality standards, unless it is less editable than its source. In principle, the higher the quality of the MT output, the less human effort needed for post-editing and hence the higher the productivity of translation.

The evaluation of MT/CAT deals with the issue of quantifying their effectiveness. In a broad sense, it is intended to systematically assess the quality, success, and efficacy of any aspect of an MT/CAT system that gives rise to a concern about the degree of the system's usefulness. It has been developed into a unique discipline in the field despite the diversity of evaluation in terms of purposes and corresponding criteria used. Nevertheless, the quality of MT output is always at the core of evaluation. This explains why the term *MT evaluation* has become more and more popular and become its default term. However, MT output is typically characterized by a lack of a widely recognized objective metric for quality quantification. Unlike a clear-cut correct output from a language processing system for an input, such as word spelling from a spell checker, there is hardly an ideal or 'correct' one among so many possible translations for a source text.

DOI: 10.4324/9781003168348-13

Besides, the productivity of translation with the aid of CAT facilities is also largely attributed to a user's proficiency in using them. In other words, the evaluation of MT/CAT inevitably involves the evaluation of its users. In response to the diversity and challenges of MT/CAT evaluation, different types of qualitative and quantitative measurement have been developed.

This chapter introduces the key issues and basic principles of MT/CAT evaluation, concerning MT systems with or without human intervention for finalizing translation output. It begins with a brief review of the history of MT/CAT evaluation to outline the evolution of evaluation methodology and technology, along with the development of MT/CAT over the past several decades. The highly context-dependent multi-dimensional nature of the evaluation will then be described, including various applications of system output and different evaluation purposes. Then the existing evaluation methodologies will be presented and illustrated. On the one hand, an MT/CAT system is evaluated as a piece of software in terms of general parameters such as speed and number of supported file formats, subject to existing standards and criteria. On the other hand, its evaluation becomes a matter of text quality assessment because MT outputs are essentially in the form of text. The major approaches of MT evaluation, including both manual and automatic, will be presented with discussion of their strengths and weaknesses.

A Brief History

The evolution of MT evaluation is inseparable from the development of MT technology. Historically, the first MT demonstration, held in 1954 by a joint effort of Georgetown University and IBM, not only attempted the first application of non-numerical programming ever run on a computer but also, as a matter of fact, conducted the very first MT evaluation. It had a tremendous impact immediately, raising the awareness of MT greatly, attracting a substantial amount of investment of money and research effort into this new-born field in the subsequent years, and consequently starting a mushrooming period of MT for about a decade. It was later considered highly controversial, misleading, and even deceptive, due to its simplicity, in that it used a set of 60 prepared or selected sentences, 250 lexical items merely covering these sentences, and 6 operational rules. However, we have to admit its success in achieving its preset goal to 'test' the feasibility of MT, instead of its robustness and output quality, and in arriving at the affirmative and even 'convincing' conclusion – 'Yes, we can do it!' – despite some unrooted exaggeration and unrealistic over-expectation that followed it. From the current point of view, one can hardly find any significant methodology and technology of MT and MT evaluation in this piece of initial work.

One may consider that the earliest evaluation of MT begins from the criticism of the first-generation MT 'technologies' and the MT research in the 1950s on the wrong track towards the unrealistic goal of FAHQT. The first formal, in a sense, and influential evaluation was conducted by ALPAC[1] in the mid-1960s to examine the effectiveness of the funding to support MT research at that time, covering a variety of aspects such as the translation market in the United States, the speed and cost of producing MT outputs, and their quality. The ALPAC report (1966) also quotes some statistics from a study by Orr and Small (1967: 1–10) that compares MT outputs and human translations in terms of their comprehensibility to illustrate that MT outputs are not as accurate or readable and therefore not as useful as human translations.[2] It further provides a few samples of MT output containing 'unnatural constructions and unnatural word order' to support the claim that the goal of FAHQT was not achievable. A controversy that arises from this conclusion is that such an evaluation focused too much on regarding MT only as a production tool to meet users' translation needs in the United States and did not recognize the other potentials of MT and the expanding global translation market. Nevertheless, the impact of the ALPAC report to MT/CAT evaluation is long lasting. Three of its final recommendations are made constructively to support 'practical methods for evaluation of translations', 'of quality and cost of various sources of translations', and 'of the relative speed and cost of various sorts of machine-aided translation'. (1966: 34) In addition, its evaluation methodology, as described in detail in Carroll (1966), greatly influenced many evaluation practices in subsequent years.

Despite all that, the ALPAC report did not bring about any immediate revolutionary change to MT evaluation. According to Hutchins and Somers (1992), most MT evaluations at that time were still carried out by nonprofessionals with very little or even no expertise in MT techniques. They were unable to judge what could be possible or unrealistic for MT nor to provide any useful comments on system performance or constructive recommendations for the target audiences of evaluations. On the other hand, evaluations by system developers were often performed at a minimal scale and prone to misleading results, mostly due to carefully selected evaluation data for 'demonstration' of system performance in a positive way. This kind of evaluation not only failed to adequately reveal the performance of an MT system but also hindered the advancement of the whole field by hiding the real weaknesses and potentials of the technology in use.

MT evaluation started to develop into its own discipline when a good number of research systems were developed and more and more commercial systems entered into the market to compete against one another, demanding a fair and objective assessment of their performance and usability. In the late 1970s, one of the oldest commercial MT systems, Systran, was assessed for the European Communities. The assessment results were compiled in a report (Slype 1979), presenting the first comprehensive study on MT evaluation. This report covers all existing proposals and practices of MT evaluation at that time, presenting a critical assessment of each of them. Furthermore, it provides a holistic view of MT evaluation as a multi-faceted activity, comprising a range of dimensions, including purpose, text typology, effectiveness and efficiency, micro and macro criteria, and methods. Accordingly, MT evaluation extends its boundary to encompass many more interrelated parameters for which proper settings require thorough considerations in different evaluation scenarios.

The DARPA[3] MT initiative (White and O'Connell 1994: 134–40; White *et al.* 1993: 206–10, 1994: 193–205) was a representative attempt at comparative MT evaluation in the 1990s. It was intended to assess the progress of sponsored MT research, involving a heterogeneity of language pairs, computational approaches, and potential end-uses. A suite of evaluation methodologies was accordingly formulated with ambitious goals: to be applicable to contextual diversity, economical to administer, and portable to other evaluations, with subjectivity minimized. The evaluation covered both research (on statistical, interlingual, and human-assisted MT) and commercial systems, assessing the translation quality and usability of system outputs. Furthermore, evaluation methods were studied and compared for their sensitivity of measurement, efficiency, and the expenditure of human time and effort demanded. Such dual foci on assessing both systems and evaluation methods, that is, evaluation and meta-evaluation, have been followed by many subsequent practices.

In contrast to evaluations by human judges, a paradigmatic change in MT evaluation since the 2000s is the prevalence of automatic evaluation metrics. With the aid of these metrics, large-scale evaluations can be conducted on a large number of systems and language pair combinations within a reasonable time and cost. Examples include the IWSLT[4] series (Akiba *et al.* 2004: 1–12; Eck and Hori 2005: 11–32; Fordyce 2007; Paul 2006: 1–15, 2008: 1–17, 2009: 1–18; Paul *et al.* 2010: 3–27), HTRDP (Liu *et al.* 2005: 18–22), TC-STAR (Choukri *et al.* 2007), the CESTA,[5] NIST open MT evaluation,[6] and the SMT workshop.[7] Through these evaluations, not only the performance of the state-of-the-art MT approaches but the validity and effectiveness of different evaluation methods, be they manual or automatic, are also examined.

Table 12.1 Types of translation purpose and their requirements of translation quality

Purpose of translation	Required quality of translation
Dissemination	Publishable quality
Assimilation	At a lower level of quality
Interchange	Translation between participants in one-to-one communication or of an unscripted presentation
Information access	Translation within multilingual systems of information retrieval, information extraction, database access, and so on

Source: Hutchins (2003)

Applications, Purposes, and Criteria

In essence, evaluating an MT/CAT system is to assess how well it serves what it is aimed to serve. For this goal one has to answer at least three interrelated *what* questions, that is, the intended applications of the system in question, the purposes of evaluation, and then the appropriate criteria to use, before moving ahead to deal with the matter of *how*, that is, the methodology of evaluation. Answers to these questions determine the design of an evaluation. A clearly defined application entails a specific evaluation purpose, such that a system is assessed only for what it is designed to do. This purpose guides the selection and definition of appropriate criteria, according to which suitable evaluation methodology can then be formulated.

An MT/CAT system is usually developed for a specific application. While CAT tools are for restricted uses, for example, translation memory primarily for supporting translators to reuse previous translations, MT systems have a wide range of potential applications, for example, for use as a CAT facility to provide an initial translation for further post-editing, a utility for gisting/ browsing foreign texts, a means for information dissemination, and so on. Different purposes require different levels of system performance in terms of translation quality, as in Table 12.1, generalized by Hutchins (2003: 5–26). No MT system has been able to translate any kind of text in any subject at a publishable quality level. The performance of an MT system highly depends on the subject domain(s) to which it is optimized and the knowledge with which it is equipped. METEO, a specialized MT system, was used to translate weather forecasts between English and French successfully for two decades (1981–2001), using a sublanguage with a restricted lexicon and grammar. A general MT system is only capable of delivering translations in gistable quality in most cases but can be very useful when translation quality is not the first priority (e.g. to get the rough idea or the subject of a text so as to locate information or decide whether professional human translation is needed).

Therefore, we have to bear in mind that the usability judgment of MT varies according to the intended use of system output besides translation quality. In a survey exploring the usefulness of MT from the users' perspective, Morland (2002) notes that 'those who feel comfortable with English do not want pure MT translations [from English to their native language], but those who are not as strong in English find it useful'. A fair comment from this survey is that 'pure MT is rough – often obscure, frequently humorous – but it can be useful'. MT can be chosen as a good enough solution for a particular task despite its translation quality. As discussed in Church and Hovy (1993: 239–58), a well-chosen application helps determine how to evaluate a system and make it look good. In contrast, an inappropriate intended task makes it difficult to find a suitable evaluation paradigm and may lead to bias in interpreting evaluation results.

Apart from the right application, the design of evaluation is also dependent on the purposes of interested parties to conduct the evaluation. Different parties involved in different stages of an

MT/CAT system, from research and development to procurement, installation, and operation, are interested in different aspects of a given system. Hutchins and Somers (1992) and White (2003: 211–44) discuss the special interests of typical parties in MT. For example, *researchers* would like to know whether, and to what extent, a particular method works for a hypothesis or is extendable to a new domain. *Developers* have to identify errors that can be corrected within the capacity of a system, find out the limitations of the system such as its coverage of text types and subject domains, and decide what facilities should be provided to intended users. *Lay users* are only able to access a system's output and perform a 'black box' evaluation[8] to examine its capabilities, acceptability, and cost-effectiveness in their own working environments. *Translators* are mainly concerned with the gain in productivity from using a system to help with translating, in particular, in a manner of revising MT output up to an acceptable quality standard.

Accordingly, a particular type of evaluation is needed for finding out the right kind of information to serve a specific purpose of each party. White (2003: 211–44) presents a categorization of MT evaluation including the following types. A *feasibility test* examines the possibility that a theory or method can be accomplished and its potentiality for a success after further research and implementation. *Internal evaluation* focuses on whether some components of an experimental, prototype, or pre-release system can work as planned and, if not, what causes and solutions there are to problems. *Usability evaluation* tests the usefulness of a system for end users, involving its utility and users' satisfaction with it, in terms of the extent to which it enables users to achieve their specific goals. *Operation evaluation* explores the cost benefits of a system in a particular operational environment. *Declarative evaluation* assesses the ability of a system to translate texts for actual end use. *Comparison evaluation* investigates particular attributes (e.g. translation quality) among a set of systems in order to find the best one, the best implementation, the best theoretical approach, and so on.

Once the purpose of evaluation is clear and the type of evaluation needed is determined, corresponding criteria can be defined and methodology implemented. For instance, criteria for evaluating an MT system to serve the needs of a translator may first include the quality of system output, because a system with poor output (i.e. below the required level for an intended application) is unlikely to be useful no matter how good it is in other aspects. Other criteria may include the amount and ease of work on pre- and post-editing system input and output, facilities for text editing, consistency of terminology, number of language pairs supported, cost of dictionary maintenance, and so on. In general, an MT/CAT system is evaluated on the one hand in terms of the quality of its output, and on the other hand as a piece of software, using criteria such as usability, operability, speed, and so on.

Software Evaluation

As an MT/CAT system is a computer program in nature, its evaluation can be considered a stage of software engineering, to which existing standards of software evaluation are applicable. Jointly developed by the International Organization for Standardization (ISO) and the International Electrotechnical Commission (IEC), the standard ISO/IEC 9126 (1991, 2001) provides a quality model and identifies several types of metric for software evaluation. It defines software quality as 'the totality of features and characteristics of a product or service that bear on its ability to satisfy stated or implied needs'. Six generic characteristics are identified: functionality, reliability, usability, efficiency, maintainability, and portability, each of which is further broken down into a number of sub-characteristics.[9] A sub-characteristic is composed of a set of attributes representing some verifiable or measurable features of a software product.

The ISO/IEC standard was followed by the ISLE[10] project to develop a criteria taxonomy for MT evaluation (ISLE 2001), resulting in FEMTI.[11] FEMTI gathers and systematizes all possible contexts of evaluation once suggested, in line with the corresponding ISO/IEC characteristics/ sub-characteristics and attributes, and collects all MT evaluation methods and metrics proposed so far, categorized under respective attributes. It helps practitioners of MT evaluation identify suitable evaluation methods for their own needs.

Central to the rationale of FEMTI is that MT evaluation is 'only a special, although rather complex, case of software evaluation in general' (Hovy *et al.* 2002: 43–75). Quality of a piece of software can be characterized and measured by (1) first defining the context of evaluation and corresponding characteristics, (2) then identifying attributes related to each characteristic, and (3) finally selecting appropriate methods to assess each attribute. In other words, the quality is compositional in nature. The meaning of some characteristics, like functionality, is operational and has to be specified by choices of attribute and evaluation method. Therefore, the notion of quality or any of its characteristics is ambiguous in isolation. Its semantics becomes clear only when a user has chosen what and how to evaluate, which is to be determined by factors such as purpose, task, and text genre or, in more general terms, by the context of evaluation, as discussed in the previous section.

Hence, there need to be a specific set of evaluation criteria and a corresponding methodology for each scenario of evaluation. For example, Kit and Wong (2008) present a comparative evaluation of online MT systems with a focus on finding out the best, out of those available, for lay users in legal translation. Recognizing the incapability of MT to deliver high-quality translation of legal texts without human post-editing, the purpose of this evaluation is to provide interested parties with substantial evidence for proper selection of online MT systems for different language pairs, assuming a need for practical use of MT for legal translation. Evaluation criteria then include coverage of supported language pairs (regarding how often users have to switch to another MT system), translation quality for a language pair on average (representing how well translation between languages can be done by various systems in general and how confident users can be with it), and translation quality for a language pair in particular (serving as an indicator for selecting the best MT system for a specific language pair). The evaluation of output quality is based on quantitative metrics using a large corpus of legal texts in order to properly and concretely reveal the performance of online MT systems.

Note that MT/CAT evaluation is not limited to assessing a system as a whole only. It is also applied to a system component, especially in the area of research and development. For instance, an example-based MT system typically consists of three major components respectively responsible for matching, alignment, and recombination of translation examples. Each of them can be viewed as an independent component with its own functions and data input and output and therefore has to be evaluated using different methods. For matching and alignment, measures such as precision and recall are commonly used to quantify system performance of retrieving relevant translation examples from database and mapping source-target example fragments, respectively, through comparison with a pre-defined set of gold-standard data. Evaluation of recombination is more complicated, because the recombined example fragments are final MT outputs whose quality is highly dependent on the performance of the previous stages, that is, matching and alignment.

The evaluation of CAT systems is also challenging. There is a wide diversity of system types, such as optical character recognition (OCR), project management, termbank, translation memory, interactive MT, and so on, with different designs and functionalities for different applications. Moreover, two systems of the same type may provide different kinds of features such that it may not be able to directly compare two systems feature by feature. A translation memory system may support some unique file types, while another may have proprietary technologies to match translation records. On the other hand, many CAT systems are claimed to enhance translators' productivity in comparison with not using them. However, such a productivity gain, if any, also depends on users' proficiency in system operation. Without sufficient training, an inexperienced user may not gain any significant benefit from using them or even inhibit his/her productivity. This kind of human factor has to be minimized or properly controlled in CAT evaluation.

Approaches to CAT evaluation can be categorized into two types, automatic vs. manual. Automatic evaluation uses objective metrics to quantify the measurable aspects of a system such as speed of execution and usability of system output. A widely used metric to evaluate translation memory and interactive MT systems is keystroke ratio: the ratio between (1) the number of keystrokes required to modify a given system output into a reference translation and (2) the number of characters in the reference translation. A reference translation is a human translation of the same source text in use as 'model answer'[12] for comparison with system output. The keystroke ratio helps to estimate the amount of human effort required to produce the final translation from the output of TM and/or MT. A ratio larger than 1 means that revising a system output takes more effort in number of keystrokes than typing the whole reference translation from scratch – literally speaking, the system output in question brings no productivity gain.

Manual evaluation relies on users' subjective judgments and experiences in assessing an MT/CAT system. Focus may be given to system features on their quality (e.g. how well they are designed and implemented) and suitability (e.g. to what extent they suit a user's particular needs). Typical evaluation methods of this kind include average user rating on a scale, such as a 5- or 7-point scale, and user trial involving a group of users to test a system under controlled conditions. For example, to investigate the productivity gain by using an MT/CAT system, a user trial can be carried out to measure and compare the difference of time between using and not using the system in question to translate a test set.

Quality of MT Output

As the main function of an MT system is to provide translation service, quality of MT output is of particular interest to all parties and usually regarded as a primary criterion of MT evaluation. Nevertheless, the notion of 'translation quality' was considered indefinable by some scholars (Slocum 1985: 1–17), accounting for the long-time absence of a universally accepted standard and method for its quantification. Accordingly, multiple quality criteria have been proposed, demonstrating various interpretations of the notion with a focus on different evaluation aspects.

Central to the notion is the question of how text quality is characterized. Even though MT output is still far from reaching the quality of human written text, it is grasped by readers in a similar manner as texts written by humans. Moreover, a main purpose of MT evaluation is to assess 'to what extent the makers of a system have succeeded in mimicking the human translator' (Krauwer 1993: 59–66). In other words, a piece of MT output has to show its quality in terms of its success in approximating human translation and therefore share many features with the latter, although the technical details of their assessment may be different.

Text quality can be characterized from both monolingual and bilingual perspectives. The quality of monolingual text is multifaceted, as shown in different evaluations with their own sets of criteria. For example, for language learners' writing assessment, holistic grading can be based on the general impression of their effort on writing or on the overall success of their written communication without attending to any particular individual element involved. Alternatively, a detailed assessment may use an analytical scale with multiple parameters for scoring, such as those in Diederich (1974), including ideas, organization, wording and phrasing, style, grammar and sentence structure, punctuation, spelling, and legibility of handwriting, whose weights in the final grade can be adjusted to fit different situations.

Quality of bilingual text has much in common with that of monolingual one. Both text types have to adhere to some general quality criteria such as grammaticality, readability, coherence, and so on. What distinguishes a translation from monolingual text is its correspondence with a source text in another language, demanding an equivalence relation in terms of meaning, in particular. This is a unique feature not required by other text types, and it is central to many translation theories characterizing the notion of translation quality.

Equivalence is also a controversial property of a translation, however, which has been defined and interpreted in different ways over the years. Some notable definitions include what Nida (1964) calls *formal* and *dynamic* equivalence, Catford's (1965) *textual* equivalence, and Newmark's (1982, 1988) *semantic* and *communicative* equivalence, among many others. From the perspective of evaluation, House (2009: 222–24) criticizes that many treatments of translation equivalence, such as 'faithfulness to the original' or 'the natural flow of the translated text', are 'atheoretical in nature', offering poor operationality, and solely dependent on the knowledge, intuition, and competence of a translator. It is difficult to establish general principles and develop, accordingly, a systematic procedure to assess the features needed to characterize translation relationship.

In practice, translation assessment commonly relies on an error-based grading. An example of this is the ATA[13] certification examination. Errors in a translation are identified and rated in terms of their consequence to the meaning, understanding, usefulness, and/or content of a translation. Its overall quality is graded in four dimensions, usefulness/transfer, terminology/style, idiomatic writing, and target mechanics. Each of them is further divided into four ranks for detailed characterization of performance variation.

Most evaluation of translation quality requires comprehension as a prerequisite for determining various kinds of equivalence relation and/or identifying errors in a translation. It is put forth in Hayes *et al.* (1987: 176–240) that 'reading to comprehend' is the basis of 'reading to evaluate'. These two cognitive processes differ in their purposes, in that the former attempts to construct an integrated representation of a text to understand how the ideas in the text work as a whole, while the latter aims at identifying problems in the text and sometimes also at finding solutions. It is worth noting that readers may also detect problems whilst endeavouring to understand a text, but they usually do not devote much thinking or conscious attention to them unless the problems are bad enough to hinder their reading.

Evaluation of MT output falls somewhere between reading to comprehend and reading to evaluate. Depending on the purpose of evaluation, evaluators may want to know how comprehensible an MT output is without any need to diagnose its problems or to perform a detailed error analysis to examine a system's strengths and weaknesses. However, what is complicated here is that both comprehension and evaluation of an MT output demand a judgment of its correspondence with the source text. Both of them reflect the intelligibility and fidelity of the output, two common criteria for assessing the quality of MT output, referring to the extent to which an output can be understood and is accurate in meaning, respectively. The quality of a translation may be uneven in these two aspects, because a translation may be strong in following the rules and conventions of target language but weak in preserving the meaning of its source. However, the reverse is hardly conceivable. Although one may artificially list examples that are 'perhaps optimally faithful, but far less intelligible than a translation' (White 2001: 35–37), such cases rarely occur in reality. It is reasonable to consider that evaluation of fidelity subsumes that of intelligibility, and the former cannot be isolated from the latter. In other words, determination of translation equivalence requires understanding of a text.

A more general challenge for MT evaluation lies in the idiosyncratic difference between MT and human translation. The quality of human translation is expected to be publishable in general, but the best quality of MT in the general domain is for 'gisting' only, except that of the outputs from tailor-made systems for specialized domains. It is not rare to find an MT output of extremely poor quality with unusual word choices, garbled characters, or unreadable word order, not to mention an appropriate judgment of its quality, such as the following outputs from three MT systems[14] for the same source text.

MT1: o???? face deliver information the hope resumes talk
MT2: Han to will restore the discussion towards the transmission hope the information
MT3: the rok will provide the dprk transfer hopes to resume talks and Information

It is difficult to apply to them any higher-order criteria of evaluation such as functional appropriateness or stylistic elegancy of a text. Thus, even though the ultimate goal of MT is to attain human translation quality, a different profile of evaluation criteria and methods needs to be used in order to cope with these kinds of text characteristics of MT output.[15]

Manual Evaluation

MT evaluation has relied on human judges since the birth of MT, and will inevitably continue to do so in the future. It is the end users of both MT systems and languages who determine the usefulness of an MT system and judge the quality of its output. Although human judgments of text quality are usually perceived and described as subjective and inconsistent, they are nevertheless the ultimate 'gold standard' that cannot be overridden by any automatic measure. As found in an industry survey about the preference of MT evaluation methods by buyers and vendors in the translation and localization industries, the most popular way to evaluate MT output remained manual evaluation (69%) (Doherty *et al.* 2013).

Manual evaluation of MT output entails two aspects: intrinsic and extrinsic. The former focuses on judgment of language quality, while the latter aims to test the usability of MT output in a specific task that MT is expected to facilitate.

Intrinsic

Quality Assessment

In quality assessment, evaluators are asked to rate, in terms of their intuitive judgment, the 'goodness' of a translation, which is normally presented sentence by sentence or as a sequence of even smaller syntactic constituents. Two most commonly used criteria in the assessment are *fidelity* and *intelligibility*. Fidelity is about whether the transfer of meaning from a source to a target text is accurate and adequate without loss, addition or distortion. Evaluators have to be bilingual if they need to work on both source texts and MT outputs for comparison, but they can be monolingual if human translation is available as reference. Intelligibility, on the other hand, is a monolingual attribute of target text, referring to 'the ease with which a translation can be understood' (Slype 1979), regardless of whether its content is accurately translated. It is a key indicator for how easily a reader can grasp key message from a translation.

Both fidelity and intelligibility are rated with a scale. The 5-point scale in Table 12.2 has been widely used in many open MT evaluations in the past decades. For example, in the NIST open MT evaluations, evaluators were instructed to spend no more than 30 seconds on average on assessing both the fidelity and intelligibility of a segment of MT output (LDC 2002). Their qualitative judgments need to be based on an instant intuition rather than a thorough understanding of translation candidates.

Table 12.2 The 5-point fidelity/intelligibility scale

Fidelity	Intelligibility
5 All	Flawless
4 Most	Good
3 Much	Non–native
2 Little	Disfluent
1 None	Incomprehensible

Source: LDC (2002)

Another approach to rate fidelity and intelligibility is to use a continuous scale, where evaluators give a score within the range of 0–100 for an MT output. This approach has been adopted in the annual Workshop on Statistical Machine Translation in recent years (Akhbardeh *et al.* 2021) and shown to be cost effective for large-scale, crowd-sourced evaluations (Graham *et al.* 2017).

In principle, fidelity and intelligibility are independent of each other. However, there are existing findings to show that they are in fact highly correlated (White 2001: 35–37). It is thus possible to excogitate an evaluation method by measuring just one of them, such as fidelity, and then inferring the other.

Translation Ranking

Translation ranking resorts to human preference by ranking a number of translation sentences instead of rating with respect to any of their quality attributes. Evaluators are instructed to 'rank translations from Best to Worst relative to the other choices (ties are allowed)' (Callison-Burch *et al.* 2009: 1–28), given a list of several system outputs each time. A variant of translation ranking is to pick, after a pairwise comparison, a preferred version, or none if the quality of two outputs is indistinguishable. The overall performance of an MT system is then reflected in the average number of times its outputs are ranked higher than the others. Translation ranking has been the official human evaluation method in the statistical MT workshops since 2008, replacing the conventional fidelity/intelligibility judgment (Callison-Burch *et al.* 2008).

The formulation of this method is driven by the poor inter-annotator agreement on traditional quality rating. Note that in many cases of MT evaluation, what system developers need the most is a system ranking, not the details of a system's quality in terms of particular features such as fidelity and/or intelligibility.

Error Analysis

While quality assessment appraises the 'goodness' of a translation, error analysis judges a translation from the opposite perspective, that is, measuring its 'badness'. It starts with identifying translation errors and ends with an estimation of 'the amount of work required to correct [a] "raw" MT output to a standard considered acceptable as a translation' (Hutchins and Somers 1992: 164). It seeks to pinpoint the feasibility, potentials, and limitations of a system by examining the contexts in which it is most likely to be effective or prone to failure (Lehrberger and Bourbeau 1988). It is considered a more reliable method than quality assessment, because identifying errors is in general more objective and consistent among evaluators than rating goodness of translation (Schwarzl 2001). Furthermore, its results are usually more meaningful and interpretable to interested parties like system developers and users.

Table 12.3 Excerpt of error classification

Word order	Incorrect word
Word level	Sense
– Local range	– Wrong lexical choice
– Long range	– Incorrect disambiguation
Phrase level	Incorrect form
– Local range	– Extra word
– Long range	– Style
	– Idiom

Source: Vilar *et al.* (2006: 699)

Table 12.4 Excerpt of the Multidimensional Quality Metrics framework

Type of translation quality error	Subtype of error
Accuracy	Addition
	Mistranslation
	Omission
	Untranslated
Fluency	Grammar
	Inconsistency
	Spelling
	Unintelligible
Design	Local formatting
	Missing text
Locale convention	Address format
	Date format
Style	Inconsistent style
	Unidiomatic
Terminology	Inconsistent with termbase
	Inconsistent use of terminology
Verity	Completeness
	Locale-specific content

Source: Lommel *et al.* (2015)

Errors can be classified in different ways according to the variety and complexity of MT systems, grammatical features of texts in various domains or languages, and user demands (Lehrberger and Bourbeau 1988). Table 12.3 illustrates an excerpt of error classification from Vilar *et al.* (2006), which can be used to count the numbers of error types in MT output so as to obtain an overall distribution of error frequencies. Table 12.4 presents another excerpt of the Multidimensional Quality Metrics framework which aims to provide a systematic categorization of translation quality errors (Lommel *et al.* 2015). This framework was used in the 2021 Conference on Machine Translation for annotation of errors in MT output (Freitag *et al.* 2021).

The difficulties of error analysis lie in the identification and classification of errors. First, except obvious mistakes in syntax and lexical choices, what constitutes an error is a subjective matter, involving human factors like evaluators' tolerance of imperfections in a sentence and their preference of expression. Second, classifying errors into pre-defined categories is often problematic because of the unclear boundaries of error types that are closely interlinked in nature (Arnold *et al.* 1994; Flanagan 1994). For example, a missing auxiliary verb could be classified as a missing word or an incorrect form of main verb (Trujillo 1999).

Extrinsic

Information Extraction

A typical use of MT is to aid extracting key information from foreign texts. According to a user study by Taylor and White (1998: 364–73), the kinds of information of interest to users range from name entities to relationships between participants in events presented in a text. The extent to which users can completely and correctly identify such key information in an MT output is thus a direct indicator of the usability of the output.

This idea is formulated into an evaluation metric in Lo and Wu (2011: 220–29). They defined the usability of MT as the extent to which it can help human readers successfully grasp essential event information: *who did what* to *whom, when, where, why,* and *how.* Such event information is closely associated with semantic roles (see Table 12.5) in sentences of MT output, reference translation, and source text. Human judges can compare the content of semantic roles on both sides and determine whether those ones on the MT side are correct, partially correct, or incorrect.

Table 12.5 Correspondence of semantic roles and event information

Semantic role	Event	Semantic role	Event
Agent	who	Location	where
Action	did	Purpose	why
Experiencer	what	Manner	how
Patient	whom	Degree or extent	how
Temporal	when	Other adverbial arguments	how

Source: Lo and Wu (2011: 225)

Comprehension Test

The ultimate goal of MT is to enable users to comprehend foreign texts. Their understanding of MT output can be examined by reading comprehension tests. Evaluators are given passages of MT output and human translation for the same source text to read and then a set of questions about the passages to answer. Their performance in the comprehension tests using the two types of passage reflects the degree to which MT can accurately and comprehensibly translate the source texts.

The MT evaluation reported in Tomita (1992) and Tomita *et al.* (1993) used TOFEL[16] test materials to see whether the materials translated by humans and by different MT systems resulted in different degrees of understanding by examinees in terms of the TOEFL scoring of their answers to questions. In this evaluation, TOEFL passages were rendered into Japanese by MT and human translators and TOEFL questions translated manually for a group of Japanese students to answer.

Reeder (2001a: 67–71, 2001b) presents another evaluation method based on language learner tests. Following her observation that evaluators were able to distinguish between texts written by native speakers and language learners in less than 100 words, Reeder studied their performance on differentiating 'authors' of translation, i.e., human or MT. Native speaker subjects were given a short passage to read and then identified whether it was a human or machine translation. How well the subjects recognized MT output was measured in terms of the accuracy of identification and the number of words required for a judgment.

Another evaluation method is based on the 'cloze procedure' (Somers and Wild 2000). For a passage of MT output, some words (e.g. every word in ten) are masked and subjects are asked to guess the missing words. The underlying idea of this method comes from an observation in Gestalt psychology, i.e., 'the human tendency to complete a familiar but not-quite-finished pattern . . . by mentally closing up the gaps' (Taylor 1953: 415). The quality of MT output in terms of readability or intelligibility is indicated by the ability of the subjects to guess the missing words correctly.

Post-Editing

Post-editing involves a human editor to revise an MT output up to an acceptable level of quality. Quality of MT output is assumed to have an inverse correlation with the amount of effort needed for the revision. In this way, MT is assessed as a means to raise translators' productivity in terms of the cost-effectiveness of post-editing its output as a usable initial draft. In the worst case, this draft may take a translator even longer to post-edit it than to translate its source text from scratch.

A direct measurement of post-editing effort is the amount of time required to revise an MT output. This provides a clear indication of the usability of MT output, for the cost of post-editing is directly reflected in the amount of revision time. Its drawback is also obvious, however. Post-editing time depends on many factors, especially such external ones as post-editors' concentration and working environment. It is unlikely that a post-editor can maintain the same concentration upon the revision of every sentence nor that two post-editors spend the same time on the same MT output. Therefore it is rather questionable whether different post-editors' time on post-editing can be comparable.

A more objective measure is the *edit-distance* that counts the number of changes required to revise an MT output, including addition, deletion, substitution, and transposition of words. To allow a fair comparison, the number of changes is then normalized by the number of words in the revised translation. Provided with source text or human translation for reference, post-editors are asked to carry out a minimal number of edits to make an MT output understandable and accurate in meaning.

Automatic Evaluation

Automatic evaluation of MT outputs involves the use of quantitative metrics without human intervention in runtime. It is intended to meet the demand from the MT community to overcome the shortcomings of manual evaluation, which is inevitably prone to personal biases of human judges and to inconsistency of subjective judgments. There are different views of what should be considered errors in translation and different levels of acceptability that revision has to achieve. Furthermore, manual evaluation is usually too costly in terms of time and monetary cost and can hardly cope with the enormous scale of MT evaluation, as evidenced by the common practice of the past decade in the field.[17] Automatic metrics thus serve as a desirable solution, providing a quick and cost-effective means for trustable estimation of the quality of MT output.

Text Similarity Metrics

Most automatic measures for MT evaluation rely on available human translations as reference for comparison with MT outputs. In this way MT evaluation is turned into a problem of computing monolingual text similarity. A rudimentary idea of this kind can be dated back to the 1950s. Miller and Beebe-Center (1956: 73–80) suggest that

> the fact that a grader can recognize errors [in a student's translation] at all implies that he must have some personal standard against which he compares the student's work . . . this might consist of his own written translation; more often it is probably a rather vague set of translations that would be about equally acceptable.

A primitive evaluation method for assessing 'the relation between the test translation and the criteria' is thus 'to ask if they use the same words' and 'to compare the order of the words which were common to the test and the criterion translations'. Although there is rarely only one correct translation for a source text, different versions of translations may share certain common words or phrases. This provides a basis for statistical comparison of an MT output with a reference in terms of common textual features.

BLEU and NIST

BLEU[18] (Papineni *et al.* 2001) is widely recognized as one of the first and the most influential metrics for automatic MT evaluation, well known for its rationale that 'the closer a machine translation is to a professional human translation, the better it is'. It is based on counting the number of n-grams, sequences of consecutive word(s) of varying length, co-occurring in an MT output and in one or more versions of corresponding reference, usually each in the form of a sentence. This idea is illustrated in Papineni *et al.* (2001) with the following exemplary translation candidates (*C1–2*) and references (*R1–3*) for the same source text.

> *C1*: It is a guide to action which ensures that the military always obeys the commands of the party.
> *C2*: It is to insure the troops forever hearing the activity guidebook that party direct.
> *R1*: It is a guide to action that ensures that the military will forever heed Party commands.
> *R2*: It is the guiding principle which guarantees the military forces always being under the command of the Party.
> *R3*: It is the practical guide for the army always to heed the directions of the party.

Human readers can easily identify *C1* as a better translation than *C2*. The results of n-gram matching,[19] as presented in Table 12.6, confirm that *C1* shares more n-grams than *C2* with all versions of reference, giving an evaluation result in agreement with human judgment.

Table 12.6 Number of common n-grams in translation candidates (*C1–2*) and references (*R1–3*)

	C1			*C2*		
n-gram length	1	2	3	1	2	3
R1	14	8	6	8	1	0
R2	11	4	1	5	1	0
R3	9	3	1	6	1	0

Upon counting the number of common n-grams, precision, the proportion of matched n-grams in a candidate, can then be calculated, by dividing this number by the total number of n-grams in the candidate. For an entire test set, the n-gram precision p_n is defined as

$$p_n = \frac{\sum_{c \in C} \sum_{w^n \in c} \text{match}\left(w^n\right)}{\sum_{c \in C} \sum_{w^n \in c} w^n}$$

where c refers to each sentence in the candidate set C, and w^n is an n-gram of the length n. In Papineni *et al.*'s proposal, p_n is computed for grams up to length 4 and then averaged to the geometric mean P_{avg} as

$$P_{avg} = \sum_{n=1}^{N} \alpha \log p_n$$

where the max n-gram length $N = 4$ and the weight $= 1/N$ for each p_n. As length discrepancy between candidate and reference is concerned, the n-gram precision can penalize a candidate for being longer than its reference. However, it cannot properly deal with a candidate that is too short. For this, a *brevity penalty* factor BP_{BLEU} is introduced into BLEU. It is a decaying exponential with respect to candidate length L_c and reference length L_r, defined as

$$BP_{BLEU} = \begin{cases} 1, \text{ if } L_c > L_r; \\ e^{\left(1 - \frac{L_r}{L_c}\right)}, \text{ if } L_c \leq L_r. \end{cases}$$

Then BLEU score is calculated as

$$BLEU = BP_{BLEU} \cdot \exp\left(P_{avg}\right)$$

resulting in a number between 0 and 1, with a larger one indicating a higher similarity of candidates to respective references.

NIST[20] is another metric revised from BLEU with a number of modifications (Doddington 2002: 138–45). While BLEU weights each n-gram equally, NIST gives more weight to n-grams that are more informative. The fewer occurrences of an n-gram in reference translation, the more informative it is considered. For an n-gram w^n of length n, its information weight $\text{Info}(w^n)$ is computed following the equation

$$\text{Info}\left(w^n\right) = \log_2 \frac{\sum_{r \in R} \sum_{w^{n-1} \in r} w^{n-1}}{\sum_{r \in R} \sum_{w^n \in r} w^n},$$

where r refers to a sentence in the reference set R and w^{n-1} an n-gram of length $n - 1$. In other words, it estimates the information of w^n given the first w^{n-1}. Other modifications in NIST include a revised version of brevity penalty to minimize the penalty on small variations in translation length. Furthermore, the geometric average of n-gram precision in BLEU scoring is changed into an arithmetic average to avoid possible counterproductive variance due to the low occurrence frequency of long n-grams. Accordingly, the NIST metric is formulated as

$$NIST = P_{avg} \cdot \exp\left(BP_{NIST}\right)$$

where

$$P_{avg} = \sum_{n=1}^{N} \frac{\sum_{c \in C} \sum_{w^n \in c} \mathrm{match}\left(w^n\right) \mathrm{Info}\left(w^n\right)}{\sum_{c \in C} \sum_{w^n \in c} w^n}$$

and

$$BP_{NIST} = \log_2 \min(L_c / L_r, 1).$$

In Doddington's proposal, $= -\log_2 2 / \log_2 3$ and $N = 5$.

BLEU and NIST have been widely used as *de facto* standard measures to monitor system performance in research and development, especially for comparison of systems, and adopted as official measures in many open MT evaluations, such as the NIST open MT evaluation, IWSLT, and statistical MT workshop.

METEOR

METEOR[21] is proposed in Banerjee and Lavie (2005: 65–72) as a recall–oriented evaluation metric, standing out from such precision-oriented ones as BLEU and NIST.[22] It begins with an explicit word-to-word alignment to match every word (i.e. a unigram) in a candidate with a corresponding one, if any, in a reference. To maximize the possibility of matching, it uses three word-mapping criteria: (1) exact character sequences, (2) identical stem forms of words, and (3) synonyms. After the word alignment is created, the unigram precision P and unigram recall R are calculated as

$$P = \frac{m}{L_c} \text{ and } R = \frac{m}{L_r}$$

where m is the number of matched unigrams, and L_c and L_r are the lengths of candidate and reference, respectively. A harmonic mean of P and R is then computed, with a parameter α to control their weights, as

$$F_{mean} = \frac{PR}{\alpha P + (1 - \alpha) R}.$$

There is a fragmentation penalty for each candidate sentence in a problematic word order. It is applied with respect to the number of 'chunks' in a candidate, formed by grouping together matched unigrams in adjacent positions. In this way, the closer the word order of matched unigrams between candidate and reference, the longer and fewer chunks are formed, and the lower the penalty. The fragmentation penalty is calculated as

$$Penalty = \gamma \left(\frac{ch}{m}\right)^{\beta}$$

where ch is the number of chunks, γ a parameter determining the maximum penalty ($0 \leq \gamma \leq 1$), and β another parameter determining the functional relation between fragmentation and the penalty.

The METEOR score for a candidate is computed as its word matching score after deduction of the fragmentation penalty, as

$$METEOR = F_{mean}(1 - Penalty).$$

METEOR is also characterized by its high flexibility in parameter weighting, which can be straightforwardly optimized to new training data in a different context of evaluation. In Lavie and Agarwal (2007), the parameters of METEOR are optimized to human judgments of translation adequacy and fluency, resulting in the following setting (adequacy | fluency): $\alpha = (0.82 \mid 0.78)$, $\beta = (1.0 \mid 0.75)$ and $\gamma = (0.21 \mid 0.38)$.

TER

TER[23] (Snover *et al.* 2006: 223–31) is an evaluation metric based on the quantification of edit-distance between two strings of words, that is, the minimal number of operations required to transform one string into another. It can be used to measure the needed post-editing effort to revise a candidate into a reference.

TER is formulated as the minimal number of insertions *INT*, deletions *DEL*, substitutions *SUB*, and shifts *SHIFT* (reordering) of words that are required for each word in a candidate:

$$TER = \frac{INT + DEL + SUB + SHIFT}{N}$$

where N is the average number of words in the reference(s) in use. It returns a score between 0 and 1, quantifying the difference of two sentences in the range of no difference (no edit is needed) to entirely different (every word has to be changed). A later version of TER, TER-Plus (TERP) (Snover *et al.* 2009: 259–68), further extends the flexibility of the edit beyond the surface text level to allow edit operations on word stems, synonyms, and paraphrases.

RIBES

RIBES[24] (Isozaki *et al.* 2010) is an evaluation metric based on a rank correlation coefficient for comparing the word order between a candidate and a reference. It addresses the difficulty in evaluating translation between distant language pairs such as English and Japanese for which the word order is highly different. RIBES first matches the corresponding words between a candidate and a reference. It then generates two word order lists for the matched words in the candidate and reference, respectively, and calculates the correlation between the two lists by a rank correlation coefficient such as Kendall's τ (Kendall 1938: 81–93). The correlation value is normalized to obtain a score ranged from 0 to 1:

$$NKT = (\tau + 1) / 2$$

where NKT refers to the normalized Kendall's τ. Finally, the RIBES score for a candidate is computed as

$$RIBES = NKT \cdot P^{\alpha}$$

where P refers to the unigram precision of matched words in the candidate and α a parameter $(0 \leq \alpha \leq 1)$.

RIBES has been used as one of the popular metrics for MT evaluation in recent years, such as the 2020 and 2021 statistical MT evaluation workshop (Barrault *et al.* 2020; Akhbardeh *et al.* 2021) and the annual workshop on Asian translation.[25]

ATEC

ATEC[26] (Wong and Kit 2008, 2010: 141–51, 2012: 1060–68) is a lexical-informativeness based evaluation metric formulated to quantify the quality of MT output in terms of word choice and position, two fundamental aspects of text similarity. It goes beyond word matching to highlight the fact that each word carries a different amount of information contributing the meaning of a sentence and provides a nice coverage of MT evaluation at the word, sentence, and document level.

The assessment of word choice first maximizes the number of matched words in a candidate in terms of word form and/or sense and then quantifies their significance in terms of informativeness. Words in a candidate and a reference are matched with the aid of various language techniques and resources, including stemming and phonetic algorithms for identifying word stems and homophones and thesauri and various semantic similarity measures for identifying synonyms and near-synonyms, respectively. The informativeness of each matched and unmatched word is calculated using a term information measure to estimate the significance of each bit of information in a reference that is preserved or missed in a candidate, so that a higher weight is assigned to a more informative word.

Following the observation that position similarity of matched words also critically determines the quality of a candidate, two distance measures are formulated to quantify the divergence of word positioning and ordering between a candidate and a reference. They are used to adjust, by way of penalty, the significance of the information load of matched words.

The basic formulation of ATEC is based on the precision P and recall R of the adjusted matched information $m(c,r)$ in a candidate, which are defined as follows:

$$P = m(c,r) / i(c), \ R = m(c,r) / i(r), \text{ and}$$

$$m(c,r) = i(c,r) \, Penalty(c,r)$$

where $i(c,r)$, $i(c)$, and $i(r)$ are the information load of matched words, candidate, and reference, respectively, and $Penalty(c,r)$ is defined in terms of the positioning and ordering distance, their weights, and respective penalty limits. The final ATEC score is computed as the parameterized harmonic mean of P and R with a parameter to adjust their relative weights. It differs from other *Fmean*-based metrics (e.g. METEOR) in a number of ways, including the information-based precision and recall, the penalty by word positioning and ordering distance, and other technical details of parameterization.

The ATEC formulation has undergone several versions, testing the effectiveness of different features and information measures. The version in Wong and Kit (2010), despite its *ad hoc* fashion of formulation and parameter setting, illustrates impressive performance comparable to other state-of-the-art evaluation metrics.

For evaluation at the document level, connectivity between sentences in a document is further recruited as a new feature, approximated by a typical type of cohesion: lexical cohesion. It is a factor to account for the critical difference between human translation and MT output, in that the former uses more cohesive devices than the latter to tie sentences together to form a highly structured text. The lexical cohesion measure *LC* is defined in Wong and Kit (2012) as the ratio of lexical cohesion devices to content words in a candidate. It is integrated into ATEC as

$$ATEC_{doc} = \beta \cdot LC + (1 - \beta) \cdot ATEC$$

where β is a weight to balance LC and $ATEC$. In this way ATEC extends its granularity of evaluation from the sentence to the document level for a holistic account of translation quality.

Quality Estimation

In contrast with the similarity-based MT evaluation, quality estimation (QE) is intended to 'predict' quality of MT output without reference to any human translation. The focus of prediction ranges from the quality of MT output (e.g. fidelity and intelligibility) to the effort of post-editing the output and the identification of output sentences which may contain critical errors (Specia *et al.* 2021). Potential use of QE includes providing feedback to MT developers for system tuning, selecting the best MT output from multiple systems, and filtering out poor MT outputs that can hardly be comprehended or require a considerable amount of effort for post-editing.

The rationale, or assumption, of QE is that quality of MT output is, to a certain extent, determined by a number of features of source text and source/target language. For instance, the length and the structural complexity of a source sentence usually have an inverse correlation with the quality of its output. Also, the lengths of the source and target sentence are normally close to a particular ratio, and a significant deviation from this ratio may signal problematic output. It is then possible to train a QE predictor with certain features, using available machine learning techniques to capture the relationship between these features and quality ratings of MT output in training data. The number of features may range from dozens to several hundreds, as illustrated in works by Blatz *et al.* (2003), Rojas and Aikawa (2006: 2534–37), and Specia *et al.* (2010: 39–50), among many others.

QE can be categorized into *strong* and *weak* forms according to precision of estimation. The former gives a numerical estimate of correctness as a probability or a score in a given range, whereas the latter gives only a binary classification of correctness (e.g. 'good' vs. 'bad' translations). Recent progress in QE has demonstrated comparable performance to that of commonly used automatic evaluation metrics in the field in terms of correlation with human judgments (Specia *et al.* 2010: 39–50).

Meta-Evaluation

Automatic evaluation metrics and QE measures both need to be evaluated by so-called *meta-evaluation* in order to validate their reliability and identify their strengths and weaknesses. It has become one of the main themes in various open MT evaluations. The reliability of an evaluation metric depends on its consistency with human judgments, that is, the correlation of its evaluation results with manual assessment, to be measured by correlation coefficients. Commonly used correlation coefficients for this purpose include Pearson's r (Pearson 1900: 157–75), Spearman's ρ (Spearman 1904: 72–101), and Kendall's τ (Kendall 1938: 81–93). The magnitude of correlation between evaluation scores and human judgment serves as the most important indicator of the performance of a metric.

Using the correlation rate with human judgment as objective function, parameters of an evaluation metric can be optimized. Two parameters that have been extensively studied are the amount of test data and the number of reference versions needed to rank MT systems reliably. Different experiments (Coughlin 2003: 63–70; Estrella *et al.* 2007: 167–74; Zhang and Vogel 2004: 85–94) give results to support that a minimum of 250 sentences are required for texts of the same domain and 500 for different domains. As there are various ways to translate a sentence, relying on only one version of reference may miss many other possible translations. Hence multiple references are recommended for necessary coverage of translation options. Finch *et al.* (2004: 2019–22) find that the correlation rate of a metric usually rises along with the number of references in use and becomes steady at four: No significant gain is then further obtained from more references. Furthermore, Coughlin (2003: 63–70) shows that even a single reference can yield a reliable evaluation result if the size of test data is large enough, i.e., 500 sentences or above, or the text domain is highly technical, such as computers.

Nevertheless, the reliability of evaluation metrics remains a highly disputed issue. Although the evaluation results of automatic metrics do correlate well with human judgment in most cases, there are still discordant ones. For instance, Culy and Riehemann (2003: 1–8) show that BLEU performs poorly on ranking MT output and human translation for literary texts, and some MT outputs even erroneously outscore professional human translations. Callison-Burch *et al.* (2006: 249–56) also give an example in a 2005 NIST MT evaluation exercise that a system ranked at the top in human evaluation is ranked only sixth by BLEU scoring. Thurmair (2005) attributes the unreliable performance of evaluation metrics, especially BLEU, to the way they score translation quality. Since most evaluation metrics rely heavily on word matching against reference translation, a direct word-to-word translation is likely to yield a high evaluation score, but a free translation would then be a disaster. Babych *et al.* (2005: 412–18) state that the evaluation metrics currently in use in the field cannot give a 'universal' prediction of human perception of translation quality, and their predictive power is 'local' to a particular language or text type. The Metrics for Machine Translation Challenge[27] that aims at formally evaluating existing automatic MT evaluation technology results in the following views on the shortcomings of current metrics (NIST 2010):

- They have not yet been proved able to consistently predict the usefulness, adequacy, and reliability of MT technologies.
- They have not demonstrated that they are as meaningful in target languages other than English.
- They need more insights into what properties of a translation should be evaluated and into how to evaluate those properties.

Currently, MT evaluation results based on automatic metrics are mainly used for ranking systems. They provide no other useful information about the quality of a particular piece of translation. Human evaluation is still indispensable when an in-depth and informative analysis is needed.

Summary

MT/CAT evaluation is characterized by its multi-dimensional nature. Focusing on addressing the issue of interpretation of translation 'quality', different modes of evaluation have been developed, with different criteria for different purposes, applications, and users. Methodologically they belong to the categories of software evaluation, using existing standards and criteria, and text quality assessment, using a diversity of manual and automatic methods.

A genuine challenge of evaluating MT output lies in the critical difference between MT and human translation. While the quality of human translation is expected to be publishable in general, the best quality of MT in the general domain is at most suitable for 'gisting' only, except those systems specifically tailor-made for specialized domains. Evaluation methods for human translation are not directly applicable to MT without necessary modification. Both the standard of acceptable translation quality and evaluation criteria have to be adjusted accordingly in order to avoid over-expectation from MT and to cope with the context of practical use of MT.

The current trend of MT evaluation is shifting from human assessment towards automatic evaluation using automatic metrics. Despite the overall strong correlation between automatic and manual evaluation results, as evidenced in previous works, automatic metrics are not good enough to resolve all doubts on their validity and reliability. In practice, they do not directly assess the quality of MT output. Rather, they measure how similar a piece of MT output is to a human translation reference. Theoretical support is yet to be provided for basing the evaluation on the relation between text similarity and translation quality, although there has been experimental evidence to support the correlation of these two variables. It has been in our agenda to further explore whether such a correlation would remain strong, constant, and even valid across evaluation contexts involving different language pairs, text genera, and systems.

Notes

1 ALPAC: The Automatic Language Processing Advisory Committee.
2 However, the original interpretation of the data in Orr and Small (1967) is generally positive, concluding that MT outputs 'were surprisingly good and well worth further consideration' while noting the poorer quality of MT outputs in comparison to human translations. Comparing this with the contrasting reading in the ALPAC report, we can see that the same evaluation result can be inconsistently interpreted with regard to different expectations, perspectives, and purposes.
3 DARPA: the US government Defense Advanced Research Projects Agency.
4 IWSLT: the International Workshop on Spoken Language Translation.
5 Campagne d'Evaluation de Systemes de Traduction Automatique (Machine Translation Systems Evaluation Campaign), at www.technolangue.net/article.php3?id_article=199
6 http://nist.gov/itl/iad/mig/openmt.cfm
7 Workshop on Statistical Machine Translation, at www.statmt.org
8 This term refers to the kind of system testing that focuses only on the output without any examination of the internal operations producing such an output.
9 An extended standard, ISO/IEC 25010, was released in 2011 as a replacement of ISO/IEC 9126, defining 8 quality characteristics and 31 sub-characteristics.
10 ISLE: International Standards for Language Engineering.
11 FEMTI: Framework for the Evaluation of Machine Translation in ISLE, at www.issco.unige.ch/en/research/projects/isle/femti/
12 In essence, a source text may have multiple versions of acceptable translation, and any of them can hardly be regarded as the sole 'model answer'. In practice, however, given a test set of sufficient size, using a single translation as reference usually yields reliable evaluation result.
13 American Translators Association, at www.atanet.org
14 Quoted from the Multiple-Translation Chinese (MTC) dataset part-2 (Huang *et al.* 2003).
15 This is in contrast with the early thought that MT outputs should share the same quality scale as human translations. For instance, it was once conceived in Miller and Beebe-Center (1956) that 'a scale of the quality of translations should be . . . applicable to any translation, whether produced by a machine or by a human translator'.
16 TOEFL: Test of English as a Foreign Language.
17 For example, the NIST Open MT Evaluation 2009 (www.itl.nist.gov/iad/mig/tests/mt/2009/) includes four sections, each of 31,000 to 45,000 words of evaluation data and 10 to 23 participating systems, that is, a total of 2.4 million words of MT output to evaluate, indicating the impracticality of resorting to any manual evaluation approach at a reasonable cost and in a reasonable time.
18 BLEU: BiLingual Evaluation Understudy.
19 For instance, the co-occurring n-grams in *C1* and *R1* are as follows.

> 1-gram: It, is, a, guide, to, action, ensures, that, the, military, the, commands, the, party;
> 2-gram: It is, is a, a guide, guide to, to action, ensures that, that the, the military;
> 3-gram: It is a, is a guide, a guide to, guide to action, ensures that the, that the military.

20 NIST: the National Institute of Standards and Technology.
21 METEOR: Metric for Evaluation of Translation with Explicit Ordering.

22 In general, a recall-oriented metric measures the proportion of reference content preserved in a translation candidate, whereas a precision-oriented one focuses on the proportion of candidate content matched with a reference.

23 TER: Translation Edit Rate.

24 RIBES: Rank-based Intuitive Bilingual Evaluation Score.

25 https://lotus.kuee.kyoto-u.ac.jp/WAT/

26 ATEC: Assessment of Text Essential Characteristics.

27 www.nist.gov/itl/iad/mig/metricsmatr.cfm

Bibliography

Akhbardeh, Farhad, Arkady Arkhangorodsky, Magdalena Biesialska, Ondřej Bojar, Rajen Chatterjee, Vishrav Chaudhary, Marta R. Costa-jussa, Cristina España-Bonet, Angela Fan, Christian Federmann, Markus Freitag, Yvette Graham, Roman Grundkiewicz, Barry Haddow, Leonie Harter, Kenneth Heafield, Christopher Homan, Matthias Huck, Kwabena Amponsah-Kaakyire, Jungo Kasai, Daniel Khashabi, Kevin Knight, Tom Kocmi, Philipp Koehn, Nicholas Lourie, Christof Monz, Makoto Morishita, Masaaki Nagata, Ajay Nagesh, Toshiaki Nakazawa, Matteo Negri, Santanu Pal, Allahsera Auguste Tapo, Marco Turchi, Valentin Vydrin, and Marcos Zampieri (2021) 'Findings of the 2021 Conference on Machine Translation (WMT21)', in *Proceedings of the Sixth Conference on Machine Translation*, online, Association for Computational Linguistics, 1–88.

Akiba, Yasuhiro, Marcello Federico, Noriko Kando, Hiromi Nakaiwa, Michael Paul, and Jun'ichi Tsujii (2004) 'Overview of the IWSLT04 Evaluation Campaign', in *Proceedings of the International Workshop on Spoken Language Translation (IWSLT-04)*, Kyoto, Japan, 1–12.

ALPAC (1966) *Languages and Machines: Computers in Translation and Linguistics*. A report by the Automatic Language Processing Advisory Committee, Division of Behavioral Sciences, National Academy of Sciences, National Research Council, Washington, DC: National Academy of Sciences, National Research Council, 1966.

Arnold, Doug, Lorna Balkan, Siety Meijer, R. Lee Humphreys, and Louisa Sadler (1994) *Machine Translation: An Introductory Guide*, London: Blackwells-NCC.

Babych, Bogdan, Anthony Hartley, and Debbie Elliott (2005) 'Estimating the Predictive Power of N-gram MT Evaluation Metrics across Language and Text Types', in *Proceedings of Machine Translation Summit X: 2nd Workshop on Example-Based Machine Translation*, 12–16 September 2005, Phuket, Thailand, 412–18.

Banerjee, Satanjeev and Alon Lavie (2005) 'METEOR: An Automatic Metric for MT Evaluation with Improved Correlation with Human Judgments', in *Proceedings of the ACL Workshop on Intrinsic and Extrinsic Evaluation Measures for Machine Translation and/or Summarization*, Ann Arbor, MI, 65–72.

Barrault, Loïc, Magdalena Biesialska, Ondřej Bojar, Marta R. Costa-jussà, Christian Federmann, Yvette Graham, Roman Grundkiewicz, Barry Haddow, Matthias Huck, Eric Joanis, Tom Kocmi, Philipp Koehn, Chi-kiu Lo, Nikola Ljubešić, Christof Monz, Makoto Morishita, Masaaki Nagata, Toshiaki Nakazawa, Santanu Pal, Matt Post, and Marcos Zampieri (2020) 'Findings of the 2020 Conference on Machine Translation (WMT20)', in *Proceedings of the Fifth Conference on Machine Translation*, online, Association for Computational Linguistics, 1–55.

Blatz, John, Erin Fitzgerald, George Foster, Simona Gandrabur, Cyril Goutte, Alex Kulesza, Alberto Sanchis, and Nicola Ueffing (2003) *Final Report of Johns Hopkins 2003 Summer Workshop on Confidence Estimation for Machine Translation*, Johns Hopkins University.

Callison-Burch, Chris, Cameron Fordyce, Philipp Koehn, Christof Monz, and Josh Schroeder (2008) 'Further Meta-evaluation of Machine Translation', in *Proceedings of the ACL Workshop on Statistical Machine Translation (WMT-08)*, Columbus, OH, 70–106.

Callison-Burch, Chris, Philipp Koehn, Christof Monz, and Josh Schroeder (2009) 'Findings of the 2009 Workshop on Statistical Machine Translation', in *Proceedings of the EACL Workshop on Statistical Machine Translation (WMT-09)*, Athens, Greece, 1–28.

Callison-Burch, Chris, Miles Osborne, and Philipp Koehn (2006) 'Re-evaluating the Role of BLEU in Machine Translation Research', in *Proceedings of the European Chapter of the Association for Computational Linguistics (EACL-06)*, Trento, Italy, 249–56.

Carroll, John B. (1966) 'An Experiment in Evaluating the Quality of Translations', *Mechanical Translation and Computational Linguistics* 9(3–4): 55–66.

Catford, John Cunnison (1965) *A Linguistic Theory of Translation: An Essay in Applied Linguistics*, London: Oxford University Press.

Choukri, Khalid, Olivier Hamon, and Djamel Mostefa (2007) 'MT Evaluation and TC-STAR', in *MT Summit XI Workshop on Automatic Procedures in MT Evaluation*, Copenhagen, Denmark.

Church, Kenneth W. and Eduard H. Hovy (1993) 'Good Applications for Crummy Machine Translation', *Machine Translation* 8(4): 239–58.

Coughlin, Deborah (2003) 'Correlating Automated and Human Assessments of Machine Translation Quality', in *Proceedings of Machine Translation Summit IX: Machine Translation for Semitic Languages: Issues and Approaches*, 23–27 September 2003, New Orleans, LA, 63–70.

Culy, Christopher and Susanne Z. Riehemann (2003) 'The Limits of N-gram Translation Evaluation Metrics', in *Proceedings of Machine Translation Summit IX: Machine Translation for Semitic Languages: Issues and Approaches*, 23–27 September 2003, New Orleans, LA, 1–8.

Diederich, Paul Bernard (1974) *Measuring Growth in English*, Urbana, IL: National Council of Teachers of English.

Doddington, George (2002) 'Automatic Evaluation of Machine Translation Quality Using N-gram Co-occurrence Statistics', in *Proceedings of Human Language Technology Conference (HLT-02)*, San Diego, CA, 138–45.

Doherty, Stephen, Federico Gaspari, Declan Groves, Josef van Genabith, Lucia Specia, Aljoscha Burchardt, Arle Lommel, and Hans Uszkoreit (2013) 'Mapping the Industry I: Findings on Translation Technologies and Quality Assessment', *QTLaunchPad*. Available at: https://doras.dcu.ie/19474/1/Version_Participants_Final.pdf

Eck, Matthias and Chiori Hori (2005) 'Overview of the IWSLT 2005 Evaluation Campaign', in *Proceedings of the International Workshop on Spoken Language Translation (IWSLT-05)*, Pittsburgh, PA, 11–32.

Estrella, Paula, Olivier Hamon, and Andrei Popescu-Belis (2007) 'How Much Data Is Needed for Reliable MT Evaluation? Using Bootstrapping to Study Human and Automatic Metrics', in *Proceedings of Machine Translation Summit XI*, 10–14 September 2007, Copenhagen Business School, Copenhagen, Denmark, 167–74.

Finch, Andrew, Yasuhiro Akiba, and Eiichiro Sumita (2004) 'How Does Automatic Machine Translation Evaluation Correlate with Human Scoring as the Number of Reference Translations Increases?', in *Proceedings of the 4th International Conference on Language Resources and Evaluation (LREC 2004)*, 26–28 May 2004, Lisbon, Portugal, 2019–22.

Flanagan, Mary (1994) 'Error Classification for MT Evaluation', in *Proceedings of the 1st Conference of the Association for Machine Translation in the Americas: Technology Partnerships for Crossing the Language Barrier (AMTA-94)*, Columbia, MD, 65–72.

Fordyce, Cameron S. (2007) 'Overview of the IWSLT 2007 Evaluation Campaign', in *Proceedings of the International Workshop on Spoken Language Translation (IWSLT-07)*, Trento, Italy.

Freitag, Markus, Ricardo Rei, Nitika Mathur, Chi-kiu Lo, Craig Stewart, George Foster, Alon Lavie, and Ondřej Bojar (2021) 'Results of the WMT21 Metrics Shared Task: Evaluating Metrics with Expert-based Human Evaluations on TED and News Domain', in *Proceedings of the Sixth Conference on Machine Translation (WMT)*, Association for Computational Linguistics, 733–74.

Graham, Yvette, Timothy Baldwin, Alistair Moffat, and Justin Zobel (2017) 'Can Machine Translation Systems be Evaluated by the Crowd Alone', *Natural Language Engineering* 23(1): 3–30.

Hayes, John R., Linda Flower, Karen A. Schriver, James F. Stratman, and Linda Carey (1987) 'Cognitive Processes in Revision', in Sheldon Rosenberg (ed.) *Advances in Applied Psycholinguistics, Volume II: Reading, Writing, and Language Processing*, Cambridge: Cambridge University Press, 176–240.

House, Juliane (2009) 'Quality', in Mona Baker and Gabriela Saldanha (eds.) *Routledge Encyclopedia of Translation Studies*, 2nd edition, London and New York: Routledge, 222–24.

Hovy, Eduard, Margaret King, and Andrei Popescu-Belis (2002) 'Principles of Context-based Machine Translation Evaluation', *Machine Translation* 17(1): 43–75.

Huang, Shudong, David Graff, Kevin Walker, David Miller, Xiaoyi Ma, Chris Cieri, and George Doddington (2003) *Multiple-Translation Chinese (MTC) Part 2*, Linguistic Data Consortium. https://doi.org/10.35111/ysj7-3f12.

Hutchins, W. John (2003) 'The Development and Use of Machine Translation Systems and Computer-based Translation Tools', *International Journal of Translation* 15(1): 5–26.

Hutchins, W. John and Harold L. Somers (1992) *An Introduction to Machine Translation*, London: Academic Press.

ISLE (2001) 'Evaluation of Machine Translation'. Available at: www.isi.edu/natural-language/mteval.

ISO/IEC-9126 (1991) ISO/IEC 9126:1991 (E) – Information Technology – Software Product Evaluation – Quality Characteristics and Guidelines for their Use. ISO/IEC, Geneva.

ISO/IEC-9126-1 (2001) ISO/IEC 9126-1:2001 (E) – Software Engineering – Product Quality – Part 1: Quality Model. ISO/IEC, Geneva.

Isozaki, Hideki, Tsutomu Hirao, Kevin Duh, Katsuhito Sudoh, and Hajime Tsukada (2010) 'Automatic Evaluation of Translation Quality for Distant Language Pairs', in *Proceedings of the 2010 Conference on Empirical Methods in Natural Language Processing*, Cambridge, MA, 944–52.

Kendall, Maurice George (1938) 'A New Measure of Rank Correlation', *Biometrika* 30(1–2): 81–93.

Kit, Chunyu and Tak-Ming Wong (2008) 'Comparative Evaluation of Online Machine Translation Systems with Legal Texts', *Law Library Journal* 100(2): 299–321.

Krauwer, Steven (1993) 'Evaluation of MT Systems: A Programmatic View', *Machine Translation* 8(1–2): 59–66.

Lavie, A. and A. Agarwal (2007) 'METEOR: An Automatic Metric for MT Evaluation with High Levels of Correlation with Human Judgments', in *Proceedings of the ACL Workshop on Statistical Machine Translation (WMT-07)*, Prague, Czech Republic, 228–31.

LDC (2002) 'Linguistic Data Annotation Specification: Assessment of Fluency and Adequacy in Arabic-English and Chinese-English Translations'. Available at: www.ldc.upenn.edu/Projects/TIDES/Translation/TransAssess02.pdf.

Lehrberger, John and Laurent Bourbeau (1988) *Machine Translation: Linguistic Characteristics of MT Systems and General Methodology of Evaluation*, Amsterdam and Philadelphia: John Benjamins Publishing Company.

Liu, Qun, Hongxu Hou, Shouxun Lin, Yueliang Qian, Yujie Zhang, and Isahara Hitoshi (2005) 'Introduction to China's HTRDP Machine Translation Evaluation', in *Proceedings of Machine Translation Summit X: 2nd Workshop on Example-Based Machine Translation*, 12–16 September 2005, Phuket, Thailand, 18–22.

Lo, Chi-kiu and Dekai Wu (2011) 'MEANT: An Inexpensive, High-accuracy, Semi-automatic Metric for Evaluating Translation Utility via Semantic Frames', in *Proceedings of the 49th Annual Meeting of the Association for Computational Linguistics (ACL-11)*, Portland, OR, 220–29.

Lommel, Arle, Aljoscha Burchardt, and Hans Uszkoreit (2015) 'Multidimensional Quality Metrics (MQM) Definition'. Available at: www.qt21.eu/mqm-definition/definition-2015-12-30.html.

Miller, George A. and J. G. Beebe-Center (1956) 'Some Psychological Methods for Evaluating the Quality of Translations', *Mechanical Translation* 3(3): 73–80.

Morland, D. Verne (2002) 'Nutzlos, bien pratique, or muy util? Business Users Speak out on the Value of Pure Machine Translation', in *Translating and the Computer 24*, London: ASLIB.

Newmark, Peter (1982) *Approaches to Translation*, Oxford: Pergamon Press.

Newmark, Peter (1988) *A Textbook of Translation*, New York and London: Prentice Hall.

Nida, Eugene A. (1964) *Towards a Science of Translating*, Leiden: E. J. Brill.

NIST (2010) 'The NIST Metrics for MAchine TRanslation 2010 Challenge (MetricsMaTr10): Evaluation Plan'. Available at: www.nist.gov/itl/iad/mig/metricsmatr10.cfm.

Orr, David B. and Victor H. Small (1967) 'Comprehensibility of Machine-aided Translations of Russian Scientific Documents', *Mechanical Translation and Computational Linguistics* 10(1–2): 1–10.

Papineni, Kishore, Salim Roukos, Todd Ward, and Wei-Jing Zhu (2001) 'BLEU: A Method for Automatic Evaluation of Machine Translation', *IBM Research Report RC22176 (W0109-022)*. Available at: https://dominoweb.draco.res.ibm.com/reports/RC22176.pdf

Paul, Michael (2006) 'Overview of the IWSLT06 Evaluation Campaign', in *Proceedings of the International Workshop on Spoken Language Translation (IWSLT-06)*, Kyoto, Japan, 1–15.

Paul, Michael (2008) 'Overview of the IWSLT 2008 Evaluation Campaign', in *Proceedings of the International Workshop on Spoken Language Translation (IWSLT-08)*, Hawaii, HI, 1–17.

Paul, Michael (2009) 'Overview of the IWSLT 2009 Evaluation Campaign', in *Proceedings of the International Workshop on Spoken Language Translation (IWSLT-09)*, Tokyo, Japan, 1–18.

Paul, Michael, Marcello Federico, and Sebastian Stüker (2010) 'Overview of the IWSLT 2010 Evaluation Campaign', in *Proceedings of the International Workshop on Spoken Language Translation (IWSLT-10)*, Paris, France, 3–27.

Pearson, Karl (1900) 'On the Criterion That a Given System of Deviations from the Probable in the Case of a Correlated System of Variables is Such That It Can Be Reasonably Supposed to Have Arisen from Random Sampling', *Philosophical Magazine* 50(5): 157–75.

Reeder, Florence (2001a) 'In One Hundred Words or Less', in *Proceedings of the MT Summit Workshop on MT Evaluation: Who Did What to Whom?* Santiago de Compostela, Spain, 67–71.

Reeder, Florence (2001b) 'Is That Your Final Answer?', in *Proceedings of the 1st International Conference on Human Language Technology Research (HLT-01)*, San Diego, CA.

Rojas, David M. and Takako Aikawa (2006) 'Predicting MT Quality as a Function of the Source Language', in *Proceedings of the 5th International Conference on Language Resources and Evaluation (LREC-06)*, Genova, Italy, 2534–37.

Schwarzl, Anja (2001) *The (Im)Possibilities of Machine Translation*, Frankfurt am Main: Peter Lang Publishing.

Slocum, Jonathan (1985) 'A Survey of Machine Translation: Its History, Current Status, and Future Prospects', *Computational Linguistics* 11(1): 1–17.

Slype, Georges van (1979) *Critical Study of Methods for Evaluating the Quality of Machine Translation*, Tech. rep. Bureau Marcel van Dijk/European Commission, Brussels.

Snover, Matthew, Bonnie J. Dorr, Richard Schwartz, Linnea Micciulla, and John Makhoul (2006) 'A Study of Translation Edit Rate with Targeted Human Annotation', in *Proceedings of the 7th Conference of the Association for Machine Translation in the Americas: Visions for the Future of Machine Translation (AMTA-06)*, Cambridge, MA, 223–31.

Snover, Matthew, Nitin Madnani, Bonnie J. Dorr, and Richard Schwartz (2009) 'Fluency, Adequacy, or HTER? Exploring Different Human Judgments with a Tunable MT Metric', in *Proceedings of the 4th Workshop on Statistical Machine Translation (WMT-09)*, 30–31 March 2009, Athens, Greece, 259–68.

Somers, Harold L. and Elizabeth Wild (2000) 'Evaluating Machine Translation: The Cloze Procedure Revisited', in *Proceedings of the 22nd International Conference on Translating and the Computer*, London, the United Kingdom.

Spearman, Charles Edward (1904) 'The Proof and Measurement of Association between Two Things', *The American Journal of Psychology* 15: 72–101.

Specia, Lucia, Frédéric Blain, Marina Fomicheva, Chrysoula Zerva, Zhenhao Li, Vishrav Chaudhary, and André F. T. Martins (2021) 'Findings of the WMT 2021 Shared Task on Quality Estimation', in *Proceedings of the Sixth Conference on Machine Translation*, online, Association for Computational Linguistics, 684–725.

Specia, Lucia, Dhwaj Raj, and Marco Turchi (2010) 'Machine Translation Evaluation versus Quality Estimation', *Machine Translation* 24(1): 39–50.

Taylor, Kathryn and John White (1998) 'Predicting What MT Is Good for: User Judgements and Task Performance', in *Proceedings of the 3rd Conference of the Association for Machine Translation in the Americas: Machine Translation and the Information Soup (AMTA-98)*, 28–31 October 1998, Langhorne, PA, 364–73.

Taylor, Wilson L. (1953) 'Cloze Procedure: A New Tool for Measuring Readability', *Journalism Quarterly* 30: 415–33.

Thurmair, Gregor (2005) 'Automatic Means of MT Evaluation', in *Proceedings of the ELRA-HLT Evaluation Workshop*, Malta.

Tomita, Masaru (1992) 'Application of the TOEFL Test to the Evaluation of Japanese–English MT', in *Proceedings of the AMTA Workshop on MT evaluation*, San Diego, CA.

Tomita, Masaru, Masako Shirai, Junya Tsutsumi, Miki Matsumura, and Yuki Yoshikawa (1993) 'Evaluation of MT Systems by TOEFL', in *Proceedings of the 5th International Conference on Theoretical and Methodological Issues in Machine Translation: MT in the Next Generation (TMI-93)*, 14–16 July 1993, Kyoto, Japan, 252–65.

Trujillo, Arturo (1999) *Translation Engines: Techniques for Machine Translation*, Heidelberg: Springer-Verlag.

Vilar, David, Jia Xu, Luis Fernando D'Haro, and Hermann Ney (2006) 'Error Analysis of Statistical Machine Translation Output', in *Proceedings of the 5th International Conference on Language Resources and Evaluation (LREC-06)*, Genoa, Italy, 697–702.

White, John S. (2001) 'Predicting Intelligibility from Fidelity in MT Evaluation', in *Proceedings of the MT Summit Workshop on MT Evaluation*, Santiago de Compostela, Spain, 35–37.

White, John S. (2003) 'How to Evaluate Machine Translation', in Harold L. Somers (ed.) *Computers and Translation: A Translator's Guide*, Amsterdam and Philadelphia: John Benjamins Publishing Company, 211–44.

White, John S. and Theresa A. O'Connell (1994) 'Evaluation in the ARPA Machine Translation Program: 1993 Methodology', in *Proceedings of the Workshop on Human Language Technology (HLT-94)*, Plainsboro, NJ, 134–40.

White, John S., Theresa A. O'Connell, and Lynn M. Carlson (1993) 'Evaluation of Machine Translation', in *Proceedings of the Workshop on Human Language Technology (HLT-93)*, Plainsboro, NJ, 206–10.

White, John S., Theresa A. O'Connell, and Francis E. O'Mara (1994) 'The ARPA MT Evaluation Methodologies: Evolution, Lessons, and Future Approaches', in *Proceedings of the 1st Conference of the Association for Machine Translation in the Americas (AMTA-94)*, Columbia, MD, 193–205.

Wong, Tak-Ming and Kit Chunyu (2008) 'Word Choice and Word Position for Automatic MT Evaluation', in *Proceedings of the AMTA 2008 Workshop – NIST MetricsMATR 08*, Waikiki, HI.

Wong, Tak-Ming and Kit Chunyu (2010) 'ATEC: Automatic Evaluation of Machine Translation via Word Choice and Word Order', *Machine Translation* 23(2–3): 141–51.

Wong, Tak-Ming and Kit Chunyu (2012) 'Extending Machine Translation Evaluation Metrics with Lexical Cohesion to Document Level', in *Proceedings of the Conference on Empirical Methods in Natural Language Processing and Computational Natural Language Learning (EMNLP-CoNLL)*, Jeju, Korea, 1060–68.

Zhang, Ying and Stephan Vogel (2004) 'Measuring Confidence Intervals for the Machine Translation Evaluation Metrics', in *Proceedings of the 10th Conference on Theoretical and Methodological Issues in Machine Translation (TMI-04)*, 4–6 October 2004, Baltimore, MD, 85–94.

13

THE TEACHING OF MACHINE TRANSLATION

The Chinese University of Hong Kong as a Case Study

Cecilia Wong Shuk Man

Introduction

The boost in technological development has led to a need to include the teaching of technology in traditional disciplines technically, practically and theoretically. Translation training is no exception, and occupational needs must be met to cope with the technological changes. As Ignacio (2010: 275–82) states, 'Translation education needs to give graduates not only the ability to use the technology, but also the frame through which to understand such change'.

According to Hutchins (1986), the idea of using mechanical devices to overcome language barriers was first suggested in the 17th century. However, all proposals required human translators to use the tools and involved no construction of machines. After the invention of mechanical calculators in the 19th and 20th centuries, pioneering activities were initiated by Charles Babbage. The first proposal for 'Translating Machines' appeared in 1933. Two patents for mechanical dictionaries have been issued: French: Georges Artsrouni (July 1993) and Russian: Petr Petrovich Smirnov-Troyanskii (September 1993). Georges Artsrouni's idea, 'Mechanical Brain', was a device worked by electric motor for recording and retrieving information on a broad paper band, which could store several thousand characters. Each line on the tape contained the entry word (SL word) and equivalents in other languages (TL equivalents). Perforations were coded on a second paper or metal band as a selector of correspondences. Petr Petrovich Smirnov-Troyanskii created a machine for the selection and printing of words while translating from one language into another or into several others simultaneously. He envisaged three stages in the translation process, and the machine was involved in the second stage as an 'automated dictionary'. It included both bilingual and multilingual translation and became the basic framework for subsequent machine translation systems.

In 1946–1949, an electronic digital computer was created following World War II. The start of development of the MT system was initiated by conversations and correspondence between Andrew D. Booth (a British crystallographer) and Warren Weaver of the Rockefeller Foundation in 1947. Andrew D. Booth and Richard H. Richens collaborated in developing a strict word-by-word dictionary translation by using punched card machinery on a wide variety of languages in 1948. In their approach, they segmented words into stems and endings in order to reduce the size of the dictionaries and introduce grammatical information into the system. In

DOI: 10.4324/9781003168348-14

1949, Warren Weaver suggested that 'some reasonable way could be found of using the micro context to settle the difficult cases of ambiguity'. He believed that the translation problem could largely be solved by 'statistical semantic studies' as logical structures of language with probabilistic uniformities. He thought the investigation of language invariants or universals was the most promising approach. In 1950, Erwin Reifler, head of the Department of Far Eastern and Slavic Languages and Literature at the University of Washington in Seattle, introduced the concepts of 'pre-editor' to prepare the text for input into the computer (to indicate the grammatical category of each word in SL) and 'post-editor' to resolve problems and tidy up the style of the translation (to select the correct translation from the possibilities found and rearrange the word order of the TL).

In 1951, the first full-time researcher on machine translation (MT), Yehoshua Bar-Hillel, produced a survey of the (con-)current position of MT at the end of 1951. He suggested the use of machines in different processes: (1) analyzing each word into stem and grammatical categories, (2) identifying small syntactical units and (3) transforming a sentence into another that is the logical equivalent to it. He suggested a second stage – building an explicit, programmable method for syntactic analysis. He also considered the possibilities of constructing a universal grammar or 'transfer grammars . . . in which the grammar of one language is stated in categories appropriate to some other language'. In 1952, the Rockefeller Foundation sponsored the first conference on MT, held at the Massachusetts Institute of Technology (MIT) and organized by Bar-Hillel. After the 1952 conference, an MT research team was established by Leon Dostert at Georgetown University. In collaboration with IBM, by the end of 1953, the team had developed the first MT program with Russian-English translation. Its public demonstration in January 1954 was the first real demonstration of MT on a computer. It was the first implementation of translation beyond word-for-word translation. There was no pre-editing required. In the MT system was a vocabulary of just 250 Russian words, only 6 rules of grammar and a carefully selected sample of Russian sentences. So there were limitations. It showed, however, that MT was a feasible objective for further development.

Machine translation has been developing for over sixty years. Since the start of the government-motivated and military-supported Russian-English translations in the United States in the 1950s and 1960s, there has been intensive research activity. After the Automatic Language Processing Advisory Committee (ALPAC) report, machine translation was considered a 'failure' and no longer worthy of serious scientific consideration. From the mid-1960s, machine translation research was ignored. However, in the 1970s, multilingual problems prevailed in the European Community. A change in attitude toward machine translation arose in Europe. The Commission of the European Community (CEC) purchased the English–French version of the SYSTRAN system in 1976 (a greatly improved product of the earliest systems developments at Georgetown University in Washington, DC). In the United States, the main activity concentrated on English translations of Russian scientific and technical materials. A Russian–English system, SYSTRAN (developed throughout the lean years after ALPAC), had been used by both the US Air Force (USAF) since 1970 and the National Aeronautic and Space Administration (NASA) in 1974–75. The CEC commissioned the development of a French–English version in 1977 and Italian–English version in 1979 with the World Translation Center (WTC). In 1979, the CEC began to set up the EUROTRA project, building on the work of the Groupe d'Etudes pour la Traduction Automatique (GETA) and the Saarbrücjen automatic translation system (SUSY) groups led by Serge Perschke. It aimed at producing a 'pre-industrial' multilingual MT system of advanced design (a linguistic knowledge system) for the European Community languages. In the late 1970s, the Pan American Health Organization (PAHO) began development of a Spanish-English MT system

(SPANAM). Since 1980, it has been operational. In 1978, the US Air Force funded work on the METAL system at the Linguistics Research Center (LRC) at the University of Texas in Austin to develop a German–English system for translating telecommunication and data processing texts. The TAUM group sponsored by the Canadian Research Council began a project at the University of Montreal in 1965. Results of work at the TAUM group led to the installation of the METEO system in 1977. It was an English–French system for translating public weather forecasts. In the 1980s, the story was of these initiatives and the exploitation of results in neighboring disciplines. As Japanese is an isolated language with no similarities to any other language, the need for good translation services is crucial to Japan's commercial and economic growth. Therefore, a great demand for translation from and to English and other languages led to rapid machine translation activity in Japan. In the 1980s, the Japanese 'fifth generation' project had established a major position in the future world economy. In recent years, different machine translation systems have produced readable translations.

As Hutchins (1986) stated, 'Machine Translation is the application of computers to the translation of texts from one natural language into another'. Arnold *et al.* (1994) put it as 'the attempt to automate all, or part of, the process of translating from one human language to another'. A machine translation system tends to automate all of the translation process, whereas a computer-aided translation system is a partly automatic machine translation system equipped with computational storage tools and matching algorithms for past translation reuse. The translation process requires human intervention, and the translation decisions are mainly made by humans.

Throughout the development, machine translation systems have been evolving from the first-generation direct approach – doing word-to-word translation with the computer as electronic dictionary lookup – to the practical transfer approach, putting emphasis on the differences between language pairs in translating natural languages. This evolution was primarily in systems using linguistic rules and analyses as the translation framework. On the other hand, some systems employ a corpus-based approach in order to fully utilize the information resources available through access to the World Wide Web. With the abundant text data available from the internet, through the use of statistical calculation, machine translation systems can generate usable translation results from the calculated probabilities. Alternatively, systems can also directly make use of aligned translated texts as built-in translation memory for generating new translations. With an example-based machine translation approach, machine translation systems work like a computer-aided translation system. However, the translation memory is built in by developers instead of cumulatively created by users. Various approaches were invented as relatively new techniques for machine translation. Pattern-based as well as knowledge-based approaches are examples of such techniques, and they can be considered extensions of the basic linguistic transfer rule- and/or corpus-based approach. Nowadays, most of the machine translation systems use a hybrid approach so that they can take advantage of the different methods of translation.

The Teaching of Machine Translation: The Chinese University as a Case Study

The curriculum design of the master of arts in computer-aided translation (MACAT) program at the Chinese University of Hong Kong includes both theoretical and practical courses. Emphasis is placed on both the machine translation and computer-aided translation areas. After several decades' development on machine translation, we may introduce to the students the current scenario in the field, teaching them what machine translation is nowadays and equipping them with hands-on experience of the systems. In this chapter, an account of the experience of teaching the machine translation–related courses Editing Skills for Computer Translation and Computer Translation is given.

Different Course Structures Based on Different Aims and Objectives of the Computer Translation Courses (Frameworks of the Courses)

As introduced by Chan Sin-wai (2010: 86), the master of arts in computer-aided translation at the Chinese University of Hong Kong 'is a graduate program that places equal emphasis on computer-aided translation and machine translation'. In contrast to the required course on computer-aided translation (CAT), Introduction to Computer-Aided Translation, we have the elective course, Computer Translation, for introducing basic concepts and knowledge in computer translation. Editing Skills for Computer Translation is a required course for introducing techniques in making the best use of the results generated by machine translation systems.

Computer Translation – An Elective Course

Computer Translation is set as an introductory course for teaching basic concepts and theory concerning computer translation (with another complementary course, Introduction to Computer-Aided Translation, introducing concepts concerning CAT). It therefore focuses more on knowledge transmission. According to Somers (2003: 319–40), there are different perspectives in using machine translation (what we refer to as 'computer translation' here) in the classroom depending on the type of student. The perspectives include (1) teaching about computers and translation, (2) teaching the software to trainee translators, (3) teaching languages and (4) educating end users to use machine translation software. The Computer Translation course belongs to the first perspective, teaching about computers and translation, and the fourth perspective, educating students on the use of machine translation systems.

Curriculum Design

In the curriculum design, the Computer Translation course involves both an introduction to theoretical concepts and acquisition of practical skills. Machine translation is different from computer-aided translation. The whole translation process is automatically done by the computer. The quality of the translation is highly dependent on the design and implementation of the machine translation systems. Basic concepts on how computers translate then have to be introduced in Computer Translation. Students then have an idea of the steps (including natural language processing steps) undergone within the computer when making the translations. How the source language is analyzed and how the target translation output is generated is explained. Machine translation systems generate translations through various approaches using different computational algorithms. How the systems make their translations through these approaches is also introduced in the course. Different approaches employed in the translation systems play a significant role in giving accurate translation output, which also influences the quality of the output. Through understanding the approaches, students get to know the strengths and weaknesses of the translation systems and so can use suitable software for translating different specific genres. Through taking the course, students should be able to evaluate different translation systems by their performance in various aspects, including accuracy, speed and algorithm employed. Moreover, according to their different developmental strategies and target customers, various translation systems' strengths may lay with particular types of texts. In their group presentations done at the end of the course, each group of students has to evaluate the performance of different machine translation tools on specific genres (i.e. different genres for different groups) so that they can explore various performances of the software on different genres or text types in a collaborative evaluation. Through such an evaluation, students can make an informed decision when selecting certain systems for their own use. In preparing their presentations, they would have a lot of hands-on experience on different machine translation systems provided by the program.

The topics covered in Computer Translation include the following:

Introduction to computer translation, which includes the basic concepts of computer translation and the differences between computer and computer-aided translation.

Different approaches to computer translation, which include

- Corpus-based,
- Example-based,
- Rule-based,
- Knowledge-based,
- Memory-based,
- Pattern-based and
- Statistical approaches.
- Natural language text processing in computer translation, word segmentation, part-of-speech tagging and parsing.
- Hands-on experience in translation systems in lab sessions.
- Evaluation of translation systems as the group presentation project.

Practical Hands-on Experience

Hands-on experience of machine translation software is also one of the core aspects of the course, which can help to deepen relevant knowledge acquired by the students. We provide lab sessions in class for students to work on some of the state-of-the-art machine translation systems. Coincidently, Somers (2003) also stated that hands-on experience is essential in teaching machine translation to trainee translators. Although not all of the students in our course are trainee translators, it is still of value for some of the students to try the software and have real experience in using it. They may as a result locate a suitable tool for their own use and buy a copy of it. This involves the purchase and selection of suitable licenses of translation systems. In addition, there are a lot of online versions of various machine translation systems for evaluation use. However, the quality generated varies. Although it is costly to keep updating the licenses of the translation systems, it is worth doing so in order to equip students with the necessary techniques in using machine translation systems and meeting practical needs in real life. It also encourages respect for property rights and innovation, which can also boost the exchange of information. Besides, our department also provides resources for remote accessing of some of the translation systems so that students can conveniently make use of the software to do testing and prepare their presentation at a remote location. Students can then benefit by having more hands-on experience with the systems.

Class Interactive Participation

Class exercise and discussion is another strategy used to encourage active learning through exchanges among students. By the end of the course, students have to evaluate different software and understand its weaknesses. (This is also one of Somers' suggestions on teaching trainee translators about machine translation.) The students are encouraged to think of ways in which to improve the performance of the systems so that creativity cultivation and problem-solving skills can be fostered. Furthermore, it is hoped that interest in further research in the area could be sown.

Means of Learning Activities and Assessments

A total of two and a quarter hours of combined lectures and tutorials is provided weekly. Students are given small-scale class exercises for group discussion at the end of each lesson.

Assessments are based on students' performance in class exercises, two written assignments, which ask the students to show their understanding of how a computer translates and to compare the different approaches employed in machine translation systems, as well as, through group presentation, evaluating the performance of different machine translation systems.

Research by Bisun and Huy (2006) found that South Pacific tertiary students have two main orientations when approaching study, meaning and reproducing; as Richardson stated in 1994.[1] '[S]tudents are directing their effort to understanding the materials studied, and on the other hand it is about reproducing materials for academic assessment purposes' (p. 16). The result also correlates to data found in Hong Kong.[2] Since self-motivated further study is one of the goals in tertiary education, memorization should not be advocated. Assessment by examination is avoided in both courses in order to promote active learning instead of passive memorizing.

As a whole, the course provides students with adequate knowledge in the machine translation area through understanding it, experiencing it and aiming at improving it in further study.

Editing Skills for Computer Translation – A Required Course

Editing Skills for Computer Translation, on the other hand, encourages practical implementation of editing skills on computer translation outputs. Compared with Computer Translation, it has a different content focus and a different nature. Computer Translation equips students with the techniques needed for using different computer translation systems and understanding the rationale behind them. They are able to have reasonable expectations of the patterns that particular systems generate in their translations and how the systems perform. They may even be able to anticipate certain errors in translations generated by specific computer translation systems. In Editing Skills for Computer Translation, students then learn the techniques involved in correcting those errors in an effective and efficient way, which helps them to make the best use of the outputs generated by computer translation systems.

Curriculum Design

For Editing Skills for Computer Translation, the acquisition of more practical skills is emphasized. Purposes and strategies in editing the translations generated by computer translation systems are discussed. As there is still no fully automatic high-quality computer translation output, editing is still inevitable when using computer translation applications. The course introduces the concepts and skills essential to the editing of the source and target texts before, during and after computer translation so as to optimize efficiency and translation quality. The three main types of editing processes, pre-editing, interactive editing and post-editing, are introduced. Editing skills on different aspects including various linguistic levels are described in the course. Real examples are also employed for illustration. By the end of the course, students are required to try formulating some practical editing guidelines on a specific type of text generated by any one specific computer translation system. Students will have to be able to practically apply the skills of editing the translation output generated by the computer translation software.

The topics covered in Editing Skills for Computer Translation include the following:

Computer Translation Editing: Purposes and Strategies
Editing Skills: Methods of Translation
Pre-Editing: Methods
Pre-Editing: Data Customization
Interactive Editing
Post-Editing: Lexical Aspects
Post-Editing: Grammatical Aspects
Post-Editing: Semantic Aspects
Post-Editing: Pragmatic Aspects
Post-Editing: Cultural Aspects
Computer Translation Editing and Computer-Aided Translation: An Integrated System

Practical Hands-on Experience

Hands-on experience of the machine translation systems is also encouraged in this course. Through remote accessing of the machine translation systems, students may use any of the systems provided by the department for preparation of their assignments and presentations. They may select any specific software for their translation work.

Class Interactive Participation

Group presentation is a means of encouraging practical application of editing skills on output generated by different software. At the same time, peer discussion is encouraged. Through the preparation of the presentation, students can familiarize themselves with at least one of the translation programs among those provided for their use and practically try to implement different editing skills to the output generated by the software on different genre types of text. Each group of students is responsible for a different type of text in order to compare the performance output of the systems on different types of texts. They can share their implementation results with their classmates so that the learning process of every student can be enriched by various ways of applying the skills and the specific methods used in handling a particular type of text. Experience in verifying editing guidelines is useful to them.

With Computer Translation taken in the first term and Editing Skills for Computer Translation in the second, the former prepares students for the use of different software and familiarizes them with its operations and weaknesses, while the latter helps them to overcome the weaknesses through editing skills. They are therefore supplementary to each other.

Means of Learning Activities and Assessments

As with Computer Translation, two and a quarter hours of combined lectures and tutorials are conducted each week.

Assessments are based on a written essay, class participation and group presentations showing how they apply editing skills to computer-generated translations of different genres.

Resources and Technical Support for the Courses

The MACAT program provides a variety of electronic resources to its students in order to facilitate their learning in the courses offered by the program. For the Computer Translation course, the provision of computer translation systems accessed through both in-class lab sessions and remotely is important in helping students become familiar with the use of the software. The computer terminal room of the department also serves as a venue where students can have hands-on experience of different computer translation systems installed on the machines in the laboratory. The translation software library provides user manuals and documentation on computer translation systems for students' reference. Up-to-date licensing of computer translation systems is also one of the essential components in facilitating effective teaching and learning of the courses.

In deciding which software is suitable for use in the course, the program has considered different factors as follows:

(1) The popularity of the software used in corporations and organizations can be one of the factors affecting the choice so as to help students meet their occupational needs.
(2) Translation quality can be another consideration. It is difficult to estimate, however, as the accuracy of translation results varies across different genres. Judgement on the quality of translation is highly dependent on the needs of the users.
(3) Language pairs supported by the systems and the functionality of the systems are among the concerns when selecting software for rule-based systems.
(4) Cost and maintenance of machine translation systems, including administrative costs, are concerns in the running of the courses too.

Any special offers for educational and/or remote access licenses can be another factor affecting the decision.

In our courses, we have employed software from different vendors in order to provide more variety of choices and a wider picture of the field. As a result, the following software is employed in our teaching,

(1) SYSTRAN, which provides a wide range of language pairs for translation, including most European and Asian languages, and has the longest developmental history in the field. It also provides an online version of the tool at www.systransoft.com.
(2) Dr. Eye, originating in Taiwan. This is a comprehensive language learning system with translation capability that is particularly good with literary texts.
(3) Transwhiz, originating as an English–Chinese translation tool. A special feature on parsing the tree structure of sentences can be shown in the process of translation. Its online version is provided at www.mytrans.com.tw/tchmytrans/Default.aspx.
(4) Translation Express, a dictionary-based software system for English–Chinese translation, reasonably priced and with some free download versions, such as at http://ky.iciba.com.
(5) LogoMedia Translate, specifically designed for European languages. Promt is software in their family, which is mainly designed for rapid translation for idea gisting.
(6) Yaxin, a computer-aided translation system that is, however, equipped with a comprehensive list of dictionaries for dictionary lookup and string matching even without a translation memory imported. It can therefore also be classified as a dictionary-based machine translation tool.

There are abundant resources providing online translations. However, some are backboned by several identical software engines. In our courses, we include systems like Google Translate:

http://translate.google.com/, SDL-powered FreeTranslation.com:www.freetranslation.com/, Yahoo Babelfish: http://babelfish.yahoo.com/, WordLingo: www.worldlingo.com/en/products/text_translator.html and Microsoft Translator: http://translation2.paralink.com/ or freetranslator: http://imtranslator.net/ as some of the testing software for students to choose from. We provide flexibility for students to try any online translation software as testing tools. Online systems have the advantage of having updated information included in the translation outputs. For example, newly created terms like 'bluetooth', 'unfriend' and 'sudoku' can be correctly rendered by online translation tools. Commercial versions of machine translation system sometimes may not be able to update their word lists or glossaries within the system at the same pace. On the other hand, online systems, for the same reason, may fail to translate accurately because of too-frequent updates of information from the World Wide Web fed into the systems, particularly in the case of systems supported by search engines. One example is the translation of proper names that may be changing all the time depending on the frequency of the appearance of the names found in any format of news feed. Students can benefit from assessing the performance of such different types of machine translation systems in various aspects.

Different Teaching Strategies According to Different Learning Processes

A common difficulty when setting the 'target' for the master's degree program in computer-aided translation at the Chinese University of Hong Kong is the diverse background of the students. This might be applicable to most master's degree programs at any international institutes. The diversity is not only with regard to intellectual disciplines but also regional cultures. In this section, how we try to make use of various teaching strategies aiming at striking a balance among the interests of different types of students and how we optimize the learning processes of the students are discussed.

Bloom's Taxonomy of Learning Domains

According to Bloom's Taxonomy of Learning Domains (Clark 1999), there are three types of learning: (1) cognitive: mental skills (knowledge), (2) affective: growth in feelings or emotional areas (attitude) and (3) psychomotor: manual or physical skills (skills).

Both Computer Translation and Editing Skills for Computer Translation involve learning processes in the cognitive and psychomotor domains. As a postgraduate course, it inevitably involves a development of intellectuality. Knowledge transmission is essential in both courses; therefore, cognitive learning is evoked. For the psychomotor counterpart, the skills applied in using the computer systems and editing the results are a form of skills transmission.

Cognitive Domain

With regard to cognitive learning, there are six levels: from concrete to abstract, from basic to advanced. They are (1) knowledge, (2) comprehension, (3) application, (4) analysis, (5) synthesis and (6) evaluation. In the course Computer Translation, concepts and theories in computer translation are introduced, whereas in Editing Skills for Computer Translation, previous research on how editing is done on computer translation is introduced. Such knowledge transition belongs to the first level (1: knowledge: recall data). In the written assignment, students have to show their understanding of the theories in computer translation. Examples of editing guidelines are discussed in Editing Skills for Computer Translation. Level 2, comprehension, involves understanding and interpretation of theories. Students have to be able to evaluate the performance of the computer translation systems in their group work so that they can show their application and analyze technique in the Computer Translation course. Students in the Editing Skills for Computer Translation course have to apply the relevant editing guidelines to certain texts taken from computer translation in their group works. They show their learning process through applying what they have learned in a real situation. During the group project, they also have to analyze and relate what relevant guidelines are to be applied so that they can perform the analysis stage of the cognitive learning process. The individual written assignment requires students to set up rules for computer translation systems so as to generate better translation results, to analyze an edited text and to create a set of editing guidelines based on the raw output of computer translation and the post-edited version of the text, respectively, in both the Computer Translation course and Editing Skills for Computer Translation course. The synthesis learning process takes place. In both courses, students have to evaluate computer translation systems and the editing guidelines and skills involved in computer translation. The evaluation learning process completes the cognitive learning phenomena of the two courses. In general, the courses cover every learning behavior of the cognitive domain.

Psychomotor Domain

The Computer Translation course provides opportunities for students to have extensive hands-on experience with computer translation systems in a classroom setting, which trains them with specific skills for operating the systems. With regard to skills development or training in Editing Skills for Computer Translation, practical implementation is the most crucial element. Therefore, real application of editing skills on texts done through the group presentation also provides students with essential experience of learning in a psychomotor process. The experience can on the one hand deepen the knowledge they have acquired and on the other hand enhance their enjoyment of editing. They can also show their team spirit and share their results with one another.

Outcome-Based Teaching and Learning

What is outcome-based education? Outcome-based teaching and learning has been widely adopted in various countries such as Singapore, the United Kingdom, United States of America and Australia. According to Spady (1994: 12), outcome-based education is 'clearly focusing and organizing everything in an educational system around what is essential for the students to be able to do successfully at the end of their learning experiences'.

We have to consider what abilities are important for students to have and to organize curriculum, instruction and assessment in order to make sure the learning ultimately happens.

As shown in the last section, consideration of the organization of the courses and assessment is based on Bloom's taxonomy and covering every learning behavior in the cognitive and psychomotor domains. In outcome-based teaching and learning, 'the outcomes are actions and performances that embody and reflect learner competence in using content, information, ideas, and tools successfully' (Spady 1994: 13).

Learning Outcomes of Computer Translation

In the Computer Translation course, the learning outcomes are as follows:

(1) Students can understand basic concepts and reasons for computer translation.
(2) Students have explored different grammar frameworks employed in computer translation.

(3) Students can learn what the basic text processing steps in computer translation are, specifically sentence identification, word segmentation, Part of Speech (POS) tagging and parsing.

(4) Students can understand different approaches employed in translation systems, including rule-based, knowledge-based, example-based, memory-based, pattern-based and statistical approaches.

(5) Students can understand the typical ambiguities generated in computer translation.

(6) Students can learn how to evaluate and analyze the approaches applied in different computer translation software.

(7) Students have hands-on experience in using different computer translation tools and become familiar with them.

(8) Students are able to present on the analysis of the performance of and the approach applied in different computer translation systems.

After taking the course, they should be able to identify the weaknesses and strengths of different computer translation approaches that are applied in translation systems and evaluate as well as analyze them.

Learning Outcomes of Editing Skills for Computer Translation

In general, students in the course can learn how to make the best use of the output generated by computer translation software through editing. They are required to practice editing skills on different genres translated by available translation software and present in groups. At the end of the course, they have to develop some editing guidelines on a specific text translated by a computer translation system. The learning outcomes are as follows,

(1) Students can understand the basic concepts in computer translation editing.

(2) Students can understand the purposes and basic classifications of computer translation editing.

(3) Students can understand different editing strategies for different computer translation approaches.

(4) Students can use the general rules for pre-editing on examples given to them as reference for practical uses in editing.

(5) Students can understand the concepts of pre-editing and practical ways of doing data customization in pre-editing.

(6) Students can learn how to do interactive editing.

(7) Students can understand how to do post-editing with a focus on various aspects, including lexical, grammatical, semantic, pragmatic and cultural aspects.

(8) Students can learn the differences between computer translation editing and computer-aided translation. They can explore the editing capabilities in different translation systems.

In the Editing Skills for Computer Translation course, students have to apply the relevant editing guidelines that they have learned in working on their group project. They are expected to be able to practically implement the skills they have learned.

In order to reach the optimal goal of generating a learning environment, setting appropriate learning outcomes can help to increase students' learning and ultimate performance abilities. One of the main purposes of outcome-based education as stated is, '[e]nsuring that all students are equipped with the knowledge, competence, and qualities needed to be successful after they exit the educational system' (Spady 1994: 20). In the courses, although knowledge is delivered through traditional lecturing, assessment and projects are ways of ensuring that the students are able to accomplish the learning outcomes, such as applying what they learn in real situations of computer translation systems usage and of editing computer-translated texts.

As outcome-based teaching and learning is the trend in tertiary education in Hong Kong, various universities are also beginning to adopt such a framework in their courses. Improvement in organization of the courses, curriculum definition, instruction and assessment based on outcome-based teaching are foreseeable.

Overcoming Difficulties Generated by Student Diversity

Accommodation of students' characteristics is one of the key components in the teaching-learning process. Students in courses are from diverse backgrounds with various disciplinary differences, including different subjects in arts, sciences and engineering, such as computer study, translation, communication, chemistry, language and education. Disciplinary differences mean students have different expectations for the course and have a different paces in study. Therefore, it is inevitable that a middle line be taken in setting the coverage and comprehensiveness of the course content in order to facilitate different students' interests. In addition, relatively more optional reading is provided as references if students want to pursue more reading. Extra research case studies are also suggested for students who have an interest in pursuing research studies.

On the other hand, different types of aimed-for careers (e.g. executives, teachers, officials, students, engineers, translators, speech therapists and news reporters) also influence the students' interest in different topics. However, working hands on with the software is one of the few common interests, as they will easily note the positive effect of gaining experience in using the tools. Even students from an arts-subject background, usually reluctant to get involved in technical matters, are very pleased to learn how to use new software and to have more hands-on work.

Regionally the students are mainly coming from Hong Kong, Taiwan, Macau, Singapore and Mainland China. In recent years, some have come from European countries. Though most of these regions use the same language, Chinese, both writing and speaking systems can be different. In terms of language medium, we follow the university's regulation of using English (an international language) for ease of communication. As our subject involves translation, the regional differences can sometimes be obstacles. In contrast, we can make beneficial use of the differences among the students. For example, we can benefit from regional variations among students to enrich our discussion in the classroom through encouraging them to suggest regionally different translations for culturally specific terminology.

Reminders on the Resource Provision Issue of Courses

It is worth noting that the updating of adequate licenses for computer translation systems is important in guaranteeing a hands-on experience for the students. The choosing of software is among the issues to be reviewed and reconsidered periodically so as to keep pace with the rapid development of translation technology. Adequate technical support for both teachers and students is obligatory so as to facilitate reliable provision of technological resources. In our case, a designated technician has responsibility for this.

Future Trends of Computer Translation and Teaching It

With decades of development on computer translation, it now reaches a bottleneck in further improving the accuracy and quality in translation outputs. Recent developments tend to combine the advantages of both computer translation and computer-aided translation. Taking computer translation's advantage of automation through providing computer translation results from public vendors to suggest more choices for the users' translation decision in doing computer-aided translation with tailor-made relevant high-quality translated data is one idea. Another option is to use the translation memory in computer-aided translation products to review results generated by computer translation systems. It is hoped that in the coming era, almost fully automatic high-quality translation can be achieved by combining both computer translation and computer-aided translation technologies. Alternatively, in my opinion, by combining the strengths of different translation approaches incorporated in computer translation systems, specific newly developed hybrid-approach systems, particularly designed for handling a particular genre, can practically improve the effectiveness and efficiency in the future performance of computer translation systems development. However, specific types of systems may be restricted to specific usage.

The unwelcome old idea of using feedback comments to improve the design of computer translation systems is nowadays employed extensively in different online systems, such as Google Translate. The change of attitude is driven by the improved performance of computer translation results. The extensive use of mobile devices also serves to make updating and uploading feedback for systems more convenient, which gives users greater incentive to respond to the system. A successful example is Google, which provides a rating option and 'revise translation/ suggest translation' options, making it possible for users to contribute to the improvement of the translation generated by the system. However, quality control remains an unsolved problem. Whether the reviewer is qualified or authorized to make judgments may affect the quality of translation outputs.

The rapid spread of the use of convenient mobile devices brings some controversy to Web-based, cloud-based and even open source translation technology too. Security – or we should more precisely call it intellectual property rights – still remains one of the unsettled concerns. Should something uploaded, whether it be Web-based, cloud-based or even open source, adhere to or be protected by the law regulating intellectual property rights? Does a translation carry property rights? 'A good translator is a lazy translator', as we have to maintain consistency in the use of language in our translation, specifically in professional translation. How and where should we locate the entity of translation copyright? Should we share without any requirement or regulation? Or how can we protect our own rights? How can we make it so that everything will be governed regularly? It still needs much discussion. If a translation is treated as 'art' or a 'cultural product' like the creation of works of art, such as poem creation, we should indeed show great respect for the property rights.

Conclusion

One of the main goals of tertiary education is to stimulate students' interest in self-learning or further education. Research shows that different attitudes can engender different effects/ results in the outcome. Maintaining good relationships with students can help students have a better attitude towards their learning. They are more willing to ask a question when they have one. Communication is a crucial factor in providing a good environment for the teaching and learning process. The various teaching approaches employed in the courses shown in this chapter can generate different effects in different ways. Through lecturing, knowledge is introduced, students' interest is stimulated and attention to/concern with specific aspects is aroused. Class exercises and discussion can help students brainstorm ideas and exchange information. Group presentations can address real practice and application of the knowledge acquired. An assignment can be an assessment at the same time, a real attempt to compare and evaluate state-of-the-art translation software and develop guidelines for practical editing (even for future reference). In general, different teaching strategies can be employed in different courses with different aims and intended learning outcomes. Communication, as a result, is the key for setting the appropriate intended learning outcomes for our students.

Notes

1 As quoted in Bisun Deo and Huy P. Phan (2006: 16–17). See also Richardson, John T. E. (1994) 'Cultural Specificity of Approaches to Studying in Higher Education: A Literature Survey', *Higher Education* 27: 449–68.

2 As quoted in Bisun Deo and Huy P. Phan (2006: 16–17). See also David Kember and Doris Y.P. Leung (1998) 'The Dimensionality of Approaches to Learning: An Investigation with Confirmatory Factor Analysis on the Structure of the SPQ and LPQ', *British Journal of Educational Psychology* 68: 395–407; as quoted in Bisun Deo and Huy P. Phan (2006: 16–17). See also Nai Ying Wong, W.Y. Lin, and David Watkins (1996) 'Cross-cultural Validation of Models of Approaches to Learning: An Application of Confirmatory Factor Analysis', *Educational Psychology* 16: 317–27.

Bibliography

Arnold, Doug J., Lorna Balkan, Siety Meijer, R. Lee Humphreys, and Louisa Sadler (1994) *Machine Translation: An Introductory Guide*, London: Blackwells-NCC.

Chan, Sin-wai (2010) 'A New Curriculum for the Teaching of Translation Technology: The Teaching of a Translation Project Course as a Case Study', in Chan Sin-wai (ed.). *Journal of Translation Studies: Special Issue on the Teaching of Computer-aided Translation* 13(1–2): 83–154.

Clark, Donald R. (1999) 'Bloom's Taxonomy of Learning Domains: The Three Types of Learning'. Available at: www.nwlink.com/~donclark/hrd/bloom.html.

Deo, Bisun and Huy P. Phan (2006) 'Approaches to Learning in the South Pacific Region: A Confirmatory Factor Analysis Study', in *Proceedings of the AARE 2006 International Education Research Conference: Adelaide Papers Collection*, 26–30 November 2006, Adelaide, Australia.

Google (2012, March 1) Google Translate. Available at: http://translate.google.com.; http://babelfish.yahoo.com.; http://imtranslator.net.; http://translate.google.com.; http://translation2.paralink.com.; www.freetranslation.com.; www.worldlingo.com/en/products/text_translator.html.

Hutchins, W. John (1986) *Machine Translation: Past, Present, Future*, Chichester: E. Horwood and New York: Halsted Press.

Ignacio, Garcia (2010) 'Translation Training 2010: Forward Thinking, Work Ready', in Chan Sin-wai (ed.). *Journal of Translation Studies: Special Issue on the Teaching of Computer-aided Translation* 13(1–2): 275–82.

Microsoft (2012, March 1) 'Microsoft Translator'. Available at: http://translation2.paralink.com/ OR freetranslator.imtranslator.net.

SDL (2012, March 1) 'FreeTranslation.com'. Available at: www.freetranslation.com.

Somers, Harold L. (2003) 'Machine Translation in the Classroom', in Harold L. Somers (ed.) *Computers and Translation: A Translator's Guide*, Amsterdam and Philadelphia: John Benjamins Publishing Company, 319–40.

Spady, William G. (1994) *Outcome-based Education: Critical Issues and Answers*, United States: American Association of School Administrators.

Systran (2012, March 1) Available at: www.systransoft.com.

Transwhiz (2012, April 26) Available at: www.mytrans.com.tw/tchmytrans/Default.aspx.

WorldLingo (2012, March 1) Available at: www.worldlingo.com/en/products/text_translator.html.

Yahoo (2012, March 1) 'Yahoo Babelfish'. Available at: http://babelfish.yahoo.com.

14

TEACHING TRANSLATION TECHNOLOGY

Venus Chan and Mark Shuttleworth

Introduction

Translation technology can be defined as the computer-based tools and associated resources and standards that are used within the translation industry (Shuttleworth forthcoming). As such, the concept encompasses the many ways in which computer programs can be used to 'support, enhance or partially or wholly replace the agency of human translators' (ibid.). Core applications include translation memory (TM) and computer-aided translation (CAT), machine translation (MT), terminology extraction, text alignment and translation management. As will no doubt be apparent, this is a rapidly developing area, which means that there is an ongoing need for curriculum updating, renewal and innovation.

For more than two decades, translation technology has been forming an increasingly significant component of many translation degree programmes in different parts of the world. This chapter sets out to consider relevant theoretical contexts and pedagogical approaches and to provide a snapshot of current implementations of translation technology teaching. In the first part, rationale, course content and approaches are all considered in some detail from a theoretical point of view. Following that, the second, more practical part offers an overview of different training types, enumerates the various types of technology that can most often be found in university-level curricula and ends with a brief discussion of a selection of problems and challenges with which course designers and deliverers are currently faced. Throughout the chapter the focus is mainly on university training, although other types are also briefly considered.

Background and Approaches

The role that technology plays in translation education has been discussed broadly over the past decades. There are a growing number of studies on translation technology teaching that particularly envisage courses as embedded in a traditional translation curriculum (e.g. Alotaibi 2014; Austermühl 2013; Kenny 1999, Kenny and Way 2001; Olkhovska 2017; Plaza-Lara 2016; Šanca 2018; Wong 2015). Far from being a systematic review, this section aims to consider the key questions raised in the previous literature on translation technology teaching: *why* translation technology teaching is important, *what* should be taught and *how* it should be taught.

DOI: 10.4324/9781003168348-15

Why Translation Technology Teaching Is Important

Rapid Growth in the Need for Translation Technology in the Expanding Translation Industry

Over the last few decades, translation technology has been widely used by an increasing number of translators and language service providers. Gouadec (2007) analyses some 120 translator job advertisements from around the world; on the basis of a list of employers' expectations, he finds that knowledge of specific translation tools is mentioned in the job advertisements. A survey of 538 European translation employers by the Optimizing Professional Translator Training in a Multilingual Europe (OPTIMALE) project also indicates that about 75% of the respondents consider the ability to use CAT tools important (Toudic 2012) (see also Massardo and van der Meer 2017; O'Brien and Vázquez 2020). Knowledge of translation and linguistics is no longer sufficient to fulfil the contemporary market requirements and the expectations of the future clients, and thus translation graduates need to be equipped with a wide range of technological skills (Sikora 2014; Kenny 2019). Hence, translation technology teaching has become an essential element of translation education in this technological era (Zhang and Vieira 2021).

New technologies change not only translation itself but also how we teach and learn translation practices (Pym 2012). A number of researchers (e.g. Bowker 2002; Doherty 2016; Pym *et al.* 2006) have emphasized that there is an onus on translator training and continuing professional development (CPD) to help translation students, in-service translators and translator trainers become skilful users of a wide range of translation tools. Alcina *et al.* (2007) also emphasize that translators of the 21st century are definitely expected to make an efficient use of new technologies in an ever more demanding market; thus translator trainers themselves have to acquire translation technology skills and teach translator trainees to exploit the emerging translation technology so as to prepare them for the translation industry and language-related professions.

Lack of Training in Translation Technology

When translation technology was still a relatively new topic in translation curricula, numerous researchers stated that a considerable number of translators and translation students do not seem to be sufficiently equipped with skills in the use of CAT tools. Focusing on the European context, Wheatley's (2003) TM survey-based study indicated that over one-third of translators perceived learning translation technology to be difficult, and about a quarter of them were not confident about their own translation technology competence. Similar results were found in the Chinese context. Chan (2005) investigated Hong Kong freelance translators' perceptions, experience and attitudes to translation technology and concluded that the uptake of translation technology, especially CAT, was rather low in the freelance translation community. While most of the respondents realized the potential benefits of translation technology, concern was expressed about the lack of previous training and the unavailability of relevant learning resources. Internationally, Lagoudaki (2006) reported that about 16% of language professionals found it challenging to acquire the skills required for using TM systems.

There is a growing body of research suggesting translation technology should be integrated into the curriculum (Chan 2015). While the benefits of translation technology in translator education are well established, training in translation technology is not widely incorporated in translation curricula due to various difficulties and constraints on the cognitive, procedural, attitudinal and institutional levels (Kenny and Doherty 2014). The problem of lack of resources such as translation technology software and learning materials may hinder the availability of translation technology learning, especially for self-learners.

Lack of Knowledge of Translation Technology

A number of researchers have emphasized that the knowledge of translation technology of pre- and in-service translators and even some translator trainers is far behind the rapid development of cutting-edge translation technology. For instance, Chan (2019a) finds that only 11% and 5% of Hong Kong translation students asked have some familiarity with MT software and CAT tools, respectively. Seventy percent of the respondents to her survey received little or no training in translation technology. These results reveal that trainee translators in Hong Kong have limited knowledge of translation technology, in particular CAT, and this might adversely influence their usage of translation technology and their perceptions of its accuracy. (On the other hand, it is unclear to what extent these findings can be generalized to other parts of the world.) The results also indicate a high level (93%) of willingness and a keen interest among the learners to become familiar with translation technology. Chan (2019b) also suggests that it is important for translation students and practitioners to understand the potential and limitations of translation technology and to learn how and when to use translation technology effectively in order to meet the challenges and expectations of a demanding and fast-changing market. In terms of translation trainers, the lack of qualified and adequately trained teaching staff has been reported in various contexts (e.g. Li and Xia 2013 in China and Kalantzi 2002 in Greece). It demonstrates the importance of CPD for translator trainers and the urgent need for translation technology training for not only students but also translation teachers and practitioners.

In sum, in view of the trend for the development of translation as a practice, advantages in job-hunting, powerfulness in translation technologies, activeness in interaction and cultivation of comprehensive ability, it is widely acknowledged that there is a great need for translator trainers to provide students with the translation technology competence that is indispensable in the translation industry in this era of information explosion (Rothwell and Svoboda 2019; Zhang and Zhang 2013).

What Should Be Taught in Translation Technology Teaching

Frameworks for Translation/Translator Competence

Translation/translator competence (TC) has been the focus of some translation scholars since the 1990s. While different terms have been used by researchers, such as "translation ability" (Pym 1993), "transfer competence" (Nord 1991) and "translational competence" (Chesterman 1997; Hansen 1997), TC can generally be described as the underlying system of knowledge and skills needed to be able to translate (PACTE 2000). These translation/translator competence models provide guidelines for learning content and the outcomes of translation programmes as well as the pedagogical implications of translator education (Angelelli and Jacobson 2009; Kelly 2005; Kiraly 1995).

Although the issue of translation/translator competence has been debated over the past few decades, there seems to be no single framework or model which would be universally agreed upon in the field of translation studies (Arango-Keith and Koby 2003). The earlier theoretical models seldom specifically name translation technology knowledge as one of the major translator competences. Samson (2005) stresses that computer skills and knowledge of translation technologies constitute a crucial component of an overall translator competence and hence should be integrated into translator education. However, among the componential models, the PACTE Group (2011) defines translator competence as "the underlying system of knowledge required to translate" (p. 318) and develops a comprehensive theoretical model which shows the inter-relationship of six sub-competences: bilingual, extra-linguistic, translation, instrumental, strategic and psycho-phys-iological. According to O'Brien and Vázquez (2020: 266), two of the sub-competences directly relate to the teaching of translation technology: "(i) knowledge about translation, which includes knowledge about translation practice and the work market, and (ii) instrumental and strategic competence, which explicitly mentions information and communication technologies". They emphasize that translation technology teaching should cover not only how to use the technology but also how the latest tools are used in the rapidly changing industry. Following PACTE's TC model, students taking a CAT course are expected to learn by: "(a) understanding crucial concepts and principles related to CAT tools; (b) identifying tool availability for each phase in the translation process; (c) recognizing software functionality; and (d) applying tools to complete translation tasks" (Rodríguez-Castro 2018: 357). To help students develop specific components of the translator instrumental sub-competence, researchers have generally suggested that both technical and profes-sional skills should be included in the curriculum.

Göpferich (2009) proposes a model with three competences: communicative competence in the source and the target languages, domain competence and tool and research competence, in which translators should have the skills to adopt various translation-specific conventional and electronic tools, "from reference works such as dictionaries and encyclopaedias, term banks and other databases, parallel texts, the use of search engines and corpora to the use of word processors, terminology and translation management systems as well as machine translation systems" (p. 22). In comparison with those of PACTE and Göpferich, the model proposed by the European Master's in Translation (EMT), a network of university Master's programmes in translation, specifically underlines the importance of technology-based competence which involves all knowledge and skills used to exploit translation technology, such as IT applications, corpus-based tools, CATA (computer-aided text analysis) tools, workflow software, CAT tools and MT systems (EMT 2017). The curriculum of the translation technology–related courses that formed part of the University College London (UCL) MA in translation theory and prac-tice in 2016, for example, was broadly based on the EMT competence framework (Shuttle-worth 2017). Chan (2021a) conducts a qualitative thematic analysis to explore what qualities characterize good translation teachers from students' perspectives. Three main themes are iden-tified: knowledge of teaching, knowledge of professional translation practice and knowledge of translation studies. Translator trainers are expected to keep their professional skills up to date, particularly their knowledge of translation and education technology.

Curriculum Design

After recognizing why pre- and in-service translators need to learn translation technology, the next important question is what they need to learn about. The increasing complexity of tasks and the high level of specialization demanded by the translation industry require higher and more sophisticated levels of skills, technical knowledge and subject-matter expertise. Numerous researchers (e.g. Ehrensberger-Dow and Massey 2014; García 2009; Rodríguez-Castro 2015, 2018) have emphasized the need for refining the traditional translation curriculum in order to incorporate additional technological translator competences that can bridge the gap between the classroom and authentic industry practices in this fast-changing digital age.

As there are a growing number of CAT and translation technology-related courses at both undergraduate and postgraduate levels, more attention is being paid to curriculum design. In the higher education systems of many European countries, educational institutions generally fol-low a harmonized "shared curricular structure" (Rico 2010: 90), which aims to develop learn-ers' industry-validated competence (ibid). Doherty and Kenny (2014), for example, present a localization course in Dublin that covers not only TM and cloud-based solutions but also project management skills and real-world problems and solutions. Many respondents to the EMT survey state that both theory and practice of tools are taught, and the main components of the programmes include TM, termbase use and data mining (Rothwell and Svoboda 2019). In terms of the tools themselves, greater emphasis has been placed on their use in projects, professional workflows and the industry in general and on the theoretical aspects, MT post-editing and tools as software. Unlike the European context, curricula and learning outcomes in the United States are commonly developed by the teachers, who design the syllabus themselves. In the Chinese context, Wong (2015) points out that the curriculum design of MT courses in Hong Kong emphasizes the practical use of translation tools via hands-on experience and interactive participation. Luo (2010) proposes a CAT course for English major undergraduates which adopts an application-oriented approach. Luo's course mainly focuses on the practical use of Yaxin rather than the theoretical concepts of CAT. Unlike Luo's syllabus, Sikora (2014) suggests that theoretical aspects of translation technologies should be discussed before shifting the focus to applying the tools in translation practice.

While the curriculum is generally designed by the translator trainers, there is a lack of needs analysis from other stakeholders. In terms of student perspectives, Pym and Torres-Simón (2016) gather 662 questions from over 200 translation students. The findings of the needs analysis provide useful insights into learners' preferences and expectations in terms of learning content. They suggest that translation trainees in the European setting predominantly perceive new technologies as a threat to or rival of human translators rather than as a set of aids. The students are generally interested in four main aspects related to translation tools: (1) whether translation technology will replace human translators, (2) which tools are most useful, (3) what new forms of translation these technologies will encourage and (4) what research there is on localization and machine translation (O'Brien and Vázquez 2020). Future research may focus on the needs of a wider range of stakeholders, such as freelancer translators, LSPs, employers and practitioners.

In general, the aforementioned courses are based on the pedagogical framework of competence-based training (Hurtado 2015), which is intrinsically related to PACTE's (2002, 2003, 2005, 2011) influential translation competence model in translation training. Translation technology teaching is expected to include both declarative and procedural knowledge (Shreve and Angelone 2010). Shuttleworth (2017) describes some of the training offered at University College London and states that translation technology teaching could include but perhaps not be limited to "absorbing a range of different types of technology; adopting a flexible approach to technology; creating, capturing and redeploying content; learning new tools quickly and confidently; and knowing when not to use technology" (pp. 34–35). In addition to the conceptual and theoretical understanding of translation technology, translation technology teaching should be multifaceted in order to reflect high-order metacognitive development (Shreve 2002). Austermühl (2013), for instance, emphasizes the importance of meta-competences (e.g. revision skills and documentary research skills) as well as multifunctional and transferable skills that are needed in translation practice. Similarly, Pym (2013) suggests students should be able to acquire the skills to learn how to learn. In line with these learning objectives, Bowker (2015) suggests a balanced approach that addresses the latest trends of the market and includes transferable skills (e.g. critical analysis and problem-solving skills) so as to help students to learn "not only *how* but also *when* and *why* to use a given tool" (p. 95). Another example is Rodríguez-Castro's (2018) CAT curriculum, which comprises

a) content modules that consist of project setup, terminology management, translation memory systems, post-editing and localisation tasks; (b) combined teaching methodology that highlights task-based learning and adds virtual reality simulation; and (c) a product and process-based approach to portfolio assessment.

(p. 358)

Recently, O'Brien and Vázquez (2020) also argue that students should not only "test the tools' functionalities (what)" but also "understand their relevance for the translator's work (why) and the situations in which their use could prove more beneficial (when), with the ultimate goal being to stimulate critical thinking and life-long learning" (p. 170).

Numerous researchers (e.g. Alotaibi 2014; Bowker and Marshman 2010; Clark *et al.* 2002; Kenny 2007; Samson 2005) have suggested that integrating technologies more fully across the translator training curriculum could optimize its benefits for students; however, it seems that some current translation technology courses are criticized because of their lack of integration into the translation curriculum. For instance, Bowker (2015) summarizes the lack of integration on two levels: (1) that translation technology is often incorporated in isolation rather than as part of a holistic and integrated translation environment or interactive tool suite, and (2) the tools are mainly adopted in a specific translation technology course rather than being fully integrated into other applied courses or actual translation practice. Enríquez Raído (2013) argues that translation technology teaching should be integrated into practical translation and translation courses instead of using these tools in stand-alone mode. In line with Rothwell and Svoboda's (2019) study, which suggests CAT tool training should become more closely integrated with the teaching and learning of practical translation, more recently, Zhang and Vieira (2021) also suggest CAT tool training should be linked more closely to practical translation sessions.

Translation Tools

There is a wide range of tools which are relevant for translators (Bowker 2015): office software, electronic resources, corpora, terminology management systems, MT systems, CAT tools, localization tools, speech recognition systems, translation management tools and tools for audiovisual translation. Thus, the question of what specific tools should be included in the curriculum becomes a challenge for translation trainers, particularly considering the need to deal with time and resource constraints. Based on the report on the EMT 2017 survey, all respondents state that both cost-free open source and commercial tools are taught, and the most common compulsory tools include Trados Studio (formerly SDL Trados Studio), memoQ, Phrase (formerly Memsource), Wordfast Anywhere and OmegaT (Rothwell and Svoboda 2019). In fact, no matter which software is taught, courseware has to be updated constantly, and curricula need to evolve continually (Shuttleworth 2017).

O'Brien and Kenny (2001) mention the so-called "skills versus knowledge" debate (p. 22). Instead of focusing mainly on the leading translation tools in the market, most researchers generally suggest teaching translation technology in a more generic way so as to equip students with the transferable skills to choose, to use, to evaluate and to learn such tools independently (Bowker 2015). It is generally argued that translation technology teaching should include a minimum of two to three tools, and the tools chosen should be flexible enough to adapt to evolving market needs. Lagoudaki (2006) conducts a survey of 874 TM users and suggests that the ability to use multiple tools (an average of three to four) is needed. In view of the issue of limited resources and educational budgets, Apostol (2018) conducts a case study to examine teaching CAT by using free tools, such as Wordfast Anywhere, Google Translator Toolkit and

OmegaT, and finds that translation tools such as these offer an excellent alternative to commercial translation software. The general consensus seems to be that every tool has its own strengths and drawbacks, and thus within the pedagogical context, it is suggested that greater emphasis should be placed on how they should be taught but not on which ones should be selected.

How Translation Technology Should Be Taught

Teaching Methodology and Practice

Many existing studies of CAT teaching mainly focus on curriculum design, including teaching materials, learning outcomes and assessment methods, whereas teaching methodologies are not extensively investigated, and there is a lack of empirical research (Zhang and Vieira 2021). While a variety of teaching approaches have been adopted, "context-based", "project-based", "task-based" and "situation learning" approaches, in particular, have been the subject of considerable attention (e.g. Biau Gil 2006; Bowker 2015; Gouadec 2003; Jaatinen and Immonen 2004; Kenny 2007; Kenny and Way 2001; Kiraly 2000, 2005; LeBlanc 2013). Based on the socio-constructivist pedagogical framework, translation technology teaching is expected to be "situated and context-dependent" (Risku 2010: 101) in order to help student translators to develop both instrumental and critical thinking competencies through role play as well as the recreation of quasi-real translation scenarios (González-Davies and Enríquez Raído 2016; Zhang and Vieira 2021). Adopting Alcina *et al.'s* (2007) socio-constructive task-based approach, Mileto and Muzil (2010) teach CAT and localization by means of various project-based activities, in which students are exposed to a simulated real-life workplace context. Adopting multiple innovative teaching strategies, student translators in Rodríguez-Castro's (2018) research are required to play different roles and serve as project managers by dealing with communication breakdowns that arise in virtual teams (on *Second Life*) created for localization projects. The results reveal that the task-based teaching methodology can enhance the technical expertise of students to meet the diverse expectations of the translation industry. Similarly, Killman (2018) also introduces the Trados Studio 2011 TM system by adopting a context-based approach, which he suggests may have helped introduce the students to the realities of the professional world of translation, for which student translators should be equipped with critical reflection skills and the ability to decide "when" and "why" to use a TM system and "how" to use it in a real-world setting.

In addition, several researchers have advocated the use of blended learning, that is, combining selected features of online and face-to-face training. For instance, Secară *et al.* (2009) implement blending learning in translator training by using eCoLoTrain and eCoLoMedia. Based on their observation, they suggest that face-to-face and online components should complement each other in order to address the diverse needs of students. Moreover, a number of researchers (e.g. Meinert *et al.* 2018) have recently advocated a blended Massive Open Online Course (bMOOC) which combines online learning and face-to-face interaction. While it is believed that the emerging bMOOC may combine the best features of online learning and in-class activities, its effectiveness and usability remain a relatively unexplored area, especially in the field of translation technology training. A research project led by Chan aims to examine learners' perceptions and the effectiveness of translation technology training in a blended MOOC environment (forthcoming).

In terms of teaching practice, a typical approach is to combine lecture and lab format, where traditional lectures introduce theoretical concepts and lab work provides students with hands-on practice in using the tools (O'Brien and Vazquez 2020). The EMT 2017 survey report reveals that autonomous learning from manuals and help systems is ranked very high by 55% of respondents but is not frequently used by some programmes. E-learning scored 29% for importance, while blended learning achieved 35% (Rothwell and Svoboda 2019). It appears that staff-led teaching remains the most prevalent teaching strategy in the European context (Zhang and Vieira 2021). In wider international contexts, Zhang and Vieira (2021) conduct an international survey of CAT teaching practices involving 102 participants from 112 institutions in 33 countries and regions. The results also indicate that the use of tutorials, where student translators are instructed on how to operate a CAT tool, is the most prevalent teaching method. Since trainers are often not confident that trainees can learn effectively without receiving direct instruction, instructor-led approaches are perceived by many as important. Learning-by-doing activities are also widely utilized in CAT teaching, whereas group discussions are mainly preferred by new teachers. Other preferred teaching activities include hands-on practice and project-based learning (practical sessions with real-life tasks), as well as a flipped classroom model.

Previous research has generally suggested that translator trainers should be responsive and flexible and able to adopt a variety of appropriate teaching and learning resources, pedagogical approaches and class activities based on the market's diverse needs, and students' learning styles, capabilities and contexts (e.g. availability of resources). Teachers need to establish an appropriate balance between teaching formats – "what" and "why" (lecture) and "how" (lab) (O'Brien and Vazquez 2020). It is also important to link CAT tool training more closely with practical translation sessions and to integrate translation technology teaching more fully within a holistic translation curriculum so that translation technology learning can be more intellectually stimulating. Finally, writing specifically about machine translation, Mellinger (2017) recommends that relevant methodologies should be embedded in courses across the whole translation curriculum, although it is unclear how widely this has been implemented as yet (see also Bowker 2015: 96–97; Enríquez Raído 2013: 277).

Effectiveness of Translation Technology Teaching

In general, the majority of questionnaire-based studies have demonstrated that students' attitudes to and perceptions of translation technology improve as they gain skills through practice. For example, Gaspari (2001) carries out a questionnaire-based survey among 38 trainee translators in Italy and finds that they have become more familiar with MT by the end of the course. Similarly, Mahfouz's (2018) questionnaire-based study investigates the attitudes towards CAT tools of 114 translation students and professional translators in Egypt. The results reveal an overall favourable attitude despite some mixed comments. Positive results are also reported in Alotaibi (2014), in which female Arabic translation students' perceptions and knowledge of CAT tools improve by the end of their CAT course. Adopting a mixed-method approach, Doherty *et al.* (2012) and Doherty and Kenny (2014) evaluate a new syllabus in statistical machine translation (SMT) and report that postgraduate student translators in Dublin undergo significant increases in their levels of knowledge and confidence in MT in general and SMT in particular. Nevertheless, it is worth considering that these positive findings are based on students' self-efficacy, and it is difficult to prove whether students have experienced a significant improvement in translation technology competence without any actual measurement of the skills and knowledge that they have acquired.

Doherty and Moorkens (2013) investigate the experience of translation technology labs and suggest that sessions are a practical supplement that allow students to operationalize/internalize what they have already learnt in theory via lectures. Lab sessions are found to be a positive and rewarding learning experience for learners despite initial teething problems. Olkhovska (2017) conducts a pilot experimental study to test the efficiency of the developed methodology of teaching 12 students majoring in philology to translate social and political texts from English to Ukrainian using Trados. The results indicate that the students' proficiency increases both qualitatively and quantitatively. Focusing on the evaluation of CAT tools, which has not been generally highlighted as one of the core competencies, Starlander and Morado Vazquez's (2013) case study examines the effectiveness of teaching translation students how to evaluate Trados Studio and MultiTrans Prism in Geneva by using the EAGLES seven-step protocol (EAGLES 1999), which is an evaluation framework proposed by the Evaluation of natural Language Processing Systems project (EAGLES I and II). Although there were a large number of undecided responses, the students generally agreed that this task should be included in the translation training curriculum.

In general, this research has demonstrated that translation technology teaching enhances students' technological skills and translation efficiency. Nevertheless, it is worth noticing that some of these studies do not provide a clear picture of the curriculum and pedagogies; thus it is difficult to identify what contributes to the benefits and how this enhances the effectiveness. Previous research has generally revealed positive results from translation technology teaching. Similarly, few studies have found no or a negative impact. Kalantzi (2002) examines the state of affairs with respect to teaching MT and CAT tools in Greece and reports that these are taught only marginally and that tuition is described as "poor" and "non-existent" due to the lack of adequately trained staff and appropriate infrastructure (p. 33). Similar obstacles and difficulties are also reported in the Chinese context. Li and Xia (2013), for instance, point out that much effort is needed to incorporate CAT into translation teaching because of inflexible thinking, shortage of qualified teachers and limited hardware and software resources. Furthermore, as mentioned, one common criticism of translation technology teaching is its lack of comprehensive integration with sometimes unreceptive translation programmes and contrasting real-life translation practice. From a macro perspective, according to the report of the EMT 2017 survey, a number of risks (e.g. the lack of trained staff, money, IT facilities and technical support) may hamper the success of translation technology teaching (Rothwell and Svoboda 2019).

Based on the findings of the survey, the EMT offers the following concrete examples of good practice (Rothwell and Svoboda 2019: 52):

- Increased embedding of tools in practical translation classes, including assessment (e.g. use of MT in exams);
- Increased attention to the presence of tools throughout the workflow process;
- Inclusion of related technologies such as speech recognition;
- Participation in collaborative projects (e.g. OPTIMALE, OTCT), including by distance methods;
- Increasing presence of online tools training through distance-delivery courses;
- Expansion of simulated translation bureaus, including internationally;
- Increased cooperation on translation projects with external companies and agencies, including the European Commission and NGOs;
- Collaboration with external bodies on training and standards;
- Multidisciplinary collaboration (law, medicine) on corpora and terminology;
- Crowd-sharing terminology work done in collaboration with, and for use by, companies and official agencies;
- Increased role for MT training, including engine-building and evaluation using Translation Quality Assessment metrics;
- Organization of conferences and summer schools devoted to translation technologies.

It is worth noticing that the effectiveness of teaching depends on a number of influencing factors, such as a teacher's personal characteristics, knowledge and skills (subject knowledge, technical skills and pedagogical content knowledge) and the teaching content and approaches used, as well as teacher-student relationships (Chan 2018, 2021b). In general, empirical evidence has suggested that there is no one-size-fits-all pedagogy and no single answer to the question of what the ideal approach is for teaching translation technology. The majority of studies have shown that it is difficult to meet "the specific needs of all future translators" (Bowker 2015: 96), and thus it is of critical importance to teach translation trainees "not just how to use technology, but also *when* to use specific technologies, *why* they are used, and *what* the implications of an increasingly technologized profession might be" (O'Brien and Vázquez 2020: 174). Since the success of translation technology learning depends on various factors (e.g. learners' perceptions and attitudes, curriculum design, availability of resources), translator trainers should adopt flexible strategies according to the specific circumstances. In addition, more research, especially the gathering of empirical evidence, is needed for a fuller understanding of how the effectiveness of translation technology teaching interacts with various contextual and individual factors, an issue of relevance that is currently under-researched.

OVERVIEW OF TRAINING TYPES

As demonstrated by this section, translation technology training is delivered in a number of different ways. These are discussed in what follows.

Training as Part of a University Degree

Since its clear emergence as a subject in the middle to late 1990s, translation technology (as distinct from the teaching of MT in the context of computational linguistics) has become an increasingly significant feature in university curricula to the extent that in some countries it is considered to be a more or less indispensable component of any programme of study featuring the word 'translation' in its title. At the same time, the possession of a Bachelor's or Master's in a relevant area is seen by many who are just embarking on their career as a near-indispensable prerequisite for entry into the translation industry and also as a distinct advantage for a jobseeker by those who are looking to recruit staff.

The availability of translation technology training at Bachelor's and/or Master's level varies from country to country and region to region. In the United Kingdom, for example, at the time of writing, concentrated specialist content of the type described in the next section still remains largely the preserve of courses at Master's rather than Bachelor's level. In the European Union, translation technology training at the Master's level is also very highly developed, with a total of 67 MA programmes from 22 EU countries participating in the EMT programme,[1] for which inclusion of a substantial translation technology component is a requirement (EMT Network 2017). Additionally, at the time of writing the EU also plays host to a European Master's in technology for translation and interpreting.[2] In Hong Kong the subject is becoming increasingly well represented at both Bachelor's and Master's levels across the higher education sector with dedicated programmes and streams of both types increasingly emerging. On the other hand, in some parts of the world, the subject is not really developed at all.

A detailed breakdown of the most usual components of a typical curriculum at university level is presented below.

Textbooks

Most of the textbooks currently in use in English-speaking institutions have been in existence for a number of years and still serve as respected points of reference despite the rapid advance of the topic. These include Esselink (2000), Austermühl (2001), Bowker (2002) and Quah (2006), with a much more recent addition being Rothwell *et al.* (2023). At least one of these has appeared in translation (Austermühl 2006). At least two Chinese textbooks are currently in existence, Li and Cui (2019) and Wang and Lin (2019), and it is very possible that other locally produced works are used elsewhere in the world.

Training Within the Translation Industry

The situation regarding training and CPD in translation technology offered by companies and/ or individuals within the industry is somewhat fragmented. Companies will typically provide new employees with full training in the systems that they use. It is also not uncommon for software providers to offer training to purchasers either at or after the point of sale, often in the form of a complete run-down of all the features that their system provides. Some also offer certification, either for users (e.g. RWS for Trados products) or additionally for trainers as well (e.g. Phrase and memoQ). Besides this, there are a large number of independent freelance training providers. The online translator community Proz.com, for example, hosts a selection of training courses in CAT tools and other topics.[3] Some universities mount short courses for professional translators in various software systems. As of the mid 2000s, take-up of training was relatively modest among translation professionals, with 51% of respondents reporting that they had not received any (Lagoudaki 2006: 16).

MOOCs and Other Online Courses

Four of the main providers of MOOCs – Coursera, Udemy, FutureLearn and edX – between them offer a number of courses in topics ranging from MT to localization, while a course by Peking University in CAT is available via both Coursera and edX. Some of the courses listed on these sites have to date been attended by several thousand participants.

Other universities are also creating online courses in this area. UCL, for example, hosts a total of five 'online courses' in localization, subtitling and cloud-based translation tools. At the time of writing, a new blended MOOC in translation technology is under development at Hong Kong Metropolitan University (Chan forthcoming).

Some of these courses are free, and for others participants are charged significant amounts of money.

Typical Content of University Courses in Translation Technology

For the last few years translation technology has been changing rapidly in terms of both how the individual technologies function and how they interact with each other, and this situation looks set to continue for the foreseeable future. At the time of writing, course designers will therefore typically consider including some or all of up to 12 separate elements within their curricula. These are discussed in what follows.

Terminology

It is not difficult to make out a convincing case for allowing space in the curriculum for terminology management and related terminology work. Theoretical topics might include the nature of terminology, common term base structures and different approaches to terminology extraction. Practical terminology work will typically focus on searching for and exploiting standard term bases, searching more creatively for individual terms, creating and searching specialized corpora and developing and populating term bases. Exposure to this material opens the door to a greater understanding of a typical CAT tool's terminology function and also to the use of more specialized terminology extraction tools.

Translation Memory

Translation memory has formed a major – if not the major – component of university curricula since at least the middle of the 1990s, reflecting the fact that it has become – and still largely remains, despite recent fundamental changes in the field of translation software – one of the main technologies used by professional translators. Throughout this time the market has been largely dominated by a single system, Trados Studio. For this reason some course providers focus exclusively on that one tool, aiming to provide students with a detailed knowledge of how the program functions and preparing them for work with employers who particularly value this expertise. Many training providers on the other hand prefer to include two or more TM systems in their curricula, arguing that this is a good way of ensuring that their students acquire a solid understanding of how the technology works and equipping them to master further systems at high speed should the need arise (Bowker 2015: 93–95; Shuttleworth 2017: 24). Other systems that are frequently covered include Phrase, memoQ and Wordfast, while decisions regarding inclusion and the order of presentation might reflect factors such as the range – and possible innovativeness – of features offered, the relative level of difficulty, the contrast afforded to other tools featured in the curriculum and the cost.

Machine Translation and Post-Editing

Machine translation has had a place in translation technology curricula right from the start, but with the advances made over the last few years leading to the general availability of free, relatively high-quality MT and the gradual incorporation of the technology in workflows outside its traditional stronghold of large well-funded institutions – often accompanied by post-editing, in which the raw MT output is repaired by humans – course designers have started to make room within their curricula for a greater coverage of these methodologies. Post-editing is becoming an increasingly significant part of the work of many professional translators, and so its inclusion in training curricula is a logical step to take (see O'Brien 2002).

Largely free online systems such as Google Translate and Bing Translator, although their output is still far from perfect (Benjamin 2019), have the advantage of covering large numbers of languages and language varieties (133 and 110, respectively, at the time of writing), making their use highly suitable for mixed-language classes. In addition, some online MT tools possess interfaces that allow users to post-edit their output and can now be seamlessly – but not necessarily costlessly – integrated into many CAT tools, an advance that has fundamentally changed the realities of working with both technologies. Moving on from free online translators, installable systems such as DeepL and PROMT give users access to features such as whole file translation and also to a degree of customizability. As discussed in what follows, a system such as KantanMT allows high levels of customization in the process of MT engine construction. Additionally, a piece of software such as Lilt can be used to demonstrate to students the potential of interactive, adaptive MT. Finally, mobile translation, speech recognition and speech-to-speech translation are all arguably becoming increasingly indispensable in this kind of curriculum.

In terms of theoretical content, while older architectures such as rule-based MT may be included for historical interest, the coverage of neural and statistical MT will enable students to understand how most modern systems work as well as giving them insights, for example, into why they produce the kinds of error that they do.

Exploitation of Corpora

A grasp of how to work with corpora gives students a distinct advantage in terms of their general understanding of different types of translation technology and, arguably, their ability to function effectively as professional translators. Concordance searches – sometimes conducted on corpora that have been specially created for the purpose – can be very useful in term base construction or in helping to solve problems of specialized language use that might arise when producing a translation. An understanding of concordancing also helps highlight the usefulness of searching a TM interactively. The parallel between a TM and a bilingual corpus is clear, although the contrast between how the two work can bring the limitations of current TM technology into relief and suggest some possible ways of improving it. The use of keyword lists provides a powerful technique for extracting terminology. Finally, a familiarity with corpora can give useful insights into how new approaches to MT work, while using them to study how MT output differs from human-written text can lead to the formulation of automated post-editing rules (see Rowda 2016).

Parallel Text Acquisition

One of the most significant selling points of TM systems is their ability to recycle old translations, with no realistic limit being set on the size of a TM database. At the same time, one of the major problems of teaching TM in the context of a university translation technology course is that the TMs that students work with are often very small simply because there has been no time for them to grow to a significant size. One of the consequences of this is that students may complete their course without having understood the full potential of the technology. There are a number of at least partial solutions to this: (1) integrating the use of CAT tools with the content of the rest of the degree programme (see Bowker 2015: 96–97; Enríquez Raído 2013: 277; Mellinger 2017), (2) either pooling TMs within the current group or obtaining a group's permission to reuse their TM content in subsequent years, (3) aligning existing source- and target-text pairs, (4) transferring content from one tool to the next if more than one is being focused on and (5) downloading one or more substantial TMs or corpora from an online public resource.

While the first two of these depend on the teaching staff to implement on behalf of the students, the last three can be consciously incorporated into the curriculum. Of these, text aligning and transferring resources between tools via the export and import functions, very likely in TMX format, will presumably be covered in the curriculum in any case. On the other hand, students can be specifically shown how to access substantial amounts of parallel aligned text – often in excess of 100,000 segments – from sites such as OPUS[4] or Data Marketplace[5] and then download it and import it into their TMs. Following this, searching and matching functions in the CAT tool will be greatly enhanced. Ultimately, parallel text in many ways drives translation technology (and not just TM), and so if students are shown how to create it, where to access it and how to work with it in various applications, that will greatly enhance their appreciation for the significance of this resource.

Project Management

For many years the inclusion of one or more team-based projects has been a relatively standard feature of translation technology courses. On top of this, students will typically learn how to use at least some of the project management features of the CAT tools they work with (such as job analysis). However, an increasing number of curriculum designers have been formally introducing their students to the procedures and techniques of project management – including a more detailed investigation of the relevant CAT tool functions and also in some cases the use of more specialized translation management software.

Translation Evaluation

As well as encouraging the ability to evaluate the strong and weak points of a particular system in an informal manner based on their experience, a well-designed course is likely to include content focusing on approaches to the evaluation of MT output that involve either human judgement or the use of automatic metrics such as the BLEU score as well possibly as a discussion of how to assess TM systems (see, for example, EAGLES 1995).

Customized MT Engine Construction

With the advent of new approaches such as neural and statistical MT, this technology has developed to such an extent that there are now systems that permit users who do not possess significant hard technical skills to produce their own customized MT engine. This reflects the kind of empowerment that was perhaps advocated by Kenny and Doherty (2014: 283–85).

A system such as KantanMT[6] provides an interface that allows users to create an MT engine with a specific subject focus by training it with resources in the form of bilingual term lists and both bilingual parallel and monolingual target-language text. The developing quality of an individual engine can be tracked using the BLEU score.

Localization Tools

Tasks that form part of the process of localizing websites, games, and desktop and mobile apps are frequently performed using CAT tools but can also involve the use of more specialized applications. They are sometimes included in a general course in translation technology but can also form the subject of a separate one.

Audiovisual Translation Tools

Tools for subtitling film and TV content and performing other tasks now form an indispensable component of the work of a professional active in this area. As with localization technology, these are sometimes included alongside other types of translation technology but are more frequently taught separately.

Speech Recognition and Speech-to-Speech MT

These topics are relative newcomers in translation technology curricula, but as the software improves, they are likely to make an appearance in an increasing number of courses (see Bowker

2015: 92). Typical content might not only feature a basic introduction to the technology but would also be likely to include content on how to use these methodologies alongside different types of translation technology such as TM.

Interpreting Technology

Another topic that is also featuring increasingly in university curricula, interpreting technology encompasses tools to facilitate the delivery of interpreting services (principally via videoconferencing) and to enhance interpreters' performance (mostly in the area of terminology, either to aid preparation or while performing a job). Because of the different focus of this category it is not frequently combined with many of the others within a 'general' course, although there is a clear overlap with speech recognition and speech-to-speech MT.

Problems and Challenges

It should be no surprise that training in translation technology gives rise to a number of issues that course designers and deliverers need to solve as they think best. Some of the more major ones are listed below.

The balance between theory and practice may vary considerably from one course to another. Some course designers might weight the content very much towards the practical end, although the more prevailing view is perhaps that the inclusion of theoretical content is appropriate at university level (see Sikora 2014) not only to ensure that students are challenged intellectually and gain deeper insights into the technologies that are being taught but also to add substance and academic weight to components of a degree that is perhaps being offered by a prestigious institution. Needless to say, the inclusion of theoretical content has implications for the format of the teaching sessions and the nature of at least some of the assessment.

Given the ongoing realignment of the two technologies the right balance also needs to be struck between TM and MT within the curriculum, and probably constantly reassessed. Taken together, these two technologies are likely to represent a significant proportion of most curricula and so this decision has weighty implications, whether the entire content is covered within a single course or spread across two or more interlinked ones. Following on from this, as mentioned, the range and precise selection of tools needs to be decided on. In addition, if exclusively web-based (or 'SaaS': 'software as a service') systems such as Phrase and Lilt are selected, greater flexibility is afforded both students and teachers, while on the other hand some of the best-known applications (such as Trados Studio, memoQ and Alchemy CATALYST) require local installation on individual computers, an issue that proved somewhat problematic during the COVID-19 pandemic. A related point is that major systems of both types can be costly (and some online MT systems that are otherwise free will require payment when used from inside a TM system), and academic licensing terms often vary significantly from one provider to another. Factors such as these will inevitably influence the final choice that is made (and also see below).

In the first part of 2020, as the COVID-19 pandemic took hold, course providers were forced to switch to online delivery with little or no time to prepare. While the use of virtual learning environments (VLEs) was already well established, in practical terms this meant utilizing videoconferencing software to teach groups the members of which were based remotely and sometimes scattered across different time zones. Chan (2022) developed a virtual reality mobile application for bi-directional English/Chinese consecutive and sight interpreting learning. The findings of the thematic analysis reveal six main areas of benefit: (1) interpreting and language proficiency, (2) authentic and immersive interpreting practice, (3) learning flexibility and effectiveness, (4) learning experience, (5) cognitive development and (6) affective development. At the time of writing, in some parts of the world, stabilizing conditions are facilitating a gradual return to face-to-face mode, although it remains to be seen what the medium- and long-term legacy of the unplanned adoption of remote teaching approaches will be in terms of the retention of practices facilitated by this mode (such as recording teaching sessions, obtaining instant feedback from students via polling, making a fuller use of the features of the VLE, etc.) and the exploitation of the new possibilities that it has opened up (e.g. in terms of collaboration with institutions in different countries), which have the strong potential to enrich students' learning experience.

As mentioned in the discussion about curriculum design, some authors (see Mellinger 2017; Bowker 2015: 96–97; Enríquez Raído 2013; Zhang and Vieira 2021) advocate integrating the skills taught in the technology component with the practical elements of the programme so that students are either encouraged or required to use the systems that they have learnt to carry out their translation assignments. The advantages of this approach are clear as students are likely to become more proficient, experienced users of the software (and their own TMs will grow more quickly as well), although on the other hand the prospect of their using machine translation would be likely to give rise to some concerns, and this approach has implications that would need to be thought through carefully before it was implemented. Currently, although students may often be informally encouraged to use the software for their practical assignments, the formal integration of technology content into the programme as a whole does not appear to be widespread.

Related to this, since one of the main purposes of such courses is to teach practical skills relevant to certain work contexts, various measures can be taken to help maximize their professional relevance. These might include running one or more team-based translation projects in which each student takes on a particular role (e.g. project manager, translator, terminologist, etc.), negotiating internships with translation companies and inviting professionals to come and talk to students about their experiences of working in the industry.

In some countries, all class members are likely to be working with the same language pair and in the same direction, while in others, groups will be multilingual and multidirectional. In the latter context, potential issues arise when performing software demonstrations and producing courseware that is equally accessible to all participants.

Most computer labs where translation technology is taught are equipped with Windows machines, and few of the TM systems that require installation are compatible with the Mac. However, many students work with a MacBook, which raises the question of how they, and their preferred devices, can be fully included in the course on which they are studying. Clearly, one solution is to require everyone to use the lab machines even when practising outside class time, assuming that it is possible to pursue full face-to-face mode. Another solution – the precise opposite of the first – would be to use only SaaS systems, but this would exclude well-known systems such as those mentioned above. Anything between these two arrangements that relies on installed Windows software that needs to be available outside a specific facility is potentially problematic for this group of users. Demo versions will not be available to them. Windows emulators, which effectively convert a partition of a device into a virtual Windows machine, would essentially oblige Mac users to work on their own device in an environment that at least some of them took the active decision to migrate from. Possibly the only effective solution that teachers committed to this kind of course architecture can exploit is to use a remote-desktop solution to make locally installed software available to non-local users.

Besides this, courseware can be made more friendly to Mac users, for example by providing Mac as well as Windows shortcuts wherever relevant.

Conclusion

As the previous discussion has hopefully demonstrated, there is a rich diversity of technology about which students potentially need to become knowledgeable and also no lack of theoretical reflection on what university curricula need to encompass, what the rationale is for teaching this subject and how trainers should approach the task. With new developments in the technology still occurring apace, it is vital that this reflection continues so that courses can keep preparing students adequately for work in the translation industry as well as providing them with a learning experience that is rich, stimulating, challenging and, hopefully, enjoyable.

Notes

1 https://ec.europa.eu/info/resources-partners/european-masters-translation-emt/list-emt-members-2019-2024_en
2 https://em-tti.eu/
3 https://training.proz.com/
4 https://opus.nlpl.eu/
5 https://datamarketplace.taus.net/
6 https://www.kantanai.io/

Bibliography

Alcina, A., V. Soler, and J. Granell (2007) 'Translation Technology Skills Acquisition', *Perspectives: Studies in Translatology* 15(4): 230–44.

Alotaibi, H. M. (2014) 'Teaching CAT Tools to Translation Students: An Examination of Their Expectations and Attitudes', *AWEJ: Special Issue on Translation* 5(3): 65–74.

Angelelli, C. V. and H. E. Jacobson (2009) *Testing and Assessment in Translation and Interpreting Studies: A Call for Dialogue Between Research and Practice*, Amsterdam and Philadelphia: John Benjamins Publishing Company.

Apostol, S. A. (2018) 'Teaching Computer-assisted Translation Technology: A Case Study', in *The European Proceedings of Social & Behavioural Sciences*, Helsinki: Future Academy, 964–70.

Arango-Keith, F. and G. S. Koby (2003) 'Translator Training Evaluation and the Needs of Industry Quality Training', in B. Bear and G. S. Koby (eds.) *Beyond the Ivory Tower: Rethinking Translation Pedagogy*, Amsterdam and Philadelphia: John Benjamins Publishing Company, 117–34.

Austermühl, F. (2001) *Electronic Tools for Translators*, Manchester: St. Jerome.

Austermühl, F. (2006) 《譯者的電子工具》 (*Electronic Tools for Translators*), Beijing: Foreign Language Teaching and Research Press.

Austermühl, F. (2013) 'Future (and Not-so-future) Trends in the Teaching of Translation Technology', *Revista Tradumàtica: tecnologies de la traducció* 11: 326–37.

Benjamin, M. (2019) 'Teach You Backwards: An In-Depth Study of Google Translate for 108 Languages', *Kamusi Project International*. Available at: https://teachyoubackwards.com.

Biau Gil, J. R. (2006) 'Teaching Electronic Tools for Translators Online', in A. Pym, A. Perekrestenko, and B. Starink (eds.) *Translation Technology and Its Teaching*, Tarragona: Universitat Rovira i Virgili, 89–96.

Bowker, L. (2002) *Computer-aided Translation Technology: A Practical Introduction*, Ottawa: University of Ottawa Press.

Bowker, L. (2015) 'Computer-Aided Translation: Translator Training', in S. W. Chan (ed.) *Routledge Encyclopedia of Translation Technology*, London and New York: Routledge, 88–104.

Bowker, L. and E. Marshman (2010) 'Toward a Model of Active and Situated Learning in the Teaching of Computer-aided Translation: Introducing the CERTT Project', *Journal of Translation Studies* 13(1–2): 199–226.

Chan, S. W. (ed.) (2015) *Routledge Encyclopaedia of Translation Technology*, London and New York: Routledge.

Chan, V. (2005) 'Customizing a General-Purpose MT System: A Case Study of Using SYSTRAN 5.0 Professional Premium User Dictionary and TM for Translation of English-Chinese Domain-specific Texts of Skin-Care and Makeup Products & An Investigation of Hong Kong Freelance Translators' Perceptions and Experience of MT', Unpublished Master's thesis, The Chinese University of Hong Kong.

Chan, V. (2018) 'Teaching in Higher Education: Students' Perceptions of Effective Teaching and Good Teachers', *Social Sciences and Education Research Review* 5(1): 40–58.

Chan, V. (2019a, August 12–14) 'Friend or Foe? Machine Translation in Language Learning', *10th Academic International Conference on Social Sciences and Humanities*, Oxford, the United Kingdom.

Chan, V. (2019b, July 10–12) 'Machine Translation in ESL Learning: Boon or Bane?', *International Conference on Open and Innovation Education*, Hong Kong, China.

Chan, V. (2021a, September 14–19) 'Translator Trainer Competence: Students Talk Back', *International Association for Translation and Intercultural Studies (IATIS) Conference 2021*, Barcelona, Spain.

Chan, V. (2021b) 'What Makes a Good Teacher in Vocational Education? Students Talk Back', *Journal of Technical Education* 12(1): 1–29.

Chan, V. (2022) 'Using a virtual reality mobile application for interpreting learning: listening to the students' voice', *Interactive Learning Environments.* https://doi.org/10.1080/10494820.2022.2147958.

Chan, W. M. V. (forthcoming) 'Acquisition of Translation Technology Skills Through Blended Learning'.

Chesterman, A. (1997) *Memes of Translation*, Amsterdam and Philadelphia: John Benjamins Publishing Company.

Clark, R., A. Rothwell, and M. Shuttleworth (2002) 'Integrating Language Technology into a Postgraduate Translation Programme', in B. Maia, J. Haller, and M. Ulrych (eds.), *Training the Language Services Provider for the New Millennium*, Porto: Faculdade de Letras da Universidade do Porto, 63–70.

Doherty, S. (2016) 'Impact of Translation Technologies on the Process and Product of Translation', *International Journal of Communication* 10: 947–67.

Doherty, S. and D. Kenny (2014) 'The Design and Evaluation of a Statistical Machine Translation Syllabus for Translation Students', *The Interpreter and Translator Trainer* 8(2): 295–315.

Doherty, S., D. Kenny, and A. Way (2012) 'Taking Statistical Machine Translation to the Student Translator', *Proceedings of the 10th Biennial Conference of the Association for Machine Translation in the Americas*. San Diego, https://doi.org/10.13140/2.1.2883.0727.

Doherty, S. and J. Moorkens (2013) 'Investigating the Experience of Translation Technology Labs: Pedagogical Implications', *Journal of Specialised Translation* 19: 122–36.

EAGLES (1995, September) 'Evaluation of Natural Language Processing Systems: Final Report'. Available at: www.issco.unige.ch/en/research/projects/ewg95/.

EAGLES Evaluation Working Group (1999, April) 'The EAGLES 7-Step Recipe'. Available at: www.issco.unige.ch/en/research/projects/eagles/ewg99/7steps.html.

Ehrensberger-Dow, M. and G. Massey (2014) 'Translators and Machines: Working Together. Man Vs. Machine?', *Proceedings of XXth World Congress of the International Federation of Translators*, 199–207.

EMT Network (2017) 'European Master's in Translation Competence Framework', *European Commission*. Available at: https://ec.europa.eu/info/sites/info/files/emt_competence_fwk_2017_en_web.pdf.

Enríquez Raído, V. (2013) 'Teaching Translation Technologies "Everyware": Towards a Self-Discovery and Lifelong Learning Approach', *Tradumàtica* 11: 275–85.

Esselink, B. (2000) *A Practical Guide to Localization*, Amsterdam and Philadelphia: John Benjamins.

García, I. (2009) 'Beyond Translation Memory: Computers and the Professional Translator', *The Journal of Specialised Translation* 12: 199–214.

Gaspari, F. (2001) 'Teaching Machine Translation to Trainee Translators: A Survey of Their Knowledge and Opinions', in M. L. Forcada, D. R. Pérez Ortiz, and D. Lewis (eds.) *Proceedings of the Workshop "Teaching Machine Translation"*, SciELO, 35–44.

González-Davies, M. and V. Enríquez Raído (2016) 'Situated Learning in Translator and Interpreter Training: Bridging Research and Good Practice', *The Interpreter and Translator Trainer* 10(1): 1–11.

Göpferich, S. (2009) 'Towards a Model of Translation Competence and Its Acquisition: The Longitudinal Study 'TransComp', in S. Göpferich, A. L. Jakobsen and I. Mees (eds.) *Behind the Mind: Methods, Models and Results in Translation Process Research*, Frederiksberg: Samfundslitteratur, 11–37.

Gouadec, D. (2003) 'Position Paper: Notes on Translator Training', in A. Pym, C. Fallada, J. R. Biau, and J. Orenstein (eds.) *Innovation and E-Learning in Translator Training*, Tarragona: Universitat Rovira i Virgili, 11–19.

Gouadec, D. (2007) *Translation as a Profession*, Amsterdam and Philadelphia: John Benjamins Publishing Company.

Hansen, G. (1997) 'Success in Translation', *Perspectives: Studies in Translatology* 5(2): 201–10.

Hurtado, A. A. (2015) 'The Acquisition of Translation Competence. Competences, Tasks, and Assessment in Translator Training', *Meta: Translators' Journal* 60(2): 256–80.

Jaatinen, H. and J. Immonen (2004) 'Finnish University Meets Needs of Translation Industry', *Multilingual Computing and Technology* 15(4): 37–40.

Kalantzi, D. (2002) 'Teaching MT/CAT tools in Greece: The State of the Art', in *Proceedings of the 6th EAMT Workshop: Teaching Machine Translation*, Centre for Computational Linguistics, UMIST, 33–42.

Kelly, D. (2005) *A Handbook for Translator Trainers. A Guide to Reflective Practice*, Manchester: St. Jerome.

Kenny, D. (1999) 'CAT Tools in an Academic Environment: What Are They Good For?', *Target: International Journal of Translation Studies* 11(1): 65–82.

Kenny, D. (2007) 'Translation Memories and Parallel Corpora: Challenges for the Translation Trainer', in D. Kenny and K. Ryou (eds.) *Across Boundaries: International Perspectives on Translation Studies*, Newcastle upon Tyne: Cambridge Scholars Publishing, 192–208.

Kenny, D. (2019) 'Technology and Translator Training', in M. O'Hagan (ed.) *Routledge Handbook of Translation and Technology*, London and New York: Routledge, 498–515.

Kenny, D. and S. Doherty (2014) 'Statistical Machine Translation in the Translation Curriculum: Overcoming Obstacles and Empowering Translators', *The Interpreter and Translator Trainer* 8(2): 276–94.

Kenny, D. and A. Way (2001) 'Teaching Machine Translation & Translation Technology: A Contrastive Study', in *Proceedings of the MT Summit VIII workshop Teaching Machine Translation*, Santiago de Compostela, 13–17.

Killman, J. (2018) 'A Context-Based Approach to Introducing Translation Memory in Translator Training', in B. Concepción (ed.) *Translation, Globalization and Translocation*, London: Palgrave Macmillan, 137–59.

Kiraly, D. C. (1995) *Pathways to Translation: Pedagogy and Process*, Kent: Kent State University Press.

Kiraly, D. C. (2000) *A Social Constructivist Approach to Translator Education*, Manchester: St. Jerome.

Kiraly, D. C. (2005) 'Project-Based Learning: A Case for Situated Translation', *Meta: Journal des traducteurs* 50(4): 1098–111.

Lagoudaki, E. (2006) 'Translation Memory Systems: Enlightening Users' Perspective'. Available at: http://citeseerx.ist.psu.edu/viewdoc/download?doi=10.1.1.1063.6423&rep=rep1&type=pdf.

LeBlanc, M. (2013) 'Translators on Translation Memory (TM). Results of an Ethnographic Study in Three Translation Services and Agencies', *Translation & Interpreting* 5(2): 1–13.

Li, M. and Q. Cui (eds.) (2019) 《電腦輔助翻譯簡明教程》 (*A Concise Course on Computer-aided Translation*), Beijing: Foreign Language Teaching and Research Press.

Li, Z. and M. T. Xia (2013) 'The Application of Computer-aided Translation Technology in the Translation Teaching and Research', *Applied Mechanics and Materials* 422: 255–59.

Luo, X. J. (2010) 'The Course Design of CAT for Undergraduate English Majors of Sun Yat-Sen University', *Journal of Translation Studies* 13(1–2): 251–72.

Mahfouz, I. (2018) 'Attitudes to CAT Tools: Application on Egyptian Translation Students and Professionals', *Arab World English Journal (AWEJ)*: 69–83.

Massardo, I. and J. van der Meer (2017). 'The Translation Industry in 2022: A Report from the TAUS Industry Summit'. *TAUS*. Available at: https://info.taus.net/translation-industry-2022-report-download.

Meinert, E., A. Alturkistani, J. Car, A. Carter, G. Wells, and D. Brindley (2018) 'Real-world Evidence for Postgraduate Students and Professionals in Healthcare: Protocol for the Design of a Blended Massive Open Online Course'. *BMJ Open* 8(9): e025196.

Mellinger, C (2017) 'Translators and Machine Translation: Knowledge and Skills Gaps in Translator Pedagogy'. *The Interpreter and Translator Trainer* 11(4): 280–293. https://doi.org/10.1080/1750399X.2017.1359760.

Mileto, F. and L. Muzil (2010) 'Teaching Computer-Assisted Translation and Localisation: A Project-Based Approach', in Ł. Bogucki (ed.) *Teaching Translation and Interpreting: Challenges and Practices*, Newcastle upon Tyne: Cambridge Scholars Publishing, 3–14.

Nord, C. (1991) *Text Analysis in Translation*, Amsterdam: Rodopi.

O'Brien, S. (2002) 'Teaching Post-Editing: A Proposal for Course Content', in *Proceedings of the 6th EAMT Workshop "Teaching Machine Translation"*, EAMT/BCS, 99–106.

O'Brien, S. and D. Kenny (2001) 'In Dublin's Fair City: Teaching Translation Technology at Dublin City University', *Language International* 13(5): 20–23.

O'Brien, S. and S. R. Vázquez (2020) 'Translation and Technology', in S. Laviosa and M. González-Davies (eds.), *The Routledge Handbook of Translation and Education*, London and New York: Routledge, 264–77.

Olkhovska, A. (2017) 'Testing Efficiency of the Methodology of Teaching Students Majoring in Philology to Translate Texts Using CAT-tools: A Pilot Study', *Advanced Education* 7: 37–44.

PACTE (2000) 'Acquiring Translation Competence: Hypotheses and Methodological Problems in a Research Project', in A. Beeby, D. Ensinger, and M. Presas (eds.) *Investigating Translation*, Amsterdam and Philadelphia: John Benjamins Publishing Company, 99–106.

PACTE (2002) 'Exploratory Tests in a Study of Translation Competence', *Conference Interpretation and Translation* 4(2): 41–69.

PACTE (2003) 'Building a Translation Competence Model', in F. Alves (ed.), *Triangulating Translation: Perspectives in Process Oriented Research*, Amsterdam and Philadelphia: John Benjamins Publishing Company, 43–66.

PACTE (2005) 'Investigating Translation Competence: Conceptual and Methodological Issues', *Meta* 50(2): 609–19.

PACTE (2011) 'Results of the Validation of the PACTE Translation Competence Model: Translation Problems and Translation Competence', in C. Alvstad, A. Hild, and E. Tiselius (eds.) *Methods and Strategies of Process Research: Integrative Approaches in Translation Studies*, Amsterdam and Philadelphia: John Benjamins Publishing Company, 317–44.

Plaza-Lara, C. (2016) 'Instrumental Competence in Translation and Interpreting Curricula in Spain: Pre-EHEA vs. EHEA Bachelor's Degrees', *Current Trends in Translation Teaching and Learning* 3: 258–310.

Pym, A. (1993) 'Negotiation Theory as an Approach to Translation History. An Inductive Lesson from Fifteenth-Century Castile', in Y. Gambier and J. Tommola (eds.), *Translation and Knowledge*, Turku: University of Turku, Centre for Translation and Interpreting, 27–39.

Pym, A. (2012) 'Democratizing Translation Technologies: The Role of Humanistic Research', *Language and Translation Automation Conference* 1: 14–29.

Pym, A. (2013) 'Translation Skill-sets in a Machine-translation Age', *Meta* 58(3): 487–503.

Pym, A., A. Perekrestenko, and B. Starink (eds.) (2006) *Translation Technology and Its Teaching: (with Much Mention of Localization)*, Tarragona: Intercultural Studies Group, Universitat Rovira i Virgili.

Pym, A. and E. Torres-Simón (2016) 'Designing a Course in Translation Studies to Respond to Students' Questions', *The Interpreter and Translator Trainer* 10(2): 183–203.

Quah, C. K. (2006) *Translation and Technology*, London: Palgrave Macmillan.

Rico, C. (2010) 'Translator Training in the European Higher Education Area', *The Interpreter and Translator Trainer* 4(1): 89–114.

Risku, H. (2010) 'A Cognitive Scientific View on Technical Communication and Translation: Do Embodiment and Situatedness Really Make a Difference?', *Target* 22(1): 94–111.

Rodríguez-Castro, M. (2015) 'Conceptual Construct and Empirical Validation of a Multifaceted Instrument for Translator Satisfaction', *The International Journal of Translation and Interpreting Research* 7(2): 30–50.

Rodríguez-Castro, M. (2018) 'An Integrated Curricular Design for Computer-assisted Translation Tools: Developing Technical Expertise', *The Interpreter and Translator Trainer* 12(4): 355–74.

Rothwell, A. and T. Svoboda (2019) 'Tracking Translator Training in Tools and Technologies: Findings of the EMT Survey 2017', *The Journal of Specialised Translation* 32: 26–60.

Rothwell, A., J. Moorkens, M. Fernández-Parra, J. Drugan and F. Austermuehl (2023) *Translation Tools and Technologies*, London and New York: Routledge.

Rowda, J. (2016, November 22) 'Understanding Your Data Using Corpus Analysis'. Available at: http://kv-emptypages.blogspot.co.uk/2016/11/understanding-your-data-using-corpus.html.

Samson, R. (2005) 'Computer-Assisted Translation', in M. Tennent (ed.) *Training for the New Millennium*, Amsterdam and Philadelphia: John Benjamins Publishing Company, 101–26.

Šanca, F. (2018) 'The Use of CAT Tools in University Translation Courses: A Case Study Based on Teaching with Memsource', Master's thesis, Charles University.

Secară, A., P. Merten, and Y. Ramírez (2009) 'What's in Your Blend? Creating Blended Resources for Translator Training', *The Interpreter and Translator Trainer* 3(2): 275–94.

Shreve, G. M. (2002) 'Knowing Translation: Cognitive and Experiential Aspects of Translation Expertise from the Perspective of Expertise Studies', in A. Riccardi (ed.) *Translation Studies: Perspectives on an Emerging Discipline*, Cambridge: Cambridge University Press, 150–71.

Shreve, G. M. and E. Angelone (2010) *Translation and Cognition*, Amsterdam and Philadelphia: John Benjamins Publishing Company.

Shuttleworth, M. (2017) 'Cutting Teeth on Translation Technology: How Students at University College London Are Being Trained to Become Tomorrow's Translators', *Tradução em Revista* 22: 18–38.

Shuttleworth, M. (forthcoming) *Dictionary of Translation Studies*, 2nd edition, London and New York: Routledge.

Sikora, I. (2014) 'The Need for CAT Training Within Translator Training Programmes', *TRAlinea Special Issue: Challenges in Translation Pedagogy*. Available at: www.intralinea.org/specials/article/2092.

Starlander, M. and L. Morado Vazquez (2013) 'Training Translation Students to Evaluate CAT Tools Using Eagles: A Case Study', *Aslib: Translating and the Computer* 35. Available at: https://archive-ouverte.unige.ch/unige:35622.

Toudic, D. (2012) 'The OPTIMALE Employer Survey and Consultation: Synthesis Report'. Available at: www.translator-training.eu/attachments/article/52/WP4_Synthesis_report.pdf.

Wang, H. and S. Lin (2019) 《電腦輔助翻譯概論》(*An Introduction to Computer-Assisted Translation*), Beijing: Intellectual Property Publishing House.

Wheatley, A. (2003) 'eContent Localization Resources for Translator Training'. Available at: https://www.translationdirectory.com/article450.htm.

Wong, C. (2015) 'The Teaching of Machine Translation. The Chinese University of Hong Kong as a Case Study', in S. W. Chan (ed.) *Routledge Encyclopaedia of Translation Technology*, London and New York: Routledge, 237–51.

Zhang, E. and W. Zhang (2013) 'Application of Computer-Aided Translation Technology in Translation Teaching', *International Journal of Emerging Technologies in Learning (iJET)* 8(5): 15–20.

Zhang, X. and L. N. Vieira (2021) 'CAT Teaching Practices: An International Survey', *The Journal of Specialised Translation* 36a: 99–124.

15

ARTIFICIAL INTELLIGENCE AND TRANSLATION

Liu Xueting and Li Chengze

Abstract

Artificial intelligence (AI) is a big field of studies that enables computers and machines to mimic the perception, learning, problem-solving, and decision-making capabilities of humans. More recently, with increasing computing power and data, AI has pushed the boundaries of human-like intelligence. In this chapter, we will discuss how AI can be used to understand text contents to perform translation.

The main challenge in AI-based translation comes from the difficulties in understanding the semantics of texts as well as understanding the syntactic structure of texts to translate them. We start from the traditional rule-based machine translation approach to show how human–crafted rules can be used to translate texts and illustrate their limitations. We then move on to statistical machine translation, which learns to translate automatically from text corpus without too much human intervention. After that, with the development of the big data and machine learning technologies, we further discuss the recent deep learning–based approaches in translation and show their strengths. The key component of deep learning is neural networks, which are used to extract text semantics and learn translation patterns from the training data. Importantly, we discuss the widely used attention mechanism, which enables a very deep understanding of the word-level text and sentence relationships to enable precise translation. Finally, we elaborate on the recent advances in language and translation models in the industry and discuss their potential future directions and the current limitations of machine-based translation techniques.

A Brief Introduction to Artificial Intelligence

Artificial intelligence is a big field of study which enables computers and machines to mimic the perception, learning, problem-solving, and decision-making capabilities of humans. With the fast development of AI technologies and rapid growth of AI applications nowadays, AI has already been used to develop and advance numerous fields and industries, including finance, healthcare, education, social service, transportation, and a lot more, towards different applications such as natural language processing, translation, chatbot, text recognition, speech recognition, face recognition, image processing, and so on.

The study of AI begins with mathematicians trying to figure out how machines can simulate reasoning capabilities of humans based on atomic computation units (i.e., "0" or "1") and

DOI: 10.4324/9781003168348-16

philosophers trying to understand how human brains can produce highly complex patterns based on basic neural cells. The study of mathematical logic led directly to Alan Turing's theory of computation (1937), which suggested that a machine, by shuffling symbols as simple as "0" and "1", could simulate any conceivable act of mathematical deduction. Based on mathematical logic studies, McCulloch and Pitts (1943) created a formal design for artificial neurons, which is generally recognized as the first work of AI. An artificial neuron is a mathematical function conceived as a model of biological neurons and is the elementary unit in an artificial neural network, or simply a neural network. While this model paved the way for further neural network research, it is only a simple model with binary inputs and outputs, some restrictions on the possible weights, and a flexible threshold value, which could hardly be used to solve complex real-world applications. Besides, their model also lacked a mechanism for learning, that is, how to acquire the weights and threshold of the model based on the data.

The term "artificial intelligence" was coined by John McCarthy in 1956, which is generally recognized as the official birthdate of this new science. Within the same year, the first AI program, Logic Theorist (Newell and Simon 1956), was created by Herbert Simon, Allen Newell, and John Shaw to mimic the problem-solving skills of humans and perform automated reasoning, which could prove logical theorems like a mathematician. Later, the first generation of AI researchers produced more AI programs with different human-like capabilities, such as playing checkers, solving algebra problems, and speaking English. These programs were considered astonishing by the press and the public at the time. The AI researchers were also optimistic about the future of AI and thought most of the artificial intelligence problems could be solved within a generation.

Concurrent with the development of AI concepts and AI programs to explore the capability of machines in learning, reasoning, problem-solving, and decision-making, artificial neurons were under fast development as well. In 1967, the first neural network–based computer, Mark 1 Perceptron, was built by Frand Rosenblatt based on his previous papers (1958, 1960, 1961). This model already considered more flexible weight values in the neurons and was used in machines with adaptive capabilities. A landmark book titled *Perceptrons* was published one year later by Marvin Minsky and Seymour Papert (1969), which initiated discussions of future neural network research projects. Despite the importance of this pioneering artificial neural network, its practical application was still limited given the simple model and lack of learning mechanism.

The development of artificial intelligence and artificial neural networks were both slowed in the 1970s but revived in the 1980s. Artificial intelligence research was revived because of the commercial success of *expert systems* in the 1980s, a form of AI program that simulated the decision-making ability of human experts. An expert system is divided into two subsystems: the inference engine and the knowledge base. The knowledge base represents facts and rules. The inference engine applies the rules to the known facts to deduce new facts. Expert systems were among the first truly successful forms of AI software and were used for various application scenarios, including interpretation, prediction, diagnosis, design, planning, monitoring, debugging, repair, instruction, and control. Various expert system software was considered successful towards different applications, such as Hearsay for voice recognition, MYCIN for medical diagnosis, Dendral for chemical analysis, and so on.

Artificial neural networks were also revived in the 1980s because of the rediscovery of *backpropagation*. Backpropagation, short for "backward propagation of errors", is an algorithm for supervised learning of artificial neural networks using gradient descent. The technique of backpropagation dated back to the 1960s and was independently rediscovered many times. But its general use in artificial neural networks was announced by David Rumelhart, Geoffrey Hinton, and Ronald Williams in 1986 and became popular since then. Later, Yann LeCun proposed the modern form of the backpropagation learning algorithm for neural networks (LeCun *et al.* 1988) in 1987 and further proposed the first *convolutional neural network* (CNN) architecture (LeCun *et al.* 1989) in 1989, which was the predecessor of modern deep learning techniques. This very first modern CNN is called LeNet, which demonstrates the significant success of backpropagation in a real-world application – handwritten digit recognition. Despite the success of CNN at this very early stage, its broader application was still limited due to the computational power at that time. The network could not be too complex, which greatly limited the practical usage of the CNN.

With the dominance of expert systems in the artificial intelligence field in the 1980s, researchers were still attempting to make computers automatically learn from experience and data without the need to explicitly design and input rules to the computers by the professionals. There are two reasons for doing so. First, it is not easy to build the knowledge base and design the inference engine, especially for complex problems that need a huge number of facts and rules. Second, there exist quite a lot of problems where humans are incapable of understanding the rules yet, such as genes and inheritance. Without expert knowledge, it is impossible to design expert systems. Therefore, research efforts have been made to understand the relationships between the input and output data by analyzing the patterns exhibited in the input data. This early research field was pattern recognition. Based on pattern recognition research, *machine learning* started to flourish in the 1990s as a subfield of AI research. Machine learning algorithms build a model based on sample data, known as "training data", to make predictions or decisions without being explicitly programmed to do so. Though there is still some disagreement on whether all of machine learning is AI or only the intelligent part of machine learning belongs to AI, most people agree that most of the current machine learning research belongs to AI.

From the 1990s to the early 2010s, the research of artificial intelligence, artificial neural networks, and machine learning continued to develop and grow with the increasing computational power and accessibility to data. AI systems have been applied to more and more complex and interesting read-world problems and applications. For example, Deep Blue became the first computer chess-playing system to beat a reigning world chess champion, Garry Kasparov, on 11 May 1997. In 2011, in a Jeopardy! quiz show exhibition match, IBM's question answering system, Watson, defeated the two greatest Jeopardy! champions, Brad Rutter and Ken Jennings, by a significant margin.

Another significant breakthrough to AI research was the release of AlexNet (Krizhevsky 2012) in 2012, which brought the term *deep learning*, first proposed in 1986, back into the public view. AlexNet was a CNN trained by backpropagation and was a deeper and much wider version of LeNet, thanks to the development of graphics processing unit (GPU). AlexNet demonstrated a big success in image classification and achieved significant improvement over the shallow machine learning methods. It was a significant breakthrough with respect to the previous approaches, and the current widespread application of CNNs can be attributed to this work. Since then, deep learning, as a subfield of machine learning, underwent prompt development and was applied to many real-world complex applications, such as face recognition, autonomous driving, medical synopses, voice assistants, and so on.

2015 was a landmark year for artificial intelligence, with the number of software projects that use AI within Google increasing from "sporadic usage" in 2012 to more than 2,700 projects. In March 2016, AlphaGo won 4 out of 5 games of Go in a match with Go champion Lee Sedol, becoming the first computer Go-playing system to beat a professional Go player without handicaps. This marked the completion of a significant milestone in the development of artificial intelligence, as Go is a relatively complex game, more so than chess. In a 2017 survey, one in five companies reported they had "incorporated AI in some offerings or processes". By 2020, natural language processing systems such as the enormous GPT-3 (then by far the largest artificial neural network) were matching human performance on pre-existing benchmarks, albeit without the system attaining common-sense understanding of the contents of the benchmarks. Facial recognition advanced to where, under some circumstances, some systems claim to have a 99% accuracy rate.

Artificial Intelligence and Translation

Using machines to translate could date back to 1933 when the Soviet scientist Peter Troyanskii presented "the machine for the selection and printing of words when translating from one language to another". The start of machine translation was merely a direct word-by-word translation based on a predefined dictionary without intelligence. With the appearance and flourishing of the first generation of AI systems, rule-based machine translation soon developed based on expert systems.

Rule-based machine translation is a machine translation paradigm where linguistic knowledge is encoded by an expert in the form of rules that translate from source to target language, which is built on the AI technology of the expert system. The first rule-based machine translation systems were developed in the early 1970s with the development of expert systems. Rule-based machine translation survived for a long time until the 2010s before the boom of deep learning, which can be roughly classified into three categories, direct machine translation, transfer-based machine translation, and interlingual machine translation. Direct machine translation systems first translate all words from source to target languages and then reorder or reform the words to obtain a proper sentence in the target language based on rules input by experts. Without grammatical information, the translated sentence in the target language is frequently grammatically incorrect. Transfer-based machine translation systems first obtain the grammatical structure of the sentence in the source language and then reconstruct the sentence in the target language with correct grammar based on rules. Interlingual machine translation generalizes this idea to translate between any source and target language by building up an intermediate language, so one needs to first reconstruct the intermediate language from the source language and then reconstruct the target from the intermediate. However, all rule-based machine translation systems, no matter which category they belong to, cannot produce satisfying results due to their simple rule-based nature. Language is always developing and changing, with homonyms and timely meanings. There are never enough rules to make a perfect translation, even between two specific languages, let alone between any two languages in the world. Despite the poor results of rule-based machine translation systems, they are still widely used with three advantages – morphological accuracy, reproducibility of results, and good use in specific subject areas such as weather reports where the sentences are somehow limited and fixed.

Rule-based machine learning works extremely poorly when the source and target languages have completely different language structures, such as western and Asian languages. In 1984, Makoto Nagao from Kyoto University came up with the idea of using ready-made phrases instead of repeated translation to translate between English and Japanese. The idea is to let experts input translations for frequently used phrases or even sentences directly instead of word-based translations only. Then when the system meets a similar phrase or sentence, it only needs to modify the manual translations for the different parts instead of translating the phrase or sentence from scratch. This new machine translation method is called example-based machine translation. The nature of example-based machine translation systems is still an expert system which needs the expert to input the rules for searching and modification. Example-based machine translation produces better results when similar manual translations exist, but it is still quite heuristic since the expert needs to input tens of thousands of manual translations to cover the commonly used phrases and sentences, and the manual effort is still limited without the consideration of language flexibility.

Since there is no way for expert-defined rules to cover all translation rules and customs with the flexibility of time-changing and localized meanings, a new type of machine translation system was invented in the early 1990 which knows nothing about rules and linguistics as a whole. This new type of machine translation is called statistical machine translation and is built on the AI technology of machine learning. The idea of statistical machine translation is to learn from existing manual translations between two languages and try to understand how each word is translated based on statistics. Even though the system doesn't have the dictionary between the two languages, by studying the existing translations, the system can easily identify the correlation between words from the two languages. For example, whenever the word A appears in the source language, more than 95% of the translated text in the target language contains the word B; then the system can learn that word A in the source language is very likely to be translated into word B in target language. The system is even more powerful than simply identifying the general translation for each word. By studying the other words appearing in the same sentence, the system may identify the different meanings of homonyms when appearing in different source text. With this statistical machine translation, there's no need to specifically design rules for the translation anymore, as the system will automatically learn from existing translations and translate similarly. It also avoids "hard" translations that must follow the rules. To let the system learn, the only thing needed is a large number of existing translations. Fortunately, there exist a large number of texts with multi-language versions, from governmental documents to famous books. The more texts we use, the better translation we could get.

Statistical machine translation started from word-based. For each sentence in both source and target languages, we represent it as the "bag of words", which is a list of words appearing in the sentence with frequencies. With the bag-of-words representation, we can learn the translation of each word via the machine learning method. This is called word-based statistical machine translation. In order to get better results, improved systems were proposed to consider word order and word alignment with extra fertility. However, word-based statistical machine translation is error prone without the consideration of context and syntax. Therefore, two more types of statistical machine translation approaches have been proposed – phrase-based machine translation and syntax-based machine translation. The idea of the phrase-based method is to let computers learn from not only bags of words but also a "bag of phrases". For computers, phrases mean n-grams from sentences, such as bigrams and trigrams, which may not be meaningful as human-identified phrases. With a bag of phrases, the quality of translation was significantly improved, which made phrase-based statistical machine translation methods the dominant method for machine translation from 2006 to 2016, and they were then superseded by neural machine translation. Syntax-based statistical machine translation was another attempt to incorporate the rule-based method into the statistical method and gain the advantages of both methods so that the translated text has correct syntax and maintains a certain quality based on the statistics. Unfortunately, the outcome of these integrated methods worked much below expectations and turned out to exhibit cons of both rule-based and statistical methods.

With the dominance of phrase-based statistical machine translation during the early 2010s, applying deep neural networks to machine translation was explored with the fast development of deep learning. An early research work on applying neural networks to machine translation was published in 2013, which attracted Google's attention and led to Google's neural machine translation project that can translate between nine languages and went online in 2016. Neural machine translation was a significant revolution in the machine translation field, which made the translation between any two languages possible without explicitly analyzing the statistics of the words and phrases. During the time of machine learning, the computational power of computers was much lower than that of current computers, so the learning ability of the computers was also limited. In order to let computers learn, humans need to manually summarize the features of the input and/or output so that the computers can learn from the features. In statistical machine translation, the features mean the words and phrases and their frequencies. Nowadays, with the much higher computational power, the learning ability of computers is also significantly improved, with much more complex deep learning models. So computers can directly learn from scratched data, that is, learn directly from whole input and output sentences without splitting them into words and phrases. With the capability to learn from whole sentences, the translation quality can be significantly improved. As of June 2021, Google Translate, with neural machine translation technology, can translate between 109 languages with high quality. Neural machine translation is still the state-of-the-art method as of June 2021 and is still under fast development with the continuous development of deep learning technology in the AI research field.

Neural machine translation started from the encoder–decoder deep learning network structure where the encoder was a convolutional neural network and the decoder was a recurrent neural network (RNN) in 2013. The CNN encoder encodes the input text in a source language into a state vector, which can be seen as a universal intermediate representation of all languages. The RNN decoder decodes the state vector into text in the target language. The RNN is used as the decoder to solve the problem of word reordering in long sentences. The idea was good, but the performance was not that inspiring in the beginning due to the exploding and vanishing gradient in network training. One year later, sequence-to-sequence (seq2seq) learning was proposed to use a RNN for both encoder and decoder, and long short-term memory (LSTM), a variety of RNN, was introduced for neural machine translation. LSTM could solve the word reordering problem in long sentences, but the method was still limited by the fixed-width state vector, which was further solved by the attention mechanism later. Besides, all RNN-based methods still had problems when facing really long sentences and were computationally inefficient. Most recently, the new model that was proposed to solve the machine translation problem is the transformer, which relies mostly on the attention mechanism. In each step, the transformer applies a self-attention mechanism which directly models relationships between all words in a sentence, regardless of their respective position. The transformer handles the entire input sequence at once and doesn't iterate word by word, which greatly improves training efficiency and also the quality of the translation.

Expert Systems for Rule-Based Machine Translation

Expert systems are the very first commercially successful AI technology used for machine translation. To build up an expert system, expert knowledge needs to be first formulated into formal machine facts and rules and stored in the knowledge base in the system. Here, facts are statements showing the facts needed during the translation; for example, "cat" in English is a noun, "cat" in English should be translated into "katze" in German, "katze" in German is a feminine word, and so on. Rules are statements showing the rules of translation and language construction; for example, English language uses the subject-verb-object structure, so the verb comes before the object, but Japanese language uses the subject-object-verb structure, so the object comes before the verb. In real practice, rules are usually implemented as if-else statements so that the machines can obtain different conclusions based on different conditions. This is also the most fundamental form of an AI system. But, as one may imagine, it needs a great many facts and rules to complete the translation between two languages, so a machine translation expert system is usually divided into several modules where each module completes a sub-task of the whole translation aim.

Paragraph Splitting and Word Tagging

The input text may be a long paragraph composed of multiple sentences, so the first simple but useful module is usually the paragraph splitting module, which splits the input paragraph into individual sentences, which could be naively achieved by breaking the paragraph at end-sentence punctuation marks, such as full stop, question mark, exclamation mark, and so on. After the paragraph is split into sentences, then it is important to identify the tag of each word; in other words, identify which part of the sentence the word is. For example, take an English sentence "My name is Alice Bacon". Here, "My" is a pronoun, "name" is a noun, "is" is a verb, "Alice" is a noun, and "Bacon" is a noun. Usually, word tagging is performed based on the facts if the word has only one tag in all its usages. However, the same word may have different tags; for example, "conduct" in English could be either a verb or a noun based on the usage. Therefore, that's when rules are needed in word tagging. For example, we may have a rule like "if there exists another verb in the sentence, then conduct is a noun, otherwise it is a verb". The rules in real practice could be much more complex than this one and are carefully designed by linguists. But you should be able to get a basic idea here of how an expert system module could tag the words for which parts of speech they are.

Things will become much more complicated if the text comes from speech without any punctuation marks. In this case, one needs to first identify each word as the part of a sentence, i.e., word tagging, and then split the paragraph into sentences based on the rules of the formation of a sentence with an expert system. For example, if the input is "I am a girl I like cats", the tags of the words are <noun> <verb> <preposition> <noun> <noun> <verb> <noun>. Since there are two verbs and no interjection, there is no problem for linguists to design rules to identify this input as two sentences and further design rules based on the language structures to identify the two "I"'s as <subject> and the "girl" and the "cats" as <object> for detailed word tagging. With the facts and rules on parts of speech and language structure, linguists have designed various machine-understandable rules for paragraph splitting and word tagging in different machine translation expert systems.

Proper Noun and Phrase Identification

Word-by-word translation is error prone since there exist many proper nouns and phrases which should be translated together for correct translation. A proper noun is a noun that identifies a single entity and is used to refer to that entity, such as *Albert Einstein* and *Los Angeles*. Besides, multiple words as a phrase may show completely different meanings from the individually translated version. For example, a dead duck[1] means a person or thing that is defunct or has no chance of success, not a real dead duck. Therefore, a machine translation expert system usually contains facts and rules for proper nouns and phrases so that they can be translated as a whole entity instead of individual words.

Translation

The translation module is the key module in the machine translation expert system. With the identified word tags, proper nouns, and phrases, the next step is to translate the sentence from the source language to the target language based on the facts and rules of the language structure.

The first set of rules needed for translation is for the language structure based on the word tags. The expert system will adjust the sequence of the words based on the word tags to fit the language structure of the target language. Then, the system needs to decide the translation for each word, proper noun, and phrase based on the facts input from the dictionary. In case multiple meanings exist for a single word, rules are needed to judge which meaning is most suitable based on the word tags and other words in the sentence. For example, "conduct" in English can be either a verb or a noun. These two cases have different meanings and are usually translated differently in other languages. As another example, "the" in English may be translated into "das", "der", or "die" in German. In order to know which language to apply, the system needs to examine whether the noun that follows it is neuter, masculine, or feminine. All these are indicated by carefully designed facts and rules in the expert system.

Refinement

Finally, one last step that usually follows in the machine translation expert system is a refinement module, which aims to make the output language as natural as possible. Even with the carefully designed many facts and rules for the previous processes, including paragraph splitting, word tagging, proper noun and phrase identification, and translation, the translated sentences may be unnatural even though they have the correct language structure due to the nature of word-by-word or phrase-by-phrase translation. Therefore, linguists may further design rules to insert, delete, or modify words to/from a sentence to make it more natural. One common case is that if you translate a past-tense sentence from Chinese to English, for example, "我以前不太聰明", you may easily get something like "I previously was not smart" because verbs in Chinese don't have tenses and additional adverbs are used to express the past tense. So, after translation to English word-by-word, this additional adverb will be translated to something like "previously", which is actually unneeded because "was" already expresses the past tense. Therefore, during the refinement stage, rules can be designed to remove these unneeded words to make the translated sentences more elegant.

Summary

As a short summary of expert systems, we can quickly identify the pros and cons when using expert systems for translation tasks. With carefully designed facts and rules, an expert system could produce stable and reasonable translations that meet humans' expectations. But they can never go beyond expectations to provide you surprisingly good translations because everything is hard coded. Besides, they also need extensive human and professional efforts to design and input millions of facts and rules to the system, which is extremely time consuming and labor intensive. After machine learning became popular, expert systems quickly lost their position in machine translation and are only used for task-specific translation purposes now.

Statistical Machine Translation

Statistical machine translation (SMT) generates translations using a statistical analysis of the bilingual data. It works to identify the relationship between the source and target languages.

The Statistical Translation Model

The statistical translation model aims to translate the source language to the target language. A statistical translation can be modeled with the so-called "noisy channel" model. The intuition of the noisy channel model is to assume the translation has introduced some "noise" during the process, and we would like to recover the original input signal. For example, if we have a certain noisy translation process $P(f|e)^2$, the input English sentence e will be processed and translated to the French sentence f. In statistical machine translation, if we already know the French sentence f and the translation model $P(f|e)$, we would like to recover the original signal e, which should also be the translation of the French sentence f. The determination of e can be achieved by Bayesian inference as:

$$\hat{e} = \underset{e}{\mathrm{argmax}}\, P(e \mid f)$$

$$= \underset{e}{\mathrm{argmax}}\, \frac{P(f \mid e)P(e)}{P(f)}$$

$$= \underset{e}{\mathrm{argmax}}\, \underbrace{P(f \mid e)}_{\substack{\text{Translation} \\ \text{model}}} \cdot \underbrace{P(e)}_{\substack{\text{Language} \\ \text{model}}}$$

The argmax operator means to find the sentence e in English, which reaches the highest possibility according to this equation. In this way, we can divide the translation problem into two parts: the translation model and the language model. The complex translation model can thus be subdivided into two simpler independent models.

The language model is a statistical model that predicts the next word in a sequence of words. It is the core concept in natural language processing (NLP). A good model would simulate the behavior of the real world: given the context, the model would predict the next word of the sentence in a natural, human-like way. Theoretically, the probabilities can be directly estimated by the frequency of the words in the training corpus. However, in that case, the model will be very complex due to the unlimited size of condition sentence lengths. Moreover, the model is not robust to unseen sentences, which could have very similar meanings but with different words. To cope with the problem, we usually use the n-gram model as the statistical language model. The n-gram model assumes that the probability of a word only depends on the previous n words. In other words, the probability of the word is only determined by the context of size n. The n-gram model is simple yet effective and is widely used in the field of NLP. It can be used for translation, as well as for other tasks such as text summarization, sentiment analysis, and so on.

After we talk about the language model, we will move on to the modeling the translation model $P(f|e)^3$. That is, given a large corpus of the paired translation data from English to French, how can we estimate the conditional probability of the occurrence of the French sentence f, given the English sentence e? In this section we mainly discuss the IBM alignment models, which were introduced in the 1990s. The alignment model is lexical based. Given the parallel corpus of English and French sentences, the model estimates the probability that each word in the French sentence is aligned to the corresponding word in the English sentence. Here we explain mainly the generative story of IBM Model 3 as follows, according to (Knight 1999):

1   For each word in the English sentence e, we assign a fertility value to it. The fertility value is the number of French words that can be aligned to the English word. The choice of fertility is dependent solely on the English word. It is not dependent on the other English words in the English sentence or on their fertility. The fertility value will be learned by the model.

2   Based on the fertility estimation, we rewrite the English sentence. If the word has a fertility of 0, we eliminate it in the rewriting process. If the word has a fertility of 1, we do not change it. If the word has a fertility of n, we rewrite it as n copies of the word.

3   The model computes another fertility score of an invisible NULL token. The intuition is that the target language may sometimes contain some spurious word that is not aligned to any word in the English sentence. We place the copies of the NULL token based on another statistical parameter that will be learned by the model.

4   We translate each English word in the combined rewritten sentence to the target language in a per-word manner. The selection of the target word is also based on a learnable parameter.

5   All those French words are permuted. Each French word is assigned an absolute target "position slot". For example, one word may be assigned position 3, and another may be assigned position 2 – the latter word would then precede the former in the final French sentence. The choice of position for a French word is dependent solely on the absolute position of the English word that generates it.

We illustrate the generative story of IBM Model 3 in Figure 15.1.

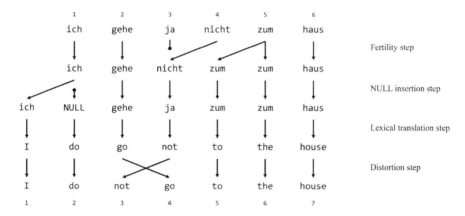

Figure 15.1   A complete translation step of IBM Model 3. The image is a visualization of a practical translation case in (Koehn 2009)

Note that in IBM Model 3, there are overall four parameters that will be learned from the training data. The parameters: a) the fertility score probability given the English word, b) the word-wise translation probability given the French word and the English word, c) the probability of the target permutation location, and d) the location of the NULL token insertion. Usually, these parameters can be obtained by the EM algorithm.

Besides the lexical-based model, there are also other types of statistical translation models, such as syntax-based or phrase-based models. Their intuitions are similar to the lexical-based model but are usually more complex and involve more parameters.

Deep Learning for Neural Machine Translation

With the recent development of machine learning techniques and efficient algorithms on vector and tensor algorithms, large-scale deep learning based machine translation is made possible. The learning-based methods for machine translation do not require explicit modeling of the translation process. Instead, the learning-based machine translation uses the translation corpus data to supervise the training of the translation model. Once the model is properly trained, it can be deployed to perform online translation. Due to the huge model capacity as well as the large size of the translation corpus, the learning-based methods reach the state of the art in terms of various translation evaluation metrics. In this section, we shall discuss several up-to-date models and techniques to perform learning-based machine translation.

Word Embeddings and word2vec Model

The motivation of word embedding is to represent the words in a vector representation. Most importantly, the vector representation can estimate the semantic similarity between words. Suppose two words have similar semantic meanings; they should also have similar word embedding vectors. With vector representation, word embeddings can also support arithmetic operations in the vector space. For example, the embedding vector of the word "king" can be roughly obtained by first subtracting the embedding of "woman" from "queen" and then adding back the embedding of "man". The semantics operation can also be on the scope of word tenses, part-of-speech, and so on, as illustrated in Figure 15.2.

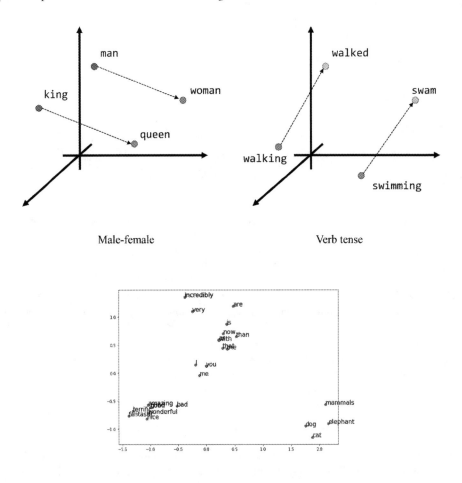

Male-female   Verb tense

Part-of-speech clusters

Figure 15.2   Semantic representation in the word embedding space. The clustering of the word embeddings is computed based on Pennington *et al.* (2014)

Moreover, traditional vector representation such as one-hot embedding encodes the word by composing the word vector of a single one and a number of zeros. The index of the single one value in the vector should be the index of the text in the dictionary (all occurring words in the text corpus). As we can see, these one-hot representations are usually very sparse and high dimensional, especially when the dictionary is large. In contrast, word embeddings generally have much lower dimensionality, as shown in Figure 15.3. This helps to reduce the computational cost of the follow-up translation tasks.

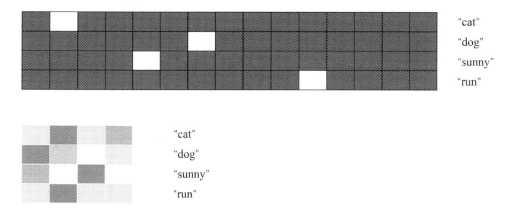

"cat"

"dog"

"sunny"

"run"

Figure 15.3 One-hot representation vs. word embeddings. One-hot representation uses only zero and one values, resulting in very sparse and high-dimensional word representations. Word embedding uses a dense vector representation and is usually learned from data

Even though the word embedding concept is proposed, it is still unclear how we can obtain the word embeddings in numerical form. It is obviously impossible for humans to extract the meaning of all words and sort them numerically into the embeddings. Yet fortunately, with the help of machine learning algorithms, we can obtain word embeddings by learning from the contexts of the word.

> You shall know a word by the company it keeps.
>
> *(J.R. Firth, 1890–1960)*

Thus, the word2vec model (Mikolov *et al.* 2013) is proposed to capture the semantic meaning of a word. The fundamental concept of the word2vec model is to infer the word semantics from its surrounding contexts. One of the most widely used models for word2vec is called continuous bag of words (CBOW). The motivation of the CBOW model is to predict the meaning of the missing word from its surroundings, as illustrated in Figure 15.4.

The structure of the CBOW model is a three-layer neural network with an input layer, a hidden layer, and an output layer. The input of the model is the *context* of the word to be predicted. The input is modeled with the bag-of-word representation by summing up the one-hot representations of the surrounding words to the word to be predicted. The hidden layer enables the model to learn the vector representation of the word through non-linearity. The output layer is a softmax layer, which is used to predict the probability of the word to be the correct word. The objective of the CBOW model is usually the cross-entropy loss to minimize the error between the predicted word and the ground truth.

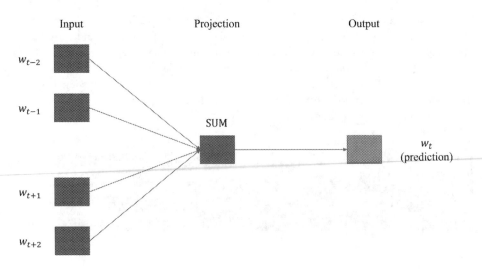

Figure 15.4   The structure of the CBOW model for word embedding estimation

Once the CBOW model is trained, we can use it to represent arbitrary words involved in training. The word embedding at the *i*th position of the input (i.e., the *i*th index in the vocabulary, as it is in the one-hot representation) can be represented by extracting all neural network weights between the *i*th neuron in the input layer and the hidden layer. The final word embedding dimension is the same as the dimension of the hidden layer, which is usually far smaller than the dimension of the input layer (the dimension of the one-hot representation could be as large as the whole dictionary!).

With the word embeddings estimated, we can further make use of these embedding for a wide variety of downstream tasks. For example, we can compute the semantic of the meanings of a long text sequence by summing up the word embeddings of the words in the sequence to form the "sentence embeddings" or "text embeddings". These embeddings can be further processed through other models and algorithms to perform the tasks such as sentence similarity, sentiment classification, and so on. Additionally, as the semantic meaning of the word is learned from the text contexts, word embedding can also be customized for certain needs (legal documents, news reports, research papers, etc.) by providing more task-specific text corpora. Word embeddings are also helpful for more complex tasks such as machine translation. In the next section, we shall discuss using the computed semantic information to perform machine translation.

Recurrent Neural Network and Sequence-to-Sequence Models

As mentioned before, we usually regard a sentence as a sequence of word tokens. In this fashion, we can formulate the machine translation problem as a generic sequence-to-sequence problem, where the input sequence is the source language sentence, and the output sequence is the target language sentence. The main challenge of this task mainly comes from the complexity of (and between) the languages. As we discussed, the languages could be very different from each other; we cannot assume the traditional language and translation model will work well in this case, as they may fail to model complicated sentence correlations. Moreover, the traditional language model assumes a limited context scope (the Markov assumption) and thus cannot fully capture the contexts during translation.

To cope with the challenges, the recurrent neural network architecture is used to solve the sequence-to-sequence problem. The RNN is a variant of a feed-forward neural network that allows sequential inputs. The "recurrent" in the name of RNN represents that the RNN can remember the past state of the network. We show an illustration of the RNN structure in Figure 15.5. As shown in the left part of the figure, the network model reads the input and processes the input from lower layers to the upper layers and finally produces the output, which shares the same behavior as traditional feed-forward neural networks. However, the key difference is that the RNN can remember the past state of the network. We usually refer to the past state as the "hidden state". With the proposal of the hidden state, the RNN is now allowed to exhibit temporal dynamic behavior, which is illustrated on the right of Figure 15.5.

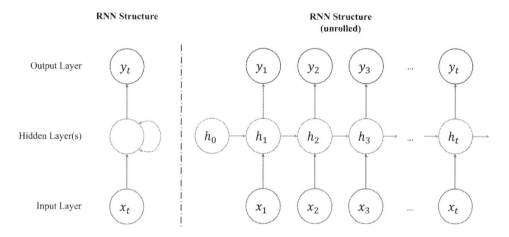

Figure 15.5 An illustration of the RNN model. Here t represents the timestep index, x represents the input, h represents the hidden state, and y represents the output. Note that the RNN model has loops. The loops can be broken by *unrolling* the model to apply the same model structure for each time step input and output while propagating the hidden state h for each time step

Taking the sentence "The cat sat on the mat" as an example, the RNN takes the word once at a time as the input. So first, at time $t = 1$, the word "the" is embedded into the input layer (usually we use the vector embedding in actual computation), and then the input embedding is passed to the bottommost feed-forward layer together with the previous hidden state to compute the new hidden state. The new hidden state is then passed to upper layers in the same manner until the output layer is reached. The output layer takes the newly computed hidden state of the uppermost feed-forward layer and makes the output. The output is usually a probability vector indicating the prediction of the next word. With the behavior of the time t defined, we shall recurrently reuse the whole network structure to process the whole sentence by feeding the following words one at a time and compute the hidden states of the network layers in the same manner.

As we already know the general structure of the recurrent neural network, one straightforward idea to use the RNN to perform the machine translation could be by a word-to-word conversion. For example, given an example English input, "I am a student", when the word "I" is input to the network, it will compute the hidden states of the network layers and output the word "je" in French (in practice, the network will output a list of probabilities of all possible

French words. We simply choose the one with the highest probabilities as the output). After that, we continue to input the word "am" into the RNN network and expect it will output the word "suis" in French, and so on. However, this kind of autoregressive use of the RNN may have several problems: First, the RNN is not trained to capture the global meaning of the whole sentence; instead, the output only depends on the "seen" words from previous steps of inputs and the current input. This will limit the translation performance, especially when the word orders may drastically change in the target language. Second, the length of the input sentence may not be the same as the output sentence. Even though the problem can be somewhat resolved by padding the sentences with the <PAD> token, the network performs very poorly.

Instead, to maximize the ability to capture the source sentence and better output the target sentence, we usually construct the sequence-to-sequence model in an *autoencoding* way. The overall model structure comprises two sub-models: the encoder and the decoder. The encoder is a RNN network that is used to encode the source sentence into a vector. The decoder is also a RNN network that is used to decode the vector to the target sentence. The encoder and the decoder are connected and trained together to minimize the translation error. We refer to this type of translation model as the *seq2seq* model (Sutskever *et al.* 2014). The overall architecture of the seq2seq model is illustrated in Figure 15.6.

When performing model training, the encoder part takes the input sentence sequence and extracts the last hidden states as the encoded vector. The decoder then takes the right-shifted target sentence sequence as the input and uses the previously extracted encoded vector as the initial hidden state. Given such settings, the objective of the decoder RNN is to predict the next word in the target sentence, given a partial translation of the target sentence. For example, if we want to train the translation of "I am a student" to "je suis étudiant" in French, in the first round of the decoding, given the input <BOS> token, the network is expected to output the word "je" in French. Then the first word, "je", of the ground truth translation is sent to the decoder

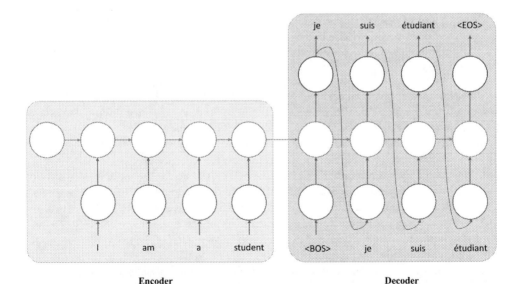

Encoder   **Decoder**

Figure 15.6   The architecture of the seq2seq model. The encoder captures the semantic meaning of the
input sentence "I am a student" and passes it to the decoder. The decoder reads the hidden
state passed to it and translates the words one at a time

as the second-round input, and the network is expected to output the next word of translation, "suis". The process continues until the network outputs a <EOS> token, which indicates the translation is finished. The model is trained by minimizing the cross-entropy loss between the target sentence and the predicted target sentence. Note that we are not feeding the network output directly as the next round input but instead using the right-shifted ground truths as the input during training. This is called the teacher forcing mechanism. The teacher forcing mechanism is used to ensure the decoder is always aware of the true target sentence and reduces the cumulative error during decoding.

During inference (i.e., actual production), the encoder works the same way as in the training phase. However, in the decoder part, as we do not obtain the ground truth translations, we must use the network output as the input to predict the next word for translation. Still, the decoding continues until the network predicts a <EOS> token to represent the end of the sentence.

With the proposed encoder-decoder structure, the seq2seq model can capture the semantics of the source sentences and manage to translate them into the target language. However, the vanilla RNN network suffers from the so-called "short-term memory problem". If the input sequence is long enough, the network would tend to forget the input information from earlier time steps. This is intuitively easy to understand, as for each timestep, the network always updates the hidden state by adding the information of the current input to the hidden state. As a result, the information of earlier time steps will contribute a much smaller portion of the hidden state when input is continuously fed into the network. To cope with the problem, two RNN cell structures, LSTM (Hochreiter and Schmidhuber 1997) and GRU (Chung *et al.* 2014), are proposed to replace the weighting layers in RNNs. GRU stands for "gated recurrent unit" while LSTM stands for "long short-term memory". These structures allow the network to learn to control how much new input information should be learned and how much previous information should be retained, allowing the network to maintain long-term memory during training and inference. When input is fed into the network, LSTM and GRU are able to learn to control the flow of information through the network, allowing them to retain important information from earlier time steps while also incorporating new input. This allows the network to maintain a more accurate representation of the input over time, improving its ability to make predictions based on long input sequences. In this way, LSTM and GRU help to overcome the problem of forgetting input information in RNNs. This layer design also helps the network learn in a smoother way by refining the gradient flows during training, according to Hochreiter (1998).

The original seq2seq paper mainly raises the previously mentioned framework in 2014, while the key ideas such as RNNs and LSTMs could be traced back to even earlier. The seq2seq model achieved state-of-the-art performance in terms of the BLEU score and some other metrics at that time. We will compare these metrics with different methods later, but keep in mind that despite the recent research such as transformers surpassing the original seq2seq model, the seq2seq model is still widely used due to its simplicity and ease of implementation. Besides machine translation, the seq2seq model is also used in a variety of other tasks such as image captioning, question answering, message quick replies, and so on.

The Attention Mechanism

While the seq2seq model can translate the source sentences into the target language, the model still has a bottleneck of the fixed representation problem. In the encoding process, the encoder must compress the whole meaning of the source sentence into a fixed-length vector representation, regardless of the length of the source sentence. In other words, the network may forget something in the input sentence. On the other hand, the decoder only sees the fixed source sentence information, but some of the words in the source language should be more important than others at each time step of target language generation.

To address this problem, the attention mechanism is first proposed in Bahdanau *et al.* (2014). It became the current standard for most of the sequence processing models. The key concept of the attention is: at different time steps of the decoding process (i.e., when the decoder outputs different words in the target language), the network is expected to focus on the most relevant information from the source sentence. Figure 15.7 is an illustrated example of the attention mechanism. The horizontal axis represents the source language sentence, while the vertical axis represents the target language sentence. The attention score is illustrated as the intensity of the matrix. For example, when the network outputs the word "like", it focuses most on the word "歡" in the source language, then the word "喜". This also happens when outputting the word "movies", where the attention mainly comes from the characters "電" and "影". The attention mechanism solves the fixed representation problem by enabling the decoder to oversee all input words to avoid the fixed vector burden. Additionally, the attention mechanism also helps the network to learn the importance of the source sentence words. Moreover, specifically in machine translation, the attention mechanism explicitly helps the network learn the "alignment" of the words, which is considered difficult in traditional statistical machine translation.

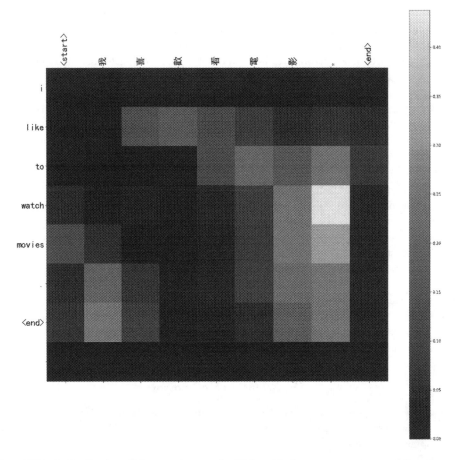

Figure 15.7 A visualization of the attention matrix. Lighter blocks mean stronger correlation between words during the attention score computation

The computation of the attention scores is performed at each timestep of the decoder RNN. After the input word is given to the decoder, the network first computes an initial hidden RNN state. After that, the hidden state will be used as the "query" to search through all source language words to find the relevance of the query word. This can be regarded as an analogy of search engine behaviors. When a keyword is input, the search engine will go through all its stored websites and compute a relevance score according to the query keywords. The relevance score is the similarity between the query and the website content. The higher the score, the more relevant the website is. What's more, those relevant websites may be uneven in content quality, so the search engine usually computes another "quality score" for each website and multiplies this score to the relevance score to get the final score, which is used to rank the websites for display. In this case, the query is the user input keywords, the keys are all the possible websites in the dataset, and the value is the quality score. The search engine first computes the relevance score from the keys and the query and afterward multiples the relevance score with the value to get the final score.

The computation of the attention score is the same as the search engine scores, where the decoder hidden states are the query, and the source language words are the keys. The attention mechanism first computes scores between the query and the keys into a probability of relevance. After that, the attention multiplies the relevance score to the values (usually computed from the keys through a feed-forward neural network or simply the same as the keys) to get the final attention score. The attention score is then summarized into a context vector, and the decoder RNN state is updated by adding the context vector to the current hidden state. Finally, the decoder uses the new hidden state to generate the next word.

By incorporating the attention mechanism, the seq2seq model has better performance than its original version. More importantly, the idea of an attention mechanism has improved to be more general and flexible to become the most recent transformer model.

Self-Attention and Transformer Model

Even though the seq2seq model, together with the attention mechanism, has had success in various fields, its recurrent nature has limited its ability to process large-scale data and information. For example, when the input sequence is very long, the recurrent model still needs to read/output the words one after another in both the encoder and the decoder actions. This behavior severely limits the scalability of processing, as the encoding and decoding cannot be parallelized. Moreover, RNNs are usually not expected to be built with a very large model capacity, which is a problem for improving the overall performance.

The transformer model is proposed in Vaswani *et al.* (2017) to address these issues. The idea of the transformer is similar to the seq2seq models, which encodes the input sequence and decodes the output sequence, but a) allows the encoder and the decoder to process very long sequences parallelly with the propositional encoding mechanism; b) enhances the attention mechanism by proposing the multi-head self-attention and the casual attention to enable internal attention within the encoder and the decoder; and c) allows the stack of the transformer blocks to make very deep models, which is another key to enable large-scale dataset training.

The general structure transformer model is similar to the seq2seq models, which contain the encoder part and the decoder part, as illustrated in Figure 15.8. However, the internal mechanism of the transformer block is rather different. First, the encoder and decoder blocks can be stacked to gain model complexity. In the encoder part, the input sequence is first embedded into the word embeddings. Then, for each word embedding, the transformer adds a positional vector to it. The positional vector follows a specific pattern to indicate the position of the word

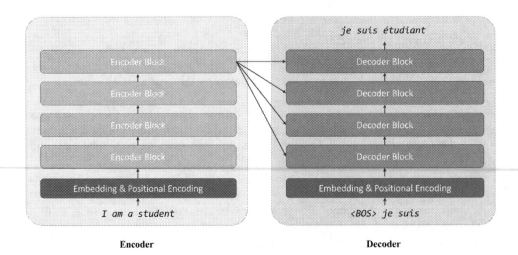

Figure 15.8   The architecture overview of the transformer model for machine translation. The model works similarly to the seq2seq model, except that it allows the sentence to be input and output as a whole

in the source sentence. After that, the composite of the word embedding and the positional vector is passed through a stack of the encoder transformer blocks. Note that these embeddings are inputted as a whole, with the ordering information inferred from the positional encoding.

The most important component of the encoder transformer block is the *multi-head self-attention* layer. Self-attention is a special kind of attention mechanism that allows the encoder to compute the attention score of the word embedding to itself. The self-attention can better reveal the contextual information of the source sentence, which is lacking in the attention-based seq2seq models. Take the sentence "The animal didn't cross the street because it was too tired" as an example; humans can easily see that the word "it" should refer to the word "animal". The self-attention aims to capture such contextual information within the input sequence for better decoding. Moreover, humans can find the reference of the word "it" by inferring from another, context "too tired" in the sentence. This means that the self-attention should not be unique but should be performed in different groups.[4] As a result, multi-head attention is proposed to allow multiple instances of self-attention computation within a single sequence. As illustrated in Figure 15.9, we can see the orange links are from one group of self-attention, and the green links are from the other group of self-attention. Finally, the self-attention scores of multiple words are summed up to get the final attention score.

Each encoder block contains a self-attention layer. After the self-attention computation, the attention scores will be added to the original embeddings. The composite vectors for each word embedding will be processed by a feed-forward neural network layer for better model generalization ability (i.e., better adapt to the training data).

After that, we move to the decoder part. For translation tasks, the decoder works similarly to the seq2seq model but is also equipped with transformer blocks to allow the output of target language translation words at once. Note that even though the decoder allows output of a whole sequence, in both the training and inference phases, the decoder actually still outputs the next word prediction instead of a whole target language sentence. In this case, the model inputs a partial target language translation sequence with a length of n and outputs a sequence of $n + 1$, where the first n words should be the same as the input, and the last word of the output is the

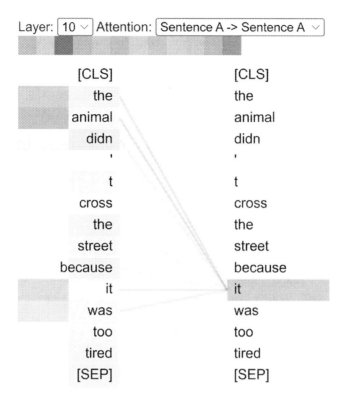

Figure 15.9 A visualization of the multi-head attention. We only show two attention heads for clearer visualization

next word prediction of the partial input translation. The decoding starts with a sequence with only a single token, <BOS>, and the decoder should output the probability prediction of the first word. After that, one can choose the word with the highest probability and concatenate it after <BOS> as the new input for the next round. The network output of this new round should be the probabilities for both the first and second words. In this case, we only care about the second word and continue choosing the one with the highest probability and concatenate the input. The process is repeated until the <EOS> token is reached from the decoder (i.e., <EOS> has the highest probability). The reason for the autoregressive decoding is that, for one source sentence, there could be multiple translations. There are no ground truth translations during the target language sentence prediction. It would be better to predict the translated sequence in an autoregressive manner, which allows the translation to be non-unique. For example, when the decoder outputs the probabilities of the next word, one can choose both the words with the highest and second-highest probabilities to create two possible partial translations for the next timestep. This is usually called *beam search*, which is a special case of autoregressive decoding.

By following the previously mentioned design goals, the decoder transformer blocks exhibit two significant differences from the encoder blocks. The first is causal attention or masked self-attention. Causal attention works similarly to ordinary self-attention computations, but it avoids the computation of the attention score for future positions. In other words, the attention is only computed in the scope of translated words. The second difference is the extra encoder-decoder attention block. The encoder-decoder attention works the same way as the encoder-decoder attention in RNN translation models, which capture the pairwise relations between the words of the source language sequence and the words of the target language sequence.

We illustrate a full transformer model for translation in Figure 15.10.

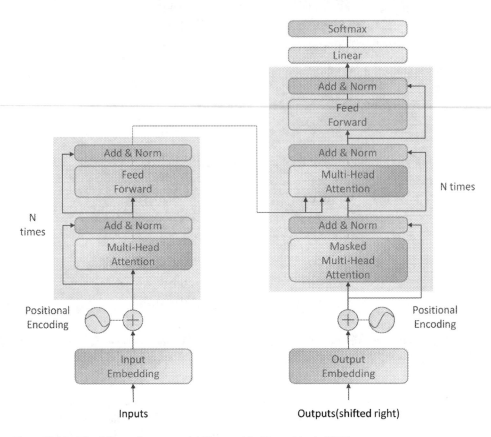

Figure 15.10   The full transformer model illustrated in Vaswani *et al.* (2017)

Note that in the recent productions of transformer models, the parameters of the transformer could be extremely large. For example, the recent transformer model for text generation, GPT-3 (Brown *et al.* 2020), uses 96 attention layers, each with 96 × 128-dimension heads, causing a monstrous model with 175 billion parameters! More surprisingly, the model is trained with a corpus of 499 billion tokens. Such a model could generate very natural text that humans cannot distinguish from human-written content. The novel structure and the model capacity of transformer models also help in the machine translation task. Google claims that with the help of the transformer architecture, it gains an average +5 BLEU score improvement over all 100+ languages than the model in one year (Google AI Blog 2020). Note that the BLEU score is the metric used to evaluate the performance of the translation by comparing the translation with a set of reference ground truth translations.

Even though the transformer model is considered very complex, it is still possible to train it with a small amount of data by fine-tuning the existing pretrained models. Thus, the transformer model has also been applied to other tasks such as question answering, text classification, image captioning, and even computer vision tasks.

Conclusions

In summary, machine translation has been evolving together with the improvement of AI technologies. At an early stage, the knowledge within machine translation must be provided by humans by explicitly defining grammar rules. With the development of statistical learning, the language model appeared to estimate the probabilities of words in a sentence. By learning with a bilingual language model, statistical machine translation can learn automatically from the text corpus. However, as the statistical model is limited in parameter size and expressive ability, it still cannot achieve satisfactory translations, especially for complex languages. In recent years, state-of-the-art deep learning models have been developed to further improve machine translation. These models feature the ability to capture the very deep semantics of the whole sentences and learn smoothly from text corpora at the terabyte scale. With the help of these models, machine translation systems nowadays can provide more accurate translation results.

Notes

1 https://dictionary.cambridge.org/dictionary/english/dead-duck.
2 $P(f \mid e)$ represents the conditional probability of the occurrence of f, conditioned by the occurrence of e.
3 $P(f \mid e)$ represents the conditional probability of the occurrence of f, conditioned by the occurrence of e.
4 One may argue that the different groups of self-attention can be summed up to form a singular attention score, but in practice, this will degrade the encoding performance, as some of the self-attention will dominate and make the network ignorant to other contexts.

Bibliography

Bahdanau, D., K. Cho, and Y. Bengio (2014) 'Neural Machine Translation by Jointly Learning to Align and Translate', *arXiv preprint arXiv:1409.0473*.

Brown, T. B., B. Mann, N. Ryder, M. Subbiah, J. Kaplan, P. Dhariwal, . . . and D. Amodei (2020) 'Language Models Are Few-Shot Learners', *arXiv preprint arXiv:2005.14165*.

Chung, J., C. Gulcehre, K. Cho, and Y. Bengio (2014) 'Empirical Evaluation of Gated Recurrent Neural Networks on Sequence Modeling', *arXiv preprint arXiv:1412.3555*.

Hochreiter, S. (1998) 'The Vanishing Gradient Problem During Learning Recurrent Neural Nets and Problem Solutions', *International Journal of Uncertainty, Fuzziness and Knowledge-Based Systems* 6(2): 107–16.

Hochreiter, S. and J. Schmidhuber (1997) 'Long Short-Term Memory', *Neural Computation* 9(8): 1735–80.

Knight, K. (1999, April) 'A Statistical MT Tutorial Workbook', in *Prepared for the 1999 JHU Summer Workshop*, 1–37. https://kevincrawfordknight.github.io/.

Koehn, P. (2009) *Statistical Machine Translation*, Cambridge: Cambridge University Press.

Krizhevsky, A., I. Sutskever, and G. E. Hinton (2012) 'Imagenet Classification with Deep Convolutional Neural Networks', *Advances in Neural Information Processing Systems* 25: 1097–105.

LeCun, Y., B. Boser, J. S. Denker, D. Henderson, R. E. Howard, W. Hubbard, and L. D. Jackel (1989) 'Backpropagation Applied to Handwritten Zip Code Recognition', *Neural Computation* 1(4): 541–51.

LeCun, Y., D. Touresky, G. Hinton, and T. Sejnowski (1988, June) 'A Theoretical Framework for Back-Propagation', in *Proceedings of the 1988 Connectionist Models Summer School*, vol. 1, Morgan Kaufmann, San Mateo, CA, 21–28.

McCulloch, W. S. and W. Pitts (1943) 'A Logical Calculus of the Ideas Immanent in Nervous Activity', *The Bulletin of Mathematical Biophysics* 5(4): 115–33.

Mikolov, T., K. Chen, G. Corrado, and J. Dean (2013) 'Efficient Estimation of Word Representations in Vector Space', *arXiv preprint arXiv:1301.3781*.

Minsky, M. and S. Papert (1969) *Perceptron: An Introduction to Computational Geometry*, Cambridge, MA: The MIT Press, expanded edition, 19(88): 2.

Nagao, M. (1984) 'A Framework of a Mechanical Translation between Japanese and English by Analogy Principle', *Artificial and Human Intelligence*: 351–54.

Newell, A. and H. Simon (1956) 'The Logic Theory Machine–A Complex Information Processing System', *IRE Transactions on Information Theory* 2(3): 61–79.

Pennington, J., R. Socher, and C. Manning (2014) 'Glove: Global Vectors for Word Representation', in *Proceedings of the 2014 Conference on Empirical Methods in Natural Language Processing (EMNLP)*. Association for Computational Linguistics.

Recent Advances in Google Translate. (2020, June 8) 'Google AI Blog'. Available at: https://ai.googleblog.com/2020/06/recent-advances-in-google-translate.html. Accessed on August 31, 2021.

Rosenblatt, F. (1958) 'The Perceptron: A Probabilistic Model for Information Storage and Organization in the Brain', *Psychological Review* 65(6): 386.

Rosenblatt, F. (1960) 'Perceptron Simulation Experiments', *Proceedings of the IRE* 48(3): 301–09.

Rosenblatt, F. (1961) *Principles of Neurodynamics: Perceptrons and the Theory of Brain Mechanisms*, Buffalo, NY: Cornell Aeronautical Lab Inc.

Rumelhart, D. E., G. E. Hinton, and R. J. Williams (1986) 'Learning Representations by Back-Propagating Errors', *Nature* 323(6088): 533–36.

Sutskever, I., O. Vinyals, and Q. V. Le (2014) 'Sequence to Sequence Learning with Neural Networks', in *Advances in Neural Information Processing Systems*, MIT Press, 3104–12.

Turing, A. M. (1937) 'On Computable Numbers, with an Application to the Entscheidungsproblem', *Proceedings of the London Mathematical Society* 2(1): 230–65.

Vaswani, A., N. Shazeer, N. Parmar, J. Uszkoreit, L. Jones, A. N. Gomez, . . . and I. Polosukhin (2017) 'Attention Is All You Need', in *Advances in Neural Information Processing Systems*, MIT Press, 5998–6008.

PART 2

National/Regional Development of Translation Technology

16

TRANSLATION TECHNOLOGY IN CHINA

Qian Duoxiu

A Historical Sketch

In 1946, the world's first practical and fully electronic computer ENIAC machine came into use at the University of Pennsylvania (Hutchins 1986: 23–24). China was then on the brink of a full-scale civil war after its anti-Japanese war ended in the previous year. In 1947, when Warren Weaver (1894–1978) came up with the idea of using computers in translation, China was divided by a civil war between forces led by Kuomintang and the Communist Party. In 1949, the war was won by the latter, and the People's Republic of China was founded. Then efforts towards industrialization and modernization began to be made in an organized and ambitious way.

Following the United States and the former Soviet Union, scholars in China started research on machine translation in 1956. China demonstrated its achievements in machine translation for the first time in 1959 and thus joined the exclusive club in this field (Dong 1995; Fu 1999). Even though Chinese character (Han Zi) output devices were not available then, this first system was for the automatic translation of twenty sentences of different syntactic structures between Russian and Chinese, with the output of Chinese characters in coded form (Chan 2004: 295).

Later, on the basis of enlarged corpora and store of structures, research for English–Chinese machine translation started. Forerunners include the Institute of Scientific and Technical Information of China (ISTIC), Harbin Institute of Technology (HIT), Beijing Foreign Studies University (BFSU), South Chinese University of Technology, and other institutions. Due to the devastating Great Cultural Revolution (1966–1976), research and development in this field entered a ten-year-long stagnation. It was only resumed in 1978 when the opening-up and reform policy was implemented.

Communication in this field began to increase. In 1980, the First Seminar on Machine Translation was held in Beijing. In 1982, the Second Seminar was held in Shanghai. There were only a few dozen participants at that time. However, since 2000, there have been more than 100 people for each Chinese Workshop on Machine Translation (CWMT). In 2011, the 7th Workshop was held in Xiamen, Fujian Province. The theme was to evaluate different systems dealing with different language pairs in different fields. Multilingualism and wide coverage of domains are now the trend (www.cas.cn/xw/yxdt/201110/t20111008_3359421.shtml). The

DOI: 10.4324/9781003168348-18

8th CWMT was held in September 2012. Its themes included MT models, techniques and systems, multi-lingual MT system evaluation, and other topics.

Communication with the outside world is also flourishing. Before its dissolution in 2011, the Localization Industry Standards Association (LISA) held its annual China Focus Forum several times. Now GALA (Globalization and Localization Association, www.gala-global.org) is involved in various activities related to localization and globalization in the Chinese context.

Besides this, academia, industry, and professional organizations have all come to realize the importance of translation technology in the process of globalization and localization. In 2009, the Localization Service Committee of the Translators Association of China (TAC) was set up. Its members are all leading translation technology and language/localization service providers (LSPs; tac-online.org.cn).

At present, with the wide application of artificial intelligence (AI) and cloud computing technology, many more parties are involved and small-scale conferences are many. In the meantime, more languages, more domains, and more approaches related to machine translation have been under research.

Though approaches in the development of translation technology in China have not been very different from those adopted in other countries, there are some distinctive features.

First, research and development in China has been chiefly sponsored by the government since the very beginning. Early in 1956, "Machine Translation/Mathematical Theories for Natural Language" was already an item listed in the government's Guidelines for Scientific Development. Later it was among the major national scientific and technical projects, such as "The Sixth Five-Year Plan", "The Seventh Five-Year Plan", and "863 Plan". Though there was a ten-year stagnation in translation research in China from 1966 to 1976, it was not because of a shortage of funding but because of political and social upheaval during the Cultural Revolution.

Second, scholars from various fields and institutions have been involved in the development of translation technology in China ever since its start. This collaboration, which is common in this field among people from computer sciences, mathematics, and linguistics, has spurred the development of translation technology greatly in China. It was also in this early period (1956–1976), not necessarily under the impact of the 1966 ALPAC Report, that people in China realized that machine-aided translation is more feasible, at least in the foreseeable future.

In the mid-1970s, translation technology research regained its original momentum and resumed its rapid growth on the basis of collective efforts of many ministries and institutions, with the Institute of Linguistics of the Chinese Academy of Social Sciences acting as the spearhead. A five-year-long collaboration yielded some rudimentary systems and helped to train many researchers, who would continue their work in places all over China. In the meantime, researchers were sent abroad to do collaborative research or recruited to do postgraduate study in this area. National conferences or seminars on translation technology were held regularly, and related journals were published.

The 1980s and 1990s witnessed the second important phase in the development of translation technology in China. During this period, two milestone practical systems came into being. One is the KY-1 English–Chinese Machine Translation System developed by the Academy of Military Sciences in 1987, which won the second prize of the National Scientific and Technical Progress Award and was later further refined into TranStar, the first commercialized machine translation system in China. The other is the IMT/EC-863 English–Chinese Machine Translation System developed by the Institute of Computing Technology of Chinese Academy of Sciences. This system won the first prize of the National Scientific and Technical Progress Award in 1995 and has brought in tremendous profits. These two systems are the children of collaborative efforts of various institutions and people. Another system worth mentioning is the MT-IR-EC developed by the Academy of Posts and Telecommunications, which is very practical in translating information service in physics, electro-technology, computer, and control (INSPEC) titles from English into Chinese. Not mentioned here are many other efforts made in this period, including the joint program between China and Japan, which introduced translation technology in the Chinese context to the outside world. This helped to train talents and promoted the transmission of technology and the accumulation of resources. Consequently, some Japanese–Chinese machine translation systems came into being, such as those developed by Tsinghua University, Nanking University, and the China University of Science and Technology. In the mid-1990s, for the first time in the world, a research group led by Yu (1993) at the Institute of Computational Linguistics of Peking University constructed a quite reliable evaluation system for translation technology.

From the 1990s onwards, translation technology in China has undergone rapid growth. Many commercial systems are available on the market. All these systems share some common features. For example, most of them are equipped with very big multi-disciplinary and domain-specific dictionaries, operational through the network and user friendly with interfaces in Chinese and other languages. New technologies, such as human–machine interfaces, began to be developed. So, in a sense, translation technology in China is not far behind in its personal computer (PC) product and network system development. The dominant technology strategy and guidelines of translation technology in the Chinese context then were not very different from those adopted in other parts of the world. They are mainly transformation based, rule based, and very practical (such as ECMT-78 developed by Liu Zhuo in 1978), and many are still in use today (for more information, see Chan 2004: 66; Feng 2007; Fu 1999).

In recent years, substantial efforts have been made in developing translation technology in China. In 1999, Yaxin CAT 1.0 was publicized. It is China's first all-in-one computer-aided translation (CAT) system which combines translation memory, human–machine interaction, and analysis. Now Yaxin CAT 4.0 is commercially available and has been popular among Chinese CAT users.

There are several academic organizations active in translation technology on the Chinese mainland. For example, the Chinese Information Processing Society (CIPSC) has organized several international and national conferences since it was founded in 1981 and is an active participant in international exchanges. However, much is still to be done given that the exchanges are mainly done in Chinese, while little effort has been made to have the conversation conducted in English in order to be recognized by a larger audience beyond the Chinese context.

To date, more than 60 years have passed since its start, and translation technology has witnessed great progress in the Chinese context (for information about Taiwan, Hong Kong, and Macau, see the related sections).

Translation Technology: Principles, Strategies, and Methodology

The basic and dominant methods in machine translation research and application in China are, not surprisingly, consistent with the approaches adopted in other countries. For example, Chinese researchers tried the transfer approach, where conversion was through a transfer stage from abstract (i.e. disambiguated) representations of SL (source language) texts to equivalent TL (target language) representations. Three stages are involved: analysis, transfer, and generation (or synthesis), such as in the KY-1 system mentioned in the previous section (for more information, see Hutchins 2005).

They also tried a rule-based approach, which was most obvious in the then-dominant transfer systems. It was also the basis of various interlingua systems, both those which were essentially linguistics oriented and those which were knowledge based, such as HansVision developed by Beijing Creative Next Technology Ltd. (Chan 2004: 94) (for more information, see Hutchins 2005).

Example-based and corpus-based approaches were later adopted as a more feasible way to tackle the problems encountered by previous approaches. These are now widely acknowledged and used as the best methods in this field in China. For example, at Beijing Foreign Studies University (BFSU), a research project on the design and construction of a bilingual parallel corpus has been going on for several years, and one of its goals is to shed some light on bi-directional translation between Chinese and English (Wang 2004). A lot more work has been done for this purpose and is briefly mentioned in the next section.

Major Participants and Achievements

There are many active participants in the research and development of machine translation (MT) and CAT. One leading organization is the Chinese Information Processing Society of China (CIPSC; www.cipsc.org.cn/index.php). It was established in June 1981, its mission being to develop methods for processing Chinese with the aid of computer technology, including automatic input, output, recognition, transfer, compression, storage, concordance, analysis, comprehension, and generation. This is to be done at different linguistic levels (character, lexical, phrasal, sentential, and textual). The field has developed into an interdisciplinary subject area in a very robust way with collaborative work by scholars from fields like philology, computer sciences, artificial intelligence, cognitive psychology, and mathematics. This organization has been in close contact with the outside world, playing a very active role in the world MT-Summits.

The Chinese Linguistic Data Consortium (CLDC; www.chineseldc.org/cldcTest.html) is an organization affiliated with CIPSC. Its mission is to build up databases of Chinese at different linguistic levels. The databases can be used in fundamental research and development in Chinese information processing. The Consortium has been supported financially by several national-level 863 research projects like General Technical Research and Fundamental Databases for a Chinese Platform (2001AA11401), Evaluation Technology Research and Fundamental Databases for a Chinese Platform (2004AA114010), a National Key 973 fundamental research project called Comprehension and Knowledge Data-mining of Image, Phonemes and Natural Language (G19980305), and many other similar endeavors.

Another purpose of this Consortium is to provide standards and regulations for Chinese language information processing to be used by different institutions both home and abroad so that they can communicate with each other with the same criteria.

For example, CLDC-2009-004 is a very large bilingual (English–Chinese) parallel corpus covering a variety of fields and text types. It contains 20,000,000 sentence pairs (www.chineseldc.org/index.html).

CLDC-LAC-2003-003 is an annotated and segmented (lexical level) Chinese corpus. There are 500 million Chinese characters in this balanced corpus, and the data are all POS tagged and segmented with human validation.

CLDC-2010-006 is also known as CIPS-SIGHAN CLP 2010 and is a corpus for evaluating lexical segmentation of simplified Chinese. The emphasis of this evaluation system is to see how well an algorithm can do segmentation of Chinese words and expressions across different fields and text types. There are four sub-corpora, literature, computer sciences, medicine, and business, each with 50,000 Chinese characters. This database also contains reference corpus, untagged training corpora (literature and computer sciences, each with 100,000 Chinese characters), evaluation guidelines, and an overall evaluation report.

CLDC-2010-005 is a bilingual Chinese–Mongolian parallel corpus of 60,000 sentences pairs. The texts belong to several types, including political, legal, daily usage, literature, and other types.

CLDC-2010-001 is an ICT web-based Chinese–English parallel corpus. The data were collected in 2009 from the web. It uses XML to mark up the information, and the encoding is UTF-8. There are 1,075,162 sentence pairs in this corpus.

Not many journals related to translation technology in China are available. The *Journal of Chinese Information Processing* was created in 1986. It is the official publication of CIPSC, co-sponsored by the China Association for Science and Technology and Institute of Software, Chinese Academy of Sciences. Papers published in this journal are all related to Chinese information processing and machine translation between Chinese and other languages. Other journals in the broad field of translation and linguistics may accept papers on this topic occasionally.

It is also worthy of note that, in this region, much attention has been paid to the teaching and study of translation technology over the past years. The world's first master of arts program in computer-aided translation was offered by the Department of Translation, the Chinese University of Hong Kong, in 2002. The enthusiasm demonstrated by students admitted into this program in the past ten years is symptomatic of the growing demand of the society at large. Later, more and more universities on the Chinese mainland began to offer programs related to this. In 2006, the Ministry of Education decided that translation and interpretation should be set up as an independent degree program. In the curricula for both undergraduates and postgraduates, it is stipulated that computer-aided translation should be either required or elective. It is believed that such programs will attract more and more talents to join this field.

Application and Mainstream Tools

Early attempts to develop practical tools were many, sponsored by either the government or private organizations. In Table 16.1 is an incomplete list of systems and their developers.

Table 16.1 Early attempts at CAT research and development

System	Developer (surname, given name)
Transtar English-Chinese MT system	Dong, Zhendong
JFY (Gaoli) English-Chinese MT system	Liu, Zhuo
IMT/EC English-Chinese MT system	Chen, Zhaoxiong
TYECT English-Chinese MT system	Wang, Guangyi
TECM English-Chinese MT system	Liu, Xiaoshu
TH (Tsinghua) English-Chinese MT system	Chen, Shengxin
NetTrans English-Chinese MT system	Wang, Huilin
SuperTran English-Chinese MT system	Shi, Xiaodong
HansBridge English-Chinese MT system	Creative Next Technology Ltd.
Ji Shi Tong English-Chinese MT system	Moon Computer Company
TongYi English-Chinese MT system	Tongyi Institute of MT Software
East Express English-Chinese MT systems	Shida-Mingtai Computer Ltd.
Yaxin English-Chinese MT system	YaxinCheng Computer Software Ltd.
FCAT system	(Feng, Zhiwei)
KEYI-1 English-Chinese system	Mars Institute
Kingsoft Powerword	Kingsoft
Oriental Express	SJTU Sunway Software Co Ltd.

Some of these tools have been further developed and successful commercially to the present day. Huajian Group (www.hjtek.com) is an example here. This now-independent high-tech enterprise was affiliated with the Chinese Academy of Sciences and is now mainly engaged in technological research, product development, application integration, and technical services in the field of computer and language information processing. It has provided the government, businesses, and individuals with solutions to computer information system applications such as computer information processing, systems integration, and information services. It has developed around 60 translation tools. Solutions like multi-lingual application service have been adopted by many domestic organizations.

The core technologies of the Huajian series include solutions to the problem of translation quality and knowledge acquisition. They combine the advantages of rule-based and corpus-based methods; a multi-level attributive character system; an integrated semantic and case (SC) syntax system, pre-analysis, and feedback in rule-based contextual testing; integrated analysis of grammar, semantics, and general knowledge in multi-route dynamic selection; solutions to polysemy using special rules; real mode expression based on multi-level abstract characteristics; semantic similarity calculation based on compatibility of multi-level characteristics; and intelligent machine translation technology.

The original interactive hybrid-strategy machine translation method is adopted in most of its systems, and system implementation algorithms are independent of specific languages and open development platforms with a multi-user consistency protection mechanism. There are nine translation systems dealing with seven languages (Chinese, English, Japanese, Russian, German, French, and Spanish). In this way, a massive multilingual language information and corpus has been accumulated (www.hjtek.com).

Since the early 1990s, tools with different brand names developed locally have become commercially available. More recently, there are Youdao, Lingoes, and Iciba (PowerWord), among others, which are leading online and offline tools for automatic translation based on a corpus.

Computer-aided translation technology has been developed mainly by several leading companies. Two mainstream tools are introduced here.

One is the Yaxin CAT series, developed by Beijing Orient Yaxin Software Technology Co., Ltd., in 1997. It has been regarded as one of the best professional translation tools produced by a domestic developer. Its products include a single-user version (English–Chinese and multilingual version), office-aided translation teaching system (multilingual two-way), and computer-aided translation teaching system (multilingual two-way). The products have the following major advantages:

- combination of machine translation with computer-aided translation;
- improving translation speed and quality by pre-translation, in-translation, and post-translation processing;
- built-in term banks based on more than eighty domain-specific dictionaries; and
- working from bilingual corpora to multilingual translation suggestions;
- integration of embedded, external, and stand-alone translation systems; and operating from single-user and network-based processing to cloud service.

The other one is TRANSN (www.transn.com). Its cloud translation technology combines cloud computing with traditional translation technology, and it is an internationally advanced fourth-generation language processing technology. The core technology includes the following components:

fragmentation cloud translation technology, which is based on cloud computing;

large-scale high-speed parallel processing of translation tasks;

workflow technology capable of infinitely flexible translation process configuration and carrying out different forms of automatic translation workflow control;

fuzzy TM engine technology to improve precision in fuzzy TM matching and raise efficiency more than threefold;

synchronized translation technology;

real-time synchronization technology which provides technical support for internet-based collaborative translation;

corpus processing technology to help realize large-scale and low-cost corpus processing;

data-mining technology based on a dashboard model and high-speed data engines to produce translation data reports that meet requirements at different levels;

search engine technology that offers translators maximum support in obtaining authentic interpretations for difficult terms and expressions; and

machine translation technology.

Since 2017, TRANSN has collaborated with Langboat (langboat.com) to provide fully automatic MT results to clients based on large sets of trained language data.

Discussions on Translation Technology

There are many discussions on translation technology in the Chinese context. With his numerous publications, Chan Sin-wai (2002, 2004, 2008, 2009) from the Chinese University of Hong Kong has been regarded as one of the doyens. The works authored or edited by him provide a panoramic picture, as well as helpful resources, for anyone interested in this topic. Publications by Feng (1999, 2004, 2007) and Qian (2005, 2008a, 2008b, 2009, 2011a, 2011b) can also be taken as useful references for the research, application, and teaching in this field.

More specifically, according to Wen and Ren (2011), there are 126 articles in all on CAT collected by China National Knowledge Infrastructure (CNKI) from 1979 to 2010. They can be divided into four major categories – theory, teaching, technology and tools, and industry. In early 2022, a simple title search with "translation technology" as the key item at the same database yields a total of 254 journal articles on this topic (in the 1979–2022 period), demonstrating the ongoing interest in this area.

When theory is concerned, three aspects are the focus of attention, namely, explanation and differentiation of terms (Zhang and Yu 2002), comparison of MT and CAT (Liang 2004), and attempts to use a multi-modal approach to CAT (Su and Ding 2009). In recent years, principles and operational guidelines for post-editing have become a prominent topic, as it can be frequently seen to be one of the major themes at some national conferences in this field.

Articles on CAT teaching are many, noteworthy among which are the pioneering ideas of setting up CAT courses at the tertiary level (Ke and Bao 2002), pedagogical reflections on curriculum design of CAT as a course (Qian 2009, 2010) and master program in engineering with CAT as its orientation (Yu and Wang 2010). According to a CNKI search with "translation technology + teaching" as the key items in abstracts in early 2022, there were 227 journal articles on this specific topic, demonstrating the emerging pedagogical interest at different educational levels.

Technology and tools are what CAT is both theoretically and practically about. People from both fields have contributed to this topic. MT, together with translation memory (TM) and its history, development, application, limitations, and prospects, are discussed in many papers (e.g. Qian 2005; Su 2007). A corpus-based approach is recognized as the most promising method in MT and CAT (Zhuang 2007). As for tools, there is an array of papers, mostly on a single tool or on CAT tools in general.

Industry has always played the key role in the research and development of MT and CAT. Though publications in this aspect are mainly about conferences and news reports, they provide important information on the latest activities in industry-related research and development of translation technology. A recent example is Langboat (https://en.langboat.com). Since its creation in 2021, it has collaborated with Huawei, Transn, and DataStory to provide them with commercialized multilingual translation engines, including dedicated engines for finance, engineering, manufacturing, and other vertical domains. All this is made possible because of its rapid vertical field adaptation technology, high-precision term recognition and translation, efficient vertical domain, and term mining techniques and supported by its large-scale industry translation data and glossary.

Prospects

Rapid growth and remarkable achievements, however, don't mean that the technologies involved are quite mature. The history of MT research and development indicates that MT and CAT require the collective efforts of people from various fields. In the past, induction was done manually and was time consuming and very costly. It is also problematic because consistency is very difficult to arrive at. Once new rules are added to improve the translation of certain sentences, it would be very difficult to handle other sentences which didn't present any problems before the addition. New errors would appear when new formations were made, which has led to the growing complexity of the system and growing difficulty in maintenance. This has been a universal bottleneck for MT systems in the past several decades.

For Chinese, another problem is word segmentation, which is the first yet a key step in Chinese information processing. So far, there has not been a perfect solution, though many advances have been made (Sun 2001; Yu 2002). On the one hand, research conducted at Peking University demonstrates that there is no need for an absolute definition of word boundary for all segmenters and that different results of segmentation shall be acceptable if they can help to reach a correct syntactic analysis in the end (Duan *et al.* 2003). On the other hand, the testable online tool it has developed cannot yet segment words with ambiguous meanings in most cases. In recent years, however, this problem has been largely solved with the tool developed on the basis of huge amounts of language data and continuously upgraded by a group of researchers led by Dr. Huaping Zhang (see ictclas.nlpir.org for details) since 2012.

Translation technology is a fast-developing area. With mobility and innovation becoming the keywords of this era, it is no wonder that new tools emerge every now and then and activities are multi-faceted and based in different places. Take the Dr.eye suite of tools (www.dreye.com/en, Su 1997) as an example. It is originally from Taiwan but now has its headquarters based in Shanghai. Like other mainstream tools, it includes an instant dictionary, translation engine, multilingual voices, multilingual dictionary provided by Oxford University Press, and many other user-friendly functions. Similar tools are many, such as Lingoes (www.lingoes.cn), Youdao (www.youdao.com), and PowerWord (www.iciba.com), to name only a few.

With the rapid growth of internet technology, the future of MT and CAT research and development is quite promising, and more advancements are to be expected. But, as pointed out in the previous sections, the quality of MT translations has not been substantially improved. One thing that is clear is that MT is not only a problem of language processing but also one of knowledge processing. Without the accumulation of knowledge and experience over the years, it is hardly possible to develop an MT system which is practical. The short cycle of development at present is the result of many years' hard work and the accessibility of shared resources.

When one looks forward, one will see there is still a long way to go before MT can truly meet the demands of users. Generally speaking, issues for both MT and CAT research and development between Chinese and other languages should include the following:

(1) Though the notion of a "text" has been lost because the translation tools now available operate primarily at the sentential level (Bowker 2002: 127), the analysis of the source language (Chinese in most cases) should be done in the context beyond the present sentential level, which is isolated and based on comprehension of the original. Future analysis should take the sentence cluster or even the entire text into consideration. While analysis today seeks to find the syntactic relationship tree or the semantic relationship of the concepts involved at most, future analysis should be on the textual meaning instead. Once this is arrived at, meaning transfer could be done more accurately than what is done by the present systems (Dong 1999).

(2) Basic research needs to be deepened and strengthened, especially the construction of common-sense databases. Scholars have even suggested that a knowledge dictionary should be built to facilitate comprehension-based analysis, such as the one developed by Dong Zhendong, a leading Chinese scholar in MT, and his colleagues (Dong 1999), which has shed some light on comprehension-based analysis and explorations of disambiguation.

(3) The stress of research and development should be more and more on the parameterized model and a corpus-based, statistically oriented, and knowledge-based linguistic approach. Accumulation of bilingual and multilingual language data/corpora will make it more feasible to develop more fully automated domain-specific machine translation systems. Efforts should be made to develop a method for semantic disambiguation and an objective evaluation of it. Automatic learning (acquisition, training) strategies of the computer and a bi-directional system design should be strengthened. A more user-friendly feedback control function should be developed so that the user can adjust the behavior of the system.

(4) As pointed out by Hutchins (1999) and applicable to MT and CAT in the Chinese context, translation software now available is still expensive. How to develop an efficient system that is low cost, has high reliability, and requires less work on constructing translation memory for individual translators is another emerging problem. Translation systems into minor and spoken languages should also be further explored.

(5) It is necessary for scholars in the Chinese context to learn from and exchange with others and to have closer contact with the industry. The collaboration, led by Yu Shiwen from the Institute of Computational Linguistics, Peking University, between Peking University and Fujitsu has been fruitful. They have managed, to a great extent, to produce a tagged corpus of 13,000,000 Chinese characters in order to find statistical rules and parameters for processing this language. Organizations in China have made efforts to have their voices heard by joining the international community. For example, EC Innovations (www.ecinnovations.com) is now a member of the Translation Automaton User Society (TAUS; www.translationautomation.com), which held its 2012 Asia Translation Summit in Beijing.

(6) Attention should be paid to "spoken language translation", which still eludes us and could be a very ambitious project (Somers 2003: 7). Now there are several tools commercially available (such as iflytek by domestic developer xfyun; https://fanyi.xunfei.cn/index), but the output still needs much revision.

(7) Attention should also be paid to network teamwork from stand-alone systems so that multiple users can share the same resources.

Translation technology is now the trend in every aspect of the industry. One manifestation of this is that training programs of varying durations have been offered, while more universities on the Chinese mainland are starting to have courses on translation technology in degree programs. Topics for the programs cover approaches to CAT and MT, localization, tools, translation project management, and so on. The total number of trainees enrolled is on the rise. There are strong reasons to believe that translation technology will have a promising future.

Bibliography

Bowker, Lynn (2002) *Computer-aided Translation Technology: A Practical Introduction*, Ottawa: University of Ottawa Press.

Chan, Sin-wai (ed.) (2002) *Translation and Information Technology*, Hong Kong: The Chinese University Press.

Chan, Sin-wai (2004) *A Dictionary of Translation Technology*, Hong Kong: The Chinese University Press.

Chan, Sin-wai (2008) *A Topical Bibliography of Computer (-aided) Translation*, Hong Kong: The Chinese University Press.

Chan, Sin-wai (2009) *A Chronology of Translation in China and the West*, Hong Kong: The Chinese University Press.

Dong, Zhendong (1995) 'MT Research in China', in Dan Maxwell, Klaus Schubert, and Toon Witkam (eds.) *New Directions in Machine Translation*, Dordrecht-Holland: Foris Publications, 85–91.

Dong, Zhendong (1999) 'Review of MT in China in the 20th Century'. Available at: http://tech.sina.com.cn.

Duan, Huiming, Bai Xiaojing, Chang Baobao, and Yu Shiwen (2003) 'Chinese Word Segmentation at Peking University', Available at: http://acl.upenn.edu/w/w03/w03-1722.pdf.

Feng, Zhiwei (1999) 'Translation Technology in China: Past, Present and Future', in Huang Changning and Dong Zhendong (eds.) *Essays on Computational Linguistics*, Beijing: Tsinghua University Press, 335–40.

Feng, Zhiwei (2004) *Studies on Machine Translation*, Beijing: China Translation and Publishing Corporation.

Feng, Zhiwei (2007) *Machine Translation: Past and Present*, Beijing: Language and Culture Press.

Fu, Aiping (1999) 'The Research and Development of Machine Translation in China', *Machine Translation Summit VII*, 13–17 September 1999, Singapore.

Hutchins, John (1986) *Machine Translation: Past, Present, Future*, Chichester, England: Ellis Horwood Ltd.

Hutchins, John (1999) 'The Development and Use of Machine Translation Systems and Computer-aided Translation Tools', in *International Symposium on Machine Translation and Computer Language Information Processing*, 26–28 June 1999, Beijing, China.

Hutchins, John (2005) 'Chapter 27 Machine Translation: General Overview', R. Mitkov (ed.) *The Oxford Handbook of Computational Linguistics*, Oxford: OUP.

Ke, Ping and Chuanyun Bao (2002) 'Translation Majors and Research Institutions in Overseas Universities', *Chinese Translators Journal* (6): 7.

Liang, Sanyun (2004) 'A Comparison of MT and CAT', *Technology Enhanced Foreign Language Education* (6): 42–45.

Qian, Duoxiu (2005) 'Prospects of Machine Translation in the Chinese Context', *Meta* 50.

Qian, Duoxiu (2008a) 'Localization and Translation Technology in the Chinese Context', in *Proceedings of XVIII FIT World Congress* (Shanghai), 4–7 August 2008.

Qian, Duoxiu (2008b) *Computer-aided Quality Assessment in Scientific and Technical Translation – The Pharmacopoeia of the People's Republic of China as a Case Study*. Changchun: Jilin University Press.

Qian, Duoxiu (2009) 'Pedagogical Reflection on the Design of a Course in Computer-aided Translation', *Chinese Translators Association Journal* 4.

Qian, Duoxiu (2010) 'Pedagogical Reflections on Computer-aided Translation as a Course', *Journal of Translation Studies* 13(1–2): 13–26.

Qian, Duoxiu (2011a) *Computer-aided Translation: A Coursebook*, Beijing: Foreign Languages Teaching and Research Press.

Qian, Duoxiu (2011b) 'Applications of Translation Technology in Interpreting', *Minority Translators Journal* 4: 76–80.

Somers, Harold (2003) 'Introduction', in Harold Somers (ed.), *Computers and Translation: A Translator's Guide*, Amsterdam and Philadelphia: John Benjamins Publishing Company, 1–12.

Su, Keh-yih (1997) 'Development and Research of MT in Taiwan'. Available at: www.bdc.com.tw/doc/twmtdvp.gb.

Su, Mingyang (2007) 'Translation Memory: State of the Art and Its Implications', *Foreign Languages Research* 5.

Su, Yangming and Shan Ding (2009) 'Unit of Translation and Its Implications for CAT', *Foreign Languages Research* (6): 84–89.

Sun, Maosong (2001) 'New Advances in the Study of Automatic Segmentation of Chinese Language', in *Proceedings of the Conference of the 20th Anniversary of CIPSC*, Beijing: Tsinghua University Press, 20–40.

Wang, Kefei (2004) 'The Design and Construction of Bilingual Parallel Corpus', *Chinese Translators' Journal* 6: 73–75.

Wen, Jun and Yan Ren (2011) 'Review of Computer-aided Translation (1979–2010) in China', *Computer-assisted Foreign Language Education* 5: 58–62.

Yu, Jingsong and Huilin Wang (2014) 'Certificate Examination of Translation Technology: Design and Experiment', *Chinese Translators Journal* (4): 73–78.

Yu, Shiwen (1993) 'Automatic Evaluation of Output Quality for Machine Translation Systems', *Machine Translation* 8: 117–26.

Yu, Shiwen (ed.) (2002) *CJNLP 2002, The Second China-Japan Natural Language Processing Joint Research Promotion Conference Proceedings*, Beijing: Institute of Computational Linguistics, Peking University.

Zhang, Zhizhong and Yu Kehuai (2002) 'Machine Translation or Machine-aided Translation? Some Thoughts on Machine Translation', *Journal of Dalian University of Technology (Social Sciences)* 3.

Zhuang, Xiaoping (2007) 'The Integration of Machine Translation and Human Translation', *Journal of Yibin University* 8.

17

TRANSLATION TECHNOLOGY IN CANADA

Elliott Macklovitch

Introduction

Technology – understood here as machinery and equipment developed from the application of scientific knowledge for the solution of practical problems[1] – is clearly an evolving and historically conditioned notion. As our scientific knowledge advances, new technologies are routinely developed that render previous technology obsolete. The devices that were considered 'high-tech' for one generation may often wind up as quaint antique store objects in the succeeding generation. Allow me to illustrate with a little bit of personal history.

Although I had previously trained and worked as a linguist, I accepted a job as a translator with the Canadian Translation Bureau[2] in 1981. The Bureau is the largest employer of language professionals in the country and the government's principal centre of expertise on all matters involving translation and linguistic services. Upon my arrival at the Bureau, the equipment I was given to support me in my work was an electric typewriter. Compared to the manual machines that had long been in use, this was considered a significant technological advance. Powered by a humming electric motor, it produced cleaner, more even copy and demanded less manual force on the part of the typist. Moreover, my machine had a self-correcting key which allowed me to backspace and white over incorrect characters. And of these, there were a great many in my first texts, because I had never learned how to type. Seeing that my salary depended on the number of words I produced each day, it wasn't long before I purchased a teach-yourself-to-type manual and eventually became a semi-proficient typist.

Not all my colleagues at the Translation Bureau in those years used a typewriter to draft their target texts. A fair number preferred to dictate their translations, using a hand-held recording device commonly known as a dictaphone.[3] Once the translator had finished dictating her target text, she handed over the resulting cassette to a typist for transcription. The women in the typing pool had another set of impressive skills: not only were they speed typists, but they also needed to have a strong mastery of the spelling and grammar of the target language in order to transform the spoken translation on the recording into a correctly transcribed written version.[4] And they too worked with specialized equipment: headphones and a tape player they could control with a foot pedal. The dictating translators were among the most productive at the Bureau, even when the time and cost of transcription were taken into account.

DOI: 10.4324/9781003168348-19

Aside from these two basic pieces of equipment, the dictaphone and the electric typewriter, Canadian translators, as far as I could tell, had access to very little else in the way of technology at the time. The section of the Translation Bureau I worked in was ringed with rows of filing cabinets in which all our past translations were stored and in which we routinely rummaged in an effort to locate texts similar to the new ones we were assigned, this with varying degrees of success. And in our section library, there was a large card index containing drawers full of file cards on which we were urged to record the results of our terminological research. There too, searching for a term equivalent was frequently a hit-or-miss affair, since translators did not always have the time between assignments to register new terms. And even when they did, each concept rarely received more than one record, making it nearly impossible to locate the appropriate equivalent via a synonymous, alternative or abbreviated term. In short, the practice of translation in Canada some thirty years ago benefited very little from what we would consider technology today.

The Advent of the First Computerized Tools

Things began to change just a few years later, with the arrival at the Translation Bureau of the first dedicated word processing machines. These bulky monsters, which were actually invented by a Canadian,[5] featured a keyboard and a video screen and were dedicated in the sense that word processing was all they were designed to do, unlike the general-purpose programmable microcomputers that later supplanted them. Nevertheless, this early word processing technology proved invaluable to the employees in the Bureau's typing pools, greatly simplifying the job of introducing corrections into the final version of the text to be delivered. But perhaps these machines' most significant technical innovation was the removable magnetic disk on which texts were stored. Not only did these 8-inch disks greatly reduce the space required to store the Bureau's enormous production volume, they also made it much easier to locate and retrieve previous texts. If one had the right disk in hand, the operator simply had to type in the file name on the keyboard – far more efficient than rummaging through countless paper files.

The other technological innovation that had a significant impact on Canadian translators in the mid-1980s was facilitated access to Termium, the government's large computerized terminology bank. Originally developed at the University of Montreal in the early 1970s, Termium was acquired by the government of Canada in 1975 in an effort to help standardize the technical terminology and official appellations in the officially bilingual federal public service. Shortly after its acquisition, the government began a major scale-up of the database, as well as a fundamental revamping of the underlying software. By the time Termium III was released in 1985, the bank contained over a million records, and its network of users numbered about 2500 people, the great majority of whom were government translators and other civil servants.[6] In the translation section I worked in, the arrival of a single dedicated terminal which allowed us direct access to the term bank, without having to address our requests to an overtaxed team of terminologists, was a major event, although by today's standards, interaction with the bank was anything but convivial.

Mention was made in the previous paragraph of the fact that the public service in Canada is officially bilingual. Before pursuing our examination of translation technology, it may be worthwhile to clarify just what this means, since official bilingualism has had extremely important consequences for the translation industry in this country. In 1969, the Canadian Parliament passed the Official Languages Act, which consecrated English and French as the country's two official languages, both having equal status. As a result of this Act, all Canadians have the right to services from the federal government in the official language of their choice, and all federal public servants have the right to work in one or other official language.[7] Furthermore, all the laws, regulations and official documents of the federal government must be published simultaneously in both official languages, and both versions of these documents have equal weight before the law. Since it was first passed in 1969, the Official Languages Act has fuelled much heated debate, and it underwent significant amendments in 1988. But one indisputable consequence of the legislation was to vastly increase the demand for English–French translation in Canada. Indeed, the federal government became, and today still remains, the largest source and client of translation in the country, and for a long time, the Translation Bureau, the agency responsible for translation, interpretation and official terminology in the federal public service, was one of the largest translation services in the world.[8] Yet even when its workforce surpassed a thousand full-time employees, the Bureau still had difficulty in meeting the continually rising demand for translation while limiting its operating costs. In an effort to find solutions to both aspects of this problem, the Translation Bureau was impelled to search for innovative ways of streamlining the translation process, and it soon became an active partner in the development and evaluation of translation technology.

Machine Translation

Before joining the Translation Bureau in 1981, I worked for four years at the TAUM group, TAUM being an acronym for Traduction Automatique de l'Université de Montréal, or machine translation at the University of Montreal. At the time, TAUM was one of the foremost MT research groups in the world. A year before I arrived at the university, TAUM had delivered to the federal government a first operational version of an MT system specifically designed for the translation of weather bulletins. Known as TAUM-Météo, this system was long considered one of the great success stories in machine translation, and to this day, the successor of Météo continues to translate the weather bulletins published by Environment Canada at a rate of more than 5 million words a year.[9] What exactly were the factors responsible for this unprecedented success?

To begin with, the weather bulletins published by the government's meteorological service constitute a highly restricted sublanguage that employs a small number of short sentence patterns and a limited vocabulary of a few thousand words (including place names). In itself, this serves to eliminate many of the ambiguities that are so pervasive in ordinary texts and which make machine translation such a difficult task. What's more, TAUM-Météo was designed to handle only the telegraphic portion of the bulletins describing weather conditions in specific localities of the country. It wasn't meant to translate the synopses that introduce these short bulletins, which describe major meteorological developments in larger regions, using a language that is far more free-ranging in form. These synopses were left to the Bureau's translators, who were also asked to revise the Météo system's output. The translators were more than willing to do this, for two reasons: first, the quality of the machine translations was generally quite good, with less than 5% of the system's output requiring modification, and second, the translators were actually grateful to be relieved of such a boring and repetitive translation task. As for the Bureau, the introduction of the Météo system meant that it was able to meet the client department's requirements for rapid turnaround time of a large volume of text without having to incur the cost of hiring a large number of translators.[10]

Shortly after TAUM-Météo was delivered, the Translation Bureau was advised of another enormous translation task that it would be receiving. The government was about to purchase a new coastal patrol aircraft and, in accordance with the Official Languages Act, it would be required to translate into French the training and maintenance manuals not just for the airplane but for all the sophisticated tracking equipment it carried as well. Flush from the success of the Météo project, the Bureau turned to the TAUM group and asked it to develop a new machine translation system that would help it handle this daunting workload. TAUM agreed to take on this challenge, although retrospectively some group members now view that decision as foolhardy, or at least somewhat naïve. This was the birth of the TAUM-Aviation project, on which I came to work as an English-language linguist in 1977.

What was it that made TAUM-Aviation such an ambitious project – perhaps even an overly ambitious one? For one thing, the aviation manuals that we were undertaking to translate by machine bore absolutely no resemblance to the simple syntax and limited vocabulary of weather bulletins. These manuals may have belonged to a well-defined sublanguage; that is, they did exhibit certain recurrent characteristics that distinguished them from ordinary, everyday English.[11] That said, this sublanguage was an exceedingly complex one, the description of which required the creation of very large dictionaries and a full computational grammar of English for the analysis of the texts to be translated. In no way could the linguists and lexicographers working on the project rely on the sublanguage to simplify their task, as their colleagues had been able to do on the Météo project.

Grammars and dictionaries had to be developed for TAUM-Aviation because we were of course working in the rule-based paradigm of machine translation; no other paradigm was available at the time, except perhaps for simplified word-for-word translation, which was clearly not up to the task. More precisely, TAUM-Aviation could be characterized as a second-generation, rule-based system. Unlike earlier MT systems, those of the second generation proposed higher-level formal languages designed specifically for linguistic descriptions, and these descriptions of linguistic knowledge were clearly distinguished from the programming languages used to actually implement the system. Furthermore, second-generation systems broke down the translation operation into three distinct linguistic phases: source-language analysis, which generated a syntactico-semantic representation of the text to be translated; bilingual transfer, which mapped that representation into its target-language equivalent; and a monolingual generation phase, which transformed the target-language tree structure into a correctly ordered and inflected target sentence. Details aside, what is important to realize is that all this linguistic description had to be undertaken by human specialists. In order to have the system map a source-language sentence into its target-language equivalent, they needed to hand-craft hundreds, if not thousands, of linguistic rules. Like other types of expert systems (as they were called at the time), we were endeavouring to formalize and implement what we understood to be the mental operations of a qualified human translator. The problem, however, is that a qualified human translator, in grappling with the pervasive ambiguities inherent in natural language, routinely draws on vast amounts of linguistic and extra-linguistic knowledge – far more that we could ever hope to code into an MT system.[12] We slowly came to realize this on the TAUM-Aviation project. We rationalized it by telling ourselves that while our system was not meant to replace human translators, it might nevertheless render them more productive by providing them with a first draft of reasonable quality, which they could post-edit cost-effectively.

Such at least was our hope. Over the four years of the Aviation project, I believe it is fair to say that we succeeded in developing one of the most sophisticated MT systems in existence at the time.[13] When the system finally came to be evaluated, however, it was found to fall well short of its ambitious objectives. The translations produced by TAUM-Aviation were generally judged to be of very good quality, based as they were on a deep linguistic analysis. The problem, unfortunately, was that for too many sentences, the system produced no output at all, usually because the input didn't conform in some way to Aviation's analysis grammar or to the lexical information contained in its dictionaries. These had been developed through the painstaking study of what was deemed a representative corpus: a 70,000-word hydraulics manual. But when tested on material from outside the hydraulics domain, the system simply didn't generalize gracefully; which is another way of saying that it wasn't robust enough. Moreover, extending Aviation's deep linguistic analyses to new domains would require a significant investment of time and effort; i.e., a full-fledged system based on this approach would turn out to be exceedingly costly. In 1981, the TAUM-Aviation project was concluded, and, unable to find other sources of funding, the TAUM group was forced to disband.

As it happens, the weaknesses of the system developed on the TAUM-Aviation project were shared by most, if not all, MT systems in the late 1970s and 80s, including the major commercial systems that were trying to break into the translation market in the United States. The best of these systems were far too expensive for individual translators and could only be afforded by large corporations or translation services. Moreover, the quality of their output was not consistently good enough to allow for the cost-effective production of translations destined for publication or broad dissemination.[14] The federal Translation Bureau conducted trials of several such systems in the 1980s, but none was able to satisfy its requirements. The effort to create wide-ranging, general-purpose MT systems through the rule-based approach was simply too difficult a challenge for computational linguistics at the time. A radically different approach to the problem was required, and it finally emerged in the early 1990s with the advent of statistical machine translation (SMT), as we will see.

Machine-Aided Human Translation

Yehoshua Bar-Hillel, who was the first full-time MT researcher in history, was also the first to demonstrate (1960: 45–76) that fully automatic, high-quality machine translation of unrestricted texts – sometimes abbreviated as FAHQTUT – is in fact impossible. The ingenious thought experiment by which he arrived at this conclusion need not concern us here; however, we can invoke the three parameters of his famous acronym to help characterize the state of the art in MT in the late 1980s and early 1990s. For MT's ultimate objective encompasses just these parameters: full automation, high quality and general applicability. In the period under consideration, it was often said that, while the ultimate goal remained unattainable, it was still possible to develop systems which achieved two of these three desiderata. Fully automatic MT systems could produce high quality, but only in restricted domains, as demonstrated by the Météo system. Otherwise, when fully automatic systems were applied to unrestricted texts, it was high quality that would have to be forfeited. On the other hand, if high quality were a *sine qua non*, particularly for the translation of texts in wide-ranging domains, then a compromise would have to be made on full automation. To achieve this last sub-set of the desiderata, the only reasonable approach was to develop sub-optimal systems designed to assist – and not replace – the human translator.

The demand for high-quality translation was growing dramatically during this period, which was a time of expanding globalization, to the point that many professional translators were having increasing difficulty in coping with larger workloads and shorter timelines. Not surprisingly, many of their large-scale corporate clients began to look to machine translation, hoping to find in that technology a solution to their pressing practical problems. It was in this context that Martin Kay (1980) published his seminal paper, 'The Proper Place of Men and Machines in Language Translation', in which he reiterated Bar-Hillel's arguments on the unfeasibility of FAHQTUT and advanced instead a more modest program of machine-aided human translation. While this may not have been the message that many of the large clients of translation wanted to hear, it was also the approach adopted by the research group directed by Pierre Isabelle at the Canadian Workplace Automation Research Centre in Montreal,[15] where I went to work in 1984. Like Martin Kay (1980), Pierre contended that research on machine translation was fully justified and indeed necessary in advancing our understanding of natural language processing. But this remained a *research* goal, and, as such, it was unlikely to provide practical solutions for working translators in the short term. For this problem, Pierre's group took a radically different, extremely original approach, setting as its goal the development of a whole new generation of computer-assisted translator tools.

Before turning to the CITI's program in machine-aided translation, allow me a short digression on statistical machine translation. As we mentioned at the end of the preceding section, the advent of SMT represented a revolutionary paradigm shift. It was first proposed by a team of researchers at IBM (Brown *et al.* 1990: 79–85) who were intent on applying to translation the same statistical techniques which had proven so successful in automatic speech recognition. A key feature of this new 'empirical' approach was its reliance on large amounts of previously translated text. This was the data from which their machine learning algorithms automatically acquired its translation knowledge, as opposed to the traditional, rationalist approach, in which linguists and lexicographers relied on their intuitions to craft declarative rules. It is interesting to note that the translated corpus that proved critical to the IBM group – both because of its size and its quality – came from the Canadian House of Commons, where all debates were required by law to be translated into the other official language. Electronic versions of those debates had in fact existed for some time. What allowed the IBM group to actually exploit that data was the development of automatic alignment programs, which calculate formal links between corresponding sentences in two files, one containing the source text and the other its translation. Texts that are linked in this way were first called *bitexts* by Brian Harris, a professor of translation at the University of Ottawa, who was also among the first to appreciate their potential usefulness for human translators. (See Harris 1988: 8–11.) For the machine learning algorithms used in SMT to work effectively, the bitexts to which they are applied must be extremely large – in the millions of words – far more than anyone could ever align by hand.

In terms of the quality of the translations they produced, the early SMT systems did not really achieve a great leap forward; it wasn't until several years later that they finally overtook the traditional rule-based systems in the public competitions organized by the US government. What they did do, however, was radically reduce the time and effort required to develop a new MT system, for their automated learning algorithms could be applied to any language pair for which sufficient translation data were available. But even then, it seemed clear that SMT was not yet the panacea that struggling translators and their overwhelmed clients were hoping for. This is why Pierre Isabelle's team at the CITI, while pursuing its own research into statistical MT, also undertook two major projects in machine-*aided* translation, designed to provide shorter-term solutions to the hard-pressed corps of professional translators, both in Canada and elsewhere.

The first of these was called Translator's Workstation project, and it was developed with the support of the federal Translation Bureau. Its goal was to integrate, within a user-friendly interface, various off-the-shelf programs, some of which were not even intended for translators. This may sound simple enough today, but it must be remembered that at the time most translators had only recently migrated to personal computers, whose hardware and operating system imposed serious limitations on the sharing and transfer of data between different applications. Following the suggestion made by Martin Kay in his 1980 paper, the central component of the successive workstations that were developed at the CITI remained a word processing program, to which a number of ancillary applications were added, including programs for glossary management, grammar and spell-checking, French verb conjugation, file comparison and so on.[16] Attempts were also made to provide translators with a full-page monitor and to link their workstations together in a local area network. For further details on the Workstation project, the historically curious reader is referred to Macklovitch (1991).

The CITI's other major project in machine-aided translation was more original and certainly more ambitious, in that it set out to develop a whole new set of translator support tools. The project's starting point, or credo, was famously formulated by Pierre Isabelle as follows: 'existing translations contain more solutions to more translation problems than any other available resource' (Isabelle *et al.* 1993: 205). The challenge, of course, is how to make all that knowledge readily available to working translators, and the answer, it turned out, lay in the recently discovered concept of bitextuality. In 1993, William Gale and Kenneth Church (1993: 75–102), two brilliant researchers at AT&T Bell laboratories, published a paper containing an algorithm for automatically aligning sentences in large, parallel corpora, that is, for creating arbitrarily large bitexts. At the CITI, Pierre Isabelle, George Foster and Michel Simard improved on the Gale-Church algorithm by exploiting the presence of cognates in the set of parallel texts (Simard *et al.* 1993: 1071–82). And the CITI researchers went one big step further: they developed an interface and a database structure that allowed users to query the resulting bitext – the queries, in the case of translators, normally corresponding to a translation problem. TransSearch, as the resulting system was called, would retrieve all sentences containing the submitted query; and because this was a *bitextual* database, along with each retrieved sentence came the corresponding sentence in the other language, where the translator could often find the solution to his problem.[17] In 1996, the CITI made a version of TransSearch freely available on the Internet. It included a parallel corpus composed of tens of millions of words of Canadian Parliamentary debates; once again, that same data on which SMT had been spawned. The system proved so popular with translators that it was soon transferred to a private-sector partner, who now manages subscriptions that are sold at a very reasonable price and ensures that the databases are regularly updated. Other bilingual concordancers have since become available – imitation is often said to be the ultimate compliment – but TransSearch was the first such tool that allowed translators to take advantage all the richness that up to then had lain dormant in past translations.

The CITI's two other projects in translator support tools did not meet with the same commercial success as TransSearch, although they were probably even more innovative. The TransCheck project, as its name suggests, set out to develop a translation checker: similar in conception to a spelling or grammar checker, with the important difference that TransCheck focussed on *bilingual* errors, that is, errors of correspondence between two texts that are mutual translations.[18] The system began by automatically aligning the sentences in the source and target files, and then it verified each aligned sentence pair to ensure that it respected certain obligatory translation correspondences while containing no prohibited correspondences. An example of a prohibited correspondence would be an instance of source language interference, such as a deceptive cognate. (TransCheck incorporated an open list containing many common translation interdictions between English and French.) An example of a compulsory correspondence would the correct transcription of numerical expressions (including dates, monetary expressions, measurements, etc.) or certain terminological equivalences which had to be respected. Terminological consistency, however, turned out to be much more difficult to enforce than we had anticipated, owing to pronominalization, natural omissions and other forms of translator licence. This was probably one of the principal reasons TransCheck never achieved widespread adoption.[19]

The TransType project proposed a radically new type of editing environment for the translator, designed to reduce the time and effort required to key in a target text by exploiting the proposals made by an embedded SMT system. The way the system operated was basically as follows. For each source sentence, the SMT system, operating in the background, would generate a host of potential translations. When the user began to type her translation of a given sentence, the system would select, among its automatically generated candidates, the most likely of those that were compatible with the prefix the user had keyed in and propose an extension to the user's draft. The user could either accept that proposal, ignore it by continuing to type or modify it in some way. With each new keystroke the user entered, however, the system would immediately revise its predictions and propose a new compatible extension. These interactions between the user and the system would continue until a satisfactory target equivalent for the sentence was generated. Shortly after the CITI's MT group moved to Université de Montréal (where it became the RALI Laboratory), the TransType project was awarded a European Commission research grant, allowing several prominent research groups to join the TransType2 research consortium. Two translation companies, one in Canada and one in Spain, also participated in the project, providing invaluable end-user feedback to the developers. The TT2 project was pursued until 2005, developing a series of sophisticated prototypes for a number of language pairs and exploring intriguing research questions – such as how an SMT engine can learn from the user's interactions in real time – for which practical solutions are only now beginning to emerge.[20]

The Current Situation

At this point, I want to shift the perspective somewhat, moving away from a historical account in order to focus on the current situation of translation technology in Canada. But first, a few words on the translation market in this country and the place of Canadian translators in it.

For a country with a relatively small proportion of the world population – about 0.5% – Canada accounts for a surprisingly large proportion of the world's translation production: approximately 10%, according to a recent study by PricewaterhouseCoopers (2012). It is difficult to obtain recent, accurate figures on the number of Canadian translators, but one federal government website mentions an average of 10,250 persons (including terminologists and interpreters) between the years 2008 and 2010.[21] Another government study puts the number of firms working in this sector at about 800, with most of these employing five or fewer people. The government's own Translation Bureau is by far the largest service in the country, with over 1200 full-time employees. And the great bulk of translation that is done in Canada is still between the two official languages, English and French. Finally, translators are relatively well paid in Canada compared to their colleagues in other countries; the Service Canada website cites their average annual income at $50,000. So, in principle, Canadian translators can afford to invest modestly in technology. But do they?

Once again, there is not a great deal of recent and reliable data available on this question, but we can begin by looking to our neighbours to the south. In 2008, the American Translators Association published a study which showed that the three most commonly used technology tools among its members were word processing applications (98% usage), translation memory applications (47% usage) and terminology management software (27% usage).[22] I strongly suspect the situation is quite similar among Canadian translators, but we can sharpen the picture somewhat by examining the results of a smaller-scale survey conducted by AnneMarie Taravella in 2011 for the Language Technologies Research Centre (LTRC) in Gatineau, Quebec. Almost all of the 380 respondents to this survey were translators, terminologists or students enrolled in a translation program, and there was some disagreement among them as to whether word processing belonged to the category of language technologies or whether the latter should be restricted to technologies that are used only by language professionals. On the other hand, virtually everyone surveyed used a word processor. Moreover, 97% of the respondents said they regularly consulted what Mme Taravella called a 'passive' language technology, that is, terminology banks like Termium and *le Grand dictionnaire terminologique*,[23] correctors like Antidote, or bilingual concordancers and online dictionaries like Linguee. And much like their American counterparts, 54% of the Canadian respondents claimed to use at least one 'active' language technology, these being essentially various types of translation memory. In short, the picture that emerges from this survey is that, as a group, Canadian translators are certainly computer literate today. To this, I would add my own personal observation that those who work in larger translation services or companies are even more likely than their freelance colleagues to work with a translation memory tool. Mme Taravella also asked her respondents to assess their use of language technologies:

> 97% of the respondents who indicated that they used language technologies claimed that they helped save time, 90% claimed that they improved the quality of their work and 90% claimed that they increased the uniformity of their work. 44% of the respondents . . . claimed that it was a requirement of their employer or their clients.
>
> *(10)*

Looking briefly at the supply side of the equation, the Canadian language industry boasts a number of small but innovative companies that develop various types of translation technology. Perhaps the best known of these market translation memory systems; they include MultiCorpora (and its MultiTrans product), Terminotix (and its highly regarded LogiTerm system) and JiveFusion. Several Canadian companies have developed sophisticated systems for managing translation workflow, including MultiCorpora's Prism Flow and Logosoft's TransFlow. The latter company also offers a bilingual concordancer called Tradooit, while Terminotix has developed Synchro-Term, a bilingual term extraction tool, as well as AlignFactory, an automatic alignment program that facilitates the creation of bitexts.

Returning to Mme Taravella's survey, it is interesting to note that none of her respondents mentioned machine translation, which is now used by millions of persons every day on public websites like Google Translate and Microsoft Translator. But what of MT for the production of publication-quality translation? The PricewaterhouseCoopers report (2012) has the following to say on the question:

> Machine translation, although a key productivity enhancing tool, is generally not considered to produce a level of quality sufficient to correctly convey a full message in another language, and its output must be reviewed by a qualified translator. As a result of the significant post process editing, machine translation is not widely adopted. It is generally used for large volume translations with an accuracy rate of 75% to 85%.
>
> *(19)*

The Canadian Translators, Terminologists and Interpreters Council (CTTIC) is cited as the source of the opinion in the first sentence; no source is cited for the startling across-the-board figures given in the final sentence. If it were indeed true that MT systems were capable of achieving 85% accuracy on arbitrary texts,[24] I'm quite sure that there would be tremendous interest in the technology, given the ever-increasing demand for translation worldwide and the strong market pressure to lower costs and shorten turnaround times. As for the need to have the MT output reviewed by a qualified human translator, this in itself is not sufficient reason to discard the technology. Rather, the real question today is the following: given the impressive improvements in statistical MT in recent years and the possibility of training such systems for well-defined domains where large volumes of past translation are now available, has the performance of such specialized engines reached a level where their output can be cost-effectively post-edited? We are hearing more and more evidence from various quarters that the answer to this question may well be yes. In Canada, the largest private-sector translation provider has been using Portage, the NRC's highly regarded SMT system, for over two years to help it produce some of its technical translations, and other major translation firms are actively exploring the possibility of integrating machine translation into their operations.

Another promising technology which hasn't yet been mentioned is automatic speech recognition (ASR). As we stated in the introduction, dictation used to be the preferred mode of text entry for many translators in Canada, preferred not only because it is fast – everyone speaks faster than they can type – but also because it allows the translator to focus on her specialization, relegating such mundane matters as layout and format to a typist. Two factors combined to change this situation in the mid-1980s: the advent of the personal computer, equipped with sophisticated word processing programs, and the increasing difficulty of finding competent typists who knew their grammar and spelling well enough to produce an error-free text from a recording. In many services, translators were instructed to turn in their dictaphones and were told that henceforth they would have to type their own target texts on a PC. Moreover, this was often presented as the inevitable march of progress, although for many translators – particularly those who were not proficient typists – the concrete benefits were not immediately obvious.

In May 2011, I conducted a series of consultation sessions with the employees of the federal Translation Bureau which focused on the technologies they were currently using and those they would ideally like to have. In the course of those sessions, I was surprised to discover that a fair number of translators continue to dictate their texts. These included older employees who had never given up their dictaphone, as well as younger translators who were using commercial ASR systems (almost always Dragon NaturallySpeaking), some in response to health problems. In principle, this technology has the potential to resolve the difficulties alluded to in the previous paragraph. For the translator, it allows a return to the more comfortable mode of dictation; only now, instead of having to wait for the typist to complete the transcription, the target text magically appears on the computer screen almost as fast as she can speak it. And for the translation manager, the elimination of the typist should help lower operating costs.

Except that we're not quite there yet. . . . Between this idealized scenario and the real-world performance of the best of today's ASR systems, there remains a gap that is populated by speech recognition errors which the translator is obliged to correct, thereby reducing her productivity. These systems have made remarkable progress in recent years, and that gap is certainly closing, but for many translators, particularly those who work in languages other than English, the word error rates remain too high to allow automatic dictation to be cost effective. This situation is likely to improve in coming years, as will the other major problem with ASR: the fact that the technology is not yet satisfactorily integrated with the other support tools that translators have come to rely on, particularly translation memory systems.

Notes

1 Definition drawn from the online version of the Oxford English Dictionary.
2 https://www.tpsgc-pwgsc.gc.ca/bt-tb/index-eng.html.
3 Dictaphone was actually the registered trademark of an American company, but I am employing the term informally here to refer to any tape recorder used in translation.
4 In fact, transcription often involved several iterations of correction between typist and translator.
5 Stephen Dorsey, the founder of AES and later Micom Data Systems.
6 For more on *Termium* at the time, see Landry (1987).
7 The application of the latter clause is subject to certain geographical restrictions, i.e. to areas where the minority language has a certain minimum density.
8 Until it was overtaken by the European Commission's translation service.
9 The volume used to be higher. It has declined somewhat in recent years, since Environment Canada is now generating in parallel certain bulletins that used to be drafted in one language and then translated.

10 For a short article on the development of the *Météo* system, see Kittredge (2012: 19–20).

11 See Lehrberger (1982: 81–106) for a detailed discussion of this sublanguage question.

12 It wasn't just the number of rules that was problematic; the rules often conflicted with one another in unpredictable ways.

13 For a detailed description and assessment of *TAUM-Aviation*, see Isabelle and Bourbeau (1985: 18–27).

14 On the other hand, they could and were used for other purposes, notably for information gathering by military and intelligence services.

15 The centre later changed its name to the CITI. Several members of the machine-aided translation team there, including Pierre Isabelle, had previously worked at the TAUM group at Université de Montréal.

16 At the time, many of these components were not yet included within the word processing programme.

17 For a detailed description of *TransSearch*, see Macklovitch *et al.* (2000: 1201–08).

18 For more on *TransCheck*, see Macklovitch (1995).

19 Although some commercial products now exist which do offer a similar type of bitextual quality assurance, for example, *ErrorSpy* by D.O.G. GmbH.

20 For more on the TT2 project, see Casacuberta *et al.* (2009: 135–38).

21 www.servicecanada.gc.ca/eng/qc/job_futures/statistics/5125.shtml. Of this number, about 74% are said to work full-time.

22 These figures are cited in PricewaterhouseCoopers (2012).

23 Like so many other linguistic resources, these two large-scale term banks are now accessible over the Internet. According to the Internet World Stats site, Internet penetration in Canada was about 83% in 2012.

24 Although much depends on the linguistic units these accuracy figures are applied to. If 85% of the *sentences* in a machine translation are accurate, then this would undoubtedly enhance production; if it's 85% of the *words*, then the impact on productivity is far less certain. (My thanks to Pierre Isabelle for pointing this out to me.)

Bibliography

Bar-Hillel, Yehoshua (1960) 'The Present Status of Automatic Translation of Languages', in *Advances in Computers 1*, New York: Academic Press (Reprinted in Sergei Nirenburg, Harold L. Somers, and Yorick Wilks (eds.) *Readings in Machine Translation*, Cambridge, MA: MIT Press, 45–76).

Brown, Peter, John Cocke, Stephen A. Della Pietra, Vincent J. Della Pietra, Fredrick Jelinek, John Lafferty, Robert L. Mercer, and Paul S. Rossin (1990) 'A Statistical Approach to Machine Translation', *Computational Linguistics* 16(2): 79–85.

Casacuberta, Francisco, Jorge Civera, Elsa Cubel, Antonio L. Lagarda, Guy Lapalme, Elliott Macklovitch, and Enrique Vidal (2009) 'Human Interaction for High-quality Machine Translation', *Communications of the ACM – A View of Parallel Computing* 52(10): 135–38.

Gale, William A. and Kenneth W. Church (1993) 'A Program for Aligning Sentences in Bilingual Corpora', *Computational Linguistics* 19(1): 75–102.

Harris, Brian (1988) 'Bi-text, a New Concept in Translation Theory', *Language Monthly* 54: 8–11.

Isabelle, Pierre and Laurent Bourbeau (1985) 'Taum-aviation: Its Technical Features and Some Experimental Results', *Computational Linguistics* 11(1): 18–27.

Isabelle, Pierre, Marc Dymetman, George Foster, Jean-Marc Jutras, Elliot Macklovitch, Francois Perrault, Xiaobo Ren, and Michel Simard (1993) 'Translation Analysis and Translation Automation', in *Proceedings of the 5th International Conference on Theoretical and Methodological Issues in Machine Translation*, Kyoto, Japan, 201–17.

Kay, Martin (1980) *The Proper Place of Men and Machines in Language Translation*, Xerox Corporation (Reprinted in Sergei Nirenburg, Harold L. Somers, and Yorick Wilks (eds.) *Readings in Machine Translation*, Cambridge, MA: MIT Press, 221–32).

Kittredge, Richard (2012) 'Reflections on TAUM-MÉTÉO', *Circuit* 117: 19–20.

Landry, Alain (1987) 'The Termium Termbank: Today and Tomorrow', in Catriona Picken (ed.) *Proceedings of the 9th Translating and the Computer Conference*, London: ASLIB, 130–44.

Lehrberger, John (1982) 'Automatic Translation and the Concept of Sublanguage', in Richard Kittredge and John Lehrberger (eds.) *Sublanguage: Studies of Language in Restricted Semantic Domains*, Berlin: de Gruyter, 81–106.

Macklovitch, Elliot (1991) 'The Translator's Workstation . . . in Plain Prose', in *Proceedings of the 32nd Annual Conference of the American Translators Association*, 16–19 October 1991, Salt Lake City, UT.

Macklovitch, Elliot (1995) 'TransCheck – Or the Automatic Validation of Human Translations', in *Proceedings of MT Summit V*, 10–12 July 1995, Luxembourg, Geneva: EAMT European Association for Machine Translation.

Macklovitch, Elliot, Michel Simard, and Philippe Langlais (2000) 'TransSearch: A Free Translation Memory on the World Wide Web', in *Proceedings of LREC 2000*, 31 May–2 June 2000, Athens, Greece, 1201–08.

Nirenburg, Sergei, Harold L. Somers, and Yorick Wilks (2003) *Readings in Machine Translation*, Cambridge, MA: MIT Press.

PricewaterhouseCoopers LLP (2012) 'Translation Bureau Benchmarking and Comparative Analysis: Final Report'. Available at: www.btb.gc.ca/publications/documents/rapport-report-benchmarking-eng.pdf.

Simard, Michel, George Foster, and Pierre Isabelle (1993) 'Using Cognates to Align Sentences in Bilingual Corpora', *Proceedings of the 1993 Conference of the Centre for Advanced Studies on Collaborative Research: Distributed Computing* 2: 1071–82.

Taravella, AnneMarie (2011) 'Preliminary Summary Report on the Results of the Survey Conducted among Users of Language Technologies in April–May 2011'. Available at: www.crtl.ca/publications_LTRC.

18

TRANSLATION TECHNOLOGY IN FRANCE

Sylviane Cardey

Introduction

In respect of natural language processing, machine translation is without doubt the application which requires the most in terms of knowledge at all the linguistic levels (lexico-morpho-syntactic), and this without talking of oral machine translation, which is even more difficult and which we mention succinctly here.

Languages when confronted with machines have already been the object of much research and criticism in respect of their analysis. Languages are codes which transmit information 1) by 'words' present in dictionaries (words are here between quotation marks, as we do not have a precise definition of this concept even if it is regularly used to describe all sorts of phenomena) and which are the conventional way of representing things and ideas, 2) by inflexions which add information to the message constituted by the uninflected word and 3) also by the rules of syntax which add precision in their turn in respect of the individual meaning of words and their role in relation to other words. Problems concerning variously homophony, homography, polysemy, all the ambiguities that are possible at the levels of lexis, syntax and, above all, composition from the least to the most frozen are still far from being solved for processing by machine.

> One can say that translation is only possible by means of an analysis of all the linguistic elements used to represent meaning – semantic values, inflexions and grammatical values, syntactic values – which are entangled in the words and the relations between them. This analysis is followed by the synthesis of the linguistic elements of language B, or output language, chosen because they enable expressing approximately the same content and are combined according to language B's own laws.
>
> *(translated from Delavenay 1959)*

Brief History

The first translation machines appeared in the 1930s, notably with the work of the Russian scientist Troyanskji. The first experiments in machine translation involving computers date from 1948 in Britain and the United States; the USSR started in 1954, and Italy followed in 1959 (Léon 1998).

DOI: 10.4324/9781003168348-20

The Beginnings of Machine Translation in France

France started MT research in 1959–60 with the creation of the Association pour l'étude et le développement de la Traduction Automatique et de la Linguistique Appliquée (ATALA) in 1959 and the Centre d'Études pour la Traduction Automatique (CETA) in December 1959 within the Institut Blaise Pascal (IBP) with two sections, one in Paris directed by Aimé Sestier (CETAP) and the other in Grenoble directed by Bernard Vauquois (CETAG).

One wonders why France started so late, that is, thirteen years after the first MT demonstration on a computer in New York in January 1954 at the instigation of the Georgetown University team directed by Léon Dostert (who was French) and above all after the Bar-Hillel report (1959–1960) and subsequently the ALPAC report in 1966. Effectively, it was in 1967 that the CETA organized its second conference on natural language processing, where the first effective demonstration of French-Russian translation by computer was presented.

The End of the 1950s

In 1954, there were no computers in France, whilst there were several in Britain. 'Informatique' (computer science) was unknown at the epoch (the term only appearing in 1962, coined by Ph. Dreyfus), and one talked simply of experiments in the United States. In this context, Sestier, who became director of the Centre école des troupes aéroportées (CETAP, not to be confused with the CETAP previously appearing in this chapter) was one of the rare persons in the defence sector who was interested in computing.

The various companies working with the French Ministry of Defence on electronic and high-precision mechanical problems had all refused to take the technological risk of starting to build a French computer. The only company which had accepted undertaking technology studies was IBM. After two unhappy attempts to construct a French computer, France purchased a British machine in 1955, an Elliot 402, for the IBP. Also, despite the presence of A.D. Booth, one of the British pioneers of machine translation, this latter subject was not discussed at a conference organized by the IBP in January 1951 entitled 'Les machines à calculer et la pensée humaine' (Computing machines and human thought); machine translation did not appear to be echoed in France. It has to be noted that French linguists manifested no specific interest in formal languages.

However, E. Delavenay (founder of the ATALA), because of his responsibility for translation and editing services at the United Nations, New York, up to 1950, took a close interest in the problems of translation at the international level. Thus, it is not surprising that he was the instigator of MT in France; in his memoirs (1992) Delavenay evokes the lack of receptivity by linguists and academics in general concerning the idea of creating MT systems in France. However, a MT work group was constituted around Delavenay which kept abreast with progress in the work of the Americans, the British and the Russians. This group took the name 'groupe international d'études sur la traduction automatique' and met regularly at UNESCO; the group was at the origin of the ATALA. In 1953, UNESCO took stock of the growing global need for scientific and technical translations, reporting the lack of training of translators and the excessive costs of translation. Finally, numerous MT papers were presented at the first International Federation for Information Processing (IFIP) congress organized by UNESCO in Paris in June 1959. The creation of the CETA at the IBP resulted in associating MT closely with the development of numerical methods, computers and automated documentation. An important role was given to the interaction between applied mathematics, formal languages and linguistics. As in many countries, the defence sector was the stakeholder in the development of this discipline, where mathematicians, engineers and linguists worked together in the CETA from 1961 onwards. The language on which the work was done was Russian.

The Sestier Report (1959)

However, for Sestier, mass production of translations was the priority, and he thought the CETA ought to offer certain services: rough translations and studies on indexing and automatic extraction. Sestier also proposed the name *Centre d'études et d'exécution de traductions automatiques*, which underlined the centre's vocational response to social needs. The method recommended by the Sestier report is especially centred on analysis of the source language, this being Russian like for most of the US research, and the task to be achieved was the translation of scientific and technical articles. The objectives were in fact linked in part to defence and to counter-espionage.

The report pointed out the lack of personnel provided with a 'fundamental' linguistic training. Grenoble was made responsible for morphology and Paris syntax. The Grenoble group decided to take on lexical polysemy problems as well. This decision was declared a temporary and unstable step at the first Scientific Council meeting held 20 February 1960. Martinet and Benveniste, members of the Council, were sharply critical of this division between morphology and syntax. They said that it was not pertinent when the objective was to compare two structures; it would be more interesting to start from a solution which is less graphical and more linguistic. As well as this, this division very rapidly became irksome. The pretexts concerning it were due as much to differences in computers as differences in methods. According to Sestier (July 1960), the Grenoble group developed a morphological system uniquely for a binary machine, which was thus strictly unusable by the CETAP, which was using a decimal machine with a small memory. Furthermore, for Sestier, the CETAG system appeared unnecessarily complicated. The Parisians thus decided to take on the morphological analysis. The members of the CETAG showed in their project report their intention also to do research in syntax concerning translations in Russian-French, Japanese-French (M. Nagao was invited) and German-French, adopting the model Sydney Lamb had developed at the University of California, Berkeley.

In 1963, Bernard Vauquois, very interested in formal languages and with a Russian group of which Igor Mel'cuk was a member, was working on an intermediary language which he called a pivot language (Vauquois 1975).

Bar-Hillel's report became known in 1962. The CETAP was dissolved, and Maurice Gross and Yves Gentilhomme went back to the Laboratoire de calcul numérique of the Institut Blaise Pascal. Following this crisis, the name of the ATALA was changed to *Association pour le Traitement Automatique des Langues* and its review *La Traduction Automatique* to *TA Informations, Revue internationale des applications de l'automatique au langage*.

The applied mathematics section of the IBP encouraged linguists and logicians to collaborate in carrying out a detailed and accurate study of natural languages. In other words, problems in MT are due variously to linguistics, to logic, to electronics and to programming. As for research, it was the development from 1963 onwards of a syntactic rules language, then from 1965 of a pivot language which constituted the most original research by the CETA which thus opted for a MT method using an intermediate language. The pivot language, a syntactico-semantic model, ensured independence of the translation process's analysis and synthesis phases. By 1970, as for most MT endeavours, the CETA considered MT the transfer of the meaning of a text written in a source language to a target language. In this epoch, pivot languages were an attempt to formalize this intermediate level that was called the 'semantic level'.

Bernard Vauquois, Maurice Gross and Yves Gentilhomme have all, in one way or another, contributed to current MT research.

Machine Translation in France at the Present Time

Methodologically one can say that linguists, computer scientists and statisticians share the MT scene. Although they have not been used to working together, we find more and more cooperation. This is to be compared with the outset of MT when mathematicians and linguists perhaps succeeded better in collaborating.

There is a great need for translation; in addition, the point is to know how the different types of translation are divided. Three types can be distinguished:

1 Rapid and crude translation in view of knowing very approximately the content of some document. This type concerns scientific and industrial organizations where researchers and engineers, not being able to read texts in the original language, need to inform themselves of research or other work conducted elsewhere. The users, who are familiar with their proper scientific domains, do not require perfect quality. This type of translation is also relevant for multilingual organizations when working documents of a temporary nature are involved.
2 Translations of texts of a general or specialized scope which have to be of good quality.
3 Accurate translations; this concerns, for example, standards, prescriptive texts of multilingual organizations or safety and security critical domains as we will see with Centre Tesnière's work at Besançon.

There also exist a range of tools such as translator aids and dictionaries.

We present here three research centres and one company which are currently active in France in MT, each with its methodology and products.

Centre Tesnière

We start with the Centre de recherche en linguistique et traitement automatique des langues, Lucien Tesnière (in brief Centre Tesnière), which is a research laboratory in the Université de Bourgogne Franche-Comté, Besançon. Since its foundation in 1980, research has been and continues to be done by linguists, mathematicians and computer scientists working together. The Centre was created by Professor Yves Gentilhomme and has been directed since 1994 by Professor Sylviane Cardey.

Centre Tesnière has many MT systems involving particular methodologies. Two of them, Korean-French and Chinese-French (Cardey *et al.* 2003), use the transfer method with very fine-grained linguistic analyses. Another, French-Arabic (Cardey *et al.* 2004) uses a double pivot and gradual generation involving both languages at the same time. A third methodology, pivot + transfer (Cardey *et al.* 2008), has been developed which involves controlled French to variously controlled Arabic, Chinese, English and Thai and controlled French too (identity translation).

All these machine translation systems are based on Centre Tesnière's constructive micro-systemic linguistic analysis approach in which traceability is inherent (systemic quality model) (Cardey 2013). The systemic approach which has been mentioned here is based on logic, set theory, partitions and relations and also the theory of algorithms. A theoretical approach which is mathematically based, whatever it is, ought to be able to accept linguistic formalisms. For this reason, such an approach has to be sufficiently flexible so as to enable the construction of models themselves founded on model theory using a constructive logic approach. These models must adapt themselves as the analysis proceeds and when new problems are uncovered (Cardey 2015). The linguistic approach involves the delimitation of sets by choosing only and uniquely those elements which serve to solve the problem, the sets so involved being able to function together in terms of relations.

As Centre Tesnière works with safety-critical domains which cannot admit any error, in their pivot + transfer methodology, the source has to be written in controlled language and must not only conform to normal controlled language constraints, but it must also be able to be machine translated, without manual pre- or post-editing (there is no time available during emergencies) to target controlled languages which are themselves controlled. The methodology is based on linguistic norms and a supporting mathematical model for the construction of a single source-controlled language to be machine translated to specific target controlled languages.

1   The source and target languages are controlled as controlled languages per se, that is for human use, the traditional raison d'être for controlled languages.
2   The source and target languages are controlled in a mutual manner so as to ensure reliable machine translation. The authors of the messages only know the source language.

The first step thus consists in detecting what is common and what is divergent in the languages concerned. Equivalence tables are established in micro-system form in order to solve divergence problems and for finding the 'equivalent form' for each concept in the other languages. This presents a real challenge, as texts have to be machine translated without error into several target languages and without post-editing.

As well as for end user applications, such computational processing can also be useful, for instance, for the mechanical verification of linguistic data representations, for grammatical concordances and traceability as well as automated case based benchmark construction and so on.

Given a defined domain and a specific need to be processed, the equivalences and divergences between the languages concerned can be represented in the following way.

With three (or more) languages, whatever they are, the systems which are common to the three languages in question are constructed; to these are added the systems which are common to all the pairs of languages and finally the systems specific to each language (see Figure 18.1).

Certain of the systems will be common with inflexional languages, others with agglutinative languages and still others with isolating languages.

As said at the outset, Centre Tesnière's model can be applied to all languages. Figure 18.2 illustrates the potential for extraction from ข้อต่ออร-อง (Thai). This is the sort of problem that can be solved using their methodology.

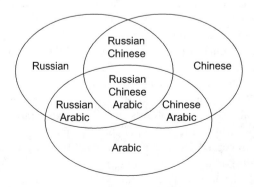

Figure 18.1   Common and specific systems between languages

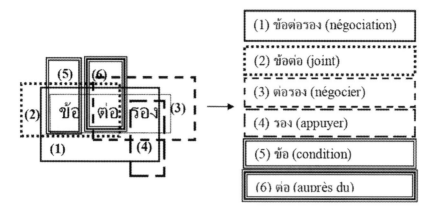

Figure 18.2 Illustration of the potential for extraction from ข้อต่อรอง (Thai)

Centre Tesnière's methodology working in intension allows the detection, tagging and disambiguation of neologisms and also automatic acronym detection. For example, the Interreg (France-Suisse) DecRIPT project, 2020–2022, dealing with detecting how information is represented in texts for personal data protection between others, is coordinated by Centre Tesnière. A standard has been developed: ISO 24620-5 Language resource management – Controlled human communication (CHC) – Part 5: Lexico-morpho-syntactic principles and methodology for personal data recognition and protection in texts (DataPro).

Centre Tesnière has also coordinated amongst others the French (ANR) project LiSe (Linguistique et Sécurité) project and the European Message project, which concern security in general and in particular where communication involving humans ought to be rapid and correct. Generation of information without ambiguity, rapidly and in several languages being the need in the case of emergencies and crises, using micro-systemic linguistic analysis, Centre Tesnière has classified and organized the language equivalences and divergences in the form of a compositional micro-system structure expressed in a declarative manner by means of typed container data structures together with their contents so as to be incorporated in the machine translation process.

The controlled languages mirror each other. The architecture of the machine translation system is thus based on the variants being divergences between the controlled target languages and the canonical controlled French source language, these divergences being organized in such a manner as to effect the translations during the translation process.

The same methodology working in intension as opposed to extension has been used to create oral controlled languages for translation and others for safety-critical application domains.

This has resulted in a model based on language norms and divergences with inherent tracing which has been used to produced an AFNOR and ISO standard for oral controlled languages (Cardey, S., Greenfield, P, ISO standard 24620-3: 2021) where 14 languages are represented as examples and where any of the languages could be source or target.

SYSTRAN

Let us turn now to an industrial machine translation system, one of the very few companies created at the very beginning of machine translation still in operation.

SYSTRAN is the supplier covering the largest range of machine translation solutions in France and has a global presence in the defence and security sector and for large enterprises looking for tailored solutions.

The company was founded in 1968 in La Jolla, California, by Peter Toma. It was acquired by Gachot S.A., a French company in 1986, was listed on the Euronext market and then was purchased by Korean investment funds in 2014.

SYSTRAN's headquarters and R&D centre is located in Paris. It has subsidiaries in San Diego, California, Seoul, Tokyo and Mexico. SYSTRAN has over 100 employees worldwide and through a very large partner network had a commercial presence in more than 50 countries in 2021.

SYSTRAN is famous for having launched Babelfish, the first ever free translation solution on the Internet in 1997 in partnership with Altavista.

The initial SYSTRAN systems were rule-based systems; however, over the decades, its development has always been driven by pragmatic considerations, progressively integrating many of the most efficient MT approaches and techniques. In 2010–2015, SYSTRAN invented hybrid machine translation combining the power of statistical machine translation and the accuracy of rule-based systems. In 2016, SYSTRAN had fully transitioned to neural machine translation (Crego *et al.* 2016) by co-developing an Open Source framework OpenNMT (Klein *et al.* 2017) – which is today the most-used framework for machine translation both by academics (more than 1000 citations on academic papers early 2021) and by industrial entities.

With a long history in language description, SYSTRAN is keeping a unique edge on the market, providing a full solution aimed at the translator and the professional – co-existing with CAT tools, complex existing system integration, multimodal input and so on while maintaining language description at the core of its development.

Thus the user dictionary, which is the ability for the end user to introduce their own terminology, has been a key component of all generations of the SYSTRAN engine, with a full support of morphology and disambiguation (Michon *et al.* 2020).

Also, while translators are making use of translation memory for productivity, SYSTRAN has developed technology for combining translation memory and machine translation (Pham *et al.* 2020).

While open source has allowed state-of-the-art neural technology to be adopted by all machine translation providers, the key remaining differentiator in quality is the training data and language expertise.

While it has in its catalogue over 250 language combination for multiple domains, SYSTRAN has been pushing the limits further by opening development of more models to third-party trainers with the SYSTRAN marketplace. This marketplace is a unique platform allowing trainers (language experts, data owners) to provide specialized translation to end users.

SYTSRAN Model Studio provides trainers with key-turn tools for training neural models on their own data; the models are then directly available for end users for testing and purchasing through a cloud service. The trainers can then monetize their expertise and knowledge, and users can find the largest offering on the market. The goal of this marketplace is to extend the reach of machine translation to lower-resourced languages and contribute to language diversity preservation.

LIMSI

In this section we review the activities of the Laboratoire d'Informatique pour la Mécanique et les Sciences de l'Ingénieur (LIMSI),[1] with François Yvon (CNRS) as principal investigator.

LIMSI's MT research mostly takes part within the Spoken Language Group, a component of the Human Language Technology Department, and focuses on corpus-based, statistical and neural translation modelling and more generally on structured learning problems in natural language processing. Other relevant activities are developed within the Information Langue Ecrite et Signée (ILES) group, notably focusing on automatic translation for sign language, but will not be further discussed in this review.

In recent years, machine translation technologies have gone through a major change, with the rapid development of new statistical tools based on so-called "neural models", which have not only deeply changed the way MT systems are designed, built and trained but also opened new perspectives and applications.

Just like statistical machine translation (SMT) models, neural models (NMT) are trained with machine learning algorithms from parallel corpora containing examples of source texts aligned with their translation(s). High-quality bitexts therefore remain essential in the development process. However, and contrarily to SMT, it is no longer necessary to compute sub-sentential alignments; this is because NMTs are simultaneously doing two things: 1) learning numerical representations of variable-length sequences representing the source and the target words and sentences and 2) using these representations, to learn the best continuation of a target language prefix of a source sentence. Such models can be viewed as the direct heirs of neural language and translation models (LMs) that were already used with the last generation of SMTs developed by the group during the period 2011–2015.

In this context, LIMSI has been developing research activities in three main directions: 1) to develop methods to address well-known limitations of SMT in the context of NMT, 2) to transfer the advances of NMT research into tools that could help professional translators and 3) to revisit the problem of MT evaluation in the face of improved automatic outputs.

Regarding theme 1), LIMSI has notably contributed to using linguistically informed word representations in NMT. More recently, fundamental statistical problems related to data sparsity or data mismatch have been looked at: Burlot and Yvon (2018) study ways to take advantage of non-parallel monolingual corpora to boost the performance of NMT systems; Pham *et al.* (2021) study multi-domain NMT, that is, systems aimed at translating optimally for several domains, under multiple angles. This problem is related to domain adaptation and also to an emerging theme: multilingual machine translation. Also worth mentioning are attempts to better use bilingual dictionaries and translation memories (TMs) (Pham *et al.* 2020) in NMT.

Such resources are basic tools in the translator workbench, which leads us to theme 2): developing methods targeting high-quality NMT aimed at publication rather than assimilation. Sentence alignment, TM cleaning and automatic word alignment, which help extract bilingual dictionaries from bilingual corpora, have been the subject of several studies. Ive *et al.* (2018) attempt to automatically detect and pre-translate difficult segments, phrases and terms instead of post-editing them. Finally, the design of new devices aimed at improving the reading experience for parallel texts is studied in Yvon *et al.* (2016).

All these innovations brought by neural models need to be diagnosed and evaluated, and significant efforts are devoted to the issue of quality measurements of MT output [theme 3]. LIMSI's systems have thus taken part in several international MT evaluation campaigns. This includes yearly participation in the WMT evaluation series, with a focus on translation into French in the bio-medical domain, a task LIMSI also helps to organize. The group has also contributed work on improving automatic metrics and to the creation of (semi)-automatic challenge sets (Burlot and Yvon 2017) dedicated to assessing the ability to handle morphological phenomena when translating from English.

While all these activities are a continuation of their past work, it is also worth mentioning the emergence of a new theme focusing on computational language documentation, which is explored in collaboration with field linguists. The goal of this research is to repurpose MT (and more generally NLP) tools to speed up language documentation. This has notably led to developing new corpora for under-resourced languages and studying the task of automatic word discovery from speech (Godard *et al.* 2018). It is likely that this theme will continue to grow in the future.

Finally, LIMSI is involved in a number of national and international projects with both academic and industrial partners.

LIUM

Activities in machine translation at the LIUM laboratory started in 2007. Since then, the LIUM has worked extensively in multiple facets of the machine translation area, including low-resource language processing, domain adaptation and multimodal machine translation. Using both statistical and neural methods, the LIUM has participated in several national and international projects. This has allowed the LIUM to develop impressive machine translation systems which are systematically classed amongst the best in numerous international evaluations, notably OpenMT 2008, 2009 and 2012; WMT 2014 and 2018 (Bougares *et al.* 2019); and IWSLT 2011, 2019 and 2020 (Nguyen *et al.* 2020).

Using both statistical and deep neural machine translation techniques, the LIUM laboratory has developed multiple translation systems for multiple languages and different domains. For instance, the LIUM participates in developing translation systems in the framework of the DARPA GALE and BOLT as well as the French DGA project PEA TRAD[2] (in collaboration with Airbus Defense and Space) programmes for Arabic–English and Chinese–English language pairs. Regarding domain-specific translation systems, the LIUM carries out much research exploring various model adaptation and specialization techniques to particular domains, using comparable corpora (Abdul-Rauf and Schwenk 2011) and corrective learning with automatic post-editing.

More recently and within the recent advances afforded by the success of deep learning methods for machine translation (end of 2013), the LIUM has continued its research activities with innovative and promising ideas including the integration of linguistic knowledge to neural translation systems (), as well as multimodal (Caglayan *et al.* 2019) and multilingual (Bardet *et al.* 2019) machine translation systems, developed in the framework of the European Chist-ERA M2CR project.

The LIUM laboratory is also developing lifelong learning methods for machine translation in the framework of the EU Chist-ERA ALLIES project. Within this framework, the LIUM aims to develop autonomous translation systems which automatically evaluate and adapt themselves to the incoming stream of documents to be translated (Barrault *et al.* 2020).[3]

Conclusion

In reality, what is interesting in France is that different technologies as well as quite different hybrid technologies are used, giving prominence either to both linguistic and mathematical models or to statistical and neural machine translation models and techniques. Sometimes we even have a mixture of linguistic, statistical and neural techniques now. We also see the will in progressing to obtain better results together with the curiosity of researchers looking at other methodologies according to the domain and public addressed by their systems.

Notes

1 As of January 2021, LIMSI has been discontinued and its activities have been merged in a larger laboratory, Laboratoire Interdisciplinaire des Sciences du Numérique (LISN), yielding significant restructuring and changes among research groups. For convenience, the older name is used throughout.
2 See www.defense.gouv.fr/content/download/324708/4453034/file/dp_forum_innovation_dga_2.pdf
3 See also http://statmt.org/wmt20/lifelong-learning-task.html

Bibliography

Abdul-Rauf, S. and H. Schwenk (2011) 'Parallel Sentence Generation from Comparable Corpora for Improved SM', *Machine Translation* 25(4): 341–75.

Bardet, A., F. Bougares, and L. Barrault (2019) 'A Study on Multilingual Transfer Learning in Neural Machine Translation: Finding the Balance Between Languages', in *International Conference on Statistical Language and Speech Processing*, 59–70, https://link.springer.com/chapter/10.1007/978-3-030-31372-2_5

Barrault, L., M. Biesialska, M. R. Costa-jussà, F. Bougares, and O. Galibert (2020) 'Findings of the First Shared Task on Lifelong Learning Machine Translation', in *International Conference on Machine Translation*, https://aclanthology.org/2020.wmt-1.2.pdf

Bougares, F., J. Wottawa, A. Baillot, L. Barrault, and A. Bardet (2019) 'LIUM's Contributions to the WMT2019 News Translation Task: Data and Systems for German-French Language Pairs', in *Proceedings of the Fourth Conference on Machine Translation (Volume 2: Shared Task Papers, Day 1)*, Association for Computational Linguistics, Florence, Italy, 129–33.

Burlot, F. and F. Yvon (2017) 'Evaluating the Morphological Competence of Machine Translation Systems', in *Proceedings of the Second Conference on Machine Translation, Volume 1: Research Papers*, Copenhagen, Denmark, 43–55.

Burlot, F. and F. Yvon (2018) 'Using Monolingual Data in Neural Machine Translation: A Systematic Study', in *Proceedings of the Third Conference on Machine Translation*, Brussels, BE, 144–55.

Caglayan, O., P. Madhyastha, L. Specia, and L. Barrault (2019) 'Probing the Need for Visual Context in Multimodal Machine Translation', in *Conference of the North American Chapter of the Association for Computational Linguistics: Human Language Technologies, Volume 1 (Long and Short Papers)*, Association for Computational Linguistics, Minneapolis, Minnesota, 4159–70.

Cardey, S. (2013) *Modelling Language*, Amsterdam: John Benjamins Publishing Company.

Cardey, S. (2015) 'Norm and Controlled Language for Machine Translation', in Chan Sin-wai (ed.) *The Human Factor in Machine Translation*, Routledge Studies in Translation Technology, London and New York: Routledge, 30–51.

Cardey, S. and P. Greenfield (2021) 'Standard, Language Resource Management – Controlled Human Communication (CHC) – Part 3: Basic Principles and Methodology for Controlled Oral Communication (COralCom)', ISO 24620-3:2021.

Cardey, S., P. Greenfield, R. Anantalapochai, M. Beddar, D. Devitre, and G. Jin (2008) 'Modelling of Multiple Target Machine Translation of Controlled Languages Based on Language Norms and Divergences', in *Proceedings of ISUC2008*, 15–16 December 2008, B. Werner (ed.), Osaka, Japan, IEEE Computer Society, 322–29.

Cardey, S., P. Greenfield, and M.-S. Hong (2003) 'The TACT Machine Translation System: Problems and Solutions for the Pair Korean – French', *Translation Quarterly* 27: 22–44, Hong Kong: The Hong Kong Translation Society.

Cardey, S., P. Greenfield, and X. Wu (2004) 'Designing a Controlled Language for the Machine Translation of Medical Protocols: The Case of English to Chinese', in *Proceedings of AMTA-2004 The 6th Conference of the Association for Machine Translation in the Americas, Georgetown University*, September 28–October 2, 2004, Washington DC, [Machine Translation: From Real Users to Research LNAI 3265], R. E. Frederking and K. B. Taylor (eds.), Berlin, Heidelberg: Springer-Verlag, 37–47.

Crego, J., J. Kim, G. Klein, *et al.* (2016) 'Systran's Pure Neural Machine Translation Systems', *arXiv preprint arXiv:1610.05540.*

Delavenay, E. (1959) *La machine à traduire*, Paris: PUF.

Godard, P., M. Zanon Boito, L. Ondel, A. Bérard, F. Yvon, A. Villavicencio, and L. Besacier (2018) 'Unsupervised Word Segmentation from Speech with Attention', in *Proceedings of the International Conference on Speech Technologies*, Hyderabad, India.

Ive, J., A. Max, and F. Yvon (2018) 'Reassessing the Proper Place of Man and Machine in Translation: A Pre-translation Scenario', *Machine Translation* 32: 279–308, Springer.

Klein, G., Y. Kim, Y. Deng, *et al.* (2017) 'OpenNMT: Open-Source Toolkit for Neural Machine Translation', in *ACL (System Demonstrations)*, Vancouver, Canada: Association for Computational Linguistics, 67–72.

Léon, J. (1998) 'Les débuts de la traduction automatique en France (1959–1968): à contretemps? Modèles linguistiques tome XIX', *fascicule* 2: 55–86, OpenEdition.

Michon, E., J. M. Crego, and J. Senellart (2020) 'Integrating Domain Terminology into Neural Machine Translation', in *Proceedings of the 28th International Conference on Computational Linguistics*, (Online), International Committee on Computational Linguistics, Barcelona, Spain, 3925–37.

Nguyen, H., F. Bougares, N. A. Tomashenko, Y. Estève, and L. Besacier (2020) 'Investigating Self-Supervised Pre-Training for End-to-End Speech Translation', *Interspeech 2020*, https://hal.archives-ouvertes.fr/hal-02962186

Pham, M. Q., J. Crego, and F. Yvon (2021) 'Revisiting Multi-domain Machine Translation', *Transactions of the Association for Computational Linguistics* 9: 17–35.

Pham, M. Q., J. Xu, J. M. Crego, F. Yvon, and J. Senellart (2020) 'Priming Neural Machine Translation', in *Proceedings of the Fifth Conference on Machine Translation*, 516–27, Online, https://hal.archives-ouvertes.fr/hal-03013196.

Vauquois, B. (1975) *La traduction automatique à Grenoble*, Paris: Dunod.

Yvon, F., Y. Xu, M. Apidianaki, C. Pillias, and P. Cubaud (2016) 'Transread: Designing a Bilingual Reading Experience with Machine Translation Technologies', in *Proceedings of the 2016 Conference of the North American Chapter of the Association for Computational Linguistics: Demonstrations*, San Diego, CA, 27–31.

19

TRANSLATION TECHNOLOGY IN HONG KONG

Chan Sin-wai, Ian Castor Chow and Billy Wong Tak Ming

Introduction

Translation technology includes typically machine translation (MT), computer-aided translation (CAT) and a wide array of supporting tools and computational techniques to facilitate translation. It has been deemed the solution to the ever-increasing amount of information waiting to be translated between languages, especially in recent decades as advances of information technologies have significantly reduced the cost of information dissemination and promoted international communication.

Hong Kong is a multicultural region in the world where inter-language interaction is prevalent, leading to a great demand for translation and a huge volume of available texts in different language versions. As a multilingual city, Chinese and English are the official languages in Hong Kong, and a number of Asian languages are spoken by various communities.[1] Furthermore, the two character sets of written Chinese in use, i.e., traditional and simplified, are different not only in graphemes of characters but also preferred vocabularies and syntactic structures due to the regional and cultural differences between Hong Kong and Mainland China. Nowadays the provision of governmental and commercial documents online in traditional/simplified Chinese and English bilingual version is essential, such as the Bilingual Laws Information System on the website of the Department of Justice,[2] which contains a comprehensive collection of the laws of Hong Kong. In some cases multilingual versions covering a number of languages are also available.[3] They provide a huge number of multilingual texts serving as a valuable resource of translation technology, for instance, for developers of MT to perform system training, or users of CAT to build up translation memory.

A typical genre of translation in Hong Kong is practical writing, covering various fields such as governmental, legal and business. It is characterized by the use of domain-specific terminology, and highly repetitive wording and sentence patterns resulting from the requirement of standardized written style. Texts having these features are suitable to be processed by CAT tools like termbanks and translation memory systems to store standard and repeated entries for future reuse for the sake of consistency and efficiency.

The translation market in Hong Kong poses other challenges for translators and prepares an appropriate environment for the growth of translation technology. As pointed out in Au (2001: 185–192), for instance, financial documents are commonly either prepared in a hurry or revised frequently with stringent deadlines, leaving translators very limited time to work and to deal

DOI: 10.4324/9781003168348-21

with the different versions while maintaining the translation quality, not to mention the linguistic challenges of specific terminology and syntactic structures. This is where technologies can be utilized to take over the routine and mechanical tasks for which they are designed.

This chapter describes the development of translation technology in Hong Kong. We use the term 'translation technology' to refer to all kinds of language technology which aids translation directly and indirectly, including, in addition to MT and CAT, those for Chinese language processing such as traditional-simplified Chinese translation and word segmentation, those for corpus construction and so on. So far their development mainly focuses on research and teaching in tertiary institutes.[4] The former covers a wide range of topics and is conducted by scholars from three main disciplines: translation, computational linguistics and computer science and engineering. The latter includes programmes and courses offered in various universities. In addition, there are a few, though limited, number of applications worth mentioning.

Research and Academic Activities

Research and academic activities related to translation technology have been actively carried out in Hong Kong. Most of the universities have different kinds of ongoing or completed works in this area, including the establishment of research centres, the organization of international conferences, publication of academic journals, encyclopaedias and a large number of research outputs.

The Chinese University of Hong Kong (CUHK)

The Hung On-To Research Laboratory for Machine Translation (1960s–1970s), Machine Translation Laboratory (1999) and Centre for Translation Technology (2006), Department of Translation at the Chinese University of Hong Kong were the first tertiary institutions to conduct research into translation technology. As early as in 1969, an MT system, the Chinese University Language Translator (CULT) (Loh 1972), was developed by the Hung On-To Research Laboratory for Machine Translation. According to Chan (2001: 205–18), translation output of CULT was found to be satisfactory for Chinese-to-English translation of scientific writings given some pre-editing techniques. CULT was later redesigned as an interactive online MT system with the construction of a new Chinese keyboard.

The Machine Translation Laboratory (MTL) was set up by the Department of Translation in 1999. It has five goals to achieve:

1 to serve as a centre for the collection of computer-related materials;
2 to serve as a centre for the study of the application and analysis of the existing software available in the market;
3 to build up a communication network of MT centres throughout the world and of active researchers in the field;
4 to propose interdepartmental, interfaculty or even intercollegiate projects that will contribute significantly to the scholarship in the field or meet the needs of the local community; and
5 to build up terminological databases for various subjects or professions that will help to achieve standardization in the translation of specialized vocabularies.

(Chan 2001: 205–18)

An MT system, TransRecipe (Chan 2002a: 3–22), was developed by the MTL for translating Chinese cookbooks into English. It combines in its system design corpus-based, example-based, pattern-based and rule-based approaches. More importantly, it adopts a 'translational approach' to have translation methods coded into the system, in addition to linguistic and computational concepts, such that human translators can contribute their expertise in the process of MT development.

The Centre for Translation Technology (CTT) was established by the same department in 2006 for carrying out research into translation technology, making practical translation tools to serve the industry through collaboration with translation companies and sister institutions and promoting the use of translation technology in society. In particular, the goals of CTT include:

1　the building of domain-specific translation corpora;
2　the construction of a database of works on computer-aided translation;
3　the creation of a software library; and
4　the organization of seminars on translation technology.

(Chan 2006: 12)

Besides, CTT also supports the teaching of the CAT Programme offered by the department, in terms of creating supporting resources to teaching, which include:

1　CAT literature archive – including monographs, anthologies, conference proceedings, academic journals and electronic magazines, published since 1984, which are classified into categories and reposited in easy-to-read electronic format;
2　CAT system user manual archive – including manuals of more than 200 CT and CAT systems, which can be accessed and searched easily;
3　CAT system operation video archive – including a series of videos to demonstrate the operation of the various systems; and
4　CAT project archive – including the CAT projects conducted by the students of the MACAT programme.

(Chan 2008b: 2)

The Department of Translation also publishes different kinds of scholarly works related to translation technology. The *CAT Bulletin* is published regularly to facilitate dissemination of information about the MACAT programme to targeted readers. It includes information on the most updated programme structure, course contents, staff profiles, academic activities, public seminars, staff publications and research findings. It also provides information on the new advances in CAT delivered through conference proceedings, seminar speeches and students' translation projects.

The *Journal of Translation Studies* is a peer-reviewed international journal dedicated to the publication of research papers in all areas of translation. A special issue (Volume 13, Numbers 1 and 2, 2010) on the teaching of CAT was published covering practical experience, systems and facilities, curriculum and course design and the future of CAT teaching.

The *Journal of Translation Technology* is the first international journal of this kind in Hong Kong. It serves to promote the scholarly study of translation technology, publish academic articles on the history, theory and practice of the discipline and review articles of books on the field.

Other publications include a book, *Translation and Information Technology* (Chan 2002b), which brings together experts from different disciplines to discuss how new technologies work on translator education and translation practice, as well as the conceptual gaps raised by the interface of human and machine. *A Dictionary of Translation Technology* (Chan 2004) is the first dictionary in the field, covering in total 1,375 entries and serving as a comprehensive reference for general readers as well as specialists in translation technology. *A Topical Bibliography of Computer(-Aided)*

Translation (Chan 2008a) provides a wide variety of information on the literature in the field, i.e., 8,363 entries of works written either in English or Chinese by 5,404 authors between 1948 and 2006 in the forms of journal articles, conference papers, book chapters, project reports, software reviews and newsletter features on or about documentary and speech MT/CAT. There are also conference presentations such as Chow (2012), which discusses how Web 2.0 and hybridity of MT-CAT change the design and use of translation tools, and Siu (2012), which illustrates an automatic pre- and post-editing approach to MT.

In the past decade a series of conferences oriented to translation technology were hosted by the department, including:

- 2012 – The 10th Anniversary Conference of the MA in Computer-aided Translation Programme: New Trends in Translation Technology;
- 2009 – International Conference: The Teaching of Computer-aided Translation;
- 2006 – International Conference: Computer-aided Translation: Theory and Practice;
- 2004 – International Conference: Translation Software – The State of the Art; and
- 2000 – International Conference: Translation and Information Technology.

These conferences drew together scholars, translation practitioners and software developers from different countries to exchange their knowledge, experiments and visions of various themes of translation technology.

The Human-Computer Communications Laboratory (1999) and the Microsoft-CUHK Joint Laboratory for Human-Centric Computing and Interface Technologies (2005), Department of Systems Engineering and Engineering Management

The Human-Computer Communications Laboratory (HCCL)[5] was established in 1999 with a mission to 'foster interdisciplinary research and education in human-centric information systems'. It supports research areas including but not limited to speech recognition, spoken language understanding, speech generation, conversational systems development, audio information processing, multimodal and multimedia interface development, intelligent agents, mobile computing and computer-supported collaborative work. Some representative research works related to translation technology conducted by HCCL include Chinese-English MT based on semi-automatic induced grammars (Siu and Meng 2001: 2749–2752; Siu *et al.* 2003: 2801–2804) and translingual speech retrieval (Lo *et al.* 2001: 1303–1306; Meng *et al.* 2004: 163–179).

The Microsoft-CUHK Joint Laboratory for Human-Centric Computing and Interface Technologies[6] was established in 2005. This laboratory was recognized as a Ministry of Education of China (MoE) Key Laboratory in 2008. It conducts basis research and technology development in five strategic areas: (1) computer vision, (2) computer graphics, (3) speech processing and multimodal human-computer interaction, (4) multimedia processing and retrieval and (5) wireless communications and networking. Research on name entity translation matching and learning was conducted (Lam *et al.* 2007: 2).

The Hong Kong University of Science and Technology

Human Language Technology Center

The Hong Kong University of Science and Technology is the only university in Hong Kong that does not offer a translation programme. However, considerable research on language and speech technology has been conducted in the Department of Computer Science and Engineering and Department of Electronic and Computer Engineering. Led by the faculty members of both departments, the Human Language Technology Center (HLTC)[7] was found in the 1990s, specializing in research on speech and signal processing, statistical and corpus-based natural language processing, machine translation, text mining, information extraction, Chinese language processing, knowledge management and related fields. A number of systems have been built at HLTC, including automated language translation for the Internet, speech-based web browsing and speech recognition for the telephone.

Two of the HLTC members, Professors Dekai Wu and Pascale Fung, have been extensively involved into the research of translation technology. Professor Wu is renowned for his significant contributions to MT, especially the development of inversion transduction grammar (Wu 1995: 69–82, 1996: 152–158, 1997: 377–404; Wu and Wong 1998: 1408–14), a syntactically motivated algorithm for producing word-level alignments of parallel sentences, which pioneered the integration of syntactic and semantic models into statistical MT. Some of his recent representative works include semantic-based statistical MT (Wu and Fung 2009: 13–16; Wu *et al.* 2010: 236–52) and an automatic MT evaluation metric based on semantic frames named MEANT (Lo and Wu 2011: 220–29; Lo *et al.* 2012: 243–52).

Professor Fung is the founding director of InterACT[8] at HKUST, a joint research and education centre between the computer science departments of eight leading universities in this field worldwide. One of their projects is EU-BRIDGE,[9] aiming at 'developing automatic transcription and translation technology that will permit the development of innovative multimedia captioning and translation services of audiovisual documents between European and non-European languages'. Fung also conducted research in Chinese MT (Fung 2010: 425–54), translation disambiguation (Cheung and Fung 2005: 251–73), speech MT (Fung *et al.* 2004), term translation (Fung and McKeown 1996: 53–87, 1997: 192–202) and so on.

City University of Hong Kong

Department of Linguistics and Translation

The Department of Linguistics and Translation at City University of Hong Kong (CityU) is one of the university departments in Hong Kong most actively involved in the research and teaching of translation technology. A number of funded projects have been conducted, covering various aspects of translation technology, such as the following:

Example-Based Machine Translation (EBMT) for Legal Texts *(PI: Jonathan J. Webster)*

This project applies the 'example-based' approach to the translation of the specialized language of legislation and legal documents . . . Research into the application of the example-based approach will be based on an aligned parallel corpus representing the work of top professionals in legal translation.

A Pilot Study of Learning From Examples to Translate Better *(PI: Kit Chunyu)*

This project will explore advanced technologies and practical methodology to implement an online machine translation (MT) system that can learn to translate better. By providing an online translation service with a bilingual editor for manual post-editing, the system acquires translation knowledge from translators to enrich its example base and language models. . . . A unique feature of this system is that it adapts its translation towards translators' expertise via learning.

Construction of an On-Line Platform for Computer-Aided Teaching and Learning of Bilingual Writing and Translating in/Between English and Chinese *(PI: Chunshen Zhu)*

[T]his project proposes to build an electronic platform for on-line teaching/(self-) learning of bilingual writing and translation in/between English and Chinese (traditional and simplified). . . . The products . . . help alleviate the pressure on the teaching of labor-intensive courses of translation and (bilingual) writing/editing.

The research of CityU on translation technology is also fruitful. For example, Kit *et al.* (2002: 57–78) critically review the major stages of example-based MT and present a lexical-based text alignment approach for example acquisition. Kit *et al.* (2005: 71–78) illustrate how English–Chinese parallel texts of the laws of Hong Kong can be harvested on the Web and aligned at the subparagraph level. Song *et al.* (2009: 57–60, 2010: 62–65) propose a new method for transliteration of name entities based on statistical MT technology. Kit and Wong (2008: 299–321), Wong and Kit (2008, 2009a: 337–344, 2009b: 141–155, 2010: 360–364, 2011: 537–544, 2012: 1060–1068) and Wong *et al.* (2011: 238–242) conduct a series of works on developing an automatic metric, Assessment of Text Essential Characteristics (ATEC), for MT evaluation and how automatic evaluation metrics can be used to aid MT users to opt for a proper MT system. Seneff *et al.* (2006: 213–222) present techniques to combine interlingua translation framework with statistical MT. Zhu (2005, 2007a, 2007b) demonstrate a computer platform, ClinkNotes, for assisting translation teaching.

The Education University of Hong Kong

Research Centre on Linguistics and Language Information Sciences

The Research Centre on Linguistics and Language Information Sciences (RCLIS), which was founded in 2010, aims to 'foster interdisciplinary research in the diverse areas of linguistics, natural language processing and information science'. It also provides a forum for scholars from the same or different institutes to work on problems of language and information technology in Chinese speech communities. The research of RCLIS is focused on

(1) the structures, as well as encoding and decoding, of information in the context of natural language, through which human beings acquire, and (2) mak[ing] use of knowledge, and . . . computational techniques to study and simulate the processes involved.

Over the years, RCLIS has conducted a number of projects funded by different agencies, such as the Research Grants Council of HKSAR, the Commerce and Economic Development Bureau's Innovation Technology Fund and the Judiciary, as well as private funding sources. Those projects related to translation technology include:

* Parallel Classical-Colloquial Chinese Alignment Processing and Retrieval Platform
* A Computational Lexicon Based on Intrinsic Nature of Word Senses: A Bilingual Approach
* BASIS (project on Chinese Lexical Data Mining) Part of Speech POS Tagging to Simplified and Traditional Chinese Texts

- Bilingual Reference System
- Chinese Semantic Networks & Construction of a (Pan) Chinese Thesaurus.

The research outputs of RCLIS range from computer system and language resources to publications. For instance, an online platform, ACKER,[10] was developed for Chinese language teaching and learning. It aligns classical Chinese texts with their modern Chinese counterparts and provides a search engine that enables bi-directional retrieval of the processed texts. Also, a Chinese–English parallel corpus of patent documents was constructed and used as a benchmark for the international competition on Chinese–English MT jointly organized by RCLIS and the National Institute of Information and Communication Technology (NICT) in Tokyo in 2010. Other relevant research includes anaphora resolution for MT (Chan and Tsou 1999: 163–190) and MT between Chinese and other languages (Lu *et al.* 2011: 472–479; Tsou 2007a, 2007b; Tsou and Lu 2011).

The Hong Kong Polytechnic University

The research of translation technology is conducted in various departments at The Hong Kong Polytechnic University (PolyU), including the Department of Chinese and Bilingual Studies, Department of Computing and Department of Electronic and Information Engineering. The related projects include:

- Cantonese-Putonghua Inter-Dialect Machine Translation and its Integration with the World Wide Web
- Evolving Artificial Neural Networks to Measure Chinese Sentence Similarity for Example-Based Chinese-to-English Machine Translation
- Building up a Computerised Mechanism for General Translation Business.

The relevant research outputs cover a number of topics. Lau and Zhang (1997: 379–382), Zhang (1998: 499–506, 1999: 40–47), Zhang and Lau (1996: 419–429) and Zhang and Shi (1997: 225–231) conduct a series of works to explore the design of an inter-dialect MT system particularly for the Cantonese–Mandarin dialect pair, which involves two dialects widely used in Chinese speech communities but with considerable differences in pronunciation, vocabulary and syntactic rules. Liu and Zhou (1998: 1201–1206), Wu and Liu (1999: 481–486) and Zhou and Liu (1997a: 65–72, 1997b: 520–525) present a hybrid MT model integrating rules and automatically acquired translation examples and a resulting system prototype PolyU-MT-99 designed for Cantonese–English translation. Wang *et al.* (2004: 97–102) propose a rule-based method for English-to-Chinese MT. Zhang (2005: 241–245) illustrates the design of what he calls the ABCD concordancer and discusses its application to translation.

The University of Hong Kong

The Pattern Recognition and Computer Vision Laboratory, Department of Computer Science

The Pattern Recognition and Computer Vision Laboratory[11] at the Department of Computer Science has several focused areas, including Chinese computing and MT. It has an ongoing project on MT (i.e. Marker Identification in Example-Based Machine Translation) and is developing an English–Chinese MT system using a combination of knowledge- and example-based approaches.

Caritas Institute of Higher Education

The School of Humanities and Languages at Caritas Institute of Higher Education (CIHE) has been actively developing research in translation technology. Its research development features an interdisciplinary approach to facilitate collaboration. The Techno-Humanities Research Centre[12] was established in 2021 to promote the use and development of technology in humanities research, in which 'techno-translation' is one of the research focuses. There is also the Distributed Artificial Intelligence Laboratory[13] at CIHE to support relevant research with artificial intelligence facilities and techniques. The relevant academic events held by the school in recent years include:

- Online Lecture Series on Computing Knowledge for Translators in 2021
- Conference in Building a Techno-Humanities Culture in Hong Kong in 2022.

The related projects include:

- Creating an Automatic Football Commentary System with Image Recognition and Cantonese Voice Output
- VisualRecipe: An online visual translation system for Chinese cookbooks.

Hang Seng University of Hong Kong

The School of Translation and Foreign Languages at Hang Seng University of Hong Kong (HSUHK) has identified translation technology as one of its strategic research areas.[14] There is the Deep Learning and Cognitive Computing Centre[15] in HSUHK to promote research in translation technology, such as MT, with the support of a cloud computing environment for deep learning. Relevant studies focus on the context of business and financial translation, with research outputs such as Luo *et al.* (2018) on the use of neural MT for translating financial documents and Siu (2015) on a hybrid approach to computerized translation of initial public offering prospectuses.

The related projects include:

- A Hybrid Approach to the Translation of Government Press Releases: Integration of Translation Memories and Neural Machine Translation
- HSUHK Business Translation Index.

Teaching

The teaching of translation technologies in Hong Kong is delivered within the disciplines of computer science and engineering, as well as arts and social sciences. The former focuses on algorithmic, programming, modelling and software engineering aspects and the latter more on translation practices utilizing MT/CAT systems and the general understanding of computational processing of languages.

Courses of translation technologies are usually elective ones, particularly in the curriculum at the undergraduate level. Surveying the translation technology courses offered at the higher institutions in Hong Kong, the teaching of this subject can be categorized into two modes – *specific* and *overview*. The specific mode takes translation technology as the core subject matter. It covers more in-depth issues concerning computer and translation and usually provides tutorials or workshops of translation tool applications. Hands-on experience of translation tools and a deeper academic exploration of the subject can be anticipated. The overview mode takes a general approach to introduce different advanced strategies in the use of computer technology to tackle linguistic issues, in which translation technology is one of the selected topics of the entire course. This type of general language technology courses usually introduces the basic concepts and background of translation technology, but actual practice of translation tools may not be included.

The following outlines the overall situation of translation programmes and translation technology courses in the universities and higher institutions in Hong Kong, which is also summarized in Table 19.1.

At present there are 22 degree-awarding universities and higher education institutions in Hong Kong.[16] Eight of them are government funded, with six universities – CityU, CUHK, HKBU, LU and PolyU – offering bachelor degree programmes which major in translation and four – CityU, CUHK, HKBU and PolyU – offering taught master degree programmes in translation. The other universities and institutions are either self financing or publicly funded. For translation major programmes, CIHE, HKMU and HSUHK offer a bachelor's degree, while HKMU and HSUHK also offer a taught master's degree. At HKUST, language or translation technology–related courses are offered from the computer science perspective by the Department of Computer Science and Engineering.

At undergraduate level, CIHE, CityU, CUHK, HSUHK and EduHK include translation technology in their translation, linguistics or language degree programmes. The BA (Hons) programme in translation technology at CIHE highly focuses on translation technology in both concepts and practices of MT and CAT applications. HKUST teaches the subject from the computer programming perspective for students majoring in computer science.

At postgraduate level, most taught master's degree translation programmes include computer technology related courses in their curriculum. CityU, CUHK, HSUHK and PolyU offer translation technology specific courses and HKBU has a technology related translation course.

Table 19.1 Translation technology–related courses at universities and higher institutions in Hong Kong.

	Translation technology–specific course		Language technology or translation technology overview course	
	Undergraduate	Postgraduate	Undergraduate	Postgraduate
CIHE ⋆	✓		✓	
CityU ⋆ ^	✓	✓	✓	✓
CUHK ⋆ ^	✓	✓	✓	✓
EdUHK				✓
HKBU ⋆ ^				✓
HKMU ⋆ ^				
HKU ⋆				
HKUST		✓	✓	
HSUHK ⋆	✓			
LU ⋆				
PolyU ⋆ ^		✓		
SYU				
UOWCHK #			✓	

Notes:
\# Offering associate degree programme in translation
⋆ Offering bachelor's degree programme in translation
^ Offering taught master's degree programme in translation

HKMU does not offer any course in this subject area at the undergraduate or postgraduate level. EduHK offers a language technology course which overviews translation technology in a taught master's degree programme. The postgraduate translation technology courses at HKUST are offered to research degree students at the Department of Computer Science and Engineering.

Besides the mentioned universities and institutions, the post-secondary institute UOW College Hong Kong (UOWCHK) offers a translation technology overview course in its associate degree programme in translation. Table 19.1 outlines the translation technology–related courses at different universities and institutions in Hong Kong.

There are currently two Master of Arts programmes majoring in translation technology. The Department of Linguistics and Translation at CityU offers a Master of Arts in Language Studies, which provides four optional specializations, including translation with language information technology. The School of Translation and Foreign Languages at HSUHK also offers the Master of Arts in Translation (Computer-Aided Translation). These programmes specialize in close attention to subject classification concerning different aspects of translation technologies, with the main focus of each individual course ranging from theoretical to practical issues. The Department of Translation at CUHK offered the Master of Arts in Computer-aided Translation from 2002 to 2016. It is the first master's degree programme of this scope in the world.

The following sections enumerate the courses in translation technologies at different universities and higher institutions in Hong Kong.

School of Humanities and Languages, Caritas Institute of Higher Education

The School of Humanities and Languages at Caritas Institute of Higher Education offers the first and only undergraduate programme in Hong Kong that specializes in translation technology. The programme features a wide coverage – translation of textual, audio, visual, graphic, verbal and photographic materials. Its courses related to translation technology provide academic and skills training in a broad range of areas, including artificial intelligence, computer-aided translation, computing skills, data and terminology, localization, machine translation, natural language processing and speech translation, resulting in many employment and education pathways for graduates of this programme.

Required Courses

Introduction to translation technology
Computing knowledge for translators
Computer-aided translation
Machine translation
Localization
Speech translation
Artificial intelligence and translation
Data and translation technology
Natural language processing
Speech processing

Elective Courses (Computer–Aided Translation)

Computer-aided translation systems
Translation project management
Terminology and translation memory management

Elective Courses (Machine Translation)

Machine translation systems
Editing in machine translation
Machine translation evaluation

Elective Courses (Localization)

Localization systems
Software and games localization
Audio-visual localization

Elective Courses (Speech Translation)

Speech translation systems
Speech dialogue technology
Speech recognition

Department of Translation, The Chinese University of Hong Kong

The Department of Translation (TRAN)[17] at the Chinese University of Hong Kong is the pioneer of translation technology. It offered the world's first MA programme in computer-aided translation (MACAT) from 2002 to 2016. Translation technology–related elective courses are offered in the MA and BA translation programmes.

At undergraduate level, the department offers two elective courses for BA students majoring or minoring in translation.

TRAN2610 Introduction to Computer-Aided Translation
TRAN3610 Machine Translation

At postgraduate level, there are three elective courses related to translation technology.

TRAN6601 Introduction to Computer-Aided Translation
TRAN6821 Computer Translation
TRAN6823 Terminology Management

Department of Linguistics and Translation, City University of Hong Kong

The Department of Linguistics and Translation (LT)[18] at City University of Hong Kong offers BA and MA programmes focused on language technology. The BALLA[19] programme – Bachelor of Arts in Linguistics and Language Applications, though not centrally focused on translation technology, aims to produce language professionals who are familiar with language-related application of computers. A number of language technology and computational linguistics courses are offered for students major or minor to this profession. Translation technology–related courses are also offered as elective courses in the Bachelor of Arts in Translation and Interpretation (BALT) programme. There are two core language technology–related courses in the curriculum.

Undergraduate language technology courses at the Department of LT, CityU:

Required Courses

LT2231 Introduction to Language Technology
LT3233 Computational Linguistics

The department offers a wide range of elective courses with orientations towards language technology, applied linguistics or language studies. Elective courses specialized to language technology and computational linguistics are listed in the following:

Elective Courses

LT3210 Electronic Publishing
LT3220 Corpus Linguistics
LT3224 Computational Lexicography
LT3554 Computer-Aided Translation
LT4218 Advanced Topics in Computational Linguistics
LT4225 Computer Assisted Language Learning

These courses involve the use of computer technology in different language issues. Courses such as Computational Linguistics, Corpus Linguistics and Computational Lexicography provide fundamental training and background concepts in translation technology. The translation technology–specialized course LT3224 Computer-Aided Translation is offered to both linguistics and translation students as an elective course.

At the postgraduate level, the Department of LT offers a Master of Arts in Language Studies (MALS)[20] programme, which provides four streams for the study and a number of translation technology–related courses.

Postgraduate translation technology courses at the Department of LT, CityU:

LT5411 Computational Linguistics
LT5421 Corpus Linguistics
LT5457 Computational Lexicography
LT5628 Human-Machine Interactive Translation

School of Translation and Foreign Languages, Hang Seng University of Hong Kong

The Bachelor of Translation with Business (BTB)[21] offered by the School of Translation and Foreign Languages at Hang Seng University of Hong Kong is another undergraduate programme in Hong Kong which provides the teaching and learning of computer-aided translation. The school offers three CAT courses. The courses TRA3105 Computer and Business Translation 1[22] and TRA4104 Computer and Business Translation 2[23] are designed as a series such that a deeper level of exploration and analysis is demanded in the second course. The course TRA3107 Mobile Application Design and Development for Translators[24] focuses on the knowledge and skills for the design and development of mobile applications to support translation.

TRA3105 Computer and Business Translation 1
TRA3107 Mobile Application Design and Development for Translators
TRA4104 Computer and Business Translation 2

At the postgraduate level, the school offers the Master of Arts in Translation (Computer-Aided Translation) programme. The courses relevant to CAT are categorized under the areas of professional language services (computer-aided) and translation technology, where students can choose to have more development either in translation practice supported by technology or translation technology itself.

Required Courses

TRA6001 Translation Technology: Knowledge and Skills
TRA6002 Professional Language Services: Skills and Strategies
TRA6004 Professional Workshop for Online Collaborative Translation

Elective Courses – Professional Language Services (Computer-Aided)

TRA6103 Electronic Tools for Translators of Philosophical, Historical and Literary Texts

Elective Courses – Translation Technology

TRA6201 Localisation and Bilingual Web Development
TRA6202 Technology for Bilingual Digital Marketing
TRA6203 Natural Language Processing for Translators
TRA6204 Technology for Translation Research
TRA6205 Advanced Topics in Translation Technology
TRA6206 Technology for Interpreting

Department of Chinese and Bilingual Studies, The Hong Kong Polytechnic University

The Department of Chinese and Bilingual Studies (CBS)[25] at The Hong Kong Polytechnic University offers a translation programme at both the undergraduate and postgraduate levels. Similar to CUHK, translation technology–related courses are offered as elective courses but at the undergraduate level only at PolyU.

Undergraduate Courses

CBS4844 Machine Aided Translation
CBS4962 Corpus and Language Technology for Language Studies

Department of Computer Science and Engineering, The Hong Kong University of Science and Technology

The teaching and learning of language technology at the Hong Kong University of Science and Technology is offered by the Department of Computer Science and Engineering (CSE)[26] The course Natural Language Processing is designed from the perspectives of programming and engineering. The teaching focus is hence very different from the previously mentioned cases at other universities, which are designed for students without a computer science background and emphasize the strategic utilization of translation systems in translation practices. There are one undergraduate course and one postgraduate courses in the scope of computational linguistics at the CSE department.

Undergraduate Course

COMP4221 Introduction to Natural Language Processing

Postgraduate Course

COMP5221 Natural Language Processing

Department of Translation, Interpreting and Intercultural Studies, Hong Kong Baptist University

The BA and MA translation programmes at the Department of Translation, Interpreting and Intercultural Studies of HKBU[27] offer a number of translation technology courses, especially at postgraduate level. According to the BA programme course description,

> Students can also take courses in Localization and Translation Technology (including computer-aided translation tools) – both important in the industry today. . . . The ITT Lab where interpreting and technology classes take place is regularly upgraded with the latest translation technology and interpreting software.[28]

The MA Translation programme has a Translation Technology stream which 'provide[s] a formal focus on new technology-based approaches to translation including translation memory, machine translation, localization and audiovisual translation and to make the programme available to applicants who have no knowledge of Chinese'.[29]

Undergraduate Courses

TRAN3035 Introduction to Translation Technology
TRAN3046 Introduction to Localization

Postgraduate Courses

TRA7140 Corpus-Based Approaches to Translation
TRA7520 Translation Technology I
TRA7550 Localization
TRA7570 Translation Technology II
TRA7580 Audiovisual Translation
TRA7600 Translation and the Web
TRA7610 Introduction to Natural Language Processing

The course TRA7600 Translation and the Web introduces a 'broad area of translation as it is implemented, enabled, supported, promoted, reflected, discussed and made available over the World-wide Web' and 'is believed to be one of the few on this topic to be offered at university level anywhere in the world'.[30]

Department of Linguistics and Modern Language Studies, The Education University of Hong Kong

The Education University of Hong Kong does not offer a translation programme, but the MA in educational linguistics and communication sciences[31] offers a course, LIN6008 Computer

Technology for Language Studies, which focuses on the use of computer in language processing. According to the course information,[32] it covers a number of language technology topics, including 'natural language processing applications such as machine translation . . . and evaluation of relevant software. [Students] will also learn how to cultivate language corpus for linguistic analysis'.

Department of English Language and Literature, Hong Kong Shue Yan University

The Hong Kong Shue Yan University (SYU) does not offer a translation degree programme, but the teaching and learning of translation are provided to BA students majoring in English. The curriculum of BA in English,[33] offered by the Department of English Language and Literature, includes a number of translation courses. The role of technology in the translation industry and its influence on the translation industry are included as selected topics in the course ENG440 Translation and Globalization.

Others

According to the information from the course lists and descriptions of the academic programmes, there is no translation technology course offered by the Translation Department of Lingnan University (LU) or the Translation Programme at the University of Hong Kong and the School of Arts and Social Sciences of Hong Kong Metropolitan University (HKMU).

In the scope of associate degree and higher diploma programmes offered by major institutions in Hong Kong, only one case of translation technology education is identified, the Associate of Arts Programme in Translation and Interpretation[34] offered by the Faculty of Arts and Humanities at UOW College Hong Kong. The curriculum includes a translation technology–specific course, LAC14406 Translation in the Digital Age, which covers an introduction to relevant translation tools.

Applications of Translation Technology

This section reviews the applications of translation technologies in Hong Kong in three areas: translation service providers, translation software companies and translation technology practices.

Translation Service Providers

It is very difficult to survey the use of translation tools within the translation industry in Hong Kong. Translation companies may not explicitly state their use of translation tools in the company description or on the official website. Some of them, however, provide services such as software and website localization or terminology extraction and standardization, implying that translation tools are utilized. Besides, as the option for a translation tool may be determined by translators, translation companies claiming the use of translation technology may not state explicitly which software is used. For international language service providers, it is also arguable whether they should be categorized as part of the Hong Kong translation industry even if Hong Kong is one of their serving markets. The following companies are a few, if not all, of the translation service providers which are identified with explicit statement of the use of translation tools at their official website and have a serving office or have registered in Hong Kong.

Chris Translation Service Company Limited[35] uses Trados as its CAT tool. According to the website, 'with 110 licenses for using Trados, a translation support tool, we respond adequately to translation and localization needs in the information and telecommunications technology industry that require translation memory control and a large volume of translation'. The company also uses Trados SDK to develop different tools 'to check translations for breaches of style rules and a tag search tool'.[36]

KERN Global Language Services[37] uses a number of translation software systems and software localization tools including Across, Trados, Transit, DejaVu, APIS-FMEA, Visual Localize, Passolo and Catalyst. Besides translation and localization, its language services also include terminology database service with software-supported terminology extraction.

INTLINGO Global Language Solutions[38] uses SDL Trados, Passolo and Wordfast. Besides multimedia production and desktop publishing, its services also include software and website localizations.

CTC Translation & Localization Solutions Limited[39] has an extensive list of software tools in terminology management, CAT, QA and localization on its technology webpages. The software tools include SDL Trados, SDL Multiterm, IBM Translation Manager, Termstar, Wordfast, Language Weaver PET, Microsoft Localization Studio, Passolo, SDLX, Lingobit Localizer and so on.

BEAUHORSE Professional Translation Ltd does not state explicitly which CAT tool is used. It is noted at its website[40] that '[their] translation system is refined and backed up by a strong database and Translation Memory System built up over years and computer-aided translation software to ensure quality and a prompt turnaround time'.

TranslateMedia offers the STREAM[41] service, which integrates translation memory and glossary management. The software tool used by the company is not made explicit.

Devon Financial Translation Services Limited[42] uses 'a combination of the latest translation technology, a unique project management system, and a multi-stage quality assurance scheme'. Its staff is trained in 'leveraging the latest in translation and localization technology'. The software tool used by the company is not made explicit.

Translation Software Companies

Two software developers in Hong Kong are identified for providing translation software.

KanHan Technologies Limited[43] 'is an information technology solution provider targeting Hong Kong and China market'. It has developed the HanWeb software for webpage translation between traditional and simplified Chinese.

Heartsome Technologies Ltd.[44] 'specialize[s] in language translation technologies'. It is a company registered in Hong Kong with branches in South Korea, Singapore and China. It is also the only CAT developer with its corporate headquarter situated in Hong Kong. Its CAT products include Heartsome Translation Studio, Heartsome TMX Editor and Heartsome Dictionary Editor.

Translation Technology Practices

There are not many salient examples of translation projects in Hong Kong emphasizing the use of translation tools. The utilization and acceptability of translation tools in large-scale translation projects seems yet to attain an acknowledgeable status. The following are two examples identified where translation software system was used significantly.

Traditional and Simplified Chinese Website Translation – HanWeb

With increasing collaboration between Hong Kong and the mainland China, there is a growing demand for websites from Hong Kong providing both Traditional and Simplified Chinese versions. The demand is especially significant in the official information dissemination by the government and other public sectors. The previously mentioned HanWeb Server[45] is a software application for webpage translation among Traditional Chinese, Simplified Chinese, Unicode and Cantonese Braille. HanWeb operates as a real-time translation server which performs machine translation as well as the generation of resulting webpages. This software system is used by the HKSAR government and many NGOs, public utilities, institutions and companies.

Chinese Bible Translation – The CSB Translation Project

The Chinese Standard Bible[46] (CSB) by the Asia Bible Society and Holman Bible Publisher is a recent translation project which highlights the application of computer technology in aiding the translation process. As stated on its website,

> a customized set of software tools was developed to create, revise and manage the translation at each stage. The revisions were aligned to the original language to facilitate cross-checking and consistency during the translation process – something never before done with a Bible translation.

Wu and Tan (2009) list a number of tree-based techniques supporting the CSB translation project:

- Tree alignment
- Tree-based translation memory
- Tree-based concordance
- Tree-based interlinear view
- Probabilistic Hebrew synonym finder
- Probabilistic similar verse finder.

Summary

Several decades have elapsed since the first MT system was invented in Hong Kong at the Chinese University of Hong Kong in 1969. What has been achieved so far in translation technology can be deemed substantial, at least in terms of research and teaching, notably starting from the late 1990s. A number of research centres were set up, a series of international conferences were hosted and plenty of research projects were funded and conducted. They have brought forth a wide variety of research outputs covering various aspects of translation technology, particularly in MT, including system development, approaches, evaluation and so on, and other specialized related areas such as CAT, terminology, lexicon and semantic networks, parallel text retrieval and alignment.

Education of translation technology is well developed in both postgraduate and undergraduate level. The launch of the world's first master's degree programme majoring in CAT in 2002 significantly highlights this increasing academic pursuit and the demand for knowledge and practical skills in this profession. Translation technology has now become a typical elective course in the curricula of translation programmes at different tertiary institutes. Different related courses on computational linguistics, language technology and computer sciences and engineering have also prepared graduates with various specializations to support the research and development and the use of translation technology.

Although the use of translation technology is not highly prevalent among translators according to available information, there are a number of translation companies employing MT and CAT in their production and several software developers producing CAT tools adopted by commercial and governmental sectors. As more and more institute graduates have received professional training in translation technology, it is to be expected that what they learnt will be somehow put into practice.

Translation technology is a multidisciplinary area involving translation, linguistics, computer science, information engineering and human technology. Both research and teaching in this subject area may be expensive in terms of computer resources and academic staff with multidisciplinary backgrounds. Interdisciplinary and intercollegiate collaborations should be encouraged, as we envisage, to foster knowledge exchange rather than isolated efforts, such that duplication of expenses can be avoided and resources can be spent on the more important and significant issues in the realm of translation technology.

Notes

1 According to the Hong Kong 2021 Population Census results (www.censtatd.gov.hk/en/EIndexby-Subject.html?pcode=B1120106&scode=600), the population in Hong Kong other than Chinese constitutes about 8% of the whole; within that, 2.7% are Filipino, 1.9% are Indonesian and 1.4% are South Asian (e.g. Indian, Nepalese and Pakistani).
2 www.legislation.gov.hk
3 For instance, other than traditional/simplified Chinese and English, the website of the Hong Kong Trade Development Council (www.hktdc.com) provides 11 language versions, German, Spanish, French, Italian, Portuguese, Russian, Czech, Polish, Arabic, Japanese and Korean, and the website of The Hong Kong Tourism Board (www.discoverhongkong.com) provides language versions of Dutch, French, German, Spanish, Russian, Arabic, Indonesian, Japanese, Korean, Thai and Vietnamese. They represent the origins of major trade partners and visitors of Hong Kong, respectively.
4 There are currently eleven universities in Hong Kong: in alphabetical order, City University of Hong Kong (CityU), Hang Seng University of Hong Kong (HSUHK), Hong Kong Baptist University (HKBU), Hong Kong Metropolitan University (HKMU), Hong Kong She Yan University (HKSYU), Lingnan University (LU), the Chinese University of Hong Kong (CUHK), the Education University of Hong Kong (EdUHK), the Hong Kong Polytechnic University (PolyU), the Hong Kong University of Science and Technology (HKUST), and the University of Hong Kong (HKU). All of these are government funded except HKMU, HKSYU and HSUHK, which are self financed. There are also a number of institutes and colleges involved in research and teaching of translation technology, including Caritas Institute of Higher Education (CIHE), the Chinese University of Hong Kong – Tung Wah Group of Hospitals Community College (CUTW) and UOW College Hong Kong (UOWCHK).
5 www.se.cuhk.edu.hk/facilities/lab_hcc.html
6 http://sepc57.se.cuhk.edu.hk
7 www.cs.ust.hk/~hltc/
8 http://interact.ira.uka.de
9 www.eu-bridge.eu
10 Aligned Chinese Knowledge Exchange Repository, at https://acker.chilin.hk/
11 www.cs.hku.hk/research/pr.jsp
12 www.cihe.edu.hk/en/schools-and-offices/schools-and-departments/school-of-humanities-and-languages/techno-humanities-research-centre/index.html
13 https://cis.cihe.edu.hk/AI.html
14 https://research.hsu.edu.hk/research-areas-and-centres/strategic-research-areas/
15 https://dlc.hsu.edu.hk/
16 www.edb.gov.hk/en/edu-system/postsecondary/local-higher-edu/institutions/index.html
17 http://traserver.tra.cuhk.edu.hk/
18 https://lt.cityu.edu.hk/
19 https://lt.cityu.edu.hk/Programmes/334/2021/balla/
20 https://lt.cityu.edu.hk/Programmes/mals/2022/
21 https://stfl.hsu.edu.hk/en/programmes-2/bachelor-of-translation-with-business-btb/
22 https://stfl.hsu.edu.hk/en/your-study-plan-2/examples-of-elective-modules/?shortname=TRA3105&cid=270

23 https://stfl.hsu.edu.hk/en/your-study-plan-2/examples-of-elective-modules/?shortname=TRA4104&cid=406
24 https://stfl.hsu.edu.hk/en/your-study-plan-2/examples-of-elective-modules/?shortname=TRA3107&cid=2398
25 www.polyu.edu.hk/cbs/
26 www.cse.ust.hk
27 https://tiis.hkbu.edu.hk/en/
28 https://tiis.hkbu.edu.hk/en/undergraduate/overview/
29 https://tiis.hkbu.edu.hk/en/taught_postgraduate/programme_structure/
30 https://tiis.hkbu.edu.hk/en/taught_postgraduate/courses/
31 www.ied.edu.hk/maelacs/
32 www.ied.edu.hk/maelacs/view.php?secid=3140
33 www.hksyu.edu/english/BA_in_English.html
34 www.uowchk.edu.hk/study-at-uowchk/find-programmes/programmes-by-study-area/languages-and-communication/associate-of-arts-in-translation-and-interpretation/
35 www.chris-translate.com/english/technology/
36 www.chris-translate.com/english/technology/support.html
37 www.e-kern.com/en/translations/software-formats.html
38 http://intlingo.com/technologies/
39 www.ctc-china.com/index.asp
40 www.beauhorse.com/en/strengths.html
41 www.translatemedia.com/stream-translation-workflow-technology.html
42 www.devonhk.com/en/index.php
43 www.kanhan.com/en/about-us.html
44 www.heartsome.net/EN/home.html
45 www.kanhan.com/en/products-services/hanweb-server.html
46 www.chinesestandardbible.com/translation.html

Bibliography

Au, Kim-lung Kenneth (2001) 'Translating for the Financial Market in Hong Kong', in Chan Sin-wai (ed.) *Translation in Hong Kong: Part, Present and Future*, Hong Kong: The Chinese University Press, 185–92.

Chan, Samuel and Benjamin Tsou (1999) 'Semantic Inference for Anaphora Resolution: Toward a Framework in Machine Translation', *Machine Translation* 14(3–4): 163–90.

Chan, Sin-wai (2001) 'Machine Translation in Hong Kong', in Chan Sin-wai (ed.) *Translation in Hong Kong: Past, Present and Future*, Hong Kong: The Chinese University Press, 205–18.

Chan, Sin-wai (2002a) 'The Making of TransRecipe: A Translational Approach to the Machine Translation of Chinese Cookbooks', in Chan Sin-wai (ed.) *Translation and Information Technology*, Hong Kong: The Chinese University Press, 3–22.

Chan, Sin-wai (ed.) (2002b) *Translation and Information Technology*, Hong Kong: The Chinese University Press.

Chan, Sin-wai (2004) *A Dictionary of Translation Technology*, Hong Kong: The Chinese University Press.

Chan, Sin-wai (2006) 'Centre for Translation Technology', *CAT Bulletin* 5: 12.

Chan, Sin-wai (2008a) *A Topical Bibliography of Computer(-aided) Translation*, Hong Kong: The Chinese University Press.

Chan, Sin-wai (2008b) 'CAT Teaching Resources at the Centre for Translation Technology', *CAT Bulletin* 9: 2.

Cheung, Percy and Pascale Fung (2005) 'Translation Disambiguation in Mixed Language Queries', *Machine Translation* 18(4): 251–73.

Chow, Ian Castor (2012) 'Technology Mashup for Translation – MT, CAT and Web 2.0: New Trends in Translation Tool and Website Localization', in *New Trends in Translation Technology: The 10th Anniversary Conference of the Master of Arts in Computer-aided Translation Programme*, Hong Kong: The Chinese University of Hong Kong.

Fung, Pascale (2010) 'Chinese Machine Translation', in Nitin Indurkhya and Fred J. Damerau (eds.) *The Handbook of Natural Language Processing*, 2nd edition, Boca Raton, FL: Chapman and Hall/CRC Press, 425–54.

Fung, Pascale, Yi Liu, Yongsheng Yang, Yihai Shen, and Dekai Wu (2004) 'A Grammar-based Chinese to English Speech Translation System for Portable Devices', in *Proceedings of the 8th International Conference on Spoken Language Processing*, Jeju Island, Korea.

Fung, Pascale and Kathleen McKeown (1996) 'A Technical Word and Term Translation Aid Using Noisy Parallel Corpora Across Language Groups', *Machine Translation, Special Issue on New Tools for Human Translators* 12(1–2): 53–87.

Fung, Pascale and Kathleen McKeown (1997) 'Finding Terminology Translations from Non-parallel Corpora', in *Proceedings of the 5th Annual Workshop on Very Large Corpora*, Hong Kong, 192–202.

Kit, Chunyu, Xiaoyue Liu, King Kui Sin, and Jonathan J. Webster (2005) 'Harvesting the Bitexts of the Laws of Hong Kong from the Web', in *Proceedings of the 5th Workshop on Asian Language Resources (ALR-05)*, Jeju Island, Korea, 71–78.

Kit, Chunyu, Haihua Pan, and Jonathan J. Webster (2002) 'Example-based Machine Translation: A New Paradigm', in Chan Sin-wai (ed.) *Translation and Information Technology*, Hong Kong: The Chinese University Press, 57–78.

Kit, Chunyu and Tak-Ming Wong (2008) 'Comparative Evaluation of Online Machine Translation Systems with Legal Texts', *Law Library Journal* 100(2): 299–321.

Lam, Wai, Shing-Kit Chan, and Ruizhang Huang (2007) 'Named Entity Translation Matching and Learning: With Application for Mining Unseen Translations', *ACM Transactions on Information Systems* 25(1): 2.

Lau, Chun-fat and Xiaoheng Zhang (1997) 'Grammatical Differences and Speech Machine Translation between Chinese Dialects', in *Proceedings of the 17th International Conference on Computer Processing of Oriental Languages (ICCPOL '97)*, Hong Kong, 379–82.

Liu, James N. K. and Lina Zhou (1998) 'A Hybrid Model for Chinese-English Machine Translation', in *Proceedings of IEEE International Conference on Systems, Man, and Cybernetics (SMC'98)*, San Diego, CA, 1201–06.

Lo, Chi-kiu, Anand Karthik Tumuluru, and Dekai Wu (2012) 'Fully Automatic Semantic MT Evaluation', in *Proceedings of the 7th Workshop on Statistical Machine Translation*, Montreal, Canada, 243–52.

Lo, Chi-kiu and Dekai Wu (2011) 'MEANT: An Inexpensive, High-accuracy, Semi-automatic Metric for Evaluating Translation Utility via Semantic Frames', in *Proceedings of the 49th Annual Meeting of the Association for Computational Linguistics: Human Language Technologies (ACL HLT 2011)*, Portland, OR, 220–29.

Lo, Wai-Kit, Patrick Schone, and Helen Meng (2001) 'Multi-Scale Retrieval in MEI: An English-Chinese Translingual Speech Retrieval System', in *Proceedings of the 7th European Conference on Speech Communication and Technology*, Aalborg, Denmark, 2: 1303–06.

Loh, Shiu-chang (1972) 'Machine Translation at the Chinese University of Hong Kong', in *Proceedings of the CETA Workshop on Chinese Language and Chinese Research Materials*, Washington, DC.

Lu, Bin, Ka Po Chow, and Benjamin K. Tsou (2011) 'The Cultivation of a Trilingual Chinese-English–Japanese Parallel Corpus from Comparable Patents', in *Proceedings of Machine Translation Summit XIII*, Xiamen, China, 472–79.

Luo, Linkai, Haiqin Yang, Sai Cheong Siu, and Francis Yuk Lun Chin (2018) 'Neural Machine Translation for Financial Listing Documents', in *Proceedings of International Conference on Neural Information Processing*, Springer, 232–43.

Meng, Helen, Berlin Chen, Sanjeev Khudanpur, Gina-Anne Levow, Wai-Kit Lo, Douglas Oard, Patrick Schone, Karen Tang, Hsin-Min Wang, and Jianqiang Wang (2004) 'Mandarin-English Information (MEI): Investigating Translingual Speech Retrieval', *Computer Speech and Language* 18(2): 163–79.

Seneff, Stephanie, Chao Wang, and John Lee (2006) 'Combining Linguistic and Statistical Methods for Bi-directional English-Chinese Translation in the Flight Domain', in *Proceedings of the 7th Conference of the Association for Machine Translation in the Americas (AMTA-06)*, Cambridge, MA, 213–22.

Siu, Kai-Chung and Helen Meng (2001) 'Semi-Automatic Grammar Induction for Bi-directional English-Chinese Machine Translation', in *Proceedings of the 7th European Conference on Speech Communication and Technology*, Aalborg, Denmark, 2749–52.

Siu, Kai-Chung, Helen Meng, and Chin-Chung Wong (2003) 'Example-based Bi-directional Chinese-English Machine Translation with Semi-automatically Induced Grammars', in *Proceedings of the 8th European Conference on Speech Communication and Technology*, Geneva, Switzerland, 2801–04.

Siu, Sai Cheong (2012) 'Automated Pre-editing and Post-editing: A Hybrid Approach to Computerized Translation of Initial Public Offering (IPO) Prospectuses', in *New Trends in Translation Technology: The 10th Anniversary Conference of the Master of Arts in Computer-aided Translation Programme*, Hong Kong: The Chinese University of Hong Kong.

Siu, Sai Cheong (2015) 'A Hybrid Approach to Computerized Translation of Initial Public Offering (IPO) Prospectuses', *Journal of Translation Technology* 1(1): 25–46.

Song, Yan, Kit Chunyu, and Xiao Chen (2009) 'Transliteration of Name Entity via Improved Statistical Translation on Character Sequences', in *Proceedings of the 2009 Named Entities Workshop: Shared Task on Transliteration (NEWS 2009)*, Suntec, Singapore, 57–60.

Song, Yan, Kit Chunyu, and Hai Zhao (2010) 'Reranking with Multiple Features for Better Transliteration', in *Proceedings of the 2010 Named Entities Workshop*, Uppsala, Sweden, 62–65.

Tsou, Benjamin K. (2007a) 'Salient Linguistic and Technical Gaps between Chinese and other Asian Languages Relevant to MT', in *Translation Automation User Society (TAUS) Exec Forum*, Beijing, China.

Tsou, Benjamin K. (2007b) 'Language Technology Infrastructure for MT', in *Translation Automation User Society (TAUS) Exec Forum*, Beijing, China.

Tsou, Benjamin K. and Bin Lu (2011) 'Machine Translation between Uncommon Language Pairs via a Third Common Language: The Case of Patents', in *Proceedings of Translating and the Computer Conference 2011 (ASLIB-2011)*, London.

Wang, Rongbo, Zheru Chi, and Changle Zhou (2004) 'An English-to-Chinese Machine Translation Method Based on Combining and Mapping Rules', in *Proceedings of Asian Symposium on Natural Language Processing to Overcome Language Barriers*, Sanya, China, 97–102.

Wong, Billy and Kit Chunyu (2008) 'Word Choice and Word Position for Automatic MT Evaluation', in *Proceedings of AMTA 2008 Workshop: MetricsMATR*, Waikiki, HI.

Wong, Billy and Kit Chunyu (2009a) 'Meta-Evaluation of Machine Translation on Legal Texts', in *Proceedings of the 22nd International Conference on the Computer Processing of Oriental Languages (ICCPOL-09)*, Hong Kong, China, 337–44.

Wong, Billy and Kit Chunyu (2009b) 'ATEC: Automatic Evaluation of Machine Translation via Word Choice and Word Order', *Machine Translation* 23(2): 141–55.

Wong, Billy and Kit Chunyu (2010) 'The Parameter-optimized ATEC Metric for MT Evaluation', in *Proceedings of the Joint Fifth Workshop on Statistical Machine Translation and MetricsMATR*, Uppsala, Sweden, 360–64.

Wong, Billy and Kit Chunyu (2011) 'Comparative Evaluation of Term Informativeness Measures for Machine Translation Evaluation Metrics', in *Proceedings of Machine Translation Summit XII*, Xiamen, China, 537–44.

Wong, Billy and Kit Chunyu (2012) 'Extending Machine Translation Evaluation Metrics with Lexical Cohesion to Document Level', in *Proceedings of the 2012 Joint Conference on Empirical Methods in Natural Language Processing and Computational Natural Language Learning (EMNLP-CoNLL 12)*, Jeju Island, Korea, 1060–68.

Wong, Billy, Cecilia F. K. Pun, Kit Chunyu, and Jonathan J. Webster (2011) 'Lexical Cohesion for Evaluation of Machine Translation at Document Level', in *Proceedings of the 7th International Conference on Natural Language Processing and Knowledge Engineering (NLP-KE 2011)*, Tokushima, Japan, 238–42.

Wu, Andy and Randall Tan (2009) 'Tree-Based Approaches to Biblical Text', in *BibleTech Conference*, Seattle, Washington.

Wu, Dekai (1995) 'Trainable Coarse Bilingual Grammars for Parallel Text Bracketing', in *Proceedings of the 3rd Annual Workshop on Very Large Corpora*, Cambridge, MA, 69–82.

Wu, Dekai (1996) 'A Polynomial-Time Algorithm for Statistical Machine Translation', in *Proceedings of the 34th Annual Meeting of the Association for Computational Linguistics (ACL 1996)*, Santa Cruz, CA, 152–58.

Wu, Dekai (1997) 'Stochastic Inversion Transduction Grammars and Bilingual Parsing of Parallel Corpora', *Computational Linguistics* 23(3): 377–404.

Wu, Dekai and Pascale Fung (2009) 'Semantic Roles for SMT: A Hybrid Two-Pass Model', in *Proceedings of Human Language Technologies: The 2009 Annual Conference of the North American Chapter of the Association for Computational Linguistics (NAACL HLT 2009)*, Boulder, CO, 13–16.

Wu, Dekai, Pascale Fung, Marine Carpuat, Chi-kiu Lo, Yongsheng Yang, and Zhaojun Wu (2010) 'Lexical Semantics for Statistical Machine Translation', in Joseph Olive, Caitlin Christianson, and John McCary (eds.) *Handbook of Natural Language Processing and Machine Translation: DARPA Global Autonomous Language Exploitation*, New York: Springer, 236–52.

Wu, Dekai and Hongsing Wong (1998) 'Machine Translation with a Stochastic Grammatical Channel', in *Proceedings of the 36th Annual Meeting of the Association of Computational Linguistics (ACL) and 17th International Conference on Computational Linguistics (ACL-COLING 1998)*, Montreal, Canada, 1408–14.

Wu, Yan and James Liu (1999) 'A Cantonese-English Machine Translation System PolyU-MT-99', in *Proceedings of Machine Translation Summit VII*, Singapore, 481–86.

Zhang, Xiaoheng (1998) 'Dialect Words Processing in Cantonese-Putonghua Text Machine Translation' (粵-普書面語機器翻譯中的方言詞處理), in *Proceedings of International Conference on Chinese Information Processing* (1998中文資訊處理國際會議論文集), Beijing: Tsinghua University Press, 499–506.

Zhang, Xiaoheng (1999) 'Words Processing in Cantonese-Putonghua Machine Translation' (粵-普機器翻譯中的詞處理), *Journal of Chinese Information Processing* (中文資訊學報) 13(3): 40–47.

Zhang, Xiaoheng (2005) '上下文索引程式ABCD及其在語言翻譯中的應用 (The ABCD Concordancer and Its Application to Language Translation)', in Li Yashu 李亞舒, Zhao Wenli 趙文利, and An Qin 晏勤 (eds.) *Informationization in Science and Technology Translation* (科技翻譯資訊化), Beijing: Science Press 科學出版社, 241–45.

Zhang, Xiaoheng and Chun-fat Lau (1996) 'Chinese Inter-Dialect Machine Translation on the Web', in *Proceedings of the Asia-Pacific World Wide Web Conference and the Second Hong Kong Web Symposium: Collaboration via The Virtual Orient Express*, Hong Kong, 419–29.

Zhang, Xiaoheng and Dingxu Shi (1997) 'Chinese Inter-Dialect Machine Translation', in Chen Liwei 陳力為 and Yuan Qi 袁琦 (eds.) *Language Engineering* (語言工程), Beijing: Tsinghua University Press, 225–31.

Zhou, Lina and James Liu (1997a) 'An Efficient Algorithm for Bilingual Word Translation Acquisition', in *Proceedings of the 2nd Workshop on Multilinguality in Software Industry: The AI Contribution (MULSAIC'97)*, Nagoya, Japan, 65–72.

Zhou, Lina and James Liu (1997b) 'Extracting More Word Translation Pairs from Small-sized Bilingual Parallel Corpus – Integrating Rule and Statistical-based Method', in *Proceedings of International Conference on Computer Processing of Oriental Languages (ICCPOL-97)*, Hong Kong, 520–25.

Zhu, Chunshen (2005) 'Machine-Aided Teaching of Translation: A demonstration', in *META 50: For a Proactive Translatology*, Montreal, Canada.

Zhu, Chunshen (2007a) 'ClinkNotes: A Corpus-based, Machine-aided Tool for Translation Teaching', in *International Symposium on Applied English Education: Trends, Issues and Interconnections*, Kaohsiung, Taiwan.

Zhu, Chunshen (2007b) 'ClinkNotes: Possibility and Feasibility of a Corpus-based, Machine-aided Mode of Translation Teaching', in *Conference and Workshop on Corpora and Translation Studies*, Shanghai, China.

20

TRANSLATION TECHNOLOGY IN JAPAN

Hitoshi Isahara

Introduction

Various services, such as information retrieval and information extraction, using natural language processing technologies trained by huge corpora have become available. In the field of machine translation (MT), corpus-based machine translations, such as statistical machine translation (SMT) (Brown *et al*. 1993: 263–311) and example-based machine translation (EBMT), are typical applications of using a large volume of data in real business situations. Thanks to the availability of megadata, current machine translation systems have the capacity to produce quality translations for some specific language pairs. Yet there are still people who doubt the usefulness of machine translation, especially when it applies to translation among different families of languages, such as Japanese and English. A study was conducted to examine the types of machine translation systems which are useful (Fuji *et al*. 2001) by simulating the retrieval and reading of web pages in a language different from one's mother tongue. Research on the technologies which make MT systems more useful in real-world situations, however, is scanty.

The problems facing developers of Japanese-to-English and English-to-Japanese machine translation systems are more serious than those encountered by developers for machine translation systems for, say, English-to-French translation. This is because Japanese is very different in syntax and semantics from English, so we often need some context to translate Japanese into English (and English into Japanese) accurately. English uses a subject-verb-object word order, while in Japanese, the verb comes at the end of the sentence, that is, a subject-object-verb order. This means that we have to provide more example sentence pairs of Japanese and English compared to translating most European languages into English, as they also use a subject-verb-object order. The computational power required for Japanese to come up with accurate matches is enormous, and accuracy is particularly necessary for businesses selling their products overseas, which is the reason it is necessary to help Japanese companies provide better-translated manuals for their products.

Faced with such obstacles, Japanese researchers conduct research on quality improvement of MT engines, which include a five-year national project on the development of a Japanese–Chinese machine translation system (Isahara *et al*. 2007). In parallel with this kind of MT research, we can take a three-step approach to improve MT quality in real-life environments: simplifying the Japanese source text (controlled language), enriching the lexicon, and enhancing the post-editing process (Figure 20.1).

DOI: 10.4324/9781003168348-22

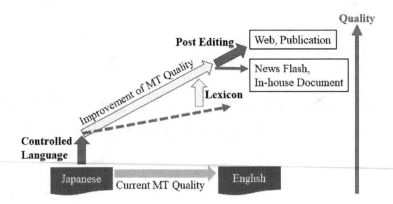

Figure 20.1 Quality improvement during translation procedure

In this chapter, a historical overview of research and development (R&D) of machine translation systems in Japan is given first. It goes on to discuss one of the latest government-funded MT projects, research activities related to pre- and post-editing, the development of linguistic resources utilized by MT systems, and research on the evaluation of MT systems.

History of MT R&D in Japan

The Dawn of the MT Age

Efforts to have a computer understand natural language began almost at the same time as computers were invented. In 1933, Petr Petrovich Smirnov-Troyanskii in Russia applied for a patent for a machine which selected and printed words during the process of translation. The first proposal of automatic translation using a computer was made by Warren Weaver in 1947 (1955).

Modern MT research began in the 1950s. As a result of the so-called Sputnik crisis in 1957, R&D of machine translation became popular, especially in the United States. In Japan, the Electrotechnical Laboratory developed the Yamato English–Japanese machine translation system, which was presented at the first International Conference on Information Processing held in Paris in June 1959. As there was no electronic computer with a large memory capacity at that time, a dedicated machine which had a large storage for a dictionary for translation was fabricated.

In the past, the implementation of machine translation adopted a range of approaches, including the transfer and interlingua methods. For the transfer method, the input text in the original language is first analysed, and then the sentence structure is mapped out in accordance with the grammar of the original language. This sentence structure is then converted into that of the target language using transfer rules to create a corresponding sentence. For the interlingua method (pivot method), the input sentence undergoes a deeper analysis and is converted into an expression described in an intermediate language that is independent of any specific language. The sentence in the target language is then created based on the structure of the intermediate expression. Since the interlingua method generates a translation from the identification of meaning, it allows for a more liberal translation and results in more natural phrasing. However, this demands that processing provide a deeper understanding of meaning while at the same time handling massive volumes of information. On the other hand, the transfer method requires the description of a great number of conversion rules, which results in a proportional increase in the number of required rules when multiple languages are involved. Both methods involve compilation from various sources (grammar rules, lexicons, thesaurus, etc.), which must be performed manually, and the establishment of a coherent approach to this task of compilation is extremely difficult. Recently, statistical machine translation (SMT) has been widely studied and shows promising features. However, its capability to handle pairs of languages with very different grammatical and/or lexical structures is still questionable.

In contrast, it is believed that when a human performs translation, he or she is not strictly applying such knowledge but is instead translating sentences through combinations of recollected phrases in the target language. Based on this hypothesis, Makoto Nagao of Kyoto University proposed an example-based machine translation in 1981 (Nagao 1984: 173–80). In an example-based machine translation system, translation is executed based on the similarity between the input sentence and an example contained in a huge parallel corpus. When EBMT was proposed, the capacity of computers was insufficient to produce a practical system with this approach. In recent years, with rapid improvements in computer performance and the development of a method for judging similarity between examples (through reference to a database of syntactically analysed sentences accumulated in the system), the foundation for the establishment of a practical example-based machine translation system has been laid.

The Golden Age of MT in Japan

In the 1980s, machine translation studies in Japan became popular, and Japan led the world in MT research. This had a lot to do with the Mu Project, which started in 1982 and ended in 1985. The Mu Project aimed to develop a Japanese–English and English–Japanese machine translation system for translating abstracts of scientific and technical papers. One of the factors that accounted for the creation of the Mu Project was the storage of scientific and technological information at the Japan Information Center of Science and Technology (JICST) in those days, and some of the items necessary for the development of a machine translation system, such as a documents database including the abstract, dictionaries, and thesaurus, were adequate. In addition, as Japanese technology was as good as that of Europe and the Americas, the United States and other countries started to criticize Japan, insisting that Japan utilized a large number of technologies from overseas. Another factor that facilitated the development of machine translation systems was the availability of computer systems, such as Japanese word processors, which could handle the Japanese language with Kanji characters. What is more important was the leadership of distinguished scholars, such as Professor Makoto Nagao of Kyoto University, who proposed, launched, and conducted national projects on natural language processing, especially machine translation.

Many Japanese companies participated in the Mu Project, and the knowledge gained from the project contributed to the study of machine translation in companies, creating the golden age of machine translation study in Japan. Following the release of ATLAS-I, which was the first commercial MT system on a mainframe computer in Japan by Fujitsu in 1984, MT vendor companies, such as Bravice International, NEC, Toshiba, Hitachi Ltd., Mitsubishi Electric, Sharp, and Oki Electric Industry, released their machine translation systems. Among them, Toshiba started to sell its MT system working on a 'mini-computer', and Bravice started to sell the system on a personal computer in 1985. In the same year, some of these systems were demonstrated at the International Exposition, Tsukuba, Japan, 1985 (Tsukuba Expo '85). At major international conferences, such as the International Conference on Computational Linguistics (COLING), a large number of research papers on machine translation were presented by researchers from Japanese companies and universities. The first Machine Translation Summit

(MT Summit), which is one of the major biannual conferences related to MT, was held in 1987 at Hakone, Japan. These conferences have since been held in Asia, Europe, and North America.

In 1986, the Advanced Telecommunications Research Institute (ATR) was established and started research on speech translation. In 1987, the Japanese Ministry of International Trade and Industry (MITI) launched its multilingual machine translation project (MMT project), which aimed to develop machine translation systems for translation among Japanese, Chinese, Thai, Malay, and Indonesian, and Japanese MT companies, such as NEC and Fujitsu, joined this project. The MMT project ended in 1996.

The 90s and Beyond

In the 1990s, there was considerable improvement in the performance of machine translation systems, with their output quality reaching the practical use level if the domain of input text was properly restricted.

The Asia-Pacific Association for Machine Translation was established in 1991, initially with the name of the Japan Association for Machine Translation. To expand its operations, the name was subsequently changed to the Asia-Pacific Association for Machine Translation (AAMT). AAMT is one of three regional associations, with the European Association of Machine Translation (EAMT) and the Association of Machine Translation in the Americas (AMTA), both of the International Association of Machine Translation (IAMT), which organize MT Summits.

For translation services, browsers interlocked with machine translation systems, such as PENSEE for Internet by Oki Electric, became commercially available in 1995. This shows that the development of MT systems was on the same pace with the expansion of the internet and world wide web, which boosted the MT industries. The Japan Patent Office (JPO) opened the Industrial Property Digital Library (IPDL) in 1999. At the beginning, abstracts of patents were translated manually. In 2000, IPDL started to use MT systems to translate Japanese patents into English in full. As the first free translation site on the internet (Excite) was launched in 2000, information acquisition via network and utilization of MT became popular.

As regards the prices of software, MT software priced at less than 10,000 JPY was released in 1994. The software market then became very competitive. In 1996, personal computers with bundled MT software merged, and software practically became cost free for customers. MT software for less than 5,000 JPY appeared in 2002, and less than 2,000 JPY in 2003. As free online translation services became popular, the survival of companies selling packaged MT software became critical.

During this period, people began to have a better understanding of machine translation, and a number of MT systems received awards from various organizations, such as the Good Design Award in 2001.

As for research projects, there have been a few large-scale projects on text translation since the Mu Project and the MMT project. In 2006, a five-year project on Japanese–Chinese machine translation using the example-based approach received funding from the Japan Science and Technology Agency.

Government-Funded Projects for Developing a Chinese–Japanese and Japanese–Chinese Machine Translation System

In 2006, the National Institute of Information and Communications Technology (NICT) of Japan, the Japan Science and Technology Agency (JST), the University of Tokyo, Shizuoka

University, and Kyoto University launched a five-year government-funded project on the development of a Chinese–Japanese machine translation system for scientific documents.

This project conducted research on augmented example-based machine translation as a verification of high-performance resource-based NLP, which was based on cutting-edge research on computational linguistics and natural language processing. It was found that, unlike what is happening in the West, the distribution of information in English in Asia is difficult. It is necessary for Asian countries to develop machine translation systems for Asian languages. As the first step in this endeavour, Japan started to develop a machine translation system for scientific and technological materials in Chinese and Japanese so as to keep pace with the significant progress that has been made in various fields.

As mentioned, the construction of such a system serves as the first step in building systems which cover a wide variety of Asian languages. As China has made remarkable progress in science and technology, this Japanese–Chinese translation system had several objectives:

- to make scientific and technological information in China and other Asian countries easily usable in Japan;
- to promote the distribution of documents to China and other countries Japan's cutting-edge science and technology; and
- to contribute to the development of science and technology in Asian countries with the help of the information available through machine translation.

The goal of this project was to develop, within a period of five years, a practical machine translation system for translation between the Japanese and Chinese languages, focusing on scientific and technological materials. In this endeavour, researchers adopted the example-based approach, which provided a better reflection of the linguistic structures and syntactic information used in a number of parts in the translation engines.

Figure 20.2 presents an outline of the system under development. Their target domains were information science, biological science, and environmental science.

EBMT requires the accumulation of a large number of examples; accordingly, researchers planned to develop a parallel corpus of around 10 million sentences. They extracted parallel

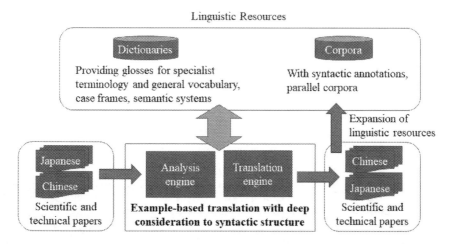

Figure 20.2 System overview

sentences from existing comparable texts and aligned words and phrases semi-automatically. They also planned to make the best use of existing linguistic resources and language processing technology owned by them.

In this five-year project, there were goals for the third year and the fifth year.

- Goal for the third year: Evaluate the Japanese–Chinese machine translation prototype system for specific target domains.
- Goal for the fifth year: Improve the Chinese analysis performance and complete demonstration experiments on the Japanese–Chinese and Chinese–Japanese machine translation prototype system

Even during the course of the project, researchers publicized the language resources (such as the corpus) to the fullest extent for research purposes. They also publicized the contents and results of their research widely as part of their outreach activities.

EBMT systems basically generate sentences in the target language by extracting and combining examples in parallel text databases whose source language sentences are similar to the input sentence. A specific feature of the previous system was the utilization of the deep syntactic analysis. Parallel texts in the example database were analysed syntactically and aligned with words using syntactic information. In the translation phase, the system analysed the input sentence syntactically, extracted parts of sentences from the example database, and combined them to generate sentences in the target language by considering their syntactic structures. At the last stage, the ordering of words in a sentence was made by using the information extracted from the monolingual corpora.

Practical Use of Machine Translation – Pre- and Post-Editing for Multilingual Information Outbound

Some major international companies use machine translation to meet their daily practical needs. These companies started to use English–Japanese MT at their branches in Japan to translate documents originally written in English into Japanese. To achieve their purposes, the performance of the MT engine and the support of the translation process are crucial. As the documents are frequently revised and reused, it is important to develop a translation environment for text input, the retrieval and display of parallel text (translation memory), dictionary lookup, MT, and formatting documents.

Japanese–English translation in Japan is mainly used for information dispatch, and high-quality translation is needed for such information dispatch from industries. Due to the linguistic features of Japanese, such as the omission of the subject, computational treatment of Japanese text is more difficult than that of other languages, such as English. The performance of Japanese–English MT is therefore not as good as that of English–Japanese MT. The editing of the output from a MT system is difficult task for a non-native speaker of English.

To overcome this difficulty, control language and crowdsourcing post-editing have been proposed.

Control Language

The output quality of MT depends heavily on the quality of the analysis of input sentences. It is mostly very difficult for automatic analysers to output proper structures for long and complex sentences in syntax and semantics. Restricting the structure of the input text is therefore beneficial to MT systems to achieve high-quality translation. Research has been carried out to address this issue by investigating the feasibility of developing a 'controlled Japanese' with explicit restrictions on vocabulary, syntax, and style when authoring technical documentation. An example was the research project which was being conducted in collaboration with an automobile-related company, an MT vendor, and a university in Japan.

This project aimed to raise translation awareness within a global Japanese company where non-professional authors are called upon to write 'global job manuals' for internal dissemination. Following an analysis of the current practice, researchers devised a document template and simple writing rules, which were tested experimentally with MT systems. Sentences violating the rules were extracted from the original data and rewritten in accordance with respective rules. The original and rewritten sentences were then translated by MT systems, and the input and output were submitted to human evaluation. Overall, native-speaker judges found that the quality of the Japanese was maintained or improved, while the impact on the raw English translations varied according to MT systems. Researchers explained their template and rules to employees of the company and asked them to write their manuals using the know-how in the template and rules. They investigated their documents to identify the most promising avenues for further development (Tatsumi *et al.* 2012: 53–56; Hartley *et al.* 2012: 237–44). Table 20.1 lists the 20 problem features from the corpus they experimented with. These gave rise to 28 pre-editing rules formulated as 'Omit . . .', 'Replace with . . .' or 'Add . . .'.

An alternative to controlled (or simplified) language is the translation between two languages, both of which are properly controlled. If we train SMT with a parallel controlled language corpus, it can translate controlled input into controlled output with high quality. Some multilingual MT systems are combinations of MT engines for two languages and translations between non-English languages are performed via English. Such cascade translation usually amplifies errors during translation. Using controlled English as a pivot would be a promising solution to this problem.

There are several activities relating to controlled languages in Japan. The Technical Japanese Project, which was funded by the Japan Patent Information Organization (JAPIO), has conducted several activities on technical Japanese, a restricted language for business purposes.

Table 20.1 'Avoid' features of manual writing guidelines

F1	Long sentences (> 50 characters)
F2	Sentences of 3 or more clauses
F3	Negative expressions
F4	Verb + nominaliser こと
F5	Nominaliser もの
F6	Verb + ように ('it is suggested that')
F7	Topicalizing particle は
F8	Coordinating conjunction または ('or')
F9	Modal れる・られる ('can')
F10	Verb 見える ('can be seen')
F11	Compound noun strings
F12	Particle など ('and so on')
F13	Single use of conjunction たり ('either')
F14	Katakana verbs
F15	Suffix 感 ('sense of')
F16	Verb かかる ('start')
F17	Verb 成る ('become')
F18	Verb 行う ('perform')
F19	Case-marking particle で ('with', 'by')
F20	Verb ある・あります ('exist')

Its activities are divided into two parts: technical Japanese for general purposes and technical Japanese for patent documents. As for technical Japanese for patent documents, its committee comprises specialists on intellectual property, patent, natural language processing, machine translation, and patent translation. Their output includes a patent writing manual, guideline for human writers, format for patent ontology, and a patent writing support system. The Japan Technical Communicators Association (JCTA) published a book on writing guidelines for technical communicators who are mainly writing business documents. The Association of System Documentation Quality (ASDoQ) has created a list of terms and technologies related to system documentation and has collected example sentences, both good and bad.

Crowdsourcing Post-Editing

With the use of properly controlled input sentences and substantial dictionaries, the current MT systems are useful, for example, for quick translations, such as news flashes and in-house translations (Figure 20.1).

For documents which need higher quality, post-editing is required. Post-editing, however, can be costly and time consuming and is not affordable to everybody. There is a preliminary investigation by Toyohashi University of Technology (TUT) in Japan on the impact of crowdsourcing post-editing through the so-called Collaborative Translation Framework (CTF) developed by the Machine Translation team at Microsoft Research (Aikawa *et al.* 2012: 1–10). Crowdsourcing translation has become increasingly popular in the MT community, and it is hoped that this approach can shed new light on the research direction of translation.

To study this issue, researchers used foreign students at TUT and asked them to post-edit the MT output of TUT's websites (www.tut.ac.jp/english/introduction) via Microsoft Translator into their own languages using the CTF functionalities. Though they did not expect the students to have the same degree of accuracy from the professionals, they did note that students had a better understanding of the context, and this kind of collaboration could improve and reduce the cost of the post-editing process.

TUT completed the first experiment with its foreign students attending our university to post-edit the MT output of the English version of the university's web site into their own languages. TUT also conducted an experiment with Japanese students with more precise settings, such as the ordering of post-editing. The experimental results show that it was possible to reduce the cost of post-editing drastically.

Development of Linguistic Resources

As the current mainstream of MT research is the resource-based MT system, the development of linguistic resources is obviously one of the main considerations in MT technology.

Parallel or Multilingual Corpora

A parallel corpus is a collection of articles, paragraphs, or sentences in two different languages. Since a parallel corpus contains translation correspondences between the source text and its translations at a different level of constituents, it is a critical resource for extracting translation knowledge in machine translation. In the development of MT systems, the example-based and statistics-based approaches have been widely researched and applied. Parallel corpora are essential for the growth of translation studies and development of practical systems. The raw text of a parallel corpus contains implicit knowledge. If we annotate its information, we can get explicit

Table 20.2 Details of the current version of NICT Multilingual Corpora

Corpora	Total	Original	Translation
Japanese–English Parallel Corpus	38,383 sentence pairs; (English 900,000 words)	Japanese (38,383 sentences, *Mainichi* newspaper)	English Translation
		English (18,318 sentences, *Wall Street Journal*)	Japanese Translation
Japanese–Chinese Parallel Corpus	38,383 sentence pairs; (Chinese 1,410,892 characters, 926,838 words)	Japanese (38,383 sentences, *Mainichi* newspaper)	Chinese Translation

knowledge from the corpus. The more information that is annotated on a parallel corpus, the more knowledge we can get from the corpus.

NICT started a project to build multilingual parallel corpora in 2002. This project focuses on Asian language pairs and the annotation of detailed information, including syntactic structures and alignment at the word and phrase levels. The corpus is known as the NICT Multilingual Corpora. A Japanese–English parallel corpus and a Japanese–Chinese parallel corpus were completed following systematic specifications. Details of the current version of the NICT Multilingual Corpora are listed in Table 20.2.

EDR Lexicon

Though current research on NLP and MT utilizes the machine-learning mechanism based on a huge amount of linguistic data, human coded lexical resources are still very important.

The EDR Electronic Dictionary was developed for advanced processing of natural language by computers and has eleven sub-dictionaries, which include, among others, a concept dictionary, word dictionaries, and bilingual dictionaries. The EDR Electronic Dictionary is the result of a nine-year project (from 1986 to 1994) aiming at establishing an infrastructure for knowledge information processing. The project was funded by the Japan Key Technology Center and eight computer manufacturers.

The EDR Electronic Dictionary is a machine-tractable dictionary that catalogues the lexical knowledge of English and Chinese (the Word Dictionary, the Bilingual Dictionary, and the Co-occurrence Dictionary) and has unified thesaurus-like concept classifications (the Concept Dictionary) with corpus databases (the EDR Corpus). The Concept Classification Dictionary, a sub-dictionary of the Concept Dictionary, describes the similarity relation among concepts listed in the Word Dictionary. The EDR Corpus is the source for the information described in each of the sub-dictionaries. The basic approach taken during the development of the dictionary was to avoid a particular linguistic theory and to allow for adoptability to various applications.

The EDR Electronic Dictionary, thus developed, is believed to be useful in the R&D of natural language processing and the next generation of knowledge processing systems. In addition, it will become part of an infrastructure that provides new types of activities in information services.

A Universal Format for the User Dictionary

The development of a lexicon is normally very costly. Sharing lexicons among groups and/or reusing lexicons between the previous system and the current system are key technologies for the development of efficient MT systems and translation procedures.

As there was no widely used standard for user dictionaries in the Japanese/English MT market, AAMT developed a common format for lexicons for machine translation and opened it as UPF (Universal PlatForm) in 1997. Currently its new format is available as Universal Terminology Exchange (UTX) (http://aamt.info/english/utx/index.htm).

UTX is a common format for the user dictionary. In 2009, AAMT established the UTX-Simple (later renamed UTX), which was an open format in a tab-delimited text. UTX greatly improves the accuracy of translation software by sharing the knowledge of terminology through dictionaries in a bilingual format. The goal of UTX is to create a simple, easy-to-make, easy-to-use dictionary from a user's perspective, not from that of a developer. A user can easily convert a UTX dictionary into various formats. With or without such conversion, the content of the same UTX dictionary can be used with various translation software or computer-aided translation tools. In addition, a UTX dictionary can also be used as a glossary without involving translation software.

An example of UTX is shown in Table 20.3.

#UTX-S 1.00; en-US/ja-JP; 2008-03-15T10:00:00Z+09:00; copyright: AAMT, license: CC-by 3.0

#src	tgt	src:pos	src:plural	src:3sp	src:past	src:pastp	src: presp	src:comp	src:super
new	新規の	adjective						newer	newest
fast	高速な	adjective						faster	fastest
# prosody should be uncountable									
prosody	韻律	noun	prosodies						
save	保存する	verb		saves	saved	saved	saving		
good evening	今晩は	sentence							

Table 20.3 Example of English-to-Japanese Dictionary in UTX

Evaluation

The Japan Electronic Industry Development Association (JEIDA) formulated three criteria for evaluating MT systems: (1) technical evaluations by users; (2) financial evaluations by users, and (3) technical evaluation by developers. JEIDA has since 1992 developed a method to evaluate quality for the developers of machine translation systems so that they can easily check the imperfections in their systems. In 1995, JEIDA's two test-sets (English-to-Japanese and Japanese-to-English) were completed and made publicly available. During the development of these test-sets, JEIDA laid down the following two types of objectivity:

(1) Objectivity in the evaluation process; and
(2) objectivity in the judgment of the evaluation results.

In an evaluation method such as the one proposed in the ALPAC report, 'fidelity' and 'intelligibility' are employed as evaluation measures, though they are dependent on subjective human judgment. Consequently, the results may differ according to who makes the evaluations, which means they do not satisfy the objectivity criterion (1). Theoretically, the evaluation method in the ALPAC report satisfies criterion (2) since the evaluation results are given as numbers. The system developers, however, fail to recognize which items cannot be handled in their own system. This is because the test example in question covers various kinds of grammatical items. Their interpretation of the evaluation result for further improvement of their system is therefore still subjective, which, for practical purposes, does not satisfy criterion (2).

On the other hand, JEIDA created test-sets that can satisfy both criteria. JEIDA explains how to evaluate individual examples by posing yes/no questions which enable system developers to make an evaluation just by answering them. With this method, everyone can evaluate MT systems equally, as his/her answers require only a simple yes or no. Even for imperfect translation results, judgment will not vary widely among evaluators. In addition, JEIDA assigned to each example an explanation which gives the relationship of the translation mechanism to the linguistic phenomenon, thus enabling the system developer to know why the linguistic phenomenon in question was not analysed correctly. Consequently, with JEIDA's test-set method, the evaluation results can be utilized for improving MT systems.

In JEIDA's test-sets, we have systematically sampled the grammatical items that ought to be taken up, and listed some examples for each item. The test-sets clearly describe what linguistic phenomenon should be evaluated in each example so that the developers can easily understand the problems they need to solve in their systems. The system developer can then identify causes of translation failures.

Following JEIDA's test-set for MT evaluation, AAMT has continued its development of an MT evaluation method. Its aim is to establish a satisfactory evaluation method to provide an objective criterion, reduce person-hour costs, and identify weaknesses of MT systems. It followed the previous approach by JEIDA, which was a binary classification evaluation in which judgment was conducted via yes/no answers for grammatical questions. So far, AAMT has developed approximately 400 test sentences (46 grammatical items) for Japanese–English/Chinese MT. (Figure 20.3)

After some experiments using these test-sets, AAMT found that test-set–based evaluation needed less than half the time than the conventional method and its test-set–based evaluation gave a higher score to Japanese–English MT than Japanese–Chinese MT, which reflects the true state of MT technology.

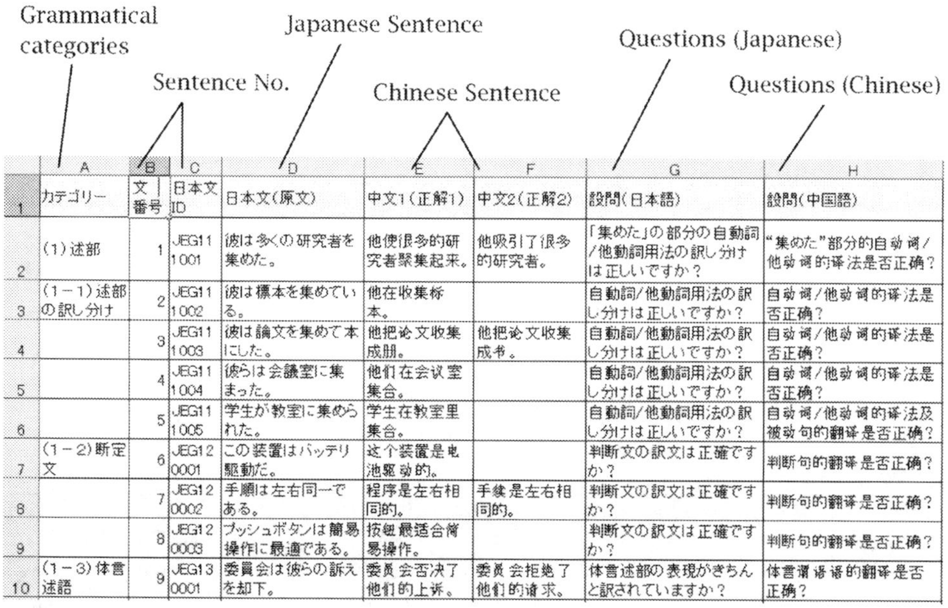

	A	B	C	D	E	F	G	H
1	カテゴリー	文番号	日本文ID	日本文(原文)	中文1(正解1)	中文2(正解2)	設問(日本語)	設問(中国語)
2	(1)述部	1	JEG11 1001	彼は多くの研究者を集めた。	他使很多的研究者聚集起来。	他吸引了很多的研究者。	「集めた」の部分の自動詞/他動詞用法の訳し分けは正しいですか?	"集めた"部分的自动词/他动词的译法是否正确?
3	(1-1)述部の訳し分け	2	JEG11 1002	彼は標本を集めている。	他在收集标本。		自動詞/他動詞用法の訳し分けは正しいですか?	自动词/他动词的译法是否正确?
4		3	JEG11 1003	彼は論文を集めて本にした。	他把论文收集成册。	他把论文收集成书。	自動詞/他動詞用法の訳し分けは正しいですか?	自动词/他动词的译法是否正确?
5		4	JEG11 1004	彼らは会議室に集まった。	他们在会议室集合。		自動詞/他動詞用法の訳し分けは正しいですか?	自动词/他动词的译法是否正确?
6		5	JEG11 1005	学生が教室に集められた。	学生在教室里集合。		自動詞/他動詞用法の訳し分けは正しいですか?	自动词/他动词的译法及被动句的翻译是否正确?
7	(1-2)断定文	6	JEG12 0001	この装置はバッテリ駆動だ。	这个装置是电池驱动的。		判断文の訳文は正確ですか?	判断句的翻译是否正确?
8		7	JEG12 0002	手順は左右同一である。	程序是左右相同的。	手续是左右相同的。	判断文の訳文は正確ですか?	判断句的翻译是否正确?
9		8	JEG12 0003	プッシュボタンは簡易操作に最適である。	按钮最适合简易操作。		判断文の訳文は正確ですか?	判断句的翻译是否正确?
10	(1-3)体言述語	9	JEG13 0001	委員会は彼らの訴えを却下。	委员会否决了他们的上诉。	委员会拒绝了他们的请求。	体言述部の表現がきちんと訳されていますか?	体言谓语语的翻译是否正确?

Figure 20.3 Example of Japanese–Chinese test set by AAMT

Bibliography

Aikawa, Takako, Kentaro Yamamoto, and Hitoshi Isahara (2012) 'The Impact of Crowdsourcing Post-editing with the Collaborative Translation Framework', in *Proceedings of the 8th International Conference on Natural Language Process (JapTAL2012)*, 22–24 October 2012, Kanazawa, Japan, 1–10.

Brown, Peter F., Stephen A. Della Pietra, Vincent J. Della Pietra, and Robert L. Mercer (1993) 'The Mathematics of Statistical Machine Translation: Parameter Estimation', *Computational Linguistics* 19(2): 263–311.

Fuji, Masaru, N. Hatanaka, E. Ito, S. Kamei, H. Kumai, T. Sukehiro, T. Yoshimi, and Hitoshi Isahara (2001) 'Evaluation Method for Determining Groups of Users Who Find MT Useful', in *Proceedings of the Machine Translation Summit VIII: Machine Translation in the Information Age*, 18–22 September 2001, Santiago de Compostela, Spain.

Hartley, Anthony, Midori Tatsumi, Hitoshi Isahara, Kyo Kageura, and Rei Miyata (2012) 'Readability and Translatability Judgments for "Controlled Japanese"', in *Proceedings of the 16th Annual Conference of the European Association for Machine Translation (EAMT-2012)*, 28–30 May 2012, Trento, Italy, 237–44.

http://aamt.info/english/utx/index.htm.

Isahara, Hitoshi, Sadao Kurohashi, Jun'ichi Tsujii, Kiyotaka Uchimoto, Hiroshi Nakagawa, Hiroyuki Kaji, and Shun'ichi Kikuchi (2007) 'Development of a Japanese–Chinese Machine Translation System', in *Proceedings of MT Summit XI*, 10–14 September 2007, Copenhagen, Denmark.

Nagao, Makoto (1984) 'A Framework of a Mechanical Translation between Japanese and English by Analogy Principle', in Alick Elithorn and Ranan Banerji (eds.) *Artificial and Human Intelligence*, New York: Elsevier North-Holland Inc., 173–80.

Tatsumi, Matsumi, Anthony Hartley, Hitoshi Isahara, Kyo Kageura, Toshio Okamoto, and Katsumasa Shimizi (2012) 'Building Translation Awareness in Occasional Authors: A User Case from Japan', in *Proceedings of the 16th Annual Conference of the European Association for Machine Translation (EAMT-2012)*, 28–30 May 2012, Trento, Italy, 53–56.

Weaver, Warren (1955) *'Translation (1949)': Machine Translation of Languages*, Cambridge, MA: MIT Press.

www.tut.ac.jp/english/introduction.

21

TRANSLATION TECHNOLOGY IN SOUTH AFRICA

Gerhard B. van Huyssteen, Martin Puttkammer, Cindy McKellar
and Marissa Griesel

Introduction

South Africa has a rich and diverse multilingual culture with eleven official languages, two Germanic languages (English and Afrikaans), four Nguni languages (isiNdebele [Ndebele], Siswati [Swati], isiXhosa [Xhosa] and isiZulu [Zulu]), three Sotho languages (Sepedi [Northern Sotho or Sesotho sa Lebo], Sesotho [Southern Sotho] and Setswana [Tswana]) and two other Bantu languages (Xitsonga [Tsonga] and Tshivenḓa [Venda]). These languages are granted official status in chapter one of the Constitution of the Republic of South Africa (6 of 1996), stating that 'the state must take practical and positive measures to elevate the status and advance the use of these languages'. To this effect, the Pan South African Language Board (PanSALB) was established in terms of the Pan South African Language Board Act (59 of 1995), with the goal to promote multilingualism in South Africa. Recently, the Use of Official Languages Act (12 of 2012) was promulgated, in which various conditions for the use of the official languages by government and other institutions are set in order to further a truly multilingual society. In addition to these acts, various other acts and industry regulations also contribute to create a progressive regulatory environment prescribing the use of multiple official languages. These include, inter alia, the Code of Banking Practice (2004) and the National Consumer Protection Act (68 of 2008).

Despite the fact that English is only the sixth most-used language in South Africa (with 9.6% of speakers indicating English as their home language in the 2011 South African National Census[1] and 8.3% in the 2016 Community Survey;[2] see Table 21.1), information in the business, health and government sectors is generally available only in English. Coupled with the fact that only a small portion of official South African government websites are available in all the South African languages (De Schryver and Prinsloo 2000: 89–106), it becomes clear that language practitioners and translators working with South African languages need all the help they can get to create texts in the South African languages as efficiently as possible.

Machine translation (MT) offers an attractive and viable option that is being explored on a wider level in South Africa. However, as is well known, the quality of automated translation is not yet at a level, even internationally, to replace human translators for the translation of documents; human involvement in post-process editing of generated translations is still of the utmost importance. This is even more true in the South African context where MT quality still reflects the early days of such MT systems. However, machine-aided human translation (where a human

DOI: 10.4324/9781003168348-23

Table 21.1 South African languages[3]

South African languages			
2011 Census			*2016 Community Survey*
Language	*Number of speakers*	*% of total*	*% of total*
Afrikaans	6,855,082	13.5%	12.1%
English	4,892,623	9.6%	8.3%
isiNdebele	1,090,223	2.1%	1.6%
isiXhosa	8,154,258	16%	17%
isiZulu	11,587,374	22.7%	24.6%
Sepedi	4,618,576	9.1%	9.5%
Sesotho	3,849,563	7.6%	8%
Setswana	4,067,248	8%	8.8%
Sign language	234,655	0.5%	0.0%
Siswati	1,297,046	2.5%	2.6%
Tshivenḓa	1,209,388	2.4%	2.4%
Xitsonga	2,277,148	4.5%	4.2%
Other	828,258	1.6%	0.9%
TOTAL	50,961,443	100%	100%

is responsible for the translation but uses different technologies to ease and assist with the process) is already very useful and attainable in the South African context.

This chapter focuses on the history and state of the art of MT research and development in South Africa for South African languages.[4] We will first provide an overview of the lead-up to MT development in South Africa, highlighting some related research, as well as the development of tools and data that could support MT in South Africa indirectly. Thereafter we give an overview of the first initiatives by the South African government to support the development of MT for South African languages. We then discuss individual research and development projects on MT for South African languages before describing in more detail the Autshumato project, South Africa's first consolidated national MT project for South African languages. We conclude with a look-ahead to post-Autshumato initiatives and possibilities for MT in South Africa.

Background: Linguistics and Language Technology in South Africa

Linguistic research in all eleven South African languages has always been a rich field of study. Different aspects of the grammars of most of the languages have long since been described in various scholarly publications; for instance, as early as 1862, Bleek compared aspects of the different Bantu languages. However, various political, socio-economic and socio-linguistic factors have slowed down processes of grammatical and lexical standardisation, as well as the development of terminology in domains where higher functions are being required (e.g. business, the judiciary, science and technology, mainstream media, etc.). Nonetheless, over the past twenty years, more and more specialised dictionaries and terminology lists have been developed through the establishment of government-supported national terminology units (not-for-profit companies) for each language. In addition, the national language bodies of PanSALB are responsible for language standardisation and the development of orthographies for each of the eleven official languages.

The Bible Fellowship of South Africa has also contributed greatly, albeit unintentionally, to standardisation of the South African languages – the Bible is available in all official languages, plus a few local variants like Fanagalo (a pidgin artificially created to support communication between English settlers and the local people, used extensively in the mines of South Africa, and incorporating words and structures from many different languages [Adendorff 2002: 179–98]). Professional language practitioner forums, like the South African Translators Institute or ProLingua, have become hubs of both knowledge in human translation practice as well as sources for data such as personal wordlists and translation memories. These organisations have also become key partners in empowering freelance translators with tools to incorporate electronic resources like translation memories, electronic dictionaries and term banks into translation practice.

Spelling checkers, like those developed by the Centre for Text Technology (CTexT) at the North-West University (NWU) in South Africa, can also contribute greatly to the usefulness of an MT system by providing spelling variants or checking the validity of generated constructions. Languages with conjunctive orthographies (like Afrikaans and isiZulu) form new words (and even phrases) by combining words and morphemes; spelling and grammar checkers could play an important role in validating such combinations in the context of MT.

Another related development has been the creation and expansion of wordnets for five South African languages. A good-quality wordnet could add valuable linguistic information to any MT system or be used for MT evaluation, as it includes various semantic relations, definitions and usage examples. The Afrikaans wordnet (Kotzé 2008: 163–84; Botha *et al.* 2013: 1–6) currently has more than 25,000 synsets and is modelled to the standards set in the Princeton WordNet and the Balkanet project. A joint effort by the University of South Africa (UNISA) and the NWU, funded by the South African Department of Arts and Culture (DAC), also saw the development of wordnets for Sepedi, Setswana, isiXhosa and isiZulu, with more than 5,000 synsets in each of these wordnets. The project received renewed funding from UNISA to expand these wordnets even further and to add another South African language from 2012 to 2014. Since 2017, the South African Centre for Digital Language Resources (SADiLaR) has contributed considerably to the sustainability of the wordnet projects at UNISA. Open access to the African Wordnet data is bound to have a significant impact not only on the promotion of African languages but also on the further development of natural language processing applications such as interlingual information retrieval and question-answering systems as well as machine translation.[5]

With a view to automated speech translation in the future, the principal groups in South Africa are the Meraka Institute at the Council for Scientific and Industrial Research (CSIR), Multilingual Speech Technologies (MuST) at the North-West University, as well as a research group at the University of Stellenbosch. These groups have been the driving force behind many projects to create core speech technologies and resources that could eventually be used for spoken MT. These include, inter alia, grapheme-to-phoneme conversion, speech recognition and speech synthesis, as well as large-scale data collection efforts in various projects.

The human language technology (HLT) fraternity in South Africa has also become an important enabler, addressing some of the needs of translators and language practitioners. Initial development started from individual researchers as part of smaller research projects and post-graduate studies; for example, automatic part-of-speech (POS) taggers utilising different machine learning techniques have been developed for Afrikaans (Pilon 2005), Sepedi (Heid *et al.* 2009: 1–19), lemmatisers for Afrikaans (Groenewald and van Huyssteen 2008: 65–91) and Setswana (Brits *et al.* 2006: 37–47), morphological analysers for isiZulu (Pretorius and Bosch 2003: 191–212; Spiegler *et al.* 2008: 9–12) and so on. (see Sharma Grover *et al.* [2011: 271–88] for an overview of technologies and resources available for the South African languages). Over the past two decades through continued support from the South African government, several HLT-related text (and speech) projects have generated NLP resources in the form of data, core technologies, applications and systems that are immensely valuable for the future development of the South African languages (Puttkammer *et al.* 2018). These initiatives are described in more detail in the following section.

The South African Government and HLT

The establishment of HLT as a viable industry in South Africa has a history extending back to 1988, with the publication of the LEXINET Report by the Human Sciences Research Council (Morris 1988). This report highlighted the importance of technological developments to foster communication in a multilingual society.

From the 1990s, South Africa was consumed with more pressing political matters, and the next government report to mention HLT explicitly only appeared in 1996. The final report by the Language Plan Task Force of the then Department of Arts, Culture, Science and Technology (DACST) included both short- and long-term action plans for language equality in South Africa (LANGTAG 1996). As a direct result of this report, a steering committee on translation and interpreting, as part of PanSALB, was established in 1998. A second steering committee, in collaboration with DACST, was formed in 1999, and was tasked to investigate and advise regarding HLTs in South Africa. The report by this joint steering committee was released in 2000, and a ministerial committee was established to develop a strategy for developing HLT in South Africa. The ministerial committee's report appeared in 2002, at which stage DACST split into two sections, the Department of Arts and Culture (DAC) and Department of Science and Technology (DST), with DAC retaining the primary responsibility for the development of HLT. In June 2019, the DAC was merged into the Department of Sport, Arts and Culture (DSAC). For an overview of the early history of HLT in South Africa, see Roux and du Plessis (2005: 24–38).

Following the recommendations of a ministerial advisory panel on HLT in 2002, three major research and development projects were funded subsequently by DAC, a speech project to foster information access via interactive voice response systems (the Lwazi project), a project to develop spelling checkers for the ten indigenous languages and a project to develop MT systems for three language pairs – the Autshumato project (see the section on the Autshumato project later for details).

Based on a decision taken by the South African cabinet on 3 December 2008, the National Centre for Human Language Technology (NCHLT) was established in 2009. As one of its first large-scale projects, the NCHLT announced a call for proposals to create reusable text and speech resources that are to serve as the basis for HLT development, to stimulate national interest in the field of HLT and to demonstrate its potential impact on the multilingual South African society. CTexT, in collaboration with the University of Pretoria (UP) and language experts across the country, was designated as the agency responsible for the development of various text resources in several phases of the project.

For each language, text corpora (1 million words for each language) from government domain sources were collected, and a subset (50,000 words for each language, aligned on the sentence level) was annotated for part of speech tagging, morphological analysis and lemmatisation (NCHLT Text phase I; Eiselen and Puttkammer 2014), as well as named entity recognition and phrase chunking (NCHLT II; Eiselen 2016a and Eiselen 2016b).

In addition to the annotated corpora, associated core technologies were also developed for each language. These technologies were sentence separators, tokenisers, lemmatisers, morphological decomposers and POS taggers during the NCHLT Text I project (Eiselen and Puttkammer 2014) as well as named entity recognisers, phrase chunkers and a language identifier during NCHLT Text II (Eiselen 2016a and Hocking 2014). A third phase of the NCHLT Text project saw the development of optical character recognition (OCR) models as well as improving access to all the technologies through the development of web services[6] (Puttkammer *et al.* 2018).

Given all these projects funded by the government, it soon became clear that a central repository should be established to manage multilingual digital text and speech resources for all official languages in a sustainable manner in order to ensure the availability and reusability of these data for educational, research and development purposes. In 2011, CTexT was appointed to set up the so-called Resource Management Agency (RMA); the RMA worked in close co-operation with the Dutch TST-Centrale. Data hosted by the RMA included broad categories such as text, speech, language-related video and multimodal resources (including sign language), as well as pathological and forensic language data. It was required that all past, current and future HLT projects funded by the government will have to deliver project data to the RMA in order to prevent loss of data and to promote reusability of the data. The RMA also aimed to position South Africa strategically through collaboration with other similar agencies worldwide, with the long-term vision of becoming the hub for language resource management in Africa. In 2017, the RMA was transferred to the newly established centre for South African Digital Language Resources (SADiLaR), a national centre funded by the governmental Department of Science and Innovation (DSI) as part of the new South African Research Infrastructure Roadmap (SARIR).

SADiLaR has an enabling function, with a focus on all official languages of South Africa, supporting research and development in the domains of language technologies and language-related studies in the humanities and social sciences. The Centre supports the creation, management and distribution[7] of digital language resources, as well as applicable software, which are freely available for research purposes through the Language Resource Catalogue.[8] Recent projects funded by SADiLaR include improving available core technologies, the development of text, speech and learner corpora, wordnets and digitisation of printed linguistic resources. Most of the available core technologies have yielded good results and can, for instance, be used in pre- and post-processing to improve machine translation output quality.

Early MT Projects in South Africa

Since the beginning of this century, when the South African government made it clear that it would be investing in and supporting initiatives for developing HLTs for South African languages, numerous research projects with smaller goals began exploring the possibilities that MT could hold for the South African community. One of the earliest projects (established in 2002 at the University of Stellenbosch) concerned the development of an experimental South African Sign Language MT system (van Zijl and Barker 2003). We could unfortunately not find any details on the performance of the system – from the latest publication from the project, it seems as if it might still be under development (van Zijl and Olivrin 2008: 7–12).

As Afrikaans has the most available resources (data and core technologies) compared to the other indigenous languages (Sharma Grover *et al.* 2011: 271–88), most of the early developments in MT research for South African languages have had Afrikaans as either the source or target language. Ronald and Barnard (2006: 136–40) showed that, even with very limited amounts of data, a first MT system for translation from English to Afrikaans was indeed possible using a statistical MT approach. They used a parallel corpus of only 40,000 sentences and achieved a BLEU score (Papineni *et al.* 2002: 311–18) of 0.3. Their study also included systems with even smaller datasets (3,800 sentences per language pair), translating from English to Setswana (BLEU = 0.32), isiXhosa (BLEU = 0.23) and isiZulu (BLEU = 0.29). This study set the scene for machine translation in South Africa and made it very clear that data collection was a big part of the effort needed to improve the quality of translation output.

Another early project, established in 2003 at the University of the Free State (UFS), was the EtsaTrans project, which built on a rule-based legacy system, Lexica. The EtsaTrans system used example-based MT for domain-specific purposes (i.e. for meeting administration at UFS). Initially, it provided only for English, Afrikaans and Sesotho, but later developments also aimed to include isiXhosa and isiZulu (Snyman *et al.* 2007: 225–38).

Another independent study is that of Pilon *et al.* (2010: 219–24), which investigated the possibility to recycle (port/transfer/re-engineer) existing technologies for Dutch to the benefit of Afrikaans, a language closely related to Dutch. They convert (i.e. as a basic form of translation) Afrikaans text to Dutch so that the Afrikaans text resembles Dutch more closely. After conversion, they use Dutch technologies (e.g. part-of-speech taggers) to annotate or process the converted text, resulting in the fast-tracking of resources for Afrikaans. Their conversion approach is similar to grapheme-to-phoneme conversion, in the sense that transformations are only applied on the graphemic level, and not, for instance, changing word order and so on. Similarities and differences between these two languages are captured as rules and wordlists and require very little other resources (like large datasets and probability estimations usually used in statistical MT methods). Although their recycling approach holds much promise for resource development for closely related languages, as an MT approach it is, of course, inefficient, since it does not deal with translation units larger than words. Pilon *et al.* (2010: 219–24) reported a BLEU score of 0.22 for converting Dutch to Afrikaans (compared to Google Translate's 0.40) and a BLEU score of 0.16 for Afrikaans to Dutch (compared to Google Translate's 0.44).

The Autshumato Project

As mentioned earlier, the Autshumato project was the first investment of the South African government to make MT a reality for South African languages. The aim of the project was to develop three MT systems (English to Afrikaans, English to Sepedi, and English to isiZulu), an integrated translation environment (incorporating the MT systems in a user-friendly editing environment) and an online terminology management system. It was explicated that all resources and systems should be released in the open-source domain.[9] The project was funded by the DAC and executed by CTexT in collaboration with UP.

The biggest portion of the budget and time for the MT subproject was spent on a drive to gather high-quality parallel corpora for the three chosen language pairs. These efforts commenced in early 2008 and included web crawling (mostly the government domain [gov.za], as this was to be the primary application domain), as well as acquiring personal translation memories, glossaries and other parallel text data from freelance translators and translation companies. Data collection was an ongoing effort for the duration of the project and proved a more difficult task than anticipated. Web crawling was largely ineffective for especially isiZulu and Sepedi, as there simply are not that many parallel texts in these languages available on the web. Translators were also sceptical to share their parallel corpora because of privacy concerns related to their clients. Subsequently the project team at CTexT developed an anonymiser that replaces names of people, places, organisations, monetary amounts, percentages and so on in order to ensure that confidential information is not included in the parallel corpora; this proved an effective measure to convince some translators and companies to make their data available to the project. As a last resort, the project team decided to commission translations and create a custom corpus. This method is by no means ideal and was costly but delivered excellent-quality data, as they were translated professionally.

While data collection continued, development of the three MT systems commenced in 2009 with the English-Afrikaans system. Based on the research of Ronald and Barnard (2006: 136–40), statistical MT has seemed to be viable option, and it was decided that the Autshumato systems would be based on the Moses statistical MT toolkit.[10] Data resources for all three systems include aligned units (sentences), wordlists and translation memories.

Since isiZulu is a morphologically rich language with a conjunctive orthography, it poses many challenges for the development of HLTs in general. The English–isiZulu system incorporated a very basic, rule-based morphologic analyser, but as it was still in early stages of development, it hindered development more than it helped. Although Sepedi is to some degree easier to process morphologically, the performance of the English–Sepedi system was only slightly better than that of the English–isiZulu system; see Table 21.2 for a comparison of the three systems.

All three systems include a pre-processing module to improve performance (Griesel *et al.* 2010: 205–10). In later stages of the project, the English–Afrikaans pre-processing module was further adapted to manipulate the syntactic structure of the English source sentences to be more similar to the Afrikaans target structure, thereby eliminating some of the translation divergences before automatic translation (Griesel 2011). Since data were such a precious commodity in this project, efforts by McKellar (2011) to manipulate available data and selecting the best possible candidate sentences for human translation were invaluable.

To make these MT systems practically available to translators, an integrated translation environment (ITE) was developed in a second subproject, which commenced in 2010. This computer-assisted translation (CAT) tool supports the translation workflow by incorporating the MT systems, glossaries, translation memories and spellcheckers in a single, easy-to-use editing application. The ITE is based on the OmegaT platform,[11] an internationally recognised base for CAT tools. The ITE was designed and developed with continual inputs and evaluations by translators working for government, ensuring that the application would fit well in an everyday working environment. Since one of the functionalities of the ITE is to update translation memories and glossaries as you translate, these valuable resources are also currently being used to continually improve the MT systems.

Table 21.2 Comparison of three MT systems

Language pair	# of aligned units	BLEU score
English–Afrikaans	470,000	0.66
English– Sepedi	250,000	0.29
English–isiZulu	230,000	0.26

The third subproject in the Autshumato project was the development of a terminology management system (TMS). One of the important functions of translators working for government is to keep a log of terminology that they come across while translating school books, government documents and pamphlets. This log serves as a way to standardise terms and encourage their use. The TMS is used for the development and management of a database of terms, including their various translations (in the eleven official languages), definitions, usage examples, images, sounds, mathematical equations and additional notes by terminologists. The database is continually expanded, while quality checks are performed regularly to ensure that the term base remains of a high standard.

In the course of these three subprojects, needs also arose for the development of various other tools, either for use by developers or by translators. These include a pdf-to-txt convertor, language identifiers for all eleven official languages, text anonymisers (described earlier) and a graphical user interface for alignment of parallel texts on sentence level. These tools were also released on the official project website (see endnote 10) under open-source licences.

The first phase of the Autshumato project was completed in 2011, and the lessons learned by the development team served future projects well. Except for the scientific and technology benefits of the project, one of the most important accomplishment of the project was the engagement of the translation community in the development and eventual up-take of this new technology as an essential part of their workflow.

During the second phase of the project (Autshumato II; 2013–2014), an English into Xitsonga MT system was developed, and a dedicated Helpdesk was set up to assist Autshumato users with the use of the software and to provide training through workshops. In the third iteration (Autshumato III; 2015–2018), the Helpdesk was extended and online services[12] to provide access to the MT systems where users can translate text, documents or other web pages and a word-for-word translation service for the DAC website were developed. A translation memory and glossary integration system, with the aim to unify distributed translation resources between government language units across the country, and another MT system for English into Setswana (Wilken *et al.* 2012) were also developed.

The next phase of the project (Autshumato IV; 2017–2019) focused on the development of evaluation data for all South African languages, which resulted in an evaluation suite that makes all MT systems for the South African languages directly comparable. The project also developed a new MT system for English into Sesotho translation.

Autshumato V (2018–2021) started with research into new developments in the field of machine translation, specifically neural machine translation, and their usefulness for the improvement of MT for the South African languages. The project also includes data and machine translation development for English–isiNdebele and English–Tshivenḓa. The scores of the MT systems currently available as well as the number of aligned translation units and word counts are provided in Table 21.3. All of the systems were evaluated on a parallel evaluation set consisting of 500 source sentences and four target translations for each sentence (McKellar and Puttkammer 2020).

Table 21.3 Scores of Autshumato MT systems

Language pair	Data			Scores	
	Aligned lines	EN words	Other words	NIST	BLEU
English–Afrikaans	908,772	11,424,637	11,211,526	9,9929	0,5213
English–isiZulu	241,591	2,794,084	1,975,583	4,977	0,1271
English–Sepedi	79,615	1,293,640	1,658,137	8,6933	0,401
English–Sesotho	126,000	2,004,971	2,401,868	8,8874	0,4124
English–Setswana	159,000	2,037,173	2,596,023	8,8376	0,4026
English–Xitsonga	450,000	3,461,089	4,328,407	8,7356	0,3879
English–isiNdebele	128,382	2,067,749	1,490,423	6,0769	0,1741
English–Tshivenḓa	124,791	2,003,583	2,523,402	9,6704	0,4782

The Autshumato VI extension[13] is scheduled to start at the end of 2021 and will include maintenance on existing Autshumato MT systems and software as well as the reversal of the MT systems to translate from the other languages back into English. These new systems will be available by the end of 2024.

Conclusion: The Future of MT in South Africa

The fact that the tools available in the Autshumato ITE are available for free in the open-source domain also leads to the development of a community of language practitioners using more sophisticated computer-based translation aids. Training workshops played a vital role in this regard and also served as a marketing mechanism to draw the attention of businesses and other government departments. Through these workshops it has also become apparent that one of the biggest needs is for customisation of translation memories and glossaries.

A few independent research projects and the government-funded Autshumato project have marked the entry of South Africa in the global MT field. Since the conclusion of the first phase of the Autshumato project in 2011, research and development of MT systems and tools for other language pairs gained momentum. Recent advances in the field of neural machine translation (NMT) showed that NMT can outperform SMT systems, if enough data are available. The research problem of building these generally resource-intensive systems with far less data than what is available for mainstream languages is currently getting a lot of interest from the local as well as international research community. One such Africa-based group is the Masakhane group,[14] an open-source, continent-wide, distributed, online research effort for machine translation for African languages (∀ *et al.* 2020). This group has published results for MT systems for 38 African languages,[15] including for all the South African languages. The Autshumato project team is also investigating the viability of porting the existing SMT systems to NMT systems.

Resource scarcity is certainly the most pressing drawback for HLT and specifically MT development for the South African languages. As HLT and MT hold the potential to facilitate human-human and human-machine interaction through natural language, the continued investment by government in this budding industry is of vital importance. The South African government's commitment in this regard is illustrated through DSAC's and SADiLaR's funding of the development of MT systems from 2013 onwards. It is an important step by the South African government to ensure the momentum created in the Autshumato project does not go to waste and to further establish MT as an area of interest for researchers, developers and end-users.

Notes

1 www.statssa.gov.za/?page_id=3839
2 http://cs2016.statssa.gov.za/
3 www.southafrica.info/about/people/language.htm#.Ugo-V5LTw6A
4 We do not give an overview of machine translation aids developed internationally for South African languages. In this regard, suffice to mention that Google Translate included Afrikaans as one of its first fifty languages and that performance has increased significantly during the first few years. In September 2013 isiZulu was released in Google Translate as well as Sesotho and isiXhosa in the following years.
5 https://sadilar.org/index.php/en/about/sadilar-nodes/unisa-node
6 www.hlt.nwu.ac.za
7 https://repo.sadilar.org
8 All resources developed through the NCHLT projects are also available in this repository.
9 http://autshumato.sourceforge.net
10 www.statmt.org/moses
11 http://omegatplus.sourceforge.net
12 https://mt.nwu.ac.za/
13 Funded by SADiLaR.
14 www.masakhane.io/
15 As of May 2021.

Additional Resources

http://autshumato.sourceforge.net.
http://cs2016.statssa.gov.za/.
http://omegatplus.sourceforge.net.
http://rma.nwu.ac.za.
https://mt.nwu.ac.za/.

https://repo.sadilar.org.
https://sadilar.org/index.php/en/about/sadilar-nodes/unisa-node.
www.southafrica.info/about/people/language.htm#.Ugo-V5LTw6A.
www.statmt.org/moses.
www.statssa.gov.za/?page_id=3839.

Bibliography

Adendorff, Ralph (2002) 'Fanakalo – A Pidgin in South Africa', in Ralph Adendorff (ed.) *Language in South Africa*, Cambridge: Cambridge University Press, 179–98.

Banking Association South Africa (2004) 'Code of Banking Practice'. Available at: www.banking.org.za.

Bleek, Wilhelm Heinrich Immanuel (1862) *A Comparative Grammar of South African Languages*, London: Trübner & Co.

Botha, Zandré, Roald Eiselen, and Gerhard B. van Huyssteen (2013) 'Automatic Compound Semantic Analysis Using Wordnets', in *Proceedings of the 24th Annual Symposium of the Pattern Recognition Association of South Africa*, 3 December 2013, University of Johannesburg, Johannesburg, South Africa, 1–6.

Brits, J. C., Rigardt Pretorius, and Gerhard B. van Huyssteen (2006) 'Automatic Lemmatisation in Setswana: Towards a Prototype', *South African Journal of African Languages* 25: 37–47.

De Schryver, Gilles-Maurice and D. J. Prinsloo (2000) 'The Compilation of Electronic Corpora, with Special Reference to the African Languages', *Southern African Linguistics and Applied Language Studies* 18(1–4): 89–106.

Eiselen, Roald (2016a) 'Government Domain Named Entity Recognition for South African Languages', in *Proceedings of the Tenth International Conference on Language Resources and Evaluation (LREC 2016)*, European Language Resources Association (ELRA), 3344–48.

Eiselen, Roald (2016b) 'South African Language Resources: Phrase Chunking', in *Proceedings of the Tenth International Conference on Language Resources and Evaluation (LREC 2016)*, European Language Resources Association (ELRA), 689–93.

Eiselen, Roald and Martin Puttkammer (2014) 'Developing Text Resources for Ten South African Languages', in *Proceedings of the Ninth International Conference on Language Resources and Evaluation (LREC 2014)*, European Language Resources Association (ELRA), 3698–703.

Griesel, Marissa (2011) 'Sintaktiese herrangskikking as voorprosessering in die ontwikkeling van Engels na Afrikaanse statistiese masjienvertaalsisteem (Syntactic Reordering as Pre-processing in the Development of English to Afrikaans Statistic Machine Translation)', Unpublished MA dissertation, Potchefstroom: North-West University.

Griesel, Marissa, Cindy McKellar, and Danie Prinsloo (2010) 'Syntactic Reordering as Pre-processing Step in Statistical Machine Translation from English to Sesotho sa Leboa and Afrikaans', in Fred Nicolls (ed.) *Proceedings of the 21st Annual Symposium of the Pattern Recognition Association of South Africa (PRASA)*, 22–23 November 2010, Stellenbosch, South Africa, 205–10.

Groenewald, Handré J. and Gerhard B. van Huyssteen (2008) 'Outomatiese Lemma-identifisering vir Afrikaans' (Automatic Lemmatisation for Afrikaans)', *Literator: Journal of Literary Criticism, Comparative Linguistics and Literary Studies: Special Issue on Human Language Technology for South African Languages* 29(1): 65–91.

Heid, Ulrich, Danie J. Prinsloo, Gertrud Faasz, and Elsabé Taljard (2009) 'Designing a Noun Guesser for Part of Speech Tagging in Northern Sotho', *South African Journal of African Languages* 29(1): 1–19.

Hocking, Justin (2014) 'Language Identification for South African Languages', Puttkammer and Eiselen (eds.), in *Proceedings of the 2014 PRASA, RobMech and AfLaT International Joint Symposium*, 27–28 November 2014, Cape Town, South Africa, 307.

Kotzé, Gideon (2008) 'Development of an Afrikaans Wordnet: Methodology and Integration', *Literator: Journal of Literary Criticism, Comparative Linguistics and Literary Studies: Special Issue on Human Language Technology for South African Languages* 29(1): 163–84.

LANTAG (1996) *Towards a National Language Plan for South Africa: Final Report of LANTAG*, Pretoria: Department of Arts, Culture, Science and Technology.

McKellar, Cindy (2011) 'Dataselektering en – manipulering vir statistiese Engels–Afrikaanse masjienvertaling (Data Selection and Manipulation for Statistical English-Afrikaans Machine Translation)', Unpublished MA dissertation. Potchefstroom: North-West University.

McKellar, Cindy and Martin Puttkammer (2020) 'Dataset for Comparable Evaluation of Machine Translation between 11 South African Languages', *Data in Brief* 29, ISSN 2352-3409. https://doi.org/10.1016/j.dib.2020.105146.

Morris, Robin (1988) *LEXINET and the Computer Processing of Language: Main Report of the LEXINET Programme, LEXI-3*, Pretoria: Human Sciences Research Council.

Papineni, Kishore A., Salim Roukos, Todd Ward, and Zhu Wei-Jing (2002) 'BLEU: A Method for Automatic Evaluation of Machine Translation', in *Proceedings of the 40th Annual Meeting of the Association for Computational Linguistics, ACL-2002*, 7–12 July 2002, University of Pennsylvania, Philadelphia, PA, 311–18.

Pilon, Suléne (2005) 'Outomatiese Afrikaanse Woordsoortetikettering (Automatic Afrikaans Part-of-speech Tagging)', Unpublished MA dissertation. Potchefstroom: North-West University.

Pilon, Suléne, Gerhard B. van Huyssteen, and Liesbeth Augustinus (2010) 'Converting Afrikaans to Dutch for Technology Recycling', in *Proceedings of the 21st Annual Symposium of the Pattern Recognition Association of South Africa (PRASA)*, 22–23 November 2010, Stellenbosch, South Africa, 219–24.

Pretorius, Laurette and Sonja E. Bosch (2003) 'Finite-state Computational Morphology: An Analyzer Prototype For Zulu', *Machine Translation* 18: 191–212.

Puttkammer, Martin, Roald Eiselen, Justin Hocking, and Frederik Koen (2018) 'NLP Web Services for Resource-Scarce Languages', in *Proceedings of the 56th Annual Meeting of the Association for Computational Linguistics-System Demonstrations*, Melbourne, Australia, 15–20 July 2018, 43–49.

Ronald, Kato and Etienne Barnard (2006) 'Statistical Translation with Scarce Resources: A South African Case Study', *SAIEE Africa Research Journal* 98(4): 136–40.

Roux, Justus and Theo du Plessis (2005) 'The Development of Human Language Technology Policy in South Africa', in Walter Daelemans, Theo du Plessis, Cobus Snyman, and Lut Teck (eds.) *Multilingualism and Electronic Language Management: Proceedings of the 4th International MIDP Colloquium*, 22–23 September 2003, Bloemfontein, South Africa, Pretoria: Van Schaik, 24–38.

Sharma Grover, Aditi, Gerhard B. van Huyssteen, and Marthinus Pretorius (2011) 'The South African Human Language Technology Audit', *Language Resources and Evaluation* 45(3): 271–88.

Snyman, Cobus, Leandra Ehlers, and Jacobus A. Naudé (2007) 'Development of the EtsaTrans Translation System Prototype and Its Integration into the Parnassus Meeting Administration System', *Southern African Linguistics and Applied Language Studies* 25(2): 225–38.

Spiegler, Sebastian, Bruno Golenia, Ksenia Shalonova, Peter Flach, and Roger Tucker (2008) 'Learning the Morphology of Zulu with Different Degrees of Supervision', in Sinivas Bangalore (ed.) *Proceedings of the 2008 IEEE Workshop on Spoken Language Technology (SLT 2008)*, 15–18 December 2008, Goa, India, 9–12.

van Zijl, Lynette and Dean Barker (2003) 'A Machine Translation System for South African Sign Language', in *Proceedings of the 2nd International Conference on Computer Graphics, Virtual Reality, Visualisation and Interaction in Africa, Afrigraph 2003*, 3–5 February 2003, Cape Town, South Africa, 49–52.

van Zijl, Lynette and Guillaume Olivrin (2008) 'South African Sign Language Assistive Translation', in Ronald Merrell (ed.) *Proceedings of the 4th Annual IASTED International Conference on Telehealth/Assistive Technologies*, 16–19 April 2008, Baltimore, MD, 7–12.

Wilken, Ilana, Marissa Griesel, and Cindy McKellar (2012) 'Developing and Improving a Statistical Machine Translation System for English to Setswana: A Linguistically-motivated Approach', in Alta de Waal (ed.) *Proceedings of the 23rd Annual Symposium of the Pattern Recognition Association of South Africa (PRASA)*, 29–30 November 2012, Pretoria, South Africa.

∀, Iroro Fred Onome Orife, Julia Kreutzer, Blessing Sibanda, Daniel Whitenack, Kathleen Siminyu, Laura Martinus, Jamiil Toure Ali, Jade Abbott, Vukosi Marivate, Salomon Kabongo, Musie Meressa, Espoir Murhabazi, Orevaoghene Ahia, Elan van Biljon, Arshath Ramkilowan, Adewale Akinfaderin, Alp ktem, Wole Akin, Ghollah Kioko, Kevin Degila, Herman Kamper, Bonaventure Dossou, ChrisEmezue, Kelechi Ogueji and Abdallah Bashir (2020) 'Masakhane – Machine Translation for Africa', arXiv preprint arXiv:2003.11529. https://doi.org/10.48550/arXiv.2003.11529.

22

TRANSLATION TECHNOLOGY IN TAIWAN

Tracks and Trends

Shih Chung-ling

Introduction

Living in a technological world, a growing number of people conduct their daily work using the technological tools afforded by computers, the Internet and advanced information technologies in diverse sectors of life. These persons are closely connected to cloud mining, cloud rating and cloud information exchange and knowledge sharing in the Internet context on a daily basis. However, in creating a user-friendly, highly communicative Internet environment, translation plays a key role because it helps people break through language barriers and boost their bi/multi-lateral understandings and dialogues across borders. More importantly, diverse translation technologies (TT) can be used to help enlarge the translation scope and increase the efficiency and cost-effectiveness of language services. All modern professional translators are well aware of the business profits of TT in the translation industry, but their reception towards it are different in different countries in different times. Still, translation scholars and instructors have learned the crucial part and/or function of TT in the contemporary translation workflow, but their reception and intentions to incorporate it into their research and teaching are also different in different countries at different times. For this reason, departing from Taiwan, a research report will be given on the application and teaching of TT in both theory and practice through an empirical investigation. However, before this, the landscape of TT development in Taiwan will be introduced to show its differences from other countries, and a general TT picture can be delineated as the background framework to support the findings in this research.

Today, machine translation (MT) development with technological advances has rekindled worldwide users' interest in it, and the development of integrated MT-TM systems, such as Trados, has boosted professional translators' confidence in translation technology applications. However, Taiwan started later and also made slower progress in TT development and application than did the United States and Europe.[1] A multilingual MT system, Systran, has been used by the Commission of the European Communities (CEC) since 1976, and the 'TAUM METEO system [has been] implemented since 1978 by the Canadian Weather Service for routine translation of weather forecasts from English into French' (O'Hagan 1996: 30). Furthermore, many companies, such as Boeing, BMW, General Motors and Caterpillar Inc., have developed controlled English checkers to help author technical texts for effective MT application and/or efficient post-MT editing (Torrejón and Rico 2002: 108). Also, the cost economics of MT

DOI: 10.4324/9781003168348-24

and TM has been supported by statistical reports from WTCC (World Translation Company of Canada), Systran Institute and Webb (1998–1999).[2] However, when European and/or American companies are enjoying the profits of using MT and MT tools, the majority of translation agencies, technological companies and governmental institutions in Taiwan still rely on human translators to perform daily translation tasks, although the scenario has slowly undergone some transformations.

Scantier use of translation technologies in Taiwan can be attributed to the great linguistic differences between Chinese and Indo-European languages. MT between Chinese and Indo-European languages is poorer than those involving some Indo-European languages. Furthermore, Taiwan's translation industry is less robust and/or less prosperous than Europe's, and there is no urgent need to use technological tools to increase translation efficiency and productivity. It was not until 1985 that an English–Chinese MT project started through joint efforts between the Department of Electrical Engineering of National Tsing Hua University and Behavior Tech Computer Corporation. This research resulted in the development of Behavior Tran,[3] which is now exclusively used to aid in the translation service offered to clients by the Behavior Design Corporation (BDC). Subsequently, some graduate institutes of computer science and information engineering in Taiwan's universities engaged in MT research and computational linguistics, and the ROC Computational Linguistics Society was formally established in March 1990, assuming responsibility for organizing events or conferences related to information technology subjects.

Taiwan's translation software market did not gain public attention until the late 1990s, nearly thirty years behind their counterparts in the United States, Europe and Russia (Shih 2002). A chain of MT software emerged in the local market, such as Dr Eye[4] in 1996, JinXlat 1.0 and JinXlat 3.0 in 1998, TransWhiz in 2000, TransBridge in 2001 and others. Dr Eye's affordable price propelled sales to the 200,000 unit level in just one year (Shih 2002), but the poor quality of its automatic translation limited its product lifespan only to two years in the TT market. In 2001, TransWhiz debuted as Taiwan's first MT+TM system, developed by Otek Company. However, after the debut of corpus/statistics-driven MT systems such as Google Translate and the import of Trados (a renowned TM system) from Germany, TransWhiz immediately gave way. Otek offered a free online MT service (Yi-Yan-Tang), but its Chinese–English translations were not as accurate as Google Translate's, so most MT users in Taiwan prefer Google Translate. Furthermore, the companies who use TM tools favor SDL Trados.[5]

To understand the current status and role of MT and TM applications, surveys have been conducted to investigate the differences before and after 2000 in Taiwan's translation industry, university language education and academic research. Some of these investigations aim to detect the gap among translator training in Taiwan's universities, translation research concerns and professional translation in domestic translation agencies and technological companies. These three aspects embody interactive relations, because translator training would affect their reception of TT application. Whether professional translators use translation technologies is connected to the adequacy of their training in TT at school. Inadequate learning of TT at school often makes professional translators turn their backs on TT. Furthermore, research subjects often pertain to the instructor/scholar's teaching, and TT application in industry also affects the content of TT teaching at school. The interactive relations among school, research and industry in TT are inevitable, so this investigation focuses on the three areas. Three research questions (RQs) are raised as follows.

RQ1. What are the differences in TT and human translation (HT) courses offered in both MA and BA programs before and after 2000 in Taiwan's universities?

RQ2. What are the differences in TT research in terms of subjects, quantity and publication media before and after 2000 in Taiwan, and what has caused these differences?

RQ3. What are the differences in TT application in Taiwan's translation agencies and technological companies before and after 2000, and what accounts for these differences?

RQ1 asks how far translator training has been modified by integrating TT components, such as MT and TM, into conventional translation teaching at Taiwan's universities. RQ2 examines the evolution of translation research on TT in research subjects over the past several decades. RQ3 explores the ways in which Taiwan's translation agencies and technological companies have integrated TT into their daily workflow.

Translator Training in TT

To arrive at a sense of MT/TM teaching in institutions of higher language education in Taiwan, a 2012 survey of curriculum online[6] was conducted by examining TT teaching at both MA and BA levels. This survey can be measured against a website survey of the pre-2000 curriculum conducted by Shih (2002) in her research. The subjects investigated include the graduate institutes and departments of translation and interpretation (T&I), English and/or applied linguistics (E/AL), foreign languages and literature (FLL) and applied foreign languages (AFL). The number of graduate institutes in the post-2000 investigation increased to 30 because Taiwan's government approved of the establishment of many new MA programs after 2000 under the policy of promoting high education in Taiwan. The finding showed that in the pre-2000 BA programs, MT/TM took up 2.4% and HT 88.1%, but in the MA programs, MT/TM had a slight rise, 7.7%, and HT had a slight fall, 69.2%. In contrast, in the post-2000 BA programs, MT/TM doubled its former position (14.3%) and HT became essential, reaching 100%, but in the MA program, HT fell to 73.3% and MT/TM rose slightly to 16.7%. Figure 22.1 shows different percentages of TT and HT courses among the departments of T&I, E/AI, FLL and AFL at both BA and MA levels before and after 2000.

As Figure 22.1 indicates, TT (MT/TM) in MA and BA programs in the pre-2000 survey shows a lower average percentage (3.6%) than HT (83.6%). This case holds true in the post-2000 survey, in which only 15.3% of MA and BA programs together offer TT courses and 87.5% offer HT courses. However, there is a higher percentage of TT teaching in both MA and BA programs in the post-2000 survey than in the pre-2000 survey. This phenomenon suggests that although some language instructors recognize the importance of translation and view translation as the fifth language skill in addition to the four skills of speaking, listening, reading and writing in foreign language education, they still do not accept technology-enabled translation,

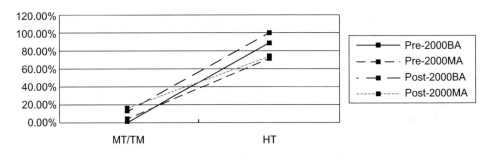

Figure 22.1   A survey of TT and HT courses before and after 2000

nor do they identify computer-aided translation as a specialized subject in translation that is not only fit for translation specialists but also good for language majors. Most language instructors in Taiwan's universities do not learn TT when they receive education for the PhD, so they find it easier to teach HT than CAT. Furthermore, many language or translation instructors in Taiwan do not have a clear notion of TT or adequate knowledge about CAT and thereby do not incorporate it into their teaching. One more important reason is that translation instructors are TT-phobic. Miss Hwang, Taiwan's exclusive agent of Trados in early times, told me that she regretted seeing that many of Taiwan's translation instructors were lazy learning Trados or other TT although they knew these tools were useful aids to professional translators.

Academic Research on TT

In addition to identifying the trends in TT education, there is a need to map out the evolutionary line in TT-related academic research by conducting an online survey of TT research. The collection includes 8 books, 42 journal papers, 20 conference papers and 42 theses. The survey results serve as an index to the growing profession-oriented concerns with TT either at school or in industry. The subjects under investigation fall into three categories: (1) TT system design and language engineering; (2) MT/TM use, MT error analysis and pre/post-MT editing; and (3) TT teaching. For each category, there are three sub-categories: MT, TM and MT plus TM. The finding showed that TT system design and language engineering held the highest frequency (53.56%), with 49.10% of MT research and 4.46% of TM research. TT application held the second highest (28.56%), with 14.28% of MT research, 13.39% of TM research and 0.89% of MT plus TM research. TT teaching showed the lowest frequency (17.8%), with 7.14% of MT research, 5.35% of TM research and 5.35% of MT plus TM research. Figure 22.2 shows the results of a website survey of TT-related research published in books and journals and presented in conferences and theses. SDLE represents system design and language engineering; APP means application TT and TEA teaching of TT.

Generally viewed, the most frequently studied area is system design and language engineering, doubling that of the other two. The main reason is that a distinct high percentage of theses discuss the issue of MT system design and language engineering. In Taiwan, there are more graduate institutes of computer science and information engineering than those of interpreting and translation, and among 42 theses investigated online, a total of 32 address the subject of technological design and computational linguistics. Those graduate students who major in translation and interpretation are not masters of computer programming and cannot deal with technological problems and MT/TM system development. They can only handle pedagogical and practical issues pertaining to TT under the supervision of instructors who are not masters

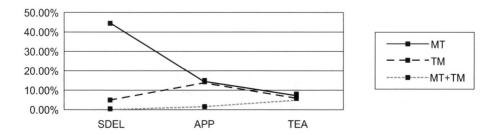

Figure 22.2 A subject-oriented investigation of TT-specific research

of language engineering. Thus, there is a clear division between two camps, with one focusing on information retrieval from the corpus or MT system design with quality improvement solutions and the other emphasizing the identification of pre/post-MT editing rules for better MT performance and the relevance of MT errors and/or TM alignments to text types and linguistic problems. Only one thesis deals with an online survey of how freelance and a few in-house translators apply TM systems and term bases.

In addition, the highest frequency of SDLE can be attributed to the majority of journal papers dealing with the development of MT systems and computing linguistics. It is found that journal papers are evenly split, with 21 papers discussing MT system design and engineering and 21 other papers handling MT editing or error analysis and teaching. Interestingly, there are slightly more papers addressing MT/TM teaching than those on editing and error analysis. My inference is that after more master's programs of translation and interpretation were offered in universities after 2000[7] in Taiwan, more translation instructors noticed the importance of TT and thereby started to propose TT-aided translation teaching. The result of their teaching research is presented at some conferences and finally published in journal papers. Scanning the papers on TT application, we find that a wide range of topics cover contrastive analysis of MT systems, development of knowledge-based MT systems, sentence-based statistical MT model, production and consumption of MT, impacts of the technological turn, teaching text types with MT error analysis and post-MT editing, teaching the concept of equivalence using TM tools, shifts in controlled English norms for different MT systems and corpus-based study of differences in explication between literature translations for children and for adults, a teaching challenge for TM, the constructivist educational effectiveness of TM-aided specialized translation and others.

Another reason for the highest ranking of SDLE is that 50% of books in the survey address MT or TM system design and engineering, and the other half pertain to editing, error analysis and teaching. Four books in the area of SDLE provide a historical sketch of MT system design, approaches and developments with an introduction to the basic functions, practical problems and strengths and weakness of TT application. One of them is a translated book by W. John Hutchins, *Machine Translation: The Past, Present and Future* (1993), published by BDC. It was translated by the MT system Behavior Trans and post-edited by in-house translators. This case suggests that although nonfiction is the right text type for MT application, MT output still requires editing prior to publication. Books in the areas of application and teaching include *Computer-Aided Translation* (Shih 2004) and *Helpful Assistance to Translators: MT and TM* (Shih 2006). These two books shift the main focus from technical issues to pedagogical ones, although they also give a brief overview of MT/TM functions and operational procedures. *Computer-Aided Translation* elaborates on three-stage MT editing in register, discourse and context areas with supportive examples and provides some exercises for student practice. The other supplements theoretical discussions and reports case studies of applying MT and TM in a translation class, such as 'Using Trados TagEditor in the Teaching of Web Translation', 'Using the Tool of Trados WinAlign to Teach the Translation Equivalence Concept', 'The Use of TM as the Scaffold in Translation Teaching' and others.

Two books, *Real-Time Communication through Machine-Enabled Translation: Taiwan's Oracle Poetry* (Shih 2011) and *New Web Textual Writing: Fast Communication across Borders* (Shih 2013), discuss cost-effective benefits of editing source texts in controlled Chinese for multilingual machine translations, with the former using Taiwan's oracle poetry as examples and the latter web texts on Taiwan's festivals, folk culture and company profile as examples. A set of pre-editing rules is designed based on the linguistic differences between Chinese and English, such as clarifying the grammatical features of words by using *–de* before an adjective and *–di* before an adverb, using an article or quantifier, using more passive voice than active voice and others. Idiomatic expressions must be adapted in controlled Chinese, and Chengyu and/or fixed four-character phrases must be paraphrased. The finding shows that oracle poetry and allusive stories have dramatically improved semantic clarity, grammatical accuracy and pragmatic appropriateness for multilingual machine translations after controlled editing. In the two books, Shih (2011) emphasizes that controlled Chinese is a new concept in the Chinese community and its use could meet some opposition, but this new language was designed for machine-friendly application and MT-enabled communication, not for daily writing. Just as we can have multiple choices for daily necessities, we can also be allowed to choose one language customized to optimize the effectiveness of MT application on the Internet.

In addition to a subject-oriented survey, the statistical result of varied channels of publicizing TT research needs to be reported. In all publications before and after 2000, journal papers and theses that address TT showed the highest percentage (37.5%); conference papers and/or presentations ranked second (17.8%) and books third (7.1%). Figure 22.3 shows the statistical result of TT-related research published in different media from the past to now in Taiwan.

The high percentage of journal papers is attributed to the result of a website survey. Many authors of journal articles in Taiwan are asked by publishers to endorse an agreement to have papers digitalized online for public access and information sharing. In contrast, conference papers are only collected in the proceedings and are not published with a copyright or ISBN. If conference papers are not uploaded by conference organizers, they cannot be accessed by this online survey. Furthermore, theses on TT hold the same high percentage as that of journal papers because Taiwan's Ministry of Education (MOE) requires all theses in Taiwan to be uploaded onto the website of National Digital Library of Theses and Dissertations. In short, theses and journals are two main sources of TT data in Taiwan. However, the contents of the theses cannot be accessed without the permission of the authors.

Regardless of varied ways of publicizing TT research results, the publications showed a difference in different times; therefore a chronological survey was needed. The findings showed that in the post-2000 period, the number of journal papers on TT had a great rise from 8 to 34, conference presentations and papers from 1 to 19 and theses from 16 to 26. In the pre-2000 period, books on TT took up 13.79% (4/29), journals 27.58% (8/29), conferences 3.44% (1/29) and theses 55.2% (16/29). In contrast, books on TT took up 4.8% (4/83), journals 40.96% (34/83), conferences 22.89% (19/83) and theses 31.32% (26/83) after 2000. The distinctive difference was that theses on TT ranked first before 2000, but journal papers on TT showed the highest percentage after 2000. Furthermore, conferences on TT showed the lowest percentage before 2000, but books on TT showed the lowest after 2000. Figure 22.4 shows the result of a chronological survey of TT research before and after 2000.

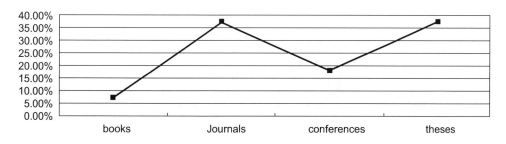

Figure 22.3 Media-oriented investigation of research on TT

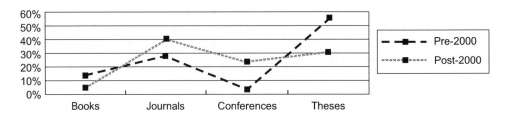

Figure 22.4 A chronological investigation of TT publications before and after 2000

In spite of the different TT publications before and after 2000, the average percentage in the post-2000 period remains higher than that in the pre-2000 period. Apparently, the concept of TT and its application before 2000 was not widespread and research issues on TT were limited to MT or relevant ones, but after 2000, the TM issue is supplemented and therefore the amount of research doubled. More importantly, more satisfying MT performance due to technical improvements has increased users' faith and rekindled their interest. This reason accounts for an increase in the amount of TT research and publications, particularly on the subject of controlled language and effective MT editing for the creation of comprehensible multilingual machine translations. Overall, this phenomenon suggests that many translators, scholars and translation instructors in Taiwan have started to realize some benefits of technology-enabled translation in recent years.

Professional Application of TT

An investigation of professional application of TT after 2000 targets 19 translation agencies and 4 technological translation companies, such as Otek International Incorporation, Fohigh Technological Translation Company, Shinewave International Incorporation and Syzygy Information Services Company in Taiwan. The finding shows that there were 14 users of MT tools and 11 users of TM tools. These companies used MT tools for different purposes. For example, BDC used Google Translate for quality assessment against the Behavior Trans system; Syzygy Company used Google Translate for accuracy tests; and Ests Company, Otek International Incorporation and Ya-Hsin Company used Google Translate or TransWhiz for gist translation and post-MT editing. Nine users viewed MT systems, such as Google Translate, as online dictionaries for specialized term lookup and did not rely on the quality of MT outputs. Figure 22.5 shows different purposes of using MT tools.

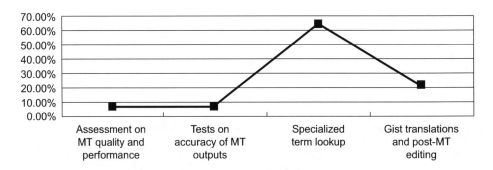

Figure 22.5 Different purposes of using MT in Taiwan's translation agencies and companies in the 2012 survey

The figure shows that over half of MT users view MT tools as an alternative to dictionary and do not use MT outputs as the scripts for post-MT editing. Their opinion is that current Chinese–English MT performance is not good enough for gist translation and post-MT editing. In light of this limitation, Shih (2011) has proposed pre-MT editing for effective MT application, particularly for the creation of multilingual translations.

With respect to TM application, the most frequently used tools are Trados, TM/Win and localization software programs such as Catalyst, Passolo, RCWin Trans, Microsoft Helium, Microsoft LosStudio, Logoport and others. Since quality assurance is a key part in the project management of localization industry, ApSIC Xbencg 2.9 serves as a favorable and helpful tool, free and accessible on the Internet. When TM users were asked to evaluate the performance of SDL Trados in my telephone interviews, six users gave 80 points, two users 85, two users 70 and one user, 90. The average score was 81. This statistical result suggests that the majority of TM users in Taiwan are satisfied with TM performance, but they also expect some technical improvements and reduction in price. One user complained that the speed was slow when the processed file was extremely large, and negative responses involved occasional breakdown, inadequate fuzzy matches, high price, no entire textual translation and complex procedures of operation. Lower capital investment and friendly hands-on experience are users' primary concerns.

Another finding showed that among the 11 agencies and companies that did not use TM tools, six (6/11 = 54.5%) held that artificial intelligence could never compete with the human brain, so human translation would always be more reliable. Two of them (2/11 = 18.2%) claimed that they handled only small amounts of translation and thereby did not need TM or a corpus. Four (4/11 = 36.4%) maintained that their translations were not highly repetitive in content and/or sentence patterns, so human translation was faster. It is noted that most of the subjects in the present investigation are small translation agencies, and for this reason, they think it is not worth an investment in the costly TM software.

A comparison between the 2012 survey and the 2001 survey of TT application (Shih 2002) shows that the percentage of MT and TM users about 11 years ago (28.6%) is lower than what it was in 2012 (54.34%). In the 2001 survey on pre-2000 MT and TM use, there were six MT users (6/14 = 42.9%) and two TM users (2/14 = 14.3%). In contrast, the 2012 survey on post-2000 MT and TM use shows that MT users rose from 6 to 14 and TM users from 2 to 11. Furthermore, the gap between MT and TM users in the 2001 survey (28.6%) was higher than that in the 2012 survey (13.1%), giving evidence to an increase in the number of professional MT and TM users in recent years. Figure 22.6 shows the difference in the results of the two surveys.

Although the average percentage of TT users after 2001 was higher than before, the percentage of MT users in both surveys was higher than that of TM users. One possible reason is that MT tools are much less expensive than TM tools, and Google Translate offers a free automatic

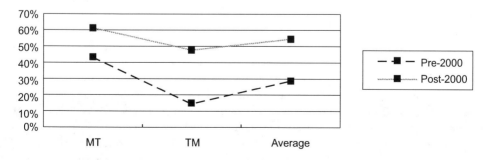

Figure 22.6   The differences in MT and TM use between 2001 and 2012 surveys

translation service. In contrast, sophisticated TM tools such as SDL Trados are costly, and post-sale training is also needed because of their complicated operational procedures.

In Shih W-M's (2007) survey, the percentage of TM tools used by Taiwan-based translators is lower (16%) than in Shih's 2012 survey (47.8%) but higher than her 2001 survey (14.3%). This implies that from 2007 to 2012, there are a growing number of freelance translators or translation agencies willing to invest in costly TM tools even though they handle only small amounts of translation. However, TT application remains inadequate in Taiwan's translation industry, suggesting that the disconnection from the international translation world has blinded professional translators to the fast-changing international translation market. The narrow scope of text type and limited language pairs of translations they handle on a regular basis is a key barrier to the use of TM tools in daily translation work. In addition, many of Taiwan's local enterprises are not internationally marketed, and their user manuals, product instructions and relevant documents do not have to be multilingual. For this reason, they do not resort to the localization company for the service of multilingual translations. Some renowned international companies such as Asus have a branch localization company (e.g. Shinewave International Incorporation) to help handle multilingual translations, and they also try to customize their own TM for their clients. Their TM is confidential and is not released on the market.

Conclusion and Suggestions

A combination of TT surveys in the areas of application, research and teaching has shown some tracks and trends, including: (1) optional TT training, not required; (2) research preferences for technical TT, not TT-aided training; (3) misconceptions and ignorance about MT and TM education; and (4) underdeveloped localization industry. These weaknesses can be diagnosed and improved with some possible solutions as follows.

Joint Lectures and On-the-Job TT Training

In answer to RQ1 about TT courses offered at Taiwan's universities, the result indicates that translator training generally uses the conventional method of HT, and most MT and TM courses are electives, not required. This suggests that most T&I instructors still view technology-enabled translation as a supplementary course, not as a necessity for translation and language majors. This is partly due to the instructors' negligence of the international trend of technology-enabled translation in the real working scenario and partly to their identification of translation as a linguistic subject or an art rather than a practical, professional science that requires market-oriented training.[8]

Seeing the low percentage of TT training in language and translation education in universities, some solutions are proposed and prepared to take action for a change of the *status quo*. Taiwan's MOE sponsors Excellence-in-Teaching projects at universities and encourages the joint-lecture practice. When grant-funded projects are in force, TT professionals in the translation industry can be invited to lecture in class as the translation instructor's partner. Shih (2006: 357) proposed that sales managers or technicians 'could be invited from software companies to teach translation [students] how to operate MT and TM tools'. As follow-up cooperation, instructors and professional translators in the localization industry can work together to design technology-enabled translation software. In the translation classes at Lunghwa University of Science and Technology, National Sun Yat-sen University and National Kaohsiung First University of Science and Technology, project managers and professional translators were invited from localization companies to give lectures, and all students were positive about the joint lectures, agreeing that this teaching method provided them with a window on the real translation world. Understanding the employment requirements for translation professionals is a catalyst to motivate them to learn the practical TT tools at school and push them to pursue internships outside class. Training in TT gives students market-oriented expertise and enhances their employment prospects in the international translation market.

Additionally, 'local governments could consider funding and sponsoring some in-service training activities on MT and TM', and 'the school or technological companies could organize seminars and conferences on the issues of MT and TM to disseminate the knowledge of technology-enabled translation' (Shih 2002: 358). The Taiwan Association of Translation and Interpretation provided training in SDL Trados to the public in October 2012, and many translation instructors and freelancers participated in the event with much ardor. Nevertheless, the training time was too short to give the participants adequate practice, and some teachers complained abut the complicated procedures of operating the TM tool. Since this was the first time providing free training in TT to the public audiences in Taiwan, its flaws can be corrected and future ones could be more rewarding and receive positive reception. Furthermore, 'internship or on-the-job training programs' can be provided by collaborating with software or technological companies (Shih 2002: 358). However, many technological or localization companies do not want to take interns because of the confidentiality of company documents, and some clients also forbid them to do so. Finally, the publication of more books on TT-related pedagogy is encouraged. Sufficient teaching resources on TT would encourage more teachers to teach TT in their translation and/or language classes.

Regular MT/TM Conferences With the Help of Government Grants

In response to RQ2 concerning differences in translation research before and after 2000, it is gratifying to see that the quantity and scope of TT-related research has increased since 2000. This means that an increasing number of translation scholars and/or instructors have shown greater interest in TT and are more devoted to TT research than before. However, the percentage of research on language engineering and technical solution remains overwhelmingly higher than that of TT teaching. Many language and translation instructors continue to assume that TT is immature and unacceptable and that they cannot trust the accuracy and quality of computer-aided translation. Since many language instructors still view translation as art, they devalue translations created with the aid of technology as unreadable.

To strengthen confidence in language and translation instructors and change their bias about TT, some conferences on MT/TM technology can be regularly organized in Taiwan's universities with the help of government grants. Adequate information input about TT can change language and translation instructors' concepts, and this can urge them to introduce TT to their students. Finally, instructors will be more willing to study technology-enabled translation and teach it in class. Academic research needs a connection to the global translation world, but most scholars lack the momentum to act upon the concept. One more important point that translation scholars must know is that translation pedagogy with the help of TT is not a rejection of conventional translation teaching; rather it enriches its teaching context through integration of old and new.

TT Education as One of the Criteria for University Evaluation

With respect to the evolution of TT application in translation industry, the percentage of MT and TM use in the 2012 survey was higher than the corresponding percentages in the 2005 and

2001 surveys, and the rate of TT application remains inadequate in current Taiwan's translation industry. This phenomenon can be attributed to less internalization or globalization of Taiwan's local businesses, and they consider using TT less to help handle their translation. Furthermore, far less use of MT tools than TM tools results from the role Taiwan's localization companies have been playing as a single language vendor (SLV), not a multiple language vendor (MLV). Since their service scope is limited to Chinese to/from English translation, they do not think of using controlled language (CL) and MT application to promote translation efficiency. Many European companies act as MLVs, but Taiwan's localization companies do not because they find it very hard to get competent multilingual translators in Taiwan. Several languages spoken by different regions in Europe share similar linguistic features, as they belong to the same Indo-European linguistic system, and the European multilingual environments easily develop native speakers into those who are able to simultaneously use two or three languages. In contrast, the limited language environment plus inadequate training in the translation of non-English languages at universities results in a severe shortage of multilingual translators in Taiwan. Various factors support that the development and application of MT tools receive ongoing concern from translation professionals in Europe, but the majority of translators in Taiwan have been mistrusting and overlooking MT application.

In Taiwan, one reason for the severe shortage of MT education is that many instructors have a misconception of MT and think MT training is useless because MT tools cannot be used to translate literary works. Thus, MT education should be first given to instructors, making them understand that no dish can be washed using the washing machine. As dish can only be washed using the dishwasher: an MT tool can only be used to translate informative texts, such as user's manuals, product instructions and relevant others, for effective communication, not for aesthetic appreciation or replication of the author's creative style. MT education should emphasize the use of controlled language for improved MT performance and the use of customized post-MT editing skills to meet diverse functions of translations. In this respect, it is important to educate translation and language instructors about MT and TT-relevant knowledge. One effective way is the government's intervention by including TT education as one of the criteria for university evaluation. This instrumental purpose will motivate school to stress TT education, and instructors will teach students the functions, strengths and weaknesses of MT, TM and others. After TT education gains popularity, governmental policy can be modified and its intervention can be reduced or eliminated.

Government Incentives to Boost the Growth of Localization Industry

With regard to the use of TM tools, cost, complicated operational procedures and lack of training are common factors that hinder wide application. To raise the application rate, TT can be technically improved on one hand, and users must also learn how to use it appropriately on the other. If employees in industrial companies or translation agencies have not already received TT training in school, they must receive in-service or on-the-job training. After they learn the genuine benefits of using TT, professional translators would cease to resist it. However, many companies in Taiwan would not invest in costly training, and therefore they cannot employ qualified TT experts for their work. The localization industry is shrinking in Taiwan, and the number of localization companies (less than 10) is fewer than in China (about 20) and European countries.

To boost Taiwan's localization industry, the government can offer some incentives such as tax reduction, favorable loan interest rates and others. Also, the government can intervene to set up an official committee for the localization industry so translation professionals can have a venue for exchanging their TT experiences and relevant information. Currently, localization companies in

Taiwan maintain a competitive relationship without any interactions or dialogue, not to mention cooperation. Domestic competition only makes their business decline. The government should do something to help the local translation industry convert to international scale, and the promotion of their business status would compel them to notice TT application. I would contend that if more of Taiwan's localization businesses, upon the request of international clients, have to create product instruction in multiple languages, the use of MT and TM tools would gain increasing attention, and more professional translators would apply TT tools to their daily work.

In fact, MT and TM tools are not a panacea, but their use can help to cope with an increasing quantity of translations. The economic profits of TT application are doubtless acknowledged. Perkins Engines has 'saved around 40000 pounds on each diesel engine manual translation using the Weidner system to translate technical documentation' (Hatim and Munday 2004: 216), and as of 1990, Mètèo 'was regularly translating around 45,000 words of weather bulletins every day' (Ibid.). Use of MT/TM systems is really a cost-effective gateway to the professional world of localization. Insofar as technological trend has swept through the international translation market, I think Taiwan's local professional translators, even without the help of the government, must find a way to integrate TT into their workflow to enhance their future competitive edge under the mantle of globalization.

At a conference organized by Taiwan's National Academy for Educational Research, Lin (2012) presented a report entitled 'A Study of Translation Development Strategies in Taiwan' and spoke of the development of diverse bilingual corpuses as one of the important and practical strategies for boosting Taiwan's translation industry. This proposal in the governmental blueprint for Taiwan's future translation industry shows upper management's increasing attention to the importance of TT application. It is expected that translation practitioners and professionals can benefit from corpus use to enhance their service quality and strengthen their image of professionalization. Lin's proposal concurs with Chen's (2012) finding in his lecture on '2012 Taiwan Translation and Interpretation Industry Survey Report' when he claimed that more than 80% of Taiwan's respondents in his survey expected Taiwan's government to provide them with diverse bilingual corpora for free use. This case suggests that since no specialized English to/from Chinese bilingual corpora are released on the local market, professional translators only seek help and support from the government. Governmental intervention is also expected to help solve the problem of textual copyrights when huge noncommercial corpora are developed for public use.

Actually, no approaches or options, however sophisticated, can provide a once-for-all solution to all problems arising from the shortage of TT professionals and TT-relevant teaching and research in Taiwan. Remodeling and modification are confronting and challenging translators, instructors and scholars. According to Abaitua (2002), the information technology and localization industries are evolving rapidly, and translators need to evolve with them. Bostad claimed that 'if you could not beat [translation technologies], join them', and 'if you cannot strike [translation technologies], connect them' (qtd. in Budiansky 1998: 84). Thus, a greater concern for and more dedication to TT application and development is urgently required in Taiwan.

Notes

1 European countries, the United States and Canada are far ahead of Taiwan in developing MT and TM systems and integrating them into the real translation work setting for time and cost benefits. A litany of MT success stories include the TAUM METEO system in the Canadian Weather Service, Systran in France, the US Air Force and Xerox in America and Logos by Lexi-tech in France and others (O'Hagan 1996; qtd. in Shih 2002).

2 "WTCC (World Translation Company of Canada) released the results of the English–French Systran II's application in 1980, [claiming] that the HT cost for 100 words was US\$ 16.50, but the MT cost for the

same 100 words was US$ 8.56" (Chen and Li 1991; qtd. in Shih 2002: 214). Systran Institute Gmbh's estimate maintained that 'the HT cost of 100 words was US$9.53 whereas the MT cost of the same 100 words was US$3.39' (Chen and Li 1991; qtd. in Shih 2002: 214). As Lynn E. Webb (1998–1999: 32 and 35) put it, 'company savings after using TM tools' were $3,360 for 'the translation of 40,000 words' and 'translation agency savings' were '$3,503 to $5,215' for the same amount of words.

3 Behavior Tran, not commercially released on Taiwan's market, has been used by BDC in translating computer manuals, user guidelines and books or articles on electrical engineering, mechanical engineering, aviation and psychology (Zhang and Chen 2001; qtd. in Shih 2002: 49).

4 Dr Eye was sold at prices ranging from NT$399 to NT$ 900 and thereby caused a big sale, roughly one unit for every 100 Taiwan residents around 1997–1998. The price of TransWhiz was higher: NT$2990 without TM and NT$78000 with TM embedded in the MT system (Shih 2002).

5 Trados users take up more than 70% of companies worldwide according to LISA's report (2002–2004).

6 Among various forms of survey, a survey of curriculum design online is the easiest method, but it is hard to identify some courses in which TT training is only a part of the content and is not shown as the course title suggests. Thus, the course whose title does not give any clue is deemed to only use the HT method without MT or TM teaching.

7 Before 2000, there are only two MA programs in translation and interpretation offered by universities such as Fu-Jen Catholic University and Taiwan Normal University. After 2000, five MA programs in T&I are offered by universities such as Taiwan University, Kaohsiung First University of Science and Technology, National Changhua University of Education, Chang Jung Christian University and Wenzao Ursuline College of Languages. MA programs in applied foreign language and literature have also dramatically increased in Taiwan since 2000.

8 It needs to be clarified that if translation achieves the goal of aesthetic appreciation, it serves as art. In contrast, if great amounts of translation need to be processed for information communication, it can be viewed as science, and the use of technological tools would shorten the turnaround time of translation and boost its productivity. Other benefits include terminological consistency and no need to translate similar or identical sentences again.

Bibliography

Abaitua, Joseba (2002) 'Is It Worth Learning Translation Technology?', in *Proceedings of the 3rd Forum on Translation in Vic. Training Translators and Interpreter: New Directions for the Millennium*. Available at: http://sivio.deustro.es/abaitua/konzeptu/ta/vic.htm.

Behavior Design Corporation, Centre for Translation and Publication 致遠科技股份有限公司翻譯出版中心 (tr.) (1993) 《機器翻譯：過去、現在、未來》 (*Machine Translation: The Past, Present and Future*), Hsinchu: Behavior Design Corporation.

Budiansky, Stephen (1998) 'Lost in Translation', *The Atlantic Monthly* 282(6): 80–84.

Chen, Han-Bin (2009) 'Learning Bilingual Linguistic Reordering Model for Statistical Machine Translation', Unpublished Master's thesis, Department of Computer Science, National Tsing Hua University, Taiwan.

Chen, Pin-chi (2006) 'A Study of the Fuzzy Match Function in CAT Software Used in Technical Translation in Taiwan', Unpublished Master's thesis, Department of Applied Foreign Language, National Taiwan University of Science and Technologies, Taiwan.

Chen, Tze-Wei (2012) '〈2012臺灣翻譯產業調查分析〉(2012 Taiwan Translation and Interpretation Industry Survey Report)', Paper presented at *2012 International Conference on Translation and Interpretation: Quality Enhancement and Professionalization (2012臺灣翻譯研討會-翻譯專業發展與品質提升)*, 23 November 2012, Development Centre for Compilation and Translation, National Academy for Educational Research.

Chen, Zi'ang 陳子昂 and Li Weiquan 黎偉權 (1991) '〈機器翻譯系統現況與展望〉(Current Status and Prospects of Machine Translation Systems)', 《CIO資訊傳真周刊》 (*CW Infopro Weekly*) 143: 166–74.

Hara, Hiroyuki (2001) 'The Difference within the Sameness: A Comparative Study of MT Translatability across Medical Genres', Unpublished Master's thesis, Graduate Institute of Translation and Interpreting, National Kaohisung First University of Science and Technology, Taiwan.

Hatim, Basil and Jeremy Munday (2004) *Translation: An Advanced Resource Book*, London and New York: Routledge.

Hsieh, Hung-Chen 謝紅貞 (2008) '〈電腦輔助翻譯軟體之翻譯記憶及匹配功能應用在西班牙文與中文新聞翻譯之可能性〉 (The Possibility of Using Translation Memory and Alignment as Computer-assisted Translation Tools for Spanish and Chinese News Text Translation)', Unpublished Master's thesis, Department of Spanish Language and Literature, Providence University, Taiwan.

Hutchins, W. John (1986) *Machine Translation: The Past, Present and Future*, West Sussex: Ellis Horwood Limited.

Lee, Jason 李家璿 (2009) '〈全自動機器翻譯加後編輯與人工翻譯之比較〉 (A Comparative Study of Fully Automatic Machine Translation with Post-editing and Human Translation)', Unpublished Master's thesis, Graduate Institute of Interpreting and Translation, National Taiwan Normal University, Taiwan.

Lin, Ching-Lung 林慶隆 (2012) '〈臺灣翻譯發展策略之探討〉 (A Study of Translation Development Strategies in Taiwan)', in *Proceedings of 2012 International Conference on Translation and Interpretation: Quality Enhancement and Professionalization*, Development Centre for Compilation and Translation, National Academy for Educational Research, Taipei, Taiwan, 1–21.

Lin, Chuan-Jie 林川傑 (1997) '〈國語-閩南語機器翻譯系統之研究〉 (The Study of a Mandarin-Taiwanese Machine Translation System)', Unpublished Master's thesis, Department of Computer Science and Information Engineering, National Taiwan University, Taiwan.

Liu, Sheng-Liang 劉聖良 (1996) '〈機器翻譯中多字動詞問題之研究〉 (A Study on the Problems of Multi-word Verbs in Machine Translation)', Unpublished Master's thesis, Department of Computer Science and Information Engineering, National Taiwan University, Taiwan.

O'Hagan, Minako (1996) *The Coming Industry of Teletranslation: Overcoming Communication Barriers Through Telecommunication*, Bristol: Multilingual Matters Ltd.

Shih, Chung-ling (2002) *Theory and Application of MT/MAHT Pedagogy*, Taipei: Crane Publishing Co., Ltd.

Shih, Chung-ling 史宗玲 (2004) 〈電腦輔助翻譯: *MT & TM*〉 *Computer-aided Translation MT and TM*, Taipei: Bookman Books Ltd.

Shih, Chung-ling (2006) *Helpful Assistance to Translators: MT and TM*, Taipei: Bookman Books Ltd.

Shih, Chung-ling 史宗玲 (2011) 《機器翻譯即時通：臺灣籤詩嘛ㄟ通》 (*Real-time Communication Through Machine-enabled Translation: Taiwan's Oracle Poetry*), Taipei: Bookman Books Ltd.

Shih, Chung-ling 史宗玲 (2013) 《網頁書寫新文體：跨界交流「快譯通」》 (*New Web Textual Writing: Fast Communication across Borders*), Taichung: White Elephant Ltd., Company.

Shih, Wei-Ming 施偉銘 (2007) '〈台灣地區筆譯工作者運用翻譯工具之現況〉 (Translation Tools: A Survey of Their Adoption by Taiwan-based Translators)', Unpublished Master's thesis, The Graduate Institute of Translation and Interpretation in National Taiwan Normal University, Taiwan.

Torrejón, Enrique and Celia Rico (2002) 'Controlled Translation: A New Teaching Scenario Tailor-made for the Translation Industry', in *Proceedings of the 6th EAMT Workshop – Teaching Machine Translation*, Centre for Computational Linguistics, UMIST, Manchester, the United Kingdom, 107–16.

Webb, Lynn E. (1998–1999) 'Advantages and Disadvantages of Translation Memory: A Cost/Benefit Analysis', Unpublished thesis, German Graduate Division of Monterey Institute of International Studies.

Yu, Jian-Heng 余鍵亨 (2005) '〈機器翻譯系統為本之雙語網頁對應〉 (Automatic Alignment of Bilingual Web Pages Using Machine Translation Systems)', Unpublished Master's thesis, Department of Computer Science, National Tsing Hua University, Taiwan.

Zhang, Jingxin 張景新 and Chen Shujuan 陳淑娟 (2001) '〈機器翻譯的最新發展趨勢〉 (The Latest Trend in Machine Translation)'. Available at: http://nlp.csie.ncnu.edu.tw/~shin/bdc/doc/INTRO.201.

23

TRANSLATION TECHNOLOGY IN THE NETHERLANDS AND BELGIUM

Leonoor van der Beek and Antal van den Bosch

Introduction

The Netherlands and Belgium share a history in translation technology research and an interest in Dutch, the language spoken by most of the inhabitants of the Netherlands and by about 60% of Belgium's population, mostly concentrated in the Dutch-speaking region of Flanders. Translation technology research and development came, went, and came back again in a span of three decades. Early Dutch and Belgian computational linguistics research was boosted significantly by roles that researchers and teams took in national and international knowledge-based machine translation system development programmes in the 1980s. Industrial spin-offs were created, remainders of which can still be found in present-day industrial translation technology providers. Currently, research follows the typical trends in translation technologies: statistical machine translation and hybridizations with linguistic knowledge and business-oriented translation process automation.

In this overview we begin with a historical listing of the most visible machine translation projects in the two countries: the international projects Eurotra and METAL and the Dutch industrial projects DLT and Rosetta. We then sketch the current state of affairs in academic research in the Netherlands and Belgium. Much of the current work focuses on statistical machine translation systems and translating between closely related languages such as Frisian and Afrikaans, but there is also work on building translation memories from monolingual corpora and bilingual lexica and usability of translation tools such as post-editing software. We look at industry and observe that most current industrial activity is located in Belgium, offering translation, terminology, and localization services.

We end our overview with a note on the position of the Dutch language in present-day translation technologies. It occurs as a language in about 15% of currently commercially available machine translation systems listed in the EAMT software compendium. Being one of the official languages of the European Union, there are a considerable amount of public parallel data available. With several research teams working on machine translation and with a host of active SMEs, translation technology for Dutch is in good shape given its approximate 23 million speakers and its ranking in the low top 30 of numbers of native speakers of languages worldwide.

DOI: 10.4324/9781003168348-25

Early Days

Dutch and Belgian academics were not among the global pioneers in translation technology. Mathematics professor Adriaan van Wijngaarden did advocate a collaboration between mathematicians and linguists in order to jointly develop automated translation systems as early as 1952, just months after the very first workshop on machine translation at the Massachusetts Institute of Technology, organized by Yehoshua Bar-Hillel. "'Cinderella Calculation" should try to charm "Prince Linguistics" to establish this new field', he claimed (Wijngaarden 1952), but his words fell on barren ground.

The required computing power was not available: there was not one working computer in the Netherlands. The first Dutch computer, the ARRA I, had been demoed a couple of months earlier but had never been able to do another calculation since. At the same time the field of linguistics was dominated by structuralism. Formal linguistics was banned from the linguistic departments, publications, and conferences. On top of that, Van Wijngaarden's PhD student Hugo Brandt Corstius, who by many is considered the founder of computational linguistics in the Netherlands and to whom the professor had given the responsibility to investigate the feasibility of machine translation, developed into a profound and well-spoken opponent. Brandt Corstius did develop a procedure for automated translation of numbers in the 1960s, but he shared Bar-Hillel's opinion that in order to perform high-quality open domain machine translation, extensive encyclopaedic knowledge was required (Battus 1973; Brandt Corstius 1978) – a problem which he did not believe could be solved any time soon. Meanwhile in Leuven, Flanders, professor Flip Droste had also reached the conclusion that fully automated high-quality machine translation was not feasible in the near future (1969). These fundamental issues added to the argument that there was no economic ground for machine translation, as formulated in the American ALPAC report (ALPAC 1966).

The adverse conditions and negative opinions meant that very little happened in the field of machine translation in the Netherlands and Belgium until the 1980s. Between 1963 and 1965, another Amsterdam-based mathematician, Evert Willem Beth, secured some of the Euratom funds for machine translation research, but this was mostly spent on allowing linguists to develop their interest in formal linguistics (van der Beek 2001: 1–60). In 1980 the sentiment towards MT changed. Professor Bondi Sciarone of Delft Technical University was asked to represent the Netherlands in the European MT project Eurotra, and after some investigation, he stated in his inaugural lecture that the conditions that led to the pessimistic view of the ALPAC report no longer applied to the then-current situation in Europe and that the time was ripe for a large-scale investigation of machine translation (Sciarone 1980): computing power was increasing rapidly, and while the cost of human labour was increasing, the cost of computing was going down. In the same period the European Union recognized an increase in the need for translation technology. With Eurotra the Netherlands and Belgium saw their first large-scale MT project.

Eurotra

Three groups represented the Dutch language within the Eurotra consortium: the Belgian group in the Flemish city of Leuven, and Dutch groups in Delft and Utrecht. The University of Leuven was the first to get involved: computational linguist Dirk Geens already participated in the steering group that prepared the official start of the Eurotra project in the late 70s. In 1980, Bondi Sciarone became the first representative of the Netherlands, soon followed by Steven Krauwer and Louis des Tombe from the University of Utrecht. The Flemish and the Dutch divided the money and the workload in a ratio of 2:1 (two thirds for The Netherlands, one third for Flanders). As Flanders was the first to join, they had the first pick of the foreign languages to work with. They chose English and German, leaving the teams from the Netherlands with French, Danish, Spanish, Portuguese, Greek, and Italian.

The real impact of the Dutch teams on the Eurotra project, however, was not in the language-specific work packages but in the thematic central committees. Geens and his students Frank Van Eynde and Lieven Jaspaerts, as well as Krauwer and Des Tombe, gained positions in various central teams, which had their own funding. Sciarone, on the other hand mostly, worked on language-specific study contracts. By 1984 most countries had signed their official participation contracts with Eurotra, and the first wave of language-specific contracts stopped. It took the Netherlands until 1986 before they secured their contracts, but Sciarone, not eligible for additional funding from central committees, had no budget for Eurotra work anymore and decided to withdraw from the project, leaving it to the larger group in Utrecht to complete the Dutch work.

As members of the Eurotra committee for linguistic specifications, Des Tombe and Jaspaerts advocated a more solid linguistic base. They argued that more linguistic research was required and an agreed-upon, well-founded linguistic basis was needed before any implementation could be done. Krauwer meanwhile pled for more solid system specifications. Both Krauwer and Des Tombes were strong advocates of the <<C,A>,T> or CAT framework (Debille 1986). This system was Eurotra's response to the rise of unification-based grammars. Eurotra had originally been based on transformational grammar, which at the start of the project was considered a novel and state-of-the-art approach. However, during the programme, unification-based grammars such as generalized phrase structure grammar (GPSG), head-driven phrase structure grammar (HPSG), and lexical-functional grammar (LFG) gained ground and proved well suited for computational implementations. Rather than adopting one of these frameworks, the committee for linguistic specifications created a new one, which incorporated some of the insights from unification-based grammars. The group in Utrecht actively collaborated with researchers in Essex on this topic and even built a working pilot system. It was called MiMo, as Eurotra leader Serge Perschke had derogatively called it a 'Micky Mouse system'. Neither the system nor the ideas behind it were implemented in the larger Eurotra project, but the group was quietly allowed to continue its development. This eventually led to MiMo II, a working translation system for a subset of Dutch, English, and Spanish – although the final system was completely unification based and had very little to do with the original Eurotra design (Noord *et al.* 1990).

Just like the Dutch-speaking region of Belgium – Flanders – contributed to the development of the Dutch components of Eurotra, the French speaking region – Wallonia – contributed to the French components: the University of Liège was contracted to work on the monolingual French components, totalling 8% of the French work. The bilingual components were covered by the groups in Paris (southern languages) and Nancy (northern languages). The main focus of the group in Liège, headed by professor Jacques Noël, was in fact on computational lexicography and terminology. Noël, a professor of English linguistics, had access to a digital version of the *Longman Dictionary of Contemporary English* since the mid-1970s, from which the group developed a more general interest in the reusability of resources for MT. The team did not gain much influence in the Eurotra organization, and their most important proposal for the integration of terminology in the Eurotra framework was never accepted.

The Eurotra project was unprecedented in its scale and funding. The impact of this enormous project on MT in Belgium and the Netherlands differs per group. For French, there was an official Eurotra demo. For Dutch, the best demo was the unofficial MiMo system. Yet the Dutch groups both in Leuven and Utrecht benefitted greatly from the project, as they were able to acquire hardware for future research and set up programmes for teaching MT (and, more broadly, computational linguistics) to a new generation of researchers. Perhaps most importantly, the project helped them establish strong ties with other MT researchers in Europe. This network had a long-lasting effect on MT and NLP research in Flanders and the Netherlands. Liège, on the other hand, never fully integrated in the project, and did not benefit from it in the same way.

METAL

In Leuven, Flanders, a second group was working on MT in the second half of the 1980s: Herman Caeyers set up a team for the French–Dutch and Dutch–French translation pairs of the American–German METAL project. METAL originated in Austin, Texas, and was based on the work of Jonathan Slocum and Winfield Bennett (Bennett and Slocum 1985: 111–21). The METAL research at the University of Austin was heavily sponsored by Siemens, the German company, and focused on translation between English and German. Siemens wanted to move all research and development to München, but when the Belgium government made a big deal with Siemens, they required Siemens to invest in research and development in Belgium. Hence the one type of research which could not easily be done in Germany moved to Belgium: dictionary development (Mons) and grammar writing (Leuven) for machine translation between Dutch and French.

In contrast to Eurotra, which focused on full translation, METAL aimed at translation support tools. It did not have the ambition to cover complex infrequent linguistic structures. Rather, it focused on building a working prototype that would cover as many as possible of the most common and frequent constructions. The group in Leuven, which included computational linguists Rudi Gebruers and Geert Adriaens, made important contributions to the base system, which had not been designed with Romance languages like French in mind. Caeyers reports apologies from the US development team for having assumed that every 'foreign' language had a case system (van der Beek 2011). Among other things, the group built a valence system that recognized the syntactic role of phrases without relying on case marking. Building on their expertise, Adriaens was able to secure European funding later on in 1995 with the Simplified English Grammar Checker and Corrector (SECC) project, in which a grammar front-end for MT was built.

Eventually, Siemens sold the rights to METAL to GSM for the C++ version for the consumer market and the Lisp version of the English–Dutch and French–Dutch translation pairs to Caeyer's company Lant, which later merged into Xplanation, which still runs a translation support tool including the original METAL product.

DLT

Besides two international projects in which the Dutch and Flemish participated, there were also two Dutch MT projects: Distributed Language Translation (DLT) and Rosetta. DLT was an industrial project that ran at the Dutch company Buro voor Systeem Ontwikkeling (BSO) – System Development Office from 1980 until 1990. In contrast to Eurotra and METAL, DLT was not transfer based but instead worked with a remarkable interlingua: Esperanto. The project was initiated by Toon Witkam, an aeronaut by training who worked on automation projects for BSO before dedicating himself to DLT.

The main argument for using an interlingua is well known: it reduces the number of translation pairs drastically. This comes at the cost of having to specify in the interlingua every distinction made in any of the languages translated to or from. The arguments for using Esperanto as interlingua, according to Witkam, were that Esperanto could be encoded compactly due to its regularity, that its degree of lexical ambiguity is supposed to be a lot lower than in other languages, and that it is a fully understandable and accessible language independent of any other language (van der Beek 2011).

The efficient encoding was important because of the envisaged application: in contrast to Eurotra, which focused on batch processing of documents, resulting in acceptable (though imperfect) translations which would then be post-edited, DLT aimed at an interactive translation system, which required the translator to disambiguate any ambiguities in the input. The disambiguated representation in the interlingua would then be distributed to work stations, where translation into the target language were to take place. The output would be clean translations that would not require post-editing.

DLT started out as a personal project of Toon Witkam. He presented the outline of his plan to the heads of the company in 1980, but even though the reactions were 'very positive' according to Witkam, no budget was allotted. An application for Dutch funding was also refused. Witkam then recruited an intern and reduced his paid work week to four days in order to work on his plan. In 1982 he turned lucky: the European Union sponsored an investigation into the feasibility of his plan with 250,000 Dutch guilders. The final report of this feasibility study was well received and lead to substantial follow-up funding of 8 million guilders from the Dutch Ministry of Economic Affairs and 8 million guilders from BSO in 1984.

Witkam proceeded to appoint Esperanto specialists Klaus Schubert, who focused on syntax, and Victor Sadler, who focused on semantics. A supervisory board of three was appointed, referred to as ABK, after the last names of the members: Bernhard Al (Van Dale lexicography), Harry Bunt (professor of computational linguistics at Tilburg University), and Gerard Kempen (professor of psycholinguistics at the University of Nijmegen). DLT adopted the dependency grammar of Tesnière as the syntactic framework. The system was originally designed to be knowledge based, with dependency grammars for source and target languages, and an enriched version of Esperanto in the middle, which would allow for an unambiguous representation of the input.

In order to disambiguate the source language input, external knowledge sources such as taxonomies were used. However, after the COLING conference of 1988, where Witkam was first introduced to statistical machine translation (Brown *et al.* 1988: 71–76), the design of DLT changed significantly. The team switched from a knowledge-based system to a corpus-based design, where disambiguation was achieved through bilingual knowledge banks (BKBs). Although DLT continued to use Esperanto as interlingua in order to reduce the number of BKBs necessary, it was no longer considered a key element (Witkam 2006). A second important development in the project was the switch of focus from general, informative texts to simplified English as was used in maintenance manuals and technical documentation of the (now-defunct) Dutch aerospace company Fokker.

Although there were some superficial contacts between DLT and other MT projects in the Netherlands and Flanders, the project was generally met with scepticism by peers. This was mainly caused by two factors: the choice for Esperanto as an interlingua, which was considered eccentric, and the bold claims made in the press. In 1990, when the project was running out of funds, BSO launched a media campaign in order to find new external investors for the project. 'Computer speaks every language' it said in one newspaper, and 'Computer translates any language in any language' in another.

Witkam estimated at the end of the project that it would require a tenfold of the earlier funds to build the actual translation product. BSO could not or was not willing to supply those funds, and new investors were never found. At the end of the project, in 1990, the results of the programme were a demo from 1987 (from before the introduction of the corpus-based approach) and an estimated 1,800 pages of documentation, mostly in a series of books published by Foris Publications (Dordrecht, The Netherlands).

Rosetta

Rosetta was a machine translation project that ran throughout the eighties at Natlab, a research institute at the Technical University of Eindhoven and a subsidiary of Philips. The design of the system was due to Jan Landsbergen, who had previously worked on the question answering system PHLIQA. He had come up with a new grammar formalism for PHLIQA which was called M-grammar. PHLIQA was discontinued before he could implement it, but Landsbergen already envisaged another application of M-grammar: machine translation.

M-grammar is based on Montague grammar (1973: 221–42), a generative grammar that regards all sentences as compositionally built from basic expressions of intentional formal logic. Landsbergen applied a number of changes to this basic setup to avoid overgeneration and to allow for the reverse process, parsing, in addition to generation. M-grammar generally allows for transformations in addition to the concatenations of traditional Montague grammar. These transformations were crucially reversible: fit both for parsing and for generation. The powerful rules with transformations would overgenerate, but Landsbergen prevented this by applying them to constituent structures instead of unstructured sentences – an extension already suggested by Barbara Partee (1976: 51–76). A context-free grammar was written to provide the constituent structures to which M-grammar was applied.

The key idea behind Rosetta is that for each language, an M-grammar is developed that can parse (in conjunction with the context-free grammar) a sentence in the source language and output some expression in intentional logic that captures the semantics of it but that can also generate a sentence (or multiple sentences) in the target language from the expression in intentional logic. It is crucial that the M-grammars be isomorphic: for each lexical entry, phrase, or rule in one language, there is a corresponding entry, phrase, or rule in all of the other languages. A successful parse then guarantees a successful translation. This setup means that most work for developing the system is in developing the M-grammars for all languages. It also means that although the logical expressions can be viewed as an interlingua, the system is not a pure interlingual system, as it is not possible to develop the modules for each language independently of the other languages.

Landsbergen proposed his ideas for a machine translation system to the Philips management in 1979 and got approval to spend one year on the project, together with engineer Joep Rous. One year later they were able to demo a pilot system for Dutch, English, and Italian: Rosetta I, named after the Rosetta stone. The demo was received with enthusiasm. Although Natlab was not willing to employ any linguists, Landsbergen did manage to get some extra hands on board through his contacts with the Eurotra group in Utrecht: Natlab was willing to pay the University of Utrecht to employ linguists to work at Natlab. An elaborate project proposal was put together for funding from the Dutch Ministry of Economic Affairs. The proposal talked of a collaboration between Natlab, the University of Utrecht, and Bondi Sciarone's group in Delft. Each group would contribute five participants. Utrecht would focus on grammar writing, Delft on lexicon development. However, the subsidy was granted to DLT instead of Rosetta. Philips then decided to step in and fund the project, although not quite to the full extent of the proposal and on the condition that all work was to take place at Natlab. Due to those two constraints, Delft stepped out, and Natlab and Utrecht continued together. Italian was replaced by Spanish as a target language.

The original plan was to develop Rosetta II, a version with greatly extended lexicons and grammars and a much larger coverage. The experience accumulated during the development and testing of this version would then lead to a third version, in which fundamental changes could be applied to the framework and formalism. Yet lexicon extension was delayed as a result of Delft leaving the consortium and the lack of consistent electronic databases of lexical information.

The team could make use of the tapes of leading dictionary publisher Van Dale, but they turned out to contain large numbers of inconsistencies. It also took more time than anticipated to develop the supporting software needed for an efficient large-scale system. In the meantime the linguists developed ideas to treat more complex constructions. The planning was adapted, and instead of generating grammar rules and dictionaries, the team developed a new version of the system, Rosetta III, which was more advanced but also more complex. A new type of transformation was introduced that did not change the semantics of a phrase and that did not need to have a counterpart in other languages. This transformation allowed for the treatment of many new and more complex syntactic phenomena. As a result, Rosetta is famous for being able to correctly translate complex sentences with the notoriously complex Dutch pronoun *er*, but it was unable to handle most sentences of newspaper text or a corpus of hotel reservations.

The project was funded until 1991, but as early as 1987 Philips started pressing for concrete applications. Although various options were researched – from integration in electronic type-writers to Philips' interactive CD (CD-i) – no well-suited application was found. The most vexing bottleneck remained the high costs associated with the development of large-scale dictionaries. When the project ended, it was not renewed. Rosetta IV, the version that would have been made for a specific application, was never built. No working version of the software remains, but the project did result in a number of PhD theses and the publication of compositional translation (Rosetta 1994), in which Rosetta is explained in detail.

Statistical and Hybrid Machine Translation Research

When IBM presented its corpus-based MT methods in the late 1980s, the Dutch MT community's reactions were sceptical. Steven Krauwer refused to report on IBM's Peter Brown's session at the TMI conference in 1989, because he thought the proposal ridiculous. DLT did embrace the new approach, but the project came to an end in 1990, before the statistical MT (SMT) revolution really took off. When the large knowledge-based projects also ended in the early 90s, they were not replaced by SMT projects. Instead, MT research in the Netherlands fell silent, while in Belgium it reduced to a trickle. The one Dutch MT project in the 90s was still knowledge based. In Nijmegen, Albert Stoop built a system based on professor Jan van Bakel's AMAZON-parser. The name of his thesis, completed in 1995, illustrates the predominant sentiment regarding MT in the Netherlands in the 1990s: 'TRANSIT: A Linguistically Motivated MT System'.

The turn to SMT was only made ten years later, when a next generation of computational linguists got public funding for research proposals in MT. Partly encouraged by the success of the open source SMT software package Moses (Koehn *et al.* 2007: 177–80) and the increasing availability of parallel corpora, Dutch researchers developed their own brands of SMT systems. In Amsterdam, research projects headed by Khalil Sima'an, Rens Bod, and Christof Monz followed the probabilistic trail. A common thread in the works of Sima'an and Bod is the inclusion of linguistically motivated features, such as tree structure (Bod 2007: 51–57; Mylonakis and Sima'an 2011: 642–52). Monz has been an active co-organizer of the Workshop on Statistical Machine Translation (WMT) series.[1] With his colleagues he has also been active in the IWSLT shared task (Martzoukos and Monz 2010: 205–08; Yahyaei and Monz 2010: 157–62), a joint and open benchmarking effort that has pushed international MT research forward and lowered the bar of entering the field of MT research, together with the advent of more public parallel corpora, open source machine translation tools, and ever-faster computers equipped with ever more memory.

The increased availability of parallel corpora can to some extent be attributed personally to Jörg Tiedemann, who, in co-operation with Lars Nygaard, initiated the Opus Corpus.[2]

Tiedemann expanded the corpus while working at the University of Groningen, the Netherlands, in the second half of the 2000s. The Opus Corpus gathers publicly and freely available parallel corpora such as the proceedings of the European Parliament and documents of the European Medicines Agency (EMEA) and offers automated preprocessing and alignment at the sentence level (Tiedemann 2012: 2214–18). While in Groningen, Tiedemann also published on transliteration and translation of closely related languages (2009: 12–19).

In the same period, a group of researchers at Tilburg University developed memory-based machine translation (MBMT) (van den Bosch and Berck 2009: 17–26; Canisius and van den Bosch 2009: 182–89; Van Gompel *et al.* 2009: 17–26). MBMT is a hybrid of SMT with example-based machine translation (EBMT), a data-driven approach that predates SMT (Nagao 1984: 173–80; Carl and Way 2003). The Tilburg group furthermore adopted SMT for paraphrasing by treating paraphrasing as monolingual translation and using aligned headlines of articles covering the same news story as parallel data (Wubben *et al.* 2011: 27–33; Wubben *et al.* 2012: 1015–24). Both the Tilburg group leader van den Bosch and Amsterdam's Sima'an became active as international collaborators of the Irish Centre for Next-Generation Localization (CNGL),[3] advising CNGL PhD students (Hassan *et al.* 2008; Haque *et al.* 2011: 239–85).

The computational linguistics research group in Leuven that had been active in the METAL and SCC projects on grammar, syntax, and resource development in the late 1990s returned to machine translation with the METIS (2001–2004) and METIS-II (2004–2007) EU projects.[4] The METIS projects were carried out with project coordinator ILSP in Athens, Greece, and project partners in Spain and Germany. METIS, full name Statistical Machine Translation Using Monolingual Corpora, was aimed at developing an SMT system without the typical but sometimes unrealistic starting condition of having a (large) parallel corpus. The METIS method involves the search for text subsequences (syntactic chunks, word n-grams) in monolingual corpora; the statistical alignment of these subsequences using bilingual lexica; and the use of these alignments in example-based MT, SMT, or directly as translation memory in TM systems (Dirix *et al.* 2005: 43–50). The Leuven group focused on hybridizing the statistical alignment of subsequences with linguistic knowledge, such as automatically computed part-of-speech tags. When computed on both sides of a language pair, part-of-speech tags are helpful in translating ambiguous high-frequency words such as the Dutch word *zijn*, which as a verb translates to *to be*, while as a pronoun, it translates to *his*.

In Belgium, MT also found a place in academia outside Leuven in the new LT[3] (Language Translation and Technology Team) at the University College Ghent. Besides NLP and text analytics, the group's expertise relevant for translation technologies is in terminology, usability of translation tools such as post-editing software, and machine translation. The group organized a shared task on cross-lingual word sense disambiguation at the SemEval 2010 workshop (Lefever and Hoste 2010: 15–20), raising the intriguing suggestion that word sense disambiguation, when seen as a subtask of translation, is more grounded than in the case when monolingual sense distinctions come from a lexical semantic resource (Lefever *et al.* 2011: 311–22). Another focus of the group is business-oriented multilingual terminology extraction; it attracted public funding for the 2011–2012 project TExSIS (Terminology Extraction for Semantic Interoperability and Standardization).

Recent and Current Translation Technology Industry

There has been relatively little activity in Dutch translation technology industry since the high-ambition projects that wound down in the 1990s. In the *Compendium of Translation Software: Directory of Commercial Machine Translation Systems and Computer-Aided Translation Support Tools*,[5] an updated reference guide to software compiled by W. John Hutchins and Declan Groves, two

Dutch translation technology companies are listed: Syn-Tactic, a spin-off of the Dutch printing and copying hardware company Océ, specializing in localization of software and translation of technical manuals, and Lingvistica, now an OEM for products of LEC (Language Engineering Company LLC). A third company, Linguistic Systems BV, has been developing a multilingual thesaurus initially called PolyGlot, now called EuroGlot. Founded in 1985, the Nijmegen-based company chose to build a multilingual thesaurus from scratch and re-implemented this over time to keep up with standard requirements. EuroGlot is concept based; when the user selects one of the possible conceptual spaces of an ambiguous words, its concept-specific translations are shown. Domain-specific add-ons are available.

Belgium continues to host more translation technology industry than its northern neighbour country. The aforementioned Xplanation (which took over the METAL/Siemens spin-off Lant, later Lantmark and Lantworks) offers human translation services supported by Tstream, an suite of in-house developed tools for terminology extraction and resource management, translation memories, document processing formats, and tools. The original METAL LISP software, ported to Linux, now part of Tstream, still receives occasional dictionary updates but continues to use the same grammars. Occasionally the company employs SMT software to train MT systems on customer-specific translation memories.

Lernout and Hauspie, the former Flemish language and speech technology company, also developed activities in translation technology in the late 1990s, mostly through its acquisition of the GlobaLink company and its GTS MT system, which was renamed to Power Translator, a software package that still exists and is now a product of LEC. Lernout and Hauspie's acquisition of the translation bureau Mendez led to the development of a hybrid translation division that turned out quite successful. An online free 'gist-quality' MT service gave the user the option to have the output post-edited by professional human translations for a fee (Sayer 2000).

LandC (Language and Computing) was another Belgian company offering translation services in the medical domain; LandC is now part of Nuance. The current Ghent-based company CrossLang, formerly Cross Language, specializes in optimizing business translation processes, employing both existing technology and developing custom SMT systems. Notably, they coordinate the Bologna Translation Services project (2011–2013), which specializes in translation services in higher education. A second currently active Ghent company is Yamagata, offering QA Distiller, an automatic tool for the detection and correction of errors and inconsistencies in translations and TMs. Together with the LT³ group, Ghent is the current capital of translation technology in the Low Countries.

Dutch in Current Translation Technology

Dutch is the first language of an estimated 23 million people worldwide. It is spoken by the majority of the population in the Netherlands and an estimated 60% of the populations of Belgium (mostly in the Flanders region) and Surinam. It is the eighth language in the European Union in terms of the number of speakers.[6] Dutch has been among the most frequently included languages in academic and industrial translation technology projects worldwide but has been losing ground due to the global rise of interest in growing-economy languages such as Chinese, (Brazilian) Portuguese, and Korean. In the EAMT software compendium, Dutch is listed as a source or target language in about 15% (66 out of 447) of the mentioned commercially available translation technology products. In MT systems Dutch is most frequently paired with its geographical and historical linguistic neighbours English (39 systems), French (26 systems), and German (12 systems). Other frequent pairings are with Spanish (11), Italian (9), Russian (9), and Chinese (9).

As one of the official European languages, Dutch is present in the larger public European parallel corpora such as those in the Opus Corpus or the JRC Acquis corpus[7] (Steinberger *et al.* 2006). This allows SMT systems to easily include Dutch paired with other official European languages. Recent academic work in Ghent, Leuven, and Tilburg has used Dutch as one of the languages. When the Tilburg translation group moved to Radboud University, Nijmegen, the Netherlands, in 2011 they developed and launched an online Dutch-Frisian SMT system called Oersetter.nl.[8] The West-Frisian variant of Frisian, another West-Germanic language that shares its origin with English and Dutch, is spoken mostly in the Dutch province of Friesland. A similar effort with a historically related language, Afrikaans, is the works by the CTEXT lab at Northwest University, Potchefstroom, South Africa, where rule-based methods for transliteration and word reordering are developed to directly convert Dutch to Afrikaans (Pilon and van Huyssteen 2009: 23–28).

Notes

1 www.statmt.org/wmt12
2 http://opus.lingfil.uu.se
3 www.cngl.ie
4 www.ilsp.gr/metis2
5 www.eamt.org/soft_comp.php – consulted in August 2012.
6 http://taalunieversum.org/taal/feiten_en_weetjes/#feitencijfers
7 http://langtech.jrc.it/JRC-Acquis.html
8 http://oersetter.nl

Bibliography

ALPAC (1966) 'Languages and Machines: Computers in Translation and Linguistics', *A Report by the Automatic Language Processing Advisory Committee, Division of Behavioral Sciences, National Academy of Sciences*, National Research Council, Washington, DC: National Academy of Sciences, National Research Council.

Battus (1973) *De vertaalmachine*, Holland Maandblad.

Bédard, Claude (1991) 'What Do Translators Want?', *Language Industry Monitor* 4: 1–3.

Beek, Leonoor van der (2001) 'Van Beth tot Van Benthem: de opkomst van de Nederlandse semantiek', *Tabu* 31(1–2): 1–60.

Beek, Leonoor van der (2011) 'Van Rekenmachine to Taalautomaat'. Available at: http://linqd.nl/book.html.

Bennett, Winfield S. and Jonathan Slocum (1985) 'The LRC Machine Translation System', *Computational Linguistics* 11(2–3): 111–21.

Bod, Rens (2007) 'Unsupervised Syntax-based Machine Translation: The Contribution of Discontiguous Phrase', in Bente Maegaard (ed.) *Proceedings of the Machine Translation Summit XI*, 10–14 September 2007, Copenhagen Business School, Copenhagen, Denmark, 51–57.

Brandt Corstius, Hugo (1978) *Computer-taalkunde*, Muiderberg: Dirk Coutinho.

Brown, Peter, John Cocke, Stephen A. Della Pietra, Vincent J. Della Pietra, Fredrick Jelinek, Robert L. Mercer, and Paul S. Roossin (1988) 'A Statistical Approach to Language Translation', in *Proceedings of the 12th Conference on Computational Linguistics*, Association for Computational Linguistics, Morristown, NJ, 1: 71–76.

Canisius, Sander and Antal van den Bosch (2009) 'A Constraint Satisfaction Approach to Machine Translation', in *Proceedings of the 13th Annual Conference of the European Association for Machine Translation (EAMT-2009)*, 14–15 May 2009, Barcelona, Spain, 182–89.

Carl, Michael and Andy Way (eds.) (2003) *Recent Advances in Example-based Machine Translation*, Dordrecht: Kluwer Academic Publishers.

Debille, L. (1986) *Het basismodel van het EUROTRA-vertaalsysteem*, Leuven: Automatische vertaling aan de K.U.

Dirix, Peter, Ineke Schuurman, and Vincent Vandeghinste (2005) 'Metis II: Example-based Machine Translation Using Monolingual Corpora – System Description', in *Proceedings of the Example-based Machine*

Translation Workshop Held in Conjunction with the 10th Machine Translation Summit, 16 September 2005, Phuket, Thailand, 43–50.

Droste, Flip G. (1969) *Vertalen met de computer; mogelijkheden en moeilijkheden*, Groningen: Wolters-Noordhoff.

Haque, Rejwanul, Sudip Kumar Naskar, Antal van den Bosch, and Andy Way (2011) 'Integrating Source-language Context into Phrase-based Statistical Machine Translation', *Machine Translation* 25(3): 239–85.

Hassan, Hany, Khalil Sima'an, and Andy Way (2008) 'Syntactically Lexicalized Phrase-based Statistical Translation', *IEEE Transactions on Audio, Speech and Language Processing* 16(7).

Koehn, Philipp, Hieu Hoang, Alexandre Birch, Chris Callison-Burch, Marcello Federico, Nicola Bertoldi, Brooke Cowan, Wade Shen, Christine Moran, Richard Zens, Chris Dyer, Ondřej Bojar, Alexandra Constantin, and Evan Herbst (2007) 'Moses: Open Source Toolkit for Statistical Machine Translation', in *Proceedings of the 45th Annual Meeting of the Association for Computational Linguistics Companion Volume: Proceedings of the Demo and Poster Sessions*, Association for Computational Linguistics, 25–27 June 2007, Prague, Czech Republic, 177–80.

Lefever, Els and Veronique Hoste (2010) 'Semeval-2010 Task 3: Cross-lingual Word Sense Disambiguation', in *Proceedings of the 5th International Workshop on Semantic Evaluation*, Association for Computational Linguistics, Uppsala, Sweden, 15–20.

Lefever, Els, Veronique Hoste, and Martine De Cock (2011) 'Parasense or How to Use Parallel Corpora for Word Sense Disambiguation', in *Proceedings of the 49th Annual Meeting of the Association for Computational Linguistics: Human Language Technologies*, Association for Computational Linguistics, Portland, OR, 317–22.

Martzoukos, Spyros and Christof Monz (2010) 'The UvA System Description for IWSLT 2010', in *Proceedings of the 7th International Workshop on Spoken Language Translation (IWSLT-2010)*, 2–3 December 2010, Paris, France, 205–08.

Montague, Richard (1973) 'The Proper Treatment of Quantification in Ordinary English', in Patrick Suppes, Julius Moravcsik, and Jaakko Hintikka (eds.) *Approaches to Natural Language*, Dordrecht: Springer Verlag, 221–42.

Mylonakis, Markos and Khalil Sima'an (2011) 'Learning Hierarchical Translation Structure with Linguistic Annotations', in *Proceedings of the 49th Annual Meeting of the Association for Computational Linguistics: Human Language Technologies*, Association for Computational Linguistics, 19–24 June 2011, Portland, OR, 642–52.

Nagao, Makoto (1984) 'A Framework of a Mechanical Translation between Japanese and English by Analogy Principle', in Alick Elithorn and Ranan Banerji (eds.) *Artificial and Human Intelligence*, Amsterdam: North-Holland Publishing Company, 173–80.

Noord, Geertjan van, Joke Dorrepaal, Pim van der Eijk, Maria Florenza, and Louis des Tombe (1990) 'The MiMo2 Research System', in *Proceedings of the 3rd International Conference on Theoretical and Methodological Issues in Machine Translation of Natural Languages*, Austin, TX, 213–33. Available at: www.let.rug.nl/~vannoord/papers.

Partee, Barbara H. (1976) 'Some Transformational Extensions of Montague Grammar', in Barbara H. Partee (ed.) *Montague Grammar*, New York: Academic Press, 51–76.

Pilon, Suléne and Gerhard B. van Huyssteen (2009) 'Rule-based Conversion of Closely-related Languages: A Dutch-to-Afrikaans Convertor', in *Proceedings of the 20th Annual Symposium of the Pattern Recognition Association of South Africa (PRASA)*, 30 November–1 December 2009, Stellenbosch, South Africa, 23–28.

Rosetta, M. T. (1994) *Compositional Translation*, Dordrecht: Kluwer Academic Publishers.

Sayer, Peter (2000) 'Lernout and Hauspie Translates Free', *PCWorld*, 2 October 2000.

Sciarone, A. C. (1980) *Over Automatisch Vertalen*, Inaugural Address.

Steinberger, Ralf, Bruno Pouliquen, Anna Widiger, Camelia Ignat, Tomaž Erjavec, and Dan Tufiş (2006) 'The JRC-Acquis: A Multilingual Aligned Parallel Corpus with 20+ Languages', in *Proceedings of the 5th International Conference on Language Resources and Evaluation (LREC '2006)*, 2142–47.

Tiedemann, Jörg (2009) 'Character-based PSMT for Closely Related Languages', in Lluís Márquès and Harold Somers (eds.) *Proceedings of 13th Annual Conference of the European Association for Machine Translation (EAMT'09)*, 14–15 May 2009, Barcelona, Spain, 12–19.

Tiedemann, Jörg (2012) 'Parallel Data, Tools and Interfaces in OPUS', in Khalid Choukri, Thierry Declerck, Mehmet Uğur Dogan, Bente Maegaard, Joseph Mariani, Jan Odijk, and Stelios Piperidis (eds.) *Proceedings of the 8th International Conference on Language Resources and Evaluation (LREC '12)*, European Language Resources Association (ELRA), 21–27 May 2012, Istanbul, Turkey, 2214–18.

van den Bosch, Antal and Peter Berck (2009) 'Memory-based Machine Translation and Language Modeling', *The Prague Bulletin of Mathematical Linguistics* 91: 17–26.

van Gompel, Maarten, Antal van den Bosch, and Peter Berck (2009) 'Extending Memory-based Machine Translation to Phrases', in Mikel L. Forcada and Andy Way (eds.) *Proceedings of the 3rd International Workshop on Example-based Machine Translation*, 12–13 November 2009, Dublin City University, Dublin, Ireland, 79–86.

Wijngaarden, A. van (1952) *Rekenen en vertalen*, Delft: Uitgeverij Waltman.

Witkam, Toon (2006) 'History and Heritage of the DLT (Distributed Language Translation) Project'. Available at: www.mt-archive.info/Witkam-2006.pdf.

Wubben, Sander, Antal van den Bosch, and Emiel Krahmer (2012) 'Sentence Simplification by Monolingual Machine Translation', in *Proceedings of the 50th Annual Meeting of the Association for Computational Linguistics (Volume 1: Long Papers)*, Association for Computational Linguistics, 8–14 July 2012, Jeju Island, Korea, 1015–24.

Wubben, Sander, Erwin Marsi, Antal van den Bosch, and Emiel Krahmer (2011) 'Comparing Phrase-based and Syntax-based Paraphrase Generation', in *Proceedings of the Workshop on Monolingual Text-to-text Generation*, Association for Computational Linguistics, 24 June 2011, Portland, OR, 27–33.

Yahyaei, Sirvan and Christof Monz (2010) 'The QMUL System Description for IWSLT 2010', in *Proceedings of the 7th International Workshop on Spoken Language Translation (IWSLT-2010)*, 2–3 December 2010, Paris, France, 157–62.

24

TRANSLATION TECHNOLOGY IN THE UNITED KINGDOM

Christophe Declercq

Introduction

The European Association for Machine Translation (EAMT)[1] might very well be registered in Switzerland;[2] the organization is an official supporter of Translating and the Computer Conferences, held by the Association for Information Management (ASLIB) in London each year. The former president of EAMT and noted machine translation authority W. John Hutchins himself resides in Norwich, England. His *Compendium of Translation Software* is close to being the Bible of what actually is covered by the concept 'translation software' and arguably one of the most sensible approaches to the concept 'translation technology'.

Translation software largely covers two subcomponents. Automatic translation systems, on the one hand, are machine translation systems of various kinds (rule-based, statistical, online/standalone . . .) and for various purposes (from enterprise over professional to website and mobile). Translation support systems, on the other hand, range from electronic dictionaries over localization support and alignment tools to translation workstations with a translation memory at their core. Basically, the two approaches distinguish between language technology and translation technology. However, language technology increasingly is paired with translation technology (see 'Editing in Translation Technology'). Therefore, this chapter covers translation software use in the United Kingdom.

Peculiar Relations

Peculiarly, this chapter depicts the role and position of translation and more in particular translation technology in a society which has a special relationships with its neighbouring countries, the EU and the United States. And each time the English language serves as a unique currency.[3]

With the widespread uptake of the English language in former British colonies and with British English acting as one of the three main working languages in the European Union (and de facto the ultimate working language?), the United Kingdom finds itself in a peculiar position when the role of translation, and technology in support of it, is concerned. In stark contrast to many of its fellow EU member states, British society has never had an historical urge to accommodate translation needs. On the contrary, English as a global lingua franca steers translation itself. English has a well-established tradition of acting as a source language, from which translation happens, or

DOI: 10.4324/9781003168348-26

as a target language.[4] And even if English is not involved as such, then it most likely acts as a relay language. Moreover, as a member of the United Nations Security Council, the European Union (EU), the Commonwealth of Nations, the Council of Europe, the G7, the G8, the G20, NATO, the Organisation for Economic Co-operation and Development (OECD) and the World Trade Organization (WTO), the United Kingdom most certainly finds itself amidst intense political and economic communication. This not only triggers translation into or out of English[5] but also sees excellent communication happen across language barriers.

Education

Sampled from a dozen people using Google Advanced within the space of a few days and performing the same search (*'translation technology' site:uk*), a few interesting results appeared. First and for all, Imperial College London's MSc in Scientific, Medical and Technical Translation with Translation Technology accounted for half the top ten results.[6] Joined by university courses at Swansea University, UCL, SOAS and elsewhere, the straightforward online search provided an important overall insight into translation technology and British web pages: according to Google, translation technology is mainly an academic field. In order to maintain a sustainable translation turnover, the United Kingdom needs a substantial continued stream of translation students on the one hand and an awareness that active mastering languages is beneficial to professional development and career progress on the other hand. Here, the United Kingdom confirms its status as the odd one out. Nowhere else in Europe is the presence of languages in education, both secondary and higher education, under threat as in the United Kingdom.

Despite continued efforts of government and institutions such as the British Academy and frequent attention by most of the quality newspapers, languages in the United Kingdom decline at the secondary education level. This is evident from these headlines:

- Languages in state schools 'decline further' (Sellgren, BBC News 27 January 2011)
- GCSE results set records but spark row over decline in modern languages (*Huffington Post* 25 August 2011)
- A-level foreign languages decline alarms examiners (Vasagar, *The Guardian* online, 16 August 2012)
- Anti-European attitudes 'turning pupils off languages' (Paton, *The Daily Telegraph* online, 20 March 2013)
- How to encourage students to pursue languages at GCSE and A-level (Drabble, *The Guardian* online, 17 May 2013)
- How can schools encourage students to take languages further? (Drury, *The Guardian* online, 3 July 2013)
- UCAS stats reveal languages decline (Matthews, Times Higher Education online, 23 July 2013)

In contrast with falling language numbers in secondary education, language learning summer courses or language evening classes continue to spike. But more often than not, this hunger for languages comes from non-native English speakers. This most peculiar situation, which in many aspects is the opposite of other EU member states, is mirrored in the specific situation of translation technology in the United Kingdom too. Whereas in many other EU member states professional translators and translation students alike are served by a local subsidiary of a translation technology software developer, the United Kingdom, more specifically in London, attracts other-lingual translators and students.

In higher education, the situation does not seem to improve much, either. Despite the substantial influx of non-UK students, translation and language departments have been curtailed on an ongoing basis. From Imperial College London over City University London to Salford University,[7] language sections of humanities departments have been scrapped along with their translation units.

It is very difficult to count the number of master's degrees in translation in the United Kingdom. Often, a new master is created by recreating most of another one, by changing core modules to optional modules, or by adding one or two new modules. Despite shifting relevance, it can be argued that translation software features heavily in virtually all translation studies courses. One of the features that sets particular master's apart from others is the EMT label granted by the European Commission's Directorate-General for Translation to higher-education institutions offering master's level translation programmes: European Master's in Translation. The quality label is granted to 'university translation programmes that meet agreed professional standards and market demands' and that answer to an elaborate 'translator competence profile, drawn up by European experts' (EMT online 2013). Transferable skills in project management and using translation software feature prominently in the EMT competences.[8] The following UK universities offer a master's course in translation that has been granted the label.

Aston University	MA in Translation in a European Context
Durham University	MA in Translation Studies
University of Surrey	MA in Translation
Imperial College London	MSc in Scientific, Technical and Medical Translation with Translation Technology (MscTrans)
London Metropolitan University	MA Applied Translation Studies
Roehampton University	MA in Audiovisual Translation
University of Westminster	MA in Technical and Specialised Translation
University of Manchester	MA in Translation and Interpreting Studies
University of Portsmouth	MA in Translation Studies
University of Salford	MA in Translating
Swansea University	MA in Translation with Language Technology

Sampling from translation software module descriptions, differences between the various EMT universities become clear. Whereas the MA at Aston University clearly keeps an open perspective on translation studies by incorporating media translation, MT, dubbing and subtitling, the MA at Birmingham retains a corpus linguistics approach ('using the Internet to search for terminology, comparable and parallel texts; using translation forums and other specialized translation resources websites', University of Birmingham 2013). Teaching audio-visual translation technology has increased substantially in the last few years (Roehampton, Surrey, Imperial College . . .), and a convergence in text and speech technology can be expected even more in the near future. The courses at Imperial and Swansea have a clear and open link with technology; the latter even offers a Postgraduate Certificate in Translation Technology for freelance translators who need to step up their technological skills.

However, when it comes to translation programmes in the United Kingdom, at least three non-EMT ones come to mind. The University of Bristol runs a straightforward computer-aided translation module, in which students gain 'an understanding of and familiarity with translation software applications and develop a practical competence in the range of functionalities offered' (University of Bristol 2013). This module is supplemented by 'The Translation Industry', in which ethics and quality assurance issues are coupled with insight into the wider business context of translation technology. The business of translation, in which technology features heavily, is indeed often lacking from translation technology modules, which frequently focus on utilizing a variety of tools. Heriot Watt University offers an MSc in Translation And Computer-Assisted Translation Tools, but arguably the mother of including technology in translation studies is the University of Leeds, which uses 'an unrivalled range of software tools that are widely used by leading translation companies – Déjà Vu X, LTC Worx, MemoQ, OmegaT, Passolo, SDL Trados, STAR Transit, and Wordfast' and whose module 'is driven by multilingual group projects, which provide valuable experience of translation project management' (University of Leeds 2013).

And yet the United Kingdom has so much more to offer the world of translation technology than just university courses on a master's level. Arguably the most striking element on the assumed fully English native soil of the United Kingdom, is the – albeit – limited presence of other languages that are recognized officially.

Devolution and Translation Technology

The United Kingdom (which reads in full: the United Kingdom of Great Britain and Northern Ireland) consists of England, Wales, Scotland and Northern Ireland. Other than England, each of the constituent nations has devolved powers. When it comes to translation software and using technology to cross linguistic barriers, Wales arguably is the most special case.

Even though the percentage of the Welsh population able to speak, read and write Welsh decreased by 1.5% in the period 2001–2011, there are still nearly half a million people[9] who master the other official language of Wales besides English. That bilingual nature of Wales drives the difference in translation technology usage between Wales and its fellow constituent UK nations. Driven by the Welsh Assembly and central authorities many associations, bodies and events have taken place in the past years that have not had an equivalent in England or Scotland.

In 2005, the Welsh Government's Translation Service was established, supporting the Assembly Government in the delivery of bilingual public services. The services were the prolongation of services that already had been running since 1999. Whereas the focus lay with terminology (Prys 2006: 50) and translation provision in the early to mid-2000s, this shifted more to translation technology later on. In 2009, the report 'Improved Translation Tools for the Translation Industry in Wales' was published, written by Delyth Prys, Gruffudd Prys and Dewi Jones. The report highlighted the significance of the translation industry for the Welsh economy and even stressed that the sector was an important employer of women and was located in any possible area of the country (urban, rural, semi-rural). The report focused on the twofold provision of the translation industry: it served the bilingual services in Wales and aided 'other sectors of the Welsh economy market in the export of their goods and services in the global marketplace'. Also, 'translation technology tools, regardless of the languages translated' (Prys *et al.* 2009: 3), were seen to be underused in Wales. In 2009, core benefits of using translation technology in Wales were considered the following:

- increasing capacity by 40%, and saving 20% in administrative time without any increase in staffing levels by appropriate use of translation technology
- 50% further growth in the sector through expanding capacity to meet domestic demand, and 300% growth in attracting translation business from outside Wales
- increasing export opportunities for customers and potential customers by 19% by making appropriate use of translation and multilingual services.

(Prys et al. 2009: 3)

However, a clear threat was seen in competition from companies from other parts of the United Kingdom and EU, which could possibly 'only be countered by equipping the industry within Wales with the means to become more technologically competent themselves'. In order to better face future threats from competitors, 'a demonstrator centre for the translation industry' (Prys *et al.* 2009: 3) was sought to be established and compiling relevant tools into a toolkit[10] for industrywide use in Wales was advocated.

The Language Technologies Unit (LTU) and more specifically SALT Cymru (Speech and Language Technology) at Bangor University now assume that role of demonstrator centre.[11] With research project and resources such as a Welsh Basic Speech Recognition Project, CEG (an electronic corpus of the Welsh language) and Maes-T (a web interface for the online development of terminology databases), SALT Cymru covers a wide variety of translation software such as

- speech technology: speech recognition, speaker recognition, text-to-speech techniques, speech coding and enhancement, multilingual speech processing
- written language input: optical character recognition, handwriting recognition
- language analysis, understanding and generation: grammar, semantics, parsing, discourse and dialogue
- document processing: text and term extraction, interpretation, summarization
- machine translation: including computer-aided translation, multilingual information retrieval
- multimodality: gesture and facial movement recognition, visualisation of text data
- language resources: written and spoken corpora, lexica, terminology
- evaluation: of all of the above.

(SALT 2010)[12]

What was retained from Hutchins' *Compendium of Translation Software* might not have been elaborate as the previous, but that does not mean that the *Compendium* did not go at similar lengths. It also means that albeit independently an MT expert from Norwich and a European-funded University in Wales think along the same lines.

An outcome of the report was the creation of a national terminology portal for Wales. Another outcome of the report was an event in January 2011, organized by the Universities of Bangor and Swansea,[13] to showcase how translation technology could support companies in reaching new markets but also to service further needs of Wales' bilingual communities. No surprise then that the Welsh Minister for Heritage, Alun Fred Jones, who opened the conference, reiterated that developing expertise in the translation industry was a win–win situation for Wales[14] (Bangor University 2011).

The focus on translation technology and Welsh does not only come from inside the Welsh borders. Google Translate added Welsh to its languages in August 2009; Microsoft (2011) produces many Welsh user interfaces for its applications and regularly updates its Welsh Style Guide for localization purposes; and already in 2004, Harold Somers, Centre for Computational Linguists at the University of Manchester, produced a report for the Welsh Language Board about the possibilities of machine translation for Welsh. Aptly called 'The Way Forward', Somers focused mainly on three items: language technology provision for Welsh at that time, three types of machine translation (SMT, RBMT, EBMT)[15] and their possible contribution to support Welsh language provision, and a comparison with minority languages elsewhere in Europe (such as Irish, Basque, Catalan and Galician). The contrast with Northern Ireland and Scotland, where only a very small number of people speak a language different from English or Irish or Scottish English, let alone England, could not be bigger.

The relative success in Wales of translation technology in government, executive associations and companies can hardly be replicated in Scotland.[16] The number of speakers of Scottish Gaelic simply is of a different proportion.[17] However, a study by Commun na Gaidhlig found that businesses that use Gaelic in their visual marketing stood out to consumers. Even though several groups of people strive for more prominence of Scottish Gaelic in the Western Isles, utilizing translation technology to help those people who do not speak that language has been made (Language Insight 2011). The attempt seems to find difficulty in establishing momentum beyond its own fragmented geographical area, which can be seen in the fact that the translation memory service for Scottish Gaelic is confined to the University of the Highlands and Islands alone,[18] whereas language technology efforts in Wales are shared across various HEI and governmental organizations.

Most definitely a much more striking Scottish presence in the world of translation software is provided by the University of Edinburgh and its machine translation research and development. Several years in the making and fully released to the world in 2007 and 2008, the Moses Open Source Toolkit for Statistical Machine Translation[19] provided for much of the seismic power of the shift in language technology use at the time (most of the other seismic shock of the time was attributed to Google Translate). It is not fair to lay credit for Moses with Edinburgh solely; half a dozen of other institutions such as MIT and Aachen also provided substantial R&D and financial input. However, Philippe Koehn, Hieu Hoang, Alexandra Birch and Chris Callison-Burch are names that still stand out in the field of MT.

Especially the case of translation technology use in Wales has seen a government-backed and EU-supported move to team up local authority, education and companies. It is therefore the purpose of the following section to provide an overview of British organizations and companies working in the field of translation technology.

Translation Technology Companies

The United Kingdom is one of the key players in translation technology. One of the homes of the global lingua franca, the United Kingdom also has London, Europe's biggest city and one of the world's financial centres.

With widely respected British television channels, especially the BBC, and newspapers,[20] the United Kingdom is an important centre for printed and broadcast media. Television and technology go hand in hand. In order to further accessibility to the media, subtitling, live captioning and audio description are increasingly used.[21] It should therefore not be a surprise that the United Kingdom is also a hub for translation technology.

Among the companies that have their headquarters in the United Kingdom are Applied Language Solutions, ArabNet, ATA Software, ITR (International Translation Resources), LTC, Network Translation, Prolingua, Screen Systems, SDL, Software Partners, Translation Experts, Translution, Wizart, Wordbank and XTM. With SDL, based in Maidenhead (and offices in Sheffield and Bristol), one of the giants of the translation software industry, the United Kingdom is provided for very well. Among the notable translation software companies that have a main base elsewhere but an important UK hub are ABBYY, LionBridge, TEMIS and Worldlingo. Overall, these companies offer software provision that is shifting towards a more diverse platform or customisable applications that includes language technology, translation technology, project management, quality assurance, collaborative aspects and the like.

Just how diverse translation software and management of translation projects have become is clear from Figure 24.1, a screenshot from SDL's Products homepage. In fact, some of its resources aren't even fully referenced in the list. BeGlobal Trainer, the functionality to customize SDL's BeGlobal MT component, is not overtly included here, nor are Contenta, the

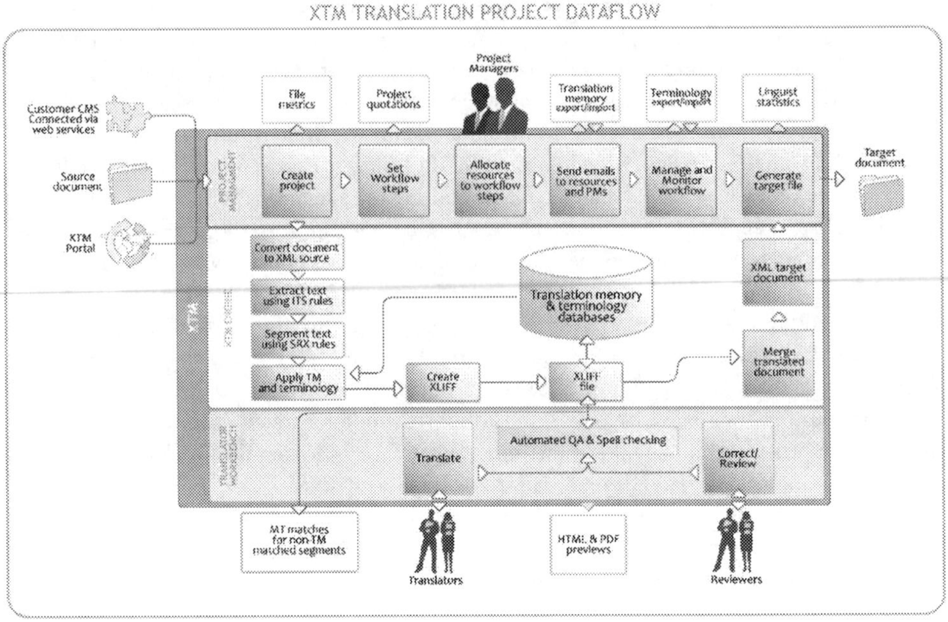

XTM TRANSLATION PROJECT DATAFLOW

Figure 24.1 Overview of SDL products

Source: SDL online

customizable XML solution, and LiveContent, which is also XML related. Although the days of a handful of translation memory tools are over and the concept of 'new kid on the block' no longer applies in an era of apps, crowd, and cloud, XTM International and their XTM modules offer a range of tools, including XTM Cloud, which is software as a service (SaaS). It has provided Figure 24.2.

Although the representation itself might be XTM International's, the workflow is very familiar to any company working with translation software. SDL and XTM differ in their approach in that SDL covers this workflow with some of their tools, whereas XTM's tools concern technology at various steps in this workflow only (a logical difference between an international corporation on the one hand and an emerging technology company on the other). But it can be argued that a workflow including project managers, translators and reviewers on the one hand and XLIFF, HTML and PDF files on the other is a more traditional workflow with translation technology involved.

Nataly Kelly, formerly of Common Sense Advisory fame, now Smartling, confirms that in the translation industry, 'prevailing business models are exactly the same as they were two decades ago' and that change is necessary, an emergence of 'technological advances that impact the translation market at large, including the hundreds of thousands of professional translators out there' (Kelly 2013). Kelly advocates the position that MT and crowdsourcing 'do not begin to touch most of the market activities yet' and that they might not do so soon but that the translation industry is losing out on a major opportunity. This drive towards new opportunities is clear from SDL's approach but not yet from XTM's. However, in the competitive and open market that is the translation software world in the United Kingdom, both models keep feeding into one another. This makes for British translation technology remaining solid at the base without losing sight of future opportunities that are not catered to yet.

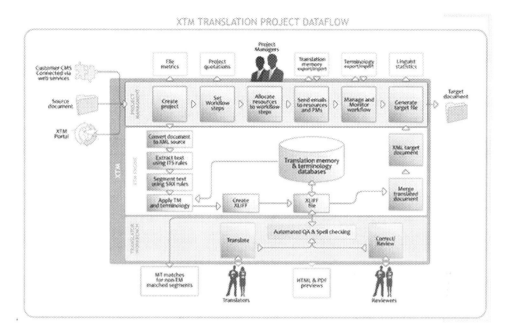

Figure 24.2 Typical XTM project dataflow

Source: XTM Online

It is true that pervasive use of social media and MT, the emergence of the crowd and the crucial role of utilizing big data have put language technology before a new paradigm. If the current age is not the time for that translation technology entities to open up to the wider information technology world, then when is? And if the United Kingdom, in particular London, is not the one place for translation technology as it is where teaching, learning and experts come and work together, then where is?

Acknowledgements

Many thanks to several members of the former Translation Unit at Imperial College London (which has now transferred to UCL) and a dozen of selected LinkedIn contacts for providing me with screenshots of Google Advanced search results. Bettina Bajaj, Rocio Banos Pinero, Lindsay Bywood and Jorge Díaz-Cintas also provided input about what makes the United Kingdom stand out in the field of translation technology.

Notes

1 The current president is Andy Way, also UK. The EAMT oversees European R&D groups active in the field of machine translation. Of the 30 groups, 3 are located in the United Kingdom: the Statistical Machine Translation Group (University of Edinburgh), Machine Intelligence Laboratory (Cambridge University) and Information Retrieval Group (Queen Mary, University of London).

2 Similarly, the International Organization for Standardization (ISO) is registered in Switzerland as well (like EAMT in Geneva too). ISO was established in 1947, after 'delegates from 25 countries met at

the Institute of Civil Engineers in London and decided to create a new international organization "to facilitate the international coordination and unification of industrial standards'" (ISO 2012).

3   It is an old adage among London cabbies that they do not need to learn a language because the world comes to London and speaks English there.

4   A noted exception to this in the field of translation software concerns Galician and Catalan, core to the many language pairs covered by both Apertium, Lucy and Translendium, open source MT and online MT services.

5   The United Kingdom is also home to diverse organizations such as the International Mobile Satellite Organisation, the International Maritime Organisation, Unicef UK, Amnesty International, PEN International, UN's Save the Children, European Bank for Reconstruction and Development, BP . . . the list is very long. Also, international assocations such as the International Cocoa Organisation, the International Grains Council and International Sugar Organisation are based in London. Sadly enough, it cannot be the scope of this contribution to be analysing translation needs and translation technology use among these institutions and associations.

6   From 2013/14 onwards, this MSc is organized at University College London.

7   At the time of writing, the Translation Studies Unit at Imperial College will be discontinued for the subsequent academic year. The unit was negotiating a transfer deal at the level of ongoing implementation meetings. At London City University, the MA in audiovisual translation no longer ran from September 2013 onwards. In June 2013, the University of Salford confirmed its plans to close all courses in modern languages, despite the fact that it leads the National Network for Translation.

8   Another European project, called OPTIMALE (Optimising Professional Translator Training in a Multilingual Europe), focuses on the training of trainers. Eight UK translation programmes are part of OPTIMALE, and educators have been taking part in workshops that eyed best practice in training students language and translation technology.

9   Wales has a population of nearly 3.1 million people.

10 'The toolkit will comprise an illustrative integration of translation memories, terminologies, language proofing tools and workflow managers in an attractive translation environment. The toolkit will be generic and exemplary to avoid licensing issues with commercial software providers, and will include trial versions of new solutions under development at the LTU' (TIKEP, no date).

11 In earlier different forms, the LTU has been active since the early 1990s.

12 In many ways both Hutchins and SALT honour the 1996 *Survey of the State of the Art in Human Language Technology*, only they take it 15 years further.

13 Swansea University also meets the individual needs of freelance translators who remain undecided as to which translation memory to use or how to apply term recognition and to that end offers a Postgraduate Certificate in Translation Technology (University of Swansea 2013). Bangor and Swansea are not the only universities in Wales that deal with language technology. Aberystwyth University, for instance, holds the Centre for Welsh Language Services.

14 The European Regional Development Fund co-funds a lot of the research and development activities.

15 Statistical machine translation, rule-based machine translation, phrase-based machine translation.

16 However, increasingly minority languages are included in language technology conferences, such as 'Language in Minority/ised Language Media' held in July 2013 at the University of Aberystwyth.

17 In 2001, it was estimated that hardly 1.2% of the Scottish population could only speak some Gaelic. That is 10% of all the Welsh people who speak, read and write Welsh.

18 On 29 May 2013, the University of Glasgow announced that among 20 funded collaborative PhD studentships with industry partners, one of their research projects concerned translation technology. (Pittock, *Herald Scotland* 2013)

19 The article with the same title has a Google reference of nearly 2000 citations (data 1 July 2013). The core arguments of the paper concerned (a) support for linguistically motivated factors, (b) confusion network decoding, and (c) efficient data formats for translation models and language models (Koehn *et al.* 2007: 177)

20 In a list of global newspapers ranked according to their circulation, 8 British newspapers feature among the top 40 (source: IFABC, 2011)

21 In September 2012, London-based Red Bee Media landed an exclusive deal to provide the BBC with subtitling, signing and audio description services for the subsequent seven years. (Laughlin 2012) Other Red Bee clients include Channel 4, Canal+ and Discovery Channel.

Bibliography

About ISO (2012) Available at: www.iso.org/iso/home/about.htm.

Apertium. Available at: www.apertium.org.

ASLIB's Annual Conference Translating and the Computer. Available at: www.aslib.co.uk/conferences/tcc/index.htm.

'Can Translation Technology Rescue Scottish Gaelic' (2011) *Language Insight*. Available at: www.language-insight.com/blog/2011/10/25/can-translation-technology-rescue-scottish-gaelic.

Cole, Ronald A. (1996) *Survey of the State of the Art in Human Language Technology*, Cambridge: Cambridge University Press. Available at: www.cslu.ogi.edu/HLTsurvey.

Drabble, Emily (2013) 'How to Encourage Students to Pursue Languages at GCSE and A-level', *The Guardian* online, 17 May 2013. Available at: www.guardian.co.uk/teacher-network/teacher-blog/2013/may/17/languages-schools-students-gcse-alevels-mfl.

Drury, Emma (2013) 'How Can Schools Encourage Students to Take Languages Further?', *The Guardian* online, 3 July 2013. Available at: www.guardian.co.uk/teacher-network/teacher-blog/2013/jul/03/schools-encourage-students-languages-advanced-level.

'EAMT: European Association for Machine Translation'. Available at: www.eamt.org.

'EMT: European Master's in Translation'. Available at: http://ec.europa.eu/dgs/translation/programmes/emt/index_en.htm.

GCSE (2011) 'Results Set Records But Spark Row Over Decline', *Modern Languages*, Huffington Post online, 25 August 2011. Available at: www.huffingtonpost.co.uk/2011/08/25/gcse-results-spark-row-over-languages-decline_n_936006.html.

Hutchins, W. John (2010) 'Compendium of Translation Software'. Available at: www.hutchinsweb.me.uk/Compendium-16.pdf.

IFABC: International Federation of Audit Bureaux of Circulations (2011) 'National Newspapers Total Circulation'. Available at: www.ifabc.org/site/assets/media/National-Newspapers_total-circulation_IFABC_17-01-13.xls.

Kelly, Nataly (2013) 'Why I Joined Smartling'. Available at: www.smartling.com/blog/2013/04/04/joined-smartling.

Koehn, Philip, Hieu Hoang, Alexandra Birch, Chris Callison-Burch, Marcello Federico, Nicola Bertoldi, Brooke Cowan, Wade Shen, Christine Moran, Richard Zens, Chris Dyer, Ondrej Bojar, Alexandra Constantin, and Evan Herbst (2007) 'Moses: Open Source Toolkit for Statistical Machine Translation', in *ACL '07: Proceedings of the 45th Annual Meeting of the ACL on Interactive Poster and Demonstration Sessions*, Prague, Czech Republic, 177–80. Available at: http://acl.ldc.upenn.edu/P/P07/P07-2045.pdf.

Kwik Translator. Available at: www.lucysoftware.com.

'Language in Minority/ised Language Media'. (2013) Available at: www.aber.ac.uk/en/tfts/latest-news/news-article/title-137696-en.html.

Laughlin, Andrew (2012) 'Red Bee Media Wins New Seven Year Subtitling Deal', in *DigitalSpy*. Available at: www.digitalspy.co.uk/media/news/a404168/red-bee-media-wins-new-seven-year-bbc-subtitling-deal.html.

Matthews, David (2013) 'UCAS Stats Reveal Languages Decline', *Times Higher Education* online, 23 July 2013. Available at: www.timeshighereducation.co.uk/news/ucas-stats-reveal-languages-decline/2005890.article.

Microsoft (2011) 'Welsh Style Guide'. Available at: http://goo.gl/m2k1EB.

OPTIMALE. 'Optimising Professional Translator Training in a Multilingual Europe'. Available at: www.translator-training.eu.

Paton, Graeme (2013) 'Anti-European Attitudes "Turning Pupils off Languages"'. *The Daily Telegraph* online, 20 March 2013. Available at: www.telegraph.co.uk/education/educationnews/9943592/Anti-European-attitudes-turning-pupils-off-languages.html.

Pittock, Murray (2013) 'Agenda: Our Culture Can Boost the Economy', *Herald Scotland* online, 29 May 2013. Available at: www.heraldscotland.com/comment/columnists/agenda-our-culture-can-boost-the-economy.21177340.

Proficiency in Welsh (2012) '2011 Census: Key Statistics for Wales, March 2011', *Office for National Statistics*. Available at: http://ons.gov.uk/ons/dcp171778_290982.pdf.

Prys, Delyth (2006) 'Setting the Standards: Ten Years of Terminology Work', in Pius Ten Hacken (ed.) *Terminology, Computing and Translation*, Tübingen: Gunter Narr Verlag, 41–57.

Prys, Delyth, Gruffudd Prys, and Dewi Jones (2009) 'Improved Translation Tools for the Translation Industry in Wales: An Investigation'. Available at: www.catcymru.org/wordpress/wp-content/uploads/Final%20ReportHE06fspRevised.pdf.

Prys, Gruffud, Tegus Andrews, Dewi B. Jones, and Delyth Prys (2012) 'Distributing Terminology Resources Online: Multiple Outlet and Centralized Outlet Distribution Models in Wales', in *Proceedings of CHAT 2012: The 2nd Workshop on the Creation, Harmonization and Application of Terminology Resources*, 22 June 2012, Madrid, Spain, Linkoping: Linkoping University Electronic Press, Linkopings Universitet, 37–40. Available at: www.ep.liu.se/ecp/072/005/ecp12072005.pdf.

SALT Cymru (2010) 'SALT Definition'. Available at: www.saltcymru.org/wordpress/?p=80&lang=en#0 38;lang=en.

SDL Products (2013). Available at: www.sdl.com.

Sellgren, Katherine (2011) 'Languages in State Schools "Decline Further"', *BBC News*, 27 January 2011. Available at: www.bbc.co.uk/news/education-12288511.

Somers, Harold L. (2004) *Machine Translation and Welsh: The Way Forward*, A Report for the Welsh Language Board. Available at: http://mti.ugm.ac.id/~adji/courses/resources/doctor/MT_book/Machine%20Translation%20and%20Welsh%20%28PDF%29.pdf.

Translation Industry Knowledge Exchange Project (TIKEP, no date) Bangor University/Welsh Assembly.

Translation Service (2010) 'Welsh Government'. Available at: http://cymru.gov.uk/about/civilservice/directorates/ppcs/translationservice/?lang=en.

Bangor University (2011) 'Translation Technology Helps Welsh Industry'. Available at: www.bangor.ac.uk/news/full.php.en?nid=3206&tnid=3206.

University of Birmingham (2013) 'Translation Studies MA Details'. Available at: www.birmingham.ac.uk/students/courses/postgraduate/taught/arts-law-inter/translation-studies.aspx#CourseDetailsTab.

University of Bristol (2013) 'MA in Translation'. Available at: www.bris.ac.uk/sml/courses/postgraduate/ma-translation.html.

University of Leeds (2013) 'MA in Applied Translation Studies'. Available at: www.leeds.ac.uk/arts/info/125053/centre_for_translation_studies/1803/taught_programmes/2.

University of Swansea (2013) 'Postgraduate Certificate in Translation Technology'. Available at: www.swansea.ac.uk/artsandhumanities/artsandhumanitiesadmissions/translationstudies/postgraduatedegrees/postgraduatecertificateintranslationtechnology.

Vasagar, Jonathan (2013) 'A-level Foreign Languages Decline Alarms Examiners', *The Guardian* online, 16 August 2012. Available at: www.guardian.co.uk/education/2012/aug/16/alevel-foreign-languages-decline.

XTM Workflow Diagram (2013). Available at: www.xtm-intl.com/files/content/xtm/images/XTM_Workflow_diagram.png.

25

A HISTORY OF TRANSLATION TECHNOLOGY IN THE UNITED STATES

Jennifer DeCamp

The evolution of translation technology in the United States has included developments not only in machine translation (MT) and computer-assisted translation (CAT) but also in automatic speech recognition (ASR), speech generation, optical character recognition (OCR), information retrieval (IR), natural language understanding (NLU), and technologies Combinations of these technologies produced speech-to-text translation (STT), speech-to-speech translation (STS), text-to-speech translation (TTS), cross-lingual information retrieval (CLIR), cross-lingual chat, social media analysis, computer-assisted language learning (CALL), and other capabilities for processing speech and text for communication between humans or between humans and technology. Innovation also occurred in hardware and software, making capabilities affordable and available to a much broader user base and massively increasing computing power. The Defense Advanced Research Projects Agency (DARPA), the Intelligence Advanced Research Projects Activity (IARPA), the National Institute for Standards and Technology (NIST), universities and research centers drove development, as did pressing needs. Translation has always been an to support government efforts to provide humanitarian assistance and resolve political conflicts and to support commercial efforts to expand markets. exceptionally international field, and the extraordinary sharing not only of ideas, software, and data but also of skilled professionals enabled rapid development of programs and capabilities worldwide. While many countries pursued similar goals and many collaborated closely with the US, this chapter focuses on innovation in the United States and is a complement to other chapters in *The Routledge Encyclopedia of Translation Technology* (2023). The chapter includes a discussion of influences, a decade-by-decade history, predictions, and a detailed timeline.

Influences on the Development of Translation Technology

Technology achievements in World War II (1939–1945) – particularly the Manhattan Project and successes with decrypting enemy messages – reinforced the deep belief held in the United States in the ability of technology innovation to ensure the security of the nation and its allies. In response to the start of the Cold War (1947–1989) and the Korean War (1950–1953), the US government created institutions such as the National Science Foundation (NSF) in 1950 and the Defense Advanced Research Projects Agency in 1957 to foster the development of new technologies to meet military needs. This innovation and development required extensive testing, accomplished by DARPA and the National Institute for Standards and Technology (NIST). Development and testing in turn drove the need for data, for which DARPA established the Linguistic Data Consortium at the University of Pennsylvania in 1972 (Hutchins 1986). The jihadist bombing of the World Trade Center and the Pentagon on 11 September 2001 (known as '9–11') resulted in the Uniting and Strengthening America by Providing Appropriate Tools Required to Intercept and Obstruct Terrorism (USAPATRIOT) Act, which provided further funding for machine translation research and development. In the Cold War and the War on Terrorism, the United States supported international military and humanitarian relief efforts with extensive foreign language requirements.

Starting in the early 1970s, US industry began to use word processing and MT to translate documentation and training materials into the languages of their foreign customers, a process that became known as 'localization'. In 1972, Wang introduced the first word processors in the United States. In 1973, Xerox introduced the Alto, the first personal computer with a graphical user interface and support for multiple languages, which was used by the company's translation department for producing foreign language (i.e. localized) versions of its photocopier material. In 1978, Xerox became the first company to use MT, adopting Systran machine translation and working with the Xerox Palo Alto Research Center (PARC) to create pre-processing and post-editing software, including confidence measures and the ability to identify and mark certain types of potential errors. Localization evolved into 'internationalization', with new processes to more efficiently provide translations of documents and computer interfaces in multiple languages. Internationalization evolved into 'globalization', with multiple departments and third parties involved in the process of providing products and documentation for foreign markets. The need for simultaneous shipping ('simship') of products to multiple countries – and later applications such as MT support for marketing, help desks, chat, search, and social media – drove a need for translation in real time or near real time. Other multinational corporations soon followed suit, including US technology companies such as IBM, Microsoft, and Google.

Meanwhile, churches, particularly the Church of Jesus Christ of Latter-day Saints (also known as the 'LDS Church' or the 'Mormon Church'), were pursuing means of automating the translation of religious texts to support their overseas missionary work. Members of the LDS Church at Brigham Young University (BYU) developed software for multilingual text processing and interactive machine translation, as well as linguistic analysis, standards, and translation data In 1977, developers associated with BYU founded the Weidner Communications Corporation to implement and market MT capabilities. In 1980, some of the developers formed (Melby 2013; Richardson 2022). In 1980, the project's leaders founded automated language processing systems (ALPS) to continue work on MT-related technologies, Other non-governmental organizations (NGOs) such as the Pan American Health Organization (PAHO) adopted MT to produce materials for use across the languages, dialects, and cultures of the Western Hemisphere. In 1985, PAHO produced an English-to-Spanish system (Vasconcellos).

Because of the pressures of the Cold War and market expansion, and because of the sheer excitement of the waves of innovation in machine translation and its parent field of artificial intelligence, the field of MT grew rapidly. As Arle Lommel of CSA Research described in his MT Summit 2021 presentation, 'Responsive MT', rule-based MT (RBMT, 1950 to 2000) was extensively superseded by SMT (Statisical Machine Translation) (2000 to 2015), which was extensively superseded by NMT (Neural Machine Translation) (2015 to 2021), which is now being further enhanced by metadata-enriched NMT. RBMT depended on hard-coded rules. SMT depended on the statistical frequency of terms or longer text used in past translations. NMT depends on neural algorithms (a cutting-edge area of artificial intelligence and machine learning). Metadata-enriched MT uses metadata to shape and constrain the MT output and thus to improve fluency and accuracy. These new tools are enabling domain (i.e. subject-specific) MT, custom human-enriched MT, augmented translation, adaptive/assistive natural language processing, and a new generation of responsive MT. This evolution has produced a wider range of tool practices, including rules, classical linguistic knowledge, lexicons, translation memories, machine learning, linguistic feedback, simple metadata, document context, and content enrichment. It has driven flexibility, adaptability, relevance, resonance, and quality (Lommel 2021). There of course have been users such as Xerox who adopted certain tools and processes far earlier and users such as PAHO who continue to employ technologies that are older technology but have been well adapted to their needs.

The United States has continued to achieve technology breakthroughs, including the development of mainframe and personal computers; multilingual text processing; pre-editing and post-editing of MT; confidence measures for MT; translation memories (segments of text paired with past translations of that text) and translation memory systems; translation management systems; RBMT; SMT; NMT; and integration of MT into translator tools, search, chat, and many other applications. The United States has developed or participated in the international development of a wide range of standards and software protocols critical for MT and CAT, including the Unicode Standard, which has provided a system of character encodings that has enabled people to efficiently work with multiple languages in the same document, database, or other tool. This early involvement in the development of translation technologies and standards has enabled the United States to shape capabilities, including through work in the international Expert Advisory Group on Language Engineering Standards (EAGLES), the International Standards for Language and Engineering (ISLE), and the International Organization for Standardization (ISO) Technical Committee on Terminology and Language 37.

In the United States, machine translation was an obsession not only in universities and development labs but also in the general public. In 1956, Robby the Robot in the movie *The Forbidden Planet* offered visitors flawless translation assistance in British or American English and in '187 other languages along with their various dialects and sub-tongues' (Internet Movie Database 2021). This tradition continued through dozens of movies, television shows, and books, most notably the Universal Translator in *Star Trek* and C-3PO in *Star Wars*, and still influences requirements for machine translation. MT also benefited from the excitement of AI triumphs, including IBM Watson beating humans in Jeopardy in 2001, and Microsoft's AI group announcing that its NMT had reached parity with professional human translators in 2018. Such coverage increased the optimism of funders, researchers, developers, and users in achieving technological excellence and in solving some of the hard problems of this application. It also generated extensive debate and criticism, resulting in a general acknowledgement that there was still more to learn about what constituted 'parity'.

This degree of academic and media hype regarding MT and the parent field of AI may have been partly responsible for a backlash in the government, including the publication of the Automatic Language Processing Advisory Committee (ALPAC) report in 1966 and a cessation of most government research funding for these technologies in the 1960s and 1970s. However, even during what has been called the 'AI Winter', industry, NGOs, and academia continued to achieve technology breakthroughs in machine translation. This level of interest and dedication was extraordinary given the low quality of MT at that time, the difficulty in showing return on investment (ROI), and the general lack of focus on the financial potential of the technology. It was not until 1987 when Lernout & Hauspie (a Belgian company) began buying up machine translation and related technology companies that community awareness began to grow of MT as a viable investment.

The intense focus on machine translation by the press and research organizations also alienated many professional translators, who were frustrated by the low quality and concerned about their careers in an increasingly automated world. The widening void in the United States between these communities resulted in a lack of understanding by many of the researchers of translation requirements and processes and a lack of understanding of the technology by the many of the practitioners. The tools were often expensive and difficult to learn, resulting in their use by large organizations and language companies but less commonly by independent translators. Meanwhile, development of CAT tools was dominated by Trados and then by SDL, which acquired Trados and was based out of Europe (DeCamp and Zetzsche 2015).

To help bridge this gap, the American Translators Association and the Association for Machine Translation in the Americas in 2010 began a multi-year effort of providing co-located conferences, joint programming, and liaisons. Systran and other MT companies incorporated post-editing tools for translators to improve the work of MT. SMT and NMT were based on the high-quality translations produced by professional translators, terminologists, and editors. Microsoft Research began looking at ways to better incorporate MT and other tools into the translator environment, including enabling translators to continuously update MT with new translation memories. Prominent MT researchers such as Alon Lavie started MT companies, many became involved with language services providers, and the void began to be filled with a new generation of developments and practices. Thanks in great part to efforts by the American Translators Association, translators and interpreters achieved significantly higher professional status.

Use of specialized translation memories and terminologies resulted in substantial gains in accuracy and consistency. Open-source CAT tools such as OmegaT and open-source MT tools such as OpenNMT enabled translators to experiment with CAT and MT and to adapt the software to new applications. In 2015, Spence Green established the new US company Lilt, providing and integrating NMT, predictive MT, and other technologies to increase the productivity of translators. With the exponentially increasing amount of work to be translated and with increasing awareness of the value of humans in the translation process, translators have not lost their jobs but rather have increased their focus on post-editing, on translation in languages and genres not well covered by MT, or on projects where accuracy is critical.

History of Translation Technology in the United States by Decade

The history of translation technology is described in the following section by decade, including information on the environment, MT, and CAT, as well as on standards and professional organizations. A timeline is provided at the end of this chapter, including additional events and milestones.

1940s: Military Focus

Environment

The concept of MT dates back to at least the year 800 (Wikipedia, 'Machine Translation'). However it was first articulated in the United States in 1945 by American author William Fitzgerald Jenkins (under the pen name of 'Murray Leinster'), who introduced the idea of the 'universal translator' in his novella 'First Contact' (Wikipedia, 'First Contact'). The concept also appeared in later science fiction works, notably *Star Trek* in the 1960s – and helped form the public's requirements and expectations for machine translation (e.g. for the Phraselator in the 1980s).

World War II (1939–1945), including the Manhattan Project, reinforced a belief in technical superiority to ensure national and international security. Experiences decrypting messages from foreign enemies shaped much of the early thinking about machine translation. For instance, Warren Weaver, Director of the United States Natural Sciences Division at the Rockefeller Center, in his 1949 'Memorandum on Translation', described an experience decrypting a Turkish message, observing: 'The most important point . . . is that the decoding was done by someone who did not know Turkish, and did not know that the message was in Turkish' – a requirement experienced in processing intelligence information in World War II but diametrically opposed to the needs of organizations or individuals producing translations for disseminating information. Weaver addressed other issues involved in translation, including the diversity of meanings for a single term. His approach to looking at past translations formed the basis for the concept of translation memory. He also explored the idea of possible language universals, which helped shape research into creating an interlingua or common form into which all other languages could be converted and raised the area of technical writing as an application (Hutchins 1980).

In 1949, the Cold War began. That year, the Board of Directors of the Bulletin of Atomic Scientists created the highly publicized Doomsday Clock. The clock's hands were set at seven minutes to midnight, with midnight designating nuclear annihilation. In this high-threat environment, a high priority for the US government was to monitor technical journals—machine translated from Russian—from the Soviet Union in order to identify developments related to weaponry (Vasconcellos).

1950s: Military Innovation

Environment

In 1950, the Korean War started, lasting through 1953. In response, the US government in 1950 created the National Science Foundation, which funded extensive research in MT, and the National Security Education Act (NSEA), which funded research and training in mathematics, science, and languages and later in translation technology.

That year, British mathematician and cryptanalyst Alan Turing proposed his 'Thinking Machine', submitting machine translation as a possible application. In 1952, he proposed the Turing Test, a test of whether a computer could imitate human conversation so well that an observer could not tell the difference between the machine and a person (*New Scientist*). This challenge of artificial intelligence and machine translation has significantly shaped MT research and development.

The 1950s saw considerable ground-breaking research in related technologies. In 1951, Marvin Minsky and Dean Edmonds built the first neural network machine, which became critical in the next century as the basis for NMT. In 1952, the United States developed some of the first machine learning programs, which were critical to SMT and particularly to NMT. In 1957, Noam Chomsky published 'Syntactic Structures', laying the groundwork for the design of rule-based MT systems.

In 1958, Russia launched the Sputnik satellite, which increased US concern about being militarily and economically competitive, which in turn increased funding for machine translation. DARPA was established the same year, which decades later enabled the growth of industry and academic research regarding machine translation and related technologies.

MT

The research field of machine translation grew quickly, first in the United States and then in other countries. Georgetown University in Washington, DC, established the first full-time research position in 1951, filled by Yehoshua Bar-Hillel. The following year, the university established the first MT research center and held the first MT conference. In 1954 the *Journal of Machine Translation* was launched. That year, Georgetown University and IBM conducted the first demonstration of MT, which obtained extensive media attention and, as Hutchins observed, helped elicit government funding (2006). In 1957, the software developed at Georgetown University was installed by the Air Force Foreign Technology Division to translate technical materials from Russian to English.

In 1958, the National Academy of Sciences set up the Automatic Language Processing Advisory Committee (ALPAC) to review the state of MT.

1960s: Research to Operations

Environment

Throughout the 1960s, the media explored issues of artificial intelligence and language technology, popularizing concepts and shaping expectations and requirements. From 1962 to 1963, the television series *The Jetsons* showed Rosie the robot maid and Astro the robot dog processing and understanding English. In 1965, the novel *Dune* by Frank Herbert portrayed the extraordinary ability of MT to work even in the absence of computers (computers having been banned by the government). From 1966 through 1969, the television show *Star Trek* extensively explored issues of machine translation, including systems interoperability and the translation of metaphors. It also popularized the idea of a universal translator.

MT

Criticism increased for MT and for AI in general. In 1960, Bar-Hillel published a report, 'The Present Status of Automated Translation of Language', questioning the feasibility of providing fully automated high-quality translation (FAHQT) and advocating the use of post-editing. Hutchins (1980) observed that Bar-Hillel was also critical of the idea that an interlingua (a common pivot point between languages being translated) would be a simpler approach to MT.

In 1966, ALPAC published 'A Demonstration of the Non-Feasibility of Fully Automatic High Quality Translation', which concluded: 'There is no immediate or predictable prospect of useful machine translation'. It recommended funding research in computational linguistics as a basic science that 'should not be judged by any immediate or foreseeable contribution to practical translation'. It also recommended investments in the improvement of human translation, specifically:

1   Practical methods for evaluation of translations
2   Means for speeding up the translation process
3   Evaluation of quality and cost of various sources of translations
4   Investigation of the utilization of translation to guard against production of translations that are never read
5   Study of delays in the overall translation process, and means for eliminating them, both in journals and in individual items
6   Evaluation of the relative speed and cost of various sorts of machine-aided translation
7   Adaptation of existing mechanized editing and production processes in translation

8   Analysis of overall translation process
9   Production of adequate reference works for the translator, including the adaptation of glossaries that now exist primarily for automatic dictionary lookup in machine translation.

The ALPAC Report not only curtailed most government funding for MT research but also failed to stimulate funding or interest in pursuing its own recommendations in the United States. In addition, the Mansfield Amendment, passed in 1969, required DARPA to fund 'mission-oriented direct research, rather than basic undirected research' (National Research Council 1999).

Despite the ALPAC report and the AI Winter, MT continued to thrive in other venues. In 1961, the University of Texas at Austin established the Linguistics Research Center. The following year, the Association for Machine Translation and Computational Linguistics (later known as the Association for Computational Linguistics) was created, and the Air Force adopted the Mark II MT system, developed by IBM and Washington University. In 1963, Euratom and the Oak Ridge National Laboratory installed the Georgetown University systems for Chinese–English MT.

In 1962, one of the Georgetown MT researchers, Peter Toma, established the private computer company Computer Concepts. The software, AUTOTRAN, and the marketing arm, Language Automated System and Electronic Communications (LATSEC), became Systran ('System Translation') in 1968. Systran continued to develop RBMT, expanding its customer base to industry, which presented new requirements and challenges. Hutchins (1980) noted that the software was adopted by the United States Air Force in 1970.

1970s: Commercial MT and CAT

Environment

In the 1970s Logos obtained contracts from the US government to develop MT to translate weapons documentation for Vietnamese and Persian. Logos provided the capability for users to interact with machine translation to clarify the meaning of a source sentence (Hutchins 1986). This process-interactive MT in the United States was designed primarily to support users without expertise in the target language (the language into which the document is to be translated), consistent with the objectives set out by Weaver in his 1949 memorandum.

In 1972, Wang, a company headquartered in Lowell, Massachusetts, introduced the first word processors to the United States. Word processors enabled translators to edit without retyping the entire page or document. Later, word processing combined with the Kermit protocol and, still later, email or file transfer protocol (FTP), enabled the transmission of documents electronically, which greatly facilitated the work of human translators and later of users of machine translation (Wright). In 1973, Xerox developed the ALTO computer. It was the first personal computer but was never marketed or implemented outside of Xerox and beta sites, but its multilingual word processing capabilities enabled significant advances in translation technology by the company's document translation division.

MT

In 1971, Bar-Hillel defined the practical roles of MT as '(1) machine-aided human translation; (2) human-aided machine translation, and (3) low-quality autonomous machine translation', a taxonomy that is still used with minor variations, although two working groups in ASTM's Language Services and Products Committee are currently revisiting this work. Bar-Hillel also observed: 'A translation which is of good quality for a certain user in a certain situation might be of lesser quality for the same user in a different situation or for a different user, whether in the same or in a different situation. What is satisfactory for one need not be satisfactory for another'. This observation has been the basis for extensive work in standards and evaluations.

From 1972 to 1979, Brigham Young University Translation Sciences Institute (BYU-TSI) developed the Interactive Translation System (ITS). The system interacted with a human operator to resolve lexical and structural ambiguities in English and then produce a translation automatically in multiple target languages.

In 1978, Xerox Corporation adopted Systran machine translation to translate photocopier documentation from English into the languages of its foreign customers, an application that Weaver in 1949 had postulated might be a good application. Hutchins (1980) noted that Xerox was the first commercial company to use MT. In 1977, according to Melby (2015), Bruce Wyndner and Stephen Weidner at BYU, but not affiliated with TSI, formed Weidner Communication to develop and market the Weidner Machine Translation System. see 3

CAT

In 1980, a subgroup of the BYU project founded the Automatic Language Processing Systems (ALP Systems, later changed to 'ALPNET') to provide technology and translation services. This company was purchased by the British translation and technology provider SDL International in 2001 and its technology incorporated into SDL products (Slocum, Melby, Richardson).

In 1974, Xerox developed Bravo, the first 'what you see is what you get' (WYSIWYG) editor, which had fonts for multiple languages. It was significantly easier for translators to use for creating, editing, printing, and emailing documents.

In 1978, Weidner Communication launched its multi-lingual word processing, which was credited by the Wall Street Journal as 'quadrupling translation volume' and by the Deseret News as 'halving translation costs and increasing output by at least 400 percent', probably the earliest estimates of ROI for CAT.

1980s: SMT, Post-Editing, CAT Tools

Environment

US involvement in the Iran–Iraq War (1980–1988) drove the development of MT applications for new languages and dialects. In 1987, Lernout & Hauspie was established and started buying and integrating machine translation and related language technology companies. Their success raised awareness of the potential profitability of machine translation and spurred general investment.

MT

In 1980 Muriel Vasconcellos and her team began developing and using machine translation at the Pan American Health Organization (PAHO), implementing their ENSPAN system for English to Spanish translation in 1985. The system was rule-based, focusing on combinations of English, Spanish, and Portuguese in the health domain. Like Xerox, PAHO made important contributions to the development of post-editing procedures. The PAHO Machine Translation System (PAHOMTS) is still in use and has demonstrated significant productivity gains when compared to manual translation (Aymerich and Camelo 2009).

In 1983, NEC Corporation provided the first demonstration of MT integrated with automatic speech recognition (ASR) and natural language generation (NLG). These applications had a significant impact on applications such as recording speech and providing automated interpreting.

Developers, including those at Carnegie Mellon University (CMU), found ways to make components more modular and thus reusable, with rules defining the source language, the target language, and/or the transfer from the source to the target. CMU conducted experiments with data-driven MT, a concept first described by Weaver in 1949.

In 1985, the University of Texas launched the Mechanical Translation and Analysis of Languages (METAL, formerly the 'Linguistics Research System'). It was marketed by Siemens-Nixdorf through 1992 (University of Texas). The availability of an increasing volume of digital translation memories enabled developers to analyze the frequency of terms or phrases to determine the statistical likelihood of the correct translation, including by specific subject area. This analysis evolved into SMT. In 1986, Peter Brown and his colleagues at IBM presented their experiments on SMT, sparking widespread interest in this approach. That year, Xerox developed TOVNA, a pilot of an example-based data-driven MT system designed for production (TAUS). Also that year, Systran was sold to a French company, although it maintained a wholly owned US subsidiary.

To help bridge the gap between MT output and the minimal acceptable quality for customer use, companies began limiting the input to what the MT system could handle well. In the mid-1980s, Xerox Corporation in Rochester, New York, in conjunction with the Xerox Palo Alto Research Center (PARC), developed tools that checked the original English documentation for terminology, punctuation, and sentence construction, as well as alerting the writers and/or pre-editors to make changes. In addition, Xerox developed post-editing tools that highlighted sections of the output where there was low confidence in the translation (e.g. which contained not-found words or complex sentence constructions), thus focusing the efforts of translators and editors. In the late 1980s and early 1990s, Xerox marketed a combination of its pre-editing and post-editing tools, its confidence measures, Systran, and METAL MT, all running on a new small IBM mainframe, together known as 'DocuTrans'.

This development was far ahead of its time. For instance, Jaap van der Meer, founder of the Translation Automation User Society, characterized the 1980s as a time when industry worldwide focused on paper documents with no use of technology. He characterized the 1990s as the beginning of localization focusing on digital content, the 2000s as the beginning of globalization focusing on providing simultaneous shipping, and the 2010s as a time of integrating MT into enterprise systems (2021).

CAT

In 1984, Trados was established in Germany. It quickly became the leading source of technology for CAT in the United States and in the world, and it was a reseller of early CAT tools developed by the Dutch company INK. The same year, Melby partnered with Leland Wright to create the MTX tool (a.k.a. 'Mercury' and then 'Termex'), which enabled translators to compile their own glossaries as a separate task or while working in documents. This tool employed a Machine-Readable Terminology Interchange Format (MARTIF), which was based on SGML. In 1985, Voice of America started using the Xerox 8010 Information System for translation foreign language document creation (DeCamp 2022).

Professional Organizations

Vasconcellos worked extensively with the American Translators Association (ATA) and later with the Association for Machine Translation in the Americas (AMTA, formed in 1994), including as president of both associations, to help people understand the new technology and processes.

1990s: Personal Computers, DARPA, Evaluation, CAT Tools

Environment

Through the decade, AI and MT continued to capture the public imagination. In1995, IBM's Deep Blue beat world chess champion Kasparov. Machine translation appeared in the best-selling novel *Timeline* by Michael Crichton in 1999, where machine translation was misleadingly depicted as translating an as-yet-unknown dialect without training materials.

MT

The 1990s saw rapid growth of MT programs and services, particularly through the establishment of several DARPA programs, including the Translation Initiative in 1990 under Allen Sears, and then Charles Wayne that was carried forward by George Doddington and Tom Crystal. The DARPA Machine Translation Initiative started in 1991 and funded diverse approaches from universities and industry, including Pangloss (from Carnegie Mellon University, the University of Southern California, and New Mexico State University), Candide (from IBM), and LINGSTAT (from Dragon Systems) This initiative also produced the Machine Translation Evaluation Program, where testing was conducted in collaboration with NIST. To provide data for development and testing, DARPA funded the establishment of the Linguistic Data Consortium at the University of Pennsylvania. DARPA then established the Babylon program for improving translation of speech

In 1991, Lernout & Hauspie continued its acquisition of translation tools and other language technology, including acquiring METAL wi (ibid.) th investments from Microsoft. In 1996 Systran began offering free web-based translation, the first available service of that kind in the United States, though the company had offered a similar but for-fee service in the 1980s in France. The next year, Systran integrated its software with the then widely used search engine AltaVista to create the cross-lingual search tool Babelfish, enabling users to easily and freely experiment with MT. This integration also accelerated a move from a production-centric approach (e.g., submitting search requests and documents to a translation office) to a user-centric one, where users could do their own searches and translations.

In 1996, Pangloss-lite was demoed for translating continuous speech.

CAT

The mid- to late 1990s saw the development of translation management systems in the United States. The earliest of these companies, Uniscape, built the first translation portal in 1999 for posting translation jobs for bids. In 1994, Trados released MultiTerm for terminology management and Workbench for translation memory management. The same year, IBM released the CAT tool Translation Manager (TM/2) and Software, Translation, Artwork, Recording (STAR) released its Transit Translation Memory system. The new fuzzy match capability enabled users to search not just on exact matches but on similar items (KantanAI). In 1997 another large-scale

TMS product, Ambassador Suite, was launched by GlobalSight Corporation. In 1998, Idiom launched WorldServer.

Standards

In 1990 the Localization Industry Standards Association (LISA) was founded in Switzerland to take on challenges of providing international standards for localization, internationalization, and globalization. In 1991 the first version of the Unicode Standard was published, based on the work of Joe Becker from Xerox Corporation and Lee Collins and Mark Davis from Apple Computing. This widely implemented standard – a subset of which became the International Organization for Standardization/International European Commission (IEC) 10646 Universal Coded Character Set – provided a single computer encoding system for a wide range of languages and writing systems, with subsequent versions adding to this global coverage. This common standard was critical for creating, managing, printing, and emailing text in multiple languages.

Translation also became more oriented towards conveying information in a format appropriate and appealing to specific cultures, a process aided by the Unicode Consortium's Common Locale Date Repository (CLDR) and later the Unicode Locale Data Markup Language (LDML). These resources provided programming-accessible information on locale or country-specific conventions, such as formatting of time, numbers, calendar information, telephone codes, and sorting rules.

Professional Organizations and Publications

This decade was also a time of extensive national and international sharing of information. In 1994, AMTA, EAMT, and AAMT held their first conferences, all with US participation. In 1998, the European Language Resources Association (ELRA) held its first international Language Resources and Evaluation Conference (LREC), with US participation. In 1999, ACL started providing considerable conference programming on machine translation and related technologies. That year, Jost Zetzsche started the free online newsletter *The Translator's Toolbox: A Computer Primer for Translators*, which has helped educate language professionals on CAT.

2000s: SMT, DARPA, SDL

Environment

On 11 September 2001, jihadists flew planes into the Twin Towers in New York and the Pentagon in Virginia, an event now known as '9–11'. The US response to 9–11 and to anthrax attacks the same year was the Global War on Terror, including the USA PATRIOT Act of 2001. This act funded MT research and development. It also established the National Virtual Translation Center (NVTC) to provide human translation services to the government. The NVTC under Everette Jordan's leadership created technology to support both users and customers.

Technology was developed to get the user data to wherever the translators were available. The Translators Online Network was created to receive requests for translation, support the translators with tools, and deliver timely finished products to the various government customers.

In 2001, Lernaut & Hauspie declared bankruptcy, which caused concern by developers and investors about the profitability of investing in language technology. It also disrupted numerous research efforts. However, SDL continued its rapid acquisition of tools and companies related to CAT.

In 2003, Google's Alpha Go beat an unhandicapped professional human player, reinforcing government and public optimism about the possibilities for AI, including MT. In 2018, Microsoft's artificial intelligence group issued a press release claiming its NMT had achieved 'human parity' with work done by humans (specifically by professional human translators). The publication was widely read and debated, raising issues about what constituted 'human parity'.

MT

DARPA established programs focusing on languages and applications to support new military and humanitarian relief efforts. In 2000, DARPA started the Translingual Information Detection, Extraction, and Summarization (TIDES) program, headed by Allen Sears, Charles Wayne, and then Bonnie Dorr. In 2005, DARPA established the Global Autonomous Language Exploitation (GALE) program under Joseph Olive, which continued and substantially expanded the research started in TIDES (ibid.) In 2006, it established the Spoken Language Communication and Translation System for Tactical Use (TRANSTAC) program under Mari Maeda, to enable automated medical interpreting (Kakaes) and the Effective Affordable Reusable Speech-to-Text (EARS) program. DARPA established the Multilingual Automatic Document Classification Analysis and Translation (MADCAT) program in 2008, under Olive. In 2010, DARPA established the Robust Automatic Transcription of Speech (RATS), also under Olive, which improved transcription of conversational speech.

In response to needs for testing and evaluation in the DARPA program, NIST began its annual MT testing, a process that spurred the development of better machine translation and better MT evaluation methods. IBM produced the Bilingual Evaluation Understudy (BLEU), which provided automatic scoring of machine translation output against reference translations but has been highly controversial in the evaluation community. Numerous alternative systems evolved, such as the MT Metric for Evaluation of Translation with Explicit Ordering (METEOR), that better reflect human assessment and that account for differences in the impact of certain errors.

In 2002 Microsoft used MT to translate support knowledge base articles, demonstrating a broader set of tasks that could be accomplished with machine translation. That year Kevin Knight and Daniel Marcu founded Language Weaver, based on SMT.

The increasing quantity of parallel corpora (i.e. of source documents paired with translations) enabled statistical analysis of the probability of a particular translation for a given term (e.g. translating 'bank' as a financial institution rather than the land abutting a river). In 2003, Philipp Koehn, Franz Och, and David Marcu published their work on phrase-based machine translation. This analysis evolved into SMT. In 2003, Franz-Josef Och won the DARPA competition for speed of MT with an SMT engine, thus launching a revolution in machine translation from rule-based MT to SMT. Och later became head of machine translation at Google. In the late 2000s various companies, including Apptek and Systran, released hybrid MT systems using rule-based MT and SMT.

In 2003, Yahoo acquired AltaVista BabelFish and incorporated MT into its search engine. In 2005, Google launched free online machine translation, which made a wider range of MT easily and freely available to the public. In 2007 Google replaced Systran with its own SMT engine, and Microsoft launched its free online MT offering that used Microsoft's own SMT for technical texts and Systran for more general texts. Also in 2007, Philip Koehn and his team produced the MOSES SMT toolkit. One of the first of several open source toolkits for SMT, the zero cost and easy availability encouraged development and experimentation by a broader user base.

In 2009, SYSTRAN released a version of its own server-based software using post-editing capabilities, as described by Melby (2015).

CAT

In 2001, Google pioneered the use of crowdsourcing for translation as part of its Google in Your Language (GIYL) campaign, which translated Google Search into 118 languages. In 2007, Facebook started employing crowdsourcing to translate the application. Other organizations have employed the same model, including WordNet and Wikipedia. Amara started using crowdsourcing for translating video subtitling, and Duolingo for language learning and website translation (DeCamp and Zetzsche 2015).

In 2002, MITRE Corporation established a laboratory to evaluate the impact of different kinds of tools, including interactive MT, entity tagging, electronic dictionaries, and automatic transliteration. The lab recorded all keystrokes of the translators to provide objective analysis.

That year, Trados established its headquarters in the United States and acquired Uniscape, thus improving its ability to provide tools and services to the US market. In 2005, Trados was acquired by SDL and most development and support was moved to Europe. In 2005, Idiom started a program to give away fully functional free licenses to qualifying language service providers, causing many translators to experiment with this technology. In 2008 Idiom was bought by SDL, which incorporated this capability into its product offerings.

In 2006, the first US CAT tool, Lingotek, was launched. In 2008, SDL purchased ALPNET and Transparent Language software and incorporated the technology into its products, creating a substantially richer set of tools for translators (Wikipedia, machine translation). In 2009, Madcap Lingo was launched, Google released its own CAT tool (Google Translator Toolkit), and Welocalize released an open-source product based on Globalsite. In addition, as described, Systran added post-editing capabilities. In 2010, the LDS Church launched Fluency and MadCap Lingo (DeCamp and Zetzsche 2015). While translators in the United States used many foreign-produced CAT tools, Lingotek, Fluency, and MadCap Lingo were the only US products during this decade.

Standards

In 2001, the Society of Automotive Engineers (SAE) committee published the SAE Standard J2450 Quality Metric for Language Translation of Service Information, the first standard to provide guidelines for the structured evaluation of translation quality based on a statistical identification of translation error types and the assignment of error severity levels to the individual error instances, thus producing a quality metric rather than just guidelines. This standard was the first effort to provide detailed guidelines for translations in a specific domain into any target language (see DeCamp 2022).

In 2002, Eduard Hovy, a South African researcher at Carnegie Mellon University, and Margaret King, a British researcher at the University of Geneva, published the Framework for Machine Translation Evaluation in ISLE or FEMTI. This framework included input from multiple countries, drawing on (Hovy and King 2003; ISLE 2021), work from the Executive Advisory Group on Language Engineering Standards

Professional Organizations

In 2002, the Globalization and Localization Industry Standards Association (GALA) was established. In 2005, the Translation Association User Society was founded by Jaap van der Meer in Europe, with US participation.

New organizations began holding competitions for machine translation. ACL held its first annual Workshop on Statistical Machine Translation Shared Task in 2005, continuing through 2014. NIST developed the NIST Metrics for Machine Translation Challenge (MetricsMATR) website and provided challenges for MT metrics in 2008 and 2010.

ATA continued its work on text-based evaluation in order to provide translator certification for its members. A detailed method of hand scoring that was based on a numerical metric was developed. Each text was scored by multiple raters.

2010s: NMT, OpenMT, Microsoft Translator Hub, Lilt

Environment

The decade started with an earthquake in Haiti, where both Google and Microsoft demonstrated that they could create a new MT language pair within days, drawing on research and data from DARPA and other programs. In 2011, IBM's Watson beat humans in Jeopardy, thus achieving the AI goal of a machine doing as well or better than a human and raising interest and optimism for achieving this goal for MT. In 2019, the Persian Gulf Crisis resulted in needs for additional languages and dialects. Moreover, the United Nations Educational, Scientific, and Cultural Organization (UNESCO) declared 2019 the Year of Indigenous Languages, promoting the digitization of indigenous languages and dialects and the development of MT capabilities in order to help preserve them.

The availability of high-quality translations drove improvements in CAT and MT. TAUS established the Human Language Project and the European Community established MyMemory, which both provided translation memories for translator use or MT development. In addition, the Jehovah's Witnesses made their Bible parallel corpora (i.e. translations and the original text) for over 300 languages publicly available, supplying CAT and MT with data for additional languages for which there has been little MT development to date, often referred to as 'long-tail' languages (Richardson).

MT

In 2010, IBM launched Fluent, including post-editing.

In 2011, DARPA established the Broad Operational Language Translation (BOLT) program and in 2012, the Deep Exploration and Filtering (DEFT) program, building on the work of GALE. These programs – both under Bonnie Dorr – addressed diversity of languages, dialects, and registers, including in social media. To address these challenges, DARPA began to combine new translation techniques with conversational analysis (Dorr 2012). That year, NIST established the Open Handwriting Recognition and Translation (OpenHaRT) testing. In 2012, IARPA established the BABEL program under Mary Harper and later Mari Maeda for speech translation and generation. In 2014, DARPA established the Low Resource Languages for Emergent Incidents (LORELEI) Program under Boyan Onyshkevych and later William Corvey to improve MT for low-resource languages. In 2016, IARPA launched the Machine Translation for English Retrieval of Information in Any Language (MATERIAL) program under Carl Rubino to 'build Cross-Language Information Retrieval (CLIR) systems that find speech and text content in diverse lower-resource languages, using English search queries' (IARPA 'MATERIAL').

In 2014, Systran was acquired by the Center for the Study of Language and Information (CSLI), founded by Stanford University, SRI International, and the Palo Alto Research Center (formerly Xerox).

That year, at the Workshop on Machine Translation (WMT) 14, an international team at Google headed by Yonghui Wu, Mike Shuster, Zhifeng Chen, Quoc V. Le, and Mohammand Norouzi, demonstrated an average 60% reduction in translation errors with neural machine translation compared to their phrase-based system. This achievement sparked considerable interest in this new approach. NMT not only reduced translation errors but also could be quickly and inexpensively trained, thus enabling the development of machine translation for additional languages and dialects and for domains (e.g. investment, medical). In 2016, Google released its first version of Google NMT (GNMT), based on direct translation from Language A to Language B (known as 'zero-shot') rather than with translation first to English, as was formerly the case with Google Translate. In 2016, the Harvard Natural Language Processing group and Systran started OpenNMT. This tool supplied free access for developers and thus encouraged experimentation with NMT (NIST). In 2017, Google's NMT was installed in the European Patent Office.

Machine translation evaluation has continued to be a key issue. In 2015, DARPA initiated TIDES MT evaluations. NIST provided Open MT evaluations and introduced an MT Challenge. In 2016, an LREC panel concluded that

> Current approaches to machine translation or professional translation evaluation, both automatic and manual, are characterized by a high degree of fragmentation, heterogeneity and a lack of interoperability between methods, tools and data sets. As a consequence, it is difficult to reproduce, interpret, and compare evaluation results.

At this workshop, Lommel presented rigorous experiments with BLEU, concluding that:

> The results of these experiments, conducted on a Chinese>English news corpus with eleven human reference translations, bring the validity of BLEU as a measure of translation quality into question and suggest that the score differences cited in a considerable body of MT literature are likely to be unreliable indicators of system performance due to an inherent imprecision in reference-based methods. Although previous research has found that human quality judgments largely correlate with BLEU, this study suggests that the correlation is an artefact of experimental design rather than an indicator of validity.

In 2017, Marie Benjamin, Atsushi Fujita, and Raphael Rubino presented their paper, 'Scientific Credibility of Machine Translation Research: A Meta-Evaluation of 769 Papers', with similar findings. They noted that 'at least 108 metrics claiming to be better than BLEU have been proposed'.

CAT

In 2012, Microsoft Research developed the Microsoft Translator Hub. This software leveraged CAT and MT capabilities, where translators selected from a variety of resources, including terminologies, translation memories, multiple MT engines, and the general internet. The users could then use the translations (paired with the original text) to tailor their SMT engines or to build new MT engines. Microsoft also experimented with a broad range of tools to improve translation quality, such as providing confidence measures based on the resources used for the translation (e.g. a terminology vs. a translation memory vs. an MT engine). It also experimented with assigning weights to translators and editors to automate the prioritization of conflicting editing decisions.

In 2011, Google released the Google Translator Toolkit and IBM released TM/2 as open source in the Open TM2 CAT tool. That year, SDL acquired Language Weaver and integrated it with its CAT tools. SDL also included a confidence measure in the product, alerting translators and editors to areas that might need post-editing. It soon added access to additional MT engines, as have most other providers of CAT tools. In 2015, Lilt was founded by Spence Green to provide a new generation of integrated tools for translators, including customized NMT. The easy user interface and high degree of customer care encouraged translators to employ tools such as interactive MT.

While assessments on the ROI of tools have been conducted for decades, the late 2010s saw improvements in the analysis of the measurement of translation productivity. These studies segmented the types of translation, translators, and tools and provided more rigorous standards for evaluation (DeCamp and Zetzsche 2015).

Standards

In 2010, the ASTM F43 Committee on Language Products and Services was established, pulling together language-related standards work from multiple committees, as well as the Technical Advisory Group on the work from the International Organization for Standardization Committee Technical Committee on Language and Terminology. In 2010, ATA and AMTA co-located their conferences and provided joint programming, leading to increased communication across these communities.

2020s: Accuracy and the Role of Translators

Environment

The early 2020s were extensively shaped by the COVID-19 epidemic. In response to quarantine restrictions, professional organizations – including AMTA, the MT Summit, and ATA – held conferences and meetings remotely over videoconferencing software. With no travel, international collaboration (e.g. at the MT Summit in 2021) became both easier and more affordable. In addition, more conferences began posting recordings and papers from presentations for free public access. ACL expanded its free online archive to include presentations and papers from its own conferences as well as from other MT and related events. This convenient and free access to conference proceedings and research papers facilitated education and global sharing of information.

In 2021, van der Meer forecast the 'singularity', where MT combined with extensive publicly available data would completely replace human translators. This idea that humans would be completely replaced from all translation workflows was hotly debated and widely refuted in the translation community (Melby and Katz).

MT

COVID-19 also resulted in a new domain with extensive documentation produced in many languages. TAUS was one of many organizations that collected this data, making it free to the community for development and testing of translation tools. Systran used this data to test the impact of using domain data, finding a 28% improvement when training its NMT with this corpus.

TAUS, an international organization with US participation, developed a broad test set of source documents and translations segmented by language, domain, and genre. INTENTO, a Berkeley Skydeck startup, tested commercial MT engines against this data set, providing scores by these factors. TAUS and INTENTO offered this segmented data to the public for testing of other engines.

In 2020, Wendt provided a keynote presentation at AMTA where he described the potential and challenges of NMT. The presentation encouraged researchers to address means of constraining the translation (e.g. through metadata). However, the 'catastrophic' errors in NMT did not appear to slow the rapid adoption of the new technology, particularly given the extensive press coverage not only of NMT but also of artificial intelligence, machine learning, and neural technologies.

In 2020, Systran was acquired by the South Korean firm STIC Investments.

CAT

In 2020, SDL was acquired by the British firm RWS.

In the early 2020s, researchers continued to experiment with natural language processing tools to improve CAT and MT. The success in 2021 of Hugging Face in raising $40 million for its open source natural language processing library encouraged researchers and developers of extensive NLP resources for experimentation and development.

Standards

Remote work continued rapidly on standards, including *ASTM Standard New Practice for Analytic Evaluation of Translation Quality* and *ASTM Standard Practice for Quality Assurance in Translation*. Work progressed on standards on sign language translation, helped in part by a strong movement in the United States to provide citizens equal access and equity to resources. Standards work began on translation of speech and captioning.

Future

Environment

In 2018, the International Data Corporation (IDC) predicted that the total global digital content generated each year would increase from 33 to 175 zetabytes in 2025. As translation technology extends to more languages and dialects and to more applications, and as MT quality and capabilities increased, there would be a rising percentage of the global digital content that would be translated and thus more access by groups inside and outside the United States to information in their languages and dialects of choice. Van der Meer predicted that the 2020s would see real-time customized MT in sixty languages at 'near-zero' cost. He predicted that the 2030s would see 'ubiquitous' and 'unlimited' content MT in more than 150 languages.

However, in 2022, there is still significant content that cannot be translated by MT or at least, not translated reliably. In extensive surveys by Lommel and CSA, 41% of language service providers reported 'pressure to use MT in inappropriate situations', and 23% reported they had experienced 'unrealistic expectations'. Respondents indicated a 'perception that current generation MT is not responsive enough and does not meet business and technical requirements'. There is a need to improve the accuracy and fluency of many language pairs and to add new languages and dialects able to translate new domains, genres, and types in specific registers and styles.

MT

As Wendt pointed out in 2020, NMT produces errors that are rare but have significant repercussions, including negatives as positives, changed numbers or units of measurement (including currencies), lack of translation of parts of the source document, introduction of offensive language, people or symbols inaccurately placed in negative contexts, bias, and introduction of material in the translation that was not in the source document (known as 'hallucinations'). He urged that researchers, developers, and users find ways to prevent these errors in MT or at least to reliably identify them for post-editing. He called for greater awareness of the document context and more real-world knowledge in order to have translations with the more discriminating word choice shown by expert translation professionals. In addition, he called for increasing the extent of localization and for finding ways to publish raw MT, implementing feedback, customizing, and making greater use of business intelligence to conduct checks on content. He also called for systems that are more context aware.

To provide this responsiveness and reliability, better evaluation is needed, particularly automated evaluation that can help identify problems and rapidly route text to appropriate tools and expertise. More consistency of terminology and practice is also needed in order to use translation evaluations for comparisons, including for acquisition decisions. Standards and guidelines are still needed for comparing alternative approaches with fully automated versus human translation or CAT.

CAT

Increased capability and use of MT will impact the roles of human translators. Gartner Group in a 2020 report estimated that by 2025, 75% of translation work would shift from developing translations to 'reviewing and editing translation output'. Lommel in 2021 also predicted a decrease in 'traditional written human language services', but foresaw a greater overall increase in jobs due to more work in spoken language services, in traditional post editing services, and in 'augmented translation, content enrichment, and other intelligence multilingual service'. These new roles for translators will require tools beyond the current CAT capabilities.

While MT researchers and developers are exploring means of producing MT for a rapidly expanding number of language pairs at a rapidly increasing accuracy, there are still the occasional catastrophic or embarrassing errors that would probably be caught by expert translators and editors. There are also types of translation, such as translation of literature, where 'useful' is not good enough.

For the foreseeable future, there will most likely be an increasing amount of material translated by machine but still some material that needs human translation and/or review. With new technical capabilities and new roles, there will be a need to continually assess and communicate the right technology and expertise for specific tasks. There will also be a need to develop technology to increase the productivity of humans and the accuracy and reliability of machine translation.

Timeline of History of Translation Technology in the United States

1943	Warren McCulloch and mathematician Walter Pitts develop first neural model
1944	
1945	Murray Leinster introduces the concept of the 'universal translator' in his novella *First Contact*

1946   A.D. Booth and Warren Weaver propose using digital computers for translation
1947   The Cold War begins, lasting until 1989
        The International Organization for Standardization (ISO) Technical Committee 37 on Terminology and Language (ISO TC37) is established
1948
1949   Warren Weaver, director of the Natural Sciences Division at the Rockefeller Center, publishes his 'Memorandum on Translation', outlining issues and directions for machine translation
1950   Turing proposes a 'Thinking Machine' and proposes machine translation as a possible application
        The Korean War begins, lasting until 1953
1951   Yehoshua Bar-Hillel at Georgetown University becomes the first full-time MT researcher
        Marvin Minsky and Dean Edmonds build the first neural network machine
1952   The Georgetown MT Research Center is established
        The first conference on MT is held at Georgetown University
        The United States develops some of the first machine learning programs
        Alan Turing proposes the Turing Test
1953
1954   The Georgetown–IBM Experiment generates significant media coverage
        The Journal of Machine Translation is launched
1955   US Government Interagency Language Roundtable is formed, including a committee on translation and later on translation and translation technology
        John McCarthy coins the term 'artificial intelligence'
1956   The movie *The Forbidden Planet* popularizes MT with Robby the Robot
1957   The Russians launch Sputnik
        Noam Chomsky publishes 'Syntactic Structures', creating the foundations for the design of rule-based MT systems
        The United States Air Force starts using Russian-to-English MT for scientific work
        The American Translators Association is established
        Bar-Hillel publishes 'The Status of Automated Translation of Language'
1958   Frank Rosenblatt develops the first artificial neural network, called Perceptron
        DARPA is established
1959
1960   Bar-Hillel publishes 'Demonstration of the Nonfeasibility of Fully Automatic High-Quality Translation', concluding that 'there is no immediate or predictable prospect of useful machine translation' and recommending investments in improving human translation
1961   The Linguistics Research Center (LRC) is founded at the University of Texas at Austin
1962   The United States Air Force adopts the Mark II system developed by IBM and Washington University
        The Association for Machine Translation and Computational Linguistics (later known as the Association for Computational Linguistics) is established
        The television series *The Jetsons* (1962–1963) popularizes speech technologies with Rosie the Maid
1963   Georgetown University systems for Chinese–English MT are established in Euratom and at Oak Ridge National Laboratory

1964

1965   US troops are sent to Vietnam

The novel *Dune* by Frank Herbert is published, depicting the extraordinary ability of MT to work even in the absence of computers

1966   The television show *Star Trek* (1966–1969) explores machine translation with the Universal Translator

The National Academy of Sciences publishes the *Automatic Language Processing Advisory Committee (ALPAC) report*, recommending that research for MT be discontinued

1967

1968   The first MT company (Language Automated Translation, System, and Electronic Communications or LATSAC) becomes SYSTRAN

1969   Logos is founded to work on MT for the US government

1970   The United States Air Force adopts SYSTRAN software

Eldon Lytle, Daryl Gibb, Alan K. Melby, Steve Richardson, and others start to develop Interactive Translation System at Brigham Young University

1971   Bar-Hillel defines roles of MT and makes the distinction that translation quality depends on the particular users and their situations

1972   Wang launches the first office word processor in the United States

Caterpillar introduces Caterpillar Fundamental English

1973   Xerox develops the Alto computer, the first personal computer, although it was never marketed or implemented outside of Xerox and beta sites

1974   Xerox develops Bravo, the first WYSIWYG editor, which has fonts for multiple languages

1975   The US Air Force develops the QUINCE Chinese-to-English MT system and starts work on a German-to-English model

1976   Logos starts developing English-to-Persian MT to support sales of military systems to the Shah of Persia

1977   Weidner Communications Corporation is founded to produce computer-assisted translation

Smart Al Inc. is established for controlled language

The movie *Star Wars* introduces C-3PO and R2-D2, robots outfitted with machine translation

1978   Xerox starts using SYSTRAN to translate technical manuals

Weidner Communications produces Weidner Machine Translation and Weidner Multilingual Word Processing systems

1979

1980   The Iran–Iraq war begins, lasting through 1988

ALPS was founded with people from the BYUTSI project

Linguatech develops MTX, a standalone terminology tool

Caterpillar launches Caterpillar Technical English

NEC demonstrates speech translation

Xerox develops the Xerox Character Code Standard, which forms the bases for the Unicode Standard

Weidner Multi-Lingua Word Processing software is sold to Siemens

1981   Xerox begins marketing the 8010 Information System (also known as the 'Xerox Star', the first commercially available personal computer with a graphical user interface

1982   ITS is shut down and technology is taken over by ALPS

1983	NEC Corporation provides the first demonstration of MT integrated with automatic speech recognition and natural language generation
1984	Trados is established in Germany
	The movie *Dune* popularizes the idea that MT can work, even in the absence of computers
1985	Voice of America starts to use the Xerox 8010 Information System for translation and transcreation in multiple languages
	The Pan American Health Organization implements ENSPAN for English- to-Spanish translation
	The Mechanical Translation and Analysis of Languages (METAL, formerly the Linguistics Research System or LRS) is marketed by Siemens-Nixdorf through 1992
1986	The Center for Machine Translation Systems is established at Carnegie Mellon University, focused on knowledge-based MT
	Xerox develops the first data-driven MT system
	SYSTRAN is sold to a private French company
1987	The first Machine Translation Summit is held
	The Unicode project begins
	Lernout & Hauspie established, buying and integrating multiple language technology companies
	NIST starts the ten-year series of Message Understanding Conferences (MUC)
1988	The Iran–Iraq War ends
	Globalink is founded, providing the first personal MT software and the first MT web services
	Peter Brown reports on experiments with statistical MT
	Xerox starts marketing its pre- and post-editing capabilities, tied to SYSTRAN and METAL MT on an IBM mainframe
	Joe Becker at Xerox drafts a proposal for a multi-language character encoding system, which becomes known as Unicode
	Peter F. Brown, John Cocke, Stephen A. Della Pietra, Vincent J. Della Pietra, Fredrick Jelinek, John D. Lafferty, Robert L. Mercer, and Paul S. Roossin from the IBM Thomas J. Watson Research Center publish 'A Statistical Approach to Machine Translation'
1989	The Localization Industry Standards Association is founded
	IBM runs a research & development project in statistical machine translation (Wikipedia, machine translation)
1990	IBM launches the first PC
	Trados, a German company, releases its first commercial product, MultiTerm
1991	The Gulf War begins
	The Unicode Consortium is formed
	The first version of the Unicode Standard is released
	The International Association for Machine Translation and the Association for Machine Translation in the Americas, as well as the European Association for Machine Translation and the Asian Association for Machine Translation, are founded
	DARPA starts the MT Initiative
	Xerox starts marketing DocuTrans, combining SYSTRAN and METAL on an IBM mini-mainframe, with pre-processing and post-processing software and confidence measures from Xerox
	NIST starts a nine-year program

1992	The Bosnian Civil war begins, ending in 1995
	DARPA establishes the Human Language Technology Program, including the Machine Translation Evaluation Program
	The Linguistic Data Consortium is founded with a grant from DARPA
	DARPA establishes the Babylon program
	NIST and IARPA start the Text REtrieval Conference (TREC), which includes Cross Lingual Information Retrieval (CLIR)
	IBM releases CAT tool Translation Manager (TM/2)
	Trados releases its first translation memory application, Workbench
	Caterpillar and Carnegie Mellon University launch Caterpillar's Automated Machine Translation
	The second volume of the Unicode standard, including Han characters, is published
1993	
1994	The Association for Machine Translation in the Americas holds its first conference
1995	Bosnian War ends
	Lernout & Hauspie acquire translation and other language technology, including METAL, with investments from Microsoft
1996	SYSTRAN offers free translation on the Internet in the United States (having offered a similar service in France in the 1980s)
	Uniscape is founded
	The movie *Mars Attacks* warns of problems with incorrect translations
	Carnegie Mellon University, New Mexico State University, and the University of Southern California experiment with multiple MT engines in their Pangloss system
1997	The United States sends humanitarian relief for the Albanian Civil War
	AltaVista Babelfish is launched using SYSTRAN software
	GlobalSight launches Ambassador Suite
	Robert Palmquist develops the first translation system for continuous speech
	IBM's Deep Blue beats world chess champion Kasparov
1998	Idiom launches WorldServer
	The Association for Computational Linguistics organizes the North American Chapter of the Association for Computational Linguistics
1999	Jost Zetzsche starts the free online newsletter for translators: *The Translator's Tool Box: A Computer Primer for Translators*
	The C-Star2 Consortium demonstrates speech-to-speech translation
	Michael Crichton's novel *Timeline* set unrealistic expectations that MT could easily be used to translate as-yet-unknown languages with no parallel corpora
	The US war with Afghanistan begins
2000	The US Department of Labor recognizes translation and interpreting as its own career field with a category in the 2000 Census
	DARPA establishes the Translingual Information Detection, Extraction, and Summarization (TIDES) program, headed by Allen Sears and then by Charles Wayne
2001	The September 11 attacks on the Twin Towers and the Pentagon ignite extensive MT requirements for Middle Eastern languages to and from English
	Lernout & Hauspie declare bankruptcy
	SDL purchases ALPNET and Transparent Language software and incorporates the technology into its products
	DARPA starts the TIPSTER Text Program, a nine-year program to improve the handling of multilanguage text

2002	Microsoft uses MT to translate support knowledge base articles
	The Globalization and Localization Industry Standards Association is established
	IBM creates BLEU automated MT evaluation tool
	Language Weaver is founded
	The SMT entry from a University of Southern California's Information Sciences Institute headed by Franz-Josef Och wins the DARPA/NIST MT competition
	Trados establishes its headquarters in the United States
	Trados acquires Uniscape
	The MITRE Corporation creates a translation laboratory to test translator preferences and productivity gains in using machine translation and other NLP tools
2003	Yahoo! acquires AltaVista Babelfish
	The International Standards for Language Engineering develops the Framework for MT Evaluation to evaluate the best MT engines for specific applications
	The movie *Timeline* popularizes the idea that MT can be developed on the fly with no rules or corpora
	Philipp Koehn, Franz Och, and Daniel Marcu publish on phrase-based machine translation
	The National Virtual Translation Center is established
	The Translation Association User Society is founded and holds its first forum
	C-STAR organizes the International Workshop on Spoken Language Translation
2004	C-STAR establishes the International Workshop on Spoken Language Translation
2005	DARPA establishes the Global Autonomous Language Exploitation program
	Satanjeev Banerjee and Alon Lavie publish paper on Metric for Evaluation with Explicit Ordering to address issues in BLEU
	Google launches free online MT, making MT widely available
	Alon Lavie and his team develop METEOR, improving automated evaluation of MT
	Idiom starts a program to give away fully functional free licenses to qualifying language service providers
2006	Lingotek is founded
	DARPA establishes the Spoken Language Communication and Translation System for Tactical Use program
2007	Johns Hopkins University Human Language Technology Center of Excellence is founded
	Microsoft launches its free online translator using both internal SMT engines and Systran
	Facebook starts its translation crowdsourcing application
	Google replaces Systran with its own statistical MT engine
	Philip Koehn and his team produce the MOSES SMT toolkit
2008	Welocalize acquires Transware
	Microsoft replaces Systran in its online translator with its own MT
	SDL acquires Idiom
	NIST develops the NIST Metrics for Machine Translation Challenge website and provides challenges for MT metrics in 2008 and 2010
	DARPA starts the Multilingual Automatic Document Classification Analysis and Translation
2009	MadCap Lingo is launched
	SYSTRAN releases a version of its own server-based software using post-editing capabilities

Google releases its own CAT tool, Google Translator Toolkit

Welocalize releases an open-source product based on GlobalSight

Apptek launches a hybrid MT system using SMT and RBMT

SYSTRAN releases version 7, which provides a hybrid version of RBMT and SMT as well as a post-editing module

2010   An earthquake hits Haiti; Google and Microsoft use materials collected by a team at Carnegie Mellon University and other sources to release a version of a Haitian Creole <-> English MT engine within days

IBM launches Fluent, including post-editing

ATA and AMTA hold first co-located conferences

Asia Online launches Language Studio, including MT and post-editing

Language Weaver launches quality confidence measure

SDL acquires Language Weaver

TM/2 – developed by IBM – is released as open source in Open TM2 CAT tool

Fluency is launched

DARPA establishes the Robust Automatic Transcription of Speech (RATS) program

The ASTM F43 Committee on Language Products and Services is established

DARPA provides TIDES MT evaluations

NIST provides Open MT evaluations

2011   ASTM F43 establishes subcommittee to focus on translation standards

DARPA establishes the Broad Operational Language Translation (BOLT) program

IBM's Watson beats humans in Jeopardy

2012   Microsoft launches the Microsoft Translator Hub, enabling self-service online MT customization. The Collaborative Translation Framework is also launched, enabling translation groups to assign and prioritize editors for new additions to the MT systems.

Yahoo! replaces Babelfish with Microsoft Bing Translator

IARPA establishes the BABEL program for speech translation and generation

The Localisation Industry Standards Association is disbanded

NIST begins its annual MT benchmarking

IBM launches WebSphere

The Phraselator speech-to-speech translation system is tested in Afghanistan

DARPA initiates the Deep Exploration and Filtering of Text program, building on the work of GALE

2013   The Iraq War starts, ending in 2017

SDL establishes a wholly owned US subsidiary

2014   Google demonstrates a 60% reduction in translation errors with NMT compared to its phrase-based system

The first paper on NMT is published

Systran is acquired by the Center for the Study of Language and Information, founded by Stanford University, SRI International, and the Palo Alto Research Center (formerly Xerox)

DARPA launches the Low Resource Languages for Emergent Incidents program

2015   Lilt is founded

OpenMT introduced an MT Challenge, which included an NMT system

Microsoft launches the Skype translator for video calls translated in real time

The unified error typology is created from TAUS Dynamic Quality Framework and DFKI Multidimensional Quality Metrics (funded by the European Commission in the QTLaunchPad and QTLeap projects)

WMT
2016 The Harvard NLP group and SYSTRAN start OpenNMT

Work begins on *ASTM Standard WK46396: New Practice for Analytic Evaluation of Translation Quality*

Google's Alpha Go beats an unhandicapped professional human player

A Language Resources Evaluation Conference panel concludes that 'current approaches to Machine Translation (MT) or professional translation evaluation, both automatic and manual, are characterized by a high degree of fragmentation, heterogeneity and a lack of interoperability between methods, tools and data sets. As a consequence, it is difficult to reproduce, interpret, and compare evaluation results'

Google, Microsoft, and Systran produce NMT

IARPA launches the Machine Translation for English Retrieval of Information in Any Language program under Carl Rubino

2017 The Iraq War ends

Google's NMT is installed in the European Patent Office

Microsoft starts the Turing Project to build large language models to support applications such as machine translation

ACL holds the First Workshop on Neural Machine Translation

Benjamin Marie, Atushi Fujita, and Raphael Rubino present a large-scale meta-evaluation of MT evaluation practices

2018 Microsoft launches the MS Custom Translator – the NMT version of the MS Translator Hub.

Google launches AutoML for customizing its MT systems

Microsoft's AI Group claims its MT has achieved parity with humans, including professional human translators

2019 The United Nations Educational, Scientific, and Cultural Organization declares 2019 the Year of Indigenous Languages, spurring efforts to develop MT for indigenous languages

The Persian Gulf Crisis (2019–2020) results in needs for additional MT and translation

The Jehovah's Witnesses make parallel corpora available for over 300 languages

The National Institute for Standards and Technology launches its first MT competition

2020 The COVID-19 epidemic results in quarantines and disruptions worldwide for more than two years

TAUS provides a set of data for translation of materials related to COVID-19, which enables new testing with domain

Systran provides free MT models based on the TAUS COVID-19 data

Systran is acquired by the South Korean company STIC Investments

SDL is acquired by the British company RWS

2021 Hugging Face receives $40 million in investments to build and test NLP models for an open source library

TAUS, with European Commission funding, provides a test bed segmented by language, domain, and genre, enabling testing of machine translation engines bay INTENTO and others against these factors

Jaap van der Meer publishes an article in *Multilingual Computing* predicting a 'singularity' when free and ubiquitous raw MT will be completely replace human translators and editors; his predictions are hotly debated in the translation community

Microsoft introduces Translation at Scale, a plan to use language models to rapidly provide translation in 10,000 language pairs

Facebook produces the Facebook Low Resource (FLORES) multilingual model with 101 languages. At the WMT workshop in November, Facebook won the large news competition using a multilingual neural model while all its competitors were using bilingual ones – the first time this ever happened! And in 2022, we've seen huge updated multilingual models from Facebook, Microsoft, and Google

2023 The *ASTM Standard New Practice for Analytic Evaluation of Translation Quality* anticipated for publication

The *ASTM Standard Practice for Translation Quality Assurance* anticipated for publication

Acknowledgments

The author would like to thank W. John Hutchins and Harold Somers. for their detailed collection of data and their analysis of the early history of MT (Hutchins 1997, 1986, 2000, 2005, 2006; Hutchins and Sommers 1992). She would like to thank organizations that provided timelines and data, including TAUS, Systran, and Wikipedia. She would also like to thank Jost Zetzsche, her co-author on a 2016 shorter version of this chapter. who provided review comments. Thanks go to Steve Richardson, Chris Wendt, Kathleen Egan, and Alan K. Melby for their input and to Sue Ellen Wright, Arle Lommel, Jen Doyon, and Madalena Sánchez Zampaulo for their input and review.

Bibliography

ASTM (2022) 'ASTM Standard New Practice for Analytic Evaluation of Translation Quality', *Draft Standard*. Available at: www.astm.org/workitem-wk46396.

ASTM (2022) 'ASTM Standard Practice for Translation Quality Assurance', *Draft Standard*. Copies available from ASTM Project Leader.

Automatic Language Processing Advisory Committee (ALPAC) (1966) 'Language and Machines: Computers in Translation and Linguistics', *Report by the Automatic Language Processing Advisory Committee, Division of Behavioral Sciences, National Academy of Sciences*, National Research Council, Washington, DC, National Academy of Sciences.

Aymerich, Julia and Hermes Camelo (2009, August 26) 'The MT Maturity Model at PAHO', in *Proceedings of the Conference for the International Association for Machine Translation (IAMT)*, Ontario, Canada.

Banerjee, S. and A. Lavie (2005) 'METEOR: An Automatic Metric for MT Evaluation with Improved Correlation with Human Judgments', in *Proceedings of Workshop on Intrinsic and Extrinsic Evaluation Measures for MT and/or Summarization at the 43rd Annual Meeting of the Association of Computational Linguistics (ACL-2005)*, Ann Arbor, Michigan, June 2005.

Bar-Hillel, Yehoshua (1971) 'Some Reflections on the Present Outlook for High-quality Machine Translation', Linguistics Research Center: The University of Texas at Austin. Available at: www.mt-archive.info/LRC-1971-Bar-Hillel.pdf.

Brown, Peter, John Cocke, S. Della Pietra, V. Della Pietra, Frederick Jelinek, Robert L. Mercer, and P. Roossin (1988) 'A Statistical App Model Approach to Language Translation', *Coling'88, Association for Computational Linguistics* 1: 71–76.

Chen, Stanley, Brian Kingsbury, Lidia Mangu, Daniel Povey, Geroe Saon, Hagen Soltau, and Geoffrey Zweig (2006) 'Advances in Speech Transcription at IBM under the DARPA EARS Program'. Available at: www.danielpovey.com/files/ieee_trans_ears_2006.pdf.

Chomsky, Noam (1957) 'Syntactic Structures', The Hague: Mouton.

CSA Research (2021, April 7) 'Releases 2021 Language Services and Technology Market Growth Scenarios'. Available at: www.seagate.com/files/www-content/our-story/trends/files/idc-seagate-dataage-whitepaper.pdf.

Day, David, Galen Williamson, Alex Yeh, Keith Crouch, Sam Bayer, Jennifer DeCamp, Angel Asencio, Seamus Clancy, and Flo Reeder (2006, May 22) 'A Platform for the Empirical Analysis of Translation Resources, Tools and their Use', *Presentation at the Language Resources Evaluation Conference*, Genoa, Italy. Available at: www.lrec-conf.org/proceedings/lrec2006/.

DeCamp, Jennifer (2022). 'Thoughts on the History of Machine Translation in the United States.' In *Proceedings of the 15th Biennial Conference of the Association for Machine Translation in the Americas (Volume 2: Users and Providers Track and Government Track)*, pages 427–437, Orlando, USA. Association for Machine Translation in the Americas.

DeCamp, Jennifer and Jost Zetzsche (2015) 'The History of Translation Technology in the United States', in Chan Sin-wai (ed.) *Routledge Encyclopedia of Translation Technology*, London and New York: Routledge, 375–92. Available at: http://dspace.vnbrims.org:13000/xmlui/bitstream/handle/123456789/4402/Routledge%20Encyclopedia%20of%20Translation%20Technology.pdf?sequence=1&isAllowed=y.

Defense Advanced Research Projects Agency (2021) 'Broad Operational Language Translation (BOLT)'. Available at: www.darpa.mil/program/broad-operational-language-translation.

Defense Advanced Research Projects Agency (2021) 'Low Resource Languages for Emergent Incidents (LORELEI)'. Available at: www.darpa.mil/program/low-resource-languages-for-emergent-incidents.

Defense Advanced Research Projects Agency (2021) 'Multilingual Automatic Documentation Classification Analysis and Translation (MADCAT)'. Available at: www.darpa.mil/program/multilingual-automatic-document-classification-analysis-and-translation.

Defense Advanced Research Projects Agency (2021) 'Robust Automatic Transcription of Speech (RATS)'. Available at: www.darpa.mil/program/robust-automatic-transcription-of-speech.

Dillet, Romain (2021, March 11) 'Hugging Face Raises $40 Million for Its Natural Language Processing Library', *Venture Beat*. Available at: https://venturebeat.com/2021/03/11/hugging-face-triples-investment-in-open-source-machine-learning-models/.

Dorr, Bonnie J. (2012) 'Language Research at DARPA: Machine Translation and Beyond', in *Proceedings of the 10th Biennial Conference for the Association for Machine Translation in the Americas (AMTA)*, 28 October–1 November 2012, San Diego. Available at: https://aclanthology.org/2012.amta-keynotes.3/.

Expert Advisory Group on Language Engineering Standards (EAGLES; 2021), European Commission. Available at: https://cordis.europa.eu/project/id/LE34244.

Hassan, Hany, Anthony Aue, Chang Chen, Vishal Chowdhary, Jonathan Clark, Christian Federmann, Xuedong Huang, Marcin Junczys-Dowmunt, William Lewis, Mu Li, Shujie Liu, Tie-Yan Liu, Renqian Luo, Arul Menezes, Tao Qin, Frank Seide, Xu Tan, Fei Tian, Lijun Wu, Shuangzhi Wu, Yingce Xia, Dongdong Zhang, Zhirui Zhang, and Ming Zhou (2018, March 14) 'Achieving Human Parity on Automatic Chinese to English News Translation'. *Microsoft Web Site*. Available at: final-achieving-human.pdf (microsoft.com).

Hutchins, W. John (1986) *Machine Translation: Past, Present, Future*, Chichester: Ellis Horwood.

Hutchins, W. John (1997) 'From First Conception to First Demonstration: The Nascent Years of Machine Translation, 1947–1954. A Chronology', *Machine Translation* 12: 195–252. https://doi.org/10.1023/A:1007969630568.

Hutchins, W. John (2000) *Early Years in Machine Translation: Memoirs and Biographies of Pioneers*, Amsterdam and Philadelphia: John Benjamins.

Hutchins, W. John (2005) 'The History of Machine Translation in a Nutshell'. Available at: http://hutchinsweb.me.uk/Nutshell-2005.pdf.

Hutchins, W. John (2006) 'Machine Translation: History', in Keith Brown (ed.) *Encyclopedia of Languages and Linguistics*, 2nd edition, Oxford: Elsevier, 7: 375–83.

Hutchins, W. John and Harold Somers (1992) *An Introduction to Machine Translation*, London: Academic Press Limited.

IBM Press Release (1954) '701 Translator', *IBM Website*. Available at: www-03.ibm.com/ibm/history/exhibits/701/701_translator.html.

Intelligence Advanced Research Projects Agency (2016) 'Machine Translation for English Retrieval of Information in Any Language (MATERIAL)'. Available at: www.iarpa.gov/research-programs/material.

International Electrical Engineering Task Force (2022) 'Weidner Multi-Lingual Word Processing System', *IEEE Bushy Tree*. Available at: Weidner Multi-Lingual Word Processing System | IEEE Bushy Tree | Fandom.

International Organization for Standardization (ISO; 2022) 'ISO/TC3 37 Language and Terminology'. Available at: www.iso.org/committee/48104.html.

International Standards On Language Engineering (2021) *ISLE Web Page*. Available at: www.ilc.cnr.it/EAGLES/isle/right.html.

Internet Movie Database (2021) 'Forbidden Planet Quotes'. Available at: www.imdb.com/title/tt0049223/quotes.

Irving, Arnold (1978, October 31) 'Provo Researchers Help Perfect Computer Translator', *Deseret News*.

ISLE (2022) 'Framework for Machine Translation in ISLE', *ISLE Web Page*. Available at: www.ilc.cnr.it/EAGLES/isle/femti.htm.

Johnson, Khari (2021, March 11) 'Hugging Face Triples Investment in Open Source Machine Learning Models', *Venture Beat*. Available at: Hugging Face triples investment in open source machine learning models | VentureBeat.

Kamprath, Christine, Eric Adolphson, Teruko Mitamura, and Eric Nyberg (1998). 'Controlled Language for Multilingual Document Production: Experience with Caterpillar Technical English', in *Proceedings of the 2nd International Workshop in Controlled Language Applications*, Carnegie-Mellon University, Pittsburgh, PA. Available at: www.researchgate.net/publication/2284766_Controlled_Language_for_Multilingual_Document_Production_Experience_with_Caterpillar_Technical_English.

KantanAI (2013, November 28) '#t9n and the Computer', *KantanMT News, Machine Translation Trends*. Available at: #T9N and the Computer – KantanAI – Machine Translation – Neural Language Technology – AI – Localization Technology – Customer Support Solutions (kantanmtblog.com).

Knowlson, James (1975) *Universal Language Schemes in England and France, 1600–1800*. University of Toronto Press. ISBN 978-0-8020-5296-4.

Koehn, Phillip, Franz J. Och, and Daniel Marcu (2003) 'Statistical Phrase-Based Translation', in *Proceedings of HLT-NAACL 2003*, 48–54. Available at: N03-1017.pdf (aclanthology.org).

Konstantin Kakaes (2012, May 11) 'Why Computers Still Can't Translate Languages Automatically', *Slate* website. Available at: https://slate.com/technology/2012/05/darpas-transtac-bolt-and-other-machine-trnslation-programs-search-for-meaning-of-words.

Localisation Industry Standards Association (Philipp Koehn, Franz J. Och, Daniel Marcu) (2003). 'Statistical Phrase-Based Translation', in *Proceedings of the 2003 Human Language Technology Conference of the North American Chapter of the Association for Computational Linguistics*.

Lommel, Arle (2016) 'Blues for BLEU: Reconsidering the Validity of Reference-Based MT Evaluation', in *Proceedings of the LREC 2016 Workshop 'Translation Evaluation – From Fragmented Tools and Data Sets to an Integrated Ecosystem*, Georg Rehm, Aljoscha Burchardt *et al.* (eds.). Available at: www.cracking-the-language-barrier.eu/wp-content/uploads/Lommel.pdf.

Lommel, Arle (2021) 'Responsive MT: Level Up for Machine Translation', Keynote Presentation at the MT Summit 2021, in *Proceedings of the online MT Summit 2021*.

Macklovich, Elliott (2006, May) 'TransType2: The Last Word', in *Proceedings of the Fifth International Conference on Language Resources and Evaluation (LREC'06)*. Available at: https://aclanthology.org/L06-1008/.

Marie, Benjamin, Atsushi Fujita, and Raphael Rubino (2017) 'Scientific Credibility of Machine Translation Research: A Meta-Evaluation of 769 Papers', in *Proceedings of the First Workshop on Neural Machine Translation*, Vancouver. Available at: arXiv:2106.15195 [cs.CL].

Melby, Alan (2013) Telephone interview with Jennifer DeCamp.

Melby, Alan (2022) Email correspondence with Jennifer DeCamp.

Melby, Alan and Christopher Kurz (2021, September 24) 'Letters to the Editor: Rebuttal to Jaap van der Meer', *Multilingual Computing.com*. Available at: Letters to the editor: rebuttal to Jaap van der Meer | Multilingual.

Melby, Alan and Terry Warner (1995) *The Possibility of Language: A Discussion of the Nature of Language, with Implications for Human and Machine Translation*, Amsterdam and Philadelphia: John Benjamins Publishing Company.

Microsoft (2020, February 13) 'Turing-NLG: A 17-Billion-Parameter Language Model by Microsoft', *Microsoft Research Blog*. Available at: www.microsoft.com/en-us/research/blog/turing-nlg-a-17-billion-parametr-language-model-by-microsoft.

Microsoft Translator (2021, November 22) 'Multiingual Translation at Scale: 10000 Language Pairs and Beyond', *Microsoft Translator Blog*. Available at: Multilingual translation at scale: 10000 language pairs and beyond – Microsoft Translator Blog.

National Institute for Standards and Technology (2021) 'Machine Translation', *Projects/Programs* website. Available at: www.nist.gov/programs-projects/machine-translation.

National Research Council (1999) 'Developments in Artificial Intelligence', in *Funding a Revolution: Government Support for Computing Research*, Washington, DC: National Academy Press. Available at: www.microsoft.com/en-us/research/blog/turing-nlg-a-17-billion-parameter-language-model-by-microsoft/.

Olive, Joseph, Caitlin Christianson, and John Mccary. (2011) 'DARPA Global Autonomous Language Exploitation', in *Handbook of Natural Language Processing and Machine Translation*, Springer Publishers. ISBN-13: 978-1-4419-7712-0, ISBN: 1-4419-7712-0.

Onyshkevych, Boyon (2016, October 28) 'DARPA Human Language Technology Programs', in *Proceedings of the Association for Machine Translation in the Americas Conference 2016*, presented by Doug Jones. Available at: Jones-AMTA-2016-Keynote-DARPA-HLT.pdf (amtaweb.org).

Open Mind (2021) 'Alan Turing and the Dream of Artificial Intelligence', *OpenMind*. Available at: www. bbvaopenmind.com.

Press, Gil (2021, May 31) 'The State of Data, May 2021', *Forbes*. Available at: www.forbes.com/sites/ gilpress/2021/05/31/the-state-of-data-may-2021.

Public Law (2001) 'USA Patriot Act'. Available at: www.govinfo.gov/content/pkg/PLAW-107publ56/ html/PLAW-107publ56.htm.

Rehm, Georg, Aljoscha Burchardt, Ondˇrej Bojar, Christian Dugast, Marcello Federico, Josef van Genabith, Barry Haddow, Jan Hajic, Kim Harris, Philipp Koehn, Matteo Negri, Martin Popel, Lucia Specia, Marco Turchi, and Hans Uszkoreit (2016, May 24) 'Translation Evaluation: From Fragmented Tools and Data Sets to an Integrated Ecosystem', in *Workshop Held at Language Resources Evaluation Conference (LREC)*, 24 May 2016. Available at: cfp-mteval.pdf (lrec-conf.org).

Reinsel, David, John Gantz, and John Rydning (2018, November) 'Data Age 2025: The Digitization of the World from Edge to Core', in *IDC White Paper Sponsored by Seagate*. Available at: www.seagate.com/ files/www-content/our-story/trends/files/idc-seagate-datage-whitepaper.pdf.

Richardson, Stephen (2021, November 4) Telephone interview with J. DeCamp.

Shaffer, Richard (1978, October 24) 'California Firm to Unveil a Computer that Processes Words for Translators', *Wall Street Journal*.

Slocum, Jonathan (1985) 'A Survey of Machine Translation: Its History, Current Status, and Future Prospects', *Computational Linguistics* 11(1): 1–17.

Society of Automotive Engineers (SAE, 2001) 'SAE Standard J2450 Quality Metric for Language Translation of Service Information'. Available at: www.sae.org/standardsdev/j2450p1.htm.

Stanford University. 'Neural Networks', *Stanford History* Website. Available at: https://cs.stanford.edu/ people/eroberts/courses/soco/projects/neural-networks/History/history1.html.

Translation Automation User Society (2010) 'A Translation Automation Timeline'. Available at: www.taus. net/timeline/a-translation-automation-timeline.

Unicode Consortium (2021) 'Unicode', Website. Available at: www.unicode.org.

Van der Meer, Jaap (2021, August 3) 'A Journey into the Future of the Translation Industry', *TAUS Blog*. Available at: https://blogtaus.net/author/jaap-van-der-meer.

Vasconcellos, Muriel (1996) 'Trends in Machine Translation and the Forces that Shaped Them', in *Proceedings of the 2nd Conference of the Association for Machine Translation in the Americas*, 2–5 October 1996, Montreal, Canada, 1–10.

Weaver, Warren (1949) 'Memorandum on Translation'. Available at: www.mt-archive.info/Weaver-1949. pdf.

Wendt, Chris (2020) 'Factor 1000: Better MT, More Content, and What We Can Do with It', in *Presentation at Virtual Meeting of the Association for Machine Translation in the Americas*. Available at: https:// amtaweb.org/wp-content/uploads/2020/11/AMTA-K3-Wendt-Factor1000-201008.pdf.

Wendt, Chris (2021, November 4) Telephone interview with J. DeCamp.

Wikipedia Contributors (2022) 'First Contact (Novelette)', *Wikipedia*, the Free Encyclopedia. Available at: https://en.wikipedia.org/wiki/Cold_War.

Wikipedia Contributors (2022) 'Machine Translation'. Available at: https://en.wikipedia.org/wiki/ machine_translation.

Wikipedia Contributors (2022, January 20) 'Robby the Robot', *Wikipedia*, The Free Encyclopedia. Available at: https://en.wikipedia.org/wiki/Robby_the_Robot.

Wikipedia Contributors (2022) 'Star Wars', *Wikipedia*, The Free Encyclopedia. Available at: https:// en.wikipedia.org/wiki/Star_Wars.

Wikipedia Contributors (2022) 'Timeline of United States Military Operations', *Wikipedia*, The Free Encyclopedia. Available at: https://en.wikipedia.org/wiki/Timeline_of_United_States_military_operations.

Wu, Yonghui, Mike Schuster, Zhifeng Chen, Quoc V. Le, Mohammad Norouzi, Wolfgang Macherey, Maxim Krikun, Yuan Cao, Qin Gao, Klaus Macherey, Jeff Klingner, Apurva Shah, Melvin Johnson, Xiaobing Liu, Łukasz Kaiser, Stephan Gouws, Yoshikiyo Kato, Taku Kudo, Hideto Kazawa, Keith Stevens, George Kurian, Nishant Patil, Wei Wang, Cliff Young, Jason Smith, Jason Riesa, Alex Rudnick, Oriol Vinyals, Greg Corrado, Macduff Hughes, and Jeffrey Dean (2018) 'Google's Neural Machine Translation System: Bridging the Gap between Human and Machine Translation', *CoRR*, vol. abs/1609.08144. Research at Google. Available at: https://research.google.com/pubs/pub45610.html.

PART 3

Specific Topics in Translation Technology

26
ALIGNMENT

Lars Ahrenberg

The Alignment Concept

In the context of translation, alignment refers to a process of relating parts of a source text to parts of a target text. As with the term translation itself, alignment may also refer to a product, the outcome of an alignment process.

The purpose of alignment is to capture relations of equivalence or correspondence in a translation. As these notions have no generally agreed definitions and can be interpreted in different ways, it must be recognized that there often cannot exist a single, correct alignment. Instead, as with translations themselves, different alignments can be judged as more or less appropriate, given some relevant criteria for their intended use.

Historically, the notion of alignment in translation technology is intimately bound up with the interest in parallel corpora, or *bitexts*, that emerged in the last half of the 1980s as a way to deal with the shortcomings of the then-existing technologies for machine translation and translation aids. Isabelle (1992: 76–89) attributes the idea of alignment, or 'methods for reconstructing correspond-ences in pre-existing translations', to Martin Kay, who used the term in a 1988 precursor to the article 'Text-Trans-Lation Alignment' (Kay and Röscheisen 1993: 121–42).

In some works (e.g. Simard *et al.* 1992: 67–81; Melamed 2001), a distinction is upheld between alignment and correspondence. Alignment is then restricted to relations that are monotonic, so that if $<s_i, t_j>$ is a pair of aligned units, then a source unit $s_k < s_i$ can only be aligned to a target unit t_l if $t_l \leq t_j$. In this chapter, the term 'alignment' is used in the wide sense, as is currently normal, and modifiers such as 'monotonic' or 'functional' are used for alignments that are restricted in the relevant sense.

Alignment processes are classified according to the size of the units that are to be related. We talk of *sentence alignment* when the minimal unit is a sentence, or some text unit of equivalent status, and of *word alignment* when the minimal unit is a word. Aligning units in between words and sentences is called *sub-sentential alignment* or *phrase alignment*. The latter term, alongside *tree alignment*, is also used when source and target sentences have been assigned syntactic analyses in the form of trees, and the alignment relates nodes of the source tree to nodes of the target tree. This topic is not covered here.

DOI: 10.4324/9781003168348-29

Definitions and Notation

It is common in the literature to call the two sides of a parallel corpus the foreign and English side, respectively, using the letters *f* and *e*, in various incarnations, to denote their parts. Here this convention will be followed. It is also common to regard one of the sides as the source side, usually the foreign side, and the other, English, as the target side. The following notational conventions will be used:

$P = <F, E>$ is a parallel corpus with the two halves F and E.

$F = <F_1, F_2, \ldots F_K>$ is the foreign half divided into K sentence-level text units. Similarly, E is divided into L units $<E_1, E_2, \ldots E_L>$.

$A = <A_1, A_2, \ldots A_S>$ is an alignment of P into S pairs, and we can write $P(s) = <f(s), e(s)>$. We will refer to this alignment as a sentence alignment and the pair itself as a *sentence pair*.

$\mathbf{f} = f_1, f_2, \ldots, f_J$ is a foreign sentence with J words.

$\mathbf{e} = e_1, e_2, \ldots, e_I$ is an English sentence with I words.

An alignment $\mathbf{a}$ of $\mathbf{f}$ and $\mathbf{e}$ is a subset of the Cartesian product of their word positions: $\mathbf{a} \in \{<j,i>: j = 1, \ldots, J; I = 1, \ldots, I\}$. A pair $<j,i>$ is called a *link*. A matrix with J rows and I columns where each element can be either 1, to indicate a link, or 0, to indicate no link, is called an alignment matrix for the pair $<\mathbf{f}, \mathbf{e}>$. The alignment problem can then be defined as a search for the best alignment(s) from the space of 2_{JI} possible alignments.

The Alignment Task

Alignment algorithms have to solve several problems. A first problem concerns how alignment characteristics are to be modeled. This is usually done by some sort of statistical model. More often than not, several models are used and then one must also decide how to combine them, for instance, by assigning a weight to each model that indicates its importance for solving the problem.

A second problem is determining values for the model parameters, and, if weights are used, their values. This can be done by fiat, such as giving equal weights to all models, by direct computation on available data, or by a statistical learning process.

Third, there is the search problem: how to find the best alignment according to the models. This problem is intimately bound up with the other two. Without restrictions on the models, the candidate alignments are just too many, and exhaustive search is out of the question. Restrictions on the models can be set as hard constraints, for example, by only considering functional or monotonic alignments. Even without such restrictions, learning the parameters and finding the best alignments will often be done iteratively by using learning schemes such as expectation–maximization (EM) (Dempster *et al.* 1977: 1–38). Approximative search regimes, such as beam search, are also commonly used. In those regimes, partial alignments are compared based on their likelihood, or scores, and those that have too low scores are not considered further. This may happen if they are not among the N best alternatives or if their relative score, compared to the best alternative, falls below a given threshold.

Evaluation

Alignment is a prerequisite for many tasks relating to translation technologies, including statistical machine translation, terminology extraction, population of bilingual lexicons, and search in translation corpora. For this reason extrinsic evaluation is important for alignment systems.

However, not least for the sake of system comparisons, intrinsic evaluation is also motivated and much used.

Precision (P) and recall (R) are basic metrics for intrinsic evaluation. These require comparisons with a gold standard. With L the set of links produced by a system, G the set of links in the gold standard, and $|X|$ indicating the cardinality of set X, we have

$$P = \frac{|L \cap G|}{|L|}$$

$$R = \frac{|L \cap G|}{|G|}$$

As usual these two metrics can be combined using F-measures, where the parameter a, $0 \le a \le 1$, determines the relative weights of precision and recall ($a = 0$ gives the precision and $a = 1$ the recall).

$$F_{\alpha} = \frac{P \star R}{\alpha P + (1 - \alpha) R}$$

Another combination is the alignment error rate (AER) defined as follows:

$$\text{AER} = 1 - \frac{2 \star |L \cap G|}{|L| + |G|}$$

Given the subjective and use-dependent nature of alignment, it has been argued that systems should not be punished for proposing links that human evaluators disagree on. Thus, if such links are classed as Possible, while those that humans agree on are termed Sure, a metric that considers the difference may be useful. Och and Ney (2003) suggested that precision should be computed on the basis of recovered Possible links, while recall could be based on Sure links. This affects AER as follows, where S stands for Sure links and P for Possible links:

$$\text{AER} = 1 - \frac{|L \cap S| + |L \cap P|}{|L| + |S|}$$

Note that Sure links are considered a subset of the possible links and that this definition coincides with the previous one if S and P are identical.

While the revised AER has been a popular metric, it has been criticized for being a weak predictor of extrinsic measures, for instance, in the case of translation performance as measured by BLEU (Fraser and Marcu 2007: 293–303). Instead, it is argued that a suitably weighted F-measure is preferable.

The AER can be particularly misleading when the number of Possible links is high compared to the number of Sure links. This will contribute to a low error rate, but when the Possible links emerge out of human disagreement, it is uncertain what is really measured.

Precision and recall at the level of links are problematic as well when multiword units are present. Aligning the English word *gold ring* with its German translation *Goldring* should arguably result in two links. A system proposing only one of them, say <*gold, Goldring*>, will still be credited with a point which is valid both for precision and recall. This is reasonable for statistical translation but not if the task is bilingual lexicon generation or terminology extraction. In those cases it is arguable that alignments should have transitive closure (Goutte *et al.* 2004: 502–09), which means that if <*j,i*>, <*j,i'*>, and <*j',i*> are non-null links, then <*j',i'*> is also a link. Søgaard and Kuhn (2009) call such clusters translation units and define the translation unit error rate, TUER, as

$$\text{TUER} = 1 - \frac{2 \star |U \cap G|}{|U| + |G|}$$

Here, U are the translation units produced by the system and G the translation units of the gold standard. The TUER is usually higher than the AER by several points.

Sentence Alignment

Nowadays, if a bitext is included in a parallel corpus collected for research and/or distribution, we can expect it to be sentence aligned and the sentence alignment to have high accuracy.

The performance of a sentence alignment system is clearly dependent on properties of the corpus, such as the presence of unambiguous sentence boundaries and the nature of the translation, in particular the frequency of non-translated, or extra, sentences and the occurrence of sentences that have been reordered, aggregated, or split during translation. Sometimes large sections may even be missing from one of the texts or moved from their original position, a situation which can be handled by reorganizing the data into smaller parts.

If the bitext is reasonably well behaved, however, it can be sentence aligned with quite simple methods. We consider a bitext well behaved if it is monotonic, or almost so, and sentence unit boundaries can be detected with high levels of accuracy. If so, the elements of a sentence pair <**f**, **e**>, could be

- single units
- up to *n* contiguous text units, where *n* is often set in advance, sometimes as low as 2
- A symbol such as 0 or *e*, indicating absence of a corresponding unit.

The type of a pair is the number of units that it covers. Types are indicated as 1–1, 1–2, 1–0, 2–2, and so on.

All sentence alignment algorithms exploit statistical tendencies in well-behaved bitexts. These are of four basic kinds:

- Distribution of matches on types. 1–1 sentence pairs tend to account for some 90% or more of all matches and 1–2 or 2–1 types for most of the remainder.
- Monotonicity. A bitext may be represented as a matrix with rows and columns representing tokens or characters (Melamed 2001). Matches, and token associations, tend to occur near the diagonal of that matrix with only local deviations from strict monotonicity.

- Length, measured as number of characters (Gale and Church 1993) or number of words (Brown *et al.* 1993: 263–311; Moore 2004). A short sentence tends to yield a short translation, a long sentence a long translation.
- Token associations, obtained by some association measure (Kay and Röscheisen 1993), from a dictionary (Brown *et al.* 1993; Varga *et al.* 2005: 90–596), or from string comparisons (Simard *et al.* 1992: 67–81). A token association signals the occurrence of a non-null pair of text units related under translation, and pairs that correspond under translation tend to contain more token associations than pairs that are not related under translation.

The first two tendencies are illustrated in Figure 26.1. Almost all sentences are part of a link, and the links follow one another monotonically. The large majority are 1–1 matches, here interleaved with isolated occurrences of other types (2–1, 1–0, 1–5).

The tendencies can be exploited in different ways. A common approach is to assign a score to each pair based on measures of one or more of the statistical tendencies. By assuming independence, the score for any complete or partial alignment can then be computed as a product of the scores for its individual matches:

$$score(A) = \prod_{i=1}^{N} score(A_i)$$

The best alignment, $\hat{A}$, is then taken to be the one with the highest score:

$$\hat{A} = \underset{A}{\operatorname{argmax}}\ score(A)$$

It is usual to apply (negative) logarithms to both sides of Equation (1) so that computations can be performed more efficiently, and the score becomes a cost measure. The best alignment is then the one with the lowest cost.

Gale and Church (1993) showed character length to be a very powerful feature for the language pairs English–French and English–German and used no token associations at all. Exploiting the independence assumption, they used dynamic programming to find the best alignment. Simard *et al.* (1992) showed that the length-based algorithm could be improved upon by applying token associations, in their case cognate based, in a second pass for cases where Gale and Church's algorithm had about equal scores for the best and second-best alternatives.

Similarly, Melamed's algorithm (2001), implemented in the geometric mapping and alignment system, which has token associations as a base, asks Gale and Church's algorithm for a second opinion on any match which is not 1–1.

Other approaches that combine length-based metrics and token associations first attempt to establish a subset of 1–1 matches that have very high scores and then work from there. This approach is more robust in the face of sentences and paragraphs that only appear on one side of the bitext. Moore (2005) finds such matches near the diagonal using a length-based statistic, while the *hunalign* system (Varga *et al.* 2005: 590–96) finds them based on a score combining length similarity and dictionary information. Moore's algorithm then creates a dictionary from the 1–1 matches found in the first pass and use it to find more matches, while hunalign has this as an option in the absence of a dictionary. Hunalign, unlike Moore's algorithm, has a final pass in which initial matches are expanded to $1 - n$ matches, for arbitrary n, if certain conditions are met.

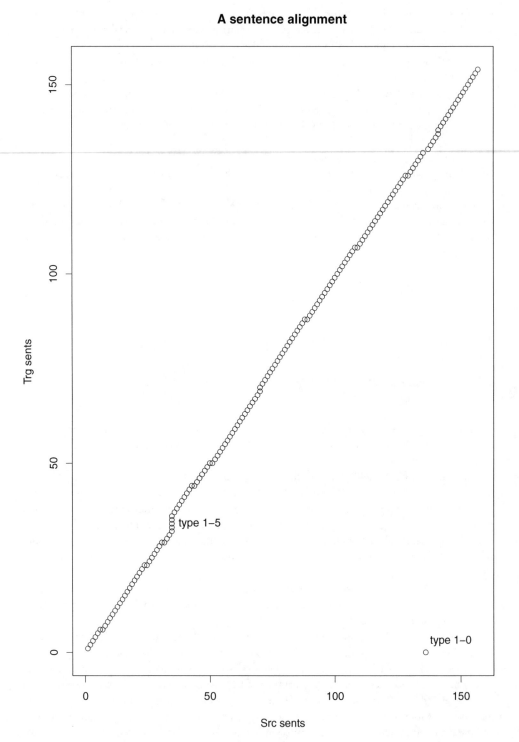

A sentence alignment

Figure 26.1 A sentence alignment from a Swedish-English novel translation with 157 source sentences

Note the Occurrence of a Null Match (Lower Right Corner) and Match of Type 1–5

Word Alignment

Word alignment is usually performed on sentence-aligned bitexts, although good results may also be reached on bitexts that have been chopped up into equal-sized arbitrary parts (Fung and Church 1994: 1096–102). On large bitexts, a limit is often set on sentence length, say, 20 or 100 words, to reduce the size of the search space.

Word alignment as a computational problem is harder than sentence alignment. Many-to-many matches are more abundant, and matches may involve sets of words that are not adjacent. Moreover, null matches are generally more frequent, as is reordering. An example is shown in Figure 26.2.

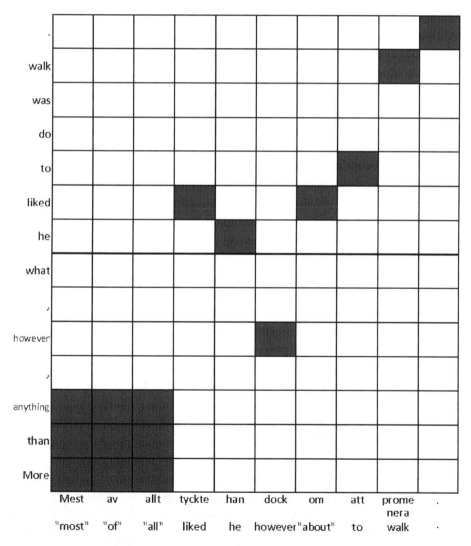

Figure 26.2 Word alignment of an English–Swedish sentence pair with null links, many-to-many links, and reordered and discontinuous translation units

Word alignments are also harder to establish for humans than sentence alignments. One reason is that structure and meaning differ between languages. One language may employ prepositions to express what another uses case endings for, as in (1), or require an extra word to express some function in comparison with another language, as in (2).

(1)

> EN: *and they came to Bethlehem.*
> FI: *ja he saapuivat Beetlehemiin.*
> GLOSS: *and they came Bethlehem+Case*

(2)

> EN: *they did not come*
> SE: *de kom inte.*
> GLOSS: *they came not.*

In these cases one can argue either for not aligning the prepositions or the extra verb form 'did', since they have no non-bound counterparts. On the other hand, one can argue that they should be aligned to the word that carries the function, although it does so morphologically.

In addition, translation is not always meaning preserving, and the semantic difference is often a matter of degree. Thus, the decision whether two words or phrases should be aligned is essentially subjective. Still, there are many sentence pairs for which human experts can agree on the best alignment, and agreement can be improved if training and guidelines are used to harmonize judgements (Melamed 2001). Remaining disagreements can be solved by voting or, as was described previously for sentence alignment, be registered explicitly.

Statistical Tendencies

While word alignment is harder than sentence alignment, similar statistical tendencies can be seen in the data.

- Distribution of matches on types. Often, a majority of matches, at least 50%, will be of type 1–1, and figures around 90% have been reported for some corpora. Other types will, however, be more common than for sentence alignments and, in particular, include more null matches.
- Monotonicity. For many languages, especially if they are genetically related or of the same typological kind, the word order of a translation tends to follow that of the source. Thus, for the majority of links $<j,i>$, i tends to be close to j, and the difference $|i-j|$ tends to have a frequency maximum near or close to 0.
- Token associations. If the words associated with position $<j,i>$ often co-occur in the sentence pairs of the bitext, this increases the chances that $<j,i>$ in the specific sentence pair is a link. Similarly, the chances are increased if the words can be found in a bilingual dictionary.
- String similarity. If the strings occupying position $<j,i>$ are identical or similar, this increases the probability that the element $<j,i>$ is a link. For languages using different alphabets, simple string comparisons are not helpful, but comparisons can be made by conversion to phonetic strings.
- Class-based associations. Given that the two sentences have been tagged or parsed, comparisons can be made on the basis of syntactic similarity. In general, if the words at $<j,i>$ have the same part of speech or the same grammatical relation, the chances are higher that they form a link. Classes can also be learnt automatically with clustering methods (Och and Ney 2003: 19–51)

These tendencies have been modeled in different ways, and in different combinations, and there is a rich literature of alternative proposals. Here, only a small subset of them can be covered. For a comprehensive overview, see Tiedemann (2011).

Methods Without Learning

Since 1–1 matches are the most common, one idea is to find as many of these as possible and then continue from there. This restricts the number of possible alignments considerably and thus simplifies search.

A particularly efficient instance of this idea is the *competitive linking algorithm* (Melamed 1997). Association metrics for the words of the bitext are computed and are used to score the positions of the alignment matrix. Positions of the matrix are then selected, starting with the highest-scoring ones and eliminating all positions belonging to rows or columns that have had a position selected. The greedy search comes to a halt when a threshold value is reached. The process may be iterated or supplemented with post-processes to extend the coverage to one–many or many–many matches. Melamed (2001) provides an extensive account of such algorithms.

Another efficient method is presented by Lardilleux and Lepage (2009). They observe that what they call 'perfect alignments', pairs of words or phrases having the same frequency n, and occurring in n sentence pairs of a bitext, are good link candidates, and this also when n is as low as 1. Based on this observation, they devise a method for principled generation of small subcorpora of a given bitext and extract the pairs that are perfect alignments in those subcorpora. The sampling process is fast, and the same links are generated several times. Also, different links for the same word are derived, enabling computation of translation probabilities. Moreover, by arranging data not in pairs but in sequences, they can generate links for three or more languages at once in all directions. This method is implemented in a system called *anymalign*.

Generative Alignment Models

From a given alignment, as in Figure 26.2, we can imagine the target words having been generated from the associated source words and then rearranged. Conversely, given a sentence pair from a bitext, we can look for an alignment as an explanation for how one sentence was translated from the other.

In this framework, the task of translation is modeled as follows:

$$\hat{\mathbf{e}} = \underset{e}{\text{argmax}}\, p(\mathbf{e}|\mathbf{f}) = \underset{e}{\text{argmax}}\, \frac{p(\mathbf{f}|\mathbf{e})\, p(\mathbf{e})}{p(\mathbf{f})}$$

The best translation, $\hat{\mathbf{e}}$, is the English string that has the highest probability given the foreign string, $\mathbf{f}$. Since $p(\mathbf{f})$ does not depend on $\mathbf{e}$, it can be removed. Alignments are introduced as hidden variables in the equation, and there may be many alignments that produce the same end result. With A representing the set of all possible alignments, we have

$$\underset{e}{\text{argmax}} \sum_{\mathbf{a} \in \mathbf{A}} p(\mathbf{f}, \mathbf{a}|\mathbf{e})\, p(\mathbf{e})$$

The alignment we are interested in is the one with the highest probability, that is, the one that can give us the most likely explanation for f as an encoding of e. Thus,

$$\hat{\mathbf{a}} = \underset{\mathbf{a} \in \mathbf{A}}{\text{argmax}}\ p(\mathbf{f}, \mathbf{a} \mid \mathbf{e})$$

As the alignment of individual sentence pairs can be considered independent, taking the union of the best alignments for all pairs will give us the best alignment for the whole bitext.

A simple account of how a foreign sentence is derived from an English one is the following: (1) Decide on the number of positions of the foreign string. (2) Associate each foreign position with at most one English position. This means that the alignment will be functional and that there may exist words in the foreign strings that have no match in the English string. (3) Pick a foreign word for each foreign position.

To turn this into a stochastic model, we need some probability distributions. A simple case, referred to as IBM Model 2, is the following: (1) length probabilities, $lgth(J \mid I)$, which are usually regarded as uniform and not necessary to estimate. (2) Alignment probabilities, $a(i \mid j, I, J)$, where $i = a(j)$ is a function of the foreign positions and $i = 0$ represents the case where a foreign word has no correspondent in the English sentence. (3) Translation probabilities, $e_{a_j} t$, which express the dependence of a foreign word on the English word in the aligned position.

To solve the search problem, Brown *et al.* (1993) proposed to start by learning a simple word-based alignment model and then introduce increasingly more complex models. This first model, IBM Model 1, is the special case of Model 2 where the alignment probabilities $a(.)$ are considered uniform. Thus, sentences are essentially treated as sets. As the alignment is functional in the direction from foreign to English, a foreign word f_j is associated with at most one English word, $e_{a(j)}$, and an alignment can be represented as an assignment of English positions to foreign positions. A specific null token e_0 is used to represent foreign words that are not aligned with any English word.

Starting from a uniform assignment of probabilities to the parameters, the probability of any alignment can be computed. This is the first E-step of the EM algorithm. Then, in the M-step, weighted counts are collected for new estimates of the probabilities, where the weights are based on the probabilities of the alignments in which the pair occurs. These steps are iterated a few times, yielding new estimates for word translation probabilities $t(f \mid e)$ and alignment weights. In the next phase, Model 2 alignment probabilities $a(i \mid j, I, J)$ conditioned on the position of the foreign word and the lengths of the two sentences are also estimated. An alternative to Model 2 using relative rather than absolute position is the so-called hidden Markov model (HMM) introduced by Vogel *et al.* (1996). Here the probability of a position in the English string is conditioned on the position of its predecessor. Often a uniform distance-based probability is used so that $a(a_j a_{j-1}, J)$ is the same for all $i = a_j$, and $i = a_{j-1}$ with the same distance $|i - i'|$.

While the alignment is functional in the direction from foreign to English in Models 1 and 2, there is nothing to prevent two (or more) foreign words to be matched with the same English word. Models 3, 4, and 5 handle the tendency of English words to be associated with one, more, or no foreign words. This property of a word is termed its fertility.

In Model 3, fertility probabilities $n(k \mid e)$ for $k = 0, 1, 2, \ldots$ are computed for English words. The case $e = e_0$ is treated separately by a single parameter, p_1, as the number of foreign words that have no English correspondent are assumed to depend on the length of the input. While keeping to the initial assumption that alignment is functional in the direction from foreign to English, the generative story for the alignment is now reversed. Starting from the English side, each word (and position) is assigned a fertility. In some cases the fertility will be 2 or more, and extra positions are introduced. Extra foreign words are introduced according to probability p_1. Then foreign words are introduced to fill positions according to their translation probabilities with the associated English words. Finally, the foreign string is reordered according to absolute position probabilities. However, in this case, with the reversed orientation, the probability of positions are modeled in the direction from English to foreign and termed distortion probabilities.

Model 4 adds more parameters for the distribution of words within and between phrases. Similarly to the HMM model, these probabilities are based on relative positioning and also on classes.

Models 3 and 4 are deficient in the sense that they allow impossible alignments. This is because the fertility and positioning of one word are assumed to be independent of the fertilities and positioning of other words. Model 5 is basically a non-deficient version of Model 4. However, it is computationally more complex, and for this reason, Model 4, although not giving quite as good results, is used more often in practice.

A freely available implementation of the IBM models is the system Giza++ (Och and Ney 2003). In addition, it includes the HMM-model. For almost a decade, Giza++ has been the most heavily used alignment system in practice. A multi-threaded reimplementation, MGIZA++ (Gao and Vogel 2008: 49–57), is also in wide use.

While IBM-style generative models have dominated the field, they are not without drawbacks. They are inherently asymmetric, as the foreign and English halves have different roles, and cannot produce many-to-many translation units. They are also hard to extend with additional models, as the generative framework must explain how one half can be generated from the other. Moreover, they are prone to overfitting to the training data and often propose many incorrect links for rare words such as numbers or proper names, a phenomenon called 'garbage collection' (Moore 2004: 518–25).

Symmetrization

The asymmetry and functional character of the IBM models make it hard to derive many-to-many links. Also, if the roles of the two sides are reversed the associations found to have positive probabilities may be very different, especially for low-frequency words.

An obvious solution to this problem proposed already in Och and Ney (2003: 19–51) is to perform two alignments, reverting the roles of the two halves in a second round. From these two alignments, it is possible to take the intersection as well as the union. The intersection will only contain 1–1 links, whereas the union can have many different types. Naturally, the intersection will have a high precision but a low recall, while the situation for the union is the opposite. It has been found empirically that adding matches from the union to those of the intersection in a principled manner can increase recall substantially without sacrificing precision too much. Growing the intersection by adding neighbouring matches from the rows and columns is usually a good strategy, as long as the additions are not in conflict with existing matches. Growing along the diagonals may improve performance further (Och and Ney 2003: 19–51; Köhn *et al.* 2003).

Liang *et al.* (2006) describe extensions to Model 2 and the HMM model that perform joint estimation of the parameters for both directions. This means that symmetrzation is performed on the go. The algorithm is implemented in the Berkeley Aligner. In another system, SyMGiza++ (Junczys-Dowmunt and Szal 2012), the M-steps are modified by weighing the alignments on an average of the parameters for both directions, and the heuristic symmetrization steps after model training are incorporated in the general system flow.

A proposal for handling many-to-many relations as first class objects in a generative model was presented by Marcu and Wong (2002). They view the corpus as the result of simultaneous generation of a foreign and English string, where the primitive pairs are not just word pairs but possibly phrase pairs. In this model there is no need for fertilities, but on the other hand, it is difficult to train. They could show, however, that the model produced better word alignments than IBM Model 4 on 100,000 sentence pairs from the French–English Hansard corpus.

Discriminative Models

Discriminative models combine an arbitrary number of information-giving functions, h_n, usually called feature functions. Each function is supplied with a weight, w_n, that indicates its importance. The combination is in most cases linear, which gives the following decision rule:

$$\hat{\mathbf{a}} = \underset{\mathbf{a} \in \mathbf{A}}{\mathrm{argmax}} \sum_{n=1}^{N} w_n h_n \left(\mathbf{f}, \mathbf{e}, \mathbf{a} \right)$$

To learn values for the weights, it is necessary to have access to reliable reference data, which makes them semi-supervised. It has been shown that the required amounts need not be very large; a common figure is a few hundred sentence pairs. Generative models are in principle unsupervised, which means that they optimize their parameters without recourse to any information about human perspectives on alignments. This is mostly considered an advantage, but, on the other hand, if a system can make use of existing manual alignments performed according to some standards, it would be in a better position to produce alignments that agree with those standards. Such data, however, will never exist in large quantities, as they take large efforts to produce. For this reason, unaligned data are still required in large quantities.

Discriminative models have the advantage that any tendency observed in parallel corpora can be taken into account. Not only that, they can also use alignments produced by a generative model.

Central to the success of a discriminative system is the selection of feature functions. All systems use one or more features that capture token associations. Such feature functions can be based on association statistics such as the Dice coefficient, the log-likelihood ratio, the c^2-statistic, or translation probabilities from one of the IBM models. These are *local features* in the sense that their values depend only on the pair of words. Other local features may concern string similarity, parts of speech, and properties of neighboring words.

Global features, on the other hand, consider the alignment as a whole. For instance, the sum of all association scores for an alignment is a global feature. Other global features would relate to monotonicity or distortion. There is nothing that prevents using several features that relate to the same aspect. Moore (2005: 81–88) used both the number of backward jumps in an alignment and the sum of their magnitudes. Liu *et al.* (2010: 303–39) used neighbour count, the number of links for which both $j - j'$ and $i - i'$ equals one, and Cross count, the number of link pairs $<j,i>$ and $<j',i'>$ for which the product $(j - j') \times (i - i')$ is negative. For a monotonic alignment, this feature would have the value zero, while the value would be larger the more reorderings there are. Other features relating to the topology of the alignment can be concerned with the number of non-linked words and the number of words that are linked to one or more than one word. The value of these features can be taken as a sign of the normality of the alignment. Yet other features can refer to external resources; an indicator feature could register whether the words of a link can be found in a bilingual dictionary, and there may be features indicating whether other aligners have proposed a given link (Ayan and Dorr 2006: 96–103).

As with generative frameworks, a discriminative framework may perform search in several steps, using different features in different steps. For instance, Moore (2005: 81–88) used a two-step approach. In the second step, the global translation probability feature based on token associations computed with the log-likelihood ratio were replaced with conditional link probabilities. These were estimated as the ratio of co-occurring word pairs that were actually linked in the first step.

The use of global features has the drawback that one has to resort to approximate methods in training and search. Alternative methods that have been used are average perceptron learning (Moore 2005: 81–88), support vector machine training (Moore *et al.* 2006), and minimum error rate training (Liu *et al.* 2010: 303–39). With only local features or first-order dependencies, globally optimal parameters can be obtained. Ayan and Dorr (2006) used generalized iterative scaling, and Blunsom and Cohn (2006: 65–72) used forward-backward inference on two linear-chain conditional random fields (CRF), one for each language direction.

Improved Statistical Learning

While discriminative systems have performed better on many corpora, the difference from Giza++ symmetrized alignments is not extreme. More recent work on generative modeling has approached the problem of overfitting by using regularization, that is, by adding restrictions or penalties that favour smooth distributions. Graça *et al.* (2010: 481–504) used posterior regularization to enforce constraints of bijectivity and symmetry on alignments in the expectation step of an HMM model and showed that it works well on six language pairs where manual alignments have a high percentage (over 90%) of 1–1 links. The main advantage of their method is that learning is tractable. Dyer *et al.* (2011: 409–19) devised a general model where only two parameters, the regularization strength and the learning rate, were learned from manually alignments, whereas features and weights were learned from the full unannotated bitext. They demonstrated clear improvements on Czech–English data compared with symmetrized Model 4 alignments. Vaswani *et al.* (2012: 311–19) proposed using a prior in the M-step to optimize translation probabilities with the effect that garbage collection behavior is much reduced. The set of translation parameters is optimized for each target word separately.

Using Syntax

It has been debated whether linguistic structure is helpful for alignment. However, for some applications, it can clearly be. Macken *et al.* (2008) describes a system for terminology extraction which aligns so called anchor chunks on the basis of lexical association and part-of-speech patterns for chunking. Given a sentence pair partially aligned with anchor chunks, further chunk pairs can be found in gaps between anchor chunks. There is also evidence that parsing one of the sides may help. Riesa and Marcu (2010) showed, for an Arabic–English corpus within a discriminative framework, that a search regime guided by a single phrase structure parse for the English sentences led to better performance than symmetrized IBM 4 alignments. Fossum *et al.* (2008: 44–52) could demonstrate improvements for Chinese–English data.

Bibliography

Ayan, Necip Fazil and Bonnie J. Dorr (2006) 'A Maximum Entropy Approach to Combining Word Alignments', in *Proceedings of the Human Language Technology Conference of the NAACL*, New York, 96–103.

Blunsom, Phil and Trevor Cohn (2006) 'Discriminative Word Alignment with Conditional Random Fields', in *Proceedings of the 21st International Conference on Computational Linguistics and 44th Annual Meeting of the ACL*, 20 July 2006, Sydney, Australia, 65–72.

Brown, Peter F., Vincent J. Della Pietra, Stephen A. Della Pietra, and Robert L. Mercer (1993) 'The Mathematics of Statistical Machine Translation: Parameter Estimation', *Computational Linguistics* 19(2): 263–311.

Dempster, Arthur P., Nan M. Laird, and Donald B. Rubin (1977) 'Maximum Likelihood from Incomplete Data via the EM Algorithm', *Journal of the Royal Statistical Society Series B* 39(1): 1–38.

Dyer, Chris, Jonathan Clark, Alon Lavie, and Noah A. Smith (2011) 'Unsupervised Word Alignment with Arbitrary Features', in *Proceedings of the 49th Annual Meeting of the Association for Computational Linguistics*, 19–24 June 2011, Portland, OR, 409–19.

Fossum, Victoria, Kevin Knight, and Steven Abney (2008) 'Using Syntax to Improve Word Alignment Precision for Syntax-based Machine Translation', in *Proceedings of the 3rd Workshop on Statistical Machine Translation*, 19 June 2008, Ohio State University, Columbus, OH, 44–52.

Fraser, Alexander and Daniel Marcu (2007) 'Measuring Word Alignment Quality for Statistical Machine Translation', *Computational Linguistics* 33(3): 293–303.

Fung, Pascale and Kenneth W. Church (1994) 'K-vec: A New Approach for Aligning Parallel Texts', in *Proceedings of the 15th International Conference on Computational Linguistics (COLING-94)*, 5–9 August 1994, Kyoto, Japan, 1096–102.

Gale, William A. and Kenneth W. Church (1993, March) 'A Program for Aligning Sentences in Bilingual Corpora', *Computational Linguistics* 19(1).

Gao, Qin and Stephen Vogel (2008) 'Parallel Implementations of Word Alignment Tool', in *Proceedings of Software Engineering, Testing, and Quality Assurance for Natural Language Processing*, June 2008, Columbia, OH, 49–57.

Goutte, Cyril, Kenji Yamada, and Eric Gaussier (2004) 'Aligning Words Using Matrix Factorization', in *Proceedings of the 42nd Annual Meeting of the Association for Computational Linguistics*, 21–26 July 2004, Barcelona, Spain, 502–09.

Graça, João V., Kuzman Ganchev, and Ben Taskar (2010) 'Learning Tractable Word Alignment Models with Complex Constraints', *Computational Linguistics* 36(3): 481–504.

Isabelle, Pierre (1992) 'Bi-textual Aids for Translators', in *Proceedings of the 8th Annual Conference of the UW Centre for the New OED and Text Research*, University of Waterloo, Waterloo, Canada, 76–89.

Junczys-Dowmunt, Marcin, and Arkadiusz Szal (2012) 'SyMGiza++: Symmetrized Word Alignment Models for Machine Translation', in Bouvry, P., Kłopotek, M.A., Leprévost, F., Marciniak, M., Mykowiecka, A., Rybiński, H. (eds) *Security and Intelligent Information Systems (SIIS)*, volume 7053 of *Lecture Notes in Computer Science*, Berlin: Springer, 379–390.

Kay, Martin and Martin Röscheisen (1993) 'Text-translation Alignment', *Computational Linguistics* 19(1): 121–42.

Köhn, Philipp, Franz Josef Och, and Daniel Marcu (2003) 'Statistical Phrase-Based Translation', in *Proceedings of HLT-NAACL*, 48–54.

Lardilleux, Adrian and Yves Lepage (2009) 'Sampling-based Multilingual Alignment', in *Proceedings of Recent Advances in Natural language Processing (RANLP)*, Borovets, Bulgaria, 214–18.

Liang, Percy, Ben Taskar, and Dan Klein (2006) 'Alignment by Agreement', in *Proceedings of the Human Language Technology Conference of the {NAACL}, Main Conference*, 104–111.

Liu, Yang, Liu Qun, and Lin Shouxin (2010) 'Discriminative Word Alignment by Linear Modeling', *Computational Linguistics* 36(3): 303–39.

Macken, Lieve, Els Lefever, and Veronique Hoste (2008) 'Linguistically-based Sub-sententential Alignment for Terminology Extraction from a Bilingual Automotive Corpus', in Donia Scott and Hans Uszkoreit (eds.) *Proceedings of the 22nd International Conference on Computational Linguistics-Volume 1*, 18–22 August 2008, Manchester, the United Kingdom, 529–36.

Marcu, Daniel and William Wong (2002) 'A Phrase-based Joint Probability Model for Statistical Machine Translation', in *Proceedings of the Conference on Empirical Methods in Natural Language Processing (EMNLP)*, 6–7 July 2002, vol. 10, University of Pennsylvania, Philadelphia, PA, 133–39.

Melamed, I. Dan (2001) *Empirical Methods for Exploiting Parallel Texts*, Cambridge, MA: MIT Press.

Melamed, I. Dan (1997) 'A Word-to-word Model of Translational Equivalence', in *Proceedings of the 35th Conference of the Association for Computational Linguistics*, 7–10 July 1997, Madrid, Spain.

Moore, Robert C. (2004) 'Improving IBM Word Alignment Model 1', *Proceedings of the 42nd Annual Meeting of the Association for Computational Linguistics*, Barcelona, Spain, 518–25.

Moore, Robert C. (2005) 'A Discriminative Framework for Bilingual Word Alignment', in *Proceedings of Human Language Technology Conference and Conference on Empirical Methods in Natural Language Processing (HLT/EMNLP)*, 6–8 October 2005, Vancouver, British Columbia, Canada, 81–88.

Moore, Robert C., Yih Wen-tau, and Andreas Bode (2006) 'Improved Discriminative Bilingual Word Alignment', in *Proceedings of the 21st International Conference on Computational Linguistics and 44th Annual Meeting of the ACL*, July 2006, Sydney, Australia, 513–20.

Och, Franz Josef and Hermann Ney (2003) 'A Systematic Comparison of Various Statistical Alignment Models', *Computational Linguistics* 29(1): 19–51.

Riesa, Jason and Daniel Marcu (2010) 'Hierarchical Search for Word Alignment', in *Proceedings of the 48th Annual Meeting of the Association for Computational Linguistics*, Uppsala, Sweden, 157–66.

Simard, Michel, George F. Foster, and Pierre Isabelle (1992) 'Using Cognates to Align Sentences in Bilingual Corpora', in *Proceedings of the 4th International Conference on Theoretical and Methodological Issues in Machine Translation*, Montreal, Canada, 67–81.

Søgaard, Anders, and Jonas Kuhn (2009) 'Empirical Lower Bounds on Alignment Error Rates in Syntax-Based Machine Translation', in *Proceedings of SSST-3 Third Workshop on Syntax and Structure in Statistical Translation*, June, Boulder, CO, 19–27.

Tiedemann, Jörg (2011) *Bitext Alignment*, San Rafael, CA: Morgan and Claypool Publishers.

Varga, Daniel, Laszlo Németh, Peter Halácsy, Andras Kornai, Viktor Trón, and Viktor Nagy (2005) 'Parallel Corpora for Medium Density Languages', in *Proceedings of the International Conference RANLP 2005 (Recent Advances in Natural Language Processing)*, 21–23 September 2005, Borovets, Bulgaria, 590–96.

Vaswani, Ashish, Huang Liang, and Avid Chiang (2012) 'Smaller Alignment Models for Better Translations: Unsupervised Word Alignment with the 10-norm', in *Proceedings of the 50th Annual Meeting of the Association for Computational Linguistics*, 8–14 July 2012, Jeju Island, Korea, 311–19.

Vogel, Stephen, Hermann Ney, and Christoph Tillmann (1996) 'HMM-based Word Alignment in Statistical Translation', in *Proceedings of the 16th International Conference on Computational Linguistics (COLING)*, 5–9 August 1996, Centre for Sprogteknologi, Copenhagen, Denmark, 836–41.

27

BITEXT

Alan K. Melby, Arle Lommel and Lucía Morado Vázquez

History of Bitext

The term bitext was coined by Brian Harris in an article written in December 1987, while Harris was in Africa on leave from the University of Ottawa, and later published in *Language Monthly* (Harris 1988: 8–10). Harris described bitext (initially spelled with a hyphen, bi-text) as designating a new concept in translation theory, with its primary nature being psycholinguistic, even though it was seen to have applications in translation technology. According to Harris (ibid.), a bitext is a source text and its corresponding target text as they exist *in the mind of a translator*. As Harris points out, a human does not translate an entire text in one fell swoop but rather a segment at a time. Each segment of a source text is mentally linked to a corresponding segment of target text to form a cognitive translation unit. Segments can be phrases, clauses, or larger stretches of text. Together, the translation units of the bitext constitute the entire source and target texts 'laminated' to each other.

In an unpublished 1988 memo to some colleagues, Harris continued to discuss the notion of bitext and provided a concrete example:

SAMPLE OF INTERLINEAR BITEXT [English to French]
| The Board of PAC unanimously confirms the PAC mandate and concept.
| *Le Conseil est unanime dans sa confirmation du mandat et du concept fondamental du PAC.*

| This includes support to long-term development through the strengthening of African NGOs;
| *Le concept comprend un appui au développement à long terme par le renforcement des ONG africaines;*

supporting African awareness in Canada
| *un appui aux activités de sensibilisation du public canadien*

| which focusses on African abilities and strengths
| *qui accentuent les forces et habiletés africaines*

| and the root causes of current problems;
| *et examinent les causes profondes de la crise;*

DOI: 10.4324/9781003168348-30

| encouraging partnerships based on a recognition and respect for mutual roles
| *l'encouragement de partenariats basés sur le respect mutuel*

| and confirmation of Africans as the agents of their own development;
| *et la reconnaissance que les Africain(e)s sont les premiers agents de leur développement;*

| supporting networking and linkage efforts both in Africa and in Canada.
| *l'appui à la création de liens et de réseaux en Afrique et au Canada.*

| PAC's emphasis is on African priorities
| *Le PAC met d'abord l'accent sur les priorités des Africain(e)s*

| and on activities which evolve out of the African context.
| *et les activités qui émanent du contexte africain.*

| Networking and linkages have been identified as priority areas for PAC
| *La promotion de liens et la formation de réseaux sont des domaines prioritaires pour le PAC*

| and are essential to developing true partnership relationships.
| *et sont essentiels pour la mise en oeuvre de relations de partenariat*

(Note [from Harris]: [The vertical bar] marks translation unit boundaries. A search for any word, or combination of words, in the source text retrieves the segment containing it together with the corresponding translation segment (printed here in italics). This enables other translators, or the same translator at some future time, to perceive reusable translations like 'unanimously confirms/*est unanime dans sa confirmation du*' and 'awareness in Canada/*sensibilisation du public canadien*', which would not appear in the dictionaries or term banks because they are context specific, but which help get away from word-for-word equivalences.)

A bitext can be presented visually in various ways. Harris originally anticipated that the preferred presentation would be interlinear, with a segment of target text appearing directly beneath a segment of source text. However, a side-by-side display of source and target segments is currently more common due to the influence of computer translation tools.

As can be seen in this example, some segments of this bitext are entire sentences, others are independent clauses, and some are phrases, depending on what the creator of the bitext considered likely units of thought for a human translator.

Whatever its size and however it is identified, each segment of source text must be linked to its corresponding segment of target text. This segmentation and alignment process allows future reuse of a bitext.

Note that Harris uses 'translation unit' to refer to either a segment of source text or a segment of target text. However, in translation memory systems, generally in translation technology, and in the rest of this article, a translation unit is two segments, a source-text unit and its corresponding target-text segment, together with the link between them.

Interlinear translation has long been a part of literary studies but is not exactly a bitext. For example, an interlinear translation of Chaucer into modern English is superficially similar to a bitext but consists of a literal translation created specifically for the purpose of studying an important text. (See Interlinear 2013.)

A predecessor to bitext was part of a bilingual concordance system in Melby (1981), where segment pairs were identified by a human marking them in source texts and their corresponding translations. The term 'bitext' was not used at that time. After the translation units were marked by a human, software identified all the words in the source text and, for each word, located all the translation units containing that word. This allowed a report of how that word was translated in various contexts. For example, the entry for 'cease' in Melby (1981: 457–66) lists three occurrences in the bitext corpus:

MRD0148 But when the echoes had fully <ceased>,
Mais quand l'écho s'était tout à fait évanoui,

MRD0024 And then the music <ceased>, as I have told;
Alors, comme je l'ai dit, la musique s'arrêta;

CMO0321 when the motion of the hellish machine <ceased>,
que le mouvement de l'infernale machine cessa,

The particular bitext from which this bilingual concordance entry was derived consisted mostly of Edgar Allen Poe stories and their translations into French by Baudelaire. The identifier at the beginning of the line indicated the translation unit. For example, MRD0148 was the 148th translation unit of the bitext of *The Masque of the Red Death*. For the reader who is not familiar with French, the three translation units retrieved for the word 'cease' show three different ways of translating it that are not fully interchangeable. In the first translation unit, an echo is ceasing and the French verb selected by the translator is typically used to translate 'to faint', with the image that the echoes faded away and eventually became inaudible. In the second and third translation units, 'cease' corresponds to different French verbs (*s'arrêter* and *cesser*) that are synonyms but are not used with the same frequency. Thus, this early bilingual concordance, derived from a bitext, fulfilled the hope that Harris expressed: 'to [help the translator] perceive reusable translations . . . which would not appear in the dictionaries or term banks because they are context specific, but which help get away from word-for-word equivalences', but this bilingual concordance system was not further developed at the time, and the idea of a bitext remained dormant until Harris independently proposed it and coined the term seven years later.

Using current translation technology, a bitext such as the examples proposed by Harris and Melby could not be constructed automatically from the source and target texts in question. When a bitext is constructed automatically, one segment size is chosen in advance. Typically, sentence-length or paragraph-length segments are used, as they can be automatically identified by segmentation software. Manual creation of large bitexts is too laborious. The notion of a bitext has strayed from its original conception by Harris as a reflection of the mental units used by a human translator and has instead become the result of a mechanical process applied to source texts and their translations.

Note that source texts and their translations are often called parallel texts in the computational linguistics community. However, the term 'parallel texts' has a different meaning in translation studies, where it refers to texts in different languages and in the same domain that are not necessarily translations of each other. This additional sense of 'parallel texts' is linked to the term 'comparable texts' in computational linguistics. Thus, a bitext corpus can be automatically derived from parallel texts in the computational linguistics sense but not in the translation studies sense of comparable texts.

As another terminological note, in the article on translation memory in the present encyclopedia, the distinction between mental units and mechanical units is described as 'cognitive' vs. 'formal' units.

Bitext in Current Translation Technology

In its application to translation technology, a bitext is ideally created segment by segment while a translator is in the act of translating. However, Harris also allows for the possibility of re-creating a bitext from a source text and a completed translation of it. Clearly, in the case of a bitext reconstructed after the fact, it is impossible for a third party to determine the segmentation that was performed in the mind of the translator. In addition, the initial translation may have been modified by a reviser or reviewer. Thus, there are two common cases: (1) a bitext created incrementally during the translation process and (2) a bitext reconstructed from separate source and target texts, typically using automatic segmentation and alignment (often with additional manual correction of misalignments).

In current practice, most translation tools pre-segment the source text using a segmentation algorithm, primarily on sentence boundaries, and the translator is expected to translate one pre-defined segment at a time. Translation technology, by pre-defining segments and presenting them to the translator, may be changing the way humans think as they translate, but addressing this issue is beyond the scope of the present chapter. The original conception of a bitext as a reflection of the mental process lives on in translation studies, where eye tracking and keystroke capture studies are providing insight into how translators actually do their work (Christensen 2011: 137–60).

Once a bitext is available, it can be converted into a traditional translation memory, which usually involves eliminating duplicate translation units, some degree of normalization of the segments, and combining unordered sets of translation units from a number of source and target texts into an indexed database. Thus, the process of creating a traditional translation memory from a set of bitexts is a non-reversible process in the sense that the original source and target texts cannot be re-created solely from a classic translation memory database without access to the source text. Some translator tools blur the distinction between translation memory and bitext by retaining sufficient information in a translation memory database to reconstruct the original source and target texts. Recently, due to increasing interest in context in machine translation, preservation of full texts has become desirable as some information cannot be reliably recovered from a deduplicated translation memory database (Lommel 2021; Lommel and DePalma 2021).

As indicated in the historical section of the chapter on translation memory, the first commercial translation memory software system was released in 1986 by ALPS, about a year before Harris wrote his first article on bitext. However, Harris did not know about the ALPS system in 1987 (personal communication). Thus, bitext and translation memory can be considered concurrent, independent developments in the history of translation technology, each with a different original focus. The focus of the first translation memory systems was to retrieve entire sentences that had been previously translated, while the focus of a bitext corpus, as envisioned by Harris, was to assist a human translator in doing research on how other translators have dealt with particular words and phrases. With the recent rise of subsegment retrieval in translation memory systems, and the addition of more information in a translation memory database to indicate how a translation unit fits into the source and target texts from which it was derived, the distinction between translation memory and a bitext system is blurring.

Three standards that are highly relevant to bitext are SRX (Segmentation Rules eXchange), XLIFF (XML Localization Interchange File Format), and TMX (Translation Memory eXchange).

SRX provides a formal mechanism for describing how a text is to be segmented, and XLIFF provides a standard format for representing a bitext. See Appendix 1 and Appendix 2, respectively, for more information about SRX and XLIFF.

Monotonicity

TMX was developed in order to represent a translation memory database consisting of an unordered set of translation units, but sometimes TMX is used to represent a bitext by assuming that the order of the segments in the source text is identical to the order of the segments in the target text.

A strict segment-by-segment, typically sentence-by-sentence, correspondence between a source text and its translation is somewhat imposed on a translator using typical tools, sometimes called TEnTs (translation environment tools) or computer-assisted translation (CAT) tools, where the source text is presented to the translator in a two-column table with a segment of source text on the left and a space for the corresponding segment of target text on the right. However, this segment-to-segment correspondence does not necessarily result in the most natural translation. It is based on the assumption that translations are monotonic; that is, segments of source and target text will progress in parallel, with no need for lines that link source and target segments to cross each other.

As pointed out by Quan *et al.* (2013: 622–30, citations in original omitted), this assumption is not necessarily valid:

> [M]ost existing approaches to sentence alignment follow the monotonicity assumption that coupled sentences in bitexts appear in a similar sequential order in two languages and crossings are not entertained in general (Langlais *et al.* 1998; Wu 2010). Consequently the task of sentence alignment becomes handily solvable by means of such basic techniques as dynamic programming.
>
> In many scenarios, however, this prerequisite monotonicity cannot be guaranteed. For example, bilingual clauses in legal bitexts are often coordinated in a way not to keep the same clause order, demanding fully or partially crossing pairings. . . . Such monotonicity seriously impairs the existing alignment approaches founded on the monotonicity assumption.

Consider the following invented source text consisting of five sentences, designed to illustrate non-monotonicity in a simple fashion.

S1 – I was looking at dresses in the store.
S2 – I decided to buy the blue dress for several reasons.
S3 – I hate green, so the green dress was out.
S4 – The yellow dress was too expensive.
S5 – That was a week ago, and I am happy with the blue dress.

Suppose that the translation into some other language, viewed in English using back translation, consists of six sentences:

T1 – I was looking at dresses in the clothing store.
T2 – I hate green, so the green dress was not seriously considered.
T3 – The yellow dress was too expensive.
T4 – Therefore I decided to buy the blue dress.
T5 – That was a week ago.
T6 – I am happy with my purchase.

How could this non-monotonic translation be represented in a bitext without changing the sentence order of either the source text or the target text?

The fact that the fifth sentence of the source text becomes two sentences in the target text is not a problem. However, the rhetorical difference of introducing the conclusion early in the source text (in segment 2) but later in the target text (in segment 4), does cause difficulties for representation in a bitext.

The correlation of the translation units (source–target segment pairs) is as shown here:

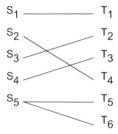

This reordering and crossed sequencing is not a problem for a translation memory that consists of unordered translation units; although, it may complicate its creation from previously translated content. However, a bitext is expected to represent the order of segments as found in the original source text and the original target text.

One way to deal with this problem is to make the segment unit a paragraph instead of a sentence and define S1–S5 and T1–T6 as one pair of paragraphs that correspond. However, there can be more dramatic ordering problems that would make this approach infeasible. Or there may be reasons to keep the segment size at the sentence level.

The most common format for representing a bitext outside any particular software application is XLIFF.

Non-monotonic segment order is handled differently in XLIFF 1.2 and 2.0/2.1:

> In XLIFF 1.2, segments are represented by <mrk mtype='seg'> elements that are set within both the source and the target contents. Each of these markers has an ID, so the markers can be in different physical order in the source and target content while they are still linked by ID value.

(See http://docs.oasis-open.org/xliff/v1.2/os/xliff-core.html#Struct_Segmentation for more information.)

Here is how the dress-buying example would be represented in XLIFF 1.2:

```
<trans-unit id= "1">
<source>I was looking at dresses in the store. I decided to buy the blue dress for several
    reasons. I hate green, so the green dress was out. The yellow dress was too expensive.
    That was a week ago, and I am happy with the blue dress</source>
<seg-source>
<mrk mtype="seg" mid="1">I was looking at dresses in the store.</mrk>
<mrk mtype="seg" mid="2">I decided to buy the blue dress for several reasons.</mrk>
<mrk mtype="seg" mid="3">I hate green, so the green dress was out.</mrk>
<mrk mtype="seg" mid="4">The yellow dress was too expensive.</mrk>
<mrk mtype="seg" mid="5">That was a week ago, and I am happy with the blue dress.</mrk>
</seg-source>
<target>
<mrk mtype="seg" mid="1">I was looking at dresses in the store.</mrk>
```

```
<mrk mtype="seg" mid="3">I hate green, so the green dress was not seriously
    considered.</mrk>
<mrk mtype="seg" mid="4">The yellow dress was too expensive.</mrk>
<mrk mtype="seg" mid="2">Therefore I decided to buy the blue dress.</mrk>
<mrk mtype="seg" mid="5">That was a week ago.</mrk>
<mrk mtype="seg" mid="5">I am happy with my purchase.</mrk>
</target>
</trans-unit>
```

Many TeNTs have implemented XLIFF 1.2. However, few have implemented the use of IDs on segments in order to represent non-monotonic translations.

In the most recent versions of XLIFF (2.0 and 2.1), segments are directly represented within the translation units. And each segment element includes its own source and target elements. A segment reordering mechanism was defined in these new versions: the optional attribute 'order' indicates the order of the target segments, while the physical order of the elements tells us the order of the source.

See http://docs.oasis-open.org/xliff/xliff-core/v2.0/xliff-core-v2.0.html#segorder for more information.

One reason why it is important to consider non-monotonic translation in bitext, besides the fact that it occurs in real translations, is to avoid imposing a monotonic mindset on translators. Languages use a variety of rhetorical structures. See, for example, the seminal work of Kaplan (1966: 1–20). We thus come full circle back to the origin of bitext as a reflection of the mental process of a human translator, not an imposition on the mind of a translator intended to reduce diversity among languages.

Applications of Bitext

Bitext has become highly influential in translation technology.

The major common applications of bitext are currently:

(1) A method of keeping source and target texts aligned throughout the entire translation process, including quality control steps;
(2) An intermediate stage toward the creation of a translation memory database; and
(3) A source of training data for statistical machine translation systems.

However, there are other uses for a bitext. Among them are:

• The study of 'shifts' in human translation (Cyrus 2006: 1240–45), such as:

    • Passivization and depassivization;
    • Number change (e.g. plural to singular);
    • Explicitation and generalization.

• Terminology research:

    • TransSearch (Macklovitch *et al.* 2000 and www.terminotix.com);
    • Termight (see Dagan and Church 1994: 34–40);
    • Identifying concept relations (not just terms): (Marshman 2012: 30–56).

• Word sense disambiguation (Diab and Resnik 2002: 255–62).

- Inducing transfer rules (Lavoie *et al.* 2001: 17–24 for rule-based machine translation, and Graham and van Genabith 2009: 1–10 for transfer-based statistical machine translation).

Conclusion

Although bitext is an idea from the 1980s that was originally intended to primarily assist human translators in retrieving instances of words and phrases as treated by other human translators, it has also turned out to be the basis for many other aspects of translation technology, from translation memory to machine translation. In a sense, it has evolved from a purely descriptive mechanism to a framework for translation that makes it difficult to break out of a sentence-by-sentence correspondence between source and target languages. One is led to wonder what effect bitext is having on language. Despite the undeniable benefits of bitext, has it reduced the richness of translation by imposing the sequence of source-language segments on the target language?

APPENDIX 1

Segmentation Rules eXchange Format

Note: SRX is closely related to the chapter on segmentation.

One significant problem that arises in building bitext (and multitext) corpora stems from segmentation, the division of texts into segments generally considered equivalent to sentences. Segmentation would pose little problem if there were an unambiguous character for marking sentence boundaries; but the full stop (.) character that indicates sentence boundaries for most Western languages is highly ambiguous. Besides ending sentences, it serves to mark abbreviations (e.g. 'etc.', 'Dr.', 'Mr.'), indicate decimals (in some languages) or serve as the thousands separator (in others) and is used for special purposes in certain areas (e.g. as the prefix for file-type extensions in many computer operating systems or to separate sections of numerical IP addresses). All of these uses mean that a full stop, by itself, is not a reliable indicator of sentence boundary.

At the same time, additional characters may serve as segment boundaries for Western languages. The following are some common examples:

- Carriage returns are frequently used to terminate list items or after titles and headings that do not end in periods. At the same time, carriage returns are frequently used to force formatting line breaks that do not end sentences.
- Semicolons (in English at least) are frequently used to separate (grammatically) full sentences that have a closer logical relationship than would be implied if they were separated by a period. But semicolons are used for other purposes that do not end segments. (Semicolons are particularly problematic when aligning English texts with source or target texts in other languages where the other language uses two distinct segments in place of one in English.)
- Other punctuation marks, such as the exclamation point (!) and question mark (?), when followed by capital letters are, for most text types, generally unambiguous segment boundary markers when followed by a space and a capital letter, but they have special uses in some text domains (such as information technology and mathematics) that may render them ambiguous.
- Tab characters may be used to separate items in tabular data, but interpreting segment boundaries in tab-delimited data is frequently highly problematic since the tabs may be combined with carriage returns, spaces, and other characters in complex fashions.

All of these issues make accurate segmentation difficult from a machine-processing perspective. While parsing and data-driven approaches can help disambiguate text and identify correct segment boundaries, most commercial applications have tended instead to use regular-expression–based iterative processes that search a text for potential segment boundaries and then check them against exception lists to determine whether segmentation is appropriate.

Leaving Western languages, the situation may be better or worse, depending on the language. Chinese, Japanese, and Korean, for example, are much easier to segment accurately at the sentence level than Western languages because the sentence-terminating punctuation tends to be used exclusively for the purpose of terminating segments. The orthography of Thai, on the other hand, poses special problems for both word- and sentence-level segmentation because Thai generally lacks inter-word white space but does use space characters to mark segment boundaries and in some other circumstances. Modern Hebrew and Arabic tend to be fairly simple to segment by comparison. (This chapter cannot address the specifics of world languages and focuses primarily on the orthographic challenges of Western languages written in Latin, Greek, and Cyrillic scripts.)

The Unicode Consortium in Unicode Standard Annex (UAX) 29 describes a process for segmenting text based on a standard algorithm. This approach, however, does not account for language-specific issues (and specifically notes that it cannot handle them). As a result, text segmented according to this specification is likely to contain errors. For example, UAX#29 rules would break this text:

On Friday we saw Mr. Smith at the theater.

into two segments:

On Friday we saw Mr.
Smith at the theater.

Such problems are quite common and pose a particular challenge for segmenting and aligning text. Early research conducted by a group of IT companies found that they lost between 5% and 10% of translation memory matches in technical text due to incorrect or differing segmentation. The largest offender was abbreviations that end in full-stop characters, such as 'Mr.' and 'Prof.' (in English), 'Mme.' (French), and 'z.B' (German). Certain abbreviations that can be termed 'prefixing abbreviations' are particularly likely to be followed by capital letters (thus triggering a simple segmentation boundary condition): these are abbreviations for titles and names. Other abbreviations, by contrast, such as 'etc.', are relatively less likely to be followed by capital letters outside of segment boundary conditions but still may be followed by them in some cases (e.g. 'I saw the camels, donkeys, horses, etc. John had brought to market').

In response to these findings, the Localization Industry Standards Association developed the Segmentation Rules eXchange format (LISA 2008, available at GALA 2012). SRX allows users to declare regular-expression–based sets of rules for segmentation. In particular, it allows them to create rules for breaking text and rules for preventing breaks in a standard XML format. SRX files specify a regular expression that defines the text that occurs before the possible break and a regular expression that defines the text after the possible break. For example, the following rule:

```
<rule break='no'>
<beforebreak>\sMr\.</beforebreak>
<afterbreak>\s</afterbreak>
</rule>
```

indicates that no segment boundary should occur after the text 'Mr.', thus overriding the default UAX#29 algorithm. By contrast, the following rule:

```
<rule break='yes'>
<beforebreak>[\.\?!]+</beforebreak>
<afterbreak>\s+[A-Z]</afterbreak>
</rule>
```

states that if a full stop, question mark, or exclamation point is followed by one or more whitespace characters and a capital letter, the text should be broken after the terminal punctuation.

SRX allows for the creation of general and language-specific sets of rules. In practice, these rule sets tend to consist of a list of rules that account for abbreviations that should not trigger a segmentation break, followed by a list of general break conditions. Each location in the file is evaluated against the rules sequentially. If a no-break condition is met, then the processing engine ceases to examine at that point and moves on to the next inter-character position in the file. If no no-break condition is met then breaking conditions are evaluated and, if one is met, the text is segmented. If no breaking condition is found, then the processor moves to the next position.

SRX rules are generally quite easy to interpret for individuals familiar with regular expressions. Complex regular expressions can be used. As mentioned, most SRX files focus on exceptions to general rules triggered by abbreviations, since these account for most segmentation faults. However, they may also address specific conditions related to specific text domains or text types. For example, if an input file is 'hard wrapped' (that is, uses new-line characters at the end of lines within a paragraph), an SRX file can specify that new line characters, which would generally indicate a segment boundary, should be ignored unless they occur after a full stop or other trailing punctuation and are followed by a capital letter. (And this behavior, in turn, may be overridden by specific rules for abbreviations or other conditions.)

SRX serves a valuable function by allowing tools to declare how they segmented text to allow other tools to emulate or understand that behavior. Because of domain and text-type differences, there is no single segmentation algorithm that will suffice for all conditions. Furthermore, users of natural language processing (NLP) tools frequently 'tweak' segmentation engines to account for issues encountered in the text with which they work. SRX provides a way to document these modifications and specific functions to ensure interoperability between segmentation engines. In addition, by correcting for segmentation faults that might otherwise confuse NLP tools, SRX files can help improve automatic alignment results.

One usage scenario for SRX with benefit for working with bitexts involves using SRX to allow bitexts to be dynamically resegmented to allow interoperability between processes that work on bitexts. In this scenario a bitext could be segmented to match multiple existing translation memory databases to identify the best matches or a new text could be segmented to match an existing bitext for which the appropriate segmentation method has been declared in SRX. Without SRX such dynamic analysis would be much more difficult and would require the creation of one-off segmentation routines that would offer little flexibility. Instead SRX permits researchers and commercial developers to implement effective segmentation rules to meet their needs without the worry that segmentation choices will negatively impact future activities due to incompatibilities.

SRX plays an important role in bitext applications, particularly in translation memory, by providing a formal mechanism to declare the specific segmentation rules used to generate a corpus. This transparency helps reduce incompatibility between bitext tools and can assist users in understanding how particular results were achieved.

SRX is recognized as the standard for segmentation rules and a number of TEnTs have implemented it (including XTM, CafeTran, MemoQ, and Swordfish)[1] and it is included the open-source Okapi, OmegaT, SRXEditor, and LanguageTool projects. A modified version of SRX is utilized by the widely used Trados to permit export of segmentation information, but this version is not compliant with the SRX specification and Trados segmentation files require modification to be used with SRX processors.

Some basic sets of SRX rules for major languages have been made publicly available (see GALA 2012), but segmentation rules depend on domain and organization and it is not possible to generate universal rule sets since specific segmentation cases may directly conflict depending on specific instances.

Given that segmentation into a TM is often a non-reversible process, SRX cannot address the problem of interoperability for unordered translation memories that were previously segmented using different rules. In other words, it cannot directly 'fix' the segmentation of heterogeneous TM resources. However, if full texts are preserved as bitexts rather than reduced to TM databases, SRX can be used to adjust segmentation as needed.

In cases where segmentation differences impede interoperability, SRX may be more productively used to resegment complete texts to ensure compatibility moving forward while treating previously segmented resources as a fall-back for match purposes. This lack of the ability to directly address previously segmented legacy texts converted to TM databases has proved a barrier to greater adoption of SRX within the TM community. However, the ability to work with bitexts and SRX to allow dynamic resegmentation is an argument for greater use of bitexts instead of traditional TM resources.

SRX plays an important role in the open standards landscape, allowing easier and more reliable movement between translation tools for use of language resources with heterogeneous segmentation processes. Such scenarios are of considerable importance for businesses with significant bitext resources and SRX can have a major business impact, especially in cases where organizations are required to merge language resources (e.g. in merger and acquisition scenarios).

APPENDIX 2

XLIFF

Introduction

The XML Localization Interchange File Format is a tool-neutral data container that allows the interchange of localization data and metadata during the localization process. It is currently being developed by the Organization for the Advancement of Structured Information Standards (OASIS). The standard was first created under the name of DataDefinition group by members of three software companies, Novell, Oracle, and Sun Microsystems, in Dublin in the year 2000 (Jewtushenko 2004). Their aim was to develop a single format that would allow the interchange of localizable data between tools during the localization process without loss or corruption of data. Two years later, XLIFF 1.0 was officially approved as a Committee Specification within OASIS XLIFF Technical Committee (XLIFF TC 2003). Since then, many software companies, TEnT developers, localization companies, and academicians have joined the OASIS XLIFF TC to work on its development and maintenance; four more versions (1.1, 1.2, 2.0, and 2.1) have already been approved; and the XLIFF TC is working on the next one. Task-specific subcommittees have also been created to work on specific aspects of the standard, for example, the Promotion & Liaison subcommittee that, since its creation, has maintained relationships with other related standardization bodies and has carried out different promotional activities, such as the organization of yearly international symposia on XLIFF that took place between 2010 and 2017.

Extraction-Merge Principle in XLIFF

XLIFF is based on an extraction–merging concept (Savourel 2003), which can be explained as a three-step localization mechanism: in the first step, it relies on the extraction of the localization-related data from an original format and its conversion to a valid XLIFF file. The second step involves the manipulation of that file by any TEnT that supports the standard. The manipulation would always depend on the specific localization project being converted and could include some typical localization tasks such as translation, reviewing, or QA checking. After finishing all the required processes, the XLIFF file can be declared as final. The third step involves merging the manipulated data into the original file to create a localized version in another language. As observed in this three-step mechanism, XLIFF was originally designed as a temporary format to be used during the localization process and discarded after the final merging process; however, it is now seen as a long-term representation of a text and its translation. Even after a translation or localization project has been completed, an XLIFF file can be used to generate a traditional translation memory, for reuse in XLIFF aware tools, and for various research tasks based on bitexts, as previously described in this chapter.

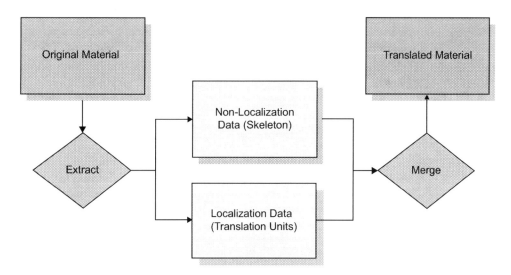

Figure 27.1   Extraction/merge principle of XLIFF (XLIFF TC 2003: 10)

The most popular version of the standard is still XLIFF 1.2; it has been widely implemented in the TEnT ecosystem (Filip and Morado Vázquez 2012) since its approval in 2008. The main criticism that this version received was the permissiveness of the specification in some points. This has resulted in some cases of different interpretations and tool-specific implementations of the standard, which could jeopardize the main feature of the standard: interoperability between tools. The XLIFF TC listened to the feedback and suggestions for improvement and designed version 2.0 and 2.1 with them in mind.

XLIFF 2.0 and 2.1

XLIFF 2.0 was approved in 2014, it differed substantially from the previous version (1.2), and introduced the core and module concepts for the first time. The core consists of

> the minimum set of XML elements and attributes required to (a) prepare a document that contains text extracted from one or more files for localization, (b) allow it to be completed with the translation of the extracted text, and (c) allow the generation of *Translated* versions of the original document.
>
> (XLIFF TC 2014)

The core concept shares some similarities with the 'minimal XLIFF' that was present in version 1.2. As well as the core, eight specific modules were designed in that version to store extra information about specific localization processes: Translation Candidates, Glossary, Format Style, Metadata, Resource Data, Change Tracking, Size Restriction, and Validation. Each of them was designed with a specific process in mind; they have their own pre-defined XML elements and attributes in an individual XML schema and namespace (XLIFF TC 2014). XLIFF 2.1 was approved four years later, in 2018, and it maintained the exact same core structure as 2.0. The difference between the versions is essentially found on the associated modules: on the one hand, the Change Tracking module was demoted, on the other hand, a new ITS (Internationalization Tag Set) module was introduced (XLIFF TC 2018).

From this version on, if a TEnT wants to be declared as XLIFF compliant, it would need to support at least the XLIFF core. Checking and certifying if a tool is truly XLIFF compliant is out of the scope of the XLIFF TC; however, this clear core-module distinction would help tool developers to concentrate their efforts on supporting at least the reduced set of XML elements and the attributes of the core. Depending on the nature of the specific TEnT and its needs, developers might also decide to implement some of the modules proposed in the 2.0 or 2.1 specifications; for example, the Translation Candidates module where alternative translation proposals can be stored. The Translation Candidate module substitutes the <al-trans> element that was present in the previous version (1.2).

The following is an example of a basic (and valid) XLIFF 2.0 file which only contains core elements and attributes. The root element is <xliff>, which can contain one or more <file> elements. Please note that the structural elements <header> and <body> are no longer present in this version. Inside the file element, we find the <unit> element where one or more elements can be included. A compulsory <source> element was placed in the unit that stores the text to be translated, followed by an optional <target> element that stores the translated version.

```
<xliff version="2.0" srcLang="en" trgLang="es">
<file>
<unit id="1">
<segment>
<source> Hello World! </source>
<target> ¡Hola, mundo! </target>
</segment>
</unit>
</file>
</xliff>
```

A new version of XLIFF, most likely 2.2, is under development. One of the current topics under discussion is the division of the current specification between core and modules information, and their publication as individual documents. This new publication strategy would present the essential information of the standard (i.e., the core) in a single and more accessible document that could help tool implementers to support it.

Note

1 This list of TEnTs and the following lists of implementations are not intended to be comprehensive.

Bibliography

Christensen, Tina Paulsen (2011) 'Studies on the Mental Processes in Translation Memory-assisted Translation – The State of the Art', *trans-kom. Zeitschrift für Translationswissenschaft und Fachkommunikation* 4(2): 137–60.

Cyrus, Lea (2006) 'Building a Resource for Studying Translation Shifts', in *LREC 2006: Proceedings of the International Conference on Language Resources and Evaluation*, 24–26 May 2006, Genoa, Italy, 1240–45.

Dagan, Ido and Kenneth W. Church (1994) 'Termight: Identifying and Translating Technical Terminology', in *Proceedings of the 4th Conference on Applied Natural Language Processing*, 13–15 October 1994, Morgan Kaufmann Publishers, Stuttgart, Germany, San Francisco, 34–40.

Diab, Mona and Philip Resnik (2002) 'An Unsupervised Method for Word Sense Tagging Using Parallel Corpora', in *Proceedings of the 40th Annual Meeting of the Association for Computational Linguistics*, 7–12 July 2002, University of Pennsylvania, Philadelphia, PA; Morgan Kaufmann Publishers, San Francisco, 255–62.

Filip, David and Lucía Morado Vázquez (2012) 'XLIFF Support in CAT Tools: Results of the Survey, January 2012', in *XLIFF Promotion and Liaison Subcommittee*, OASIS.

GALA (2012) 'LISA OSCAR Standards'. Available at: www.gala-global.org/lisa-oscar-standards.

Graham, Yvette and Josef van Genabith (2009) 'An Open Source Rule Induction Tool for Transfer-based SMT', *The Prague Bulletin of Mathematical Linguistics: Special Issue: Open Source Tools for Machine Translation* 91: 1–10.

Harris, Brian (1988) 'Bi-text, A New Concept in Translation Theory', *Language Monthly* 54: 8–10.

Interlinear (2013) Available at: http://sites.fas.harvard.edu/~chaucer/teachslf/tr-index.htm.

Jewtushenko, Tony (2004) 'An Introduction to XLIFF', in *IV International LRC Localisation Summer School 2004*, 2 June 2004, LRC, University of Limerick, Ireland.

Kaplan, Robert B. (1966) 'Cultural Thought Patterns in Inter-cultural Education', *Language Learning* 16(1–2): 1–20.

Lavoie, Benoit, Michael White, and Tanya Korelsky (2001) 'Inducing Lexico-structural Transfer Rules from Parsed Bi-texts', in *Association for Computational Linguistics: 39th Annual Meeting and 10th Conference of the European Chapter: Workshop Proceedings: Data-driven Machine Translation*, 6–11 July 2001, Toulouse, France, 17–24.

LISA (Localization Industry Standards Association) (2008) *Segmentation Rules eXchange (SRX)*, Féchy, Switzerland: Localization Industry Standards Association.

Lommel, Arle, and Donald A. DePalma (2021) 'Responsive Machine Translation'. Cambridge MA: CSA Research. Available at: https://insights.csa-research.com/reportaction/305013336/Toc.

Lommel, Arle (2021) 'Responsive Machine Translation: The Next Frontier for MT'. Available at: https://csa-research.com/Blogs-Events/Blog/responsive-MT-Test.

Macklovitch, Elliott, Michel Simard, and Philippe Langlais (2000) 'TransSearch: A Free Translation Memory on the World Wide Web', in *LREC 2000: Proceedings of the International Conference on Language Resources and Evaluation*, 31 May–2 June 2000, Athens, Greece, 1201–1208.

Marshman, Elizabeth, Julie L. Gariépy, and Charissa Harms (2012) 'Helping Language Professionals Relate to Terms: Terminological Relations and Termbases', *Journal of Specialized Translation* 18: 30–56.

Melby, Alan K. (1981) 'Linguistics and Machine Translation', in James Copeland and Philip W. Davis (eds.) *The Seventh Lacus Forum*, Columbia, SC: Hornbeam Press, 457–66.

Quan, Xiaojun, Kit Chunyu, and Yan Song (2013) 'Non-monotonic Sentence Alignment via Semi-supervised Learning', in *Proceedings of the 51st Annual Meeting of the Association for Computational Linguistics*, 4–9 August 2013, Sofia, Bulgaria, 622–30. Available at: http://aclweb.org/anthology/P/P13/P13-1061.pdf.

Savourel, Yves (2003) 'An Introduction to Using XLIFF', *Multilingual Computing & Technology* 14(2): 28–34.

XLIFF TC (2003) 'A White Paper on Version 1.1 of the XML Localisation Interchange File Format (XLIFF)'. Available at: http://www.oasis-open.org/committees/download.php/3110/XLIFF-core-whitepaper_1.1-cs.pdf.

XLIFF (2008) 'XLIFF Version 1.2, OASIS Standard, 1 February 2008'. Available at: http://docs.oasis-open.org/xliff/v1.2/os/xliff-core.html.

XLIFF TC (2014) 'XLIFF Version 2.0, OASIS Standard'. Available at: http://docs.oasis-open.org/xliff/xliff-core/v2.0/os/xliff-core-v2.0-os.pdf

XLIFF TC (2018) 'XLIFF Version 2.1, OASIS Standard'. Available at: http://docs.oasis-open.org/xliff/xliff-core/v2.1/os/xliff-core-v2.1-os.pdf

28

COMPUTATIONAL LEXICOGRAPHY

From the Electronic to Digitalized Age

Zhang Yihua

Introduction

The term "computational lexicography" can be interpreted as the study of lexicographical theory and practice by means of computational technology. Thus, computational lexicography should certainly function within the framework of traditional lexicography, but with the focus on a new lexicographical methodology based on modern technology created in the digital age. Undoubtedly, the development of computer information technology, multi-media, and media convergence provide excellent tools for lexicographical study and practice.

In fact, the computer creates favourable conditions for such aspects of lexicography as data storage, extraction, analysis, transmission, and exchange, as well as corpus construction and dictionary compilation and publication.

Origin and Development of Computational Lexicography

Relationship Between Computational Lexicography and Machine Translation

Computational lexicography is an outcome of the combination of lexicography and computer technology, and the primary symbol is the electronic dictionary. The earliest and most direct integration of dictionaries with computers can be traced back to the late 1940s. It began with the research on machine translation (MT) or natural language processing (NLP) by British engineer A.D. Booth and American scientist W. Weaver, since one of the core elements of a machine translation system (MTS) is a bilingual electronic dictionary (machine dictionary: MD). As Feng (1994: 231) said, "the basic information of the MT comes from the MD. Without a good MD, machine translation means nothing, and cannot run at all" (Feng 2001: 99).

Relationship Between Electronic Dictionary and Machine Dictionaries

Due to the limitations of computer hardware and application software at that time, the MT and related dictionaries experienced a long period of difficult exploration. It was not until the end of the 1970s that Canada and the European Union launched the Weinder and Eurotra translation systems, respectively. The mid–late 1980s to the early 1990s saw a rapid development of machine

DOI: 10.4324/9781003168348-31

dictionaries, and some of them turned into electronic dictionaries for human use, widely available on the market for many years. To some extent, modern electronic dictionaries originated from the research and development of MT or NLP.

From this perspective, the purpose of computational lexicography is to deal with the design, compilation, and use of machine readable dictionaries (MRDs) in natural language processing and then to turn them into human-readable versions for human use.

Dictionary-making is a very time-consuming and laborious task. Since the major purpose of both MDs and human-oriented dictionaries is to interpret the meanings of entry words and to find their corresponding equivalents in target languages, it is wise to make a dictionary accessible for both humans and machines. But it should be noted that the methods of organization and representation of lexicographical data are different in human- and machine-readable dictionaries.

Humans can look up and understand the information in dictionaries by association to their prior knowledge or relying on their linguistic intuition. The lexical representation is informal, and some of the items can be highlighted for their visual sense by capital, bold, italic, flashing, and coloured graphemes, which help users to quickly find the information they need. As for machine-readable dictionaries, they need to have unified codes for the morphological, syntactic, and semantic information of the lexical unit, encoded in various formulae, so that the machine can understand the dictionaries and undertake automatic processing.

Transformation From Paper to Electronic Dictionaries

As there exists major commonality between MDs and human-oriented dictionaries, it is a good idea to make full use of traditional dictionaries to make machine-readable dictionaries. Since the beginning of the 1980s, the major English learners' dictionaries, such as the *Oxford Advanced Learner's Dictionary* (OALD) and *Longman Dictionary of Contemporary English* (LDOCE), have been transformed into MDs used for NPL because of their fine classification of lexical information and well-established grammatical patterns and lexical collocations extracted from repeated instances of corpora.

On the other hand, the adoption of computer technology can be seen in the compilation of these English learners' dictionaries in the late 1970s, when MDs began to make use of information from printed versions. *OALD, LDOCE*, and *Collins Cobuild (Advanced Learner's) English Dictionary* (COBUILD) are good examples representing the different stages of the development of electronic dictionaries.

At the end of the 1970s, the *OALD* turned the printed version into machine-readable form. A computer was not involved in the actual lexicographical preparation of the dictionary, such as corpus-based sense division, (grammatical/lexical) pattern-analysis, exemplification, and so on. Basically it was a typesetting of ready-made dictionaries, rendering the printed version machine readable.

In the early 1980s, an electronic version of the *LDOCE* was made available. A computer was not involved in the lexicographical preparation but in checking the wordlist and entry texts so as to ensure consistency of word definitions. What's more, some lexical or grammatical information (or columns), which wasn't available in the printed version, was provided for special use. This can be referred to as the first computer-aided MRD.

In the mid-1980s, *Collins COBUILD English Dictionary* was written for advanced English learners. It can be said that the first edition of the dictionary was not compiled but "generated" on the basis of a powerful corpus of 73 million words. The computer was involved in the whole process, including data collection, entry selection, word sense definitions, entry arrangement, and so on, and a special writing system could automatically check the consistency and completeness of each entry. This can be referred to as the first corpus-based MRD.

Computational Lexicography: Theoretical Research

The combination of dictionary and computer technology has opened up a new area of study: computational lexicography. The theoretical research on computational lexicography began as early as the 1960s, when the *American Heritage Dictionary* started the lexicographical preparation with the help of the Brown Corpus. In the early 1960s, Brown University collected and analyzed a large number of written materials, and built the first computer-readable general corpus – the Standard Corpus of Present-Day Edited American English (the Brown Corpus), which contains over 1 million words of running text (500 sample essays of 2000+ words each in 15 styles or genres). *The American Heritage Dictionary* used computers to count word frequencies in the corpus, determine their genres, and define their meanings based on the contextual distributions or grammatical patterns of each word in combination with its frequency.

However, it was not until the mid-1980s that a great breakthrough was made in the academic field of computational lexicography. With the publication of the corpus-based dictionary (COBUILD), the annual journal *Lexicographica* published a special issue, *Computational Lexicography and Computational Linguistics*, in 1988, and Boguraev and Briscoe put out a book entitled *Computational Lexicography for Natural Language Processing* in 1989. These mean that the theoretical framework of computational lexicography took shape, and the research scope or task became specifiable.

Some years later, Atkins and Zampolli's *Computational Approaches to the Lexicon* (1994) and van Eynde and Gibbon's *Lexicon Development for Speech and Language Processing* (2000) both gave deep insights into the issues concerning computational lexicography, and articles on computational lexicography became available in many journals and online media.

Meanwhile, writings on corpus lexicography coming off the press attracted lexicographers' attention. *Corpus, Concordance, Collocation* (Sinclair 1991) and *Computer Corpus Lexicography* (Ooi 1998) are two examples. With the advent of the 21st century, a somewhat systematic framework of computational lexicography was put forward by Zhang in his books *Computational Lexicography and New Dictionaries* (2004) and *Computational Lexicography* (2013).

In short, computational lexicography covers the computational approaches and tools to assist in various lexicographical tasks, including the collection of language data, extraction of linguistic evidence, preparation or editing of lexical entries, construction of lexicographical definitions, typesetting of lexicographical texts, and dissemination of finished products.

In recent years, the world community has entered a digital age. Digitized information and Internet communications through new media have been highly integrated into all levels of social development, and media convergence has become an inevitable trend in data processing and dissemination of dictionaries. Digitization of dictionaries in converged media environments will also be an inevitable choice for lexicographers. In fact, people's reading habits have changed a lot with the widespread use of new media; printed and traditional e-dictionaries have lost the position of "first consultation" for foreign language learners, and instead mobile phones, iPads, tablet PCs, and so on have become their preference for consulting dictionaries. Furthermore, in terms of dictionary-assisted language teaching, traditional literacy based on reading and writing is not adequate in the multimedia era (Hu 2007). Educators, government bodies, and employers have acknowledged the need for modern learners to acquire 21st-century skills using information and communication technologies to personalize student learning (Keane *et al.* 2016). Multiliteracies are gaining more and more attention in foreign language teaching, and multimodal pedagogy will gradually become a general trend in second language teaching (Zhang and Wang 2010; Zhang and Ding 2013). Thus, learners' dictionaries specially designed for second language learning must adapt to changes in learners' needs and adopt multimodality in the representation of word meaning. It will be seen that research on multimodal dictionaries from the perspective of media convergence will soon become a new hot spot for computational lexicography.

It is worth mentioning that in 1990, a conference on computational lexicography (COMPLEX) was initiated by the Research Institute for Linguistics of the Hungarian Academy of Sciences. In principle, it was held every two years. The first COMPLEX conference took place in 1990 in Balatonfiired with mainly French and Hungarian participants. Very soon, however, it became more and more international. But, towards the late 1990s, the interest in a special meeting for computational lexicography started to diminish due to the fact that the original function of COMPLEX was taken over in part by the EURALEX conferences and in part by the COLING meetings (cf. Kiefer 2005). Thus, the 8th COMPLEX meeting, which was held in Budapest in June 17–18, 2005, became the last conference. The COMPLEX conferences certainly played an important role in the past and have contributed a great deal to the development of the computational lexicography.

Computational Lexicography: Main Study Fields

Computational lexicography is technologically related to computational linguistics and theoretically to computational lexicology. The former focuses mainly on computer-aided NLP, including the technology of information processing in various aspects or layers of both written and oral languages. The achievements in computational linguistic research can only contribute to the practice of dictionary making when they are well integrated into lexicography. The latter studies the application of computers to lexicon research, especially the computational representation of the lexicon, methods of lexical data calculation, and the relation between the computerized lexicon and various parts of the system of NLP. As a cross-disciplinary field of study, computational lexicography has developed into a relatively independent subject through serial research over a rather long time, with a set of methodologies and clear research objectives.

Corpus Lexicography

Lexicography is the second major field where corpus linguistics not only introduced new methods but also extended the entire scope of research (Teubert 2001). The combination of corpus and lexicography constitutes an effective merger of three notions: computational linguistics, computational lexicography, and corpus linguistics. Corpus linguistics proposes a new train of thought that linguistic research and NLP can be done based on computer corpora, which provides a new way for the lexicographer to compile contemporary learners' dictionaries and large-scale comprehensive dictionaries and thus satisfy the requirements of current dictionary users. Corpus linguistics has its function and research focus as follows: (a) language performance, (b) language description, (c) quantitative and qualitative modelling of language, and (d) experimentalism (Leech 1992: 107). Therefore, corpus-based theoretical research and practice of lexicography can justify being called corpus lexicography.

Main Characteristics of Corpus Lexicography

The application of corpora can be seen in almost every branch of linguistics in which research can be done based upon corpora. As for corpus lexicography, the scope of study falls into three aspects:

1   The construction of corpora, including the collection, input, segmentation, lemmatization, tagging, arrangement, and storage of language materials; the management of corpora, supplementation and updating of language materials.

2   The use of corpora, including the word frequency count, language data query, generation of wordlists, generation of example repository, extraction of examples and usages, and the statistics of corpus data.

3   The datafication of corpora, including corpus pattern analysis, word sketches, collocate extraction based on word frequency, and lexicon or database building based on corpora for general or specialized dictionaries.

Sinclair (1985: 81–94) and Atkins (1991: 167–204) put forward a new methodology, which Atkins termed corpus lexicography, to evaluate instances of language performance by means of running texts in an attempt to build a more complete, coherent, and consistent set of language data compared to the traditional lexicon. Language data can be regarded as the representation of linguistic/lexical knowledge, which can be subdivided into two levels, the conceptual structure and the computational structure (Kim 1991: 129). The former is a format comprehensible by human beings, and the latter is readable by machines. Computational structure is characterized by its clear formulation and can directly reflect the conceptual structure of defined words, while conceptual structure facilitates the compilation of general language dictionaries.

Construction and Application of Corpora

Since the construction of the Brown Corpus in the early 1960s, the first representative computerized mega-corpus, numerous corpora have been built around the world. Especially in Britain, a series of dictionary corpora have been built and put into use during the 1980s and 1990s, such as The Bank of English, Longman Corpus Network, British National Corpus (BNC), Longman Learner's Corpus, Longman Written American Corpus, Longman Spoken American Corpus, Longman Lancaster English Language Corpus, Cambridge International Corpus, and International Corpus of English.

In the new century, with the tremendous increase in online publication, language materials on the Internet become more and more abundant, and linguists and lexicographers have begun to think about using online resources to substitute for printed matter. In this way, the acquisition of language materials becomes much easier, and the corpora expand increasingly in size; corpora of more than 1 billion, or even 10 billion words have appeared one after another, for example, the enTenTen Web-based corpus included in the Word Sketch Engine, in which the "TenTen" means the corpus has a capacity of 10 to the 10th power of words. In fact, enTenTen-15 has reached 13.2 billion words. In addition, the COCA corpus cluster of the United States has also gathered some Web-based corpora, such as the Global Web-Based English (1.9 billion), News on the Web (13.5 billion+), and the Intelligent Web-based Corpus (14 billion). This greatly enriches the theoretical concepts and user experience of the corpus.

Corpus building should take into consideration the following aspects: first, the basic features of the corpus; that is, a corpus is usually designed for a specific purpose or for general use, the language materials collected must be authentic and typical, and the lexical data encoding and decoding must be standardized and machine readable. Second, the function of the corpus; that is, a dictionary corpus should have the function of data management, indexing, statistics, tagging, speech analysis, and lexical data extraction. Third, the types of corpora; that is, different types of corpora can be classified from the perspective of a specific purpose, languages involved, language forms, language use, text type distribution, degree of processing, and storage media (cf. Zhang 2013: 48–66).

Since the late 1970s, the corpus first began to be used in the compilation of English learners' dictionaries; especially the five best-known learners' dictionaries: Longman, Oxford, Cambridge, Collins COBUILD, and Macmillan are all based on corpora.

The *OALD* pays special attention to the syntactic pattern of verbs to illustrate the usage of defined words. The *LDOCE* uses special defining vocabularies to define words. All these are authenticated and controlled by computer programs. The first edition of the *COBUILD* was fully based on corpus. The language data extracted from corpora are practical and reliable. It is noticeable that, at present, these dictionaries make full use of computers to complete the data processing stages that must be done manually in traditional lexicography: data collection, headword selection and establishment, and arrangement, as well as entry compilation.

Digitalization and Datafication of Corpora

In the early days of corpus development, lexicographers evaluated the roles of corpora. It seems that with a corpus, all the problems of dictionary-making can be solved: it provides a solid basis for sense division and lexicographical definition, the syntactic patterns and collocational relation of words can be easily found, illustrative examples are always ready, and thus the compilation of the dictionary is highly efficient. The only concern of lexicographers is to enlarge the size of corpora. Therefore, the corpera quickly went from 1 million to 100 million, and finally Collins' Bank of English reached an unprecedented nearly 500 million words in the 1980s. At that time, the lexicographers suddenly recognized that searching for desired information became very difficult, because a simple query would hit tens of thousands of concordances, and the display interface was full of different instances of this word. A choice of the right data is like finding a needle in a haystack. Therefore, Western linguists and lexicographers have started working on datafication and pre-processing of corpora since the late 1990s, and have attained good achievements.

The datafication of corpora is mainly, through tagging and processing programs, to make the massive and disordered corpus orderly and searchable and provide relatively accurate information and language evidence according to the needs of users. For example, the Corpus of Contemporary American English has designed more than 150 tags on the basis of the CLAWS Tagset and tagged all 450 million words. Then a set of index elements and search syntax are provided for users: **[pos] [vvg]** for precise part of speech, **[pos*] [v*]** for various parts of speech, **[lemma] [word]** for all variant of a lexeme, **[=word]** for synonyms, **word | word** for comparison of two words, ***xx** for words beginning with a certain prefix, and so on. Using these syntactic components and tags, various syntactic structures can be formulated to meet the various needs of users for accurate search.

Pre-processing is to have pattern analysis and description of words in the corpus through the Word Sketch Engine, which has the following main functions:

1   Sketch of word features: Providing grammatical relationships and lexical collocations through statistical analysis, including object, subject, modifier, and prepositional phrases.
2   Comparison of word sketches: Comparing different linguistic attributes or distributional patterns to search and discriminate among synonyms, such as <object, drink, beer> and <object, drink, wine> are similar in distribution and features, and thus "beer" and "wine" can be regarded as synonyms.
3   Significance of word collocations: Calculating the significance of collocations through the occurrence frequencies of each words and their co-occurrence frequency as well as their mutual information in the corpus.

Whole-corpus tagging and pre-processing, with a complete set of search syntax and a well-established indexing system, can considerably facilitate lexicographical activities and meet various needs of lexicographical research and dictionary compilation. Especially, the use of the special indexing tool Word Sketch Engine can greatly improve the use of the corpus.

Electronic Dictionaries: From CD-ROM to New Media

The concept of the electronic dictionary came into being in the late 1940s when Americans began the research on MT (or NLP), and it attracted people's attention in the middle 1950s and 1960s. However, it came to a standstill mainly because no progress was made in computer technology and machine readability. Then the development of electronic dictionaries became unprecedentedly active with the popularization of personal computers and the resurgence of MT in the 1980s

The electronic dictionary is so called in contrast to the printed dictionary: the storage media ranges from the magnetic disk to the optical disk, magneto-optical disk, flash disk, and IC card (chip). It can be queried and read through a microprocessor and related facilities. Hartmann and James (2000) define *electronic dictionary* as "a type of reference work which utilizes computers and associated facilities to present information on-screen". Electronic dictionaries can be classified into two types according to their function: (a) encoded computer-language dictionary for MT and NLP and (b) non-coding natural language dictionary available for human users.

The non-coding dictionary is input, stored, displayed, and read through computers with natural language as its text form. The encoded dictionary stores and transmits natural language by means of computer language code and is specially designed for MT or NLP. A MT system needs the support of various encoded dictionaries, including a monolingual dictionary, a bilingual dictionary, a collocation dictionary, a concept dictionary, and so on.

The electronic dictionary refers to all dictionaries which are stored in a electronic media, including magnetic media, optical media, chip media, and online media. Here are some typical types of electronic dictionaries:

1   *CD-ROM dictionaries* are those on compact disc, including DVD. In the late 1980s and early 1990s, the CD and DVD were the main forms of the electronic dictionary. It can be read by a computer or an electronic book player. There were a large number of CD-ROM dictionaries on the market; mainstream printed dictionaries are usually sold with a CD version, including the dictionary series published by Oxford, Longman, Cambridge, Collins COBUILD, Macmillan, Webster, Larousse, and Robert.

2   *Hand-held e-dictionaries* are compact, lightweight, portable, and suitable for school and college students. The first handheld electronic dictionary, the Instant-Dict EC-1000 developed by China Group Sense Ltd., came out in 1983. Since then, many hand-held electronic dictionaries have appeared on the market with ever-increasing functional ability, such as handwriting input, updating from the Internet, and interactive search; some of them are provided with electronic versions of various printed dictionaries.

3   *Online dictionaries* can be divided into four categories according to their functionality and configuration:

    a   A single dictionary, which is usually attached to a website and can be consulted at any time. When users log on to the website, they can use the dictionary to look up words. Many online dictionaries appeared in such a form in the 1990s.

    b   A dictionary group, which gathers tens and hundreds of dictionaries in different languages and subjects on one website. This is often set up by a dictionary publishing house such as

Oxford, Longman, Larousse, and so on or such independent sites as yourdictionary.com, onelook.com, vocabulary.com, 1000Dictionaries.com, thesaurus.com, and so on.

c A dictionary website, which provides a special web dictionary or translation software based on various dictionaries. It may be used either for looking up words or for text translation, for example, babylon.com, translate.google.cn, translate.iciba.com, china-fanyi.com, and fanyi.baidu.com. In recent years, some have included dictionary series of Oxford and COBUILD, and others, like iciba.com and dict.youdao.com.

d An integrated dictionary portal, which is a user interface that provides access to a set of standalone online dictionaries with the aim of helping users (human and/or machine) to retrieve lexical entries in one or various dictionaries. There are various types of access, such as external (dictionaries), outer (articles within the dictionaries), or inner access (data items within entries). The layout of the portal can be uniform or different, but cross-references can be made among dictionaries.

Computer-Aided Dictionary Compilation and Database

The most direct, typical, and revolutionary development of computer-aided dictionary compilation (CADC) is the application of machine-readable corpora in dictionary making. What is important is that the lexical data created by special writing systems can be used to generate electronic lexicons and dictionaries through specific processing programs.

Computer-Aided Dictionary Compilation Tools

CADC tools are found in a special word processing platform and management system designed mainly for the compiling, editing, and revising of dictionaries. The CADC system differs from general word processing tools (e.g. Microsoft Word) in that the input and display interface is designed especially to conform with dictionary microstructure and the user's needs for lexicographic data processing, including example extraction, corpus pattern analysis, semantic disambiguation, entry arrangement, text editing, and typesetting.

The CADC system has incorporated some well-known Dictionary Writing Systems (DWSs), which have been widely used across the world. Some representatives are: Dictionary Production System (DPS) by IDM (in France), ABBYY Lingvo Content by ABBYY (in Russia), TshwaneLex by TshwaneDJe (in South Africa), Lexique Pro by SIL International, and so on.

These DWSs are designed for creating, updating, and managing lexical or lexicographical data for various types of monolingual and bilingual dictionaries. They may, to a certain degree, satisfy the requirements of dictionary authors and publishers, providing them with a multifunctional template for dictionary compilation.

Lexical Databases for Various Uses

Since the 1970s, American scholars have established large-scale lexicons that could make semantic descriptions automatic and began to put them into practice in the mid-1980s. Some scholars in China also made an attempt to build a Chinese lexicon in the 1990s. The best-known lexicons to us include WordNet, MindNet, FrameNet, HowNet, Integrated Linguistic Database, VerbNet, PropBank, and the common-sense knowledge base of CYC.[1] Moreover, English and American lexicographers put out lexical databases and interface software aimed at corpus datafication, such as Dante Database, Word Sketch Engine, Corpus Pattern Analysis, and the Wordlist and Frequency Dictionary of American English.

WordNet uses synonym sets (synsets) to represent lexical concepts and describe the lexical matrix, which builds a mapping between the form and meaning of words and classified nouns, verbs, adjectives, and adverbs into sets of cognitive synonyms, each set representing a different concept.

MindNet uses Microsoft's broad-coverage parser to automatically analyse the dictionary definition and thus obtain linguistic knowledge. There are 24 relationships presented in MindNet, including the attribute, possessor, co-agent, deep-object, deep-subject, domain, material, source, goal, cause, purpose, manner, means, subclass, and synonym.

FrameNet is a knowledge base built with the help of lexicographic definitions and corpora within frame semantics. A frame is a basic way to describe the meanings of lexical units and organize lexical knowledge. Each frame has a number of frame elements, which represent a precise semantic role.

WordNet, FrameNet, and MindNet are all characterized by describing mental representation through semantic frames, valences, and selected restrictions of frame elements, including semantic class and lexical aspect, or the relations within the language system, such as synonymy, antonymy, hyponymy, meronymy, and entailment.

VerbNet doesn't define lexical units as precisely as FrameNet, but it relates them more closely in terms of syntactic structures. PropBank is an annotated corpus which was developed with the idea of serving as training data for machine learning-based systems.

HowNet extracts all semantic relationships implied in the knowledge system of natural language, forms various relational tables, and then describes the intrinsic relationships among and between concepts and features, as well in the knowledge system, and eventually constructs a reticular knowledge and information structure system.

Research on lexical databases mainly focuses on the mental representation of language for NLP. In his "Generative Lexicon", Pustejovsky (1991: 419) provides a kind of mechanism that roughly satisfies the requirements for this purpose. It consists of four levels of representations: argument structure, event structure, qualia structure, and lexical inheritance structure.

The lexical database is a dictionary knowledge base that is built in light of the principle and method of data organization in the mental lexicon and in conformity with dictionary macro- and microstructure. It is beneficial for dictionary compilation and revision, as well as the (semi-) automatic generation of dictionaries.

Lexicographical Databases for Dictionary Generation

A database is a collection of interrelated data stored in digital form and compiled in a specific structure or format. The main purpose is to assemble all kinds of data required for various dictionaries; these data are not simply piled together but organized according to a certain frame structure and logical relationship.

The data in the database are generally stored in tables consisting of records and fields. A field is a basic information item that can be recognized in a data record. A record is a data item that combines multiple related fields to meet the requirements of data processing; it is an entity unit with practical significance. A table stores all the records for a certain dictionary.

As for a dictionary with a complex microstructure, it can be divided into several relatively independent tables based on related fields. The information items of each table have the same structure, such as spelling and pronunciation table, basic annotations table, syntax patterns table, definitions table, and examples table. It is based on these structure levels that the micro-data in the lexicographical database are constructed. The following characteristics of the database should be considered during the construction process:

1   The data should record and describe the commonality and specialties in the microstructure of different dictionaries, constituting an ideal configuration (including text, video, audio, etc.) of printed and/or digitalized dictionaries.
2   Each data field and record have a specific lexicographical significance and related labels, and various relationships among data items must be clearly marked to form a logically closely related data set.
3   The data processing adopts a self-sufficient and diversified module approach, which can provide data query and processing of key word in context or bilingual parallel citations and make good use of Web resources through data mining technology.
4   The management program can perform task assignment, text modification, acceptance check, work log preparation, and personal information maintenance in the process of lexicographical data production. The backstage program can automatically mark and access data in order to generate dictionaries.

New Developments of Computational Lexicography in the Digital Age

Language Big Data and Dictionary Compilation

In the era of the digital economy, implementation is accelerated in the digitization of all trades and professions. A major feature of digitization is to transform various complex and changeable information into measurable digits and data for storage, transmission, and dissemination. This in turn has promoted the development of the digital economy, which is achieved by human beings through the identification, selection, filtering, storage, and use of big data (digital information) for the rapid optimization of resource allocation and renewal.

With the development of the digital economy and language big data, the channels and methods for obtaining the language information required for dictionary compilation have greatly changed. The traditional lexicographer usually starts with the collection and sorting out of language materials and the building of the corpus and then compiles the dictionary with the support of the corpus. The compilation is highly dependent on corpus processing and the role of the editor. Nowadays, the Internet is full of language resources needed for dictionary making in sufficient quantity and variety; it can be regarded as a very large language repository.

Provided you make good use of IT (e.g. indexing technology, Web crawler data collection technology, data mining technology, etc.) and do a good job of data sorting, statistics, and analysis, you can directly extract the required lexicographical information from language big data and turn it into lexicographical data. As Zhan (2013: 76) said, in the era of big data, linguists play the role of mining, sorting, and representation of language data. Usually, the backstage management system of the dictionary can be designed to dynamically crawl web pages in real time and use mass storage technology to continuously update language resources to form a dictionary database with automatic expansion and no upper limit.

As mentioned, in the context of big data, the traditional processes of data collection, analysis, and processing for dictionary-making, and even the generation of dictionaries, can now be handed over to computers, and the editors only need to make appropriate adjustments and editing. For example, large websites such as Google, Baidu, NetEase, and Tencent started to attach importance to the application of language big data technology more than 10 years ago. These companies successively launched web-based big data dictionaries and MT systems and expanded user terminals from PCs to various mobile devices.

1   *Bing* in oblique by Microsoft: It functions on the basis of the Bing search engine in com-
    bination with big data and cloud computing technology. The system has an integrated
    translation program and various dictionaries on one service platform, and the core module
    of the system is a lexicographical database with abundant entries and reliable examples, pro-
    viding free dictionary and translation services. The dictionary consists of two discrete parts;
    one of them is a dictionary generated based on millions of points of Web data, with a rich
    example sentence repository. The query terminal can be a PC, a mobile phone, a tablet,
    and so on, and it is compatible with Android and iOS.

2   *QQ Dictionary* by Tencent: It is based on Web big data for entry-word selection and inclu-
    sion, providing rich definitions, including lexicographical definitions, Internet definitions,
    illustrative examples, and encyclopaedia information. Agile Screen Retrieval is provided; if
    you want to search a new word while reading through the interface of web pages, Office,
    and so on, you simply use a mouse or finger to click on that word, and a query result will
    be displayed immediately. The pop-up window disappears automatically after the query is
    completed, which does not have any impact upon the users' normal reading.

3   *Youdao Dictionary* by NetEase: It is based on big data thinking and methodology, using
    NetEase's powerful Internet search technology to obtain massive amounts of data from
    billions of web pages. In addition, *Youdao Dictionary*'s built-in backstage search engine can
    continuously crawl web pages in real time, constantly updating and expanding the data with
    latest web publication so as to provide users with rich web explanations. You may search
    in Chinese or English, and multiple definitions can be displayed according to your choice,
    such as web explanations, professional English–Chinese definitions, and English definitions.

Media Convergence Technology and Digital Dictionary Compilation

In the era of digitization, media convergence has become the main approach to the production,
organization, and transmission of information. Dictionaries rooted in textual information will
inevitably embark on the development path of converged media.

The core of media convergence for lexicography is connecting all aspects of dictionary-
making through a cross-media digital platform, including construction of language resources and
the production of lexicographical texts and the methods and media of dissemination. That is, the
dictionary data, once produced on one single platform, can be widely disseminated through multiple publishing channels or media and delivered to every end user (Zhang 2019, 2021a, 2021b).

1 Convergence of Dictionary Production Resources

The actual activities of dictionary making involve human resources (e.g. professional lexicographical talents), language resources, and lexicographical data resources, which are the prereq-
uisites for dictionary-making and dissemination.

A CONVERGENCE OF HUMAN RESOURCES

The convergence of dictionary and mass media puts forward higher requirements for lexicographical talents. Apart from mastering the knowledge of lexicography, they must also have
awareness of digitalization, informatization, and media convergence, as well as cross-disciplinary
knowledge and good planning and organization skills for cross-media dictionaries. There are
few such "all-rounders", and necessary training takes time. A feasible way is to converge the
talents of relevant specialists in lexicography for this purpose.

B CONVERGENCE OF LANGUAGE RESOURCES

The corpus is an essential resource for lexicographical practice. The media convergent platform can integrate various stock resources and use data mining and Web crawling technologies to extract useful multimedia data such as text, picture, audio, and video information through the World Wide Web and social media in order to redesign and build a large multimodal corpus for media converged dictionaries.

C CONVERGENCE OF LEXICOGRAPHICAL DATA RESOURCES

Dictionary publishing institutions have to integrate the stock printed and electronic dictionaries, as well as lexical data repositories such as word pronunciation lexicons, language attribute lexicons, and multimedia information, in order to prepare an all-purpose language resource bank. Then a special platform for resource convergence and filtering should be built, which would facilitate the transformation of these resources into a large comprehensive dictionary database, providing a more mature digital resource for the media converged dictionary.

2 Convergence of Lexicographical Text

Media converged dictionaries involve the multi-modalization of information representation, the digitization of information organization, and the polarization of dictionary types. This is the essential content of lexicographic innovation.

A MULTIMODALITY OF LEXICOGRAPHICAL TEXTS

Media converged technology provides actual support for "multiliteracy" (New London Group 1996), and visual, auditory, and tactile sensations can all participate in language interpretation. The convergent mechanism can effectively help lexicographers to establish multi-modal scenarios for lexicographical definitions; especially virtual mode, virtual reality (VR), and augmented reality (AR) technologies can enable the dictionary to have more vivid multi-modal effects and successfully improve the literacy ability of language learners (cf. Kress and Van Leeuwen 1996/2006).

B POLARIZATION OF DICTIONARY TYPES

The reading habits of potential dictionary users have shifted from printed media to various new media, so they prefer to use online dictionaries. Numerous network users at very different levels result in much more detailed requirements for dictionary types. This will push dictionaries to develop to two extremes: one is a dictionary for a single subject or purpose, and the other a large-scale lexicographical database for all subjects with all-inclusive information and multiple purposes to meet the needs of all new-media users.

C DATAFICATION OF LEXICOGRAPHICAL TEXTS

The detailed subdivision of media dissemination forms and the fragmented data needs of users have prompted dictionary writing to shift from entry based to entry metadata based, or language attribute based, and the various information contained in the defined words is comprehensively described in the form of multimodal representations according to "blocks" of microstructure items. Finally, these data are organized and stored in accordance with database structures and formats such as SQL (Structured Query Language) and NoSQL (Not Only SQL).

3 Convergence of Dictionary and Digital Technology

The omni-mediazation of lexicographical text transmission, the intelligentization of dictionary queries, and the human-computer interaction are technical guarantees for the innovation of lexicography. These three elements are interdependent and integrated.

A OMNI-MEDIAZATION OF TEXT TRANSMISSION

The publication of media converged dictionaries is "intangible", and dictionary knowledge will only be presented to users in the form of fragments after inquiries. Media convergence ensures that the dictionary's multi-modal information such as texts, graphics, and sounds is expressed in the form of images, animations, videos, and so on and is delivered to dictionary users through various new media terminals, such as mobile phones, tablets, and smart watches.

B INTELLIGENTIZATION OF DICTIONARY QUERIES

The dictionary can estimate users' needs according to their query settings, retrieve relevant information from the database according to their needs, and display it in categories. Such intelligentization is based on the datafication of dictionary information, the structuration of information storage, and the modularization of information retrieval. The degree of intelligence depends on the fineness or granularity of the algorithm and the learning ability of the system.

C HUMAN–COMPUTER INTERACTION

The dictionary has changed from being statically consulted to being able to respond or interact dynamically according to users' learning tasks. In order to achieve this function, a multimodal graphical user interface (GUI) must be set up on the database application platform in accordance with the convergent media transmission mechanism, and all the built-in information of the dictionary is linked in the form of "function keys" so that users can choose desired items to search. In addition to text query, sound-text query and graphics-text query can also be set.

Conclusion

Computational lexicography has gone through decades of development and has acquired a distinct theoretical framework. Many achievements have been made in theoretical and practical research concerning computational lexicography. Unquestionably, computer technology has contributed greatly to the development of lexicographical studies and dictionary making, and more than 40 years' experience has been accumulated for the building and use of corpora. The development of lexicographical databases and the use of computer-aided compiling systems have achieved noticeable success. Nowadays, with the development of information and communication technology and the application of digital media and big data in the compilation of dictionaries, multimodal and converged media dictionaries have become a hot topic in lexicographical circles. Big data creates a better environment and richer language resources for dictionary-making, digitization provides a major opportunity for the digital transformation of printed dictionaries, and media convergence technology can integrate various modalities for data display so that dictionaries can meet the needs of all-media publishing and various users to the greatest extent.

Note

1 CYC comes from "en**cyc**lopedia", which is a valid registered trademark of Cycorp in Austin, Texas, USA.

Bibliography

Atkins, Sue T. (1991) 'Building a Lexicon: The Contribution of Lexicography', *International Journal of Lexicography* 3: 167–204.

Atkins, Sue T. and Antonio Zampolli (eds.) (1994) *Computational Approaches to the Lexicon*, Oxford: Oxford University Press.

Boguraev, Bran and Ted Briscoe (eds.) (1989) *Computational Lexicography for Natural Language Processing*, London: Longman Science and Technology.

Feng, Zhiwei 馮志偉 (1994)《自然語言機器翻譯新論》(*New Landscape of Machine Translation*), Beijing: Language and Culture Press 語文出版社.

Feng, Zhiwei 馮志偉 (2001)《計算語言學基礎》(*Fundamentals of Computational Linguistics*), Beijing: The Commercial Press 商務印書館.

Hartmann, Reinhard R. K. & Gregory James (2000) *Dictionary of Lexicography*. Foreign Language Teaching and Research Press.

Hu, Zhuanglin 胡壯麟 (2007) '〈社會符號學研究中的多模態化〉(Multimodalization in Social Semiotics)', *Language Teaching and Research*《語言教學與研究》1: 1–9.

Keane, Therese, William F. Keane, and Aaron S. Blicblau (2016) 'Beyond Traditional Literacy: Learning and Transformative Practices Using ICT', *Education and Information Technologies* 21: 769–781.

Kiefer, Ferenc (2005) 'Preface', in Ferenc Kiefer, Gábor Kiss, and Júlia Pajzs (eds.) *Papers in Computational Lexicography: COMPLEX 2005 (Proceedings of the 8th International Conference on Computational Lexicography)*, Budapest: Hungarian Academy of Sciences.

Kim, Steven H. (1991) *Knowledge Systems Through Prolog: An Introduction*, Oxford: Oxford University Press.

Kress, Gunther, Théo Van Leeuwen, and Jean-Jacques Boutaud (1996/2006) *Reading Images: The Grammar of Visual Design*, London and New York: Routledge.

Leech, G. (1992) 'Corpora and Theories of Linguistic Performance', in Jan Svartvik (ed.) *Directions in Corpus Linguistics*, Berlin: Mouton de Gruyter, 105–222.

Ooi, Vincent B. Y. (1998) *Computer Corpus Lexicography*. Edinburgh: Edinburgh University Press.

Pustejovsky, James (1991) 'The Generative Lexicon', *Computational Linguistics* 17(4): 409–41.

Sinclair, John (1985) 'Lexicographic Evidence', in Robert Illson (ed.) *Dictionaries, Lexicography, and Language*, Oxford: Pergamon Press in Association with the British Council, 81–94.

Sinclair, John (1991) *Corpus, Concordance, Collocation*, Oxford: Oxford University Press.

Teubert, Wolfgang (2001) 'Corpus Linguistics and Lexicography'. *International Journal of Corpus Linguistics* 6:125–153.

Van Eynde, Frank and Dafydd Gibbon (eds.) (2000) *Lexicon Development for Speech and Language Processing*, Dordrecht: Kluwer Academic Publishers.

Zhan, Weidong 詹衛東 (2013) '〈大資料時代的漢語語言學研究〉(Chinese Linguistics in The Era of Big Data)', *Journal of Shanxi University: Philosophy and Social Science*《山西大學學報: 哲學社會科學版》5: 70–77.

Zhang, Delu 張德祿 and Wang Lu 王璐 (2010) '〈多模態話語模態的協同及在外語教學中的體現〉(The Synergy of Different Modes in Multimodal Discourse and Their Realization in Foreign Language Teaching)', *Foreign Language Research*《外語學刊》2: 97–102.

Zhang, Delu 張德祿 and Ding Zhaofen 丁肇芬 (2013) '〈外語教學多模態選擇框架探索〉(Exploration on the Framework of Multimodal Choice in Foreign Language Teaching Selection of Multimodality in Foreign Language Teaching)', *Foreign Language World*《外語界》3(3): 39–47, 56.

Zhang, Yihua 章宜華 (2004)《詞算詞典學與新型詞典》(*Computational Lexicography and New Dictionaries*), Shanghai: Shanghai Lexicographical Publishing House 上海辭書出版社.

Zhang, Yihua 章宜華 (2013)《詞算詞典學》(*Computational Lexicography*), Shanghai: Shanghai Lexicographical Publishing House 上海辭書出版社.

Zhang, Yihua 章宜華 (2019) '〈論融媒體背景下辭書編纂與出版的創新〉(On the Innovation of Dictionary Compilation and Publication in the Context of Media Convergence)', *Chinese Journal of Language Policy and Planning*《語言戰略研究》6: 79–89.

Zhang, Yihua 章宜華 (2021a) '〈融媒體英語學習詞典的設計理念與編纂研究〉 (Design Conception of Multimodal-lexicographical Texts from the Perspective of Convergent Media)', *Technology Enhanced Foreign Language Education*《外語電化教學》 3: 102–08.

Zhang, Yihua 章宜華 (2021b) '〈融媒體視角下多模態詞典文本的設計構想〉 (Design Conception of Multimodal-lexicographical Texts from the Perspective of Convergent Media)', *Lexicographical Studies*《辭書研究》 2: 20–32.

29

CONCORDANCING

Federico Zanettin

What Is a Concordance?

A concordance is an index of all the contexts in which a word appears in a given text or corpus. Concordancing involves retrieving all the instances of a specific word or expression from the corpus and displaying them in such a way that they provide context-based information.

Long before the advent of computers, concordances were manually produced as lists of words arranged alphabetically with indications to enable the inquirer to find the passages of the text where the words occurred. The first concordances were produced in 1230 by Dominican friars from the Vulgate, the Bible in Latin used in the Middle Ages. It was simply an index to the positions of a word in the text but was later expanded to include the complete quotations of the passages indicated. These concordances did not of course contain all the words in the Bible but only those deemed most important, and they quoted enough from a passage for one familiar with it to recall it to memory. Bible concordancing continued during the centuries, and concordances were produced for the Hebrew and Greek Bible (the Septuagint), as well as for their translations into English and other languages. Near completion, sometimes with reference to different versions, was achieved at the price of considerable bulk and weight (Herbermann 1913). The production of concordances was time-consuming scholarly work and was typically carried out only for important books such as sacred and literary texts, with the notable exception of Otto Käding, who based his 1897 frequency dictionary of German on a manually collected 11 million–word corpus of legal and commercial texts (Těšitelová 1992: 90).

The first computer-generated concordances were produced by Father Roberto Busa in 1951 after he had created a machine-readable version of the works of Saint Thomas Aquinas in order to carry out its lemmatization, known as the Index Thomisticus. Computers allow us to carry out consistent and quick indexing and retrieval of any text available in electronic format, and this prompted the first studies of language based on corpora, undertaken in the United States and Europe in the 1960s (see, e.g., Kučera and Francis 1967; Quirk *et al.* 1972). Corpus linguistics established itself as a full-fledged discipline and methodology starting from the late 1980s, when research focused on language as a social rather than a psychological phenomenon, and approaches to the study of language based on actual textual products rather than on abstract linguistic competence became mainstream. The development of concordancing and corpus linguistics techniques more in general has been consequential to progress in computational power

DOI: 10.4324/9781003168348-32

and storage capacity. Starting from the 1990s, 'second generation' large 'reference' corpora of up to around 100 million words were created, while 'third generation' very large corpora consisting of billions of words have been compiled since the 2000s. Corpora and concordancing, once the domain of a few linguists, have become a resource at hand for translators, terminologists, and other language services professionals alike.

McEnery and Hardie (2012: 36–48) distinguish between four generations of concordancers, as corpus analysis tools are often referred to, which largely correspond to four different phases of information and communication technology (ICT) development. First-generation concordancers were programs running on large mainframe computers which could generally produce key word in context (KWIC) concordances, that is, printouts of all the occurrences of a word in a corpus, displayed in the middle of the page or screen and accompanied on each side by enough context to fill a line. This basic display format is still usually the default option for all concordancers (Figure 29.1).

Left context ↑	KWIC	Right context
mutant, where 650 bp including the first ATG codon used for N-Oct 3	translation	are missing. In vitro transcription/translation of this mutant (Figure
omparable among the Greeks, I hesitate to attribute to royal initiative a	translation	so clearly born within the precincts of the synagogue. The LXX ren
ate, word-perfect familiarity with Horace, and whether he also added a	translation	. How far did he go? The entire fifty-two lines? Or only down as far
the county again in Mary I's third and Elizabeth I's first Parliaments. A	translation	of Cato's precepts dedicated to Cawarden praised him as the emb
source it is. All this is disclosed in a special 'dance', the discovery and	translation	of which is one of the great achievements of modern ethology. It w
consequences was the beginning of active co-operation with the Bible	translation	societies, whose work had hitherto been boycotted by Catholics. (c
AX or Mips users move to Alpha platforms, DEC has developed binary	translation	tools which can recompile programs for Alpha without using source
ation of synthetic oligonucleotide primers and subclones. The deduced	translation	is shown beneath the DNA sequence. The putative signal peptide
ists Jimmy Pike, Doris Gingingara and Clifford Possum. the ties depict	translations	of ancient cave and skin paintings. The first batch of designs for su
d large commercial and industrial clients. TRANSLATIONS Discursive	translation	is a lawyer's defining skill. Even a simple conveyance of a newly b
ound which the isolated chain under consideration must wriggle during	translation	, in practice the network 'knots' would also be in motion. The conto
enaeus saw a key word in this - anakepbalaiosis - which in the English	translation	means 'to unite all things'. However, the word can equally be transl
res for her research into essential oils and cosmetology. In the English	translation	from the French of her book entitled The Secret of Life and Youth
ay has been celebrated most reverently every year, and the day of her	translation	has been particularly blessed. Our most dutiful and saintly brother
ionymous ('I chuse to be concealed'), she set her name in 1806 to her	translation	from German of Johann Martin Miller's Siegwart and then, 'with the
al Church Council meeting, supper organized. And then, there was her	translation	. Paid by the page, Anna translated German and French technical
its first appearance in English in 1382 when John Wyclif used it in his	translation	of the Old Testament (Genesis VI. 19). 'Of alle thingis havynge so
nt in Proust is nothing more than the elaboration of his initial imperfect	translation	. Yet the aporia reached between" at least two mutually exclusive r
given over to legitimate theatre. British fiction, whether in original or in	translation	. often dominates sales across the world, and in a manner that mig
the most fascinating aspects of grammar and the most problematic in	translation	. It reflects the tenor of discourse and can convey a whole range of

Figure 29.1   A KWIC concordance of the word 'translation'

Source: The Sketch Engine

Second-generation concordancers were the first such programs available when personal computers started to become a commodity for the corpus linguist. While these concordancers included features which previously had to be performed by external programs, such as the possibility to sort results according to the alphabetical order of the words surrounding the search word (for instance, the concordance in Figure 29.1 is sorted according to the first word to the left of the search word), generate a wordlist, and compute some basic descriptive statistics, they had less processing power than mainframe programs. However, they allowed interested researchers to undertake corpus-based studies without needing to be part of a dedicated team or possess programming skills. Third-generation concordancers are stand-alone applications for corpus analysis and are still currently available. As opposed to those of the previous generation, these concordancers 'were able to deal with large datasets . . . had bundled in with them a wider range of tools . . . gave access to some meaningful statistical analyses [and] effectively supported a range of writing systems' (McEnery and Hardie 2012: 40). Finally, fourth-generation concordancers have become available as a result of Web 2.0 ICT infrastructural developments. They are based on a client–server architecture, meaning that search processing is done by a server application, while the input for a search is received from and the output is displayed on the client application, using a common browser as an interface. Whereas standalone concordancers work with a corpus residing on the same machine or local network, online concordancing software and services interact with a corpus located on a remote machine, potentially available and searchable from any computer.

While some basic concordancers only work with plain text corpora, more sophisticated applications can also process text that has previously been linguistically annotated and indexed. Annotation refers to the enrichment of running text with explicit linguistic labels, as regards, for instance, lemmatization and part-of-speech (pos) tagging. Labels for lemmas allow the researcher to include in the results of a search different forms of the same basic lemma, for instance, singular and plural forms of nouns and inflected forms of verbs. Pos labels allow one to distinguish between homographs belonging to different word classes, for instance, between the word 'go' as a verb and the same word form used as a noun. Indexing refers to the fact that searches are not conducted on the fly, as usually happens with stand-alone concordancers, but on a database containing information about the position and frequency of each word in the corpus. Indexing allows more flexible and quicker retrieval of even very large and heavily annotated corpora, since information about word position and annotation is stored separately from the texts themselves.

What Can Concordancing Do for Translators?

Translation practitioners and professionals have at their disposal several computational tools and resources to help them perform translation tasks and jobs, ranging from online dictionary and reference sources, to dedicated forums and social networks, to specialized software tools and services. Corpora and corpus analysis software play an important role as they allow translators to tap into linguistic and textual knowledge in a way which no other resource can offer. By analyzing concordance lines, translators can derive information about how words are used in actual texts, be they source language texts to better understand the language they are translating from or target language texts to confirm candidate translations and find unforeseen solutions to translation problems.

Concordancing software is clearly of no use without corpora. Translators, as well as other language professionals and learners, have two options available; that is, they can resort to existing corpora or create new ones to suit their needs. In the first case, they can either access corpora available online through a Web-based interface or download already compiled corpora and analyze them through a local concordancer. Online services which offer access to one or more corpora through a concordancing application include, for instance, Mark Davies' interface to a range of English corpora (www.english-corpora.org/), comprising among others the 1 billion–word Corpus of Contemporary American English (COCA), a 15 billion–word corpus of news texts (NOW), and a 1.9 billion–word corpus of Wikipedia texts (Davies 2009; Davies and Kim 2019); a subscription to the Sketch Engine (app.sketchengine.eu/) provides access to a range of pre-loaded corpora in over 100 languages and several specialized domains (Kilgarriff *et al.* 2004; Kilgarriff *et al.* 2014). These corpora, which also include parallel corpora, can amount to several billion words in size. Some of the corpora available at English-Corpora.org and Sketch Engine can also be downloaded for local use. Some 'national' corpora such as the British National

Corpus (BNC), the American National Corpus (ANC), the Czech National Corpus (CNC), the German National Corpus (DeReKo, Deutsches Referenzkorpus), and others are accessible through dedicated Web sites.

The large and very large corpora available online for free or at a fee are very useful resources, but sometimes a translator may be better off, corpus-wise, with a smaller but more specialized corpus relating to a specific translation task to be performed. Some specialized corpora can be found at language resource repositories such as the European Language Resource Depository (ELRA, www.elra.info/) and the Linguistic Data Consortium (LDC, www.ldc.upenn.edu/) and can in principle be downloaded and used by translators, though the choice of genres, topics, and text types offered by these archives is ultimately restricted. Furthermore, many of these corpora were often created for use in machine translation or other automated technologies rather than for manual analysis through concordancing software and may thus prove impractical and difficult to set up and exploit. Thus, translators may find it worthwhile to build their own corpora, turning to the Internet as a source of suitable texts. To build their own DIY corpus, translators can use corpus creation software such as the freely available BootCaT (bootcat.dipintra.it/), which allows the user to compile a corpus semi-automatically from a set of Internet texts meeting specific criteria. These corpora can then be analyzed using a concordancer of choice. Alternatively, translators can resort to an online service such as the Sketch Engine, which allows the user to create a corpus (using an inbuilt version of BooTCaT), as well as to annotate and analyze it using the system's standard interface.

Translators may avail themselves not only of monolingual but also of bilingual corpora, that is, corpora comprising two components or subcorpora, one in the source and one in the target language, to compare lexical and grammatical features across two languages. A first type of bilingual corpus is the comparable bilingual corpus, created by putting together two sets of texts in different languages, paired on the basis of design similarity. In this sense, two general reference corpora with roughly the same composition can be used as a comparable corpus. Specialized comparable bilingual corpora are, however, not easily found for many language pairs, and this is where translators may have to create their own DIY corpora. When using a comparable bilingual corpus, search techniques and display options are the same for the two (sub)corpora, though the user will have to consider differences in writing systems, text segmentation, and structural linguistic features.

A more specific type of bilingual corpus is the parallel corpus, comprising a set of source texts in one language and their translations in the other, or two sets of texts in the two languages which are held to be 'equivalent', for instance, the different language versions of EU legislation. Parallel corpora can be equally difficult to create, as they require a non-straightforward process of alignment, that is, the pairing of source and target 'equivalent' segments, on a sequential basis. In order to take advantage of aligned parallel corpora, specific search and display functions must be made available in addition to those found in monolingual concordancers (see subsequently).

The usefulness of corpora and concordancing over more traditional tools may be assessed by comparing them with dictionaries. Both corpora and dictionaries can be consulted to help understand the source text and compose the target text. Large reference corpora can be seen as analogous to general language dictionaries, while smaller specialized corpora play a function similar to that of specialized monolingual dictionaries. Parallel corpora can instead be compared to bilingual dictionaries, as they both provide a direct link between lexical items in two languages.

Dictionaries, on paper and in electronic format, offer information about words which has already been distilled by lexicographers, often based on corpus evidence. While dictionaries favor a synthetic approach to lexical meaning via a definition, and by necessity condense and simplify the complexity of lexis, corpora allow for an analytic approach via multiple usage contexts. In selecting a target language equivalent from a monolingual dictionary, a translator has to appraise the appropriateness of the translation candidate to the new context by consulting a definition and a few examples. However, translators often need to understand precise senses of meaning and nuances of use, and corpus concordancing provides access to a range of examples of actual language use which no dictionary can offer. Clearly, the added comprehensiveness has a cost, which is that translators must make out by themselves the solution to their problems by exploring and interpreting a very large quantity of raw textual data. To this end, they must be able to take advantage as much as possible of corpus concordancing techniques, including concordancers' data search and display options.

Dictionaries are primarily accessed by looking up basic word forms (lemmas), though some electronic dictionaries also allow for searching within definitions and examples. Corpora instead allow searching for specific (groups of) word forms as well as (variable) phrases in the context of other words or expressions. Sinclair (1991) has argued that the meaning of a word is determined by the patterns in which it occurs and that lexis and grammar cannot be treated separately. Rather, each word has its own specific grammar, which comprises the structures it appears in as well as its collocations. By observing lexicogrammatical patterns resulting from the distributional profile of words in texts, translators can get a better understanding of the meaning and usage of a word or expression they find in the source text and assess the appropriateness of a translated word or expression in the target context. Close observation of corpus concordances and collocations can unveil syntactic and semantic patterns of lexis as occurring in natural language, as well as information related to text type and textual organization. Specialized corpora can be especially useful in providing information on lexical, syntactic, and rhetorical structures of a specific text type or genre. For instance, by concordancing even a very small corpus of medical articles, translators can be helped to make well-informed choices on medical phraseology (Gavioli and Zanettin 2000) or find out whether a given expression is typically used in the first or in the last part of research articles (Aston 1997).

General and specialized bilingual dictionaries are repertories of lexical equivalents established by dictionary makers which are offered as translation candidates. Parallel corpora are repertoires of translation equivalents as well as of strategies past translators have resorted to when confronted with problems similar to the ones that have prompted a search. Parallel corpora provide information that bilingual dictionaries do not usually contain, since while the former supply lexical equivalents, the latter also offer examples of lack of direct equivalence. A parallel corpus can, in fact, provide evidence of how actual translators have dealt with cases where there is no easy equivalent for words, terms, or phrases across languages (Zanettin 2002). Some online language service platforms such as Reverso (www.reverso.net/), however, try to combine the advantages of bilingual dictionaries and concordances, as well as offering other translation aids.

Corpora and concordancing have also changed terminological practice, that is, the way terminological entries are compiled and used. According to Bowker (2011), as personal terminology management systems have largely replaced large institutional data banks, terminological work has moved from an onomasiological to a semasiological approach. That is, rather than using a conceptual ontology to map the terms used in a specific domain, personal term banks are usually compiled from lists of words obtained from corpora. Furthermore, terminological entries do not necessarily fit into the traditional definition of terms as nominal constructs, as they may consist of frequent combinations of words belonging to different word classes. They are often recorded in their most frequent rather than in the base form, and synonyms may be registered as different entries. The entries will often contain basic information, that is, target language equivalent(s) and selected concordance examples.

Translators can resort to monolingual and bilingual corpora and corpus analysis software to find information about terms, phraseology, and textual patterns in both source and target languages and to parallel corpora to find solutions to translation problems based on previous translational experience. Large, general monolingual corpora are now available for many languages, and translators can create their own small corpora from the Web by downloading and processing documents retrieved using search engines and compiled through semi-automatic routines implemented by ad hoc programs and online services. Like the use of dictionaries, the use of corpus concordancing has to be learnt (Frankenberg-Garcia 2010), and proficiency in corpus concordancing skills and procedures has become an indispensable part of the translator's professional competence. The usefulness of concordancing depends on the corpus, on the software, and on the user. Users must be aware of what a corpus contains and to what extent observations derived from it are relevant, reliable, and applicable to a specific translation task. They must also be able to understand the potentialities and limitation of the software which is used to interrogate a corpus and to interpret the results of a search appropriately.

Search and Display Options

Corpus software includes applications which are used to perform the various tasks associated with corpus construction and analysis: acquire, process, manage, query, and display corpus data. While translators may need to become involved in corpus compilation, this chapter focuses on corpus analysis and on concordancing more in particular. Concordancers can offer different functionalities and features, each having their advantages and disadvantages. A collaboratively compiled and updated comprehensive list of available commercial and public domain software and services is available at the Tools for Corpus Linguistics website (corpus-analysis.com/). While such a list would be too long to include here, some of the most commonly used concordancers are mentioned in the discussion, and bibliographical references are provided (see also Zanettin 2012 for a more in-depth discussion).

A search is typically carried out by typing a search string, that is, a typographical word or sequence of words in a search box, much as happens with a general-purpose search engine. There are, however, decisive differences between general search engines like Google or Bing and concordancers, regarding both search and display facilities. Furthermore, the Internet can only be considered a corpus to a certain extent, inasmuch as it is an open-ended depository, and even though a search can be restricted to specific sectors of the WWW (e.g. a newspaper archive, a mailing list or a forum, Facebook, Twitter, Google Books, etc.) search and display functions of search engines are not fully within the control of the user. However, while first- and second-generation corpora were composed of printed texts typewritten or scanned in and OCRed, most corpora are currently made up of 'native' electronic texts, often downloaded from the Internet through semi-automated procedures.

Concordancers may be assessed according to the options available for data search and display. These may vary depending on whether the concordancing application is the only or main tool of a corpus analysis software or a component of a different piece of software, for instance, a translation memory management system. Both stand-alone programs and online services may include, besides the concordancing function proper, other options for displaying corpus data.

Search Options

A simple search for a word or a phrase in a concordancer will retrieve all instances of that word or phrase in all the texts in the corpus. More advanced searches are generally based on regular expressions resembling those of programming languages and allow for the retrieval of variable textual patterns. Non-alphabetic characters are attributed special meanings, some acting as wildcards. For instance, an asterisk ★ is used by some concordancing programs to represent one or more trailing characters, while the escape \ character is used to invoke alternative interpretations of subsequent characters in a sequence or to introduce a list of alternative characters, depending on the software used. For instance, in Wordsmith Tools (Scott 2020), an asterisk can be used to retrieve all words beginning or ending with a specified sequence, so that 'go★' will retrieve 'go', 'going', 'Godzilla', and so on, while '★go' will retrieve 'embargo', 'forgo', 'tango', and so on. The escape character can be used to provide alternatives; for instance, the string 'go\goes\going\gone' can be used to retrieve all the forms of the verb. Thus, while in a simple search, precision is ensured by retrieving all and only the citations containing the exact search string specified, in an advanced search, different characters can be used to increase recall by allowing for variation.

Regular expressions can be used to conduct highly complex searches. For instance, a search using the regular expression

\bha[vs]e?\W\w{4,}e[nd]\b.

in MonoConc Pro (Barlow 2004b) will retrieve all instances of 'has' or 'have' followed by an -*en*/-*ed* form: The metacharacter \b is used to indicate word beginning and end, and alternative characters are enclosed in square brackets. The question mark indicates an optional preceding character, while '[t]he part of the search query that we hope will match the participle is "padded" with alphanumeric characters (\w) to eliminate shorter words ending in -*en* or -*ed* such as ten and bed' (Barlow 2004a: 62). As Barlow explains, regular expression (regex) searches allow for very complex queries, though caution must be exerted:

> some good hits such as seen will also be omitted by this search query and in cases like this it is up to the user to formulate the search query in such a way as to get the right balance between a good retrieval rate and a high percentage of desired forms in the concordance results. The specification of a minimum of four letters in the participle in the search query above has the effect of increasing the percentage of good "hits" in the results, at the cost of missing some instances of the present perfect that occur in the corpus.
>
> *(ibid.: 70)*

Annotated corpora can be used to both fine-tune and simplify a search. In a corpus which has been lemmatized and pos-tagged, a search can be carried out not only in the running text but also in the content of the labels attached to words. For instance, a search for verb forms in the present perfect in the English corpus, which is part of the Leeds collection of Internet corpora (Sharoff 2006, corpus.leeds.ac.uk/internet.html), is formulated as follows:

[lemma="have"] [pos="V.★"]

The search syntax specifies that the concordances returned must contain all forms of the lemma 'have' followed by any verb.

The Sketch Engine online concordancing service, which is similarly based on the IMS Corpus Workbench, a standard platform for corpus indexing and management, offers a more sophisticated and user-friendly interface. Figure 29.2 shows how the same search can be performed

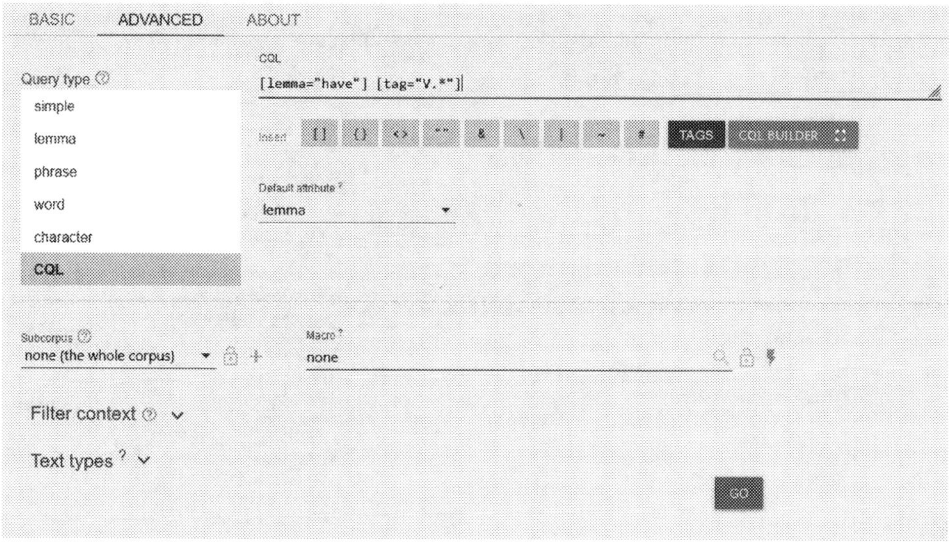

Figure 29.2 A search for the lemma 'have' immediately followed by a verb

Source: The Sketch Engine

by using the Corpus Query Language (CQL) builder function in the Advanced search input form, which allows the user to select the contents of the annotation (the tag attributes) from a predefined set of options in drop-down menus.

The interface to Mark Davies' annotated corpora also allows the user access to variable phraseological expressions. Figure 29.3, for instance, shows the output of a search for all phrases containing a verb followed by the phrase 'one's way' followed by a preposition by carrying out a search for the string

> VERB one's way PREP

in the 1.9-billion-word Wikipedia corpus. Concordances for each expression are then displayed by clicking on the lines in the table.

A graphical user interface (GUI) makes queries more user friendly, though expert users can still run searches using the regular expression search syntax.

Additional annotation regarding text or discourse features can also be exploited if available. For instance, both the Sketch Engine and Mark Davies' corpus interface allow the user to create subcorpora, and therefore retrieve more accurate data, by filtering out unwanted texts from a larger corpus using specifications based on metalinguistic annotation concerning genre, text type, date, author, and so on.

A parallel concordancer allows the user to perform a search in either of the two subcorpora which make up a bilingual parallel corpus and retrieve, together with the lines or sentences containing the word, phrase, or variable expression searched for in one language, the corresponding segments in the other language. In addition, some parallel concordancers allow one to specify search criteria in both languages and return only those results from the texts in one language for which the paired target segments contain the expression specified in the other language. For instance, a search in an English–Italian parallel corpus can be made to include in the results only

Figure 29.3 'Verb + own's way + preposition' constructions in the 1.9-billion–word Wikipedia English
corpus

Source: www.english-corpora.org/wiki/

those occurrences of the English word 'run' contained in sentences for which the corresponding
aligned sentences in Italian contain a form of the verb 'correre'.

Statistical information about word frequency and position can be used to (semi-)automatically
retrieve the most likely translations for a given word or expression. For instance, the ParaConc
stand-alone parallel concordancer (Barlow 2003) has a 'hot words' function which allows the user
to select from a list of 'possible translations and other associated words (collocates) . . . suggested
by the program itself' (Barlow 2004c) on the basis of how frequently these words appear in target
segments which translate source text segments. Annotated corpora may provide additional information with which more precise bilingual (semi-)automated searches can be performed.

A special type of parallel corpora are translation memories (TMs), which are created by
translation memory management systems (TMMSs) as a by-product of the translation process. As translations are carried out, source and target text segments are stored together in
the system's 'memory'. In the TM database, each translation unit (TU), that is, each aligned
text segment pair, is archived together with administrative information and retrieved by the
system in order to be considered again as a candidate for future translations. TMs are usually
proprietary; that is, they belong to individual translators or translation companies, but they
can also be created from publicly available parallel corpora. For instance, some very large
multilingual parallel corpora, including the Europarl corpus (the proceedings of the European
Parliament from 1996 to 2011, consisting of up to 50 million words for each official language
of the European Union) and the Acquis Communautaire (the entire body of EU legislation,
consisting of 1 billion words all together), are available both as aligned parallel corpora and in
standard TM format.

Most TMMSs offer a way to generate parallel concordances from a word or expression in the
source text, that is, a list of all the translation units in the memory in which this word or expression occurs, together with the target segments. Such applications are usually less sophisticated

than most stand-alone bilingual concordancers. As opposed to the former, the latter allow more control both over what is searched by letting the user perform more flexible pattern searches and over how results are displayed by letting the user sort the results and access the wider context of a given segment (Bowker and Barlow 2008). Though translation memory search engines allow for 'fuzzy' matches, that is, to search for target segments which only partly match the new source text, the text retrieval system is often not geared to perform complex searches such as those described previously, and results are not liable to be manipulated regarding the order and the format in which they are displayed (see subsequently). Some hybrid tools, however, allow for the integration of the functions of TMMSs and parallel concordancers (ibid: 20).

Data Display Options

General search engines typically return the results of a search by listing document extracts containing the search word(s), together with the documents' URL and title. Results are ordered according to commercial rather that linguistic criteria, and they can be browsed in the order of retrieval but not sorted or otherwise manipulated by the user. Though the usefulness of general search engines and of the WWW as a corpus for linguistic purposes should not be underestimated, especially when it comes to finding uncommon or long phrases (Zanettin 2009; Zanettin 2018), concordancers and corpora specifically compiled for linguistic purposes offer a number of advantages regarding display options and usually allow the user to view the results of a search in several formats. The most common of these is the KWIC format illustrated in Figure 29.1, with the possibility of enlarging the context around the search word to more than one line. Most concordancers also allow the user to switch between line and sentence view, sentence boundaries being derived either from punctuation marks or explicit annotation. The occurrences shown can be limited to a random selection in order to make the analysis more manageable. Results can be filtered according to contextual restrictions, that is, by including only those where a given word of phrase occurs within a given right or left word span. In order to highlight linguistic patterns, concordance lines can be ordered alphabetically by sorting them according to the 'node' word(s) or according to the words to the right or left of them, establishing different sorting criteria if desired. Colour coding and typeface can be used as further visual aids. Concordances may also be categorized according to user-decided criteria by manually marking occurrences or using existing mark-up such as lemma or pos tags if the corpora have been previously annotated. Sorting concordance results according to linguistic patterns and visualizing them in a clear and memorable way allows the user to acquire important information about how words and phrases are used in actual texts and contexts.

Concordancers sometimes include facilities which, on the basis of statistical analysis, provide information about the frequency of occurrence of words in relation to each other and in the corpus as a whole which would be otherwise impossible to recover. Thus, for instance, WordSmith Tools can not only generate concordances but also give access to information about Collocates, Plots (the dispersion of words in the texts in the corpus), Patterns, and Clusters. The Patterns view shows collocates of a given word visually organized in terms of frequency. The Clusters view displays all recurrent groups of words which appear more frequently around the search word or expression, for example, clusters of between three and six words, with a frequency of at least five occurrences. Greaves' (2009) CongCgram was created to specifically 'identify all of the co-occurrences of two or more words irrespective of constituency and/or positional variation in order to account for phraseological variation and provide the raw data for identifying lexical items and other forms of phraseology' (Greaves 2009: 2). ConcGram displays concordance lines with all the words in a 'concgram' equally highlighted, and concordance output can be sorted and centred alternatively around any of these words.

Further options for the display of collocational data, which rely to an even greater extent on visual and graphic features, include 'collocate clouds', in which collocates are listed alphabetically, while frequency information is displayed as font size and collocational strength as text brightness, and 'concordance mosaics' (Luz and Sheehan 2014), in which the data are displayed in a tabular structure which 'preserves the relative position of each word and scales the rectangles they occupy proportionally to word occurrence probabilities or collocation statistics' (Luz 2022: 377) (Figure 29.4).

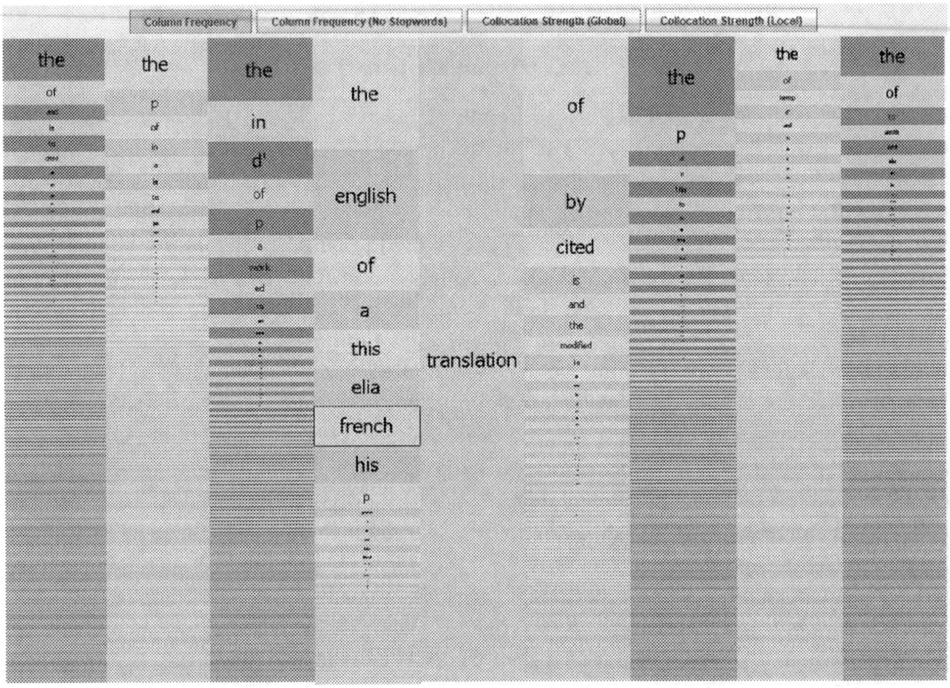

Figure 29.4　Mosaic concordance of the word 'translation' in the Genealogies of Knowledge corpus

Source: Luz's ModNLP, genealogiesofknowledge.net/software/

Linguistic annotation can be used to sort collocational patterns on the basis of the relations between words, their grammatical class, and their position and to obtain automated summaries of such relations. Thus, the Sketch Engine provides for the creation of a 'word sketch', that is, 'a one-page summary of the word's grammatical and collocational behavior' (www.sketchengine. eu/guide/word-sketch-collocations-and-word-combinations/) in which collocates are grouped according to the type of relation they entertain with a given word (e.g. object, subject, modifier, etc.). This highlights collocation between word class and grammatical function rather than simply between words. Collocates can be shown in tables listing different types of word categories but also displayed in a graphic using colour, position in space, and size to highlight collocational strength and type of relation (Figure 29.5).

Annotated corpora can also be used to generate automated thesauruses of words that tend to occur in similar contexts in terms of grammatical and collocational behavior.

Finally, bilingual concordances can be arranged on the screen either along the vertical or the horizontal axis: in the vertical display, alignment units are arranged side by side; in the horizontal

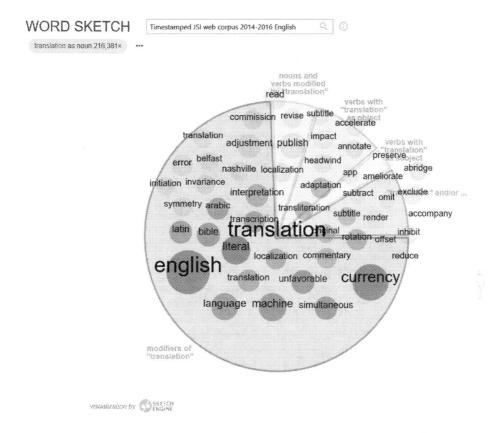

Figure 29.5 Word Sketch of 'translation' in the timestamped JSI web corpus 2014–2016 English

Source: The Sketch Engine

display, concordance lines can either be presented as alternating sentences/segments in different languages, or the screen can be split into an upper and a lower window, one containing the output for the search expression in the source language and the other containing the aligned target segments. Within each presentation display, results can be shown in KWIC format, with concordance lines centered around the search expression either or both in the source and target language or in any other format usually available in monolingual concordancers.

Figure 29.6 shows a KWIC bilingual concordance in a horizontal split-screen display in which concordances are sorted according to target language order. The link between segment pairs in different languages is not provided by spatial proximity, with segment pairs displayed in adjacent columns or lines, but by sorting order and highlighting. Source text segments and their translations are arranged in the same sequence, and concordance lines are highlighted in pairs. When the results in one language are re-sorted or otherwise manipulated, much as they are with a monolingual concordancer, aligned units in the other language are re-ordered accordingly.

Different display formats are useful for focusing on different aspects of bi-textual correspondences. The KWIC display in split-screen format allows a better visualization of linguistic patterns, whereas the sentence-by-sentence interlinear format is more efficient for comparing correspondences at sentence level.

Federico Zanettin

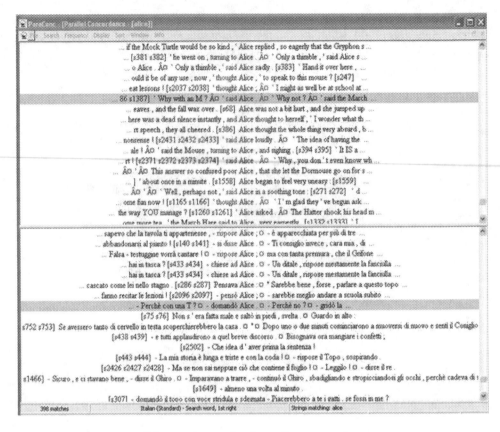

Figure 29.6 ParaConc, parallel concordance ordered according to target language

Source: Barlow's ParaConc

Bibliography

Aston, Guy (1997) 'Small and Large Corpora in Language Learning', in B. Lewandowska-Tomaszczyk and P. J. Melia (eds.) *PALC 97: Practical Applications in Language Corpora*, Łodz: Łodz University Press, 51–62.

Barlow, Michael (2003) *ParaConc*, Houston, TX: Athelstan.

Barlow, Michael (2004a) *Concordancing and Corpus Analysis with MP2.2*, Houston, TX: Athelstan.

Barlow, Michael (2004b) *MonoConc Pro 2.2*, Houston, TX: Athelstan.

Barlow, Michael (2004c) 'Parallel Concordancing and Translation', in *Translating and the Computer 26*, London: Aslib.

Bowker, Lynne (2011) 'Off the Record and On the Fly: Examining the Impact of Corpora on Terminographic Practice in the Context of Translation', in A. Kruger, K. Wallmach, and J. Munday (eds.) *Corpus-Based Translation Studies: Research and Applications*, London and New York: Continuum, 212–36.

Bowker, Lynne and Michael Barlow (2008) 'A Comparative Evaluation of Bilingual Concordancers and Translation Memory Systems', in E. Yuste-Rodrigo (ed.) *Topics in Language Resources for Translation and Localisation*, Amsterdam and Philadelphia: John Benjamins Publishing Company, 1–22.

Davies, Mark (2009) 'The 385+ Million Word Corpus of Contemporary American English (1990–2008+). Design, Architecture, and Linguistic Insights', *International Journal of Corpus Linguistics* 14(2): 159–90.

Davies, Mark and Jong-Bok Kim (2019) 'The Advantages and Challenges of "Big Data": Insights from the 14 Billion Word iWeb Corpus', *Linguistic Research* 36(1): 1–34.

Frankenberg-Garcia, A. (2010) 'Raising Teachers' Awareness of Corpora', *Language Teaching* 1(1): 1–15.

Gavioli, Laura and Federico Zanettin (2000) 'I corpora bilingui nell'apprendimento della traduzione. Riflessioni su un'esperienza pedagogica', in S. Bernardini and F. Zanettin (eds.) *I corpora nella didattica della traduzione. Corpus Use and Learning to Translate*, Bologna: CLUEB, 61–80.

Greaves, Chris (2009) *ConcGram 1.0. A Phraseological Search Engine*, Amsterdam and Philadelphia: John Benjamins Publishing Company.

Herbermann, Charles (ed.) (1913) 'Concordances of the Bible', in *Catholic Encyclopedia, Vol. 4*, Robert Appleton Company, 195–96. Available at: http://en.wikisource.org/w/index.php?title= Catholic_Encyclopedia_(1913)/Concordances_of_the_Bible&oldid=2168065.

Kilgarriff, Adam *et al.* (2014) 'The Sketch Engine: Ten Years On', *Lexicography* 1(1): 7–36.

Kilgarriff, Adam, Rychly Pavel, Pavel Smrž, and David Tugwell (2004) 'The Sketch Engine', in *Proceedings of Euralex, Lorient, France, July 2004*, 105–16. Available at: http://www.euralex.org/elx_proceedings/ Euralex2004/011_2004_V1_Adam%20KILGARRIFF,%20Pavel%20RYCHLY,%20Pavel%20 SMRZ,%20David%20TUGWELL_The%20%20Sketch%20Engine.pdf.

Kučera, Henry and Nelson W. Francis (1967) *Computational Analysis of Present-Day American English*, Providence, RI: Brown University Press.

Luz, Saturnino (2022) 'Computational Linguistics and Natural Language Processing', in F. Zanettin and C. Rundle (eds.) *The Routledge Handbook of Translation and Methodology*, Abingdon and New York: Routledge, 373–91.

Luz, Saturnino and Shane Sheehan (2014) 'A Graph Based Abstraction of Textual Concordances and Two Renderings for Their Interactive Visualisation', in *Proceedings of the 2014 International Working Conference on Advanced Visual Interfaces*, 27 May 2014, Association for Computing Machinery, New York, NY, 293–96.

McEnery, Tony and Andrew Hardie (2012) *Corpus Linguistics: Method, Theory and Practice*, Cambridge: Cambridge University Press.

Quirk, Randolph, Sidney Greenbaum, Geoffrey Leech, and Jan Svartvik (1972) *A Grammar of Contemporary English*, London: Longman.

Scott, Mike (2020) *WordSmith Tools Version 8*, Stroud: Lexical Analysis Software.

Sharoff, Serge (2006) 'Creating General-Purpose Corpora Using Automated Search Engine Queries', in M. Baroni and S. Bernardini (eds.) *WaCky! Working Papers on the Web as Corpus*, Bologna: GEDIT, 63–98.

Sinclair, John (1991) *Corpus, Concordance, Collocation*, Oxford: Oxford University Press.

Těšitelová, Marie (1992) *Quantitative Linguistics*, Amsterdam and Philadelphia: John Benjamins Publishing Company.

Zanettin, Federico (2002) 'Corpora in Translation Practice', in E. Yuste-Rodrigo (ed.) *Language Resources for Translation Work and Research LREC 2002 Workshop Proceedings, University of Las Palmas de Gran Canaria*, ELRA, 10–14.

Zanettin, Federico (2009) 'Corpus-Based Translation Activities for Language Learners', *The Interpreter and Translator Trainer* 3(2): 209–24.

Zanettin, Federico (2012) *Translation-Driven Corpora. Corpus Resources for Descriptive and Applied Translation Studies*, Manchester: St Jerome.

Zanettin, Federico (2018) 'Electronic Tools and Resources for Translating and Writing in the Digital Age', *inTRAlinea* 20. Available at: www.intralinea.org/specials/article/2295.

30

CONTROLLED LANGUAGES

Rolf Schwitter

Introduction

Natural languages are the primary mode of human communication. In their textual form they constitute the most widely used medium for storing human knowledge. Natural languages are also the most expressive knowledge representation languages that exist, far more expressive than any machine-processable formal language. While natural languages allow humans to deal with most aspects of everyday life, their expressive power can create problems for both humans and machines. Sometimes, it is difficult for humans who have only limited knowledge of an official language that is used in a work environment to read and understand technical documents. It is also often difficult for machines to process full natural language for a given task because of its inherent ambiguity and complexity.

Controlled natural languages tackle these kinds of problems by restricting the size of the grammar and vocabulary in order to reduce or eliminate ambiguity and complexity inherent in natural languages. Kuhn (2014) proposed a formal model to classify controlled languages with a focus on the inherent properties of controlled languages and the environment for which these languages were designed and used for. These properties are organised with the help of a classification scheme, named PENS, on a discrete scale on the dimensions of precision (P), expressiveness (E), naturalness (N), and simplicity (S). The dimension of precision subsumes aspects of ambiguity, predictability, and formality of a controlled language. The dimension of expressiveness describes the range of propositions a controlled language can express. The dimension of naturalness indicates how close the controlled language is to a natural language in terms of readability and understandability, and finally, the dimension of simplicity assesses the complexity of a controlled language with respect to an implementation of the language in form of a computer program. The PENS scheme is usually used together with nine general (partly overlapping) properties that can be used to describe the goal of the controlled language, its intended application environment, and its origin.

In contrast to Kuhn's fine-grained classification scheme, this chapter classifies controlled languages into four major groups according to the problem these languages are supposed to solve. We observe that one group of controlled languages have been created to improve the communication between humans who do not share a common native language. A second group of controlled languages have been developed to make it easier for non-native speakers to read and understand technical documentation written in a foreign language. A third group

DOI: 10.4324/9781003168348-33

of controlled languages aim to improve the quality of machine translation and to reduce the post-editing effort. And finally, a fourth group of controlled languages have been designed as high-level interface languages for semantic systems where different forms of automated reasoning are used to make inferences from knowledge expressed in controlled language, in particular to answer questions about this knowledge.

Controlled Languages for Human Communication

Historically, the most famous controlled language for human communication is Basic English (Ogden 1930), which was created as an international auxiliary language to help non-native speakers learn English as a second language and use the language for general and technical communication. Basic English derives its vocabulary and grammar from Standard English and eliminates those words (mainly verbs) that can be reconstructed by using simpler words and a number of prescribed grammar rules.

The core vocabulary of Basic English is very small. It consists of only 850 words: 600 of them are nouns (e.g., *act, hour, milk, town, tooth*); 150 are adjectives (e.g., *angry, conscious, loud, quiet, true*), including 50 opposites; and 100 are words that are called operations (e.g., *come, enough, for, he, some, or*). This last category includes verbs, adverbs, prepositions, pronouns, quantifiers, and conjunctions: words that are used to put other words in statements into "operation". The size of the vocabulary of Basic English is kept small by using only 18 verbs (*come, get, give, go, keep, let, make, put, seem, take, be, do, have, say, see, send, may, will*). These verbs are also called operators and operator-auxiliaries in Basic English. The reduction to this subset is based on the assumption that irregular verb forms of English are difficult to learn for non-native speakers and that all important verbs can be expressed by more basic constructions. These alternative constructions use the 18 basic operators as a starting point and combine them with prepositions to express the intended meaning. For example, instead of the verb *approach* in *approach (a town)*, the operator *come* is used together with the preposition *to*; this results in the basic construction *come to (a town)*. Another example is the construction *take out (a tooth)* instead of *extract (a tooth)*.

To address the need of a particular work environment, the core vocabulary of Basic English is augmented by 100 words for any general environment (e.g., science or trade) and 50 words for any specific field in that environment. The resulting vocabulary of 1000 words is further enriched by a list of international words (e.g., *hotel, electricity, university*) that are presumed to be widely understood without additional instructions. According to the advocates of Basic English, this vocabulary is sufficient for any form of business communication or publication that is required for international use.

The grammar of Basic English follows the accepted rules of English but is subject to a number of restrictions. For example, compound nouns can be formed by combining two basic nouns (e.g., *footnote*) or an adjective and a noun (e.g., blackberry), and derivatives can only be constructed by using a specific group of suffixes (-ed, -er, -ing, -ly, -s) and one single prefix (un-).

The following is a short excerpt of the Atlantic Charter written in Standard English as well as in Basic English (Ogden 1968):

Standard English

The President of the United States and the Prime Minister, Mr. Churchill, representing His Majesty's Government in the United Kingdom, being met together, deem it right to make known certain common principles in the national policies of their respective countries on which they base their hopes for a better future for the world.

First, their countries seek no aggrandizement, territorial or other.
Second, they desire to see no territorial changes that do not accord with the freely expressed wishes of the peoples concerned. . . .

Basic English

The President of the United States and the Prime Minister, Mr. Churchill, acting for His Majesty's Government in the United Kingdom, being now together, are of the opinion that it is right to make public certain common ideas in the political outlook of their two countries, on which are based their hopes for a better future for all nations.
First, their countries will do nothing to make themselves stronger by taking more land or increasing their power in any other way.
Second, they have no desire for any land to be handed over from one nation to another without the freely voiced agreement of the men and women whose interests are in question. . . .

As this example illustrates, the simplification of the vocabulary is achieved at the expense of longer sentences that include sometimes lengthy paraphrases. Although experience showed that Basic English was easy to learn to read, it turned out that it was difficult to rewrite a given text in Basic English so as to preserve the original meaning.

A modified form of Basic English, known as Simple English, is nowadays used to write articles for Simple English Wikipedia,[1] an online encyclopaedia that uses fewer words and a simpler grammar than the ordinary English Wikipedia. This simplified encyclopaedia is designed for people who are learning English or who have special needs (e.g., for children, students, and adults with learning difficulties). Most Simple English articles are not new Wikipedia articles; instead, their content has been borrowed from ordinary English Wikipedia articles, and these articles have been rewritten in order to make them simpler and easier to understand. Simple English does not specify strict rules that prescribe which words or grammatical structures can be used. However, the writing guidelines[2] suggest that articles should only consist of the 1000 most common basic words of English. These guidelines also acknowledge that articles on scientific topics sometimes need complex words and that these words should be explained on a new web page. There are no specific rules about vocabulary, tense, or suffixes for Simple English, but it is recommended that the sentence structures be simple and the resulting sentences short. Like Basic English, the use of Simple English does not result in shorter articles, although these articles often use shorter sentences than the original Wikipedia source. It is not uncommon that a Simple English article requires between 25% and 50% more words than the original Wikipedia article. However, we can observe an interesting shift between the early use of Basic English and Simple English: the guidelines of Simple English focus more on the use of simpler grammatical structures and shorter sentences compared to the guidelines of Basic English, where the focus is on the control of the vocabulary. The guidelines of Simple English recommend, for example, the use of the following sentence patterns to reduce syntactic complexity:

1   Subject – Verb – Direct Object.
2   Subject – Verb – Indirect Object.
3   Subject – Verb – Direct Object – Indirect Object.
4   Subject – Verb – Direct Object – Subordinate Clause.
5   Subject – Verb – Direct Object – Indirect Object – Subordinate Clause.

The guidelines also discuss several techniques that illustrate how complex sentence structures can be simplified; for example, by removing conjunctions:

Non-SE: *John Smith walked his dog but later he was tired.*
SE: *John walked his dog. Later, he was tired.*

or by reconstructing sentences that contain multiple subordinate or dependent clauses. It is recommended that this can be done by changing the order of the constituents in the sentence and by introducing filler words:

Non-SE: *John Smith walked his dog, which made him angry because the dog always cut into ongoing traffic, which, in turn, made the drivers angry at John, not the dog.*
SE: *John Smith was angry while walking his dog. This was because the dog would always cut into on-coming traffic. This, in turn, made the drivers irritated at John not the dog.*

Again, rewriting and simplifying does not necessarily mean using fewer words, since improving the structure may require additional words. Shorter sentences clearly improve the readability and increase comprehension. However, it is clear that readability is not only a property of the text but also depends on the level of education, expertise, and the type of reader (O'Brien 2010, 2019).

Controlled Languages for Technical Documentation

Many controlled languages are used in industry to improve the readability of technical documentation, often with the additional benefit to improve the (semi)-automatic translation of these documents (see O'Brian 2019 for a recent overview). A typical controlled language for technical documentation uses a (more or less well-defined) subset of a grammar and lexicon of the language and adds domain-specific terminology. Sometimes the rules that govern these controlled languages are precise, but sometimes they are informal and difficult to check automatically by a machine.

The most successful controlled language for technical documentation is ASD Simplified Technical English (ASD-STE100). Simplified Technical English (STE), formerly known as AECMA Simplified English, was first created for the aerospace industry to help readers easily understand maintenance documentation. Due to its success, STE is also used today in other industries (ASD-STE100 2021). Most technical documentation in these industries is written in English and used in multi-national programs. However, many readers of this documentation have only limited knowledge of English and are often overwhelmed by complex sentence structures and the number of meanings and synonyms of English words. STE was developed to address these issues with the aim of improving the quality of procedural and descriptive texts in maintenance documentation so that human errors can be reduced during maintenance tasks in the aerospace and other industries.

The STE specification consists of two parts: a set of 53 writing rules and a controlled dictionary of about 875 approved words for writing technical documents. The writing rules are about grammar and style. The dictionary specifies the words that are most frequently used in technical writing. If a word is not in the STE dictionary, then it is not approved and cannot be used in a technical document, unless it is a manufacturer-specific word that qualifies as a technical name or a technical verb and fits into one of the categories listed in the STE specification.

The words in the STE dictionary were chosen for their simplicity and ease of recognition. In general, there exists only one part of speech for one word and only one word for one meaning. For example, the word *test* is approved only as a noun but not as a verb, and the verb *follow* has only the approved meaning *come after, go after* but not *obey*. The writing rules of STE cover aspects of grammar and style and regulate mainly the use of word forms, grammatical voice, sentence lengths, and layout. Some of the writing rules are easy to check automatically, for example:

RULE: 5.1 Write short sentences. Use a maximum of 20 words in each sentence.

Other writing rules are difficult or even impossible to check automatically, since they rely on domain-specific knowledge and on human experience:

RULE: 6.1 Give information gradually.

Writing correctly in STE is not an easy task, since it requires a good command of English together with detailed knowledge of the domain and familiarity with the STE specification. There exist commercial word and rule checkers that support the writing process of STE, and flag unapproved and unknown words and violations of rules. However, these checkers are no replacement for training in STE authoring, since these tools cannot do the hard work and transform a non-STE compliant text automatically into a compliant one.

Although STE was not intended for use as a general writing standard, STE has been successfully adopted by other industries for their documentation needs, including the defence, construction, and medical industries. It turned out that STE is not only beneficial for those who do not have English as their first language but also for native speakers, since simple and unambiguous texts can improve the readability and comprehensibility of documents for all users and as a consequence limit human factor risk, in particular in safety-critical domains.

Another benefit of writing in STE is that documents are easier to translate into other languages, although this is not the primary objective of STE. In some cases, translation of safety-critical documentation is not even allowed by national regulations.

Controlled Languages for Machine Translation

Machine translation (MT) is another interesting application area for controlled languages. Various controlled languages have been used in industry to improve the quality of MT output using different MT architectures (Mitamura and Nyberg 1995; Hayes *et al.* 1996; Rychtyckyj 2002; Winkler *et al.* 2014; Ranta *et al.* 2020). The primary objective of using controlled language for MT is to limit lexical ambiguity in the source language and to rule out complex sentence structures to ease processing and achieve better translation results. The overall quality of the translation depends on the rule set that restricts the input language, the availability of tools that help authors comply with this rule set, and the architecture of the MT system that is used in the translation process.

Traditionally, MT systems used either a rule-based or a corpus-based approach to translate a document. While rule-based machine translation (RBMT) systems (Nirenburg 1989) use lexical and grammatical rules to govern the translation process, statistical machine translation (SMT) systems (Koehn 2010) use statistical models derived from bilingual text corpora to find the best translation. Often hybrid machine translation (HMT) systems (Costa-Jussa and Fonollosa 2015) are in practical use and combine the strengths of the first two approaches by post-processing the output of RBMT systems using statistical methods or by pre-processing the input or output of STM systems with the help of rules. In recent years, neural machine translation (NMT) systems (Vaswani *et al.* 2017) which model the direct mapping between source and target languages using deep neural networks (based on a transformer architecture) have achieved excellent results and can be considered the de facto paradigm for machine translation.

Most commercial MT systems have been designed for processing full natural language but provide mechanisms for domain customisation. This means that the input to the MT system is often restricted in a specific form by human intervention to improve the translation quality. Controlled languages can help to optimise this customisation process in a systematic and linguistically motivated way for a particular application domain. The restrictions on the source language for MT are often stricter than those for writing technical documentation, since the main goal is the reduction of ambiguity in input sentences for an MT system and not the improvement of readability for a human reader; however, these simplifications may work not only for machines but also for humans. However, caution is advised if the controlled language that is used to write the source text for MT becomes too restrictive. This is because sentences that are not stylistically adequate will not be accepted by technical writers, and this can lead to usability and productivity problems (O'Brien 2019).

Many of these special requirements to controlled language processing for MT have been addressed in the KANT system (Mitamura and Nyberg 1995; Mitamura 1999) and the KANTOO project (Nyberg and Mitamura 2000). The KANT system is designed as a large-scale, practical translation system for technical documents. It uses a controlled vocabulary and grammar for each source language and semantic models for each technical domain.

It is still instructive to have a closer look at this rule-based system since it tightly integrates controlled language checking and multilingual translation. The input language to the KANT system, KANT Controlled English, specifies lexical and grammatical restrictions. It turns out that the most effective way to improve the translation accuracy of the KANT system is to limit lexical ambiguity. In most cases, the lexicon of the KANT system encodes only a single meaning for each word/part-of-speech pair and alternative terms are used if a lexical item has more than one potential meaning in a domain. If a term must absolutely carry more than one meaning, then interactive lexical disambiguation is carried out during source language analysis. Other lexical restrictions concern the use of function words, modal verbs, participle forms, acronyms/abbreviations, and orthography.

The grammar of KANT Controlled English is based on two types of grammatical constraints: phrase-level constraints and sentence-level constraints. Phrase-level constraints govern the use of phrasal verbs; for example, particles of phrasal verbs are often ambiguous with prepositions, and these verbs should therefore be replaced by single-word verbs. Note that this is in contrast to Basic English, where a small number of verbs that function as operators are combined with prepositions. Other phrasal-level constraints govern the use of coordinated verb phrases and conjoined prepositional phrases, since these constructions can result in ambiguity. Sentence-level constraints ensure that two parts of a conjoined sentence are of the same type, that relative clauses are always introduced by a relative pronoun, and that the use of ellipsis is ruled out whenever possible. To guarantee that a source text is compliant with the rules of KANT Controlled English, an interactive checker is used that performs vocabulary and grammar checking. The checker parses each sentence in the source text and supports interactive disambiguation of lexical and structural ambiguities. If no analysis can be found, then the sentence must be rewritten. The KANT system was successfully used in the heavy equipment industry. In particular, the combination of constraining the domain lexicon and the grammar together with interactive disambiguation by the authors resulted in a dramatic reduction in the number of parses per sentence (from 27.0 to 1.04) and improved the resulting translations.

Instead of using a specialised MT system such as KANT, researchers have tried to identify those controlled language rules that have a high impact on the translation quality of commercial MT systems (O'Brien and Roturier 2007; Aikawa *et al.* 2007). Implementing only rules that have a high impact on the resulting translation is an interesting idea, since authoring in a controlled language with a large rule set can be time-consuming. A comparative study of two commercial rule-based MT systems found that a small set of high-impact rules can considerably reduce the post-editing effort and improve the comprehensibility of the MT output (O'Brien and Roturier 2007). Interestingly, these rules are relatively simple to apply; they govern misspelling, misuse of punctuation, long sentences (more than 25 words), and personal pronouns without an immediate antecedent. The hypothesis that a small set of rules can reduce the post-editing effort and improve MT quality has also been confirmed for statistical MT (Aikawa *et al.* 2007). In this study, it was found that in particular style restrictions on lexical and phrasal items, correct spelling and capitalisation had the greatest cross-linguistic effects on four typologically different languages (Dutch, Chinese, Arabic, French). While the outcome of this research is promising, it is important to note that these high-impact rules depend on the capabilities of the MT system and that language-specific rules are equally important to achieve good results. For example, in a multilingual MT scenario, prepositional attachment ambiguity is a special problem for Chinese but not so much for French because this form of ambiguity can usually be preserved between English and French but not between English and Chinese.

In two recent comparative studies (Marzouk and Hansen-Schirra 2019; Marzouk 2021), the authors showed the positive impact of a controlled language rule set on the quality of the output of RBMT, SMT, and HMT systems for German-to-English translation. However, it turned out that the same rule set did not have the same kind of impact on a NMT architecture. The NMT system showed the lowest number of errors before and after applying the controlled language rule set but the quality of the translation decreased after applying the rule set. That means the application of controlled language rules appears to become obsolete for the latest state-of-the-art NMT-based system architectures that deliver significantly better results than earlier MT system architectures.

Controlled Languages for Semantic Systems

Another group of controlled languages have been designed and used as general-purpose knowledge to knowledge representation languages and interface languages to knowledge systems, in particular to the semantic web, and as specification languages for business rules (Schwitter 2010; Kuhn 2014). These controlled languages can often be translated unambiguously into a formal target language and then be used for automated reasoning. Since these controlled languages correspond closely to a formal target language, their design is driven by theoretical considerations that require a careful balance between the expressive power of the language and computational complexity (Pratt-Hartmann 2010).

Controlled Languages for Knowledge Representation

While there are many proposals for representing knowledge in the context of automated reasoning, by far the most dominant approach is first-order logic or one of its variants. Unlike English, the language of first-order logic is completely formal. This enables software engineers to write precise and unambiguous specifications in this notation. However, formal notations are difficult to understand by domain specialists, who often do not have training in formal logic. This makes it difficult for them to check if a formal specification fulfils the intended purpose in a specific application domain. There exist a number of general-purpose controlled languages that can serve as high-level specification languages (Schwitter 2010; Kuhn 2014). These controlled languages can be translated into a version of first-order logic or into a non-monotonic logic and can then be used for automated reasoning tasks including question answering.

Attempto Controlled English

Attempto Controlled English (ACE) is a controlled natural language that has been designed as a specification and knowledge representation language (Fuchs and Schwitter 1996; Fuchs *et al.* 2008). It covers a well-defined subset of English and allows users to specify their knowledge about an application domain in form of a text. ACE texts are computer processable and can be unambiguously translated into discourse representation structures (DRSs) (van Eijck and Kamp 2011). These DRSs are a variant of first-order logic and serve as an interlingua that can be translated into various other formal notations for the purpose of automated reasoning.

ACE is defined by a small number of construction rules that specify admissible sentence structures and a small number of interpretation rules that disambiguate constructs that might appear ambiguous in full English. Simple ACE sentences have the following form:

subject + verb + [complements] + {adjuncts}

Complements depend on the verb and are required to complete a sentence, while adjuncts are optional modifiers of the verb. Composite ACE sentences can be built recursively from simpler ACE sentences through coordination, subordination, quantification, and negation.

The vocabulary of ACE consists of predefined function words (e.g., determiners, conjunctions, and pronouns), some predefined fixed phrases (e.g., *there is*, *it is false that*), and approximately 100,000 content words (nouns, proper names, verbs, adjectives, and adverbs). Users can import additional content word lexicons, prefix unknown words in a sentence by their word class, or let the ACE parser guess the word class.

ACE supports language constructs such as:

- active and passive verbs (incl. modal verbs);
- strong negation (e.g., *no*, *does not*) and weak negation (e.g., *it is not provable that*);
- subject and object relative clauses;
- declarative, conditional, interrogative and imperative sentences; and
- various forms of anaphoric references to noun phrases (e.g., *he*, *himself*, *the man*, *X*).

To make it easier to write in ACE, authors can use a predictive text editor that can help to construct a text in controlled language.

The following example shows Lewis Carroll's *Grocer puzzle* in ACE:

1: Every honest and industrious person is healthy. 2: No grocer is healthy. 3: Every industrious grocer is honest. 4: Every cyclist is industrious. 5: Every unhealthy cyclist is dishonest. 6: No healthy person is unhealthy. 7: No honest person is dishonest. 8: Every grocer is a person. 9: Every cyclist is a person.

Given this text, the ACE reasoner RACE (Fuchs 2012) can prove that a conclusion such as:

No grocer is a cyclist.

can be derived from the premises expressed in the text. The reasoner proves this conclusion and gives a justification for the proof in ACE. For our example, RACE finds the following minimal subset of premises that entail the conclusion:

1: Every honest and industrious person in healthy.
2: No grocer is healthy.

3: *Every industrious grocer is honest.*
4: *Every cyclist is industrious.*
8: *Every grocer is a person.*

Variations of this reasoning process allow for consistency checking in an ACE text, as well as question answering. Some proofs require domain-independent linguistic and mathematical knowledge that is expressed in the form of additional auxiliary axioms.

It is important to note that ACE texts are not decidable and therefore the search for a proof might not terminate. RACE controls undecidability by a time limit for a proof. However, there are decidable fragments of ACE. One of these fragments can be translated into the web ontology language OWL2 and covers almost all of OWL2 (apart from some data properties).

ACE has been used for several applications, including software and hardware specifications, agent control, legal and medical regulations, and ontology construction.

Recently, the RACE reasoner of ACE has been extended to deal with default logic and to reason with the law of inertia using auxiliary axioms (Fuchs 2021a). Furthermore, the reasoner has also been extended to reason with mathematical and functional constructs. The mathematical extension offers a solution for arithmetic problems and linear equations, and the functional extension provides a solution to operate recursively on list, set and string constructs (Fuchs 2021b).

Processable English

Processable English (PENG) is a controlled language that is similar to ACE but adopts a more lightweight approach in that it covers a smaller subset of English (White and Schwitter 2009). The language processors of ACE and PENG are both implemented in Prolog and based on grammars that are written in a definite clause grammar (DCG) notation. These DCGs are enhanced with feature structures and are specifically designed to translate declarative, conditional, and interrogative sentences into a first-order logic notation via a discourse representation structure (DRS).

In contrast to the original version of ACE that uses the DCG directly and resolves anaphoric references only after a DRS has been constructed, the language processor of PENG transforms the DCG into a format that can be processed by a top-down chart parser and resolves anaphoric references during the parsing process. PENG was the first controlled language to be supported by a predictive editor (Schwitter *et al.* 2003). This editor provides text- and menu-based writing support and partially removes the burden of learning and memorising the constraints of the controlled language. The editor enforces the grammatical restrictions of the controlled language via look-ahead information while a text is written and displays a paraphrase that clarifies the interpretation of each sentence. For each word form that the user enters, look-ahead information is generated by the chart parser that informs the user how the current input can be completed. These restrictions ensure that the text follows the rules of the controlled language so that it can be translated unambiguously into a DRS and then be further transformed in order to be processed by an automated reasoner.

PENG has been used as a high-level interface language to specify dynamic scenarios and the relevant background knowledge that is required to reason about direct and indirect effects of events as well as about continuous change (Schwitter 2011).

PENG has been used as an interface language to Answer Set Programming (ASP) (Lifschitz 2008). Instead of writing a problem specification in ASP, the specification can be expressed directly in PENG and then translated automatically into an ASP program to compute stable models for question answering (Schwitter 2012). The latest implementation of the PENG[ASP] system supports semantic round-tripping between a specification written in controlled language and an executable ASP program and vice versa (Schwitter 2020). Furthermore, temporal expressions are now allowed in a PENG^{ASP} specification and temporal reasoning is supported with the help of a linguistically motivated version of the event calculus (Shanahan 1999; Schwitter 2019).

Computer Processable Language

Computer Processable Language (CPL) is a controlled language for knowledge representation that has been developed at Boeing Research and Technology (Clark *et al.* 2005). In contrast to ACE and PENG where all syntactic constructions have a default interpretation, CPL allows for ambiguous constructions, but to a lesser extent than full natural languages. In CPL multiple interpretations of a sentence are possible, and the task of the language processor is to find the best parse and interpretation using additional external knowledge sources. The CPL parser relies on a preference mechanism to resolve attachment ambiguities. During parsing a simplified logical form is generated by rules that are parallel to the grammar rules. This logical form does not contain explicit quantifier scoping. Additional disambiguation decisions are performed during the generation of the logical form, while other decisions are deferred and handled during the translation of the logical form into the underlying frame-based knowledge representation language KM (Clark and Porter 1999). Each CPL sentence is interpreted interactively, and new sentences are added incrementally to the knowledge system. The interpretation of the system is then displayed to the user in paraphrased English. Furthermore, the KM system uses an inference mechanism that allows for reasoning about actions and dynamic worlds.

CPL accepts three types of sentences: ground facts, questions, and rules. In the case of ground facts, a basic CPL sentence takes one of the following three forms:

There is | **are** NP
NP verb [NP] [PP]★
NP **is** | **are** passive-verb [**by** NP] [PP]★

The nouns in noun phrases can be modified by other nouns, prepositional phrases, and adjectives. The verbs can include auxiliaries and particles. CPL accepts five forms of questions; the two main ones are:

What is NP?
Is it true that Sentence?

In the case of rules, CPL accepts sentence patterns of the form:

IF Sentence [**AND** Sentence]★ **THEN** Sentence [**AND** Sentence]★

CPL has been used in the AURA system (Chaudhri *et al.* 2009) that is part of the project Halo (Gunning *et al.* 2010). This project is an effort to develop a reasoning system that enables domain specialists in a broad range of scientific disciplines to author knowledge bases in controlled language and allow a different group of users to ask novel questions against the given knowledge bases. As the following example illustrates, the question answering process may involve a short scenario (1) and a question (2) against this scenario:

1   *A car accelerates from 12 m/s to 25 m/s in 6.0 s.*
2   *How far did it travel in this time?*

In order to answer the question, the user first reformulates the scenario and the question in CPL. This results in our case in the following specification:

A car is driving.
The initial speed of the car is 12 m/s.
The final speed of the car is 25 m/s.
The duration of the drive is 6.0 s.
What is the distance of the drive?

If a CPL guideline is violated during this reformulation process, the AURA system responds with a notification of the problem and gives advice about how to rephrase the input. In addition to this advice, the user has access to a vocabulary list that contains all words that the system understands and a searchable database of good CPL examples. If the input is a valid CPL sentence, then the AURA system displays its interpretation in graphical form so that the interpretation can be validated by the user.

Controlled Languages for the Semantic Web

A number of controlled languages have been proposed as interface languages to the semantic web, such as Attempto Controlled English (Kaljurand and Fuchs 2007), Lite Natural Language (Bernardi *et al.* 2007), Rabbit (Hart *et al.* 2008), OWL Simplified English (Power 2012), SQUALL (Ferré 2013), and Sparklis (Ferré 2017). Most of these controlled languages have been used with the support of predictive authoring tools in systems for authoring and verbalising ontologies of the description logic-based OWL family (Krötzsch *et al.* 2012).

Let us have a closer look at OWL Simplified English, since this language has a number of interesting features that have been introduced to simplify the learning and use of the language at the expense of its expressiveness (Power 2012). This adjustment is supported by an empirical study of a large ontology corpus of about 500,000 axioms. This study revealed interesting details about the information structure and the semantic complexity of these axioms (Power and Third 2010). Some logical patterns occur with high frequency in the axioms of these ontologies, while others are very rare. For example, 99.8% of terms that occur as the first argument of an axiom (subject position) are atomic, and only 0.2% consist of complex subject terms. Furthermore, names of individuals, classes, and properties have distinctive features. This makes it possible to define formation rules that allow a parser to determine with high accuracy where an entity name begins and ends and then classify them accordingly. Therefore, the authoring tool of OWL Simplified English requires only the specification of verbs; all other words can be automatically classified as long as they follow the formation rules. Another interesting finding of this study was that complex OWL expressions are invariably right branching; this allows for verbalisations that are structurally unambiguous and can be described efficiently by a finite-state grammar.

The linguistics patterns that are used for expressing common axiom and class constructors in OWL Simplified English are similar to other controlled languages (Schwitter *et al.* 2008). However, OWL Simplified English considerably restricts the structure of complex sentences. Only three strategies are allowed for constructing complex sentences: noun-phrase lists (1), verb-phrase lists (2), and verb-phrase chains (3):

1   *London is a city and a capital and a tourist attraction.*
2   *London is capital of the UK and has as population 15000000.*
3   *London is capital of a country that is governed by a man that lives in Downing Street.*

These constructions are free of ambiguity and can be combined in a systematic way to form more complex sentences, for example (4):

4   *London is a city that has as population 15000000 and is capital of a country that is governed by a man that lives in Downing Street.*

Note that OWL Simplified English does not allow the use of *and/that* and *or* in the same sentence, since this would result in ambiguous structures. Furthermore, only three forms of negation are allowed in this language, and these forms can only occur in predicates: negating a simple class (*is not a* Class), negating a simple restriction (*does not* Property *a* Class), and negating the second term of a simple intersection (*is a* Class1 *that is not a* Class2).

Controlled Languages for Business Rules

Another interesting application domain for controlled languages is the domain of business rules. Business rules are statements in natural language that describe how a person or a machine can perform a specific action in an organisation. The process of writing useful business rules is a difficult task, since these business rules need to be understood by humans and need to be processable by machines. Business rules fall into two main categories: (1) behavioural business rules that indicate how things can or cannot be done in an organisation and (2) definitional business rules that indicate how things must be interpreted in a particular context. For example, the first rule below is a behavioural rule, and the second rule is a definitional one, both written in plain English (Firas *et al.* 2003):

(1) *If a car is returned to a location other than the agreed drop-off branch, a drop-off penalty is charged.*
(2) *The end date of the rental must be before any scheduled booking of the assigned car for maintenance or transfer.*

In contrast to behavioural business rules, definitional business rules cannot be violated, but they can be ill-formed or inappropriate. Because of these characteristics, it is important that business rules be written in a precise and unambiguous manner so that they are easy to validate for businesspeople and easy to verify automatically for consistency.

The Semantics of Business Vocabulary and Business Rules (SBVR) is a standard that allows businesspeople to document the semantics of business vocabularies and business rules in a clear and unambiguous way for exchange between organisations and software tools (OMG 2019). While the SBVR specification is interpretable in predicate logic with a small extension that relies on modal operators and aligned with Common Logic (International Organization for Standardization 2018), the specification is mainly designed for businesspeople rather than for automated processing by machines.

SBVR specifies a meta-model for describing the meaning of business vocabularies, facts, and rules of natural language expressions and sentences in any natural language. The core idea of the SBVR approach is that rules build on facts, and facts build on concepts that are expressed by terms. SBVR does not standardise a particular surface notation, but SBVR meta-models can be rendered in graphical from, textual form, or a combination of both.

SBVR Structured English is a controlled language that has a particular mapping to SBVR structures of meaning. To avoid confusion between behavioural business rules and definitional business rules, SBVR Structured English uses key phrases that denote either deontic or alethic modalities to distinguish between these rules. On the one hand, SBVR Structured English uses deontic key phrases (with possible negation) for expressing behavioural business rules that embed exactly one logical formulation (*p*), for example:

> It is (not) obligatory that *p*
> It is (not) permitted that *p*
> It is permitted but not obligatory that *p*

Note that a conjunction of permission and non-obligation can be used to express optionality to pre-empt the application of behavioural rules that might be assumed to exist (e.g., for advising that it is not obligatory that a renter show a picture id when picking up a rental car).

On the other hand, SBVR Structured English uses alethic key phrases (with possible negation) for describing definitional business rules that embed exactly one logical formulation (*p*), for example:

> It is (not) necessary that p
> It is (not) possible that p
> It is possible but not necessary that p

Note that a conjunction of possibility and non-necessity can be used to express contingency to pre-empt the application of definitional rules that might be assumed to exist (e.g., for advising that it is not necessary for a qualified diver to be over 21).

The specification of a business rule in SBVR Structural English usually takes a vocabulary entry of a fact type (= verb concept) as a starting point, for example:

> branch owns rental car

This is a binary fact type that uses two designations (*branch* and *rental car*) for the noun concepts and one designation (*owns*) for the verb concept. Vocabulary entries of fact types usually use singular, active forms of verbs; other forms of verbs are implicitly usable in business rules. For the specification of a behavioural business rule, a suitable deontic key phrase is selected and added to the representation of the fact type. Additionally, the grammatical voice is fixed and this results, for example, in the following sentence:

> *It is obligatory that rental car is owned by branch.*

In the next step quantifiers are added to the designations of the noun concepts:

> *It is obligatory that <u>each</u> rental car is owned by <u>exactly one</u> branch.*

The specification of a definitional business rule works in a similar way but uses an alethic key phrase, for example:

> *It is necessary that each rental has exactly one requested car group.*

This business rule is based on the following supporting fact type:

> rental has requested car group

SBVR does not provide a special semantic notation for representing tenses or for different ways states and events can relate to each other with respect to time. However, fact types can be turned into objects by giving these objects a name. This process is called objectification. Objectification can be used to identify a state of affairs (event, activity, situation, or circumstance) and relate this state of affairs to times and durations or to other verb concepts. For example, in the following sentence:

> *It is obligatory that each car assignment of a rental occurs before the pick-up date of the rental.*

the designation *car assignment* represents the objectification of the following fact type:

> car is assigned to rental

By defining this objectification and using the following fact types:

> car assignment objectifies car is assigned to rental
> car assignment is a state of affairs
> state of affairs occurs before point in time
> state of affairs$_1$ occurs before state of affairs$_2$ occurs

the state of affairs (*car assignment*) can be related to a time point (*pick-up date*) with respect to time (occurring before or after that time point).

The SBVR business rules introduced so far prefix a statement with key phrases which convey the intended modality. SBVR Structured English uses an alternative style to communicate the modality. This alternative embeds a keyword (in front of verbs) within rule statements, for example:

> *Each rental car <u>must</u> be owned by exactly one branch.*
> *Each rental <u>always</u> has exactly one requested car group.*

This embedded keyword style is the preferred style for expressing modalities in RuleSpeak (Ross 2003), an existing business rule notation that related to SBVR and has been used by businesspeople in large-scale projects.

Despite the existence of a formally grounded notation, SBVR lacks a logical formalisation which would allow a reasoning tool to automatically check the consistency of a set of business rules. This is because SBVR uses very expressive constructs for which it is known that a sound and complete reasoner cannot be constructed. Research into logic-based reasoning support for subsets of SBVR using a specific first-order deontic-alethic logic (Solomakhin *et al.* 2013) and into rule verification techniques for anomaly detection in business rules (Mitra *et al.* 2018) are important research contributions to increase acceptability of SBVR.

Conclusion

As we have seen, there exist several application areas that can benefit from restricting the expressivity of natural language in a systematic way in order to improve communication between humans, comprehensibility and processing of documents or interaction between humans and machines. Controlled languages achieve these improvements by carefully restricting the size of the grammar and vocabulary for a specific application area with the aim of reducing or eliminating ambiguity and complexity of full natural language. We have identified four main application areas in this chapter: controlled languages for human communication, controlled languages for technical documentation, controlled languages for machine translation, and controlled languages for semantic systems. Each of these areas has specific requirements to the design of a controlled language, and even within an area there often exist competing but formally equivalent linguistic constructions, and it is not always clear which one works best. Without doubt there is a lot of room for comparative evaluations in this domain to determine which constructions work best for a particular user group.

Controlled languages have been used successfully in many industries over the last thirty years as a method to improve the readability of technical documents or to make these documents easier to translate into the language of their customers. Authoring support is essential to produce texts and documents in controlled language, since human writers need to be able to judge whether a sentence or a paragraph complies with the rules of the controlled language and whether an expression belongs to the approved vocabulary or not. In the future, we will see more companies using controlled languages for document production and producing their own controlled language standards. We expect to see many more semantic systems that will use controlled languages as high-level interface languages that allow humans and machines to communicate in a truly cooperative way without the need to formally encode the relevant knowledge.

Notes

1 http://simple.wikipedia.org/wiki/Main_Page
2 https://simple.wikipedia.org/wiki/Wikipedia:How_to_write_Simple_English_pages

Bibliography

Aikawa, T., L. Schwartz, R. King, M. Corston-Oliver, and C. Lozano (2007) 'Impact of Controlled Language on Translation Quality and Post-editing in a Statistical Machine Translation Environment', in *Proceedings of MT Summit XI*, 1–7. Available at: https://aclanthology.org/2007.mtsummit-papers.1.pdf.

ASD (2021) *ASD Simplified Technical English*, Specification ASD-STE100, International Specification for the Preparation of Maintenance Documentation in a Controlled Language, Issue 8, April 30.

Bernardi, R., D. Calvanese, and C. Thorne (2007) 'Lite Natural Language', in *Proceedings of the 7th International Workshop on Computational Semantics (IWCS-7)*. Available at: https://www.inf.unibz.it/~calvanese/papers-html/IWCS-2007.html.

Chaudhri, V. K., P. E. Clark, S. Mishra, J. Pacheco, A. Spaulding, and J. Tien (2009) 'AURA: Capturing Knowledge and Answering Questions on Science Textbooks', *Technical Report*, SRI International.

Clark, P., P. Harrison, T. Jenkins, J. Thompson, and R. Wojcik (2005) 'Acquiring and Using World Knowledge Using a Restricted Subset of English', in *The 18th International FLAIRS Conference* (FLAIRS'05). Available at: https://ai2-website.s3.amazonaws.com/team/peterc/publications/flairs.pdf.

Clark, P. and B. Porter (1999) 'KM – The Knowledge Machine 2.0: Users Manual', *Technical Report*, AI Lab, University Texas at Austin.

Costa-Jussa, M. R. and J. A. Fonollosa (2015) 'Latest Trends in Hybrid Machine Translation and Its Applications', *Computer Speech and Language* 32(1): 3–10.

Eijck van, J. and H. Kamp (2011) 'Discourse Representation in Context', in J. van Benthem and A. ter Meulen (eds.) *Handbook of Logic and Language*, 2nd edition, Amsterdam: Elsevier, 181–52.

Ferré, S. (2013) 'SQUALL: A Controlled Natural Language as Expressive as SPARQL 1.1', in *Natural Language Processing and Information Systems. NLDB 2013*. Lecture Notes in Computer Science, vol. 7934, Berlin, Heidelberg: Springer, 114–25.

Ferré, S. (2017) 'An Expressive Query Builder for SPARQL Endpoints with Guidance in Natural Language', *Semantic Web* 8: 405–18.

Frias, L., A. Queralt, and A. Olive (2003) 'EU-Rent Car Rentals Specification', *Research Report*, 56.018 UPC E-Prints, Polytechnic University of Catalonia.

Fuchs, N. E. (2012) 'First-Order Reasoning for Attempto Controlled English', in *Proceedings of the Second International Workshop on Controlled Natural Language (CNL 2010)*, Springer, Berlin, Heidelberg.

Fuchs, N. E. (2021a) 'The Law of Inertia and the Frame Problem in Attempto Controlled English', in *Proceedings of the Seventh International Workshop on Controlled Natural Language (CNL 2020/21)*, Amsterdam, Netherlands, September.

Fuchs, N. E. (2021b) 'Reasoning in Attempto Controlled English: Mathematical and Functional Extensions', in *Proceedings of the Seventh International Workshop on Controlled Natural Language (CNL 2020/21)*, Amsterdam, Netherlands, September.

Fuchs, N. E., K. Kaljurand, and T. Kuhn (2008) 'Attempto Controlled English for Knowledge Representation', in C. Baroglio, P. A. Bonatti, J. Maluszynski, M. Marchiori, A. Polleres, and S. Schaffert (eds.) *Reasoning Web, Fourth International Summer School 2008*, LNCS 5224, Berlin, Heidelberg: Springer, 104–24.

Fuchs, N. E. and R. Schwitter (1996) 'Attempto Controlled English (ACE)', in *Proceedings of CLAW 96*, Leuven, Belgium: University of Leuven, March, 124–36.

Gunning, D., V. K. Chaudhri, P. Clark, K. Barker, S.-Y. Chaw, M. Greaves, B. Grosof, A. Leung, D. McDonald, S. Mishra, J. Pacheco, B. Porter, A. Spaulding, D. Tecuci, and J. Tien (2010) 'Project Halo Update – Progress Toward Digital Aristotle', *AI Magazine* 31(3): 33–58.

Hart, G., M. Johnson, and C. Dolbear (2008) 'Rabbit: Developing a Control Natural Language for Authoring Ontologies', in S. Bechhofer, M. Hauswirth, J. Hoffmann, and M. Koubarakis (eds.), *ESWC 2008*, LNCS 5021, Berlin, Heidelberg: Springer, 348–60.

Hayes, P., S. Maxwell, and L. Schmandt (1996) 'Controlled English Advantages for Translated and Original English Documents', in *Proceedings of CLAW 1996*, 84–92. Available at: https://aclanthology.org/www.mt-archive.info/90/CLAW-1996-Hayes.pdf.

International Organization for Standardization (2018) *Information Technology – Common Logic (CL) – A Framework for a Family of Logic-Based Languages* (ISO/IEC 24707), 2nd edition, Geneva, July.

Kaljurand, K. and N. E. Fuchs (2007) 'Verbalizing OWL in Attempto Controlled English', in *Proceedings of OWL: Experiences and Directions*, CEUR-WS, vol. 258, Innsbruck, Austria.

Koehn, P. (2010) *Statistical Machine Translation*, Cambridge: Cambridge University Press.

Krötzsch, M., F. Simančik, and I. Horrocks (2012) 'A Description Logic Primer', *CoRR*, abs/1201.4089. Available at: https://arxiv.org/abs/1201.4089.

Kuhn, T. (2014) 'A Survey and Classification of Controlled Natural Languages', *Computational Linguistics* 40(1): 121–70.

Lifschitz, V. (2008) 'What is answer set programming?', in *Proceedings of the 23rd National Conference on Artificial Intelligence,* vol. 3, AAAI Press, Menlo Park, CA, 1594–97.

Marzouk, S. (2021) 'An In-depth Analysis of the Individual Impact of Controlled Language Rules on Machine Translation Output: A Mixed-Methods Approach', *Machine Translation* 35: 167–203.

Marzouk, S. and S. Hansen-Schirra (2019) 'Evaluation of the Impact of Controlled Language on Neural Machine Translation Compared to Other MT Architectures', *Machine Translation* 33: 179–203.

Mitamura, T. (1999) 'Controlled Language for Multilingual Machine Translation', in *Proceedings of MT Summit VII*, 46–52. Available at: https://aclanthology.org/www.mt-archive.info/90/MTS-1999-Mitamura.pdf.

Mitamura, T. and E. Nyberg (1995) 'Controlled English for Knowledge-based MT: Experience with the KANT System', in *Proceedings of the Sixth International Conference on Theoretical and Methodological Issues in Machine Translation, TMI* vol. 95, 158–72. Available at: https://aclanthology.org/1995.tmi-1.12.pdf.

Mitra, S., K. Anand, and P. K. Chittimalli (2018) 'Identifying Anomalies in SBVR-based Business Rules using Directed Graphs and SMT-LIBv2', in *Proceedings of the 20th International Conference of Enterprise Information Systems (ICEIS) 2018*, vol. 2, 215–22. Available at: https://www.scitepress.org/papers/2018/66698/66698.pdf.

Nirenburg, S. (1989) 'Knowledge-Based Machine Translation', *Machine Translation* 4(1): 5–24.

Nyberg, E. and T. Mitamura (2000) 'The KANTOO Machine Translation Environment', in *Proceedings of ATMA 2000: Envisioning Machine Translation in the Information Future,* Springer, Berlin, Heidelberg, 192–95.

Object Management Group (OMG) (2019) *Semantics of Business Vocabulary and Business Rules (SBVR)*, Version 1.5. Specification, OMG (October).

O'Brien, S. (2010) 'Controlled Language and Readability', in *Translation and Cognition*, Amsterdam and Philadelphia: John Benjamins Publishing Company, 143–65.

O'Brien, S. (2019) 'Controlled Language and Writing for an International Audience', in *Translation and Localization*, London and New York: Routledge.

O'Brien, S. and J. Roturier (2007) 'How Portable are Controlled Languages Rules? A Comparison of Two Empirical MT Studies', in *Proceedings of MT Summit XI*, 345–52. Available at: https://aclanthology.org/2007.mtsummit-papers.46.pdf.

Ogden, C. K. (1930) *Basic English: A General Introduction with Rules and Grammar*, London: Paul Treber and Co., Ltd.

Ogden, C. K. (1968) *Basic English: International Second Language*, New York: Harcourt, Brace and World.

Power, R. (2012) 'OWL Simplified English: A Finite-State Language for Ontology Editing', in T. Kuhn and N. E. Fuchs (eds.) *CNL 2012*, LNCS 7427, Springer, 44–60.

Power, R. and A. Third (2010) 'Expressing OWL Axioms by English Sentences: Dubious in Theory, Feasible in Practice', in *Proceedings of the 23rd International Conference on Computational Linguistics*, 1006–13. Available at: https://aclanthology.org/C10-2116/.

Pratt-Hartmann, I. (2010) 'Computational Complexity in Natural Language', in A. Clark, C. Fox, and S. Lappin (eds.) *The Handbook of Computational Linguistics and Natural Language Processing*, Hoboken, NJ: Wiley-Blackwell, 43–73.

Ranta, A., K. Angelov, N. Gruzitis, and P. Kolachina (2020) 'Abstract Syntax as Interlingua: Scaling up the Grammatical Framework from Controlled Languages to Robust Pipelines', *Computational Linguistics* 46(2): 425–86.

Ross, R. G. (2003) *Principles of the Business Rule Approach*, Boston, MA: Addison-Wesley.

Rychtyckyj, N. (2002) 'An Assessment of Machine Translation for Vehicle Assembly Process Planning at Ford Motor Company', in *Proceedings of AMTA 2002*, LNAI 2499, 207–15. Available at: https://aclanthology.org/2002.amta-studies.3/.

Schwitter, R. (2010) 'Controlled Natural Languages for Knowledge Representation', in *Proceedings of COLING 2010*, Beijing, China, 1113–21.

Schwitter, R. (2011) 'Specifying Events and Their Effects in Controlled Natural Language', in N. A. Aziz, K. Hasida, A. W. A. Rahman, and H. Saito (eds.) *Computational Linguistics and Related Fields*, Procedia – Social and Behavioral Sciences, Amsterdam: Elsevier, 12–21.

Schwitter, R. (2012) 'Answer Set Programming via Controlled Natural Language Processing', in *Proceedings of CNL 2012*, LNCS 7427, Springer, 26–43.

Schwitter, R. (2019) 'Augmenting an Answer Set Based Controlled Natural Language with Temporal Expressions', in A. C. Nayak and A. Sharma (eds.) *PRICAI 2019: Trends in Artificial Intelligence*, LNAI 11670, Cham: Springer, 500–13.

Schwitter, R. (2020) 'Lossless Semantic Round-Tripping in PENG ASP', in *Proceedings of the Twenty-Ninth International Joint Conference on Artificial Intelligence (IJCAI-20)*, Demonstrations Track, Yokohama, Japan, 5291–93.

Schwitter, R., K. Kaljurand, A. Cregan, C. Dolbear, and G. Hart (2008) 'A Comparison of Three Controlled Natural Languages for OWL 1.1', in *OWL Experiences and Directions, 4th International Workshop*, Washington, DC.

Schwitter, R., A. Ljungberg, and D. Hood (2003) 'ECOLE – A Look-ahead Editor for a Controlled Language', in *Proceedings of EAMT-CLAW03*, Dublin City University, Ireland, 141–50.

Shanahan, M. (1999) 'The Event Calculus Explained', in *Artificial Intelligence Today*, Berlin, Heidelberg: Springer, 409–30.

Solomakhin, D., E. Franconi, and A. Mosca (2013) 'Logic-based Reasoning Support for SBVR', *Fundamenta Informaticae* 124(4): 543–60.

Vaswani, A., N. Shazeer, N. Parmar, J. Uszkoreit, L. Jones, A. N. Gomez, L. Kaiser, and I. Polosukhin (2017) 'Attention is All You Need', in *Advances in Neural Information Processing Systems* 30.

White, C. and R. Schwitter (2009) 'An Update on PENG Light', in *Proceedings of ALTA 2009*, Sydney, Australia, 80–88.

Winkler, K., T. Kuhn, and M. Volk (2014) 'Evaluating the Fully Automatic Multi-language Translation of the Swiss Avalanche Bulletin', in *Proceedings of CNL 2014: Controlled Natural Language*, LNAI 8625, Springer, Cham, 44–54.

31

CORPORA

Li Lan and Ye Meng

Introduction

The word *corpus* (plural *corpora*) originally came from Latin. According to the *Oxford English Dictionary*, its sense of "body of a person" started in the mid-15th century, and the meaning of "collection of facts or things" occurred later in 1727. The year 1956 saw its meaning extended to "the body of written or spoken material upon which a linguistic analysis is based". A large number of index cards used by early dictionary compilers were, in fact, human-readable language corpora. As Leech (1992) observed, corpora of text collection had been used by linguists and grammarians for the study of language long before the invention of the computer; therefore, he believes that "computer corpus linguistics" would be a more appropriate term for studies based on language database today. Brookes and McEnery (2020) note that corpus linguistics embraces a wide range of approaches such as frequency, keyword analysis and collocation. The concept of corpus in linguistics is a large collection of machine-readable text compiled with a specific purpose that can be retrieved with particular computer software for different linguistic research.

Corpus-based translation study (CTS) is defined as the use of corpus linguistic technologies to inform and elucidate the translation process (Baker 1995). In tandem with rapid development in computational power and availability of electronic texts, the corpus approach has become a truly empirical approach to language and translation studies (Granger 2003). Based on the statistical analysis of corpora, it mainly handles "the features of translation and translation norms" (p. 1), aiming to identify the relationship between translation and social realities (Hu 2016). Applications of the approach have including professional human translation to machine translation, from descriptive linguistic and translation research to language teaching and translator training.

Development and Typology of Corpora

The landmark of modern corpora is generally thought to be the Brown Corpus of Standard American English. It consists of 500 text samples (2,000 words each) distributed in 15 categories, forming a 1-million-word selection of American English from a wide variety of sources. The corpus was compiled in the 1960s and was used in the analysis of linguistics, language teaching, psychology, statistics and sociology (Kucera and Francis 1967). It was used as a foundation for the famous Survey of English Usage, and the outcome, *A Comprehensive Grammar of*

DOI: 10.4324/9781003168348-34

the English Language Longman (Quirk *et al.* 1985), is regarded as one of most important English grammar books in the English language.

In addition, the Brown Corpus also provided support to the 1969 edition of the *American Heritage Dictionary* (AHD). The AHD took the innovative step of combining prescriptive elements (how language *should* be used) with descriptive information (how it actually *is* used). Currently, the corpus is considered small but is still used in studies of English for specific purposes. The corpus is used to investigate linguistic features in non-native maritime communication (John *et al.* 2017). After an exciting start, corpus linguistics in North America seemed to enter a rather dormant phase throughout the 1980s and 90s until fairly recently, when a number of freely available online mega-corpora were introduced to the public domain. These mega-corpora include the 400-million-word Corpus of Contemporary American English (COCA), 200-million-word Time Corpus, COHA, Google Books and the latest release of the 1.9-billion-word GloWbE, all by Mark Davis at Brigham Young University. The free mega-corpora have percolated through different types of corpus research. As the compiler predicts, COHA, TIME, COCA and Google Books can be used for historical or diachronic studies of the English language studies; COCA and BYU-BNC are for genre studies; and GloWbE, which consists of subcorpora of English used in 20 countries, will contribute to the exploration of a variety of Englishes in the world.

The first corpus of British English was London-Lund, built in 1965, which also contributed to the Survey of English and *A Comprehensive Grammar of the English Language.* The late 1980s and 1990s saw corpus linguistics flourishing in Great Britain. A number of famous linguists entered the area of corpus linguists and made great contributions in terms of developing its theoretical premise and methodological application, John Sinclair and Geoffrey Leech making particularly notable contributions to the field. Under the leadership of Sinclair, the Bank of English, or the COBUILD corpus, has served a large number of dictionaries, grammar books and ELT teaching materials. The project started in 1991 and has been growing, reaching a total of 650 million running words in 2012. The corpus is held both at HarperCollins Publishers and the University of Birmingham and is open only to paid academic institutions in Europe. Another influential standard corpus is the British National Corpus (BNC), a collection of standard British English. The compilation lasted from 1991 to 1994. It is a balanced corpus with 100 million words of both spoken and written data with part of speech (POS) tagging. Since its publication, the BNC has been used as a reference corpus for many linguistic studies, including general English versus specialized English, standard English versus a variety of English and native English versus non-native or learner English. A recent update of BNC is BNC2014. The spoken component of the corpus includes 11.5 million words and is composed of transcripts of recorded informal conversations of British citizens. The corpus has been employed to explore features in contemporary British speech, such as intensifiers (Aijmer 2021) and politeness variations used by the public (Culpeper and Gillings 2018). The compilation of written BNC2014 is ongoing. As stated by the compiler, the 100-million-token corpus will reveal use in modern-day British English.

Although these monolingual English corpora are non-translational, they can be used in translation training to strengthen students' knowledge of target language patterns and improve the quality of translation (Bowker 1999; Kenny 2001), to help with the extraction of enormous terminology (Pearson 1996; Hu 2016) and "to allow patterns observed in a source or target text to be set off against what is known about the language in general" (Kenny 2001: 58).

The development of English corpora, together with fast development of computer technology, has inspired corpora of different languages in many parts of the world. To date, more than 30 languages have built their own corpora, big or small, general or specific. Although a huge amount of data is available online today, it is important to note the difference between corpora and archives of electronic texts: Building a corpus requires not only a large quantity of data but also an information retrieval operation in order to locate relevant and reliable documents, while an archive is only a repertory of electronic texts (Granger 2003). In this sense, representativeness is significant in corpus compilation. It is defined as "what type of speaker/variety/discourse is the corpus meant to represent" (Ädel 2020: 4). Many monolingual corpora (e.g. BNC) mainly cover a general type of discourse and a large population, whereas there are quite a few specific corpora (e.g. Thai Literature corpora, TLC and the Coronavirus corpus).

Table 31.1 lists some influential monolingual non-English corpora from recent publications. Their websites can be easily googled on the internet. The application of these data in translation will be discussed later in this chapter.

Compared to the English mega corpora, these linguistic databases may not be as standard and representative, but they have been used for national and international linguistic studies. It is obvious that the development of corpus study across languages is not balanced; as Granger noticed, "less widespread language may not have any corpus resources at all or access to them may be severely limited" (Granger 2003: 22).

The Role of Corpus in Language Study

The role of corpus in language study offers new perspectives, allowing us "to see phenomena that previously remained obscure because of the limitation of our vintage points" (Kenny 2001: xiii). John Sinclair (2003) believes that natural language use constitutes the best source of linguistic evidence. Such use can only be found in authentic communicative texts. He claims one of the main aims of creating the corpus Bank of English was to retrieve evidence in support of the learning of the English language (Sinclair 1991) and lead the COUBUILD team to compile one of the earliest learner's dictionaries drawing on the data from the Bank of English.

Wallis and Nelson (2001) propose 3A perspectives for data processing:

- *Annotation* consists of the application of a scheme to texts. Annotations may include structural markup, part-of-speech (POS) tagging, parsing, and numerous other representations.
- *Abstraction* consists of the translation (mapping) of terms in the scheme to terms in a theoretically motivated model or dataset. Abstraction typically includes linguist-directed search but may include, for example, rule-learning for parsers.
- *Analysis* consists of statistically probing, manipulating, and generalizing from the dataset. Analysis might include statistical evaluations, optimization of rule-bases, or knowledge discovery methods.

A corpus approach to language studies can be corpus-driven or corpus-based (Biber *et al.* 1998; Tognini-Bonelli 2001). A corpus-based approach is a top-down methodology "that uses corpus evidence mainly as a repository of examples to expound, test or exemplify given theoretical statements" (Tognini-Bonelli 2001: 10). A corpus-driven approach involves a bottom-up methodology, beginning by selecting random examples from the corpus, identifying their shared and individual features, and then grouping them for different purposes. Researchers observe language facts from corpus data, formulate a hypothesis to account for these facts, make a generalization based on corpus evidence of the repeated patterns and then unify these observations in a theoretical statement (ibid, pp. 14–18). Given that translation studies are, after all, a linguistic study, both corpus-driven and corpus-based approaches can contribute to providing linguistic and cultural evidence and improving the quality of translation.

In language study as well as in translation study, dictionaries and corpora are indispensable tools. The difference between the two lies in the way they are used. Dictionaries provide word

Table 31.1 Monolingual non-English corpora

Language	Title	Span of compilation	Span of data production	Size	Host institution	Website
European languages						
Swedish	The Swedish Treebank	2008	Post-1970	0.35 million	Uppsala University; Växjö University	http://stp.lingfil.uu.se/~nivre/swedish_treebank/
	Swedish Web 2014 (svTenTen14)	2014	2014	3 billion	Masaryk University and Sketch Engine	www.sketchengine.eu/svtenten-swedish-corpus/
	COW web corpora (SVCOW14)	2014	2012–2014	4.8 billion	Roland Schäfer from Humboldt-Universität	https://corporafromtheweb.org/svcow14/
Danish	Korpus 2000	2000	1990–2000	56 million	Society for Danish Language and Literature	http://ordnet.dk/korpusdk_en
	Danish Web 2014 (daTenTen)	2014	Not known	2 billion	Masaryk University and Sketch Engine	www.sketchengine.eu/datenten-danish-corpus/
	Danish Corpus	Not known	Post-1960	10 million	University of Southern Denmark	https://corp.hum.sdu.dk/corpuseye.da.html
Spanish	Corpus de Referencia del Español Actual (CREA) v 3.0	2021	1975–2004	200+ million	REAL ACADEMIA ESPAÑOLA	http://corpus.rae.es/creanet.html
	Spanish Web corpus (esTenTen)	2014	2018–2011	7.4 billion	Masaryk University and Sketch Engine	www.sketchengine.eu/estenten-spanish-corpus/#toggle-id-3
	Corpus Diacrónico del Español (CORDE)	Not known	Post-1974	300 million	University of Nevada Las Vegas	http://corpus.rae.es/cordenet.html
	Corpus del Español del Siglo XX	2021	2001–2015	175 million	US National Endowment for the Humanities	https://apps2.rae.es/CORPES/view/inicioExterno.view;jsessionid=8208D485A5EF5EF555030F4239D004B9
French	French Treebank	Since 1997	1989–1995	1 million	Laboratoire de Linguistique Formelle	www.llf.cnrs.fr/Gens/Abeille/French-Treebank-fr.php
	Corpus of the French Web	2017	Not known	5.7 billion	Masaryk University and Sketch Engine	www.sketchengine.eu/frtenten-french-corpus/
	WikipediaFR2008 Corpus	2008	2008	262 million	Université Toulouse 2/5	http://redac.univ-tlse2.fr/corpora/wikipedia_en.html
German	Deutsches Referenzkorpus (DEREKO)	2004	1999–2002	200 million	The Institut für deutsche Sprache (IDS) in Mannheim, the Seminar für Sprachwissenschaft (SfS) in Tübingen, and the Institut für Maschinelle Sprachverarbeitung (IMS) in Stuttgart	www.sfs.uni-tuebingen.de/dereko/

	German WebCorpus (deTenTen)	2019	2018	5.3 billion	Masaryk University and Sketch Engine	www.sketchengine.eu/detenten-german-corpus/
	Deutscher Wortschatz Project	Since 1998	Not known	500 million	Deutscher Wortschatz	https://wortschatz.uni-leipzig.de/en
	The Hamburg Dependency Treebank	2015	1996–2001	261.821 sentences	Hamburger Zentrum für Sprachkorpora	https://corpora.uni-hamburg.de/hzsk/de/islandora/object/treebank:hdt
	Limas Corpus	2014	1970s	1 million	University of Duisburg-Essen	https://korpora.zim.uni-duisburg-essen.de/Limas/
Scottish	The Scottish Corpus of Texts and Speech (SCOTS)	2004	12th century onward	5.4 million	The School of Critical Studies at Glasgow University	www.scottishcorpus.ac.uk/corpus/search/
	The Corpus of Modern Scottish Writing (CMSW)	2004	1970–present	5.5 million	The School of Critical Studies at Glasgow University	www.scottishcorpus.ac.uk/cmsw/
Welsh	Cronfa Electroneg o Gymraeg	2001	Post-1970–2001	1 million	University of Wales, Bangor	www.bangor.ac.uk/canolfanbedwyr/ceg.php.en
	Corpws Cenedlaethol Cymraeg Cyfoes (CorCenCC) (National Corpus of Contemporary Welsh)	2020	Not known	11 million	Cardiff University	https://corcencc.org/
Irish	TOBAR NA GAEDHILGE	2019	1885–1995	3.5 million	The University of the Highlands and Islands	www.smo.uhi.ac.uk/~oduibhin/tobar/index.htm#history
	The New Corpus for Ireland	Not known	Not known	30 million	Lexical Computing Ltd.	http://focloir.sketchengine.co.uk/run.cgi/index
	Irish Syllabic Poetry	2008	1200–1650	0.3 million	The University of Dublin	www.tcd.ie/Irish/research/bardic-guide.ga.php
Portuguese	The CETEMPúblico Corpus	2000	1991–1998	180 million	Portuguese Ministry for Science and Technology (MCT)	www.linguateca.pt/cetempublico/
	The Corpus do Português	2016–2018	1920–2019	2.5 billion	National Endowment for the Humanities	www.corpusdoportugues.org/
	Corpus of the Portuguese Web (ptTenTen)	2014	Not known	3.8 billion	Masaryk University and Sketch Engine	www.sketchengine.eu/pttenten-portuguese-corpus/

(Continued)

Table 31.1 (Continued)

Language	Title	Span of compilation	Span of data production	Size	Host institution	Website
Czech	The Prague Dependency Treebank	2012–2013	1991–1995	4.3 million	Institute of Formal and Applied Linguistics (ÚFAL)	http://ufal.mff.cuni.cz/pdt2.0/
	Corpus of the Czech Web (csTenTen17)	2015–2017	Not known	10.5 billion	Masaryk University and Sketch Engine	www.sketchengine.eu/cstenten-czech-corpus/
	Czech National Corpus (CNC)	Since 1994	Not known	100+ million	Charles University	www.korpus.cz
Croatian	Croatian National Corpus	Since 1998	1998–2013	234 million	University of Zagreb	www.hnk.ffzg.hr/default_en.htm
	Croatian corpus from the web (hrWaC)	2014	Not known	1.2 billion	European Commission University of Zagreb	www.sketchengine.eu/hrwac-croatian-corpus/
Russian	BOKR (The Russian Reference Corpus)	Since 2002	2001–2011	100 million	Leeds University	http://bokrcorpora.narod.ru/index-en.html
	Russian National Corpus	Since 2003	Posts 2004	300+ million	Russian Academy of Sciences	https://ruscorpora.ru/old/en/index.html
	Russian Corpus for SKELL (ruSKELL)	2016	Not known	1 billion	Sketch Engine	www.sketchengine.eu/russian-skell-corpus/
	Russian corpora	Not known	Not known	281 million	University of Leeds	http://corpus.leeds.ac.uk/ruscorpora.html
	Computer corpus of Russian newspaper texts of the late 20th century	Not known	Late 20th century	1 million	University of Moscow	www.philol.msu.ru/~lex/corpus/
Serbian	Corpus Of Serbian Language (CSL)	1996	12th century–contemporary times	11 million	Institute for Experimental Phonetics and Speech Pathology, Belgrade; Laboratory for Experimental Psychology, University of Belgrade	http://serbian-corpus.rs/eindex/digest.html
	Serbian corpus from the web (srWaC)	2014	Not known	476 million	Jožef Stefan Institute	www.sketchengine.eu/srwac-serbian-corpus/
Polish	The National Corpus of Polish	2012	1921–2010	20 million	Polish Ministry of Science and Higher Education	http://nkjp.pl/index.php?page=15&lang=1
	The Polish Web Corpus	2012	2012	7 billion	Sketch Engine	www.sketchengine.eu/pltenten-polish-corpus/
	Timestamped JSI web corpus	2017	2014–2016	720+ million	Sketch Engine	www.sketchengine.eu/jozef-stefan-institute-newsfeed-corpus/

Language	Corpus					URL
Turkish	METU Turkish Corpus	2017	Post-1990	2 million	Middle East Technical University	https://ii.metu.edu.tr/metu-corpora-research-group
	Corpus of the Turkish Web (trTenTen)	2011–2012	2011–2012	3.3 billion	Masaryk University and Sketch Engine	www.sketchengine.eu/trtenten-turkish-corpus/
	Turkish corpus from the web (trWaC)	2012	2010	32 million	Sketch Engine	www.sketchengine.eu/trwac-turkish-corpus/
Asian languages						
Hebrew	Wikipedia 2013 Corpus	2003–2013	2013	100,000 articles	Israel Ministry for Science and Technology	https://mila.cs.technion.ac.il/resources_corpora_wikipedia_2013.html
	Hebrew General Corpus (HebrewGC)	2017	Modern times	150+ million	Hebrew University	www.sketchengine.eu/hebrewgc-hebrew-general-corpus/
	Hebrew web corpus (hebWaC)	2010	Modern times	47 million	Sketch Engine	www.sketchengine.eu/hebwac-hebrew-corpus/
Arabic	Buckwalter Arabic Corpus	2002	1986–2003	2.5–3 million	Tim Buckwalter	www.qamus.org/wordlist.htm
	ArabiCorpus	Not known	Not known	30 million	Brigham Young University	https://arabicorpus.byu.edu/
	Corpus of the Arabic Web (arTenTen)	2012	2012	5.8 billion	Masaryk University and Sketch Engine	www.sketchengine.eu/artenten-arabic-corpus/
Chinese	CCL (simplified Chinese)	Not known	Not known	477 million	Peking University	http://ccl.pku.edu.cn:8080/ccl_corpus/
	Chinese Treebank 8.0	2013	Not known	1.5 million	University of Pennsylvania	https://catalog.ldc.upenn.edu/LDC2013T21
	The Modern Chinese Language Corpus	2014	1919–2002	19 million	The National Languages Committee, *China*	http://corpus.zhonghuayuwen.org/
	Academia Sinica Tagged Corpus of Early Mandarin Chinese	2001	Ancient China	Not known	Academia Sinica	http://lingcorpus.iis.sinica.edu.tw/cgi-bin/kiwi/pkiwi/kiwi.sh?ukey=1672298496&qtype=-1
	BLCU Corpus	2019	Not known	15 billion characters	Beijing Language and Culture University	http://bcc.blcu.edu.cn/
	New Era People's Daily Segmented Corpus (NEPD)	2015–2018	2015–2018	35 million characters	Nanjing Agricultural University	http://corpus.njau.edu.cn/ (need to application for corpus downloading)

(Continued)

Table 31.1 (Continued)

Language	Title	Span of compilation	Span of data production	Size	Host institution	Website
Japanese	Balanced Corpus of Contemporary Written Japanese	2018	1976–2006	100 million	National Institute for Japanese Language (NIJLA), Communications Research Laboratory (CRL), and Tokyo Institute of Technology (TITech)	https://ccd.ninjal.ac.jp/bccwj/en/
	Japanese WebCorpus (jaTenTen)	2013	Not known	8 billion	Masaryk University and Sketch Engine	www.sketchengine.eu/jatenten-japanese-corpus/
	jpWaC Corpus	2009	Not known	300 million	Jožef Stefan Institute	www.sketchengine.eu/jpwac-japanese-corpus/
Korean	Korean National Corpus	2004	Post-1910	57 million (as of 2002)	The Ministry of Culture and Tourism	www.sejong.or.kr/gopage.php?svc=intro.eintro
	koTenTen 2018: Corpus of the Korean Web	2017–2018	Not known	1.7 billion	Masaryk University and Sketch Engine	www.sketchengine.eu/kotenten-korean-corpus/
	National Institute of the Korean Language Corpus	2005	Not known	80 million	National Institute of Korean Language	www.kaggle.com/rtatman/national-institute-of-the-korean-language-corpus
Malay	Malay Concordance Project	Not known	1770–1940	5.8 million	Australian National University	http://mcp.anu.edu.au/
	Malaysian Web (MalaysianWaC)	2010	2010	230 million	Masaryk University and Sketch Engine	www.sketchengine.eu/malaysianwac-malaysian-corpus/
Mongolian	The Multi-dialectal speech corpus of Mongolia (MDSCM)	2008	1998–2006	27 hours of speech	Waseda University and ATR of Japan	http://universal.elra.info/product_info.php?cPath=37_39&products_id=2222
	Mongolian Web Texts 2016 (mnWaC16)	2016	2016	6 million	Sketch Engine	www.sketchengine.eu/mongolian-wac-corpus/
Thai	Thai National Corpus	2007	Not known	80 million	Chulalongkorn university	www.arts.chula.ac.th/ling/tnc/
	HSE Thai Corpus	Not known	Not known	50 million		http://web-corpora.net/ThaiCorpus/search/
	Thai Literature Corpora (TLC)		Not known	59 million	Chulalongkorn University	https://attapol.github.io/tlc.html

Language	Corpus name			Size	Institution	URL
South Asian languages	EMILLE (Enabling Minority Language Engineering)	2019	2003	97 million	Lancaster University	www.emille.lancs.ac.uk/
Nepali	Nepali Grammar Project	2006	2004–2006	Not known	Lancaster University	www.lancs.ac.uk/staff/hardiea/nepali/index.php
Bengali	SHRUTI Bengali Continuous ASR Speech Corpus	Not known	Not known	22,012	Society for Natural Language Technology Research	http://cse.iitkgp.ac.in/~pabitra/shruti_corpus.html
	The Bangla webCorpus (bnWaC)	2010	Not known	11 million	Sketch Engine	www.sketchengine.eu/bnwac-bengali-corpus/
African languages						
Swahili	The Helsinki Corpus of Swahili (HCS)	2016	2004–2006	25 million	University of Helsinki	https://metashare.csc.fi/repository/browse/helsinki-corpus-of-swahili-20-hcs-20-annotated-version/232c1910b9eb11e5915e005056be118e59fb2e920f1f4c0cafc94915fc6f5cac/
	Leipzig Corpora Collection – Swahili	2017	2017	5 million	Leipzig University	https://corpora.uni-leipzig.de?corpusId=swa_community_2017
Zulu	Ukwabelana	2010	1995–2013	30,000 sentences	University of Bristol	www.cs.bris.ac.uk/Research/MachineLearning/Morphology/resources.jsp#corpus
	Leipzig Corpora Collection–Zulu	2017	2017	2 million	Leipzig University	https://corpora.uni-leipzig.de/en?corpusId=zul_community_2017
Amharic	Amharic corpus from the web (amWaC)	2016	2013–2017	210,000 words	Sketch Engine	www.sketchengine.eu/amwac-amharic-corpus/
	Amharic Speech Corpus	2014–2020	Not known	0.15 million	Addis Ababa University	http://tekstlab.uio.no/ethiopia/
	Amharic web corpus	2016	2013–2016	17 million	Sketch Engine	https://corpora.fi.muni.cz/habit/run.cgi/corp_info?corpname=amwac16
Somali	Corpus Somali WaC [2016]	2016	2016	79 million	Ministry of Education, Youth and Sports, Czech Republic	https://corpora.fi.muni.cz/habit/run.cgi/corp_info?corpname=sowac16
Tigrinya	Tigrinya WaC [2016]	2016	2016	2 million	Ministry of Education, Youth and Sports, Czech Republic	https://corpora.fi.muni.cz/habit/run.cgi/corp_info?corpname=tiwac16
Oromo	Oromo WaC [2016]	2016	2016	5 million	Ministry of Education, Youth and Sports, Czech Republic	https://corpora.fi.muni.cz/habit/run.cgi/corp_info?corpname=orwac16

meanings or target language equivalents directly. Corpora, or rather the concordance lines from the data, require translators' judgement to choose proper information to meet the needs of translation.

Cross-Linguistic Corpora for Translation

Cross-linguistic corpora are becoming increasingly available for a large number of languages and have been used for theoretical generalizations in a range of linguistic disciplines – from contrastive linguistics (Giugliano and Keith 2021; Granger 2010) to functional and cognitive linguistics (Croft 2010), todialectometry (Grieve *et al.* 2011), and neural machine translation (Duan *et al.* 2021; Islam *et al.* 2021). However, the most important use of translation corpora is for translation (Baker 1993, 1995). After three decades, it is quite common now for translation researchers to use corpora to verify, refine, or clarify theories that had little or no empirical support and to achieve a higher degree of descriptive adequacy. In recent years, translation corpora are commonly used datasets to train machine translation models. However, as in many new scientific fields, the terms of the cross-lingual corpus have not received general consensus leading to a great deal of confusion.

The field of translation turned to corpus when corpus linguistics began to thrive in the 1990s. Mona Baker initialized corpus-based translation studies (Baker 1993) and started building the Translational English Corpus (TEC) for studying translated English at the University of Manchester (see Baker 1999). The TEC corpus consists of written texts translated by native speakers of English from four genres: fiction, biography, newspaper articles, and in-flight magazines. The collection constantly expanded with fresh materials from a range of source languages and reached a total of 10 million words in 2003. The TEC corpus is freely available on the internet and has stimulated a number of publications on translation patterning of translated text and non-translated text in the same language and stylistic variation across individual translators.

As a comparatively new area, corpus-based translation study has not secured a chain of consistent terminology. Granger (2003) argues the confusion of the terms is caused by two different linguistic branches: translation studies (TS) and contrastive linguistics (CL). Translation researchers use the terms *translation corpus*, *parallel corpus*, and *comparable corpus* to refer to various types of cross-linguistic texts. The terms are used interchangeably and can be confusing. Contrastive linguists, according to Johansson and Hasselgård (1999) and Kenning (2010), have different definitions:

(1) *Translation corpora:* corpora consisting of original texts in one language and their translations into one or more other languages.
(2) *Comparable corpora:* consist of original texts in two or more languages, matched by criteria such as the time of composition, text category, intended audience, and so on. As with translation corpora, comparable corpora include texts of a wide range of genres, registers and historical periods.

The term *translation* (or *translational*) *corpus* refers to the corpus of translated texts (Baker 1999). Translational data conveys the same semantic content and therefore is an ideal resource for establishing equivalence, terminology, and phraseology between languages. Translation corpora may bear many extralinguistic features, such as the translator's status or the direction of the translation process. The main drawback of translation corpora, however, is that they can hardly have balanced genres. It is easy to get translation pairs of copyright-free texts such as documents from the UN, EU, or bilingual societies such as Hong Kong; some older masterpieces of literature; film transcripts; and standard company letters, most of which the source and target languages are hard to find, though source text is a major variable for translation studies. It is unlikely to collect bilingual email messages; internal and external communications are not usually translated. Accessing translated news reports is also rare, as news reporters mostly write in their own language. In addition, there are a few bi-directional translation corpora because the majority of translations are in one direction, such as from English to another language.

The term *parallel corpus* has been used to refer to different types of cross-linguistic corpora. In much early work, it is understood, in the broadest possible sense, as any collection of texts in different languages and language varieties conveying similar information produced under similar pragmatic conditions (Aijmer 2008). In recent studies, it refers to a translation (translational) corpus. (Aijmer and Lewis 2017; Kenning 2010). The ParaConc software designed by Barlow (2009) names translated texts as parallel corpora and has influenced many of its users; the users have to align the translated text at the sentence level, making it parallel, before using the software. According to Aijmer and Lewis (2017), the corpora embrace the feature of translation directions, thus being categorized as unidirectional (e.g. English texts and their translation in French) and bi-directional corpora (e.g. texts in English and the translation in Chinese, alongside texts in Chinese and the translation in English). Parallel corpora have been applied extensively in recent translation studies (Giugliano and Keith 2021; Kajzer-Wietrzny *et al.* 2021), since they include different language pairs. However, the limitation lies in small size and English as a dominant source language. It is thus necessary to use comparable corpora in translation research. A typical case is comparing seldom-translated lexicogrammatical and discourse items (Aijmer and Lewis 2017). In sum, parallel corpora are currently used interchangeably with translation corpora and employed sometimes in combination with comparable corpora.

Comparable corpora, according to Granger (2003) and Aijmer and Lewis (2017), are not translational. They represent original texts in different languages. Produced by native speakers of the languages under comparison, the texts are, in principle, free from the influence of other linguistic systems. In the case of translation corpora, the original source text is in a different language and will naturally impose some influence over the translated text. The main drawback of comparable corpora lies in the difficulty of establishing comparability of texts. Johansson and Hasselgård (1999) and Kenning (2010) mentioned time, categories, audience, genres, and time spans in comparable corpora but seemed to have overlooked an important item: theme. When compiling trilingual business corpora at Hong Kong Polytechnic University, we defined the three sub-corpora as thematically parallel, because the texts were collected at the same time in the same genre and had similar topics, although they were not translated texts. In an early article, Baker used *comparable corpus* to mean translation corpus: "the term *comparable corpus* is used to refer to 'two separate collections of texts in the same language: one corpus consists of original texts in the language in question and the other consists of translations in that language from a given source language or languages" (Baker 1995: 234). More recently, comparable and translation have been clearly distinguished by researchers. In short, comparable corpora are thematically parallel non-translational corpora.

To sum up, the term *translation* corpora has been explicitly defined, but *parallel* and *comparable* corpora may refer to any type of multilingual corpora, translational or non-translational. Granger (2003) attributes the difference to the two cross-linguistic approaches: comparative linguistics and translation studies. Apart from the terminological difference, she thinks there is a more fundamental discrepancy. In the TS framework, translated texts are considered texts in their own right, which are analysed in order to "understand what translation is and how it works" (Baker 1993: 243). It is added that translated texts are an elusive presence of the translator (Kenny 2008). In the CL framework, they are often presented as unreliable as the cross-linguistic similarities and differences that they help establish may be "distorted" by the translation process. This may be the

Table 31.2 Translation corpora

Corpus name	Languages	Span of compilation	Span of data production	Compiler	Link	Size	Coding
The English-Norwegian Parallel Corpus (ENPC)	English Norwegian	1997–2001	Not known	University of Oslo	www.hf.uio.no/ilos/english/services/knowledge-resources/omc/enpc/	100 English texts and 100 Norwegian texts aligned at the sentence level, in all approximately 2.6 million words	√ POS
Academia Sinica Balanced Corpus of Modern Chinese	Chinese English	1997–2010	Not known	Academia Sinica, Taiwan	http://godel.iis.sinica.edu.tw/CKIP/engversion/onlinesystem.htm	15 million	√
PELCRA Parallel Corpora	English Polish	1997–2013	Not known	University of Łódź Lancaster University	http://pelcra.pl/new/engpol_18	40 million English and 35 million Polish words	Not known
Parallel Corpus Project: The Bible	12 languages	1999	Not known	University of Maryland	www.umiacs.umd.edu/~resnik/parallel/bible.html	Not known	√ according to the Corpus Encoding Standard
Babel Chinese-English Parallel Corpus	Chinese English	2001–2004	Not known	Institute of Computational Linguistics, Peking University	www.icl.pku.edu.cn/icl_groups/parallel/default.htm	544,095 words	√
MLCC Multilingual and Parallel Corpora	9 European languages	2005	1986–1994	European Language Resources Association	http://catalog.elra.info/product_info.php?products_id=764	Not known	Not known
Hunglish Corpus Version 2.0	Hungish English	2005–2013	Not known	Budapest University of Technology and Economics; Hungarian Academy of Sciences Institute of Linguistics	http://mokk.bme.hu/resources/hunglishcorpus/	120 million	Not known
The BAF corpus	English French	2006	Not known	University of Montreal campus	http://rali.iro.umontreal.ca/rali/?q=fr/BAF	0.4 million words in each language	Not known

Corpus	Languages	Year	Date range	Institution	URL	Size	Annotation
The ZJU Corpus of Translational Chinese (ZCTC)	English Chinese	2008	1991–2001	Lancaster University	www.lancaster.ac.uk/fass/projects/corpus/ZCTC/	1 million words	√ annotated using ICTCLAS 2008
An English-Inuktitut Parallel Corpus	Inuktitut-English	2008	1999–2007	Institute for information technology, Canada	www.inuktitutcomputing.ca/NunavutHansard/en/index-VX.html	3,432,212 English words; 1,586,423 Inuktitut words	Not known
Urdu-Nepali-English Parallel Corpus	Urdu Nepali English	2009	Not known	Center for Research in Urdu Language Processing (CRULP)	www.cle.org.pk/software/ling_resources/UrduNepaliEnglishParallelCorpus.htm	100,000 words	√, POS
MultiUN: Multilingual UN Parallel Text 2000–2009	English French Spanish Arabic Russian Chinese German	2011	2000–2009	Language Technology Lab in DFKI GmbH (LT-DFKI), Germany	www.euromatrixplus.net/multi-un/	Not known	Not known
The Kyoto Free Translation Task (KFTT)	English Japanese	2011–2012	Not known	Nara Institute of Science and Technology (NAIST); Kyoto University	www.phontron.com/kftt/	Not known	√
IDENTIC	Indonesia English	2011–2012	Not known	Charles University in Prague	http://ufal.mff.cuni.cz/~larasati/identic/#Introduction	Not known	√, see http://ufal.mff.cuni.cz/~larasati/identic/annotation.html
CzEng 2.0 (Czech-English Parallel Corpus, version 2.0)	English Czech	2011	Not known	Institute of Formal and Applied Linguistics (ÚFAL)	http://ufal.mff.cuni.cz/czeng/czeng1 https://ufal.mff.cuni.cz/czeng	233 million English and 206 million Czech tokens	√
CLUVI Parallel Corpus	Galician English French Spanish	2012	Not known	Universidade de Vigo. Grupo de investigación TALG	http://repositori.upf.edu/handle/10230/20051	23 million	Not known

(Continued)

Table 31.2 (Continued)

Corpus name	Languages	Span of compilation	Span of data production	Compiler	Link	Size	Coding
The Babel English-Chinese Parallel Corpus	Chinese English	2012	2000–2001	Lancaster University	http://114.251.154.212/cqp/ ID and password: test	121,493 English tokens and 135,493 Chinese tokens	√ POS and aligned at the sentence level
European Parliament Proceedings Parallel Corpus (Europarl)	21 European languages	2012	1996–2011	EuroMatrixPlus	www.statmt.org/europarl/	Around 60 million words per language	√ Processed with TreeTagger tool
BangorTalk	Welsh English Spanish intermediate	2013–2019	Not known	University of Wales Bangor	http://bangortalk.org.uk/	0.9 million words	√ annotated using the CHAT and CLAN applications
DGT-Translation Memory	24 European languages	2014	Not known	The European Commission	www.sketchengine.eu/dgt-translation-memory/	Not known	Not known
English–Nepali Parallel Corpus	English Nepali	2014	Not known	ELRA (European Language Resources Association)	https://catalog.elra.info/en-us/repository/browse/ELRA-W0077/	27,060 English words; 21,756 Nepali words	Not known
QTLP English-Greek Corpus for the MEDICAL domain	English Greek	2014	Not known	Common Language Resources and Technology Infrastructure	http://qt21.metashare.ilsp.gr/repository/browse/qtlp-english-greek-corpus-for-the-medical-domain/665f3832a93211e3b7d8000155dbc02011906d5402fc4d3b497aa9dcd7a4892/	62,452 pairs of sentences	Not known

Name	Languages	Year	Date range	Source	URL	Size	Annotation
The Europarl parallel corpus (DCEP)	21 European languages	2015	2007–2011	A list of universities involved in EuroMatrixPlus Project	www.sketchengine.eu/europarl-parallel-corpus/	60 million per language	√ POS
United Nations Parallel Corpus	Arabic, Chinese, English, French, Russian and Spanish	2015	1990–2014	United Nations	https://conferences.unite.un.org/UNCORPUS/en/DownloadOverview#download	98 million, 19 million per language	Not known
TED speeches (TCSE)	29 languages	2015	Not known	Yoichiro Hasebe at Doshisha University	https://yohasebe.com/tcse/	1000 talks	√ POS
German-French website parallel corpus	German French	2015	2013–2015	Federal Foreign Office Berlin, EU	https://data.europa.eu/data/datasets/elrc_42?locale=en	11,852 pairs	Not known
The EUR-Lex Corpus	24 official languages of the European Union	2016	1958–2016	European Union	www.sketchengine.eu/eurlex-corpus/#toggle-id-1	12 billion	√
The EUR-Lex judgments corpus	23 languages	2016	Around 2000	European Union	www.sketchengine.eu/eurlex-judgments-corpus/	Not known	Not known
English-Czech Corpus from Wikipedia	English Czech	2016	Not known	Masaryk University	https://lindat.mff.cuni.cz/repository/xmlui/handle/11234/1-1932	7.5 million words	Not known
OPUS2 parallel corpus	40 languages	2017	Not known	Jörg Tiedemann	https://opus.nlpl.eu/	Not known	√
Korean-English parallel corpus	Korean English	2017	2010–2011	University of Ulsan	https://sites.google.com/site/koreanparalleldata/	96,982 sentences	Not known
THUMT	English Chinese	2017–2018	Not known	Tsing Hua University	http://thumt.thunlp.org/#Introduction	2.85 million pairs of sentences	Not known
TRAD Chinese French Parallel Text	French Chinese	2018	Not known	Linguistic Data Consortium, ELDA	https://catalog.ldc.upenn.edu/LDC2018T17	33,571 Chinese characters and French reference translation contains 22,424 words	Not known

result of interference from the source texts (Granger 2003: 34). About the caveat of translated texts, Aijmer and Lewis (2017) construe that social-cultural institutions and practices between SL and TL cannot be precisely identical. The "equivalent" can be routinely applied in different genres between two or more languages. Despite the discrepancies, recent years have witnessed linguists use different types of parallel corpora and employ new methodological approaches to cross-linguistic studies quantitatively and qualitatively. Corpus translation studies have been enriched with more empirical methods after a long reign of generative approaches to lexicogram-mar and largely intuitive judgement on grammaticality and lexicality (Wulff and Gries 2011).

Quantitative and Qualitative Research in Corpus-Based Translation Study

The application of the corpus approach has enabled the interplay of quantitative and qualitative methodologies used in translation studies, based on the concept that "linguistic system as well as idiolectal uses is commensurable to a degree" (Lakoff 1987). Many different quantitative and qualitative methods have been used in translation studies, but they are largely tentative with limited construction and testing methods for theoretic models of translation, which in turn has hindered the expansion of the field (Oakes and Ji 2012: vii).

Things have changed in recent years. Quantitative methods are preceded from the research-er's ideas and hypotheses about observed dimensions to calculable and measurable parameters. Frequency occurrence of a language form, its combinations with other items in discourse as well as patterns of semantic similarity, oppositeness and inclusion all contribute to a language specific character of SL and TL forms. In her report on the interplay of quantitative and qualitative analysis of Polish and English cross-lingual corpora, Lewandowska-Tomaszczyk (2012) proposed general methods to conduct the explanatory analysis in translation studies:

1   Comparison of two or more translations of an original text (to study stylistic differences);
2   A comparison of translation and monolingual corpora in the same languages as the transla-tion (to study linguistic features of the translation as compared to the reference text in the same language as the translation).

(Lewandowska-Tomaszczyk 2012: 4)

Lewandowska-Tomaszczyk clearly described how lexical profiles of the TL and SL can be compared, how the keyness of certain grammatical patterns can be generated with a large refer-ence corpus of the same language, and how collocation patterns of TL and SL can be presented statistically. The typology of translational quantitative criteria of resemblance in two languages is summarised in Table 31.3.

Table 31.3 The typology of translational quantitative criteria of resemblance

i. Frequencies of occurrence of lexical units
ii. Keyness
iii. Frequencies of syntactic patterns (complex/simple constructions, sentence types and sentence patterns)
iv. Frequencies of classes of lexical-semantic patterns
v. Frequencies of types of figurative extensions (frequency of Source Domain and Target Domain patterns)
vi. Quantitative cross-correspondence of concepts from the same conceptual cluster
vii. Distributional criteria

(Lewandowska-Tomaszczyk 2012:32)

Statistical analysis of translation texts has revealed some interesting findings. The first aspect of studies explores lexico-grammatical features in literary translation. Ji and Oakes (2012) compared three versions of early English translations of *Honglongmeng*, a masterpiece of Chinese literature, and demonstrated in detail that "a set of bivariate statistics, commonly used for the comparison of corpora, can be applied in translation studies" (176). The statistical analysis of sentence length, positive and negative emotional words, value words, idioms, and phrases used, presents stylistic differences of the translators, showing that "text and linguistic features can be demonstrated by the validity and productivity of statistics in the study of translation corpora" (Ibid, p. 206). More recently, Giugliano and Keith (2021) identified the relationship between three repetitive patterns in the novel *The Years* and two early Catalan translations carried out by Maria-Antònia Oliver. It was found that the translator used more translation variations when the repetition is shorter and frequently occurring. Nevertheless, Oliver keeps very close to the source text when translating long phrases and sentences with prominent stylistic features of the novelist.

The second aspect of quantitative CTS focuses on the interplay between translation and sociolinguistics. There is research on translations and national images, democratic campaigns, and so on. The national image in translation is commonly explored by parallel concordance analysis. Turzynski-Azimi (2021) found strong domestication in translating culture-specific items in Japanese tourism texts. Non-lexicalized borrowing is frequent in the discourse of Japanese history and food. Li and Pan (2021) compared Chinese political discourse and the English translation published by the Chinese government, drawing on appraisal system. What is striking in the findings is a less positive construction of China in TL than SL, which suits a governing principle of Chinese diplomacy. Regarding the democratic campaign, Jones (2020) explored the revelation of Jowett's democratic stance in his 1881 translation of Thucydides using keyword analysis. It is claimed that the translation highlights hierarchical divisions in Greek democracy, echoing his political viewpoint.

While quantitative research investigates relations between a few variables in larger samples, qualitative research deals with relations between many variables that can be investigated in smaller samples. Qualitative study is based on interpretations of resemblance between the concepts presented in the original SL and TL translation from the experiences, actions, and observations of individuals. The key skill in this new area, according to Sinclair is "to be able to interrogate the corpus efficiently – to ask the right sort of questions, to refine the first responses and to control the retrieval process so as to reveal the way in which meaning and pattern interact in text" (2003: 3). These activities also need support from various computer programs.

Multilingual computer tools can work on different corpora concurrently and generate bilingual or multilingual concordance lines at the same time. Some commonly used multilingual tools for non-computer scientists are Multi-Concord (Woolls 2002), AntPConc, (Anthony 2017), ParaConc (Barlow 2009), and Sketch Engine (Lexical Computing Limited 2021). ParaConc and is a bilingual or multilingual concordancers that can be used with translated texts in contrastive analyses, language learning, and translation studies. The ParaConc website shows that since its birth in 1990, it has been used at a variety of institutions for about 16 language pairs, such as English–Arabic, English–Chinese, English–French, English–Japanese, English–Korean, English–Russian, and so forth. Sketch Engine is a corpus manager and text analysis software. It contains many mega parallel corpora listed in Table 31.2, such as Europarl, Euro-Lex, and OPUS. A parallel concordance tool in the software helps users to search for the translation of items in context.

Computer software can generate paralleled concordance lines in both SL and TL, but it cannot explain them. Analysing and interpreting keywords in context cannot be conducted completely without human intelligence. The linguistic approaches to corpus study by John Sinclair may also apply to translation studies. The five co-selections are the core, collocation, colligation, semantic prosody, and semantic preference. Collocations are word relations. They are "the co-occurrence of words with no more than four intervening words" (Sinclair 2004: 34). Colligational patterns are lexicogrammatical realizations and are relations between words and grammatical categories. Semantic preference is "the restriction of regular co-occurrence to items which share a semantic feature, e.g. about sport or suffering" (ibid, p. 141). Semantic prosody is the relation between words and lexical sets and refers to a particular attitude or a particular point of view of a writer. Sinclair explains that "the initial choice of semantic prosody is the functional choice which links meaning to purpose; all subsequent choices within the lexical item relate back to the prosody" (ibid, p. 34). In other words, it is the semantic prosody selected by the speaker or writer that determines the semantic preference. The semantic preference then determines the collocational and colligational patterns. The five linguistic parameters can help establish textual profiles of both source language and target language and further categorize the text's function and its communicative purposes.

Corpus analysis enables translators to compare the original text and the translated text with a number of criteria, namely perceptual, functional, emotional, axiological, ideological, logical, and associative (Lewandowska-Tomaszczyk 2012: 32). To realize these goals, the choice of qualitative and/or quantitative methods has to be taken in line with particular research questions. Both methods have advantages and limitations, but each can contribute to translation in a different manner. In practice, translators and researchers have to use combined approach: qualitative data are in many cases also annotated and counted, and quantitative data are interpreted and explained. There is no universally "best way" to combine methods.

Topics of Corpus Approach in Translation Studies

Translation memories and statistical machine translation have changed the way translated texts are generated. Improved alignment techniques at the word, phrase, and sentence level provide increasingly important resources for the proper use of both source language and target language. At the same time, theoretical and descriptive corpus-based research has investigated topics such as translation universals (Baker 1996; Laviosa 2002; Mauranen and Kujamäk 2004), translation ideology (Li and Pan 2021; Jones 2020; Turzynski-Azimi 2021), translator style (Baker 2000; Burrows 2002, 2007; Giugliano and Keith 2021; Rybicki 2012), and translated/interpreted language (Granger 2003; Ji and Oakes 2012).

The corpus approach can investigate translation universals in that large amount of data can better represent linguistic features of a particular language than individuals' intuitive judgements. Despite the argument on whether translation is universal across different languages (Hu 2016), research has proved some universal features in translation such as simplification, convergency, explicitation, disambiguation, over-representation, and conservatism. Baker defines simplification as "a translator's attempt to make things easier for the reader, but not necessarily more explicit" (Baker 1996: 182). Laviosa-Braithwaite's study showed that simplification has at least three types: syntactic, stylistic, and lexical, making translated texts simpler and easier to understand than non-translated texts (Laviosa-Braithwaite 1997: 533). In view of convergence, universal, translated texts are found to be more similar to each other than non-translated texts (Mauranen and Kujamak 2004). Explicitation indicates that some translated texts avoid extremes in translation and may generate a target language text with many more redundancies (Laviosa 2008; Moropa 2011). Additionally, there is another categorization of translation universals that help to explain linguistic features in translated texts. S-universals refer to divergences between translated and the source texts, whereas T-universals are understood as differences between translated and the comparable non-translated texts in TL (Laviosa 2008). Baker summarized that universal features can be seen as a product of constraints which are inherent in the translation process itself, and this accounts for the fact that they are universal. They do not vary across cultures. Other features have been observed to occur consistently in certain types of translation within a particular socio-cultural and historical context.

(1993: 246)

The manifestation of ideology in translation has become an increasingly important issue in translation studies. According to Baker (2006), translation ideology aims to contribute to the broader discussion of a set of ideas, beliefs, and codes of behaviour that govern a community. Some translation studies have compared ideological phenomena such as group interest, dominance, and power relations in source and target language (Petrescu 2009; Li and Pan 2021; Mac Giolla Chríost *et al.* 2016). Others are more interested in the phenomenon of how translators implant their own viewpoints in translated texts (Jones 2020; Turzynski-Azimi 2021). Not only questions of politics but also reflections upon gender, sexuality, religion, secularity, and technology provide a strong argument that such diversity of perspectives is highly desirable for good translation.

Translation style deals with a number of measurable features of style such as sentence length, vocabulary richness and various frequencies of words, word lengths and word forms, and so on. There are numerous applications in authorship attribution research. Statistical analysis of conscious and unconscious elements of personal style can help detect the true author of an anonymous text, which means stylistic fingerprints can betray the plagiarist with more or less sophisticated statistical methods (Rybicki 2012). Burrows (2002) applied z-scores to establish a Delta system to evaluate the differences between the most frequent words in two corpora. The system, while the accuracy is challenged (Hoover 2004; Rybicki 2012), was used as a simple and intuitively reasonable method for traceable differences between texts. Additionally, a bulk of stylistic research focuses on authorship in literary translation. The aforementioned study discussed the translation strategies of a novelist's use of repetitions (Giugliano and Keith 2021). Likewise, by analysing the Dutch translation of *One Flew over the Cuckoo's Nest*, Dorst (2019) argues that translating metaphors and mind styles are not straightforward. The sacrifice of metaphors helps to maintain stylistic coherence.

Corpora form a basis in machine language translation. Corpora are databases in machine translation studies, while the research foci lie in developing algorithms and models that allow computers to automatically produce quality translated texts. In the studies, parallel corpora are desirable but not available for all languages. Researchers instead employ pseudo parallel corpora (Imankulova *et al.* 2020; Zin *et al.* 2021) and non-related monolingual corpora (Marie and Fujita 2018) and compile parallel corpora for machine language translation (Seresangtakul and Unlee 2019). Corpora are also essential to machine translation services in the current market, such as the Europarl corpus in Google Translate and Linguee (a multilingual corpus) in DeepL.

Conclusions

The rapid growth of data and technology innovation has made corpora a convenient tool for translation professionals and translation students. The main benefits of corpora in translation are summarized by Granger (2003) as a great resource for content information, terminology, phraseology, a large quantity and good coverage of genres and texts, and improved operation of retrieving linguistic and contextual information. While the success of machine translation systems relies on automation and data quantity, descriptive applications rely on manual analysis and data quality. The availability of suitable tools and resources are key to corpus-based translation studies, but user-friendly tools and balanced translation corpora are yet to be produced. Given that the necessary steps to prepare corpus may be technically complex or time consuming in terms of manual labour required, it is necessary for those with technical expertise, such as programmers and computational linguists, to team up with linguists and translation scholars who are willing to contribute their time and efforts with corpus texts.

As Granger noticed, "many corpus-based descriptive translation investigations suffer from a piecemeal, fragmentary and tentative approach; the variety of data sets, methods and tools used do not combine into a single overall framework and the results are often hardly commensurable" (2003: 22). In order to improve the quality of resources and make them available and accessible and realize the fuller potential of corpus linguistic methodologies, scholars of corpus-based translation studies need high-quality, easy-to-use linguistic resources and tools to bridge the gap between source language and target language.

Bibliography

Ädel, A. (2020) 'Corpus Compilation', in M. Paquot and S. T. Gries (eds.) *A Practical Handbook of Corpus Linguistics*, Cham: Springer, 3–24.

Aijmer, K. (2008) *English Discourse Particles: Evidence from a Corpus*, Amsterdam and Philadelphia: John Benjamins Publishing Company.

Aijmer, K. (2021) "'That's Well Good"': A Re-emergent Intensifier in Current British English', *Journal of English Linguistics* 49(1): 18–38.

Aijmer, K. and D. Lewis (2017) 'Introduction', in K. Aijmer and D. Lewis (eds.) *Contrastive Analysis of Discourse-Pragmatic Aspects of Linguistic Genres*, Cham: Springer, 1–13.

Anthony, L. (2017) 'AntPConc (Version 1.2.1)' [Computer Software]. Available at: www.laurenceanthony.net/software/antpconc/.

Baker, M. (1993) 'Corpus Linguistics and Translation Studies. Implications and Applications', in M. Baker, G. Francis, and E. Tognini-Bonelli (eds.) *Text and Technology*, Amsterdam and Philadelphia: John Benjamins Publishing Company, 233–50.

Baker, M. (1995) 'Corpora in Translation Studies: An Overview and Some Suggestions for Future Research', *Target* 7(2): 223–43.

Baker, M. (1996) 'Corpus-based Translation Studies: The Challenge that Lies Ahead', in H. Somers (ed.) *Terminology, LSP, and Translation: Studies in Language Engineering*, Amsterdam and Philadelphia: John Benjamins Publishing Company, 175–88.

Baker, M. (1999) 'The Role of Corpora in Investigating the Linguistic Behaviour of Professional Translators', *International Journal of Corpus Linguistics* 4(2): 281–98.

Baker, M. (2000) 'Towards a Methodology for Investigating the Style of a Literary Translator', *Target* 12(2): 241–66.

Baker, M. (2006) *Translation and Conflict: A Narrative Account*, London and New York: Routledge.

Barlow, M. (2009) 'Contrastive Patterns Contrastive Patterns Patterns Contrastive Patterns Contrastive'. Available at: https://paraconc.com/

Biber, D., S. Conrad, and R. Reppen (1998) *Corpus Linguistics: Investigating Language Structure and Use*, Cambridge: Cambridge University Press.

Bowker, S. (1999) 'The Design and Development of a Corpus-based Aid for Assessing Translations', *Teanga* 18: 11–24.

Brookes, G. and T. McEnery (2020) 'Corpus Linguistics', in S. Adolphs and D. Knight (eds.) *The Routledge Handbook of English Language and Digital Humanities*, London and New York: Routledge, 378–404.

Burrows, J. (2002) "'Delta": A Measure of Stylistic Difference and a Guide to Likely Authorship', *Literary and Linguistic Computing* 17: 267–87.

Burrows, J. (2007) 'All the Way Through: Testing for Authorship in Difference Strata', *Literary and Linguistic Computing* 22: 27–47.

Croft, W. (2010) 'Language Structure in Its Human Context: New Directions for the Language Sciences in the Twenty-First Century', in P. Hogan (ed.) *Cambridge Encyclopedia of the Language Sciences*, Cambridge: Cambridge University Press, 1–11

Culpeper, J. and M. Gillings (2018) 'Politeness Variation in England: A North-South Divide?', in V. Brezina, R. Love, and K. Aijmer (eds.) *Corpus Approaches Contemporary British Speech: Social Linguistic Studies of the Spoken BNC2014*, London and New York: Routledge, 55–89.

Dorst, A. G. (2019) 'Translating Metaphorical Mind Style: Machinery and Ice Metaphors in Ken Kesey's *One Flew Over the Cuckoo's Nest*', *Perspectives: Studies in Translation Theory and Practice* 27(6): 875–89.

Duan, G., H. Yang, K. Qin, and T. X. Huang (2021) 'Improving Neural Machine Translation Model with Deep Encoding Information', *Cognitive Computation* 1.

Giugliano, M. and V. A. Keith (2021) 'Repetition and Variation in the Catalan Translation of Virginia Woolf's the Years: A Corpus-Based Approach', *Perspectives: Studies in Translation Theory and Practice* 30(2): 242–57.

Granger, S. (2003) 'The Corpus Approach: A Common Way Forward for Contrastive Linguistics and Translation Studies?', in S. Granger, J. Lerot, and S. Petch-Tyson (eds.) *Corpus-based Approaches to Contrastive Linguistics and Translation Studies*, Amsterdam and Atlanta: Rodopi, 17–28.

Granger, S. (2010) 'Comparable and Translation Corpora in Cross-linguistic Research. Design, Analysis and Applications', *Journal of Shanghai Jiaotong University* 2: 14–21.

Grieve, J., D. Speelman, and D. Geeraerts (2011) 'A Statistical Method for the Identification and Aggregation of Regional Linguistic Variation', *Language Variation and Change* 23: 193–221.

Hoover, D. (2004) 'Testing Burrows's Delta', *Literary and Linguistic Computing* 19(4): 453–75.

Hu, K. B. (2016) *Introducing Corpus-based Translation Studies*, Shanghai, London, and New York: Shanghai Jiaotong University Presss and Springer.

Imankulova, A., T. Sato, and M. Komachi (2020) 'Filtered Pseudo-parallel Corpus Improves Low-resource Neural Machine Translation', *ACM Transactions on Asian and Low-Resource Language Information Processing* 19(2): 1–16.

Islam, M. A., M. S. H. Anik, and A. B. M. A. A. Islam (2021) 'Towards Achieving a Delicate Blending Between Rule-Based Translator and Neural Machine Translator', *Neural Computing and Applications*: 1–27.

Ji, M. and M. Oakes (2012) 'A Corpus Study of Early English Translations of Cao Xueqin's Hongloumeng', in M. Oakes and M. Ji (eds.) *Quantitative Methods in Corpus-based Translation Studies: A Practical Guide to Descriptive Translation Research*, Amsterdam and Philadelphia: John Benjamins Publishing Company, 177–208.

Johansson, S. and H. Hasselgård (1999) 'Corpora and Cross-Linguistic Research in the Nordic Countries', in S. Granger *et al.* (eds.) *Contrastive Linguistics and Translation*, Amsterdam and Atlanta: Rodopi, 145–62.

John, P., B. Brooks, and U. Schriever (2017) 'Profiling Maritime Communication by Non-Native Speakers: A Quantitative Comparison Between the Baseline and Standard Marine Communication Phraseology', *English for Specific Purposes* 47: 1–14.

Jones, H. (2020) 'Jowett's Thucydides: A Corpus-Based Analysis of Translation as Political Intervention', *Translation Studies* 13(3): 333–51.

Kajzer-Wietrzny, M., I. Ivaska, and A. Ferraresi (2021) '"Lost" in Interpreting and "Found" in Translation: Using an Intermodal, Multidirectional Parallel Corpus to Investigate the Rendition of Numbers', *Perspectives: Studies in Translation Theory and Practice* 29(4): 469–88.

Kenning, M. M. (2010) 'What Are Parallel and Comparable Corpora and How Can We Use Them?', in A. Anne O'Keeffe and M. McCarthy (eds.) *The Routledge Handbook of Corpus Linguistics*, London and New York: Routledge, 487–500.

Kenny, D. (2001) *Lexis and Creativity in Translation: A Corpus-Based Study*, Manchester: St. Jerome.

Kenny, D. (2008) 'Corpora', in B. Mona and G. Saldanha (eds.) *Routledge Encyclopedia of Translation Studies*, London and New York: Routledge, 59–62.

Kucera, H., and W. N. Francis (1967). *Computational Analysis of Presentday American English*. RI: Brown University Press.

Lakoff, G. (1987) *Women, Fire and Dangerous Things: What Categories Reveal about the Mind*, Chicago: Chicago University Press.

Laviosa, S. (2002) *Corpus-based Translation Studies. Theory, Findings, Applications*, Amsterdam and New York: Rodopi.

Laviosa, S. (2008) 'Universals', in M. Baker and G. Saldanha (eds.) *Routledge Encyclopedia of Translation Studies*, London and New York: Routledge, 306–10.

Laviosa-Braithwaite, S. (1997) 'Investing Simplification in an English Comparable Corpus of Newspaper Articles', in K. Klaudy and J. Kohn (eds.) *Transferre Necesse Est. Proceedings of the 2nd International Conference on Current Trends in Studies of Translation and Interpreting*, Budapest: Scholastica, 531–40.

Leech, G. (1992) '100 Million Words of English: The British National Corpus (BNC)', *Language Research* 28(1): 1–13.

Lewandowska-Tomaszczyk, B. (2012) 'Explicit and Tacit an Interplay of the Quantitative and Qualitative Approaches to Translation', *Studies in Corpus Linguistics* 51: 3–34.

Lexical Computing Limited (2021) 'Sketch Engine'. Available at: www.sketchengine.eu/.

Li, T. and F. Pan (2021) 'Reshaping China's Image: A Corpus-based Analysis of the English Translation of Chinese Political Discourse', *Perspectives: Studies in Translation Theory and Practice* 29(3): 354–70.

Mac Giolla Chríost, D., P. Carlin, and C. H. Williams (2016) 'Translating y Cofnod: Translation Policy and the Official Status of the Welsh Language in Wales', *Translation Studies* 9(2): 212–27.

Marie, B. and A. Fujita (2018) 'Phrase Table Induction Using Monolingual Data for Low-Resource Statistical Machine Translation', *ACM Transactions on Asian and Low-Resource Language Information Processing* 17(3): 1–25.

Mauranen, A. and P. Kujamäk (eds.) (2004) *Translation Universals: Do They Exist?* Amsterdam and Philadelphia: John Benjamins Publishing Company.

Moropa, K. (2011) 'A Link Between Simplification and Explicitation in English-Xhosa Parallel Texts: Do the Morphological Complexities of Xhosa Have an Influence?', in A. Kruger, K. Wallmach, and J. Munday (eds.) *Corpus-based Translation Studies: Research and Applications*, London: Continuum, 259–81.

Oakes, M. and M. Ji (eds.) (2012) *Quantitative Methods in Corpus-based Translation Studies: A Practical Guide to Descriptive Translation Research*, Amsterdam and Philadelphia: John Benjamins Publishing Company.

Pearson, J. (1996) 'Electronic Texts and Concordances in the Translation Classroom', *Teanga* 16: 85–95.

Petrescu, C. (2009) 'Translation and Ideology', *Professional Communication and Translation Studies* 2(1–2): 93–96.

Quirk, R., S. Greenbaum, G. Leech, and J. Svartvik (1985) *A Comprehensive Grammar of the English Language*, London: Longman.

Rybicki, J. (2012) 'The Great Mystery of the Invisible Translator: Stylometry in Translation', in M. Oakes and M. Ji (eds.) *Quantitative Methods in Corpus-based Translation Studies: A Practical Guide to Descriptive Translation Research*, Amsterdam and Philadelphia: John Benjamins Publishing Company, 231–58.

Seresangtakul, P. and P. Unlee (2019) 'Thai-Isarn Dialect Parallel Corpus Construction for Machine Translation', in *2019 11th International Conference on Knowledge and Smart Technology (KST)*, IEEE, 121–25. Available at: https://ieeexplore.ieee.org/document/8687534.

Sinclair, J. (1991) *Corpus, Concordance, Collocation*, Oxford: Oxford University Press.

Sinclair, J. (2003) *Reading Concordances: An Introduction*, Harlow: Pearson and Longman.

Sinclair, J. (2004) *Trust the Text*, London: Routledge.

Tognini-Bonelli, E. (2001) *Corpus Linguistics at Work*, Amsterdam and Philadelphia: John Benjamins Publishing Company.

Turzynski-Azimi, A. (2021) 'Constructing the Image of Japan as a Tourist Destination: Translation Procedures for Culture-specific Items', *Perspectives: Studies in Translation Theory and Practice* 29(3): 407–25.

Wallis, S., and G. Nelson (2001) 'Knowledge Discovery in Grammatically Analysed Corpora', *Data Mining and Knowledge Discovery* 5: 305–35.

Woolls, D. (2002) 'Multiconcord: The Lingua Multilingual Parallel Concordancer for Windows'. Available at: http://artsweb.bham.ac.uk/pking/multiconc/l_text.htm.

Wulff, S., and S. T. Gries (2011) 'Corpus-driven Methods for Assessing Accuracy in Learner Production', in P. Rovinson (ed.) *Second Language Task Complexity: Researching the Cognition Hypothesis of Language Learning and Performance*, Philadelphia, PA: John Benjamins Publishing Company, 61–87.

Zin, M., T. Racharak, and N. Le (2021) 'Construct-Extract: An Effective Model for Building Bilingual Corpus to Improve English-Myanmar Machine Translation', *Proceedings of the 13th International Conference on Agents and Artificial Intelligence* (2): 333–42. Available at: https://pdfs.semanticscholar.org/e5ac/9a53aaeb9c3561def6b5428bd9d281ec3c97.pdf.

32

EDITING IN TRANSLATION TECHNOLOGY

Christophe Declercq

Language and Translation Technology

With the emergence of translation memory technology in the early to mid-1990s,[1] the translation profession underwent a true technological turn that had been eagerly awaited by those working on machine translation systems since the 1950s. At the core of the translation memory systems (TMSs) was a database of human translations, aided by the machine: machine-aided human translation (MAHT) or computer-aided translation (CAT). With the segment-based approach of re-use of previously translated material, traditional concepts and workflows changed dramatically too. Other than language skills and writing abilities, translation of texts included an increasing use of computer technology. Processes such as editing, revision and proof-reading should follow suit, but to date translators are struggling to cope with the speed of translation technology uptake.[2]

In the last few years, that uptake has assumed the shape of machine translation (MT), especially statistical machine translation (SMT), which has taken the translation industry by storm. Yet, it would not be accurate to brand MT as new. In fact, MT is into its seventh decade. Nonetheless, deeply rooted reservations about quality output of translation engines remain commonplace among translators. Yet that scepticism among many translators is overcome by the daily dependency of millions of users on Google Translate or Microsoft's Bing Translator and by the incorporation of thousands of customized translation engines the world over.

An in-depth analysis of 'editing and translation today' therefore not only looks into the more traditional workflow of using a translation memory (TM) and its processes of verification such as editing and proof-reading but also looks into the emerging convergence of translation technology (in particular translation memories) and language technology (especially machine translation).[3] This merging movement becomes clear from any description of the term translation technology. Translation technology (TT) concerns the applied use of any computer application that supports the translation process as performed by a human translator (HT). But even then the description is flawed as any machine translation output for each no match in a translation project that is performed in a translation memory system is in fact language technology (LT), human language generated automatically by a computer system.

As no clear delineation can be established between translation technology and language technology,[4] this chapter therefore aims to include any automated means of facilitating

DOI: 10.4324/9781003168348-35

productivity and/or quality of human translation. The following overview will therefore provide an insight into 21st-century translation whereby the benefits of technology at the disposal of translators lies in the balance with a further acceptance of post-editing both TM and MT output.

'Traditional' Translation Technology and Editing

Traditional translation technology has at its core the translation memory system and is likely to be supported further with a terminology database.[5] The TM application which re-uses segments that matches previously translated material has also been described as machine-aided human translation, computer-aided translation or translation environment tools (TEnTs). Whatever the acronym and whatever the definition of a TMS, besides re-use of previously translated segments (or translation units), a key feature is often overlooked by translators themselves: TM systems allow translators to deal with complex file formats they have not necessarily mastered themselves.[6] They receive and deliver files in their native formats without interfering with the underlying code such as cross-references or mark-up language.[7] Typical material concerns FrameMaker or InDesign but also DITA XML or Microsoft .NET files. As such, a main benefit of any TMS is that it allows translators to translate and edit much more material than in any typical word processing environments. With the translation interface, the user interface of any TM environment in which translators visually see the text on screen as they edit it (Biau Gil 2007), translating and editing also converge.

Not all types of matches from a TM occur in just any translation project. In Figure 32.1, the fourth and last segment still need translating from scratch, and no source was copied across there. All the 100% matches are re-used from the TM. Whether the perfect matches need editing should depend on the quality of the TM results, the formatting and quality assurance settings, the project requirements and the experience of the translator. However, this is often limited to contractual obligations that urge the translator not to alter any perfect match. Note that the named entities make up about 35% of the overall word count. Copying across the source segments with added shortcut expertise to be jumping across words in the target segment most certainly constitutes an increase in productivity (especially for this text type, i.e. sports).

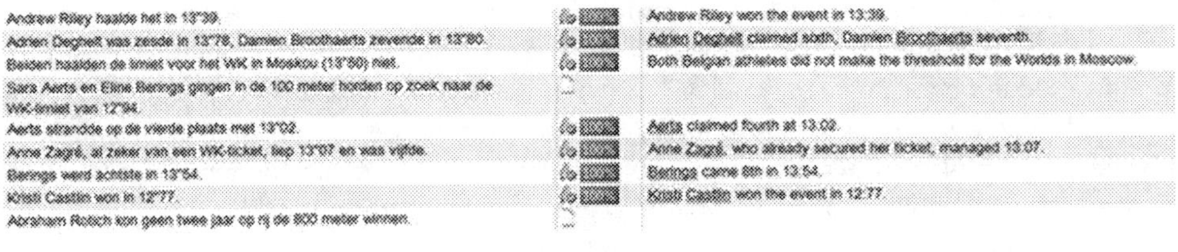

Figure 32.1 Detail of the editor environment of SDL Trados Studio 2011 (SP1), with 3 + 1 + 4 + 1 units

However, beyond those stipulations, each degree of matching requires different cognitive processes of the translator. Whereas often minor brief additions or alterations might improve a segment to the level that it is acceptable for the purpose for which it is used,[8] research on how translators maintain their awareness of possible flaws while re-using translation units from the TM might be relevant to analyses of editing MT output too.

Cognitive Processes and Editing

Lagoudaki (2006) is a reference work about translators' perception and use of technology, but translation environments have moved on.[9] Among others, the pervasive use of SMT has effectuated a new paradigm in that perception of language and translation technology. More importantly, in the last few years, translation memory systems have broken away from the – admittedly often preferred by translators – environment of word processors and moved to standalone applications and online software as a service (SaaS). However, what has remained ever since the increased uptake of TM systems in the 1990s is widespread concern about translating and editing in a TMS. Based on an empirical study, Dragsted (2008) proved that any TM's segmentation into units, usually sentences, creates a strong focus on those segments, which affects the overall quality of the translation as a final product.

With a text that is presented in a TMS in various segments or units, a sentiment of alienation lies in the balance with a steady pace and a structured approach. In fact, with translation technology as a form of human–computer interaction, it is very difficult to differentiate formal benefits/disadvantages from holistic ones.

Table 32.1 Benefits and disadvantages of segmentation in translation memory systems

Benefits (of segmentation in) a TM	*Disadvantages (of segmentation in) a TM*
• A sense of control on the segment level • Similar pace • Close reading, no interference of non-verbal elements • Added value of term recognition • No formatting issues • Increased accuracy and consistency • Being able to monitor progress • Auto-propagation • Possible copying across of the source segment	• The layout of the source text is lost • No feeling of overall view and alienation from the context • Lack of non-verbal elements affects quality and productivity (Biau Gil 2007) • Lack of control • Formatting sometimes still requires editing • A tendency to more literal translation

Whether segmentation leads to an increased tendency towards more literal translation remains a matter for scholars to discuss and for further empirical studies. In the debate about the consequences of segmentation, experience and maturity are often overlooked, along with the need for increased productivity. In fact, in his pilot study, Biau Gil proves that subject-matter knowledge is more relevant than visual information (2007: 7). Taking this finding across the TM/MT threshold, this is a further argument that post-editors should above all be knowledgeable about the subject topic.

Forms of Editing Other Than Translating

Editing in projects that involves translation technology run along two axes. The first axis ranges from TM to MT. The second axis then concerns editing, ranging from pre-editing to post-editing. As pre-editing and controlled language are discussed elsewhere in this encyclopaedia, post-editing is broken down into more sub-concepts. Editing, revision and proof-reading are fundamental elements in translation projects, and as a consequence, their validity in MAHT projects is equally important.

Translation service providers (TSPs, sometimes also referred to as language service providers [LSPs]) adhere to the translation/editing/proof-reading (TEP) model. However, in marketing their services, the added value, especially of proof-reading, is often sold as a separate service. In the next section, the differentiation between the various forms of going over a text other than translating is effectuated in a sense of best practice, not in an academic overanalysing of terminological diffusion.[10] Publications and/or guidelines on editing, revision and proof-reading often concern a mere modal framework, 'how revisers *ought* to go about their jobs or what jobs they *could* use' (Mossop 2007a: online), and eventually best practices or workflows for revisers are often based on experience anyway.

Comparing the translation with the original text and ensuring that there are no errors left such as spelling mistakes, grammatical errors, omissions or ambiguities, is a well-established practice by the Translation Bureau of the Public Works and Government Services Canada. In their style guide, long lists of possible errors in both writing and editing are produced. However, much of this list is aimed at text production and not necessarily at translation projects in computerized setting. The error categorization by the Canadian Translation Bureau proves that translation technology increases the speed of how editing (of errors) and translation merged: translation memory tools started to elaborate on their proprietary quality assurance functionalities (such as verification in SDL Trados Studio 2011). Companies have been working towards this trend, too, as can be seen with Yamagata Europe's QA Distiller.

Whether in QA Distiller, Studio or any other TMS, detection of possible errors has become very much an automated feature of translation projects too. This greatly enhances the consistency of translator's output as well as his/her ability to submit a formally flawless target file, but it also provides a learning curve for translators to become more experienced in translation quality assurance and as such set themselves apart for those who do not.

In order to distinguish between the various forms of editing and the various identities editing can assume, a practical overview is reproduced in the following, whereby the various forms of editing are in fact allocated a position in the workflow.

Source files		Translated files		Final files	
Formal QA	Non-formal QA	Formal QA	Non-formal QA	Formal QA	Non-formal QA
Manual check QA software	Editing Controlled language Authoring memory, etc.	Manual check QA software	Proofreading Editing	Manual check QA software	In-country review

Figure 32.2   Editing stages in an overall quality assurance approach

Source: Makoushina and Kockaert (2008: 3)

Makoushina and Kockaert (2008) place editing of the translated files along proof-reading and deem it a non-formal form of quality assurance. With this approach, editing 'after' the translation (either HT or MT), 'post-editing', and editing of source files, 'pre-editing', are differentiated clearly as stages in the translation workflow. As mentioned earlier, pre-editing and controlled language are not within the scope of this chapter, as they are dealt with elsewhere, but (post-)editing still needs to be set apart from proof-reading.

Editing, Revision and Proof-Reading

In 2006, the European Committee for Standardisation (CEN) published the EN15038 standard,[11] developed for translation service providers. The standard aimed to cover the entire translation process, including quality assurance. The standard offered TSPs and their clients a breakdown of the entire translation provision in accurate definitions and standard description. Most importantly, the European standard required both a translator and a reviewer for each translation and differentiated between the two. Under EN15038, only translators with the appropriate background and competences can translate documents, and it is the task of that translator to check the translation themselves.[12] A reviewer then is a subsequent person in the translation workflow who examines 'a translation for its suitability for the agreed purpose, and respect for the conventions of the domain to which it belongs' and recommends corrective measures, if necessary. A review can be distinguished from a revision in that in the case of the latter, a translation is examined with both source and target texts compared. According to the European standard, proof-reading is limited to checking of proofs.[13]

Figure 32.3   Segment status in SDL Trados Studio 2011

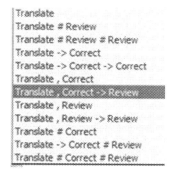

Figure 32.4   Various translation workflows possible in XTM Cloud

These concepts and their allocated positions in the translation workflow are often mimicked by the translation tools themselves. In the Editor window of SDL Trados Studio 2011, the status of each translated segment can be altered, including being translated and reviewed. This is similar to what XTM Cloud offers. Across Systems (2011) takes this a step further and includes buttons for the various steps in the translation process and aligns them with the EN15038 standard.[14]

In EN15038, editing in any form (copy-editing, pre-editing, post-editing) is included in an appendix only, as an added value service, but just how editing differs from review, revision and

Table 32.2 How EN15038 could possibly set editing apart from review, revision and proof-reading

Elements editing shares with EN15038 stipulations of review, revision and proof-reading	*Elements editing does not share with EN15038 stipulations of review, revision and proof-reading*
• Altering a translation for its suitability for the agreed purpose • Matching the translation to the conventions of the domain to which it belongs • A level of comparing source and target text is involved	• Checking of proofs (even though it can be argued editing shares elements of checking of proofs on screen) • Recommendation of corrective measures (even though it can be argued editing pro-actively ensures these measures)

proof-reading is not very clear.[15] It can, however, be easily deduced from the descriptions what editing is and what it is not.

Still, as already indicated by the various forms of editing, these stipulations do not entail a set of practical guidelines on how editing is used in translation projects, be it in the strictest sense by means of a translation memory system or in a broader interpretation of translation technology. This then not only includes machine translation but also social media (crowd-sourced translations or community translations), and sometimes both are even combined (as if often the case with projects posted on platforms such as Transifex). But most importantly, editing alongside translation and/or language technology takes the shape of post-editing machine translation.

Post-Editing and Machine Translation

Post-editing machine translation concerns the practical answer to the longstanding quest for the Holy Grail: machine-translated material that is substantially good enough for communication and/or dissemination.[16] A valid example of how practical post-editing MT can be is Jeff Allen's Creole MT,[17] a publicly available MT system for the purpose of relief during the 2010 Haiti earthquake and its aftermath.

Understanding the choices translators make while working with translation technology such as translation memories can be of significant relevance to how to approach the influence of translation provided by machine translation. Even when translation scholars have considered the 'black box' of machine translation in the past, it was in opposition to Holmes's 'little black box of the translator's mind' (1972: 72). However, especially when post-editing machine translation (PEMT) is concerned, the two in fact are more in juxtaposition and will be converging still more in the future. Above all, post-editing should be seen as a process of improving a machine-generated translation through modification (rather than revision), often eyeing a minimum of effort on behalf of the post-editor.[18] The quicker the turn-around needs of a translation, the more likely the PEMT

Source Text	Raw MT
Un vaste réseau qui piratait les codes de déverrouillage des téléphones portables a été démantelé, ont annoncé, dimanche 26 septembre, les enquêteurs.	A vast network hacked unlock codes for mobile phones has been dismantled, announced Sunday, Sept. 26, investigators.
Example of Light Post-Edit	A vast network which hacked unlock codes for mobile phones has been dismantled, it was announced Sunday, Sept. 26, by investigators.
Example of Full Post-Edit	A vast network which hacked security codes for mobile phones has been dismantled, according to an announcement by investigators on Sunday, Sept. 26.

Figure 32.5 Light and full post-editing of raw MT output

effort will be a fast one, also known as 'light post-editing'. More thorough modifications, with less time urgency, aims for better quality and is often known as 'full post-editing'. The latter category is the more common one, not least because it aims to obtain a quality level that is the same as if the entire text had been translated from scratch by the human translator.

The quality of a translation is a hotly debated issue, let alone the quality of a translation in which MT played a part and subsequent post-editing. O'Brien rightly argues that quality expectations differ depending on where a particular person is involved. Developers are very interested in automated quality metrics such as Bilingual Evaluation Understudy (BLEU), Translation Edit Rate (TER) or Word Error Rate (WER).[19] They are also very keen on getting usage feedback from the translator, improving the system they have developed with valuable input.[20] Buyers allocate PEMT projects to translators or TSPs because they hope for a faster turnaround. The overall translation cost might be similar to HT; if the PEMT approach saves time, then that is a major benefit for the buyer already. The translators or TSPs hope that by increasing their productivity, they can also increase their client portfolio and/or market share. Two categories that are often overlooked are the project managers[21] and the account executives or sales. These people do not necessarily need to be included in the list just now, but they are crucial in the communication chain with the client and its subsequent users and as such cannot afford to create false expectations. In the end, much of the success of post-edited machine translations depends on how the users perceive the quality of what was disseminated or communicated.

In the entire debate of considering raw MT output fuzzy matches so as to gauge the probable workload for post-editors properly, Guerberof (2009) analysed findings of a small-scale research project that are very interesting. Translators were asked to post-edit TM segments of 80–90% fuzzy matching on the one hand and SMT output on the other hand, as well as to translate anew. In an analysis of all the errors produced in each of the three categories, new segments accounted for roughly 1 error in 5. Intriguingly, a similar amount of words to be post-edited triggered not many more errors. In fact, the errors in the final translation produced with the aid of a translation memory accounted for half of all the errors; that is, editing fuzzy matches in a TMS triggers double the amount of errors compared to post-editing raw MT output.[22] Similarly, using the TM even slowed down productivity by 2.5%, whereas MT increased it by 24.5%, a combined difference of 27%, or nearly a third.

The re-usable nature of raw MT output has been confirmed by Fontes (2013), chair of the European Commission's machine translation user group (MTUG). In a survey across the Directorate-General for Translation, experienced translators were asked to rate MT output quality. Of the 643 ratings of language pair combinations, 200 confirmed that they had used MT for more than 75% of their translation jobs. Asked to rate the output of the respective engines on a 0–4 scale, 726 ratings were delivered; 185 people rated the MT quality as 4 or 3, in which most segments were considered re-usable. Asked for the reasons MT should be used, three of the five answers[23] (MT is a typing aid, MT is a source of inspiration for alternative translations available in the translation memory and a quick draft) imply subsequent use of post-editing.

Post-Editing Guidelines

The Translation Automation User Society (TAUS) is one of the most authoritative sources on post-editing machine translation. Crucial to raising the awareness with users of PEMT about the various issues involved, it has highlighted recommendations and post-editing guidelines.

On the recommendation of tuning your engine appropriately, TAUS (2010) distinguishes between rule-based or statistical engines, whereby a high-level dictionary and linguistic coding are crucial for rule-based machine translation, and clean, high-quality, domain-specific data are key to data-driven systems. The second TAUS recommendation is to ensure that the source text is written well, preferably even written with later MT in mind. As mentioned earlier: there is no post-editing machine translation without including pre-editing the source material.

One of the most obvious recommendations by TAUS (2010) is to train post-editors in advance. However, there is a major difference between training people to act as post-editors for a specific job with project-specific data and guidelines on the one hand and linguists on the other hand, who receive more basic training because they work across projects and therefore need to adhere more to a common denominator. Moreover, including post-editing in the curriculum of higher education has proven difficult.[24]

Table 32.3 TAUS post-editing guidelines versus quality assurance in SDL Trados Studio 2011

Selected guidelines for post-editing (TAUS 2010)	Quality assurance in SDL Trados Studio 2011
'Ensure that no information has been accidentally added or omitted'.	QA Checker 3.0: Segment verification • Check for forgotten and empty translations • Check for segments where source and target are identical • Check for segments which are x% shorter/longer • Segments to exclude
'Basic rules about spelling, punctuation and hyphenation apply'.	QA Checker 3.0: • Inconsistencies (repeated words in target, unedited fuzzy matches) • Punctuation • Numbers, times, dates, measurements
'Ensure that key terminology is correctly translated and that untranslated terms belong to the client's list of "Do Not Translate" terms'.	QA Checker 3.0: Word List and Regular Expression Terminology Verifier (with a term base open)
'Ensure that formatting is correct'.	Any TMS strives towards maintaining exactly the same formatting between source and target. Most TMS also include warning messages in cases where there are differences

Providing generic guidelines for achieving quality that is in line with the project stipulations and the agreed-upon expectations is not easy, as TAUS (2010) proves. Most guidelines, twice half a dozen of bullet points only, remain very tentative and do not immediately constitute a checklist. However, in line with the quality assurance capacities of translation memories mentioned earlier, several guidelines can in fact be dealt with in the automated environment of a TMS.

In a combined approach of the previous, the text segment represented in the following, which could have been reproduced in many other TMS, too, requires actions on both levels: in the TMS of Wordfast Anywhere (WFA), formatting has not been reproduced appropriately by Google Translate. A post-editor would need to restore the tags. However, this would be picked up on already by the verification feature of WFA. The post-editor would have to restore some cultural elements to the source text, and this example indeed triggers the copying across of the source segment.

①Le Monde② ③Télérama④ ⑤Le Monde diplomatique⑥ ⑦Le Huffington Post⑧ ⑨Courrier international⑩ ⑪La Vie⑫ ⑬au Jardin⑭

The World①② ③④ ⑤Télérama Le Monde diplomatique The Huffington Post⑥ ⑦⑧ ⑨⑩ ⑪Courrier international Life in the Garden⑫ ⑬⑭

Figure 32.6 Tag differences returned by Google Translate in Wordfast Anywhere (text by Le Monde)

So far, no proprietary environment for post-editing alone has been mentioned, and even though they are around (such as PET by Wilker Aziz and Lucia Specia), it should be clear that post-editing can happen very well in the environment of a TMS. It should be noted that post-editing is also required in platforms for crowd-sourced translations such as Transifex, live subtitling with speech recognition or subtitling editors such as dotsub and YouTube Subtitler.

With post-editing material that has been provided by a translation memory, machine translation or even speech recognition, pricing methods are a tricky business. Three common options apply. Other than having a linguist available in-house (for public broadcasting and live captioning, for instance), either a nominal fee is paid based on the time spent or a word rate is agreed on, differentiating between re-use from the TM (see earlier categories of matches) and machine translation (which differs based on the training data and the input). Eventually PEMT is paid along the lines of fuzzy matching.

Conclusion

While on the Eurostar into London, the author wanted to joke with friends who also use Road Bike, a cycling app. After travelling at about 285 km/h on average for 5 minutes, the live tracking was stopped, and as the 20,660 kcal were about to be sent via Gmail, the app, which had been installed in Dutch along with the operating language of its Android 4.1 system, neatly indicated 'U gaat wel erg snel. Wellicht heeft u de verkeerde sport gekozen' [*You are going very fast. Perhaps you have chosen the wrong sport.*, MT by Google Translate]. It would be very difficult to find out whether this segment had been localized into Dutch by a translator (who might have used machine translation for draft output and treated it as fuzzy matches), by machine translation *tout court* or by a community of users who had mastered Dutch. Such a community can use a platform such as Transifex, which in turn can have community members who base their work on machine translation. Although this anecdotal instance does not prove much, it will be recognized by millions of users, 99.9% of whom are not translators or linguists. The world of translation technology, language technology, mobile technology and social media (the people networks, the cloud and the crowd, and subsequently the feed of social data, too) are converging.

With that rapid uptake of machine translation at a low entry level, but also on mobile phones and on tablets, the perception of translation from the global user's perspective is changing dramatically. The main problem in overcoming that threshold fear by translators of incorporating machine translation in their workflow, and therefore post-editing, is that translators deem the process of translation sacred, whereas eventually the target text is only a product with a purpose that is relevant to a world outside their own. If the wider translation profession does not see the opportunity to maintain a much-cherished art and profession, too many users will discard human translators and resort to MT output that has been post-edited by either a native speaker or someone who knows the subject really well. The latter can very well be someone who is trusted within the (online) user community.

Editing in translation technology applications is an elementary step in the well-sought increase in productivity. Any target text that is the product of a translation process should be considered complete only after careful revision and editing. Reviewing segment after segment that has been produced by a computer application can indeed be more cumbersome than editing a human translation. However, if translation as a process and the means to an end product, whether by a human, a machine or hybrid, needs post-editing and this is not mastered by human translators themselves, then who will fight in the corner of the added value of humans here?

Arguably most clashes between quality expectations and deliverables can be overcome beforehand. By examining raw MT output quality, an appropriate price needs to be negotiated and an agreement needs to be reached about the final quality of the information to be post-edited. Even though these two recommendations are included in those by TAUS (2010), they in fact constitute common practice in projects that involve HT only or HT+TM. However, it is very true that the ongoing new paradigm of pervasive use of MT can indeed act as a technological turn that triggers an awareness HT has not been able to for decades. Including MT output in translation projects offers an opportunity to start negotiating this awareness anew. It would be lethal to miss out on that.

Notes

1 Any historical review of translation memory systems will point to Trados MultiTerm and IBM Translation Manager emerging in 1992, Atril's Déja Vu in 1993 and Trados Workbench in 1994. The concept, however, emerged much earlier, with Peter Arthern already in 1979 stipulating that the use of unrestricted machine translation at the European Commission might very well be too early still but that there was 'scope for post-edited machine translation of a restricted range of texts' (Hutchins 1998: 293).

2 Crucial in the perception of language and translation technology is Google Translate, which more than a year after it became a paid service, still had more than 200 million people using it monthly. By April 2012, the daily total number of words equalled that of 1 million books (Kerr 2012). The influence of Google Translate, for instance, goes well beyond the albeit limited online tool and Google Translator Toolkit. With a free Website Translator plugin, websites can be made available in more than 60 languages. In fact, Google's Website Translator allows users to edit and improve their websites themselves.

3 For an appreciation of the history of post-editing machine translation, see Ignacio Garcia 2012.

4 For instance, re-use from a large TM on the basis of aligned source and equivalent target texts or MT output from an SMT that has been trained on the same or similar corpus of equivalent texts are perhaps distinctively different in technology but closely related in use.

5 Although terminology management and the inclusion of term recognition in TM systems is not discussed here, it should be made clear that terminology is not only key to the HT but also to MT. A combined hybrid TM/MT + terminology management allows for increased quality assurance and, if maintained successfully, also increased consistency and thus quality. Also, dictionary compilation is a skill crucial in the development of translation engines.

6 From here onwards, this contribution does not allocate much space to defining several of its key concepts, let alone analysing the differences between respective definition variants. The applied field of translation technology itself, a world of increased productivity, does not warrant such ponderings.

7 Biau Gil, however, attests that translators' perfomance is improved by an environment whereby the nonverbal elements of a text or its native format are visible in an interface that is similar to WYSIWYG, what you see is what you get: 'texts translated using WYSIWYG translation interfaces include fewer errors than those translated using non-WYSIWYG interfaces', and 'when translators use WYSIWYG translation interfaces they work faster than when they use non-WYSIWYG interfaces' (2007: 7).

8 One such purpose is to maintain the standard or open format in which the translation memory is contained. XML Localization Interchange File Format (XLIFF) allows users of translation technology to pass on data between various tools during the translation or localization process. XLIFF editors can be found among more familiar providers of translation technology tools such as MultiTrans as well as through less-known freeware, such as Transolution. Other file formats that drive the translation editing environment are, for instance, Poedit, which allows translators and users to edit cross-platform gettext catalogs (PO files). SRT Translator provides a translation memory in which Google Translate produces draft translations of subtitles.

9 The Copenhagen Business School has been particularly active in researching the cognitive processes while translating using a TM and the effects of segmentation on the productivity and quality of the translator. Dragsted 2004, Dragsted 2008, Jakobsen 2009, Christensen and Schjoldager 2010 and Christensen and Schjoldager 2011 are but a selected few. Other people who have

contributed to this field are Bowker 2005, Guerberof 2009, O'Brien 2008, O'Brien 2011 and Pym 2011.

10   In analogy to doctors being the worst patients, translators have a similar ailment: perennial analysis of concepts and their definitions and denotations and a subsequent ongoing debate about slight differences.

11   Even though it was published in 2006, already EN 15038 has been gaining acceptance. It was accepted by 28 nations (all EU member states, except Bulgaria and Croatia, but it was accepted by non-EU Iceland, Norway and Switzerland) after its inception and acted as a benchmark in the European Union.

12   This check by the translator is also called self-editing.

13   The Language Resource Centre of Aalborg University refers to proof-reading as follows: the process where 'we focus exclusively on orthography, typing errors, grammar and punctuation'. Vocabulary and spelling are proof-read so as to make them consistent. For English-language texts, 'either British or American spelling is used, and not a mixture of the two varieties of English'. In the case of an ambiguous translation, a comment is inserted explaining the problem, but the text itself will never be re-phrased (LRC 2009, online).

14   Across Systems uses a slightly different terminology: the corrector and reviewer ensure checking, revision, reviewing and verification.

15   According to Mossop 2007, in editing a translation project, corrections and improvements are made whereby the purpose and the given readership of the text are prioritized. Revising is a very similar task, but this is then applied to draft translations. Trying to rename all the PEMT, post-editing machine translation, as PRMT (post-revision?) seems not immediately feasible. In light of Mossop 2007, it could be argued that post-editors first revise the MT segments and edit the text in its entirety next. In practice, this would hardly happen, and texts are translated and subsequently edited on a segment-by-segment basis. These corrections to a translation in order to increase its quality are also known as quality assurance (QA), whereas any correction round to detect flaws in a translation after it has been submitted is often referred to as quality control (QC). For an appreciation of QA and QC, see Makoushina and Kockaert 2008, Rasmussen and Schjoldager 2011 and European Union 2012.

16   W. John Hutchins differentiates between MT for the purpose of communication (light post-editing required only) and dissemination (full post-editing required) (2013).

17   For an appreciation of the language technology effort for distress relief in Haiti, see Munro 2010.

18   The description of post-editing is a combination of two definitions: post-editing is 'the process of improving a machine-generated translation with a minimum of manual labour' (TAUS 2010) and 'a process of modification rather than revision'.

19   For an appreciation of machine translation evaluation metrics, see Snover 2006. Users can compare users Google Translate or Bing Translator through iBLEU.

20   This is where pre-editing re-emerges: by comparing the raw MT output with the source text, errors can be found and arguably a system behind types of errors, too. Other than leaving things as they are, developers have two options: boost the engine by training it on new data or allowing document authors to pre-edit their source material so as to have increased raw MT output quality.

21   For an appreciation of machine translation and project management, see Guerberof 2010.

22   When Guerberof categorized the errors according to five types (mistranslation, accuracy, terminology, language and consistency), post-editing raw MT output produced very similar numbers of errors for language and consistency as the new segments did. With double the errors for mistranslation and accuracy, it should then come as no surprise that re-using and editing fuzzy matches from the TM in fact landed more than half the errors for the three approaches together, whereas MT only has a quarter.

23   Other responses referred to an increase in productivity and a gain in time for more thorough research.

24   For an appreciation of teaching post-editing, see Allen 2001, Kenny and Way 2001, O'Brien 2002, Belam 2003 and Kliffer 2008.

Bibliography

Across Systems (2011) 'The EN 15038 Standard Workflow'. Available at: www.across.net/documentation/onlinehelp/across_en/acrossHaupt648.htm.

Allen, Jeff (2001) 'Post-editing: An Integrated Part of a Translation Software Program', *Language International*, April, 26–29.

Aziz, Wilker and Lucia Specia (2012) 'PET: A Tool for Post-editing and Assessing Machine Translation', in *Proceedings of the 16th Annual Conference of the European Association for Machine Translation*, 28–30 May 2012, Trento, Italy, 99. Available at: www.lrec-conf.org/proceedings/lrec2012/pdf/985_Paper.pdf.

Belam, Judith (2003) 'Buying up to Falling Down: A Deductive Approach to Teaching Post-editing', in *Proceedings of Machine Translation Summit IX: Machine Translation for Semitic Languages: Issues and Approaches*, 23–27 September 2003, New Orleans, LA. Available at: www.dlsi.ua.es/t4/proceedings.html.

Biau Gil, José Ramon (2007) 'What You See Is What You Get? A Pilot Experiment on Access to Visual Information in Translation Interfaces', *Paper presented at the 12th Annual Internationalisation and Localisation Conference*, 26–28 September 2007, Dublin, Ireland. Available at: www.localisation.ie/resources/conferences/2007/presentations/Biau_LRC_XII/LRC_XII_slides.pps.

Bowker, Lynn (2005) 'Productivity vs. Quality: A Pilot Study on the Impact of Translation Memory Systems', *Localisation Focus* 4(1): 13–20.

Canada Translation Bureau (1997) 'The Canadian Style: A Guide to Writing and Editing'. Available at: http://bt-tb.tpsgc-pwgsc.gc.ca/btb.php?lang=eng&cont=791.

Christensen, Tina Paulsen and Anne Schjoldage (2010) 'Translation-Memory (TM) Research: What Do We Know and How Do We Know It?', *Journal of Language and Communication Studies* 44: 89–101.

Christensen, Tina Paulsen and Anne Schjoldage (2011) 'The Impact of Translation-Memory (TM) Technology on Cognitive Processes: Student-translators' Retrospective Comments in an Online Questionnaire', in Bernadette Sharp, Michael Zock, Michael Carl, and Arnt Lykke Jakobsen (eds.) *Proceedings of the 8th International NLPCS Workshop: Special Theme: Human-Machine Interaction in Translation*, 20–21 August 2011, Copenhagen, Denmark, 119–30.

Crabbe, Stephen (2010) 'Controlled Languages for Technical Writing and Translation', in Ian Kemble (ed.) *The Changing Face of Translation: Proceedings of the 9th Annual Portsmouth Translation Conference 2009*, 7 November 2009, University of Portsmouth, Portsmouth, the United Kingdom, 48–62. Available at: http://tinyurl.com/b8truqo.

Dotsub. Available at: http://dotsub.com.

Dragsted, Barbara (2004) *Segmentation in Translation and Translation Memory Systems: An Empirical Investigation of Cognitive Segmentation and Effects of Integrating a TM System into the Translation Process*, Copenhagen: Copenhagen Business School.

Dragsted, Barbara (2008) 'Computer-aided Translation as a Distributed Cognitive Task', in Itiel Dror and Stevan Harnad (eds.) *Cognition Distributed: How Cognitive Technology Extends Our Minds*, Amsterdam and Philadelphia: John Benjamins Publishing Company, 237–56.

European Quality Standard EN-15038: 2006. Available at: http://qualitystandard.bs.en-15038.com/. Accessed February 1, 2013.

European Union (2012) *Quantifying Quality Costs and the Cost of Poor Quality in Translation: Quality Efforts and the Consequences of Poor Quality in the European Commission's Directorate-General for Translation*, Luxembourg: Publications Office of the European Union.

Fontes, Hilàrio Leal Fontes (2013) 'Evaluating Machine Translation: Preliminary Findings from the First DGT-wide Translators' Survey', in *Language and Translation: Machine Translation*, European Commission. Available at: http://goo.gl/66H3a.

Garcia, Ignacio (2012) 'A Brief History of Postediting and of Research on Postediting', *Revista Anglo Saxonica* 3(3): 291–310.

Google Translator Toolkit. Available at: translate.google.com/toolkit.

Google's Website Translator. Available at: http://translate.google.com/manager/website/?hl=en.

Guerberof, Ana (2009) 'Productivity and Quality in the Post-editing of Outputs from Translation Memories and Machine Translation', *Localisation Focus* 7(1): 11–21.

Guerberof, Ana (2010) 'Project Management and Machine Translation', *Multilingual*, April/May. Available at: http://isg.urv.es/library/papers/2010_guerberof.pdf.

Holmes, James S. (1972) 'The Name and Nature of Translation Studies', *Third International Congress of Applied Linguistics*, Copenhagen. Available at: www.universita-mediazione.com/wp-content/uploads/2012/02/Materiale_Prof_Donadio_31_01_2012.pdf.

Hutchins, W. John (1998) 'The Origins of the Translator's Workstation', *Machine Translation* 13(4): 287–307.

Hutchins, W. John (2013) 'History and Methods of MT', in *Visiting Seminar, Imperial College London's Translation Unit*, 27 February 2013.

ITR (2013) 'Document Translation'. Available at: www.itr.co.uk/documentation-translation.

Jakobsen, Arnt Lykke (2009) 'Instances of Peak Performance in Translation', *Lebende Sprachen* 50(3): 111–16.

Kenny, Dorothy and Andy Way (2001) 'Teaching Machine Translation and Translation Technology: A Contrastive Study', in *Proceedings of the Machine Translation Summit VII, Teaching MT Workshop*. Available at: http://doras.dcu.ie/15830/1/Teaching_Machine_Translation_%26_Translation_Technology.pdf.

Kerr, Dara (2012) 'Google Translate Boasts 64 Languages and 200M Users', *CNET Internet and Media News*, 26 April 2012. Available at: http://news.cnet.com/8301-1023_3-57422613-93/google-translate-boasts-64-languages-and-200m-users.

Kliffer, Michael (2008) 'Post-editing Machine Translation as an FSL Exercise', *Porta Linguarum* 9: 53–67.

Lagoudaki, Elina (2006) 'Translation Memory Systems: Enlightening Users' Perspective. Key Finding of the TM Survey 2006 Carried out during July and August 2006', Unpublished doctoral dissertation, Imperial College London.

Lagoudaki, Elina (2009) 'Translation Editing Environments', in *Proceedings of the 12th MT Summit*, 26–30 August 2009, Ottawa, Ontario, Canada. Available at: http://goo.gl/sQHxS.

LionBridge (2013) 'Language Services'. Available at: https://en-gb.lionbridge.com/translation-localization/language-quality.htm.

Madnani, Nitin (2013) 'iBLEU'. Available at: https://code.google.com/p/ibleu.

Makoushina, Julia and Hendrik Kockaert (2008) 'Zen and the Art of Quality Assurance: Quality Assurance Automation in Translation: Needs, Reality and Expectations', in *Proceedings of the 13th International Conference on Translating and the Computer*, 27–28 November 2008, ASLIB, London. Available at: http://goo.gl/l08EJ.

Mendez, José (1986) 'Machine Translation in Bureau Service', *Terminologie et Traduction* 1: 48–53.

Mossop, Brian (2006) 'Has Computerization Changed Translation?', *Meta* 51(4): 787–93. Available at: www.erudit.org/revue/meta/2006/v51/n4/index.html.

Mossop, Brian (2007a) 'Empirical Studies of Revision: What We Know and Need to Know', *Journal of Specialised Translation* 8. Available at: www.jostrans.org/issue08/art_mossop.pdf.

Mossop, Brian (2007b) *Revising and Editing for Translators*, 2nd edition, Manchester: St. Jerome Publishing.

Multitrans XLIFF Editor. Available at: http://multicorpora.com/products-services/options-and-add-ons/xliff-editor.

Munro, Robert (2010) 'Crowdsourced Translation for Emergency Response in Haiti: The Global Collaboration of Local Knowledge', in *Proceedings of the 9th Conference of the Association for Machine Translation in the Americas*, 31 October–4 November 2010, Denver, CO. Available at: http://amta2010.amtaweb.org/AMTA/papers/7-01-01-Munro.pdf.

O'Brien, Sharon (2002) 'Teaching Post-editing: A Proposal for Course Content', in *Proceedings of 6th EAMT Conference Workshop: Teaching Machine Translation*, 14–15 November 2002, Manchester, the United Kingdom, 99–106. Available at: http://mt-archive.info/EAMT-2002-OBrien.pdf.

O'Brien, Sharon (2008) 'Processing Fuzzy Matches in Translation Memory Tools: An Eye-tracking Analysis', in Susanne Göpferich, Arnt Lykke Jakobsen, and Inger M. Mees (eds.) *Looking at Eyes: Eye Tracking Studies of Reading and Translation Processing*, Copenhagen: Copenhagen Business School, 79–102.

O'Brien, Sharon (ed.) (2011) *Cognitive Explorations of Translation*, London: Bloomsbury Publishing.

Och, Franz (2012) 'Breaking Down the Language Barrier – Six Years in', *Online Blog Post, Google Official Blog*. Available at: http://googleblog.blogspot.be/2012/04/breaking-down-language-barriersix-years.html.

PoEdit. Available at: http://sourceforge.net/projects/poedit.

Pym, Anthony (2011) 'What Technology Does to Translating', *The International Journal for Translation and Interpreting Research* 3(1): 1–9. Available at: www.trans-int.org/index.php/transint/article/viewFile/121/81.

QA Distiller. Available at: www.qa-distiller.com.

Rasmussen, Kirsten Wölch and Anne Schjoldager (2011) 'A Survey of Revision Policies in Danish Translation Companies', *Journal of Specialised Translation* 15: 87–120. Available at: www.jostrans.org/issue15/art_rasmussen.pdf.

SDL Trados Studio (2011). Available at: www.sdl.com/products/sdl-trados-studio.

Snover, Matthew and Bonnie J. Dorr (2006) 'A Study of Translation Edit Rate with Targeted Human Annotation', in *Proceedings of the 7th Biennial AMTA Conference*, 8–12 August 2006, Cambridge, MA, 223–31. Available at: http://goo.gl/33Et1.

Somers, Harold L. (2003) *Computers and Translation: A Translator's Guide*, Amsterdam and Philadelphia: John Benjamins Publishing Company.

Somers, Nick (2001) 'Revision – Food for Thought', *Translation Journal Online* 5: 1. Available at: https://sites.google.com/site/penidea/revision%E2%80%94foodforthought.

SRT Subtitler. Available at: http://sourceforge.net/projects/srt-tran/?source=directory.

TAUS (2010) 'MT Post-editing Guidelines'. Available at: www.translationautomation.com/images/stories/guidelines/taus-cngl-machine-translation-postediting-guidelines.pdf.

TAUS. Available at: www.translationautomation.com.

Transifex. Available at: www.transifex.com.

Transolution XLIFF Editor. Available at: http://sourceforge.net/projects/eviltrans.

Transperfect (2013) 'Human Translation Services'. Available at: www.transperfect.com/services/translation.html.

van de Poel, Kris, W. A. M. Carstens, and John Linnegar (2012) *Text Editing: A Handbook for Students and Practitioners*, New York: Academic and Scientific Publishing.

Verbeke, Charles A. (1973) 'Caterpillar Fundamental English', *Training and Development Journal* 27(2): 36–40.

Yamagata Europe (2013) 'Quality Assurance'. Available at: www.yamagata-europe.com/en-gb/page/520/iso-certification.

Youtube Subtitler. Available at: http://yt-subs.appspot.com.

33

EDITING IN AUDIOVISUAL TRANSLATION (SUBTITLING)

Alejandro Bolaños García-Escribano and Christophe Declercq

Through the use and application of technology in producing and editing target text segments, the translation industry, the translation profession and translation studies have developed a strong focus on translation technology – especially computer-aided translation tools (CAT) such as translation memories (TMs) but also subtitling systems and platforms allowing for crowdsourcing translations – and language technology on the other hand, typically machine translation (MT).[1] Language and translation technology support and frame the interlingual transfer of rendering source-language text strings into the target language with as much productivity as possible. Productivity here is not only driven by the re-use of already translated material and by the translators' efficiency when handling technologies, but it is also determined by the amount of editing that must happen in order for the target-language production to be deemed successful, that is, fit for the purpose of the target text. The quality of the translation relies on the quality of the content with which the translator has to work when using TM and MT tools. Amending TM or MT string suggestions is often referred to as post-editing effort (Krings 2001), and this has been the focus of much of the editing-related research in recent years (including O'Brien 2005; Specia and Farzindar 2010; Garcia 2011; O'Brien 2011; Koponen 2016; Toral *et al.* 2018; Alvarez *et al.* 2020). Effort can be understood from several angles, but scholars seem to agree on Krings's (2001) classification: temporal, technical and cognitive effort. Research also shows that these cognitive efforts correlate among them (Moorkens *et al.* 2015), can be considered relatively linear and do not require much consideration beyond the text level.

For other localisation processes – involving more complex files such as apps, video games or multimedia content – focus on the editing process is less linear as one takes into consideration other modes than purely textual ones, such as audiovisual translation (AVT). Yet these additional modes are crucial for the effectiveness of the respective translation practices of audiovisual source content, and they are often also seen as the threshold of referring to rendering processes as localisation instead of merely translation. Therefore, this chapter aims to provide an overarching description of concepts and issues involved with editing forms of AVT, particularly subtitling.

AVT Modes and Practices

AVT is an academic discipline and professional field of expertise that involves localising audiovisual media content employing different language transfer practices. With spoken text

DOI: 10.4324/9781003168348-36

mainly, but also some body language, gestures and sounds such as sighs and pants, AVT sees different modes converge into a single target-language textual dimension, be it written for subtitling (e.g. interlingual subtitling, captioning) or spoken again for revoicing (e.g. voiceover, dubbing). Audiovisual texts can be considered acts of communication involving sounds and images, in which four different types of signs – audio-verbal, audio-nonverbal, visual-verbal and visual-nonverbal – are complementary and equally important in the process of meaning production (Delabastita 1989). Audiovisual texts are thus predetermined insofar as they combine two complementary channels and meaning codes whose signs interact and build a semantic composite of a complex nature (Zabalbeascoa 2001; Sokoli 2005). The inner challenges of translating audiovisual texts (e.g. spatial and temporal limitations, visual information on screen) establish an umbilical connection with translation technologies (e.g. dubbing and subtitling systems), which increasingly have a more comprehensive presence in translators' workstations as AVT practices have diverged and, at times, become more complex (Chaume 2018; Díaz-Cintas and Massidda 2019).

Localising media content requires awareness of this coexistence of the acoustic and visual communication channels, together with the presence of verbal and nonverbal information. The AVT profession and industry has dramatically multiplied and diversified since the advent of digitisation at the end of the twentieth century, which in turn led to a growth of academic interest in the complex semiotic texture of audiovisual texts (Gambier and Gottlieb 2001; Pérez-González 2014, 2018; Bogucki and Deckert 2020). This was amplified even more, on the one hand, with the emergence of captioning capabilities that happened through crowdsourced efforts (such as TED) or in an automated fashion through speech recognition in freely available online platforms such as YouTube and, on the other hand, through the omnipresent visibility of AVT through streaming networks such as Netflix.[2]

AVT, as an umbrella term, subsumes a wide range of language transfer modes that differ in the nature of their linguistic output and the translational techniques they imply (Gambier 2003), as well as on how they are ultimately consumed by the target audience. This consumption is framed by spatial and temporal constraining factors, or restrictions, that have been thoroughly theorised in the past (Mayoral *et al.* 1988) and which include, for example, the maximum number of characters that a translation can accommodate and the fact that words ought to mirror the source material, while aiming for the most appropriate reading speed for the target audience. For linguists to focus on the output that is most suited for the purpose and the target audience, dedicated AVT software tools will often help with the technical dimension.

It has traditionally been agreed that there are two main types of AVT practices: revoicing and subtitling (de Linde and Kay 1999).[3] Generally speaking, revoicing consists of replacing the original dialogue soundtrack with a newly recorded or live soundtrack in the target language (Chaume 2006), whereas subtitling operates by displaying written chunks of text that correspond to synchronised translations of the original aural utterances as well as some of the visual input contained in the source programme (Gambier 2006). In broad terms, subtitling is fast, inexpensive, flexible and easy to produce when compared to revoicing. It also allows for (relatively) easy editing as soon as a template with timestamps is available and for a much swifter turnaround if minor updates or changes are required. These are some of the essential qualities that make it the perfect translation ally of globalisation and the preferred mode of AVT on the world wide web (Díaz-Cintas 2012). In this sense, subtitling can be said to represent the most successful and economical accomplice of the current processes of internetisation, digitalisation and audiovisualisation of communication (Díaz-Cintas 2015). Perhaps this is also the reason technological advances have been patently more prominent in subtitling than in dubbing. In this chapter, the discussion will solely revolve around the editing of subtitles.

Subtitling

According to whether they are in the same or a different language to the one heard in the audiovisual production, subtitling can be either interlingual or intralingual. Sub-varieties exist, though, depending on the language combination and whether they can be removed from the screen. When produced in advance for recorded programmes, in what is known in the industry as pre-prepared subtitles, they take the form of pop-on or pop-up text; however, subtitles can also be produced online for (semi)live or real-time events, in which case they are usually rolled up or scrolled. In the 1980s, laser techniques were introduced whereby subtitles were burnt onto celluloid, especially for theatrical releases, therefore allowing for minor post-synchronisation changes. Electronic subtitles, which were initially utilised in film festivals, have become the most common type, as they do not require the burning of subtitles. Instead, the subtitles are projected onto the film copy and can be easily edited if need be.

With the expansion of subtitled material on social media, video games and streaming platforms, the very concept of subtitling is now being diluted, as videos can be found without sound but can include subtitles; also, some multimedia products contain textual instructions that resemble standard subtitles. The changes have also had a knock-on effect on the terminology used in the industry, with companies like Netflix referring to this activity as text timing (Netflix 2020). Even corporate communication and maintenance manuals increasingly take on an audiovisual format, allowing for easier dissemination in other languages through subtitling, though more recently, revoicing is emerging as a more common AVT trend in the English language, too (Spiteri-Miggiani 2021; Sánchez-Mompeán 2021). The 2020 global pandemic has also brought about a paradigm shift in online meeting practices and has drastically expanded, among others, the use of video for learning and teaching purposes, for example, capturing speech to text or (machine) translated dialogue during online sessions using platforms such as Zoom. The pervasive presence of audiovisual texts has provided a parallel plethora of opportunities but also a similarly increasing demand for the accurate and appropriate formal rendering of audiovisual texts in other languages (Díaz-Cintas 2015).

Subtitle Editing

Editing can refer to various practices and, when combined with technologies, it brings about even more understandings to the same concept (see Declercq's Chapter 32 in this volume). In AVT, there are at least six types of editing that are often performed in the industry before, during or after the translation process – although most often performed during the post-production phase.[4] This chapter contends that one more type supersedes all levels and can be considered a supra-element of editing.

The term (1) *pre-editing* typically refers to reviewing a source text so that MT should or might be able to produce a more useful target output that requires less editing in the target language. For AVT, however, pre-editing, equally a verification of the source text, adds a technical dimension to the linguistic one. Audiovisual source texts such as dialogue lists and subtitle templates need to be adequate (for templates, the timings need to be accurate, for instance) but also compliant with minimum quality standards. The application of (2) *post-editing* in AVT as a localisation practice has an added dimension compared to more linear translation (focusing on main text only, see earlier). Apart from amending suggested target-language text strings, regardless of their origin, post-editing AVT output becomes more complicated whenever automated speech recognition (ASR) and MT are involved; in other words, post-editing would mean amending an auto-generated timed text file (e.g. master template), which can be either an intralingual version (e.g. verbatim transcript) or a translation (e.g. machine-translated subtitle template) of the original, to guarantee its compliance with the linguistic and technical demands of the project. Just like in localisation, however, AVT demands additional levels of possible editing. By comparing the translated text to the source text in the post-translation phase, (3) *revision* adds to post-editing the dimension of the relation with the source text, also known as bilingual review. Monolingual review, or (4) *proofreading*, however, refers to checking the translated text on its own to guarantee it reads naturally and contains no grammatical or lexical infelicities (including typos). Without necessarily evaluating the translation or language used, scrutinising (a sample of) the technical dimensions of the localised file (e.g. subtitle template) – to make sure it complies with the client's specifications – is AVT's (5) *quality control* or *quality assurance* (QC or QA, respectively).[5] Similar to videogame testing and final checking of localised software, testing or simulation of the AVT is needed: (6) *post-QC viewing* of the localised product needs to rule out any errors that may still be present after the editing process is finalised. Apart from these types of editing, we would like to argue that each AVT mode requires additional editing tasks, which may well take place during any phase in which linguists are involved. For instance, when the linguistic make-up of subtitles needs to be adjusted (because of time limitations, for example), there may be alterations to the original translation (Díaz-Cintas and Remael 2020). In the same vein, when dialogue writers adjust translated scripts so as to synchronise target-language output with the original actors' utterances (e.g. lip synchrony), they can introduce substantial changes when close-up shots are involved and are a reason instances of dubbese are still common nowadays (Spiteri-Miggiani 2019). Therefore (7) *truncation*, particularly the total or partial reduction or substitution of dialogue in translated speech or subtitles, is a supra-editing AVT-specific type of editing that can occur at any point during the localisation process. The different types of editing have shown that the concept of editing is not clearly defined, which is why several standards have attempted to do so.

There are supranational agreements in terms of the terminology used for editing-related work in the translation industry (e.g. ISO 18587:2017, ISO/IEC 20071-23:2018, BSI EN ISO 17100:2015+A1:2017 and the European Quality Standard EN-15038:2006), but neither definitions nor practical applications are shared among all academics and practitioners with ease. Even if long-established works advocate for further homogeneity in editing practices among translation academics (e.g. Mossop 2001), some practices are often known differently in different industry sectors and poorly reflect the AVT professional reality. For instance, in subtitling workflows, many stakeholders equate editing to QC, referring to all components that can help a translation reflect quality standards (i.e. revision, proofreading and technical checks). Some companies may also advertise *subtitle editing* tasks when, in fact, they are looking for subtitle post-editors to manually edit timecodes (i.e. fixing or retiming ASR-generated templates) or translations (i.e. MT-generated subtitles) or both simultaneously. In some practices, such as respeaking, editing is simultaneous to the production of rolling captions utilising speech-to-text tools, since the voice-recognition software is not fault proof and the respeaker may have to elicit, add or amend information while producing the subtitles live.

Despite or perhaps because of the variations in application in terms of definitions, subtitles are governed by norms (Pedersen 2011), which can take multiple forms. In the professional subtitling industry, "in-house guidelines are the most common product-oriented quality tools that many companies have" (Pedersen 2017: 213–14). In most cases, the recommendations differ from one to another, irrespective of whether they have been created in academic or commercial circles. The rules of the subtitling and editing game do not always follow logic or consensus. In the academic sphere alone, there are various contributions to subtitling guidelines, including, in descending order, Díaz-Cintas and Remael (2020), Torralba-Miralles *et al.* (2019), Díaz-Cintas and Remael (2007), Díaz-Cintas (2001, 2003), Karamitroglou (1998, 2000), Ivarsson and Carroll (1998), Ivarsson (1992), Luyken (1991) and Laks (1957/2013). However, academic norms and industry practices relate to their respective relationships with linguistic and technical considerations when translating and localising audio-visual texts, that is, while editing AVT. Technical considerations in the context of subtitling refer to those aspects that define this professional practice and which usually derive from the multisemiotic nature of audiovisual texts (e.g. synchronising text with soundtrack and visuals) and the technological component (e.g. subtitling software). The two main technical dimensions of subtitling concern spatial and temporal features.

Technical Considerations (Space)

Subtitles should be displayed in the least distracting manner to avoid detracting from the visuals in general and from the plot in particular. The spatial dimension is usually characterised in terms of visibility (i.e. subtitles appear at a specific on-screen location), legibility (i.e. subtitles can be read against the background) and readability (i.e. subtitles are well segmented and inviting to read).

The traditional way of displaying interlingual subtitles is centred, both horizontally and vertically, and placed at the bottom of the screen. Subtitles ought to be placed at the top of the screen when they risk being illegible because the background is too light at the bottom or whenever meaningful action or essential data appear in the said position (such as opening credits or already existing subtitles because the audiovisual source text temporarily switches to another language). Regardless of the position, it is common practice to leave at least a 10% safe area at the top, bottom, right-hand side and left-hand side of the screen. Subtitles traditionally comprise one or two lines, although it is also common to come across three-liners, and even four-liners, especially in programmes captioned for people who are d/Deaf or hard-of-hearing.[6] The font should be non-serif (often Arial or Helvetica), and although the size varies across different pieces of software, the range is between 25 and 40 points, the most common being 30. Despite little variation in subtitling guidelines of streaming platforms such as Netflix, considerations in terms of location of subtitles on the screen, font type and font size become more varied, as they are localised using input from users (Pedersen 2018).[7]

Ever since electronic subtitles emerged, laser subtitles – always white and burnt on onto the celluloid – are increasingly less produced. Because they are projected onto the images, electronic subtitles also allow for different colours. These can vary depending on the commission, though yellow and mainly white are preferred in interlingual subtitling. Subtitle characters are almost always shadowed or black contoured so that they stand up against the images. Should there be legibility problems with very light backgrounds, they may be encased in a grey or black box.

The pixels occupied by subtitles have a direct implication on the number of characters, including spaces, that subtitle lines can accommodate. Díaz-Cintas and Remael (2020) argue that, with the arrival of digital media, subtitling editors have been enhanced and have started working with proportional lettering or variable-width fonts, thus allowing for more significant rationalisation of the space available. Therefore, subtitlers can now write as much text as possible as long as the output is contained within the limits of the area that is deemed safe and appropriate according to industry practice. Today, industry guidelines still impose maximum character-per-line (CPL) values on subtitlers; for instance, Netflix (2020) advocates for 42-character lines (i.e. two-line subtitles of up to 84 spaces) across their whole range of languages, except for some like Chinese (16 characters), Korean (16), Japanese (16 horizontal and 11 vertical) and Russian (39).

The spatial dimension of the technical features co-occurs with the temporal dimension. Both drive the linguistic considerations of editing AVT, but they are also intrinsically connected.

Technical Considerations (Time)

With regard to temporal parameters, one key element is, first and foremost, understanding how the timing of a clip is calculated. Every single frame of a given clip can be identified with a unique reference number, called a timecode, which is a sequence of numeric codes generated at regular intervals by a timing synchronisation system and recorded by the time code reader or recording (TCR) display. The TCR assigns an eight-digit figure (hours, minutes, seconds and frames) to every single frame of any given clip and is available in most video players and subtitling programs (e.g. 00:00:01:14 –> 00:00:03:11).[8] Each subtitle, therefore, has two timecodes that indicate when it starts (e.g. 00:00:01:14) and when it ends (e.g. 00:00:03:11). Spotting (also known as authoring, mastering, text timing or cueing) consists of setting the in and out times of the subtitles so that they appear and disappear in synchrony with the spoken dialogue and what is being shown on screen as well as in a visually appealing fashion that does not distract the viewer's and listener's attention from the visuals. The spotting ought to mirror the rhythm of the film and the actors' performance and be mindful of pauses, interruptions and other prosodic features of the original speech, allowing for the smooth reading of the subtitles. These prosodic features also belong to the linguistic characteristics of subtitling and its editing but are driven by temporal aspects of the film's rhythm.

The reading speed, also known as subtitle speed or display or presentation rate (Pedersen 2011; Sandford 2015), is understood as the relationship that exists between the quantity of text contained in a subtitle and the time that it remains on screen. The reading speed is calculated by dividing the total number of characters by the time they remain on screen. Subtitles ought to have a minimum duration of one second (usually 24, 25 or 30 frames) and a maximum duration of four to seven seconds depending on the number of lines. Generally speaking, the fewer characters in a subtitle, the lower the reading time will be, whereas the more characters in a subtitle, the higher the display rate will be. The reading speed is calculated in words per minute (WPM) or characters per second (CPS), the latter quickly becoming more common in the industry for all languages, as seen in professional guidelines such as the ones distributed by Netflix (2020). The duration of a two-line subtitle typically varies between four to seven seconds (cfr. infra), but the most commonly known 'rule' is the six second one, which equals about 140–150 words per minute or 12 characters per second (Karamitroglou 1998; Díaz-Cintas and Remael 2020).

Subtitling systems use algorithms to calculate reading speed values, which are usually displayed on each subtitle along with its duration as well as the start and end timecodes. Nonetheless, as not all subtitling systems use the exact same algorithms, reading speed values can differ when exporting subtitle files from one tool and importing them into a different one (González-Iglesias 2011; Martí-Ferriol 2013). Furthermore, the display rate value calculation depends on whether the blank spaces that separate words are counted. For the viewer to be able to perceive that a subtitle is different from the next and hence register that a change of written material has occurred, the two subtitles should be separated by a minimum gap consisting of at least two to four frames. When subtitles are separated by a small number of frames, usually 12 or less (Netflix 2020), a spotting strategy is to chain them, that is, spot them close to each other and maintain only the minimum gap of two frames rather than, say, five or nine frames.

Linguistic Considerations

Just like some technical considerations directly impact the leeway subtitlers have to produce the most accurate and adequate subtitles, linguistic considerations are shaped by those spatial and temporal limitations. When dividing dialogue, narrations and other content that needs to be translated into subtitles, the ensuing target text can be ideally written over the two available lines of a subtitle, as one of the golden rules in the profession is that, when possible, each subtitle should contain a complete idea. If too long, the target text can spread over several subtitles. The line breaking within subtitles and the segmentation across subtitles ought to be done according to syntactic and grammatical considerations rather than aesthetic rules, since the ultimate objective is to facilitate the reading and understanding of the message in the little time available.

An essential factor in the readability of subtitles across ideas and rules concerns punctuation. As in other types of written text, punctuation signs in subtitling are utilised to convey paralinguistic information. Punctuation in subtitling can also inform about the prosody of the speech, for example, rhythm, tone, pauses, hesitations, orality markers and intonation.[9] Yet the traditional and most frequently used approach in the industry rests on the assumption that the fewer punctuation signs used, the better, since they take up space on the screen, which would be better used for the actual message. All signs ought to be used following the rules of the target language grammar, although exceptions may be made in cases where some may acquire a particular expressive role in subtitling, such as the use of hyphens to indicate that lines come from two different speakers.

According to Díaz-Cintas and Remael (2007, 2020), the main linguistic parameters that affect interlingual subtitling are text reduction, cohesion and coherence on the one hand and segmentation and line breaks on the other.[10] Subtitles must afford viewers not only enough time to read and understand what is written at the bottom of the screen but also to watch and listen to what is happening. As a rule of thumb, subtitles ought to be syntactically and grammatically self-contained and flawless, as they serve as a model for literacy by reflecting idiomaticity, culture and register.

The inscription of the original dialogue in the form of written subtitles in the target language is often accompanied by the deployment of truncation or reduction techniques, which may be total (i.e. omission) or partial (i.e. condensation). There are many ways to reduce information, although "no steadfast rules can be given as to when to condense and reformulate, or when to omit" (Díaz-Cintas and Remael 2020: 150) on account of the many technical constraints and conventions (see previously), each of which might differ slightly because of guidelines, client demands, regional conventions and the like. It is important to highlight that truncation also takes place intralingually, in particular for subtitles for deaf and hard-of-hearing audiences, as these often require lower display rates when produced for specific audiences (Zárate 2021). Table 33.1 shows an example taken from J. Lynn's *Clue* (1985), showing an extract from a translation distributed on Netflix following American captioning standards (e.g. three-liners and left/right alignment, among other features,

Table 33.1 Source and captioned dialogue of an excerpt from J. Lynn's *Clue* (1985)

Source Dialogue	*Captioned Dialogue*
~~Well,~~ someone's got to break the ice, ~~and it might as well be me. I mean,~~ I'm used to being a hostess; ~~it's part of my husband's work, and~~ it's always difficult when a group of new friends meet together for the first time ~~to get acquainted, so~~ I'm ~~perfectly~~ prepared to start the ball rolling. ~~I mean,~~ I have ~~absolutely~~ no idea what we're ~~doing here, or what I'm doing here,~~ or what this ~~place~~ is about, but I am determined to enjoy myself ~~and~~ I'm very intrigued ~~and oh, my,~~ this soup's delicious isn't it?	Someone's got to break the ice. I'm used to being a hostess. It's always difficult when a group of new friends meet together for the first time. I'm prepared to start the ball rolling. I have no idea why we're here or what this is about, but I am determined to enjoy myself. I'm very intrigued. This soup's delicious, isn't it?
100 words – 511 characters (with spaces)	61 words – 327 characters (with spaces)

were present). This example does not contain timecodes, as an emphasis is put on the quantity of information that can be delivered, within the same space of time, in spoken dialogue as opposed to written subtitles. The amount of the information supplied in writing is 36% smaller if we count the total number of spaces present in each version.

In the translation industry, estimations exist of how much a target language relates to a source language in terms of the number of characters, typically expressed in percentages. If an English source text is translated into other Latin-script languages, then the target text will be characterised by a text swell of about 10% to 20%, if not more (Esselink 2000; Declercq 2011; Scriptis 2021). However, these proportional relations concern text translations or localisation of websites and software, not multimodal translations such as those needed for video games, movies, televised or streamed content. In fact, AVT is driven so much through reduction that subtitles from English to Dutch, for instance, often see the opposite occur, with fewer characters. Table 33.2 includes an example of that reverse swell can be seen in the opening subtitles, in English and Dutch, of the 2001 Dreamworks movie *Shrek*.

Table 33.2 Opening subtitles of A. Adamson and V. Jenson's *Shrek* (2001) for Dutch and English, with their overall total word and character counts

English captions	Dutch subtitles	[Literal backtranslation]
Once upon a time there was a lovely princess.	Er was eens een mooie prinses.	[There was once a fine princess]
But she had an enchantment upon her of a fearful sort . . . which could only be broken by love's first kiss.	Maar er rustte een vreselijke betovering op haar, die enkel gebroken kon worden door de eerste kus der liefde.	[But a terrible spell rested on her,] [which could only be broken by love's first kiss]
29 words – 146 characters (with spaces)	25 words – 135 characters (with spaces)	

The first English subtitle has 9 words and 44 characters; Dutch uses only 6 words and 30 characters. The second subtitle has 11 words (55 spaces) for English and 8 words (47 spaces) for Dutch, but the third has 9 words (46 spaces) compared to 11 words (58 spaces) in the Dutch version. This exemplifies the leeway that always exists concerning the reduction of information in intralingual and interlingual subtitling; decisions vary depending on each subtitle, and transferring (and reducing) information are part of the subtitler's style, skill and creativity, among other factors.

Whilst truncating, in order for subtitlers to reformulate information adequately and purposefully, they may resort to the works of translation studies scholars on traditional translation strategies and techniques (e.g. Molina and Hurtado-Albir 2002), although this might fall short in certain practices such as subtitling. In the latter, micro-level techniques to better fit the target content within the temporal and spatial limitations are called for (Díaz-Cintas and Remael 2020). These practices play out at both word level and beyond (clause or sentence), with some examples shown in Table 33.3.

The different reduction procedures in subtitling provide a plethora of techniques that can be applied in the many forms of subtitling: subtitle production in the source language, in the target language and the editing of both when relevant. As for omission in subtitling, some elements are typically subject to removal, such as speech hesitations and false starts of utterances, among others. Unfinished sentences allow for reduction by the further omission of elements or even compensating by adding fewer elements to a previous or following sentence and therefore deleting the formal equivalent of the unfinished sentence from the source text. When on-screen

Table 33.3 Frequent condensation procedures in subtitling

word level	1. simplifying verbal periphrases
	2. generalising enumerations
	3. using a shorter near-synonym or equivalent expression
	4. using simple rather than compound tenses
	5. changing word classes
	6. exploiting short forms and contractions
clause or sentence level	1. changing negations or questions into affirmative sentences or assertions
	2. transforming indirect questions into direct ones
	3. simplifying modal verbs, turning direct speech into indirect speech
	4. changing the subject of a sentence or phrase
	5. manipulating the theme and rheme
	6. turning long or compound sentences into simple sentences
	7. switching from active to passive voice or vice versa
	8. using pronouns and other deictics to replace substantives or noun phrases
	9. merging two or more phrases or sentences into one

visually present information is highly relevant for the understanding of a particular passage but appears together with considerable amounts of dialogue, shorter references can be used in writing (e.g. deictics). Figures of speech and idiomatic expressions in the source language might be equivalent in the target language but omitted altogether (proper elimination) or compensated for by replacing them with a shorter, near-equivalent solution (omission-compensation).

Equally a form of reduction is the partial omission and compensation or complete elimination of features in the source language that take on forms that are difficult to render in another language, either because the equivalent does not trigger the same response or sentiments, or because the source language element is not considered appropriate in the target language: dialect, taboo language and slang.[11] This changing of those features, often by eliminating, is seen as a third type of reduction (Antonini 2005: 213–14). Still, because of the shared characteristic of full or partial elimination, this chapter envisages this type of rendering as aligned with omission. With all the limitations and considerations in place now, the technology comes into the picture, that is, the tools used to produce subtitles and to edit them.

Subtitle Editing and Translation Technologies (Computer-Aided Tools)

AVT workstations have experienced multiple shifts and transformations over the last few decades. The multimedial nature of audiovisual texts has often made it difficult to use certain computer-aided translation tools, such as TM, in professional subtitling. Words, expressions and sentences in written texts take on or trigger many additional forms (e.g. social implications, metaphorical values and implicit meaning, to mention but a few), but the number of possible added dimensions increases substantially with the incorporation of image and sound. These added layers have traditionally been a stumbling block in the use of TMs in the translation of audiovisual texts (Díaz-Cintas 2005). Nowadays, though, TM tools are being timidly integrated into AVT with the aim of increasing AVT productivity and reducing costs. Despite the criticism that CAT tools impose constraints on the cognitive and textual processes translators carry out (Jiménez-Crespo 2013: 213), Athanasiadi (2017) concluded in her study of current practices in the freelance subtitling industry that subtitlers were very eager to utilise subtitling tools with functions like TM to improve their efficiency.

In this respect, the TM system memoQ launched an add-on in 2018 that allows users to watch a clip when translating in the TM interface. Some months later, in September 2019, SDL, now

RWS, released a similar video plugin for its flagship translation software, then called SDL Studio, now Trados Studio. The pluginprovides features for previewing subtitle captions within the video while translating in the existing editor and – according to the company's selling points – includes QC checks for validating subtitle content. Other developers have also followed suit, and the cloud-based tool Transifex now offers an editor tool that supports video preview to help translate subtitles whilst being able to watch the clip within the same interface. Having said that, no CAT tools on the market allow users to spot clips, which still constitute a quintessential part of the subtitling process. Instead, they assume that translators will be working with timed templates, as this is common practice in the AVT industry (Nikolić 2015; Georgakopoulou 2006, 2012).

Some cloud-based tools are now experimenting with incorporating TM (and also MT) into their interfaces. Some even combine ASR for the transcription of dialogue and neural MT (NMT) as well as TM features for the translation and editing of dialogue within the same interface. Some of these platforms also consider project management so that the work can be better distributed among translators and thus streamline workflows on cloud ecosystems (Bolaños-García-Escribano and Díaz-Cintas 2020). At the time of writing, there are large AVT service providers that are further exploiting ASR and NMT to produce semi-automatic subtitle templates, thereby commissioning post-editing tasks to their pools of translators in an attempt to increase their efficiency but also with the anticipation to cut back production cycle time and therefore costs. Similarly, several media distributors have carried out practically oriented research on subtitle translation production employing NMT (Mehta *et al.* 2020) as well as on human-introduced translation error identification using pre-trained language models (Gupta *et al.* 2021).

Subtitle Editing and Language Technology (Machine-Generated Subtitles)

Little scholarly attention has been paid to the editing of material that has been captioned and subtitled automatically by means of an application. There are two main technologies that allow for the automation of subtitle production: ASR and MT. ASR enables the recognition and translation of spoken language into text by computers; it can either facilitate the production of live subtitles to a human linguist (e.g. respeaking) or produce subtitles automatically (e.g. automatic captioning). The latter is usually done intralingually, meaning the dialogue and other utterances in a particular programme are automatically transcribed by the machine; however, there is an ever-increasing number of tools that incorporate MT engines to enable the automatic translation of video material in subtitles. The most widespread and well-known platform that uses ASR and then machine-translates that ASR output is Google's YouTube.

MT necessarily calls for yet a new understanding of quality, as the raw output is generally of a lesser quality than human translations (Läubli and Orrego-Carmona 2017). Therefore, to comply with (high) quality standards, machine-translated raw output ought to be post-edited. Post-editing is a task that involves revising MT output (BSI 2015: 1), hence overlapping revision, albeit differing in many aspects, such as the type of errors encountered and the final level of quality expected. As Allen (2005) highlights, post-editing guidelines in the market tend to be individually elaborated for each institution, thus leading to a general lack of homogeneity. Still, many academic and professional post-editing guidelines mainly differentiate between two main degrees of post-editing: (1) light post-editing, from which an understandable and usable text is produced even if it is not linguistically or stylistically perfect, and (2) full post-editing, which pursues human-like quality by producing text that is stylistically appropriate and linguistically correct (Hu and Cadwell 2016)).

When it comes to applying MT, AVT poses a number of challenges (Burchardt *et al.* 2016), but, despite these hurdles, a number of EU-funded research projects have looked into the possibility of merging MT and AVT over the years, among which are MUSA (Multilingual Subtitling of MultimediA content, 2002–2004), eTitle (2003–2004), SUMAT (2011–2014, Subtitling by Machine Translation) and EU-BRIDGE (2012–2015). Originally funded by the EU, TransLectures (Transcription and Translation of Video Lectures, 2011–2014) is a cloud-based tool that utilises ASR and MT systems to localise academic video lectures.[12] In such a flurry of technological advances and increasing hybridisation, it can only be expected that automation will make deeper, far-reaching inroads into subtitling in the upcoming years. Still, whatever the level of automation, the ultimate test for a subtitle is its usability per its purpose, that is, the editing of the target language has achieved an accurate level of quality: accurate equivalence is in place both formally (spatial/temporal) and linguistically.

Editing and Quality

According to the British Standards Institute (BSI 1995: 5), quality is "the totality of characteristics of an entity that bear on its ability to satisfy stated and implied needs", where an entity represents textual products of any nature. Evaluating the quality of a translation, irrespective of its type, depends on internal and external factors that go undeniably far beyond mere words. Furthermore, "there is no such thing as absolute quality. Different jobs will have different quality criteria because the texts are meeting different needs" (Mossop 2001: 6). Research on translation quality, however, has almost solely focused on the linguistic aspects of rendering texts from one language to another, thus obliterating the paratextual and paralinguistic dimension of certain translation types like AVT (Kuo 2020).

Because of its multimodal nature, AVT challenges traditional approaches to the study of translation quality, which tend to focus on the linguistic dimension only. Quality evaluation models, such as House (1977, 2015), are of limited use in AVT, where the multisemiotic nature of the translated texts calls for alternative assessment methods. Neither do proofreading and revision guidelines help much, as translations for subtitling and other AVT modes are often curtailed and consciously handled to abide by the given technical constraints, per the guidelines and protocols explained in the previous sections.

When it comes to interlingual subtitling, companies have their own in-house quality processes, but information about them is scarce as translation companies and language service–providing companies (LSPs) tend to be zealous guardians of their own workflows and QC models. Nonetheless, there are some exceptions with large media providers, such as Netflix (2020), offering comprehensive documents underlining QC workflows and conventions, from which trainers and students can benefit.[13] From an academic perspective, however, few theoretical constructs are available, and the FAR model proposed by Pedersen (2017) is arguably the only subtitling quality model available as such. Drawing heavily on Romero-Fresco's (2009) NER model for respeaking,[14] the FAR proposal constitutes a reasonably comprehensive attempt to categorise pre-prepared, interlingual subtitling errors. Pedersen's (2017) model identifies three main error categories whose initials name the FAR model: functional equivalence, acceptability and readability. Functional equivalence errors can be semantic (e.g. mistranslations, false friends, inaccuracies) or stylistic (e.g. inappropriate register). Acceptability errors are those that affect grammar, spelling and naturalness. Readability includes errors closely related to the technical dimension and has to do with spotting, synchronisation, segmentation, line breaking, line lengths and punctuation, as well as display rates.

Whereas the functional and acceptability types of errors could potentially be extrapolated to other translation domains because they concentrate primarily on the linguistic dimension, the readability classification can be said to be unique to subtitling, as it focuses on the technical dimension that characterises the production of subtitles, as previously expounded earlier in this chapter.

Final Remarks and Future Avenues

Editing can come in many different shapes in AVT practices. This chapter has served as an introduction to some practices and technologies involved in AVT editing, with an emphasis on subtitling. We have identified at least six different types of editing that traditionally take place in the AVT industry – i.e. pre-editing, post-editing, revision, proofreading, QC and post-QC viewing – and have discussed the additional editing-related complexity posed by the localisation of media programmes. We have proposed a seventh type of editing, processes acting on a 'supra' level. It would also be worth noting that revoicing tools encompass different workflows and that media accessibility[15] modes would also require alternative editing tasks to the ones mentioned previously, which means that the previous list is far from exhaustive.

It can be argued that the audiovisual nature of media evidently poses additional challenges to the editing of translation output, be it human or machine generated. In AVT, not only does the linguist handle linguistic output, which is heavily affected by the audio and visual information transferred on screen, but also technical aspects, such as timecodes, need to be closely considered too. When it comes to the use of automation tools in AVT, such as the combination of ASR and MT engines to produce automatically timed subtitle templates in languages other than those of the source text/video, the complexity of the editing tasks is significantly greater. In a subtitle post-editing scenario, for instance, the linguist is expected to assess both the linguistic and the technical quality of the machine-generated work. First, technical editing is then carried out by looking at aspects such as timings, position, number of characters, display rate, synchronisation and segmentation. Secondly, linguistic editing looks at the effectiveness of the (multisemiotic) meaning transfer by means of comparing the translated subtitles not only with the original dialogues but also with the visuals, as it is highly plausible that language-based MT engines have missed out on visual references affecting nuance. Research on how practitioners perceive the editing of machine-generated translations in the form of subtitles is not promising (Koponen *et al.* 2020a), even where productivity might indeed be higher in such cases (Koponen *et al.* 2020b). Future research efforts could be devoted to the analysis of machine-timed subtitles combined with machine-generated subtitles, especially with regard to the cognitive effort involved in such practices as well as their long-term applicability in light of rapidly evolving industry conventions and standards.

Notes

1 The scope of the relevant literature is substantial, but includes, for instance, Wagner (1985), Esselink (2000), Krings (2001), Bowker (2002), O'Brien (2007), Garcia (2009), Guerberof (2009), Quah (2006), Garcia (2011), Yamada (2011), Declercq (2015), Koponen (2016), Daems *et al.* (2017), Vieira (2019).

2 *Speech recognition* and *voice recognition* are often used without any differentiation, but in a strict approach, usage of the latter term should be limited to recognising the voice only (speaker identification, separating a specific voice from the surrounding noise) and the former to recognising the words that are being spoken. Both terms actually refer to two different functionalities that often operate in conjunction in order to obtain spoken words in written format through automated speech recognition.

3 Media accessibility practices are also understood to fall under either two categories according to how the transfer is accomplished (i.e. oral or written output).

4 This language- and translation-related *editing* should not be confused with the editing of the programme, i.e. the manipulation and arrangement of video shots, which takes place during the production phase.

5   Quality assurance is a comprehensive and often proactive process in order to ensure that the quality of a localisation project is in line with the requirements stipulated by the client and/or demanded by the target users. Quality control is reactive and typically happens at the end of the translation phase of a more linear project and of the localisation phase for more complex projects. Whereas the prime aim of QA is to prevent errors, QC is primarily looking to correct them (or a sample that is deemed representative of the entire project).

6   For a discussion on two or three lines, see Gerber-Morón and Szarkowska (2018).

7   For a discussion on how conventional subtitling can affect image composition and how subtitles can still help preserve the artistic qualities of the original image and sound, see Fox (2018).

8   Milliseconds are rarely used in the industry but are common when working with free open-source cross-platform subtitle editing tools like Aegisub, Subtitle Workshop, Subtitle Edit, Sub Station Alpha, Sabbu and JacoSub, all of them very popular among fansubbers.

9   The main punctuation conventions that ought to be observed for English-language subtitling can be found in either Díaz-Cintas and Remael (2007, 2020), in the academic sphere, or Netflix (2020), in the professional sphere.

10 In a less structured fashion, Ivarsson and Carroll (1998) also make reference to linguistically related good subtitling practices, which regard grammar, word order, condensation, coherence and consistency.

11 Due to word limitations, no attention is given to the difficult relationship between reduction, omission, rendering and compensation as a form of normalising domestication, and possibly a form of censorship too.

12 For more on the respective project see their EU pages: MUSA (https://cordis.europa.eu/project/id/IST-2001-38299), eTitle (https://cordis.europa.eu/project/id/22160), SUMAT (https://cordis.europa.eu/project/id/270919) and EU-Bridge (https://cordis.europa.eu/project/id/287658). All pages accessed 1 September 2021.

13 For a discussion on quality control of subtitles, see Nikolic (2021).

14 N for number of words in the respoken subtitles, E for editing errors, R for recognition errors (Romero-Fresco 2009: 32–33). This model has also been further developed in later publications such as Romero-Fresco and Martínez-Pérez (2015) and Romero-Fresco (2016) for live captioning and Romero-Fresco and Pöchhacker (2017) for interlingual live subtitling.

15 Media accessibility has often been used as an umbrella term to subsume certain translation practices that aim at making media accessible to users with sensory disabilities, and more specifically has traditionally referred to two main practices: subtitling for the deaf and the hard-of-hearing as well as audio description (Orero 2004). However, as explained by Greco (2018), media accessibility modalities can also include audio subtitling, sign language interpreting and any other practices that aim to overcome sensory barriers linguistically (Baños 2017).

Bibliography

Allen, Jeff (2005) 'What Is Post-Editing?', *Translation Automation Newsletter* 4.

Alvarez, Sergi, Antoni Oliver, and Toni Badia (2020) 'Quantitative Analysis of Post-editing Effort Indicators for NMT', in *Proceedings of the 22nd Annual Conference of the European Association for Machine Translation*, EAMT, Lisbon, 411–20. Available at: https://aclanthology.org/2020.eamt-1.44.

Antonini, Rachele (2005) 'The Perception of Subtitled Humor in Italy', *Humor. International Journal of Humor Research* 18(2): 209–25. https://doi.org/10.1515/humr.2005.18.2.209.

Athanasiadi, Rafaella (2017) 'The Potential of Machine Translation and Other Language Assistive Tools in Subtitling: A New Era?', in Łukasz Bogucki (ed.) *Audiovisual Translation – Research and Use*, Oxford: Peter Lang, 29–49.

Baños, Rocío (2017) 'Audiovisual Translation', in Kristina Bedjis and Christina Maaß (eds.) *Manual of Romance Languages in the Media*, Berlin: De Gruyter, 471–88. https://doi.org/10.1515/9783110314755-021.

Bogucki, Łukasz and Mikołaj Deckert (eds.) (2020) *The Palgrave Handbook of Audiovisual Translation and Media Accessibility*, London: Palgrave Macmillan.

Bolaños-García-Escribano, Alejandro and Jorge Díaz-Cintas (2020) 'The Cloud Turn in Audiovisual Translation', in Łukasz Bogucki and Mikołaj Deckert (eds.) *The Palgrave Handbook of Audiovisual Translation and Media Accessibility*, London: Palgrave Macmillan, 519–44. https://doi.org/10.1007/978-3-030-42105-2_26.

Bowker, Lynne (2002) *Computer-aided Translation Technology: A Practical Introduction*, Ottawa: University of Ottawa Press.

BSI (1995) *Quality Management and Quality Assurance – Vocabulary*, London: British Standards Institute.

BSI (2015) *Translation Services – Post-editing of Machine Translation – Requirements*, London: British Standards Institute.

Burchardt, Aljoscha, Arle Lommel, Lindsay Bywood, Kim Harris, and Maja Popović (2016) 'Machine Translation Quality in an Audiovisual Context', *Target* 28(2): 206–21. https://doi.org/10.1075/target.28.2.03bur.

Chaume, Frederic (2006) 'Dubbing', in Keith Brown (ed.) *Encyclopedia of Language and Linguistics*, Amsterdam: Elsevier, 6–9.

Chaume, Frederic (2018) 'Is Audiovisual Translation Putting the Concept of Translation up Against the Ropes?', *The Journal of Specialised Translation* 30: 84–104. www.jostrans.org/issue30/art_chaume.pdf.

Daems, Joke, Sonia Vandepitte, Robert J. Hartsuiker, and Lieve Macken (2017) 'Identifying the Machine Translation Error Types with the Greatest Impact on Post-editing Effort', *Frontiers in Psychology* 8(1282): 1–20. https://doi.org/10.3389/fpsyg.2017.01282.

Declercq, Christophe (2011). 'Advertising and Localization', in Kirsten Malmkjaer (ed.) *The Oxford Handbook of Translation Studies*, Oxford: Oxford University Press, 262–74.

Declercq, Christophe (2015). 'Translation Technology in the UK', in Chan Sin-wai (ed.) *The Routledge Encyclopedia of Translation Technology*, Oxford and New York: Routledge, 364–74.

Delabastita, Dirk (1989) 'Translation and Mass-Communication: Film and T.V. Translation as Evidence of Cultural Dynamics', *Babel* 35(4): 193–218. https://doi.org/10.1075/babel.35.4.02del.

de Linde, Zoé and Neil Kay (1999) *The Semiotics of Subtitling*, Manchester: St Jerome.

Díaz-Cintas, Jorge (2001) *La traducción audiovisual: el subtitulado*, Salamanca: Almar.

Díaz-Cintas, Jorge (2003) *Teoría y práctica de la subtitulación inglés/español*, Barcelona: Ariel Cine.

Díaz-Cintas, Jorge (2005) 'El subtitulado y los avances tecnológicos', in Raquel Merino-Álvarez, Eterio Pajares-Infante, and José Miguel Santamaría-López (eds.) *Trasvases Culturales: Literatura, Cine, Traducción*, vol. 4, Guipuzkoa: UPV, 155–75.

Díaz-Cintas, Jorge (2012) 'Clearing the Smoke to See the Screen: Ideological Manipulation in Audiovisual Translation', *Meta: Journal Des Traducteurs* 57(2): 279–93. https://doi.org/10.7202/1013945ar.

Díaz-Cintas, Jorge (2015) 'Technological Strides in Subtitling', in Chan Sin-wai (ed.) *The Routledge Encyclopedia of Translation Technology*, Oxford and New York: Routledge, 632–43.

Díaz-Cintas, Jorge and Aline Remael (2007) *Audiovisual Translation: Subtitling*, Manchester: St. Jerome.

Díaz-Cintas, Jorge and Serenella Massidda (2019) 'Technological Advances in Audiovisual Translation', in Minako O'Hagan (ed.) *The Routledge Handbook of Translation and Technology*, London and New York: Routledge, 255–70.

Díaz-Cintas, Jorge and Aline Remael (2020) *Subtitling: Concepts and Practices*, London and New York: Routledge.

Esselink, Bert (2000) *A Practical Guide to Localization*, Amsterdam and Philadelphia: John Benjamins Publishing Company.

Fox, Wendy (2018) *Can Integrated Titles Improve the Viewing Experience? Investigating the Impact of Subtitling on the Reception and Enjoyment of Film Using Eye Tracking and Questionnaire Data*, Berlin: Language Science Press. Available at https://library.oapen.org/handle/20.500.12657/29550.

Gambier, Yves (2003) 'Introduction: Screen Transadaptation: Perception and Reception', *Translator* 9(2): 171–89. https://doi.org/10.1080/13556509.2003.10799152.

Gambier, Yves (2006) 'Subtitling', in Keith Brown (ed.) *Encyclopedia of Language and Linguistics*, Elsevier Science, 258–63. Available at: www.sciencedirect.com/science/article/pii/B0080448542004727.

Gambier, Yves and Henrik Gottlieb (2001) 'Multimedia, Multilingua: Multiple Challenges', in Yves Gambier and Henrik Gottlieb (eds.) *(Multi) Media Translation: Concepts, Practices and Research*, Amsterdam and Philadelphia: John Benjamins Publishing Company, viii–xx. https://doi.org/10.1075/btl.34.01gam.

Garcia, Ignacio (2009) 'Beyond Translation Memory: Computers and the Professional Translator', *Journal of Specialised Translation* 12: 199–214.

Garcia, Ignacio (2011) 'Translating by Post-Editing: Is It the Way Forward?', *Machine Translation* 25(3): 217–37. https://doi.org/10.1007/s10590-011-9115-8.

Georgakopoulou, Panayota (2006) 'Subtitling and Globalisation', *The Journal of Specialised Translation* 6: 115–20. Available at: www.jostrans.org/issue06/art_georgakopoulou.php.

Georgakopoulou, Panayota (2012) 'Challenges for the Audiovisual Industry in the Digital Age: The Ever-changing Needs of Subtitle Production', *The Journal of Specialised Translation* 1(17): 78–103. Available at: www.jostrans.org/issue17/art_georgakopoulou.pdf.

Gerber-Morón, Olivia and Agnieszka Szarkowska (2018) 'Line Breaks in Subtitling: An Eye Tracking Study on Viewer Preferences', *Journal of Eye Movement Research* 11(3). https://doi.org/10.16910/jemr.11.3.2.

González-Iglesias, Juan David (2011) 'Análisis diacrónico de la velocidad de presentación de subtítulos para DVD', *Trans* 15: 211–18.

Greco, Gian Maria (2018) 'The Nature of Accessibility Studies', *Journal of Audiovisual Translation* 1(1): 205–32. Available at: www.jatjournal.org/index.php/jat/article/view/51.

Guerberof, Ana (2009) 'Productivity and Quality in the Post-editing of Outputs from Translation Memories and Machine Translation', *International Journal of Localization* 7(1): 11–21.

Gupta, Prabhakar, Ridha Juneja, Anil Nelakanti, and Tamojit Chatterjee (2021, April) 'Detecting Over/under-Translation Errors for Determining Adequacy in Human Translations', *ArXiv.* http://arxiv.org/abs/2104.00267.

House, Juliane (1977) *A Model for Translation Quality Assessment*, Tübingen: Narr.

House, Juliane (2015) *Translation Quality Assessment: Past and Present*, London and New York: Routledge.

Hu, Ke and Patrick Cadwell (2016) 'A Comparative Study of Post-Editing Guidelines', *Baltic Journal of Modern Computing* 4(2): 346–53. Available at: www.bjmc.lu.lv/fileadmin/user_upload/lu_portal/projekti/bjmc/Contents/4_2_23_Hu.pdf.

Ivarsson, Jan (1992) *Subtitling for the Media: A Handbook of an Art*, Stockholm: Transedit.

Ivarsson, Jan and Mary Carroll (1998) *Subtitling*, Simrishamn: TransEdit HB.

Jiménez-Crespo, Miguel Ángel (2013) *Translation and Web Localization*, London and New York: Routledge.

Karamitroglou, Fotios (1998) 'A Proposed Set of Subtitling Standards in Europe', *Translation Journal* 2(2). Available at: http://translationjournal.net/journal/04stndrd.htm.

Karamitroglou, Fotios (2000) *Towards a Methodology for the Investigation of Norms in Audiovisual Translation: The Choice between Subtitling and Revoicing in Greece*, Amsterdam: Brill Rodopi. Available at: https://brill.com/view/title/27730.

Koponen, Maarit (2016) 'Is Machine Translation Post-editing Worth the Effort? A Survey of Research into Post-Editing and Effort', *The Journal of Specialised Translation* 25: 131–48.

Koponen, Maarit, Umut Sulubacak, Kaisa Vitikainen, and Jörg Tiedemann (2020a) 'MT for Subtitling: Investigating Professional Translators' User Experience and Feedback', in Michael Denkowski and Christian Federman (eds.) *Proceedings of the 14th Conference of the Association for Machine Translation in the Americas, October 6–9, 2020, 1st Workshop on Post-Editing in Modern-Day Translation*, AMTA, 79–92. Available at: https://aclanthology.org/2020.amta-research.pdf.

Koponen, Maarit, Umut Sulubacak, Kaisa Vitikainen, and Jörg Tiedemann (2020b) 'MT for Subtitling: User Evaluation of Post-Editing Productivity', in André Martins, Helena Moniz, Sara Fumega, Bruno Martins, Fernando Batista, Luisa Coheur, Carla Parra, Isabel Trancoso, Marco Turchi, Arianna Bisazza, Joss Moorkens, Ana Guerberof, Mary Nurminen, Lena Marg, and Mikel L. Forcada (eds.) *Proceedings of the 22nd Annual Conference of the European Association for Machine Translation*, Lisbon: EAMT, 115–24. Available at: www.aclweb.org/anthology/2020.eamt-1.13.

Krings, Hans (2001) *Repairing Texts: Empirical Investigations of Machine Translation Post-Editing Processes*, Sarah Litzer (ed.) and Geoffrey S. Koby, Gregory M. Shreve, and Katja Mischerikow (trans.), Kent, OH: Kent University Press.

Kuo, Arista Szu-Yu (2020) 'The Tangled Strings of Parameters and Assessment in Subtitling Quality: An Overview', in Łukasz Bogucki and Mikołaj Deckert (eds.) *The Palgrave Handbook of Audiovisual Translation and Media Accessibility*, London: Palgrave, 437–58. https://doi.org/10.1007/978-3-030-42105-2_22.

Laks, Simon (1957/2013) *Le sous-titrage de films : sa technique, son esthétique*, Paris: L'Écran traduit, Hors-série 1 (2013), 4–46.

Läubli, Samuel and David Orrego-Carmona (2017) 'When Google Translate is Better than Some Human Colleagues, Those People Are No Longer Colleagues', in João Esteves-Ferreira, Juliet Macan, Ruslan Mitkov, and Olaf-Michael Stefanov (eds.), *Translating and the Computer, London, 16 November 2017*, Geneva: Tradulex, 59–69. Available at: www.zora.uzh.ch/id/eprint/147260/.

Luyken, Georg-Michael (1991) *Overcoming Language Barriers in Television: Dubbing and Subtitling for the European Audience*, Manchester: The European Institute for the Media. Available at: www.opengrey.eu/item/display/10068/523211.

Martí-Ferriol. José Luis (2013). 'Subtitle Reading Speed: A New Tool for Its Estimation'. *Babel*, 59(4): 406–20.

Mayoral, Roberto, Dorothy Kelly, and Natividad Gallardo (1988) 'Concept of Constrained Translation: Non-Linguistic Perspectives of Translation', *Meta* 33(3): 356–67. https://doi.org/10.7202/003608ar.

Mehta, Sneha, Bahareh Azarnoush, Boris Chen, Avneesh Saluja, Vinith Misra, Ballav Bihani, and Ritwik Kumar (2020) 'Simplify-Then-Translate: Automatic Preprocessing for Black-Box Machine Translation', *ArXiv*, May. http://arxiv.org/abs/2005.11197.

Molina, Lucía and Amparo Hurtado-Albir (2002) 'Translation Techniques Revisited: A Dynamic and Functionalist Approach', *Meta* 47(4): 498–512. https://doi.org/10.7202/008033ar.

Moorkens, Joss, Sharon O'Brien, Igor Antônio Lourenço da Silva, Norma Fonseca, and Fabio Alves (2015) 'Correlations of Perceived Post-Editing Effort with Measurements of Actual Effort', *Machine Translation* 29(3–4): 267–84. https://doi.org/10.1007/s10590-015-9175-2.

Mossop, Brian (2001) *Revising and Editing for Translators*, 1st edition, London and New York: Routledge.

Netflix (2020) 'English Template Timed Text Style Guide – Netflix | Partner Help Center'. Available at: https://partnerhelp.netflixstudios.com/hc/en-us/articles/219375728-English-Template-Timed-Text-Style-Guide.

Nikolić, Kristijan (2015) 'The Pros and Cons of Using Templates in Subtitling', in Rocío Baños and Jorge Díaz-Cintas (eds.) *Audiovisual Translation in a Global Context. Mapping and Ever-Changing Landscape*, Basingstoke: Palgrave Macmillan, 192–202.

Nikolić, Kristijan (2021) 'Quality Control of Subtitles: A Study of Subtitlers, Proofreaders, Quality Controllers, LSPs and Broadcasters/Streaming Services', *Journal of Audiovisual Translation* 4(3): 66–88. https://doi.org/10.47476/jat.v4i3.2021.182.

O'Brien, Sharon (2005) 'Methodologies for Measuring the Correlations between Post-editing Effort and Machine Translatability', *Machine Translation* 19(1): 37–58. https://doi.org/10.1007/s10590-005-2467-1.

O'Brien, Sharon (2007) 'An Empirical Investigation of Temporal and Technical Post-Editing Effort', *Translation and Interpreting Studies* II(I): 83–136. https://doi.org/10.1075/tis.2.1.03ob.

O'Brien, Sharon (2011) 'Towards Predicting Post-editing Productivity', *Machine Translation* 25(3): 197–215. https://doi.org/10.1007/s10590-011-9096-7.

Orero, Pilar (2004) 'Introduction: Audiovisual Translation. A New Dynamic Umbrella', in Pilar Orero (ed.) *Topics in Audiovisual Translation*, Amsterdam: John Benjamins Publishing Company, vii–xiii. https://doi.org/10.1017/CBO9781107415324.004.

Pedersen, Jan (2011) *Subtitling Norms for Television: An Exploration Focussing on Extralinguistic Cultural References*, Amsterdam and Philadelphia: John Benjamins Publishing Company.

Pedersen, Jan (2017) 'The FAR Model: Assessing Quality in Interlingual Subtitling', *The Journal of Specialised Translation* 28: 210–29. Available at: www.jostrans.org/issue28/art_pedersen.pdf.

Pedersen, Jan (2018) 'From old tricks to Netflix: How Local are Interlingual Subtitling Norms for Streamed Television?' *Journal of Audiovisual Translation* 1(1): 81–100. Available at: https://jatjournal.org/index.php/jat/article/view/46/5.

Pérez-González, Luis (2014) *Audiovisual Translation: Theories, Methods and Issues*, London and New York: Routledge.

Pérez-González, Luis (ed.) (2018) *The Routledge Handbook of Audiovisual Translation*, London: Routledge.

Quah, Anne C. K. (2006) *Translation and Technology*, London: Palgrave Macmillan.

Romero-Fresco, Pablo (2009) 'A Corpus-based Study on the Naturalness of the Spanish Dubbing Language: The Analysis of Discourse Markers in the Dubbed Translation of Friends', PhD thesis, Heriot-Watt University. Available at: www.ros.hw.ac.uk/handle/10399/2237.

Romero-Fresco, Pablo (2016) 'Accessing Communication: The Quality of Live Subtitles in the UK', *Language and Communication* 49: 56–69. https://doi.org/10.1016/j.langcom.2016.06.001.

Romero-Fresco, Pablo and Juan Martínez Pérez (2015) 'Accuracy Rate in Live Subtitling: The NER Model', in Rocío Baños and Jorge Díaz-Cintas (eds.) *Audiovisual Translation in a Global Context: Mapping and Ever-Changing Landscape*, Basingstoke: Palgrave Macmillan, 28–50.

Romero-Fresco, Pablo and Franz Pöchhacker (2017) 'Quality Assessment in Interlingual Live Subtitling: The NTR Model', *Linguistica Antverpiensia* 16: 149–67.

Sánchez-Mompeán, Sofia (2021) 'Netflix Likes It Dubbed: Taking on the Challenge of Dubbing into English', *Language and Communication* 80: 180–90. https://doi.org/10.1016/J.LANGCOM.2021.07.001.

Sandford, James (2015) *White Paper WHP 306. The Impact of Subtitle Display Rate on Enjoyment under Normal Television Viewing Conditions Digital*, London: BBC.

Scriptis (2021) *Text Expansion and Contraction during Localization*. Available at: https://scriptis.com/wp-content/uploads/2021/03/expansion-chart-1.pdf.

Sokoli, Stavroula (2005) 'Temas de investigación en traducción audiovisual: la definición del texto audiovisual', in Patrick Zabalbeascoa, Laura Santamaría-Guinot, and Frederic Chaume-Varela (eds.) *La traducción audiovisual. Investigación, enseñanza y profesión*, Granada: Comares, 177–85.

Specia, Lucia and Atefeh Farzindar (2010) 'Estimating Machine Translation Post-editing Effort with HTER', in *Proceedings of the Second Joint EM+/CNGL Workshop: Bringing MT to the User: Research on Integrating MT in the Translation Industry*, 33–43. Available at: https://aclanthology.org/2010.jec-1.5.

Spiteri-Miggiani, Giselle (2019) *Dialogue Writing for Dubbing: An Insider's Perspective*, Basingstoke: Palgrave Macmillan.

Spiteri-Miggiani, Giselle (2021) 'English-Language Dubbing: Challenges and Quality Standards of an Emerging Localisation Trend', *The Journal of Specialised Translation* 36: 2–25. Available at: www.jostrans. org/issue36/art_spiteri.php.

Toral, Antonio, Martijn Wieling, and Andy Way (2018) 'Post-editing Effort of a Novel with Statistical and Neural Machine Translation', *Frontiers in Digital Humanities* 5: 1–11. https://doi.org/I:10.3389/fdigh.2018.00009.

Torralba-Miralles, Gloria, Ana Tamayo-Masero, Laura Mejías-Climent, Juan José Martínez-Sierra, José Luis Martí-Ferriol, Julio de los Reyes-Lozano, Irene de Higes-Andino, Frederic Chaume, and Beatriz Cerezo-Merchán (eds.) (2019) *La traducción para la subtitulación en España: mapa de convenciones*. Castellò de la Plana: Publicacions de la Universitat Jaume I.

Vieira, Lucas Nunes (2019) 'Post-editing of Machine Translation', in Minako O'Hagan (ed.) *The Routledge Handbook of Translation and Technology*, London and New York: Routledge, 319–35.

Wagner, Elisabeth (1985) 'Rapid Post-Editing of Systran', in *Proceedings of Translating and the Computer 5: Tools for the Trade*, 10–11 November 1983. Available at: https://aclanthology.org/1983.tc-1.23.pdf.

Yamada, Masaru (2011) 'Can College Students be Post-Editors? An Investigation Into Employing Language Learners in Machine Translation Plus Post-Editing Settings', *Machine Translation* 29(1): 49–67. https://doi.org/I:10.1007/s10590-014-9167-7.

Zabalbeascoa, Patrick (2001) 'La traducción de textos audiovisuales y la investigación traductológica', in Frederic Chaume-Varela and Rosa Agost-Canós (eds.) *La traducción en los medios audiovisuales*, Castelló de la Plana: Publicacions de la Universitat Jaume I, 49–56.

Zárate, Soledad (2021) *Captioning and Subtitling for d/Deaf and Hard of Hearing Audiences*, London: UCL Press.

34

POST-EDITING OF MACHINE TRANSLATION

May Li

Introduction

In natural language processing, post-editing is mostly associated with machine translation (MT), being referred to as MT's 'human partner' (Bar-Hillel 1951: 230). It entails more correction of the pre-translated text than translation from scratch (Wagner 1985). The task of the post-editor, according to Allen (2003), is to 'edit, modify and/or correct pre-translated text that has been processed by an MT system from (a) source language into a target language(s)' (García 2012). Despite differences in the description of post-editing, it is generally acknowledged that post-editing is an integral part of the translation process whereby editing, revision or correction is performed after the target language text is generated by the MT system.[1]

Post-editing has been a long-time ally of MT since the inception of MT technology, though it remained an unnoticed, behind-the-scenes activity due to the low quality of MT for decades. The first time that post-editing was brought to public attention was when the Automatic Language Processing Advisory Committee (ALPAC) published the best-known report in the history of MT in November 1966, which led to a collapse of confidence in the research and development of MT. The report concluded that MT 'serves no useful purpose without postediting' and that 'with postediting the over-all process is slow and probably uneconomical' (ALPAC 1966: 24). The message conveyed by the report to the general public and the research community was clear: that MT is hopeless and the role of post-editing highly unconvincing.

Notwithstanding the initial negative reports which cast doubt on the usefulness of post-editing (Beyer 1965; ALPAC 1966), production of post-edited MT texts occasionally resumed by the 1980s (Hutchins 1992; Vasconcellos and León 1985). The quality improvement of statistics-based MT (SMT) over rule-based MT (RMT) turned post-editing into an effective means of translating a large quantity of text at reduced cost in translation workflow (Moorkens 2018). People turn to MT for help because they wish to increase the speed of translation without compromising the quality of the translation. This can only be achieved when MT has reached a quality so high that post-editing the MT output becomes economical and practical; that is, the post-edited MT text is comparable to human translation in terms of quality and is achieved in a more resource-efficient manner.

The sweeping increase in internet use has accelerated the pace of globalization, which renders it impossible for human translators to cope with the overwhelming and huge demands for

DOI: 10.4324/9781003168348-37

translation (Gambier 2014; Doherty 2016; Accenture 2020). Meanwhile, steady improvement has been made in MT quality (Plitt and Masselot 2010), especially since Google announced its free online neuro-based Google Translate in 2016. The translation accuracy of MT is reported to have reached as high as 75% in specific domains, language pairs and content types (Zong 2020; Memsource 2021).

All this has boosted the application of MT both in our working and social lives. For example, a click on the choice of language on a Google page online, powered by Google Translate, allows us to surf the net in our own language, no matter what the source language is. However, despite the improvement in quality of MT-generated texts, it remains unlikely that MT can produce output which is as good as translations carried out by humans. Therefore, the practice of post-editing high-quality MT outputs is turning out to be an effective way of increasing translation productivity and has gradually become a standard practice in the language service industry in recent years (Guerberof 2009; Plitt and Masselot 2010; Bonet 2013; Koponen 2016; Li 2021).

Post-Editing Guidelines

When a post-editor, in carrying out post-editing, starts to interact with the machine, he or she has to take a number of factors into consideration with regard to the MT system, language pairs and domains which he or she would otherwise not do when translating from scratch. Other factors such as the post-editing process and his or her experience as a post-editor also affect how the raw MT output can be improved. Herein lies the question of how far the post-editor is supposed to intervene in editing the text produced by the machine. In fact, the extent to which the post-editor intervenes into the raw MT output depends largely on the purpose of the translation task at hand and the quality requirements placed by the client, in addition to the factors mentioned previously. Sometimes the request for post-editing is substantial: to correct MT errors as much as possible so that the final translation product reflects accurately the meaning of the source text, and other times, post-editing is intended for suitable improvement of the MT output without the need to make it perfect.

Over the years, many post-editing approaches have been adopted to tailor to various individual or organizational needs, which are reflected in the different levels of post-editing proposed in guidelines for distinct industrial settings. These levels vary in number and are categorized under different labels. At the initial stage, when post-editing was practiced at the European Commission, 'rapid' and 'full' post-editing levels were cited, the difference in which lay between the time spent on the task and the quality of the final product (Wagner 1985; O'Brien 2010; Mesa-Lao 2013). In the seminal work by Allen, a 'minimal' post-editing level is proposed as fuzzy and wide ranging (2003) between the two popular categories of 'rapid' and 'full' post-editing. Different levels of post-editing are required and provided for specific needs of translation. For instance, minimum post-editing is applicable where major errors are corrected without 'fine-tuning' the translation (Allen 2003). In addition, 'no post-editing' is also included as a post-editing level (Allen 2003; Krings 2001; Kovačević 2014). These levels of post-editing are boiled down to two generally accepted levels of 'light' and 'full' post-editing (for more details, see the following discussions of the Translation Automation User Society [TAUS] 2010 Report), whereby the previous 'rapid' or 'minimum' post-editing is categorized mostly under 'light' post-editing. The notion of 'no post-editing' has been largely dismissed today (Hu and Cadwell 2016).

Specific guidelines are needed for every post-editing project to guide post-editors in properly completing the post-editing work in order to meet the needs of the clients, on the one hand, and, on the other, for clients and language service providers (LSPs) to set their expectations. This would make the nature of the productivity to be achieved clear to both sides. However, organizations set their own rules as guidelines in accordance with their own individual needs (Krings 2001; Allen 2003; Groves and Schmidtke 2009; Rico and Torrejón 2012; Hu and Cadwell 2016). As noted by Kovačević (2014), the guidelines from corporations and institutions as cited in Allen (2003) vary considerably, and those developed by Microsoft may not be readily applicable to the Pan American Health Organization (PAHO). As an example of the diverse set of guidelines in operation, the SAE J2450 standard metric for translation quality is used by post-editors at General Motors whereby seven categories and two subcategories of errors are prioritized, while the European Commission Translation Service prescribes 'dos' and 'don'ts' to their post-editors. As there are no professionally or internationally adopted post-editing standards, the post-editor is often faced with a major challenge in deciding which ones to follow.

In response to this, TAUS released the report *Postediting in Practice* in March 2010 jointly with the Centre for Next Generation Localization (CNGL) as a result of their five-year research on post-editing advances and best practices based upon information collected from a range of organizations, including Dublin City University, the European Commission, Lionbridge, Microsoft, SAP, SDL and Systran. In this report, post-editing guidelines are proposed for organizations to use as a baseline and tailor them for their own purposes. This is the first attempt to produce industry-focused post-editing guidelines which are available online to the general public. In the report, post-editing is categorized under the two 'degrees'[2] of 'light post-editing' and 'full post-editing', with the former resulting in 'an understandable document' where terminology is correctly translated and meaning explicitly, though not elegantly, expressed and the latter 'a publishable document', the quality of which is comparable to that by a human translator. It is interesting to note that the report minimalizes light post-editing, as it seems unnecessary, with hardly any application for it to deliver a distinct quality of translation in practice. It is almost impossible to provide detailed guidelines where a demarcation line is so clearly drawn between the two 'degrees' or levels of post-editing (TAUS 2010: 7–8). This distinction of the two levels of post-editing is further supported in the ISO (2017) where only requirements for full post-editing are included in the body text of *Translation Services – Post-Editing of Machine Translation Output – Requirements* (ISO 2017), while light post-editing appears as Annex B of the same document (ISO 2017).

Therefore, it comes as no surprise when the influential *MT Post-Editing Guidelines* were released by TAUS later in 2016, where two levels of expected quality are defined instead of simply differentiating between guidelines for light and full post-editing. Under these guidelines, light post-editing is applicable in producing acceptably 'understandable' documents, the quality of which is referred to as 'good enough'. Full post-editing will be appropriate to achieve 'publishable', high-quality target text comparable to human translation. 'Good enough' is defined as 'comprehensible and accurate without being stylistically compelling', where 'comprehensible' means one can understand the essential part of the message in the target text, and 'accurate' means the content of the source text's meaning is retained (Massardo *et al.* 2016). This differentiation is echoed in ISO (2017) standard's interpretation of light and full post-editing by which the output of light post-editing shall be 'comprehensible and accurate but need not be stylistically adequate', and the output of full post-editing is 'indistinguishable from human translation output'. When post-editing is fast becoming a mainstream offering in the language service industry, it is encouraging for both academia and industry to see TAUS (2016) and ISO (2017) share a common understanding of the two levels of post-editing. In addition, they almost agree in what post-editors may follow as guidelines for both levels of post-editing to achieve translation at different levels of expected quality. Table 34.1 compares the light post-editing guidelines as issued by TAUS (2016) and ISO (2017).

As shown in the table, ISO (2017) is similar to TAUS (2016) in focusing the post-editor's attention on getting the gist of the source text. However, TAUS (2016) provides more details on

Table 34.1 Guidelines for light post-editing from TAUS (2016) and ISO (2017)

TAUS (2016) (selected)	ISO (2017)
1. Aim for semantically correct translation;	N/A
2. Ensure that no information has been accidentally added or omitted;	Ensuring that no information has been added or omitted;
3. Edit any offensive, inappropriate or culturally unacceptable content;	Editing any inappropriate content;
4. Use as much of the raw MT output as possible	Using as much of the raw MT output as possible;
5. Basic rules regarding spelling apply;	N/A
6. No need to implement corrections that are of a stylistic nature only;	N/A
7. No need to restructure sentences solely to improve the natural flow of the text.	Restructuring sentences in the case of incorrect or unclear meaning.

Table 34.2 Guidelines for full post-editing provided by TAUS (2016) and ISO (2017)

TAUS (2016)	ISO (2017)
1. Aim for grammatically, syntactically and semantically correct translation. (D)	A. Ensuring that no information has been added or omitted. (3)
2. Ensure that key terminology is correctly translated and that untranslated terms belong to the client's list of "Do Not Translate" terms. (E)	B. Editing any inappropriate content. (4)
3. Ensure that no information has been accidentally added or omitted. (A)	C. Restructuring sentences in the case of incorrect or unclear meaning.
4. Edit any offensive, inappropriate or culturally unacceptable content. (B)	D. Producing grammatically, syntactically and semantically correct target language content; (1)
5. Use as much of the raw MT output as possible.	E. Adhering to client and/or domain terminology. (2)
6. Basic rules regarding spelling, punctuation and hyphenation apply. (F)	F. Applying spelling, punctuation and hyphenation rules. (6)
7. Ensure that formatting is correct. (H)	G. Ensuring that the style appropriate for the text type is used and that stylistic guidelines, provided by the client are observed.
	H. Applying formatting rules. (7)

semantic, stylistic dimensions and even refers to spelling. Table 34.2 provides a clear view of the similarities in the full post-editing guidelines between ISO (2017) and TAUS (2016).

In the table, the letter in brackets at the end of an instruction under TAUS (2016) indicates its corresponding instruction listed under ISO (2017). Likewise, the number in brackets at the end of an instruction under ISO (2017) indicates its corresponding instruction listed under TAUS (2016). The dotted lines inserted under text in both columns indicate that instructions for full post-editing are the same as or similar to those for light post-editing as shown in Table 34.1. It is clear to conclude that ISO (2017) corresponds with TAUS (2016) in almost all respects except on an additional instruction in style.

The guidelines shown in Tables 34.1 and 32.2 are conceptualized and general, from which post-editors may select and use basic guidelines to carry out post-editing at two defined quality levels, tailored to their organization-specific needs or to the particular needs of their clients. Given that MT quality has reached such a high level, post-editing, as standard practice for the language service industry, can be applied to increase productivity for better, quicker and cheaper translation. In operational terms, a research project was conducted to test TAUS post-editing guidelines (2010) on students by Flanagan and Christensen. From their research, they adopted the TAUS guidelines for light post-editing and established their own guidelines for full post-editing to satisfy their own teaching needs through revising the TAUS baseline (Flanagan and Christensen 2014).

From the guidelines formulated in recent years, we can see that the evolution of post-editing is strongly linked with the development of technology. For example, both Allen (2003) and Densmer (2014) list the factors for determining post-editing levels, yet they show that the determinant factors of the latter are more related to modern technology. In the case of translation memory, Allen's list includes such traditional factors as translation time, life expectancy and perishability of the information, while Densmer's list includes 'factual correctness' and 'good enough' for light post-editing, which adhere to the TAUS guidelines (Hu and Cadwell 2016). Indeed, as the pursuit of greater productivity is behind the application of MT, post-editing can be seen to go hand in hand with the development of the technology which is intended to achieve high quality at high speeds and low cost.

Post-Editing Productivity

The motivation for post-editing raw MT output, an incomplete or unfinished half-product of translation, is built on the conviction that incorporating the MT system into the translation process will result in productivity gain. However, few tests or experiments have been undertaken to estimate the productivity of post-editing as compared to human translation from scratch in the last century (Allen 2003). Earlier post-editing research was mainly involved in validating whether post-editing was indeed faster than traditional translation by humans. This was vindicated by the observation that the initial translated target text produced by SMT, let alone RMT prior to SMT, failed to attain a level of quality that justified the use of post-editing as a means to save time and reduce cost of translation. The situation has changed since the start of the 21st century, especially since the advent of neuro-based MT (NMT). Now that NMT is able to deliver MT output with much higher quality, growing interest has focused on conducting experiments to test the productivity of post-editing both from academia and industry. Research results from these experiments show greater post-editing productivity gain than loss (Plitt and Masselot 2010; Kovačević 2014; Daems *et al.* 2017). In recent years, increasing research has probed into the post-editing process to examine issues related to productivity, for example, comparison in speed between post-editing and translation from scratch, contrasts in quantity of material translated through post-editing vs human translation and the quality achievable through post-editing (Plitt and Masselot 2010; Carl *et al.* 2011; Koponen and Salmi 2015). Following are some cases demonstrating experiments carried out in relation to productivity testing.

In an eight-month international research project, TransType2, over the period 2002–2005, six professional translators were asked to translate sections of between 2000–2500 words from English to Spanish, German and French using TransType, supplemented by post-editing over five rounds. The research reported a productivity figure of 16.75 words per minute, totaling 1,005 words per hour in their best performance over Round 4. An average MT post-editing productivity gain of 20% was achieved on texts composed of singleton sentences as compared to human translation

(Macklovitch 2006). In another experiment conducted in 2009, a combination of the LISA QA Model and the GALE post-editing guidelines were used as a typology for classifying post-editing changes made by six post-editors from English to French and Spanish. They extrapolated the values for post-editing productivity and expected the average productivity at 5,000 words per day, whereas the actual productivity calculated for the two fastest post-editors was as high as 9,600 and 8,592 words per day. The extrapolated productivity values were much higher than the average productivity normally expected for human translation, which stood between 2,000 and 2,500 words per day (Almeida and O'Brien 2010). Guerberof (2009) reported a mean productivity gain of between 13% and 25% from MT over human translation as the result of an experiment on productivity and quality in MT post-editing. His experiment also showed that MT turned out to be faster than human translation by 16 %, whereby the speed for post-editing was 13.86 words per minute and that for human translation from scratch was 11.87 words per minute. This would translate to hourly values of 831.6 words for post-editing and 712 words for from-scratch human translation. The figures obtained from the experiments provide solid evidence for a post-editing productivity gain as compared to from-scratch translation, especially in terms of speed. In all these experiments, the post-edited texts were supposed to reach the quality standard expected from human translation.

Such research findings are significant because it is now generally accepted that post-editing MT output with high quality can save time and reduce the cost of translation without compromising the quality of translation, hence enhancing productivity, especially in the technical domain (Plitt and Masselot 2010; Zong 2020). Conversely, post-editing MT content with poor quality will take a longer time and require greater effort than human translation and is therefore not viable. (Guerberof 2009; García 2010; Specia 2011; Koponen 2012, 2016). On the other hand, research results showed that post-editing was faster than human translation, but not always significantly so (Carl *et al.* 2011; García 2011, Daems *et al.* 2017). Researchers also noted that the productivity figures are subject to a number of uncertain factors, including the experience of post-editors, nature of projects, type of source texts and language pairs as well as the MT system itself (Guerberof 2009, 2010; García 2011).

Productivity of post-editing has been measured by different methodologies, both objective and subjective, and for diversified purposes over the years. Allen (2003) predicted that easy-to-use post-editing tools which are integrated into standard word processing applications could become translation productivity boosters. His prediction has turned out to be true with the development of flourishing post-editing tools that are either incorporated into word processing systems or stand alone. As reported by Groves and Schmidtke (2009), a methodology based on a translator's logging time was developed at Microsoft for productivity tracking on Microsoft's Treelet MT engine (Quirk *et al.* 2005), with the intent to benefit both their translation system and post-editors. A series of experiment results, compounded with data, were obtained, some of which are shown in Tables 34.3 and 34.4. Standard dynamic programming techniques were then designed to calculate the edit distance (to be explored in detail later in this chapter) between the MT and post-edited MT strings to assess productivity (Levenshtein 1965).

Research results at Microsoft show that the MT quality improved over time and the related productivity increased as translators became more familiar with MT and post-editing. As demonstrated in Table 34.3, these improvements resulted in an increase in productivity gain from 6.1% (Czech) to 28.6% (Danish) depending on selected languages. As displayed in Table 34.4, analysis of the quantifiable data on what changes were made during post-editing, as a result of the tracking methodology, provided useful information for Microsoft to improve its MT system and to assess the suitability of MT for a specific project. It also strengthened the understanding of what it took to make post-editing successful.

Table 34.3 Productivity gain between languages with
sentence lengths given in words

Language	Productivity Gain
Danish	28.6%
Brazilian	20.0%
Dutch	14.7%
French	14.5%
Swedish	8.0%
Czech	6.1%

Table 34.4 Details of data sets

		GERMAN	FRENCH
# Sentences		9,454	5,400
	SOURCE	138,578	67,924
# Words	MT	124,831	82,497
	PEMT	135,728	84,364
Min. Sent. Length		1	1
Max. Sent. Length		74	81
	SOURCE	14.66	12.58
Avg. Sent. Length	MT	13.20	15.28
	PEMT	14.36	15.62

Guerberof (2014) conducted an investigation on perception of post-editing productivity on the SurveyMonkey platform. He gathered a group of 24 translators and 3 reviewers and asked them to complete a questionnaire. According to his research results, 40% of the participants reported that their productivity increased over time when using post-editing, while 45% remarked that their productivity remained constant over time. As they gained more experience of post-editing, 55% found it easier to detect MT errors, and 30% felt that their experience did not have any effect on their productivity. When asked about post-editing effort, 30% felt that MT post-editing required the same effort as checking human translations, 40% felt that more effort was needed when post-editing MT-generated texts than when checking human translations and only 20% felt that less effort was needed when post-editing MT output than when checking human translations.

Daems *et al.* (2017) conducted an experiment in which post-editing processes were logged via eye tracking and keystrokes to find out more about translation speed, cognitive load and the use of external resources for MT post-editing of general text types, as performed by student translators and professional translators. They concluded that post-editing proved faster than human translation not only for technical texts, as proposed by Plitt and Masselot (2010), but also significantly faster statistically for general text types. However, no significant differences were found to exist between student and professional translators in terms of speed, which concurred with Jääskeläinen's observation that professional translators do not necessarily translate faster than students (1996). In addition, they found it necessary to look at the cognitive aspects of post-editing apart from speed, because even if post-editing wins the upper hand over human translation in terms of speed, if it is more cognitively demanding, and post-editors will become exhausted sooner than translators who carry out regular translations from scratch, this would lead to decreased productivity in the long run.

The author of this chapter is carrying out a research project to measure the productivity of post-editing with an intention to help LSPs with post-editing pricing, an issue that has long perplexed both translation providers and clients. In this research, productivity is calculated in the three dimensions of edit distance, cognitive load and processing difficulty, among which edit distance is to be achieved by optimizing the results from regular MT evaluation metrics such as BLEU, Meteor and TER; cognitive load estimates by means of eye-tracking and keylogging; and processing difficulty assessed through analysis of post-editing error patterns. Three functions will be formulated based on data collected from edit distance, cognitive load and processing difficulty to ascertain the correlation among them. Of these, the processing difficulty is examined on the basis of earlier research on the error analysis of post-editing from English to Chinese (Luo and Li 2012; Li and Zhu 2013a) which aimed at identifying MT error patterns to help with development of an automated post-editing tool. In the research, which used 100,000 English–Chinese sentence pairs from car maintenance manuals, MT errors detected by comparison between raw MT output and post-edited versions were classified into lexical, syntactic and typographic categories. The lexical category was further put into seven subcategories including terminology, abbreviations and conjunctions, while the syntactic category was put into further seven subcategories including word order, verb phrases and infinitive clauses. Statistics based upon the error pattern analysis showed that lexical errors were as high as 70.84%, syntactic errors 26.84% and typographic errors 2.32%, among which 42% of lexical errors are found with terminology and 35.84% syntactic errors with word order (Li and Zhu 2013b). The research findings provide insight into the effort made by humans during post-editing and the different difficulty levels to be encountered by human post-editors in making post-editing changes when amending draft MT-produced translations.

In general, productivity gain or loss is mostly indispensable from time and quality, among which the former determines the speed of post-editing, and the latter shapes the final translation product. At this stage, it is necessary to mention the well-known '2-second decision benchmark' proposed by Microsoft in analyzing and measuring postediting productivity. According to this benchmark, a post-editor gets to decide whether the MT output text is suitable for post-editing within 2 seconds; otherwise, productivity gain is out of the question. The feasibility of implementing the benchmark remains controversial, as it seems impossible in the first instance, despite the fact that the benchmark is the result of Microsoft's decade-long R&D program on MT that paved the way for the Microsoft Translator service of today. Interested readers are referred to the TAUS technology briefing on Microsoft Translator (TAUS 2010: 30).

Note that quality in productivity has been largely ignored in our previous discussions. The reality is that in calculating productivity, quality is mostly measured in isolation from time. Following this is the question of whether post-edited MT quality is as good as that of human translation in satisfying client expectations. An experiment on post-editing quality conducted by Koponen and Salmi (2017) shows that 9% of post-editing is incorrect, and of the remaining 91% which is correct, 61% of correction is necessary and 38% unnecessary. Combining the 9% incorrect correction and the 38% unnecessary correction provides a total of 47%. Will this alarming figure cut into the quality credibility of MT post-editing? The potential productivity improvement brought by MT would be undermined if post-editing failed to deliver post-edited texts at the quality comparable to human translation. How quality can be taken into proper account in the productivity measure is certainly an issue that deserves more attention from academia and industry. In measuring post-editing productivity, it is evident that the means by which quality evaluation is administered deserves greater attention.

A shift to the post-editing effort emerges amid the increasing interest in research on processes in recent years (Ortiz-boix and Matamala 2016; DePalma *et al.* 2019). Researchers are especially attentive to the cognitive effort based upon the belief that insight into the human mind will lead to in-depth understanding of the factors that affect the productivity of post-editing in the long run. Measurement of post-editing effort is significant in that it helps not only with the identification of translation difficulty but also with the pricing of post-editing (Vieira 2014), without which post-editing can never be realized as an independent alternative for translation.

Post-Editing Effort

Though post-editing has been integrated into the translation workflow by increasing LSPs, only a few of these provide post-editing as an independent service. This is mainly because there are too many uncertainties involved in the post-editing process. These can include, for example, the level of quality that MT-generated texts should attain before being acceptable for post-editing and, most notably, how to determine or estimate the human effort needed to improve the text generated by MT as part of the general translation process. In evaluating human effort, both the cognitive effort made to detect and determine the amendments to be made to the MT texts, as well as the manual or technical effort to actually activate the amendments, should be taken into account. Krings (2001) proposes three ways of measuring post-editing effort (for which much research has been carried out since): temporal, technical and cognitive.

Temporal effort refers to the time at which the post-editor takes to complete a post-editing task, which is often measured by words per second/minute or per day. Technical effort relates to the number of actual edits or changes made to the text (such as additions, deletions and cut and paste) performed by the post-editor. These changes, also known as 'edit distance' between the MT-produced text and the post-edited text, can be calculated by using either keystroke logging software or evaluation metrics, such as Levenshtein edit distance (Levenshtein 1965) or the translation edit rate metric (Snover *et al.* 2006), among others (Krings 2001; O'Brien 2005; Aikawa *et al.* 2007). Cognitive effort represents the mental processing behind editing decisions, which cannot be directly observed but can be estimated through certain methods such as standard cognitive metrics like Think-Aloud Protocols (TAPs), Choice Network Analysis (CAN), pause measurement, MT error analysis and, increasingly in recent years, keyboard logging and eye-tracking technology (Krings 2001; Timnikova 2010; Moorkens 2018).

Post-editing research has centered on both temporal and technical effort for many years, the research results of which have given rise to the introduction of post-editing in the workplace. The temporal effort has been explored in detail in our discussion of post-editing productivity in the previous section. For the technical effort, edit distance has been widely accepted by LSPs as a way of measuring the workload of the post-editor and used as an important reference in the remuneration of the translation. In recent years, keystroke logging has become an effective way to record the edit distance, because keystroke information, measuring the total number of keystrokes made by the post-editor, including insertions, deletions and cut and paste, reflects the real and tangible linguistic changes made in the post-editing of MT text. The underlying assumption is that the larger the amount of edit distance, the more changes made and the greater effort required during post-editing (Koglin 2015; Huang and Carl 2021). In more recent research, Huang and Carl (2021) developed the word-based human edit rate (WHER) as a measure to assess the post-editing effort at the lexical level by using eye-tracking and keystroke-logging devices. WHER, derived from HTER for measurement of the minimum edit distance at the sentence level (Snover *et al.* 2006), is an extension of HER which maps the edit operations of the target language word to the corresponding source text positions through word-alignment. Their experiment engaged 21 student translators who were asked to post-edit audiovisual texts from English to Chinese. During their post-editing, keystroke information was collected as indicators of the real amount of technical effort. WHER measures the number of minimum Chinese target text edit operations per English source text word to assess the extent to which WHER correlates with post-editing behavior and thus may be suitable for estimating post-editing effort (Huang and Carl 2021).

Cognitive effort, which had been measured in translation process research (TPR) since the early 1980s, was not related to post-editing until Krings (2001) introduced it as a measurement for post-editing effort. He used TAP (post-editors commenting on their decisions out loud) to discover the 'type and extent of cognitive processes' required to 'remedy a given deficiency' in MT (Moorkens 2018). However, one significant problem with TAP is that it impacts on efficiency, as the processing speed without TAP was assessed as being roughly 30% faster (Shreve and Diamond 1997; Krings 2001). Therefore, alternative approaches are desirable for assessing cognitive effort. With the development of modern technology, more and more technological tools are applied in the research on cognitive effort, including keystrokes and eye-tracking, functional magnetic resource imaging (fMRI) and electroencephalography, which are used either alone or in combination with other methods (Chang 2009; Dragsted 2010; Moorkens 2018).

Eye-tracking has become popular for research in translation studies in recent years, in particular for measuring post-editing effort, since O'Brien (2006a) published her pilot study on fuzzy match editing and post-editing effort.[3] Since the human ratings of post-editing efforts can be very subjective and affected by the previous rating, as well as 'fatigue or boredom' (O'Brien 2011), the employment of eye-tracking makes it possible to measure post-editing effort from temporal, technical and/or cognitive aspects in an objective manner. This is further proved true in the experiments referred to later where data were collected from eye-tracking for post-editing effort analysis. In an experiment involving 24 translators who were asked to post-edit Google Translate output texts from English to German on the Casmacat interface, comparison between human translation and the post-edited texts showed that all participants were more efficient with regard to temporal, technical and cognitive effort in post-editing, even though they all claimed they had no post-editing experience and would prefer to translate from scratch. The research results demonstrated that source text complexity had more of an impact on processing effort when translating from scratch than when post-editing (Carl *et al.* 2015). In another experiment, based on an investigation into whether estimates of post-editing effort were accurate predictors of the work that was actually carried out, a conclusion was drawn that 'human ratings of post-editing effort do not correlate strongly with the actual time required during post-editing'. A moderate correlation was found between measurements of post-editing effort and mean user ratings, which suggested the link between the categorized 'traffic light' color scheme and the measurement of temporal and technical effort as participants moved along the texts to be post-edited (Moorkens *et al.* 2015). These experiments suggest that the use of technological tools such as keystroke logging and eye-tracking provides a more accurate and reliable assessment of post-editing effort, which could otherwise be misinterpreted by human perception.

In addition, MT error analysis has also turned out to be an important measure of post-editing effort. Plenty of research findings demonstrate that post-editing effort, be it temporal, technical or cognitive, is affected by MT errors to some extent (Temnikova 2010; Koponen *et al.* 2012; Daems *et al.* 2017; Carl and Cristina 2019).

Vilar *et al.* (2006) classifies MT errors into four categories: missing words, word order, incorrect words and punctuation errors. Based on this MT error classification, Baddeley's working memory theory (Baddeley and Hitch 1974) and a cognitive model of reading (Harley 2008), Temnikova (2010) proposes a 'cognitive MT error ranking' whereby Vilar's MT error types are enriched with information encoded with the cognitive effort of post-editors in identifying and correcting the MT errors. Errors are ranked in order of difficulty based on error type and the sentence span, as illustrated in Table 34.5 with (1) being the easiest and (10) the most difficult.

This new evaluation approach allows an in-depth look into the postediting cognitive process, especially on how much effort post-editors put into correcting the different kinds of MT errors. This approach has been further tested by a good number of interested researchers (Koponen *et al.* 2012; Lacruz and Martín 2014; Hu 2020). Hu (2020) carried out an experiment which involved eight participants who were asked to post-edit texts generated by Baidu Translate, a state-of-the-art NMT system from English to Chinese. This was to test the cognitive MT error ranking, as shown in Table 34.5, by using two indicators of cognitive postediting effort: the pause to word ratio (PWR) and the average pause ratio (APR). Analysis of the pause data shows that the cognitive effort spent on amending the MT errors correlates positively with the stretch of text in which the error is embedded, thus yielding the following correlation ranking: postediting cognitive effort demanded by punctuation errors < lexical errors < syntactic errors. A different perspective of the MT errors takes us on to another approach to post-editing: monolingual post-editing, during which post-editors perform their task with no access to the source text. The objective behind this monolingual post-editing approach is multifold: to investigate whether an MT system can generate output texts with quality good enough to convey the information in the source text appropriately depending on the translation requirements, to ascertain the competence of post-editors in carrying out post-editing; and to assess the post-editing effort required of the post-editor. Krings (2001) comments that MT does not lead to the expected reduction in cognitive effort during post-editing and that post-editing MT texts takes more cognitive effort than translation from scratch, independent of varying MT quality. He observes that the only

Table 34.5 Cognitive MT error ranking (Temnikova 2010: 3488)

Morphological level	1. Correct word, incorrect form
Lexical level	2. Incorrect style synonym
	3. Incorrect word
	4. Extra word
	5. Missing word
	6. Idiomatic expression
Syntactic level	7. Wrong punctuation
	8. Missing punctuation
	9. Word order at word level
	10. Word order at phrase level

reported decreased cognitive effort for post-editing tasks takes place without access to the source text (Koponen and Salmi 2015). His observation that post-editing without access to the source text requires less cognitive effort sounds reasonable. But how reliable can the quality of post-edited texts without source text be?

According to Koehn (2010), the student post-editors who participated in his experiment did not seem to be attentive to the MT language errors, because he found quite a few cases where not all errors in a sentence were corrected and cases where the errors simply went unnoticed. To make things worse, the post-editors themselves contributed to language errors that were not even in the raw MT output. The low quality of the MT texts could be held responsible for such unsatisfactory post-editing results, as students complained about the number of MT errors which made their post-editing cumbersome and onerous. Mitchell *et al.* (2013) also noted that post-editing with and without the source text did not make much difference to post-editors with regard to fluency and comprehensibility, but monolingual post-editing without the source text led to less fidelity, implying that the post-editors were not able to fully comprehend the message conveyed by the source text. Koponen and Salmi (2015) conducted an experiment where 48 student translators were asked to post-edit MT texts from English into Finnish without access to the source text in order to examine the extent to which the post-editors could decipher the meaning of the source text. It turned out that the post-editors were successful at deducing the correct meaning for about half of the sentences they post-edited and that it was easier to amend errors in word forms and mangled relations as comprehended from the context but more difficult to assemble the meaning from mistranslated idioms and missing content. For post-edited sentences, 29.5% were judged fully correct with regard to both meaning and language. This result is comparable to prior studies, where results for different systems and language pairs have ranged from 26% to 35% (Koehn 2010). Furthermore, mistakes were found in some post-edited sentences where no errors were present in the MT texts. This experiment also revealed the quality of the raw MT output: only six of the 120 sentences (5%) were evaluated as fully correct, and a further 24 sentences (20%) were evaluated as correct with regard to meaning but with language errors (Koponen and Salmi 2015: 125). It should be noted that all the experiments reported here were conducted before the emergence of NMT, which has given rise to substantial quality improvement to the MT output. A more recent comparative experiment was carried out by Li (2021) to explore the effort made by post-editors with and without access to the source text during post-editing. A total of 42 professional translators were asked to post-edit texts generated by NMT systems: Google Translate from English to Chinese and Baidu Translate from Chinese to English. All the edits made by the post-editors were categorized and labeled with reference to the benchmark indicators, as shown in Table 34.6, using two levels of edits in analyzing the difficulty of different MT errors and measuring the productivity of the post-editors.

Table 34.6 MT post-editing benchmark indicators (Li 2021: 95)

Level 1	Accuracy	Comprehensiveness	Style
Level 2	terminology grammar punctuation spelling format	syntax semantics	stylistic features

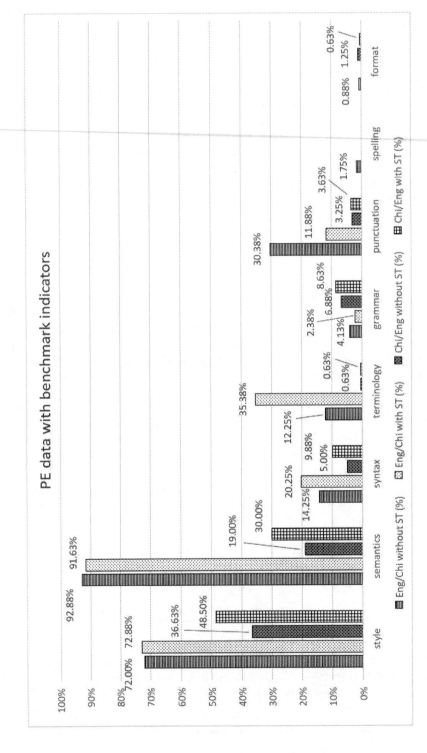

Figure 34.1 Comparison of post-editing effort with and without access to ST

Statistics from this comparative experiment demonstrate that post-editing with or without the source text has little impact on post-editors both in terms of time and the quality of the post-edited output but that language direction impacts post-editing effort more, as illustrated in Figure 34.1. Contrastive analysis demonstrates that the post-editor becomes less dependent on the source text as the quality of the MT text improves. This research result is encouraging in that post-editing without access, or at least with little reference to the source text, is proved feasible, which would theoretically lessen the post-editing effort temporally, technically and cognitively both on a short-term basis and in the long run. The research also reveals that the higher quality of the NMT output enables the post-editor to focus more on stylistic improvement rather than on correction of grammar and spelling errors. This repudiates the previous report that even if monolingual post-editors are able to improve the language, MT quality has not been good enough to reliably convey the meaning of the source text (Krings 2001: 139).

As shown in Figure 34.1, edits made for the category of Accuracy, under which are terminology, grammar, punctuation and spelling indicators, were very limited, and syntactic changes under Comprehensiveness were few, whereby post-editors made greater efforts in correcting basic and annoying MT errors in grammar and spelling. In contrast, for post-editing from English to Chinese, in the Comprehensiveness category, edits recorded in semantics made up 92.88% without access to the source text and 91.63% with access to the source text, while edits under the Style category were 72% without access to the source text and 72.88% with access to the source text (Li 2021: 97).

There is one further factor that plays a significant part in the performance of the post-editor: his or her competence. What is the skillset with which a good post-editor can arm himself/herself in the goal of achieving a quality translation product with reduced time and cost? It is generally acknowledged that the post-editor shares most of the skills of a good translator. In addition, however, there is one vital skill that is especially required for a post-editor: the ability to decide whether the MT-generated text is suitable for post-editing, as reflected by the 2-second decision benchmark proposed by Microsoft in our earlier discussion on post-editing guidelines. It will make the post-editor's job even more efficient if he or she knows which MT system produces the better translation for a certain domain. Almeida and Obrian (2010) proposed three skills for a good post-editor: the ability to identify the problems with the raw MT output and make 'Essential Changes', the ability to carry out post-editing at an average speed of 5,000 words per day and the ability to follow the post-editing guidelines to make 'Preferential Changes'. We suggest that a competent post-editor should be able to: a) make a quick decision about whether to use an MT output or disregard it, b) keep as much of the MT output as possible and c) make the changes necessary to meet the expected quality. Due to the word limit of this chapter, we will not dwell upon this issue at length. Interested readers are referred to Offersgaard *et al.* (2008), Almeida and Obrian (2010), Guerberof (2014), TAUS (2010), ISO (2017) and the references cited in these papers.

Measuring the effort involved in post-editing is important because it plays a decisive role in determining its productivity, which will, in turn, regulate its pricing, without which post-editing is less likely to become an independent practice in the localization workflow. This would take full advantage of the remarkable technological advances of NMT in improving the quality of translation.

Notes

1 A look into how post-editing is defined over the years reveals the change of perception on the concept and workflow in the language service profession with the translation technology uptake. At the early stage of MT, post-editing is linked mostly with semantic and stylistic deals, as pointed out

by Bar-Hillel (1951: 230): the main business of a post-editor would be 'elimination of semantical ambiguities, in addition to stylistic smoothing'. Post-editing is defined as 'examination and correction of the text resulting from an automatic or semi-automatic machine system (machine translation, translation memory) to ensure it complies with the natural laws of grammar, punctuation, spelling and meaning, etc.' in the Draft of European Standard for Translation Services (Brussels 2004). In the European Standard for Translation Services EN-15038 (2006), post-editing is listed a an added value translation service with no definition provided for it. According to TAUS, post-editing is 'the process of improving a machine-generated translation with a minimum of manual labor'. (2010: 7). More recently, in 2017, ISO 18587 states that post-editing is 'performed on MT output for the purpose of checking its accuracy and comprehensibility, improving the text, making the text more readable, and correcting errors' (p. 5).

2 Compare the different terms used by TAUS (2010) and ISO (2017) in distinguishing light post-editing from full post-editing. The former uses the term 'degree' and the latter 'level'.

3 According to Huang and Carl (2021), eye movements reflect reading behavior on the source text and target text. According to the eye-mind hypothesis, fixations are usually linked to attention (Just and Carpenter 1980) such that the attention follows eye movements. Empirical translation studies have shown that the average fixation duration and the number of fixations per word correlate with other effort indicators such as the pause-to-word ratio and production duration per word (Vieira 2016). Also, the first fixation duration and the total fixation duration are used as indicators of effort (Schaeffer *et al.* 2019). Research show that differences are observed in post-editors' fixation behavior, with TT usually attracting more attention than ST (Sanchis-Trilles *et al.* 2014; Vieira 2014).

Bibliography

Accenture (Ed.) (2020). *Technology Vision 2020 We, The Post-Digital People Can your enterprise survive the "tech-clash"?* https://www.accenture.com/content/dam/accenture/final/a-com-migration/custom/_acnmedia/thought-leadership-assets/pdf-2/Accenture-Technology-Vision-2020-Full-Report.pdf#zoom=100

Aikawa, T., L. Schwartz, R. King, M. Corston-Oliver, and C. Lozano (2007) 'Impact of Controlled Language on Translation Quality and Post-editing in a Statistical Machine Translation Environment', *Machine Translation Summit* XI: 10–14.

Allen, J. (2003). Post-editing. In H. Somers (Ed.), *Computers and Translation. A Translator's Guide* (297–317). Benjamins Translation Library, 35. https://doi.org/10.1075/btl.35.19all

Almeida, G. D. , & Brien, S. . (2010). Analysing Post-Editing Performance: Correlations with Years of Translation Experience. *Proceedings of the 14th Annual conference of the European Association for Machine Translation*. European Association for Machine Translation.

ALPAC. (1966) 'Languages and Machines: Computers in Translation and Linguistics. A Report by the Automatic Language Processing Advisory Committee', *Division of Behavioral Sciences*, National Academy of Sciences, National Research Council.

Baddeley, A. D. and G. Hitch (1974) 'Working Memory', in G. H. Bower (ed.) *The Psychology of Learning and Motivation: Advances in Research and Theory*. Academic Press.

Bar-Hillel, Y. (1951) 'The Present State of Research on Mechanical Translation', *American Documentation* 2(4): 229–37.

Beyer, R. T. (1965) 'Hurdling the Language Barrier', *Physics Today* 18(1): 46–52.

Bonet, J. (2013) 'No Rage Against the Machine', *Languages and Translation* 6: 4–5. Available at: http://ec.europa.eu/dgs/translation/publications/magazines/languagestranslation/documents/issue_06_en.pdf.

Carl, M. and T. B. Cristina (2019) 'Machine Translation Errors and the Translation Process: A Study Across Different Languages', *Journal of Specialised Translation* 31: 107–32.

Carl, M., B. Dragsted, J. Elming, D. Hardt, and L. J. Arnt (2011) 'The Process of Post-Editing: A Pilot Study', in B. Sharp, M. Zock, M. Carl, and J. A. Lykke (eds.) *Proceedings of the 8th International NLPCS Workshop. Special Theme: Human-Machine Interaction in Translation*, Samfundslitteratur, 131–42.

Carl, M., S. Gutermuth, and S. Hansen-Schirra (2015) 'Post-Editing Machine Translation: Efficiency, Strategies, and Revision Processes in Professional Translation Settings. Psycholinguistic and Cognitive

Inquiries into Translation and Interpreting', in A. Ferreira and J. W. Schwieter (eds.) *Psycholinguistic and Cognitive Inquiries into Translation and Interpreting*, Amsterdam and Philadelphia: John Benjamins Publishing Company, 145–74.

Carl, M. and J. A. Lykke (2010) 'Towards Statistical Modeling of Translators' Activity Data', *International Journal of Speech Technology* 12(4): 124–46.

Chang, V. C. (2009) 'Testing Applicability of Eye-tracking and fMRI to Translation and Interpreting Studies: An Investigation into Directionality', Doctoral dissertation, Imperial College London.

Daems, J., S. Vandepitte, R. Hartsuiker, and L. Macken (2017) 'Translation Methods and Experience: A Comparative Analysis of Human Translation and Post-editing with Students and Professional Translators', *Meta* 62(2): 245–70. https://doi.org/10.7202/1041023ar.

Densmer, L. (2014) 'Light and Full MT Post-Editing Explained'. Available at: http://info.moravia.com/blog/bid/353532/Light-and-Full-MT-Post-Editing-Explained.

DePalma, D., H. Pielmeier, and P. O'Mara (2019) 'Who's Who in Language Services and Technology: 2019 Rankings', *Common Sense Advisory*. Available at: https://insights.csa-research.com/reportaction/305013039/Marketing.

Doherty, S. (2016) 'The Impact of Translation Technologies on the Process and Product of Translation', *International Journal of Communication* 10: 647–69.

Dragsted, B. (2010) 'Coordination of Reading and Writing Processes in Translation: An Eye on Uncharted Territory', in G. M. Schreve and E. M. Angelone (eds.) *Translation and Cognition*, Amsterdam and Philadelphia: John Benjamins Publishing Company, 41–62.

Flanagan, M. and T. P. Christensen (2014) 'Testing Post-Editing Guidelines: How Translation Trainees Interpret them and How to Tailor them for Translator Training Purposes', *The Interpreter and Translator Trainer* 8(2): 257–75.

Gambier, Y. (2014) 'Changing Landscape in Translation', *International Journal of Society, Culture and Language* 2(2): 1–12.

García, I. (2010) 'Is Machine Translation Ready Yet?', *Target* 22(1): 7–21.

García, I. (2011) 'Translating by Post-Editing: Is it the Way Forward?', *Machine Translation* 25(3): 217–37.

García, I. (2012) 'A Brief History of Postediting and of Research on Postediting', in A. Pym and A. A. Rosa (eds.), *New Directions in Translation Studies. Special Issue of Anglo Saxonica* 3(3): 292–310.

Groves, D. and D. Schmidtke (2009) 'Identification and Analysis of Post-editing Patterns for MT', in *MT Summit XII Proceedings of the Twelfth Machine Translation Summit*, 429–36. Available at: www.researchgate.net/publication/228789664.

Guerberof, A. (2009). Productivity and quality in MT post-editing. In M. Goulet et al. (Eds.), *Beyond Translation Memories Workshop*. MT Summit XII, 39, 137–144. http://www.mt-archive.info/MTS-2009-Guerberof.pdf

Guerberof, A. (2010) 'Project Management and Machine Translation', *Multilingual* 21(3): 1–4.

Guerberof, A. (2014) 'The Role of Professional Experience in Post-editing from a Quality and Productivity Perspective', in S. O'Brien, L. W. Balling, M. Carl, M. Simard, and L. Specia (eds.), *Post-editing of Machine Translation: Processes and Applications*, Newcastle upon Tyne: Cambridge Scholars Publishing, 51–76.

Harley, T. A. (2008) *The Psychology of the Language: From Data to Theory*, Psychology Press.

http://bridge.cbs.dk/projects/seecat/material/hand-out_post-editing_bmesa-lao.pdf.

Hu, K. K. (2020) 'How MT Errors Correlate with Postediting Effort: A New Ranking of Error Types', *Asia Pacific Translation and Intercultural Studies*. http://doi.org/10.1080/23306343.2020.1809763.

Hu, K. K. and P. Cadwell (2016) 'A Comparative Study of Post-editing Guidelines', *Baltic Journal of Modern Computing* 4(2): 346–53.

Huang, J. and M. Carl (2021) 'Word-based Human Edit Rate (WHER) as an Indicator of Post-editing Effort', in M. Carl (ed.) *Explorations in Empirical Translation Process Research, Machine Translation: Technologies and Applications*, Switzerland AG: Springer Nature, 39–55. https://doi.org/10.1007/978-3-030-69777-8_2

Hutchins, W. J. (1992) 'Météo', in W. J. Hutchins and H. L. Somers (eds.) *An Introduction to Machine Translation*, Academic Press, 207–20.

Hutchins, W. J. (1996) 'ALPAC: The (In)famous Report', *MT News International* 14: 9–12.

ISO 18587 (2017). *Translation Services-Post-editing of Machine Translation Output-Requirements*. https://www.iso.org/standard/62970.html.

Jääskeläinen, R. (1996) 'Hard Work Will Bear Beautiful Fruit. A Comparison of Two Think- Aloud Protocol Studies', *Meta* 41(1): 60–74.

Just, M. A. and P. A. Carpenter (1980) 'A Theory of Reading: From Eye Fixations to Comprehension', *Psychological Review* 87(4): 329–54.

Kevin, Hu (2020) 'How MT Errors Correlate with Postediting Effort: A New Ranking of Error Types', *Asia Pacific Translation and Intercultural Studies*. http://doi.org/10.1080/23306343.2020.1809763.

Koehn, P. (2010) 'Enabling Monolingual Translators: Post-editing vs. Options', in *Proceedings of NAACL HLT 2010: Human Language Technologies*, 537–45. Available at: http://aclweb.org/anthologynew/N/ N10/N10-1078.pdf. Accessed 12 September 2014.

Koglin, A. (2015) 'An Empirical Investigation of Cognitive Effort Required to Post-edit Machine Translated Metaphors Compared to the Translation of Metaphors', *Translation and Interpreting* 7(1): 126–41.

Koponen, M. (2012) 'Comparing Human Perceptions of Post-editing Effort with Post-editing Operations', in C. Callison-Burch *et al.* (eds.), *7th Workshop on Statistical Machine Translation, Proceedings of the Workshop*, Association for Computational Linguistics, 181–90.

Koponen, M. (2016) 'Is Machine Translation Post-Editing Worth the Effort? A Survey of Research in to Post-Editing and Effort', *Journal of Specialised Translation* 25: 131–48.

Koponen M. Aziz W. Ramos L. & Specia L. (2012). Post-editing Time as a Measure of Cognitive Effort. In O'Brien S, Simard M, Specia L. (eds). *AMTA 2012 Workshop on Post-editing Technology and Practice (WPTP)*, 11-20. Available at: http://amta2012.amtaweb.org/AMTA2012Files/html/13/13_paper.pdf.

Koponen, M. and L. Salmi (2015) 'On the Correctness of Machine Translation: A Machine Translation Post-Editing Task', *Journal of Specialised Translation* 23: 118–36.

Koponen, M. and L. Salmi (2017) 'Post-editing Quality: Analysing the Correctness and Necessity of Post-editor Corrections', *Linguistica Antverpiensia, New Series–Themes in Translation Studies* 16: 137–48.

Kovačević, M. (2014) 'Post-editing of MT Output with and Without Source Text', *Hieronymus* 1: 82–104.

Krings, H. P. (2001) *Repairing Texts: Empirical Investigations of Machine Translation Post-Editing Processes*, G. S. Koby (tr. and ed.), Kent: The Kent State University Press.

Lacruz, I. and R. M. Martín (2014) 'Pauses and Objective Measures of Cognitive Demand in Postediting', in *Proceedings of the American Translation and Interpreting Studies Association Conference*, New York.

Levenshtein, V. I. (1965) 'Binary Codes Capable of Correcting Spurious Insertions and Deletions of Ones', *Problems of Information Transition* 1: 8–17.

Li, M. (2021) 'Impact of Source Text on Translators in MT Post-Editing', *Foreign Language Teaching* 42(4): 93–99.

Li, M. and X. Zhu (2013a) 'Exploration of Post-editing Automation of English Chinese Machine Translation', *Chinese Translators Journal* 34(1): 83–87.

Li, M. and X. Zhu (2013b) 'English Chinese Machine Translation Error Patterns and Their Statistical Data Analyses', *Journal of University of Shanghai for Science and Technology* 35(3): 201–07.

Luo, J. and M. Li (2012) 'Error Analysis of Machine Translation Texts', *Chinese Translators Journal* 33(5): 84–89.

Macklovitch, E. (2006). TransType2: The Last Word. In *Proceedings of the Fifth International Conference on Language Resources and Evaluation* (LREC'06), Genoa, Italy. European Language Resources Association (ELRA), 167-172. http://www.lrec-conf.org/proceedings/lrec2006/pdf/14_pdf.pdf

Massardo, I., J. Meer, S. O'Brien, F. Hollowood, N. Aranberri, and K. Drescher (2016) 'MT Post-Editing Guidelines', Translation Automation User Society.

Memsource (Ed). (2021). Machine Translation Report Q2/2021: 14-16. https://phrase.com/resources/ machine-translation-report/

Mitchell, L., J. Roturier, and S. O'Brien (2013) 'Community-based Post-editing of Machine-translated Content: Monolingual vs. Bilingual', in S. O'Brien, M. Simard, and L. Specia (eds.) *Proceedings of the MT Summit XIV Workshop on Post-editing Technology and Practice WPTP-2*, 35–44. Available at: http:// doras.dcu.ie/20030/.

Moorkens, J. (2018). Chapter 4 Eye-Tracking as a Measure of Cognitive Effort for Post-Editing of Machine Translation. *Eye Tracking and Multidisciplinary Studies on Translation*. Benjamins Translation Library 143, 55–69. http://dx.doi.org/10.1075/btl.143.04moo

Moorkens, J., A. Toral, S. Castilho, and A. Way (2018) 'Translators' Perceptions of Literary Post-editing Using Statistical and Neural Machine Translation', *Translation Spaces* 7(2): 240–62. https://doi. org/10.1075/ts.18014.moo

O'Brien, S. (2005) 'Methodologies for Measuring the Correlations between Post-editing Effort and Machine Translatability', *Machine Translation* 19(1): 37–58.

O'Brien, S. (2006a) 'Pauses as Indicators of Cognitive Effort in Post-editing Machine Translation Output', *Across Languages and Cultures* 7(1): 1–21. http://doi.org/10.1556/Acr.7.2006.1.1.

O'Brien, S. (2006b) 'Eye-tracking and Translation Memory Matches', *Perspectives: Studies in Translatology* 14(3): 185–205.

O'Brien, S. (2007) 'An Empirical Investigation of Temporal and Technical Post-editing Effort', *Translation and Interpreting Studies* II: I.

O'Brien, S. (2010) 'Introduction to Post-Editing: Who, What, How and Where to Next?'. Available at: http://amta2010.amtaweb.org/AMTA/papers/6-01-ObrienPostEdit.pdf.

O'Brien, S. (2011) 'Towards Predicting Post-Editing Productivity', *Machine Translation* 25(3): 197–215.

O'Brien, S. (2016) 'Post-Editing and CAT', *EST Newsletter* 48.

O'Brien, S. and R. Fiederer (2009) 'Quality and Machine Translation: A Realistic Objective?', *Journal of Specialised Translation* 11.

O'Brien, S. and Alessandra Rossetti (2021) 'Neural Machine Translation and Evolution of the Localisation Sector, Implications for Training', *Journal of Internationalization and Localization* 7(1–2): 95–121.

Offersgaard, L., Povlsen, C., Almsten, L. K., & Maegaard, B. (2008). Domain specific MT in use. In J. Hutchins, & W. v.Hahn (Eds.), EAMT 2008: *12th annual conference of the European Association for Machine Translation*, 150-159. HITEC e.V, Vogt-Kölln Strasse 30, Hamburg, Germany.

Ortiz-boix, C. and A. Matamala (2016) 'Post-Editing Wildlife Documentary Films: A New Possible Scenario?', *Journal of Specialised Translation* 26: 187–210.

Plitt, M. and F. Masselot (2010) 'A Productivity Test of Statistical Machine Translation Post-Editing in a Typical Localisation Context', *The Prague Bulletin of Mathematical Linguistics* 93: 7–16. Available at: http://ufal.mff.cuni.cz/pbml/93/art-plitt-masselot.pdf.

Quirk, C., Menenzes, A., & Cherry, C. (2005). Dependency Treelet Translation: Syntactically Informed Phrasal SMT. In *Proceedings of the 43rd Annual Meeting of the Association for Computational Linguistics* (ACL'05), 271–279. Ann Arbor, Michigan. Association for Computational Linguistics.

Rico, C. and E. Torrejón (2012) 'Skills and Profile of the New Role of the Translator as MT Post-editor', *Revista tradumàtica* 10: 166–78.

Sanchis-Trilles, G., V. Alabau, C. Buck, *et al.* (2014) 'Interactive Translation Prediction Versus Conventional Post-Editing in Practice: A Study with the CasMaCat Workbench', *Machine Translation* 28: 217–35.

Schaeffer, M. and Michael Carl (2017) 'A Minimal Cognitive Model for Translating and Post-editing', in Sadao Kurohashi and Pascale Fung (eds.) *Proceedings of MT Summit XVI vol. 1*, Nagoya, Japan, September 18–22, 144–55. Available at: http://aamt.info/app-def/S-102/mtsummit/2017/conference-proceedings/. Accessed 1 December 2018.

Schaeffer, M., J. Nitzke, A. Tardel, *et al.* (2019) 'Eye-Tracking Revision Processes of Translation Students and Professional Translators', *Perspectives* 27(4): 589–603.

Shreve, G. M. and B. Diamond (1997) 'Cognitive Processes in Translation and Interpreting: Critical Issues', in J. H. Danks, G. M. Shreve, S. B. Fountain, and M. K. McBeath (eds.), *Cognitive Processes in Translation and Interpreting*, Sage Publications, 233–51.

Snover, M., Dorr, B., Schwartz, R., Micciulla, L., Makhoul. J. (2006). A Study of Translation Edit Rate with Targeted Human Annotation. In *Proceedings of the 7th Conference of the Association for Machine Translation in the Americas: Technical Papers*, 223–231. Cambridge, Massachusetts, USA. Association for Machine Translation in the Americas.

Specia, L. (2011). Exploiting Objective Annotations for Minimising Translation Post-editing Effort. In *Proceedings of the 15th Annual conference of the European Association for Machine Translation*, 73–80. Leuven, Belgium. European Association for Machine Translation. https://aclanthology.org/2011.eamt-1.12

TAUS (ed.) (2010) 'MT Post-editing Guidelines'. Available at: www.taus.net/academy/best-practices/postedit-best-practices/machine-translationpost-editing-guidelines.

TAUS (ed.) (2016) 'TAUS Post-Editing Guidelines'. Available at: www.taus.net/think-tank/articles/postedit-articles/taus-post-editing-guidelines.

Temnikova, I. (2010). Cognitive Evaluation Approach for a Controlled Language Post-Editing Experiment. In *Proceedings of the Seventh International Conference on Language Resources and Evaluation* (LREC'10), Valletta, Malta. European Language Resources Association (ELRA). http://www.lrec-conf.org/proceedings/lrec2010/pdf/437_Paper.pdf

Vasconcellos, M. and M. León (1985) 'SPANAM and ENGSPAN: Machine Translation at the Pan American Health Organization', *Computational Linguistics* 11: 122–36.

Vieira, L. N. (2014) 'Indices of Cognitive Effort in Machine Translation Post-Editing', *Machine Translation* 28(3): 187–216.

Vieira, L. N. (2016) 'How Do Measures of Cognitive Effort Relate to Each Other? A Multivariate Analysis of Post-editing Process Data', *Machine Translation* 30: 41–62.

Vieira, L. N. (2019) 'Post-editing of Machine Translation', in M. O'Hagan (ed.) *Routledge Handbook of Translation and Technology*, London and New York: Routledge, 319–35.

Vilar, D., Xu, J., D'Haro, L., Ney, H. (2006). Error Analysis of Statistical Machine Translation Output. In *Proceedings of the Fifth International Conference on Language Resources and Evaluation* (LREC'06), 697–702. Genoa, Italy. European Language Resources Association (ELRA). http://www.lrec-conf.org/proceedings/lrec2006/pdf/413_pdf.pdf

Wagner, E. (1985) 'Post-editing Systran – A Challenge for Commission Translators', *Terminologie et Traduction* 3: 1–7.

Zong, C. (2020) 'Technology Prospect of Human Language', *China Association for Artificial Intelligence* 1: 2–3.

35

INFORMATION RETRIEVAL AND TEXT MINING

Kit Chunyu and Nie Jian-Yun

Information retrieval

Introduction

Anyone who has ever looked for any information via a web search has in fact experienced the most popular and powerful means of information retrieval ever available in human history. The World Wide Web has become the largest source of information on earth. Without a powerful web search engine for access to such a massive volume of data, one would find no way out of the problem of the information explosion in this information era. The information retrieval first envisioned by Bush (1945) as 'an enlarged intimate supplement' to a user's memory that 'may be consulted with exceeding speed and flexibility' has become part of our daily life that is characterized by extensive use of the World Wide Web (Berners-Lee *et al.* 1992).

Although web users search through the Web for required content in various kinds of media, including text, graphics, audio and video, canonical information retrieval deals only with texts. Other types of content apart from text are usually retrieved through their associated (or surrounding) texts, such as title, author, caption and/or other kinds of description. The term *information retrieval* (IR) was first coined by Mooers in his 1948 MIT master's thesis and subsequently introduced into the literature of documentation (Mooers 1950; Swanson 1988; Garfield 1997). However, IR as is generally recognized today deals with full text search instead of reference retrieval relying merely on certain specific types of information such as author, title and some keywords about a document (Sparck Jones 1981). The field started much later in the late 1950s, marked by the International Conference on Scientific Information held in Washington in 1958. IR can be defined in slightly different ways using similar terms. For example,

> Information retrieval is often regarded as being synonymous with document retrieval and nowadays, with text retrieval, implying that the task of an IR system is to retrieve documents or texts with information content that is relevant to a user's information need.
>
> *(Sparck Jones and Willett 1997)*

DOI: 10.4324/9781003168348-38

Information retrieval (IR) is finding material (usually documents) of an unstructured nature (usually text) that satisfies an information need from within large collections (usually stored on computers).

(Manning et al. 2008)

Information need is what a user intends to look for and a *query* is an (approximate) expression of information need in the form of free text to be input into an IR system to begin a search.

The development of IR so far can be divided into three stages. The first, roughly from the late 1950s to the mid-1970s, is a period of hatching and testing key ideas and basic techniques, including various IR models. The second, from the mid-1970s to the emergence of commercial search engines on the Web in the early 1990s, develops and advances operational systems that can cope with a massive volume of texts growing alongside computer capacity in terms of both storage and computing power, and puts them in large-scale evaluation in a competitive manner (Harman 1993; Voorhees and Harman 2005). The third, from the mid-1990s onward, is featured by the development of a web search for practical use on the Web, especially those search engines relying more on term-weighting schemes based on the cross-linkage of web pages, e.g., HITS (Kleinberg 1998) and PageRank (Brin and Page 1998), the most famous one.

General architecture of an IR system

The key components in the general architecture of an IR system are illustrated in Figure 35.1. The goal of IR is to find in a document collection what a user intends to find according to the information need expressed in an input query. A non-trivial task preceding that is to acquire

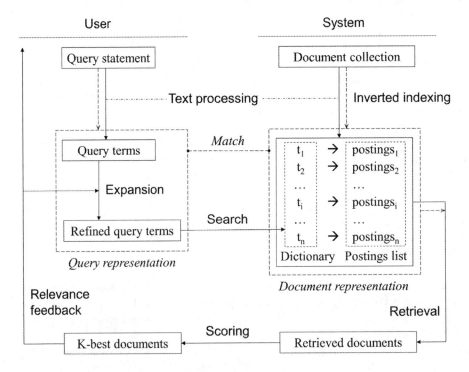

Figure 35.1   Key components of information retrieval system

and maintain a document collection of a certain size that demands automated means of crawling, e.g., the collection of all webpages from the Web. It certainly demands adequate computing power and sufficient storage space besides advanced techniques (e.g., text processing and web crawling) for support. To focus on the core issues of IR, however, one may assume – as most researchers did in the past – the availability of such a document collection as the starting point of IR. There have been a good number of standard test collections of very large size for IR evaluation since the small but pioneering Cranfield collection, among which the most influential ones include TREC,[1] NTCIR,[2] and CLEF.[3]

Conceptually, an IR system achieves its goal by matching a user query statement against each document in the document collection, as depicted by dash lines in Figure 35.1. In order to facilitate such matching, necessary text processing has to be first applied to turn the texts in question into a comparable representation. The simplest and most popular form of such representation is called the *bag of words* model, which represents a text as a set of words, known as *index terms*. Even so, however, matching a query, as a bag of words, against each document, as another bag of words, one after another in a sequential manner throughout a large document set, is of too low efficiency to make a practically usable IR system. A technique generally used from a very early stage of IR (Firth 1958a, b; Nolan 1958; Leibowitz *et al.* 1958; as cited in Moore 1961) is to construct an *inverted index*, also known as *inverted file* or *inverted list*. An inverted index stores a list of documents (postings) for each index term, as we will see in more detail in the following subsection. With such an inverted index, the matching for a query is realized by combining the postings of different query terms, as depicted by solid lines in Figure 35.1. As a user's query statement is usually a very short description of the information needed (to be convinced of this, one only has to think about the two to three word queries generally used in web searches), *query expansion* or *query reformulation/rewriting* can be performed in order to enrich the query so as to retrieve more relevant documents that do not contain the same words as the query. Another way to refine the query is *relevance feedback*, which is aimed at formulating a better expression of information need by incorporating into the current query a few related terms extracted from the documents that are judged relevant by the user, or retrieved in the top of the first round of retrieval.

Indexing and inverted index

As mentioned before, search in IR has to be efficient given a very large number of documents. Inverted index, hailed as 'the first major concept in information retrieval' by Manning *et al.* (2008), was specifically devised to address this issue.

Given a document set, an inverted index can be built in a way as simple as compiling a list of postings for each index term recording all documents that contain it. The result of this compilation gives two parts of an inverted index: a *dictionary* consisting of all index terms, and a set of *postings lists*, each of which is associated to a particular term, as illustrated in Figure 31.1. In practice, a postings list is used to hold much more information than a list of bare document IDs, including, for instance, the number of occurrences of the term in each document that contains it, known as term frequency *tf*, their positions in the document (used in modern IR to calculate the proximity of query terms in a document), the total number of its occurrences in the whole document collection, known as collection frequency *f*, the number of documents that contains the term, known as its document frequency *df*, and so on. A postings list for position index may take a form as this:

$$term \rightarrow \{f, df : [ID_1, tf_1:(pos_1^1, pos_2^1, \cdots)]; [ID_2, tf_2:(pos_1^2, pos_2^2, \cdots)]; \cdots\}$$

Accordingly, to search for documents containing two given terms is to intersect their postings lists for a set of common document IDs, and if needed, to determine whether they form a phrasal index term by examining their adjacency according to their positions.

Given the large scale of data in the dictionary and the postings list, a really efficient way of index construction and compression is needed for practical IR. Witten *et al.* (1999) provide a comprehensive coverage of these topics. Some more advanced treatments can be found elsewhere in the literature, e.g., the single-pass in-memory indexing (SPIMI) in Heinz and Zobel (2003) and a number of efficient storage allocation schemes, especially, the arrival rate scheme, in Luk and Lam (2007). Zobel and Moffat (2006) is recommended by Manning *et al.* (2008) 'as an in-depth and up-to-date tutorial on inverted indexes, including index compression'.

An important question in indexing is to determine which terms are to be kept as index terms. Not all the words in a language are deemed meaningful, i.e. bearing semantic meaning. Typical examples are function words that exist in any natural language. For example, we have 'a', 'an', 'the', 'to' etc. in English. A simple way to exclude these words from the index is to put them into a *stop list*.

Another important issue in natural language is that words in different forms may have the same or a similar meaning. For example, 'computer' and 'computing' are related to similar concepts. Therefore, one needs to normalize the word forms found in documents and queries. Lemmatization and stemming are two specific forms of normalization to reduce morphological variants. The former maps inflectional variants of a word to its *base form* or *lemma*, e.g., {'go', 'went', 'gone', 'goes', 'going'} to 'go'. The latter reduces words to their stems by removing their affixes, particularly, their suffixes, conflating a family of derivationally related words into an equivalence class – their stem, e.g., {'stems', 'stemming', 'stemmer', 'stemmers', 'stemmed'} to 'stem'. Computer programs for these kinds of processing are known as *lemmatizers* and *stemmers*, respectively. In principle, accurate morphological analysis is needed in order to support accurate identification of the lemma or the stem of a given word. In practice, however, stemming can be done by conditional transformation rules that successively transform or remove suffixes, as in the Porter stemmer[4] (Porter 1980), which is the most popular stemmer for English. This method has been extended to a number of other languages.

Term weighting and IR models

An IR model defines the representation of query and document, e.g., as a bag of words or even a graph with words as vertices, and the way the relevance of a document to a query is quantified or determined. The *Boolean model* represents a text as a conjunction of terms and a query as a Boolean expression of terms, e.g., a query q = *inverted* AND *file* AND (NOT *inverse*), and accordingly Boolean retrieval is to return documents that satisfy a given query, involving no term weighting in principle, and no document ranking. In practical uses of IR, document ranking is crucial and a good IR system should rank documents according to their relevance to the query.

An intuitive way of scoring the relevance of a document to a query is that the more term matches between them, the more relevant the document should be. However, not all the terms are equally meaningful, or representative of important and specific content. A widely held intuition for term weighting is to assume that frequent terms in a document (or a query) are important, and terms that do not appear in many other documents are specific. The *tf-idf* weighting schema combines both factors as follows:

$$tf - idf_{t,D} = tf_{t,D} \times idf_t$$

$$idf_t = log \frac{N}{df_t}$$

where $tf_{t,D}$ – term frequency – is the frequency of term t in document D;[5] N is the total number of documents in the collection in question, df_t the document frequency of t (i.e., the number of documents that contain t), and idf_t the inverse document frequency (Sparck Jones 1972). A simple document scoring function can be defined as follows:

$$score(Q,D) = \sum_{t \in Q} tf_{t,Q} \times tf - idf_{t,D}$$

Many other IR models have been developed, in which documents are scored in different ways according to different principles.

The *vector space model* (Salton *et al.* 1975) treats queries and documents each as a vector in a high dimension space, in which each term is weighted using *tf-idf*. The relevance of a document to a query is estimated according to the similarity of their vectors: the greater their similarity, the greater the relevance. The *cosine similarity* may be adopted as a measure for this purpose:

$$sim(Q, D) = \frac{\vec{V}(Q) \cdot \vec{V}(D)}{|\vec{V}(Q)| \, |\vec{V}(D)|} = \vec{v}(Q) \cdot \vec{v}(D)$$

where the *dot* (or *inner*) *product* of two vectors, say, of k dimensions, is defined as $\vec{x} \cdot \vec{y} = \sum_{i=1}^{k} x_i y_i$, the *length* of a vector as $|\vec{x}| = \sqrt{\sum_{i=1}^{k} x_i^2}$, and a unit vector as $\vec{v}(x) = \vec{V}(x) / |\vec{V}(x)|$.

A *probabilistic model* aims at estimating the probability of relevance of a document to a query. The simplest probabilistic model is the *binary independence model* (BIM) (Robertson and Sparck Jones 1976; van Rijsbergen 1979), which assumes that terms are mutually independent of each other. Then, a document is ranked with the log *odds* of the event that the document is relevant (R) to a query vs. its being irrelevant ($\bar{R}$).

$$logO(R| Q, D) \doteq log \frac{P(R | Q, D)}{P(\bar{R} | Q, D)}$$

By the Bayes rule, we have

$$logO(R| Q, D) = \frac{P(D| Q, R) P(R | Q)}{P(D| Q, \bar{R}) P(\bar{R} | Q)} \propto log \frac{P(D | Q, R)}{P(D | Q, \bar{R})},$$

for $\frac{P(R|Q)}{P(\bar{R}|Q)}$ is a constant. Assuming independence between terms, a document can be represented as a set of independent events – the presences and absences of terms. Let p_t and u_t represent respectively $P(t \text{ is present in } D | Q, R)$ and $P(t \text{ is present in } D | Q, \bar{R})$, and assume that only terms appearing in the query have an impact on the document's relevance, we have

$$logO(R | Q, D) \propto log \frac{\prod_{t \in Q \cap D} p_t \cdot \prod_{t \in Q \setminus D} (1 - p_t)}{\prod_{t \in Q \cap D} u_t \cdot \prod_{t \in Q \setminus D} (1 - u_t)}$$

Table 35.1 Contingency table of term occurrences

Number of documents	Relevant	Irrelevant	Total
Containing t	R	$df_t - r$	df_t
Not containing t	R $-$ r	$N - df_t - (R - r)$	$N - df_t$
Total	R	$N - R$	N

Adding a document-independent constant $\log(\Pi_{t \in Q} \frac{1-u_t}{1-p_t})$, we turn it into a neater form as follows.

$$\log O(R \mid Q, D) \propto \log \frac{\prod_{t \in Q \cap D} p_t \cdot \prod_{t \in Q \cap D} (1 - u_t)}{\prod_{t \in Q \cap D} u_t \cdot \prod_{t \in Q \cap D} (1 - p_t)} = \sum_{t \in Q \cap D} \log \frac{p_t (1 - u_t)}{u_t (1 - p_t)}$$

The logarithm in the sum is the term weight wt for term t in the model. Given the contingency table of document counts in Table 35.1, we have $p_t = r / R$ and $u_t = (df_t - r)/(N - R)$. Accordingly, we have the following term weight, where 0.5 is added for smoothing (Robertson and Sparck Jones 1976).

$$w_t = \log \frac{r(N - df_t - (R - r))}{(df_t - r)(R - r)} \cong \log \frac{(r + 0.5)(N - df_t - R + r + 0.5)}{(df_t - r + 0.5)(R - r + 0.5)}$$

Some more sophisticated probabilistic models than BIM can be found in the literature, e.g., van Rijsbergen (1979) and Fuhr (1992). In practice, the contingency table is rarely available. To cope with this problem, Croft and Harper (1979) assume that p_t is the same for all query terms and hence $p_t / (1 - p_t)$ is a constant, and that almost all documents in a large collection are irrelevant to a query, giving an estimation of u_t by df_t/N (for t appears in df_t irrelevant documents among N). Accordingly, we have the following scoring function, with 0.5 for smoothing, which appears to be a variant of *idf* weighting.

$$\log O(R \mid Q, D) \propto \sum_{t \in Q \cap D} \log \frac{N - df_t}{df_t} \cong \sum_{t \in Q \cap D} \log \frac{N - df_t + 0.5}{df_t + 0.5}$$

As summarized in Robertson and Sparck Jones (1994), '[t]he idea of term weighting is selectivity: what makes a term a good one is whether it can pick any of the few relevant documents from the many non-relevant ones', and there are three kinds of data source available for weighting: (1) collection frequency: N, df_t and their combination into $idf_t = \log N / df_t$; (2) term frequency: $tf_{t,D}$; and (3) document length: $|D|$ and its ratio to average document length $|D|/L_{ave}$. They can be combined into a combined weight

$$w_{t,D} = \frac{idf_t \times (k_1 + 1) tf_{t,D}}{k_1 \left((1 - b) + b \frac{|d|}{L_{ave}} \right) + tf_{t,D}}$$

with the tuning parameters k_1 and b to calibrate the scaling of term frequency and document length, respectively. The idf_t certainly can be substituted with another one of its variants, e.g., the one above with 0.5 for smoothing. Among many options for term weighting, two widely used scoring schemes, namely, the *Okapi weighting* (Robertson *et al.* 1999) and the *pivoted normalization weighting* (Singhal *et al.* 1996, 1999), opt for the following term weights, and then combine three factors with the aid of the constant tuning parameters k_1 (between 1.0 and 2.0), b (usually 0.75), k_3 (between 0 and 1000) and s (usually 0.2) for scaling purpose.

$$\text{Okapi:} \quad \sum_{t \in Q \cap D} \log \frac{N - df_t + 0.5}{df_t + 0.5} \times \frac{(k_1 + 1)tf_{t,D}}{k_1\left((1-b) + b\frac{|D|}{L_{ave}}\right) + tf_{t,D}} \times \frac{(k_3 + 1)tf_{t,Q}}{k_3 + tf_{t,Q}}$$

$$\text{Pivoted normalization:} \quad \sum_{t \in Q \cap D} \log \frac{N + 1}{df_{t,D}} \times \frac{1 + \ln\left(1 + \ln tf_{t,D}\right)}{(1-s) + s\frac{|D|}{L_{ave}}} \times tf_{t,Q}$$

In contrast to heuristic term weighting, *language modeling* provides a more principled approach to IR (Zhai 2008). Exploring the effective use of various language models in IR has been an active area of research since Ponte and Croft (1998). Instead of estimating document relevance, this approach aims at ranking documents according to the likelihood of a document D being what is looked for given a query Q, i.e.,

$$P(D|Q) = \frac{P(Q|D)P(D)}{P(Q)} \propto P(Q|D)P(D)$$

where $P(Q)$ is a constant. The document prior $P(Q)$ can be used to favor some special text features or simply assumed, for the sake of simplicity, to be a uniform distribution. Thus, $P(Q|D)$ becomes the choice of scoring for ranking. If we opt for a unigram model, this probability can be decomposed, by the independence assumption, into that of each query term, which is then estimated by $P(t|\theta_D)$ with a language model θ_D derived from D. A popular choice for parameter estimation is the maximum likelihood estimator (MLE), which starts from using the relative frequency of a term in given data. In this way, we have

$$P(Q|D) = \prod_{t \in Q} P(t|D) \cong \prod_{t \in Q} P_{ML}(t|\theta_D) = \prod_{t \in Q} \frac{tf_{t,D}}{|D|}$$

where $|D|$ denotes document length in number of words. This is called the *query likelihood model*, which ranks documents according to the probability that a query is generated by the model of each document. Accordingly, we can take its logarithm as a scoring function. Since a document is usually not large enough to train reliable parameters, an issue known as the *data sparseness* problem, smoothing is inevitably one of the most critical issues in language modeling for IR. Appropriate smoothing handles not only the zero probability of a query term unseen in a document but also the problem of overestimated probability for low-frequency terms, especially those occurring only once mostly by chance. A typical method for this is *linear interpolation*, also referred to as Jelinek-Mercer smoothing, to mix a document model θ_D with the collection model θ_C that is trained on the whole document collection:

$$P(t \mid D) = \lambda\, P_{\mathrm{ML}}(t \mid \theta_D) + (1 - \lambda)\, P_{\mathrm{ML}}(t \mid \theta_C)$$

where $0 < \lambda < 1$. The setting of λ is critical and has to be carefully tuned through training. Then, we have the following estimation for how likely a document is what a user looks for with a particular query:

$$P(D \mid Q) \propto P(D) \prod_{t \in Q} [\lambda\, P_{\mathrm{ML}}(t \mid \theta_D) + (1 - \lambda)\, P_{\mathrm{ML}}(t \mid \theta_C)]$$

A more general probabilistic similarity model for retrieval is formulated using the Kullback-Leibler (KL) divergence between the respective *query* and *document likelihood models* as follows:

$$-D(\theta_Q \mid\mid \theta_D) = -\sum_{t \in V} P(t \mid \theta_Q) \log \frac{P(t \mid \theta_Q)}{P(t \mid \theta_D)} \propto \sum_{t \in V} P(t \mid \theta_Q) \log P(t \mid \theta_Q)$$

where V is the vocabulary involved. The simplification made in the last step is due to the fact that $\sum_{t \in V} P(t \mid \theta_Q) \log P(t \mid \theta_Q)$ is a document-independent constant and can be ignored for document ranking. This model comparison approach is reported to outperform the approaches that use only a document or query model (Lafferty and Zhai 2001). Another language model is the *translation model* introduced into IR by Berger and Lafferty (1999) to deal with the problem of expression deviation (e.g., the use of synonyms) between queries and documents. It facilitates retrieval of documents containing alternativee terms with similar meanings to query terms by incorporating into the IR model a translation model, namely, a conditional probability $T(\cdot \mid \cdot)$ between terms:

$$P(Q \mid \theta_D) = \sum_{t \in Q} \prod_{w \in V} P(w \mid \theta_D)\, T(t \mid w)$$

This model is widely used in IR to incorporate relationships between terms, including in cross-language IR in which terms t and w are in two different languages.

In the traditional IR, each document is considered in isolation and its score to a query is only determined by its content words. The prior of a document (i.e. $P(D)$) is assumed to be uniform. This is counterintuitive, especially in the context of web searches. Some documents may be more popular, of higher quality or authority, than others, and therefore are preferred by users. Hyperlinks between web documents provide a way to estimate a document's popularity or authority: Each link to a document can be considered a vote in favor of it; the more votes a document receives, the more it is weighted. This idea is cast in the following PageRank algorithm (Brin and Page 1998): Assuming that a document d_i has links from a set $IN(d_i)$ of documents, its PageRank score $PR(d_i)$ is determined by

$$PR(d_i) = \frac{1 - d}{N} + d \sum_{d_j \in M(d_i)} \frac{PR(d_j)}{L(d_j)}$$

where d is a dumping factor, which is usually set at 0.85, N the total number of documents, and $L(d_j)$ the number of outbound links from d_j. This formula is used to update the PR scores (initially set to $1/N$) of documents (or pages) iteratively until reaching a stationary point. The resulting score $PR(d_i)$ can be used to estimate the prior of a document $P(d_i)$.

In a similar way, HITS (Kleinberg 1998) computes two scores for a page: authority and hub. The former estimates the value of the content of a page in terms of how many other pages (or hubs) link to it, and the latter the value of its links to other pages. An authoritative page means a page with many other pages referring to it, while a hub a directory page with many links to other authoritative pages. Starting with an initial value 1 for each page, the scores of authority and of hub are calculated as follows in a mutual recursion:

$$Auth(d_i) = \alpha \sum_{d_j \in IN(d_i)} Hub\left(d_j\right)$$

$$Hub(d_i) = \beta \sum_{d_j \in OUT(d_i)} Auth\left(d_j\right)$$

where $IN(d_i)$ and $OUT(d_i)$ denote the inlink and outlink pages of d_i, respectively, and α and β are two normalization factors. That is, for a page, its authority/hub score is determined by the sum of the hub/authority scores of its inlink/outlink pages.

In addition to content words and hyperlinks, a number of additional factors can also be utilized in a web search. For example, clickthrough data (the click behavior of users for a given query) is proven to be a useful resource that encodes some relevance relationship between a query and a (clicked) document. It is difficult to incorporate all these factors into a formal IR model. An alternative way is to consider them as defining features for use in combination to predict the relevance score of a document for a query. This has led to the new direction of *learning to rank* (L2R) (Liu 2009; Li 2011). Its original idea comes from Fuhr (1989, 1992), who tried to generalize the earlier probabilistic IR models by using a learning method to learn a probabilistic ranking model. The last decade has witnessed a significant progress in both research and applications of L2R. In general, L2R makes use of known relevance information to train a learning model to optimize the ranking in terms of a loss function, in a way to minimize the expected loss. Various machine learning methods (e.g. SVM) have been adapted for IR problems by transforming a desired ranking order to a list of binary preferences between documents or between document lists. The availability of relevance data from web search, especially, search log data from search engines, has made this supervised approach not only practically feasible but particularly appealing. A particularly strong advantage of this approach is that it treats a document as a bag of features (vs. a bag of terms) in its discriminative (vs. generative) learning. In theory, any useful feature conceivable can be integrated into a learning model for optimization on a large volume of training data with true answers, so as to yield a generalized IR model that subsumes classic IR weighting schemes as its features, especially those already proven to be particularly informative, e.g., *tf*, *idf*, normalized document length, PageRank and HITS scores. Interested readers may find a detailed description of L2R in Liu (2009) and Li (2011).

Evaluation

Comprehensive evaluation of an IR system is more complicated than one thinks at first glance, especially when subjectivity has to be involved in the judgment of document relevance to a user need. Nevertheless, the core of IR evaluation is to measure the retrieval effectiveness of an IR system, which is mostly conducted following the Cranfield paradigm using a *test set* consisting of (1) a set of queries as expressions of information needs and (2) a collection of documents in company with (3) relevance judgments specifying relevant documents to each query, namely, the *gold standard* or true answers. Besides, a *development test set* may be provided for tuning system parameters towards expected performance. There have been a good number of standard test collections, including the most influential ones mentioned above (in the subsection 'General architecture of IR system').

Table 35.2 Contingency table of retrieved documents

Number of documents	Relevant	Irrelevant	Total
Retrieved	true positive: *tp*	false positive: *fp*	*tp* + *fp*
Not retrieved	false negative: *fn*	true negative: *tn*	*fn* + *tn*
Total	*tp* + *fn*	*fp* + *tn*	

The two most fundamental measures in IR evaluation are precision and recall. *Precision* and *recall* are the proportions of retrieved relevant documents to, respectively, all retrieved documents and all relevant documents. Given the contingency in Table 35.2, we have

$$P = \frac{tp}{tp + fp}, R = \frac{tp}{tp + f}$$

Sometimes, we also use *F-measure*, which is the weighted harmonic mean of precision and recall:

$$F = \frac{1}{\alpha\frac{1}{P} + (1 - \alpha)\frac{1}{R}} , \text{ or } F = \frac{(\beta^2 + 1)PR}{\beta^2 P + R} \text{ with } \beta^2 = \frac{1 - \alpha}{\alpha}$$

where $\alpha \in [0, 1]$ and accordingly $\beta^2 \in [0, \infty]$. With $\beta^2 = 1$ (equivalently $\alpha = 0.5$), we have the default balanced F-measure (also called F1-measure) as follows:

$$F_{\beta=1} = \frac{2PR}{P + R}$$

As an IR system returns a ranked list, precision and recall change according to the number (k) of documents one picks from the list. A common practice is to draw a precision–recall curve by considering more and more documents. As k gets larger, we get more relevant documents included in the top-k and a lower precision, resulting in a curve descending along recall: the larger the recall, the lower the precision. To provide a single measure on the quality of IR systems, average precision at 11 points of recall is often used, i.e. the average of the precisions at 0.0, 0.1, ..., 1.0 recall (Teufel 2007). Another widely used measure, the *mean average precision* (MAP), is defined as follows:

$$\text{MAP}(Q) = \frac{1}{|Q|}\sum_{q \in Q}\frac{1}{|D_q|}\sum_{d \in D_q}P(R_d)$$

where Q is a query set, D_q the set of documents relevant to $q \in Q$, and R_d the set of top-k ranked retrieved documents up to d.

In the scenario of using multiple levels (or labels) of relevance judgment, e.g., {perfect, excellent, good, fair, and bad} each with a score (say, 4–0), as used in most recent works on learning to rank, a popular performance measure is the *normalized discounted cumulative gain* (NDCG) introduced by Järvelin and Kekäläinen (2000, 2002). The NDCG at position k (i.e., over the top-k retrieved documents) for a set of queries Q is defined as

$$NDCG(Q, k) = \frac{1}{|Q|} \sum_{q \in Q} Z_{k,q} \sum_{d \in \text{top-}k} \frac{2^{scr(q,d)} - 1}{\log_2(1 + \text{pos}(d))}$$

where $\text{pos}(\cdot)$ is the position of a document in the top-k list in question, $Z_{k,q}$ is a normalization factor calculated to ensure that the *NDCG* at k for a perfect ranking is 1, and the numerator and denominator of the inner fraction are the *gain* and the *position discount* function, respectively.

Query expansion and relevance feedback

An initial query from a user is often not a good enough expression of information need. One of the main reasons for this is that the same thought can be paraphrased in different ways using different words. The words used in a user query are not always the only and the best search terms used in relevant documents. The goal of query expansion is to extend an original query by incorporating other related terms that could be used in relevant documents. Towards this goal, two key issues need to be dealt with: how to select related terms for addition to a query, and how to combine these terms with those already in the query.

The first obvious way to find related terms to expand a q uery is to use a manually constructed thesaurus. For many language analysis tasks, one needs relations between words or terms. Among the available resources of this kind that are readily useable for IR, a typical example is WordNet[6] (Miller *et al.* 1990) which provides various semantic relations between words and compound terms (e.g. synonymy, hyponymy, hypernymy, etc.). For example, 'data processing system' is a synonymous term with 'computer', which has 'PC' (a-kind-of 'computer') as a hyponym. Using such a resource, one can append synonyms or other types of related term to initial query terms to form an expanded query, e.g., expand the query 'computer' with 'data processing system' and 'PC'. Voorhees (1993, 1994) first attempted to use WordNet in IR experiments on TREC collections, but the expected advantages did not concretize, in that when related terms were added to expand a query, retrieval effectiveness was degraded rather than increased. Careful analyses revealed that coverage and ambiguity were the two main problems that limit the usefulness of this kind of resource in IR. Like other lexical resources, WordNet has only a partial coverage of concepts and terms used in documents and queries, missing many others, and it does not deal with term ambiguity either. For example, 'computer' has two meanings in WordNet: as a machine or as a human expert. When a query containing 'computer' is expanded with all its meanings in WordNet, a certain amount of noise (i.e., unrelated terms) is unavoidably brought in. Some later studies (Mandala *et al.* 1999; Cao *et al.* 2005) obtained positive results by means of selecting or weighting related WordNet terms with the aid of corpus statistics.

Another approach to query expansion, which is widely used in IR, exploits term co-occurrences in the document collection in question (Qiu and Frei 1993), based on the assumption that two terms that co-occur often are likely to be related. It helps improve retrieval effectiveness significantly. Since it is also a topic in text mining for IR, we will present its details later in the section on text mining.

The above approaches, one relying on general lexical knowledge and the other on query-independent co-occurrence statistics, are two typical *global expansion* methods. However, it is often observed that a strong co-occurring term in the collection in question is not always appropriate for use to expand a given query. Consider, for instance, a query on 'Java hotel' and a collection mainly consisting of computer science documents. Most co-occurring terms with 'Java' are Java language related terms, which are inappropriate for use to expand this query. A way to remedy this is to perform local analysis, extracting expansion terms only from top-ranked retrieved documents (Xu and Croft 2000). More specifically, the first round of retrieval identifies a small set of documents, from which a set of related terms are extracted and used as expansion terms. Compared to global methods, this method benefits from a filtering of the documents retrieved with an initial query. In general, the top documents so retrieved are more likely to be related to the query than others in the same collection, and thus the expansion terms extracted from them are more related to the topic of the query.

In contrast to global expansion that may use any other resources, a *local expansion* method expands a query using only documents retrieved for this particular query. Typically, it selects a set of strongly related terms only from top-ranked retrieved documents, using various criteria such as *tf*, *idf*, etc., or co-occurrences with query terms. Since user judgment of relevance is rarely available, the best one can do is to assume the relevance, the so-called pseudo relevance, of a few top-ranked retrieved documents and incorporate their terms into a query. Query expansion carried out this way is called *pseudo* (or *blind*) *relevance feedback*. Experiments confirm that local expansion of this kind outperforms global expansion. However, it has a drawback of performing two rounds of retrieval, which may not be practical in a real situation, e.g., web search.

In general, query expansion may exploit all available relations between terms (e.g., thesaurus, ontology) and all possible connections between queries and documents (e.g., user relevance judgments, clickthrough data) or between documents (e.g., hyperlinks). A special case is *relevance feedback*, in which a user is asked to judge the relevance (or irrelevance) of some returned documents for a query, such that the query can be extended to a new one by incorporating some terms extracted from relevant documents while excluding those from irrelevant documents. As mentioned above, true relevance feedback is usually unavailable, and the best we can resort to is pseudo-relevance feedback, which assumes the relevance of top-ranked documents. User clickthrough is another form of implicit relevance feedback from users: when choosing to click on a document, a user often (although not always) considers it to be potentially relevant. A simple way to exploit clickthrough data is to assume that terms in clicked documents are related to those in the query in question. This idea has motivated a number of studies on mining term relationships from clickthrough data (Wen *et al.* 2001; Cui *et al.* 2002; Baeza-Yates and Tiberi 2007; Gao *et al.* 2010), which will be presented in more detail in the section on text mining. Similarly, anchor texts pointing to a document also reflect some relations of them with the terms in the document.

The next key issue in query expansion is how to combine selected expansion terms with original ones in a query. Most approaches are based on, or derived from, the Rocchio formula (1965/1971) popularized by the SMART system (Salton 1971), which was developed for relevance feedback to a vector space model. Given an initial query vector $\vec{q}_0$, a set R of relevant documents and a set $\bar{R}$ of irrelevant documents (as judged by users), the new query vector to be produced by the relevance feedback with these documents is defined as:

$$\vec{q}_1 = \alpha \, \vec{q}_0 + \frac{\beta}{|R|} \sum_{\vec{d} \in R} \vec{d} - \frac{\gamma}{|\bar{R}|} \sum_{\vec{d} \in \bar{R}} \vec{d}$$

where α, β, and γ are the weights to balance the three vectors in reflecting the true use need. The meaning of this formulation is straightforward: it moves the query closer towards the centroid of relevant documents and away from that of the irrelevant documents, in hopes that there are more relevant documents around the former centroid than any other place and hence more of them can be retrieved by the new query. To reflect the observation that relevant documents are more useful than irrelevant ones, most IR systems have $\alpha=1$ and $\beta>\gamma$ (e.g., $\beta=0.75$ and $\gamma=0.15$).

The same formula has been used for pseudo-relevance feedback, with top-k retrieved documents as R, and no irrelevant document (i.e. $\gamma=0$). Unlike true relevance feedback that usually leads to improved retrieval effectiveness, pseudo-relevance feedback often produces less consistent results: when top retrieved documents are truly related to an initial query, it often yields better effectiveness; otherwise, a query drift phenomenon (i.e., the resulting new query departures from the original intent of the initial query) is often observed. An example to illustrate this problem is the query 'Java public transportation', which may retrieve many documents about 'Java programming language'—using the terms in these documents for query expansion inevitably makes the resulting query drift away from the originally intended information need.

In the framework of probabilistic IR, when true relevance feedback is available, it is used to build (or update) the contingency table so as to obtain more precise probability estimations. When pseudo-relevance feedback is used, it may be exploited as follows: Let $\mathcal{R}$ be the set of top-ranked documents that are retrieved from the document collection C, of size N, and $\mathcal{R}_t \subset \mathcal{R}$ be the subset of documents containing term t, and assume that the remaining $N-|R|$ documents in the collection are irrelevant, the pt and ut defined above can be estimated as

$$p_t = \frac{|\mathcal{R}_t|}{|\mathcal{R}|}, \; u_t = \frac{\mathrm{df}_t - |\mathcal{R}_t|}{N - |\mathcal{R}|}$$

Accordingly, the term weight for t is

$$w_t = \log\frac{p_t\left(1-u_t\right)}{u_t\left(1-p_t\right)} = \log\frac{|\mathcal{R}_t|}{|\mathcal{R}|-|R_t|} \cdot \frac{N-|\mathcal{R}|-\left(\mathrm{df}_t - |R_t|\right)}{\mathrm{df}_t - |R_t|}$$

Since $N \gg |\mathcal{R}|$ and $\mathrm{df}_t \gg |\mathcal{R}|$, it can be approximated as follows, with 0.5 for smoothing (as we did before):

$$w_t \cong \log\frac{|\mathcal{R}_t|+0.5}{|\mathcal{R}|-|\mathcal{R}_t|+0.5} + \log\frac{N-df_t+0.5}{df_t+0.5}$$

where the second log may be further approximated by $idf_t = \dfrac{N}{df_t}$, assuming $N \gg df_t$. Then, comparing it with $\log O(R\,|\,Q,D)$ formulated earlier, we can see that relevance feedback adds the first log to t's weight.

Query expansion and pseudo-relevance feedback have also been widely used in language models for IR. Recall that in the formulation using KL-divergence, a language model is built, respectively, for a query and for a document. Query expansion aims at building a new language model for a user query. It is typically implemented as an interpolation between an original query model θ_{Q_0} and a feedback (or expansion) model $\theta_{\mathcal{R}}$ that accommodates new terms from top-ranked documents or a thesaurus:

$$P(t \mid \theta_{Q1}) = (1 - \alpha)P(t \mid \theta_{Q0}) + \alpha P(t \mid \theta_{\mathcal{R}})$$

where $\alpha \in [0,1]$ is a parameter to control the contribution of the two models.

There are various ways to formulate an expansion model $\theta_{\mathcal{R}}$. If a set of term relationships have been determined (e.g., extracted from a document collection or obtained from a thesaurus), and let the relationship between two terms ti and t be expressed as a probability function $P(t \mid t_i)$, then the model $\theta_{\mathcal{R}}$ can be defined as:

$$P(t \mid \theta_{\mathcal{R}}) = \sum_{t \in V} P(t \mid t_i)P(t_i \mid \theta_{Q0})$$

In theory, this formulation could also be applicable to pseudo-relevance feedback, using the set of top-ranked documents to construct the model $\theta_{\mathcal{R}}$, say, using MLE. However, it does not work well, because top-ranked documents contain many terms that are not necessarily related to the query in use. In addition, they also contain many terms that are generally frequent in a language and hence ineffective in the discrimination of relevant documents from irrelevant ones. A better way to construct $\theta_{\mathcal{R}}$ is to isolate a part of term distribution mass in feedback documents that is different from a general language model, i.e., specific to the query. This idea is implemented in the mixture model (Zhai and Lafferty 2001), which assumes that the feedback documents $\mathcal{R}$ are generated by a mixture of two models: a query-specific feedback (or topic) model $\theta_{\mathcal{R}}$ and a general (or background) language model, which is usually approximated by the collection model θ_C. The log likelihood of R under this model is

$$\log P(\mathcal{R} \mid \theta_{\mathcal{R}}) = \sum_{t \in V} f_t, \mathcal{R} \log[(1 - \lambda)P(t \mid \theta_{\mathcal{R}}) + \lambda P(t \mid \theta_C)]$$

where $f_t, \mathcal{R}$ is the frequency of t in $\mathcal{R}$, and $\lambda \in [0,1]$ the weight for the background model. With λ set to a constant, the topic model $\theta_{\mathcal{R}}$ can be trained in a way to use the Expectation-Maximization (EM) algorithm to maximize the above log likelihood (see Zhai and Lafferty (2001) for detailed EM updates).

Alternatively, their divergence minimization method pursues a $\theta_{\mathcal{R}}$ as close to the language model of each document in R and as far away from the background model θ_C as possible, using C as an approximation of the set of nonrelevant documents:

$$\theta_{\mathcal{R}} = \arg\min_{\theta} \frac{1}{|\mathcal{R}|} \sum_{d \in \mathcal{R}} D(\theta \mid\mid \theta_d) - \lambda D(\theta \mid\mid \theta_C)$$

where $\lambda \in [0,1]$ is a weighting parameter. Once determined, this $\theta_{\mathcal{R}}$ can be interpolated with θ_{Q_0} to produce a new query model θ_{Q_1} for ranking documents.

However, it is showed in Cao et al. (2008) that terms extracted by the above methods are not always beneficial when added to a query. A case study on three TREC collections reveals that only about 17 percent of terms so extracted are truly useful, while about 30 percent of them are harmful, i.e. lowering retrieval effectiveness. It is thus necessary to perform a further selection or reweighting of expansion terms among all candidates. A classification method, based on a set of features, can be used to determine if a candidate term is a good one, in order to further improve retrieval effectiveness.

Another well-known method to incorporate feedback documents is the *relevance model* (Lavrenko and Croft 2001). Its basic idea is to consider top-ranked retrieved documents to be i.i.d. (independent and identically distributed) samples of relevance. Using these samples, a relevance model $\theta_{\mathcal{R}}$ is defined as follows:

$$P\left(t \mid \theta_{\mathcal{R}}\right) = P\left(t \mid Q, \mathcal{R}\right) = \sum_{d \in \mathcal{R}} P(t \mid \theta_d) P(\theta_d \mid Q) \propto \sum_{d \in \mathcal{R}} P(t \mid \theta_d) P(Q \mid \theta_d) P\left(\theta_d\right)$$

where $P(Q \mid \theta_d)$ is indeed the original ranking score of a document. One may further assume a uniform $P(\theta_d)$ for simplification.

There are a number of other approaches to query expansion derived from the above ones. Interested readers can refer to Carpineto and Romano (2012) for a comprehensive survey of them. A few representative ones by means of text mining will be discussed later in the text mining section. In practice, query expansion techniques can be used in alternative forms, including query suggestion, query rewriting, and query reformulation, all of which are intended to suggest a better query formulation. Besides the resources mentioned above for query expansion, the search history of a user can also be analyzed for use to determine which query formulation is preferable. Nonetheless, technical details on these related tasks are not permitted in this chapter due to limited space.

Cross-language information retrieval

A special form of information retrieval is *cross-language information retrieval* (CLIR), which aims at retrieving documents in a language different from that of a query. CLIR research started in the early 1970s (e.g., Salton (1970)) and has been an active area of research since the late 1990s when TREC introduced a cross-language track in 1997 involving English, French and German. NTCIR started CLIR experiments between English and Asian languages (mainly Chinese, Japanese and Korean) in 1999 and CLEF for European languages in 2000. On top of traditional monolingual IR, CLIR has a language barrier, an extra difficulty, to overcome by some means of *translation*, in order to bring documents and queries into a comparable representation as if they were in the same language. One may opt to perform either query translation or document translation. Experiments (Franz *et al.* 1999; McCarley 1999) show that either achieves a comparable level of effectiveness. Nevertheless, query translation is more commonly adopted, for its flexibility in adapting to new languages of interest and the efficiency of translating a smaller amount of texts.

Translation can be performed in several ways using different resources and methods (Oard and Dorr 1996; Nie 2010). The simplest way is to use a bilingual dictionary to turn each query word into its translation words as stored in the dictionary, or into a selection of the translation words based on some coherence criteria (Grefenstette 1999; Gao *et al.* 2001; Liu *et al.* 2005; Adriani and van Rijsbergen 2000). It is certainly very convenient to use a machine translation (MT) system, if available, to translate a query simply as a text into a target language (Franz *et al.* 1999; McCarley 1999; Savoy and Dolamic 2009), so that it can be used as a query in monolingual IR. CLIR is typically cast as a problem of MT + monolingual IR, although several recent studies have started to investigate IR-specific translation, with a focus on examining the utility of MT results (Türe *et al.* 2012; Ma *et al.* 2012; Türe and Lin 2013). Another option is to use parallel and/or comparable texts more directly. From a large corpus of parallel texts, translation relations can be extracted automatically with a statistical translation model for use in CLIR (Nie *et al.* 1998; Nie *et al.* 1999; Kraaij *et al.* 2003). The simplest way to do so is to train an IBM model 1 (Brown *et al.* 1993), which assumes that word alignment between two parallel sentences is independent of word order and position. This assumption is certainly invalid for translation in general, but it corresponds well to the traditional word-bag model of IR, whose retrieval results are also independent of word order and position. This assumption has been questioned in both IR (Metzler and Croft 2005; Bendersky *et al.* 2010; Shi and Nie 2010) and CLIR (Türe *et al.* 2012; Türe and Lin 2013; Ma *et al.* 2012). It turns out that a more sophisticated phrase-based translation model can produce better query translations and hence lead to better cross-language retrieval results.

In addition to parallel texts, comparable texts (i.e., bilingual or multilingual texts about the same topics) that are available in an even larger amount can also be utilized, e.g., Wikipedia (or news) articles in different languages about the same concepts (or events). A number of studies have attempted to exploit comparable texts to facilitate query translation (Sheridan and Ballerini 1996; Franz *et al.* 1999; Braschler and Schäuble 2000; Moulinier and Molina-Salgado 2003). In general, it is unrealistic to apply the same word alignment process for parallel texts to comparable texts. A more flexible cross-language similarity function is instead needed. However, it is also unrealistic to expect it to work as well as a translation model, as shown in CLIR experiments. Nevertheless, comparable texts can be used not only as a last means for rough translation of user queries, especially in the scenario of no parallel text available, but also as complementary resources to available parallel texts for additional gain in CLIR (e.g., Sadat *et al.* 2003). The use of Wikipedia is a special case of exploiting comparable texts to facilitate CLIR (Nguyen *et al.* 2008): in addition to text contents on similar topics in different languages, its organization structure and concept descriptions can also be utilized to further enhance the mining of translation relations.

Query translation for CLIR is not merely a translation task. It is intended to produce a query expansion effect by means of including multiple and related translation words (Oard and Dorr 1996; Nie 2010). This has been proven useful for both general IR (Carpineto and Romano 2012) and CLIR. Simple use of MT to translate user queries is often not a sufficient solution. A number of recent studies (Türe *et al* 2012; Türe *et al.* 2013; Ma *et al.* 2012) have shown that opening the MT 'blackbox' to allow the use of multiple translation candidates and their appropriate weighting in CLIR is indeed more advantageous than using a single best translation. Last but not least, however, whatever approach to CLIR is opted for, there is an acute need to infer translation relations between words and/or phrases, towards which a very first step is to mine parallel/comparable texts from the Web. A number of attempts to do such mining will be presented in a later section.

Text mining

Text mining (TM) is also known as *knowledge discovery in texts* (KDT; Feldman and Dagan 1995) or *text data mining* (TDM; Hearst 1999), referring to the process and/or the study of the (semi) automated discovery of novel, previously unknown information in unstructured texts. Both TM and IR are aimed at facilitating our access to information, but they differ in a number of ways. What IR returns to a user is some known and overt information that can be directly read off from the documents it retrieves in relevance to the user's query, and the relevance is estimated by computing the similarity of a document and a query or the likelihood that a document is looked for with a query. Unlike IR, TM is not for locating any wanted information in a large collection of texts in response to a query. Instead, the goal of TM is to infer new knowledge, mostly as covert information about facts, patterns, trends or relationships of text entities, which is hidden in, and hence inaccessible via the comprehension and literary interpretation of, texts. Despite no query being involved, TM serves a certain information need, in the sense that the novel knowledge it uncovers needs to be of good quality for use to serve a particular purpose or application, e.g., term correlation information to facilitate query expansion in IR, and term translation options and respective probabilities to enable statistical machine translation (SMT) and CLIR. If we refer to the content that can be obtained from a text by reading as overt information and to the rest that cannot be so obtained as covert, a clear-cut boundary between IR and TM is that IR accesses the former and TM the latter. It is thus conceivable that any information access to texts beyond the reach of fully fledged IR may have to be facilitated by TM. Serving the general goal of TM to make the covert visible, the development of visualization tools has been an indispensable and popular sub-area of TM since the very beginning.

TM is considered a variation or extension of *data mining* (DM), which is also known as *knowledge discovery in database* (KDD) and whose goal is to find implicit, previously unknown, and non-trivial information, of potential use for certain purpose or interest, from large structured databases. Instead of working on databases, TM works on unstructured texts. The view of TM as a natural extension of DM can be found in the early work by Feldman and Dagan (1995), that once a certain structure or relation can be imposed onto text entities of interest, e.g., a conceptual hierarchy, traditional DM methodologies can be applied. A typical DM process can be conceptually divided into three stages: (1) pre-processing, (2) mining and (3) result validation. The first stage is to prepare a set of target data for a mining algorithm to work on, mostly focusing on data selection, necessary transformation and noise filtering. For the purpose of validation, available data is usually divided into a training and a test set, so that the patterns of interest mined by a mining algorithm from the training set are evaluated on the test set. A common practice of evaluation is to apply the mined patterns to a target application that the mining is aimed at bettering, and then measure the performance gain of using the mined patterns. As in language modeling, a common problem in TM is over-fitting, that the patterns found in training data have a rare or too low a chance to present elsewhere, such as in test data. Drawing on statistical inference and machine learning, a mining approach may fall into one of the following categories:

1 regression, to model data with the least amount of error;
2 anomaly/deviation detection, to identify unusual records or trends in data, e.g., deviations from normal credit card usage, revealing possible frauds;
3 association/dependency modeling, to detect relationships between variables, e.g., customers' purchasing habits, such as items customarily bought together;
4 clustering, to find groups (or categories) and/or structures in data in terms of a certain similarity;
5 classification, to assign known (or predefined) categories or structures to new data;
6 summarization, to infer a more compact representation for data, usually by means of finding regularities in data or estimating the importance of data; and
7 sequencing or sequence pattern mining, to infer significant co-occurring patterns of data items in a data stream.

This names a few among many others. Several representative ones are presented below for a bird's eye view of the whole field.

Categorization, clustering and information extraction

Considering TM as a natural extension of DM, we have text categorization, text clustering and information extraction as typical TM tasks. Interestingly, however, not all scholars agree with this view. For example, Hearst (1999, 2003) holds a purist position against this view while defining what TM is, for the reason that these tasks do not lead to any genuine discovery of new, heretofore unknown information, in the sense that anything in a text already known to its author is not new! She points out that 'mining' as a metaphor to imply 'extracting precious nuggets of ore from otherwise worthless rock' mismatches the real essence of TM. The best known example of real TM is Swanson's (1987, 1991) work on deriving novel hypotheses on causes of rare diseases from biomedical literature, e.g., the hypothesis of magnesium deficiency as a possible cause of migraine headache. Besides the aforementioned TM tasks, what she also puts under the label of mining-as-ore-extraction include automatic generation of term associations from existing resources (such as WordNet) for IR query expansion (Voorhees 1994) and automatic acquisition of syntactic relations from corpora (Manning 1993).

The gap between Hearst's definition and the work by many researchers in the field suggests that two issues concerning the word 'new' are worth examining: (1) the continuum of newness (or the degree of novelty), e.g., wholly vs. partly new, and (2) new to whom, e.g., to everyone vs. to a particular user (or agent). To avoid too narrow a scope of research, it is necessary to relax the definition of TM to this weaker one: the (semi)automated acquisition of information from texts to enrich or add to an existing pool of information (or knowledge), which at the beginning can be empty or the whole of human knowledge. In this way, Hearst's purist definition becomes a special case, and the two meanings of the term 'text mining', namely, mining texts (or text nuggets) from some resources (e.g., large corpora) and mining hidden (i.e., not directly readable) information from texts, are covered, corresponding to two different types of TM that resort to different methodologies.

The former, that mines text nuggets for critical information or special knowledge, is more fundamental and popular, and relies more on basic text processing operations for recognition of surface string patterns. A simple and typical example of this is to extract strings of particular patterns from texts (such as e-mail addresses, phone numbers, URLs, and so forth from webpages) that are new to an interested user. Information extraction (IE) to find targeted types of information to fill in predefined slots (e.g., an event frame: who did what to whom, where, when, how, why, and so forth) and mining personal data to compose or complement a personal profile are other two examples involving natural language processing of various degrees of complexity. In particular, *named entity recognition* (NER) to identify names of various types (e.g., person, organization, place, and so forth) and their variants (e.g., full names, nicknames, abbreviations, etc.) plays a critical role in IE, underlain by basic natural language processing techniques, e.g., part-of-speech (POS) tagging. Associating a recognized name with its true referent, e.g., 'Ford' with a company or a person, and differentiating concepts under the same word or term may be tackled by means of categorization or clustering, depending on the availability of candidate entities, which usually resorts to advanced statistical inference.

The latter type of TM to dig out concealed information in texts is more challenging and attracts a more serious research effort. It needs to go beyond the basic language processing that supports the former, and rely more on logical reasoning and/or statistical inference. Swanson's aforementioned work demonstrates the effectiveness of logical reasoning. For statistical inference, the starting point is to derive (co-)occurrence frequencies of text units (e.g., words) from a large corpus (i.e., a collection of texts), for use in statistical measurement, test, and/or distribution modeling. In the case of using a machine learning model, the features in use need to be extracted from text units with regard to their context, to produce training data for model training. No matter what methodologies are employed, the two types of TM manifest their common and different characteristics clearly in specific tasks in almost all popular areas of TM in recent years.

Summarization

In language technology, many undertakings that are now viewed as typical branches of TM in fact originated independently of DM and developed into standalone disciplines before the emergence of, or in parallel with, TM. For example, originating from Luhn (1958), *text summarization*, also known as *automatic summarization*, has developed into a popular research area for exploration of various approaches (mainly in two categories: extraction vs. abstraction) to producing various types (e.g., indicative, informative, vs. critical) of summaries with different orientations (i.e., query-based vs. query-independent) in one of two major dimensions (i.e., single- vs. multi-document). Three stages are identified in a full process of summarization (Sparck Jones 1999; Hovy and Lin 1999; Hovy 2005):

1   *topic identification*, to identify the key content of the text(s) to be summarized by identifying the most important text units (including words, phrases, sentences, paragraphs, etc.) in terms of some predefined criterion of importance and returning the *n* best ones in respect to a requested summary length;
2   *interpretation*, to fuse and then represent the identified topics in an abstract representation or formulation (e.g., event template, lexical chain, concept network/relation, etc.), using prior domain knowledge and involving other words or concepts than those in the input text(s); and
3   *summary generation*, to turn the unreadable abstract representation to a coherent summary output in human-readable text form using language generation techniques.

The involvement of interpretation distinguishes an abstraction from an extraction approach. The latter simply extracts the most important portions (e.g., key phrases, sentences, etc.) of text and combines them into a summary through a 'smoothing' process to eliminate such dysfluencies as redundant repetitions of nouns, name entities and even clauses. The popularly used criteria for topic identification include frequency, position (e.g., such locations as headings, titles, first paragraphs/sentences, etc.), cue phrases, query and title, lexical connectedness, discourse structure, and combined scores of various models. All these can be used as features, together with other textual ones (e.g., uppercases, sentence length, proper names, dates, quotes, pronouns, etc.), in a classifier or a machine learner for estimating the probabilities of text portions for inclusion into a summary (Kupiec *et al.* 1995; Lin 1999). In particular, Lin (1999) shows that the most useful summary length is 15–35 per cent of that of an original text. In another dimension, multi-document summarization has to deal with more challenges beyond single documents, including cross-document overlaps and inconsistencies, in terms of both timeline and thematic content.

Summarization evaluation is complicated and remains one of the greatest challenges in this area. The common practice is to compare machine generated summaries against ideal ones prepared by human (e.g., evaluators). ROUGE (Lin and Hovy 2003; Lin 2004) is the most popular metrics for this purpose, which is defined to quantify the quality of a candidate summary in terms of its n-gram overlaps with a reference summary. Besides, two widely used measures, namely, *compression ratio* (CR) and *retention ratio* (RR), are defined respectively as the proportions of the length and information of a summary to its original text(s). In general, we assume that the smaller the CR and the larger the RR, the better the summary.

Sequence mining

Good examples of sequencing include DNA sequence analysis, stock trend predication, and language pattern recognition; and a good example of the latter is unsupervised lexical learning to model how language learners discover words from language data from scratch without a priori knowledge and teaching (Olivier 1968; Brent and Cartwright 1996; Brent 1999; Kit 2000, 2005; Venkataraman 2001). The basic idea is to segment a sentence into chunks, namely word candidates, that yield the greatest probability of the whole sentence, computed as the product of some conditional probability of each chunk. Theoretically, most existing works follow the *minimum description length* (MDL) principle (Solomonoff 1964; Rissanen 1978, 1989; Wallace and Boulton 1968; Wallace and Freeman 1987).[7] Technically, the learning becomes an issue of mining string patterns, mostly by means of formulating an optimization algorithm (e.g., the EM algorithm) to infer a probabilistic model (i.e., a set of candidate chunks and respective probabilities) on a given set of child-directed speech data (i.e., a set of utterances transcribed into speech transcription or plain text), such that the optimal chunks into which an utterance is segmented by the model coincide with what we call words. Alternatively, *description length gain* (DLG) is formulated as an empirical goodness measure for word candidates in terms of their compression effect (Kit and Wilks 1999) and later applied to simulate the manner of lexical learning that pre-verbal infants take to acquire words, by means of pursuing an optimal sum of compression effect over candidate chunks (Kit 2000, 2005). This approach is particularly successful in simulating language learning infants' two basic strategies to acquire new words that are widely recognized in psycholinguistics: a bottom-up strategy combines speech elements (or characters) into a word candidate, and a top-down strategy first recognizes clumps of frequently co-occurring words as word-like items and then divides them into smaller candidate chunks recursively when upcoming evidence favors this division, e.g., leading to further description length gain.

Biomedical text mining

Biomedical text mining is one of the most active areas of TM, having formed the biggest community of researchers and developed the largest volume of specialized resources:

1   MEDLINE/PubMed[8] database of journal citations and abstracts, and the Medical Subject Headings (MeSH),[9] maintained by the U.S. National Library of Medicine (NLM);
2   a good number of datasets derived from this primary one over various periods or special areas, e.g., the OHSUMED test collection,[10] the TREC Genomics Track[11] data, the GENIA[12] corpus of annotated MEDLINE abstracts, the BioCreAtive[13] collections, and the PennBioIE[14] corpus; and
3   many knowledge resources, e.g., the Metathesaurus[15] and the Semantic Network[16] of Unified Medical Language System (UMLS)[17] of NLM that unify over 100 controlled vocabularies such as dictionaries, terminologies and ontologies, the Pharmacogenomics Knowledge Base (PharmGKB),[18] the Neuroscience Information Framework,[19] and the Gene Ontology.[20]

This field has undergone rapid development in response to the exponentially growing volume of biomedical literature and data, including clinical records. Its general purpose is to facilitate information access, beyond ordinary IR, to the massive volume of specialized texts, e.g., retrieving explicitly expressed relations, facts or events of interest, and further exploit such texts for discovery of unrecognized hidden facts, via the generation of hypotheses for further investigation. Its main tasks include NER, extraction of relations and events, summarization, question answering, and literature-based discovery. Grouped together with the extraction of relations and events under the banner of IE, NER is in fact the very initial step for almost all biomedical text processing, conceptually corresponding to the tokenization phase of general-purpose NLP but practically requiring to go beyond, whilst also based on, morphological processing to tackle a more complicated problem of identifying names (and terms) of various types in the biomedical domain, including gene and protein names, disease names and treatments, drug names and dosages, and so forth, most of which are compounds composed of several words. The main challenges in NER come not only from the growth of new names alongside the rapid growth of scientific discoveries but also from our slack use of existing names, giving rise to many problems such as synonyms (several names referring to the same entity) and polysemous acronyms and abbreviations (one abbreviated name referring to more than one entity or concept). Thus, NER is not merely to identify the boundaries of a name entity in the text, but to further carry out *entity normalization* to map a recognized entity to its canonical, preferred name (i.e., its unique concept identifier). The main approaches to NER can be grouped into the following categories (Krauthammer and Nenadic 2004; Leser and Hakenberg 2005; Simpson and Demner-Fushman 2012):

1   dictionary-based approach, which demands a comprehensive list of names and also has to resort to approximate string matching to deal with various kinds of variants;
2   rule-based approach, which uses a set of man-made rules or string patterns to describe the structures of names and their contexts;
3   statistical approach, especially machine learning, which exploits a classifier (e.g., support vector machine) or a sequencing model (e.g., hidden Markov model, maximum entropy model, or conditional random fields) to predict the position (e.g., beginning (B), inside (I) and outside (O)) of a word in a name entity, trained on annotated data with various kinds of lexical information (e.g., orthographical characteristics, affix, POS) as features; and
4   hybrid approach, which integrates (1) or (2) with (3) above, or combines several machine learning models.

Approaches of these categories are also applied to extracting pair-wise relations between two entities, including interactions between protein and protein, genes and proteins, genes and diseases, proteins and point mutations, and so forth, and relations of diseases and tests/treatments. The starting point of relation extraction is that a high co-occurrence frequency of two entities indicates a higher chance of a relation (or association) between them, e.g., the association between diseases and drugs, and then other means are applied to determine the type and direction of the relation. Besides rule-based approaches, which use rules or patterns manually prepared by experts or automatically derived from annotated corpora, machine learning approaches are commonly used to identify and classify these relations of interest, especially those between diseases and treatments. Nevertheless, further advances certainly have to count on advanced NLP techniques such as syntactic and semantic parsing, especially dependency parsing and semantic role labeling, to enable the utilization of specific syntactic patterns and/or semantic roles of words in predicate-argument structures.

Event extraction is to identify event structures, each of which consists of a verb (or nominalized verb, e.g., 'expression'), termed a *trigger*,[21] that specifies an event of some type (e.g., binding, positive regulation),[22] and one or more than one name (or another event) as event *argument* of some role (e.g., cause, theme). For example, in a nested event like '*X* gene expression is activated by *Y*', we have 'activated' as a trigger, and *Y* and another event 'expression' (with '*X* gene' as theme) as its cause and theme, respectively. In general, an event extraction procedure goes through three stages, namely, trigger detection to identify trigger words, argument detection and role assignment to determine if a name entity or trigger is an argument and what role it plays, and event construction to form an event structure for a trigger using available arguments. This works in a similar way as semantic parsing via semantic role labeling: identifying predicates, their argument candidates and respective roles, in such a way as to form well-instantiated predicate-argument structures. Usually, a machine learning model is trained for each stage. However, to cope with the problem of cascading errors, i.e., an error in an earlier stage resulting in many in a later stage, the joint prediction of triggers and arguments is necessary, following the common practice of semantic parsing in this direction.

Unlike question answering that is basically to extend existing IR techniques to retrieving highly specialized information, via extracting relevant snippets of text as candidate answers and then returning the top-ranked ones, *literature-based discovery* is a genuine TM task beyond extraction of relations and events to uncover hidden, previously unknown or unrecognized relationships between entities (or concepts) in scientific literature. It was pioneered by a series of Swanson's prototypical examples of hypothesis generation, based on his observation of the 'complementary structures in disjoint literatures' (Swanson 1991). This series of manually generated hypotheses include the hidden connections between fish oil and Raynaud's syndrome (Swanson 1986), migraine and magnesium (Swanson 1988), somatomedin C and arginine (Swanson 1990), and also the potential use of viruses as biomedical weapons (Swanson *et al.* 2001). A prototypical pattern to generalize these discoveries is: given a known characteristic *B* (e.g., stress, spreading cortical depression, high platelet aggregability, and so forth) of a disease *C* (e.g., migraine) presented in a body of literature and the effect(s) of a substance *A* (e.g., magnesium) on *B* in another 'complementary but disjoint' body of literature, we can infer a hidden *A*–*C* relationship, i.e., *A* may be a potential medication for *C*. What bridges such a hidden connection is a shared co-occurrent *B* of two terms *A* and *C* in two disjoint literatures. Two modes of discovery for this kind of second-order association (vs. the first-order relation between two co-occurring entities) are further distinguished by Weeber *et al.* (2001), namely, closed vs. open discovery: the former to find *B* term(s) to bridge a hypothesized *A*–*C* connection and the latter to find *B*–*C* relations (in another domain) given some *A*–*B* relations already known. Existing approaches to automatic literature-based discovery can be categorized into three categories:

1   co-occurrence based, which relies on the statistics (e.g., frequency, log likelihood, or some information theoretic score) of second-order (or shared) co-occurrences of two biomedical entities (e.g., gene symbols, concepts);
2   semantic based, which further builds on (1) above by applying semantic information (e.g., UMLS semantic types) to filter out uninteresting or spurious candidate relations; and
3   graph based, which constructs a graph representation for various kinds of association among biomedical entities (e.g., gene-disease) to allow uncovering indirect associations along paths in the graph.

Literature-based discovery systems are evaluated in terms of how well they can replicate known discoveries (e.g., Swanson's ones or those in recent publications), as measured by precision and recall. Comprehensive reviews of existing research in this field can be found in Cohen and Hersh (2005), Zweigenbaum *et al.* (2007) and Simpson and Demner-Fushman (2013).

Opinion mining

Opinion mining, also known as *sentiment analysis* and many other names in literature, has been another very active research area of TM since around the turn of this century. It aims at analyzing and collecting, from unstructured opinionated texts such as those from social media websites, people's subjective evaluations, views or opinions, in the form of expressing certain sentiment, attitude, emotion, mood or other type of affect,[23] towards entities, issues or topics of interest (e.g., products, services, events, individuals, organizations, etc.) and/or their aspects or attributes. Effective access to mainstream social opinions or public sentiment has a profound impact on decision making in many domains, especially politics, the economy, business and management. A good number of recent studies using Twitter data have demonstrated this from various perspectives. For example, a 'relatively simple' analysis of Twitter sentiment by O'Connor *et al.* (2010) replicates highly similar results of traditional polls (e.g., consumer confidence and presidential job approval polls), illustrating a strong correlation of the two, and Bollen *et al.* (2011) show that the GPOMS Calm time series lagged by 3 days exhibit an amazing congruence with the DJIA closing values.[24]

The goal of opinion mining is to detect opinions in real texts (e.g., product reviews). An opinion is a claim (or statement) in the form of verbal expression held (1) by someone, called *opinion holder* or *source*, (2) about something (e.g., a movie, product, service, event or individual, formally referred to as an *entity* or *object*), called *topic* or *opinion target*, (3) at some time (4) associated with certain semantic orientation or (sentiment) *polarity*, which may be positive, negative or neutral, or of some strength or intensity (e.g., represented by 1 to 5 stars or some other numeric rating score) (see Kim and Hovy 2004; Wiebe *et al.* 2005; Liu 2010, 2012; among many others). It is described in Kim and Hovy (2004) as a quadruple [Topic, Holder, Claim, Sentiment]. However, a common situation is that an opinion is specifically targeted at some particular (sub)part(s) or attribute(s)/feature(s) of an entity. With *aspect* as a general term to refer to the (sub)parts and attributes in the hierarchical decomposition of an entity, an opinion is defined in Liu (2012) as a quintuple (e, a, s, h, t), where s is the sentiment on the aspect a of the target entity e,[25] h the holder of the opinion, and t the time that the opinion is expressed. The sentiment may be expressed by a categorical and/or a numerical value for its polarity and/or intensity, respectively. Accordingly, the general task of opinion mining can be divided into subtasks to identify these components of the quintuple in an opinionated document. Since the early works by Hatzivassiloglou and McKeown (1997), Turney (2002), and Pang *et al.* (2002) on detecting the polarity of adjectives, product reviews and movie reviews, respectively, there has been so large a volume of literature in the field on opinion holders' attitudes towards topics of interest that sentiment analysis is equated with the detection of attitudes, mostly represented in terms of polarities and/or intensity scores (instead of a set of types as in Scherer's typology).[26]

Most existing works on sentiment analysis can be categorized into two types, namely, text-oriented vs. target-oriented. The former focuses on identifying the sentiment polarities, or predicting the rating scores, of opinionated/subjective text units of various sizes, ranging from documents to sentences, phrases and words. Since it is formulated as a classification problem, various supervised and unsupervised machine learning approaches have been applied, including naïve Bayes, MaxEnt, SVM, CRFs, etc. Conceptually, one may conceive two levels of classification, one to detect whether a text carries any opinion, i.e., opinionated (vs. factual) or subjective (vs. objective), and the other to determine a text's sentiment polarity or score (e.g., 1 to 5 stars), although the latter subsumes the former in principle. Extracting features from input text for machine learning of such classification is a critical task after sentiment-aware tokenization and POS tagging to deal with the irregularities of web texts (e.g., Twitter) and retain useful tags, expressions and symbols (e.g., emoticons).[27] Many special forms of verbal expression, such as negation and subjunctive mood, known as *sentiment shifters*, that critically deflect the sentiment of lexical items, require special treatment, e.g., marking negated words (in between a negation word and the next punctuation) with 'NOT_' (Das and Chen 2001). Besides known sentiment words and phrases, the most important features, other effective features include n-grams (and their frequencies), POS tags (especially adjectives, adverbs (e.g., *hardly* and *barely*) and negation words (e.g., *never*, *neither* and *nobody*)), syntactic dependency, and rules of opinion (e.g., negation of positive means negative and vice versa, mentioning a desirable fact implies positive; see Liu (2010) for more). Interestingly, however, it is shown in Pang *et al.* (2002) that using unigrams outperforms bigrams and using their presence outperforms their frequencies in classifying movie reviews with naïve Bayes and SVM models.

Certainly, this does not necessarily imply the denial of the significance of (co-) occurrence statistics. The Turney (2002) algorithm is a successful demonstration of this in inferring the *semantic orientation* (SO) of extracted phrases (by a set of predefined POS tag patterns and constraints) in terms of their *pointwise mutual information* (PMI), with one positive and one negative reference word (namely, 'excellent' and 'poor') as

$$SO(\text{phrase}) \equiv PMI(\text{phrase, ``excellent''}) - PMI(\text{phrase, ``poor''}),$$

where the PMI of two terms to measure their association is

$$PMI(x,y) = \log \frac{P(x,y)}{P(x)P(y)}.$$

Then, a review is classified into positive ('recommended') or negative ('not recommended') in terms of the average SO over all its phrases. This early work not only illustrated an unsupervised approach to sentiment document classification, but also inspired many subsequent works on mining sentiment lexicons, by utilizing statistics of co-occurrence (in various co-occurring patterns) with a seed set of polarity-labeled words. Before this, Hatzivassiloglou and McKeown (1997) followed the intuition, that adjectives in *and/but* conjunctions have a similar/different semantic orientation, to mine adjective polarity by means of supervised learning: first, expanding a seed set of adjectives with predetermined polarities to conjoined adjectives, predicting their polarity (dis)similarity using a log–linear regression model, and then clustering the resulting graph (with hypothesized polarity links between adjectives) in two groups, namely, positive vs. negative. Starting from a seed set of words with known polarities, a basic corpus-based strategy is to follow available hints (e.g., syntactic patterns) to enlarge this set with their synonyms and antonyms iteratively until no more are available (Hu and Liu 2004). In contrast, a dictionary-based approach compiles sentiment words from existing dictionaries (e.g., WordNet) that provide tractable relations of synonyms and antonyms.

Unlike text-oriented sentiment analysis that assumes a default (or unconcerned) target for a text (document) under analysis, aspect-oriented sentiment analysis is conducted at a much finer level of granularity to pinpoint the exact aspect (or feature) of a target entity that an opinion is about, and its sentiment polarity or strength. Specifically, it involves two main subtasks, namely, identification of opinion target, mostly by aspect extraction, and classification (or quantification) of aspect sentiment. The rules of thumb to follow include the assumptions that every piece of opinion has a target and that an opinionated text usually focuses on one opinion target and hence mentions its aspects in a more prominent way than other texts.

A simple but effective strategy to extract explicitly mentioned aspects is to take frequent nouns and noun phrases, by means of POS tagging and frequency thresholding, and the nearest (infrequent) ones to a sentiment word (Hu and Liu 2004). This strategy can be further enhanced by other statistical means or constraints, e.g., PMI between a candidate and known hints (such as meronymy discriminators for a target entity) (Popescu and Etzioni 2005), occurrence in a subjective sentence or co-occurring with sentiment words (Blair-Goldensohn *et al.* 2008), and dependency relations (Zhuang *et al.* 2006). The fact that sentiment words and aspects tend to co-occur with each other is commonly exploited by researchers, e.g., Ghani *et al.* (2006) and Qiu *et al.* (2011). Starting from a seed set of sentiment words, Qiu *et al.* extended the bootstrapping method to *double propagation* of both sentiment words and aspects along their dependency relations, combining sentiment lexicon acquisition and aspect extraction into one. Aspect extraction can also be tackled as an information extraction problem with supervised learning, using sequential labeling models such as HMM and CRFs. Also in this direction of research, Li *et al.* (2010) extended the linear-chain CRFs to a few variants, namely, skip-chain, tree and skip-tree CRFs, so as to exploit rich structure features to facilitate extraction of both aspects and opinions. Other kinds of syntactic or semantic information can be exploited as well, e.g., semantic role (Kim and Hovy 2006) and coreference (Stoyanov and Cardie 2008). Topic modeling (Hofmann 1999; Blei *et al.* 2003), which outputs a probability distribution over words (of certain semantic coherence) as a topic, is a principled statistical method of conceptual and mathematical elegance that many researchers have followed to attempt unsupervised extraction of aspects and sentiment words, but its weaknesses (e.g., hard to tell apart aspects and sentiment words, insensitive to locally frequent but globally infrequent words) needs to be overcome in order to have more practical use in sentiment analysis (Liu 2012). Besides *explicit* aspects, *implicit* aspects are perhaps more challenging to detect, because they have no overt form, but are only implied by certain expressions, especially adjective phrases (e.g., 'heavy' indicates weight and 'expensive' price). Their detection becomes a task of mapping sentiment words to explicit (or known) aspects. Co-occurrence association is usually the primary criterion for this mapping using various strategies, e.g., clustering (Su *et al.* 2008; Hai *et al.* 2011).

Extraction of opinion holder and time is also an NER problem. Usually, the author and publishing (or posting) time of a text (such as a review or blog) are, respectively, the default holder and time of an opinion extracted from the text, unless they are explicitly stated. The latter case is a typical NER issue to be tackled by strategies of various complexity, including (1) heuristics, e.g., only consider person and organizations as candidates (Kim and Hovy 2004), (2) sequential labeling, e.g., using CRFs with surrounding words' syntactic and semantic attributes as key features (Choi *et al.* 2006), and (3) other machine learning models, e.g., using MaxEnt to further rank heuristically selected candidates (Kim and Hovy 2006) or using SVM to classify them (Johansson and Moschitti 2010). SRL is also an effective means to facilitate this task (Bethard *et al.* 2004; Kim and Hovy 2006), especially in joint recognition of opinion holders and expressions.

Since, in different domains, not only are opinions expressed with different words, but the same words may express different sentiments, a sentiment model trained with opinion data (labeled or unlabeled) in one domain, called the *source* domain, is usually not directly applicable or adaptable to another, called the *target* domain. The purpose of *domain adaptation* is to enable this with minimum resources. Towards this goal, Gamon and Aue (2005) illustrated the outperformance of semi-supervised learning with EM training over a number of other strategies using SVM. Typically, this learning approach uses a small amount of labeled data combined with a large amount of unlabeled data, both from a target domain, for training. Most subsequent research by others focused on selecting domain independent features (words) to enable the adaptation. Yang *et al.* (2006) selected highly-ranked features in labeled data from two domains as common features for across-domain transfer learning, so as to facilitate sentence-level opinion detection in a target domain that lacks labeled training data. Blitzer *et al.* (2006, 2007) applied structural correspondence learning (SCL) to cross-domain sentiment analysis, first choosing a set of *pivot* features (in terms of their frequency and mutual information with a source label) and then establishing a feature correspondence between two domains by computing the correlation of pivot and non-pivot features.

Cross-language sentiment analysis looks to be an issue of adaptation across two languages as if they were two domains, but is argued to be qualitatively different from the usual cross-domain adaptation caused by domain mismatch (Duh *et al.* 2011). It aims to utilize both monolingual and bilingual tools and resources to accomplish sentiment analysis in another language. Given that most available sentiment analysis tools and resources are developed for English, one strategy to achieve this aim is to convert English resources into a foreign language to analyze foreign texts, and the other is to have foreign texts automatically translated into English for analysis. Mihalcea *et al.* (2007) found that projecting sentiment annotation from English into Romanian by virtue of a parallel corpus is more reliable than translating a sentiment lexicon with the aid of bilingual dictionaries. To leverage English resources for Chinese sentiment analysis, Wan (2008) opted to work on multiple MT outputs, and then combined their sentiment analysis results with ensemble methods. Wan (2009) further demonstrated a co-training approach that makes use of labeled English texts, unlabeled Chinese texts, and their MT output counterparts in the other language, to train two SVM classifiers and combine them into one for Chinese sentiment classification. Besides, other approaches can be applied to tackle this problem too, e.g., transfer learning using the SCL method (Wei and Pal 2010). In a multilingual setting, unsupervised methods such as topic modeling can be used to create multilingual topics (Boyd-Graber and Resnik 2010) or mulitlingual aspect clusters (i.e., semantic categories of product-features) (Guo *et al.* 2010).

Besides the key issues briefly introduced above, there are many others in the field that cannot be accommodated in this short subsection, such as discourse analysis for sentiment analysis, comparative opinion mining, summarization and presentation/visualization of mined opinions, opinion spam detection, and estimation of opinion/review quality/sincerity, to name but a few. Interested readers may refer to the books/surveys by Shanahan *et al.* (2006), Pang and Lee (2008) and Liu (2012) for a more detailed discussion. Pang and Lee (2008) also provide plenty of information about publicly available resources and evaluation campaigns, including:

1   annotated datasets, such as Cornell Movie-Review Datasets[28] (Pang *et al.* 2002; Pang and Lee 2004, 2005), Customer Review Datasets[29] (Hu and Liu 2004; Ding *et al.* 2008), and MPQA Corpus[30] (Wiebe *et al.* 2005);
2   past evaluations, such as TREC Blog Track[31] and NTCIR-6~-8[32] (on multilingual opinion analysis tasks (MOAT) in Japanese, English and Chinese);
3   lexical resources, such as General Inquirer[33] (Stone 1966), OpinionFinder's Subjectivity Lexicon[34] (Wilson *et al.* 2005) and SentiWordNet[35] (Esuli and Sebastiani 2006; Baccianella *et al.* 2010); and
4   a few pointers to online tutorials and bibliographies.

Besides, there are also language resources and open evaluations for other languages than English, e.g., NTU Sentiment Dictionary[36] (Ku *et al.* 2006) and COAE[37] (Zhao *et al.* 2008; Xu *et al.* 2009) for Chinese.

Text mining for IR—mining term relations

TM has long been applied to IR, focused on deriving term relationships (or association) to facilitate query expansion. Assuming that a relationship between terms t_1 and t_2 can be found and expressed as $P(t_2 \mid t_1)$, measuring the extent to which t_1 implies t_2, a new query representation can then be built upon an old one by adding a set of expansion terms which are related to its terms. In language modeling, this means the construction of a new query model θ_{Q_1} by interpolating an existing query model θ_{Q_0} with another one, constructed with selected expansion terms $\theta_{\mathcal{R}}$. In a similar manner of expanding a user query to a new model using feedback documents, we can further build an expansion query model using term relations mined from available texts.

The relation most widely used in IR is the term co-occurrence (Crouch 1990; Qiu and Frei 1993; Jing and Croft 1994). Its underlying assumption is that the more frequently two terms co-occur, the more closely they are related. In general, such term relationships can be quantified by the following conditional probability (or a similarity measure following the same idea):

$$P\left(t_i \mid t_j, t_k\right) = \frac{cooc\left(t_i, t_j, t_k\right)}{\sum_{t \in V} cooc\left(t_i, t_j, t_k\right)}$$

where *cooc* means the frequency of co-occurrence within a certain context. Various types of context can be used to derive co-occurrence statistics, e.g., within the same text, paragraph, sentence, or a text window of some fixed size (such as 10 words). Too large a context (e.g. the same text) could bring in much noise—unrelated terms are extracted, while too narrow a context may miss useful relations. In IR experiments, it turns out that a relatively small context (such as sentence or a text window of 10 words) works well. In addition to the above conditional probability, one can also use other measures to quantify the relationship between terms such as mutual information, log-likelihood ratio, χ-square statistics, and so on.

To extract many other useful relations such as synonyms that cannot be extracted this way (because many synonyms are rarely used in the same context), we need to resort to second-order co-occurrences: two terms are deemed to be related if they occur in similar contexts, i.e., co-occur with similar words. This idea was practiced in Lin (1998) in a way to define word context in terms of certain syntactic relations (e.g., verb–object): two words are considered related if they are linked to similar words within a similar syntactic context. In this way, words in the same category (e.g., clothes, shoes, hat, etc., that appear as objects of the verb 'wear') can be extracted. In Bai *et al.* (2005), this idea was incorporated into *information flow* (IF): the context of a word is defined by its surrounding words, and two words are considered similar if their context vectors are similar. Word relations extracted this way by means of information flow were successfully applied to query expansion, achieving a large performance improvement. More specifically, the following document scoring function is used:

$$\mathrm{score}\left(Q, D\right) = \sum_{t \in O} P_{\mathrm{ML}}\left(t \mid \theta_Q\right) \log P(t \mid \theta_D) + \left(1 - \lambda\right) \sum_{t \in V} P_{\mathrm{IF}}\left(t \mid \theta_Q\right) \log P\left(t \mid \theta_Q\right)$$

where $P_{\mathrm{IF}}\left(t \mid \theta_Q\right) = \sum_{q \subseteq Q} P_{\mathrm{IF}}\left(t \mid \theta_q\right) P\left(q \mid \theta_Q\right)$, with q to be a subset of query terms and $P_{\mathrm{IF}}(\bullet \mid \bullet)$ to be defined in terms of the degree of information flow.

To tackle the noise problem with co-occurrence relation (i.e., frequently co-occurring terms are not necessarily truly related) and word ambiguity (e.g., the relation between 'java' and 'language' does not apply to a query on 'java tourism'), phrases are used instead of words in relation extraction. Multi-word phrases are in general less ambiguous, and thus a term (word or phrase) related to a phrase in a query has a higher chance of being truly related to the query. Among the several studies following this idea, Bai *et al.* (2007) extended the *context-independent* co-occurrence relation between single words to the *context-dependent* co-occurrence relation of a word to a set of words. This idea can be traced back to Schütze and Pedersen (1997). Using more than one word as a context to determine related words imposes a stronger contextual constraint, resulting in words in a less ambiguous relation (e.g., the relation between 'java, program' and 'language' is more certain than the one between 'java' and 'language', in that a query containing both 'java' and 'program' is more likely to be related to 'language'). In Bai *et al.* (2007), the number of context words was restricted to two, so as to minimize the complexity of the extraction process. Accordingly, the above conditional probability can be extended to estimate the strength of a word–words relation, as follows:

$$P\left(t_i|t_j,t_k\right)=\frac{cooc\left(t_i,t_j,t_k\right)}{\sum_{t\in V}cooc\left(t_i,t_j,t_k\right)}$$

Experiments on several TREC collections show that this word–words relationship brings in more performance gain than the word–word one. According to the survey of Carpineto and Romano (2012), this is one of the best performing methods for query expansion.

Among the long list of query expansion methods surveyed in Carpineto and Romano (2012), all four best performing ones (including the above two) on TREC collections utilize some forms of context-dependent relation. (1) Liu *et al.* (2004) rank documents first by *phrase* similarity and then *word* similarity, using (a) machine-learned distances of window size for identifying phrases of different types, (b) WordNet for query expansion, (c) a combination of local and global correlations for pseudo relevance feedback, and (d) a variant of *Okapi* weighting (with document length replaced by L2-norm, i.e., the vector length, of a document) for similarity scoring. (2) Bai *et al.* (2005) integrate a set of information flow relationships of terms into language modeling with KL-divergence for document scoring as mentioned above. (3) Bai *et al.* (2007) further generalize the above query model by the following interpolation:

$$P\left(t|\theta_Q\right)=\sum_{i\in X}\alpha_iP\left(\theta_Q^i\right),\text{ with }\sum_{i\in X}\alpha_i=1$$

where α_i are mixture weights. It integrates a set of component models X={0,F,Dom,K}, including the original query model θ_Q^0, the feedback model θ_Q^F on retrieved documents, a domain model θ_Q^{Dom} on predefined domain documents, and a knowledge model θ_Q^K on the *context dependent* relations of terms in the form $P(t_i|t_j,t_k)$ as above. Each model has a scoring function defined as:

$$\text{score}\left(Q,D\right)=\sum_{i\in X}\alpha_i\,\text{score}_i\left(Q,D\right)=\sum_{i\in X}\alpha_i\sum_{i\in V}P(t|\theta_Q^i)\log P\left(t|\theta_D\right)$$

With other language models trained on respective data, say, using the EM algorithm, the knowledge model is defined as:

$$P\left(t|\theta_Q^K\right)=\sum_{\left(t_j,t_k\right)\in Q}P\left(t_i|t_jt_k\right)P(t_jt_k|\theta_Q)=\sum_{\left(t_j,t_k\right)\in Q}P\left(t_i|t_jt_k\right)P(t_j|\theta_Q)P(t_k|\theta_Q)$$

where $\left(t_j t_k\right) \in Q$ and $P(t_i \mid t_j, t_k)$ is defined as above. (4) Metzler and Croft (2005, 2007) generalize the relevance model into a general discriminative model, using the Markov random field (MRF) model to integrate a large variety of scoring schemes as its arbitrary features (such as *tf* and *idf* of word and phrase, document length, and PageRank, among many others) for scoring a document with respect to a query, and utilizing term dependencies by combining the scoring of unigrams, bigrams and collocations (i.e., co-occurring words within a small fixed-size window) into expansion term likelihood computation on feedback documents. These four methods all demonstrate the power of effective use of term dependencies, regardless of the difference of their scoring schemes.

Besides a document collection, modern search engines also benefit from rich interactions with users, which are recorded in *query logs*. Data items in query logs usually include, among others, user ID (or IP address), submitted query, time, search results (usually URLs plus some key information) presented to, and a few of them clicked by, a user. User clickthrough information preserved in the last item is of particular importance, for there is reason to assume that a user must have a certain preference for clicked documents over unclicked ones, meaning that the former ones are more likely to be relevant to the query in question than the latter ones (Joachims 2002). The more such clickthrough by users, the stronger the signal of the relevance.

Clickthrough information can be exploited to facilitate IR in several ways. (1) It can be used to identify similar queries to a given query following the 'co-click' assumption, that queries sharing the same or similar clicked documents are similar (Wen *et al.* 2001; Baeza-Yates and Tiberi 2007; Craswell and Szummer 2007). Implicit relations of this kind between queries have been widely used in commercial search engines to suggest alternative queries to users. (2) A large number of user clicks on a document may imply a certain semantic relatedness between the query terms in use and the terms in the clicked document. However, it is risky to assume that such a query term is related to any term in the document, for it would result in false relationships between unrelated query and document terms. A more common (and safer) practice is to assume that trustable relations only exist between terms in a query and in a document title, and then estimate their relation probability (Cui *et al.* 2002), or train a statistical translation model for this, taking a query and a clicked document title as a pair of parallel texts for the training (Gao *et al.* 2010). (3) Other useful features can also be extracted from clickthrough data to help document ranking, in a way to favor the popularly clicked documents (or similar ones) in the ranked list output for a query (Joachims 2002).

Several sets of query log data have been made available for IR experiments: MSN query logs,[38] Sogou query logs in Chinese,[39] Yandex query logs,[40] MSRBing image retrieval challenge,[41] and the AOL query logs, which was the first publicly released dataset of this kind but later retracted. However, larger amounts of query logs and clickthrough information beyond these datasets are only available within search engine companies. To simulate this kind of large-scale clickthrough, Dang and Croft (2010) used anchor texts and links in webpages, assuming the former as queries and the latter as clicked documents. Their experiments showed that even such simulated data can bring some nice improvements to IR effectiveness, but certainly not on a par with true clickthrough data.

Text mining for CLIR—mining cross-language term relations

CLIR imposes a strong demand for translation relations between terms (words or phrases) across languages. In the sense that such cross-language relations encode translation knowledge, i.e., how likely a word (or phrase) in one language is to be the translation for a word (or phrase) in another language, inferring them from parallel texts can be considered a kind of bilingual text mining. A principled way to do this is to resort to an SMT model in the series, called IBM models, defined in Brown *et al.* (1993), which provides a mathematical foundation for all SMT methods. It is assumed that an IBM model generates a translation (i.e., a target sentence) from a source sentence by (1) first determining its length, (2) then determining the position alignment between the two sentences, and (3) finally filling appropriate translation words into the slots in the target sentence.

The most popular translation model used in CLIR is IBM model 1, or IBM 1 for short, thanks to its underlying assumption that a word is translated in isolation from its context, i.e., independently of its position and other words in a sentence. This is an assumption that does not hold for human translation but which corresponds so well to the bag-of-words assumption for IR. The IBM model 1 is formulated as follows for a source sentence S and a target sentence T:

$$P(S \mid T) = \frac{\in}{(l+1)^m} \prod_{j=0}^{m} \sum_{i=0}^{l} P(s_j \mid t_i)$$

where l and m are, respectively, the length of T and S, $\in$ is a constant meaning the probability to produce a sentence of m words from T, and $P(s_j \mid t_i)$ is the lexical translation probability between two words t_i and s_j. Note that in SMT we choose the translation $\hat{T}$ that maximizes $P(T \mid S)$, i.e.,

$$\hat{T} = \arg \max_T P(T \mid S) \propto \arg \max_T P(S \mid T) P(T)$$

where $P(T)$ is a language model to estimate the likelihood of T in target language, and $P(T \mid S)$ the translation model from T to S; and that a lexical translation model $P(s_j \mid t_i)$ is usually trained on a large set of parallel sentences using the EM algorithm, in a way to maximize the translation likelihood of the parallel sentences.

While fully fledged SMT demands a more sophisticated translation model than IBM 1, in order to take into account word order and word position, CLIR has relied on IBM 1 successfully so far, thanks to the fact that the state-of-the-art IR is largely rooted in the word-bag model, sharing similar assumptions as IBM 1. Several experiments have shown that such a simple translation model trained on large scale parallel data can be competitive to high-performance MT systems in supporting CLIR (e.g., Kraaij *et al.* 2003).

As query translation does not need as strict a translation as MT, translation relationships to be utilized in CLIR can be relaxed to *cross-language co-occurrence*. The idea is that the more often a pair of source and target words co-occurs in parallel sentences, the stronger the translation relationship they have. Accordingly, this relationship can be estimated as:

$$P(S \mid t) \propto \frac{cooc(s,t)}{\sum_s cooc(s,t)}$$

However, this estimation has an innate weakness: when s is a frequent term (e.g., a function word), $P(s \mid t)$ will be too strong, lowering CLIR effectiveness. In contrast, the alignment of t with a frequent s in IBM 1 is gradually weakened along EM iterations. Even so, many other measures effectively used in monolingual text mining can be extended to the bilingual case without iterative training, e.g., mutual information, log-likelihood ratio, etc.

Moreover, this less strict co-occurrence measure can be straightforwardly applied to comparable texts, on which an IBM model can hardly be trained. As mentioned before, less strict translation (or cross-language) relations of this kind trained on comparable texts can improve CLIR to some extent, as shown in the experiments of Sheridan and Ballerini (1996) and Braschler and Schäuble (2000), although their effectiveness is lower in comparison with an IBM model trained on parallel texts. However, when parallel texts are not available, they can be used as a second-choice substitute. Even when parallel texts are available, translation relations trained on comparable texts can also be used as a beneficial complement (Sadat *et al.* 2003).

Mining bilingual texts from the Web

The training of statistical MT models critically depends on the availability of a large amount of bilingual parallel texts (or bitexts). For resource-rich languages such as European languages, many manually compiled large-scale parallel corpora are available, including the Canadian Hansard, the earliest large parallel corpus in English and French, popularly used in MT, and the European Parliament documents in several European languages. In contrast, however, bitexts are inadequately available for many other languages such as Arabic, Chinese, Indian languages, and so on. This was, and to a great extent still is, the case. A possible way out from this situation seems to be allowed by the flourishing of the Web, where more and more websites provide information in several languages, mostly through bilingual or parallel webpages. The Web has been a huge repository of various kinds of texts, including parallel texts (Grefenstette 1999; Kilgarriff and Grefenstette 2003; Resnik and Smith 2003). What we need to do is to identify and then extract available parallel texts automatically via web mining.

A good number of attempts have been made in this direction to illustrate the feasibility and practicality of automatically acquiring parallel corpora from bilingual (or multilingual) websites, resulting in respective web miners for parallel texts, including STRAND (Resnik 1998, 1999; Resnik and Smith 2003), BITS (Ma and Liberman 1999), PTMiner (Nie *et al.* 1999; Chen and Nie 2000), PTI (Chen *et al.* 2004), WPDE (Zhang *et al.* 2006), the DOM tree alignment model (Shi *et al.* 2006), PupSniffer (Kit and Ng 2007; Zhang *et al.* 2013), PagePairGetter (Ye *et al.* 2008), and Bitextor (Esplà-Gomis and Forcada 2010).

The basic strategy they follow is to utilize the characteristic organization patterns of parallel webpages, including inter-page links, similarity of intra-page structures, file and URL naming conventions, and other features that reveal any such pattern. For example, many parallel pages are either linked to from a common entry page or to each other mutually. An entry page usually contains many close links with anchor texts (such as 'English version' and 'Version française') to indicate the language of a linked-to page, providing strong hints about parallel pages. This structure is exploited in STRAND (Resnik 1998, 1999). Another common structure is that parallel pages contain mutual links to each other, pointing to their counterparts in the other language, with an anchor text to indicate language (e.g., 'English version'). This structure is used in PTMiner (Nie *et al.* 1999; Chen and Nie 2000).

Also, two parallel pages are often found to have similar names or URLs, e.g., 'www.xyz.org/intro_en.html' vs. its French counterpart 'www.xyz.org/intro_fr.html'. Their only difference is the segments indicating their languages, i.e. their URL pairing pattern 'en:fr'. This kind of widespread characteristic of parallel pages was widely used in the previous attempts to determine possible parallel pages in a bilingual website, relying on predefined pairing patterns such as {'e:c', 'en:ch', 'eng:chi', …} for English–Chinese. A problem with such an *ad hoc* method is that hand-crafted heuristics can never exhaust all possibilities, leaving many true parallel pages untouched.

Automatic discovery of URL pairing patterns of this kind was attempted in Kit and Ng (2007) and further extended in Zhang *et al.* (2013). Among the fundamental tasks involved in web mining for parallel texts, namely, (1) identifying bilingual (or multilingual) websites and retrieving their webpages, (2) matching retrieved webpages into parallel pairs, and (3) extracting parallel texts from matched pairs for alignment at a finer level of granularity. Since there have been matured techniques of web crawling and text alignment to deal with (1) and (3) respectively, (2) is the most vital one at the core of the whole mining process. Compared to similarity analysis of HTML structure and/or webpage content, it is preferable to match candidate webpages by pairing up their URLs using automatically inferred URL pairing patterns (or keys). The basic idea to achieve this is as follows: given two sets of URLs for webpages in a bilingual website, each in a language, a candidate key is generated from each pair of candidate URLs by removing their common prefix and suffix, and then its linking power, defined as the number of URL pairs that it can match, is used as the objective function to search for the best set of keys that can find the largest number of webpage pairs within the website. A best-first strategy to let candidate keys compete, in a way that a more powerful key matches URLs first, results in correct discovery of 43.7 percent true keys (at precision 67.6 percent) that matches 98.1 percent true webpage pairs (at precision 94.8 percent), with the aid of an empirical threshold to filter out weak keys (Kit and Ng 2007). Later, this approach is extended to work on a large set of bilingual websites, digging out more webpage pairs by extending the notion of linking power to global credibility to rescue many weak (but true) keys, uncovering bilingual webpages from the deep web by generating crawler-unreachable counterparts of unmatched URLs using found keys, and also incorporating PageRank based analysis of bilingual website relationship into this framework for discovery of more bilingual websites beyond an initial seed set for mining more bitexts. This automatic approach is simple and effective, but it is not designed to deal with machine-generated webpages, e.g., from a (text) database, whose URLs are randomly generated without any pairing patterns.

Notes

1   At http://trec.nist.gov/data.html.
2   NII Test Collections for IR system, at http://research.nii.ac.jp/ntcir/data/data-en.html.
3   The CLEF Initiative – Conference and Labs of the Evaluation Forum, formerly known as Cross-Language Evaluation Forum, at http://www.clef-initiative.eu.
4   http://tartarus.org/martin/PorterStemmer.
5   However, it is questionable whether a term ten times more frequent than another in a document would really make a ten times more significant contribution to the relevance of the document. Different scaling strategies can be applied to adjust the above term weighting, e.g., using the logarithm of term frequency 1+logtf (or 0, if tf=0), the probabilistic idf:max$\{0,\log[(N-dft)/dft]\}$. A systematic presentation of a good number of principal weighting schemes can be found in Salton and Buckley (1988), Singhal *et al.* (1996), and Moffat and Zobel (1998).
6   http://wordnet.princeton.edu.
7   See Grünwald (2007) for an extensive introduction to the MDL principle.
8   http://www.ncbi.nlm.nih.gov/pubmed, with a resources guide at http://www.nlm.nih.gov/bsd/pmresources.html.
9   http://www.nlm.nih.gov/mesh/meshhome.html.
10   http://trec.nist.gov/data/t9_filtering.html.
11   http://ir.ohsu.edu/genomics.
12   http://www.nactem.ac.uk/aNT/genia.html.
13   http://biocreative.sourceforge.net.
14   http://bioie.ldc.upenn.edu.
15   http://www.nlm.nih.gov/research/umls/knowledge_sources/metathesaurus/index.html.
16   http://www.nlm.nih.gov/research/umls/knowledge_sources/index.html#semantic.
17   http://www.nlm.nih.gov/research/umls.
18   http://www.pharmgkb.org.
19   http://www.neuinfo.org.

20 http://www.geneontology.org.
21 Obviously it corresponds to *predicate* or *semantic head* in semantic parsing.
22 Nine event types are listed in the BioNLP Shared Task 2011 GENIA Event Extraction (GENIA) site, at https://sites.google.com/site/bionlpst/home/genia-event-extraction-genia.
23 See Scherer (1984) for a typology of affective states, including emotion, mood, interpersonal stances, attitudes, and personality traits.
24 GPOMS: Google-Profile of Mood States, which measures mood in terms of six dimensions, namely, Calm, Alert, Sure, Vital, Kind and Happy. DJIA: the Dow Jones Industrial Average.
25 A conventional aspect *a=general* is reserved for an opinion targeted on an entity as a whole.
26 'Attitudes: relatively enduring, affectively colored beliefs, preferences, and dispositions towards objects or persons (*liking, loving, hating, valuing, desiring*)' (Scherer 1984).
27 More technical details (and source codes) are available from Christopher Potts' Sentiment Symposium Tutorial at http://sentiment.christopherpotts.net/ and from CMU's Twitter NLP and Part-of-Speech Tagging site at http://www.ark.cs.cmu.edu/TweetNLP/.
28 http://www.cs.cornell.edu/people/pabo/movie-review-data/.
29 http://www.cs.uic.edu/~liub/FBS/sentiment-analysis.html.
30 http://www.cs.pitt.edu/mpqa/.
31 http://ir.dcs.gla.ac.uk/wiki/TREC-BLOG/.
32 http://research.nii.ac.jp/ntcir/index-en.html.
33 http://www.wjh.harvard.edu/~inquirer/.
34 http://www.cs.pitt.edu/mpqa/.
35 http://sentiwordnet.isti.cnr.it/.
36 http://nlg18.csie.ntu.edu.tw:8080/opinion/.
37 Chinese Opinion Analysis Evaluation 2008–2012 at http://ir-china.org.cn/Information.html and COAE 2013 at http://ccir2013.sxu.edu.cn/COAE.aspx.
38 http://research.microsoft.com/en-us/um/people/nickcr/wscd09/.
39 http://www.sogou.com/labs/dl/q.html.
40 http://switchdetect.yandex.ru/en/datasets.
41 http://web-ngram.research.microsoft.com/GrandChallenge/.

References

Adriani, Mirna and Keith van Rijsbergen (2000) 'Phrase Identification in Cross-Language Information Retrieval', in *Proceedings of the 6th International Conference on Computer-Assisted Information Retrieval (Recherche d'Information et ses Applications) (RIAO 2000)*, 520–528.

Aggarwal Charu C. ChengXiang Zhai (eds) (2012) *Mining Text Data*. New York: Springer.

Baccianella, Stefano, Andrea Esuli, and Fabrizio Sebastiani (2010) 'SentiWordNet 3.0: An Enhanced Lexical Resource for Sentiment Analysis and Opinion Mining', in *Proceedings of the 7th Conference on Language Resources and Evaluation (LREC 2010)*, 2200–2204.

Baeza-Yates, Ricardo and Alessandro Tiberi (2007) 'Extracting Semantic Relations from Query Logs', in *Proceedings of the 13th ACM SIGKDD International Conference on Knowledge Discovery and Data Mining (ACM SIGKDD 2007)*, 76–85.

Bai, Jing, Dawei Song, Peter Bruza, Jian-Yun Nie, and Guihong Cao (2005) 'Query Expansion Using Term Relationships in Language Models for Information Retrieval', in *Proceedings of the 14th ACM International Conference on Information and Knowledge Management (CIKM 2005)*, 688–695.

Bai, Jing, Jian-Yun Nie, Hugues Bouchard, and Guihong Cao (2007) 'Using Query Contexts in Information Retrieval', in *Proceedings of the 30th Annual International ACM SIGIR Conference on Research and Development in Information Retrieval (SIGIR 2007)*, 15–22.

Bendersky, Michael, Donald Metzler, and W. Bruce Croft (2010) 'Learning Concept Importance Using a Weighted Dependence Model', in *Proceedings of the 3rd ACM International Conference on Web Search and Data Mining (WSDM2010)*, 31–40.

Bethard, Steven, Hong Yu, Ashley Thornton, Vasileios Hatzivassiloglou, and Dan Jurafsky (2004) 'Automatic Extraction of Opinion Propositions and their Holders', in *Proceedings of 2004 AAAI Spring Symposium on Exploring Attitude and Affect in Text*, 22–24.

Berger, Adam and John Lafferty (1999) 'Information Retrieval as Statistical Translation', in *Proceedings of the 22nd Annual International ACM SIGIR Conference on Research and Development on Information Retrieval (SIGIR 1999)*, 222–229.

Berners-Lee, Tim, Robert Cailliau, Jean-François Groff, and Bernd Pollermann (1992) 'World-Wide Web: The Information Universe', *Electronic Networking: Research, Applications and Policy* 1(2): 74–82.

Blair-Goldensohn, Sasha, Kerry Hannan, Ryan McDonald, Tyler Neylon, George A. Reis, and Jeff Reynar (2008) 'Building a Sentiment Summarizer for Local Service Reviews', in *Proceedings of WWW Workshop on NLP in the Information Explosion Era (NLPIX 2008)*.

Blei, David M., Andrew Y. Ng, and Michael I. Jordan (2003) 'Latent Dirichlet Allocation', *Journal of Machine Learning Research* 3: 993–1022.

Blitzer, John, Ryan McDonald, and Fernando Pereira (2006) 'Domain Adaptation with Structural Correspondence Learning', in *Proceedings of the 2006 Conference on Empirical Methods in Natural Language Processing (EMNLP 2006)*, 120–128.

Blitzer, John, Mark Dredze, and Fernando Pereira (2007) 'Biographies, Bollywood, Boom-boxes and Blenders: Domain Adaptation for Sentiment Classification', in *Proceedings of the 45th Annual Meeting of the Association of Computational Linguistics (ACL 2007)*, 440–447.

Bollen, Johan, Huina Mao, and Xiaojun Zeng (2011) 'Twitter Mood Predicts the Stock Market', *Journal of Computational Science* 2(1): 1–8.

Boyd-Graber, Jordan and Philip Resnik (2010) 'Holistic Sentiment Analysis Across Languages: Multilingual Supervised Latent Dirichlet Allocation', in *Proceedings of the 2010 Conference on Empirical Methods in Natural Language Processing (EMNLP 2010)*, 45–55.

Braschler, Martin and Peter Schäuble (2000) 'Using Corpus-based Approaches in a System for Multilingual Information Retrieval', *Information Retrieval* 3(3): 273–284.

Brent, Michael R. (1999) 'An Efficient, Probabilistically Sound Algorithm for Segmentation and Word Discovery', *Machine Learning* 34(1–3): 71–105.

Brent, Michael R. and Timothy A. Cartwright (1996) 'Distributional Regularity and Phonological Constraints Are Useful for Segmentation', *Cognition* 61(1–2): 93–125.

Brin, Sergey and Larry Page (1998) 'The Anatomy of a Large-scale Hyper-textual Web Search Engine', *Computer Networks and ISDN Systems* 30(1–7): 107–117.

Brown, Peter E., Stephen A. Della Pietra, Vincent J. Della Pietra, and Robert L. Mercer (1993) 'The Mathematics of Statistical Machine Translation: Parameter Estimation', *Computational Linguistics* 19(2): 263–311.

Bush, Vannevar (1945) 'As We May Think', *The Atlantic Monthly* 176: 101–108.

Cao, Guihong, Jian-Yun Nie, and Jing Bai (2005) 'Integrating Word Relationships into Language Models', in *Proceedings of the 28th Annual International ACM SIGIR Conference on Research and Development on Information Retrieval (SIGIR 2005)*, 298–305.

Cao, Guihong, Jian-Yun Nie, Jianfeng Gao, and Stephan Robertson (2008) 'Selecting Good Expansion Terms for Pseudo-relevance Feedback', in *Proceedings of the 31st Annual International ACM SIGIR Conference on Research and Development on Information Retrieval (SIGIR 2008)*, 243–250.

Carpineto, Claudio and Giovanni Romano (2012) 'A Survey of Automatic Query Expansion in Information Retrieval', *ACM Computing Surveys* 44(1): Article 1, 50 pages.

Chen, Jisong, Rowena Chau, and Chung-Hsing Yeh (2004) 'Discovering Parallel Text from the World Wide Web', in *Proceedings of the 2nd Workshop on Australasian Information Security, Data Mining and Web Intelligence, and Software Internationalisation*, 157–161.

Chen, Jiang and Jian-Yun Nie (2000) 'Automatic Construction of Parallel English-Chinese Corpus for Cross-language Information Retrieval', in *Proceedings of the 6th Applied Natural Language Processing Conference (ANLP-NAACL 2000)*, 21–28.

Chen, Jiang and Jian-Yun Nie (2000) 'Parallel Web Text Mining for Cross-language IR', in *Proceedings of the 6th International Conference on Computer-Assisted Information Retrieval (Recherche d'Information et ses Applications) (RIAO 2000)*, 62–77.

Choi, Yejin, Eric Breck, and Claire Cardie (2006) 'Joint Extraction of Entities and Relations for Opinion Recognition', in *Proceedings of the 2006 Conference on Empirical Methods in Natural Language Processing (EMNLP 2006)*, 431–439.

Cohen, Aaron M. and William R. Hersh (2005) 'A Survey of Current Work in Biomedical Text Mining', *Briefings in Bioinformatics* 6(1): 57–71.

Craswell, Nick and Martin Szummer (2007) 'Random Walks on the Click Graph', in *Proceedings of the 30th Annual International ACM SIGIR Conference on Research and Development in Information Retrieval (SIGIR 2007)*, 239–246.

Croft, W. Bruce and D.J. Harper (1979) 'Using Probabilistic Models on Document Retrieval without Relevance Information', *Journal of Documentation* 35(4): 285–295.

Crouch, Carolyn J. (1990) 'An Approach to the Automatic Construction of Global Thesauri', *Information Processing and Management* 26(5): 629–640.

Cui, Hang, Ji-Rong Wen, Jian-Yun Nie, and Wei-Ying Ma (2002) 'Probabilistic Query Expansion Using Query Logs', in *Proceedings of the 11th International Conference on World Wide Web (WWW 2002)*, 325–332.

Dang, Van and Bruce W. Croft (2010) 'Query Reformulation Using Anchor Text', in *Proceedings of the 3rd ACM International Conference on Web Search and Data Mining (WSDM 2010)*, 41–50.

Das, Sanjiv and Mike Chen (2001) 'Yahoo! for Amazon: Extracting Market Sentiment from Stock Message Boards', in *Proceedings of the 8th Asia Pacific Finance Association Annual Conference (APFA)*, 37–56.

Ding, Xiaowen, Bing Liu, and Philip S. Yu (2008) 'A Holistic Lexicon-based Approach to Opinion Mining', in *Proceedings of the 2008 International Conference on Web Search and Data Mining (WSDM 2008)*, 231–240.

Duh, Kevin, Akinori Fujino, and Nagata, Masaaki (2011) 'Is Machine Translation Ripe for Cross-lingual Sentiment Classification?' in *Proceedings of the 49th Annual Meeting of the Association for Computational Linguistics: Human Language Technologies (ACL-HTL 2011)*, 429–433.

Esuli, Andrea and Fabrizio Sebastiani (2006) 'SentiWordNet: A Publicly Available Lexical Resource for Opinion Mining', in *Proceedings of the 5th Conference on Language Resources and Evaluation (LREC 2006)*, 417–422.

Esplà-Gomis, Miquel and Mikel L Forcada (2010) 'Combining Content-based and URL-based Heuristics to Harvest Aligned Bitexts from Multilingual Sites with Bitextor', *The Prague Bulletin of Mathematical Linguistics* 93: 77–86.

Feldman, Ronen and Ido Dagan (1995) 'Knowledge Discovery in Textual Databases (KDT)', in *Proceedings of the First International Conference on Knowledge Discovery (KDD-95)*, 112–117.

Firth, Frank E. (1958a) 'An Experiment in Mechanical Searching of Research Literature with RAMAC', in *Proceedings of the May 6–8, 1958, Western Joint Computer Conference: Contrasts in Computers (IRE-ACM-AIEE '58 (Western))*, 168–175.

Firth, Frank E. (1958b) *An Experiment in Literature Searching with the IBM 305 RAMAC*, San Jose, California: IBM.

Franz, Martin, J. Scott McCarley, and Salim Roukos (1999) 'Ad hoc and Multilingual Information Retrieval at IBM', in *Proceedings of the 7th Text REtrieval Conference (TREC-7)*, 157–168.

Fuhr, Norbert (1989) 'Optimum Polynomial Retrieval Functions Based on the Probability Ranking Principle', ACM *Transactions on Information Systems* 7(3): 183–204.

Fuhr, Norbert (1992) 'Probabilistic Models in Information Retrieval', *The Computer Journal* 35(3): 243–255.

Gamon, Michael and Anthony Aue (2005) 'Automatic Identification of Sentiment Vocabulary: Exploiting Low Association with Known Sentiment Terms', in *Proceedings of the ACL Workshop on Feature Engineering for Machine Learning in Natural Language Processing*, 57–64.

Gao, Jianfeng, Jian-Yun Nie, Endong Xun, Jian Zhang, Ming Zhou, Changning Huang (2001) 'Improving Query Translation for Cross-language Information Retrieval Using Statistical Models', in *Proceedings of the 24th Annual International ACM SIGIR Conference on Research and Development on Information Retrieval (SIGIR 2001)*, 96–104.

Gao, Jianfeng, Xiaodong He, and Jian-Yun Nie (2010) 'Clickthrough-based Translation Models for Web Search: From Word Models to Phrase Models', in *Proceedings of the 19th ACM International Conference on Information and Knowledge Management (CIKM 2010)*, 1139–1148.

Garfield, Eugene (1997) 'A Tribute to Calvin N. Mooers, A Pioneer of information Retrieval', *Scientist* 11(6): 9–11.

Ghani, Rayid, Katharina Probst, Yan Liu, Marko Krema, and Andrew Fano (2006) 'Text Mining for Product Attribute Extraction', *ACM SIGKDD Explorations Newsletter* 8(1): 41–48.

Grefenstette, Gregory (1999) 'The World Wide Web as a Resource for Example-based Machine Translation Tasks', in Translating and the computer 21: *Proceedings of the 21st International Conference on Translating and the Computer*, London: Aslib.

Grünwald, Peter D. (2007) The Minimum Description Length Principle. Cambridge, MA: MIT Press.

Guo, Honglei, Huijia Zhu, Zhili Guo, Xiaoxun Zhang, and Zhong Su (2010) 'OpinionIt: A Text Mining System for Cross-lingual Opinion Analysis', in *Proceedings of the 19th ACM International Conference on Information and Knowledge Management (CIKM 2010)*, 1199–1208.

Hai, Zhen, Kuiyu Chang, and Jung-jae Kim (2011) 'Implicit Feature Identification via Co-occurrence Association Rule Mining', in *Proceedings of the 12th International Conference on Computational Linguistics and Intelligent Text Processing (CICLing 2011)*, LNCS 6608, Springer, 393–404.

Harman K. Donna (ed.) (1993) *The First Text REtrieval Conference* (TREC-1), NIST Special Publication 500–207, Gaithersburg, MD: National Institute of Standards and Technology.

Hatzivassiloglou, Vasileios and Kathleen R. McKeown (1997) 'Predicting the Semantic Orientation of Adjectives', in *Proceedings of the 35th Annual Meeting of the Association for Computational Linguistics (ACL 1997)*, 174–181.

Heinz, Steffen and Justin Zobel (2003) 'Efficient Single-pass Index Construction for Text Databases', *Journal of the American Society for Information Science and Technology* 54(8): 713–729.

Hearst, Marti A. (1999) 'Untangling Text Data Mining', in *Proceedings of the 37th Annual Meeting of the Association for Computational Linguistics on Computational Linguistics* (ACL 1999), 3–10.

Hearst, Marti (2003) 'What is Text Mining?', unpublished essay, UC Berkeley, available at http://people.ischool.berkeley.edu/~hearst/text-mining.html.

Hofmann, Thomas (1999) 'Probabilistic Latent Semantic Indexing', in *Proceedings of the 22nd Annual International ACM SIGIR Conference on Research and Development on Information Retrieval (SIGIR 1999)*, 50–57.

Hovy, Eduard (2005) 'Text Summarization', in R. Mitkov (ed.), *The Oxford Handbook of Computational Linguistics*, Oxford: Oxford University Press, 583–598.

Hovy, Eduard and Chin-Yew Lin (1999) 'Automated Text Summarization in SUMMARIST', in Inderjeet Mani Mark T. Maybury (eds), *Advances in Automatic Text Summarisation*, Cambridge, MA: MIT Press, 81–97.

Hu, Minqing and Bing Liu (2004) 'Mining and Summarizing Customer Reviews', in *Proceedings of ACM SIGKDD International Conference on Knowledge Discovery and Data Mining (KDD-2004)*, 168–177.

Järvelin, Kalervo and Jaana Kekäläinen (2000) 'IR Evaluation Methods for Retrieving Highly Relevant Documents', in *Proceedings of the 23rd Annual International ACM SIGIR Conference on Research and Development in Information Retrieval (SIGIR 2000)*, 41–48.

Järvelin, Kalervo and Jaana Kekäläinen (2002) 'Cumulated Gain-based Evaluation of IR Techniques', *ACM Transactions on Information Systems* 20(4): 422–446.

Jing, Yufeng and W. Bruce Croft (1994) 'An Association Thesaurus for Information Retrieval', in *Proceedings of the 4th International Conference on Computer Assisted Information Retrieval (Recherche d'Informations Assistee par Ordinateur) (RIAO1994)*, 146–160.

Joachims, Thorsten (2002) 'Optimizing Search Engines Using Clickthrough Data', in *Proceedings of the 8th ACM SIGKDD International Conference on Knowledge Discovery and Data Mining (KDD 2002)*, 133–142.

Johansson, Richard and Alessandro Moschitti (2010) 'Reranking Models in Fine-grained Opinion Analysis', in *Proceedings of the 23rd International Conference on Computational Linguistics (COLING 2010)*, 519–527.

Kilgarriff, Adam and Gregory Grefenstette (2003) 'Introduction to the Special Issue on the Web as Corpus', *Computational Linguistics* 29(3): 333–347.

Kim, Soo-Min and Eduard Hovy (2004) 'Determining the Sentiment of Opinions', in *Proceedings of the 20th International Conference on Computational Linguistics (COLING 2004)*, 1367–1373.

Kim, Soo-Min and Eduard Hovy (2006) 'Extracting Opinions, Opinion Holders, and Topics Expressed in Online News Media Text', in *Proceedings of COLING-ACL 2006 Workshop on Sentiment and Subjectivity in Text*, 1–8.

Kim, Jin-Dong, Tomoko Ohta, Yuka Teteisi, and Jun'ichi Tsujii (2003) 'GENIA Corpus–A Semantically Annotated Corpus for Bio-textmining', *Bioinformatics* 19 (suppl. 1): i180–i182.

Kit, Chunyu (2000) *Unsupervised Lexical Learning as Inductive Inference*, PhD thesis, University of Sheffield.

Kit, Chunyu (2005) 'Unsupervised Lexical Learning as Inductive Inference via Compression', in James W. Minett William S-Y. Wang (eds) *Language Acquisition, Change and Emergence: Essays in Evolutionary Linguistics*, Hong Kong: City University of Hong Kong Press, 251–296.

Kit, Chunyu and Jessica Y. H. Ng (2007) 'An Intelligent Web Agent to Mine Bilingual Parallel Pages via Automatic Discovery of URL Pairing Patterns', in *Proceedings of the 2007 IEEE/WIC/ACM International Conferences on Web Intelligence and Intelligent Agent Technology – Workshops: Workshop on Agents and Data Mining Interaction (ADMI 2007)*, 526–529.

Kit, Chunyu and Yorick Wilks (1999) 'Unsupervised Learning of Word Boundary with Description Length Gain', in Miles Osborne Erik T. K. Sang (eds) CoNLL99: *Computational Natural Language Learning*, 1–6.

Kleinberg, Jon M. (1998) 'Authoritative Sources in a Hyperlinked Environment', in *Proceedings of ACM-SIAM Symposium on Discrete Algorithms*, 668–677. An extended version was published in *Journal of the*

Association for Computing Machinery 46(5): 604–632. Also as IBM Research Report RJ 10076, May 1997.

Kraaij, Wessel, Jian-Yun Nie, and Michel Simard (2003) 'Embedding Web-based Statistical Translation Models in Cross-language Information Retrieval', *Computational Linguistics* 29(3): 381–420.

Krauthammer, Michael and Goran Nenadic (2004) 'Term Identification in the Biomedical Literature', *Journal of Biomedical Informatics* 37(6): 512–526.

Ku, Lun-Wei, Yu-Ting Liang, and Hsin-Hsi Chen (2006) 'Tagging Heterogeneous Evaluation Corpora for Opinionated Tasks', in *Proceedings of the 5th International Conference on Language Resources and Evaluation (LREC 2006)*, 667–670.

Kupiec, Julian, Jan Pedersen, and Francine Chen (1995) 'A Trainable Document Summarizer', in *Proceedings of the 18th Annual International ACM SIGIR Conference on Research and Development in Information Retrieval (SIGIR 1995)*, 68–73.

Lafferty, John and Chengxiang Zhai (2001) 'Document Language Models, Query Models, and Risk Minimization for Information Retrieval', in *Proceedings of the 24th Annual International ACM SIGIR Conference on Research and Development on Information Retrieval (SIGIR 2001)*, 111–119.

Lavrenko, Victor and W. Bruce Croft (2001) 'Relevance-based Language Models', in *Proceedings of the 24th Annual International ACM SIGIR Conference on Research and Development on Information Retrieval (SIGIR 2001)*, 120–127.

Leibowitz, Jacob, Julius Frome, and Don D. Andrews (1958) *Variable Scope Patent Searching by an Inverted File Technique*, Patent Office Research and Development Reports No. 14, U. S. Department of Commerce, Washington, DC, 17 November 1958.

Leser, Ulf and Jörg Hakenberg (2005) 'What Makes a Gene Name? Named Entity Recognition in the Biomedical Literature', *Briefings in Bioinformatics* 6(4): 357–369.

Li, Hang (2011) *Learning to Rank for Information Retrieval and Natural Language Processing*, Synthesis Lectures on Human Language Technologies, Morgan & Claypool Publishers, 4(1): 1–113.

Li, Fangtao, Chao Han, Minlie Huang, Xiaoyan Zhu, Ying-Ju Xia, Shu Zhang, and Hao Yu (2010) 'Structure-aware Review Mining and Summarization', in *Proceedings of the 23rd International Conference on Computational Linguistics (COLING 2010)*, 653–661.

Lin, Chin-Yew (1999) 'Training a Selection Function for Extraction', in *Proceedings of the 8th International Conference on Information and Knowledge Management (CIKM 1999)*, 55–62.

Lin, Chin-Yew (2004) 'ROUGE: A Package for Automatic Evaluation of Summaries', in *Proceedings of the ACL-04 Workshop on Text Summarization Branches Out*, 74–81.

Lin, Chin-Yew and Eduard H. Hovy (2003) 'Automatic Evaluation of Summaries Using N-gram Co-occurrence Statistics', in *Proceedings of the 2003 Human Language Technology Conference of the North American Chapter of the Association for Computational Linguistics (HLT-NAACL 2003)*, 71–78.

Lin, Dekang (1998) 'Automatic Retrieval and Clustering of Similar Words', in *Proceedings of the 36th Annual Meeting of the Association for Computational Linguistics and 17th International Conference on Computational Linguistics (COLING-ACL 1998)*, 768–774.

Liu, Bing (2010) 'Sentiment Analysis and Subjectivity', in Nitin Indurkhya Fred J. Damerau (ed.) *Handbook of Natural Language Processing*, 2nd edition, Boca Raton, FL: Chapman & Hall/CRC, 627–666.

Liu, Bing (2012) *Sentiment Analysis and Opinion Mining*. San Rafao, CA: Morgan & Claypool Publishers.

Liu, Shuang, Fang Liu, Clement Yu, and Weiyi Meng (2004) 'An Effective Approach to Document Retrieval via Utilizing WordNet and Recognizing Phrases', in *Proceedings of the 27th Annual International ACM SIGIR Conference on Research and Development in Information Retrieval (SIGIR 2004)*, 266–272.

Liu, Tie-Yan (2009) 'Learning to Rank for Information Retrieval', *Foundations and Trends in Information Retrieval* 3(3): 225–331.

Liu, Tie-Yan, Xu Jun, Tao Qin, Wenying Xiong, and Hang Li (2007) 'LETOR: Benchmark Dataset for Research on Learning to Rank for Information Retrieval', in *Proceedings of SIGIR 2007 Workshop on Learning to Rank for Information Retrieval (LR4IR 2007)*, 3–10.

Liu, Yi, Rong Jin, and Joyce Y. Chai (2005) 'A Maximum Coherence Model for Dictionary-based Cross-language Information Retrieval', in *Proceedings of the 28th Annual International ACM SIGIR Conference on Research and Development on Information Retrieval (SIGIR 2005)*, 536–543.

Luhn, Hans Peter (1958) 'The Automatic Creation of Literature Abstracts', *IBM Journal of Research and Development* 2(2): 159–165.

Luk, Robert W. P. and Wai Lam (2007) 'Efficient In-memory Extensible Inverted File', *Information Systems* 32(5): 733–754.

Ma, Xiaoyi and Mark Liberman (1999) 'BITS: A Method for Bilingual Text Search over the Web', in *Proceedings of Machine Translation Summit VII*, 538–542.

Ma, Yanjun, Jian-Yun Nie, Hua Wu, and Haifeng Wang (2012) 'Opening Machine Translation Black Box for Cross-language Information Retrieval', in *Information Retrieval Technology: Proceedings of the 8th Asia Information Retrieval Societies Conference* (AIRS 2012), Berlin/Heidelberg: Springer, 467–476.

Mandala, Rila, Takenobu Tokunaga, and Hozumi Tanaka (1999) 'Combining Multiple Evidence from Different Types of Thesaurus for Query Expansion', in *Proceedings of the 22nd Annual International ACM SIGIR Conference on Research & Development on Information Retrieval (SIGIR 1999)*, 191–197.

Manning, Christopher D. (1993) 'Automatic Acquisition of A Large Sub Categorization Dictionary From Corpora', in *Proceedings of the 31st Annual Meeting of the Association for Computational Linguistics (ACL 1993)*, 235–242.

Manning, Christopher D., Prabhakar Raghavan, and Hinrich Schütze (2008) *Introduction to Information Retrieval*, Cambridge University Press.

McCarley, J. Scott (1999) 'Should We Translate the Documents or the Queries in Cross-language Information Retrieval?' in *Proceedings of the Proceedings of the 37th Annual Meeting of the Association for Computational Linguistics (ACL 1999)*, 208–214.

Metzler, Donald and W. Bruce Croft (2005) 'A Markov Random Field Model for Term Dependencies', in *Proceedings of the 28th Annual International ACM SIGIR Conference on Research and Development in Information Retrieval (SIGIR 2005)*, 472–479.

Metzler, Donald and W. Bruce Croft (2007) 'Latent Concept Expansion Using Markov Random Fields', in *Proceedings of the 30th Annual International ACM SIGIR Conference on Research and Development in Information Retrieval (SIGIR 2007)*, 311–318.

Mihalcea, Rada, Carmen Banea, and Janyce Wiebe (2007) 'Learning Multilingual Subjective Language via Cross-lingual Projections', in *Proceedings of the 45th Annual Meeting of the Association of Computational Linguistics (ACL 2007)*, 976–983.

Miller, George A., Richard Beckwith, Christiane Fellbaum, Derek Gross, and Katherine J. Miller (1990) 'WordNet: An Online Lexical Database', *International Journal of Lexicography* 3(4): 235–244.

Moffat, Alistair and Justin Zobel (1998) 'Exploring the Similarity Space', SIGIR Forum 32(1): 18–34.

Moore, Robert T. (1961) 'A Screening Method for Large Information Retrieval Systems', in *Proceedings of the Western Joint IRE-AIEE-ACM Computer Conference (IRE-AIEE-ACM'61 (Western))*, 259–274.

Mooers, Calvin E. (1950) 'Coding, Information Retrieval, and the Rapid Selector', *American Documentation* 1(4): 225–229.

Moulinier, Isabelle and Hugo Molina-Salgado (2003) 'Thomson Legal and Regulatory Experiments for CLEF 2002', in C.A. Peters (ed.), *Advances in Cross-Language Information Retrieval: 3rd Workshop of the Cross-Language Evaluation Forum (CLEF 2002)*, Berlin/Heidelberg: Springer, 155–163.

Nguyen, Dong, Arnold Overwijk, Claudia Hauff, Dolf R. B. Trieschnigg, Djoerd Hiemstra, and Franciska De Jong (2008) 'WikiTranslate: Query Translation for Cross-lingual Information Retrieval Using only Wikipedia', in *Evaluating Systems for Multilingual and Multimodal Information Access: 9th Workshop of the Cross-Language Evaluation Forum (CLEF'08)*, Berlin/Heidelberg: Springer, 58–65.

Nie, Jian-Yun (2010) *Cross-Language Information Retrieval*, Synthesis Lectures on Human Language Technologies, San Rafael, CA: Morgan & Claypool Publishers, 3(1): 1–125.

Nie, Jian-Yun, Pierre Isabelle, and George Foster (1998) 'Using a Probabilistic Translation Model for Cross-language Information Retrieval", in *Proceedings of the 6th Workshop on Very Large Corpora*, 18–27.

Nie, Jian-Yun, Michel Simard, Pierre Isabelle, and Richard Durand (1999) 'Crosslanguage Information Retrieval based on Parallel Texts and Automatic Mining of Parallel Texts from the Web', in *Proceedings of the 22nd Annual International ACM SIGIR Conference on Research and Development on Information Retrieval (SIGIR 1999)*, 74–81.

Nolan, J.J. (1958) *Principles of Information Storage and Retrieval Using a Large Scale Random Access Memory*. San Jose, CA: IBM.

Oard, Douglas and Bonnie J. Dorr (1996) *A Survey of Multilingual Text Retrieval, Research Report* UMIACS-TR-96-19 CS-TR-3615, 31 pages, University of Maryland.

O'Connor, Brendan, Ramnath Balasubramanyan, Bryan R. Routledge, and Noah A. Smith (2010) 'From Tweets to Polls: Linking Text Sentiment to Public Opinion Time Series', in *Proceedings of the 4th International AAAI Conference on Weblogs and Social Media (ICWSM 2010)*, 122–129.

Olivier, Donald Cort (1968) *Stochastic Grammars and Language Acquisition Mechanisms*, PhD thesis, Harvard University.

Pang, Bo and Lillian Lee (2004) 'A Sentimental Education: Sentiment Analysis Using Subjectivity Summarization Based on Minimum Cuts', in *Proceedings of the 42nd Annual Meeting of the Association for Computational Linguistics (ACL 2004)*, 271–278.

Pang, Bo and Lillian Lee (2005) 'Seeing Stars: Exploiting Class Relationships for Sentiment Categorization with Respect to Rating Scales', in *Proceedings of the 43rd Annual Meeting of the Association for Computational Linguistics (ACL 2005)*, 115–124.

Pang, Bo and Lillian Lee (2008) 'Opinion Mining and Sentiment Analysis', *Foundations and Trends in Information Retrieval* 2(1–2): 1–135.

Pang, Bo, Lillian Lee, and Shivakumar Vaithyanathan (2002) 'Thumbs up? Sentiment Classification Using Machine Learning Techniques', in *Proceedings of the 2002 Conference on Empirical Methods in Natural Language Processing (EMNLP 2002)*, 79–86.

Ponte, Jay M. and Croft, W. Bruce (1998) 'A Language Modeling Approach to Information Retrieval', in *Proceedings of the 21st Annual International ACM SIGIR Conference on Research and Development on Information Retrieval (SIGIR 1998)*, 275–281.

Popescu, Ana-Maria and Oren Etzioni (2005) 'Extracting Product Features and Opinions from Reviews', in *Proceedings of Human Language Technology Conference and Conference on Empirical Methods in Natural Language Processing (HLT-EMNLP 2005)*, 339–346.

Porter, Martin F. (1980) 'An Algorithm for Suffix Stripping', *Program* 14(3): 130–137.

Qiu, Guang, Bing Liu, Jiajun Bu, and Chun Chen (2011) 'Opinion Word Expansion and Target Extraction through Double Propagation', *Computational Linguistics* 37(1): 9–27.

Qiu, Yonggang and Hans-Peter Frei (1993) 'Concept based Query Expansion', in *Proceedings of the 16th Annual International ACM SIGIR Conference on Research and Development on Information Retrieval (SIGIR 1993)*, 160–169.

Resnik, Philip (1998) 'Parallel Strands: A Preliminary Investigation into Mining the Web for Bilingual Text', in D. Farwell L. Gerber E. Hovy (eds) *Machine Translation and the Information Soup: 3rd Conference of the Association for Machine Translation in the Americas (AMTA 1998)*, Springer, 72–82.

Resnik, Philip (1999) 'Mining the Web for Bilingual Text', in *Proceedings of the 37th Annual Meeting of the Association for Computational Linguistics (ACL 1999)*, 527–534.

Resnik, Philip and Noah A Smith (2003) 'The Web as a Parallel Corpus', *Computational Linguistics* 29(3): 349–380.

Rissanen, Jorma (1978) 'Modeling by Shortest Data Description', *Automatica* 14(5): 465–471.

Rissanen, Jorma (1989) *Stochastic Complexity in Statistical Inquiry Theory*, River Edge, NJ: World Scientific Publishing.

Robertson, Stephen E. and Karen Sparck Jones (1976) 'Relevance Weighting of Search Terms', *Journal of the American Society for Information Science* 27(3): 129–146.

Robertson, Stephen E. and Karen Sparck Jones (1994) *Simple, Proven Approaches to Text Retrieval*, Technical Report UCAM-CL-TR-356, Computer Laboratory, University of Cambridge.

Robertson, Stephen E., Stephen Walker, and Micheline Hancock-Beaulieu (1999) 'Okapi at TREC–7: Automatic Ad Hoc, Filtering, VLC and Filtering Tracks', in *Proceedings of the 7th Text REtrieval Conference (TREC-7)*, 253–264.

Rocchio, J.J. (1965/1971) 'Relevance Feedback in Information Retrieval', reprinted in Gerald Salton (ed.) (1971) *The SMART Retrieval System – Experiments in Automatic Document Processing*, Englewood Cliffs, NJ: Prentice Hall, 313–323.

Sadat, Fatiha, Masatoshi Yoshikawa, and Shunsuke Uemura (2003) 'Learning Bilingual Translations from Comparable Corpora to Cross-language Information Retrieval: Hybrid Statistics-based and Linguistics-based Approach', in *Proceedings of the 6th International Workshop on Information Retrieval with Asian Languages (IRAL)*, 57–64.

Salton, Gerard (1970) 'Automatic Processing of Foreign Language Documents', *Journal of the American Society for Information Science*, 21(3): 187–194.

Salton, Gerard (ed.) (1971) *The SMART Retrieval System – Experiments in Automatic Document Processing*. Englewood Cliffs, NJ: Prentice Hall.

Salton, Gerard and Christopher Buckley (1988) 'Term-weighting Approaches in Automatic Text Retrieval', *Information Processing and Management* 24(5): 513–523.

Salton, Gerald, Anita Wong, and Chung-Shu Yang (1975) 'A Vector Space Model for Automatic Indexing', *Communications of the ACM* 18(11): 613–620.

Savoy, Jacques and Ljiljana Dolamic (2009) 'How Effective is Google's Translation Service in Search?', *Communications of the ACM* 52(10): 139–143.

Scherer, Klaus R. (1984) 'Emotion as a Multicomponent Process: A Model and Some Cross-cultural data', *Review of Personality and Social Psychology* 5: 37–63.

Schütze, Hinrich and Jan O. Pedersen (1997) 'A Co-occurrence-based Thesaurus and Two Applications to Information Retrieval', *Information Processing and Management* 33(3): 307–318.

Shanahan, James G., Yan Qu, and Janyce Wiebe (2006) *Computing Attitude and Affect in Text: Theory and Applications*, the Information Retrieval Series, Vol. 20, New York: Springer.

Sheridan, Páraic and Jean Paul Ballerini (1996) 'Experiments in Multilingual Information Retrieval Using the SPIDER System', in *Proceedings of the 19th Annual International ACM SIGIR Conference on Research and Development on Information Retrieval (SIGIR 1996)*, 58–65.

Shi, Lixin and Jian-Yun Nie (2010) 'Using Various Term Dependencies according to their Utilities', in *Proceedings of the 19th ACM International Conference on Information and Knowledge Management (CIKM 2010)*, 1493–1496.

Shi, Lei, Cheng Niu, Ming Zhou, and Jianfeng Gao (2006) 'A DOM Tree Alignment Model for Mining Parallel Data from the Web', in *Proceedings of the 21st International Conference on Computational Linguistics and 44th Annual Meeting of the Association for Computational Linguistics (COLING-ACL 2006)*, 489–496.

Simpson, Matthew S. and Dina Demner-Fushman (2012) 'Biomedical Text Mining: A Survey of Recent Progress', in Charu C. Aggarwal Chengxiang Zhai (eds) *Mining Text Data*, New York: Springer, 465–517.

Singhal, Amit, Chris Buckley, and Mandar Mitra (1996) 'Pivoted Document Length Normalization', in *Proceedings of the 19th Annual International ACM SIGIR Conference on Research and Development on Information Retrieval (SIGIR 1996)*, 21–29.

Singhal, Amit, Gerard Salton, and Chris Buckley (1996) 'Length Normalization in Degraded Text Collections', in *Proceedings of the Annual Symposium on Document Analysis and Information Retrieval (SDAIR 1996)*, 149–162.

Singhal, Amit, John Choi, Donald Hindle, David Lewis, and Fernando Pereira (1999) 'AT&T at TREC-7', in *Proceedings of the 7th Text REtrieval Conference (TREC-7)*, 239–252.

Solomonoff, Ray J. (1964) 'A Formal Theory of Inductive Inference', *Information Control*, 7: 1–22 (part 1), 224–256 (part 2).

Sparck Jones, Karen (1972) 'A Statistical Interpretation of Term Specificity and its Application in Retrieval', *Journal of Documentation* 28(1): 11–21; reprinted in *Journal of Documentation* 60(5): 493–502.

Sparck Jones Karen (ed.) (1981) *Information Retrieval Experiment*. London: Butterworths.

Sparck Jones, Karen (1999) 'Automatic Summarising: Factors and Directions', in Inderjeet Mani Mark T. Maybury (eds) *Advances in Automatic Text Summarisation*, Cambridge, MA: MIT Press, 1–12.

Sparck Jones, Karen and Peter Willet (1997) *Readings in Information Retrieval*. San Francisco: Morgan Kaufmann.

Stone, Philip J. (1966) *The General Inquirer: A Computer Approach to Content Analysis*. Cambridge, MA: MIT Press.

Stoyanov, Veselin and Claire Cardie (2008) 'Topic Identification for Fine-grained Opinion Analysis', in *Proceedings of the 22nd International Conference on Computational Linguistics (COLING 2008)*, 817–824.

Su, Qi, Xinying Xu, Honglei Guo, Zhili Guo, Xian Wu, Xiaoxun Zhang, Bin Swen, and Zhong Su (2008) 'Hidden Sentiment Association in Chinese Web Opinion Mining', in *Proceedings of the 17th International Conference on World Wide Web (WWW 2008)*, 959–968.

Swanson, Don R. (1986) 'Fish Oil, Raynaud's Syndrome, and Undiscovered Public Knowledge', *Perspectives in Biology and Medicine* 30(1): 7–18.

Swanson, Don R. (1987) 'Two Medical Literatures That Are Logically but Not Bibliographically Connected', *Journal of the American Society for Information Science* 38(4): 228–233.

Swanson, Don R. (1988) 'Migraine and Magnesium: Eleven Neglected Connections', *Perspectives in Biology and Medicine* 31(4): 526–557.

Swanson, Don R. (1988) 'Historical Note: Information Retrieval and the Future of an Illusion', *Journal of the American Society for Information Science* 39(2): 92–98.

Swanson, Don R. (1990) 'Somatomedin C and Arginine: Implicit Connections between Mutually Isolated Literatures', *Perspectives in Biology and Medicine* 33(2): 157–186.

Swanson, Don R. (1991) 'Complementary Structures in Disjoint Science Literatures', in *Proceedings of the 14th Annual International ACM SIGIR Conference on Research and Development on Information Retrieval (SIGIR 1991)*, 280–289.

Swanson, Don R., Neil R. Smalheiser, and A. Bookstein (2001) 'Information Discovery from Complementary Literatures: Categorizing Viruses as Potential weapons', *Journal of the American Society for Information Science and Technology*, 52(10): 797–812.

Teufel, Simone (2007) 'An Overview of Evaluation Methods in TREC Ad-hoc Information Retrieval and TREC Question Answering', in Laila Dybkjaer Holmer Hemsen Wolfgang Minker (eds) *Evaluation of Text and Speech Systems*, Dordrecht: Springer, 163–186.

Türe, Ferhan, Jimmy J. Lin and Douglas W. Oard (2012) 'Combining Statistical Translation Techniques for Cross-language Information Retrieval', in *Proceedings of the 24th International Conference on Computational Linguistics (COLING 2012)*, 2685–2702.

Türe, Ferhan and Jimmy J. Lin (2013) 'Flat vs. Hierarchical Phrase-based Translation Models for Cross-language Information Retrieval', in *Proceedings of the 36th Annual International ACM SIGIR Conference on Research and Development on Information Retrieval (SIGIR-2013)*, 813–816.

Turney, Peter (2002) 'Thumbs up or Thumbs down? Semantic Orientation Applied to Unsupervised Classification of Reviews', in *Proceedings of the 40th Annual Meeting of the Association for Computational Linguistics (ACL 2002)*, 417–424.

van Rijsbergen, Cornelis Joost (1979) Information Retrieval, 2nd edition. London: Butterworths.

Venkataraman, Anand (2001) 'A Statistical Model for Word Discovery in Transcribed Speech', *Computational Linguistics* 27(3): 351–372.

Voorhees, Ellen M. (1993) 'Using WordNet to Disambiguate Word Senses for Text Retrieval', in *Proceedings of the 16th Annual International ACM SIGIR Conference on Research and Development on Information Retrieval (SIGIR 1993)*, 171–180.

Voorhees, Ellen M. (1994) 'Query Expansion Using Lexical-semantic Relations', in *Proceedings of the 17th Annual International ACM SIGIR Conference on Research and Development in Information Retrieval (SIGIR 1994)*, 61–69.

Voorhees Ellen M. Donna K. Harman (eds) (2005) *TREC: Experiment and Evaluation in Information Retrieval*. Cambridge, MA: MIT Press.

Wallace, C. S. and D. M. Boulton (1968) 'An Information Measure for Classification', *Computer Journal* 11(2): 185–194.

Wallace, C. S. and P. R. Freeman (1987) 'Estimation and Inference by Compact Coding', *Journal of the Royal Statistical Society*, Series B, 49(3): 240–265.

Wan, Xiaojun (2008) 'Using Bilingual Knowledge and Ensemble Techniques for Unsupervised Chinese Sentiment Analysis', in *Proceedings of the 2008 Conference on Empirical Methods in Natural Language Processing (EMNLP 2008)*, 553–561.

Wan, Xiaojun (2009) 'Co-Training for Cross-lingual Sentiment Classification', in *Proceedings of the Joint Conference of the 47th Annual Meeting of the ACL and the 4th International Joint Conference on Natural Language Processing of the AFNLP (ACL-IJCNLP 2009)*, 235–243.

Weeber, Marc, Henny Klein, Lolkje T. W. de Jong-van den Berg, and Rein Vos (2001) 'Using Concepts in Literature-based Discovery: Simulating Swanson's Raynaud–Fish Oil and Migraine–Magnesium Discoveries', *Journal of the American Society for Information Science and Technology* 52(7): 548–557.

Wei, Bin and Christopher Pal (2010) 'Cross Lingual Adaptation: An Experiment on Sentiment Classifications', in *Proceedings of the 48th Annual Meeting of the Association for Computational Linguistics (ACL 2010)*, 258–262.

Wen, Ji-Rong, Jian-Yun Nie, and Hong-Jiang Zhang (2001) 'Clustering User Queries of a Search Engine', in *Proceedings of the 10th International Conference on World Wide Web (WWW 2001)*, 162–168.

Wiebe, Janyce, Theresa Wilson, and Claire Cardie (2005) 'Annotating Expressions of Opinions and Emotions in Language', *Language Resources and Evaluation* 39(2–3): 165–210.

Wilson, Theresa, Janyce Wiebe, and Paul Hoffmann (2005) 'Recognizing Contextual Polarity in Phrase-level Sentiment Analysis', in *Proceedings of Human Language Technology Conference and Conference on Empirical Methods in Natural Language Processing (HLT-EMNLP 2005)*, 347–354.

Witten, Ian H., Alistair Moffat, and Timothy C. Bell (1999) *Managing Gigabytes: Compressing and Indexing Documents and Images*, 2nd edition, San Francisco: Morgan Kaufmann Publishers.

Xu, Hongbo, Tianfang Yao, Xuanjing Huang, Huifeng Tang, Feng Guan, and Jin Zhang (2009) 'Overview of Chinese Opinion Analysis Evaluation 2009', in *Proceedings of the 2nd Chinese Opinion Analysis Evaluation (COAE 2009)*. (In Chinese.)

Xu, Jinxi and W. Bruce Croft (2000) 'Improving the Effectiveness of Information Retrieval with Local Context Analysis', *ACM Transactions on Information Systems* 18(1): 79–112.

Yang, Hui, Luo Si, and Jamie Callan (2006) 'Knowledge Transfer and Opinion Detection in the TREC2006 Blog Track', in *Proceedings of the 15th Text REtrieval Conference (TREC 2006)*.

Ye, Sha-ni, Ya-juan Lv, Yun Huang, and Qun Liu (2008) 'Automatic Parallel Sentence Extraction from Web', *Journal of Chinese Information Processing* 22(5): 67–73. (In Chinese.)

Zhai, ChengXiang (2008) *Statistical Language Models for Information Retrieval*, Synthesis Lectures on Human Language Technologies, Morgan & Claypool Publishers, 1(1): 1–141.

Zhai, Chengxiang and John Lafferty (2001) 'Model-based Feedback in the Language Modeling Approach to Information Retrieval', in *Proceedings of the 10th International Conference on Information and Knowledge Management (CIKM 2001)*, 403–410.

Zhang, Chengzhi, Xuchen Yao, and Chunyu Kit (2013) 'Finding more Bilingual Webpages with High Credibility via Link Analysis', in *Proceedings of the 6th Workshop on Building and Using Comparable Corpora (BUCC 2013)*, 138–143.

Zhang, Ying, Ke Wu, Jianfeng Gao, and Phil Vines (2006) 'Automatic Acquisition of Chinese-English Parallel Corpus from the Web', in *Advances in Information Retrieval, Proceedings of 28th European Conference on IR Research (ECIR 2006)*, Springer, 420–431.

Zhao, Jun, Hongbo Xu, Xuanjing Huang, Songbo Tan, Kang Liu, and Qi Zhang (2008) 'Overview of Chinese Opinion Analysis Evaluation 2008', in *Proceedings of the 1st Chinese Opinion Analysis Evaluation (COAE 2008)*, 1–20. (In Chinese.)

Zhuang, Li, Feng Jing, and Xiaoyan Zhu (2006) 'Movie Review Mining and Summarization', in *Proceedings of the 15th ACM International Conference on Information and Knowledge Management (CIKM 2006)*, 43–50.

Zobel, Justin and Alistair Moffat (2006) 'Inverted Files for Text Search Engines', *ACM Computing Surveys* 38(2): Article 6.

Zweigenbaum, Pierre, Dina Demner-Fushman, Hong Yu, and Kevin B. Cohen (2007) 'Frontiers of Biomedical Text Mining: Current Progress', *Briefings in Bioinformatics* 8(5): 358–375.

36

LANGUAGE CODES AND LANGUAGE TAGS

Sue Ellen Wright

Introduction

Most people are unaware that every time they log onto the web or use a computer program, watch a TV program, or use a cell phone, they invoke a language code. Sometimes the codes become visible even to the inexperienced user if a colleague who works mostly in another language sends a word-processing file that starts generating spelling errors because it is checking English text against a dictionary for a different language. Resolving links that used non-ASCII characters (e.g. Japanese or Chinese) in a Western European computing environment was once a serious problem that has improved significantly with the implementation of the World Wide Web Consortium's (W3C) Internationalization Tagset (W3C 2013) and layered handling of multilingual web addresses (W3C 2008).

Language and script identifiers enable users to use keyboards to type in a variety of languages using multiple scripts and both standard and specialized fonts. Identifiers facilitate the generation of screen displays and drive printers to render those scripts on physical media, such as paper. The critical *language tag* specifies both language and region. It consists of a simple string of characters that provides the information fuel that keeps the engine of the web running: for instance, en-US, zh-ZH, deu-CHE, esp-MEX – American English, Mainland Chinese, Swiss German, or Mexican Spanish. If something goes wrong, as mentioned, adjusting one of these elements may be required to rectify problems in the computing environment.

This chapter will examine what a human language is, as well as other related concepts, such as language families and groups, language varieties, and dialects. The first part of the chapter provides an outline-like reference to the many stakeholders and standards used to encode or otherwise characterize languages and language varieties, while the second part of the chapter provides a more detailed review of the history and future directions affecting the creation, maintenance, and application of language identifiers, codes, and tags.

Language Codes – What Is a Human Language?

Printed text relies on humans to intuit the language of the text, and spoken discourse assumes (or fails to achieve) interlocutor understanding. Every translator experiences how difficult this can be for non-linguists - for instance, when uninformed clients send a Catalan text to a Spanish

DOI: 10.4324/9781003168348-39

translator. Computers, however, need to be "told" explicitly what to expect, although utilities exist for parsing text to determine its probable language. Protocols governing content representation, especially in web environments, "declare" language, locale (country or region), script, and other related information using a *language code* or a *language tag*. At one time presented in a six-part series, language identifiers are slated to be, as of 2023, governed by a single unified code as specified in a new, single *ISO 639 Code for the Representation of Individual Languages and Language Groups – General Principles, Rules and Guidelines*. The new standard defines *human language* as quoted in the short vocabulary at the end of this chapter. The notion of a human language is profiled, among other distinctions, with language *varieties* and *dialects*. While these concepts are widely accepted, the principles for assigning a particular manner of speaking (writing or thinking) to one or the other designation are not always transparent.

There may be general agreement that, for instance, English, German, Japanese, and Russian, are separate languages, but as soon as the view moves away from the most common idioms, the certainty of what a language is can stand on shaky ground. Speakers of English and Chinese who have not studied each other's languages can be quite clear on the distinction: their respective speech conventions are mutually unintelligible. This notion of non-intelligibility is often used, even by linguists and in the code standards, to distinguish languages from dialects, but the assertion itself can be tenuous.

Speakers of Norwegian and Swedish, for instance, can chat together, each speaking their own language, but understanding most of what is said and delighting in their shared heritages. In contrast, Croatian and Serbian are also mutually intelligible, but they are traditionally represented by different scripts (Latin and Cyrillic, respectively), and for political and historical reasons, linguists and ordinary speakers alike have worked hard to profile what was once designated as a single language in ways that underscore differences. This/these language(s) is/are (depending on one's perspective) consciously split apart, invoking linguistic particularism in response to political schism.

Should this trend sound regrettable or even bizarre, it is not unprecedented. After the American Revolution at the beginning of the 19th century, American lexicographers and linguists consciously introduced the spelling "reforms" that today distinguish written American English from its British cousin. Nevertheless, with some degree of change in lexis (word and term usage) and pronunciation over the course of two and a half centuries, American; Canadian; British; and even Australian, Indian, and South African English(es) remain more or less mutually comprehensible varieties of the same language. Although experts do indeed define dialects and varieties of English (Spanish, Russian, Arabic), these huge speech communities are classified as recognized varieties of the same mother tongues, the same macrolanguages.

By the same token, although German asserts itself as a single individual language with many dialects, a speaker of a so-called "low German" dialect in Hamburg finds the everyday speech of a Bavarian mountaineer quite incomprehensible. The "high" German learned carefully throughout the German school system and spoken by educated people across Germany, Austria, and even, with some stress and strain, parts of Switzerland (as well as part of Belgium and in pockets of a German-speaking diaspora scattered about the world), originated as an artificial construct painstakingly fashioned at the end of the 18th and the beginning of the 19th century in an effort both to quell French influence and to unify a splintered nation with no single dominant political center. (Göttert 2010) The situation with Italian is similar. Chinese is even more dramatic. Although it claims a highly portable, unified writing system, actual spoken varieties differ even more dramatically than spoken dialects of German or Italian.

So if intelligibility or the lack thereof is not the determining criterion for defining a language, what is? An often quoted Yiddish definition claims *"a shprakh iz a diyalekt mit an armey un a flot"* (a language is a dialect with an army and a navy), despite the fact that the Yiddish language itself has never had either.[1] All joking aside, the distinction between the two concepts is essentially colored by historical and geo-political precedents. When all is said and done, a language variety is a *language* (as opposed perhaps to a *dialect*) if its speakers – or perhaps even some external researchers – have decided this is so, with the result that some mutually intelligible languages, like the Scandinavian languages already cited, or, for instance, Portuguese and some dialects of Spanish, are classified as individual languages, while some unintelligible dialects are nonetheless considered dialects of larger macrolanguages. National boundaries may be cited as dividing lines in some cases, but idioms such as Basque, Catalan, and Kurdish, for instance, assert themselves as languages that straddle national and provincial borders and throughout their checkered histories have experienced both ethnic and linguistic suppression from various sides. Other languages like Yiddish, Ladino, and the language varieties of the Roma distinguish themselves as borderless migrant languages, ever in motion and often subject to discrimination and persecution.

In some cases, external influences related to the global history of colonialism and various waves of cultural and political hegemony affect the choice of language identification. Current Iranian preference for "Persian" as the name of their language, in rejection of "Farsi", reflects a negative reaction to both Arabic (from which the latter stems) and western misunderstandings. Some may argue that these distinctions are political and not warranted as "scientific" linguistic factors, but personal, historical, and political forces play a significant role in defining both language and in some cases national identity. Nevertheless, even the most vehement nationalist positions on language as incontrovertibly associated with specific nation states are dangerously untenable in the long term. Even French, with its valorization of a single variety (the language of the Île de France) must at the pragmatic level tolerate the existence of regional dialects. Spain under Franco and Libya under Gadhafi promoted the ascendance of a single national language within their borders, only to see repressed regional languages and dialects break free at the first opportunity. Hence the juxtaposition of language with country should not be interpreted as an immutably aggregated entity but rather as a theme with determiner – French *as spoken in Canada* – and nothing more. Nor dare we view the tendency of languages like blood to seep across boundaries to penetrate deep into the tissue of neighboring lands as an extension of the sovereignty of the mother country, an error that can have serious consequences if taken too literally, as evidenced by the history of Germany in the 20th century, or, alas, Russia's insistence on a mythologized Russian identity of Ukraine in the 21st.

How then, if it is so difficult to determine what a language is, or what a dialect is, when and by whom have languages been classified and coded? What is the range of application for these codes? What determines their form and content?

Stakeholders and Standards

Despite the ignorance of language identifiers on the part of the general public described in the introduction, there are several communities of practice (CoPs) that have a strong vested interest in naming and citing languages, as well as assigning designators to them, commonly called *language codes* and *language tags*. These CoPs have traditionally been dedicated to the maintenance and stability of the codes as well as to responding to changing insights and attitudes, both scholarly and political. The following section groups these CoPs together with their original standards and resources in order to provide a roadmap designed to traverse a potentially forbidding landscape.

The first three groups in this list are closely associated with the International Organization for Standardization (ISO), TC 37, *Language and Terminology,* Sub-committee 2 for *Terminology Workflow and Language Coding*, which has published the ISO 639 series of standards. Current work is focusing on issuing a new single-part ISO 639 *Code for the Representation of Individual Languages and Language Groups: General Principles, Rules and Guidelines*, which as of this writing is slated to replace the earlier ISO 639, Parts 1–3 and 5.

Terminologists: ISO TC 37 and InfoTerm together have traditionally maintained a Registration Authority for

- *ISO 639-1:2002, Codes for the Representation of Names of Languages – Part 1: Alpha-2 Code,*[2] which becomes *Set 1* of the language identifiers specified as part of the language code in the new standard.

Alpha-2 codes are represented in lowercase and are for the most part formed mnemonically based on the name of a language as it is expressed in that language, for example, *en, es, de* for English, Spanish (español), and German (Deutsch). The current Alpha-2 identifiers comprise 136 language identifiers.

Librarians and Information Scientists: ISO TC 46, *Information and Documentation*, and the US Library of Congress (LoC) have maintained the Registration Authority for

- ISO 639-2:1998, *Codes for the Representation of Names of Languages – Part 2: Alpha-3 Code*, which becomes *ISO 639, Set 2*, and for
- ISO 639-5:2008, Codes for the representation of names of languages – Part 5: Alpha-3 code for language families and groups, which becomes *ISO 639, Set 5*.

Set 2 Alpha-3 codes are formed mnemonically where possible, with the note that there are some English-based forms that exist in parallel with native-tongue forms, such as *eng, fra/fre, spa/esp, ger/deu.* The collection comprises 464 language identifiers.

The LoC has traditionally published information on these codes (including 639-1 two-letter codes) in its ISO 639-2 Registration Authority page, www.loc.gov/standards/iso639-2/, and in the *MARC Code List for Languages*, www.loc.gov/marc/languages/.

OCLC (originally the Ohio College Library Center) specifies procedures for entering MARC language codes in various fields of the OCLC search record in its *OCLC Bibliographic Formats and Standards 047, Language Code (R)*, available at www.oclc.org/bibformats/en/0xx/041.html.

Translators and Field Linguists: SIL International has maintained the Registration Authority for

- ISO 639-3:2007, *Codes for the Representation of Names of Languages – Part 3: Alpha-3 Code for Comprehensive Coverage of Languages*, which becomes *ISO 639, Set 3*.

The Set-3 identifiers follow the same pattern as Set 2, with exception that there are no ambiguous English-based designators. Set 3 provides language identifiers for over 7,150 languages.

SIL International maintains an easy-to access and interpret table documenting all four sets at *ISO 639 Code Tables*, www-01.sil.org/iso639-3/codes.asp?order=639_2&letter=a and provides detailed information (subject to a subscription fee) on each individual code point at www.ethnologue.com/world.

The United Nations and The International Organization for Standardization (ISO): together under the auspices of the ISO 3166 Maintenance Agency in Geneva, Switzerland, administer

- ISO 3166-1:2020, *Codes for the Representation of Names of Countries and Their Subdivisions – Part 1: Country Codes; Part 2: Country Subdivision Code, and Part 3: Code for Formerly Used Names of Countries.*

Country codes are often (but not always) expressed with capital letters to distinguish them from language codes and are available as Alpha-2, Alpha-3, and three-digit numerical forms, such as *BE, BEL, 056, Belgium.*

Computer scientists, internationalization specialists, Internet and World Wide Web designers, under the auspices of the following entities, maintain a variety of standards and normative recommendations:

The *World Wide Web Consortium* specifies that web pages and online resources shall utilize the *lang* (HTML) and *xml:lang* (XML) attributes to identify the language of web content. W3C does not specify the form of these elements; it only requires them, as stated in:

- W3C, *The Global Structure of an HTML Document,* Chapter 8.1, "Specifying the Language of Content: the *lang* Attribute", www.w3.org/TR/html401/struct/dirlang.html#adef-lang
- W3C, *Extensible Markup Language (XML)* 1.0 (Fifth Edition); W3C Recommendation 26 November 2008. www.w3.org/TR/REC-xml/

The *Internet Engineering Task Force (IETF, BCP 47)* specifies the syntax for creating language tags in:

- *Tags for Identifying Languages,* https://tools.ietf.org/html/bcp47 (current edition as of 2013–12: IETF RFC 5646, Addison Phillips and Mark Davis, editors).

Language tags can be as simple as a single two-letter code or may indicate additional information, such as language, variety, script, region, such as *zh-cmn-Hans-CN (Chinese, Mandarin, Simplified script, as used in (Mainland) China).* (See Figure 36.1.)

The *Internet Assigned Numbers Authority (IANA)* assigns and maintains a

- *Registry of Language Subtags* designed to meet the private needs of individuals for whom the standard language tags do not reflect a particular desired level of specificity, www.iana.org/assignments/language-subtag-registry/language-subtag-registry

The *Unicode Consortium* began as a mirror to the parallel ISO standard: *ISO 10646, Information Technology – Universal Coded Character Set (UCS).* These standards provide "a character coding system designed to support the worldwide interchange, processing, and display of the written texts of the diverse languages and technical disciplines of the modern world", including support for classical and historical texts of many written languages.

Unicode encoding replaced earlier incompatible encoding formats developed in various computing environments. It also supersedes the old *American Standard Code for Information Interchange (ASCII)* standard (ANSI_X3.4-1968/1986) and its multipart ISO companion ISO/IEC 8859 family of standards, which attempted to provide encoding for individual languages. The advantage of the Unicode approach is that it provides encoding for every character used in every registered language, enabling the encoding of multiple languages in the same text or computing space. Unicode maintains an extensive website providing access to codes, as well as a wealth of other information, at: https://home.unicode.org/

The standard itself is available at: www.unicode.org/versions/Unicode14.0.0/. Unicode also maintains:

- ISO 15924, *Codes for the Representation of Names of Scripts* and

- The *Common Locale Data Registry (CLDR)*, which augments the language tags with locale-related information needed in computing environments, particularly on the web.

These *locale IDs* can be used to implement a variety of information, such as currencies, time related information, region-specific spelling and capitalization rules, transliteration rules, keyboard layouts, and more, expressed using Unicode's *UTS #35: Unicode Locale Data Markup Language (LDML)*. Primary resources are available at:

- https://cldr.unicode.org/ and www.unicode.org/reports/tr35/, respectively.

Proprietary Code Variants

Although the current CLDR configuration provides a rich and powerful set of tools for invoking language tags in computing environments, a number of proprietary code sets evolved historically during the development of today's approaches. These modalities remain as legacy threads in the fabric of today's web.

Microsoft posts its [MS-LCID]: *Windows Language Code Identifier (LCID) Reference* on the MSDN Microsoft Developer Website, with links to detailed data repositories on GitHub for purposes of identifying specific languages and varieties used in localizing software for particular languages and cultures (Constable and Simon 2000; Constable 2000a, 2002b). They were designed originally to specify formatting for dates, times, and numbers, as well as sorting based on language elements. The list is posted at: http://msdn.microsoft.com/en-us/library/cc233965.aspx. The original list specifies Set 1 identifiers but over time has come to expand to accommodate Set 3 identifiers not included in Set 1.

IBM's original short list of National Language Codes, using what appear to be country code conventions (all caps), powers the familiar drop-down lists used in many multilingual

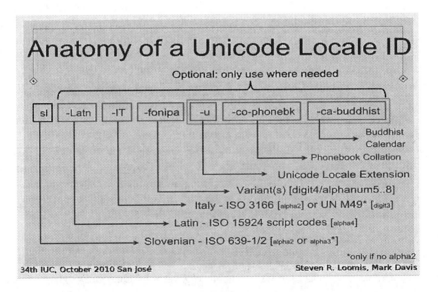

Figure 36.1 Unicode Locale ID taken from the CLDR, where the code implies:

Slovenian | represented in Latin script | as spoken in Italy | classified by the variant code fonipa | assigned the Unicode Locale Extension − u | collated according to phonebook rules | [and whimsically] subject to the Buddhist calendar conventions

Figure 36.2   Sub-languages drop-down menu, MultiTerm 2011

Figure 36.3   Language keyboard selection menu, Microsoft Word

computing applications, such as the selection of specific keyboard layouts, or the specification of regional language varieties used to classify machine translation or translation memory resources.

Google Web Interface and Search Language Codes were designed to specify a search in a specific language (as opposed to using the advanced search features provided by the standard search interface). Limited to 56 major languages (with a small number of indigenous entries like Cherokee and Telugu), the list is based solely on Set 1, reflecting the original reliance of web environments on ISO 639-1, and was designed for indicating language as the value of the *customer.language* tag. https://developers.google.com/admin-sdk/directory/v1/languages

Historical Development

Historically speaking, the language codes as we know them today evolved out of a need to save space and time within the framework of both terminology documentation and library cataloguing procedures in an era when both terminographers and lexicographers on the one hand and library cataloguers on the other recorded documentary information about terms or library holdings (books and other objects) on relatively small paper or cardboard fiche or catalogue cards. Terminologists working at Infoterm and in similar environments developed a system of two-letter codes (ISO 639 Set 1) as identifiers for a relatively limited set of "familiar" languages. Even with the best of intentions, this collection was nonetheless limited to the number of languages it could accommodate because of the simple mathematical principle afforded by the possible arithmetic permutations of the number "2" coupled with the 26 letters of the Latin alphabet. The alpha-2 identifiers were the first to be standardized, and they set the base width for language identifier fields in many legacy computing environments.

Librarians, both at the US Library of Congress and across Europe, were confronted with a broader collection of languages than required by the early terminologists. Viewed from the mathematical perspective, their three-letter-code solution immediately provides for a broader range of values and became the current ISO 639, Set 2. The introduction of this new collection caused some consternation, particularly in the computing community. First of all, the introduction of three-letter codes was problematic for systems built on two-character data fields. Needless to say, cries against expansion of the two-letter codes as an alternative were met with the logical admonition "to do the math". A further complication involves the presence of several instances of ambiguity: the original LoC designators were developed for use in English in the United States, with a resulting set of mnemonic codes that reference the English names for languages, a practice that is countered in the European library community with parallel identifiers specified mnemonically according to the native-language name for those languages. There are 21 of these items, referred to as the *Bibliographic* (B) and the *Terminological* (T) codes, with the latter preferred for non-bibliographical purposes. For instance, B identifiers *fre, ger,* and *spa* correspond to T counterparts *fra, deu,* and *esp* for French (français), German (Deutsch), and Spanish (español), respectively.

Although 639 Set 2 is not necessarily limited by numerical permutations, it imposes its own constraints in that it comprises identifiers for languages for which "a significant body of literature" exists. The requirements for requesting a new code specify the holding of at least 50 documents in the language by one to five "agencies" (ISO 639). This stipulation rules out the inclusion of spoken languages without any tradition of written literature, and actually poses the danger of becoming a Catch-22 clause in an environment where it becomes increasingly difficult to publish anything without assigning a language identifier to it, a factor of particular concern in web environments.

ISO Set 2 also includes a number of so-called "collective language identifiers" designed for assignment to documents in language groups "where a relatively small number of documents exist or are expected to be written, recorded or created". ISO 639 Set 5 represents a refinement of sorts of this approach by providing a segregated list of Alpha-3 identifiers for language families and groups, which provides broad classifiers for languages that did not have their own three letter identifiers in Set 2 or for which it is sometimes expedient to cite related sublanguages as an aggregate. While this approach might work for library collections, it can cause sincere distress when the identifier is used to classify, for instance, the mother tongue of school children when a family finds itself classified with a designator that would more properly refer to a despised ethnic rival language.

Another concept introduced with respect to 639 Set 2 is the notion of the "macrolanguage", with Arabic cited as a primary example. In this case, the macro-language designation reflects the overriding notion of Arabic, both the classical language of the Koran and so-called Modern Standard Arabic (MSA, *al-fusha*), being the common language across the Arabic-speaking region, in much the same way that standard German is a common language in an essentially diglossic area where everyone speaks both the "high" form of the literary and school language, as well as their own local dialect. An essential difference here, however, is that High German is indeed mastered, written, and spoken by the vast majority of individuals identified as German speakers. MSA in contrast is a written language that is not really spoken and that is not mastered outside the ranks of the highly educated, while the spoken vernaculars are many and varied across the region. The upshot of these concerns is that collective and macrolanguages must be carefully scrutinized on an individual basis when using the identifiers for pragmatic applications.

Whereas the first two sets of identifiers in ISO 639 included major world languages used in technical publications requiring terminological documentation or that have significant bodies of catalogable literature, Set 3 continues the three-letter identifier tradition with the intent to "support a large number of the languages that are known to have ever existed". Administered by SIL International, the collection treats languages living, dead, and endangered. In contrast to the earlier, shorter standards, which published their full identifier sets "on paper", Part 3 is backed up by the substantial Ethnologue database, which includes data fields documenting the population of language speakers, geographical location, language maps showing geographic distribution, status, classification, dialects, use, resources, writing system, and other comments. With the exception of the language family designators, the three sets are configured such that Sets 1 and 2 are subsets of Set 3.

As illustrated, the ISO language identifiers combine with other related standards to form locale-specific two-or multi-part language tags that reflect geographical varieties. From the outset, the original ISO 639-1 already provided for regional encoding by combining the Alpha-2 language codes with Alpha-2 country codes taken from ISO 3166-1, yielding the example: *elevator (en-US), lift (en-GB)*. In like manner, 639-2 specified the combinatory pattern: spool of thread (eng-US), bobbin of cotton (eng-GB). Obviously, this principle informs the generation of more complex language identifiers and CLDR notations, as outlined previously.

IETF RFC 1766 (1995), *Tags for the Identification of Languages* (Alvastrand), specified the use of a language tag consisting of either a two-letter language code or the five-character locale string (ex.: en-GB) suggested in the original 639-1. Already RFC 1766 allowed for the expansion of the language code to include not only the country code but also dialect or variety information, codes for languages not listed in 639-1, and script variations. At that time, anyone wishing to use a language identifier for any language not present in the then valid 639-1 could apply to the Internet Assigned Numbers Authority to receive an alpha-3 code that could be used for this purpose. When 639-3 (2007) was adopted, all extra IANA assigned three-letter codes rolled over to 639-3 identifiers. This initial IETF language tag standard specified the values used for the SGML *lang* attribute (Standard Generalized Markup Language, the parent standard that has spawned both HTML and XML).

In February 1998 the World Wide Web Consortium published the first edition of the Extensible Markup Language (XML) standard, which specified that the *xml:lang* attribute shall be used to identify language information in XML documents, citing IETF 1766. The present Fifth Edition was updated in February 2013 to comply with the currently valid version of the IETF language tag standard, now referenced as BCP 47, which has replaced all previous versions of the document. BCP 47 is a stable designation for the IETF's language tag standard. As shown, according to this version of the standard, the language tags can become quite complicated (and expressive) and can cover a wide range of applications and scenarios. It also provides rules for negotiating the alpha-2/alpha-3 anomaly in order to protect legacy data while at the same time facilitating the use of the newer three-letter codes specifically for languages and countries that do not have two-letter codes.

The value assigned to the *lang* attribute is scaffolded, so that simple language codes (for instance, *ja* for Japanese) are used as the language tag if they are never ambiguous, but locale identifiers comprising language and country codes are used to designate regional language varieties within the same language family. For example, the attribute <. . . lang="en-UK"> is used in headers or within the body of documents to identify the locale or language of a current document, but <. . . hreflang ="en-UK"> is generally used in localization environments to indicate the language and locale of a targeted URI in order to support search engine optimization (SEO).

The Unicode Common Locale Data Repository (CLDR) is based on Unicode's UTS # 35 Locale Data Markup Language (Unicode LDML), which is designed for the interchange of locale data. The CLDR provides a broad range of information designed to supply software applications with machine-parsable data associated with different languages and regions, such as formatting and parsing for language and country names, dates, times, numbers, and currency values; scripts used with specific languages; pluralization rules, language-specific collation, writing direction and transliteration rules; calendar preference, postal and telephone codes, and much more. Selected sets of relevant information can be downloaded from the Unicode website in LDML format free of charge and can be accessed via GitHub utilities (Unicode October 2022a).

Indigenous Languages and Languages of Limited Distribution

Oblique to and in many cases, before, the rigorous and formal procedures introduced by ISO, IETF, and the CLDR, various entities over the years launched efforts to list and codify languages, including indigenous languages (See Figure 36.4). Although much of this work is still accessible, active maintenance has in any cases ceased, producing accessible, but static and outdated repositories.

"Voluntary transnational researchers" working under the auspices, sequentially, of Linguasphere and the Observatoire linguistique, developed

- ISO 639-6, 2009, *Codes for the Representation of Names of Languages – Part 6: Alpha-4 Code for Comprehensive Coverage of Language Variants*

This document attempted to describe procedures for documenting Alpha-4 codes representing dialects and varieties, but has been withdrawn due to complaints that the data were not always accurate (Linguasphere 1998, 2018).

At one time, the *Research Data Alliance Working Group on Standardisation of Data Categories and Codes* launched an effort to expand codes for the identification of languages and language varieties, together with categories for describing the content of resources, but it is not apparent that they have made significant progress in the meantime (Musgrave 2014).

The Linguists List MultiTree resource, which provided an intriguing view of both ancient and modern language families and relations, still displays valuable but dated information. However, the interactive language trees that were once served up are no longer accessible due to lack of funding to upgrade the complicated system to modern programming environments (http://multitree.org/).

The Open Language Archives Community (OLAC), an international partnership of institutions and individuals created a worldwide virtual library of language resources (closely affiliated with the Linguists List), attempted a system for tagging syntax for use in encoding both the language of a document and the language discussed in a document using 639 Set 3 identifiers together with Linguist List extensions, as specified in: www.language-archives.org/REC/language.html. This system has not been updated since 2008.

Glottolog 4.5 was created originally by the Max Plank Institute Psycholinguistics, Nijmegen, with the goal of maintaining a comprehensive reference resource for the world's languages, especially the lesser-known languages. The currently available system represents a now familiar theme: a once active system exists now as a static resource that is no longer updated (https://glottolog.org/).

The *Digital Endangered Languages and Musics Archives Network* (DELAMAN) is an international network of archives of data on linguistic and cultural diversity, in particular for small languages and cultures under pressure. Unlike some of the earlier efforts to archive information in a central repository, DELAMAN is configured as an advisory body and clearing house for groups working on their own to collect, archive, and potentially digitize linguistic and cultural resources (www.delaman.org/).

UNESCO, in response to issues involving languages of limited distribution (LLD), has declared the period 2022–2023 the International Decade of Indigenous Languages, with a goal of identifying, preserving, and empowering indigenous peoples to preserve their languages and cultures. In response, the *Translation Commons Language Digitization Initiative* (https://translation-commons.org) has responded with an international effort to provide support for the digitization of languages so that speakers can access tools for implementing their languages in computerized and web environments. So far the LDI group of volunteer linguists and computer specialists has created a number of guidelines under the rubric *0 to Digital* designed to enable speakers of indigenous languages and their supporters to create scripts and fonts (where necessary), facilitate their digitization, implement keyboards, and achieve other aspects of the digitization process so that they can produce and read texts in their languages using their unique scripts.

Unlike earlier efforts that proposed identifiers and attempted central repositories, DELAMAN and Translation Commons endeavor to support the creation of digital archives in the relevant communities, which often starts by helping them register new identifiers in existing ISO or IANA systems so that the new languages can function via the CLDR.

Against this background, ISO TC37/SC 2 is introducing the three-part ISO 21636 family of standards under the title: *Language Coding – A Framework for Language Varieties* with Part 1: Terminology, Part 2: Description of the Framework, and Part 3: Implementation. The core of the framework proposes eight dimensions of linguistic variation: space (essentially geographic), time, social group, medium (e.g. spoken, written, signed), situation, individual speaker, proficiency, and communicative function. The goal is not to create a new registry as much as to provide a framework for identifying dialects and varieties within existing resources, such as IANA.

Definition of key terms (Definitions reflect wording in the new ISO 639.)

human language   means of communication characterized by a systematic use of sounds, visual-spatial signs (by movements or gestures), characters or other written symbols or signs that can be combined to express or communicate meaning or a message between humans (Clause 3.1.1)

language variety   largest subset of an individual language that is internally consistent with regard to both an external criterion for linguistic variation and a structural criterion for linguistic variation, and that can be identified and named (3.2.4)

dialect   language variety specific to speakers from a given location or region (3.2.5)

language code   code that maps individual languages or language groups, represented by their unique language reference name, to language identifiers (3.7.3)

language identifier   string of characters assigned to an individual language or a language group for the purpose of identifying it uniquely (3.7.10)

language tag   sequence of one or more subtags indicating a language indicator, plus optionally a subtag or subtags indicating, for example, script, region (locale), variant or other possible details describing a language or group of languages

Note: The *lang* attribute specifies language tags in HTML and the *xml:lang* attribute specifies them for XML. (See W3C Internationalization, *Language Tags in HTML and XML*, www. w3.org/International/articles/language-tags/)

locale   unique combination of parameters consisting at a minimum of identifiers for a language and a region

Note: Optionally, a locale tag or ID can also specify the other cultural, administrative or technical preferences of a given community (ISO 22274:2013, 3.20)

macrolanguage   individual language that for the purpose of language coding may be subdivided into two or more other individual languages (ISO 639-4, 3.1.1)

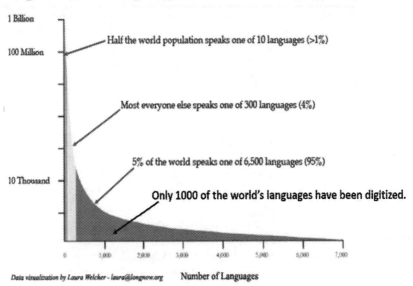

Indigenous Languages and the Long Tail

Figure 36.4   The long tail of endangered languages (Buszard-Welcher)

Notes

1 The Wikipedia entry http://en.wikipedia.org/wiki/A_language_is_a_dialect_with_an_army_and_navy points to the many varied versions of this statement and its uncertain provenance.

2 ISO standards are available as downloadable PDF files for purchase from the ISO Store, www.iso.org/iso/home/store.htm, or from national standards bodies. As noted, however, specific language identifier, country code, and language tag information is available online at the official web addresses cited in the bibliography. Users should be cautioned to seek out official websites because the many secondary postings found online are frequently outdated or otherwise incorrect or incomplete. The new ISO 639 consolidates the standards framework for the three sets, but users should reference the online resources for information on specific identifiers.

Bibliography

Buszard-Welcher, Laura. 'The Long Tail'. Available at: www.longnow.org. Last accessed 12 January 2023.

Constable, Peter (2002a) 'An Analysis of ISO 639: Preparing the Way for Advancements in Language Identification Standards', *SIL International*. Available at: www.sil.org/resources/publications/entry/7847.

Constable, Peter (2002b) 'Toward a Model for Language Identification: Defining an Ontology of Language-related Categories SIL Electronic Working Papers', *SIL International*. Available at: www-01.sil.org/silewp/abstract.asp?ref=2002-003.

Constable, Peter and Gary Simons (2000) 'Language Identification and IT: Addressing Problems of Linguistic Diversity on a Global Scale', *SIL International*. Available at: www-01.sil.org/silewp/2000/001/SILEWP2000-001.pdf.

Google. 'Google Web Interface and Search Language Codes'. Available at: https://developers.google.com/admin-sdk/directory/v1/languages.

Göttert, Karl Heinz (2010) *Deutsch: Biografie einer Sprache*, Berlin: Ullstein Verlag.

IETF. (2009) 'BCP (Best Common Practices) 47', *IETF*. Available at: https://tools.ietf.org/search/bcp47.

ISO 639 (2022) *Code for the Representation of Individual Languages and Language Groups – Part 4: General Principles, Rules and Guidelines*. Geneva: ISO (In process, to replace ISO 639, Parts 1–3 and 5).

ISO 15924 (2022) *Information and Documentation – Codes for the Representation of Names of Scripts*, Geneva: ISO.

ISO 22274 (2013) *Systems to Manage Terminology, Knowledge and Content – Concept-Related Aspects for Developing and Internationalizing Classification Systems*, Geneva: ISO.

ISO 3166-1 (2020) *Codes for the Representation of Names of Countries and Their Subdivisions – Part 1: Country Codes; Part 2: Country Subdivision Code, and Part 3: Code for Formerly Used Names of Countries*, Geneva: ISO.

Linguasphere (1998, 2018) 'The Linguasphere Register of the World's Languages and Speech Communities'. Available at: www.linguasphere.info/jr/index.php?l1=home&l2=welcome.

LoC. 'MARC Code List for Languages'. Available at: www.loc.gov/marc/languages/.

Microsoft (2021, June 21) '[MS-LCID]: Windows Language Code Identifier (LCID) Reference'. Available at: https://docs.microsoft.com/en-us/openspecs/windows_protocols/ms-lcid/70feba9f-294e-491e-b6eb-56532684c37f.

Musgrave, Simon (2014) 'Improving Access to Recorded Language Data'. *D-Lib Magazine*, 20(1/2). http://doi.org/10.1045/january2014-musgrave.

Unicode (2015) 'UTS #35: Unicode Locale Data Markup Language (LDML)'. Available at: www.unicode.org/reports/tr35/.

Unicode (2022a, October) 'CLDR Release 41'. Available at: https://github.com/unicode-org/cldr/tree/release-41.

Unicode (2022b, May) 'Unicode Standard'. Available at: https://home.unicode.org/unicode-cldr-version-41-released/.

W3C (2008) 'An Introduction to Multilingual Web Addresses'. Available at: www.w3.org/International/articles/idn-and-iri/.

W3C (2013) 'HTML <link> hreflang Attribute'. Available at: www.w3schools.com/tags/att_link_hreflang.asp.

W3C (2013) 'Internationalization Tag Set (ITS) Version 2.0'. W3C Recommendation 29 October 2013. Available at: www.w3.org/TR/its20/.

37

LOCALIZATION

Keiran J. Dunne

Localization is an umbrella term that refers to the processes whereby digital content and products developed in one locale are adapted for sale and use in one or more other locales. Although the term 'localization' has been in use since the early 1980s, confusion persists as to what exactly it means. To understand localization, it is necessary to consider when, why and how it arose; the ways it has changed over time; and its relationship to translation and internationalization. Thus, this chapter will examine localization and its evolution from the 1980s to present.

The practice of translation remained relatively unchanged from the dawn of writing until the commoditization of the PC and the advent of mass market software ushered in the digital revolution in the 1980s. As increasing numbers of computers appeared in homes and business offices, 'typical users were no longer professional computer programmers, software engineers or hardware engineers' (Uren *et al.* 1993: ix). US-based software companies quickly realized that by developing products such as spreadsheet programs and word processors that average people could use for work or leisure, they could sell to a vastly larger potential market. Targeting average users instead of computer professionals was not without challenges, however.

> While experienced professionals had become adept in detecting bugs and working around them, the new users expected, indeed demanded, that they software they bought operate exactly as described in the manuals. Benign acceptance of anomalies in the operation of software could no longer be tolerated.
>
> *(Uren et al. 1993: x)*

Initial efforts by software publishers to develop this embryonic mass market thus focused on improving software reliability and user-friendliness.

US-based software companies soon broadened the scope of their marketing efforts beyond the domestic market to target international users. Expansion into international markets required that software publishers offer products in languages other than English. 'For a software product to have wide market acceptance in an non-English-speaking environment, it was essential to convert the software so that users saw a product in their own language and firmly based in their own culture' (Uren *et al.* 1993: x). Software publishers thought that adapting their products for international markets was merely a matter of 'translating' software. As a result, initial attempts to adapt software for international users were characterized as 'translation on the computer for the

DOI: 10.4324/9781003168348-40

computer' (van der Meer 1995). However, it soon became clear to practitioners that this work was 'related to, but different from and more involved than, translation' (Lieu 1997). Indeed, the scope of the undertaking was not confined to translation of text in the user interface but rather encompassed all target market requirements for culturally dependent representation of data, including but not limited to the following:[1]

- character sets, scripts and glyphs for the representation of various writing systems
- encodings to enable the storage, retrieval and manipulation of multilingual data
- text comparison, searching and sorting (collation)
- line and word breaking
- calendars (e.g. Buddhist, Coptic, Gregorian, Hebrew lunar, Hijri, Japanese Emperor Year, Julian, Year of the Republic of China and Tangun Era calendars)
- date formats (MM/DD/YYYY, DD/MM/YYYY, YYYY-MM-DD, etc.; for example, 5/11/2014 would be read as May 11, 2014, in the United States but as November 5, 2014, in Italy)
- time formats (12-hour vs. 24-hour clock; use of AM and PM)
- number formats, digit groupings and decimal separators (period vs. comma)
- paper sizes (A3, A4, legal, letter)
- units of measurement (metric vs. imperial)

In software engineering, these local market requirements are referred to using the hypernym 'locale'. Locales are expressed as language-country pairs. Thus, 'French-Canada is one locale, while French-France is another' (Cadieux and Esselink 2002). The need to account not only for translation but also for 'locale' explains why and how the process of adapting software for international markets came to be known as 'localization' in the early 1980s. The scope and scale of this new activity expanded so rapidly that within less than a decade localization was perceived as an industry unto itself, as reflected by the creation of the Localization Industry Standards Association in 1990 (Lommel 2007: 7).

The costs of adapting software products for other locales seemed like a small price to pay given the sizable international markets and potential revenues to which localized products could enable access. Software publishers approached localization in different ways: some performed the work using in-house teams, and some outsourced the work to specialized service providers, whereas others assigned responsibility for localization to in-country subsidiaries or distributors (Esselink 2003b: 4). Despite the ostensible differences between these approaches, they all shared one fundamental characteristic: in each case localization was performed apart from, and subsequent to, the development of the original, domestic-market products. 'This separation of development and localization proved troublesome in many respects', observes Esselink (2003b: 4).

First, the software provided to localization teams often could not be localized because it lacked certain fundamental capabilities, such as the ability to display target-language scripts and writing systems. In such cases, the localization teams had to send the software back to the development teams for implementation of the necessary capabilities, such as support for the display of Asian languages or of right-to-left scripts for languages such as Arabic and Hebrew. Second, translatable text was typically embedded in the software source code. Identifying and locating translatable text was very difficult for localization teams that had not participated in the development of the software (see Figure 37.1). Finally, and perhaps most critically, localization required that changes be made directly to the source code of the software. To understand why and how working directly in source code caused problems, it is important to note that software source code is the raw material from which the running copy of a program is created. In other words, source code must be compiled, or built, into a machine-readable (binary) executable file, which in turn must be tested (and debugged, if any bugs are found) before the software can be released for use (see Figure 37.2).

```
IDD_PEN_WIDTHS DIALOG  0, 0, 203, 65
STYLE DS_SETFONT | DS_MODALFRAME | WS_POPUP | WS_VISIBLE | WS_CAPTION |
    WS_SYSMENU
CAPTION "Pen Widths"
FONT 8, "MS Sans Serif"
BEGIN
    DEFPUSHBUTTON    "OK",IDOK,148,7,50,14
    PUSHBUTTON       "Cancel",IDCANCEL,148,24,50,14
    PUSHBUTTON       "Default",IDC_DEFAULT_PEN_WIDTHS,148,41,50,14
    LTEXT            "Thin Pen Width:",IDC_STATIC,10,12,70,10
    LTEXT            "Thick Pen Width:",IDC_STATIC,10,33,70,10
    EDITTEXT         IDC_THIN_PEN_WIDTH,86,12,40,13,ES_AUTOHSCROLL
    EDITTEXT         IDC_THICK_PEN_WIDTH,86,33,40,13,ES_AUTOHSCROLL
END
```

Figure 37.1   Source-code representation of the dialog box shown in Figure 37.5a

Identifying translatable text can be difficult for non-programmers. In the example shown in Figure 37.1, items in quotation marks are translatable except for the name of the default font (MS Sans Serif). Each group of four digits separated by commas represents layout coordinates.

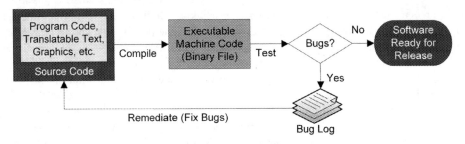

Figure 37.2   Because source code must be compiled and tested anew whenever it is modified, localizing directly in source code is labor intensive

Working directly in source code had profound ramifications for localization. Indeed, the adaptation of software products for other locales did not merely entail a few changes to compiled, tested and debugged versions of programs that had already been released to the domestic market. Instead, localization of a given program required that a separate set of source code be maintained and that a different executable be compiled, tested and debugged for each target locale. Consequently, creating N localized versions of a program required that the publisher maintain N + 1 sets of source code: one for each target locale plus one for the domestic market. In addition, each set of source code had to be localized, compiled, tested, debugged, updated and managed separately (Luong *et al.* 1995: 3). For instance, a US-based publisher that wanted to market a product in three international locales, such as German-Germany, French-France and Japanese-Japan, was required to manage four different versions of source code in parallel, one set for the domestic English-United States locale plus one set for each of the three international locales (see Figure 37.3). The process of compiling and testing localized software products as distinct from source-locale versions is called localization engineering (Esselink 2002).

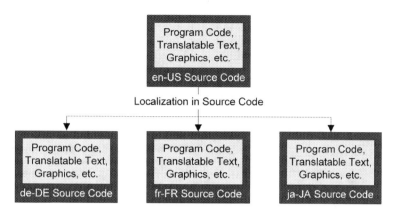

Figure 37.3   When localization is performed in the source code, it is necessary to maintain a separate set of code for each target locale plus one set for the domestic market

Creating, maintaining and supporting multiple localized versions in parallel proved time-consuming and expensive. Testing and debugging software was inherently labor intensive and costly even without adding localization as a variable. Seminal work on software engineering economics by Boehm had demonstrated that 'uncorrected errors become exponentially more costly with each phase in which they are unresolved' (1981: 8). The exponential cost increase of error correction was exacerbated by the *post hoc* approach to localization in which the adaptation of software for other locales – and thus the discovery of localization bugs – did not begin until the development of the domestic-market versions had been completed. This cost multiplier problem was compounded by the management of a distinct set of source code for each target locale, since a bug discovered in one set of code might need to be fixed in all other sets. Indeed, localization engineering has traditionally involved 'quite a bit of bug fixing', as Esselink observes (2002: 4). Not surprisingly, complexity soon established itself as a hallmark of localization (Esselink 2000b). Ultimately, most of the problems posed by early localization efforts stemmed from a single root cause: the failure to effectively plan for the re-use of software source code across multiple locales.[2]

Most software and hardware companies that made forays into international markets quickly concluded that localization and translation were not an integral part of their business. As Esselink (2000a: 5) observes, '[t]he increasing size and complexity of localization projects soon forced companies to an outsourcing model. Most software publishers simply did not have the time, knowledge or resources to manage multilingual translation or localization projects'. As a result, most companies decided that it would be more efficient to outsource the adaptation of software products for international markets to external language service providers as project work. In addition to the adaptation of the software application, a typical software localization project might also involve the translation and/or adaptation of various other components such as sample files, demos and tutorials, Help systems and printed and online user documentation, as well as marketing collateral (see Figure 37.4). The fact that these components were authored in a variety of digital formats, some of which needed to be compiled and tested prior to release, meant that localization involved a number of new forms of work in addition to traditional translation, including software and online Help engineering and testing, conversion of documentation to different formats, translation memory creation and management, as well as project management (Esselink 2000b; Esselink 2003a: 69; Dunne and Dunne 2011). Localization thus required that translators possess strong instrumental and technical skills in addition to traditional translation and domain expertise. 'Throughout the 1990s, the localization industry tried to turn translators into semi-engineers', recalls Esselink (2003b: 7).

Figure 37.4   The scope of a traditional software localization project may encompass a number of components in addition to the software application itself

Source: Adapted from Esselink 2000a: 10

Outsourcing shifted the challenges of managing complex multilingual localization projects to external service providers but did not address the fundamental problem of the duplication of effort required to manage multiple sets of source code in parallel. Faced with the challenge of controlling the complexity and cost of the localization process, software publishers in the late 1980s and early 1990s began to realize that 'certain steps could be performed in advance to make localization easier: separating translatable text strings from the executable code, for example. This was referred to as *internationalization* or *localization-enablement*' (Cadieux and Esselink 2002). Internationalization is an engineering process that precedes localization and entails the separation of '[a]ll the culturally and linguistically sensitive software components . . . from the core of the application' (Hall 1999: 298). In practice, the scope of internationalization is typically confined to the linguistic and culturally dependent contents of the user interface that may require adaptation, which are collectively designated using the hypernym 'resources'. When a piece of software is properly internationalized, '[t]here is no programming code in the [resources] nor is there any [translatable] text in the program code' (Uren *et al.* 1993: 60). Resources in a typical desktop software application may include the following:

- Accelerators: keyboard shortcuts that enable direct execution of commands. Accelerators are typically associated with a function key or with a combination of the Ctrl key plus a specific keyboard letter. For example, pressing the F1 function key in a typical Windows application launches the Help, while pressing Ctrl+C executes the Copy command.
- Dialog boxes: secondary windows that allow the user to perform a command and/or that ask the user to supply additional information (see Figure 37.5a). Common examples include the 'Save As' and 'Print' dialog boxes. Dialog box resources also contain the coordinates that govern the layout and display of the user interface (see Figure 37.1).
- Icons: images that symbolize and provide clickable shortcuts to programs, files and devices (see Figure 37.5b1 and 37.5b2).
- Menus: lists of options or commands that display at the top of the main program window (see Figure 37.5c). Secondary menus, called 'context' or 'popup' menus, display when the user clicks the right-hand mouse button.

- String tables: 'string' is short for 'string of characters', and designates any text that is stored and manipulated as a group. Strings include button captions, dialog box titles, error messages, menu items, tool tips and so on. Menu and dialog box strings can often be visually represented in a what you see is what you get (WYSIWYG) editor during localization, whereas string tables typically cannot (see Figure 37.5d).

- Toolbars: raster graphics that contain toolbar button images, typically in bitmap (*.bmp) or Portable Network Graphics (*.png) format (see Figure 37.5e).

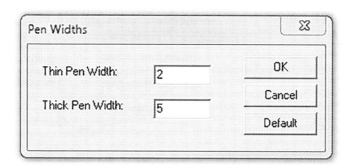

(a)

(b1) **(b2)** **(c)**

Value	Caption
57632	Erase the selection\nErase
57633	Clears the drawing
57634	Copy the selection and put it on the Clipboard\nCopy
57635	Cut the selection and put it on the Clipboard\nCut
57636	Find the specified text\nFind
57637	Insert Clipboard contents\nPaste
57640	Repeat the last action\nRepeat

(d) **(e)**

Figure 37.5 Typical resources in a software application include (a) one or more dialog boxes, (b) a program icon and a document icon (left and right images, respectively), (c) one or more menus, (d) a string table and (e) one or more toolbars.[3] See also Figures 37.8 and 37.9

The creation of a standardized way to represent culturally dependent user interface material and store it independently from the functional program code greatly facilitated the localization process. No longer was it necessary to modify the source code or to compile, test and debug each target version of a program separately (Luong *et al.* 1995: 3). Instead, the development team could simply extract the resources from the binary executable file, provide them to a localization team that would translate the text and perform all other necessary modifications and then return the target resources to the developers, who would integrate them into copies of the binary executable file to create the necessary target version or versions (see Figure 37.6). This extraction-adaptation-integration process is one of the defining characteristics of localization.

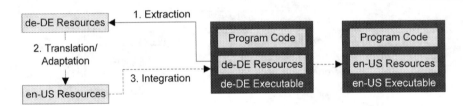

Figure 37.6   Internationalization enables the logical separation of the culturally dependent contents of the user interface from the functional core of the program, transforming localization into a simpler process of resource replacement

By enabling the use of a single set of source code to support multiple target locales, internationalization diminished the effort and cost associated with localization and increased the speed and accuracy with which it can be accomplished (Schmitz 2007: 51). It soon occurred to software developers that they could not only embed resources in a program's executable file and bind them directly to the application code but also externalize the resources, store them in a dedicated file called a satellite assembly and dynamically link this external resource file to the application. To localize an application developed using this internationalization strategy, one simply creates a localized version of the resource file(s) for each target locale. For example, a publisher that created a program for the German-Germany locale and wanted to market localized versions in the United States and the People's Republic of China would create a localized version of the resource assembly for each locale (see Figure 37.7).

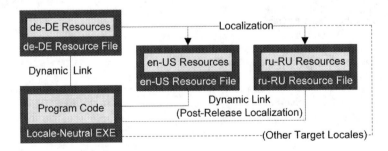

Figure 37.7   Externalizing resources, storing them in dedicated files and linking them dynamically to a locale-neutral program core is the logical culmination of software internationalization strategies

The advent of software internationalization coincided with, and was facilitated by, the broad shift from procedural and structured programming to object-oriented programming in the 1980s and the 1990s. Procedural and structured programming languages, which predominated during the 1960s and 1970s, were adequate for small, relatively simple standalone applications. However, as applications expanded in terms of size, complexity and the degree of interaction with other systems, procedural and structured languages began to show their limitations (Clark 2013: 2–5). The larger a program became, the harder it was to maintain, and it was difficult to modify one aspect of existing functionality without negatively impacting the system as a whole. Programmers needed a comprehensive understanding of how a program worked and could not focus their efforts on discrete functions. In addition, the absence of standardized notational ways to represent and encode functions hindered the portability and reusability of software's source code, with the result that programs were typically built from scratch.

Object-oriented programming effectively resolved these problems. In object-oriented programming, data and functions that use those data are grouped and encapsulated in logical structures named objects. One object's encapsulated data and functions can be used, or invoked, by other functions or programs. Communication between objects in a program is carried out through messages. An object's interface is defined by the messages that it can send and receive. In object-oriented programming, sending a message to an object is also called setting a property of that object. Objects are defined by classes, which determine their code, data and the messages they can send and receive (i.e. their properties). Individual objects inherit all of the properties and functions of the class to which they belong. Inheritance enables the creation of 'child' objects and subclasses that inherit all of the properties and functions of the original class of the 'parent' object. Inheritance facilitates software maintenance, updates and debugging because a change made to one instance of an object is applied to all instances of objects in that class. Objects can also be reused in and across programs, which simplifies the development of new programs.

Object-oriented programs are not written but rather drawn in integrated WYSIWYG development environments using a variety of objects including menus, dialog boxes; forms; and user controls such as command buttons, check boxes and text labels, among others. From the standpoint of object-oriented programming, internationalization standardizes the representation, definition and storage of the inventory of user interface objects as classes of resources. It follows that localization is properly understood as the modification of the properties of objects. For example, translating a command button caption entails the modification of the Caption property of the Button object (see Figure 37.8).

Internationalization not only eliminated the need to maintain a separate set of source code for each supported locale but also clarified the respective roles of programmers, engineers and translators.

> [Internationalization] allows programmers and engineers to focus on code and translators to focus on translation. It means the software with all its complex logic does not have to be touched just because you want to add another language; all you have to do is translate some files.
>
> *(Uren et al. 1993: 63)*

Indeed, most locale-dependent aspects of data storage, retrieval, manipulation and presentation can be managed today through internationalization capabilities built into host operating systems and/or by using development frameworks and runtime environments that offer robust support for internationalization, such as Java (Deitsch and Czarneki 2001) or Microsoft's .NET Framework (Smith-Ferrier 2007). If a program has been properly internationalized and all translatable text has been externalized from the source code, the localizer works only on resource files and cannot access or modify the program's functional code. Consequently, the nuts-and-bolts work of software localization now primarily involves the translation of strings in menus,

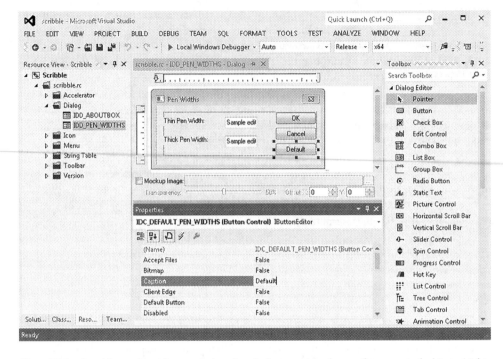

Figure 37.8 An object-oriented program interface is drawn using classes of user control objects (right-hand pane), composite interface objects are defined and stored as resources (left-hand pane); localization of object-oriented software is properly understood as the modification of the properties of objects, such as the command button caption 'Default' (upper and lower middle panes)

dialog boxes and string tables. Dialog boxes and user controls such as buttons and labels may also require resizing to account for translation-related string expansion or shrinkage, depending on the source and target languages involved. Visual localization tools facilitate these tasks by enable localizers to view resources in context and by enabling them to use translation memory and terminology databases as they work (see Figure 37.9).

Internationalization and the use of satellite resource files allow software publishers to proactively address potential locale-related problems during the software development process, well in advance of localization. This state of affairs begs the question of how – and perhaps even if – localization differs from translation today. The fact that the translation of strings makes up the bulk of the work in current practice suggests that the term 'localization' has come full circle and once again essentially means 'translation on the computer, for the computer'. The blurring of the boundaries between translation and localization can also be seen as evidence of a convergence of these processes as authoring and publishing undergo an evolution similar to that of software localization (Esselink 2003b).

Authoring and publishing were generally separate processes and professions until the 1980s and 1990s, when the advent of digital authoring tools such as word processors turned authors into desktop publishers who were able not only to create digital content but also to control the manner of its presentation (Rockley *et al.* 2003: 165). However, the desktop- and document-based approach to authoring and publishing hindered content reuse in much the same way as early localization efforts that required modifications to source code. Repurposing content stored

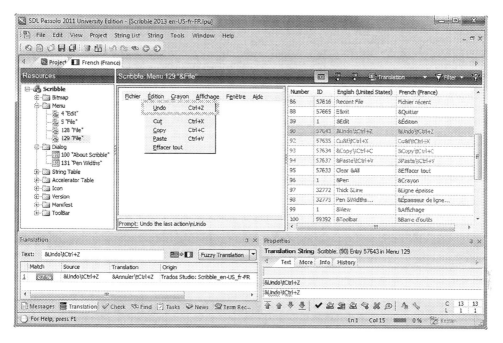

Figure 37.9 Localization of a sample application named Scribble using a visual localization tool. The left-hand pane displays the resource tree, the middle pane displays the selected resource in WYSIWYG mode and the right-hand pane displays the corresponding source and target strings in tabular format

in documents created using word processors and other traditional desktop publishing software is generally a labor-intensive, manual process. A common rule of thumb is that technical communicators who use word processors and document-based authoring tools spend as much as half of their time formatting documents (e.g. Bartlett 1998). 'To reuse the content, authors must apply formatting that is appropriate for each output. Stripping and reapplying formatting is tricky and usually not 100% effective. Format conversions always require correction by hand or complicated scripting' (Rockley *et al.* 2003: 165). Further complicating content reuse efforts was the need to manage multiple versions of document source files in parallel. Practitioners soon discovered that file management and version control become exponentially more complex as the number of parallel versions of source files and the number of target language increase. These problems were exacerbated by the Web and its widespread adoption as an enterprise communication platform. Desktop-based authoring and publishing could not keep up with the speed of change on the Web, nor could it meet demand for content in an increasingly wide range of formats for use on an expanding array of devices, from PCs and laptops to PDAs, tablets and smart phones.

The challenges of document-based content reuse were very similar to those associated with early software localization efforts. Thus it is perhaps unsurprising that the strategies adopted to facilitate content reuse are very similar to strategies developed to facilitate software localization. Just as internalization simplified localization by logically separating the culturally and linguistically dependent aspects of the user interface from the functional core of a program, content reuse strategies are predicated on the separation of content from presentation. This approach is called *single sourcing*: 'Single sourcing implies that there is a single source for content; content is written once, stored in a single source location, and reused many times' (Rockley *et al.* 2003: 15).

The implementation of single sourcing typically involves eXtensible Markup Language (XML)-based authoring strategies (Savourel 2001: 7; Rockley *et al.* 2003: 159–71). XML is a meta-markup language that provides a universal, application-independent mechanism for representing text in a structured format. XML was created in response to the challenges of content reuse associated with large-scale digital publishing. As stated in a December 1997 World Wide Web Consortium Press release announcing the publication of version 1.0 of XML as a proposed recommendation,

> XML is primarily intended to meet the requirements of large-scale Web content providers for industry-specific markup, vendor-neutral data exchange, media-independent publishing, one-on-one marketing, workflow management in collaborative authoring environments, and the processing of Web documents by intelligent clients.
>
> *(W3C 1997)*

Whereas HTML is a presentational markup language that specifies how content should be displayed, XML is a semantic markup language that specifies what content means. Because XML provides a structured, semantic representation of content and does not focus on the presentational aspects of document, authoring of content in XML is often referred to as *structured authoring*. Formatting of XML in documents is specified by style directives stored in separate files and applied dynamically in response to user demand. In this way, the same content can be processed and output in any format for which the organization has a defined set of style rules, such as webpages (HTML), PDF documents and Word documents, as well as Eclipse Help, HTML Help, Java Help and WebHelp, to cite but a few examples. Today, the single sourcing of technical and procedural documentation is often implemented using the XML-based Darwin Information Typing Architecture (DITA) standard (Bellamy *et al.* 2012).

The implementation of single sourcing also often involves the use of content management systems (Rockley *et al.* 2003: 178–91), which are centralized, server-based repositories 'designed to manage "information chunks" (generically known as "content"), usually no longer than a couple of paragraphs' (Biau Gil and Pym 2006: 11). Information chunks, such as DITA topics, are dynamically assembled into documents in response to user requests, typically via a web interface. As is the case with XML-based authoring, content stored in a content management system (CMS) can generally be output in various formats.

Single sourcing, structured authoring and 'chunking' can be thought of as applications of the concepts of object orientation and internationalization in the fields of authoring and publishing. Once written, a given information object can be reused systematically; once translated, the target language versions of that same information object can also be reused systematically. Because content is separated from form, it can be processed using as many different style directives as needed to publish it in the desired output formats (e.g. print, help, web and mobile devices) without having to modify the content. Just as object orientation and internationalization facilitated the modularization and reuse of software, single sourcing, structured authoring and chunking facilitate the modularization and reuse of content.

Translation of XML content and of information chunks is not 'localization' as the process has been traditionally understood, because it does not entail modification of the properties of objects in a software user interface. Nevertheless, 'content translation projects are now often considered as localization projects simply because of the complex environments in which the content is authored, managed, stored and published', as Esselink has pointed out (2003b: 7).

Complexity was once a defining characteristic of software localization projects but now characterizes large-scale translation projects as well.

At a more fundamental level, the complexity of software localization and content translation is due largely to the fact that translators and localizers do not work on *linear* text but rather on decontexualized text strings or chunks. Working on text without context not only complicates the translation decision-making process but arguably calls into question the very possibility of understanding the text as a whole and the pragmatic act of communication of which it is an ostensible artifact. 'In understanding text, a reader must not only be able to integrate information within sentences but also make connections across sentences to form a coherent discourse representation', as Rayner and Sereno observe (1994: 73). However, it is not always possible for translators to make connections across sentences while working on software strings. 'Due to their non-linear structure and lack of narrative thread, software programmes cannot be 'read' in the same way as [traditional documents]' (Dunne 2009: 197). This also holds true for XML content and information chunks. In single sourcing projects, the 'document' does not exist until it is created dynamically in response to a user request (typically from an end-user). On a surface level, the translation of strings and information chunks may seem technologically simpler than traditional localization because translators do not have to compile or test target files. However, the translation of strings and information chunks is cognitively more complex because reading and comprehending text without context and 'texts without ends' (Biau Gil and Pym 2006: 11) requires translators to construct a situation model of a text that does not yet exist. In other words, the industry is no longer trying to turn translators into semi-engineers, but translators still need to understand the architecture of the components from which software localization project deliverables are created, such as software resource files, and Help topics, tables of contents and indexes. As Esselink observes, 'it looks likely that while translators will be able and expected to increasingly focus on their linguistic tasks . . . the bar of technical complexity will be raised considerably as well' (2003b: 7).

Notes

1 For more information on target-market requirements, see Giammarresi 2011, especially 39–40.
2 For a case study that illustrates some of the problems that can occur in the absence of an organized approach to internationalization, see Margulies 2000.
3 These resources are derived from a sample application called Scribble developed by the author using Visual Studio 2010 C++ sample files. MSDN Archive, Visual C++ MFC Samples for Visual Studio 2010, http://archive.msdn.microsoft.com/vcsamplesmfc (accessed Sep. 8, 2012).

Bibliography

Bartlett, P. G. (1998) 'The Benefits of Structured XML Authoring for Content Management', in Graphic Communications Association (U.S.), Organization for the Advancement of Structured Information Systems (OASIS) (ed.) *XML 98 Conference Proceedings*, 15–18 November 1998, Chicago, IL, New York: Graphic Communications Association. Available at: www.infoloom.com/gcaconfs/WEB/chicago98/bartlett.HTM.

Bellamy, Laura, Michelle Carey, and Jenifer Schlotfeldt (2012) *DITA Best Practices: A Roadmap for Writing, Editing, and Architecting in DITA*, Upper Saddle River, NJ: IBM Press.

Biau Gil, Jose Ramon and Anthony Pym (2006) 'Technology and Translation (A Pedagogical Overview)', in Anthony Pym, Alexander Perekrestenko, and Bram Starink (eds.) *Translation Technology and Its Teaching*, Tarragona, Spain: Intercultural Studies Group, Universitat Rovira I Virgili, 5–19.

Boehm, Barry W. (1981) *Software Engineering Economics*, Englewood Cliffs, NJ: Prentice-Hall.

Cadieux, Pierre and Bert Esselink (2002) 'GILT: Globalization, Internationalization, Localization, Translation', *Globalization Insider* 11. Available at: www.lisa.org/globalizationinsider/2002/03/gilt_globalizat.html.

Clark, Dan (2013) *Beginning C# Object-Oriented Programming*, N.p.: Apress.

Deitsch, Andy and David Czarnecki (2001) *Java Internationalization*, Sebastopol, CA: O'Reilly.

Dunne, Keiran J. (2009) 'Assessing Software Localization: For a Valid Approach', in Claudia V. Angelelli and Holly E. Jacobson (eds.) *Testing and Assessment in Translation and Interpreting Studies*, Amsterdam and Philadelphia: John Benjamins Publishing Company, 185–222.

Dunne, Keiran J. and Elena S. Dunne (2011) *Translation and Localization Project Management: The Art of the Possible*, Amsterdam and Philadelphia: John Benjamins Publishing Company.

Esselink, Bert (2000a) *A Practical Guide to Localization*, revised edition, Amsterdam and Philadelphia: John Benjamins Publishing Company.

Esselink, Bert (2000b, January 15) 'Translation versus Localization', *Tranfree* 10. Available at: www.translationtips.net/tranfreearchive/tf10-localization-one.html.

Esselink, Bert (2002) 'Localization Engineering: The Dream Job?', *Revista Tradumàtica* 1(October): 2–5. Available at: www.fti.uab.es/tradumatica/revista/articles/besselink/besselink.PDF.

Esselink, Bert (2003a) 'Localisation and Translation', in Harold L. Somers (ed.) *Computers and Translation: A Translator's Guide*, Amsterdam and Philadelphia: John Benjamins Publishing Company, 67–86.

Esselink, Bert (2003b) 'The Evolution of Localization', *The Guide to Localization*, Supplement to *Multilingual Computing and Technology* 14(5): 4–7. Available at: www.multilingual.com/downloads/screenSupp57.pdf.

Giammarresi, Salvatore (2011) 'Strategic Views on Localization Project Management: The Importance of Global Product Management and Portfolio Management', in Keiran J. Dunne and Elena S. Dunne (eds.) *Translation and Localization Project Management: The Art of the Possible*, Amsterdam and Philadelphia: John Benjamins Publishing Company, 17–49.

Hall, Patrick A. V. (1999) 'Software Internationalization Architectures', in Gregory E. Kersten, Zbigniew Mikolajuk, and Anthony Gar-On Yeh (eds.) *Decision Support Systems for Sustainable Development in Developing Countries: A Resource Book of Methods and Applications*, Boston: Kluwer Academic Publishers, 291–304.

Lieu, Tina (1997) 'Software Localization: The Art of Turning Japanese', *Computing Japan* 4(12). Available at: www.japaninc.com/cpj/magazine/issues/1997/dec97/local.html.

Lommel, Arle (2007) *The Globalization Industry Primer*, Romainmôtier, Switzerland: Localization Industry Standards Association.

Luong, Tuoc V., James S. H. Lok, David J. Taylor, and Kevin Driscoll (1995) *Internationalization: Developing Software for Global Markets*, New York: John Wiley & Sons.

Margulies, Benson I. (2000, May 1) 'Your Passport to Proper Internationalization', *Dr Dobb's*. Available at: http://drdobbs.com/your-passport-to-proper-internationaliza184414603.

Rayner, Keith and Sara C. Sereno (1994) 'Eye Movements in Reading: Psycholinguistic Studies', in Morton A. Gernsbacher (ed.) *Handbook of Psycholinguistics*, San Diego, CA: Academic Press, 57–81.

Rockley, Ann, Pamela Kostur, and Steve Manning (2003) *Managing Enterprise Content: A Unified Content Strategy*, Indianapolis, IN: New Riders.

Savourel, Yves (2001) *XML Internationalization and Localization*, Indianapolis: Sams Publishing.

Schmitz, Klaus-Dirk (2007) 'Indeterminacy of Terms and Icons in Software Localization', in Bassey Edem Antia (ed.) *Indeterminacy in Terminology and LSP*, Amsterdam and Philadelphia: John Benjamins Publishing Company, 49–58.

Smith-Ferrier, Guy (2007) *NET Internationalization: The Developer's Guide to Building Global Windows and Web Applications*, Upper Saddle River, NJ: Addison-Wesley.

Uren, Emmanuel, Roberet Howard, and Tiziana Perinotti (1993) *Software Internationalization and Localization: An Introduction*, New York: Van Nostrand Reinhold.

van der Meer, Jaap (1995) 'The Fate of the Localization Industry and a Call to Action', *The LISA [Localization Industry Standards Association] Forum Newsletter* 4(4): 14–17. Available at: www.lisa.org/globalizationinsider/1995/10/the_fate_of_the.html.

W3C (World Wide Web Consortium) (1997, December 8) 'W3C Issues XML1.0 as a Proposed Recommendation', *World Wide Web Consortium Press Release*. Available at: www.w3.org/Press/XML-PR.

38

NATURAL LANGUAGE PROCESSING

Olivia Kwong Oi Yee

Introduction

Natural language processing (NLP) concerns the handling and understanding of human languages by computers with two major goals. One is to enable human–computer interaction with human languages as the medium. The other is to build language application systems that require considerable human language abilities and linguistic knowledge. NLP thus focuses on the design and implementation of practical systems with textual natural language as input and output. It is closely related to computational linguistics, which is more theoretically oriented and works on formal models, as well as speech recognition and synthesis, which deals with the analysis and understanding of speech sounds to allow human-computer interaction by voice. They are often considered together under the larger umbrella of speech and language processing (e.g. Jurafsky and Martin 2009).

Among the many applications, machine translation (MT) is apparently the most well-known example that has been typically associated with translation technology, although the latter has a much broader scope. In fact, MT has a critical role in NLP research from day one, as projects in the 1950s set out with the ambition to build systems that were capable of automatically translating texts from one language into another. The efforts unfortunately turned sour upon the release of the famous ALPAC report[1] in 1966. Noted by Charniak and McDermott (1985) as the "sad story of machine translation", the report pronounced the failure of MT research thus far and recommended further funding should support more basic research in computational linguistics and down-to-earth studies toward the improvement of translation. Despite the unfavourable outcome, at least two important lessons were learned. On the one hand, translations produced entirely by lexicon lookup and simple syntactic methods can hardly meet even minimal practical needs. On the other hand, language processing requires vast and diverse knowledge, and it is much more complicated than once imagined for computers to do it. Without satisfactorily addressing the smaller, intermediate sub-problems, it is hard to expect good performance on more sophisticated and demanding tasks like translation.

It turns out that research on MT came under the spotlight again after about two decades, during which research on a variety of other NLP problems has yielded some important progress and insight. The increasing availability of digitised texts and large electronic corpora during the 1980s opened up a path to semi-automatic knowledge extraction as well as probabilistic language models. Especially with the development of the first statistical machine translation (SMT)

DOI: 10.4324/9781003168348-41

system (Brown *et al.* 1990), it marked the significance of statistical approaches in NLP, and with its widespread use since the 1990s, MT and many other NLP areas embarked on a fast track of development. The fast-growing web technology in the 2000s, accompanied by the advance in big data technologies, further boosted the demand and supply of NLP research. The rise of neural network models and deep learning during the last decade had a great impact on most NLP tasks, and neural machine translation (NMT) systems brought particularly salient changes to the field.

Importance of Corpus Data

One of the foremost notorious problems in NLP is often known as the knowledge acquisition bottleneck. Language understanding typically needs different kinds of knowledge, including not only linguistic knowledge but also extensive general knowledge. This leads to three questions: What knowledge is necessary? How should knowledge be represented for computational purposes? Where can we adequately obtain such knowledge? Knowledge crafting and representation in early systems were in an artificial intelligence (AI) fashion. To balance between the details required and the time and labour incurred, this was often limited in scale and domain. For instance, the classic SHRDLU system was designed to communicate with the user and perform accordingly but only within the pre-defined "blocks world" (Winograd 1973). Knowledge represented in the form of plans and scripts is often situated in specific domains and scenarios (e.g. Schank and Abelson 1977). Realising the limitation, in the 1980s, researchers went for automatic or semi-automatic means of extracting knowledge, particularly lexico-semantic knowledge, from existing language resources such as machine-readable dictionaries (e.g. Boguraev and Briscoe 1989). With the availability of large electronic text corpora, such as the Brown Corpus and the British National Corpus in the 1960s and 1990s, respectively; structurally annotated corpora like the Penn Treebank later; and the even larger gigaword corpora available soon after the new millennium, lexical information can be more conveniently gathered at large scale, capitalising on the occurrence patterns of words exhibited in corpora. This has given rise to an area of research on automatic lexical acquisition, aiming to acquire a variety of lexical information, including domain-specific monolingual and bilingual lexicons, significant collocations, subcategorisation information, semantic similarities, selectional preferences, and others (e.g. Church and Hanks 1990). In addition to knowledge acquisition, large corpora are often directly used for training statistical NLP systems for estimating the probabilities of particular linguistic phenomena.

As far as translation is concerned, bilingual lexicons as a major knowledge source may be manually constructed or automatically acquired, and SMT systems are essentially trained on bilingual or multi-lingual corpora. Parallel corpora, referring to the same textual content existing simultaneously in two languages in the form of real translation, are particularly valuable. Typical early examples include bilingual government documents like the Canadian Hansard[2] and the Hong Kong Hansard.[3] The Europarl corpus consists of parallel texts in 11 languages extracted from the proceedings of the European Parliament published on the web and used as training data for SMT systems[4] (Koehn 2005). Other than government and legal documents, bilingual texts from patent documents (Goto *et al.* 2011), newswire and broadcast sources (Strassel *et al.* 2011), IT translation, and biomedical translation[5] have also been used in MT research. There is also the OpenSubtitles corpus consisting of parallel texts from movie and TV subtitles (Lison and Tiedemann 2016).

The internet has also become an important source for mining parallel texts, especially for less common language pairs (e.g. Resnik and Smith 2003). Much larger-scale parallel corpora mined from the web are more available, such as the ParaCrawl Corpus[6] consisting of translated sentences covering all official European languages (Bañón *et al.* 2020). Given the relative scarcity of parallel corpora, comparable corpora provide an important supplement. Unlike parallel corpora, the bilingual or multilingual textual data in comparable corpora only cover similar contents or topics but are not translations of each other. The BUCC workshop series focuses on the building of comparable corpora and their application in NLP tasks.[7]

Dominance of Statistical and Machine Learning Algorithms

Another notorious problem for NLP is the handling of ambiguity which exists at different levels of linguistic analysis. For tasks like translation, which definitely require a thorough understanding of a text, the ambiguity problem is particularly relevant. Lexical ambiguities such as part-of-speech and word sense ambiguity, as well as higher-level syntactic and semantic ambiguities, which exist for most NLP tasks in general, also need to be handled in MT. For cases where there are lexical gaps in one language, such as when the target language has lexical distinctions which are absent in the source language, disambiguation becomes even more critical to arrive at a correct lexical choice in the target language during translation. NLP tools and applications must be able to robustly process different input texts and resolve various kinds of ambiguities therein.

As demonstrated in the second edition of the *Handbook of Natural Language Processing*, approaches in NLP are often categorised into the more classical symbolic approaches and the more contemporary empirical and statistical approaches (Indurkhya and Damerau 2010). Symbolic approaches mostly follow the AI tradition, with manually crafted procedural knowledge. They were later developed into more general knowledge-based or rule-based approaches, for which knowledge may be in the form of rules, or more declarative as in semantic lexicons like WordNet (Miller 1995), ontologies like SUMO (Pease *et al.* 2002), and so on, which may be handcrafted or (semi-)automatically acquired from existing language resources. Empirical and statistical approaches, also known as stochastic approaches, are data driven. They often require large annotated corpora as training data for estimating the probabilities of various linguistic units or phenomena with respect to particular statistical language models. According to Charniak (1993), a statistical approach in its purest form is to note statistical regularities in a corpus. Statistical methods thus evaluate different possible outcomes probabilistically and output the one with highest value as the result. Statistical language models, however, may assume different levels of complexity with different dependency assumptions. An important group of algorithms is based on machine learning, which attempts to learn patterns for classification from a set of linguistic features extracted from texts. Learning can be supervised, with annotated data, or unsupervised, with no or just minimal annotated data to start with.

As large text corpora became more accessible, machine learning became the dominant approach in many NLP tasks during the 1990s. In many cases, hybrid methods were adopted, with machine learning algorithms at the core, supplemented by post-processing the results with rules. Statistical methods have an advantage with their scalability. Their general coverage regardless of the frequency or rarity of individual linguistic phenomena overcomes the severe limitation of rule-based systems, as the efforts involved in crafting the rules often confine the resulting systems to toy systems. Statistical methods remove this hurdle, although they do not necessarily model human cognitive processes. Allen (1995) gives detailed descriptions of symbolic approaches to NLP, while a comprehensive account of statistical NLP can be found in Manning and Schütze (1999).

Web Technology as a Catalyst

The development of web technology has to a certain extent catalysed the development of statistical NLP. On the one hand, the use of XML as a standard protocol for data markup and document encoding has made it easier to share data over the internet and improved interoperability of language resources. On the other hand, the global popularity of the internet has made the sharing of resources much more convenient and allowed crowdsourcing for data preparation or even annotation (e.g. Chklovski and Mihalcea 2002). Web 2.0 has led to a surge of user-generated content over the World Wide Web, and web-crawling techniques have enabled quick collection of mega-size textual data. With such facilities just at our fingertips (e.g. Baroni and Bernardini 2004), mining the web for large corpora has thus formed a trend, beating traditional corpus compilation in terms of time, quantity, and variety, although materials gathered from the web have to be considerably cleaned and used with caution (Kilgarriff and Grefenstette 2003). In addition, cloud computing has enabled storage of virtually unlimited data and running of applications without confinement to specific physical locations, and the evolution of web and mobile applications has brought about more different modes of deployment of language technology, accessible to a great many users.

The almost unlimited supply of text data by the web is both a blessing and a challenge to NLP. On the one hand, machine learning loves data, the more the better. For something as complicated as human language, there simply can never be enough data for machines to learn a perfectly comprehensive representation of its nature and features. Web texts remove the size limit of hand-constructed corpora, and machine learning is expected to benefit from the data boom. For instance, the ParaCrawl corpora mentioned previously is now providing the largest publicly available parallel corpora for many European language pairs to train MT systems (Bañón *et al.* 2020). On the other hand, systems also have to be prepared to handle raw and noisy data, as well as the many unpredicted and uncontrolled elements therein. Data processing capacity in terms of speed and storage must advance simultaneously. With the arrival of the big data era, computing hardware and software are catching up swiftly, giving an advantage for neural network models to be feasibly used with deep learning in NLP, which has become the state of the art after the 2010s. Nevertheless, it is the high-resource languages that are getting most of the benefits in this trend, while low-resource languages are still craving systems and resources to be developed by the language community, which is a major limitation of NLP today (Hirschberg and Manning 2015).

State of the Art: Neural Networks and Deep Learning

Neural network (NN) models in computing is not entirely a new idea, except that the complexity of a model and the practicability to train it in reality have been much enhanced in recent years. Modern neural networks contain a network of small computing units. Each unit takes a vector of input values and produces a single output value. As there are usually many layers of such units, a deep network is formed, and the approach is known as deep learning. NN does not use rich hand-derived features but takes raw words as inputs and learn to induce features as part of the process. Young *et al.* (2018) provide a succinct summary of the recent trends of using deep learning in natural language processing. Charniak (2019) and Nielsen (2019) give a comprehensive introduction to deep learning.

The rise of NN and deep learning has completely changed the way NLP applications are done. On the one hand, the traditional knowledge representation issue has almost gone. In the past, one needed to sort out what kinds of knowledge should be included and how. Even for supervised machine learning, specific features had to be annotated and learned. With deep learning, however, no hand-derived features are used and a system is left to induce the informative and useful features all by itself. But the consequence is: no one knows what exactly these features turn out to be. On the other hand, NN and deep learning have made most NLP tasks an end-to-end learning process. Conventionally, an NLP task like machine translation had to be broken into a sequence of sub-tasks typically starting with tokenisation, part-of-speech tagging, parsing, and so on. Such individual components in the pipeline are no longer distinguished in modern NN approaches, as everything is taken care of by a single deep neural network model implicitly within the learning process.

NLP Tasks and Translation Technology

In this section, we will take a look at selected NLP tasks and applications bearing on translation technology in the broadest sense.

Common Text Pre-Processing Tasks

In most natural language processing applications, one of the first steps is to tokenise the input text, that is, to locate word boundaries in the input text and break it into basic token units. This tokenisation process is relatively less demanding for Indo-European languages like English and French, as words in the texts are already delimited by spaces. Despite this, the process is not always straightforward, as certain punctuation and symbols could have multiple functions depending on the context of their individual occurrences (Mikheev 2003). For example, a period amidst digits should be considered part of the decimal number instead of a token delimiter. In other cases multi-word expressions might be more properly considered a single unit. For instance, New York may more intuitively be treated as one unit instead of two. The definition and boundary of tokens are further blurred with most web texts where emoticons and informal spellings are abundant.

Tokenisation is much more important for processing many Asian languages where word boundaries are implicit. In the case of Chinese, the notion of word has always been under debate, and there is no standard definition for what constitutes a Chinese "word". Various criteria are usually considered, including syntax (e.g. bound/free morphemes and word structures), semantics (e.g. fixed phrases, idioms, and emergent meanings), frequency, length, and so on. In practice, disyllabic words apparently dominate. The maximum matching algorithm is a simple knowledge-based method for Chinese word segmentation, which requires only a dictionary containing all legitimate words in the language to start with. During the process, the input text is compared against the dictionary to find the longest matching word, and the word boundary is thus marked. Sproat *et al.* (1996) used a statistical method together with finite-state techniques for the purpose. Other approaches include hybrid methods and character-based segmentation with machine learning (e.g. Xue and Converse 2002). System performance is often measured in terms of in-vocabulary and out-of-vocabulary segmentation scores, as in the SIGHAN International Chinese Segmentation Bakeoffs[8] (Sproat and Emerson 2003). A comprehensive review of the development of Chinese word segmentation research during the decade before 2007 can be found in Huang and Zhao (2007). During the following decade, deep learning has been increasingly applied to Chinese word segmentation, although neural network–based methods have not yet shown an obvious advantage over previous machine learning methods (Zhao *et al.* 2019).

Recent approaches also tend to tackle the out-of-vocabulary problem by performing tokenisation at the subword level. One of the most popular algorithms is adapted from the data compression technique called byte pair encoding (BPE) (Gage 1994) and uses an iterative process to learn a subword vocabulary from a corpus. The algorithm is employed in many neural machine translation models to enable open-vocabulary translation (e.g. Sennrich *et al.* 2016).

Equally important is part-of-speech tagging, which assigns the most appropriate lexical category label from a tagset to individual words in a text. Traditional rule-based tagging relies on a dictionary containing all possible part-of-speech tags for individual words and a large set of manually devised disambiguation rules for eliminating incompatible tags (Greene and Rubin 1971). Transformation-based tagging, also known as Brill tagging, is data-driven in the sense that the input text is first tagged with the most frequent tag for each word, followed by applying a large set of transformation rules in a particular order to modify the tags under particular contexts. These transformation rules were learned from a large set of training data (Brill 1995). Probabilistic methods for such a sequence labelling task include generative approaches like those based on the hidden Markov model (e.g. Church 1989) and discriminative approaches like those using conditional random fields (e.g. Lafferty *et al.* 2001). Modern taggers are shifting to the deep learning architecture (e.g. Huang *et al.* 2015).

Sentence structures are often worked out as a next step for subsequent processing. The process of analysing a sentence in terms of its syntactic structure is known as parsing, which may follow different grammar formalisms. For example, phrase-structure parsing refers to a set of context-free grammar rules and renders a sentence into a tree of phrasal constituent structures, whereas dependency parsing delineates the structure of a sentence in terms of the binary grammatical relations among the words in it. The main challenge in parsing is to resolve structural ambiguities in sentences. SIGPARSE[9] organises biennial conferences on parsing technologies, and CoNLL[10] has held shared tasks on multi-lingual parsing and dependency parsing from 2006 to 2009. Parsing results are useful for machine translation, especially for reordering to improve the fluency of the translation output.

Word Sense Disambiguation and Lexical Semantics

Word sense disambiguation (WSD) refers to the process of identifying word meanings in a discourse for words which have multiple form-meaning possibilities. The importance of disambiguating word senses had already been realised by the time MT emerged as ambitious projects in the 1950s. On the one hand, a thorough understanding of the source text is needed to resolve the word sense ambiguities therein, and vice versa. On the other hand, word sense ambiguities often surface as translation differences. For example, "duty" in English should be translated to "devoir" or "droit" in French depending on whether the word is used in its "obligation" or "tax" sense, respectively (e.g. Gale *et al.* 1992). Automatic WSD largely depends on the knowledge sources capturing the various semantic (and possibly other) relations among words available to a system and subsequently its ability to uncover and deploy these relations among words in a text.

WSD is often treated as a classification task. Systems thus attempt to assign the most appropriate sense among those given in a particular sense inventory, typically some dictionary or lexical resource, to individual words in a text. As for many NLP tasks in general, WSD methods are conventionally classified into AI-based, knowledge-based, and corpus-based methods, corresponding closely with the predominant kind of lexical resources during various historical periods. The survey by Ide and Veronis (1998) documents the development of WSD before the end of the last millennium. Knowledge-based approaches, supervised approaches, and unsupervised approaches are discussed in details in Mihalcea (2006), Màrquez *et al.* (2006) and Pedersen (2006) respectively. Navigli (2009) gives detailed technical descriptions of various algorithms.

The performance evaluation of WSD systems has been more or less standardised with the Senseval and SemEval exercises[11] (e.g. Edmonds and Cotton 2001). It turns out that top systems are mostly based on combinations of multiple classifiers, and voting schemes combining several learning algorithms outperform individual classifiers (Mihalcea *et al.* 2004). Notwithstanding the many encouraging results, WSD methods may need to take specific real language processing applications into account to be effective in practice (Specia *et al.* 2006).

Lexical semantic representation in the form of word vectors used for machine learning in the past is now taken over by word embedding. Previous word vectors are often sparse, long vectors with dimension corresponding to the number of words in the vocabulary, whereas word embeddings are short, dense vectors, with dimension in the range of 50 to 1000. The reduction in dimensionality, however, is accompanied by the lack of clear interpretation of the individual dimensions, unlike the specifically defined features as in previous word vectors. Common word embedding models include Word2Vec (Mikolov *et al.* 2013) and GloVe (Pennington *et al.* 2014). Such static embedding is further developed into dynamic contextual embedding as the ELMo (Peters *et al.* 2018) and BERT (Devlin *et al.* 2018) representations. Recent research shows that the best performing algorithms for WSD often use simple neural networks with contextual embedding (e.g. Melamud *et al.* 2016; Loureiro and Jorge 2019).

Automatic Transliteration

Transliteration takes a name in a source language and renders it in a target language in a phonemically similar way. Proper names, including personal names, place names, and organisation names, make up a considerable part of naturally occurring texts, and even the most comprehensive bilingual lexicon cannot capture all possible proper names. The accurate rendition of personal names thus means a lot to machine translation accuracy and intelligibility, and cross-lingual information retrieval, especially between dissimilar languages such as English and Chinese, English and Japanese, and English and Hindi. There are basically two categories of work on machine transliteration: one is to acquire transliteration lexicons from parallel corpora and other resources (e.g. Kuo *et al.* 2008) and the other is to generate transliteration for personal names and other proper names.

Traditional systems for transliteration generation often consider phonemes the basic unit of transliteration (Knight and Graehl 1998). Li *et al.* (2004) suggested a grapheme-based joint source-channel model within the direct orthographic mapping framework, skipping the middle phonemic representation in conventional phoneme-based methods, and modelling the segmentation and alignment preferences by means of contextual n-grams of the transliteration units. Their method was shown to outperform phoneme-based methods. In fact, transliteration of foreign names into Chinese is often based on the surface orthographic forms, as exemplified in the transliteration of Beckham, where the supposedly silent h in "ham" is taken as pronounced. Some models combine phonemic and graphemic features (e.g. Oh and Choi 2005), while temporal, semantic, and tonal features have also been found useful in transliteration (e.g. Tao *et al.* 2006; Li *et al.* 2007; Kwong 2009).

The shared task on transliteration generation organised by the Named Entities Workshop (NEWS) series suggested that an appropriate transliteration should meet three criteria, phonemic equivalence between the source name and the target name, conformity of target name to the phonology of the target language, and user intuition considering cultural and orthographic conventions in the target language (Zhang *et al.* 2011). A decade ago, two popular approaches dominated: phrase-based statistical machine transliteration and conditional random fields (Li *et al.* 2010). State-of-the-art systems tend to use neural network approaches or a combination of multiple systems (Chen, Banchs *et al.* 2018).

The task of transliteration can be quite mechanical on the one hand, but can also be highly variable on the other. In the case of English-to-Chinese transliteration, for instance, homophones are abundant in Chinese and the choice and combination of characters for the Chinese rendition is relatively free. Besides linguistic and phonetic properties, many other social and cognitive factors such as dialect, gender, domain, meaning, and perception also play a role in the naming process. Evaluating systems based on a given set of "correct" transliterations may therefore not be entirely satisfactory, as there might be options outside this set which are also acceptable. Nevertheless, effective systems developed under such a paradigm should be helpful to organisations like news agencies and mass media, which are likely to encounter many new foreign names every day.

Text Alignment

Automatic text alignment refers to taking two parallel texts, or bitexts, as input, segmenting them at different granularities such as sentences or words, and identifying the corresponding segments between the two texts as output. It is closely related to translation lexicon extraction and machine translation research.

The extraction of translation lexicons from parallel corpora depends, to a certain extent, on parallel text alignment at the word level. In addition, together they provide foundational resources for machine translation research. The relation between parallel text alignment and machine translation, especially SMT, is even more intimate, as the alignment model often forms part of an SMT model. Bilingual word alignment and thus extraction of translation lexicons were usually carried out statistically or via lexical criteria. The former relies on large corpora to be effective, and the latter depends on existing bilingual dictionaries which often only cover general terms.

Bilingual sentence alignment on Indo-European language pairs has conventionally based statistically on sentence length (e.g. Gale and Church 1991) or lexically on cognates (e.g. Simard *et al.* 1992) and correspondence of word position (e.g. Kay and Röscheisen 1993). For other language pairs like English–Chinese, the length criterion may be supplemented with lexical criteria, such as identifying fixed words or phrases with consistent translations first (e.g. Wu 1994). Word alignment is often done statistically, leveraging the translation association or token co-occurrences between the source language and the target language (e.g. Melamed 1997). In practice, sentence alignment is not always distinctly separated from word alignment. In fact, apart from Gale and Church's length-based method, most others also simultaneously tackle word alignment to some extent. More technical details and comparisons of different alignment models can be found in Och and Ney (2003) and Wu (2010).

With the rise of neural networks and deep learning, alignment is often taken as an integrated part in the process of machine translation. For instance, to address the bottleneck imposed by fixed-length vectors, Bahdanau *et al.* (2015) extended the encoder-decoder model to learn to align and translate jointly. When the model generates a word in a translation, it searches for a set of positions in a source sentence for the most relevant information, thus finding a soft alignment between a source sentence and the corresponding target sentence.

Translation Lexicon and Terminology Extraction

Parallel corpora, aligned or otherwise, are important resources for extracting translation lexicons. One may start by acquiring monolingual collocations before extracting their translation equivalents based on certain statistical association criteria (e.g. Wu and Xia 1995; Smadja *et al.* 1996). Existing lexical resources like bilingual dictionaries may be leveraged in the process, although the coverage could be limited even when several are used in combination (e.g. Huang and Choi 2000). Using a third, pivot language as a bridge in word alignment could be an alternative, especially for Slavic and Indo-European languages (e.g. Borin 2000; Mann and Yarowsky 2001). Hybrid methods may produce better results. For instance, Piperidis *et al.* (1997) first aligned sentences statistically, and then used a variety of information, including part-of-speech categories, noun phrase grammars, and co-occurrence frequency, to identify translation equivalents at word or multi-word level. Instead of parallel corpora, Fung (1998) tried to extract bilingual lexicons from comparable corpora. The context vector of a given English word was compared with the context vectors of all Chinese words for the most similar candidate, and a bilingual dictionary was used to map the context words in the two languages. About 30% accuracy was achieved if the top-one candidate was considered, reflecting the inferiority of non-parallel corpora for bilingual lexicon extraction. Later studies along this line have focused on improving the quality of the comparable corpora, using better association measures for comparing the context vectors, and addressing the polysemy problem with the bilingual dictionary used in the process, amongst others (e.g. Laroche and Langlais 2010; Li and Gaussier 2010; Bouamor *et al.* 2013).

While general translation lexicon extraction does not particularly address domain specificity, terminology extraction would need to consider "termhood" in addition to simply "unithood" (Kageura 1996). In computational terminology, this could be done by filtering the extraction results (from a domain-specific corpus) against a general dictionary or lexicon extracted from a general corpus (e.g. Resnik and Melamed 1997). This is not only a means to measure termhood but also a way to reduce the amount of noise in the output. Like many other NLP tasks, methods for automatic term extraction are generally categorised as linguistic (e.g. Bourigault 1992), statistical (e.g. Daille and Morin 2005), or hybrid (e.g. Daille 1996; Drouin 2003), and, as with most NLP tasks, machine learning and deep learning approaches have been pushing back the frontiers of terminology extraction without exception (e.g. Wang *et al.* 2016; Hazem *et al.* 2020).

Machine Translation

Machine translation has always been considered one of the most important and typical applications of natural language processing. This type of sophisticated language processing tasks is often described as "AI-complete" (e.g. Rich and Knight 1991), which means all difficult problems identified in artificial intelligence are relevant and the task can only be achieved when these problems are resolved. For a task like translation, which is sometimes more an art than a science, it requires deep understanding of the source language and the input text, and a sophisticated command of the target language. One may also need to possess a poetic sense and be creative for literary translation. In addition to basic linguistic (lexical, syntactic, semantic, pragmatic, and discourse) knowledge, common sense and encyclopaedic knowledge are particularly difficult to quantify and adequately represent. To produce high-quality translation without human intervention, which is the original and ambitious goal of MT research, was soon found to be unrealistic. The goals thus have to be toned down, such as aiming only at rough translation to be post-edited by humans and limiting the content to small sublanguage domains.

Traditional wisdom of MT depicts several levels of intermediary representation between the source text and the target text: direct translation, transfer approach, and interlingua approach. There are thus three phases in MT: analysis, transfer, and generation. Direct translation does little analysis but simply word-to-word translation from a source language to a target language. Lexical transfer considers the contrastive lexical differences between the source and target languages. Syntactic transfer considers the contrastive syntactic differences between the source and target languages. The source sentence is analysed according to the source language syntactic representation, which is converted to the corresponding target language syntactic representation, and the target sentence is generated accordingly. The interlingua approach uses a somewhat language-independent semantic representation to bridge the source sentence analysis and target sentence generation.

The first statistical machine translation system by Brown *et al.* (1990) offered a new perspective to view the MT problem. Based on an aligned parallel corpus, automatic translation is achieved by finding the best translation, that is, the translation giving the highest conditional probability $P(T|S)$, where T is the target sentence and S is the source sentence. Fitting it into the noisy-channel model, this is equivalent to finding the translation which gives the highest value for $P(S|T)P(T)$. These two terms analogously quantify two important criteria in translation: faithfulness and fluency, respectively. The faithfulness model and the fluency model can be of different complexity or sophistication. Subsequent research on SMT has developed the original word-based model into phrase-based models (e.g. Marcu and Wong 2002; Koehn *et al.* 2003). Despite the apparent superiority and dominance of the statistical approach, traces of the transfer models are found in contemporary SMT research, such as the syntax-based translation model (e.g. Liu *et al.* 2006) as well as the SMT model incorporating predicate-argument structures (e.g. Zhai *et al.* 2012). As Costa-jussà *et al.* (2013) remarked, there was a clear trend toward hybrid MT, with more linguistic knowledge incorporated into statistical models and data-driven methods combined with rule-based systems.

Modern MT systems, mostly following neural network models, apply encoder-decoder networks (also called sequence-to-sequence networks) that are capable of generating contextually appropriate output sequences of arbitrary lengths. The memory consumption is also much less than the SMT models. Common NMT architectures include recurrent neural network (RNN) (Cho *et al.* 2014) and transformer (Vaswani *et al.* 2017). The attention mechanism (Bahdanau *et al.* 2015), on which the transformer model is based allows dynamic production of a context vector for each token during decoding to get information from all hidden states of the encoder, instead of just the last hidden state. Moreover, systems are often now designed to go further beyond literal translation and to accommodate more semantic elements and meaning preservation. Semantic machine translation (e.g. Song *et al.* 2019) and evaluation (e.g. Lo 2020) have become a major direction in MT research. Simultaneous machine translation (or simultaneous speech translation) is also seen as one of the next significant challenges in MT research (e.g. Cho and Esipova 2016; Alinejad *et al.* 2018). Combining techniques in speech recognition, machine translation, and text-to-speech synthesis, speech-to-speech translation systems are beginning to be deployed in everyday mobile devices (Jia *et al.* 2019).

As mentioned, the availability of large corpora had brought significant breakthroughs to MT research. For instance, at some point there was also example-based machine translation, which has been an important empirical method enabled by large corpora (e.g. Sato and Nagao 1990). Maturing corpus processing techniques as well as statistical and hybrid approaches to various subtasks have again led to large projects and investments on machine translation and related language technology (e.g. Olive *et al.* 2011). An account of early MT can be found in Hutchins and Somers (1992), and a comprehensive account of SMT and NMT is discussed in Koehn (2010) and Koehn (2020), respectively.

NLP and Computer-Aided Translation

Computer-aided translation (CAT) started from the idea of integrating various translation tools like online dictionaries, terminology banks, and translation memory into the translator's workstation (see e.g. Hutchins 1998). Conventionally, CAT mainly refers to the use of translation memory and terminology management systems in its narrow sense. The former relies mostly on string matching of the surface forms with some sort of edit distance measurement, and the latter employs much database management techniques. NLP had little role to play in both. The weakness of the first generation translation memory, which lacks semantic knowledge, soon becomes obvious. Segments with similar meanings but different surface forms can hardly be matched. The retrieval of useful target segments is thus much hindered. At the same time, source segments with similar surface syntactic forms may not always warrant a similar translation. In view of this inadequacy, some NLP processing (such as syntactic analysis and use of paraphrases) was introduced in the research of the second- and third-generation translation memory (Planas 2005; Gupta *et al.* 2016). As for terminology management, most commercial term extraction systems tend to rely primarily on n-gram statistics, the noisy output of which often deters translators from using them. More effective knowledge transfer from computational terminology research to application tools targeting translators is needed (Kwong 2021). In the broader sense of CAT, NLP can be applied to enhance any tools that might be used in the process of human translation. For instance, NMT techniques and word embeddings may be used to enhance information access in bilingual dictionaries to provide examples and navigational means in addition to the context-free equivalents available in existing dictionaries to assist human translators in their lexical choices for achieving better fidelity and fluency (Chen, Kwong *et al.* 2018; Kwong 2020).

Concluding Remarks

The progress and development in NLP and MT are undeniably remarkable in the last few decades. Not only has MT development made significant progress, managing to fulfil basic demands like gisting and reducing post-editing efforts, the application of NLP techniques in translation technology has also led to more useful tools to assist human translators in professional translations for various purposes. The once-narrow view of replacing human translators with MT is gradually replaced by greater acceptance of translation technology in a much broader sense, and the unrealistic expectation of high-quality fully automated translation by machine is giving way to more practical endeavours for useful application tools to benefit translators in various aspects. The road ahead is still wide open, with plenty of room for development and improvement. NLP will continue to play a significant role in translation technology, as it has something to offer to both machine translation and human translation, with more substantial contributions and results to be expected in the future.

Notes

1 The ALPAC report, titled "Language and Machine: Computers in Translation and Linguistics", was issued in 1966 by the Automatic Language Processing Advisory Committee established by the US government.
2 The Canadian Hansard consists of records of the proceedings of the Canadian parliament in both English and French.
3 The Hong Kong Hansard consists of records of the proceedings of the Legislative Council of Hong Kong in both English and Chinese.
4 www.statmt.org/europarl/
5 WMT started as the Workshop on Statistical Machine Translation in 2006. The workshop series went on until 2015, and it continued as the First Conference on Machine Translation in 2016. See, for example, the website of the Sixth Conference (WMT21) at http://statmt.org/wmt21/index.html. The WMT workshops organised a recurring news translation shared task since 2006, and since 2016, when it became a conference series, the tasks were expanded to other domains such as IT and biomedical translation.
6 https://paracrawl.eu/
7 BUCC is the Workshop on Building and Using Comparable Corpora, which started in 2008. See, for example, the website of the 14th BUCC at https://comparable.limsi.fr/bucc2021/
8 SIGHAN is the Special Interest Group on Chinese Language Processing of the Association for Computational Linguistics. The Chinese word segmentation bakeoffs, organised at its workshops during 2003 to 2008, have provided a common platform for evaluating system performance.

9 SIGPARSE is the Special Interest Group on Natural Language Parsing of the Association for Computational Linguistics.
10 CoNLL is the series of Conference on Computational Natural Language Learning, organised by the Special Interest Group on Natural Language Learning (SIGNLL) of the Association for Computational Linguistics.
11 Organised by the Special Interest Group on the Lexicon (SIGLEX) of the Association for Computational Linguistics, Senseval started in 1998 as the first evaluation exercise for word sense disambiguation. It has run from Senseval-1 to Senseval-3 and became SemEval in 2007 which continues to be an ongoing series of computational semantic analysis system evaluation, including many other semantic tasks deemed appropriate as the field progresses, such as semantic role labelling, sentiment analysis and paraphrases. SemEval is under the umbrella of both SIGLEX and SIGSEM (Special Interest Group on Computational Semantics).

Bibliography

Alinejad, Ashkan, Maryam Siahbani, and Anoop Sarkar (2018) 'Prediction Improves Simultaneous Neural Machine Translation', in *Proceedings of the 2018 Conference on Empirical Methods in Natural Language Processing*, Brussels, Belgium, 3022–27.

Allen, James (1995) *Natural Language Understanding*, 2nd edition, Redwood City, CA: The Benjamin/Cummings Publishing Company, Inc.

Bahdanau, Dzmitry, KyungHyun Cho, and Yoshua Bengio (2015) 'Neural Machine Translation by Jointly Learning to Align and Translate', *arXiv:1409.0473v7*.

Bañón, Marta, Pinzhen Chen, Barry Haddow, Kenneth Heafield, Hieu Hoang, Miquel Esplà-Gomis, Mikel Forcada, Amir Kamran, Faheem Kirefu, Philipp Koehn, Sergio Ortiz-Rojas, Leopoldo Pla, Gema Ramírez-Sánchez, Elsa Sarrías, Marek Strelec, Brian Thompson, William Waites, Dion Wiggins, and Jaume Zaragoza (2020) 'ParaCrawl: Web-Scale Acquisition of Parallel Corpora', in *Proceedings of the 58th Annual Meeting of the Association for Computational Linguistics (ACL 2020)*, Online Conference, 4555–67.

Baroni, Marco and Silvia Bernardini (2004) 'BootCaT: Bootstrapping Corpora and Terms from the Web', in *Proceedings of 4th International Conference on Language Resources and Evaluation (LREC 2004)*, Lisbon, Portugal, 1313–16.

Boguraev, Bran and Ted Briscoe (eds.) (1989) *Computational Lexicography for Natural Language Processing*, London: Longman.

Borin, Lars (2000) 'You'll Take the High Road and I'll Take the Low Road: Using a Third Language to Improve Bilingual Word Alignment', in *Proceedings of the 18th International Conference on Computational Linguistics*, Saarbrucken, Germany, 97–103.

Bouamor, Dhouha, Nasredine Semmar, and Pierre Zweigenbaum (2013) 'Context Vector Disambiguation for Bilingual Lexicon Extraction from Comparable Corpora', in *Proceedings of the 51st Annual Meeting of the Association for Computational Linguistics (Volume 2: Short Papers)*, Sofia, Bulgaria, 759–64.

Bourigault, Didier (1992) 'Surface Grammatical Analysis for the Extraction of Terminological Noun Phrases', in *Proceedings of the Fourteenth International Conference on Computational Linguistics (COLING '92)*, Nantes, France, 977–81.

Brill, Eric (1995) 'Transformation-Based Error-Driven Learning and Natural Language Processing: A Case Study in Part-of-Speech Tagging', *Computational Linguistics* 21(4): 543–65.

Brown, Peter F., John Cocke, Stephen A. Della Pietra, Vincent J. Della Pietra, Fredrick Jelinek, John D. Lafferty, Robert L. Mercer, and Paul S. Roossin (1990) 'A Statistical Approach to Machine Translation', *Computational Linguistics* 16(2): 79–85.

Charniak, Eugene (1993) *Statistical Language Learning*, Cambridge, MA: The MIT Press.

Charniak, Eugene (2019) *Introduction to Deep Learning*, Cambridge, MA: The MIT Press.

Charniak, Eugene and Drew McDermott (1985) *Introduction to Artificial Intelligence*, Reading, MA: Addison-Wesley.

Chen, Nancy, Rafael E. Banchs, Min Zhang, Xiangyu Duan, and Haizhou Li (2018) 'Report of NEWS 2018 Named Entity Transliteration Shared Task', in *Proceedings of the Seventh Named Entities Workshop*, Melbourne, Australia, 55–73.

Chen, Qi, Oi Yee Kwong, and Jingbo Zhu (2018) 'Detecting Free Translation in Parallel Corpora from Attention Scores', in *Proceedings of the 32nd Pacific Asia Conference on Language, Information and Computation (PACLIC 32)*, Hong Kong, 89–97.

Chklovski, Timothy and Rada Mihalcea (2002) 'Building a Sense Tagged Corpus with Open Mind Word Expert', in *Proceedings of the Workshop on Word Sense Disambiguation: Recent Successes and Future Directions*, Philadelphia, PA, 116–23.

Cho, Kyunghyun and Masha Esipova (2016) 'Can Neural Machine Translation Do Simultaneous Translation?', *arXiv:1606.02012v1*.

Cho, Kyunghyun, Bart van Merrienboer, Dzmitry Bahdanau, and Yoshua Bengio (2014) 'On the Properties of Neural Machine Translation: Encoder-Decoder Approaches', *arXiv:1409.1259v2*.

Church, Kenneth Ward (1989) 'A Stochastic Parts Program and Noun Phrase Parser for Unrestricted Text', in *Proceedings of International Conference on Acoustics, Speech, and Signal Processing (ICASSP '89)*, Glasgow, Scotland, 695–98.

Church, Kenneth Ward and Patrick Hanks (1990) 'Word Association Norms, Mutual Information, and Lexicography', *Computational Linguistics* 16(1): 22–29.

Costa-jussà, Marta R., Rafael E. Banchs, Reinhard Rapp, Patrik Lambert, Kurt Eberle, and Bogdan Babych (2013) 'Workshop on Hybrid Approaches to Translation: Overview and Developments', in *Proceedings of the Second Workshop on Hybrid Approaches to Translation*, Sofia, Bulgaria, 1–6.

Daille, Béatrice (1996) 'Study and Implementation of Combined Techniques for Automatic Extraction of Terminology', in Judith L. Klavans and Philip Resnik (eds.) *The Balancing Act: Combining Symbolic and Statistical Approaches to Language*, Cambridge, MA: MIT Press, 49–66.

Daille, Béatrice and Emmanuel Morin (2005) 'French-English Terminology Extraction from Comparable Corpora', in R. Dale, K.-F. Wong, J. Su, and O. Y. Kwong (eds.), *Natural Language Processing – IJCNLP 2005*, Lecture Notes in Artificial Intelligence, vol. 3651, Berlin, Germany: Springer-Verlag, 707–18.

Devlin, Jacob, Ming-Wei Chang, Kenton Lee, and Kristina Toutanova (2018) 'BERT: Pre-training of Deep Bidirectional Transformers for Language Understanding', *arXiv:1810.04805v2*.

Drouin, Patrick (2003) 'Term Extraction Using Non-Technical Corpora as a Point of Leverage', *Terminology* 9(1): 99–115.

Edmonds, Philip and Scott Cotton (2001) 'SENSEVAL-2: Overview', in *Proceedings of the Second International Workshop on Evaluating Word Sense Disambiguation Systems (SENSEVAL-2)*, Toulouse, France, 1–6.

Fung, Pascale (1998) 'A Statistical View on Bilingual Lexicon Extraction: From Parallel Corpora to Non-parallel Corpora', in *Lecture Notes in Artificial Intelligence*, vol. 1529, Springer, 1–17.

Gage, Philip (1994) 'A New Algorithm for Data Compression', *The C Users Journal* 12(2): 23–38.

Gale, William A. and Kenneth W. Church (1991) 'A Program for Aligning Sentences in Bilingual Corpora', in *Proceedings of the 29th Annual Conference of the Association for Computational Linguistics (ACL'91)*, Berkeley, CA, 177–84.

Gale, William A., Kenneth W. Church, and David Yarowsky (1992) 'One Sense Per Discourse', in *Proceedings of the Speech and Natural Language Workshop*, San Francisco, CA, 233–37.

Goto, Isao, Bin Lu, Ka Po Chow, Eiichiro Sumita, and Benjamin K. Tsou (2011) 'Overview of the Patent Machine Translation Task at the NTCIR-9 Workshop', in *Proceedings of the NTCIR-9 Workshop Meeting*, Tokyo, Japan, 559–78.

Greene, Barbara B. and Gerald M. Rubin (1971) *Automatic Grammatical Tagging of English*. Providence, RI: Department of Linguistics, Brown University.

Gupta, Rohit, Constantin Orăsan, Marcos Zampieri, Mihaela Vela, Josef van Genabith, and Ruslan Mitkov (2016) 'Improving Translation Memory Matching and Retrieval Using Paraphrases', *Machine Translation* 30: 19–40.

Hazem, Amir, Mérième Bouhandi, Florian Boudin, and Béatrice Daille (2020) 'TermEval 2020: TALN-LS2N System for Automatic Term Extraction', in *Proceedings of the 6th International Workshop on Computational Terminology (COMPUTERM 2020)*, 95–100. Available at: https://aclanthology.org/2020.computerm-1.13.pdf.

Hirschberg, Julia and Christopher D. Manning (2015) 'Advances in Natural Language Processing', *Science*, New Series 349(6245): 261–66.

Huang, Chang-ning and Hai Zhao (2007) 'Chinese Word Segmentation: A Decade Review', *Journal of Chinese Information Processing* 21(3): 8–19.

Huang, Jin-Xia and Key-Sun Choi (2000) 'Chinese-Korean Word Alignment Based on Linguistic Comparison', in *Proceedings of the 38th Annual Meeting of the Association for Computational Linguistics (ACL-2000)*, Hong Kong, 392–99.

Huang, Zhiheng, Wei Xu, and Kai Yu (2015) 'Bidirectional LSTM-CRF Models for Sequence Tagging', *arXiv:1508.01991v1*.

Hutchins, John (1998) 'The Origins of the Translator's Workstation', *Machine Translation* 13(4): 287–307.

Hutchins, John and Harold L. Somers (1992) *An Introduction to Machine Translation*, London: Academic Press.

Ide, Nancy and Jean Veronis (1998) 'Introduction to the Special Issue on Word Sense Disambiguation: The State of the Art', *Computational Linguistics* 24(1): 1–40.

Indurkhya, Nitin and Fred J. Damerau (2010) *Handbook of Natural Language Processing*, 2nd edition, Boca Raton, FL: Chapman & Hall.

Jia, Ye, Ron J. Weiss, Fadi Biadsy, Wolfgang Macherey, Melvin Johnson, Zhifeng Chen, and Yonghui Wu (2019) 'Direct Speech-to-Speech Translation with a Sequence-to-Sequence Model', *arXiv:1904.06037v2*.

Jurafsky, Daniel and James H. Martin (2009) *Speech and Language Processing: An Introduction to Natural Language Processing, Computational Linguistics, and Speech Recognition*, 2nd edition, Upper Saddle River, NJ: Prentice-Hall Inc.

Kageura, Kyo (1996) 'Methods of Automatic Term Recognition – A Review', *Terminology* 3(2): 259–89.

Kay, Martin and Martin Röscheisen (1993) 'Text-Translation Alignment', *Computational Linguistics* 19(1): 121–42.

Kilgarriff, Adam and Gregory Grefenstette (2003) 'Introduction to the Special Issue on the Web as Corpus', *Computational Linguistics* 29(3): 334–47.

Knight, Kevin and Jonathan Graehl (1998) 'Machine Transliteration', *Computational Linguistics* 24(4): 599–612.

Koehn, Philipp (2005) 'Europarl: A Parallel Corpus for Statistical Machine Translation', in *Proceedings of the Tenth Machine Translation Summit (MT Summit X)*, Phuket, Thailand, 79–86.

Koehn, Philipp (2010) *Statistical Machine Translation*, Cambridge: Cambridge University Press.

Koehn, Philipp (2020) *Neural Machine Translation*, Cambridge: Cambridge University Press.

Koehn, Philipp, Franz Josef Och, and Daniel Marcu (2003) 'Statistical Phrase-based Translation', in *Proceedings of the 2003 Human Language Technology Conference of the North American Chapter of the Association for Computational Linguistics*, Edmonton, 48–54.

Kuo, Jin-Shea, Haizhou Li, and Chih-Lung Lin (2008) 'Mining Transliterations from Web Query Results: An Incremental Approach', in *Proceedings of the Sixth SIGHAN Workshop on Chinese Language Processing (SIGHAN-6)*, Hyderabad, India, 16–23.

Kwong, Oi Yee (2009) 'Homophones and Tonal Patterns in English-Chinese Transliteration', in *Proceedings of the ACL-IJCNLP 2009 Conference Short Papers*, Singapore, 21–24.

Kwong, Oi Yee (2020) 'Translating Collocations: The Need for Task-driven Word Associations', in *Proceedings of the Workshop on the Cognitive Aspects of the Lexicon*, Online, 112–16. Available at: https://aclanthology.org/2020.cogalex-1.14.pdf.

Kwong, Oi Yee (2021) 'User-Driven Assessment of Commercial Term Extractors', *Terminology* 27(2): 179–218. https://doi.org/10.1075/term.20032.kwo.

Lafferty, John, Andrew McCallum, and Fernando C. N. Pereira (2001) 'Conditional Random Fields: Probabilistic Models for Segmenting and Labeling Sequence Data', in *Proceedings of the 18th International Conference on Machine Learning (ICML 2001)*, Williams College, Williamstown, MA, 282–89.

Laroche, Audrey and Philippe Langlais (2010) 'Revisiting Context-Based Projection Methods for Term-Translation Spotting in Comparable Corpora', in *Proceedings of the 23rd International Conference on Computational Linguistics (COLING 2010)*, Beijing, China, 617–25.

Li, Bo and Eric Gaussier (2010) 'Improving Corpus Comparability for Bilingual Lexicon Extraction from Comparable Corpora', in *Proceedings of the 23rd International Conference on Computational Linguistics (COLING 2010)*, Beijing, China, 644–52.

Li, Haizhou, A. Kumaran, Min Zhang, and Vladimir Pervouchine (2010) 'Report of NEWS 2010 Transliteration Generation Shared Task', in *Proceedings of the 2010 Named Entities Workshop*, Uppsala, Sweden, 1–11.

Li, Haizhou, Khe Chai Sim, Jin-Shea Kuo, and Minghui Dong (2007) 'Semantic Transliteration of Personal Names', in *Proceedings of the 45th Annual Meeting of the Association for Computational Linguistics*, Prague, Czech Republic, 120–27.

Li, Haizhou, Min Zhang, and Jian Su (2004) 'A Joint Source-Channel Model for Machine Transliteration', in *Proceedings of 42nd Meeting of the Association for Computational Linguistics (ACL'04)*, Barcelona, Spain, 159–66.

Lison, Pierre and Jörg Tiedemann (2016) 'OpenSubtitles2016: Extracting Large Parallel Corpora from Movie and TV Subtitles', in *Proceedings of the Tenth International Conference on Language Resources and Evaluation (LREC'16)*, Portorož, Slovenia, 923–29.

Liu, Yang, Liu Qun, and Shouxun Lin (2006) 'Tree-to-String Alignment Template for Statistical Machine Translation', in *Proceedings of the 21st International Conference on Computational Linguistics and 44th Annual Meeting of the Association for Computational Linguistics*, Sydney, Australia, 609–16.

Lo, Chi-kiu (2020) 'Extended Study on Using Pretrained Language Models and YiSi-1 for Machine Translation Evaluation', in *Proceedings of the 5th Conference on Machine Translation (WMT)*, Online, 895–902. Available at: https://aclanthology.org/2020.wmt-1.99.pdf.

Loureiro, Daniel and Alípio Jorge (2019) 'Language Modelling Makes Sense: Propagating Representations through WordNet for Full-Coverage Word Sense Disambiguation', in *Proceedings of the 57th Annual Meeting of the Association for Computational Linguistics (ACL 2019)*, Florence, Italy, 5682–91.

Mann, Gideon S. and David Yarowsky (2001) 'Multipath Translation Lexicon Induction via Bridge Languages', in *Proceedings of the 2nd Meeting of the North American Chapter of the Association for Computational Linguistics (NAACL 2001)*, Pittsburgh, PA, 151–58.

Manning, Christopher D. and Hinrich Schütze (1999) *Foundations of Statistical Natural Language Processing*, Cambridge, MA: The MIT Press.

Marcu, Daniel and Daniel Wong (2002) 'A Phrase-Based, Joint Probability Model for Statistical Machine Translation', in *Proceedings of the 2002 Conference on Empirical Methods in Natural Language Processing*, Prague, 133–39.

Màrquez, Lluís, Gerard Escudero, David Martínez, and German Rigau (2006) 'Supervised Corpus-Based Methods for WSD', in Eneko Agirre and Philip Edmonds (eds.) *Word Sense Disambiguation: Algorithms and Applications*, Dordrecht, The Netherlands: Springer.

Melamed, I. Dan (1997) 'A Word-to-Word Model of Translational Equivalence', in *Proceedings of the 35th Conference of the Association for Computational Linguistics and 8th Conference of the European Chapter of the Association for Computational Linguistics (ACL/EACL'97)*, Madrid, Spain, 490–97.

Melamud, Oren, Jacob Goldberger, and Ido Dagan (2016) 'Context2vec: Learning Generic Context Embedding with Bidirectional LSTM', in *Proceedings of the 20th SIGNLL Conference on Computational Natural Language Learning (CoNLL 2016)*, Berlin, Germany, 51–61.

Mihalcea, Rada (2006) 'Knowledge-based Methods for WSD', in Eneko Agirre and Philip Edmonds (eds.), *Word Sense Disambiguation: Algorithms and Applications*. Dordrecht, The Netherlands: Springer.

Mihalcea, Rada, Timothy Chklovski, and Adam Kilgarriff (2004) 'The SENSEVAL-3 English Lexical Sample Task', in *Proceedings of SENSEVAL-3, the Third International Workshop on the Evaluation of Systems for the Semantic Analysis of Text*, Barcelona, Spain, 25–28.

Mikheev, Andrei (2003) 'Text Segmentation', in Ruslan Mitkov (ed.) *The Oxford Handbook of Computational Linguistics*, Oxford: Oxford University Press, 201–18.

Mikolov, Tomas, Kai Chen, Greg Corrado, and Jeffrey Dean (2013) 'Efficient Estimation of Word Representations in Vector Space', *arXiv:1301.3781v3*.

Miller, George A. (1995) 'WordNet: A Lexical Database for English', *Communications of the ACM* 38(11): 39–41.

Navigli, Roberto (2009) 'Word Sense Disambiguation: A Survey', *ACM Computing Surveys* 41(2): 1–69.

Nielsen, Michael A. (2019) *Neural Networks and Deep Learning*, Free online book available at: http://neuralnetworksanddeeplearning.com/.

Och, Franz Josef and Hermann Ney (2003) 'A Systematic Comparison of Various Statistical Alignment Models', *Computational Linguistics* 29(1): 19–51.

Oh, Jong-Hoon and Key-Sun Choi (2005) 'An Ensemble of Grapheme and Phoneme for Machine Transliteration', in Robert Dale, Kam-Fai Wong, Jian Su, and Oi Yee Kwong (eds.), *Natural Language Processing – IJCNLP 2005*, LNAI, vol. 3651, Berlin, Germany: Springer, 451–61.

Olive, Joseph, Caitlin Christianson, and John McCary (eds.) (2011) *Handbook of Natural Language Processing and Machine Translation: DARPA Global Autonomous Language Exploitation*, New York: Springer.

Pease, Adam, Ian Niles, and John Li (2002) 'The Suggested Upper Merged Ontology: A Large Ontology for the Semantic Web and its Applications', in *Working Notes of the AAAI-2002 Workshop on Ontologies and the Semantic Web*, Edmonton, Canada.

Pedersen, Ted (2006) 'Unsupervised Corpus-Based Methods for WSD', in Eneko Agirre and Philip Edmonds (eds.) *Word Sense Disambiguation: Algorithms and Applications*, Dordrecht, The Netherlands: Springer.

Pennington, Jeffrey, Richard Socher, and Christopher D. Manning (2014) 'GloVe: Global Vectors for Word Representation', in *Proceedings of the 2014 Conference on Empirical Methods in Natural Language Processing (EMNLP)*, Doha, Qatar, 1532–43.

Peters, Matthew E., Mark Neumann, Mohit Iyyer, Matt Gardner, Christopher Clark, Kenton Lee, and Luke Zettlemoyer (2018) 'Deep Contextualized Word Representations', in *Proceedings of the 2018*

Conference of the North American Chapter of the Association for Computational Linguistics: Human Language Technologies (NAACL-HLT 2018), New Orleans, LA, 2227–37.

Piperidis, Stelios, S. Boutsis, and Iason Demiros (1997) 'Automatic Translation Lexicon Generation from Multilingual Texts', in *Proceedings of the 2nd Workshop on Multilinguality in Software Industry: The AI Contribution (MULSAIC'97)*, Nagoya, Japan.

Planas, Emmanuel (2005) 'SIMILIS: Second-Generation Translation Memory Software', in *Proceedings of the 27th International Conference on Translating and the Computer (TC27)*, London, 331–39.

Resnik, Philip and I. Dan Melamed (1997) 'Semi-Automatic Acquisition of Domain-Specific Translation Lexicons', in *Proceedings of the Fifth Conference on Applied Natural Language Processing*, Washington, DC, USA, 340–47.

Resnik, Philip and Noah A. Smith (2003) 'The Web as a Parallel Corpus', *Computational Linguistics* 29(3): 349–80.

Rich, Elaine and Kevin Knight (1991) *Artificial Intelligence*, New York: McGraw-Hill Book Company.

Sato, Satoshi and Makoto Nagao (1990) 'Toward Memory-based Translation', in *Proceedings of the 13th International Conference on Computational Linguistics*, Helsinki, 247–52.

Schank, Roger C. and Robert P. Abelson (1977) *Scripts, Plans, Goals and Understanding: An Inquiry into Human Knowledge Structures*, Hillsdale, NJ: Lawrence Erlbaum.

Sennrich, Rico, Barry Haddow, and Alexandra Birch (2016) 'Neural Machine Translation of Rare Words with Subword Units', in *Proceedings of the 54th Annual Meeting of the Association for Computational Linguistics (Volume 1: Long Papers)*, Berlin, Germany, 1715–25.

Simard, Michel, George F. Foster, and Pierre Isabelle (1992) 'Using Cognates to Align Sentences in Bilingual Corpora', in *Proceedings of the Fourth International Conference on Theoretical and Methodological Issues in Machine Translation (TMI-92)*, Montreal, Canada, 67–81.

Smadja, Frank, Vasileios Hatzivassiloglou, and Kathleen McKeown (1996) 'Translating Collocations for Bilingual Lexicons: A Statistical Approach', *Computational Linguistics* 22(1): 1–38.

Song, Linfeng, Daniel Gildea, Yue Zhang, Zhiguo Wang, and Jinsong Su (2019) 'Semantic Neural Machine Translation Using AMR', *Transactions of the Association for Computational Linguistics* 7: 19–31.

Specia, Lucia, Maria das Graças Volpe Nunes, Mark Stevenson, and Gabriela Castelo Branco Ribeiro (2006) 'Multilingual versus Monolingual WSD', in *Proceedings of the EACL-2006 Workshop on Making Sense of Sense: Bringing Psycholinguistics and Computational Linguistics Together*, Trento, Italy, 33–40.

Sproat, Richard and Thomas Emerson (2003) 'The First International Chinese Word Segmentation Bakeoff', in *Proceedings of the Second SIGHAN Workshop on Chinese Language Processing*, Sapporo, Japan, 133–43.

Sproat, Richard, William Gales, Chilin Shih, and Nancy Chang (1996) 'A Stochastic Finite-State Word-Segmentation Algorithm for Chinese', *Computational Linguistics* 22(3): 377–404.

Strassel, Stephanie, Caitlin Christianson, John McCary, William Staderman, and Joseph Olive (2011) 'Data Acquisition and Linguistic Resources', in Joseph Olive, Caitlin Christianson, and John McCary (eds.) *Handbook of Natural Language Processing and Machine Translation: DARPA Global Autonomous Language Exploitation*, New York: Springer.

Tao, Tao, Su-Youn Yoon, Andrew Fister, Richard Sproat, and ChengXiang Zhai (2006) 'Unsupervised Named Entity Transliteration Using Temporal and Phonetic Correlation', in *Proceedings of the 2006 Conference on Empirical Methods in Natural Language Processing*, Sydney, Australia, 250–57.

Vaswani, Ashish, Noam Shazeer, Niki Parmar, Jakob Uszkoreit, Llion Jones, Aidan N. Gomez, Lukasz Kaiser, and Illia Polosukhin (2017) 'Attention is All You Need', *arXiv:1706.03762v5*.

Wang, Rui, Wei Liu, and Chris McDonald (2016) 'Featureless Domain-specific Term Extraction with Minimal Labelled Data', in *Proceedings of Australasian Language Technology Association Workshop*, Melbourne, Australia, 103–12.

Winograd, Terry (1973) 'A Procedural Model of Language Understanding', in Roger C. Schank and Kenneth Mark Colby (eds.) *Computer Models of Thought and Language*, San Francisco, CA: Freeman, 152–86.

Wu, Dekai (1994) 'Aligning a Parallel English-Chinese Corpus Statistically with Lexical Criteria', in *Proceedings of the 32nd Annual Meeting of the Association for Computational Linguistics (ACL-94)*, Las Cruces, NM, USA, 80–87.

Wu, Dekai (2010) 'Alignment', in Nitin Indurkhya and Fred J. Damerau (eds.) *Handbook of Natural Language Processing*, 2nd edition, Boca Raton, FL: Chapman and Hall.

Wu, Dekai and Xuanyin Xia (1995) 'Large-Scale Automatic Extraction of an English-Chinese Translation Lexicon', *Machine Translation* 9(3–4): 285–313.

Xue, Nianwen and Susan P. Converse (2002) 'Combining Classifiers for Chinese Word Segmentation', in *Proceedings of the First SIGHAN Workshop on Chinese Language Processing*, Taipei, 63–69.

Young, Tom, Devamanyu Hazarika, Soujanya Poria, and Erik Cambria (2018) 'Recent Trends in Deep Learning Based Natural Language Processing', *arXiv:1708.02709v8*.

Zhai, Feifei, Jiajun Zhang, Yu Zhou, and Chengqing Zong (2012) 'Machine Translation by Modeling Predicate Argument Structure Transformation', in *Proceedings of the 24th International Conference on Computational Linguistics*, Mumbai, India, 3019–36.

Zhang, Min, Haizhou Li, A Kumaran, and Ming Liu (2011) 'Report of NEWS 2011 Machine Transliteration Shared Task', in *Proceedings of the 3rd Named Entities Workshop (NEWS 2011)*, Chiang Mai, Thailand, 1–13.

Zhao, Hai, Deng Cai, Changning Huang, and Kit Chunyu (2019) 'Chinese Word Segmentation: Another Decade Review (2007–2017)', *arXiv:1901.06079v1*.

39

ONLINE TRANSLATION

Federico Gaspari

Overview

This chapter concerns key aspects related to online translation and focuses on the relationship between translators and the web. The introduction offers an overview of the first internet-based communication channels used by the early online communities of language and translation professionals and charts their subsequent evolution. The section 'The Ecosystem of Online Translation' presents a range of web-based resources for translators, including online (meta-)dictionaries, glossaries, terminology databases and shared translation memories, highlighting their key features. The following part covers online translation tools and internet-based translation environments, such as browser-based applications that support translation projects from start to finish, allowing the deployment of communal or proprietary translation memories and glossaries, as well as the integration of online machine translation (MT) for subsequent post-editing to boost productivity. The chapter continues with a description of the key features of the most popular online translation marketplaces, given their growing importance in creating business opportunities for translators.

Finally, the section 'Online Translation in the Web 2.0' is devoted to the latest developments of user-generated translation in the Web 2.0 scenario and reviews high-profile online collaborative translation projects as well as crowdsourcing efforts. This leads to an assessment of the translation crowdsourcing model, in which volunteer (amateur) translators are involved in projects for the localization of popular social media platforms of which they are themselves users. Each section discusses representative examples of relevant websites, online tools, web resources, internet-based projects or services, with a bias towards those available in English, which are analysed from the perspective of translators. While the inclusion or exclusion of items from the various categories does not imply any endorsement or criticism, or any implicit judgement of their quality, an attempt is made to identify common trends and interesting specific features that have played a role in the development of online translation, discussing their pros and cons.

Introduction: The Origins of Online Translation

The Gradual Impact of the Internet on Translation

As has been the case for virtually all other professions and businesses, the internet has had a profound impact on translation, dramatically accelerating the process that started in the early

DOI: 10.4324/9781003168348-42

1980s, when personal computers became widely available to translators, initially as sophisticated typewriters. This was the prelude to rapid developments in the following decades that were bound to affect the daily work of translators and, more broadly, increase the impact of technology on the ways in which translations are produced, circulated and finally used by clients and target readers (Cronin 2013). The internet affected translation only indirectly until the late 1990s, due to two main reasons: first of all, until that time the internet was not yet widely available across the globe, with the exception of relatively few users working mostly for government agencies, academic institutions, multinational companies and large organizations located in a small number of countries around the world; second, the internet still had very little to offer to translators compared to the impressive array of online resources, tools and opportunities that can be found today.

For most of the 1990s, then, one could talk of online translation only insofar as translation agencies and professionals progressively started to use email in order to receive source texts from their clients and deliver back their translations (O'Hagan 1996), with some pioneers setting up (often multilingual) websites to advertise their services. This was clearly a very limited use of the internet, which was largely confined to taking advantage of its speed and convenience for transferring files electronically and for promotional purposes. The associated benefits gradually led to the decline in the use of fax machines and floppy disks, which had been the primary means to exchange original and translated documents during the final stages of the pre-internet era. The early transition to the use of email by translators (and their clients) motivated by basic file transfer needs encouraged more and more professionals to get online towards the late 1990s. This, in turn, laid the foundation for the first online communities of translators, who started to use email and the (then rather rudimentary) internet-based communication facilities to discuss work-related issues.

Early Translation-Related Newsgroups and Online Forums

Usenet-based newsgroups were early online communities organized in hierarchical categories around topics of interest to their members, and designed to share textual messages via the nascent internet infrastructure. Users could read and post messages for their preferred categories, thus becoming part of virtual distributed communities: this made it possible for translators to exchange information among themselves and consult more knowledgeable colleagues, for instance to seek advice on terminological issues, payment practices, and so on. Members could generally sign up to these newsgroups free of charge, and it was not uncommon for individuals to be members of multiple (in some cases partially overlapping) communities, depending on their interests. This was a significant turning point for translators, as for the first time it was no longer necessary to attend conferences, workshops or meetings of translators' associations to be instantly connected to fellow professionals. Indeed, physical distance became irrelevant, and such online asynchronous discussion systems allowed the interaction of translators and interpreters over the internet across time zones, regardless of where they were based – crucially, due to their multilingual skills, international contacts of this nature were more feasible and natural for translators and interpreters than for any other professionals.

One of the first newsgroups of specific interest to translators, sci.lang.translation, was set up in late 1994 as an unmoderated newsgroup, where related postings were presented as threads. Its aims included facilitating discussion among members on professional issues such as the activities of translators' organizations, accreditation procedures, dictionaries and other useful resources, terminology problems, training opportunities, and so on. Subsequently, with the development of the internet and associated technologies, several Usenet-type newsgroups evolved into discussion forums, which had additional user-friendly features designed to make the exchange of postings smoother. Some of them subsequently migrated to more easily accessible platforms – sci.lang. translation, for example, became part of Google Groups,[1] and it still serves as a forum for discussions on a vast number of translation-related subjects. Although the volume of traffic has increasingly moved to other channels (see the section 'From Translators' Mailing Lists to Social Media'), there are still several popular online forums about translation, languages and linguistics, such as those hosted by WordReference.com (more information in the section 'Online Dictionaries and Meta-dictionaries') and others that are part of websites serving as online translation marketplaces (see the section 'Online Translation Marketplaces').

From Translators' Mailing Lists to Social Media

Around the mid-1990s, the first mailing lists for (and run by) translators started to appear. They were different from newsgroups and discussion forums in some respects: mailing lists were usually moderated, and instead of logging on to a website to view the latest threads, subscribers received the posts of fellow members directly into their email inbox, and they could also reply and send new messages to other subscribers from their email client. Mailing lists could have memberships of variable sizes, from a few dozens to several thousands, and as a consequence their email traffic varied dramatically. These email-based communication channels were no longer public, strictly speaking, in that one had to join the mailing lists to start receiving and posting messages. Mailing lists, especially those with many members and heavy traffic, adopted policies to manage the flow of information efficiently; these included conventions concerning the subject lines of emails posted to the group, allowing for quick filtering of relevant messages and management of threads, and the possibility to receive overview summaries (so-called 'digests') of messages posted during a day or a week, to avoid the constant trickle of emails on diverse topics.

One of the earliest mailing lists for translators, which still retains a sizeable international membership, is Lantra-L.[2] This is a generalist mailing list; that is, it does not impose any restriction on membership and broadly welcomes discussions on any topic related to translation and interpreting, concerning any language and language combination, although messages are predominantly in English, which in itself guarantees a large readership. Other mailing lists have chosen different approaches, adopting more restrictive criteria in terms of their membership and remit, for example, by focusing exclusively on a single target language or language pair, concentrating on specific professional areas (say, literary as opposed to technical or specialized translation), or encouraging membership from translators based in certain countries. Of course, mailing lists can also be open only to the members of an existing translators' community or organization, for instance a regional or national professional association, and as such serve as restricted communication channels among members, for example, to circulate newsletters or information on upcoming events.

Since the mid-1990s, newsgroups, online discussion forums and mailing lists have had remarkable appeal for translators, in particular because they suddenly offered an unprecedented antidote to the oft-lamented isolation and loneliness of translation professionals. These effective online communication channels created a sense of community, giving individuals access to the collective wealth of expertise of translators spread around the world, at virtually no cost once a user had a computer with internet access (Plassard 2007: 643–57; Williams 2013: 92). Wakabayashi (2002) and Alcina-Caudet (2003: 634–41) stress the importance of helping translation students and budding professionals to familiarize themselves with these email-based online communities, due to the large repository of expertise to which they give access. In a similar vein, several translators also maintain blogs to share their views on professional matters, and McDonough

Dolmaya (2011a: 77–104) analyses a convenience sample of 50 such translation blogs to discover how they are used to discuss translation-related problems, generate business contacts and socialize with colleagues around the world.

With the passing of time, however, this scenario is changing: just like the increased popularity of personal email accounts and availability of user-friendly clients boosted the success of translators' mailing lists around the turn of the 21st century, they currently seem to be losing ground due to the growing role of social media. For instance, the popular online social networking platform Facebook[3] supports the fast and easy creation of (public, restricted or private) groups and shared pages to discuss any topic and circulate information among members of the online community, encouraging cross-platform interaction. LinkedIn[4] serves a similar purpose, but with a much stronger focus on professional networking, hence its specific relevance to practising translators and players in the translation and localization industry. Finally, the microblogging site Twitter[5] allows its users to follow real-time updates on issues of interest to them, reading and exchanging brief online posts that can be organized and prioritized according to personal preferences (the section 'Crowdsourced Online Translation Projects' reviews crowdsourced online translation projects promoted by Facebook, LinkedIn and Twitter). The visibility of translation and the presence of translators on these and other social media can be expected to grow in the foreseeable future, while the activity of traditional online discussion forums and mailing lists seems to be gradually, and probably irreversibly, dwindling.

The Ecosystem of Online Translation

Online Resources for Translators

With the start of the 21st century, online translation became a reality in parallel with the gradual growth of the internet into a widely used multi-faceted environment to create, share and distribute digital contents in multiple languages for increasingly diverse audiences. In spite of all its multimedia contents (videos, graphics, sound, etc.), the web is still a heavily textual and language-intensive medium – one need only think of how search engines are used; in addition, the multilingual and multicultural nature of its growing global user population arguably makes the internet a natural environment for translation: it is therefore not surprising that a multitude of valuable online resources are available for translators, some of which are created by members of the translation community. Their actual use by, and relevance for, professionals varies depending on their working languages and specialism, but it is fair to say that hardly any translator today can afford to neglect the importance of online resources. Indeed, they are increasingly considered part and parcel of the translators' standard working environment, as traditional libraries and documentation centres are unlikely to match the quantity and diversity of relevant information that is available on the internet – as Cronin (2013: 8) puts it, 'the working practices of translators have been changed beyond recognition in terms of the access to many different kinds of knowledge that are afforded by the infrastructure of the internet'. The double challenge for translators consists in finding quickly high-quality websites and valuable online sources when they need them, and in using them properly.

Online Dictionaries and Meta-Dictionaries

At the most basic level, translators can take advantage of online resources that are made available to the general public, such as monolingual and multilingual dictionaries, some of which are of very high quality and may be available free of charge, including the online versions of leading traditional printed dictionaries for an impressive variety of languages and language pairs. Apart from these general-purpose online resources, there are others that are more specifically geared towards the needs of translators, including technical and specialized dictionaries. In addition, the web hosts a number of meta-dictionaries, which aggregate several online reference works (sometimes also including encyclopaedias) in many languages drawing on a huge amount of background information, and which support multiple simultaneous word searches.[6] A popular resource among translators is WordReference.com,[7] which was launched in 1999 and provides free online bilingual dictionaries as well as a variety of other contents of interest to translators. This website offers two main sets of online resources: first of all, bilingual dictionaries primarily of English in combination with other languages – WordReference.com also aims to serve other languages, including Spanish, French, Italian, Portuguese, and so on; second, the site also provides a wide range of language-specific and translation-related forums on a number of topics, especially concerning the meaning and translation of words, phrases and idioms in several languages (Cronin 2013: 74–75). The archives of these forums are publicly available for perusal, but some of them require registration before a user can post a question or reply to an existing message.

WordReference.com combines the traditional discussion forum format (see also the section 'Online Translation Marketplaces' for other websites offering similar virtual meeting spaces) with the constantly expanding availability of online dictionaries, thus bringing together lexico-graphic information and expert advice on usage and translation issues. One potential problem in this respect is that fellow users who volunteer answers may not be great experts of the languages or fields in question, and it might difficult for inexperienced professionals to identify forum members who can give valuable advice. On the one hand, the translators posting questions and requests for help via online discussion forums, for example concerning terminology, must provide sufficient background information and context with their queries, so that others are effectively able to provide relevant and helpful answers. On the other hand, though, the ultimate responsibility for using wisely the advice received from such mostly anonymous online com-munities rests with the translators themselves, as they are accountable to clients for the quality of their work. This underscores the need to scrutinize the trustworthiness and reliability of infor-mation obtained from internet-based sources, including via professional discussion forums and online translators' communities, due to the woeful lack of robust screening procedures linked to the professional credentials of online forum members.

Online Terminology Databases and Glossaries

There are also several online resources for translators that are vetted and made available by reputable sources following rigorous quality checks, thus providing more reliable and authorita-tive materials to translators conducting research for a specific assignment. This is the case, for example, of IATE,[8] an online multilingual terminology database that was developed from the European Union's inter-institutional terminology assets, which were built up over many years by translators, terminologists and linguists working in various EU institutions and agencies (Ball 2003). IATE started to be used internally by the EU in 2004, and the database was made publicly available online in mid-2007, following significant efforts in terminology collection, validation and standardization. Its records are constantly extended with new entries concerning EU-related terminology and jargon in all the official EU languages from a wide variety of areas, including law, agriculture, economics, computing, and so on.

IATE can be consulted online by anybody via a user-friendly interface available in all the official EU languages, which offers a number of intuitive features, including the possibility to automatically load the user's search preferences for source and target languages, a star-rating system showing how reliable an equivalent term in the target language is considered, term definitions, cross-references to the sources consulted for term validation and examples of real uses in context. In addition, users can submit queries for terms selecting specific search domains from dozens of options (ranging from 'air and space transport' to 'wood industry'). IATE is a very high-profile publicly available resource containing excellent multilingual terminological data that can be used by any translator, not only those working in or for the EU institutions.

There are countless other web-based terminological databases and online glossaries covering an extremely wide range of languages and subjects, which can be found on the internet using search engines or based on the recommendations and advice of colleagues. Of course, nothing prevents translators from mining the web directly for linguistic and terminological information, without consulting pre-compiled lexicographic online resources. A number of tools have been created to support translators in their efficient online terminology research. For example, Intelli-WebSearch[9] is a free application developed by a professional translator to speed up the search for terms on the internet when working on a translation (see also e.g. Durán Muñoz 2012: 77–92). Again, caution is required to differentiate trustworthy, valuable webpages from online sources of dubious or variable quality.

Online Shared Translation Memories and Parallel Corpora

Apart from online (meta-)dictionaries, terminological databases and glossaries, the internet also offers other language resources whose use entails a higher level of technical expertise on the part of translators, but whose benefits can be very significant. This is the case for a number of multilingual translation memory repositories that have been made available online as part of different projects. Three examples provided by the EU are reviewed here for illustration purposes, starting with the DGT-Translation Memory,[10] a large database that has been updated every year since 2007 and contains the multilingual parallel versions of the Acquis Communautaire (i.e. the entire EU legislation, including all the treaties, regulations and directives) in the official EU languages (Steinberger *et al.* 2012: 454–59). All the multilingual versions of each text are aligned at the sentence level, which results in an impressive set of combinations: more than 250 language pairs, or over 500 language pair directions; this is particularly remarkable because some of the languages covered are not particularly well supported in terms of parallel corpora or language resources (as is the case for relatively rare language combinations such as Maltese–Finnish or Estonian–Slovene). The parallel texts can be downloaded in the widely adopted Translation Memory eXchange (TMX) format, thus enabling translators to import the aligned parallel data into their preferred translation memory software.

Similarly to the case of IATE, the DGT-Translation Memory is released online as part of the European Commission's effort to support multilingualism, language diversity and the re-use of information produced within the EU institutions. These high-quality multilingual parallel texts can be used by translators when working with translation memory software, to ensure that identical segments in new source texts do not have to be retranslated from scratch several times (or to avoid that they end up being translated inconsistently into the same target language); in addition, similar past translations can be leveraged to speed up the current job, while ensuring consistency across translation projects. Collections of multilingual parallel data such as the DGT-Translation Memory can also be used for a variety of other purposes, such as training MT systems, extracting monolingual or multilingual lexical and semantic resources, developing language models for data-driven systems with a linguistic or translation component, and so on. Other similar, but smaller, parallel data sets publicly released online by the EU are the ECDC-TM,[11] which contains documents from the European Centre for Disease Prevention and Control in 25 languages, and the EAC-TM,[12] consisting of texts from the Directorate General for Education and Culture in 26 languages.

The OPUS project[13] is dedicated to assembling a growing collection of publicly available parallel corpora covering dozens of languages, including multiple domains such as law, administration (again using mostly EU texts), film subtitles, software and computing documentation, newspaper articles, biomedical papers, and so on (Tiedemann 2012: 2214–18). Overall, the parallel corpora of the OPUS collection cover nearly 4,000 language pairs, for a total of over 40 billion words, distributed in approximately 3 billion parallel translation units (aligned sentences and fragments), and the collection is constantly growing. These multilingual parallel corpora provided by the OPUS project can be downloaded from the web in different formats (native XML, TMX and plain text format), so that translators can use them with their own translation memory software.

In addition, the OPUS project website offers an online interface to directly interrogate the parallel corpora, for example to generate (multilingual aligned) concordances from the selected corpora: users can consult their chosen languages in parallel, or query a single version of a given corpus to consider one language at a time. Although it is difficult to retrieve information on which version of the parallel texts was the original one, all the translations were done by human professionals, thus guaranteeing high quality standards across languages. To accompany these online linguistic resources, the OPUS project website also makes available a range of other tools to further annotate and process the data, so that they can be used for multiple purposes, as noted previously for the DGT-Translation Memory.

These resources created by the EU institutions and by the OPUS project have been made available online to the advantage of different users and for a variety of purposes, but it is easy to see how translators in particular can benefit from them, also because they are constantly growing with updates and extensions. In addition, these translation memories and parallel corpora come from reputable sources and underwent a number of quality checks. There exist several similar online resources, which however tend to be subject to a more restrictive regime in terms of use and distribution, partly because they were created within commercial entities, and are covered by copyright and other intellectual property constraints. Moreover, in some cases, the reliability of potentially useful resources for translators found online may be unclear in terms of provenance, copyright status and quality requirements.

Online Translation Platforms, Environments and Tools

Online Platforms to Share Translation Memories

MyMemory[14] claims to be the world's largest free online translation memory, but in fact it does not limit itself to offering a collection of linguistic data, because it also provides a web platform to upload, store and manage a repository of translation memories for different language pairs and various domains. MyMemory is free to use for registered members, and its multilingual translation memories have been assembled collecting parallel texts from different institutions, including the EU and the UN, as well as from other sources, particularly crawling multilingual websites covering several domains – it should be noted that this resource is not as well documented as the ones reviewed in the section 'Online Shared Translation Memories and Parallel Corpora'. After registering with MyMemory, users can download translation memories customized to match the texts that they intend to translate, and use them in their own computer-assisted translation environments. Interestingly, when its existing translation memory databases fail to come up with relevant matches for a document to be translated uploaded by a user, MyMemory provides raw

MT output as a translation draft. Differently from the resources examined in section 'Online Shared Translation Memories and Parallel Corpora', MyMemory also invites users to directly contribute to the growth of its online repository by uploading additional translation memories or by editing existing materials via its platform, although it is not clear what guidelines or quality controls apply in such cases. In addition, MyMemory's online platform also provides the possibility of searching terms and translated segments among its resources in multiple language pairs and domains.

Online Translation Environments and Tools

Google Translator Toolkit[15] (GTT) is a web application that supports translators, not necessarily only professionals but also amateur bilinguals who wish to translate documents or webpages. GTT was released in 2009 and handles several document formats; it also includes a specific facility to import Wikipedia entries that a user wishes to translate into another language, taking care of layout and formatting issues and letting the user concentrate on the translation of the text. This browser-based translation environment, which is reported to support hundreds of source and target languages, enables users to set up translation projects and gives them the option to upload relevant glossaries and translation memories, if they so wish. Interestingly, and similarly to what was noted in the section 'Online Platforms to Share Translation Memories' for MyMemory, GTT can also be configured so that it offers a draft of the target text based on MT output provided by Google Translate,[16] which the user can then correct and improve (on the development of the early free online MT systems see Yang and Lange 1998: 275–85; Yang and Lange 2003: 191–210; Gaspari and Hutchins 2007: 199–206).

Effectively, then, GTT is a cloud-based customisable translation memory environment, with an integrated dictionary lookup function and an optional statistical MT facility supported by Google Translate, which the user can activate when no matches are found in the translation memories. One feature of interest to translators is that when the translation of a document is completed, the updated translation memory created during the project can be downloaded from the GTT online environment and imported by users in TMX format along with the finished target text, thus allowing for its reuse in subsequent projects and even with different offline translation memory tools. Since GTT was made available for free to users, there have been speculations that this might be a veiled attempt by Google to acquire high-quality glossaries and parallel texts from translators to feed its own proprietary MT system, also relying on users' corrections of the raw MT output to improve its performance (Garcia and Stevenson 2009: 16–19). It should be noted, however, that users can choose not to share the resources that they upload online into GTT when working on a translation project.

Boitet *et al.* (2005) and Bey *et al.* (2008: 135–50) describe the design and development of an online translation environment called BEYTrans. This wiki-based platform is aimed at volunteer translators working on shared projects via the internet, especially those involved in well-organized mission-oriented translation communities, say to translate the technical documentation related to free and open-source software development projects. The BEYTrans environment enables users to access and manage a range of online language tools and resources, including multilingual dictionary and glossary lookup facilities and community-specific translation memories to match the requirements of particular translation projects. In addition, this wiki-based translation platform also has an integrated facility that supports Internet searches for translated text fragments in the target language corresponding to parts of the source text. Similarly to GTT, the output of free web-based MT services can also be provided: BEYTrans users are expected to check and improve it where necessary.

Utiyama *et al.* (2009) and Kageura *et al.* (2011: 47–72) present three projects related to a Japan-based open online translation aid and hosting service called Minna no Hon'yaku.[17] This was launched in 2009, initially to facilitate voluntary translation work for NGOs and with subsequent ramifications into the commercial domain. QRedit is the translation-aid text editor of this online translation platform and was designed specifically to support the work of online distributed communities of translators (Abekawa and Kageura 2007: 3–5). The overall platform enables users to contribute to translation projects involving a set of language pairs with a strong Asian focus, offering them access to useful online language resources and translation-related tools. These include integrated dictionary lookup, a terminology management system, a bilingual concordancer and a bilingual term extraction facility. Depending on the type of project (as some of them have a more commercial, rather than philanthropic or humanitarian, nature), the platform may also be partly open to non-professional translators, who have to pass a language proficiency test before they can contribute to the translations, and then they receive payment for their work – the quality requirements are adjusted accordingly.

Online Translation Marketplaces

This section gives an overview of a small sample of particularly popular online marketplaces for translation and related services, which evolved as the distributed communities of translators (and their clients) grew over time and converged onto the web to conduct parts of their business. A long-standing and well-established online platform devoted to connecting professionals, agencies and clients specifically in the translation and localization industry is Aquarius,[18] which was launched in 1995 and aims to support the outsourcing of translation and localization projects. The site includes some features to match offer and demand, that is, a list of jobs where potential contractors can give quotes for available projects, and a directory of professionals that can be searched by clients. In addition, the Aquarius website has an area with forums where subscribers can post professional questions and elicit feedback or advice from other registered members.

Another professional networking site for translators is ProZ.com,[19] which was founded in 1999 and now gathers a large community of translators, interpreters, translation companies and clients. The ProZ.com site is a virtual marketplace where professionals can outsource and accept assignments, give feedback on their experience with clients, exchange information on their work, request help on the translation of specific terminology, be referred to training opportunities, and so on. ProZ.com has an interesting mechanism to incentivize and reward successful high-quality online interactions among its members. When someone receives help from a fellow ProZ.com member in reply to a request for assistance concerning the translation of a difficult term or phrase, the author of the most useful answer is rewarded with KudoZ points; these are favourable ratings that are used to establish the professional reputation of ProZ.com members, and subsequently to rank professionals in the directory of language service providers from which clients can pick contractors (Perrino 2009: 55–78).

TranslatorsCafé.com[20] was launched in 2002 and is another popular networking site hosting an online community and marketplace for translators. It not only provides access to a range of language- and translation-related news and resources such as online forums but also offers a platform to connect with other professionals and to contact registered translation agencies looking for translation and interpreting services. Similarly to the policy adopted by ProZ.com, TranslatorsCafé.com also encourages users to provide feedback and comments on the online activities of fellow members, in particular by rating the quality and usefulness of answers to the questions they post. McDonough (2007: 793–815) proposes a framework for categorizing and describing such online translation networks, and discusses TranslatorsCafé.com as a case study of a practice-oriented translation network; the analysis of the most typical and interesting online behaviour of its members reveals the dynamics governing this and other similar virtual professional communities, also showing that fewer than 10% of registered users ever posted a message in the discussion forum and that threads normally had many more views than replies (ibid.: 809).

There are several other portals, online translation marketplaces and networking sites specifically designed to match translators and their clients, for example, GoTranslators,[21] Langmates. com[22] and TranslationDirectory.com.[23] They all have different strengths and specific features, depending on the areas in which they specialize and on the specific types of professionals, agencies and clients that they aim to serve. Nowadays online translation marketplaces are an important arena bringing together professionals who can secure projects and clients who can source some of their service providers. Given their vital role in an increasingly fragmented and competitive industry, the significance of online translation marketplaces in matching offer and demand is likely to grow in the future.

Pros and Cons of Online Translation Resources, Tools and Services

Due to the very nature of the internet, online resources such as (meta-)dictionaries, glossaries, terminological databases, translation memory repositories, and so on are subject to constant and potentially rapid change, which presents both advantages and disadvantages. On the positive side, materials published online can be constantly updated, extended and refreshed at a fraction of the costs and time needed for their printed counterparts, also lending themselves to quick searching and further electronic processing. This helps, for example, the timely inclusion in major online dictionaries of neologisms, accepted borrowings, and so on, as well as the constant creation of new web-based glossaries, or the expansion of already existing terminological databases, translation memory and corpus repositories, covering an ever growing range of languages and specialized domains. As has been mentioned, these online resources can then be accessed very easily via web interfaces or conveniently downloaded for further offline use by professional translators.

On the other hand, however, the unstable nature of the internet means that valid information sources and online resources on which translators rely for research and documentation purposes may suddenly disappear without any warning, or the quality of their contents may deteriorate over time (e.g. by becoming obsolete, due to lack of updates or thorough quality checks, which may not always be transparent to users). Another danger is that the multitude of resources, tools and services available online to translators may make it difficult to select the reliable high-quality ones, especially for relatively inexperienced professionals working with widely used languages; as a result, the task of screening websites and online resources on the basis of their quality may turn out to be a time-consuming activity.

A final word of caution concerns the confidentiality of data circulated or shared on the web. For example, MyMemory offers a mechanism to protect privacy by removing people's and brand names from the translation memories that registered users upload onto its online platform to be shared. However, sensitive information may go beyond these details, for example, in the case of documents concerning financial matters, legal disputes or medical conditions or describing inventions, patents, industrial applications, and so on. Translators and translation agencies have a duty to protect the privacy and interests of their clients; therefore, they should carefully consider all the confidentiality issues and legal implications that may arise, before passing on texts and translation resources to third parties on the internet (Drugan and Babych 2010: 3–9).

Online Translation in the Web 2.0

Online Collaborative Translation

The Web 2.0 emphasizes the social and collaborative dimensions of the internet, with users becoming active producers of dynamic online contents distributed and shared across platforms, rather than purely passive consumers of static pages found in websites authored by others. Crucial to the achievement of this vision is the removal (or at least the reduction) of language barriers: users are not only empowered to author online contents in their preferred languages, but they also contribute to their translation (O'Hagan 2011: 11–23; Cronin 2013: 99ff). Given its diverse and multilingual nature, Wikipedia[24] epitomizes the key role of users as both authors and translators in making its entries accessible in multiple languages to communities of internet users from different national, linguistic and cultural backgrounds. What is worth noting here is that online translation is performed not only by professionals or trained translators but also more and more often by multilingual amateurs as a hobby or volunteer activity.

Désilets *et al.* (2006: 19–31) discuss the design and implementation of processes and tools to support the multilingual creation and maintenance of multilingual wiki contents; their discussion is not restricted to Wikipedia but also applies in principle to any wiki site with collaboratively created and translated multilingual contents. Désilets (2007, 2011) outlines a number of challenges for translators and consequences for translation arising from the model of massive online collaboration leading to the distributed and user-participated creation and translation of web content, especially due to the availability of open and shared online translation-oriented resources. Désilets and van der Meer (2011: 27–45) describe current best practices to manage collaborative translation projects successfully. Gough (2011: 195–217) investigates the trends that have developed in the translation industry as part of the transition towards the Web 2.0: her sample of 224 respondents reveals that professional translators have a vague awareness and limited understanding of such trends and also that they make marginal use of open online tools, engaging little in collaborative translation processes. McDonough Dolmaya (2012: 167–91) presents a survey among Wikipedia volunteer translators to explore the perception of collaborative translation efforts, also discussing the role of the organizations driving them, while Fernández Costales (2012: 115–42) illustrates the range of motivations leading volunteers to become involved in web-based collaborative translation projects.

Perrino (2009: 55–78) reviews a number of tools specifically designed to support online collaborative translation in a Web 2.0 scenario, enabling what he calls 'user-generated translation', including Traduwiki,[25] Der Mundo[26] and Cucumis,[27] in addition to WordReference.com (covered in the section 'Online Dictionaries and Meta-Dictionaries'), Proz.com and TranslatorsCafé.com (both discussed in the section 'Online Translation Marketplaces'). Perrino (2009: 68–70) has a rather negative assessment of the actual usefulness of integrating web-based MT services into these tools for online collaborative translation, even though this trend seems to be continuing in the latest online translation platforms and environments (cf. the sections 'Online Platforms to Share Translation Memory' and 'Online Translation Environments and Tools'). His conclusion is that overall web-based tools and environments supporting distributed online collaborative translation efforts are below the standards that would be expected by those translating user-generated content in the Web 2.0 era, thus pointing to the need for further developments in this area.

There have been attempts to efficiently translate and synchronize the multilingual versions of wiki sites by maximizing the impact of online MT and other state-of-the-art natural language processing techniques, such as by the European project CoSyne[28] (Gaspari *et al.* 2011: 13–22; Bronner *et al.* 2012: 1–4). Other endeavours have investigated ways in which online MT can support the creation of multilingual content for Wikipedia and other wiki sites by translating entries from English which are then checked and post-edited by users fluent in the target language, for example, WikiBhasha,[29] a multilingual content creation tool for Wikipedia developed by Microsoft Research from the previous WikiBABEL project[30] (Kumaran *et al.* 2010); the multiple language versions of Wikipedia entries thus created can also provide parallel data to develop domain-adapted MT systems.

Crowdsourced Online Translation Projects

DePalma and Kelly (2011: 379–407) address the project management issues faced by four commercial companies that pioneered voluntary community translation, including Facebook, whose crowdsourced translation effort was launched in late 2007. In early 2008 the social networking platform inaugurated its versions in Spanish and German with contents translated for free by volunteer users, and dozens of other languages were added with this crowdsourcing approach by the end of the same year. This early example of grassroots volunteer web localization applied to a major social media platform showed that enthusiastic users were willing to work for free to extend the multilingual accessibility of their online communities. Consistently with Facebook's community-focussed ethos, in the case of competing translations for specific strings and textual contents, a voting mechanism was in place to measure the popularity of alternatives and assign points to the most prolific and successful volunteer translators (Ellis 2009: 236–44). Dramatic gains in speed were reported thanks to this crowdsourcing model compared to the time that it would have taken to localize Facebook in new languages using traditional methods (Kelly *et al.* 2011: 87).

However, some control over translation quality was still retained centrally, as the whole process powered by distributed online volunteer translators was overseen and checked by professionals before Facebook released the new language versions. Using a monolingual comparable corpus methodology, Jiménez-Crespo (2013a: 23–49) shows that the interface textual units of the crowdsourced non-professionally translated version of Facebook in Peninsular Spanish are more similar to those found in 25 native social networking sites originally produced in Spain than to other social media platforms that had been professionally localized from English. This indicates the qualitative soundness of the approach adopted by Facebook: the specialist insider knowledge possessed by bilingual users of these social networking environment enabled them to produce localized versions matching the norms of the target language and meeting the expectations of the target user population, even though they were not trained or professional translators.

Crowdsourced user-driven translation projects were also successfully pursued by other major social media platforms such as LinkedIn and Twitter (Garcia 2010; Fernández Costales 2011). However, professional translators' associations and other interest groups have heavily criticized these attempts at leveraging the expertise and time of enthusiastic bilingual Internet users providing a critical mass of online amateur translators, decrying the callousness of profit-making enterprises relying on volunteers to effectively increase their revenues (O'Hagan 2013: 513). McDonough Dolmaya (2011b: 97–110) investigates the ethical issues surrounding voluntary crowdsourced translations for the web, also discussing how these projects affect the perception of translation, with a special focus on minority languages; she finds that the for-profit or not-for-profit status of the organizations behind these crowdsourced translation efforts is not the only consideration in ethical terms and places emphasis on how these projects are managed and presented to the public (see also Baer 2010).

Conclusion: The Future of Online Translation

The technological and social evolution of the internet seems to be an unstoppable process, for example with the development of the semantic web, and the role of online translation is crucial to its growth. More and more users from different countries and with a variety of linguistic and cultural backgrounds obtain online access and become active on social media and in Internet-based projects. While this extends the potential for ubiquitous collaborative translation and large-scale crowdsourcing efforts (European Commission 2012), it also raises thorny issues in terms of professionalism, quality, accountability, public perception, and so on (Sutherlin 2013: 397–409). With these trends set to continue for the foreseeable future, online translation will remain an exciting area for volunteer and professional translators, translation scholars and researchers. Jiménez-Crespo (2013b: 189) predicts 'the expansion of online collaborative translation for all types of translation', also forecasting the future growth of online crowdsourcing services and exchange marketplaces providing free volunteer translations as part of web-based projects. Whilst the current importance of online translation is there for all to see, the ways in which professional and amateur translators will be able harness its potential and maximize the opportunities that it offers still remain to be discovered.

Notes

1 https://groups.google.com/forum/#!forum/sci.lang.translation
2 http://segate.sunet.se/cgi-bin/wa?A0=LANTRA-L
3 www.facebook.com
4 www.linkedin.com
5 www.twitter.com
6 http://dictionary.reference.com, www.onelook.com and www.thefreedictionary.com
7 www.wordreference.com
8 http://iate.europa.eu
9 www.intelliwebsearch.com
10 http://ipsc.jrc.ec.europa.eu/index.php?id=197
11 http://ipsc.jrc.ec.europa.eu/?id=782
12 http://ipsc.jrc.ec.europa.eu/?id=784
13 http://opus.lingfil.uu.se/index.php
14 http://mymemory.translated.net
15 translate.google.com/toolkit
16 http://translate.google.com
17 http://en.trans-aid.jp
18 www.aquarius.net
19 www.proz.com
20 www.translatorscafe.com
21 www.gotranslators.com
22 www.langmates.com
23 www.translationdirectory.com
24 www.wikipedia.org
25 http://traduwiki.org
26 www.dermundo.com
27 www.cucumis.org
28 www.cosyne.eu
29 www.wikibhasha.org
30 http://research.microsoft.com/en-us/projects/wikibabel

Bibliography

Abekawa, Takeshi and Kyo Kageura (2007) 'QRedit: An Integrated Editor System to Support Online Volunteer Translators', in *Proceedings of the Digital Humanities 2007 Conference*, 4–8 June 2007, University of Illinois, Urbana-Champaign, IL, 3–5.

Alcina-Caudet, Amparo (2003) 'Encouraging the Use of E-mail and Mailing Lists among Translation Students', *Meta* 48(4): 634–41.

Baer, Naomi (2010) 'Crowdsourcing: Outrage or Opportunity?', *Translorial: Journal of the Northern California Translators Association – Online Edition*, February 2010. Available at: http://translorial.com/2010/02/01/crowdsourcing-outrage-or-opportunity.

Ball, Sylvia (2003) 'Joined-up Terminology – The IATE System Enters Production', in *Proceedings of the Translating and the Computer 25 Conference*, 20–21 November 2003, ASLIB, London, the United Kingdom.

Bey, Youcef, Christian Boitet, and Kyo Kageura (2008) 'BEYTrans: A Wiki-based Environment for Helping Online Volunteer Translators', in Elia Yuste Rodrigo (ed.) *Topics in Language Resources for Translation and Localisation*, Amsterdam and Philadelphia: John Benjamins Publishing Company, 135–50.

Boitet, Christian, Youcef Bey, and Kyo Kageura (2005) 'Main Research Issues in Building Web Services for Mutualized, Non-commercial Translation', in *Proceedings of the 6th Symposium on Natural Language Processing, Human and Computer Processing of Language and Speech (SNLP)*, Chiang Rai, Thailand. Available at: http://panflute.p.u-tokyo.ac.jp/~bey/pdf/SNLP05-BoitetBeyKageura.v5.pdf.

Bronner, Amit, Matteo Negri, Yashar Mehdad, Angela Fahrni, and Christof Monz (2012) 'CoSyne: Synchronizing Multilingual Wiki Content', in *Proceedings of the 8th Annual International Symposium on Wikis and Open Collaboration – WikiSym 2012*, 27–29 August 2012, Linz, Austria, 1–4. Available at: www.wikisym.org/ws2012/Bronner.pdf.

Cronin, Michael (2013) *Translation in the Digital Age*, London: Routledge.

DePalma, Donald A. and Nataly Kelly (2011) 'Project Management for Crowdsourced Translation: How User-translated Content Projects Work in Real Life', in Keiran J. Dunne and Elena S. Dunne (eds.) *Translation and Localization Project Management: The Art of the Possible*, Amsterdam and Philadelphia: John Benjamins Publishing Company, 379–407.

Désilets, Alain (2007) 'Translation Wikified: How Will Massive Online Collaboration Impact the World of Translation?', in *Proceedings of the Translating and the Computer 29 Conference*, 29–30 November 2007, ASLIB, London, the United Kingdom.

Désilets, Alain (2011) *Wanted: Best Practices for Collaborative Translation*, Montreal, Ottawa: Institute for Information Technology, National Research Council Canada. Available at: www.taus.net/downloads/finish/56-public-reports/482-wanted-best-practices-for-collaborative-translation.

Désilets, Alain, Lucas Gonzalez, Sebastien Paquet, and Marta Stojanovic (2006) 'Translation the Wiki Way', in *Proceeding of WikiSym '06 – 2006 International Symposium on Wikis*, 21–23 August 2006, Odense, Denmark, 19–31.

Désilets, Alain and Jaap van der Meer (2011) 'Co-creating a Repository of Best-practices for Collaborative Translation', in Minako O'Hagan (ed.) *Linguistica Antverpiensia: Special Issue on Translation as a Social Activity*, 10: 27–45.

Drugan, Joanna and Bogdan Babych (2010) 'Shared Resources, Shared Values? Ethical Implications of Sharing Translation Resources', in Ventsislav Zhechev (ed.) *Proceedings of the 2nd Joint EM+/CNGL Workshop Bringing MT to the User: Research on Integrating MT in the Translation Industry*, 4 November 2010, Denver, CO, 3–9. Available at: www.mt-archive.info/JEC-2010-Drugan.pdf.

Durán Muñoz, Isabel (2012) 'Meeting Translators' Needs: Translation-oriented Terminological Management and Applications', *The Journal of Specialised Translation* 18: 77–92. Available at: www.jostrans.org/issue18/art_duran.pdf.

Ellis, David (2009) 'A Case Study in Community-driven Translation of a Fast-changing Website', in Nuray Aykin (ed.) *Internationalization, Design and Global Development: Proceedings of the 3rd International Conference IDSG 2009*, 19–24 July 2009, San Diego, CA, Berlin: Springer Verlag, 236–44.

European Union, European Commission, Directorate-General for Translation (2012) *Crowdsourcing Translation: Studies on Translation and Multilingualism*, Luxembourg: Publication Office of the European Union. Available at: http://bookshop.europa.eu/en/crowdsourcing-translation-pbHC3112733.

Fernández Costales, Alberto (2011) '2.0: Facing the Challenges of the Global Era', in *Proceedings of Tralogy, Session 4 – Tools for translators/Les outils du traducteur*, 3–4 March 2011, Paris, France. Available at: http://lodel.irevues.inist.fr/tralogy/index.php?id=120.

Fernández Costales, Alberto (2012) 'Collaborative Translation Revisited: Exploring the Rationale and the Motivation for Volunteer Translation', *Forum – International Journal of Translation* 10(3): 115–42.

Garcia, Ignacio (2010) 'The Proper Place of Professionals (and Non-professionals and Machines) in Web Translation', *Revista Tradumàtica*, December 2010, Issue 08. Available at: www.fti.uab.cat/tradumatica/revista/num8/articles/02/02.pdf.

Garcia, Ignacio and Vivian Stevenson (2009, September) 'Google Translator Toolkit: Free Web-based Translation Memory for the Masses', *Multilingual*: 16–19.

Gaspari, Federico and W. John Hutchins (2007) 'Online and Free! Ten Years of Online Machine Translation: Origins, Developments, Current Use and Future Prospects', in *Proceedings of Machine Translation Summit XI*, 10–14 September 2007, Copenhagen Business School, Copenhagen, Denmark, 199–206. Available at: www.hutchinsweb.me.uk/MTS-2007.pdf.

Gaspari, Federico, Antonio Toral, and Sudip Kumar Naskar (2011) 'User-focused Task-oriented MT Evaluation for Wikis: A Case Study', in Ventsislav Zhechev (ed.) *Proceedings of the 3rd Joint EM+/CNGL Workshop Bringing MT to the User: Research Meets Translators*, 14 October 2011, European Commission, Luxembourg, 13–22. Available at: www.computing.dcu.ie/~atoral/publications/2011_jec_usereval_paper.pdf.

Gough, Joanna (2011) 'An Empirical Study of Professional Translators' Attitudes, Use and Awareness of Web 2.0 Technologies, and Implications for the Adoption of Emerging Technologies and Trends', in Minako O'Hagan (ed.) *Linguistica Antverpiensia: Special Issue on Translation as a Social Activity* 10: 195–217.

Jiménez-Crespo, Miguel A. (2013a) 'Crowdsourcing, Corpus Use, and the Search for Translation Naturalness: A Comparable Corpus Study of Facebook and Non-translated Social Networking Sites', *Translation and Interpreting Studies* 8(1): 23–49.

Jiménez-Crespo, Miguel A. (2013b) *Translation and Web Localization*, London and New York: Routledge.

Kageura, Kyo, Takeshi Abekawa, Masao Utiyama, Miori Sagara, and Eiichiro Sumita (2011) 'Has Translation Gone Online and Collaborative? An Experience from Minna No Hon'yaku', in Minako O'Hagan (ed.). *Linguistica Antverpiensia: Special Issue on Translation as a Social Activity* 10: 47–72.

Kelly, Nataly, Rebecca Ray, and Donald A. DePalma (2011) 'From Crawling to Sprinting: Community Translation Goes Mainstream', in Minako O'Hagan (ed.). *Linguistica Antverpiensia: Special Issue on Translation as a Social Activity* 10: 75–94.

Kumaran, A., Naren Datha, B. Ashok, K. Saravanan, Anil Ande, Ashwani Sharma, Srihar Vedantham, Vidya Natampally, Vikram Dendi, and Sandor Maurice (2010) 'WikiBABEL: A System for Multilingual Wikipedia Content', in *Proceedings of the Collaborative Translation Workshop: Technology, Crowdsourcing, and the Translator Perspective at the AMTA 2010 Conference*, Association for Machine Translation in the Americas, 31 October 2010, Denver, CO. Available at: http://amta2010.amtaweb.org/AMTA/papers/7-01-04-KumaranEtal.pdf.

McDonough Dolmaya, Julie (2011a) 'A Window into the Profession: What Translation Blogs Have to Offer Translation Studies', *The Translator: Studies in Intercultural Communication* 17(1): 77–104.

McDonough Dolmaya, Julie (2011b) 'The Ethics of Crowdsourcing', in Minako O'Hagan (ed.). *Linguistica Antverpiensia: Special Issue on Translation as a Social Activity* 10: 97–110.

McDonough Dolmaya, Julie (2012) 'Analyzing the Crowdsourcing Model and Its Impact on Public Perceptions of Translation', *The Translator: Studies in Intercultural Communication* 18(2): 167–91.

McDonough, Julie (2007) 'How Do Language Professionals Organize Themselves? An Overview of Translation Networks', *Meta* 52(4): 793–815.

O'Hagan, Minako (1996) *The Coming Industry of Teletranslation: Overcoming Communication Barriers Through Telecommunication*, Clevedon: Multilingual Matters.

O'Hagan, Minako (2011) 'Community Translation: Translation as a Social Activity and Its Possible Consequences in the Advent of Web 2.0 and Beyond', in Minako O'Hagan (ed.). *Linguistica Antverpiensia: Special Issue on Translation as a Social Activity* 10: 11–23.

O'Hagan, Minako (2013) 'The Impact of New Technologies on Translation Studies: A Technological Turn?', in Carmen Millán and Francesca Bartrina (eds.) *The Routledge Handbook of Translation Studies*, London and New York: Routledge, 503–18.

Perrino, Saverio (2009, July) 'User-generated Translation: The Future of Translation in a Web 2.0 Environment', *The Journal of Specialised Translation*: 55–78. Available at: www.jostrans.org/issue12/art_perrino.php.

Plassard, Freddie (2007) 'La traduction face aux nouvelles pratiques en réseaux', *Meta* 52(4): 643–57.

Steinberger, Ralf, Andreas Eisele, Szymon Klocek, Spyridon Pilos, and Patrick Schlüter (2012) 'DGT-TM: A Freely Available Translation Memory in 22 Languages', in *Proceedings of the 8th International Conference on Language Resources and Evaluation (LREC 2012)*, 21–27 May 2012, Istanbul, Turkey, 454–59.

Sutherlin, Gwyneth (2013) 'A Voice in the Crowd: Broader Implications for Crowdsourcing Translation during Crisis', *Journal of Information Science* 39(3): 397–409.

Tiedemann, Jörg (2012) 'Parallel Data, Tools and Interfaces in OPUS', in *Proceedings of the 8th International Conference on Language Resources and Evaluation (LREC 2012)*, 21–27 May 2012, Istanbul, Turkey, 2214–18.

Utiyama, Masao, Takeshi Abekawa, Eiichiro Sumita, and Kyo Kageura (2009) 'Minna no Hon'yaku: A Website for Hosting, Archiving, and Promoting Translations', in *Proceedings of the Translating and the Computer 31 Conference*, 19–20 November 2009, ASLIB, London, the United Kingdom.

Wakabayashi, Judy (2002) 'Induction into the Translation Profession Through Internet Mailing Lists for Translators', in Eva Hung (ed.) *Teaching Translation and Interpreting 4: Building Bridges*, Amsterdam and Philadelphia: John Benjamins Publishing Company, 47–58.

Williams, Jenny (2013) *Theories of Translation*, London: Palgrave Macmillan.

Yang, Jin and Elke D. Lange (1998) 'Systran on AltaVista: A User Study on Real-time Machine Translation on the Internet', in David Farwell, Laurie Gerber, and Eduard Hovy (eds.) *Proceedings of the 3rd AMTA Conference*, 21–28 October 1998, Langhorne, Philadelphia, New York: Springer, 275–85.

Yang, Jin and Elke D. Lange (2003) 'Going Live on the Internet', in Harold L. Somers (ed.) *Computers and Translation: A Translator's Guide*, Amsterdam and Philadelphia: John Benjamins Publishing Company, 191–210.

40

PART-OF-SPEECH TAGGING

Felipe Sánchez-Martínez

Introduction

Part-of-speech (PoS) tagging is a well-known problem and a common step in many natural language processing applications such as machine translation, word sense disambiguation, and syntactic parsing. A PoS tagger is a program that attempts to assign the correct PoS tag or lexical category to all words of a given text, typically by relying on the assumption that a word can be assigned a single PoS tag by looking at the PoS tags of neighbouring words.

Usually PoS tags are assigned to words by looking them up in a lexicon or by using a morphological analyser (Merialdo 1994). A large portion of the words found in a text (around 70% in English) have only one possible PoS, but there are ambiguous words that have more than one possible PoS tag; for example, the English word *book* can be either a noun (*She bought a book for you*) or a verb (*We need to book a room*).

This chapter reviews the main approaches to PoS tagging and the methods they apply to assign PoS tags to unknown words. It also elaborates on the design of the tagset to be used and reviews two different approaches that have been applied to automatically infer the tagset from corpora. Among the many different applications that PoS tagging has in natural language processing and computational linguistics, it elaborates on the use of PoS taggers in rule-based and statistical machine translation. The chapter ends by providing pointers to free/open-source implementations of PoS taggers.

Approaches to Part-of-Speech Tagging

Different approaches have been applied in order to obtain robust general-purpose PoS taggers to be used in a wide variety of natural language processing and computational linguistic applications; most of these approaches are statistical, but there are also approaches based on the application of rules. This section overviews the main approaches to PoS tagging, some of which are also reviewed by Feldman and Hana (2010), who provide a comprehensive review of the main approaches to PoS tagging with emphasis on the tagging of highly inflected languages.

DOI: 10.4324/9781003168348-43

Hidden Markov Model

Among the different statistical approaches to PoS tagging, hidden Markov model (HMM; Rabiner 1989: 257–86; Baum and Petrie 1966: 1554–63) is one of the most used. An HMM is a statistical model in which it is assumed that one can make predictions (e.g. assign a PoS tag to a word) based solely on the current (hidden) state, on the previous states (e.g. PoS tags of previous words) and on the observable output (e.g. word) emitted from the current state. In addition to PoS tagging, HMMs are used for a wide variety of applications such as speech recognition, optical character recognition, and machine translation, just to name a few.

In an HMM, states are not directly visible; only observable outputs generated by the states are visible (see Figure 40.1). Each state has a probability distribution over the possible observable outputs; therefore, the sequence of observable outputs generated by an HMM gives some information about the underlying sequence of hidden states. The parameters of an HMM are the state transition probabilities, that is, the probability of being in a hidden state at time *t* given the hidden states at previous times, and the emission probabilities, that is, the probability of generating an observable output from a hidden state.

When an HMM is used to perform PoS tagging, each HMM state is made to correspond to a different PoS tag, and the observable outputs are made to correspond to word classes, which, in general, may be any suitable partition of the vocabulary; using word classes instead of the words themselves makes it easier to collect reliable statistics. Typically a word class is an *ambiguity class* (Cutting *et al.* 1992: 133–40), that is, the set of all possible PoS tags that a word could receive. However, some frequent words may be chosen to have their own word classes (ibid.), that is, a word class holding a single word, to better deal with their distributional peculiarities across texts. Having *lexicalised* states for very frequent words is also possible (Pla and Molina 2004: 167–89; Kim *et al.* 1999: 121–27), in that case the possible PoS tags for the selected words are made to correspond to HMM states that are different to those used for the rest of words.

The PoS ambiguity is solved by assigning to each word the PoS tag represented by the corresponding state in the sequence of states that maximises, given a set of HMM parameters previously estimated, the probability of the sequence of word classes observed; this can be efficiently done by means of a dynamic programming algorithm as described by Viterbi (1967: 260–69) (Manning and Schütze 1999: 332). The model assumes that the PoS tag of each word depends solely on the PoS tag of the previous *n* words, and therefore this model is referred to as *n*th order HMMs.

The parameters of an HMM can be estimated in a supervised way from hand-tagged corpora via the maximum-likelihood estimate (MLE) method (Gale and Church 1990: 283–87). A hand-tagged corpus is a text in which each PoS ambiguity has been solved by a human expert; such tagged corpora are expensive to obtain, and therefore they may not be available. The MLE method estimates the transition and emission probabilities from frequency counts (e.g. the number of times PoS tag *si* is seen before PoS tag *sj*) collected from the hand-tagged corpus.

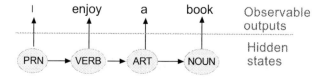

Figure 40.1 Example of state transitions (horizontal arrows) and output emissions (vertical arrows) in a hidden Markov model

When hand-tagged corpora are not available, the HMM parameters can be estimated in an unsupervised way by using untagged corpora as input to the Baum-Welch expectation-maximisation algorithm (Baum 1972: 1–8; Manning and Schütze 1999: 333). An untagged corpus (Merialdo 1994: 155–71) is a text in which each word has been assigned the set of all possible PoS tags that it could receive independently of the context. Untagged corpora can be automatically obtained if a morphological analyser or a lexicon is available; in an untagged corpus, ambiguous words receive more than one PoS tag. Baum-Welch is an iterative algorithm that needs an initial HMM which may be randomly chosen, estimated from untagged corpora (Kupiec 1992: 225–42) or obtained from a small amount of hand-tagged corpora as explained previously. Once an initial model is chosen, the method works by giving the highest probability to the state transitions and output emissions used the most. In this way a revised model that is more accurate is obtained after each iteration.

Maximum-Entropy Model

Maximum-entropy models (Berger *et al.* 1996: 39–71) allow to integrate information coming from different sources in a principled way in the form of features to build classifiers to identify the category (e.g. PoS tag) to which a new instance (e.g. word in context) belongs. Features encode any information that might help the task at hand, and may be of the form 'suffix of word at position j is "ing" and its PoS tag is VERB-GERUND'. They represent constraints imposed to the model, usually take binary values, and get activated when seen in data; that is, they equal 1 only when the condition they express is true.

Each feature has a weight associated with it that measures its contribution to the probability of an event, such as the event of a word being assigned a certain PoS tag in a given context. Training a maximum entropy model means finding the set of weights that makes the resulting probabilistic model to have the maximum entropy of all possible models that satisfy the constraints, which can be shown to be equivalent to maximising the likelihood of the training data. Having a model that maximises entropy, that is, uncertainty, means that no assumptions are made over the training data: the model maximises the likelihood of the training corpus and at the same time it has the least possible bias towards it, thus making no assumptions about the missing information in the corpus. Maximum-entropy models have been used for word sense disambiguation, text categorisation, machine translation, and language modelling, among others.

For maximum-entropy models to be used for PoS tagging one needs to specify a set of features and run a training algorithm, such as generalised iterative scaling (Darroch and Ratcliff 1972: 1470–80), over a hand-tagged corpus. Ratnaparkhi (1996: 133–42) uses a set of feature templates from which the actual features to be used are generated by scanning all pairs of contexts and PoS tags in the training corpus. These features ask yes/no questions on the context of word at position *j* and constraint the tag in that position to a certain PoS tag, like in the example shown previously.

Tagging is performed one sentence at a time. All the candidate PoS tags sequences of the sentence being tagged are enumerated and the PoS tag sequence with the highest probability is chosen. When enumerating the candidate tag sequences a lexicon providing the allowed PoS tags for each word is used to avoid generating meaningless candidates. The search for the best tag sequence is done by means of a beam search algorithm that works from left to right and maintains, as it sees a new word, a set with the N best candidate sequences up to the position of that word. To estimate how promising a candidate PoS tag sequence is, the algorithm uses the conditional probability of a PoS tag given its context. The complexity of this tagging algorithm grows linearly with the product of the sentence length, the number of allowed PoS tags, the average number of features that are activated per event (PoS tag and context) and N, the size of the beam.

Support Vector Machines

Support vector machines (SVMs; Cristianini and Shawe-Taylor 2000) are a supervised machine learning method for binary classification that learns an hyperplane in an n-dimensional space that has the largest possible distance to the nearest *training sample* and linearly separates positive samples from negative ones; a training sample is a point of n feature values like those used in maximum entropy models. The hyperplane is chosen to have the largest possible distance to the nearest training sample because this has proved to provide a good generalisation of the classification bounds. When the training samples are not linearly separable, kernel functions (Shawe-Taylor and Cristianini 2004) that map each sample into a higher dimensional space may be used in the hope that they will be linearly separable in that higher dimensional space. SVM has been used for text classification, hand-writing recognition and word sense disambiguation, just to name a few applications.

PoS tagging is a multi-class classification problem, whereas SVM are useful for binary classification: a binarisation of the problem is therefore needed for SVM to be applied for PoS tagging. Giménez and Màrquez (2003: 153–63) apply a simple binarisation approach that consists of training a different SVM per PoS tag that discriminates between that tags and all the rest; then, when tagging, they select the PoS tag most confidently predicted among all the possible ones according to the predictions provided by all the binary classifiers. For training they only consider the set of allowed PoS tags provided by a lexicon for each word and consider a word occurrence (training sample) as a positive sample for the tag assigned to it in the training hand-tagged corpus, and as a negative sample for the rest of allowed PoS tags for that word.

Transformation-Based Error-Driven Learning

Most of the approaches to PoS tagging are statistical mainly because they achieve high performance (tagging error rate on the English WSJ corpus is below 4%) without having to perform any deep analysis of the input text, and because they are easy to train from corpora; thus, allowing PoS taggers for the disambiguation of new languages or types of text to be learned when enough corpora are available. However, the knowledge learned by statistical PoS taggers is indirectly coded in large statistical tables which makes it hard, or even impossible, to fix any recurrent tagging error detected after training because it is the results of the combination of different probabilities together.

A rule-based PoS tagger achieving competitive results is described by Brill (1992: 152–55, 1995a: 543–65, 1995b: 1–13) whose transformation-based error-driven learning (TBEDL) approach is capable of acquiring a set of human-readable rules both from a small amount of tagged corpus (Brill 1992: 152–55, 1995a: 543–65) and also from untagged corpora (Brill 1995a: 543–65, 1995b: 1–13); the method may even use untagged corpora to infer a initial set of rules and then improve the tagging it provides by using a small hand-tagged corpus.

Brill's method works by first using an initial PoS tagger which makes naïve decisions such as selecting for each word the most-frequent PoS tag in a tagged corpus or no decision at all when no tagged corpus is available, thus providing for each word the set of allowed PoS tags, and then learning patching rules in an iterative process that tries to reduces the tagging error as much as possible. At each iteration a different rule candidate is evaluated and added to the set of rules learned so far; if the tagging error decreases the rule is eventually added to the final set of rules, otherwise discarded. The tagging error is easily computed over a hand-tagged corpus, or approximated from an untagged corpus by taking advantage of the distribution of non-ambiguous words over the untagged corpus. Each candidate rule is an instance of one of the rule templates provided to the TBEDL algorithm. These templates are of the form 'change tag A to tag B when the preceding (or following) word is tagged Z', for the supervised learning, and of the form 'change tag (A or B or C) to tag D when the preceding (or following) word is tagged Z' for the unsupervised learning.

One of the advantages of the TBEDL approach is that one can try as much rule templates as one can devise without affecting tagging performance, because the method only includes in the final set of patching rules those that have proved to improve tagging performance. Another advantage is that the inferred rules are easy to post-edit, and therefore it is easier than with statistical methods to fix recurrent tagging errors. A possible drawback when learning the rules from untagged corpora is that the resulting PoS tagger may not be capable of resolving the PoS ambiguity in all cases, leaving after the application of the patching rules some words with more than one PoS tag. In those cases the method just picks one, either the first one or a random one. The final set of patching rules can be coded using finite-state transducers (Roche and Schabes 1995: 227–53) which makes the complexity of the resulting PoS tagger linear with the length of the input texts, that is, faster than any of the statistical taggers described previously.

Other Approaches

There are other approaches to PoS tagging such as the one by Sánchez-Villamil *et al.* (2004: 454–63) which uses a fixed-width context window of word classes – like those used in HMM-based PoS taggers – around the word to tag. In this approach PoS tagging is performed by evaluating the probability of a given PoS given a fixed amount of word classes to the left and to the right, in addition to the word class to which the word to disambiguate belongs. The parameters of the model can be estimated either from a hand-tagged corpus (supervised training), or from an untagged corpus (unsupervised training), and the tagger can directly be implemented as a finite-state machine.

Schmid (1994: 172–76) uses a multilayer perceptron neural network in which each unit in the output layer correspond to one PoS tag, and there is a unit in the input layer per PoS tag t and context word position to take into account; the activation of an input unit represents the probability of the corresponding context word being assigned the PoS tag t; no hidden layers are used. When tagging, the unit in the output layer with the highest activation indicates the PoS tag to assign. Training is supervised: output unit activations are set to zero except for the unit which correspond to the correct tag, and a modified backpropagation algorithm is used.

Tagging Unknown Words

In the previous section we assumed that for every word the set of allowed PoS tags was known, but this is not actually the case when we face new texts in which unknown words are likely to appear. Different approaches can be applied for tagging unknown words, the most simple one consists in considering the set of all possible PoS tags as the set of allowed PoS tags for unknown words and let the tagger decide. Alternatively, one can restrict this set to the set of open categories, that is, the set of PoS tags (categories) which are likely to grow by addition of new words to the lexicon: nouns, verbs, adjectives, adverbs and proper nouns. Another option is to run a morphological guesser to reduce the set of allowed PoS tags (Mikheev 1996: 327–33) before running any specific tagging method.

More sophisticated approaches to tagging unknown words by using their lexical aspects get integrated into the specific method being used for tagging. The TnT HMM-based PoS tagger (Brants 2000) uses suffix analysis (Samuelsson 1993: 225–37) to set tag probabilities according to the ending of the words; an approach that seems to provide good results with highly inflected languages. The probability $p(t|s)$ of a tag t given a suffix s of n letters is estimated from all the words in the training hand-tagged corpus that share the same suffix; the value of n depends on the length of the word and is chosen to have the largest possible suffix from which evidence are found in the training corpus. These probabilities are then integrated through Bayesian inversion into the HMM as the emission probability $p(s|t)$ of an unknown word with suffix s being emitted from HMM state (PoS tag) t.

In the maximum-entropy approach, lexical aspects of the words to be tagged are easily integrated in the form of features to properly deal with unknown words. The feature templates used by Ratnaparkhi (1996: 133–42) differentiate between *rare* and regular words, and assumes that unknown words behave pretty much in the same way as the rare ones with respect to how their spelling help to predict theirs PoS tags. Rare words are those that occur less than five times in the training corpus. The feature templates for the rare words take into account the prefix and suffix of the word up to a length of four letters, and whether the word contains numbers, hyphens or capitalised letters. When tagging a new text, the features for the rare words are also used to help predict the PoS tag of the unknown words.

Nakagawa *et al.* (2001: 325–31) and Giménez and Màrquez (2003: 209–40) use dedicated SVMs for tagging unknown words by considering the set of open categories as the set of allowed tags for them. This dedicated SVMs make use of features specially designed for tagging unknown words, some of which are similar to the rule templates used by Brill (1995a: 543–65) and described next.

In the transformation-based error-driven learning of rules for PoS tagging discussed previously (Brill 1992: 152–55, 1995a: 543–65, 1995b: 1–13), tagging of unknown words is performed in a two-step procedure. The first step assigns a single PoS tag to each unknown word; this PoS tag is proper noun if the word is capitalised and common noun otherwise. The second step learns contextual patching rules to reduce the amount of unknown words wrongly tagged; these patching rules differ from those used for the known words because unknown words have a distributional behaviour which is quite different from that of the known ones. In addition to the rule templates used for the known words, Brill (1995a: 543–65) uses rule templates that take into account lexical aspects of the unknown word such prefix, suffix, or if the addition or removal of a suffix (or prefix) from the unknown word results in a known word.

Tagset Design

The tagset to be used may differ depending on the natural language processing application in which the PoS tagger will be integrated. While for syntactic parsing it would be sufficient to differentiate a noun from a verb, for machine translation one might need to solve the ambiguity that may occur within the same lexical category, that is, the ambiguity of words such as the Spanish word *canta*, which may refer to the third person present tense of the verb *cantar* in indicative mood or to that same verb in the imperative mood, second person. Henceforth, we will refer to those PoS tags that convey not only a lexical category but also inflection information such verb tense, mood, person, number, definitiveness, and case as fine-grained PoS tags.

If fine-grained PoS tags are directly used for disambiguation, the number of parameters, or disambiguation rules, to learn becomes considerably high, making it harder to collect reliable evidence from corpora. For instance, in first-order HMMs, the number of parameters to estimate grows as the square of the number of states (PoS tags). To avoid using such a large tagset, fine-grained PoS tags are usually manually grouped into coarse tags by following linguistic guidelines. In doing so one needs to avoid grouping tags having different syntactic roles because this would result in poor tagging results. In this regard it is important to bear in mind that, contrary to what one would expect, the relationship between tagging accuracy and tagset size is weak and is not consistent across language (Elworthy 1995: 1–9). The tagset must be carefully designed, bearing in mind the task for which the tagger will be used.

Automatic Inference of the Tagset

The manual definition of the tagset involves a human effort that would be desirable to avoid. Moreover, linguistically motivated tagsets do not guarantee better PoS tagging performance because the underlying assumption that fine-grained PoS tags having the same lexical category usually have similar probability distributions does not necessarily hold for all lexical categories. Furthermore, not all the information provided by fine-grained PoS tags is useful for disambiguation, and the amount of information that is useful because it allows to discriminate between different analyses may vary from one lexical category to another.

Brants (1995a: 1–10, 1995b: 287–89) automatically infers the grouping of fine-grained PoS tags into coarse ones by applying the HMM model merging method introduced by Stolcke and Omohundro (1994) and Omohundro (1992: 958–65), subject to some restrictions to guarantee that the information provided by the fine-grained PoS tags is preserved, that is, that even though coarse tags are used, the inflection information provided by the fine-grained tags is not lost. Model merging is an iterative method that starts with an HMM that has as many states as fine-grained PoS tags. Then, in each iteration two states are selected for merging and combined into a single state, updating the transition and emission probabilities accordingly; the states to merge are chosen by using an error measure to compare the goodness of the various candidates for merging. This methods assumes supervised training and has the advantage of finding the grouping of the fine-grained PoS tags into coarse ones at the same time the HMM parameters are estimated. The main drawback is the computational cost of finding the pair of states to merge.

Another way of finding the best grouping of fine-grained PoS tags into coarse ones is to apply the model splitting strategy (Brants 1996: 893–96) which, in contrast to model merging, selects an HMM state to be divided into two new states, updating the transitions and emission probabilities accordingly. The state selected for splitting is the one that maximises the divergence between the resulting probability distributions after splitting. The exponential growth of the number of possible splittings makes the computation of the global maximum infeasible, forcing the use of heuristics to find a local maximum.

Part-of-Speech Tagging in Machine Translation

Machine translation (MT) is one of the natural language processing applications in which PoS taggers are widely used, especially in rule-based MT (Hutchins and Somers 1992), where PoS ambiguities need to be resolved before doing any further analysis of the sentence to translate. The choice of the correct PoS tag may be crucial when translating to another language because the translation of a word may greatly differ depending on its PoS; for example, the translation into Spanish of the English word *book* may be *libro* or *reservo,* depending on the PoS tag (noun or verb, respectively). However, not all words incorrectly tagged are wrongly translated since some of them may be involved in a *free-ride* phenomenon. A free-ride phenomenon happens when choosing the incorrect interpretation for an ambiguous word in a certain context does not cause a translation error. The more related two languages are, the more often this free-ride phenomenon may occur.

The fact that in MT what really counts is MT quality rather than tagging accuracy – one may not care whether a word is incorrectly tagged at a certain point as long as it gets correctly translated – may be exploited to train PoS tagger specially tuned to translation quality (Sánchez-Martínez *et al.* 2008: 29–66; Sánchez-Martínez 2008). Sánchez-Martínez *et al.* (2008) describes a method to train HMM-based PoS taggers that are specially tuned to translation quality by using information from the source language (as any other training method) and also information from the target language and the rule-based MT system in which the PoS tagger is to be embedded. The method is completely unsupervised and incorporates information from the target language by scoring the translation of each possible disambiguation of the source-language text segments in the untagged training corpus using a statistical model of the target language;[1] these scores are then renormalised and used as fractional counts to estimate the HMM parameters in the same way the supervised training method does with counts collected from hand-tagged corpora. The resulting PoS tagger allows the MT system in which it is used to perform translations of the same quality of those produced when the PoS tagger is trained in a supervised way. PoS tagging performance is of better quality than that obtained with the unsupervised Baum-Welch expectation-maximisation algorithm, but worse than that obtained when supervised training is used.

In statistical MT (Koehn 2010), PoS taggers have been used to reduce the problem caused by the fact that pure statistical MT systems treat inflected forms of the same word (e.g. *book* and *booked*) as if they were different words, which causes translation errors when the amount of parallel corpora available to learn the translation models is scarce or the languages involved in the translation show a rich morphology. PoS taggers have been used, among other things, to annotate each word in the training corpus with its PoS tag before learning *factored translation* models (Koehn and Hoang 2007: 868–76) to better model word reorderings and local agreements; to reorder the source-language side of the training corpus, as well as the source sentences to translate; to better match the word order of the target language (Popović and Ney 2006: 12781283); and to help the automatic alignment of words with their translations in the training parallel corpus (Ayan and Dorr 2006: 96–103), a common task when building statistical MT systems.

PoS tagging has also been used for the automatic evaluation of MT to devise linguistically motivated MT quality measures (Giménez and Màrquez 2010: 209–40), for the automatic categorisation and analysis of translation errors (Popović and Ney 2011: 657–88), and for translation quality estimation (Felice and Specia 2012: 96–103; Popović 2012: 133–37).

Free/Open-Source Tools for Part-of-Speech Tagging

There are several free/open source PoS taggers freely available on the Internet; this section provides pointers to well-known implementations.

HMM-Based PoS Taggers

The FreeLing suite of language analysers (http://nlp.lsi.upc.edu/freeling/; Padró and Stanilovsky 2012: 2473–79; Carreras *et al.* 2004: 239–42) provides a classical second-order HMM-based PoS tagger.

HunPos (http://code.google.com/p/hunpos/; Halácsy *et al.* 2007: 209–12) implements a second-order HMM-based PoS tagger in which, contrary to what standard HMM implementations do, emission probabilities are based on the current state (PoS tag) and on the previous one.

The PoS tagger used by the Apertium rule-based MT platform (www.apertium.org/; Forcada *et al.* 2011: 127–44) implements a first-order HMM-based PoS tagger that can be trained using the method described in the previous section to get PoS taggers specially tuned to translation quality (Sánchez-Martínez *et al.* 2008: 29–66).

Maximum-Entropy PoS Tagger

The Stanford *log-linear* part-of-speech tagger (http://nlp.stanford.edu/software/tagger.shtml; Toutanova and Manning 2000: 63–70; Toutanova *et al.* 2003: 252–59) includes, in addition to the baseline features described by Ratnaparkhi (1996: 133–42), features for the disambiguation of the tense forms of verbs, for disambiguating particles from prepositions and adverbs, and a more extensive treatment of capitalisation for tagging unknown words.

SVM-Based PoS Taggers

SVMTool (www.lsi.upc.edu/~nlp/SVMTool/) is an free/open-source implementation of SVM that can be used to train SVM-based PoS taggers (Giménez and Màrquez 2003: 153–63). It supports feature modelling (including lexicalisation) and disambiguates thousands of words per second.

Rule-Based PoS Tagger

GPoSTTL (http://gposttl.sourceforge.net/) is an enhanced version of the rule-based PoS tagger described by Brill (1992: 152–55, 1995a: 543–65, 1995b: 1–13). The enhancement includes a built-in (English) tokeniser and lemmatiser and better handling on unknown numerals.

Note

1 A language model measures how likely it is that a given text segment represents a valid construction of the language.

Additional Resources

http://code.google.com/p/hunpos.
http://gposttl.sourceforge.net.
http://nlp.lsi.upc.edu/freeling.
http://nlp.stanford.edu/software/tagger.shtml.
www.apertium.org.
www.lsi.upc.edu/~nlp/SVMTool.

Bibliography

Ayan, Necip Fazil and Bonnie J. Dorr (2006) 'A Maximum Entropy Approach to Combining Word Alignments', in *Proceedings of the Human Language Technology Conference of the North American Chapter of the Association for Computational Linguistics*, New York, 96–103.

Baum, Leonard E. (1972) 'An Inequality and Associated Maximization Technique in Statistical Estimation of Probabilistic Functions of a Markov Process', *Inequalities* 3: 1–8.

Baum, Leonard E. and Ted Petrie (1966) 'Statistical Inference for Probabilistic Functions of Finite State Markov Chains', *The Annals of Mathematical Statistics* 37(6): 1554–63.

Berger, Adam L., Stephen A. Della Pietra, and Vincent J. Della Pietra (1996) 'A Maximum Entropy Approach to Natural Language Processing', *Computational Linguistics* 22(1): 39–71.

Brants, Thorsten (1995a) 'Estimating HMM Topologies', in *Tbilisi Symposium on Language, Logic, and Computation*, 19–22 October 1995, Tbilisi, Republic of Georgia, 1–10.

Brants, Thorsten (1995b) 'Tagset Reduction without Information Loss', in *Proceedings of the 33rd Annual Meeting of the Association for Computational Linguistics*, Cambridge, MA, 287–89.

Brants, Thorsten (1996) 'Estimating Markov Model Structures', in *Proceeding of the 4th International Conference on Spoken Language Processing*, Philadelphia, PA, 893–96.

Brants, Thorsten (2000) 'TnT – A Statistical Part-of-speech Tagger', in *Proceedings of the 6th Applied Natural Language Processing Conference and North American Chapter of the Association of Computational Linguistics Annual Meeting*, Seattle, WA, 224–31.

Brill, Eric (1992) 'A Simple Rule-Based Part of Speech Tagger', in *Proceedings of the 3rd Conference on Applied Natural Language Processing*, Trento, Italy, 152–55.

Brill, Eric (1995a) 'Transformation-based Error-driven Learning and Natural Language Processing: A Case Study in Part-of-speech Tagging', *Computational Linguistics* 21(4): 543–65.

Brill, Eric (1995b) 'Unsupervised Learning of Disambiguation Rules for Part of Speech Tagging', in *Proceedings of the 3rd Workshop on Very Large Corpora*, Cambridge, MA, 1–13.

Carreras, Xavier, Isaac Chao, Lluis Padró, and Muntsa Padró (2004) 'FreeLing: An Open-Source Suite of Language Analyzers', in *Proceedings of the 4th International Conference on Language Resources and Evaluation (LREC 2004)*, 26–28 May 2004, Lisbon, Portugal, 239–42.

Cristianini, Nello and John Shawe-Taylor (2000) *An Introduction to Support Vector Machines and Other Kernel-based Learning Methods*, Cambridge: Cambridge University Press.

Cutting, Doug, Julian Kupiec, Jan Pedersen, and Penelope Sibun (1992) 'A Practical Part-of-speech Tagger', in *Proceedings of the 3rd Conference on Applied Natural Language Processing*, Trento, Italy, 133–40.

Darroch, J. N. and D. Ratcliff (1972) 'Generalized Iterative Scaling for Log-linear Models', *Annals of Mathematical Statistics* 43: 1470–80.

Elworthy, David (1995) 'Tagset Design and Inflected Languages', in *Proceedings of the ACL SIGDAT Workshop from Texts to Tags: Issues in Multilingual Language Analysis*, 4 April 1995, Dublin, Ireland, 1–9.

Feldman, Anna and Jirka Hana (2010) *A Resource-light Approach to Morpho-syntactic Tagging*, Amsterdam and Atlanta: Rodopi.

Felice, Mariano and Lucia Specia (2012) 'Linguistic Features for Quality Estimation', in *Proceedings of the 7th Workshop on Statistical Machine Translation*, Montréal, Canada, 96–103.

Forcada, Mikel L., Mireia Ginestí-Rosell, Jacob Nordfalk, Jim O'Regan, Sergio Ortiz-Rojas, Juan Antonio Pérez-Ortiz, Flipe Sánchez-Martínez, Gema Ramírez-Sánchez, and Francis M. Tyers (2011) 'Apertium: A Free/Open-Source Platform for Rule-Based Machine Translation', *Machine Translation* 25(2): 127–44.

Gale, William A. and Kenneth W. Church (1990) 'Poor Estimates of Context Are Worse Than None', in *Proceedings of a Workshop on Speech and Natural Language*, Hidden Valley, Philadelphia, PA, 283–87.

Giménez, Jesus and Luis Màrquez (2003) 'Fast and Accurate Part-of-speech Tagging: The SVM Approach Revisited', in *Proceedings of the International Conference on Recent Advances in Natural Language Processing*, Borovets, Bulgaria, 153–63.

Giménez, Jesus and Luis Màrquez (2010) 'Linguistic Measures for Automatic Machine Translation Evaluation', *Machine Translation* 24(3–4): 209–40.

Halácsy, Peter, András Kornai, and Csaba Oravecz (2007) 'HunPos – An Open Source Trigram Tagger', in *Proceedings of the 45th Annual Meeting of the Association for Computational Linguistics (ACL 2007)*, 25–27 June 2007, Prague, Czech Republic, 209–12.

Hutchins, W. John and Harold L. Somers (1992) *An Introduction to Machine Translation*, London: Academic Press.

Kim, Jin-Dong, Sang-Zoo Lee, and Hae-Chang Rim (1999) 'HMM Specialization with Selective Lexicalization', in *Proceedings of the 1999 Joint SIGDAT Conference on Empirical Methods in Natural Language Processing and Very Large Corpora*, College Park, Madison, WI, 121–27.

Koehn, Philipp (2010) *Statistical Machine Translation*, Cambridge: Cambridge University Press.

Koehn, Philipp and Hieu Hoang (2007) 'Factored Translation Models', in *Proceedings of the 2007 Joint Conference on Empirical Methods in Natural Language Processing and Computational Natural Language Learning*, Prague, Czech Republic, 868–76.

Kupiec, Julian (1992) 'Robust Part-of-speech Tagging Using a Hidden Markov Model', *Computer Speech and Language* 6(3): 225–42.

Manning, Christopher D. and Hinrich Schütze (1999) *Foundations of Statistical Natural Language Processing*, Cambridge, MA: MIT Press.

Merialdo, Bernard (1994) 'Tagging English Text with a Probabilistic Model', *Computational Linguistics* 20(2): 155–71.

Mikheev, Andrei (1996) 'Unsupervised Learning of Word-category Guessing Rules', in *Proceedings of the 34th Annual Meeting of the Association for Computational Linguistics*, New York, NY, 327–33.

Nakagawa, Tetsuji, Taku Kudoh, and Yuji Matsumoto (2001) 'Unknown Word Guessing and Part-of-speech Tagging Using Support Vector Machines', in *Proceedings of the 6th Natural Language Processing Pacific Rim Symposium*, Tokyo, Japan, 325–31.

Omohundro, Stephen M. (1992) 'Best-first Model Emerging for Dynamic Learning and Recognition', *Neural Information Processing Systems* 4: 958–65.

Padró, Lluis and Evgeny Stanilovsky (2012) 'FreeLing 3.0: Towards Wider Multilinguality', in *Proceedings of the 8th International Conference on Language Resources and Evaluation*, Istanbul, Turkey, 2473–79.

Pla, Ferran and Antonio Molina (2004) 'Improving Part-of-speech Tagging Using Lexicalized HMMs', *Journal of Natural Language Engineering* 10(2): 167–89.

Popović, Maja (2012) 'Morpheme- and POS-based IBM1 Scores and Language Model Scores for Translation Quality Estimation', in *Proceedings of the 7th Workshop on Statistical Machine Translation*, Montréal, Canada, 133–37.

Popović, Maja and Hermann Ney (2006) 'POS-based Reorderings for Statistical Machine Translation', in *Proceedings of the 5th International Conference on Language Resources and Evaluation*, Genoa, Italy, 1278–83.

Popović, Maja and Hermann Ney (2011) 'Towards Automatic Error Analysis of Machine Translation Output', *Computational Linguistics* 37(4): 657–88.

Rabiner, Lawrence R. (1989) 'A Tutorial on Hidden Markov Models and Selected Applications in Speech Recognition', *Proceedings of the IEEE* 77(2): 257–86.

Ratnaparkhi, Adwait (1996) 'A Maximum Entropy Part-of-speech Tagger', in *Proceedings of the Conference on Empirical Methods in Natural Language Processing*, Philadelphia, PA, 133–42.

Roche, Emmanuel and Yves Schabes (1995) 'Deterministic Part-of-speech Tagging with Finite-state Transducers', *Computational Linguistics* 21(2): 227–53.

Samuelsson, Christer (1993) 'Morphological Tagging Based Entirely on Bayesian Inference', in *Proceedings of the 9th Nordic Conference on Computational Linguistics*, Stockholm, Sweden, 225–37.

Sánchez-Martínez, Felipe (2008) 'Using Unsupervised Corpus-based Methods to Build Rule-Based Machine Translation Systems', PhD Thesis, Universitat d'lacant, Spain.

Sánchez-Martínez, Felipe, Juan Antonio Pérez-Ortiz, and Mikel L. Forcada (2008) 'Using Target-language Information to Train Part-of-speech Taggers for Machine Translation', *Machine Translation* 22(1–2): 29–66.

Sánchez-Villamil, Enrique, Mikel L. Forcada, and Rafael C. Carrasco (2004) 'Unsupervised Training of a Finite-state Sliding-window Part-of-speech Tagger', in *Lecture Notes in Computer Science 3230* (Advances in Natural Language Processing), Alacant, Spain, 454–63.

Schmid, Helmut (1994) 'Part-of-speech Tagging with Neuronal Networks', in *Proceedings of the International Conference on Computational Linguistics*, Kyoto, Japan, 172–76.

Shawe-Taylor, John and Nello Cristianini (2004) *Kernel Methods for Pattern Analysis*, Cambridge: Cambridge University Press.

Stolcke, Andreas and Stephen M. Omohundro (1994) *Best-first Model Merging for Hidden Markov Model Induction*, Technical Report TR-94-003, University of California, Berkeley, CA.

Toutanova, Kristina, Dan Klein, Christopher D. Manning, and Yoram Singer (2003) 'Feature-rich Part-of-speech Tagging with a Cyclic Dependency Network', in *Proceedings of the 2003 Conference of the North American Chapter of the Association for Computational Linguistics on Human Language Technology*, Edmonton, Canada, 252–59.

Toutanova, Kristina and Christopher D. Manning (2000) 'Enriching the Knowledge Sources Used in a Maximum Entropy Part-of-speech Tagger', in *Proceedings of the Joint SIGDAT Conference on Empirical Methods in Natural Language Processing and Very Large Corpora*, Hong Kong, China, 63–70.

Viterbi, Andrew (1967) 'Error Bounds for Convolutional Codes and an Asymptotically Optimal Decoding Algorithm', *IEEE Translations on Information Theory* 13: 260–69.

41

SEGMENTATION

Freddy Y.Y. Choi

Introduction

The aim of segmentation is to partition a text into topically coherent parts. The result is a structure that resembles the table of contents of a book, where each chapter and section focuses on a specific topic within a story. This technology supports machine translation by limiting the size, scope and context of the input text. It improves translation speed by reducing the size of the input text from a complete story to a series of shorter independent text segments, thus reducing the search space and the number of candidate translations for selection. Text segments can be processed in parallel to boost speed performance in practical applications. The technology also improves translation accuracy by reducing the level of ambiguity (e.g. river *bank*, world *bank*) and the range of references (e.g. he, she, the president) in the input text, thus enabling the translation process to generate the most appropriate and specific output for the local context.

The level of improvement gained from incorporating segmentation into a machine translation process varies according to the nature of the input text. Topically fragmented input texts are common in real world applications; examples include long plain text emails and documents about multiple topics, closed caption (subtitle) text from television broadcasts, meeting minutes and interview transcripts. These input texts rarely contain any markup data about the topic boundaries; thus segmentation is applied to separate the continuous text into coherent parts prior to translation. In practical applications, the recommendation is to investigate the availability of pre-partitioned texts from the data provider where possible rather than relying on automatic text segmentation as the default solution. Common alternative data sources that provide manually segmented data include RSS news feeds and on-demand television services.

Machine translation requires domain and language independent text segmentation, where the algorithm is able to partition texts about any topic in any language. These algorithms rely on a statistical analysis of word frequency, co-occurrence and word occurrence profile to measure cohesion (Halliday and Hasan 1976) and cluster analysis to identify the location of topic boundaries by merging the related parts. This chapter shall provide an overview of domain and language independent text segmentation solutions for machine translation.

DOI: 10.4324/9781003168348-44

Background

Linguistic Foundation

Cohesion (Halliday and Hasan 1976) is a linguistic phenomenon that is observed in well-written and well-structured texts. It enables the reader to follow a story from one part to the next, recognising the change of scene and shift of focus between the different parts. Halliday and Hasan identified five observable linguistic characteristics that contribute towards cohesion: reference, ellipsis, substitution, conjunction and lexical cohesion.

Anaphora and cataphoric references (e.g. '*John* went to England.' . . . '*He* studied English.') indicate the text fragments are focusing on the same set of actors and objects and thus are likely to be about the same topic. An anaphora reference refers to a previously identified item (e.g. 'John' . . . 'He'), whereas a cataphoric reference refers to an item to be identified in the following text (e.g. 'The President' . . . 'Barack Obama').

Ellipsis is the omission of words in a cohesive text to reduce repetition and eliminate easily inferred fragments (e.g. 'What are you having for dinner?' . . . 'Burgers.', instead of '*I am having* burgers.'). Substitution is the replacement of a word with a more general word (e.g. 'Large *shops* sell lots of different products.' . . . 'Small *ones* tend to sell more interesting products.'). Conjunction is a word for specifying the association between sentences and clauses (e.g. 'and', 'however', 'therefore'). Ellipsis, substitution and conjunction give the reader a clear signal that the text fragments are parts of the same topic, as the interpretation of one is dependent on the other.

Lexical cohesion is the repetition of related words in a text (e.g. 'I like *fruits*.' . . . '*Bananas* are the best.'), thus indicating the text fragments are related to a common topic. This is a more subtle and less well-defined phenomenon, as the definition of 'related' is unclear. Examples of word relations that suggest cohesion include semantic similarity (e.g. 'Apples' . . . 'Bananas'), class and subclasses (e.g. 'mammals' . . . 'human'), synonyms (e.g. 'sofa' . . . 'couch') and antonyms (e.g. 'expensive' . . . 'cheap'). Word relations are the least consistent but also the strongest signal for cohesion. A human reader can easily recognise a topic shift from the text content, but the actual relation that signalled the shift may vary between texts.

Practical Applications

Text segmentation is a relatively new linguistic research challenge that has gained interest and popularity through the US DARPA-funded Topic Detection and Tracking (Wayne 1998) evaluations that have been running annual international competitions since 1998. The aim of the competitions is to accelerate development of core technologies for enabling access to a growing collection of unstructured free text information.

As a practical example, applying topic detection and tracking technology to RSS news streams from multiple broadcasters (e.g. BBC, ITV and CNN) will enable the human reader to monitor the development of a specific story over time without the need to read all the reports about other irrelevant topics. This is achieved by partitioning the input streams into topically coherent fragments using a text segmentation algorithm and then grouping semantically similar fragments (e.g. about a specific story or theme) using a clustering algorithm, thus making it possible to monitor the development of an individual story over time without the need to read all the irrelevant fragments.

While topic detection and tracking shall remain the main motivation for advancing text segmentation algorithms, the technology is becoming a key enabler for many large-scale information management challenges, including machine translation. Natural language processing algorithms typically work at the character and sentence levels. Tokenisation and sentence boundary disambiguation algorithms use minimal local context (e.g. less than 100 characters) to establish the token boundary and the purpose of punctuation. Part of speech tagging, shallow parsing, syntactic parsing and named entity recognition algorithms are applied to individual sentences (e.g. less than 100 tokens) to establish the grammatical structure of a sentence and extract semi-structured information (e.g. date, time, currency) and named references to world objects (e.g. people, places, events). These algorithms all work on small independent text fragments, thus making them scalable in practical applications by processing different parts of a longer text in parallel.

Natural language understanding algorithms, in contrast, tend to work at the document level. Reference resolution algorithms search the whole document to find the most probable actor or object (e.g. *John, sofa*) that is being referred to by an anaphoric or cataphoric reference (e.g. *he, it*). Summarisation algorithms find the most salient information across the whole document to generate a more concise text. Machine translation algorithms find the most appropriate transformation of the whole document to produce the same text in a different language. These algorithms are applied to the whole story and tend to utilise more and more computational resources as the story length grows; scalability is a real concern in practical applications. Topic segmentation makes it possible to partition a text into independent parts for parallel processing, thus providing a linguistically sound basis for enabling divide and conquer.

Evaluation

Problem Definition

The aim of text segmentation is to identify the existence of topic shifts in a text and the exact location of the topic boundaries. Given cohesion is a loosely defined linguistic phenomenon, the problem is defined by examples where a collection of texts is manually segmented by human readers (Hearst 1994). The challenge is to develop an automated process that finds all the segment boundaries and their exact locations according to human judgement.

The use of manually annotated example data to characterise a loosely defined linguistic phenomenon is common in linguistic research; however, the production of an example data set is labour intensive and expensive, thus providing only a limited set of examples for investigation and testing purposes. An example-driven investigation requires a large data set to generate consistently useful findings that are applicable to real situations, especially when the inter-annotator agreement levels are variable across the example data set.

Given the limitations of manually annotated example data, an alternative approach was created and adopted (Reynar 1998; Allan *et al.* 1998; Choi 2000b: 26–33) to facilitate large-scale testing. Rather than using manually annotated example data, an artificial data set is created by concatenating text fragments from different texts, thus ensuring the topic boundaries are well defined and adjacent segments are about different topics. The assumption is that a good segmentation solution must at least perform well on the artificial data set to be considered for application to real data. The use of artificial data makes it possible to conduct large-scale testing of segmentation algorithms under controlled conditions. The key variables for investigation are algorithm sensitivities associated with segment size and algorithm performance associated with document length.

Evaluation Metrics

The accuracy of a segmentation algorithm is measured by its ability to accurately identify and locate all the segment boundaries. This is computed by comparing the expected segment boundaries with the algorithm output. Given a manually annotated or artificially generated test data set, where each example document is a sequence of word tokens with known segment boundaries, accuracy is measured by a variant of precision-recall (Hearst 1994; Reynar 1998), edit distance (Ponte and Croft 1997) or cluster membership (Beeferman *et al.* 1999: 177–210).

Precision-recall metrics consider segmentation as a retrieval task where the aim is to search and retrieve all the segment boundaries. A false positive is a segment boundary that did not exist in the reference segmentation. A false negative is a segment boundary that was missed by the algorithm. The basic metric does not consider near misses; that is, the algorithm finds the boundary but not at the exact location.

Edit distance based metrics aim to remedy the near miss problem by considering segmentation a transformation task where the aim is to generate the most similar segmentation to the reference example. Similarity is measured by the minimum number of elementary operations (insert, delete) required to transform the output segmentation to the reference segmentation. A perfect result will require no transformation, a near miss will require a few operations and a poor algorithm will require many operations. The metric offers a graded result according to the level of mismatch, taking into account both near misses and complete omissions.

Cluster membership–based metrics follow a similar principle by considering segmentation as a clustering task where the aim is to group consecutive text fragments about the same topic together into a sequence of clusters. Accuracy is measured by the number of text fragments that have been placed in the correct and incorrect clusters; more specifically, the Beeferman metric (Beeferman *et al.* 1999) considers all possible pairs of text fragments across the document and tests whether they belong to the same or different clusters as defined in the reference segmentation. Once again, the metric offers a graded result that considers near misses; however, the calculation considers all cluster membership tests equal; thus it can generate unintuitive results. For instance, the separation of distant text fragments (e.g. start and end of a document) should be easier than the separation of adjacent fragments around a topic boundary, but the metric considers both decisions equally valuable.

None of these earlier metrics were perfect, and more recent works (e.g. Kazantseva and Szpakowicz 2011: 284–93) have gravitated towards the WindowDiff metric (Pevzner and Hearst 2002), which combines the concepts from the precision-recall and cluster membership metrics. It scans the text with a fixed size window and compares the number of boundaries in the output segmentation and reference segmentation. The metric penalises the algorithm whenever the number of boundaries within the window does not match. Although the metric addresses the key issues associated with the previous evaluation approaches (i.e. near misses are ignored by precision-recall metrics; all cluster membership decisions are considered equal by the Beeferman metric), the WindowDiff metric is a parameterised metric (window size), thus making direct comparison of reported results impossible if the researchers used different window sizes in the evaluation (Lamprier *et al.* 2007).

All existing evaluation metrics have different issues and undesirable characteristics. Given the main purpose of an evaluation metric is to facilitate direct comparison of algorithms in literature, the recommendation is to adopt the Beeferman metric as the standard metric for reporting segmentation performance on a common publicly available test data set, for example, the artificial test set presented in (Choi 2000b).

Solution

Architecture

All text segmentation algorithms are based on a common architecture with three key components: normalisation, cohesion metric and clustering. As an overview of the end-to-end processing chain that makes up a text segmentation algorithm, an input text is first normalised to provide the clean elementary parts for text analysis (e.g. lowercased paragraph with no punctuation). An elementary part is the smallest unit of text that may be considered a complete topic segment in an application (e.g. a sentence or a paragraph). The cohesion metric is then applied to the elementary parts to estimate the level of cohesion between the different parts. The estimates are used by the clustering algorithm to determine the optimal segmentation (i.e. each segment is a cluster of elementary parts) that maximises within cluster cohesion and minimises intra-cluster cohesion.

The result of the analysis is either a list of topic segments for linear text segmentation or a tree of segments for hierarchical text segmentation. The former is typically used in real-world applications for topic detection and tracking across news streams or to introduce scalability to natural language understanding applications such as summarisation and machine translation. Hierarchical text segmentation provides the topic structure of a text by capturing the intermediate results of the divisive (i.e. top-down) or agglomerative (i.e. bottom-up) clustering algorithm used in linear text segmentation. The topic structure is typically used as one of several linguistic cues in a natural language understanding algorithm (e.g. summarisation, table of contents generation).

Accuracy Drivers

The accuracy of a text segmentation algorithm is largely determined by (a) the accuracy of the cohesion metric, (b) the level of noise eliminated and introduced by the normalisation procedure and (c) the clustering algorithm's ability to establish the optimal segmentation granularity. The cohesion metric is fundamental to text segmentation algorithms, as it is responsible for recognising the signals (e.g. references, similarity) that suggest two texts are part of the same topic segment. Step improvements to the accuracy of an algorithm is typically achieved by changing the linguistic basis of the cohesion metric and combining multiple linguistics cues in a single metric. Intuitively, the combination of multiple cues should provide the best results, but in practice a metric that combines just the most powerful cues tend to yield the best accuracy and speed performance over a large diverse corpus (i.e. real texts in a practical application). The reason is that no single linguistic cue gives the perfect result; thus the combination of multiple cues will introduce both positive improvements and additional sources of errors to the analysis. This is managed by introducing weighted cues to ensure only the most useful cues are applied in each context and their contribution to the overall estimate is adjusted according to their accuracy in general. Both weight estimation and context recognition require a large corpus of training data to yield beneficial results; thus the recommendation is to use a simple and minimal combination of linguistic cues to boost accuracy while ensuring the combination is applicable and stable across a wide range of texts.

The normalisation procedure is responsible for filtering the input text for irrelevant signals (e.g. capitalisation, punctuation), cleaning the input (e.g. remove invalid characters) and amplifying the relevant signals (e.g. morphological variants of the same word) to support the cohesion metric. Input data cleansing is a necessity in any practical applications for ensuring the core algorithm components are not exposed to invalid input caused by common errors such as character encoding issues, carriage return and line feed characters on different operating systems and input file size limits. From an accuracy improvement perspective, the signal-to-noise ratio enhancement function offered by the normalisation procedure is the main focus. The challenge is to eliminate all the noise without removing any useful signals. For instance, the removal of closed class words (e.g. determiners such as 'the', 'a', 'some' and prepositions such as 'on', 'over', 'with') is generally a positive improvement, as these have little contribution to cohesion across multiple sentences, unless the text is about the usage and distinctions between determiners and prepositions. As for the amplification of relevant signals, the challenge is to avoid introducing errors and noise. For instance, the translation of all word tokens into word stems (e.g. 'run' instead 'running') is generally a good process for highlighting cohesion in a text to support the cohesion metric, unless the story is about the usage and distinctions between the morphological variants of a word. The examples presented here have been selected to highlight the subtle issues in normalisation rather than to give concrete examples of specific challenges, as they will differ in every practical application. The recommendation is to test and refine a text segmentation algorithm iteratively by applying the algorithm to a large corpus of actual input texts. In general, the data cleansing function will need to be refined first to enable large-scale testing over a diverse text collection without errors. For accuracy improvements, the refinement of the normalisation component is secondary to the cohesion metric, although the two components are closely coupled. Improvements to the cohesion metric tend to offer significant enhancements, whereas adjustments to the normalisation component will provide relatively smaller benefits; thus it should be applied once the cohesion metric is stable and all avenues for enhancing the metrics have been exhausted.

The clustering algorithm has both a large and small contribution to the overall accuracy of the text segmentation algorithm. The component is used to translate the cohesion estimates into an optimal segmentation by merging the most cohesive parts and splitting the least cohesive parts; thus it has minimal contribution from a linguistic perspective, as it is simply acting upon the results of the cohesion metric. The function can be performed by a wide range of common clustering algorithms. The challenge here is in knowing when to stop in a specific application (i.e. when to terminate the clustering algorithm to avoid under- or oversegmentation), to ensure the right level of granularity is being achieved by the segmentation algorithm. What constitutes a complete topic segment frequently varies across applications. For instance, the task is clearly defined for broadcast news, where the aim is to find the series of different news reports about unrelated events, whereas the segmentation of a story book may generate many equally valid results, such as chapters, sections within a chapter, themes and scenes across chapters and dialogues amongst different set of characters in the story. This aspect of the clustering algorithm has a significant and obvious impact on the overall accuracy, especially when it is being tested on a gold standard data set for comparative analysis of algorithm performance. The recommendation for comparative studies is to perform the test with known number of target segments first (i.e. the clustering algorithm knows how many segments are expected in the test text), thus making it possible to isolate the automatic termination problem and enabling the experimenter to focus on refining the cohesion metric to recognise the segments boundaries.

Normalisation

The aim of normalisation is to pre-process the input text to ensure the content is valid for processing by the cohesion metric and clustering algorithm and to enhance the content for assessing cohesion. The processing chain for a typical normalisation component comprises the following processes: input validation, tokenisation, surface feature normalisation, stemming or morphological analysis and stop word removal.

Input validation is typically implemented using a series of handcrafted regular expressions for text transformation and filtering. The process conducts basic checks on the input text to ensure the content does not contain any invalid characters (e.g. due to file corruption or encoding errors) and the size of the content is within design limits (i.e. not too long and not too short).

Tokenisation in this instance covers both the partition of a string of characters into word tokens (i.e. a series of letters, a series of digits or punctuation) and the partition of the whole document into elementary parts. For most applications, a plain text document will contain line breaks for paragraphs or sentences. These are the elementary parts that can be combined to form topic segments; in other words, the assumption is that a sentence or a paragraph is unlikely to contain more than one topic; thus the segmentation algorithm will start the analysis at this level of granularity. The key challenge in tokenisation is recognising the different uses of punctuation in words (e.g. 'I.B.M.') and structured information (e.g. date, time, currency, reference numbers). This is solved using a combination of handcrafted regular expressions (e.g. for domain-specific information such as credit card numbers) and pattern recognition algorithms for sentence boundary disambiguation (e.g. does a full stop mean the end of a sentence, or is it a part of an abbreviation?). Tokenisation is considered a solved problem as language-independent solutions are now achieving over 99.5% accuracy (Schmid 2000), and even rule-based language specific methods have achieve over 99.7% accuracy since 1994 (Grefenstette and Tapanainen 1994). For the development of text segmentation algorithms, or any complex natural language processing solutions, the recommendation is to use a simple rule-based tokenisation solution in the first instance to generate consistent input to the cohesion metric to facilitate analysis and refinement, then replace it with a more sophisticated tokenisation solution to boost accuracy once the cohesion metric is settled.

Surface feature normalisation simplifies the input text by replacing all the characters with the lower (or upper) case equivalent, removing all punctuation and optionally replacing or removing structured information with keywords (e.g. replacing a specific date with just the keyword '[DATE]'). The aim is to eliminate all the obviously irrelevant content for assessing cohesion (e.g. punctuation is unhelpful as it is used throughout the text for other purposes) and to improve string matching for recurrences of the same word (e.g. 'President' at the beginning of a sentence and 'president' in the middle of a sentence are describing the same concept, thus they should be normalised to 'PRESIDENT' to offer basic improvements in recognising cohesion). The replacement of structured information (e.g. date, time) with keywords (e.g. for describing the information type) is optional, as an application may choose to simply remove or ignore these overly specific and infrequently occurring tokens that tend to play a small part in assessing cohesion.

Stemming or morphological analysis aims to replace every word in the document with the word stem (e.g. 'running' becomes 'run') such that semantically similar words are represented by the same string to eliminate false signals for topic shifts (i.e. the use of different words suggests a topic shift). Morphological analysis performs deep analysis of a word (e.g. 'restructuring') to identify its prefixes (i.e. 're-'), suffixes (i.e. '-ing') and stem (i.e. 'structure'). This is a relatively complex and generally language specific process and thus is less desirable for machine translation applications. Stemming (Porter 1980: 130–37) is a rough kind of morphological analysis that was created to support early information retrieval applications in matching user query keywords with the text document contents. The aim here is to generate a reasonable approximation of the stem (e.g. 'running' becomes 'runn') with minimal effort and maximum speed. The process involves using a series of fixed rules to strip out all known prefixes and suffixes for a language to reveal the word stem. Although the solution is still language dependent, the linguistic resource required to construct a stemmer is simple and widely available for most languages. For the development of text segmentation algorithms, the recommendation is to use an existing stemmer where possible, or simply don't use a stemmer if one is unavailable for the target language in the initial stages as stemming generally has a positive but small impact (Choi 2000c) on segmentation accuracy.

Stop word removal uses a lookup table or word frequency analysis to eliminate semantically irrelevant words tokens in the input text, such as frequently occurring closed class words (e.g. determiners 'a', 'an', 'the'). The aim is to remove all the obviously unhelpful signals for assessing cohesion. Lookup tables are popular in existing text segmentation algorithms, but these are language specific;

thus for machine translation applications, the recommendation is to use frequency analysis to filter the most frequently occurring word tokens in a text according to Zipf's law (1949).

Cohesion Metric

Lexical cohesion can be estimated by a range of linguistic cues. These can be broadly classified into four groups: lexical repetition, semantic similarity, collocation networks and keywords. The first assumes the reoccurrence of the same word token in different text fragments implies the segments are likely to be focusing on the same topic, and a change of vocabulary signals a topic shift. Semantic similarity uses semantically related words such as synonyms, as defined in a dictionary or thesaurus, to form lexical chains across a text for use as evidence of lexical cohesion and repulsion. Collocation networks are similar to semantic similarity in principle, except related words are discovered by applying statistical analysis to a training corpus to find frequently co-occurring words within small text fragments, thus implying they are related to the same topic. Finally, keyword-based metrics use a collection of handcrafted or inferred words and phrases to detect cohesion and topic shift, for example the words 'however', 'as such' and 'furthermore' imply the next sentence is a continuation of the same topic segment, whereas phrases such as 'over to you in the studio', 'and now for the weather' are frequently used in broadcast news to signal the change of topic to the viewer or listener.

Machine translation requires language independent metrics; thus the discussion here shall focus on lexical repetition and collocation network-based metrics. Semantic similarity relies on language specific resources. Keyword-based solutions are developed and tuned for a specific language and domain. Even if they offer minor accuracy improvements over language-independent metrics in specific contexts, the overhead and additional complexity of introducing a language detection component and the use of multiple context specific models make them unattractive for practical machine translation applications.

Lexical Repetition

Lexical repetition–based metrics are all based on a statistical analysis of word token distribution in the text (e.g. Hearst 1994; Reynar 1994: 331–33; Heinonen 1998; Choi 2000b: 26–33; Utiyama and Isahara 2001), which is fast (Choi 2000b: 26–33) and as accurate as language-specific methods, achieving over 95% (Utiyama and Isahara 2001) on large test data sets. Repetition can be represented as lexical chains, a vector space model or a language model. A lexical chain in this context is simply a list of word position references for describing the occurrence of a word token in the text. A typical algorithm will start by analysing the positions of each unique token in the text to create a complete chain for each token spanning the entire text. A filter is then applied to fragment each chain according to distance; for example, occurrence of the same word just at the beginning and end of the text is unlikely to be a useful linguistic cue. Cohesion between elementary text fragments is then estimated by counting the number of chains that cross the fragment boundaries. One of the key challenges here is in adjusting the filter to apply the right level of fragmentation to the chains, as there is little linguistic basis for setting the distance threshold.

Vector space model representations of lexical repetition consider each elementary text fragment an unordered collection of word tokens. A text fragment is represented by a vector of word frequencies in the fragment. Each unique word token is a dimension in the vector space. Cohesion between two text fragments is estimated by the cosine metric, which measures the angle between the corresponding vectors. In essence, text fragments containing similar words will have similar vectors; thus the angle will be small, and they are considered cohesive, whereas fragments containing different words will have vectors that point towards very different directions; thus the angle will be large and they are not cohesive. The vector space model is a well-established solution for estimating semantic similarity in information retrieval. A simple enhancement to the basic metric adjusts the vector dimensions with weights to take into account the information value of each word in the text, for instance, using the term frequency and inverse document frequency weighting (TF–IDF) scheme (Jones 1972). Another enhancement projects the vector space according to an inferred word similarity matrix that has been generated through statistical analysis of a large corpus, for instance, using latent semantic analysis (Choi *et al.* 2001). This is in essence the same as the collocation network approach. Finally, another avenue for enhancing the metric applies smoothing and scaling to the raw estimates to improve the stability and reliability of the analysis. For instance, minor differences in the similarity estimates are meaningless when they have been calculated from short texts; thus one can only rely on the rough order of magnitude in similarity as the basis for estimating cohesion rather than the absolute value. This is the theoretical basis of the local ranking scheme (Choi 2000b: 26–33) that delivered significant improvements to segmentation accuracy.

Language model–based representations of lexical repetition consider the likelihood of word distributions to detect topic shifts. In general, existing solutions frame the text segmentation problem as one of model optimisation to find the most likely word sequences that belong together according to a probabilistic word distribution model. A word distribution model describes the most likely collection of words that belong to each topic; this is generally derived from the text itself, thus making these solutions language independent. The most probable segmentation for a text is discovered by applying dynamic programming techniques to find the optimal solution. Experiment results (Utiyama and Isahara 2001) have shown the language model–based approach delivers at least the same level of accuracy as vector space model approaches.

Collocation Networks

Collocation network–based metrics (Ponte and Croft 1997; Kaufmann 1999: 591–95; Choi *et al.* 2001; Ferret 2002) are not strictly language independent, as they rely on a domain- and language-specific model of word co-occurrence to detect cohesion. However, the model is created automatically using raw text data and thus can be applied to any language or domain; hence it is included in this discussion. From a linguistic perspective, collocation networks assume words that co-occur in a small text fragment (e.g. a paragraph) are likely to be about the same topic; thus a model of cohesion can be derived from a training corpus by analysing the word co-occurrence statistics. The result is a word distribution model for building lexical chains, enhancing the basic vector space model and providing prior probabilities for language model–based metrics.

Existing solutions are all based on some variation of latent semantic analysis where word co-occurrence statistics are collected from a training corpus to produce a frequency matrix. Eigenanalysis is then applied to the matrix to perform principle component analysis, thus identifying the most discriminating dimensions for estimating similarity and enabling filtering of the matrix to reduce the impact of noisy data and its size to reduce the computational cost of runtime calculations. Experiment results (Choi *et al.* 2001) have shown that collocation network–based metrics can outperform vector space model–based metrics by about 3%.

Discussion

Lexical repetition has established itself as one of the most reliable linguistic cues for detecting cohesion, especially in language and domain independent applications. The lexical chain approach is linguistically sound in principle, but it does not take into account the strength of each link, and there is no reliable linguistic foundation for setting the threshold for fragmenting long chains. The vector space model has consistently delivered good results, especially when enhanced with smoothing techniques to make it more resilient against sparse data issues in short texts, false cues and local variations. Language model–based approaches have delivered equally good and sometimes better results than vector space model approaches, but the solution is more complex, and the practical implementation usually requires more computational resources than vector space models. Collocation networks have been shown to deliver further improvements over vector space models and offer a similar level of accuracy as language model–based solutions.

For machine translation, the recommendation is to use vector space model–based metrics as the default solution, given the underlying technology, mathematical foundation and linguistic basis are well established and proven across a wide range of practical large-scale multilingual applications such as internet search engines. Their implementation is simple and computationally inexpensive relative to other methods. More recent works have shown that language model–based metrics are emerging as the front runners for consistently delivering the best accuracy under test conditions. Future work in text segmentation should investigate the combination of collocation networks and language models for boosting accuracy and the use of smoothing techniques to improve stability and resilience of the estimates, especially taking into account the statistical significance and linguistic basis of the estimates to ensure the interpretation is in line with what information is actually available in the source text; that is, small differences in the cohesion estimates are meaningless when the source text fragments only contain a few words.

Clustering

The clustering component analyses the cohesion estimates to establish the optimal segmentation for a text. Clustering is a well-understood process with many proven solutions. For text segmentation, there are broadly three kinds of clustering solutions: moving window, divisive clustering and agglomerative clustering. Moving window-based solutions (e.g. Hearst 1994) are not strictly clustering, as it simply involves analysing the local cohesion estimates and dividing a text when the value drops below a predefined or calculated threshold. The challenge is setting the correct threshold value to prevent over- or undersegmentation and making the value adapt all the texts in the target collection, as cohesion estimates will vary across different documents. A popular approach to setting an adaptive threshold is to take the mean value for all the cohesion estimates for a text and use the standard deviation to compute the threshold (i.e. number of standard deviations from the mean) according to a sample of test examples (Hearst 1994).

Divisive clustering considers all cohesion estimates for the whole text and performs segmentation by dividing the text recursively, selecting the candidate boundary that maximises the total cohesiveness of the resulting topic segments and repeating the process until it reaches a termination condition. Overall cohesiveness of a text is computed by the sum of cohesive estimates for all pairs of elementary segments within each topic segment (i.e. attraction within each cluster) and optionally subtracted from the sum of estimates for elementary segments in different topic segments (i.e. repulsion between clusters). The termination condition is generally estimated by a variant of the adaptive threshold scheme produced in Hearst (1994), which in this instance assesses the rate of change in the overall cohesiveness value of the segmentation. Practical implementations of divisive clustering in text segmentation have used the dot-plotting algorithm (e.g. Reynar 1994; Choi 2000b: 26–33) and dynamic programming algorithm (Utiyama and Isahara 2001). The former is generally faster but requires more working memory, whereas the latter is more computationally intensive but more memory efficient.

Agglomerative clustering is similar to divisive clustering, except it starts bottom up, merging the most cohesive consecutive elementary segments at each step until it reaches the termination condition. Practical implementations of agglomerative clustering in text segmentation have achieved better results than moving-window methods (Yaari 1997) but are less accurate than divisive clustering–based methods.

As a direct comparison of the three clustering methods, moving-window methods only consider the level of cohesion between consecutive elementary segments within a finite window. Agglomerative clustering only considers the level of cohesion between consecutive segments across the whole text. Divisive clustering considers all the estimates across the whole text between all pairs of elementary segments, thus making it possible to find the globally optimum solution, taking into account the local and global variations in cohesion. The recommendation is to use divisive clustering where possible to obtain the best segmentation to support machine translation. Although the method is the most computationally expensive and memory intensive, the resource requirement is relatively small in comparison to the key machine translation processes. The key limitation of divisive clustering is the input text length, as the method needs to build a similarity matrix for all pairs of elementary segments. For translation applications that operate on long texts, the recommendation is to either use any available macro-level segmentation (e.g. chapters) to partition the story into more manageable blocks for topic segmentation or apply the moving window-based solution with an adaptive threshold set according to maximum segment length to perform a coarse-grained segmentation before detailed analysis and topic segmentation with a divisive clustering-based algorithm.

Summary

Text segmentation enables machine translation algorithms to operate on long input texts that would otherwise be impractical due to computational constraints. It partitions a text into smaller topically independent segments for parallel processing by multiple instances of the same machine translation algorithm, thus improving throughput while ensuring the individual results are complete and the combined result is linguistically sound.

Machine translation requires language-independent linear text segmentation. This implies all the underlying processes with a text segmentation algorithm must be adapted to eliminate the need for language-specific resources. The general architecture of a text segmentation algorithm consists of three key components: normalisation, cohesion metric and clustering. A conceptual language-independent text segmentation algorithm for machine translation that combines proven parts of existing solutions shall comprise a normalisation component that uses regular expression for tokenisation (Grefenstette and Tapanainen 1994) and frequency analysis for stop word removal (Zipf 1949), a cohesion metric that uses the vector space model (Reynar 1994; Choi 2000b: 26–33), TF-IDF weighting (Jones 1972: 11–21), ranking filter (Choi 2000b: 26–33) to estimate the level of cohesion between the elementary segments and a clustering algorithm that uses the moving-window method to partition the text into more manageable sizes (Hearst 1994) and then applies a divisive clustering algorithm to perform detailed analysis (Choi 2000b: 26–33).

Bibliography

Allan, James, Jaime Carbonell, George Doddington, Jonathan Yamron, and Yiming Yang (1998) 'Topic Detection and Tracking Pilot Study Final Report', in *Proceedings of the DARPA Broadcast News Transcription and Understanding Workshop*, Computer Science Department, Paper 341.

Beeferman, Doug, Adam Berger, and John Lafferty (1997a) 'A Model of Lexical Attraction and Repulsion', in *Proceedings of the 35th Annual Meeting of the ACL*, 373–80.

Beeferman, Doug, Adam Berger, and John Lafferty (1997b) 'Text Segmentation Using Exponential Models', *Proceedings of EMNLP-2*: 35–46.

Beeferman, Doug, Adam Berger, and John Lafferty (1999) 'Statistical Models for Text Segmentation', in Claire Cardie and Raymond J. Mooney (eds.). *Machine Learning: Special Issue on Natural Language Processing* 34(1–3): 177–210.

Cettolo, Mauro and Marcello Federico (2006) 'Text Segmentation Criteria for Statistical Machine Translation', in Tapio Salakoski, Filip Ginter, Sampo Pyysalo, and Tapio Pahikkala (eds.) *Advances in Natural Language Processing: Proceedings of the 5th International Conference, FinTAL 2006*, Turku, Finland, LNCS 4139, Springer Verlag, Berlin, 664–73.

Choi, Freddy Y. Y. (2000a) 'A Speech Interface for Rapid Reading', in *Proceedings of IEE Colloquium: Speech and Language Processing for Disabled and Elderly People*, April, London, England.

Choi, Freddy Y. Y. (2000b) 'Advances in Domain Independent Linear Text Segmentation', in *Proceedings of the 1st North American Chapter of the Association for Computational Linguistics Conference*, Association for Computational Linguistics, 26–33.

Choi, Freddy Y. Y. (2000c) 'Content-based Text Navigation', PhD Thesis, Department of Computer Science, University of Manchester, the United Kingdom.

Choi, Freddy Y. Y., Peter Wiemer-Hastings, and Johanna Moore (2001) 'Latent Semantic Analysis for Text Segmentation', in *Proceedings of the Conference on Empirical Methods in Natural Lanauage Processing 2001*.

Church, Kenneth W. (1993) 'Char_align: A Program for Aligning Parallel Texts at the Character Level', in *Proceedings of the 31st Annual Meeting of the ACL*.

Church, Kenneth W. and Jonathan I. Helfman (1993) 'Dotplot: A Program for Exploring Self-similarity in Millions of Lines of Text and Code', *The Journal of Computational and Graphical Statistics*.

Eichmann, David, Miguel Ruiz, and Padmini Srinivasan (1999) 'A Cluster-based Approach to Tracking, Detection and Segmentation of Broadcast News', in *Proceedings of the 1999 DARPA Broadcast News Workshop (TDT-2)*.

Ferret, Olivier (2002) 'Using Collocations for Topic Segmentation and Link Detection', in *Proceedings of the 19th International Conference on Computational Linguistics Volume 1*, Association for Computational Linguistics.

Grefenstette, Gregory and Pasi Tapanainen (1994) 'What Is a Word, What Is a Sentence? Problems of Tokenization', in *Proceedings of the 3rd Conference on Computational Lexicography and Text Research (COMPLEX'94)*, July, Budapest, Hungary.

Hajime, Mochizuki, Honda Takeo, and Okumura Manabu (1998) 'Text Segmentation with Multiple Surface Linguistic Cues', in *Proceedings of COLING-ACL'98*, 881–85.

Halliday, Michael and Ruqaiya Hasan (1976) *Cohesion in English*, New York: Longman Group.

Hearst, Marti A. (1994) 'Multi-paragraph Segmentation of Expository Text', in *Proceedings of the ACL'94*.

Hearst, Marti A. and Christian Plaunt (1993) 'Subtopic Structuring for Full-length Document Access', in *Proceedings of the 16th Annual International ACM/SIGIR Conference*, Pittsburgh, Philadelphia, PA.

Heinonen, Oskari (1998) 'Optimal Multi-paragraph Text Segmentation by Dynamic Programming', in *Proceedings of COLING-ACL '98*.

Helfman, Jonathan I. (1996) 'Dotplot Patterns: A Literal Look at Pattern Languages', *Theory and Practice of Object Systems* 2(1): 31–41.

Jones, Karen Sparck (1972) 'A Statistical Interpretation of Term Specificity and Its Application in Retrieval', *Journal of Documentation* 28(1): 11–21.

Kan, Min-Yen, Judith L. Klavans, and Kathleen R. McKeown (1998) 'Linear Segmentation and Segment Significance', in *Proceedings of the 6th International Workshop of Very Large Corpora (WVLC-6)*, August, Montreal, Quebec, Canada, 197–205.

Kaufmann, Stefan (1999) 'Cohesion and Collocation: Using Context Vectors in Text Segmentation', in *Proceedings of the 37th Annual Meeting of the Association of for Computational Linguistics (Student Session)*, June 1999, College Park, Madison, WI, 591–95.

Kazantseva, Anna and Stan Szpakowicz (2011) 'Linear Text Segmentation Using Affinity Propagation', in *Proceedings of the 2011 Conference on Empirical Methods in Natural Language Processing*, 27–31 July 2011, Edinburgh, Scotland, the United Kingdom, 284–93.

Kozima, Hideki (1993) 'Text Segmentation Based on Similarity between Words', in *Proceedings of ACL'93*, 22–26 June 1993, Columbus, OH, 286–88.

Kurohashi, Sadao and Makoto Nagao (1994) 'Automatic Detection of Discourse Structure by Checking Surface Information in Sentences', in *Proceedings of COLING'94*, 2: 1123–27.

Lamprier, Sylvain, Tassadit Amghar, Bernard Levrat, and Frederic Saubion (2007) 'On Evaluation Methodologies for Text Segmentation Algorithms', in *Proceedings of ICTAI'07*, vol. 2.

Litman, Diane J. and Rebecca J. Passonneau (1995) 'Combining Multiple Knowledge Sources for Discourse Segmentation', in *Proceedings of the 33rd Annual Meeting of the ACL*.

Miike, Seiji, Etsuo Itoh, Kenji Ono, and Kazuo Sumita (1994) 'A Full Text Retrieval System with Dynamic Abstract Generation Function', in *Proceedings of SIGIR '94*, Dublin, Ireland, 152–61.

Morris, Jane (1988) *Lexical Cohesion, the Thesaurus, and the Structure of Text*, Technical Report CSRI 219, Computer Systems Research Institute, University of Toronto.

Morris, Jane and Graeme Hirst (1991) 'Lexical Cohesion Computed by Thesaural Relations as an Indicator of the Structure of Text', *Computational Linguistics* 17: 21–48.

O'Neil, Mark A. and Mia I. Denos (1992) 'Practical Approach to the Stereo-matching of Urban Imagery', *Image and Vision Computing* 10(2): 89–98.

Palmer, David D. and Marti A. Hearst (1994) 'Adaptive Sentence Boundary Disambiguation', in *Proceedings of the 4th Conference on Applied Natural Language Processing*, 13–15 October 1994, Stuttgart, Germany, San Francisco: Morgan Kaufmann Publishers, 78–83.

Pevzner, Lev and Marti A. Hearst (2002) 'A Critique and Improvement of an Evaluation Metric for Text Segmentation', *Computational Linguistics* 28(1): 19–36.

Ponte, Jay M. and Bruce W. Croft (1997) 'Text Segmentation by Topic', in *Proceedings of the 1st European Conference on Research and Advanced Technology for Digital Libraries*, University of Massachusetts, Computer Science Technical Report TR97-18.

Porter, M. (1980) 'An Algorithm for Suffix Stripping', *Program* 14(3): 130–37.

Press, William H., Saul A. Teukolsky, William T. Vettering, and Brian P. Flannery (1992) *Numerical Recipes in C: The Art of Scientific Computing*, 2nd edition, Cambridge: Cambridge University Press, 623–28.

Reynar, Jeffrey C. (1994) 'An Automatic Method of Finding Topic Boundaries', in *ACL'94: Proceedings of the 32nd Annual Meeting on Association for Computational Linguistics (Student session)*, 331–33.

Reynar, Jeffrey C. (1998) 'Topic Segmentation: Algorithms and Applications', PhD thesis, Computer and Information Science, University of Pennsylvania.

Reynar, Jeffrey C. (1999) 'Statistical Models for Topic Segmentation', in *Proceedings of the 37th Annual Meeting of the ACL*, 20–26 June 1999, College Park, MD, 357–64.

Reynar, Jeffrey C., Breck Baldwin, Christine Doran, Michael Niv, B. Srinivas, and Mark Wasson (1997) 'Eagle: An Extensible Architecture for General Linguistic Engineering', in *Proceedings of RIAO '97*, June 1997, Montreal, Canada.

Reynar, Jeffrey C. and Adwait Ratnaparkhi (1997) 'A Maximum Entropy Approach to Identifying Sentence Boundaries', in *Proceedings of the 5th Conference on Applied NLP*, Washington, DC.

Schmid, Helmut (2000) *Unsupervised Learning of Period Disambiguation for Tokenisation*, Internal Report, IMS, University of Stuttgart.

Utiyama, Masao and Hitoshi Isahara (2001) 'A Statistical Model for Domain-independent Text Segmentation', in *Association for Computational Linguistics: 39th Annual Meeting and 10th Conference of the European Chapter: Workshop Proceedings: Data-driven Machine Translation*, 6–11 July 2001, Toulouse, France.

van Rijsbergen, C. J. (1979) *Information Retrieval*, Newton, MA: Butterworth-Heinemann.

Wayne, Charles L. (1998) 'Topic Detection and Tracking (TDT) Overview and Perspective', in *Proceedings of the DARPA Broadcast News Transcription and Understanding Workshop*, 8–11 February 1998, Lansdowne, Virginia.

Yaari, Yaakov (1997) 'Segmentation of Expository Texts by Hierarchical Agglomerative Clustering', in *Proceedings of RANLP'97: Recent Advances in Natural Language Processing*, 11–13 September, Tzigov Chark, Bulgaria.

Youmans, Gilbert (1991) 'A New Tool for Discourse Analysis: The Vocabulary-management Profile', *Language* 67(4): 763–89.

Zipf, George K. (1949) *Human Behavior and the Principle of Least Effort*, London: Addison-Wesley Press.

42

SPEECH TRANSLATION

Lee Tan

What Is Speech Translation?

Speech translation, or more precisely speech-to-speech translation (abbreviated as S2S), is a technology that converts a spoken utterance in one language into a spoken sentence in another language. It enables natural speech communication between two persons who speak different languages. A speech translation system is a computer system equipped with an audio interface that captures what the speaker says and plays back the output speech to the listener. The translation process is realized by specially designed software installed on the computer.

In the simplest case, a speech translation system could work like a T-speaking dictionary that performs word-by-word translation without considering the grammatical relations and other linguistic properties of individual words. The technology level of such a system is relatively low, and its practical applications are very limited. Today's technology is generally expected to perform whole-sentence translation and deal with continuous speech in a conversational or enquiry setting. The translated output is required to be natural speech with high intelligibility and human-like voice quality.

Applications of Speech Translation

Communication is fundamental societal behavior. With the trend of globalization, being able to communicate with people who speak different languages has become a basic and required ability for many individuals. Learning to speak a new language takes a lot of time and effort. Human translators may not always be available and are often very costly. Computer-based speech translation technology provides a feasible and efficient solution to address many practical needs.

In business communication, telephone conversation between speakers at remote locations is often needed. A speech translation system can be integrated into the telephony system as an added-value service. This allows for interactive spoken dialogue, which is preferable for effective negotiation, lobbying, and decision-making. If the translation system is able to support multiple languages, it will help small enterprises and organizations to develop international connections at lower costs.

Military and security applications have long been one of the major driving forces for the development of speech translation technology. For example, speech translation software was

DOI: 10.4324/9781003168348-45

developed for two-way conversation in Arabic and English to support the United States military operations in the Middle East. It enabled frontline soldiers and medics to communicate efficiently with civilians when human translators were not available. Similar systems are also useful to the United Nation peacekeeping forces, which need to execute missions in different countries.

The invention of the smartphone has made revolutionary changes in our experience with personal communication devices. Smartphone provides an ideal platform for deploying and popularizing speech-to-speech translation systems because of its user-friendliness, high portability, and large customer base. A smartphone with a speech translation function would empower the user with stronger communication ability and a broader range of information sources. For example, when people travel across different countries, they are able to use smartphones to 'speak' naturally to local people and 'listen' to their responses. Users may also use the same speech translation system as a convenient tool to learn to speak another language.

It has become part of our daily life to watch and share online video and audio recordings. Traditionally sharing of media files is for entertainment purpose and within a group of connected friends. Nowadays the applications extend widely to news broadcasting, commercial advertisements and promotions, education and self-learning, and many other areas. With speech translation technology, online spoken documents would be accessible to a much wider audience.

History of Speech Translation

In the early 1980s, the NEC Corporation developed a concept demonstration system for Spanish–English automated interpretation and later extended to Japanese and French (www. nec.com/en/global/rd/innovative/speech/04.html). This system could handle only 500 words, and the processing time for each utterance was as long as several seconds. A number of large-scale research projects on speech translation and related technologies were launched in early 1990. These projects were carried out at universities and research organizations in Japan, Germany, and the United States. The major groups included the Advanced Telecommunications Research Institute International (ATR) in Japan, Carnegie Mellon University (CMU) and IBM Research in the United States, and University of Karlsruhe in Germany. ATR was founded in 1986 to carry out systematic research on speech translation technology. The ATR-ASURA and ATR-MATRIX systems were developed for speech translation in a limited domain between Japanese, German, and English (Takezawa *et al.* 1998: 2779–82). In Germany, the Verbmobil project was a major initiative of speech translation technology development. Funded by German Federal Ministry for Education and Research and multiple industrial partners, this large-scale project involved hundreds of researchers during 1992–2000 (http://verbmobil.dfki. de/overview-us.html). The Verbmobil system was built to support verbal communication in mobile environments and handle spoken dialogues in three domains of discourse, appointment scheduling, travel planning, and remote PC maintenance. JANUS was another domain-specific system developed at CMU for translating spoken dialogues between English, German, Spanish, Japanese, and Korean (Levin *et al.* 2000: 3–25).

Since the year 2000, research and development of speech translation technology have progressed gradually to deal with real-world scenarios. A wider range of application domains was explored and more realistic speaking style and acoustic conditions were assumed. The NESPOLE! (NEgotiation through SPOken Language in E-commerce) system was designed to allow novice users to make enquiries using English, French, or German about winter sports possibilities in Italy via a video-conferencing connection (Metze *et al.* 2002: 378–83). In 2004, the European Commission funded a long-term project named TC-STAR, which targeted unconstrained conversational speech domains in English, Spanish, and Chinese.

In the past decade, the Defense Advanced Research Projects Agency (DARPA) of the United States launched three influential programs on technology advancement in speech translation. They are well known by the acronyms of GALE (Global Autonomous Language Exploitation), TRANSTAC (TRANSlation system for TACtical use), and BOLT (Broad Operational Language Translation). These projects were featured by wide international collaboration among academic institutions and industrial research laboratories from the United States and western European countries. Arabic languages were the major focus of the technologies in order to support US military operations and national security actions. The TRANSTAC systems were required to be installed on portable devices for tactical use without involving visual display (www.dtic.mil/dtic/pdf/success/TRANSTAC20080915.pdf). The MASTOR (Multilingual Automatic Speech to Speech Translator) system developed by IBM Research and the Iraq-Comm system developed by the Stanford Research Institute (SRI) were computer software running on laptop computers. These systems were deployed to various US military units to support their operations in Iraq.

Development of speech translation technology for Chinese started in the late 1990s at the National Laboratory of Pattern Recognition (NLPR), Chinese Academy of Sciences (CAS). The first system, named LodeStar, supported Chinese-to-English and Chinese-to-Japanese translation in the travel domain (Zong and Seligman 2005: 113–37). The 29th Summer Olympic Games was held in Beijing, the People's Republic of China. As part of the Digital Olympics initiative, a prototype speech-to-speech translation system was developed to assist foreign tourists in making travel arrangements. The project involved joint efforts from CAS-NLPR, Universitat Karlsruhe (TH), and Carnegie Mellon University. The system supported Chinese, English, and Spanish and could run on laptop computers and PDAs with wireless connection (Stüker *et al.* 2006: 297–308).

The Asian Speech Translation Advanced Research (A-STAR) Consortium was formed in 2006 by a number of research groups in Asian countries, with the aims of creating infrastructure and standardizing communication protocols in the area of spoken language translation. In July 2009, A-STAR launched 'the first Asian network-based speech-to-speech translation system'. In 2010, A-STAR was expanded to a worldwide organization, the Universal Speech Translation Advanced Research (U-STAR) consortium (www.ustar-consortium.com). The standardizing procedures for network-based speech-to-speech translations were adopted by ITU-T. The U-STAR consortium currently has 26 participating organizations.

Architecture of a Speech Translation System

Speech translation is made possible by three component technologies: speech recognition, spoken language translation, and speech synthesis. Figure 42.1 shows the basic architecture and operation of a bi-directional speech translation system for a pair of languages A and B. The input utterance spoken in language A is first recognized to produce a textual representation, for example, an ordered sequence of words, in language A. The text in language A is then translated into an equivalent textual representation in language B, which is used to generate synthesized speech in language B. The same process is followed vice versa.

A speech translation system can be built from independently developed systems that perform speech recognition, machine translation, and speech synthesis. These component systems are loosely coupled to operate in a sequential manner. There is no mechanism of information feedback or error correction between the systems. In this approach, the performance deficiency of a preceding component may greatly affect the subsequent components, and hence degrade the performance of the entire system.

In an integrated approach, the component systems work coherently with each other with a unified goal of achieving optimal end-to-end performance. For example, the speech recognition system may produce more than one possible sentence and allow the machine translation system to choose the most suitable one according to linguistic constraints of the target language. If there exist a few translation outputs that are equally good in meaning representation, the quality and fluency of the synthesized speech outputs can be used as the basis for selection (Hashimoto *et al.* 2012: 857–66).

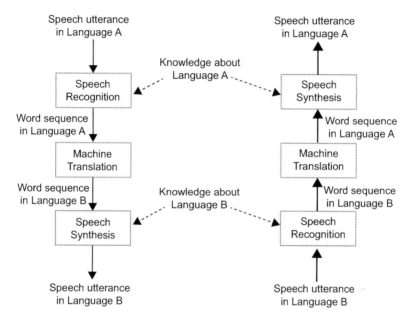

Figure 42.1 Architecture of bi-directional speech translation system

Automatic Speech Recognition

Automatic speech recognition (ASR) refers to the computational process of converting an acoustic speech signal into a sequence of words in the respective language. Statistical modeling and pattern recognition approach is widely adopted in today's ASR systems. The problem of speech recognition is formulated as a process of searching for the most probable word sequence from a large pool of candidate sequences. A general mathematical formulation is given as

$$\mathbf{W}^{\star} = \arg\max_{\mathbf{W}} P(\mathbf{W} \mid \mathbf{O}),$$

where $\mathbf{W}$ denotes a word sequence, $\mathbf{O}$ denotes a parameterized representation of the input signal, $P(\mathbf{W} \mid \mathbf{O})$ is known as the posterior probability of $\mathbf{W}$ given the observation $\mathbf{O}$. $\mathbf{W}^{\star}$ is the output of speech recognition, which corresponds to the word sequence with the highest posterior probability. By Bayes's rule, the previous equation can be re-written as

$$\mathbf{W}^{\star} = \arg\max_{\mathbf{W}} P(\mathbf{O} \mid \mathbf{W})P(\mathbf{W}),$$

where P(**O** | **W**) is the probability of observation **O** given that **W** is spoken, and P(**W**) is the prior probability of **W**. P(**O** | **W**) is referred to as the acoustic model (AM). It describes that, when **W** is spoken, how probable **O** is observed in the produced speech. P(**W**) is known as the language model (LM). It indicates how probable **W** is spoken in the language. AM and LM jointly represent the prior knowledge about the spoken language concerned as well as the intended domain of application. The models are obtained through a process of training, which requires a good amount of speech and text data. The basic architecture of an ASR system is depicted as in Figure 42.2.

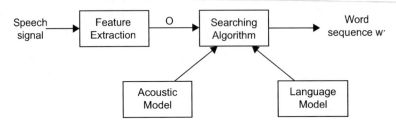

Figure 42.2 Architecture of a speech recognition system

Signal Pre-Processing and Feature Extraction

The acoustic signal is picked up by a microphone, which converts the signal into an electrical one. The electrical signal is amplified, sampled and digitized at the audio interface of a computer system. The digitized signal is a sequence of signed integer values that represent the signal amplitudes. There are typically 8,000–16,000 samples in each second of signal, depending on the application. The sample sequence is divided into short time frames within each of which the signal properties are assumed to be homogeneous. The time advancement between successive frames is 0.01 second, and each frame is 0.02 to 0.03 seconds long. In other words, neighboring frames overlap each other. A group of feature parameters is computed from each short time frame by applying prescribed signal processing procedures. These parameters form a feature vector that consists of 20 to 40 elements. Thus a digitized speech signal is represented by a temporal sequence of feature vectors, which are used in speech recognition.

Mel-frequency cepstral coefficients (MFCCs) are the most commonly used feature parameters. The computation of MFCC features starts with fast Fourier transform (FFT) of the signal samples, which results in a set of spectral coefficients that outline the frequency spectrum of the respective frame. A bank of nonlinearly spaced filters is applied to the log magnitude spectrum. The nonlinearity is designed in the way that the filter-bank simulates human auditory mechanism. The number of filters is 20 to 30, depending on the signal bandwidth. Subsequently discrete cosine transform (DCT) is applied to the filter-bank output, and the first 13 (low-order) DCT coefficients are used for speech recognition. The complete feature vector in a state-of-the-art ASR system also includes the first-order and second-order time differences between the MFCC parameters of successive frames, which characterize the temporal dynamics of the frame-based features. Other methods of feature extraction for speech recognition include perceptual linear prediction (PLP) and modulation spectrum.

Feature parameters may go through a transformation process, which maps the features into a new space of representation. The transformed feature vectors are desired to be more effective for representing and discriminating speech sounds and hence to achieve a higher recognition accuracy. Examples of such transformation are the principal component analysis (PCA), linear discriminant analysis (LDA), vocal tract normalization (VTN), and cepstral mean normalization (CMN). Some of these transformations are particularly useful in dealing with change of speaker or change of microphone.

Acoustic Modeling

Acoustic models are built for a set of speech units that are the basic constituents of the language concerned. The models are used to compute the likelihood of the input utterance with respect to a hypothesized sequence of speech units. In state-of-the-art ASR systems, the acoustic model of a speech unit $\mathbf{W}$ is in the form of a probability distribution function, denoted by $P(\mathbf{O} \mid \mathbf{W})$. $P(\mathbf{O} \mid \mathbf{W})$ is obtained via a process of statistical inference that involves a large number of incidences of $\mathbf{W}$. This process is known as model training.

The choice of modeling units is application-dependent. Word-level modeling is adequate and appropriate for small-vocabulary applications, for example, recognition of digit strings. However, this approach is difficult to be scaled up to handle thousands of words, due to the scarcity of training data for each word. Sub-word modeling is a practical choice for large-vocabulary continuous speech recognition. Since the same sub-word unit may appear in different words, better sharing of training data can be achieved. This approach also offers the capability of recognizing a word that is not covered in the training data. The definitions of sub-word units are different from one language to another. For English, there are about 40 phonemes to be modeled. For Mandarin Chinese, it is a common practice to model about 60 sub-syllable units, initials and finals, which are defined based on traditional Chinese phonology. The exact choices and definitions of modeling units are not critical to the performance of a speech recognition system, provided that the chosen units completely cover the anticipated input speech.

Context-dependent phoneme models are commonly used in large-vocabulary systems. A basic phoneme may be represented with multiple models that cater to different phonetic contexts. In the approach of tri-phone modeling, the immediately neighboring phonemes on the left and right of a basic phoneme are taken into account. Other contextual factors that can be considered include stress, lexical tone, and sentential position. Effective clustering methods, such as decision tree based clustering, can be used to control the total number of context-dependent units.

The hidden Markov model (HMM) has been widely and successfully applied to acoustic modeling of speech. HMM is an extension of observable Markov process. Each state in an HMM is associated with a probability distribution function, which is typically represented by a Gaussian mixture model (GMM). The acoustic observations, that is, feature vectors, are regarded as random variables generated by the HMM according to the state-level probability functions. As an example, the English phoneme /o/ can be modeled with an HMM with three states arranged in a time-ordered manner. Each of the states corresponds to a sub-segment of the phoneme. The state transitions reflect the temporal dynamics of speech. The training of HMMs for a large vocabulary system typically requires hundreds of hours of transcribed speech data.

Other approaches to acoustic modeling for ASR include artificial neural networks (ANN) and segmental trajectory models. ANN is a powerful technique of pattern classification. It can be used to model the state-level probability functions in an HMM. In particular, recent studies showed that deep neural networks (DNN) with many hidden layers could achieve significantly better ASR performance than using GMM.

Lexical and Language Modeling

Speech is not a random sequence of phonemes and words. It is governed by the linguistic rules of the language. The lexical and language model of an ASR system reflect the system's knowledge of what constitute a word, how individual words are arranged in order to form a sentence, and so on. The lexical model is in the form of a pronunciation dictionary, which tabulates all legitimate words and their pronunciations in terms of a sequence of phonemes. If a word has multiple pronunciations, they will be listed as separate entries in the dictionary. The language model is a statistical characterization that attempts to encode multiple levels of linguistic knowledge: syntax, semantics, and pragmatics of the language. The lexical model can be constructed from published dictionaries of the language. The language model is usually developed via a computational process with a large amount of real-world language data.

N-gram language models are widely used in large-vocabulary continuous speech recognition. Let $W = w_1, w_2, ..., w_N$ be a sequence of N words. The probability $P(W)$ can be expressed as

$$P(W) = P(w_1)P(w_2 \mid w_1)P(w_3 \mid w_1, w_2) \cdots P(w_N \mid w_1, w_2 \cdots, w_{N-1})$$

$$= \prod_{n=1}^{N} P(w_n \mid w_1, w_2, \cdots, w_{n-1})$$

$P(w_n \mid w_1, w_2, \cdots, w_{n-1})$ denotes the probability that the word W_n follows the sequence $w_1, w_2, \cdots, w_{n-1}$. It is referred to as the n-gram probability. $P(w_n)$ is called the uni-gram, $P(w_n \mid w_{n-1})$ the bi-gram, and $P(w_n \mid w_{n-2}, w_{n-1})$ the tri-gram.

N-gram probabilities are estimated by counting word occurrences. For example, the tri-gram probability $P(w_n \mid w_{n-2}, w_{n-1})$ is computed as

$$P(w_n \mid w_{n-2}, w_{n-1}) = \frac{C(w_{n-2}, w_{n-1}, w_n)}{C(w_{n-2}, w_{n-1})},$$

where $C(\times)$ is the count of occurrences of the word sequence in a given corpus.

Uni-gram language model contains information about how frequently a word is used in the language, which does not help the recognition of a word sequence. Word bi-grams and tri-grams are commonly used in continuous speech recognition because they are able to capture local grammatical properties and computationally manageable in practical applications. The process of estimating the n-gram probabilities is called language model training. If there are 10,000 words in the vocabulary, the total number of bi-grams and tri-grams will be 10^8 and 10^{12}, respectively. Reliable estimation of these probabilities requires a huge amount of training data. For a word combination that does not appear in the training corpus, the respective n-gram probability will be assigned a zero value. This may lead to an undesirable generalization that a sentence containing this word combination will never be recognized correctly. To alleviate this problem, the technique of language model smoothing is applied to make the n-gram probabilities more robust to unseen data. Another way of handling data sparseness problem is to use class n-grams. A relatively small number of classes are formed by grouping words with similar linguistic functions and grammatical properties. N-gram probabilities are estimated based on word classes instead of individual words.

Search/Decoding

The goal of continuous speech recognition is to find the optimal word sequence, which has the highest value of $P(\mathbf{W})P(\mathbf{O} \mid \mathbf{W})$. This is done via a process of search over a structured space that contains many candidate sequences. The process is also called decoding because it aims at discovering the composition of an unknown signal. The acoustic models and the language models together define the search space, which is represented by a graph with many nodes and arcs. The nodes are HMM states, and the arcs include HMM state transitions and cross-phoneme and cross-word transitions. Phoneme-level HMMs are connected to form word-level models according to the lexical model. The lexical model can be represented with a tree structure, in which words having the same partial pronunciation are merged instead of reproduced. With n-gram language models, the end state of each word is linked to many other words with probabilistic transitions. Higher-order language models require a longer word history. This makes the search space expand exponentially.

Each spoken sentence corresponds to a legitimate state-transition path in the search space. The likelihood of the sentence is computed from the state output probabilities, state transition probabilities, and word n-gram probabilities along the path. Exhaustive search over all possible paths is impractical and unnecessary. Many efficient search algorithms have been developed. Examples are the time-synchronous Viterbi search with pruning and the best-first $A^\star$ stack decoder. The search algorithm is required to find not only a single best answer but also other alternatives that may rank just below the best. This is important because the single best output of speech recognition often contains errors. Since these errors may not be recoverable in the subsequent language translation process, inclusion of a broader range of hypotheses makes the whole system more robust. The most commonly used representations of multiple hypotheses are N-best list, word graph, and word lattice.

Machine Translation

A machine translation (MT) system performs text translation from one language to another. For speech translation applications, the input text to the MT system is derived from natural speech, and the output text from the MT system is used to generate natural speech. The difference between spoken language and written language has to be well understood when applying general machine translation techniques to speech-to-speech translation.

Language translation is a knowledge-based process. A good human translator must have profound understanding of both the source and the target languages, as well as their similarities and differences. Knowledge-based machine translation starts with linguistic analysis or parsing of the input sentence. The result of parsing is a structured representation, for example, parse tree, which describes the syntactic relation between individual words in the sentence. A set of transformation rules are applied to change the syntactic structure of the source language to that of the target language. The translation of content words is done with a cross-language dictionary. This approach is referred to as rule-based translation. In the case that the parsing algorithm fails to analyze a sentence, the method of direct translation is used to produce a conservative result by performing word-for-word substitution.

The use of interlingua is an effective approach to domain-specific speech-to-speech translation in a multilingual scenario. Interlingua is a kind of meaning representation that is language independent. In other words, sentences in different languages but with the same meaning are represented in the same way. Translation is formulated as a process of extracting the meaning of the input text and expressing it in the target language. Interlingua representations are crafted manually based on both domain knowledge and linguistic knowledge. Since there is a need to determine the exact meaning of an input sentence, interlingua-based approaches require a deeper parsing than rule-based transformation.

Example-based machine translation is an empirical approach that does not require deep linguistic analysis. It is sometimes called or related to a corpus-based or memory-based approach.

An example-based system is built upon a bilingual corpus of translated examples. The translation is formulated as a process of matching fragments of the input sentence against this corpus to find appropriate examples and recombining the translated fragments to generate the output sentence (Somers 1999: 113–57). Since examples are used directly in the translation process, the generalizability is limited unless the corpus can cover everything in the language.

Statistical machine translation has become a mainstream approach in the past decade. It leverages the availability of large-scale bilingual parallel corpora and statistical modeling techniques. In a bilingual parallel corpus, each sentence in the source language is aligned with a counterpart in the target language. Typically millions of sentence pairs are required for establishing a meaningful translation model. EUROPARL is one of the well-known parallel corpora for machine translation research (www.statmt.org/europarl). It contains a large collection of recordings of the European Parliament meetings in 11 different languages.

Statistical translation follows the same principle and mathematical framework as automatic speech recognition. Let $\mathbf{F}$ denote a string of words (sentence) in the source language. Given $\mathbf{F}$, the conditional probability of a translated word string $\mathbf{E}$ in the target language is denoted as $P(\mathbf{E} \mid \mathbf{F})$. The goal of translation is to find the optimal choice of $\mathbf{E}$, which has the largest $P(\mathbf{E} \mid \mathbf{F})$, i.e.,

$$\mathbf{E}^* = \arg\max_{\mathbf{E}} P(\mathbf{F} \mid \mathbf{E})P(\mathbf{E}),$$

where $P(\mathbf{E})$ is the language model probability in the target language, and $P(\mathbf{F} \mid \mathbf{E})$ is the translation model probability (Brown *et al.* 1993).

The sentence-level probability $P(\mathbf{F} \mid \mathbf{E})$ can be computed from word-level probability $P(\mathbf{f} \mid \mathbf{e})$, in which $\mathbf{f}$ and $\mathbf{e}$ denote a pair of aligned words. Word alignment is a critical step in translation. It is done in the same way as HMM state alignment in speech recognition. To capture the dependencies between words, phrase-level alignment is performed in translation. A phrase is defined a group of words. In the training of the phrase-level translation model, each phrase in the target sentence needs to be mapped to a phrase in the source sentence. The conditional probability for each pair of phrases is estimated from the training data.

With the translation model and the language model of target language, translation is a process of search for the optimal sequence of words in the target language. Different hypotheses of target sentences are generated in a bottom-up manner. Similar to speech recognition, the techniques of A⋆ search and Viterbi beam search can be applied. However, the search algorithm has to be flexibly designed such that different word orders between the two languages are allowed. In speech recognition, the input feature vector and the corresponding phoneme sequence are aligned in the same temporal order.

Since statistical machine translation uses the same computational framework as speech recognition, an integrated approach can be developed to perform the conversion from speech input in the source language to text output in the target language. Stochastic finite-state transducers (SFTS) are commonly used to implement the integrated search.

Speech Synthesis

Speech synthesis refers to the process of generating an audible speech signal to express a given message. Usually the message is in the form of written text, and the process is called text-to-speech (TTS) conversion. A text-to-speech system consists of three modules, as shown in Figure 42.3.

The text processing module maps the textual input into a sequence of sound units. The acoustic synthesis module generates a continuous speech signal according to the sound unit

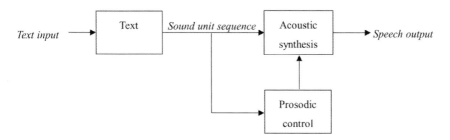

Figure 42.3　Architecture of a text-to-speech system

sequence. The prosodic control module contributes to improve naturalness of the synthesized speech (Dutoit 1997: 25–36).

Similar to the consideration in speech recognition, the selection of sound units for speech synthesis is a trade-off between generalizability and accuracy. A small number of phoneme-level units are adequate to synthesize speech of arbitrary content. However, they may not be accurate enough to represent the contextual variation in natural speech. Use of word-level or even phrase-level units is effective in capturing local co-articulation effects. This is at the expense of a large number of distinctive units that need to be processed and stored. For general-domain TTS systems, context-dependent phonemic units are most commonly used. There are also systems using variable-length units.

For most languages, phonemic symbols cannot be straightforwardly observed from written text. Grapheme-to-phoneme conversion for TTS involves linguistic analysis at lexical, morphological, and syntactic levels. The input sentence is first parsed into a list of words. Chinese written text does not have explicitly marked word boundaries. Thus word segmentation is an important problem in Chinese text processing. A pronunciation lexicon is used to map each word into a phoneme sequence. If a word has alternative pronunciations, the most appropriate one is chosen according to its linguistic context. The pronunciation of proper names, abbreviations, idiomatic expressions, numbers, date and time, and so on, cannot be covered by the lexicon, because there are too many variations of them. These items are handled specially by heuristic rules, which are application dependent.

Prosody refers to the temporal variation of rhythm, pitch, and loudness along a spoken utterance. It plays an important role in human speech communication. Prosodic phenomena in natural speech include focus, stress, accentuation, sentential intonation, pause, and many others. They are realized in acoustic signals through the variation of fundamental frequency (F0), duration, and signal intensity. The prosodic control module specifies the target values of these parameters based on the results of text analysis. Prosodic control in TTS can be rule-based, model-based, or corpus-based. Rule-based methods generate target prosody from a set of pre-determined rules that are derived by linguistic observations. Model-based approaches assume that prosody production is governed by an underlying model, usually a parametric one. Corpus-based approaches use a large amount of natural speech data to train a generative prosody model in a statistical sense.

Waveform concatenation is a predominant approach for acoustic synthesis in commercial TTS systems. It is an engineering approach that leverages the availability of low-cost computer storage. An acoustic inventory is designed to cover all basic sound units in the language. For each of these sound units, multiple waveform templates are stored to represent its contextual variations. A continuous speech utterance is produced by selecting appropriate waveform templates from the acoustic inventory and concatenating them in the time domain. The selection of waveform templates can be formulated as an optimization process. The objective is to minimize phonetic and prosodic mismatches, and signal discontinuities that are incurred by concatenation. If the acoustic inventory is well designed and comprehensive in coverage, the concatenated speech would be able to reach a high level of smoothness and naturalness. Further modification on the prosody of concatenated speech utterances can be done using pitch-synchronous overlap and add (PSOLA) technique.

HMM-based speech synthesis has been investigated extensively in recent years. It makes use of a set of context-dependent HMMs that are trained from natural speech data in the same way as in a speech recognition system. For speech synthesis, the HMMs that correspond to the desired phoneme sequence are concatenated. A temporal sequence of spectral and prosodic parameters are generated from the HMM parameters and used to synthesize the output speech. Without the need of storing original speech waveforms, an HMM-based speech synthesis system has a much lower memory requirement than a concatenation system, making it a better choice for portable and personalized applications. An appealing advantage of HMM-based speech synthesis is that it provides a good mechanism for flexible change, modification, or customization of voice characteristics. This is done by retraining and adaptation of the HMMs with a relatively small amount of new training data. It is even possible to develop a multilingual system that can speak several different languages using the same voice. This is particularly useful in speech translation.

Compared to speech recognition and language translation, speech synthesis technology is considered to be mature and ready for real-world applications. Multilingual text-to-speech capabilities are now provided in standard computer systems running Windows 8 and iOS.

Examples of Speech Translation Systems

There were many speech-to-speech translation systems developed for research demonstration purposes. Most of them worked in specific application domains. Very few general-purpose systems are available in the commercial market. One of them is the Compadre product suite of SpeechGear, Inc. It consists of a series of software modules that are designed for different modes of communication. The latest version supports bi-directional translation between English and 40 other languages. The speech recognition engine in the Compadre modules is Dragon Naturally Speaking provided by Nuance Communications, Inc.

Recently a number of smartphone apps for multilingual speech-to-speech translation have become available. This makes the technology more accessible and portable for general users. Jibbigo was initially developed by a start-up company founded by Dr. Alex Waibel, who is one of the pioneer researchers in speech translation technologies. The Jibbigo app supports about 20 languages. The online version is available for free download at Apple's AppStore and Android. The offline version charges per language pair. It can be used without an internet connection.

Simutalk is a speech-to-speech translation app developed by ZTspeech in Beijing, China. The technologies in the software are backed up by speech translation research at the Institution of Automation, Chinese Academy of Sciences. Simutalk supports bi-directional Chinese–English translation with a large vocabulary and requires internet connection. Another multilingual speech-to-speech translation app is VoiceTra4U. It is developed by the U-STAR consortium. A major feature of VoiceTra4U is that it supports many Asian languages. The software is available for free download at Apple's AppStore.

Additional Resources

www.dtic.mil/dtic/pdf/success/TRANSTAC20080915.pdf.
www.nec.com/en/global/rd/innovative/speech/04.html.

www.statmt.org/europarl.
www.ustar-consortium.com.

Further Reading

Casacuberta, Francisco, Marcello Federico, Hermann Ney, and Enrique Vidal (2008) 'Recent Efforts in Spoken Language Translation', *IEEE Signal Processing Magazine* 25(3): 80–88.
Nakamura, Satoshi (2009) 'Overcoming the Language Barrier with Speech Translation Technology', *NISTEP Quarterly Review* 31: 35–48.
Weinstein, Clifford J. (2002) 'Speech-to-Speech Translation: Technology and Applications Study', *MIT Lincoln Laboratory Technical Report*.

Bibliography

Brown, Peter, Stephen A. Della Pietra, Vincent J. Della Pietra, and Robert L. Mercer (1993) 'The Mathematics of Statistical Machine Translation: Parameter Estimation', *Computational Linguistics* 19(2): 263–311.
Dutoit, Thierry (1997) 'High-Quality Text-to-Speech Synthesis: An Overview', *Journal of Electrical and Electronic Engineering Australia* 17: 25–36.
Federico, Marcello (2003) 'Evaluation Frameworks for Speech Translation Technologies', in *Proceedings of EUROSPEECH 2003 – INTERSPEECH 2003: 8th European Conference on Speech Communication and Technology*, 1–4 September 2003, Geneva Switzerland, 377–80.
Gao, Yuqing, Bowen Zhou, Ruhi Sarikaya, Mohammed Afify, Hong-Kwang Kuo, Wei-zhong Zhu, Yong-gang Deng, Charles Prosser, Wei Zhang, and Laurent Besacier (2006) 'IBM MASTOR SYSTEM: Multilingual Automatic Speech-to-Speech Translator', in *Proceedings of the Workshop on Medical Speech Translation*, 9 June 2006, New York, NY, 53–56.
Hashimoto, Kei, Junichi Yamagishi, William Bnyrne, Simon King, and Keiichi Tokuda (2012) 'Impacts of Machine Translation and Speech Synthesis on Speech-to-Speech Translation', *Speech Communication* 54(7): 857–66.
http://verbmobil.dfki.de/overview-us.html.
Levin, Lori, Alon Lavie, Monika Woszczyna, Donna Gates, Marsal Gavalda, Detlef Koll, and Alex Waibel (2000) 'The Janus-III Translation System: Speech-to-Speech Translation in Multiple Domains', *Machine Translation* 15(1–2): 3–25.
Metze, Florion, John McDonough, Hagen Soltau, Chad Langley, Alon Lavie, Tanja Schultz, Alex Waibel, Roldano Cattoni, Gianni Lazzari, and Fabio Pianesi (2002) 'The NESPOLE! Speech-to-Speech Translation System', in Mitchell Marcus (ed.) *Proceedings of the 2nd International Conference on Human Language Technology Research*, 24–27 March 2002, San Diego, CA, 378–83.
Papineni, Kishore, Salim Roukos, Todd Ward, and Zhu Wei-Jing (2002) 'DFHJLBLEU: A Method for Automatic Evaluation of Machine Translation', in *Proceedings of the 40th Annual Meeting of the Association for Computational Linguistics, ACL-2002*, 7–12 July 2002, University of Pennsylvania, Philadelphia, PA, 311–18.
Somers, Harold L. (1999) 'Review Article: Example-Based Machine Translation', *Machine Translation* 14(2): 113–57.
Stüker, Sebastian, Chengqing Zong, Jürgen Reichert, Wenjie Cao, Guodong Xie, Kay Peterson, Peng Ding, Victoria Arranz, and Alex Waibel (2006) 'Speech-to-Speech Translation Services for the Olympic Games 2008', in Andrei Popescu-Belis, Steve Renals, and Hervé Bourlard (eds.) *Machine Learning for Multimodal Interaction: Proceedings of the 4th International Workshop, MLMI 2007*, 28–30 June 2007, Brno, Czech Republic, 297–308.
Takezawa, Toshiyuki, Tsuyoshi Morimoto, Yoshinori Sagisaka, Nick Campbell, Hitoshi Lida, Fumiaki Sugaya, Akio Yokoo, and Seiichi Yamamoto (1998) 'A Japanese-to-English Speech Translation System: ATR-MATRIX', in *Proceedings of the 5th International Conference on Spoken Language Processing, Incorporating the 7th Australian International Speech Science and Technology Conference*, 30 November–4 December 1998, Sydney Convention Centre, Sydney, Australia, 2779–82.
Zhang, Ying (2003) 'Survey of Current Speech Translation Research'. Available at: http://projectile. is.cs. cmu.edu/research/public/talks/speechTranslation/sst-survey-joy. pdf.
Zong, Chengqing and Mark Seligman (2005) 'Toward Practical Spoken Language Translation', *Machine Translation* 19(2): 113–37.

43

TECHNOLOGICAL STRIDES IN SUBTITLING

Jorge Díaz Cintas

The Audiovisualisation and Internetisation of Communication

The production and exchange of material in which written texts, images and speech are integrated and exploited through visual and auditory channels is an everyday reality in our society, which increasingly relies on these audiovisual programmes for information, entertainment, education and commerce. This type of format is appealing not only for its alluring semiotic complexity but also because thanks to today's technology, these messages can travel nearly instantly and have the potential to reach large audiences anywhere in the world. Traditionally, the flow of communication was unidirectional, through the cinema and the television, but nowadays it takes the form of bidirectional, dynamic exchanges increasingly through the world wide web.

Audiovisual exchanges are appealing because they can communicate complex messages in a ludic way. Their composite audio and visual nature gives them the edge over written communication and has triggered the audiovisualisation of our communicative environment, where sounds and visuals coalesce in a winning combination over other formats, particularly among younger generations. A situation like this is a fertile ground for the blossoming of subtitling, which has grown exponentially in the profession, has gained much deserved visibility in the academe and become the international voice of millions of bloggers and netizens.

The catalyst for this moulding of our habits towards greater audiovisual communication can be traced back to cinema in the first instance and television some decades later, though the real impact came about with the start of the digital revolution in the 1980s. Boosted by vast improvements in computing technology, it marked the beginning of the information age and the globalisation trends.

The phasing out of analogue technology and the advent of digitisation opened up new avenues not only for the production but also for the distribution, commercialisation and enjoyment of subtitles. This transition is best symbolised in the death of VHS and the upsurge of the DVD at the end of the last millennium, followed by the switch off of the analogue signal and the switchover to digital broadcasting in the early years of the 21st century. From a linguistic point of view, the cohabitation of several languages and translations on the very same digital versatile disc has provided consumers with a different viewing experience altogether, allowing them a greater degree of interactivity and more control over the language combination(s) they want to follow.

DOI: 10.4324/9781003168348-46

All these changes have favoured the audiovisualisation of translation, which has been taken to new levels thanks to the omnipresent and omnipowerful world wide web. Without a doubt, the biggest catalyst of changes in audiovisual communication and translation has been, and continues to be, the internet. Since its launch in the early 1990s, it has known phenomenal growth and has had an enormous impact on culture, commerce and education. The potential unleashed by the technology has meant that video material, once too heavy to travel through the ether, can now be transmitted and received with surprising ease virtually anywhere. This, together with the consolidation of Web 2.0 – associated with applications that facilitate participatory and collaborative activities among netizens of virtual communities as well as the production of user-generated content – have made possible that the viewing, exchange and circulation of audiovisual materials is just a keystroke away for nearly everybody. Passive viewers of the first static websites have now become prosumers and bloggers of the cyberspace, with the power of creating and distributing their own material.

This internetisation of communication, aimed at reaching commercial success and visibility on a global scale, has found its best ally in subtitling, an easy, economical and fast way of breaking language and sensory barriers by making audiovisual programmes linguistically available and accessible to the rest of the world and potential clients. Indeed, unless this material comes with translations into other languages, it risks capping its potential exposure and its reach across countries and cultures, and without subtitles most videos will be equally inaccessible to audiences with hearing impairments.

Although subtitling took its first steps soon after the invention of cinema over a century ago, its technical evolution was rather slow for many decades, focusing primarily on modernising the various methods of engraving subtitles on the celluloid (Ivarsson and Carroll 1998: 12–19). In more recent decades, the efforts of the technology manufacturers have been directed to the development of powerful software packages specifically designed for subtitling. Yet, and perhaps rather surprisingly when compared with other areas in translation (O'Hagan 2013), little attention has been paid so far to the role that computer-aided translation (CAT) tools can play in subtitling or to the potential that translation memories and machine translation can yield in this field, although the situation is changing rapidly.

When talking about CAT tools, Chan (2013: 1) states that "the history of translation technology is short, but its development is fast"; an affirmation that in the field of subtitling is particularly apparent. In fact, it could be argued that developments in subtitling are taken place at a faster pace than in any other areas of translation because of, among other reasons, the ubiquitous presence of subtitles in the cyberspace and the magnetism they seem to exert on netizens. Researchers, software developers, subtitling companies, and even amateurs are finally paying closer attention to the technical intricacies of this translation practice, as they have realised that subtitling is much more than just adding two lines at the bottom of a film and that technology holds the key for companies (and individuals) to be able to cope with the vast amounts of audiovisual material, both commercial and user-generated, that needs translating.

The audiovisualisation of communication is having a great impact not only on the nature of the translation practice – with traditional ones being reassessed (dubbing, voiceover, subtitling) and new ones entering the market (subtitling for the deaf and the hard-of-hearing, audio description for the blind and the partially sighted, audio subtitling) – but also on the working flows of companies, the technology being used, the role of the translator, the nature of the subtitling job, the formal conventions being applied in the subtitles (Díaz Cintas 2010: 105–30), and the multifarious audiovisual genres that get subtitled these days. The following sections concentrate mainly on the technical dimension.

The Commoditisation and Globalisation of Subtitling

Of the various modes of translating audiovisual programmes, subtitling is arguably the most widely used in commercial and social environments for two main reasons: it is cheap, and it can be done fast.

Subtitles are used in all distribution channels – cinema, television, DVD, Blu-ray, internet – both intra- and interlingually. The entertainment industry, and increasingly the corporate world, has been quick to take advantage of the potential offered by digital technology to distribute the same audiovisual programme with numerous subtitled tracks in different languages. On the internet, the presence of subtitles has been boosted by the development and distribution of specialist subtitling freeware, which allows fansubbers and amateur subtitlers to create their own translations and distribute them around the globe. On a more domestic note, one of the most symbolic ways in which (intralingual) subtitles have been propelled to the media centre stage has been the inclusion of a subtitle button on most TV remote controls, which takes viewers to the subtitles in an easy and straightforward manner. Legislation in many countries is also having a great impact in the total amount of subtitled hours that TV stations must broadcast to satisfy the needs of deaf and hard-of-hearing viewers, with some corporations like the BBC subtitling 100% of their output.

As subtitling projects have become bigger in the number of hours and languages that need to be translated, their budgets have also risen, making the whole operation an attractive field for many old and new companies setting up innovative businesses or expanding the portfolio of services they provide to their clients. In this highly competitive commercial environment, the role of new technologies aimed at boosting productivity is being keenly explored by many of the stakeholders.

The Technology Turn

As in many other professions, technical advancements have had a profound impact on the sub-titling praxis. The profile expected of subtitlers has changed substantially and linguistic compe-tence, cultural awareness and subject knowledge are no longer sufficient to operate effectively and successfully in this profession. Would-be subtitlers are expected to demonstrate high techni-cal know-how and familiarity with increasingly more powerful subtitling software.

The first programmes designed exclusively for subtitling started being commercialised in the mid 1970s. At the time, subtitlers needed a computer, an external video player in which to play the VHS tapes with the material to be translated, and a television monitor to watch the audiovisual programmes. The computer would have a word processor with a special subtitling programme which made it possible to simulate the subtitles against the images on screen. Some subtitlers would also need a stopwatch to perform a more or less accurate timing of the dialogue.

The situation has changed significantly and these days, with a PC, a digital copy of the video, and a subtitling programme, subtitlers can perform all pertinent tasks in front of a single screen: they can watch the video and type their translation, decide the in and out times of each of their subtitles, take due care of shot changes, monitor the reading speed and length of their subtitles, decide on the positioning and colour of the text, spell check their translation, and simulate their subtitles against the images.

The capability and functionality of most professional subtitling programs have been improved at an incredibly fast pace in recent decades, with some of the leading manufacturers being EZTi-tles (www.eztitles.com), FAB (www.fab-online.com), Spot (www.spotsoftware.nl), and Screen Systems (www.screensystems.tv), the latter developers of the program WinCaps (Figure 43.1):

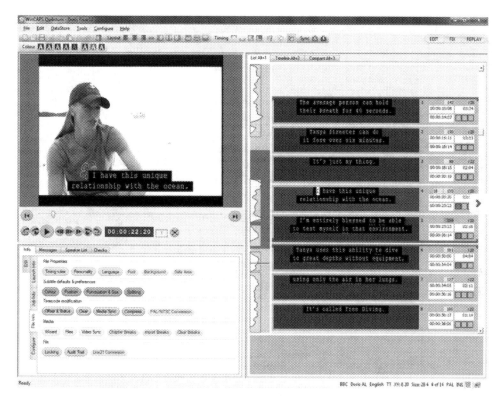

Figure 43.1 Interface of the professional subtitling program WinCaps Q4

The fact that professional subtitling software has traditionally been rather expensive and out of reach for many translators has encouraged some to take advantage of the potential offered by technology and come up with their own creative solutions, favouring the development of a vast array of free subtitling programmes, of which some of the best known are: Subtitling Workshop (https://subworkshop.sourceforge.net) – shown in Figure 43.2 –Aegisub (https://aeg-dev.github.io/AegiSite) and Subtitle Edit (www.nikse.dk/SubtitleEdit).

New Software Functionality

As time equals money, professional (but also amateur) subtitling programs are being constantly updated with a view to maximising productivity and hence reducing costs. Improved user interfaces and the automation of certain subtitling tasks, particularly at the technical level, have always been the favoured remit of software engineers, though experiments have been conducted in recent years into the potentiality of automating some steps in the linguistic transfer.

To speed up the spotting process (i.e. the synchronisation of the subtitles with the soundtrack) whilst respecting shot changes, some subtitling software applications detect shot changes in the audiovisual program automatically, displaying a timeline in which the video track and the shot change boundaries are shown, thus making it easier and quicker to set the subtitle in and out times. Another improved feature of most programs is the provision of an audio-level indication waveform, whereby changes in soundtrack volume are shown and speech presence can be detected and distinguished from music or background effects. The main benefits of these

Figure 43.2 Interface of Subtitle Workshop 6.0a, subtitling freeware developed by URUWorks

efficiency tools are twofold. First, subtitlers can skip the scenes with no speech, saving time especially during the final preview or quality check. Second, by assisting them in identifying the timing of speech points, it helps making spotting a lot easier, faster, and more accurate.

Technology can further assist subtitlers by simplifying the tasks of text input and timecode synchronisation. The automatic timing of subtitles is achieved by means of speech alignment technology: the script or transcript of the dialogue is fed to the subtitling programme, which, equipped with a speech recognition system, synchronises it with the soundtrack of the video and assigns it a given timecode, taking account of parameters such as timing rules for shot changes, reading speeds, minimum gaps between subtitles, and minimum and maximum duration of subtitles. If the script contains more textual information than just the dialogue exchanges, the latter can still be imported into the software, with a script extractor that is capable of parsing the script layout to extract dialogue or any information deemed relevant, such as speaker cues. When subtitling for the deaf and the hard-of-hearing (SDH), this information can be used in order to automatically colour the interventions of the different actors, for instance.

In the case of live subtitling, speech recognition has been instrumental in the growth of respeaking:

a technique in which a respeaker listens to the original sound of a live programme or event and respeaks it, including punctuation marks and some specific features for the deaf and hard of hearing audience, to a speech recognition software, which turns the recognized utterances into subtitles displayed on the screen with the shortest possible delay.

(Romero-Fresco 2011: 1)

Although this is a new, cost-effective alternative to conventional keyboard-based methods for live subtitling using stenotype or velotype, its very own survival is already being challenged by experiments that look into using speech recognition for subtitling directly from the voice of the TV presenter, thus doing away with the figure of the respeaker.

Reaching for the Cloud

When it comes to the production of subtitles, the traditional model of a translation company that commissions a project from professional subtitlers and pays them for their work has ceased to be the only one in existence. In today's global world, viewers are also bound to come across subtitles that nobody has commissioned or paid for (fansubs), as well as subtitles that organisations have requested from volunteers but not reimbursed (crowdsourced subtitling or crowdsubtitling).

The latter usually refers to collaborative, nonprofit subtitles powered by specific organisations or teams of volunteers. From a technical perspective, they often use applications or platforms built for the specific purpose of this task and which are very easy to learn and use, as is the case of dotSub (dotsub.com), since they usually do not allow the participants to decide the timing of the subtitles and ask them to concentrate on the linguistic transfer. The process of adding subtitles is fast and easy, and no software needs to be downloaded or installed. The final output, clips and subtitles, is shared on open websites like TED (www.ted.com), Khan Academy (www.khanacademy.org), or Viki (www.viki.com).

Fansubbers or amateur subtitlers, on the other hand, tend to operate within their own *ad hoc* groups, motivated by their ultimate belief in the free distribution on the net of subtitles made by fans for the consumption of other fans. The first fansubs date from the early 1990s, and their exponential rise in recent years has been made possible thanks to the availability of free subtitling and video-editing software. If in the early years fansubbers' drive was confined to the popularisation of Japanese anime, the reality these days is that most audiovisual programmes, including the latest US films and most popular TV series, find their way into the fansubbing circuit, raising thorny ethical considerations. As opposed to crowdsubtitling, in which both clips and subtitles are distributed with the consent of the interested parties, fansubs are technically illegal, as they are not officially licensed and, therefore, infringe the copyright of the owners of the audiovisual programme. On occasions, fansub sites have been closed by copyright enforcement agencies, as in Sweden, and in Poland, nine fansubbers were arrested by police in 2007 (Briggs 2013).

Another difference with crowdsubtitling is that fansubbers tend to work with free subtitling programs that they download from the web, such as the ones mentioned earlier in this chapter, whereas crowdsubtitling is usually done through online platforms without the need to download any software. In this sense, fansubbing can be said to be closer to professional subtitling, since the fansubber tends to be in charge of the technical as well as the linguistic tasks.

A recent trend, cloud subtitling, refers to the notion of subtitling on the cloud through collaboration among people based in different geographical locations. On the surface, the only common characteristics it has with fansubbing and crowdsubtitling is delivery on the internet, the use of teams of subtitlers for different tasks, and the relative ease in the preparation of subtitles as opposed to conventional professional subtitling. But, essentially, cloud subtitling adopts a different working model overall and resembles closely the typical chain of subtitling preparation followed by subtitling companies. The final product is no longer considered user-generated content as it is prepared by subtitlers rather than volunteers. It is a solution mostly adopted by translation companies who act as mediators between clients and vendors. The entire subtitling project is managed online through a cloud-based platform that usually incorporates a project management environment as well as a subtitling editor with a user-friendly application that operates as subtitlers' workspace. One of the advantages of working in this way is that subtitlers can manage their projects without having to buy or download software themselves. What is more, cloud-based subtitling is often provided in different formats, supporting most of the current technologies and devices in the market as well as internet applications, and deliverables are forwarded automatically to clients without any additional effort by subtitlers.

Although a very new development, cloud subtitling has made rapid inroads in the industry, opening new avenues in the provision of subtitles. Among the most prominent examples of cloud subtitling platforms are ZOOsubs (www.zoodigital.com/technology/zoosubs) by Zoo Digital and iMediaTrans (https://secure.new.lite.imediatrans.com/login) by iYuno. The former was launched in 2012 and currently offers services for subtitling and post-production in more than 40 languages, including fully visible monitoring of the subtitling process, archiving, and reviewing of the content, while the final content as well as subtitle files can be converted into several formats, and clients have the opportunity to actively participate in the workflow. iMediaTrans also replicates all the tasks involved in the subtitling industry chain, while in-house teams coordinate projects to make sure that the outcome quality within the cloud is of the standard requested by clients. These cloud platforms, also including OOONA (https://ooona.net/ooona-tools), tend to work on the basis of automatic alignment of text with audio whilst still allowing for subtitle editing with options on positioning and use of colours as well as various other technical attributes that can be set by the client or the vendor. These subtitling providers usually select their collaborators online but, unlike crowdsubtitling, they claim to employ professional subtitlers rather than volunteers and offer clients the possibility of choosing a particular subtitler to take care of their project.

This streamlining of labour management makes cloud subtitling a unique solution for saving time, money, and space in the production, editing, post-production, and delivery of subtitles. When compared with the practices followed by traditional subtitling companies, a certain degree of harmonisation can be detected, with the latter relying more than ever on freelance subtitlers and orders and project management being conducted online. What cloud subtitling notably brings is the potential for closer monitoring on the part of the clients themselves, the possibility to deliver the final product in different formats with greater ease, and the use of cloud-based applications and platforms that lower the cost of subtitling and post-production overall.

Machine Translation and Subtitling

Whilst developments in the technical dimension of subtitling have been numerous regarding, for example, spotting, shot changes, audio and speaker recognition, and automatic colouring of text, the advances on the linguistic front have been much more modest. Although some programs can facilitate text segmentation by automatically dividing the text of a script into subtitles based on linguistic rules that are set up for a specific language, the results can be rather disappointing, and the participation of the translator is crucially required.

Translation memory tools, which store previously translated sentences and allow the user to retrieve them as a base for a new translation, have had a great impact in translation, particularly in the fields of specialised and technical translation. However, their worth has been called into question in the case of subtitling because of the fictional and literary nature of audiovisual programmes. Though this might have been true in the past, when most of the materials being subtitled belonged to the entertainment genre, the situation is rapidly evolving. The fact that companies and institutions involved in selling, marketing, education, and science, to name but a few areas, are discovering the virtues of communicating audiovisually, mainly through the internet, is clearly bringing changes to this state of affairs. DVD bonus material, scientific and technical documentaries, edutainment programmes, and corporate videos tend to contain the high level of lexical repetition that makes it worthwhile for translation companies to employ assisted translation and memory tools in the subtitling process.

As one of the pioneers in this area, the Taiwanese company Webtrans Digital (www.webt rans.com.tw) has been working with a computer-assisted tool called Wados for many years now and claims that it enhances its efficiency and subtitling consistency.

A step further from computer-assisted translation in the form of memory tools is machine translation (MT). Subtitling has only recently been recognised as an area that could benefit from the introduction of statistical machine translation (SMT) technology to increase translator productivity (Etchegoyhen *et al.* 2013). Two of the first funded research projects to look into its feasibility were MUSA (MUltilingual Subtitling of multimediA content; http://sifnos.ilsp. gr/musa) and eTITLE (Oliver González *et al.* 2006). MUSA ran from 2002 until 2004 and had English, French, and Greek as the working languages. According to the information provided on the web portal, the team's highly ambitious goal was:

> the creation of a multimodal multilingual system that converts audio streams into text transcriptions, generates subtitles from these transcriptions and then translates the subtitles in other languages. . . . A state-of-the-art Speech Recognition system was enhanced and improved to meet the project settings. An innovative Machine Translation scenario combining a Machine Translation engine with a Translation Memory and a Term Substitution module was designed. Sentence condensing for subtitle generation was performed by an automatic analysis of the linguistic structure of the sentence. MUSA combined core speech and language technologies in a real-life application addressing a pan-European audiovisual audience that depends on subtitles to overcome the linguistic barriers.

Despite such high hopes, no tangible results have yet materialised from either of these two projects, one of the main reasons being the lack at the time of professional-quality parallel sub-title data, without which it is difficult to adequately train SMT systems for subtitles.

More recently, the European Commission funded the project SUMAT, an online service for SUbtitling by MAchine Translation, under its Information and Communication Technologies Policy Support Programme (https://cordis.europa.eu/project/id/270919). Run by a consortium of four subtitling companies and five technical partners from 2011 until 2014, one of its aims is to use the archives of subtitle files owned by the subtitling companies in the consortium to build a large corpus of aligned subtitles and use this corpus to train SMT systems in various language pairs. Its ultimate objective is to benefit from the introduction of SMT in the field of subtitling, followed by human post-editing in order to increase the productivity of subtitle translation procedures, reduce costs and turnaround times while keeping a watchful eye on the quality of the translation results. To this end, the consortium has built a cloud-based service for the MT of subtitles in nine languages and seven bidirectional language pairs. The service will offer users, from individual freelancers to multinational companies, the ability to upload subtitle files in a number of industry-standard subtitle formats as well as in plain text format and to download a machine-translated file in the same format, preserving all time codes and formatting information where possible (Georgakopoulou and Bywood 2013).

Although the switch from rule-based approaches to statistical translation methods has the potential to improve the accuracy of the translation output, the reality is that no current system provides the holy grail of fully automatic high-quality MT. Indeed, as foregrounded by Hunter (2010: online):

> There is scope for machine translation technology to be used in the creation of translated subtitle files, but as this is not yet a perfect science, there is a fine line between the time taken to check and edit automated content and the time taken to translate each subtitle in turn.

In the toolbox of automatic translation undertaken within the context of subtitling, TranslateTV (www.translatetv.com) has been translating English closed captions into Spanish subtitles in real time as a commercial venture in the United States since 2003. Taking advantage of the high volume of intralingual subtitles (English into English) for the deaf and the hard-of-hearing being done in the United States, Vox Frontera, Inc., offers an automatic translation service of those subtitles into Spanish, aimed primarily at the Hispanic and Latino community, who see and hear exactly what English-speaking viewers see and hear with the only difference of the added real-time Spanish subtitles.

A bolder approach in the automation of subtitling has been taken by Google and YouTube. In an attempt to boost accessibility to audiovisual programmes, primarily to people with hearing impairments, they introduced in 2006 a new feature allowing the playback of captions and subtitles (Harrenstien 2006). In 2009, they announced the launch of machine-generated automatic captions, with the firm belief that "captions not only help the deaf and hearing impaired, but with machine translation, they also enable people around the world to access video content in any of 51 languages" (Harrenstien 2009: online). Their philosophy is summarised in the following quote:

> Twenty hours of video is uploaded to YouTube every minute. Making some of these videos more accessible to people who have hearing disabilities or who speak different languages, not only represents a significant advancement in the democratization of information, it can also help foster greater collaboration and understanding.
>
> *(YouTube 2010)*

Automatic captioning, based on Google's automatic speech recognition technology and the YouTube caption system, is only available for user-generated videos where English is spoken (ibid.). For the system to work best, a clearly spoken audio track is essential, and videos with background noise or a muffled voice cannot be auto-captioned. The video owner can download the auto-generated captions, improve them, and upload the new version, and all viewers are offered the option to translate those captions into a different language by means of machine-translated subtitles (Cutts 2009), with various degrees of success.[1]

The second subtitling feature launched by the two internet giants allows for a higher degree of accuracy in the linguistic make-up of the captions. Called *automatic timing*, it permits video owners to add manually created captions to their videos by automatically cueing the words uttered in the video. All the user needs is a transcript of the dialogue and, using speech-to-text technology, Google does the rest, matching the words with the time when they are said in the audio and chunking the text into subtitles. The owner of the video can download the time-coded subtitles to modify or to use somewhere else, and the subtitles can also be automatically translated into other languages. As pointed out by Lambourne (2011: 37), "Look at Google

AutoCaps. Submit your media file and see it create automatic captions. The quality and accuracy varies from the sublime to the ridiculous but if you're deaf you may not be able to determine which is which".

Other Developments

Assistive technology and audiovisual translation have started to combine as a successful tandem to foster access services in online education, with the aim of making educational material on the web accessible for people with sensory impairments (Patiniotaki 2013). With regard to live distribution on web-based media – broadcasts, webinars, or web-supported conferences – one of the upcoming needs is that of real-time captioning for audiences with hearing impairments but also for interlingual transfer. The use of speech recognition and speech-to-text services has been explored by research groups which have developed their own platforms, like eScribe (www. escribe-europe.com) or Legion Scribe (http://legionscribe.com), both relying on crowdsourcing human transcribers (Bumbalek *et al.* 2012). Automatic speech recognition (ASR) is also being tested as a potential solution, though the quality of real-time captions created in this way is still problematic.

Other hardware developments that prove this thirst for subtitles in everyday life include Will Powell's glasses, which, inspired by Google Glass, 'provide (almost) real-time subtitles for conversations being held in foreign languages' (Gold 2012: online).

On a different note, *A Christmas Carol*, directed by Robert Zemeckis in 2009, marked a milestone in UK cinema as the first movie ever in the United Kingdom to become truly accessible in 3D to deaf and hard-of-hearing viewers and hence as the first film to show 3D intralingual subtitles. The release of *Avatar*, by James Cameron (2009), a month later in December saw the birth of interlingual 3D subtitles and set the trend of the changes to come. With the surge in interest for 3D stereographic movies, more pressure is being applied to the broadcast and entertainment industry to provide 3D content for the array of 3D media players, fifth-generation video games consoles, television, and cinema. This migration to high definition and 3D is bringing along new job profiles – like the *3D subtitle mapper*, responsible for the positioning of the subtitles – as well as fresh challenges and novel ways of working in subtitling and is bound to have an impact on the workflows and the skills required of the translators.

The need for 3D subtitles in multiple languages has become a commercial necessity since the use of traditional subtitles in a 3D environment risks destroying the 3D illusion (Yue *et al.* 2018). The main challenges derive particularly from the way the 3D subtitles are positioned on screen and how they interact with the objects and people being depicted. Any apparent conflict between an onscreen object and the subtitle text will destroy the 3D illusion and can lead to physiological side effects in the form of headaches and nausea. To address the issues raised by 3D subtitling, the British company BroadStream Solutions (https://broadstream.com/products/poliscript) has been pioneers in the development of Poliscript 3DITOR, a subtitle preparation package that helps design, display and deliver 3D subtitles.

Final Remarks

Though technology has been a defining feature of subtitling ever since its origins, the linguistic transfer has somewhat been forgotten when it comes to the use of CAT tools, perhaps because originally subtitling was used to translate audiovisual genres (i.e. films) that did not feature high levels of lexical repetition, as opposed to technical manuals, for instance. Given the commercial importance of subtitling, it is intriguing that software engineers do not seem to have made any serious attempts to develop tools, beyond the inclusion of spell checkers, that would help subtitlers with the linguistic dimension and not only with the technical tasks. For example, by integrating a search function in the interface of the subtitling software, time could be saved as subtitlers will not have to exit the program every time they need to document themselves. In addition, some of these tools could help improve consistency in terminology, especially when dealing with team translations or TV series consisting of numerous episodes; facilitate the consultation and creation of glossaries when working in specific projects; include thesauri and suggest synonyms when space restrictions are at a premium; and propose to reuse (parts of) subtitles that have been previously translated to give account of the same or very similar expressions.

This status quo may soon change, though, as the visibility of subtitling has grown exponentially around the world, including in the so-called dubbing countries where until recently this practice was rather marginal. The output has multiplied quantitatively, the outlets and screens where subtitles are displayed have proliferated and diversified, and the demand for subtitles has never been so high. Their attraction for learning and maintaining a foreign language and the ease and speed at which they are produced are some of subtitling's strongest appeal. In an audiovisualised world, subtitles have become a commodity expected by most viewers and a translation field worth of further exploration from a technical (and linguistic) perspective.

Despite this promising outlook, subtitling also faces important challenges such as the deprofessionalisation of this activity and the downward price spiral of recent years. On the industry's side, the mantra of the subtitling companies can be summarised in three key concepts: (low) costs, (speedy) turnovers, and (high) quality. The first two are being clearly addressed by the various technological advancements mentioned in the previous pages. The latter, not so much, leaving quality as one of the unresolved questions that needs to be addressed, with some professionals advocating the formation of a subtitling trade body by the industry for the industry (Lambourne 2011). The high demand for subtitles to translate both user-generated content and commercial programmes is the driving force behind most technical developments taking place in the field. Reconciling costs, time, quality, and professional satisfaction is not an easy task and, to date, there is no technology that adequately fills the gap.

Instead of looking for ways to do away with the human translator, technology should concentrate more on how subtitlers can be assisted in their work. Ultimately, the solution to the conundrum has to be the development of technology that finds synergies with the individual and relies on the participation and *savoir faire* of professional subtitlers. The key to success may not be so much in the technology itself but rather in the innovative use the industry and the subtitlers make of it.

Note

1 More information on viewing videos with automatically generated captions can be found on <www.google.com/support/youtube/bin/answer.py?hl=en&answer=100078>, and a video singing the virtues of the system is available at: <www.youtube.com/watch?v=QRS8MkLhQmM>.

Bibliography

Briggs, John (2013, July 10) 'Swedish Fan-made Subtitle Site Is Shut Down by Copyright Police', *TechCrunch*. Available at: http://techcrunch.com/2013/07/10/swedish-fan-made-subtitle-site-is-shut-down-by-copyright-police.
Bumbalek, Zdenek, Jan Zelenka, and Lukas Kencl (2012) 'Cloud-based Assistive Speech-Transcription Services', in Klaus Miesenberger, Arthur Karshmer, Petr Penaz, and Wolfgang Zagler (eds.) *Computers Helping People with Special Needs, ICCHP 2012, Part II*. Heidelberg: Springer, 113–16.

Chan, Sin-wai (2013) 'Translation Technology on the Fast Track: Computer-aided Translation in the Last Five Decades', in Rokiah Awang, Aniswal Abd. Ghani, and Leelany Ayob (eds.) *Translator and Interpreter Education and Training: Innovation, Assessment and Recognition*, Kuala Lumpur: Malaysian Translators Association, 1–11.

Cutts, Matt (2009) 'Show and Translate YouTube Captions'. Available at: www.mattcutts.com/blog/youtube-subtitle-captions.

Díaz Cintas, Jorge (2010) 'The Highs and Lows of Digital Subtitles', in Lew N. Zybatow (ed.) *Translationswissenschaft – Stand und Perspektiven, Innsbrucker Ringvorlesungen zur Translationswissenschaft VI*, Frankfurt am Main: Peter Lang, 105–30.

Etchegoyhen, Thierry, Mark Fishel, Jie Jiang, and Mirjam Sepesy Maučec (2013) 'SMT Approaches for Commercial Translation of Subtitles', in Khalil Sima'an, Mikel L. Forcada, Daniel Grasmick, Heidi Depraetere, and Andy Way (eds) *Proceedings of the 14th Machine Translation Summit*, 2–6 September 2013, Nice, France, 369–70. Available at: https://aclanthology.org/2013.mtsummit-user.10.

Georgakopoulou, Panayota and Lindsay Bywood (2013, December) 'MT in Subtitling and the Rising Profile of the Post-editor', *Multilingual*. Available at: https://multilingual.com/articles/mt-in-subtitling-and-the-rising-profile-of-the-post-editor.

Gold, John (2012, July 28) 'See Real-time Subtitles through Google Glass-like Apparatus', *Computer World*. Available at: www.computerworld.com/article/2724534/see-real-time-subtitles-through-google-glass-like-apparatus.html.

Harrenstien, Ken (2006, September 19) *Finally, Caption Playback*. Available at: http://googlevideo.blogspot.com/2006/09/finally-caption-playback.html.

Harrenstien, Ken (2009, November 19) *Automatic Captions in YouTube*. Available at: http://googleblog.blogspot.com/2009/11/automatic-captions-in-youtube.html.

Hunter, Gordon (2010, September/October) 'Services for Impaired and Disabled Users', *CSI, Cable and Satellite International*. Available at: www.csimagazine.com/csi/Services-for-impaired-and-disabled-users.php.

Ivarsson, Jan and Mary Carroll (1998) *Subtitling*, Simrishamn: TransEdit.

Lambourne, Andrew (2011) 'Substandard Subtitles: Who's Bothered?', *TVB Europe*, January, 37.

O'Hagan, Minako (2013) 'The Impact of New Technologies on Translation Studies: A Technological Turn?', in Carmen Millán and Francesca Bartrina (eds.) *The Routledge Handbook of Translation Studies*, London and New York: Routledge, 503–18.

Oliver González, Antoni, Maite Melero, and Toni Badia (2006) 'Automatic Multilingual Subtitling in the eTITLE Project', in *Proceedings of Translating and the Computer 28*, ASLIB, London. Available at: https://aclanthology.org/2006.tc-1.10.

Patiniotaki, Emmanouela (2013) 'Assistive Technology and Audiovisual Translation: A Key Combination for Access Services in Online Education', *A Global Village* 11: 52–55.

Romero-Fresco, Pablo (2011) *Subtitling Through Speech Recognition: Respeaking*, Manchester: St. Jerome Publishing.

YouTube (2010) 'The Future Will Be Captioned: Improving Accessibility on YouTube'. Available at: http://youtube-global.blogspot.com/2010/03/future-will-be-captioned-improving.html.

Yue, Guanghui, Chunping Hou, Jianjun Lei, Yuming Fang, and Weisi Ling (2018) 'Optimal Region Selection for Stereoscopic Video Subtitle Insertion', *IEEE Transactions on Circuits and Systems for Video Technology* 28(11): 3141–53. Available at: http://sim.jxufe.cn/JDMKL/pdf/Optimal%20region%20selection%20for%20stereoscopic%20video%20subtitle%20insertion.pdf.

44

TERMINOLOGY MANAGEMENT

Kara Warburton

Introduction

A frequent question raised by professionals in the information industry, such as writers and translators, is how we can optimize information for the computer medium that is so ubiquitous today. The effectiveness of an information product largely depends on how easily it can be found in online searches. The cost of producing information is related to how clear, concise, and effective the information is and how often it can be reused in different delivery media and for different purposes and audiences. There are increasing demands for information to be suitable for automated processes such as machine translation or content classification. New natural language processing (NLP) technologies such as controlled authoring software, content management systems, and computer-assisted translation (CAT) tools are becoming commonplace in documentation and translation departments. These and other technology-driven changes are transforming information into tangible digital assets that can be organized, structured, managed, and repurposed.

One of these digital information assets is *terminology*, and it can help address these new challenges. Methodologies have been developed to create, manage, and use *terminology* – or *terminological resources* – for specific aims such as to improve communication within and across disciplines, to strengthen minority languages, or to create and manage knowledge resources that are increasingly in highly structured electronic form.

The aim of this chapter is to raise awareness among information professionals about terminology as a discipline and as a valuable language resource, and to describe the work known as *terminology management*. In doing so, we will briefly describe some theoretical and methodological underpinnings. For further readings about terminology theory, see L'Homme and Faber (2022).

Terminology as a Discipline

Definition

Within the broader field of linguistics, "terminology" is the scholarly discipline that is concerned with understanding and managing terminologies, which are words and expressions that carry special meaning. To distinguish between "terminology" the discipline, and "terminology"

DOI: 10.4324/9781003168348-47

meaning a set of terms, ISO Technical Committee 37, which sets standards for language resources, recently adopted the term "terminology science" to refer to the former. Its definition of terminology science is as follows:

> science studying terminologies, aspects of terminology work, the resulting terminology resources, and terminological data.
>
> *(ISO 1087:2019)*

where *terminologies* are sets of *terms* belonging to special language (sometimes called languages for special purposes, or LSP), and *subject fields* are fields of special knowledge.

Subject fields, also called domains, are what differentiates LSPs from general language (Rondeau 1981: 30; Dubuc 1992; Sager 1990: 18). LSPs are the language used in specific subject fields. Examples of subject fields are classic disciplines such as law, medicine, economics, science, and engineering but also applied fields such as sports, cooking, and travel or commercial activities such as product development, shipping, business administration, manufacturing, and so forth.

In the field of terminology, the relationship between terms, concepts, and objects is fundamental. A *term* is the name or *designation* of a *concept* in a particular *subject field*. A concept is a mental representation of a class of objects that share the same properties or characteristics, which are known as *semantic features*. For example, the concept of 'pencil' would be a 'writing instrument' with the following properties: graphite core, wood casing, sharpened to a point for writing at one end, and often with an eraser at the other end. Essential and delimiting characteristics help in the crafting of definitions of concepts such that each concept is distinguished from all other related concepts. Figure 44.1 shows the semantic triangle, as it is known in linguistics, adapted here to incorporate the *definition* as a representation of meaning.

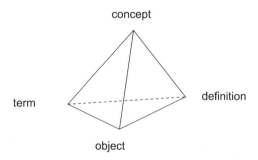

Figure 44.1 Semantic triangle

The triangle shows the relationship between an object of the real world; our mental conceptualization of that object; the term, which represents both the object and our conceptualization of it; and finally the definition, which is a verbal description of the concept and the object. The term and definition denote the object. The object and an individual's conceptualization of that object may not be perfectly equivalent; for instance, most people visualize pencils as having a yellow casing, yet they can come in any colour. Likewise, two individuals' conceptualizations of the same object may differ slightly; for instance, they may have slightly different mental images of a tree or a boat, depending on their personal experience.

In LSPs, the relationship between the term and the concept is more stable than in general language; that is, the concept is less subject to individual interpretation or variation: it is more objective.

Terms Versus Words

Association with a subject field is the feature most commonly cited to differentiate terms from so-called common or general words. In contrast to terms, words are members of the general lexicon (Pearson 1998: 36), and most do not refer to a specialized activity (Rondeau 1981: 26). A term is a lexical unit belonging to an LSP; they are *subject-field-specific lexical units*.

Terms are distinguished from words by their single-meaning relationship (called *monosemy*) with the specialized concepts that they designate and by the stability of that relationship (Pavel 2001: 19). In general, terms have a more precise, narrow meaning compared to common words.

Words are generally understood to be a sequence of characters bounded by a white space at both ends (or by punctuation).[1] However, terms are often composed of more than one word, for example, *climate change* or *sports utility vehicle*; these types of terms are referred to as multi-word units (MWUs). A sports utility vehicle is also known by the acronym *SUV*; such abbreviated forms, a phenomenon known as lexical variation, are very common in LSPs. In contrast, the lexical units one finds in a general language dictionary are usually single words, and lexical variants may not even be mentioned. Thus, both semantically and morphologically, terms exhibit certain properties that distinguish them from so-called common words.

Relation to Other Disciplines

While terminology is related to many disciplines in linguistics and in information technology, the two main ones are mentioned here: lexicography and translation.

Terminology is concerned with the language used in distinct subject fields, whereas lexicography studies the general lexicon of a language. In terminology, the *concept* is the focus of study and the central structure for organizing data, whereas in lexicology it is the *word*.

Terminologists typically create and manage a multilingual concept-oriented database, a kind of 'knowledge base', whereas lexicologists develop dictionaries, typically monolingual ones. The two professionals thus focus on different parts of the lexicon, look at the lexicon from different perspectives, and structure the data differently. They also differ in their methodologies, but this will be explained later. Both however, perform some of the same tasks such as preparing definitions and describing the usage and grammatical properties of words and terms.

The field of terminology traces its origins to the need for speakers of different languages to communicate clearly with each other in various subject fields. Therefore, it almost always takes a multilingual approach. As such, it is closely related to the field of translation, and most terminologists have a translation background. Many training programmes for translators include modules about terminology, and software programs used by translators often include functions for managing terminology.

Theoretical Evolution

The original theoretical principles that inform the development and structure of terminological resources were developed by Eugen Wüster and colleagues in Vienna in the middle of the last century (Wüster 1979). These principles, still predominant today, are referred to as the traditional theory, the general theory of terminology (GTT), the Wusterian theory, or the Vienna School. An engineer, Wüster developed his approaches while preparing a multilingual dictionary of machine tools (Wüster 1967). According to the GTT, objective communication is achieved by establishing a one-to-one relationship between a term and the concept that it designates. In other words, a term should have only one meaning, and a concept should be named by only one term. This property is referred to as *biunivocity* (L'homme 2004: 27). Synonyms and polysemes are therefore undesirable and must be eliminated. Also according to the GTT, the focus of study is the concept, to which terms are secondarily assigned as designators (Cabré Castelvi 2003: 166–67). Concepts are to be delimited *before* any of their corresponding terms are even considered, an approach referred to as *onomasiological*. The essential features of each concept are then identified, which enables the concepts, represented graphically such as by boxes, to be placed in a *concept system*, where they can be hierarchically related to other concepts (see Figure 44.2). Usually at this point one or more terms have been identified for each concept, and they are used as labels (e.g. of the boxes) in the concept system. Since the goal of the GTT is *standardization* of communication, a "preferred" term is chosen for each concept and any others discarded. Monographs based on the GTT include Cabré Castelvi (1999), Felber (1984), Rondeau (1981), Dubuc (1992), and Picht (1985).

The onomasiological approach is one of the basic tenets of the GTT. It contrasts with the *semasiological* approach, which is used in lexicography. These two approaches are fundamental for distinguishing terminology from lexicography. Lexicographers identify words that are used in a language and explain what they mean through definitions. For words that have more than one meaning – a common phenomenon in language – the corresponding dictionary entry will contain more than one definition, often numbered. In contrast, at least according to the GTT, terminologists study and describe concepts and then, only secondarily, determine how these concepts are expressed verbally by terms. And each "entry" in a terminological resource describes only one meaning, although it may contain more than one term.

Parallel to a shift from structuralist linguistics to corpus linguistics and cognitive linguistics, since the mid-1990s, the GTT has been subject to criticism. The main critique is that it does not take into account language in its authentic use (Pearson 1998; Temmerman 1997: 51–90 and 2000; L'Homme 2004 and 2005: 1112–32; Cabré Castelvi 1999; Kageura 2002). Concepts are to be studied outside of their use in real communicative settings. Consequently, several new theories emerged in recent decades that emphasize communicative, cognitive, and lexical aspects (see, for example, Cabré Castellvi, Temmerman, Sager, and L'Homme). The socio-cognitive theory and the lexico-semantic theory come to mind, exemplified by Temmerman and L'Homme respectively. The emergence of these theories was facilitated by advances in NLP technologies and the availability of large machine-readable corpora, which opened up new opportunities to study terms in their natural context.

The socio-cognitive theory views terms as expressions of meaning that are dependent on the context of communication. The lexico-semantic theory considers terms first and foremost as lexical units. The focus is on lexical structures rather than conceptual ones.

The three aforementioned theories (GTT, socio-cognitive, and lexico-semantic) diverge considerably in their definition of what constitutes a term (sometimes called *termhood*), emphasizing, respectively, the concept, cognitive aspects and communicative context, and lexical behaviour. The GTT considers membership in an objectivist, structured system of concepts a criterion of termhood, and it determines this membership status on the basis of conceptual features. In contrast, subsequent theories place more emphasis on a range of linguistic properties (morphological, syntactic, paradigmatic, etc.) of terms, properties that can be determined from the text where the term occurs. For further reading about terminology theories, see L'Homme and Faber (2022).

Terminology Management

Overview

The act of managing terminology refers to a wide range of tasks focused on terminology data, that is, terms and information about terms such as definitions, context sentences, and grammatical information. These tasks include collecting, developing, storing, reviewing, harmonizing, enhancing, and distributing terminology data. Today terminology is always managed by using computers, and terminology data are stored in a terminology database, or termbase. The person who manages terminology is referred to as a *terminologist*.

Spreadsheets are commonly used to record terminology in the initial stage, such as by a translator. However, this activity would not be considered 'terminology management', and ultimately, in order to be properly utilized, the terminology in the spreadsheet would need to be imported into a termbase that the terminologist manages with the aid of a terminology management software. This is why terminology management software programs usually provide an import function for spreadsheets.

Terminologists create and manage termbases, which are composed of terminological *entries*. They work in the language services of governments, where they play a key role in supporting the national languages; in the private sector, where they support corporate communications; and in supra-national non-governmental organizations, such as the United Nations, where they facilitate multilingual communication.

When an organization needs to communicate clearly, it examines its terminology and decides which terms to use and which terms to avoid. This decision-making process results in a prescribed set of terms, which need to then be distributed to members of the organization, often with definitions to ensure that everyone using the terms knows exactly what they mean.

Terminology resources are often created to support multilingual communication needs in specialized subject fields or domains, such as law, science, and medicine. Clarity and precision are paramount, and yet the terms can be difficult for translators who are not domain specialists. Providing semantic information about the source language terms, such as definitions, can greatly assist translators to determine the correct target language equivalents when they are translating a document. In many production settings, target language equivalents of key source language terms are determined *before* the document is translated, often by a dedicated translator, so that they can be provided to the translators as soon as they start working. This sequence of events – translate terms before translating the document – helps to reduce terminology errors and raise terminology consistency.

Terminology resources can also be developed in monolingual settings, such as to provide sets of pre-approved terminology for writers to use. A case in point is the aeronautical industry, which was an early adopter of controlled terminology in technical writing.

The Need for Terminology Management

Consistency of language (terms and various other expressions) is frequently cited as one of the key factors in information clarity and usability. Terminology consistency in an information set also has an impact on the reader's ability to find this information through search engines or online indices. When inconsistent or variable terms occur in a text, these problems often multiply in any translated versions, due to the fact that there can be several ways to translate a given term or expression. When a document or a collection of documents is divided into smaller "jobs" that are distributed to several translators, term variations and inconsistencies increase even more. In spite of this risk, the use of multiple translators has become a common strategy for getting products to global markets as quickly as possible. In industries with highly specialized terminology, such as the automotive industry, terminology inconsistencies and other terminology errors are among the most frequently occurring translation errors (Woyde 2005). In high-risk fields such as health sciences, engineering, national defence, and law, problems of ambiguity, inconsistency, or imprecision can have serious consequences. Prescribed terminology can be provided to writers and translators to help them avoid these problems.

Aside from improving the quality of information content, the benefits of terminology management can also be demonstrated from a business perspective, that is, in terms of cost, time, and productivity gains. The return on investment (ROI) needs to be separately measured for each organization, since the gains depend on its specific production environment. Nevertheless, several generic ROI evaluations have been produced, for instance Champagne (2004), Warburton (2013) and Schmitz and Straub (2010). These studies show that costs are saved by reducing wasteful duplication of work, such as when two translators research and work through the process of translating the same term, or when two technical writers create definitions for the same term in different company documents. Another area of cost savings is reducing the effort of editors and revisers to correct terminology mistakes by reducing the occurrence of such mistakes.

The purpose of managing terminology in an organization, such as a company or an NGO, is to improve the use of language across that organization. In a language planning environment, such as a branch of government responsible for protecting the national language, the mission is to strengthen the language as a whole. The latter has a social dimension, and indeed, the term *socioterminology* has been coined for this type of terminology work. There is no specific term yet for the former type of terminology management, but we could call it *institutional terminology.*

In summary, establishing and using consistent and appropriate terminology helps increase the quality of information which in turn improves the usability of related products, makes information easier to find, and lowers translation costs.

Types of Terminology Management

Onomasiological Versus Semasiological

As previously noted, the classical approach to terminology management is onomasiological, whereby the concept is the central focus. This distinguishes terminology from lexicology, which adopts a semasiological (word-based) approach. However, in many situations, terminology work is actually semasiological. Translators, for instance, often identify a handful of key terms in a document that they are translating and determine the correct translations after doing a bit of research. To save their work for future reference, they add the terms to a termbase.[2] Although they have taken care to ensure that the target language terms they choose have the same meanings as the source language terms, they spend little if any time analysing the concepts and recording conceptual information such as definitions or subject-fields, and they would never need nor have the time to produce diagrams of hierarchical concept systems. In practice, the dividing line between terminology and lexicology has become quite fuzzy.

Descriptive, Prescriptive, and Normative

Terminology management methods also vary depending on whether the goal is *descriptive, prescriptive* or *normative*. In descriptive terminology, the terminologist 'describes' the current and actual behaviour and usage of terms without making any value judgments about them. This approach is adopted for instance to record the vocabulary used in so-called minority languages or languages at risk. Normative terminology seeks to develop a 'standardized' terminology in specific subject fields; an example is the terminology found in the glossary section of ISO standards. Prescriptive terminology adopts some aspects of both the former: it documents terms in use but at the same time it is concerned about consistency and quality of terminology, and therefore it 'prescribes' terms to use and terms to avoid in cases of synonymy. The prescriptive approach is common in institutional terminology management.

Different methodologies and types of information are needed to achieve these different aims. Descriptive terminology emphasizes recording the sources of terms and context sentences. Normative terminology is the most likely type to adopt an onomasiological approach, where significant time and resources are spent on concept analysis, synonym ranking and the crafting of definitions. In fact, definitions are often mandatory and adhere to strict rules of style. Prescriptive terminology adopts the normative approach only for difficult cases of problematic synonyms or conflicting terms and for the remainder settles on basic description. Definitions are less rigorous than in normative settings and will only be present in a small proportion of the total number of entries.

When providing an aid to translators is the primary purpose of terminology work, the descriptive approach is most common. The terminologist finds source language terms that are used and puts them into the termbase, and target language equivalents are then added to the entries when they are needed. Thus, most translation companies and their clients accumulate their terminology data using descriptive methods over a period of years or even decades. Problems arise, however, if the needs for terminology move beyond the translation activity, since the nature and structure of terminology data required for other purposes can vary considerably. The organization may find that its termbase needs to be modified to handle these new uses. This issue will be further discussed in the section "Repurposing and Interoperability".

Methodology

Thematic Versus Ad-Hoc

According to the GTT, concepts should be studied systematically, that is, as members of a logical and coherent concept system (Rondeau 1981). This onomasiological approach to terminology work is also referred to as *thematic* (L'Homme 2004). The terminologist studies and then defines key concepts from a subject field by applying the rigor of Aristotelian logic, that is, naming a genus, the superordinate class that the concept belongs to, and differentiae, the semantic properties that differentiate this concept from other concepts belonging to the same class. The concepts are then represented in a diagram showing the hierarchical relations between them. Only then are terms selected to denote the concepts. Figure 44.2 shows a concept system elaborated according to the thematic method.

Concepts, represented by the grey boxes, are denoted by terms (the box labels). Concepts are numbered and arranged hierarchically to show their relations. Concepts at the same level of the hierarchy, called coordinate concepts, share the same parent, their superordinate concept. For instance, *marker*, *pencil*, and *pen* are coordinate concepts to the superordinate *writing instrument*. The white boxes represent criteria of subdivision, i.e., on what basis the subordinate concepts are differentiated from each other. For instance, what makes a *lead pencil* different from a *mechanical pencil* is the casing holding the graphite core: the former has to be removed for use (through sharpening), but for the latter it is fixed.[3] The text below the grey boxes lists the essential characteristics of the concept; one can write a definition using these characteristics. For instance:

mechanical pencil: pencil with a fixed casing

Note that it is not necessary for the definition to state 'writing instrument used for making marks that has a graphic core and a fixed casing' since all the properties except 'fixed casing' are present in the concept of *pencil*. This inheritance principle allows definitions to be quite concise. However, in order for this definition to be valid, the term *pencil* used as the genus must also be defined in the terminology resource in question.

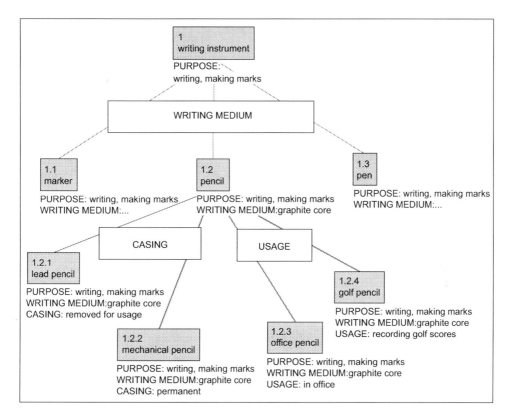

Figure 44.2 Concept system for writing instruments

Source: Courtesy of Copenhagen Business School

The thematic approach is widely recognized in the field of terminology. It is particularly well suited for developing standardized terminology, such as for nomenclatures. However, in situations where someone simply needs help deciding what term to use, a task- and text-driven approach is usually adopted. On-the-spot research is carried out in various sources depending on the problem at hand. Finding instances of the target language term in authentic contexts, where it has the same meaning as the source language term, is the only evidence required for confirming the appropriateness of a given term translation. Definitions and concept diagrams are almost never prepared. This approach is referred to as *ad-hoc* (Wright and Wright 1997: 13–24) or *punctual* (Cabré Castellvi 2003; Picht 1985) because the aim is to fulfil an immediate need and then move on to other tasks.

Between the thematic and ad-hoc approaches there are also varying degrees of combinations of the two. The terminologist may, for example, set up workflows to handle term proposals, reviews, and approvals. Terms identified through both the ad-hoc and the thematic approach may proceed through these workflows. During review and approval of ad-hoc-identified terms, for example, some elements of the thematic approach may be undertaken as a means to confirm that conceptually related terms are consistent, coherent, and harmonized with each other, or in other words, there are no glaring conflicts. For an example of a workflow, refer to the *Terminology Starter Guide* (TerminOrgs 2016).

These different methodologies have different interpretations about the notion of what constitutes a term. In the thematic approach espoused by the GTT, terms assume the more classical identity of designators of conceptual nodes in a structured concept system that represents concepts from an LSP. Real contexts may be studied to confirm the existence of these terms, but their final determination is based solely on the concept system and its semantic characteristics. The ad-hoc approach, in contrast, identifies terms through corpus analysis, and is less concerned about semantic criteria.

Corpora, Concordances, and Term Extraction

As noted earlier, terminologists frequently adopt a semasiological approach to term research and identification. Due to advances in text processing capabilities through the use of computers, terminologists can now use large bodies of text, called corpora, in their research. Using corpora as empirical evidence of terms is essential in any medium to large-scale terminology project. Due to the large size of most corpora, the task usually needs to be carried out with the assistance of technologies such as concordancing software and automatic term extraction (ATE) tools. Not only do these technologies allow terminologists to identify more terms than would be possible manually, their use also raises the correspondence between the terms in the termbase and the corpus that the terms are supposed to reflect. In other words, terms for the termbase are pulled from the corpus directly rather than resulting from a decision made by the terminologist with potentially no reference to the corpus at all. The latter results in some terms being entered in the termbase that are not useful to its users, simply because they occur rarely in practice. Since entering a term and associated information such as definitions in a termbase typically triggers a downstream process of adding translations, the wasted cost in terms of manpower of adding source language terms that have little value is multiplied, in some cases tenfold or higher.

Deciding which terms to include in a termbase to optimize its value can be a major challenge for terminologists, and nowadays, basing this decision on corpus evidence rather than strictly on semantic 'specialness' is highly recommended. Often, a corpus-based approach to term identification (i.e. termhood) reveals various lexical units that, if managed in a termbase, would enhance some process in the organization (authoring, translation, search, indexing, etc.). And yet, many such lexical units may not have a domain-specific meaning and therefore would not qualify as 'terms' according to classical theory. Terminologists working in institutional settings may have to reconcile such apparent contradictions between theory and practice. In settings where productivity is key, the classical criteria for termhood may need to be revisited. For more information about managing terminology in commercial settings, see Warburton 2021.

Terminology Databases

Explanation

A terminology database (termbase) is a collection of terms and descriptive information about these terms in electronic form, similar to yet different from a dictionary. Termbases are almost always multilingual.

Organizations of various sorts develop a termbase to serve their communication needs. Governments of countries that have more than one official language or significant populations speaking different languages may develop a termbase to store terms needed to express concepts for their various programmes, services, and industries. Examples are Canada and Switzerland. Supra-national organizations such as the European Union develop termbases to support interlingual communication which facilitates cross-border trade and collaboration. Non-governmental organizations, such as the World Health Organization, develop termbases in order to help implement their programmes effectively in different linguistic communities. Increasingly, commercial enterprises are using termbases to store multilingual terminology about their products and services; these termbases are leveraged in the authoring and translation process to increase quality, improve productivity, and save time.

Data Categories

Many termbases are quite simple, containing primarily just terms. Some, however, contain a wide range of other types of information such as definitions, usage notes, and grammatical descriptors. Some also include links between entries, which can range from simple pointers between related terms to hierarchical relations of various sorts, such as to link broader and narrower terms. These bits of information are called *data categories* by terminologists. There are hundreds of different data categories possible for a termbase. In 1999, ISO TC37 published an inventory of terminology data categories as an international standard (12620). In 2009 this standard was revised and the inventory was moved into an electronic database that is now available on the Internet (https://datcatinfo.net/).

Broadly speaking, data categories are organized into three groups: conceptual, terminological, and administrative. Conceptual data categories describe concepts; they provide semantic information. Examples are subject field values and definitions. Terminological data categories describe terms, for example, usage notes, part of speech, and context sentences. Administrative data categories include, for example, the name of the person who added some information or the date that it was added.

Structure

The structure of termbases has also been standardized by ISO TC37, through ISO 16642: *Terminological Markup Framework*. According to this standard, terminological entries are structured in three hierarchical sections: concept, language, and term. The concept section contains the conceptual data categories, which describe the concept as a whole, and thus applies to all the terms in the entry (regardless of the language). All the information pertaining to a given language is organized in a dedicated language section, which is subdivided into term sections for information about individual terms. Information that is shared by all the terms in a given language occurs at the language level, such as a language-specific definition or a comment, and information about a specific term is inserted at the term level, such as a usage note or a context sentence. A term section can contain only one term, but a language section can contain multiple term sections, and a concept section can contain multiple language sections. All the terms in the entry are synonyms. This principle is referred to as *concept orientation*.

Examples of Termbases

Some large termbases are publicly available today. The following are a few examples:

- United Nations – UNTERM: http://unterm.un.org/
- European Union – IATE: http://iate.europa.eu
- Government of Canada – TERMIUM: www.btb.termiumplus.gc.ca/
- Microsoft – www.microsoft.com/en-us/language
- Eurotermbank – www.eurotermbank.com/

Terminology Management Systems

Industry-Specific Versus Multi-Purpose

A terminology management system (TMS) is a software program specifically designed for managing terminology. When the first terminology databases were developed in the 1970s, none existed, and so the organizations responsible for these termbases developed their own in-house systems. In the 1980s and 1990s, TMSs began to emerge as part of desktop software programmes for translators, known as computer-assisted translation (CAT) tools. Today, virtually all CAT tools have functions for collecting and storing terminology.

It should be pointed out that the terminology components of CAT tools are not general purpose, since they are designed specifically for use by translators. Some are even 'locked in' to the CAT tool, making it difficult to use the terminology data they contain in any other system or application. As developers of termbases began to want to use their terminology data for purposes in addition to translation, the need for a TMS that supports a wider range of users has increased. If there is any possibility that a termbase may be needed for applications beyond computer-assisted translation, a TMS that is part of a CAT tool may not be the best choice.

Like CAT tools, controlled authoring software may include functions for recording and managing terminology. But they are designed for the needs of controlled authoring. One should be careful not to assume that such functions are suitable for developing and managing terminology resources for other purposes. ISO TC37 Sub-committee 3 has published several standards and guidelines that may be helpful when choosing a terminology management system.

Key Features

It is beyond the scope of this chapter to describe the features of terminology management systems. It is, however, essential that a TMS adhere to the international standards mentioned in this chapter. Some of the most important principles and features include:

- Web interface
- Concept orientation
- Term autonomy
- A variety of import and export formats, minimally including spreadsheets and TBX (ISO 30042: TermBase eXchange format)
- Views and layouts customizable for different user types
- Ability to record relations between terms and between concepts

Some of these topics are described in later sections of this chapter.

Push and Pull Approach

Terminology can be shared among all translators working on a project, which obviously helps to increase consistency. However, expecting translators to look up terms and obtain the prescribed translations is not effective; if they already know how to translate a term in *their* way, it will not occur to them to look for a different translation. Working under time pressures, they are not likely to check their terminology frequently.

CAT tools address this problem by providing functionality whereby if a sentence to be translated contains a term that is in the connected termbase, the corresponding entry is automatically displayed to the translator. This function is commonly known as *autolookup*. It reflects a 'push' approach, where the technology 'pushes' information to the user at the moment it is needed, as opposed to a 'pull' approach, where the user decides if and when to access the information.

This push approach applies in other user scenarios, such as in controlled authoring. A controlled authoring software normally has a terminology component for writers just as a CAT tool does for translators, only in this case, it is monolingual. The terminology function contains terms with usage information, and terms that should be avoided are clearly indicated. When a writer uses one of these deprecated terms, the function automatically highlights the incorrect term and displays another that should be used in its place. It works just like a spell checker, highlighting errors and suggesting how to correct them.

Repurposing and Interoperability

Explanation

Terminology data are a language resource that can be used for various purposes, as described in the next section. The term *repurposing* refers to using terminology data in different applications. In order to repurpose terminology, the data have to be interoperable, meaning that it must be possible to exchange the data between the termbase and other systems easily and without loss of information. This can be achieved by exporting the terminology from the termbase and then importing it into other apps or by direct real-time links between the two that are implemented programmatically such as through application programming interfaces. Repurposing requires a standard interchange format: TermBase eXchange (TBX, ISO 30042).

Applications of Terminology Resources

The performance of many NLP applications can be improved through the use of richly structured terminological resources (Cabré Castellvi *et al.* 2007). Thirty years ago, Meyer (1993) predicted that machines would become a primary user of terminological data.

> It is predicted that machines may become a category of user for terminology banks; machine translation tools, expert systems, natural-language interfaces to databases, and spelling checkers are just a few of the most obvious applications. . . . Machines will need very large quantities of explicitly represented conceptual information since they do not possess much of the basic real-world information that humans know implicitly.

Ibekwe-SanJuan *et al.* (2007) consider commercial applications of what they call 'terminology engineering'.

> Applications of terminology engineering include information retrieval, question-answering systems, information extraction, text mining, machine translation, science and technology watch, all are external fields that can benefit from the incorporation of terminological knowledge.

They further note that terminology is useful for building other types of language resources such as ontologies and aligned corpora. Numerous works describe the role of controlled terminologies for indexing (Strehlow 2001: 419–25; Buchan 1993: 69–78). Strehlow further notes that a sound strategy for the use of terminology in strategic areas of content (such as titles, abstracts and keywords) can lead to significant improvements in information retrieval. Wettengl *et al.* (2001: 445–66) describe how terminology data can help build product classification systems.

There are numerous references in the literature to applications of terminology resources: automatic back-of-the-book indexing, indexing for search engines, ontology building, content classification, content categorization, contact record analysis, search engine optimization (query expansion and document filtering), federation of heterogeneous document collections, cross-lingual information retrieval, document summarization/abstraction and keyword extraction, product classifications, automated construction of domain taxonomies and ontologies, and so forth (Park *et al.* 2002: 1–7; Jacquemin 2001; Oakes *et al.* 2001: 353–70; Cabré Castellvi 1999).

Repurposing Considerations

As shown in the previous section, the use of terminology data in an organization can change over time. We mentioned that repurposing requires a standard interchange format. But that in itself is not sufficient to prepare the data for different potential applications; the data also need to be designed so that they are usable in these systems. For instance, to reduce translation costs, an organization may deploy controlled authoring software to help raise the consistency, quality, and translatability of its source content. Controlled authoring software requires terminology data of a nature and structure that is different from that required for translation purposes. Among other types of data, it requires information about synonyms in the source language, which is frequently lacking in translation-oriented terminology resources. But even more concerning is the fact that terminology resources developed for translators are frequently not even concept oriented. This means that in addition to information about synonyms being lacking, such as usage notes and status indicators (telling which term is preferred and which is to be avoided), synonyms themselves are not even stored in the same entry. This is a serious problem for any organization wishing to use its termbase for controlled authoring.

Another problem occurs when manually prepared glossaries are imported into a TMS. Typically these glossaries lack a part-of-speech value for the terms. This particular data category is essential for any NLP-oriented application of the data. It is therefore recommended to add the part-of-speech value when importing glossaries into a TMS.

Terminology data developed for translation purposes may not be usable for other purposes without significant rework. Re-engineering the terminology resources to meet new requirements can be very difficult and cost prohibitive. If an organization anticipates that it may want to repurpose its terminology, hiring the services of a professional terminology consultant prior to purchasing a TMS or creating a database of any significant size can help to protect its investment.

Standards and Best Practices

Adhering to standards ensures that the terminology data are developed according to long-standing best practices and sound principles, some of which are described in this section.

Concept Orientation

Concept orientation is the fundamental principle whereby a terminological entry describes only one concept. This principle originates from the GTT and is still extremely relevant today even for the most practical types of terminology work. Terminology databases are usually multilingual; each language term in an entry is equivalent in meaning to the others.

And because entries are meaning based, they can contain multiple terms in a given language. Synonyms, abbreviations, and spelling variants of a term must all be placed in the same entry. One can say that terminology resources are structured more like a thesaurus than a conventional dictionary.

Term Autonomy

Term autonomy is the principle whereby each term in a terminological entry can be documented or described with the same level of detail. In other words, the TMS should not have an unbalanced structure whereby there are various fields available to describe a so-called 'main' term but fewer fields available for other terms. This unbalanced structure has been observed in some TMSs where there are a number of fields available to document the first term, such as **Part-of-speech** and **Definition**, and then only single fields for subsequent terms, such as **Synonym** and **Abbreviation**. This reflects a poor design. Instead, the TMS should use a Term type data category. For example, instead of:

Term:

    Part-of-speech:
    Definition:
    Synonym:
    Abbreviation:

One should have:
Term:

    Part-of-speech:
    Definition:
    Term type:

where the **Term type** field allows values such as *abbreviation* and *acronym*. The value *synonym* is not required since all terms in a given entry are synonyms of each other. So long as the term section shown above can be repeated in the entry, all terms can be equally described.

Data Elementarity

Data elementarity is a best practice in database management in general, and it also applies to termbases. According to this principle, there can only be one type of information in a database record or field. This means that in the termbase design, separate fields are required for different types of information, which takes careful planning to account for all types of information that may be required by the users. An example where this principle has been violated is when the **Definition** field contains not only a definition but also the source of that definition. Another example is when both the part-of-speech and gender are inserted into one field, such as 'n f' for a feminine noun. Possibly the worst case is when the **Term** field contains two terms, as this also violates term autonomy. Unfortunately this seems to occur fairly frequently, such as when a term field contains both a full form and an abbreviation, for example:

  Term: access control list (ACL)

These are two different terms. The following arrangement is better:

763

Term: access control list

    Term type: full form

Term: ACL

    Term type: acronym

Summary

Terminology is a field in applied linguistics that is experiencing rapid growth due to advances in information technology and natural language processing, economic globalization, and linguistic diversity. While terminology shares some methodology with lexicology, the two have different foci, concept description and language description, and a different scope, that is, special language and general language, respectively. Terminology resources help translators, writers, and other content producers use clear and consistent terms so that communication is most effective. These resources are created and managed in databases that reflect fundamental principles unique to the field of terminology. Nonetheless, terminology methods are changing in response to advances in computer technologies, in particular access to large-scale digital corpora.

Notes

1 This description is restricted to languages that employ spaces between words; some do not.
2 Many translators use spreadsheets rather than a proper termbase.
3 Here, we have chosen 'fixed' instead of 'permanent', as it seems more accurate. The term *permanent* frequently has a temporal meaning.

Bibliography

Buchan, Ronald (1993). 'Quality Indexing with Computer-aided Lexicography', in Helmi B. Sonneveld and Kurt L. Loening (eds.) *Terminology – Applications in Interdisciplinary Communication*, Amsterdam: John Benjamins Publishing Company, 69–78.

Cabré Castellví, M. Teresa (1999). *Terminology – Theory, Methods and Applications*, Amsterdam: John Benjamins Publishing Company.

Cabré Castellví, M. Teresa (2003). 'Theories of Terminology', *Terminology* 9(2): 163–99.

Champagne, Guy (2004). *The Economic Value of Terminology – An Exploratory Study*. (Report commissioned by the Translation Bureau of Canada). Available at: https://www.danterm.dk/docs/EconomicValu eTerminology-1.pdf.

Dubuc, Robert (1992). *Manuel pratique de terminologie*, Quebec, Canada: Linguatech.

Felber, Helmut (1984). *Terminology Manual*, Paris: United Nations Educational, Scientific and Cultural Organization: International Information Centre for Terminology.

Ibekwe-SanJuan, Fidelia, Anne Condamines, and M. Teresa Cabré Castellvi (2007). *Application-driven Terminology Engineering*, Amsterdam: John Benjamins Publishing Company.

ISO TC37/SC1 (2019). *ISO 1087: Terminology Work and Terminology Science*, Geneva: International Organization for Standardization.

Jacquemin, Christian (2001). *Spotting and Discovering Terms Through Natural Language Processing*, Cambridge, MA: MIT Press.

Kageura, Kyo (2002). *The Dynamics of Terminology: A Descriptive Theory of Term Formation and Terminological Growth*, Amsterdam: John Benjamins Publishing Company.

L'Homme, Marie-Claude (2004). *La terminologie: principes et techniques*, Montreal: Les Presses de l'Université de Montréal.

L'Homme, Marie-Claude (2005). 'Sur la notion de terme', *Meta* 50(4): 1112–32.

L'Homme, Marie-Claude and Pamela Faber (eds.) (2022). *Theoretical Perspectives on Terminology: Explaining Terms, Concepts and Specialized Knowledge*, Amsterdam: John Benjamins Publishing Company.

Meyer, Ingrid (1993). 'Concept Management for Terminology: A Knowledge Engineering Approach', in Richard Alan Strehlow and Sue Ellen Wright (eds.) *Standardizing Terminology for Better Communication*, West Conshohocken, PA: ANSI (American National Standards Institute).

Oakes, Michael and Chris Paice (2001). 'Term Extraction for Automatic Abstracting', in Didier Bourigault, Christian Jacquemin, and Marie-Claude L'Homme (eds.) *Recent Advances in Computational Terminology*, Amsterdam: John Benjamins Publishing Company, 353–70.

Park, Youngja, Roy J. Byrd, and Branimir K. Boguraev (2002). 'Automatic Glossary Extraction: Beyond Terminology Identification', in *Proceedings of the 19th International Conference on Computational linguistics*, vol. 1, Association for Computational Linguistics, 1–7.

Pavel, Sylvia, and Diane Nolet (2001). *Handbook of Terminology*, Minister of Public Works and Government Services Canada. Available at: https://publications.gc.ca/collections/collection_2007/pwgsc-tpsgc/S53-28-2001E.pdf.

Pearson, Jennifer (1998). *Terms in Context – Studies in Corpus Linguistics*, Amsterdam: John Benjamins Publishing Company.

Picht, Heribert and Jennifer Draskau (1985). *Terminology: An Introduction*, Denmark: LSP Centre, Copenhagen Business School.

Rondeau, Guy (1981). *Introduction à la terminologie*, Montreal: Centre educatif et culturel Inc.

Sager, Juan (1990). *A Practical Course in Terminology Processing*, Amsterdam and Philadelphia: John Benjamins Publishing Company.

Schmitz, Klaus-Dirk and Daniela Straub (2010). *Successful Terminology Management in Companies: Practical Tips and Guidelines: Basic Principles, Implementation, Cost-benefit Analysis and System Overview*, Stuttgart: Stuttgart TC and More GmbH.

Strehlow, Richard (2001). 'Terminology and Indexing', in Sue Ellen Wright and Gerhard Budin (eds.) *Handbook of Terminology Management*, vol. 2, Amsterdam: John Benjamins Publishing Company, 419–25.

Temmerman, Rita (1997). 'Questioning the Univocity Ideal: The Difference between Socio-cognitive Terminology and Traditional Terminology', *Hermes Journal of Linguistics* 18: 51–90.

Temmerman, Rita (2000). *Towards New Ways of Terminology Description*, Amsterdam: John Benjamins Publishing Company.

TerminOrgs (2016). 'Terminology Starter Guide'. Available at: www.terminorgs.net/Publications.html.

Warburton, Kara (2013). 'Developing a Business Case for Managing Terminology'. Available at: http://termologic.com/?page_id=56.

Warburton, Kara (2021). *The Corporate Terminologist*, Amsterdam: John Benjamins Publishing Company.

Wettengl, Tanguy and Aidan van de Weyer (2001). 'Terminology in Technical Writing', in Sue Ellen Wright and Gerhard Budin (eds.) *Handbook of Terminology Management*, vol. 2, Amsterdam: John Benjamins Publishing Company, 445–66.

Woyde, Rick (2005). 'Introduction to SAE J1930: Bridging the Disconnect Between the Engineering, Authoring and Translation Communities', in *Globalization Insider*, Geneva: Localization Industry Standards Association. Available at: www.translationdirectory.com/article903.htm.

Wright, Sue Ellen (1997). 'Term Selection: The Initial Phase of Terminology Management', in Sue Ellen Wright and Gerhard Budin (eds.) *Handbook of Terminology Management*, vol. 1, Amsterdam: John Benjamins Publishing Company, 13–24.

Wright, Sue Ellen and Leland Wright (1997). 'Terminology Management for Technical Translation', in Sue Ellen Wright and Gerhard Budin (eds.) *Handbook of Terminology Management*, vol. 1, Amsterdam: John Benjamins Publishing Company, 147–59.

Wüster, Eugen (1967). *Grundbegriffe bei Werkzeugmaschinen*, London: Technical Press.

Wüster, Eugen (1979). *International Bibliography of Standardized Vocabularies*, Munich: K.G. Saur Verlag.

45

TRANSLATION MEMORY

Alan K. Melby and Sue Ellen Wright

Introduction

A 'translation memory' (TM) is a database of paired text segments, where Segment B is a translation of Segment A. Translators use TMs to 'remember' the content of past translations. TM programs make up the prototypical function associated with so-called computer assisted translation (CAT) systems.

The term 'translation memory' is ambiguous. As noted in Macklovitch and Russell (2000: 137–46), it is sometimes used to designate a database containing a collection of paired source-language (SL)/target-language (TL) text units, but in common parlance, the term is also inaccurately used to refer to one of the software programs used to create, store, access, retrieve, and process the units contained in the TM database. Somers and Diaz (2004: 5–33) try to circumvent this ambiguity by referring to *translation memory systems* as *TMS*, although care must be taken to ensure the context is clear, since *TMS* can also stand for *terminology management system* or *translation management system*. Another ambiguous term that needs to be clarified before discussing TM technology is 'translation unit'. Early in the development of TM, it was defined as 'an entry [as in a database entry] consisting of aligned segments of text in two or more languages' (TMX Standard 1998, where it is assigned the XML tag *<tu>*, as shown in Figure 45.2). We will call this the *formal translation unit*, and the process of dividing text into segments, logically enough, is called 'segmentation'. Formal <tu>s have traditionally been automatically identified based on elements of primary punctuation, such as periods (full stops), question marks, exclamation points, and (optionally) colons and semi-colons, as well as end-of-paragraph markers. Consequently, although they may be fragments, they usually equate to full sentences or sometimes paragraphs.

The term *translation unit* is also common in translation studies, where it has undergone several shifts. Early on, Vinay and Dalbelnet (1958/1995) focused on the smallest (atomic) units of thought, essentially terminological and collocational units. Nevertheless, to many translators, the translation unit (unit of translation) is instead 'a stretch of source language text' on which the translator focuses during the cognitive translation *process*, or, viewed conversely, the corresponding target-text chunk that is the *product* of that process and that can be 'mapped onto the source-text unit' (Malmkjaer 1998: 373).

Kenny notes that the translation unit undergoes constant transformation, depending on changes in a translator's cognitive processing (2009: 304). These *cognitive translation units* may

DOI: 10.4324/9781003168348-48

vary dynamically in rank (unit level) from single terms to collocations to clauses, even to whole sentences (McTait *et al.* 1999), but do probably tend to occur at the clause level, which is confirmed in research involving *think-aloud protocols* (TAPs).

If formal <tu>s are set at the sentence or paragraph level, and cognitive <tu>s are frequently sub-sentential, there can be a cognitive disconnect between the human translator and the TM. Consequently, Reinke even asserts that the notion of the translation unit used to designate pairs of SL and TL texts is a complete misnomer. He observes that the translator's cognitive unit (regardless of rank) is actually the *expression* (*Äußerung*) of a conceptual (semantic) content, whereas the chunk the TM retrieves is just a string of matchable characters (*Satz*). Therefore, he proposes that instead of formal *translation units*, we should speak of *retrieval units* (2003: 186). Regardless of how they are defined, these retrieved segments have a coercive effect, prompting the translator to use them as is, even if the conceptual reality of the TL might dictate otherwise. Our discussion will include attempts to resolve this anomaly by integrating methods for including sub-segment identification and processing in the TM workflow.

Translation Memory and the CAT in the TEnT

CAT tool environments feature a variety of individual, often interactive, functions, including TMs, terminology management, alignment, analysis, conversion, and knowledge management. These tools may also offer project management features, spellchecking, word and line-counting, machine translation input, and the ability to output a variety of file types. Jost Zetzsche has called this combination of features and resources a *Translation Environment Tool (TEnT)* and adds code protection, batch processing, and code page conversion, among others, to the list of features (2007). Although TMs, termbases, and concordances may be separate programming functions within a TEnT, they are typically integrated at the interface level.

Traditional TM databases are created in three different modes: interactive generation of <tu>s during the translation of texts, alignment of existing parallel translations, and subsetting of existing aligned resources (Sommers and Diaz). <tu>s created interactively become immediately available for intratextual matching during the ensuing translation of the SL text in question. <tu>s are commonly stored together with a set of metadata, such as client, subject matter, and location in the source text. This means that although the full ST is not saved as such, it can be regenerated at any time. This metadata can be used to create subsets of larger TMs, which enables the creation of highly specialized, specific job-related TMs and to validate the appropriateness of specific SL/TL matches. Subordinate portions of a <tu> cannot generally be manipulated or combined, although they do contribute to so-called fuzzy matches.

An alternative approach that stores whole texts with their complete translations is called 'bitext'. When Brian Harris introduced the term in 1988, his description sounded very much like our TMs, which leads many people to use the terms as synonyms. Bowker, for instance, speaks of individual paired segments as bitexts (2010). In the larger sphere of computational linguistics, however, bitexts are complete bilingual or multilingual parallel texts that are aligned with one another. Tiedemann provides a very broad definition: 'A bitext $B=(B_{src}, B_{trg})$ is a pair of texts B_{src} and B_{trg} that correspond to each other in one way or another. . . . Correspondence is treated as a symmetric relation between both halves of a bitext' (2011: 7).

Sub-Segment Identification

At the interface, users may not be clearly aware of the differences between TM and bitext, but instead of saving matched, pre-defined text chunks in a database as individual frozen segments, bitext or full-text, bitext systems employ pattern matching algorithms to identify matched similar text chunks of any length, which introduces the possibility of working with sub-sentential 'coupled pairs' of SL–TL segments. Even in standard TMs, not all segments consist of sentences. Section headings and items in a list are examples of non-sentence segments, as are the isolated text strings that often appear in computer program interfaces. However, short segments are not at all the same thing as sub-segments. Sub-segments are automatically extracted from segments, long or short, without modifying the actual translation memory database.

Sub-segmenting can be thought of as an automatic concordance lookup in which the software automatically chooses which sub-segments to look up within a source segment and presents the <tu>s from the translation-memory database that contain each sub-segment, sometimes highlighting the probable translation(s) of the sub-segment. Clearly, if too many sub-segments are chosen within a source-text segment and presented to the translator, or if there are multiple variations in sub-segment target language matches, the translator can be overwhelmed by the amount of information presented. Another aspect of sub-segmenting is that potentially incorrect <tu>s that are rarely or never displayed using full-segment lookup can often be retrieved during sub-segment lookup, requiring increased maintenance to ensure substantially higher quality translation memory.

Macklovitch *et al.* describe sub-sentential segmentation that is based essentially on bilingual concordancing within the framework of the Canadian RALI project, while Benito, as well as McTait and Diaz, observe that traditional TMs cannot combine fragments from different translation units (<tu>s) to build new target language options based on analyzed patterns. A variety of strategies to achieve sub-sentential segmentation have been suggested in addition to concordancing, including morphological analyzers associated with example-based MT (EBMT), part-of-speech taggers used in corpus analysis, and closed class word lists designed to enhance the effectiveness of corpus-based bitexts (ibid., Rapp). Interestingly, although many proponents assert the increased recall potentially afforded by sub-sentential segmentation, Gow (2003) shows that efforts to establish statistical comparison between the two styles produce inconclusive results – with standard TM benefiting from greater certainty (matches are often confirmed during creation or editing) but shorter segments providing greater recall but also additional noise that may actually slow the translation process. Gow concludes that implementers need to weigh their options and choose the system type that best meets their needs. Nevertheless, recent upgrades in sub-segment algorithms and the enthusiasm of some current users may well inspire researchers like Gow to reassess their results.

Advantages of a TM

The ability to retrieve previously translated text enables individual translators to quickly and efficiently create the translation for a revised source text, even when the original was completed long ago. It also enables pairs or groups of translators working in networked environments or over the Internet to collaborate using the same translation memory and terminology resources. New translators can take over in the absence of initial translators and produce consistent results. Furthermore, networking among multiple translators rapidly builds the size of the TM.

An even more dramatic example of the power of translation memory is when a product is delivered simultaneously to multiple markets at the same time that the product is released in its domestic market, in each case with localized – that is, regionally adapted – documentation. This approach to localization is called *simship*, short for *simultaneous shipment*. In order to achieve simship without delaying release of the domestic version, translation into multiple languages must begin before completing the final version. Based on translation memory, versions with minor changes can be translated very quickly. In this regard, Bowker (2002) distinguishes between *revisions* (texts revised over time) and *updates* (ongoing changes during a production phase).

Translation memory is also useful even when the source text is not a revised version of a previously translated source text, so long as it is part of a collection of related documents that contain segments that are identical or very similar to previously translated segments. Applied appropriately in a translation workflow, TM can significantly enhance efficiency, time to market, and quality (O'Hagan 2009: 48–51). Used without effective quality assurance, however, TM enables the rapid and efficient replication of bad translations, giving rise to a special kind of multilingual 'garbage-in, garbage-out' exercise (GIGO), reflecting the fact that TM promotes *consistency* without necessarily having any effect on *accuracy* (Zerfass 2002).

Bowker (2002: 92–128) and O'Hagan (2009: 48–51) distinguish between *exact matches* and *full matches*. With exact (100%) matches, stored segments are identical to the new SL segment not only in string content, but also with regard to any layout features. Context matches (alternatively called *perfect matches* and *in context exact* (ICE) matches by various vendors) also ensure that the immediately preceding segment (or even both the preceding and the following segments) in the new SL is identical to that for the original document, which a growing number of database TMs and bitext systems in general can provide. *Full matches,* in contrast, are almost 100%, but may feature minor differences such as punctuation, capitalization, or dates.

The identification of *partial* equivalents supports the retrieval of so-called 'fuzzy matches' in traditional systems. Fuzzy matches are typically assigned a value indicating what percentage of a source segment matches the source segment in a retrieved <tu>. The screenshot in Figure 45.1 shows an example of a 74% fuzzy match, which resulted when the phrase 'for example our protagonist Bishop Otto von Bamberg' was modified in a second version of a previously translated text. This capability is especially powerful for frequently modified texts, such as software manuals and machine instructions. Freigang and Reinke call this value an *Ähnlichkeitswert,* something like a 'coefficient of similarity' (2005; *similarity coefficient* in Macklovitch and Russell), which corresponds to McTait *et al.,*'s 'similarity measure' (1999). Typically, the translator can assign a threshold (such as 70%) below which a fuzzy match is not displayed, since excessive fuzziness results in noise that slows translation down.

In the translation/localization industry, translator compensation is often influenced by how closely a segment retrieved from translation memory matches the current segment of source text. However, as of this writing, there is no standard method of computing the percentage of match. Some methods are word-based and some are character based. This makes it difficult to use the same threshold across multiple tools.

Two other factors can affect fuzzy-match values. One is inline markup, which consists of tags used to identify layout features such as boldface, underline, or italics. There may also be hypertext links, footnotes, or other embedded controls or operative features. These items may not end up in the same place in the target text, or in some cases it may be desirable to delete them or possibly to add something new in the target text that is not there in the original. They need to be protected on the one hand and manipulated on the other so that they will be in the right place in the finished translation. It is not necessarily uncommon for inline markup to vary from one version of a document to the next, in which case just a change in, say, a boldface command, will cause an otherwise identical passage to register as a fuzzy match.

The second kind of item that is often treated using similar strategies is the presence of so-called 'named entities'. These could be people's names or the names of institutions, countries, and the like, but in localization environments, named entities include dates, numbers, currency units, proper names, identifiers, URLs, inline graphics or other region-specific values that can be simply transferred or automatically generated according to set rules. Translators do not usually have to

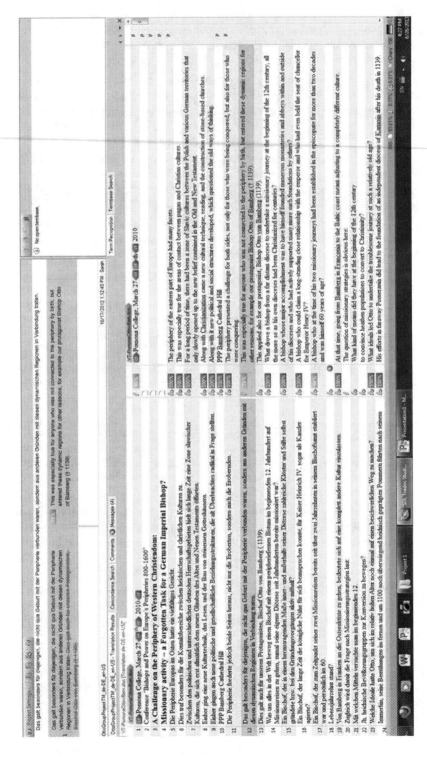

Figure 45.1 Side-by-side segment display

'translate' these items because they will either not change (in the case of people's names) or the TM will generate the proper TL form; for instance: American English 8/2/2013 (for August 2, 2013) becomes 2.8.2013 in German (for the 2nd of August 2013), which is the standard German order and notation.

Different TM applications and writers use different terms for these variables. Sometimes they are both called 'placeables' because systems typically convert native code to visual markers that appear in the TM editor and can be manipulated (placed) by the translator without breaking the original markup. (See the small pointed icons in Figure 45.1, Line 1.) Azzano calls these elements 'placeables' and 'localizables', respectively: 'Placeable elements are portions of a document which – in translation – do not change in content. Localizable elements are portions of a document which – in translation – are adapted in content to a target locale according to standard or given rules' (2011: 38). Bowker, however, uses the term *placeables* for Azzano's *localizables,* and refers to them as 'named entities', while Kenny talks about *formatting tags* and *placeables* (Bowker 2002; Kenny 2009), and Macklovitch and Russell dub them *non-translatables.*

Creating, Using, and Maintaining a TM

Although TMs may be used in multilingual computing environments, each individual TM is in most cases bilingual and directional. TMs can be created with general language pairs in mind (for instance, English → Spanish), but many are based on locale-specific SL and TL language code values, such as: en-US → es-ES (US English to Spanish [Iberian] Spanish). This choice has relative advantages and disadvantages. More general resources are more reusable if a translator or translation team encounters texts from many different locales (such as with Spanish from countries all over the Western Hemisphere).

Such TMs may also end up being larger overall because of the range of input, and TM size can accelerate return on investment (ROI) up to a certain point. However, more specific locale codes support the automatic generation of useful localizable entities, and overly large TMs may produce excess noise, require extra maintenance, and waste time. The notion of so-called 'Big Mama' TMs has inspired such efforts as the TAUS project, where individuals and companies are encouraged to pool their TMs in a single global resource; Linguee, which harvests identifiable <tu>s from across the Web; and MyMemory, which claims to house 'the World's Biggest Translation Memory'. The latter is perhaps unique in that it offers interface capability with a wide range of TM tools, in addition to offering its own API (All references 2013). Many experienced translators prefer a mixed solution, maintaining their own universal TM but actively subsetting it as needed using metadata-based filters for client, product, subject field, and text type classifications.

Regardless of how the <tu>s will be added to the database, the first step in creating a TM is to create the empty database itself. This involves making various choices, depending on the tool used, such as designating segmentation rules and stop lists, which are lists of lexical items or possibly punctuation that may cause problems during segmentation. A typical example might be abbreviations or German ordinal numbers (German *1.* = English *1st*) that end in periods, which may trigger unwanted mid-sentence segmentation.

In typical 'interactive mode', aligned translation segments are stored in the TM during the initial translation process. One or many texts for translation can be associated with the working TM, provided that the language direction of the project is also aligned with that of the TM. The greater the repetition factor, the greater the ROI from the TM. Needless to say, interactive mode requires considerable time and effort before reaching a desirable break-even point. In some cases, however, large amounts of legacy translation are available from documents that have been translated without using a TM. Users may even harvest 'Rosetta Stone' translations (existing multilingual versions of authoritative texts) from the Internet to increase recall by leveraging these texts to populate the TM. The segments contained in such legacy documents can be matched up in *batch mode* using alignment tools.

Alignment involves a series of stages: an initial automatic first-pass alignment, followed by a second pass in which a human translator 'corrects' any errors in the machine alignment. Such errors can result when, for instance, one long, possibly complicated sentence in the SL has been split into two or when two short or repetitive sentences have been combined into one in the TL. Flexible alignment tools allow human editors to move and recombine segments (including whole sentences or paragraphs) as needed to accommodate for segments that may have been moved around during translation. New material can also have been introduced that does not directly correspond to any SL segment (explicitation), or, conversely, an SL segment may be intentionally omitted (implicitation) because it is inappropriate to the target audience. Where such null segments occur, matches are most likely to be lost.

The concordance feature, if turned on during TM setup, allows users to search for a specified string wherever it occurs and provides a quick reference to its equivalent (or equivalents if it is not translated the same way in every case). By retrieving information that does not meet the validation criteria for fuzzy matching, concordance search supports translators if they have a hunch that they have seen a word or string before. Concordance lookup is not satisfying, however, for text varieties such as patents, where clauses (but not full sentences) are used intra-textually with a high degree of repetition. These cases offer a good argument for sub-sentential matches, as discussed earlier.

As the TM grows, the power of TM technology supports a pre-translation phase whereby the system-generated indexing function quickly finds paired translation segments and populates the TL with possible matches even before starting the follow-up human processing stage. Pre-translation can also predict expansion or compression rates based on average relationships for a given language pair or other calculable factors that may occur.

In this way, human knowledge and translation competence have been captured in machine-processable format, but it is important to remember that neither traditional translation memory nor bitext lookup software in any way 'understands' the translation process or the subject matter of the translated text. Nor does the software attempt to parse sentences or negotiate grammatical equivalents as some machine translation systems do, or attempt to do. Furthermore, translators need to carefully review suggestions presented by the TM to ensure they are still valid and that they fit the new micro- and macro-context, a process de Vries calls a 'sanity check' (2002). At this point the translator both enjoys the efficiency of retrieval but is also obliged to bear the previously cited GIGO principle in mind.

Layout and Interface Issues

Editor designs vary. In the past, some editors worked on the premise that most texts for translation are created in Microsoft Word. These systems enabled users to display TM functionality on the same screen while editing the actual translation as a Word document. This approach was attractive insofar as users know Word and how to use it.

By the same token, however, the interface between the TM software and Word can cause problems, especially if there are even slight differences in software versioning. File corruption is an ever-present danger. Furthermore, there are a wide range of other formats that also need to be translated (for instance, PowerPoint, InDesign, and HTML, as well as standard formats such as DITA and XLIFF). As a result, the current trend is for TMs to provide their own editing environment where most major file formats can be processed by converting native-mode text, often to XML Localization Interchange File Format (XLIFF), which is designed 'to standardize the way localizable data are passed between tools during a localization process'. (XLIFF).

Such programs process the global formatting codes accompanying the original file, strip them out, and save them as 'stand-off' markup. The translator sees more or less plain text, and placeables appear as placeholders that can be positioned correctly in the target text. This approach helps prevent broken code, but manipulating placeable markers can itself be challenging and requires additional knowledge from translators, revisers, and reviewers. Other files with special layout requirements, such as PowerPoint slides, can demand careful editing and reformatting in the TL export file because expansion and contraction in text volume can significantly affect slide design.

Separation of Data and Software

Translators become accustomed to individual TM features and interfaces, such as whether source and target language text are presented in side-by-side tables (as shown in Figure 45.1) or stacked vertically. Supplemental keyboard and mouse commands used to control program functions require a certain learning curve before users become truly proficient. Furthermore, it is often difficult to get several programs to run correctly on the same machine. Consequently, translators generally work with a limited number of applications. This leads to the need to allow multiple translation team members to use different programs. In such cases, the demand for a universal file exchange format is critical.

Soon after the appearance of multiple TM tools, it became apparent to the owners of translation memory databases that it was desirable to separate the data from the software so that a TM can be used in a different tool and so that multiple TMs created using different tools can be combined. This business need led to the development of the Translation Memory eXchange format (TMX) format, which was developed by the OSCAR special interest group of the now defunct Localisation Industry Standards Association (LISA). TMX is an XML markup formalism that 'allows any tool using translation memories to import and export databases between their own native formats and a common format', as shown in Figure 45.2. This interchange format not only allows people to work together despite different applications and platforms; it also frees up assets so that users can change systems without losing data.

Another obstacle to maximizing the re-use of information in a TM is differing methods of segmentation. If a TM is set up to segment at the sentence or sub-sentence level, and a revised version of the source text is to be translated using a different tool that segments in even just a slightly different way, it will be impossible to fully leverage the data from the original TM. These segmentation differences can keep relevant translation units from being retrieved, or exact matches can be categorized as fuzzy matches. This problem inspired the development of the Segmentation Rules Exchange Standard (SRX) for recording and transmitting information on the segmentation method used when creating either TMs or bitexts.

Special Language Support

Most TM software was created to support languages that use white space to separate words, that have relatively stable noun and verb forms with easy to manage inflections, and that track from left to right. Arabic, for instance, poses special problems in this regard. If a system is not carefully configured, bidirectional text sometimes results in bizarre behaviors, such as the actual inversion of text so that it reads in mirror image. Arabic morphology, where roots are embedded inside words,

```
<?xml version="1.0" ?>
<tmx version="1.4">
    <header creationtool="XYZTool" creationtoolversion="1.01-023"
    datatype="html" segtype= "sentence" adminlang="en-US" srclang="en" o-
    tmf-"ABCTransMem">
    </header>
    <body>
        <tu>
            <tuv xml:lang="en">
            <seg> Text in <bpt i="l">&lt;B></bpt>bold
            <ept i="l">&lt;/B></ept>.</seg>
            </tuv>
            <tuv xml:lang="fr"> <seg> Texte en
            <bpt i="l">&lt;B></bpt>gras<ept i="l">&lt;/B></ept>.</seg>
            </tuv>
        </tu>
    </body>
</tmx>
```

Figure 45.2   Sample TMX markup

and orthographic variation make it very difficult to ensure that real matches will be recognized. These problems have led many Arabic translators to eschew the use of tools.

In similar fashion, some Russian translators argue that terminology components and concordance searches are less useful because they still have a great deal of typing to do in order to account for the many inflectional forms in Russian, although many users have developed compensatory ways of dealing with these languages, such as creating multiple index terms for different forms. Other languages (Chinese and Thai, for instance) pose issues because they lack white space between 'words'. What is sorely needed in this regard is the development of special resources designed to facilitate more comfortable processing in a variety of different languages. Historical discussions often mention problems involving character sets, but these issues have been widely solved by near-universal implementation of Unicode character codes. What has not been widely implemented in TM systems is language-specific morphological processing, including word-boundary identification.

Professional Considerations

We have already discussed the advantages and disadvantages of building large global TMs, along with the merits of carefully maintained specialized smaller resources. We have not discussed related copyright issues, client confidentiality, and various knowledge management considerations, all of which frequently dictate careful segregation of resources.

Ownership of TMs and termbases is a critical factor in managing CAT tools. Technically, if translators contract with clients simply to translate text, without mentioning TM or terminology management in the job order for the project, then they may feel they have a claim on resulting resources, even though the translation produced under the agreement belongs to the client as a work made for hire. The argument has been made that translations and TMs are different works. If in doubt, it is wise to contact a copyright attorney for specific advice.

Nevertheless, in today's translation and localization markets, many language service providers (LSPs) control the copyright to TMs by asserting ownership and include statements to this effect in agreements. Many end clients in today's market, however, are increasingly realizing that they need to retain the rights to these resources as valuable intellectual property documenting enterprise knowledge assets. In any event, confidentiality issues may play a bigger role with regard to a translator's relationship to the client than actual ownership of the TM. With the advent of online TM service, where the translator never really has the TM on his or her machine, the question is rendered moot. Nevertheless, other TM owners have bought into a sharing principle as referenced early in the TAUS project, which designers hope will benefit both human and machine translation.

A further consideration that has significantly altered the translation market concerns discounted payment for full and fuzzy matches. Assuming that previously translated text segments should not be double charged, many LSPs and end clients have demanded percentage reductions for leveraged text. This may make sense provided translators enjoy improved productivity adequate to compensate for lost income. The practice is not, however, without its problems. As de Vries points out, TM maintenance itself (such as TM cleanup after subsequent editing outside the TM editor) requires effort, which is traditionally incorporated into hidden overhead but is exposed if discounts are imposed.

Fuzzy matches can require significant editing, and even full matches may suggest inappropriate solutions if the overall context has changed (2002). Failure to review the entire translation for macro-contextual coherence results in what Heyn has called the 'peep-hole' phenomenon, where translators see the text through the aperture of the individual segment (1998). In worst-case scenarios, translators only receive compiled lists of new segments for processing, without any view of the greater context. Technology aside, the business practices surrounding implementation of the tools can create environments where pressure to increase productivity at the cost of quality adversely affects professionalism and even erodes translator skills (LeBlanc 2013).

This situation contributes to the commodification of translation services and serves neither the well-being of the translator nor the quality of the final text. It also has produced a two-tier system where 'premium' translators focus on demanding jobs that require a high level of stylistic skill, while others produce 'bulk' work. The former generally turn down jobs involving discounts, while the latter work at bulk rates, producing high volumes. Durban's solution to this apparent payment issue is for translators to charge for their time instead of using traditional by-the-word rates (unpublished).

History of Translation Memory

During the early phase of research and development in translation technology (from the early 1950s until the mid-1960s), the focus was on fully automatic translation intended to replace human translators rather than increase their productivity. Probably the most influential early document on machine translation was a 1949 memo by Warren Weaver, who held an important position at the Rockefeller Foundation. The memo was later reprinted, but by then it had already had an influence on machine translation. W. John Hutchins (1999), on the occasion of the 50th anniversary of the Weaver memo, published an article about its historical context and significance. According to Hutchins:

> perhaps the most significant outcome of the Weaver memorandum was the decision in 1951 at the Massachusetts Institute of Technology to appoint the logician Yehoshua Bar-Hillel to a research position. Bar-Hillel wrote the first report on the state of the art and convened the first conference on machine translation in June 1952.

By 1960, Bar–Hillel had soured on the prospects of what he termed fully automatic high-quality machine translation (FAHQT). In an important (1960) article, he concluded that humans would need to be involved but only suggested two possible roles: pre-editor or post-editor of machine translation. The idea of translation memory would come later.

Six years later, the ALPAC report (1966) brought a halt to US government funding for translation technology, even though the report listed 'means for speeding up the human translation process' as its second recommendation (34). The ALPAC report was probably the first widely read publication recommending the use of technology to increase the productivity of human translators. This recommendation marks an important shift from a human-assisted machine translation (HAMT) perspective to a machine-assisted human translation (MAHT) perspective. Appendix 13 of the report shows what looks, at first glance, like translation memory (Figure 45.3; note the limitation to uppercase lower ASCII characters).

Despite the apparent TM 'look' in the reproduced printout, these source–target pairs were manually entered in a database, one pair at a time, by human translators to provide context for terms. A search of the database using keywords retrieved information for the purpose of terminology lookup. Although the database was not derived by processing existing source texts and their translations, it can be considered to be a precursor to translation memory. This system was developed for the European Coal and Steel Community in Luxembourg between 1960 and 1965 and thus may be the first hint at modern translation memory.

Until the late 1970s, the emphasis for the involvement of human translators with translation technology was on

(a) humans assisting machine translation systems through pre-editing, post-editing, or interactive resolution of ambiguity
(b) computers assisting humans by providing access to a terminology database
(c) humans examining a database of previously translated documents to avoid re-translating the same text.

As an example of (c), Friedrich Krollmann (1971) cited the recommendations of the ALPAC report and made several suggestions for supporting translators using technology. One suggestion, a database of entire translations to avoid translating an entire text more than once in a large organization, could be considered to be another precursor to translation memory.

(Source-text sentence containing the French term 'Jetée)

JETEE POUR LES CHARGEMENTS DE PETROLIERS

(Closest match French segment in the database)

JETEE D ACCES AVEC PLATE-FORME POUR CHARGEMENT ET DECHARGEMENT DE PETROLIERS

(Corresponding English segment (also from the database))

PIER WITH PLATFORM FOR LOADING AND UNLOADING TANKERS

Figure 45.3 Pseudo TM segment from the ALPAC Report

The first published description of translation memory as it has come to be understood was by Peter Arthern. In a 1978 presentation at the ASLIB conference on translating and the computer (published in 1979), he discussed the impact of translation technology on the Council of the European Commission, beginning with the status of machine translation. He then writes that since submitting an abstract for his ASLIB presentation, he realized that 'it is the advent of text-processing systems, not machine translation or even terminology data banks, which is the application of computers which is going to affect professional translators most directly – all of us, freelances and staff translators alike' (82).

Arthern points out that text-processing systems (currently better known as word processing systems) must be able to transmit and receive files through central computers rather than function as stand-alone machines. The first word processing system for a microcomputer, Electric Pencil (Bergin 2006), had been released in 1976 shortly before Arthern was preparing his presentation, and it was word processing on a general-purpose microcomputer with communication capabilities that led to TM tools for translators.

After a description of terminology management, Arthern presents his newly conceived proposal:

> The pre-requisite for implementing my proposal is that the text-processing system should have a large enough central memory store. If this is available, the proposal is simply that the organization in question should store all the texts it produces in the system's memory, together with their translations into however many languages are required.
>
> This information would have to be stored in such a way that any given portion of text in any of the languages involved can be located immediately, simply from the configuration of the words, without any intermediate coding, together with its translation into any or all of the other languages which the organization employs.
>
> This would mean that, simply by entering the final version of a [source] text for printing, as prepared on the screen at the keyboard terminal, and indicating in which languages translations were required, the system would be instructed to compare the new text, probably sentence by sentence, with all the previously recorded texts prepared in the organization in that language . . .
>
> Depending on how much of the new original was already in store, the subsequent work on the target language texts would range from the insertion of names and dates in standard letters, through light welding at the seams between discrete passages, to the translation of large passages of new text with the aid of a term bank based on the organization's past usage.
>
> *(94)*

Arthern's proposal is a remarkably accurate description of a modern translation tool with a translation memory function and a terminology lookup function, integrated with a text editor or word processing software.

In 1980, another visionary, Martin Kay, proposed similar features in an internal report to colleagues at Xerox PARC, Palo Alto (California) Research Center, titled 'The Proper Place of Men and Machines in Language Translation'. Kay was probably not aware of Arthern's paper, which had been published only months before. Kay's report was not officially published until 1999 but had a substantial impact year earlier on the community of translation developers who were sympathetic to the idea that post-editing raw machine translation was certainly not the only and probably not the best use of the talents of a professional human translator.

The result of proposals from Arthern, Kay, and others is what is known as a translator workstation, consisting of a personal computer and various software functions, including translation memory, that have been integrated in some way with text processor or word processing. Considerably more detail on the history of the translator workstation is available in Hutchins (1998).

Software development work on commercial implementation of translation memory began in the early 1980s, with the first commercial translation memory system being the ALPS system mentioned by Hutchins (1998). An examination of ALPS corporate documents has determined that an ALPS translator support system with a translation memory function (called 'repetitions processing') was commercially released in 1986. Shortly thereafter (1988), a translation editor called TED was developed for internal use within Trados, then a translation service provider, but not commercialized. It was not until the 1990s that other translation-memory systems, such as Trados and STAR Transit, would be offered to the public.

Most of the features of an integrated translator workstation foreseen in the early 1980s have been implemented in today's translator tools, with a few notable exceptions, such as morphological processing in terminology lookup and automatic 'quality estimation' of machine translation.

Kay (1980) foresaw translator productivity software that would be able to match on the base form of a word. This is, of course, particularly important when doing automatic terminology lookup on highly inflected languages where the form of the term in the source text is not the same as the form of the term in the termbase. As noted, most current translator tools try to work for all languages and thus have limitations when applied to morphologically complex languages such as Finnish and Arabic.

Melby (1982) foresaw the current trend in translator tools that provides multiple resources for a translator. For each segment of source text, various resources would be consulted, including terminology lookup and a database of previously translated texts. In addition, a segment of raw machine translation would be presented, but only if the machine translation system's self-assessment of quality exceeded a translator-set threshold. Automatic quality estimation (NAACL 2012) of raw machine translation did not achieve a really useful status until the early 2010s, about 30 years after Melby's proposal.

In summary, translation memory emerged from a combination of the availability of word processing and a change in perspective on the role of humans, from assistant to master of a translation technology system.

Future Developments and Industry Impact

When translation memory was introduced to the commercial translation market in the 1980s, all machine translation systems were rule based. In the first decade of the 21st century, statistical machine translation (SMT) and example-based machine translation (EBMT) rose to prominence. This led to an unanticipated connection between TM and these new forms of MT. A large TM can provide the training data for SMT and EBMT. This raises the question of where to obtain a very large TM for general-purpose machine translation. The technology currently used in the Internet was around in the 1980s, but it was used primarily by the military and selected universities. Since the 1990s, as the Internet and, in particular, multilingual websites and other online multilingual resources have blossomed, it has gradually become more feasible to automatically harvest gigantic TMs from the Internet, at least for those languages with the most online content. All this led to the improvement of the SMT version of Google Translate, for instance. It has also led to additional privacy concerns, since material submitted to Google Translate becomes available to Google for other purposes. Nevertheless, examination of online resources such as Linguee reveals the great danger in simply accepting translation segments taken out of context. Indeed, as more and more online content is produced through machine translation in the first place, automatically generated <tu>s create a kind of questionable vicious circle.

There is a further tension between massive distributed translation memories and careful terminology management. The broader the set of bitexts that are used to create a large TM, the more likely that terminological variation will be introduced, originating from multiple text types and domains, as well as from the proliferation of styles representing multiple authors. Especially in combination with sub-segment lookup, such TMs can result in inconsistent terminology across various TM suggestions to a translator as a text is translated. One possibility for addressing this problem is to combine TM lookup and terminology lookup in a more integrated fashion. This kind of integration has not yet appeared in commercial translation tools.

Melby (2006) proposes that data-driven MT may in the future converge with TM technology to improve recall and cut down on fuzziness. EBMT incorporates existing rule-based architectures (Somers) or draws on statistical probabilities that parse linguistic coherence factors in determining probable matches (Simard). This vision of the future implies that coordinating linguistic awareness through MT tools into the current relatively blind look-up capabilities of TM could result in increased coherence, consistency and accuracy (*ibid*, also Rapp, Koehn).

Creative document writing is the enemy of TM efficiency. The advent of single-source controlled authoring enables not just the reuse of translated segments but of source language chunks as well, which can be used to generate a number of text varieties, such as advertising brochures, maintenance manuals, product literature, and web pages. Here the same concerns apply as for TM leveraging in general: assembling disparate units to create a new text may not always meet audience needs.

It may be that in the future translation memory will become less visible as a separate function in a translation tool. Information from translation memory, terminology databases, and machine translation may be integrated and presented to the translator as a single suggestion in some cases, refined by automatic or explicit domain identification, with the sources of the integrated suggestion only visible to the translator upon request.

Bibliography

ALPAC (1966) 'Languages and Machines: Computers in Translation and Linguistics', *A Report by the Automatic Language Processing Advisory Committee, Division of Behavioral Sciences, National Academy of Sciences, National Research Council*, Washington, DC: National Academy of Sciences, National Research Council.

Arthern, Peter J. (1979) 'Machine Translation and Computerized Terminology Systems: A Translator's Viewpoint', in Mary Snell (ed.) *Translating and the Computer: Proceedings of a Seminar*, London, 14 November 1978, Amsterdam: North-Holland Publishing Company, 77–108.

Austermühl, Frank (2001) *Electronic Tools for Translators*, Manchester and North Hampton, MA: St. Jerome Publishing.

Azzano, Dino (2011) 'Placeable and Localizable Elements in Translation Memory Systems: A Comparative Study', PhD thesis, Ludwig Maximilian University of Munich. Available at: http://edoc.ub.uni-muenchen.de/13841/2/Azzano_Dino.pdf.

Bar-Hillel, Yehoshua (1960) 'The Present Status of Automatic Translation of Languages', *Advances in Computers* 1: 91–163.

Benito, Daniel (2009) 'Future Trends in Translation Memory', *revista tradumàtica: Traducció I Technologies de a Informació I la Comunicació*, 07 (desembre 2009).

Bergin, Thomas J. (2006, October–December) 'The Origins of Word Processing Software for Personal Computers: 1976–1985', *IEEE Annals of the History of Computing* 28(4): 32–47. http://doi.org/10.1109/MAHC.2006.76.

Bowker, Lynne (2002) 'Translation-memory Systems', in *Computer-Aided Translation Technology: A Practical Introduction*, Ottawa: University of Ottawa Press, 92–128.

Bowker, Lynne and Des Fisher (2010) 'Technology and Translation', in Carol A. Chapelle (ed.) *The Encyclopedia of Applied Linguistics*, Hoboken: Wiley-Blackwell Publishing Ltd.

Dunne, Keiran (2012a) 'Computer-assisted Translation', in Carol A. Chapelle (ed.) *The Encyclopedia of Applied Linguistics*, Hoboken: Wiley-Blackwell Publishing Ltd.

Dunne, Keiran (2012b) 'Translation Tools', in Carol A. Chapelle (ed.) *The Encyclopedia of Applied Linguistics*, Hoboken: Wiley-Blackwell Publishing Ltd.

Eurdicautom (2013) 'In: EUGRIS: Portal for Soil and Water Management in Europe'. Available at: www.eugris.info/displayresource.aspx?r=5703.

Foreign Exchange Translations (2012) 'When TMs Jump the Shark'. Available at: http://blog.fxtrans.com/2009/12/when-tms-jump-shark.html.

Freigang, Karlheinz and Uwe Reinke (2005) 'Translation-Memory-Systeme in der Softwarelokalisierung', in Detlef Reineke und Klaus-Dirk Schmitz (eds.) *Einführung in die Softwarelokalisierung*, Tübingen: Gunter Narr Verlag, 55–72.

Gow, Francie (2003) *Metrics for Evaluating Translation Memory Software*, Ottawa: University of Ottawa, Canada.

Harris, Brian (1988) 'Bi-text, A New Concept in Translation Theory', *Language Monthly* 54: 8–10.

Hutchins, W. John (1998) 'The Origins of the Translator's Workstation', *Machine Translation* 13(4): 287–307.

Hutchins, W. John (1999) 'Warren Weaver Memorandum', July 1949, *MT News International* 22: 5–6, 15.

Kay, Martin (1998/1980) 'The Proper Place of Men and Machines', *Language Translation* 12(1–2): 3–23. Hingham, MA: Klewer Acaademic Publishers.

Kenny, Dorothy (2009) 'Unit of Translation', in Mona Baker and Gabriela Saldanha (eds.) *Routledge Encyclopedia of Translation Studies*, 2nd edition, London and New York: Routledge, 304–06.

Koehn, Philipp and Jean Senellart (2010) 'Convergence of Translation Memory and Statistical Machine Translation', in *AMTA Workshop on MT Research and the Translation Industry*.

Krollmann, Friedrich (1971) 'Linguistic Data Banks and the Technical Translator', *Meta* 16(1–2): 117–24.

LeBlanc, Matthieu (2013) 'Translators on Translation Memory (TM): Results of an Ethnographic Study in Three Translation Services and Agencies', *Translation and Interpreting* 5(2): 1–13.

Linguee: 'Dictionary and Search Engine for 100 Million Translations'. Available at: http://linguee.com.

Macklovitch, Elliott and Graham Russell (2000) 'What's Been Forgotten in Translation Memory', in *AMTA '00, Proceedings of the 4th Conference of the Association for Machine Translation in the Americas on Envisioning Machine Translation in the Information Future*, Springer, London, 137–46.

Macklovitch, Elliott, Michael Simard, and Philippe Langlais (2000) 'TransSearch: A Translation Memory on the World Wide Web', in *Proceedings of LREC 2000*.

Malmkjaer, Kristen (1998) 'Unit of Translation', in Mona Baker and Kirsten Malmkjaer (eds.) *Routledge Encyclopedia of Translation Studies*, 1st edition, London and New York: Routledge, 286–88.

McTait, Keven, Maive Olohan, and Arturo Trujillo (1999) 'A Building Bocks Approach to Translation Memory', in *Translating and the Computer 21: Proceedings from the ASLIB Conference*, London.

Melby, Alan (1982) 'Multi-level Translation Aids in a Distributed System', in Jan Horecký (ed.) *Proceedings of COLING 1982*, Amsterdam: North Holland.

Melby, Alan (2006) 'MT +TM+QA: The Future Is Yours', *Traducció I Tenologies de la informació I a Comunicació*, Numero 4.

MyMemory. Available at: http://mymemory.translated.net/doc.

NAACL (2012) *7th Workshop on Statistical Machine Translation*, Shared Task: Quality Estimation, Montreal, Quebec, Canada.

O'Hagan, Minako (2009) 'Computer-aided Translation (CAT)', in Mona Baker and Gabriela Saldanha (eds.) *Routledge Encyclopedia of Translation Studies*, 2nd edition, London and New York: Routledge, 48–51.

Rapp, Reinhard (2002) 'A Part-of-speech-based Search Algorithm for Translation Memories', in *Proceedings of LREC 2002*.

Reinke, Uwe (2003) *Translation Memories – Systeme – Konzepte – Linguistische Optimierung (Systems, Concepts, Linguistic Optimization)*, Frankfurt am Main: Peter Lang.

Simard, Michel (2003) 'Translation Spotting for Translation Memories', *HLT-NAACL-PARALLEL '03: Proceedings of the HLT-NAACL 2003 Workshop on Building and Using Parallel Texts: Data-driven Machine Translation and Beyond*, 27 May–1 June 2003, Edmonton, Canada, 3: 65–72.

Somers, Harold L. and Gabriela Fernandez Diaz (2004) 'Translation Memory vs. Example-Based MT – What's the Difference?', *International Journal of Translation* 16(2): 5–33.

Stoll, Cay-Holger (1988) 'Translation Tools on PC', in Catriona Picken (ed.) *Translating and the Computer 9: Proceedings*, London: ASLIB.

Tiedemann, Jörg (2011) *Bitext Alignment*, San Rafael, CA: Morgen and Claypool.

TMX 1.4b Specification: Translation Memory eXchange format, 2005-04-26. Available at: www.gala-global. org/oscarStandards/tmx/tmx14b.html (Original: 1998).

Vinay, Jean-Paul and Jean Darbelnet (1995) *Comparative Stylistics of French and English: A Methodology for Translation (1958/1995)*, Juan Sager and Marie-Jo Hamel (trans.), Amsterdam and Philadelphia: John Benjamins Publishing Company.

Weaver, Warren (1949/1955) 'Translation', in William N. Locke and Donald Booth (eds.) *Machine Translation of Languages: Fourteen Essays*, Cambridge, MA: Technology Press of the Massachusetts Institute of Technology, 15–23.

XLIFF (XML Localization Interchange File Format). Available at: www.oasis-open.org/committees/ tc_home.php?wg_abbrev=xliff.

Zerfass, Angelika (2002) 'Evaluating Translation Memory Systems', in *Proceedings of LREC 2002*.

Zetzsche, Jost (2003) *The Translator's Tool Box: A Computer Primer for Translators*, Winchester Bay Oregon: The International Writers' Group.

46

TRANSLATION MANAGEMENT SYSTEMS

Mark Shuttleworth

Introduction and Definition

Perhaps less well known than some other types of translation technology, computerized translation management systems have been in existence since the late 1990s. This technology, which was introduced in order to enable translation companies or individual translators to remain in control of the ever-increasing volumes of content that they need to process, was designed to facilitate the monitoring of the business, process and language aspects of their translation and localization projects.

Through the reduction or almost complete elimination of manual tasks, the use of a TMS should permit translation professionals to work more efficiently and to focus on the aspects of their job that require some exercise of judgment. Given that products and services are being constantly developed and improved and new systems continue to appear, this chapter represents a snapshot of the technology as it appeared at the time of writing. It should also be pointed out that, while the terminology used to refer to different features and functions varies widely from system to system, this chapter seeks to use a nomenclature that is neutral and does not systematically follow the terminology of any one product.

The purpose of translation management tools is characterized by Chan as follows:

> Translation management systems primarily help teams reduce the need to do repetitive tasks via automating process or document hand-off. This includes process driven workflows such as assignment of documents for review, translation, editing, sign off, publishing and such. The most important job of translation management systems is to help translation teams improve consistency and efficiency.
>
> *(2021)*

While translation management functions are sometimes performed by a combination of different specialized programs, this characterization envisages the situation in which many or all of them are combined within a single application or service that permits users (who will generally be senior executives, coordinators or project managers within a translation or localization company or language service provider) to control the company's translation assets (i.e.

DOI: 10.4324/9781003168348-49

translation memories, termbases and machine translation solutions) and to monitor every aspect of workflow:

> These applications orchestrate the business functions, project tasks, process workflows, and language technologies that underpin large-scale translation activity, coordinating the work of many participants in the communications value chain, working inside, outside, and across organizations.
>
> *(Sargent and DePalma 2009: 1)*

The key advantages brought by this technology include the ability to handle an increased workflow, to accomplish more with less and to manage language service vendors better (ibid.: 20). When combined with a company's content and/or document management system (CMS and/or DMS), the result is a significantly enhanced capability in at least the first two of these three areas, as the use of a CMS (and/or DMS) will help manage the whole content life cycle, from the writing of original material, through editing work and localization to publication to multiple output formats, including, for example, PDF, HTML and RTF. Many of the functions offered by a TMS are made available to freelance translators within a desktop computer-aided translation (CAT) tool, and there is now an increasing overlap between the former and the latter in terms of functionality.

Workflow is described by Rico (2002) as including stages for commissioning, planning, groundwork (term extraction and research, text segmentation and alignment, and text preparation), translation (using translation memory, machine translation and/or localization tools) and wind-up (including consistency check, detection of missing elements, grammar check and testing). However, one might sometimes wish to include other procedures as well, such as desktop publishing engineering, reviewing feedback and so forth (see, for example, Shaw and Holland 2009: 112 for an alternative workflow scheme). Great importance is ascribed to workflow simply because defining the step-by-step procedures involved in a complex translation project helps prevent possible errors occurring. It should be added that some workflows are highly complex in nature and involve loops, parallel steps, the skipping of individual steps and the inclusion of multiple transitions in and out of each step (Peris 2012).

TMSs, which can also be referred to as globalization management systems or project management systems, can be commercial (desktop, server-based, 'software-as-a-service' or 'captive'), open source or formed on an *ad hoc* basis by combining a number of different applications if a particular company decides that none of the commercial solutions available suit their particular requirements (see Appendix).

Scope and Main Functionalities

By way of providing a rationale for this technology, Chamsi (2011) tracks the various stages in the development of a new language service provider (LSP), from start-up and growth phases to a greater maturity, in terms of the kind of translation management procedures it is likely to have in place. In the first phase, the system used is likely to be *ad hoc*, and may even be largely paper-based or may consist of a single Excel spreadsheet, although given the relatively low level of workflow such a simple system is likely to be flexible enough for the demands placed on it (53). Once the LSP starts to experience significant growth, in many cases the original basic translation management procedures will continue to be used, although by this time the system's simplicity and flexibility will both have been seriously compromised (54). If the LSP has not already taken this step, then under pressure from heavy workloads, customer or invoicing issues or reduced profitability (55), sooner or later it will be forced to make the transition to a more robust set of procedures or adopt an off-the-shelf TMS solution. Sargent and DePalma similarly argue that the alternative to adopting a TMS is to 'reach a choke-point in communication with key constituencies' (2009: 1) and observe that it is companies with a high degree of 'digital saturation' that will be likely to opt for an IT-based TMS solution (2009: 28; see also Lawlor 2007).

Translation management comes in a variety of forms. Some TMS functions (e.g. translation analytics, quality control and translator database and workflow management) are provided by many desktop CAT systems (e.g. Trados Studio, memoQ and OmegaT), while there are now also a number of Software-as-a-Service (SaaS – or, in other words, cloud-based) systems that combine translation memory (TM) functionality with more sophisticated TMS capabilities (e.g. Phrase [formerly Memsource], Wordbee and XTM Cloud). Systems that follow the SaaS model have the advantage of requiring no installation and being available in the latest version from anywhere on a 24/7 basis using browser-based access, while the implications of the phrase 'cloud-based' are that users access the cluster of software services held on the provider's server in the manner described previously and indeed entrust to them their private data, which is held securely on their behalf (see Muegge 2012). Such products are generally licensed via a subscription model, different payment plans being typically available for freelancers and translation companies of different sizes. In addition, a few systems are what are termed 'captive', or only available to a company's clients as part of a language service contract (DePalma 2007). There are also more dedicated TMSs that do not offer all the features of a typical CAT tool but provide heavy-duty support for a wide range of business and project-related tasks. For those who choose to implement their own solution (whether that be by creating a new product or configuring an existing one), this will greatly enhance the system's flexibility while not generally leading to a significant increase in costs (Stejskal 2011).

Chamsi (2011: 61–62) identifies the following list of basic characteristics that a TMS should possess. Some of these would be typical of any information system, while others are specific to the activity of project management:

> *simplicity* the system should not require users to undergo extensive training and should be as intuitive as possible, at least regarding most areas of functionality;
>
> *adaptability/flexibility* it should be possible for the system to handle a number of different processes in parallel;
>
> *scalability* the system should be able to grow as the organization also experiences expansion;
>
> *ease and security of access* since many translation projects are performed by people living in different parts of the world, the system should be securely accessible from any location;
>
> *automation of repetitive tasks* the system should enable project managers to focus on the 'value-added' (62) aspects of their work by freeing them from repetitive tasks as well as helping them to improve their productivity by allowing them to spend less time on each task; by acting as a 'productivity multiplier' (62) in this way, it will facilitate the growth of the LSP;
>
> *reduction in file management and file transfer overhead* the task of storing and transferring files should be managed automatically so that files can be made available to those who need them with a minimum of effort;
>
> *reduction of risk of mistakes* any risk, such as those intrinsic to understanding a project specification or transferring files, should be reduced through the implementation of specific pre-defined processes;
>
> *access to relevant data for decision-making* practical information such as details of suppliers and clients, project specifications and suchlike should be easily accessible within the system.

Depending on the precise needs of a particular user, some of these characteristics will be essential, while others may be less so.

According to Sargent and DePalma (2009: 6–8; see also Sargent 2012), there are four types of TMS: language-centric, business, enterprise and house. These will be considered below; as will be seen, they are distinguished to a large extent by the sophistication of the workflow management that is built in.

Language-Centric

A typical language-centric system consists of tools for project managers, translators, editors and reviewers. While these are likely to be web or server based, some will also offer a desktop translation client. The workflow management will typically only include the translation process itself rather than more peripheral functions such as desktop publishing and testing. Terminology management is also frequently included (Sargent and DePalma 2009: 6–7). This type of system is relatively widespread. It is frequently adopted because of its centralized translation memory capability and its ability to pre-process files for translation (7–8). A CAT tool with TMS functionality is only considered a TMS if it is web rather than desktop based (7). Typically, a language-centric tool can be deployed very quickly (33).

Business

The second type, business systems, comprise project, resource and finance modules and are frequently used in conjunction with a language-centric system. Once again, the workflow capabilities are relatively limited (7). Such systems tend to be favoured by LSPs (ibid.) because of the business management capabilities that they offer.

Enterprise

Enterprise systems, the third type that the authors identify, place the emphasis firmly on workflow. They combine the functionalities of language-centric and business types, although they can be weaker than business-type systems in the areas of project, resource and finance management. Workflow management is sophisticated and allows for collaborative multi-vendor scenarios and for non-core processes such as desktop publishing and testing (7).

House

Finally, house systems also focus on workflow and collaboration management. In addition to this, they provide clients with logins to enable them to access status reports, and permit online job submission and retrieval (7).

Unfortunately, Sargent and DePalma do not provide examples of each type of system.

Development of the Technology

Although individual translators and translation companies have always had to use some method for managing their various procedures, the concept of TMSs itself was first conceptualized by Melby, who envisaged two kinds of application dedicated to this area, which he referred to as 'infrastructure' and 'translation workflow and billing management', as two of eight different categories of translation technology (1998: 1–2). The former of these was intended to deal with document creation and management, the terminology database and telecommunications, while the latter handled the non–translation–specific logistics of processing translation projects. Possibly one of the earliest TMSs, GEPRO, which was used from 1985 in the European Parliament (Wilson and Carlisle 1988: 115), was essentially a 'logging system for translation jobs' (116). Three other early TMSs were GlobalSight, which was released in 1998 (see DePalma 2011); the LTC Organiser; and Projetex. SaaS systems first started appearing around 2002 (Muegge 2012: 18).

According to Sargent and DePalma (2007), by early 2006 a shift in emphasis was occurring amongst software vendors, who were repositioning themselves as translation workflow providers rather than competing with CMS producers. In 2007 Lingotek made its system available free of charge (Muegge 2012: 18), while in 2009 Google launched the Translator Toolkit, although this was chiefly intended to improve the quality of output from Google Translate (ibid.) and was in fact discontinued at the end of 2019 (Google Help 2019).

Over the last ten years there has been a continuation of the drive to automate monotonous tasks and permit project managers to focus on more creative aspects of their work through the use of increasingly intelligent software (Protemos 2020). Already of great significance for the translation industry, the role of SaaS and cloud computing has grown to some extent over the last few years. At the same time, successive versions of the major CAT tools have included increasingly substantial features designed for managing translation projects.

Common Features

Systems vary greatly in terms of the functions that they offer their users. In particular, features offered in translation memory, SaaS and dedicated desktop and server-based systems will differ from each other, as in each case a different type of user and corporate environment is generally envisaged. Similarly, many vendors offer different versions of their software for specific groups of user (e.g. freelancer, LSP, large enterprise, etc.). Here differences between versions are likely to involve the availability of a supplier module, possible connectivity to a CMS, the potential for being networked and the provision of access to the system for clients and suppliers. The price differential between the most basic and most sophisticated versions will normally be huge. In addition, it should be pointed out that there are tools that are designed to accomplish a single translation management task (e.g. Trados GroupShare for group collaboration; globalReview for reviewing and approving translations performed with Trados; TMXEditor and Transolution Xliff Editor for editing TMX and XLIFF files respectively and one2edit for managing, editing and translating InDesign documents online).

There are a wide range of features that different TMSs possess, depending on their level of sophistication. However, all TMSs will include a number of functions that are typically available in desktop CAT tools. These would include items such as file format conversion, text segmentation, formatting tag handling, text alignment, a built-in editing environment and, possibly, pretranslation. In some cases, TMS vendors will ensure a close integration with their own CAT tool. In addition, there will be at least a basic kind of workflow management, including some deadline management and mechanisms for managing translation assets. The system will also allow for connection to an SQL database or other CMS via an application programming interface (API) in order to raise the level of automation in the translation process. It will assign roles within a project (e.g. translator, reviser, desktop publishing expert) to service providers and the project itself to a project manager and will handle the submission of translated content electronically. Reports on status, deadlines, costs, workload, quality parameters and the like can be generated for clients to inspect. The system will analyse files to be translated against project TMs in order to determine the leverage that can be achieved and where possible will 'pretranslate' – or in other words compare entire source texts with TMs and automatically insert all exact and fuzzy matches that it finds – so that translators are only presented with material that needs to be processed. Some systems also have procedures to manage version control issues.

In addition to what might be termed these core functionalities, each system will typically offer many further features. These will be discussed in the following paragraphs. (It should be noted that not all these features are available in all systems.)

E-mail Many systems provide e-mail templates and permit the automatic sending of job offers, deadline reminders, payment advices and so forth. Similarly, incoming e-mails that are identified with a project number can be automatically filed under the appropriate project.

Business Many systems can store templates for purchase orders, job assignments, invoices, quotes and so on and help to control the budget. Automatic numbering of projects, currency calculations and setting of credit limits for customers are also possible features.

Project management A complete overview of the structure of a project (e.g. in tree-like view) can often be provided. Source language content can be monitored for changes. Freelancers in the database of service providers can be searched according to a range of different criteria (e.g. by job details, tool use, area of specialization or previous performance). Time management support can be offered in the form of different job statuses (e.g. Done, Due today and Overdue).

Customer front end Customers can be offered a log-in in order to enable them to track their project and documentation, upload and download files and access quotes and invoices (e.g. Cloudwords, OTM, GlobalSight).

Freelancer front end Via their own log-ins, freelancers can receive job documentation, upload and download documents and so on.

Crowd-sourcing management Some tools offer support for this new area of translation activity via integration with an open-source CMS, as well as automatic publication of translations. Greater management flexibility is required here, as translators need to be able to collect a job that they would like to work on and submit it once they are ready to do so.

Sales Systems can provide sales representatives with a simple means to ensure consistency of pricing, both in general and on a customer-specific level.

Translation Quality Assessment Tools are usually offered to permit linguistic and formal quality assessment, and job quality and sizing assessment. The tracking of freelancers' performance via indicators enables the ranking when selecting resources for a job. Finally, complaints can be managed and documented.

Standards Most tools should conform to the usual industry standards (e.g. XLIFF, TMX, TBX, SRX and GMX) as well as open standards.

Collaboration Various collaborative tools may be offered, such as collaborative post-editing.

Smartphone version Some systems (e.g. Phrase and XTM Cloud) give project managers the possibility of tracking projects via mobile devices in order to help ensure fast responses to customer requests.

The idea of a company connecting a TMS to their CMS via an API has been mentioned. There are various advantages to this. Firstly, the documents remain secure throughout the translation process. Secondly, files can be transferred automatically by the system. Thirdly, various different workflows are unified within a single process managed by the software. Fourthly, in this way it is possible to exercise strong version control, thus eliminating the risk of selecting an out-of-date version of a file (see MultiCorpora 2011).

Implementation of Different Features: Examples From Systems

In this section we will be looking at four different systems: Trados Studio 2021 SR1 as an example of a desktop TM tool that offers some translation management functionality, Phrase as a typical SaaS-type TM-cum-TMS-tool, and Transifex and Wordbee as representatives of dedicated industry-strength TMSs.

In the discussion that follows, the use of one or other application to illustrate a particular feature does not imply that that is the only or the main translation management function that the application possesses or that it performs that task particularly effectively compared to other tools.

Trados Studio 2021

As explained, as a desktop CAT tool with TMS functionality, Trados Studio 2021 is not considered a TMS. However, like many other CAT tools, it offers freelance translators and companies a range of management tools.

This application boasts extensive translation management features, ranging from quality control and workflow management to translator database management and the generation of quotations and invoices. In the case of a file analysis request, Trados Studio will produce the detailed information about the project files shown in Figure 46.1.

What this report shows the user is how many recurring segments there are and what the different match levels are. This will provide the user with an idea of the level of assistance the use of translation memory is likely to provide and consequently how much time will be needed to translate the files and what sums to charge the client and pay the translators. In the case of the analysis presented in Figure 46.1, we can see that, of the 33 segments that the file contains, 11 are repeated, while 2 have fuzzy matches, both at 95–99%.

Phrase

Phrase is a CAT tool that has existed since 2010, with a SaaS version having been launched in the following year. Like Trados Studio, it has very well-developed translation management functions, including analytics, workflow management, collaboration tools, translator database management, quality control and quote generation.

Figure 46.2 shows the interface for nominating a particular translation service provider for a job and tracking its status.

The provider can be selected from a database of translators and can if necessary be created in the system by the project manager. Once a job has been offered to a provider, the project manager can track its progress, as well as the provider's response, by assigning the appropriate status.

The Split File function is illustrated in Figure 46.3.

Phrase allows a project manager to specify precisely how a file will be split. Following this, the file will appear on the Linguist Portal of each translator to whom segments have been assigned, and when translators click on it, only the segments that have been assigned to them for translation will be visible to them.

Transifex

Transifex describes itself as a localization platform, and it is a scalable solution available in editions for enterprises of various sizes. For project managers it offers tools to facilitate workflow

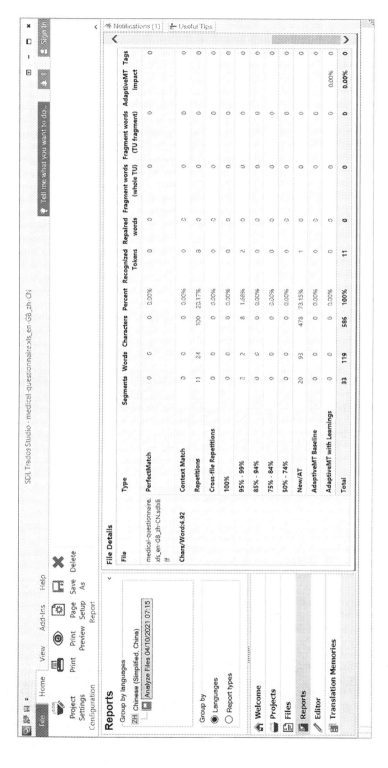

Figure 46.1 Using Trados Studio to perform file analysis

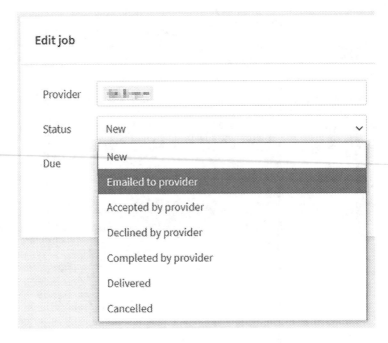

Figure 46.2 Using Phrase to assign a job to a translator

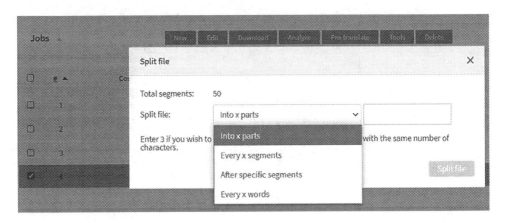

Figure 46.3 Splitting a file prior to distribution to translators in Phrase

management, translation quality control and team management. In addition, the software facil-itates the management of crowdsourced translation projects in which large numbers of trans-lators collaborate on a large-scale project (open source or otherwise), usually on a voluntary basis.

Figure 46.4 demonstrates the progress being made in the 154 project languages through the 3,896 strings that need to be translated by volunteers working on the Bitcoin Core localization project. The same interface permits users to enrol as project contributors, and the company makes the software available free of charge for participation in open source projects.

Ukrainian 100%	0 strings to translate
Indonesian 99.9%	4 strings to translate
Norwegian Bokmål 99.3%	29 strings to translate
Slovenian 100%	1 strings to translate
Finnish 98.2%	69 strings to translate
Italian 98.1%	74 strings to translate
Hungarian 97.3%	104 strings to translate

Figure 46.4 An extract from the language list for the Bitcoin Core localization project in Transifex

Wordbee Translator

This application describes itself as a translation management system, although it also has functionality that is designed for an individual translator. Translation management features include invoicing, collaboration, quality control and so on. In Figure 46.5, we see how the application permits a project manager to store a detailed client profile:

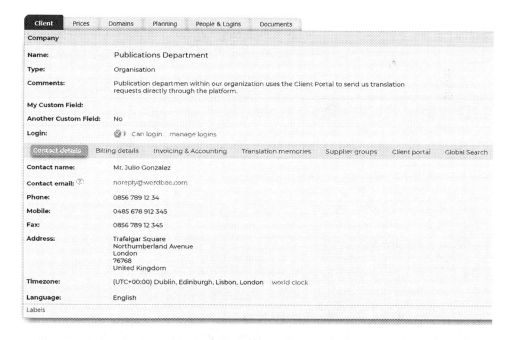

Figure 46.5 A client profile in Wordbee Translator

Besides contact details, as can be seen there are other tabs that can contain information about invoicing preferences, the availability of client TMs, access to MT via the client portal and so on.

Wordbee also allows users to break the workflow of a job into a number of discrete stages.

Figure 46.6 indicates how a job has been divided into translation and revision stages, each of which can be separately assigned to a different service provider. As seen in the figure, deadline calculation is also available.

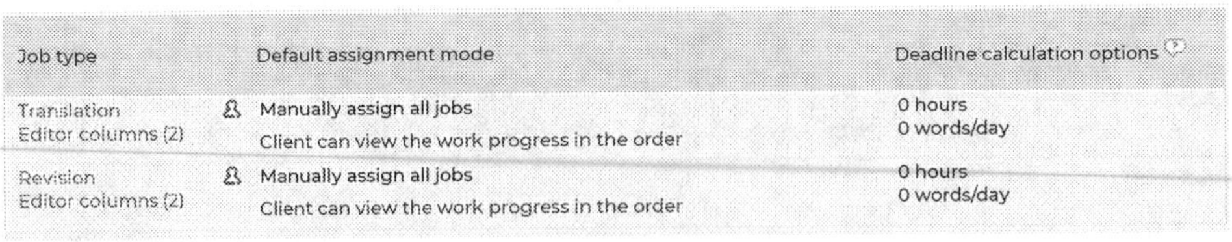

Job type	Default assignment mode	Deadline calculation options
Translation Editor columns (2)	Manually assign all jobs Client can view the work progress in the order	0 hours 0 words/day
Revision Editor columns (2)	Manually assign all jobs Client can view the work progress in the order	0 hours 0 words/day

Figure 46.6 Using Wordbee Translator to specify a workflow

Clearly, the assistance that TMS functionality can offer large and small enterprises and also individual translators is quite significant. The former group can make full use of the extensive features of an industry-level TMS system, while by and large the management functions included in CAT tools are sufficient for the needs of the latter – and, indeed, the potential offered by some such applications does in fact exceed what is likely to be required.

Future of the Technology

A number of possible directions in which the technology might develop in the short and medium terms may be discerned. These will be considered briefly below.

Firstly, building on a current tendency, it is likely that TMS functionality will continue to become increasingly prominent in CAT tools.

Secondly, a move towards greater integration between translation management and the management of translation assets would be sensible, with the purpose of allowing both processes to take place under a single roof. Indeed, it is important not to underestimate the potential significance of the role that TMSs might play as receptacles of considerable linguistic assets. As pointed out by Sargent and DePalma (2009: 39), it is essential for companies to formulate a well-thought-out corporate policy for capturing and managing terminology and TM assets that can be re-used – 'today, tomorrow, and for many years to come'. As a side effect of this, organizations that succeed in pursuing and/or further refining such a policy and gathering language assets within a TMS 'will also achieve useful MT output sooner than companies that do not' (ibid.). The authors' prediction that in the medium and long terms it will be impossible to calculate 'how much the accumulation of knowledge and fixed language assets could mean to a commercial or governmental entity' (2009: 29) continues to be true.

Thirdly, it has been predicted that increasingly complex processes will undergo automation. One likely route towards achieving this goal is via the rolling out of AI and machine learning; besides the likely continued improvement in machine translation and other types of translation technology that these approaches will bring, other possible enhancements are likely to include 'recommendations such as which documents to prioritize, plugins to offload workloads to pools of freelancers, multi-user real-time collaboration tools and many others' (Chan 2021). AI-based systems will be capable of learning on their own without being explicitly instructed to do so (Pielmeier 2018). In this way, they will be able to make predictions regarding the probable shape of a new project's timeline and the likelihood of a translation reaching a specific quality threshold based on past translator performance and behaviour (ibid.). Indeed, Pielmeier suggests that we are currently only seeing 'the tip of the iceberg' in terms of the use of AI, and that this area is likely to experience 'a complete explosion' (ibid.).

Conclusion

With new systems appearing all the time, in view of all the parameters that have been discussed, it is a potentially confusing matter for a customer to select the one that is most suited to his or her company's requirements. However, the core functions of the technology have been well defined for some years now, even though, as already stated, it is still a relatively young category of business software. As a technology, it has a number of clear strong points. Firstly, it is designed to manage complexity within translation projects, greatly facilitating the task of project managers and enabling them to focus on the more creative aspects of their work. Secondly, it will automate many tasks for project managers and will control workflow, with much the same result. Finally, as a repository of linguistic resources, it will preserve and accumulate knowledge. On the other hand, there are clear lines of development that are still in progress, with the result that much is still promised by this exciting area of translation technology.

Acknowledgements

I wish to express my gratitude to Dr Elina Lagoudaki for sharing her voluminous collection of relevant bookmarks with me early on in the project, and also to Common Sense Advisory, Inc., for making the full text of Sargent and DePalma (2009) available to me while I was preparing the first edition of this chapter. I am also grateful to RWS, Phrase, Transifex and Wordbee for permission to use screenshots from their respective systems.

APPENDIX: LIST OF TRANSLATION MANAGEMENT SYSTEMS

This list is not exhaustive but is believed to contain at least a representative cross-section of systems available during the autumn of 2021. It should be noted that the list does not include desktop CAT tools that offer some limited TMS functionality.

(1) Desktop- or server-based

    (a) Proprietary

Across Language Server (www.across.net/en) A general-purpose TM-cum-TMS tool available in versions for companies of different sizes and also in a personal edition.

Advanced International Translations Projetex (http://projetex.com) Workstation and Server versions of this tool ensure that freelance and corporate workflow management are both catered for.

Déjà Vu TEAMserver (https://atril.com/product/teamserver/) A general-purpose tool intended for companies.

QuaHill (www.quahill.com) A tool available in Basic, Premium and Enterprise versions.

    (b) Open source

GlobalSight Translation Management System (www.globalsight.com) An open-source system designed to enable companies to manage and localize global content.

Pootle (https://pootle.translatehouse.org/) A tool that has functionality for managing community-based localization projects.

(2) SaaS

(a) Proprietary

Cloudwords (www.cloudwords.com) A tool for business users.

Lokalise (https://lokalise.com/) A TMS focusing on localization and collaborative translation and available in Start, Essential, Pro and Enterprise plans.

LTC Worx (www.alphacrc.com/worx/) A company-oriented system.

ONTRAM (www.ontram.de/) For enterprise translation management; available in Basic, Advanced, Professional and Enterprise versions.

OTM – Online Translation Manager (www.lsp.net/online-translation-management.html) A system that controls and manages workflows for translation, editing, localization and desktop publishing; available in Business and Enterprise versions.

Plunet Business Manager (www.plunet.com) Available in AgencyStart, AgencyPlus, AgencyAdvanced and Enterprise editions.

Phrase (https://phrase.com/) A general-purpose tool combining translation memory, termbase and workflow modules, and intended for translators, translation companies and enterprises.

Smartcat (www.smartcat.com/) A general-purpose TMS focusing particularly on localization and aimed at freelancers, language service providers and organizations.

Smartling Translation Management System (www.smartling.com/software/translation-management-system/) A translation management tool for managing and automating the translation process.

Text United (www.textunited.com) A tool with versions aimed at both corporate and individual users.

Transifex (www.transifex.com) A translation and localization platform with workflow and crowdsourcing functionality designed for enterprises of various sizes.

Wordbee (www.wordbee.com) A general-purpose TM-cum-TMS tool intended for freelancers and businesses.

XTM Cloud (https://xtm.cloud/) A versatile TM-cum-TMS tool that is available in versions for enterprises and small groups of users.

(b) Open source

]project-open[(www.project-open.com) A general-purpose enterprise resource planning-cum-project management solution that has a module for translation.

Zanata (http://zanata.org) A system for managing localization projects.

(3) Both desktop/server-based and SaaS versions available

Lingotek Translation Management System (https://lingotek.com/translation-management-system/) A tool aimed at corporate users.

memoQ server (www.memoq.com/products/memoq-server) A general-purpose TMS.

Language Cloud Translation Management (www.rws.com/translation/language-cloud/management-system/) One of RWS's four TMS products.

MultiTrans (www.rws.com/translation/language-cloud/management-system/multitrans/) A general-purpose TMS; one of RWS's four TMS products.

Worldserver (www.rws.com/translation/language-cloud/management-system/worldserver/) A TMS that focuses on localization; one of RWS's four TMS products.

TPBox (www.tpbox.com/cgi-bin/aec.cgi) A general-purpose TMS for translation companies of different sizes.

XTRF (https://xtrf.eu/product/tms/) A system intended for companies of different sizes.

(4) 'Captive' systems that are only available as part of a language service contract. Each of these systems is a general-purpose TMS that offers clients a wide range of functionalities.

> *Crosslang* (https://crosslang.com/solutions/localization-lifecycle-management/)
> *i plus* (www.translateplus.com/technology/i-plus/)
> *Translation Management Platform* (www.lionbridge.com/our-platforms/)
> *translations.com* GlobalLink Connect and GlobalLink Enterprise (https://globallink.translations.com/products)

(5) Tools that perform a single or limited number of translation management tasks

> *Merix* (www.etranslate.com.au/technology/translation-management-system.asp) A tool that enables web developers to maintain multilingual and international websites.
> *globalReview* (www.kaleidoscope.at/en/translation/globalreview/) A tool for managing and reviewing Trados projects.
> *one2edit* (www.brandguardian.com/en/products/one2edit/) A system that manages, edits and translates InDesign documents.
> *TMXEditor* (www.maxprograms.com/products/tmxeditor.html) A tool for editing TMX files.
> *Trados GroupShare* (www.rws.com/translation/software/trados-groupshare/) A tool that facilitates collaboration between localization–translation team members; one of RWS's four TMS products.
> *Transolution Xliff Editor* (https://sourceforge.net/projects/eviltrans/files/Transolution/) A tool for editing XLIFF files.

Bibliography

Chamsi, Alain (2011) 'Selecting Enterprise Project Management Software: More Than Just a Build-or-buy Decision?', in Keiran J. Dunne and Elena S. Dunne (eds.) *Translation and Localization Project Management: The Art of the Possible*, Amsterdam and Philadelphia: John Benjamins Publishing Company, 51–68.

Chan, Erik (2021) 'What Is the Future of Translation Management Systems?', posted 5 May in *Blog*. Available at: www.translatefx.com/blog/everything-to-know-about-enterprise-translation-management-systems?lang=en?lang=en.

DePalma, Donald A. (2007) 'Managing Translation for Global Applications', *Galaxy Newsletter* 3. https://web.archive.org/web/20140112081935/www.gala-global.org/articles/managing-translation-global-applications-0.

DePalma, Donald A. (2011) 'The Attack of the TMS Patents', Lowell, Massachusetts, Common Sense Advisory, Inc. Abstract available at: https://web.archive.org/web/20120216125458/www.commonsenseadvisory.com/AbstractView.aspx?ArticleID=2171.

Google Help (2019) 'Google Translator Toolkit Has Shut Down'. Available at: https://support.google.com/answer/9464390.

Lawlor, Terry (2007) *Globalization Management Systems: Building a Better Business Case*, White Paper. Available at: www.sdl.com/products/translation-management.

Melby, Alan (1998) 'Eight Types of Translation Technology'. Available at: www.ttt.org/technology/8types.pdf.

Muegge, Uwe (2012) 'The Silent Revolution: Cloud-based Translation Management Systems', *TC World*, July 2012. Available at: www.csoftintl.com/Muegge_The_silent_systems.pdf.

MultiCorpora (2011) 'Other Available Products'. Available at: https://web.archive.org/web/20130329113230/http://www.multicorpora.com/en/products/other-available-products/.

Peris, Nick (2012) 'SDL WorldServer: Getting Started with Custom Reports'. Available at: http://localizationlocalization.wordpress.com/category/translation-management-systems.

Pielmeier, Hélène (2018) 'AI's Role in Project Management', posted 29 October. Available at: https://multilingual.com/articles/ais-role-in-project-management/.

Protemos (2020) 'The Future of Translation Project Management', posted 10 August 2020, in *Blog*. Available at: https://protemos.com/blog/the-future-of-translation-project-management.html.

Rico, Celia (2002) 'Translation and Project Management', *Translation Journal* 6(4). Available at: http://translationjournal.net/journal/22project.htm.

Sargent, Benjamin B. (2012) 'What's a TMS? And Why Isn't It a CMS?'. Available at: www.softwareceo.com/blog/entry/46120/What-s-a-TMS-And-Why-Isn-t-It-a-CMS.

Sargent, Benjamin B. and Donald A. DePalma (2007) 'How TMS Developers Pitch Their Wares to LSPs', *Galaxy Newsletter* 2007(4). Available at: https://web.archive.org/web/20110726072853/http://www.gala-global.org/articles/how-tms-developers-pitch-their-wares-lsps-0.

Sargent, Benjamin B. and Donald A. DePalma (2009) *Translation Management Takes Flight: Early Adopters Demonstrate Promise of TMS*, Lowell, MA: Common Sense Advisory, Inc.

Shaw, Duncan R. and Christopher P. Holland (2009) 'Strategy, Networks and Systems in the Global Translation Services Market', in Peter H. M. Vervest, Diederik W. van Liere, and Zheng Li (eds.) *The Network Experience: New Value from Smart Business Networks*, Berlin: Springer-Verlag, 99–118.

Stejskal, Jiri (2011) 'Translation Management System: Buy It or Build It?', *Translating and the Computer* 33, 17–18 November 2011, London, the United Kingdom. Available at: http://mt-archive.net/Aslib-2011-Stejskal.pdf.

Wilson, Barry and Alan Carlisle (1988) 'GEPRO – an Online System for Translation Management', *Terminologie et Traduction* 1, 115–18. Available at: https://op.europa.eu/en/publication-detail/-/publication/2e8184c0-2faa-4e2e-8f14-1dee52c36edd/language-en/format-PDF/source-229847173.

47

DEEP LEARNING AND TRANSLATION TECHNOLOGY

Siu Sai Cheong

Introduction

This chapter discusses deep learning and its application to translation technology. We first explain what deep learning is and how it works, with an introduction to key concepts, such as artificial neural networks, activation functions, loss functions, forward propagation, backpropagation and optimization. We then explore three approaches to machine translation with deep neural networks, which is followed by a discussion of the application of deep neural networks to speech translation, intersemiotic translation and translation memory and a review of noteworthy trends.

An Introduction to Deep Learning

Deep Learning and Artificial Intelligence

Deep learning is a type of machine learning, which is in turn an approach to artificial intelligence (Goodfellow *et al.* 2016), with common tasks such as classification, regression, tagging, denoising and sequence learning (Zhang *et al.* 2021). Loosely inspired by biological neurons (Goodfellow *et al.* 2016) and bringing together findings from such disciplines as mathematics, statistics and computer science, deep learning can learn any functions by using neural networks composed of multiple layers of artificial neurons (Zhang *et al.* 2021).

Different from other machine learning or artificial intelligence methods, deep learning focuses on the automatic identification of features (i.e. finding the right representations of the input data for downstream algorithms [Stevens *et al.* 2020]) from large amounts of training data, reducing the need for hand-crafted feature engineering (A. Zhang *et al.* 2021). The stacking of neuron layers allows the progressive identification of more complex features as the data or their intermediate representations pass through the layers (see, for example, Goodfellow *et al.* 2016).

Along with applications in computer vision (e.g. object detection [Jiao *et al.* 2019] and image classification [Algan and Ulusoy 2021]), prediction (e.g. time series prediction [Lim and Zohren 2021]) and gaming (e.g. MuZero [Schrittwieser *et al.* 2020], which masters Atari, Go, chess and shogi), deep learning has brought about dramatic changes to natural language processing, such as machine translation (e.g. Yang *et al.* 2020), speech recognition (Kumar *et al.* 2018), speech synthesis (Ning *et al.* 2019), sentiment analysis (L. Zhang *et al.* 2018), text classification (Q. Li,

DOI: 10.4324/9781003168348-50

Peng *et al.* 2020), named entity recognition (Yadav and Bethard 2018; J. Li, Sun *et al.* 2020), summarization (Dong 2018; Ma *et al.* 2020), visual question answering (Srivastava *et al.* 2019) and chatbots (H. Chen *et al.* 2017).

Recent Surge in Popularity of Deep Learning

As discussed in Goodfellow *et al.* (2016), the use of artificial neural networks can be traced back to the 1940s. Over the past decades, neural network research has emerged under different names. There was a boom in the 1940s–1960s (under the name of "cybernetics") and the 1980–1995 period (under the name of "connectionism"). It has seen a resurgence since 2006, with deep learning achieving impressive results in a number of tasks compared with other machine learning methods. The success of deep learning is attributed to the availability of larger datasets and more computational power, as well as improvements in the algorithms and software tools for the design and training of neural networks.

Main Tasks of Deep Learning

Key Components of Deep Learning

Similar to machine learning, to apply deep learning to a practical task, we need to have (1) data for training and evaluation, (2) a model for making predictions (a mathematical model specifies how the input is mapped to the output) and (3) an algorithm to measure the performance and enhance the results. In other words, to build a deep learning system, we need to collect data and design, train and evaluate models. This section further explains the tasks (see Goodfellow *et al.* 2016; Kelleher 2019; Zhang *et al.* 2021 for more information).

Data Collection

This refers to the collection of data and the building of datasets for training and evaluation. The data collected are often divided into the training set, the validation set (see "Model Training") and the test set (see "Model Evaluation"). The validation and test sets, which are used to monitor the training process, select hyperparameters or evaluate the model, should contain data not seen in the training set. For supervised learning tasks, which predict labels given input features (Zhang *et al.* 2021), the data comprise examples and labels (for a text classification task, for example, the text to be classified is an example, and the class it belongs to is a label).

Model Design

Model design is about defining the architecture of a model (in our case designing a neural network) for the mapping of the input to the output. The basic units of neural networks are neurons (Kelleher 2019), simple processing units that are interconnected to handle complex tasks or model different functions. A simple example is a perceptron, which receives multiple inputs, assigns different weights to them and computes a weighted average, which is fed into an activation function that adds non-linearity. Common activation functions include the hyperbolic tangent function and the rectified linear unit (ReLU). The output is then sent to other neurons connected to it. There are many interesting alternatives to perceptrons, and they are not necessarily analogous to biological neurons. Examples include long short-term memory and gated recurrent units (see "Recurrent Neural Networks Explained").

A network consists of multiple layers of neurons. Different neural network architectures (see, for example, the sections "Recurrent Neural Networks for Translation", "Convolutional Neural Networks for Translation" and "Self-attention Neural Networks for Translation") emerge as a result of the use of various types of neurons or processing units and the diverse ways in which they are connected. A simple example is a "multilayer perceptron" (also known as a feedforward neural network), comprising layers of perceptrons, as discussed. More specifically, we have three types of layers: The layer that receives the input is called the input layer. The one that gives the final output is the output layer. The ones between the input and output layers are the hidden layers. The word "deep" in "deep learning" signifies the use of multiple hidden layers in a network for the identification of (increasingly) complex features in the data.

Model Training

This refers to the process by which the computer "learns" from data, finding the "right" set of weights (also known as parameters) in the neurons for transforming the inputs and intermediate results into good predictions.

The first step is forward propagation. The training data, which are often divided into batches (we use the term "batch size" to denote the number of examples in each batch), are fed into the model, in which the weights are initialized randomly. The input data are processed with reference to the weights and activation functions of the neurons, and the intermediate results are processed and passed through layers of neurons until the output layer is reached for the generation of the prediction.

The second step is the computation of the loss function. The predicted values are compared with the "ground truth" (i.e. the labels in the training data) with reference to a loss function (a measure of how good the model is). For numerical prediction, we can use the squared error to calculate the difference between the predicted and true values. For classification (e.g. the output layer is a softmax function that generates a list of values representing the predicted probabilities of different classes, as in the case of machine translation), we can consider the cross-entropy loss.

The third step is to find the contribution of different weights in the network to these differences, so that we can later adjust the weights in the direction where the loss value can be reduced or minimized. This is done by backpropagation: the gradients of the loss function with respect to the weights are calculated (starting from the output layer), and by using the chain rule in multivariate calculus, they are "propagated" back to the previous layers of neurons for the computation of the corresponding gradients.

The fourth step is optimization, which is the updating of the weights based on the results of the previous step. For each weight, the actual amount of adjustment is determined by the gradient and learning rate (which indicates the size of the weight update at each step). The learning rate should be neither too large nor too small; we can have either a constant learning rate or a dynamic learning rate (e.g. a gradual increase in the learning rate at the beginning of training and a gradual decrease afterwards). There are various optimization algorithms for the adjustment of weights, such as stochastic gradient descent and ADAM (Kingma and Ba 2014).

The previous steps (i.e. forward propagation, loss calculation, gradient computation and optimization) are repeated until a predefined training criterion is satisfied, for example, when the pre-defined number of epochs (i.e. the number of times all training data are seen) or number of weight update steps is reached or when there are signs of overfitting (i.e. the model may start to "memorize" the training data and not generalize well to unseen data), such as a drop in training loss with a growing validation loss, which is computed with reference to the difference between the predicted and true values using the validation data that are not visible in the training data.

From the previous discussion, it is clear that the final results of training (or the performance of the trained model) depend on a wide range of factors, such as the training data used, network architecture (how the model is designed) and hyperparameters (e.g. the learning rate and the number of epochs or training steps). The hyperparameters are predefined before training, while the parameters are "trained" and adjusted during training with reference to the loss values and gradients.

Model Evaluation

After training, a model is ready to be used for prediction (e.g. classification of images/text or prediction of the next target text word, as in the case of machine translation). The performance of the model can be evaluated using a test dataset, with the prediction results compared with the true values of the samples in the dataset. This assessment is conducted with reference to an evaluation benchmark or metric, depending on the nature of the task in question. Common evaluation benchmarks or metrics in natural language processing include BLEU (Papineni *et al.* 2002; often used in machine translation) and GLUE (Wang *et al.* 2018; for a number of tasks relevant to natural language understanding).

An Overview of Neural Machine Translation

Popularity of Neural Machine Translation

The main application of deep learning to machine translation is neural machine translation (NMT), which encodes the source text and generates the target text by training and using deep neural networks. NMT has been popular since the mid-2010s, when it was shown to outperform its predecessors (e.g. statistical machine translation; see "NMT and Conventional Machine Translation Methods"), and major machine translation developers, such as Google, Microsoft and Baidu, began to adopt NMT in their products, along with a surging number of papers on NMT (Stahlberg 2020). Prior to the rise of NMT, early attempts explored the possibilities of incorporating neural networks into statistical machine translation systems (e.g. language modeling [Bengio *et al.* 2003; Vaswani *et al.* 2013], word alignment [Yang *et al.* 2013], phrase reordering [Li *et al.* 2014], feature score combination [Huang *et al.* 2015]), as opposed to end-to-end NMT systems mapping natural languages directly using neural networks (Deng and Liu 2018).

NMT and Conventional Machine Translation Methods

Conventionally, common approaches to machine translation are rule-based machine translation (RBMT), example-based machine translation (EBMT) and statistical machine translation (SMT) (Bhattacharyya 2015).

RBMT, an early approach to machine translation dating back to the 1950s, is about the design and application of manually designed rules for different tasks of automatic translation generation, such as the syntactic and semantic analysis of the source text and transfer of expressions and sentence structures from the source language to the target language. RBMT can be further divided into direct machine translation, transfer machine translation and interlingual machine translation (Hutchins 2007), which differ in the depth of linguistic analysis.

EBMT, first proposed by Nagao (1984), focuses on automatic translation by "analogy", which involves the retrieval and recombination of bilingual expressions, similar to the way foreign language learners translate simple sentences. More specifically, instead of using rules, it puts an emphasis on the use of bilingual examples, such as expressions, segments and sentences. Key steps include the collection of bilingual examples, the retrieval of bilingual examples based on the input and the recombination of the examples for the generation of the target text. For more information, see Hutchins (2005).

SMT, which was introduced in the late 1980s and early 1990s (Brown *et al.* 1988 and 1993) and later became the dominant approach until the mid-2010s, builds mathematical models for translation based on a large volume of linguistic data (e.g. parallel sentences). Featuring the use of language models and translation models together with language/translation features predetermined by the developer, SMT aims to find sequences of target language expressions that are most likely to be the "correct" translations by maximizing the language and translation probabilities (see Ney (2005) and Koehn (2009) for more information).

Similar to other deep learning applications, NMT does not require the manual crafting of rules. Like EBMT and SMT, NMT requires data, which are however used for the training of artificial neural networks (i.e. the "learning" of a set of weights that can generate results minimizing the loss, as discussed previously for deep learning applications in general) rather than for the retrieval and recombination of translation examples as in EMBT or for the building of models of language or translation features as in SMT. In NMT, as with other deep learning applications, we design the architecture of neural networks and specify hyperparameters instead of focusing on feature engineering.

Key Concepts of NMT

To discuss the general working principle of NMT, formally, we denote the source sentence x with m elements as $x_1,...,x_m$ and the target sentence y with n elements as $y_1,...,y_n$. NMT computes the conditional probability of translating x into y as follows:

$$p(\boldsymbol{y} \mid \boldsymbol{x}) = \prod_{t=1}^{n} p(y_t \mid \boldsymbol{y}_{<t}, \boldsymbol{x})$$

where $\boldsymbol{y}_{<t} = y_1,...,y_{t-1}$

The dominant approach to NMT is the use of the encoder-decoder architecture. More specifically, the source elements in x are represented using word embeddings, which are high-dimensional vectors in a continuous space that are intended to capture the meaning of the tokens. Such embeddings can be obtained through an embedding matrix or pre-trained word embedding models using methods such as CBOW and skip-gram (see Mikolov *et al.* 2018). The word embeddings are passed on to the encoder for the computation of the intermediate representation $\boldsymbol{z} = z_1,...,z_m$ of the source sentence. The target elements in $\boldsymbol{y}$ are generated (usually one after the other) by the decoder with reference to $\boldsymbol{z}$ and other inputs, such as the internal representation of the previous target element(s), until the production of a special end-of-sentence token.

The encoder-decoder is typically trained on parallel training corpora, with weight initialization and weight updates similar to the training process discussed in "Key Concepts of NMT". During the training process, we compute the loss (e.g. the cross-entropy loss) by comparing the predictions with the reference translations in the training data. Training stops after reaching a fixed number of steps or epochs or meeting other predefined criteria.

There are different ways to implement the encoder-decoder architecture, and they differ in how they model and compute $p(y_j \mid \boldsymbol{y}_{<j}, \boldsymbol{x})$ (Stahlberg 2020). In the next three sections

("Recurrent Neural Networks for Translation", "Convolutional Neural Networks for Translation" and "Self-attention Neural Networks for Translation"), we will discuss the following three main approaches to building the encoder-decoder: recurrent neural networks, convolutional neural networks and self-attention neural networks.

Recurrent Neural Networks for Translation

Recurrent Neural Networks Explained

Recurrent neural networks (RNNs) generalize feedforward neural networks to sequences (Sutskever *et al.* 2014) with a hidden state *h*. Formally, given a sequence of inputs *x*, at each time step *t*, the network computes the hidden state h_t based on the current input x_t and the previous hidden state h_{t-1}, which encodes the context of the previous inputs. Formally, we have

$$h_t = f\left(x_t, h_{t-1}\right)$$

where *f* is a non-linear activation function (Cho *et al.* 2014) and the output y_t can be obtained by applying a linear transformation to h_t.

The function *f* refers to a simple linear transformation with an activation function (e.g. the logistic sigmoid function) in the vanilla RNN, which may have the problem of vanishing gradients given long input sequences requiring the backpropagation of many time steps for weight updates (Koehn 2020).

To address this issue of long-term dependencies, we can define *f* as a long short-term memory (LSTM) or gated recurrent unit (GRU) network. LSTM networks (Hochreiter and Schmidhuber 1997) maintain memory states and use three gates (the input gate, the forget gate and the output gate) to regulate how much new information is accepted, how much old information (from previous time steps) is retained (or forgotten) and how the information in the memory is sent to the next layer. GRU (Cho *et al.* 2014), with only two gates (the reset gate and the update gate) and no separate memory states, is a "simpler alternative" to LSTM (Koehn 2020).

RNNs have been applied to NMT for encoding and decoding given their ability to model the dependencies between input tokens, especially after the application of LSTM and GRU networks, which facilitate the modeling of long-term dependencies. Examples include Sutskever *et al.* (2014), Bahdanau *et al.* (2015), Luong *et al.* (2015) and Wu *et al.* (2016).

Encoding With RNNs

An RNN encoder, comprising a stack of RNN (usually LSTM and GRU) layers, reads the source sentence *x* one token at a time and generates the source sentence representation *z*. The tokens of the source sentence can be read from left to right (i.e. from the beginning to the end of the sentence using a unidirectional encoder), from right to left (i.e. from the end to the beginning using a reversed unidirectional encoder) or in both directions (using a bidirectional encoder) (see, for example, Sutskever *et al.* (2014) for the use of unidirectional encoders and Bahdanau *et al.* (2015) and Wu *et al.* (2016) for the bidirectional encoder). For unidirectional encoders, the hidden states h_t (left-to-right, also known as the forward hidden states) and h_t (right-to-left, also known as the backward hidden states) at time step *t* are computed as follows:

$$\vec{h}_t = \vec{f}\left(x_i, \vec{h}_{t-1}\right)$$

and

$$\bar{h}_t = \bar{f}\left(x_i, \bar{h}_{t+1}\right)$$

where $\vec{f}$ and $\bar{f}$ are usually LSTM or GRU (Bahdanau *et al.* 2015; Stahlberg 2020). Combining the results in both directions, the bidirectional encoder computes the hidden states h_t, which consider both the past (preceding words) and future contexts, with a focus on the surrounding parts of the t th token in the source sequence (Bahdanau *et al.* 2015), as follows:

$$h_t = [\vec{h}_t^{\top}; \bar{h}_t^{\top}]^{\top}$$

where $[;]$ is vector concatenation and $\top$ is vector/matrix transpose.

For the generation of the internal representation z of x based on h_t, we have

$$z = q\left(\{h_1, \ldots, h_i\}\right)$$

where q is a nonlinear function (Bahdanau *et al.* 2015). Some RNN encoders use a fixed-length vector representing the entire sentence (e.g. Sutskever *et al.* [2014] computed z as $q\left(\{h_1, \ldots, h_i\}\right) = h_i$, i.e., the use of the hidden state of the RNN encoder at the last time step), while others use a variable-length representation that takes into account the hidden states at different time steps (e.g. Bahdanau *et al.* 2015) using an attention mechanism, which has become popular in RNN-based NMT systems and will be further discussed in the next section.

Decoding With RNNs

RNN decoders consist of a stack of RNN layers generating a hidden state s_t based on the previous hidden state s_{t-1}, an embedding of the last predicted token y_{t-1} and the source sentence representation z from the encoder. The hidden state is used for the prediction of the next target token through a probability distribution over all target output symbols that is computed by a softmax layer (Y. Wu *et al.* 2016). Depending on the form of the internal representation z, the actual design of the RNN decoder varies.

Formally, the conditional probability $p(y_t \mid y_{<t}, z)$ for predicting the next target token y_t at time step t given the source sentence representation z is modeled as follows:

$$p(y_t \mid y_{<t}, z) = g\left(s_{t-1}, y_{t-1}, z\right)$$

where the function g, which can also be defined as a function with only two parameters s_{t-1} and z (i.e. $p(y_t \mid y_{<t}, z) = g\left(s_{t-1}, z\right)$), comprises LSTM or GRU layers (typically the choice matches the encoder; see Koehn 2020) and a softmax function (and possibly other linear transformations) and computes the probability distribution.

If z is a fixed-length vector, it can be used to initialize the decoder state or fed into g for the generation of each target token (Cho *et al.* 2014). For variable-length representations, an attention mechanism is applied for the computation of z as a weighted sum of annotations $h_1, \ldots, h_i$, the weights of which are known as attention scores. The scores, which indicate how relevant an input token is to the production of the next word (Koehn 2020) and allow the decoder to focus on different parts of the source sentence when generating the target sentence (Gehring *et al.* 2017), can be computed by comparing each annotation with the previous hidden state, for example, using additive attention (Bahdanau *et al.* 2015) or dot-product attention (Luong *et al.* 2015).

Formally, the first step is to compute the attention scores. Given h_m with $m=[1,i]$, for dot-product attention, we have

$$score\left(s_{t-1}, h_m\right) = s_{t-1}^\top h_m,$$

and for additive attention, we have

$$score\left(s_{t-1}, h_m\right) = v^\top \tanh\left(Ws_{t-1} + Uh_m\right)$$

with the weight vector v and weight matrices W and U. The second step is to normalize the attention value using the softmax function so that the scores over all tokens in the source sentence add up to one (Koehn 2020). We denote the normalized score as a, as an element of a variable-length alignment vector of i dimensions:

$$a\left(s_{t-1}, h_m\right) = \frac{exp\left(score\left(s_{t-1}, h_m\right)\right)}{\sum_{k=1}^{i} exp\left(score\left(s_{t-1}, h_k\right)\right)}.$$

The third step is to compute z given the alignment vector as weights:

$$z = q\left(\{h_1, \ldots, h_i\}\right) = \sum_{m=1}^{i} a\left(s_{t-1}, h_m\right) h_m.$$

In our case here, z is also referred to as the context vector at step t. Given the context vector, the decoder produces an attentional hidden state (or attentional vector) s_t, which is passed on to the softmax layer for the predictive distribution.

Convolutional Neural Networks for Translation

Convolutional Neural Networks Explained

Convolutional neural networks (CNNs), a special family of neural networks containing convolutional layers, have been widely used in computer vision, such as image recognition and object detection (Zhang *et al.* 2021). Consisting of convolutional layers, CNNs encode input sequences by creating representations of words with their left and right contexts using a limited window (i.e. kernel). (Gehring *et al.* 2017; Koehn 2020; Zhang *et al.* 2021).

Formally, as discussed in Stahlberg (2020), given an input sequence $x = x_1, \ldots, x_i$ comprising i vectors in M dimensions (i.e. $x_d \in \mathbb{R}^M$ for $d = [1, i]$, with the d-axis and M referred to in the literature as spatial dimension and channels, respectively), a standard one-dimensional convolutional layer for the generation of a sequence of N-dimensional vector y of the same length i is defined as follows:

$$y_{d,n} = \sum_{m=1}^{M} \sum_{k=0}^{K-1} w_{kM+m,n} x_{d+k,m}$$

where K is the width of the kernel, $w_{kM+m,n}$ refers to the element in the $(kM+n)$th row and nth column of the weight matrix $W \in \mathbb{R}^{KM \times N}$ and $x_{d+k,m}$ and $y_{d,n}$ represent the mth element ($m \in [1, M]$) of the $(d+k)$th input vector and the nth element ($n \in [1, N]$) of the dth output vector, respectively. Note that the inner sum and the outer sum represent spatial dependency and cross-channel dependency respectively, and they can be factored out as pointwise and depthwise convolutions.

CNNs enable parallelization over the elements in the input sequence as they reduce sequential computation (Gehring *et al.* 2017; Stahlberg 2020). For the generation of representations of input sequences, we can increase the effective context size by stacking multiple layers, where nearby input elements interact at lower levels and distant elements at higher levels, and this hierarchical structure provides a shorter path for capturing long-term dependencies, compared with chain modelling using RNNs. (Gehring *et al.* 2017).

NMT With CNNs

CNN-driven NMT systems perform encoding and decoding with CNNs. According to Koehn (2020), Kalchbrenner and Blunsom (2013) proposed the first modern end-to-end NMT model using CNNs instead of RNNs. Their CNN model encodes the input by merging the representations of input tokens into a single vector through the iterative use of convolutional kernels and reverses the process when generating the output.

Gehring *et al.* (2017) proposed an alternative architecture for CNN-driven NMT. The model adopts CNNs and the attention mechanism. For encoding, given the word embeddings of an input sequence, position embeddings are added so that the model is aware of the position of each of the tokens. After that, the CNN encoder, which is a stack of blocks comprising a one-dimensional convolution and gated linear units (GLUs, a nonlinear function implementing a gating mechanism [Dauphin *et al.* 2017]), computes intermediate states based on a fixed number of elements in the input. For decoding, the CNN decoder, which is another stack of blocks with a linear transformation and a softmax layer for the computation of a probability distribution over the possible target tokens, features (1) the combination of the encoder states and input word embeddings, (2) the use of masks to avoid the network's access to the future context and (3) the introduction of a separate attention mechanism to each decoder layer (Koehn 2020; Stahlberg 2020).

Wu *et al.* (2019) proposed lightweight convolutions (LightConv) and dynamic convolutions (DynamicConv) for NMT. Instead of using standard convolutions, both methods adopt depthwise convolutions, which perform convolutions independently over every channel and reduce the number of parameters. LightConv uses kernels with context element weights that remain unchanged across time steps and shares certain output channels (with weights normalized across the temporal dimension using the softmax function). Built on LightConv, DynamicConv uses kernels that vary across time steps. The weights assigned to context elements change over time and do not depend on the entire context. The architecture of the CNN encoder-decoder is similar to that of self-attention models to be discussed in the next section, except that the self-attention modules are replaced by LightConv or DynamicConv modules, which (1) apply an input projection to map the input from dimension d to $2d$; (2) use a GLU, similar to Gehring *et al.* (2017); (3) perform LightConv or DynamicConv; and (4) apply an output projection to the results of LightConv or DynamicConv.

Self-Attention Neural Networks for Translation

Self-Attention NMT Explained

As discussed in "Recurrent Neural Networks for Translation", the attention mechanism can bridge the encoder and the decoder. Here, in self-attention NMT, the mechanism is also used

(1) within the encoder for the generation of z for the building of context-aware word embeddings, with reference to other words in the source sentence, and (2) within the decoder for the consideration of the current translation history (Stahlberg 2020). Such self-attention neural models, which introduce short paths between distant words and reduce the amount of sequential computation (Stahlberg 2020), were first used in the transformer (Vaswani *et al.* 2017) and have become the standard architecture for NMT because of its translation quality (Stahlberg 2020; see, for example, Barrault *et al.* 2019, 2020) and facilitated the generation of contextualized word embeddings like BERT (Devlin *et al.* 2019).

Multi-Head Attention With Queries, Keys and Values

To better understand the extension of attention to encoding and decoding, we can consider attention in terms of queries, keys and values, using the terminology of Vaswani *et al.* (2017) and Stahlberg (2020). We can view attention as a mapping of n query vectors q to their output vectors through a memory of m pairs of key vectors k and value vectors v, where q, k and v are all assumed to have the same dimension d here and can be stacked into matrices $Q \in \mathbb{R}^{n \times d}$, $K \in \mathbb{R}^{m \times d}$ and $V \in \mathbb{R}^{m \times d}$ respectively. For each q, we compute a weighted sum of the value vectors in V, and the weights are based on the similarity scores between q and the key vectors in K. Formally, the attention given Q, K and V is calculated as follows:

$$attention(Q,K,V) = (scoremat(Q,K))V$$

where $scoremat(Q,K) \in \mathbb{R}^{n \times m}$ is the matrix of similarity scores, normalized by the softmax function for each column. Using this notation, if we consider the dot-product attention we discussed previously, we can compute the score matrix as follows:

$$scoremat(Q,K) = softmax\left(QK^{\top} \cdot scale\right)$$

with $scale = 1$ for Luong *et al.* (2015, with $q = s_j$ and $k = v = h_i$) and $scale = \dfrac{1}{\sqrt{d}}$ for Vaswani *et al.* (2017), which uses scaled dot-product attention.

A noteworthy feature of the self-attention model is the use of multi-head attention: instead of having only one attention operation, we perform H attention operations (H is known as the number of attention heads). For each attention head (mathematically, $head_h \in \mathbb{R}^{n \times \frac{d}{H}}$, where $h \in [1, H]$), we apply linear transformations to Q, K and V and compute attention:

$$head_h = attention(W_Q Q, W_K K, W_V V) = attention(Q_h, K_h, V_h)$$

where $Q_h \in \mathbb{R}^{n \times \frac{d}{H}}$, $K_h \in \mathbb{R}^{m \times \frac{d}{H}}$ and $V_h \in \mathbb{R}^{m \times \frac{d}{H}}$. The output of the multi-head attention is a linear transformation of the concatenation of the heads:

$$multihead(Q,K,V) = W_{multihead}\left[head_1; head_2; ...; head_H\right]$$

with the weight matrix $W_{multihead} \in \mathbb{R}^{d \times d}$. Based on the discussion of multi-head attention with queries, keys and values, we will discuss the design of self-attention encoders and decoders in "Self-attention Encoder" and "Self-attention Decoder".

Self-Attention Encoder

Similar to CNNs, we use positional encodings to make word embeddings sensitive to position. Here trigonometric functions of different frequencies are used:

$$posenc\left(pos,dim\right) = f\left(pos \cdot 10000^{-\frac{dim}{d}}\right)$$

where *pos* is the absolute position of a word in the sentence, *d* is the size of the word embedding with $dim \in [1,d]$ and *f* is either a sine function (when *dim* is even) or a cosine function (when *dim* is odd).

The self-attention encoder is a stack of encoding blocks. Given an input matrix X_{input} of size $n \times d$, which is either the positional encodings (for the first encoding block) or the output of the previous encoding block (for the blocks thereafter), each block first performs multi-head attention with the query, key and value projections of X_{input}. The block computes $X_{intermediate}$ with (1) the layer normalization of the result of multi-head attention and (2) a residual connection:

$$X_{intermediate} = layernorm\left(multihead\left(X_{input}, X_{input}, X_{input}\right) + X_{input}\right).$$

The intermediate result is then passed to a feedforward network comprising two position-wise feedforward layers F_{x1} and F_{x2} (in the form $Wx+b$) with a ReLU activation in between, followed by layer normalization and a residual connection for the generation of the output of the encoding block. Formally, we have

$$X_{output} = layernorm(F_{x2}\left(ReLU\left(F_{x1}\left(X_{intermediate}\right)\right) + X_{intermediate}\right).$$

The output X_{output} is then passed on to the next encoding block or the decoder for further processing.

Self-Attention Decoder

The structure of the self-attention decoder is similar to that of the encoder in terms of the use of positional encodings. As a stack of multiple decoding blocks, the decoder differs from the encoder in the following ways: First, the positional encodings here are based on the target language tokens generated. Second, each of its decoding blocks comprises two self-attention modules instead of one as in the encoding block.

More specifically, given an input matrix *Y* (either the positional encodings [for the first decoding block] or the output of the previous decoding block [for the blocks thereafter]), each decoding block first performs masked multi-head self-attention with future decoder states masked to prevent computation conditioned on future tokens. The block computes the first intermediate result $Y_{intermediate(1)}$ with (1) the layer normalization of the output of the masked self-attention and (2) a residual connection:

$$Y_{intermediate(1)} = layernorm\left(multihead\left(Y_{input}, Y_{input}, Y_{input}\right) + Y_{input}\right).$$

To utilize the information from the encoder, the block performs the second multi-head self-attention using the first intermediate result $Y_{intermediate(1)}$ (for the computation of Q_h) together with the output of the self-attention encoder $X_{output(encoder)}$ (for the computation of K_h and V_h). For the computation of the second intermediate output, the second self-attention is followed by layer normalization and a residual connection:

$$Y_{intermediate(2)} = layernorm\left(multihead\left(Y_{intermediate(1)}, X_{output(encoder)}, X_{output(encoder)}\right) + Y_{intermediate(1)}\right).$$

Similar to the encoding block, the second intermediate result $Y_{intermediate(2)}$ is then passed to a two-layered position-wise feedforward network (F_{y1} and F_{y2} in the following; again, in the form $Wx+b$) with an ReLU activation in between:

$$Y_{output} = layernorm(F_{y2}\left(ReLU\left(F_{y1}\left(Y_{intermediate(2)}\right)\right)\right)) + Y_{intermediate(2)}.$$

The output Y_{output} is then passed to the next decoding block. For the last decoding block, similar to RNN and CNN decoders, a linear transformation is applied to the output, which is then passed to a softmax layer for the generation of the output probabilities.

Other Transformer Architectures

Many variants of the self-attention model have been proposed since the emergence of the transformer. For example, Transformer-XL (Dai *et al.* 2019) uses relevant positions for the computation of positional encodings. Other approaches include the use of fixed patterns, learnable patterns, memory and low-rank approximations or kernels; see Tay *et al.* (2020) for more information.

Deep Learning for Other Translation-Related Applications

In addition to text translation, application of deep learning to areas such as speech and image processing has also facilitated the development of other translation-related tools. The following are three noteworthy areas.

Deep Learning and Speech Translation

Speech translation refers to the translation of speech in the source language into text or speech in the target language, with three modes of delivery: the batch mode (translating a recorded speech as a whole), the consecutive mode (translating utterances like consecutive interpreting) and the simultaneous mode (translating an input audio stream in real time like simultaneous interpreting) (Sperber and Paulik 2020). Generally, there are two approaches to building speech translation systems: (1) cascaded systems and (2) direct systems.

Cascaded systems usually consist of three parts: (1) automatic speech recognition (ASR) for speech-to-text conversion, (2) text-to-text machine translation and (3) speech synthesis for text-to-speech conversion (applicable to speech-to-speech translation systems). Deep learning has contributed not only to machine translation, as discussed, but also to ASR and speech synthesis. For ASR, Baevski *et al.* (2020), for example, proposed a model comprising CNN and the transformer for self-supervised learning on unlabeled raw audio data, followed by fine-tuning on a small set of labelled data instead of thousands of hours of transcribed speech. There have also been encouraging results in speech synthesis, including the use of RNNs (e.g. Shen *et al.* 2018), the transformer (Ren *et al.* 2019) and generative adversarial networks (GANs, proposed by Goodfellow *et al.* [2014], which consist of a generative model capturing the data distribution and a discriminative model estimating whether a sample is from the distribution; see, for example, Kong *et al.* [2020] for their use in speech synthesis).

Cascade systems may be susceptible to error propagation (e.g. ASR errors leading to translation errors), modeling mismatches between components (e.g. spoken language modeling for ASR but written language modeling for machine translation) and loss of speech information (e.g. unawareness of prosody by machine translation) (Sperber and Paulik 2020). To help address these issues, direct systems perform end-to-end speech translation. Examples include (1) the sequence-to-sequence model proposed by Jia *et al.* (2019), which consists of an attention-based network generating target spectrograms and a vocoder converting the spectrograms to time-domain waveforms, and (2) the tandem connectionist encoding network proposed by Wang, Wu *et al.* (2020), which comprises two connected encoders and a decoder with an attention module. However, direct systems often require large-scale end-to-end datasets, which are not always readily available, and the use of augmented data may help (e.g. the use of automatic translation results or synthesized speech) (Sperber and Paulik 2020).

Deep Learning and Intersemiotic Translation

According to Jakobson (1959/2012), intersemiotic translation refers to "an interpretation of verbal signs by means of signs of nonverbal sign systems". Considering this "a change of medium" (Munday 2009), we can extend its scope by including the conversion of nonverbal signs to verbal signs, which allows us to explore the contribution of deep learning to cross-modal translation from the following perspectives:

Multimodal machine translation (MMT) refers to machine translation with multimodal inputs (e.g. given an image and its source language description, an MMT system translates the description into the target language) (Barrault *et al.* 2018). Calixto *et al.* (2017), Ive *et al.* (2019) and Yao and Wan (2020) proposed the use of RNNs (with pre-trained CNNs), the transformer and a multimodal transformer (with an "image-aware" attention mechanism instead of the direct encoding of image features), respectively. The use of cross-modal contextual input in text translation is beneficial for the translation of subtitles and manga (see, for example, Hinami *et al.* 2021).

Image captioning is the verbal description of the content of an image (Cornia *et al.* 2020). RNN, CNN and transformer-based architectures have been used for image-to-text conversion with (1) a combination of models for image understanding and text generation (Hossain *et al.* 2018) or (2) visual-language pre-training models, featuring the use of shared transformer networks for encoding and decoding (e.g. Zhou *et al.* 2020). See X. Li *et al.* (2020), Cornia *et al.* (2020) and Zhang *et al.* (2021) for more examples.

Video captioning refers to the automatic explanation of the content of video frames using natural language (Islam *et al.* 2021). Inspired by deep image captioning, deep learning-driven video captioning adopts sequence learning methods that comprise two phases similar to NMT: the encoding of visual features (e.g. using CNNs) and the decoding/generation of captions (e.g. using RNNs) (Z. Zhang *et al.* 2020; Singh *et al.* 2020).

Text-to-image conversion synthesizes images from textual descriptions. Since Mansimov *et al.* (2015), there has been much work on the creation of images conditioned on text captions using, for example, GANs (e.g. Reed *et al.* 2016). More recently, Ramesh *et al.* (2021) trained a transformer with 12 billion parameters on 250 million image-text pairs for the autoregressive modeling of text and image tokens as a single data stream.

Text-to-music conversion is music generation conditioned on lyrics. For example, Dhariwal *et al.* (2020) proposed JukeBox, adopting the VQ-VAE architecture (Razavi *et al.* 2019) and transformer with sparse attention (Child *et al.* 2019). Given inputs such as lyrics, genres and artist style, this model generates music as raw audio rather than piano rolls specifying the pitch and length of each note as in conventional symbolic generation.

Deep Learning and Translation Memories

Translation memories (TMs) (Simard 2020; Ranasinghe *et al.* 2020) consist of translation units (TUs), which are pairs of text segments (usually sentences) in the source and target languages, to facilitate the reuse of previously translated segments. First proposed in the late 1970s, TMs have become popular among translators since their commercialization in the early 1990s (Arthern 1978; Zaretskaya *et al.* 2017). TMs compute the similarity between the segments to be translated and the translation units in the database and identify the following cases: exact matches (TUs identical to the source segments are found), context matches (exact matches with identical contexts are found, often indicated by the presence of the same neighboring sentences), fuzzy matches (similar TUs are found, with similarity scores higher than the threshold) and no matches (no similar TUs are found).

Deep learning offers new ways to compute the similarity score. Conventionally, we calculate the similarity using edit distance measures, which may not be able to identify semantically similar but syntactically different segments (Ranasinghe *et al.* 2020). The generation of sentence encoding using neural networks provides an alternative: instead of directly comparing the segments to be translated with the source language segments in TUs, we compare their sentence embeddings generated by the NMT encoder.

Ranasinghe *et al.* (2020), for example, proposed the use of universal sentence encoder (Cer *et al.* 2018). One of the models provided by the sentence encoder uses the transformer. The output of the transformer encoder after multiple rounds of attention computation is a list of context-sensitive word embeddings, which are averaged for the generation of sentence-level embeddings for sentence comparison. Formally, given two source sentences A and B with sentence embeddings $a \in \mathbb{R}^n$ and $b \in \mathbb{R}^n$ respectively, the similarity score is computed using cosine similarity:

$$cossim(a,b) = \frac{a \cdot b}{|a||b|} = \frac{\sum_{i=1}^{n} a_i b_i}{\sqrt{\sum_{i=1}^{n} a_i^2} \sqrt{\sum_{i=1}^{n} b_i^2}}$$

Their experiment showed that sentence encodings outperformed simple edit distance.

Other Noteworthy Trends

In addition to the design and use of neural network architectures and the exploration of new application areas discussed previously, there has been much research on ways to enhance natural language processing, model training and inference, thus contributing to the advancement of deep learning for translation and cross-lingual communication. The following are notable examples:

Use of subwords: The division of the input sequence into subword units rather than words can help reduce the size of a translation model (by reducing the vocabulary size) and deal with rare words or out-of-vocabulary items. Possible approaches include word-piece modeling (Wu *et al.* 2016), byte-pair encoding (Sennrich *et al.* 2016b), sentence-piece modeling (Kudo and Richardson 2018) and byte-level subwords (Wang, Cho *et al.* 2020).

Multilingual NMT: Instead of building translation engines between one source language and one target language, multilingual NMT focuses on the development of a single model between "as many languages as possible", featuring exposure to diverse languages, which may result in better generalization and enhance machine translation for low-resource languages (Dabre *et al.* 2020). Recent examples include Y. Liu *et al.* (2020) and Fan *et al.* (2020).

Decoding methods: When decoding, NMT requires an effective method to search for target sentences (i.e. the "best" combinations of target language tokens) to maximize the translation probability (see Gu *et al.* 2017; Stahlberg 2020). Common ways include greedy search (using the candidate with the highest probability at each time step), beam search (keeping multiple highest scoring candidates at each step, with variants such as dynamic beam allocation [Post and Vilar 2018]) and other methods like re-ranking (Liu *et al.* 2018).

Data augmentation: There are ways to enhance NMT models using monolingual data, which are more readily available than bilingual documents (Edunov *et al.* 2018). One of these methods is back translation (Sennrich *et al.* 2016a), which augments parallel training corpora by translating monolingual target language data into the source language, probably with the addition of noise (Edunov *et al.* 2018) or tags (Caswell *et al.* 2019). This method has been used in the development of different systems, such as Ng *et al.* (2019), Meng *et al.* (2020), L. Wu *et al.* (2020) and S. Wu *et al.* (2020). Other ways of using monolingual data are discussed in Edunov (2018) and Meng *et al.* (2020).

Use of multiple models: The use of multiple translation models, as opposed to a single set of trained weights, can help improve the accuracy of translation (see, for example, Liu *et al.* 2018). Two common approaches are model ensembling and checkpoint averaging. The former involves the use of multiple neural networks by the decoder, which averages their predictions of different networks (e.g. Sutskever *et al.* 2014; Cromieres *et al.* 2016; Ng *et al.* 2019), and the latter is the combination of several recent checkpoints into a single model (e.g. Popel and Bojar 2018; Ng *et al.* 2019) to reduce small fluctuations in the training process (Stahlberg 2020).

Non-autoregressive NMT: As opposed to the generation of output words one by one (i.e.

$p(\boldsymbol{y} \mid \boldsymbol{x}) = \prod_{t=1}^{n} p(y_t \mid \boldsymbol{y}_{<t}, \boldsymbol{x})$, also known as autoregressive NMT), as discussed, non-autoregressive

NMT aims to generates target sentence tokens in parallel to reduce inference time (i.e.

$p(\boldsymbol{y} \mid \boldsymbol{x}) = \prod_{t=1}^{n} p(y_t \mid \boldsymbol{x}))$ (see Gu *et al.* 2017). Recent examples include the Levenshtein transformer

(Gu *et al.* 2019), which is a sequence generation model comprising insertion and deletion operations, and EDITOR (Xu and Carpuat 2021), which generates new sequences by introducing a reposition operation and editing hypotheses iteratively.

Deeper networks: Increasing the number of layers of the encoder and decoder may lead to better results as in many other deep learning tasks, but there may be bottlenecks for architectures like the transformer because of issues such as gradient vanishing, which can be mitigated by decreasing parameter variance in the initialization phase, reducing the output variance of residual connections, using merged attention sublayers and adopting adaptive initialization methods for the stabilization of early stage training (see Zhang *et al.* 2019; L. Liu *et al.* 2020; X. Liu *et al.* 2020).

Document-level NMT: Unlike sentence-based translation systems, which may degrade the coherence and cohesiveness of the translation as a result of neglecting the discourse connections between sentences, document-level NMT systems take into account the document context by employing methods such as sentence concatenation (Tiedemann and Scherrer 2017), hierarchical attention networks (Miculicich *et al.* 2018), capsule networks (Z. Yang *et al.* 2019) and discourse structure modeling (J. Chen *et al.* 2020).

Domain adaptation: Given that general-purpose translation systems tend to perform poorly when translating domain-specific documents (Chu and Wang 2018), domain adaptation, which focuses on the adaptation of machine translation systems to new domains (Freitag and Al-Onaizan 2016), aims to identify ways to enhance the performance of in-domain translation by leveraging out-of-domain and in-domain datasets, the latter often being less readily available in both the source and target languages (Chu and Wang 2018). A common method is fine-tuning, which trains out-of-domain models on in-domain data or on a combination of general and specialized data (see, for example, Luong and Manning 2015; Chu *et al.* 2017).

Pre-trained language models: Since the advent of the transformer, there has been a growing number of pre-trained language models such as BERT (Devlin *et al.* 2019) based on this architecture, and they provide contextual embeddings and can be fine-tuned for downstream natural language processing tasks, such as classification and question answering. The success of such models has been followed by research on their incorporation into NMT for encoding or decoding. Zhu *et al.* (2020), for example, explored BERT-generated representations that are used by each layer of the NMT encoder and decoder with attention.

Refer to Stahlberg (2020) and Zhang and Zong (2020) for other research directions.

Conclusion

Recent rapid advances in deep learning, as an approach to machine learning and artificial intelligence with an emphasis on automatic feature extraction through the training and use of multilayer artificial neural networks, have stimulated the development of translation technology in different aspects, including not only NMT using recurrent neural networks, convolutional neural networks or self-attention networks but also cascaded or end-to-end speech translation, intersemiotic translation (e.g. multimodal machine translation, image and video captioning and text-to-image/music translation) and translation memories based on sentence embeddings. We expect more progress in the future with the availability of more data, the design of novel neural architectures, the development of new approaches to training, inference and natural language processing and the innovative use of deep learning models.

Bibliography

Algan, G. and I. Ulusoy (2021) 'Image Classification with Deep Learning in the Presence of Noisy Labels: A Survey', *Knowledge-Based Systems* 215: 106771.

Arthern, P. J. (1978, November) 'Machine Translation and Computerized Terminology Systems: A Translator's Viewpoint', *Translating and the Computer: Proceedings of a Seminar, London* 14: 77–108.

Baevski, A., Y. Zhou, A. Mohamed, and M. Auli (2020) 'wav2vec 2.0: A Framework for Self-Supervised Learning of Speech Representations', *Advances in Neural Information Processing Systems* 33.

Bahdanau, D., K. H. Cho, and Y. Bengio (2015, January) 'Neural Machine Translation by Jointly Learning to Align and Translate', in *3rd International Conference on Learning Representations, ICLR 2015*. Available at: https://arxiv.org/abs/1409.0473.

Barrault, L., M. Biesialska, O. Bojar, M. R. Costa-jussà, C. Federmann, Y. Graham, . . . and M. Zampieri (2020, November) 'Findings of the 2020 Conference on Machine Translation (wmt20)', in *Proceedings of the Fifth Conference on Machine Translation*, 1–55.

Barrault, L., O. Bojar, M. R. Costa-Jussa, C. Federmann, M. Fishel, Y. Graham, . . . and M. Zampieri (2019, August) 'Findings of the 2019 Conference on Machine Translation (wmt19)', in *Proceedings of the Fourth Conference on Machine Translation (Volume 2: Shared Task Papers, Day 1)*, 1–61. Available at: https://aclanthology.org/W19-5301/.

Barrault, L., F. Bougares, L. Specia, C. Lala, D. Elliott, and S. Frank (2018, October) 'Findings of the Third Shared Task on Multimodal Machine Translation', *Proceedings of the Third Conference on Machine Translation: Shared Task Papers* 2: 308–27.

Bengio, Y., R. Ducharme, P. Vincent, and C. Janvin (2003) 'A Neural Probabilistic Language Model', *Journal of Machine Learning Research* 3: 1137–55.

Bhattacharyya, P. (2015) *Machine Translation*, New York: CRC Press.

Brown, P. F., J. Cocke, S. A. Della Pietra, V. J. Della Pietra, F. Jelinek, R. L. Mercer, and P. Roossin (1988) 'A Statistical Approach to Language Translation', in *COLING Budapest 1988 Volume 1: International Conference on Computational Linguistics*. Available at: https://dl.acm.org/doi/10.3115/991635.991651.

Brown, P. F., S. A. Della Pietra, V. J. Della Pietra, and R. L. Mercer (1993) 'The Mathematics of Statistical Machine Translation: Parameter Estimation', *Computational Linguistics* 19(2): 263–311.

Calixto, I., Q. Liu, and N. Campbell (2017, July) 'Doubly-Attentive Decoder for Multi-modal Neural Machine Translation', in *Proceedings of the 55th Annual Meeting of the Association for Computational Linguistics (Volume 1: Long Papers)*, 1913–24. Available at: https://aclanthology.org/P17-1175/.

Caswell, I., C. Chelba, and D. Grangier (2019, August) 'Tagged Back-Translation', in *Proceedings of the Fourth Conference on Machine Translation (Volume 1: Research Papers)*, 53–63. Available at: https://aclanthology.org/W19-5206/.

Cer, D., Y. Yang, S. Y. Kong, N. Hua, N. Limtiaco, R. S. John, . . . and R. Kurzweil (2018, November) 'Universal Sentence Encoder for English', in *Proceedings of the 2018 Conference on Empirical Methods in Natural Language Processing: System Demonstrations*, 169–74. Available at: https://aclanthology.org/D18-2029/.

Chen, H., X. Liu, D. Yin, and J. Tang (2017) 'A Survey on Dialogue Systems: Recent Advances and New Frontiers', *ACM Sigkdd Explorations Newsletter* 19(2): 25–35.

Chen, J., X. Li, J. Zhang, C. Zhou, J. Cui, B. Wang, and J. Su (2020, July) 'Modeling Discourse Structure for Document-level Neural Machine Translation', in *Proceedings of the First Workshop on Automatic Simultaneous Translation*, 30–36. Available at: https://aclanthology.org/2020.autosimtrans-1.5/.

Child, R., Gray, S., Radford, A., and Sutskever, I. (2019) 'Generating Long Sequences with Sparse Transformers', *arXiv preprint arXiv:1904.10509*.

Cho, K., B. van Merriënboer, C. Gulcehre, D. Bahdanau, F. Bougares, H. Schwenk, and Y. Bengio (2014, October) 'Learning Phrase Representations using RNN Encoder–Decoder for Statistical Machine Translation', in *Proceedings of the 2014 Conference on Empirical Methods in Natural Language Processing (EMNLP)*, 1724–34. Available at: https://aclanthology.org/D14-1179/.

Chu, C., R. Dabre, and S. Kurohashi (2017) 'An Empirical Comparison of Simple Domain Adaptation Methods for Neural Machine Translation', *arXiv preprint arXiv:1701.03214*.

Chu, C. and R. Wang (2018) 'A Survey of Domain Adaptation for Neural Machine Translation', *arXiv preprint arXiv:1806.00258*.

Cornia, M., M. Stefanini, L. Baraldi, and R. Cucchiara (2020) 'Meshed-Memory Transformer for Image Captioning', in *Proceedings of the IEEE/CVF Conference on Computer Vision and Pattern Recognition*, 10578–87. Available at: https://openaccess.thecvf.com/content_CVPR_2020/html/Cornia_Meshed-Memory_Transformer_for_Image_Captioning_CVPR_2020_paper.html.

Cromieres, F., C. Chu, T. Nakazawa, and S. Kurohashi (2016, December) 'Kyoto University Participation to WAT 2016', in *Proceedings of the 3rd Workshop on Asian Translation (WAT2016)*, 166–74. Available at: https://aclanthology.org/W16-4616/.

Dabre, R., C. Chu, and A. Kunchukuttan (2020) 'A Survey of Multilingual Neural Machine Translation', *ACM Computing Surveys (CSUR)* 53(5): 1–38. Available at: https://dl.acm.org/doi/abs/10.1145/3406095.

Dai, Z., Z. Yang, Y. Yang, J. G. Carbonell, Q. Le, and R. Salakhutdinov (2019, July) 'Transformer-XL: Attentive Language Models beyond a Fixed-Length Context', in *Proceedings of the 57th Annual Meeting of the Association for Computational Linguistics*, 2978–88. Available at: https://aclanthology.org/P19-1285/.

Dauphin, Y. N., A. Fan, M. Auli, and D. Grangier (2017, July) 'Language Modeling with Gated Convolutional Networks', in *International Conference on Machine Learning*, PMLR, 933–41.

Deng, L. and Y. Liu (eds.) (2018) *Deep Learning in Natural Language Processing*, Singapore: Springer.

Devlin, J., M. W. Chang, K. Lee, and K. Toutanova (2019, June) 'BERT: Pre-training of Deep Bidirectional Transformers for Language Understanding', in *Proceedings of the 2019 Conference of the North American Chapter of the Association for Computational Linguistics: Human Language Technologies, Volume 1 (Long and Short Papers)*, 4171–86. Available at: https://aclanthology.org/N19-1423/.

Dhariwal, P., H. Jun, C. Payne, J. W. Kim, A. Radford, and I. Sutskever (2020) 'Jukebox: A Generative Model for Music', *arXiv preprint arXiv:2005.00341*.

Dong, Y. (2018) 'A Survey on Neural Network-Based Summarization Methods', *arXiv preprint arXiv:1804.04589*.

Edunov, S., M. Ott, M. Auli, and D. Grangier (2018) 'Understanding Back-Translation at Scale', in *Proceedings of the 2018 Conference on Empirical Methods in Natural Language Processing*, 489–500. Available at: https://aclanthology.org/D18-1045/.

Fan, A., S. Bhosale, H. Schwenk, Z. Ma, A. El-Kishky, S. Goyal, . . . and A. Joulin (2020) 'Beyond English-centric Multilingual Machine Translation', *arXiv preprint arXiv:2010.11125.*

Freitag, M., and Y. Al-Onaizan (2016) 'Fast Domain Adaptation for Neural Machine Translation', *arXiv preprint arXiv:1612.06897.*

Gehring, J., M. Auli, D. Grangier, D. Yarats, and Y. N. Dauphin (2017, July) 'Convolutional Sequence to Sequence Learning', in *International Conference on Machine Learning*, PMLR, 1243–52.

Goodfellow, I. J., Y. Bengio, A. Courville, and Y. Bengio (2016) *Deep Learning*, Cambridge: MIT Press.

Goodfellow, I. J., J. Pouget-Abadie, M. Mirza, B. Xu, D. Warde-Farley, S. Ozair, . . . and Y. Bengio (2014) 'Generative Adversarial Networks', *arXiv preprint arXiv:1406.2661.*

Gu, J., J. Bradbury, C. Xiong, V. O. Li, and R. Socher (2017) 'Non-Autoregressive Neural Machine Translation', *arXiv preprint arXiv:1711.02281.*

Gu, J., K. Cho, and V. O. Li (2017, September) 'Trainable Greedy Decoding for Neural Machine Translation', in *Proceedings of the 2017 Conference on Empirical Methods in Natural Language Processing*, 1968–78. Available at: https://aclanthology.org/D17-1210//.

Gu, J., C. Wang, and J. Zhao (2019) 'Levenshtein Transformer', *arXiv preprint arXiv:1905.11006.*

Hinami, R., S. Ishiwatari, K. Yasuda, and Y. Matsui (2021) 'Towards Fully Automated Manga Translation', *arXiv preprint arXiv:2012.14271.*

Hochreiter, S. and J. Schmidhuber (1997) 'Long Short-Term Memory', *Neural Computation* 9(8): 1735–80.

Hossain, M., F. Sohel, M. F. Shiratuddin, and H. Laga (2018) 'A Comprehensive Survey of Deep Learning for Image Captioning', *arXiv preprint arXiv:1810.04020.*

Huang, S., H. Chen, X. Dai, and J. Chen (2015, July) 'Non-linear Learning for Statistical Machine Translation', in *Proceedings of the 53rd Annual Meeting of the Association for Computational Linguistics and the 7th International Joint Conference on Natural Language Processing (Volume 1: Long Papers)*, 825–35. Available at: https://aclanthology.org/P15-1080/.

Hutchins, J. (2005, September) 'Towards a Definition of Example-Based Machine Translation', in *Machine Translation Summit X, Second Workshop on Example-Based Machine Translation*, 63–70. Available at: https://aclanthology.org/2005.mtsummit-ebmt.9.pdf.

Hutchins, J. (2007) 'Machine Translation: A Concise History', *Computer Aided Translation: Theory and Practice* 13: 29–70, 11.

Islam, S., A. Dash, A. Seum, A. H. Raj, T. Hossain, and F. M. Shah (2021) 'Exploring Video Captioning Techniques: A Comprehensive Survey on Deep Learning Methods', *SN Computer Science* 2(2): 1–28.

Ive, J., P. S. Madhyastha, and L. Specia (2019, July) 'Distilling Translations with Visual Awareness', in *Proceedings of the 57th Annual Meeting of the Association for Computational Linguistics*, 6525–38. Available at: https://aclanthology.org/P19-1653/.

Jakobson, R. (2012) 'On Linguistic Aspects of Translation', in *Theories of Translation*, Chicago: University of Chicago Press, 144–51. (Original work published 1959)

Jia, Y., R. J. Weiss, F. Biadsy, W. Macherey, M., Chen, Z. Johnson, and Y. Wu (2019) 'Direct Speech-to-Speech Translation with a Sequence-to-Sequence Model', *Proc. Interspeech 2019*, 1123–27. Available at: https://www.isca-speech.org/archive_v0/Interspeech_2019/abstracts/1951.html.

Jiao, L., F. Zhang, F. Liu, S. Yang, L. Li, Z. Feng, and R. Qu (2019) 'A Survey of Deep Learning-Based Object Detection', *IEEE Access* 7: 128837–68.

Kalchbrenner, N. and P. Blunsom (2013, October) 'Recurrent Continuous Translation Models', in *Proceedings of the 2013 Conference on Empirical Methods in Natural Language Processing*, 1700–09. Available at: https://aclanthology.org/D13-1176.pdf.

Kelleher, J. D. (2019) *Deep Learning*, Cambridge, MA: MIT Press.

Kingma, D. P. and J. Ba (2014) 'Adam: A Method for Stochastic Optimization', *arXiv preprint arXiv:1412.6980.*

Koehn, P. (2009) *Statistical Machine Translation*, Cambridge: Cambridge University Press.

Koehn, P. (2020) *Neural Machine Translation*, Cambridge: Cambridge University Press.

Kong, J., J. Kim, and J. Bae (2020) 'HiFi-GAN: Generative Adversarial Networks for Efficient and High Fidelity Speech Synthesis', *Advances in Neural Information Processing Systems* 33.

Kudo, T., and J. Richardson (2018) 'SentencePiece: A Simple and Language Independent Subword Tokenizer and Detokenizer for Neural Text Processing', *EMNLP 2018* 66.

Kumar, A., S. Verma, and H. Mangla (2018, October) 'A Survey of Deep Learning Techniques in Speech Recognition', in *2018 International Conference on Advances in Computing, Communication Control and Networking (ICACCCN)*, IEEE, 179–85.

Li, J., A. Sun, J. Han, and C. Li (2020) 'A Survey on Deep Learning for Named Entity Recognition', *IEEE Transactions on Knowledge and Data Engineering*. Available at: https://ieeexplore.ieee.org/document/9039685.

Li, P., Y. Liu, M. Sun, T. Izuha, and D. Zhang (2014, August) 'A Neural Reordering Model for Phrase-Based Translation', in *Proceedings of COLING 2014, the 25th International Conference on Computational Linguistics: Technical Papers*, 1897–1907. Available at: https://aclanthology.org/C14-1179/.

Li, Q., H. Peng, J. Li, C. Xia, R. Yang, L. Sun, . . . and L. He (2020) 'A Text Classification Survey: From Shallow to Deep Learning', *arXiv preprint arXiv:2008.00364*.

Li, X., X. Yin, C. Li, P. Zhang, X. Hu, L. Zhang, . . . and J. Gao (2020, August) 'Oscar: Object-Semantics Aligned Pre-Training for Vision-Language Tasks', in *European Conference on Computer Vision*, Cham: Springer, 121–37.

Lim, B. and S. Zohren (2021) 'Time-series Forecasting with Deep Learning: A Survey', *Philosophical Transactions of the Royal Society A* 379(2194): 20200209.

Liu, L., X. Liu, J. Gao, W. Chen, and J. Han (2020) 'Understanding the Difficulty of Training Transformers', in *Proceedings of the 2020 Conference on Empirical Methods in Natural Language Processing (EMNLP)*, 5747–63. Available at: https://aclanthology.org/2020.emnlp-main.463/.

Liu, X., K. Duh, L. Liu, and J. Gao (2020) 'Very Deep Transformers for Neural Machine Translation', *arXiv preprint arXiv:2008.07772*.

Liu, Y., J. Gu, N. Goyal, X. Li, S. Edunov, M. Ghazvininejad, . . . and L. Zettlemoyer (2020). 'Multilingual Denoising Pre-Training for Neural Machine Translation', *Transactions of the Association for Computational Linguistics* 8: 726–42.

Liu, Y., L. Zhou, Y. Wang, Y. Zhao, J. Zhang, and C. Zong (2018, August) 'A Comparable Study on Model Averaging, Ensembling and Reranking in NMT, in *CCF International Conference on Natural Language Processing and Chinese Computing*, Cham: Springer, 299–308.

Luong, M. T. and C. D. Manning (2015, December) 'Stanford Neural Machine Translation Systems for Spoken Language Domains', in *Proceedings of the International Workshop on Spoken Language Translation*, 76–79. Available at: https://aclanthology.org/2015.iwslt-evaluation.11/.

Luong, M. T., H. Pham, and C. D. Manning (2015, September) 'Effective Approaches to Attention-based Neural Machine Translation', in *Proceedings of the 2015 Conference on Empirical Methods in Natural Language Processing*, 1412–21. Available at: https://aclanthology.org/D15-1166/.

Ma, C., W. E. Zhang, M. Guo, H. Wang, and Q. Z. Sheng (2020) 'Multi-document Summarization via Deep Learning Techniques: A Survey', *arXiv preprint arXiv:2011.04843*.

Mansimov, E., E. Parisotto, J. L. Ba, and R. Salakhutdinov (2015) 'Generating Images from Captions with Attention', *arXiv preprint arXiv:1511.02793*.

Meng, F., J. Yan, Y. Liu, Y. Gao, X. Zeng, Q. Zeng, . . . and H. Zhou (2020, November) 'WeChat Neural Machine Translation Systems for WMT20', in *Proceedings of the Fifth Conference on Machine Translation*, 239–47. Available at: https://aclanthology.org/2020.wmt-1.24/.

Miculicich, L., Ram, D., Pappas, N., & Henderson, J. (2018) 'Document-level Neural Machine Translation with Hierarchical Attention Networks', in *Proceedings of the 2018 Conference on Empirical Methods in Natural Language Processing*, 2947-2954. Available at: https://aclanthology.org/D18-1325/.

Mikolov, T., É. Grave, P. Bojanowski, C. Puhrsch, and A. Joulin (2018, May) 'Advances in Pre-Training Distributed Word Representations', in *Proceedings of the Eleventh International Conference on Language Resources and Evaluation (LREC 2018)*. Available at: https://aclanthology.org/L18-1008/.

Munday, J. (2009) 'Issues in Translation Studies', in Jeremy Munday (ed.) *The Routledge Companion to Translation Studies*, London: Routledge, 1–19.

Nagao, M. (1984) 'A Framework of a Mechanical Translation Between Japanese and English by Analogy Principle', *Artificial and Human Intelligence*: 351–54.

Ney, H. (2005) 'One Decade of Statistical Machine Translation: 1996–2005', in *IEEE Workshop on Automatic Speech Recognition and Understanding, 2005*, IEEE, 2–11.

Ng, N., K. Yee, A. Baevski, M. Ott, M. Auli, and S. Edunov (2019, August) 'Facebook FAIR's WMT19 News Translation Task Submission', in *Proceedings of the Fourth Conference on Machine Translation (Volume 2: Shared Task Papers, Day 1)*, 314–19. Available at: https://aclanthology.org/W19-5333/.

Ning, Y., S. He, Z. Wu, C. Xing, and L. J. Zhang (2019) 'A Review of Deep Learning Based Speech Synthesis', *Applied Sciences* 9(19): 4050.

Papineni, K., S. Roukos, T. Ward, and W. J. Zhu (2002, July) 'Bleu: A Method for Automatic Evaluation of Machine Translation', in *Proceedings of the 40th Annual Meeting of the Association for Computational Linguistics*, 311–18. Available at: https://aclanthology.org/P02-1040/.

Popel, M. and O. Bojar (2018) 'Training Tips for the Transformer Model', *The Prague Bulletin of Mathematical Linguistics* 110: 43–70.

Post, M. and D. Vilar (2018, June) 'Fast Lexically Constrained Decoding with Dynamic Beam Allocation for Neural Machine Translation', in *Proceedings of the 2018 Conference of the North American Chapter of the*

Association for Computational Linguistics: Human Language Technologies, Volume 1 (Long Papers), 1314–24. Available at: https://aclanthology.org/N18-1119/.

Ramesh, A., M. Pavlov, G. Goh, S. Gray, C. Voss, A. Radford, . . . and I. Sutskever (2021) 'Zero-shot Text-to-Image Generation', *arXiv preprint arXiv:2102.12092*.

Ranasinghe, T., C. Orasan, and R. Mitkov (2020) 'Intelligent Translation Memory Matching and Retrieval with Sentence Encoders', in *22nd Annual Conference of the European Association for Machine Translation*, 175–84. Available at: https://aclanthology.org/2020.eamt-1.19/.

Razavi, A., A. V. D. Oord, and O. Vinyals (2019) 'Generating Diverse High-fidelity Images with vq-vae-2', *arXiv preprint arXiv:1906.00446*.

Reed, S., Z. Akata, X. Yan, L. Logeswaran, B. Schiele, and H. Lee (2016, June) 'Generative Adversarial Text to Image Synthesis', in *International Conference on Machine Learning*, PMLR, 1060–60.

Ren, Y., Y. Ruan, X. Tan, T. Qin, S. Zhao, Z. Zhao, and T. Y. Liu (2019) 'Fastspeech: Fast, Robust and Controllable Text to Speech', *arXiv preprint arXiv:1905.09263*.

Schrittwieser, J., I. Antonoglou, T. Hubert, K. Simonyan, L. Sifre, S. Schmitt, . . . and D. Silver (2020) 'Mastering Atari, Go, Chess and Shogi by Planning with a Learned Model', *Nature* 588(7839): 604–09.

Sennrich, R., B. Haddow, and A. Birch (2016a, August) 'Improving Neural Machine Translation Models with Monolingual Data', in *Proceedings of the 54th Annual Meeting of the Association for Computational Linguistics (Volume 1: Long Papers)*, 86–96. Available at: https://aclanthology.org/P16-1009/.

Sennrich, R., B. Haddow, and A. Birch (2016b, August) 'Neural Machine Translation of Rare Words with Subword Units', in *Proceedings of the 54th Annual Meeting of the Association for Computational Linguistics (Volume 1: Long Papers)*, 1715–25. Available at: https://aclanthology.org/P16-1162/.

Shen, J., R. Pang, R. J. Weiss, M. Schuster, N. Jaitly, Z. Yang, . . . and Y. Wu (2018, April) 'Natural TTS Synthesis by Conditioning Wavenet on Mel Spectrogram Predictions', in *2018 IEEE International Conference on Acoustics, Speech and Signal Processing (ICASSP)*, IEEE, 4779–83.

Simard, M. (2020) 'Building and Using Parallel Text for Translation', in Minako O'Hagan (ed.) *The Routledge Handbook of Translation and Technology*, London: Routledge, 78–90.

Singh, A., T. D. Singh, and S. Bandyopadhyay (2020) 'NITS-VC System for VATEX Video Captioning Challenge 2020', *arXiv preprint arXiv:2006.04058*.

Sperber, M. and M. Paulik (2020, July) 'Speech Translation and the End-to-End Promise: Taking Stock of Where We Are', in *Proceedings of the 58th Annual Meeting of the Association for Computational Linguistics*, 7409–21. Available at: https://aclanthology.org/2020.acl-main.661/.

Srivastava, Y., V. Murali, S. R. Dubey, and S. Mukherjee (2019) 'Visual Question Answering Using Deep Learning: A Survey and Performance Analysis', *arXiv preprint arXiv:1909.01860*.

Stahlberg, F. (2020) 'Neural Machine Translation: A Review', *Journal of Artificial Intelligence Research* 69: 343–418.

Stevens, E., L. Antiga, and T. Viehmann (2020) *Deep Learning with PyTorch*, New York: Manning Publications Company.

Sutskever, I., O. Vinyals, and Q. V. Le (2014) 'Sequence to Sequence Learning with Neural Networks', *Advances in Neural Information Processing Systems* 27: 3104–12.

Tay, Y., M. Dehghani, D. Bahri, and D. Metzler (2020) 'Efficient Transformers: A Survey', *arXiv preprint arXiv:2009.06732*.

Tiedemann, J. and Y. Scherrer (2017, September) 'Neural Machine Translation with Extended Context', in *Proceedings of the Third Workshop on Discourse in Machine Translation*, 82–92. Available at: https://aclanthology.org/W17-4811/.

Vaswani, A., N. Shazeer, N. Parmar, J. Uszkoreit, L. Jones, A. N. Gomez, . . . and I. Polosukhin (2017, December) 'Attention Is All You Need', in *Proceedings of the 31st International Conference on Neural Information Processing Systems*, 6000–10. Available at: https://papers.nips.cc/paper/2017/hash/3f5ee243547dee91fbd053c1c4a845aa-Abstract.html.

Vaswani, A., Y. Zhao, V. Fossum, and D. Chiang (2013, October) 'Decoding with Large-Scale Neural Language Models Improves Translation', in *Proceedings of the 2013 Conference on Empirical Methods in Natural Language Processing*, 1387–92. Available at: https://aclanthology.org/D13-1140/.

Wang, A., A. Singh, J. Michael, F. Hill, O. Levy, and S. Bowman (2018, November) 'GLUE: A Multi-Task Benchmark and Analysis Platform for Natural Language Understanding', in *Proceedings of the 2018 EMNLP Workshop BlackboxNLP: Analyzing and Interpreting Neural Networks for NLP*, 353–55. Available at: https://aclanthology.org/W18-5446/.

Wang, C., K. Cho, and J. Gu (2020, April) 'Neural Machine Translation with Byte-Level Subwords', *Proceedings of the AAAI Conference on Artificial Intelligence* 34(5): 9154–60.

Wang, C., Y. Wu, S. Liu, Z. Yang, and M. Zhou (2020, April) 'Bridging the Gap Between Pre-training and Fine-Tuning for End-to-End Speech Translation', *Proceedings of the AAAI Conference on Artificial Intelligence* 34(5): 9161–68.

Wu, F., A. Fan, A. Baevski, Y. N. Dauphin, and M. Auli (2019) 'Pay Less Attention with Lightweight and Dynamic Convolutions', *arXiv preprint arXiv:1901.10430*.

Wu, L., X. Pan, Z. Lin, Y. Zhu, M. Wang, and L. Li (2020, November) 'The Volctrans Machine Translation System for WMT20', in *Proceedings of the Fifth Conference on Machine Translation*, 305–12. Available at: https://aclanthology.org/2020.wmt-1.33/.

Wu, S., X. Wang, L. Wang, F. Liu, J. Xie, Z. Tu, . . . and M. Li (2020, November) 'Tencent Neural Machine Translation Systems for the WMT20 News Translation Task', in *Proceedings of the Fifth Conference on Machine Translation*, 313–19. Available at: https://aclanthology.org/2020.wmt-1.34/.

Wu, Y., M. Schuster, Z. Chen, Q. V. Le, M. Norouzi, W. Macherey, . . . and J. Dean (2016) 'Google's Neural Machine Translation System: Bridging the Gap Between Human and Machine Translation', *arXiv preprint arXiv:1609.08144*.

Xu, W., and M. Carpuat (2021) 'EDITOR: An Edit-Based Transformer with Repositioning for Neural Machine Translation with Soft Lexical Constraints', *Transactions of the Association for Computational Linguistics* 9: 311–28.

Yadav, V. and S. Bethard (2018, August) 'A Survey on Recent Advances in Named Entity Recognition from Deep Learning models', in *Proceedings of the 27th International Conference on Computational Linguistics*, 2145–58. Available at: https://aclanthology.org/C18-1182/.

Yang, N., S. Liu, M. Li, M. Zhou, and N. Yu (2013, August) 'Word Alignment Modeling with Context Dependent Deep Neural Network', in *Proceedings of the 51st Annual Meeting of the Association for Computational Linguistics (Volume 1: Long Papers)*, 166–75. Available at: https://aclanthology.org/P13-1017/.

Yang, S., Y. Wang, X. and Chu (2020) 'A Survey of Deep Learning Techniques for Neural Machine Translation', *arXiv preprint arXiv:2002.07526*.

Yang, Z., J. Zhang, F. Meng, S. Gu, Y. Feng, and J. Zhou (2019, November) 'Enhancing Context Modeling with a Query-Guided Capsule Network for Document-level Translation', in *Proceedings of the 2019 Conference on Empirical Methods in Natural Language Processing and the 9th International Joint Conference on Natural Language Processing (EMNLP-IJCNLP)*, 1527–37. Available at: https://aclanthology.org/D19-1164/.

Yao, S. and X. Wan (2020, July) 'Multimodal Transformer for Multimodal Machine Translation', in *Proceedings of the 58th Annual Meeting of the Association for Computational Linguistics*, 4346–50. Available at: https://aclanthology.org/2020.acl-main.400/.

Zaretskaya, A., G. C. Pastor, and M. Seghiri (2017) 'User Perspective on Translation Tools: Findings of a User Survey', in Gloria Corpas Pastor and Isabel Durán-Muñoz (eds) *Trends in E-tools and Resources for Translators and Interpreters*, Leiden: Brill, 37–56.

Zhang, A., Z. C. Lipton, M. Li, and A. J. Smola (2020) *Dive into Deep Learning*. Available at: https://d2l.ai/.

Zhang, B., I. Titov, and R. Sennrich (2019, November) 'Improving Deep Transformer with Depth-Scaled Initialization and Merged Attention', in *Proceedings of the 2019 Conference on Empirical Methods in Natural Language Processing and the 9th International Joint Conference on Natural Language Processing (EMNLP-IJCNLP)*, 898–909. Available at: https://aclanthology.org/D19-1083/.

Zhang, J., and C. Zong (2020) 'Neural Machine Translation: Challenges, Progress and Future', *Science China Technological Sciences*: 1–23.

Zhang, L., S. Wang, and B. Liu (2018) 'Deep Learning for Sentiment Analysis: A Survey', *Wiley Interdisciplinary Reviews: Data Mining and Knowledge Discovery* 8(4): e1253.

Zhang, P., X. Li, X. Hu, J. Yang, L. Zhang, L. Wang, . . . and J. Gao (2021) 'VinVL: Revisiting Visual Representations in Vision-Language Models', *arXiv preprint arXiv:2101.00529*.

Zhang, Z., Y. Shi, C. Yuan, B. Li, P. Wang, W. Hu, and Z. J. Zha (2020) 'Object Relational Graph with Teacher-recommended Learning for Video Captioning', in *Proceedings of the IEEE/CVF Conference on Computer Vision and Pattern Recognition*, 13278–88. Available at: https://openaccess.thecvf.com/content_CVPR_2020/papers/Zhang_Object_Relational_Graph_With_Teacher-Recommended_Learning_for_Video_Captioning_CVPR_2020_paper.pdf.

Zhou, L., H. Palangi, L. Zhang, H. Hu, J. Corso, and J. Gao (2020, April) 'Unified Vision-Language Pre-Training for Image Captioning and VQA', *Proceedings of the AAAI Conference on Artificial Intelligence* 34(07): 13041–49. Available at: https://ojs.aaai.org/index.php/AAAI/article/view/7005.

Zhu, J., Y. Xia, L. Wu, D. He, T. Qin, W. Zhou, . . . and T. Y. Liu (2020) 'Incorporating Bert into Neural Machine Translation', *arXiv preprint arXiv:2002.06823*.

INDEX